MARRIAGE NOTICES
from the MAINE FARMER
1833–1852

Elizabeth
Keene Young

Benjamin
Lewis Keene

HERITAGE BOOKS
2012

HERITAGE BOOKS
AN IMPRINT OF HERITAGE BOOKS, INC.

Books, CDs, and more—Worldwide

For our listing of thousands of titles see our website
at
www.HeritageBooks.com

Published 2012 by
HERITAGE BOOKS, INC.
Publishing Division
100 Railroad Ave. #104
Westminster, Maryland 21157

Copyright © 1995 Elizabeth Keene Young
and Benjamin Lewis Keene

Other Heritage Books by the authors:

*Abstracts of Death Notices (1833–1852) and
Miscellaneous News Items from the* Maine Farmer *(1833–1924)*
David C. Young and Benjamin Lewis Keene

Marriage Notices from the Maine Farmer 1833
Elizabeth Keene Young and Benjamin Lewis Keene

Stackpole's History of Winthrop, Maine, with Genealogical Notes
David C. Young and Elizabeth Keene Young

Vital Records from Maine Newspapers, 1785–1820
David C. Young and Elizabeth Keene Young

All rights reserved. No part of this book may be reproduced or transmitted in any form or by any means, electronic or mechanical, including photocopying, recording or by any information storage and retrieval system without written permission from the author, except for the inclusion of brief quotations in a review.

International Standard Book Numbers
Paperbound: 978-0-7884-0373-6
Clothbound: 978-0-7884-9410-9

Contents

Foreword v
Preface vii
Alphabetical Listing of Marriage Notices from the *"Maine Farmer"* 1
List of Ministers and Justices of the Peace 469
Quaker Marriages Mentioned in this Book 481
List of Towns, Cities, and Places Named in this Volume 483

Foreword

Newspapers can be a major source of vital records for genealogical research in Maine. Elizabeth Keene Young, my wife, and Benjamin Lewis Keene, our nephew, have competed a project originally started over a half a century ago by the National Youth Administration. Working under the supervision of Clarence A. Day, Extension Service, University of Maine at Orono, the three students who did the original abstractions were: Oscar R. Martin, class of 1940; Carlton B. Payson, class of 1941; and J. Herbert Roberts, class of 1942. At that time the *Maine Farmer* was under the supervision of Mr. Louis T. Ibbetson, Librarian of the University of Maine, and Miss Theresa R. Stuart, Librarian of the Maine State Library, who deserve recognition for giving permission to copy from the issues in their possession. Special appreciation is due to the NYA authorities and Dean Arthur L. Deering of the College of Agriculture, University of Maine, for their interest and support.

The task was originally financed by the National Youth Administration, under the local direction of Philip J. Brockway. It was abondoned when funds were no longer available. At that time only the marriage records from Abbott to Patten had been compiled alphabetically. They were continued through the interest of Arthur. L. Deering, Director of Agricultural Extension Services, University of Maine. Miss Eleanor Lounsbury deserves much credit for her patient and painstaking typing.

The editors found that the original NYA typescript did not include issues for: 1848, 1851, part of 1852, and 4 July 1840 to 5 Dec 1840. It is likely they had not yet been copied when funding ran out for the NYA project. The editors have incorporated the missing records except for 6 Aug 1842 and 18 Mar 1843.

Marriage records compiled from the *Maine Farmer* cover the entire state of Maine, but most are from the Kennebec Valley. Both professional and amatuer genealogists should find them useful, not only for the information contained, but also for the clues they give to finding further information.

David C. Young
P. O. Box 152
Danville, ME
Dec. 1994

Preface

The *Maine Farmer* was established in 1833 by Dr. Ezekiel Holmes and was issued regularly for nearly a hundred years. The weekly paper was devoted to the interest of agriculture and mechanic arts. The first number was dated 21 Jan 1833, and called the *Kennebec Farmer*. The name was changed to the *Maine Farmer* on 18 Mar of the same year.

The *Maine Farmer* moved several times. It was published at Winthrop from 1833-1837, at Hallowell from 1837-1838, at Winthrop again from 16 October 1838 to the end of 1843. During the year 1842, the *Maine Farmer* was printed in Portland and Winthrop. In January 1844, the paper was moved to Augusta where it was located to the end of the period. Thus, for the reader's convenience, if an article stated that a marriage took place "in this town", the editors have substituted (in parentheses) the name of the town where the paper was being published at that time.

Most entries in the paper did not include the date of marriage. The date or dates at the end of each item is the date of the issue of the paper in which the item appeared. Accounts of gifts of wedding cake to the editor and similar references in most cases have been omitted.

The editors would like to thank Mrs. Bonnie Collins of the Maine State Library for furnishing us with a copy of the original NYA typescript, and the University of Maine Library for permission to publish this work.

We would also like to thank David C. Young, who has acted as the role of coach in this project. Nicholas Noyes of the Maine Historical Society deserves our appreciation as well.

The editors have made a great effort to be correct. We have copied the important information so there is no need to check the newspaper. However, those who require a photocopy may write to Bates College Library, Lewiston, ME. For a small fee a photocopy can be obtained. If you require a photocopy of the issues which were not microfilmed, you may be out of luck, as neither the Maine State Library nor the Maine Historical Cociety have copy services for the public.

Elizabeth Keene Young
P. O. Box 152
Danville, ME

Abbreviations

d/o   daughter of
Esq   Esquire
inst   instant (of this month)
Plt   plantantion
ult   ultimo (of the previous month)

- A -

ABBOTT/ABBOT Abby & Albert J MASON at South Berwick ME [27 June 1844]
Abiel Esq & Sarah S DAVIS at Farmington ME [23 Oct 1845]
Alex A & Margaret M BELCHER at Farmington ME [27 Sept 1849]
Anvella & John MARTIN at Rumford ME by P C VIRGIN Esq all of R [6 Mar 1835]
Clara A, d/o Jacob ABBOTT Esq, & Rev Elbridge G CUTLER of Belfast ME on 21st inst by Rev Isaac ROGERS at Farmington ME [3 June 1843]
David S & Jemima WILBUR d/o Pardon TINKHAM Esq at Albion ME on 1st ult [4 Feb 1843]
Dolly M & Marshall B COLBY of Concord NH at Rumford ME [1 Feb 1849]
Francis & Irena PIKE on Oct 12 by Rev N HOBART at Cornish ME [15 Nov 1849]
Harriet N & Cyrenius B WOLCOTT at (Augusta) ME on 11th Feb [19 Feb 1852]
Isaac & Eliza REED at Sebasticook ME on Oct 6 by Jas W NORTH Esq [19 Nov 1842]
James M of Oxford ME & Sarah J BERRY of Norway ME at Waterford ME [1 Feb 1849]
John P & Louisa DIXON at Gardiner ME [24 Jan 1850]
John S Esq of Thomaston ME & Elizabeth T d/o Wm ALLEN Jr Esq of Norridgewock ME [23 Oct 1835]
John & Betsey R WING d/o Ichobod WING Esq late of Winthrop ME, by J SPAULDING at Belgrade ME [7 Nov 1834]
Lucy W of Lowell MA & Daniel A YOUNG at Farmington ME [26 Aug 1852]
Martha & George W WILLARD at Bangor ME [11 Jul 1844]
Mary B & George W MONK at Albion by D B FULLER Esq [24 Jul 1851]
Mary Ann & Silas MOSES of Scarborough ME at Portland ME [21 Jan 1847]
Mary H & John TRUE, merchant, at Bangor ME [12 Feb 1846]
Mrs Mary J & Joel T DAMREN at Belgrade ME on 14th inst [30 Mar 1848]
Rebecca, d/o William ABBOT Esq, & Dr Thomas C BARKER at Bangor ME [4 Feb 1833]
Sam'l P Rev of Houlton ME & Hannah BARKER d/o Wm BARKER of Nottingham England by Rev Jacob ABBOT at Farmington ME [3 Jul 1841]
Sarah & Samuel WOOD of Hallowell ME at Litchfield ME [23 May 1837]
Walter & Ruth HORN in Bath ME [15 May 1845]
William A Capt of Ellsworth ME & Harriet C EMERY on Sept 24th by Rev STONE at Biddeford ME [9 Oct 1845]
William F of Belfast ME & Mary A SANBORN of Lowell MA? at Knox ME [29 Jul 1847]
William T of Farmington ME & R Brenda WHITTIER on Nov 29th by Rev J COLE at Hallowell ME [6 Dec 1849]

ABORN Frederick & Mrs Orra A PHILBROOK by Rev C F ALLEN at Augusta ME on Jan 5 [17 Jan 1850]
ACORN Mary Jane & John F SCHWARTZ at North Waldoboro ME [15 May 1851]
ACHORN Albion G & Lucy G PARTRIDGE at Thomaston ME [5 Mar 1846]
  Harriet & William FLANDERS at Waldoboro ME [4 May 1848] & on 4th inst [13 Apr 1848]
  Kate H & Dr A D NICHOLS both of Rockland ME at Albany NY [19 Aug 1852]
  Margaret E & Davis TILSON at Rockland ME [19 Aug 1852]
  Melinda & Capt William H THORNDIKE at Thomaston ME [5 Aug 1847]
  Sarah Jane & Otis LARRABEE at Thomaston ME [22 Mar 1849]
  Sarah & Josiah SIDELINGER all of Waldoboro ME [26 Feb 1846]
ACRES Eunice of Westbrook ME & Wm BARTLETT of Gorham ME at W [16 Jan 1838]
ADAMS A B & Louisa CURTIS by Wm R HERSEY Esq at Lincoln ME [16 Apr 1846]
  Albert F of Skowhegan ME & Abby W PARKER at Waterville ME [20 Mar 1851]
  Alexander & Jane MECRACKEN at Eastport ME [29 Jul 1836]
  Almira J & Wm H JONES of Saco at Lewiston ME [18 Jan 1849]
  Amos of Belgrade ME & Sarah PIPER of Winthrop ME at Gardiner ME [8 Jul 1833]
  Benj & Eliza B SAWYER at New Portland ME [16 Aug 1849]
  Benjamin Jr & Harriet MERRILL by Eld INGRAHAM on 25th ult at Hallowell ME [8 May 1838]
  Benjamin & Abby HATCH at GRAY ME [12 Sept 1844]
  Benjamin & Hannah WARREN d/o Josiah WARREN all of Norridgewock ME [27 Mar 1838]
  Cornelia P & Charles S PENNEL at Brunswick ME [30 Jan 1845]
  Daniel of Norridgewock ME & Mrs Deborah L RUSSELL at Madison ME [6 Dec 1849]
  Elijah & Cordelia KNIGHT at Portland ME [13 Mar 1845]
  Emma & John WHORFF Jr at Madison ME [14 Oct 1836]
  Esther & Simeon GILMORE of Turner at Norridgewock ME [25 Mar 1847]
  Experience B Mrs of Farmington ME & Thomas S LOCKE of Temple ME at Temple [22 Jul 1852]
  George W Rev of Newfield ME & Elizabeth MORRIS at Limerick ME [10 Oct 1837]
  Henry & Hannah ALBEE of Wiscasset ME at Boston MA [23 May 1844]
  Isaac of Gray ME & Elvira ALLEN at Portland ME [21 Jan 1847]
  James M of Anson ME & Mrs Abigail RUSSELL of Starks ME at Norridgewock ME [23 Nov 1839]
  Joanna & Francis FONTAN by D T PIKE Esq at Augusta ME [13 Dec 1849]
  Joel & Jane HUNT both of Readfield ME by Rev WEBBER [24 Jan 1834]
  John Capt of Madison ME & Vira HODSDON of Jay ME at North Anson ME [10 Jan 1850]
  John Q & Nancy A CAMPBELL at Cherryfield ME [27 May 1843]
  John R & Sarah KNOWLTON at Farmington ME [20 Dec 1849]
  John W & Mary J WISE of Topsham ME at Litchfield ME [27 Jul 1848]
  John & Roxana ADAMS in Madison ME [21 Feb 1834]

- A -

ABBOTT/ABBOT Abby & Albert J MASON at South Berwick ME [27 June 1844]
Abiel Esq & Sarah S DAVIS at Farmington ME [23 Oct 1845]
Alex A & Margaret M BELCHER at Farmington ME [27 Sept 1849]
Anvella & John MARTIN at Rumford ME by P C VIRGIN Esq all of R [6 Mar 1835]
Clara A, d/o Jacob ABBOTT Esq, & Rev Elbridge G CUTLER of Belfast ME on 21st inst by Rev Isaac ROGERS at Farmington ME [3 June 1843]
David S & Jemima WILBUR d/o Pardon TINKHAM Esq at Albion ME on 1st ult [4 Feb 1843]
Dolly M & Marshall B COLBY of Concord NH at Rumford ME [1 Feb 1849]
Francis & Irena PIKE on Oct 12 by Rev N HOBART at Cornish ME [15 Nov 1849]
Harriet N & Cyrenius B WOLCOTT at (Augusta) ME on 11th Feb [19 Feb 1852]
Isaac & Eliza REED at Sebasticook ME on Oct 6 by Jas W NORTH Esq [19 Nov 1842]
James M of Oxford ME & Sarah J BERRY of Norway ME at Waterford ME [1 Feb 1849]
John P & Louisa DIXON at Gardiner ME [24 Jan 1850]
John S Esq of Thomaston ME & Elizabeth T d/o Wm ALLEN Jr Esq of Norridgewock ME [23 Oct 1835]
John & Betsey R WING d/o Ichobod WING Esq late of Winthrop ME, by J SPAULDING at Belgrade ME [7 Nov 1834]
Lucy W of Lowell MA & Daniel A YOUNG at Farmington ME [26 Aug 1852]
Martha & George W WILLARD at Bangor ME [11 Jul 1844]
Mary B & George W MONK at Albion by D B FULLER Esq [24 Jul 1851]
Mary Ann & Silas MOSES of Scarborough ME at Portland ME [21 Jan 1847]
Mary H & John TRUE, merchant, at Bangor ME [12 Feb 1846]
Mrs Mary J & Joel T DAMREN at Belgrade ME on 14th inst [30 Mar 1848]
Rebecca, d/o William ABBOT Esq, & Dr Thomas C BARKER at Bangor ME [4 Feb 1833]
Sam'l P Rev of Houlton ME & Hannah BARKER d/o Wm BARKER of Nottingham England by Rev Jacob ABBOT at Farmington ME [3 Jul 1841]
Sarah & Samuel WOOD of Hallowell ME at Litchfield ME [23 May 1837]
Walter & Ruth HORN in Bath ME [15 May 1845]
William A Capt of Ellsworth ME & Harriet C EMERY on Sept 24th by Rev STONE at Biddeford ME [9 Oct 1845]
William F of Belfast ME & Mary A SANBORN of Lowell MA? at Knox ME [29 Jul 1847]
William T of Farmington ME & R Brenda WHITTIER on Nov 29th by Rev J COLE at Hallowell ME [6 Dec 1849]

ABORN Frederick & Mrs Orra A PHILBROOK by Rev C F ALLEN at Augusta ME on Jan 5 [17 Jan 1850]
ACORN Mary Jane & John F SCHWARTZ at North Waldoboro ME [15 May 1851]
ACHORN Albion G & Lucy G PARTRIDGE at Thomaston ME [5 Mar 1846]
  Harriet & William FLANDERS at Waldoboro ME [4 May 1848] & on 4th inst [13 Apr 1848]
  Kate H & Dr A D NICHOLS both of Rockland ME at Albany NY [19 Aug 1852]
  Margaret E & Davis TILSON at Rockland ME [19 Aug 1852]
  Melinda & Capt William H THORNDIKE at Thomaston ME [5 Aug 1847]
  Sarah Jane & Otis LARRABEE at Thomaston ME [22 Mar 1849]
  Sarah & Josiah SIDELINGER all of Waldoboro ME [26 Feb 1846]
ACRES Eunice of Westbrook ME & Wm BARTLETT of Gorham ME at W [16 Jan 1838]
ADAMS A B & Louisa CURTIS by Wm R HERSEY Esq at Lincoln ME [16 Apr 1846]
  Albert F of Skowhegan ME & Abby W PARKER at Waterville ME [20 Mar 1851]
  Alexander & Jane MECRACKEN at Eastport ME [29 Jul 1836]
  Almira J & Wm H JONES of Saco at Lewiston ME [18 Jan 1849]
  Amos of Belgrade ME & Sarah PIPER of Winthrop ME at Gardiner ME [8 Jul 1833]
  Benj & Eliza B SAWYER at New Portland ME [16 Aug 1849]
  Benjamin Jr & Harriet MERRILL by Eld INGRAHAM on 25th ult at Hallowell ME [8 May 1838]
  Benjamin & Abby HATCH at GRAY ME [12 Sept 1844]
  Benjamin & Hannah WARREN d/o Josiah WARREN all of Norridgewock ME [27 Mar 1838]
  Cornelia P & Charles S PENNEL at Brunswick ME [30 Jan 1845]
  Daniel of Norridgewock ME & Mrs Deborah L RUSSELL at Madison ME [6 Dec 1849]
  Elijah & Cordelia KNIGHT at Portland ME [13 Mar 1845]
  Emma & John WHORFF Jr at Madison ME [14 Oct 1836]
  Esther & Simeon GILMORE of Turner at Norridgewock ME [25 Mar 1847]
  Experience B Mrs of Farmington ME & Thomas S LOCKE of Temple ME at Temple [22 Jul 1852]
  George W Rev of Newfield ME & Elizabeth MORRIS at Limerick ME [10 Oct 1837]
  Henry & Hannah ALBEE of Wiscasset ME at Boston MA [23 May 1844]
  Isaac of Gray ME & Elvira ALLEN at Portland ME [21 Jan 1847]
  James M of Anson ME & Mrs Abigail RUSSELL of Starks ME at Norridgewock ME [23 Nov 1839]
  Joanna & Francis FONTAN by D T PIKE Esq at Augusta ME [13 Dec 1849]
  Joel & Jane HUNT both of Readfield ME by Rev WEBBER [24 Jan 1834]
  John Capt of Madison ME & Vira HODSDON of Jay ME at North Anson ME [10 Jan 1850]
  John Q & Nancy A CAMPBELL at Cherryfield ME [27 May 1843]
  John R & Sarah KNOWLTON at Farmington ME [20 Dec 1849]
  John W & Mary J WISE of Topsham ME at Litchfield ME [27 Jul 1848]
  John & Roxana ADAMS in Madison ME [21 Feb 1834]

ADAMS (cont.) Joseph Capt of Bowdoinham ME & Hannah DUNLAP at Brunswick ME [19 Sept 1840]
Lemuel of Farmington ME & Mrs Experience B PRESSY at Mercer ME [27 June 1844]
Louisa S & Daniel CARR at Portland ME [31 Jul 1835]
Lucinda A & Charles E HAYES at Kittery ME [27 Mar 1845]
Lucy & Jacob LUFKIN of Rumford ME at Farmington ME [11 Dec 1851]
Margaret W & Isaac ROWELL at Litchfield ME [14 May 1846]
Martha K & Wm T LIBBY of Lowell MA at Buxton ME [24 Sept 1846]
Mary E & Walter R LITTLEFIELD at Brunswick ME [19 Sept 1844]
Mr J S & Harriet A JONES at Chelsea [25 Dec 1851]
Mr L S & Ann Maria HALL at Litchfield ME on 30th ult [19 Oct 1848]
Nancy of Madison ME & Lyman CHILDS of Jay ME at Embden ME [10 Jan 1850]
Nancy & Peter CORBETT by John A WOODS Esq at Farmington ME [28 Mar 1840]
Nathan 2d & Durinda S STARBIRD at Bowdoin ME [12 June 1851]
Olive F & Samuel H WATERMAN at Thomaston ME [11 Feb 1847]
Pamelia of Kennebunkport ME & Jesse WARREN of Hollis ME at K [8 Apr 1836]
Richard & Martha ROGERS at Topsham ME [4 Jan 1849]
Roxana & John ADAMS at Madison ME [21 Feb 1834]
Rufus of Chelmsford MA & Jane G COX of Bristol ME at Boston MA [27 Aug 1846]
Sally & John BURNHAM of Parsonsfield ME at Newfield ME [25 Mar 1847]
Samuel of Hallowell & Philomela JOHNSON of Winthrop ME on Sunday last by Rev D THURSTON at the Congregational Meeting House in Winthrop ME [20 Jul 1839]
Sarah Mrs & Capt Francis PERLEY of Winthrop ME on March 8th by Rev W A DREW at Augusta ME [22 Mar 1849]
Solomon Jr of Farmington ME & Martha SAWYER at Wilton ME [19 Sept 1844]
Susan & John MAYALL at Skowhegan ME [19 Aug 1843]
Tabitha & Joseph GERALD at Clinton ME [8 Aug 1840]
William of Canaan & Paulina FITZGERALD of York ME at York [23 Oct 1845]
William & Joanna LEIGHTON all of Steuben ME by Samuel MOORE Esq at Steuben [12 Feb 1842]

ADDAMS I E of Boston MA & Susan PIKE at Saco ME [9 Apr 1846]

ADDISON Sarah W & Samuel L LYFORD of Livermore ME at Dexter ME [13 Jul 1839]

ADDITON Bethiah & Flavius J PAGE of Winthrop ME at Dexter ME [12 June 1841]
Joseph Capt of Wilton ME & Emma HINDS of Livermore ME on May day by Rev G W QUINBY at Livermore [11 May 1839]
Josiah B & Eliza A JENNINGS only d/o Perez J Esq by Rev A BARROWS at Leeds ME on 5 May [13 May 1852]

ADERTON Rachel J & Alexander RIDLEY at Bowdoinham ME [25 Sept 1851]

ADLAM Samuel Jr & Susan T CUTTER both of Gardiner ME at Newport RI on 3 June [24 June 1852]

ADLAR Catherine & Edwin CORLISS at Eastport ME [16 Aug 1849]
ADLE Cornelius of Readfield ME & Mary A DUDLEY of Augusta ME at Hallowell ME [9 Oct 1845]
AGRY George Capt & Caroline HODGES both of Hallowell ME on 8th inst at New York [25 Sept 1841]
  Harriet & Franklin SCAMMON at Hallowell ME [21 Sept 1833]
  Thomas & Mary Ann EMERY at Fairfield ME [20 Dec 1849]
AIKEN Alvin & Elizabeth S WINSLOW both of Boston at (Augusta) ME on 28 Sept [12 Oct 1848]
AILES Adelia C of Philadelphia PA & Charles H FAIRBANKS, printer, formerly of Winthrop ME, June 2nd at Philadelphia [10 Jul 1845]
AKNOS Martha & Daniel MCDONALD at Eastport ME [8 Nov 1849]
ALBEE Elizabeth & William H STARLING at Damariscotta ME [19 Feb 1852]
  Frances & James A WOODBRIDGE at Hallowell ME [30 May 1844]
  Hannah of Wiscasset & Henry ADAMS at Boston [23 May 1844]
  Harriet & John FOYE by Rev A P HILLMAN at Wiscasset ME [5 Feb 1842]
  Henry A & Martha A BRAN at Hallowell ME [10 June 1852]
  Hiram & Lucy PUSHARD at Wiscasset ME [25 Feb 1847]
  Peter H & Eliza Ann SMITH both of Winthrop ME by Rev Hiram ALBEE at Hallowell ME [29 June 1848]
  Sarah & Daniel B PERKINS at Boston MA [11 Jul 1837]
ALBY Emeline H of Bethel ME & Horace CUMMINGS at Oxford ME [26 Dec 1844]
ALDEN Darius of Augusta ME & Bethiah S NICKERSON at Strong ME [30 Nov 1839]
  Gustava & Horace HUTCHINSON at Turner ME [18 Jan 1840]
  Silas & Mary PAGE of Winthrop ME at Jay ME [15 May 1851]
  Solomon H & Caroline HOSLEY at Livermore ME [30 Nov 1839]
ALDRICH Dorcas Jane & George RIGBY at Webster ME on June 6th [17 June 1852]
  Grosvener of Uxbridge MA & Joanna H SMITH at Farmington ME [13 Sept 1849]
ALEXANDER Benjamin B & Harriet FRYE at North Haven [20 Jul 1848]
  Charles & Cecelia WINSLOW at Bath ME [5 June 1845]
  Charles Dr of Orono ME & Achsah E ALLEN of Industry ME at Bangor ME [27 Feb 1851]
  Deborah R & O T MACUMBER of Concordia Parish LA at Farmington ME [2 Sept 1843]
  Eleanor & Thomas BROWN at Harpswell ME [5 Aug 1836]
  Elizabeth F of Topsham & Gould JEWELL of Brunswick ME at Topsham ME [16 Apr 1842]
  Ezekiel H & Lucy W SAMPSON at Vinalhaven ME [22 Jan 1846]
  George & Tryphosa CARSON at Belfast ME [18 June 1846]
  John of Litchfield ME & Albina S COX by Rev GRANT at Bowdoin ME [28 Jan 1843]
  Jordan & Abigail GODDARD of Brunswick ME at Topsham ME [24 Sept 1846]
  Joseph Capt of Brunswick ME & Mary G MOSHER at Gorham ME [12 June 1845]

ALEXANDER (cont.) Lorenzo of Brunswick ME & Mrs Louisa WILSON (the young lady whose husband was murdered about two years ago) of Harpswell at Harpswell ME [19 Dec 1844]
Margaret & George BARNES at Harpswell ME [17 Feb 1848]
Mary E & Joseph S DRINKWATER at Topsham ME [6 May 1843]
Mary E & Thomas BULLOCK at Northport ME [18 Sept 1851]
Minerva H & Capt N T THOMPSON at Bowdoin ME [17 Sept 1846]
ALIFF Margaret & William NOYES at Gardiner ME [21 Aug 1845]
Ruth & James LEARD both of Gardiner at Hallowell ME [9 Aug 1849]
ALLARD Thomas & Philena F MERRILL at Lewiston ME [2 Jan 1851]
ALLEN Abigail Mrs & Daniel ALLEN of Winthrop ME at Litchfield ME. "This is the third time the loving couple have come together." [1 Apr 1833]
Abraham W & Ruhama Ann PERRY at Minot ME [20 Jan 1837]
Achsah E of Industry ME & Dr Charles ALEXANDER of Orono ME at Bangor ME [27 Feb 1851]
Alice & Samuel ROBERTS at Rome ME [11 Feb 1843]
Amanda E & Edwin NORTON at Farmington ME [3 Apr 1841]
Amanda M & Reed W POWERS at Bowdoin ME [13 Jan 1848]
Andrew L of Ellsworth ME & Harriet S EDWARDS at Belfast ME [6 Jul 1848]
Areneth of Winthrop ME & Israel WILBUR of Augusta ME on the 22d ult by Eld Samuel FOGG at Winthrop [6 June 1834]
Barnabas of St Stevens New Brunswick, Canada & Hannah WAKEFIELD of Smithfield ME at Norridgewock ME [1 Oct 1846]
Benjamin H & Mehitable J ALLEN at Bath ME [1 Feb 1844]
Benjamin Jr of Winthrop ME & Betsey G BASFORD by Rev SPAULDING at Mt Vernon ME [25 Apr 1840]
Caleb W of Somerville MA & Clarissa LEAVETT at Bath ME [18 Jul 1844]
Catherine & Ransom HINKLEY of Bradley ME at Frankfort ME [12 Feb 1846]
Charles L & Martha BEVERAGE at Thomaston ME [15 Jan 1846]
Charles of Wayne ME & Susan E RICHARDS formerly of Milo ME at Boston MA [3 Aug 1848]
Charlotte J & Capt George T HOWE at Greene ME [14 Dec 1848]
Clarissa Mrs & Jason KING at Newport RI on the 4th inst [14 Nov 1840]
Cornelius & Mary MORREL of Hallowell ME by Rev Wm A DREW at Augusta ME [21 Nov 1834]
Cynthia & Duane MOWER at Greene ME [23 June 1852]
Daniel, grandson of Capt Elijah ALLEN who remarried on this same day & Charity CURTIS of Webster ME at Bowdoin ME [14 Nov 1844]
Daniel & Ann E LITTLEFIELD at Monmouth ME [18 Jul 1837]
Daniel & Mrs Abigail ALLEN of Winthrop ME at Litchfield ME "This is the third time the loving couple have come together" [1 Apr 1833]
Deborah H & Samuel F ALLEN on 8 Jul by E SMITH Esq at Augusta ME [12 Jul 1849]
Dorcas & William JOY of Orono ME at Bangor ME on 4th inst [17 Dec 1842]
Ebenezer S & Sophia E MARR at Bath ME [17 Feb 1848]
Edmund of Hartford ME & Hannah BUCK at Sumner ME [29 Jan 1846]
Edwin & Sarah ALLEY at Dresden ME [28 March 1850]
Eleanor & Martin GAY, M.D., of Boston MA at Gardiner ME [31 Oct 1844]

ALLEN (cont.) Elijah Capt ae 78 & Mrs Mary GRANCE of Freeport ME ae 75 at Bowdoin ME [14 Nov 1844]
    Eliza A L of Poland ME & Benjamin NOYES of Falmouth ME by Rev Thomas WILLIAMS at Poland ME on 21st ult [15 Jan 1842]
    Eliza A & Col Samuel GILPATRICK at Limerick ME [20 Feb 1851]
    Elizabeth J & David E CHADWICK at Lewiston ME [23 June 1852]
    Elizabeth T, d/o Wm ALLEN Jr Esq of Norridgewock ME, & John S ABBOT Esq of Thomaston ME at Norridgewock ME [23 Oct 1835]
    Elizabeth & Cyrus H FOLSOM at Mt Vernon ME [1 Aug 1840]
    Elvira & Isaac ADAMS of Gray ME at Portland ME [21 Jan 1847]
    Emeline H of Litchfield ME & Josiah E TOWLE of Monmouth ME at Litchfield [8 Jul 1843]
    Emily J & Amos WELTS at East Winthrop ME on 10th Mar [18 Mar 1852]
    Frederick, M.D., & Charlotte WALES d/o Benj WALES Esq at Hallowell ME [18 June 1842]
    Gilbert of Fayette ME & Merriam MORSE at Carthage ME [6 Nov 1851]
    Harriet A & Luther GRAY on Dec 9 by Eld N F NASON at Plymouth [27 Dec 1849]
    Harriet ae 11 years & Master Edward TAPPAN ae 15 at Hempstead Harbor L.I. [4 Sept 1838]
    Harriett Newell, d/o the late Rev Wm ALLEN, & Rev William POOL of Whitefield ME at Jefferson ME [5 Aug 1836]
    Horatio Gates Dr of Winthrop ME & Sarah Jackson PETTINGILL at Bath ME [26 Oct 1833]
    Huldah & William P PAGE of Sidney ME on 15 Feb at Augusta ME [1 Mar 1849]
    Isadore R & Virgil SCRIBNER at Hallowell ME [28 Sept 1848]
    J S & Marietta TOLMAN at Thomaston ME [9 Oct 1845]
    James B of Hermon ME & Susan G PAGE at Monroe ME [27 May 1852]
    James & Mrs Sophilia SAVAGE at Bath ME [19 Dec 1834]
    Jane M & Isaac HACKER at Brunswick ME on the 19th inst [29 Aug 1834]
    John of Alfred & Caroline P HILL at Lyman [1 Jul 1852]
    Joseph H & Adeline D McLELLAN at Bath ME [28 Oct 1847]
    Joseph O & Mrs Mary CHICK both of Litchfield ME at Monmouth ME [21 Mar 1844]
    Lavina & Benjamin ELWELL at Windham ME [10 Aug 1848]
    Lorenzo B Pastor of the First Baptist Church & Nancy P PRINCE youngest d/o the late Hon Hezekiah PRINCE all of Thomaston ME on Weds evening Oct 19 by Rev Job WASHBURN at Thomaston [28 Oct 1842]
    Lucretia of Alexandria DC & William LEEMAN of Wiscasset ME by Rev Mr JOHNSTON at Alexandria on 24th ult [16 Jan 1841]
    Lucy T of Turner ME & Cyrus DAVENPORT by Rev C FULLER at Wayne ME [6 Sept 1849]
    Lydia J & Jos PAUL at E Thomaston ME [25 Oct 1849]
    Margaret J of Augusta ME & William K JEWETT at Portland ME [24 Oct 1844]
    Marietta M d/o Horatio G ALLEN Esq of Bath ME & Ferdinand LAMBERT at Nemours DE [12 Feb 1842]
    Mary Jane, d/o Rev John ALLEN, & Robert STUDLEY at China ME [16 May 1834]

ALLEN (cont.) Mary P of Augusta ME & Nathaniel H LOWELL of Windham ME at Augusta [13 Nov 1845]
Mehitable J & Benj H ALLEN at Bath ME [1 Feb 1844]
Miss E L, d/o late Joseph ALLEN Esq. & J C THOMPSON of Philadelphia PA by Rev Wm D HOWARD at Frankford PA [25 Jan 1849]
Nancy Ann & Capt Redford TALLMAN at Richmond ME on 6th inst [17 Oct 1844]
Newell late of Foxcroft ME & Gertrude A HALL at Parma Centre NY [21 Mar 1844]
Olive C of Freeport ME & Albion K P GILPATRICK of Webster ME at Brunswick ME [25 Feb 1843]
Samuel B & Mary A HANSON at Smithfield [5 Apr 1849]
Samuel F & Deborah H ALLEN 8 July at Augusta ME by E SMITH Esq [12 Jul 1849]
Sarah Jane & Orrin HOXIE at Fairfield ME [1 Jul 1847]
Sarah N & John APPLETON Esq of Bangor at Northfield [7 Mar 1834]
Sarah W & G W MASON at Hallowell ME on 11th inst [21 Dec 1848]
Sarah & Jefferson WILSON at Brunswick ME [11 Feb 1847]
Silas & Olive BROWN of Shad Island at Brunswick ME [3 Aug 1848]
Sophronia M & James C WATT at Lubec ME [10 Jan 1850]
Stephen Rev of NY State & Rachel STURDEVANT d/o Ephriam S Esq of Cumberland at Cumberland ME [21 Aug 1838]
Sumner & Hannah DODGE of Thomaston at Montville ME [25 May 1839]
Temperence P & George THOMAS at Belmont ME [22 Feb 1849]
Thorndike Jr & Lydia R DAMON at Stetson [20 May 1847]
William, Preceptor of Thornton Academy, & Amanda C COLE at Saco ME [6 Mar 1845]
William H, Principal of the Augusta High School, & Martha Ann RICHARDSON of Toronto at Toronto UC on the 20th ult [14 Oct 1836]
ALLENWOOD Francis F & Nancy BICKNELL at Belmont ME [12 Aug 1847]
ALLEY Hannah & G W FARR Dr at Lynn MA [28 Dec 1848]
Harriet Newell & Hezekiah BLINN both of Boston at Bath ME [13 Aug 1846]
James H of Winslow ME & Lucy R JOHNSON at Albion ME on 11 Mar by P TINKHAM Esq [20 Mar 1851]
Sarah & Edwin ALLEN at Dresden ME [28 Mar 1850]
ALLING Helen M of Salisbury CT & Hon Joseph C NOYES of Eastport ME at Washington City [24 Jul 1838]
AMBROSE George H & Elizabeth M T LITTLE at Lewiston Falls ME [28 Oct 1847]
AMEE Agnes & Eld John STEVENS of Bath ME at Gardiner ME [3 June 1847]
AMES Almira F & John W KNOWLTON both of Swanville ME at Belfast ME [29 May 1845]
Caroline H & Charles H BROWN at Clinton ME [22 Jan 1842]
Caroline S & John W WHITTEN at Hallowell ME [1 Apr 1847]
Catharine H & Russell A CUMMINGS of Winthrop ME at Hallowell ME [18 Apr 1850]
Daniel of Sangerville ME & Mrs Mary SHAW of Sebec ME at Swanville ME [26 Dec 1837]
Daniel W of Oldtown ME & Sarah E WING of Bangor ME at Lowell MA? [25 Sept 1851]

AMES (cont.) Edmund & Clarissa Ann SMITH at Norway ME [11 Feb 1847]
Eliakim of Oldtown ME & Eliza M BRAGG on Aug 9 by William BOWLER Esq at China ME [16 Aug 1849]
Elizabeth H & Rev Jos RUSSELL both of Farmington ME at Strong ME [15 Feb 1849]
Elizabeth & Charles Hubbard FOSTER at Winthrop ME on 17th June [23 June 1852]
Hannah Mrs & Bradford WINSLOW at Damariscotta ME [1 Apr 1852]
Harriet T & Alden BAILEY at Wiscasset ME [4 Mar 1847]
Henry & Mary A WELLS both of Belfast ME by Rev S G SARGENT at Belfast ME [3 Dec 1842]
Isaac & Sarah H LAMBERT at Skowhegan ME [29 Jul 1852]
John J of Calais ME & Emily BALCH at Lubec ME [20 June 1844]
Lucia Elvira & Moses L PAINE of Jay ME at Chesterville ME [4 Apr 1850]
Lucy & Clement P RING at Lewiston ME [6 Dec 1849]
Margaret E & James TODD at Belfast ME [8 Jul 1836]
Mary C & James N HALL Jr at Belfast ME [3 Sept 1846]
Mary E & Robert G HANDY by Rev BUTLER at Hallowell ME on 21st [1 Jan 1842]
Nancy P & Oliver J CONANT at Thomaston ME [6 Jan 1848]
Nancy & Charles BRIDGE at Gardiner ME on 10th inst [28 Dec 1848]
Phineas & Jemima SAUNDERS at Dover ME? [15 Aug 1844]
Prudence L & Samuel WINSLOW at Freeman ME [18 May 1848]
Rachel & John WOOD at Hallowell ME [29 Apr 1847]
Ruth & Jesse DUNBAR of Palermo ME at Jefferson ME [10 Jan 1850]
Sarah A of Jefferson ME & Edmund J SMITH of Hallowell ME on Thanksgiving Day morning by Rev JUDD at Augusta ME [9 Dec 1847]
Sarah Ann & Sylvanus PRATT at Phillips ME on Feb 15th [2 Mar 1848]
Susan of Belchertown & C W CHAPMAN Esq of NY, Foreign Agent of the Southhampton Bachelor Society, and last but one of its members at Belchertown [4 Sept 1838]
Susan & Thomas F NORTON at Farmington ME [11 Apr 1850]
Warren A & Abby CHILDS at Farmington ME [24 May 1849]

ANDERSON Belinda R & David MITCHELL at Freedom ME [3 Apr 1851]
Elijah V & Sarah F MERO of Union ME at Warren ME [29 Jul 1852]
Eliza Mrs & Jacob GARDNER Jr at Cornville ME by Elder RUSSELL [12 June 1851]
Elizabeth M & Capt D COLLINS formerly of Portland ME at Collinsville IL [2 Apr 1846]
Elizabeth M & Truman H SAWYER at Norridgewock ME [27 Jan 1848]
H J Capt & Catherine C WADLIN of Belfast ME at Brooklyn NY [5 Jul 1849]
Hannah Elizabeth of Warren ME & Capt Horace WINCHENBAUCH by Rev John DODGE at Waldoboro ME [14 Jan 1843]
John C & Mary F WINSLOW at Bath ME [5 Dec 1844]
John of Limington ME & Albarona F COFFIN at Limerick ME [22 Apr 1847]
Margaret J & J H NASH of Fall River MA at Webster ME [16 Sept 1847]
Mary A/E & Calvin P JORDEN at Ellsworth ME [9 Jul 1846]
Mary & John FAWETT at Robbinston ME [17 Apr 1835]
Thomas A & Sabrina H SMITH d/o the officiating clergyman, Rev James SMITH, on July 1st at Fayette ME [19 Jul 1849]

ANDERSON (cont.) William of Hallowell ME & Sarah TIBBITS of Augusta ME on the 21st ult by E K BUTLER Esq at Hallowell ME [2 Jan 1838]
ANDREWS Arthur & Elizabeth HOWARD at Warren ME [13 Mar 1841]
 Charles G & Ruth A HILTON at Corinna ME [28 Jan 1847]
 Charles Hon, Speaker of the House of Representatives & Persis, youngest d/o Wm SIBLEY Esq on 22nd ult by Rev John TRUE at Freedom ME [9 Jul 1842]
 Daniel G & Mercy L SMITH at Thomaston ME [7 Aug 1845]
 Everett & Mary FOY at Gardiner ME [21 Mar 1850]
 Ezekiel ae 18 & Mrs Ann C DEARBORN ae 30 at Corinna ME [11 Apr 1844]
 Horace A & Sarah PORTER at Augusta ME [18 Jul 1837]
 James H & Lucy A GREEN both of Eastport ME at Perry ME [9 Dec 1836]
 John E of Boston MA & Mary H BRIGGS at Hampden ME [14 August 1851]
 Lydia M & Thomas M BAKER at Gardiner ME [9 Jan 1851]
 M C & Elizabeth C WAKEFIELD at Thomaston ME [4 June 1846]
 Margaret B of Gardiner ME & John H RICE at Hallowell ME [12 Dec 1844]
 Martha Antenetter & Daniel RAFTER of Jefferson ME at Warren ME [13 Mar 1841]
 Martha Jane & Calvin S CHASE at Pleasant Ridge ME? [13 Dec 1849]
 Rachel E of Woodstock ME & Samuel W DUNHAM at Paris ME [22 Mar 1849]
 Sarah & John W GATCHELL both of Waldo ME at Augusta ME on 25th ult [16 Jan 1845]
 Seth & Harriet JONES at Warren ME [28 June 1849]
 Sophia of Warren ME & James VOSE of Thomaston ME at Cushing ME [4 Feb 1833]
 Stephen of Waterville ME & Emily HAYWOOD by Rev Daniel FULLER at Winthrop ME [9 Nov 1833]
 Sullivan & Olivia GRAY at Paris ME [23 May 1840]
 Susan M & Dr George L PEASLEE of Wilton ME at Rumford ME [28 June 1849]
ANGOVE Asa B & Mary D MEGUIRE both of Sebec ME at Foxcroft ME [4 Sept 1851]
 Benjamin G & Huldah MEGUIRE both of Sebec ME at Foxcroft ME [4 Sept 1851]
ANNIS Ellison & Eliza J BARTER both of Camden ME at Goose River ME [1 Apr 1852]
 John Jr & Mehitable BRIER at Goose River [29 Jan 1852]
ANTHONY George W & Mary Ann DEALAND at Hallowell ME [5 Mar 1846]
 Joseph & Jane W HUNT d/o William HUNT on Thurs eve last by Rev TAPPAN at Augusta ME [17 Oct 1844]
APPERBY Sarah & Charles P STETSON at Brunswick ME [30 Dec 1843]
APPLEBY Ann Eliza & Myrick BIBBER at Eastport ME [29 Jul 1836]
 Elizabeth & Fergus POTTER at Eastport ME [11 Nov 1847]
APPLETON Elizabeth P & Shelton L HALL Esq of Rockford IL at Portland ME [18 Sept 1845]
 John Esq of Bangor ME & Sarah N ALLEN at Northfield [7 Mar 1834]
 Sarah P d/o John W A Esq & John GOODNOW Esq of Hiram ME at Portland ME [30 Jan 1845]

ARCHABLE Jane Isabella & C L SPRAGUE at Bath ME [22 Jul 1836]
ARCHER J W & Sarah MORTON at Lincoln ME [1 Apr 1847]
AREY Ebenezer & Caska DYER at Thomaston ME [27 Apr 1848]
    James Capt & Eliza T PIERCE of Belfast ME at Frankfort ME [22 Jan 1846]
    Mary C & Richard S BLAISDELL at E Thomaston ME [8 Oct 1846]
    Nathaniel & Eliza Ann BAKER at Hampden ME [23 Dec 1836]
    Nancy T & Isaac S ELLIOTT at Belfast ME [12 Aug 1852]
ARMSTRONG Peter & Sarah A SHAW of Gardiner ME at Phipsburg ME [23 June 1852]
    Ebenezer of Portland ME & Mary L DINSMORE of Cape Elizabeth ME at Cape Eliz [23 May 1844]
    Hiram & Sarah SPRAGUE at Richmond ME [8 Aug 1844]
    Lucinda S & Eld John HOWELL at Readfield ME [9 Jul 1846]
ARNO John & Elizabeth C BLAKE both of Monmouth ME at Litchfield ME [16 Jan 1845]
ARNOLD Albion P & Harriet COURIER at Readfield ME [20 June 1834]
    Augusta & Anna BOSWORTH at Bath ME [27 May 1852]
    Columbus & Anna SEVERANCE both of Augusta at Skowhegan ME [24 Jul 1845]
    Cyrus T & Lucy A HASKELL at Farmington ME [3 Oct 1844]
    Danville A & Clara A JUDKINS on Jan 1st by Rev W A DREW at Augusta ME [10 Jan 1850]
    Eloisa G of Hope ME & Amasa SHEPHARD of Jefferson ME at Whitefield ME [14 March 1840]
    Eveline S & Stephen W LAUGHTON at Appleton ME [24 June 1847]
    Jane & Simon G WHITTEMORE both of Foxcroft ME at Dover ME [23 May 1844]
    Maria H & Weston HARDY both of Bremen ME at Thomaston ME [5 Feb 1846]
    Mary S & Rev A B ROBBINS of Muscatine Iowa at Monmouth ME [9 Oct 1851]
    Rhoda & Hiram HAMMONS at Dixmont ME [7 Jan 1847]
    Samuel D & Sarah PHILBRICK at Skowhegan ME [8 Jan 1839]
    Sarah E of Mercer ME & George W SHAW of Cincinnati OH at Norridgewock ME [15 May 1838]
ARRAS Sarah B & William HODGDON at Bath ME [23 Apr 1846]
ARRIS Julia A & Charles BAILEY by Rev C FULLER at Hallowell ME [20 Mar 1845]
    Wentworth of Lisbon ME & Mrs Martha P ATWOOD of Poland ME at Minot ME [9 Apr 1842]
ARTHUR Henry & Mary A P DOUGLASS at Hallowell ME [15 Feb 1849]
ASHFORD Anthony C & Martha HILTON June 15th by A COOMBS Esq at Windsor ME [8 Jul 1852]
    Apphia C & Isaac S HALL at Windsor ME [8 Jul 1852]
ASHLEY William of Salem ae 84 & Mrs Polly WEEKES ae 70 wid of the late Dr WEEKES of Northam England Dec 22nd at Salem [16 Jan 1841]
ASIEL Mr J of (Augusta) ME & Henrietta STOCK of (New York City) at New York City on Apr 27th [11 May 1848]
ASPENWALL Joseph C Rev of the ME Conference & Mary DAGGETT at Bangor ME [2 May 1837]

ATHERN Alice J & Capt Richard RICH at Bath ME [14 Nov 1834]
ATHEARN John & Eliza J FOLSOM by L G SMITH Esq at Starks ME on 6th Apr [13 Apr 1848]
ATHERTON Margaret W & Abiel W TINKHAM at Portland ME [7 Jan 1847]
ATKINS Charles W of Mt Vernon ME & Mary G STUART of Augusta ME at Readfield ME [24 June 1847]
    Henry & Lydia YOUNG at Corinna ME [28 Mar 1850]
    James Capt & Olive J GORHAM both of Hallowell ME by Rev D FORBES at Hallowell ME on 19th ult [8 June 1839]
    Louis [sic; see p. 346, *History of Winthrop ME*, by E.S. Stackpole, should read "Lois"] (Miss) & Calvin DEARBORN by Rev Mr FOSTER Mon evening Jul 31 at Winthrop ME [5 Aug 1843]
    Lucinda d/o Rev Charles ATKINS of Mt Vernon ME & Johnson GOVE of Readfield at Mt Vernon [13 Mar 1838]/or Moses J GOVE of Readfield at Mt Vernon [3 Apr 1838]
    Lucy & Calvin A RICHARDSON both of Winthrop ME by Rev G W QUINBY at Livermore ME [20 Jul 1839]
ATKINSON Benjamin F & Rachel HACKER at Brunswick ME [19 June 1845]
    Elisha of New Sharon ME & Lucy T CUSHING of Winthrop ME by Rev David THURSTON on Wed last at Winthrop ME [6 Feb 1835]
    Eliza Mrs of Buxton ME & Elder James SAWYER of Saco ME at Saco ME [15 May 1851]
    Ellen & Albert WILLIAMS at North Anson ME [15 Jul 1852]
    James & Martha CROSBY at Chesterville ME [16 Mar 1839]
    Maria B & Howard B WYMAN at Madison ME [30 Nov 1848]
    Mary E & Joseph W BURNS of Hollis ME at Buxton ME [15 Jul 1847]
    Mary & Samuel BALENTINE of Hallowell ME at Chesterville ME [18 Mar 1847]
    Moses & Mrs M A WILLITS at Canaan ME [30 Oct 1851]
    Nancy S & Dr William MANNING at South Berwick ME [20 Jul 1848]
    Sally & J H GOODWIN at Montville ME [16 Feb 1839]
    Susanna Mrs of Corrinna ME & Benjamin SINKLER of Levant ME at Newport ME [13 Jul 1839]
    Thomas M of Mercer ME & Mrs Mary I TOBEY of Fairfield ME at Mercer ME on 14 Jan [29 Jan 1852] & [12 Feb 1852]
    W H & Laura A BERRY at Wayne ME [24 Dec 1846]
ATWATER William & Priscilla LEIGHTON at Steuben ME [2 May 1837]
ATWOOD/ATTWOOD Adeline S of New Gloucester ME & Edwin DOW at Poland ME [16 May 1844]
    Anna & Jonah DUNN at Mt Vernon ME [5 Mar 1846]
    Charles B & Emily D IRISH at Buckfield ME [2 Sept 1847]
    George M & Emily Ann WHITTIER at Readfield ME [6 Nov 1838]
    George M & Lucy WHITTIER at Gardiner ME [30 Jan 1845]
    J J of Greenville ME & Alice P NICHOLS at Abbot ME [30 Dec 1847]
    Joanna T of Durham ME & John R WILSON Esq of Cincinnati OH at Lisbon ME [18 Sept 1845]
    John J of Greenville ME & Alice P NICHOLS at Abbot ME [20 Jan 1848]
    Margaret Ann & Harlow H SAWYER on Sunday Sept 26 by Rev C FULLER at North Wayne ME [7 Oct 1847]
    Martha Ann & Charles J LIBBY at Skowhegan ME [3 Oct 1840]

ATWOOD (cont.) Martha P of Poland ME & Wentworth ARRIS of Lisbon ME at Minot ME [9 Apr 1842]
    Sophia A & Hiram TUTTLE at Canaan ME [10 Sept 1846]
AUBENS Charity & William GODFREY at Bath ME [1 Apr 1847]
    Humphrey & Jane FOSTER of Brunswick ME at Bath ME [22 Jan 1836]
AUBINS Nancy M & Benjamin OWEN at Bath ME [26 Sept 1840]
AULD James Capt & Adaline B GREENLEAF at Westport ME [7 Jan 1847]
AUMOCK William C & Ann L HAYNES at Saco ME [20 Jul 1848]
AUSPLUND Stephen of Prospect ME & Sarah H RANA at Thorndike ME [12 Aug 1852]
AUSTIN Addison of Waldoboro ME & Mary L TEAGUE of Newcastle ME at Providence [25 Sept 1851]
    Agnes & Leonard P SMITH both of Canton ME by Rev George W QUINBY on 2nd inst at Canton [25 May 1839]
    Angeline Mrs & Henry CHAPMAN at Nobleboro ME [4 Feb 1843]
    Benjamin D & Mary Elizabeth HUNT at Augusta ME [18 Feb 1847]
    Caroline M & Charles W THOMPSON of Hartford ME at Canton ME [27 Nov 1845]
    Clorinda & Samuel CONE both of Skowhegan ME at Canaan ME [20 Sept 1849]
    Cyrus & Thankful SNOW of (Augusta) ME by Isaiah ROLLINS Esq at Belgrade ME on 18th inst [21 Sept 1848]
    Elijah H & Ruth HUSSEY at China ME [17 June 1847]
    Eliza Ann & Benjamin D SWEET at Farmington ME [18 Nov 1843]
    Eliza & Willard R PAGE at Belgrade ME [14 Dec 1833]
    Esther & Barnabas FRENCH at China ME [4 Jan 1834]
    James T & Almira L LUNT at Brunswick ME [6 Dec 1849]
    Jane C & James BURBANK by Rev A MOORE at Augusta ME on 6th inst [17 Apr 1845]
    Luther D of Salem & Philena P WILSON at Augusta ME [4 Nov 1847]
    Lydia & Michael H SCRUTON of Augusta at Belgrade ME on 21st ult [2 Oct 1845]
    M & Elenor BARTLETT at Thomaston ME [6 Mar 1838]
    Martha & Joshua LINCOLN at Newcastle ME [15 Oct 1846]
    Mary of Parkman ME & Isaac COBB of Abbot at Parkman ME [16 Nov 1833]
    Mary & Thomas PORTER at China ME [26 Feb 1846]
    Mary & William A JENKINS of Lee at Great Falls NH [25 Feb 1843]
    Mr S Harris & Louisa EATON d/o Amherst EATON Esq at Boston MA on 22 Oct [6 Nov 1851]
    Sophia & Silas BAKER of Weld ME on 30 April by Isaiah VICKERY at Parkman ME [10 May 1849]
AVERAL Charles G & Calatia CHAPMAN both of Damariscotta ME at Wiscasset ME [20 Mar 1851]
AVERILL Austin & Martha KENNEY at Newcastle ME [22 Apr 1852]
    David & Martha Ann MORTON at Portland ME [13 Mar 1845]
    Emeline K & Ebenezer DODGE at New Castle ME [27 May 1852]
    Gerry & Margaret E LOVETT at Portland ME [25 Apr 1844]
    Hannah & Loring FRENCH at Saco ME [17 Sept 1846]
    Henry of Northfield & Mehitable M BURPEE at Machias Port ME [26 Aug 1847]
    Hiram & Mary J SCOTT at Readfield ME [15 Feb 1849]

AVERILL (cont.) J Capt of San Francisco CA & Anna B FOOTE youngest d/o Hon Erastus FOOTE 4 July by Rev U BALKHAM at Wiscasset ME [15 Jul 1852]
Samuel of Northfield Washington Co ME & Mrs Eleanor A BURPEE of Eastport at Machias ME [9 Jul 1846]
AVERY Emeline P & Richard F PERKINS Esq of Augusta ME by Rev COLE at Hallowell ME [23 Dec 1843]
Emeline & Loring HARTFORD at Georgetown ME [5 Nov 1846]
Hannah E of Vienna ME & Cyrus H GRAY at Readfield ME [11 Apr 1840]
John & Mary R SHEA at Phipsburg ME [22 Apr 1852]
Julia A & Stephen P MARDEN of W Cambridge MA on 23 Sept at Whitefield ME [27 Sept 1849]
Peter & Rosanna PEPPER at Bath ME [30 Jul 1846]
Sarah of Pittston ME & Darius ROCKWOOD of Belgrade ME by Asaph R NICHOLS Esq at Augusta ME [4 June 1846]
AXTELL James & Mary Ann JONES at Augusta ME [30 Jan 1838]
AYER Almira B & John H HORR at Saco ME [10 Sept 1846]
Annice C & B B Stevens of Unity ME at Freedom ME [3 May 1849]
Benjamin of Freedom ME & Sarah FAIRBANKS on 13 Apr by Rev Daniel FULLER at Winthrop ME [9 May 1834]
Daniel of Vassalboro ME & Emily GIFFORD on 23 Jan by D Blin FULLER Esq at Albion ME [7 Feb 1850]
Eliza T & Rufus C VOSE at Palermo ME [13 June 1837]
Priscilla & Samuel H HINDS of Kingfield ME at Embden ME [8 Oct 1846]
Samuel of Embden ME & Caroline J CROSBY at Waterville ME [22 Feb 1840]
Samuel & Julia A NICHOLS at Pittston ME [23 Dec 1847]
AYRES George F of E Thomaston ME & Harriet L HOSMER at Camden ME [28 June 1849]
James & Harriet PERKINS of Bridgton ME at Salem MA [21 Jan 1847]

- B -

BABB Andrew & Lucy A BERRY at Saco ME [5 Jul 1849]
Julia A & Eph WILSON of Monmouth ME at Litchfield ME [8 Feb 1849]
Moses of Orono ME & Nancy J TIBBETTS of Harmony ME at Dexter ME [17 Jul 1845]
Rosanna & Van Rensselaer LOVEJOY of Gardiner ME at Boston MA [8 Feb 1849]
Sarah E & Samuel McLELLAN at Sacarappa ME [4 Jun 1846]
BABBAGE Deborah & Seth WEBB at Deer Isle ME [18 Feb 1847]
BABBET Isaac T of Oakham MA & Ann PACKARD at Winthrop ME [12 Jun 1838]
BABCOCK Anna E & Geo STARRETT both of Augusta ME at Providence RI 27th ult [10 May 1849]
Francis & Mary Ann SOULE at Portland ME [8 Feb 1844]
John C & Harriet N BROOKINGS at Pittston ME [31 May 1849]
Lucy Ann & William T PIERCE of Windsor at Augusta ME [7 Dec 1839]
William R Rev Rector of Christ's Church of Gardiner ME & Catherine PIERCE d/o Hon Dutee J P at Newport RI [14 Nov 1840]

BABSON Abigail & Edwin A NORTON of Portland ME at Wiscasset ME [16 Nov 1833]
　Catherine of Wiscasset ME & Wm B GRANT Jr of Gardiner ME at Wiscasset [6 Nov 1841]
BACHE Horatio & Martha HUSSEY at Biddeford ME [27 Jul 1848]
BACHELDER see **BATCHELDER**
BACHELER/BACHELLER Hannah & George CHAMBERLAIN at Fayette ME [23 Sept 1843]
　Nathan of Machias ME & Mary WILLIAMS of Mercer ME by Rev Mr FARRINGTON at Mercer ME [14 May 1842]
BACKUS Octavia J of Farmington ME & David DAVIS Esq of Edgartown MA at New York NY [20 Mar 1845]
BACON Alvan, M.D., & Mary A MAXWELL both of Biddeford ME at Worcester MA [20 Dec 1849]
　Benjamin of Greenwood & Lucy THURLOW of Poland ME at Poland ME [21 Mar 1840]
　Betsey ae 43 & Orson LANE ae 21 by John LEATHHEAD [sic] Esq 14th inst at Anson ME [26 Feb 1836]
　George of Boston MA & Olivia BUCKMINSTER d/o Samuel C GRANT Esq at Hallowell ME [9 Oct 1845]
　Harriet (Mrs) & Greenfield LOW at Lincoln [3 Aug 1848]
　Josiah Esq & Hannah BUTTERFIELD by Elijah WOOD Jr Esq 24th ult at Hartland ME [1 Jan 1836]
　Lucinda & William BEAL at (Winthrop ME) on 13 Aug [22 Aug 1840]
　Olive D of Greenwood & Hiram YOUNG of Bethel ME at Norway ME [21 Aug 1845]
　Ruth W & Gen S T STRICKLAND of Bangor ME at Buxton ME [7 May 1846]
BADGER Anne S d/o Nathanial BADGER Esq of Brunswick ME & John R HOUGHTON of Boston MA at Brunswick ME [2 Sept 1843]
　Apphia A & E Wallis HALL at Kittery ME [3 Aug 1848]
　Jane & Washington GILBERT of Saco ME at Brunswick ME [27 Jun 1844]
　Samuel Capt of Kittery ME & Lois M STRATTON of Albion ME at Newcastle ME [1 Mar 1849]
　William G of Bangor ME & Harriet Jane KINGSLEY at Boston ME [21 Nov 1844]
　William S & Susan EMERY on Nov 30 by Rev S JUDD at Augusta ME [10 Dec 1846]
BAGLEY John P Capt & Mrs Sarah P COTTRELL at Belfast ME [10 Oct 1844]
　John P Capt & Miss Myra E ROGERS at Belfast ME [23 Dec 1847]
BAILEY also see BAYLEY
　Abigail C of Minot ME & Samuel FOGG of Greene ME by Rev D T STEVENS at Minot ME [4 May 1839]
　Alden & Harriet T AMES at Wiscasset ME [4 Mar 1847]
　Almira & David WRIGHT at Windsor [25 Mar 1847]
　Andrew J & Mary E NUTTER at Wiscasset ME [3 Feb 1848]
　Anna of Auburn ME & Jeremiah COLE at Lewiston ME [24 May 1849]
　Caroline L of Pittston & Albert MARWICK of Portland ME at Pittston [2 Oct 1845]

Marriage Notices from the "Maine Farmer"

BAILEY (cont.) Charles M & Sophia D JONES at Friends meeting-house at Winthrop ME [14 Nov 1844]
Charles & Emily L SEEKINS at Windsor ME [21 Sept 1848]
Charles & Julia A ARRIS by Rev C FULLER at Hallowell ME [20 Mar 1845]
Daniel & Hannah S GAULT by Jere BURGIN Esq at Eastport ME [6 Feb 1845]
Dexter S of Foxcroft ME & Joanna A HERRING at Guilford ME [3 Jan 1850]
Eben Jr & Mrs Eliza MURRAY at (Augusta ME) on 25 Mar [8 Apr 1852]
Elizabeth & William COBURN of New Sharon ME at Farmington ME [16 Jan 1851]
Ella & Abial MAYERS at Bath ME [20 Jun 1844]
Erastus W & Mary C LITTLEFIELD at Foxcroft ME [6 May 1852]
Giles BAILEY Rev Pastor of the Universalist Church in Brunswick ME & Susan MURPHY at Alstead NH [6 Feb 1845]
Giles BAILEY Rev Pastor of the Universalist Society of Winthrop ME & Jane T DAMON of Lynn MA by Rev L WILLIS at Lynn MA [6 Jun 1840]
Harriet of Greene ME & Thomas S PULLEN of Winthrop ME at Greene ME [20 May 1836]
Henry E of Maxfield & Miss M L ELLIS at Farmington ME [2 Nov 1848]
James 2d & Sarah W SOULE at Woolwich ME [13 Jul 1848]
James T & Mary Jane HUFF at Hallowell ME [20 May 1847]
John C of Maxfield & Elizabeth HOLLOM at Sebec ME [21 Aug 1851]
Lenora V & George W STEVENS of Pittston at Gardiner ME [12 Nov 1846]
Lewis E & Mrs Julia A FENNEL at Gardiner ME [6 Jan 1848]
Louisa & Franklin RICHARDSON both of Pittston ME at Hallowell ME [18 Oct 1849]
Lydia G & Rev N B ROGERS of Hallowell ME in Hopkinton NH [25 Oct 1849]
Lydia J & Capt Abner J MOORES at Gardiner ME [14 Mar 1850]
Martin K of Cohasset & Lois S LOWELL of Farmington ME at Farmington ME [17 Jul 1841]
Mary Ann & Robert EDGECOMB both of Litchfield ME by Elder Wm O GRANT at Litchfield ME [21 Mar 1840]
Mary & William W NEVENS at Sweden ME [19 Feb 1852]
Miss & Augustus K WING at Phillips ME [3 Feb 1848]
Moses & Betsey JONES at the Friends meeting house of Winthrop ME [25 Apr 1840] & [5 Dec 1840]
Philena & Dennis MARR of Gardiner ME at Augusta ME [20 Nov 1841]
Sarah A & Luther C CUMMINGS of Eddington at Milford [1 Nov 1849]
Sarah E & Rulof DODGE at Portland ME [2 May 1837]
Sarah Jane & Wm S DONNELL at Bath ME [5 Dec 1844]
Silas of Topsfield & Lydia PENDLETON of Calais ME at Eastport ME [14 Aug 1845]
Susan J & Capt Alexander McFADDEN at Wiscasset ME [20 Feb 1845]
Timothy of Brunswick ME & Mary E MAIN at Bath ME [25 Mar 1847]
William Rev of Buxton ME & Pamela W CARTER of Parkman ME at Parkman ME [16 May 1840]
Willoughby H of Harrington ME & Nancy BRACKET of Brunswick ME at Brunswick ME [28 May 1842]

BAIRD Joanna & Hiram C MITCHELL at Canton ME [23 Oct 1851]

BAIRD (cont.) Sally & Charles FOSTER at Canton ME [3 Jun 1847]
BAIRNEE Nathaniel & Bethia SMITH at St Albans ME [16 Jan 1838]
BAKER Abigail J & Robinson A DAVIS at Farmington ME [9 Mar 1848]
    Adeline & Dr Albert PEARSON at Albion ME [24 Jun 1843]
    Ann B of Augusta ME & James WEBSTER of Orono ME at Albion ME on 30th Dec by Rev Z MANTER [23 Jan 1851]
    Ashford of Weymouth MA & Julia A HOLMES of Bangor ME at Turner ME [30 Nov 1839]
    Benjamin F Esq of Norridgewock ME & Nancy A MORRILL at Athens ME [1 May 1851]
    Caroline B & Howard D WALDRON at Buckfield ME [23 Aug 1849]
    Caroline E & Stephen L TOBEY of Waterville ME at New Sharon ME [5 Aug 1843]
    Catharine & Edgar M CHURCHILL of Augusta ME at Woolwich ME [28 Jan 1833]
    Edmund J Esq of Dorchester & Mrs Sarah H SHERMAN of Augusta ME at Springfield [16 Sept 1847]
    Edward of Hallowell ME & Harriet S OSBORN of Belfast ME at Belfast ME [8 Aug 1837]
    Eliza Ann & Henry BOND of Nobleboro ME at Sidney ME [18 Jul 1837]
    Eliza Ann & Nathaniel AREY at Hampden ME [23 Dec 1836]
    Emily & Albion TRUE at Albion ME [14 Mar 1850]
    Emma J & John A GLIDDEN both of Gardiner ME at Hallowell ME [10 Jan 1850]
    Frances A & Edward PAINE at Eastport ME [15 Jan 1846]
    George & Elizabeth PREBLE at Newcastle ME [6 Nov 1845]
    Hannah W & Dr Parmenas DYER at New Sharon ME [2 Dec 1847]
    Harriet S of Portland ME & Henry HUTCHINSON at Portland ME [13 Feb 1845]
    Harriet & Henry UPTON of Norway ME at Bridgeton ME [15 Apr 1847]
    Harrison of Bangor ME & Sarah E REED d/o John REED Esq of Augusta ME by Rev Wm A DREW the 26th inst at Augusta ME [28 May 1846]
    Henry K, editor of the *Free Press & Advocate*, & Sarah M LORD at Hallowell ME [11 Dec 1835]
    Henry & Elizabeth C WOODCOCK both of Sidney ME at Waterville ME [15 Mar 1849]
    Henry & Sarah CURRIER at Winthrop ME [4 Nov 1847]
    Jane F & Capt Mitchell L TROTT at Bath ME [12 Dec 1837]
    Jeremiah Jr of Yarmouth ME & Mary J DEARBORN at Biddeford ME [31 Jan 1850]
    Joseph Esq & Frances ROGERS at Augusta ME [20 Nov 1841]
    Josiah & Lucy Ann WATSON at Portland ME [25 Jul 1834]
    Julia A & Elbridge THOITS at N Yarmouth ME [14 Dec 1848]
    Julia Ann of Litchfield ME & John BOOKER of Bowdoin ME at Bath ME [14 May 1846]
    Lewis of Hampden ME & Grace WHEELDEN at Charleston ME? [20 Mar 1851]
    Mary A & Jonathan H FULLER of Freedom at Albion ME [4 Apr 1840]
    Mary H & Oliver YOUNG at The Forks [13 Dec 1849]
    Mary & Abel M MORSE of Starks ME by Rev C SCAMMEN at New Sharon ME [23 Oct 1841]
    Moses N of Franklin & Lucinda MOON at Hancock [22 Apr 1852]

BAKER (cont.) Samuel C & Sybil B COOK both of Danville ME at Lewiston ME [26 Feb 1852]
Samuel P cashier of the Mariner's Bank Wiscasset ME & Sophia d/o Capt Jotham PARSONS of Bangor ME at Bangor ME [5 Feb 1836]
Samuel R & Charlotte MILLIKEN both of Saco ME at Charlestown MA [11 Sept 1851]
Sarah Jane & Joel C WILSON at Minot ME [8 Jan 1839]
Sarah M & Dr J S CUSHMAN of New Gloucester ME at Portland ME [19 Nov 1846]
Silas of Weld ME & Sophia AUSTIN 30 April by Isaiah VICKERY Esq at Parkman ME [10 May 1849]
Smith of Bingham & Sarah W DUTTON at New Sharon ME [12 Nov 1846]
Susan S & Capt Jacob A MERRIMAN at Portland ME [5 Aug 1833]
Thomas M & Lydia M ANDREWS at Gardiner ME [9 Jan 1851]
Thomas of Albion ME & Rachel H JOHNSON of Freedom ME at Thorndike ME [18 Oct 1849]
Zilpha of Bingham ME & E ADDEN Esq at Embden ME [8 Apr 1843]
BALCH Eliza Greenleaf of Haverhill MA & Parker M'COBB Jr Esq at Thomaston ME [25 Apr 1844]
Emily & John J AMES of Calais at Lubec ME [20 Jun 1844]
Maria W & Elias C NASON of Augusta ME at Boston MA [7 Mar 1850]
Sophia G & Lowell G CHASE at Lubec ME [10 Oct 1840]
BALDWIN Ann E & Charles HAYES of Industry ME at New Sharon ME [31 May 1849]
William of Livermore ME & Abigail KINNEY at Westbrook ME [11 Feb 1833]
BALENTINE Samuel of Hallowell ME & Mary ATKINSON at Chesterville ME [18 Mar 1847]
BALKAM Uriah Rev of Wiscasset ME & Anne Sophia LONGFELLOW d/o Col Samuel L late of Gorham ME by Rev Dr TAPPAN at (Augusta ME) at the residence of her step-father Hon Asa REDINGTON [1 Apr 1852]
William & Maria MOORE at Thomaston ME [28 Mar 1850]
BALLARD Calvin Capt of Gardiner ME & Elizabeth S SMITH of Hallowell ME on Sunday even last by Wm A DREW at Hallowell ME [21 Aug 1838]
Eliza & Samuel SMITH at Chelsea ME [20 May 1852]
Emily H & Rev Daniel D DOLE at Gardiner ME [10 Oct 1840]
Ephraim & Mrs Phebe BROWN at Augusta ME [4 Jul 1837]
Frederic & Mrs Anna N GAY at Farmington ME [14 Nov 1844]
Job & Mitty A THURSTON at Parsonfield ME [16 Jul 1846]
Martha L & Chandler TUTTLE at Thompson CT on 14th inst [26 Oct 1848]
Mary R & Thomas L POLLARD on 16 Jan by Rev JUDD at Augusta ME [24 Jan 1850]
Sarah P & Wm A MACOMBER both of Monmouth ME at Hallowell ME [31 Jan 1850]
Sarah & Noah WOODS Esq both of Gardiner ME at Norridgewock ME [22 Feb 1844]
William S Capt & Sarah E CALL at Gardiner ME [19 Sept 1844]
BALLENTINE Eliza A & George W HOOKER both of Augusta ME at Sidney ME [3 Apr 1851]
Mary E & Harrison JOY at Waterville ME [14 Mar 1844]

BALLOU Sylvia of Turner ME & Americus CROCKETT of Abbot ME at Turner ME [1 Feb 1840]
BAMFORD John of Fayette ME & Relief WHITTIER at Readfield ME [24 Apr 1845]
BAMSFORD Elizabeth S & Henry A STANLEY at East Winthrop ME [20 May 1847]
BANCROFT George A of Readfield ME & Drusilla REED at Albion ME [25 Nov 1837]
BANE Daniel B & Rebecca McPHETERS at Bangor ME [30 Oct 1845]
BANGS Charles E & Nancy BUBIER at Auburn ME [14 Feb 1850]
   E B Dr of Saco ME & Mary J BROOKS at Limerick ME [18 Mar 1847]
   Eben & Lucy E COFFIN at Sweden ME [19 Feb 1852]
   Joshua N & Rachel H DYER at Pownal ME [27 Mar 1845]
   Lurania R & Albion R P HIGGINS of Thomaston ME at New Sharon ME [26 Nov 1846]
   Mary A & Franklin L CARY of G at Sidney ME [3 Dec 1846]
   Paulina C & Charles K SAWTELLE at Sidney ME [19 Feb 1846]
   Rebecca S & Charles MILLIKEN of Gardiner ME at Sidney ME [3 Dec 1846]
   Sarah J & Dr William YOUNG of Farmington ME at Phillips ME [3 Jul 1851]
BANKS Charles & Ellether SPINNEY at Bath ME [26 Feb 1836]
   Ebenezer C of Livermore ME & Mary Ann WOODBRIDGE of Hallowell ME at Hallowell [13 Nov 1841]
   Elias & Dorcas HOPKINS at Portland ME [19 Jun 1845]
   Eunice & Simeon CARY Esq of Hallowell ME at Boston MA [1 Jan 1846]
   Martha A & John H MARSHALL at Augusta ME [12 Jul 1849]
   Mary A & Joseph F NYE of Fairfield ME on 11th inst by Rev S ALLEN at Augusta ME [23 Sept 1847]
   Porter of Fairfield ME & Mary BURRILL at Canaan ME [29 Aug 1844]
   Sarah & Rev Luther C STEVENS of Richmond Village at Hartford ME [27 Jun 1834]
   Sharon E Mr & Caroline A POTE at Belfast ME [5 Feb 1846]
   William C of Ellsworth ME & Eliza C HILL at Bangor ME [6 Jan 1848]
BANN Mary L & Henry S SWASEY Jr of Bangor ME at New Orleans LA/MA? [11 Apr 1837]
BANNAN Lucy F & Jesse H FRYE at Belfast ME [27 May 1843]
BARBOUR Abigail R & Wm DEERING of Paris ME at Gray ME [22 Nov 1849]
BAREU Pauline of Cornville ME & Peter BUSHEY at Madison ME [18 Feb 1847]
BARKER Charles B of Norridgewock ME & Mary Jane BOYINGTON by Rev Mr ALLEN at (Augusta ME) on 1st inst [13 Apr 1848]
   Charles H, M.D., of Buxton Centre ME & Mary Ann SMALL at Cornish ME [21 Jan 1847]
   Daniel C & Frances M CLARK at Portland ME [19 Jun 1845]
   Elishia & Lydia SAWYER at Norridgewock ME [27 Apr 1848]
   Emeline S & Mr R S HIGHT at Skowhegan ME [29 Jun 1848]
   Freeman & Lucy B GUILD on 16 Dec by Rev DILLINGHAM at Augusta ME [23 Dec 1847]
   Gideon of Pittston ME & Elizabeth G LORD at China ME on 30 Jul [3 Aug 1848]

BARKER (cont.) Hannah, d/o Wm BARKER of Nottingham, England & Rev Sam'l P ABBOT by Rev Jacob ABBOT at Farmington ME [3 Jul 1841]
Harriet & Samuel GOODWIN of Dresden ME at Wayne ME [10 Sept 1846]
Isaac & Mary MALOON at Belfast ME [19 Oct 1839]
Jedediah M & Mary B MORTON at New Vineyard ME [20 May 1843]
John Jr & Martha HILL at Bangor ME [10 Jul 1835]
Lewis of Stetson & Elizabeth HILL at Exeter [13 Aug 1846]
Mark Esq of Exeter & Julia McCOBB at Orrington ME [28 Jun 1849]
Mary Ann & Joshua DUNTON of Athens ME at Cornville ME [27 Feb 1851]
Mary T & Horace P STORER of Portland ME at Limerick ME [13 May 1847]
Mary & George B MOULTON at (Augusta ME) at St Mark's Church [6 Jan 1848]
Mary & Isaac PATTERSON of Limerick ME at Cornish ME [18 Feb 1847]
Noah Esq of Exeter & Temperence B EDDY at Corinth ME [18 Jan 1840]
Samuel W of Pittston ME & Mary Jane MORRILL on Wed eve last by Rev ADLAM at Hallowell ME [6 Mar 1845]
Sarah, d/o John BARKER, Esq & Henry W HERBET Esq of England at Bangor ME [11 Jan 1840]
Sarah J of Cornish ME & Josiah F DOW of Lynn MA at Cornish ME [15 Oct 1846]
Stephen Jr of Methuen MA & Caroline H WARDWELL of Rumford ME at New York [14 Jan 1847]
Thomas C Dr & Rebecca d/o Wm ABBOT Esq at Bangor ME [4 Feb 1833]
BARNARD Eliza P & Dinsmore CLEAVELAND of Madison ME at Bloomfield ME [15 Jul 1847]
Jane Ann of Waldoboro ME & Noah E SHEPARD Esq of Union ME at N Waldoboro ME on Dec 10th by Rev H W LATHAM [18 Dec 1851]
John G & Sophronia MINK at North Waldoboro ME by Reuben ORFF Esq [25 Dec 1851]
Mahala L & W H H WHEELER of Canton ME at Dixfield ME [28 Aug 1842]
William H & Susan MORSE at Waldoboro ME [23 Jan 1838]
BARNES Asa & Catharine DEAL both of Waldoboro ME at Nobleboro ME [23 Dec 1836]
Bulah ae 14 & Thomas WILLIAMS ae 17 at Union Vale NY [21 Sept 1833]
Daniel W & Lydia F THOMPSON at Bowdoinham ME [18 Sept 1851]
George & Louisa TUCKER both of Hartland ME at H [21 Aug 1838]
George & Margaret ALEXANDER at Harpswell ME [17 Feb 1848]
Hannah J & Ezekial D GAMMON at Portland ME [22 Jan 1846]
John C & Melinda A WHITE at Solon ME [1 Jan 1846]
Louisa of Hartland ME & Thomas MERRILL of Smithfield ME at Waterville ME [23 Oct 1851] (West Waterville) [9 Oct 1851]
Mary P & David K KEITH at Thomaston ME [13 Nov 1845]
Phinehas of Waterville ME & Ann J BUTLER d/o Rev John BUTLER of N Yarmouth ME at N Yar [29 Aug 1837]
Richard T & Lydia THOMPSON at Gardiner ME [3 Apr 1845]
Robert of Hartland ME & Hannah L COOMBS of Bowdoinham ME at Topsham ME [30 Sept 1843]
William C & Charlotte WELSH at Atkinson ME [28 Feb 1850]
William & Maria KIMBALL at Greene ME [19 Mar 1846]

BARNEY Ellen H d/o Hon Charles BARNEY & W K A HANSON on 13 Jan by
E F HAMMOND Esq at Atkinson ME [8 Feb 1849]
Harriet A & James BURT at Norwick CT [18 May 1848]
Henry W & Lucy A WEEKS by Rev J P WESTON at Gardiner ME [19 Jun 1845]
William & Clarinda NELSON at Atkinson ME [16 Sept 1843]
BARRETT Amos of Camden ME & Julia TOLMAN at Rockland ME [6 Mar 1851]
Albert J & Olive E DAY at Dover ME [7 Apr 1848]
Edwin & Rosilla LOMBARD of Carthage ME by Kendall WRIGHT Esq at Weld ME [17 Jun 1852]
Louisa, d/o Capt John BARRETT of Sumner ME, & Capt James HERSEY at Sumner ME [23 Mar 1839]
Joseph Esq of Canaan ME & Pamelia WYMAN at Skowhegan ME [25 Nov 1836]
BARRON Sarah & Rev George KNOX at Topsham ME [11 Mar 1847]
BARROWS Andrew & Eliza HAYFORD at Canton ME [25 Nov 1836]
Ann R & Augustine BLAKE Esq both of Monmouth ME by Rev Jedadiah PRESCOTT at Monmouth ME [16 Mar 1839]
Elisha & Lydia ROBINSON by Rev E FREEMAN 5th ult at Augusta ME [7 May 1846]
John U & Ruth P GROVE by Rev J B PRESCOTT at Monmouth ME [23 Jan 1841]
Nancy J & Alfred P BURNELL both of Norway ME at South Paris ME [25 Apr 1844]
BARRY Amos & Roxana GETCHELL both of Marsfield ME at East Machias ME [1 Jun 1848]
Stedman of Springfield MA & Judith JONES formerly of Norridgewock ME at Lowell MA [10 Dec 1846]
BARSTOW Benjamin of Damariscotta ME & Mrs Mary COX at Gardiner ME [23 Nov 1848]
H W (Mrs) & Alonzo S Holmes at Bath ME [27 Jul 1848]
George of Hillsborough NH & Emily E SHEPLEY at Saco ME [20 Jun 1844]
Horace B & Nancy RAND at Bangor ME [20 Nov 1835]
John G Capt & Arlitta M HOLMES at Newcastle ME [3 Sept 1842]
Moses L of Brunswick ME & Mary J DONNELL of Harpswell ME at Durham ME [23 Apr 1846]
Roxana & Joseph W JORDAN at Brewer ME [23 Dec 1836]
Susan B, adopted d/o Isaac BACKUS Esq, & Arthur F DRINKWATER Esq of Bluehill ME at Canterbury CT [23 Sept 1847]
BARTELS Eduah L & Amos W DANA of Boston MA at Portland ME [8 Feb 1844]
Harriet & Dr Joseph STURTIVANT of Mechanic Falls ME at Portland ME [19 Apr 1849]
BARTER Elijah & Elizabeth D KIMBALL both of Hallowell ME by Rev Wm A DREW on 7th inst at Augusta ME [16 Sept 1847]
Eliza J & Ellison ANNIS at Goose River [1 Apr 1852]
Harriet E & Sylvanus RUSH at Bath ME [23 Dec 1847]
Jane H & Capt Frederic A SENTER master of brig *Porto Rico* by Rev DREW at Hallowell ME [13 Nov 1845]

Marriage Notices from the "Maine Farmer"

BARTLETT Amasa Jr Capt of Orrington & Sarah H NICKERSON at Skowhegan ME [15 Feb 1849] & [30 Nov 1848]
Amelia & Orrin FLY at Augusta ME on 7th Jan by Rev Z THOMPSON [23 Jan 1851]
Avery C & Hannah W COLLUM at Ellsworth ME [4 Dec 1851]
Benjamin F & Aurelia RICHARDSON both of North Anson ME at North Anson ME [9 Apr 1846]
Elenor & M AUSTIN at Thomaston ME [6 Mar 1838]
Erastus of Foxcroft & Sarah BROWN of Sebec ME at Atkinson ME [17 Jun 1852]
F H & Elmira SNOWDEAL at Thomaston ME [24 Aug 1848]
Frederick W BARTLETT of Harmony ME & Elizabeth WYMAN at Bloomfield ME [25 Jul 1844]
Gilmore C & Margaret J SOUTHWARD on 1 Dec by Asaph R NICHOLS Esq at Augusta ME [13 Dec 1849]
Isabella & Jos F GEE both of Wayne ME at Mt Vernon ME [17 May 1849]
J C (Mr) & Mary Ann D NUDD both of Waterville ME at Providence RI on 3 Sept by Rev J HOBART [18 Sept 1851]
J P & Abba W McLAUGHLIN at New Portland ME [29 Apr 1852]
Joel B of Kennebec ME & Abby R SHERBURN of Augusta ME at Hallowell ME [16 Oct 1851]
Julia A & John P GREELY of Bangor ME at Camden ME [8 May 1845]
Margaret & Beniah BROWN at Carmel ME [30 Dec 1847]
Martha W & John BOARDMAN at Bangor ME [24 Jan 1834]
Martha & John W GREELEY by Rev Theodore HILL at Mt Vernon ME [21 Feb 1850]
Mary (Mrs) of Orono ME & John BENNOCK Esq at Bangor ME [28 Aug 1838]
Moses B Esq of Bethel ME & Sarah E THOMPSON at Brunswick ME [10 Jul 1845]
Orin & Mary BUCK at Abbott ME [27 Apr 1848]
Reed formerly of Eastport ME & Harriet BLAIR at Dayton OH [29 May 1845]
Ruth & Omes FLETCHER of Augusta ME at Searsmont ME [28 May 1842]
Sarah E & Andrew McPASKIEL both of Warren ME at Thomaston ME [10 Oct 1844]
Silome T & Benj F KIMBALL both of New Portland ME at North Anson ME [7 Mar 1850]
William editor of the *Mercury* & Mercy J YOUNG at Bangor ME [22 Apr 1847]
William of Gorham & Eunice ACRES of Westbrook ME at W [16 Jan 1838]
William S Rev of Little Falls NY & Hannah M STEVENS of Pittston by Rev Wm R BABCOCK Rector Weds 9th inst at Christ Church at Gardiner [19 Jun 1841]
BARTOL Reuben & Almira EDES at Portland ME [15 Feb 1844]
BARTON A & Rev A W REED of Stetson ME at Albion ME [23 Jan 1851]
Crosby Esq of Sinney (Sidney?) & Ruby HINDS at Sebasticook ME [4 Feb 1843]
Dorcas ae 55 & George SMALL ae 80 after a courtship of one hour 26 Aug at Raymond ME [18 Sept 1841]

BARTON (cont.) Elizabeth (Mrs) of Mercer ME & John CHURCH at Farmington ME [25 Dec 1845]
George L D printer & Eunice H LONGLEY both of Paris ME at Boston MA [2 Oct 1851]
Helen A & Rev John B WHEELWRIGHT at Sidney ME [1 Jun 1848]
Hiram of Wayne ME & Elmira HAINES at Readfield ME [25 Jun 1846]
Isaac N of Boston MA & Mary C HARRICK at Alfred ME [7 Oct 1847]
Jane & John REMICK at N Anson ME [1 Mar 1849]
Lewis & Eliza Ann CALER at Centreville [3 Aug 1848]
Lydia F, eld d/o Asa BARTON Esq. & Capt John TARBOX at Garland ME [4 Jun 1842]
Maria B & Benjamin ROBERTS at Waldoboro ME [8 Feb 1840]
Martha Augusta & Thaddeus A CHICK formerly of Bangor ME 10 Sept at Augusta ME [20 Sept 1849]
Martha P & Thomas H COOMBS at Sebasticook ME [9 Mar 1848]
Percival, M.D., & Sarah C PAINE at Anson ME [9 Aug 1849]
Reuben & Mrs Mary E MILES by Rev Mr ALLEN at (Augusta ME) on 11th inst [19 Oct 1848]
Sarah E d/o Dea Gideon BARTON & W H MORSE at Windsor on Jun 29 by Rev William BOWLER [3 Jul 1851]
BARWISE John of Garland ME & Charlotte H REED at Skowhegan ME [4 Oct 1849]
Thomas & Nancy P REED of Skowhegan ME at Kenduskeag ME [22 Jul 1852]
BASFORD Betsey G & Benjamin ALLEN Jr of Winthrop ME by Rev SPAULDING at Mt Vernon ME [25 Apr 1840]
Louisa M & Gorham L BOYNTON of Bangor ME at Dixmont ME [15 May 1835]
BASS Elizabeth & Steven WINSLOW of Augusta ME at Bath ME [14 Oct 1836]
Hiram of Freeport ME & Hannah E CUMMINGS at Farmington ME [27 Jun 1844]
BASSET/BASSETT Eli D & Mary DOUGLASS at Gardiner ME [19 Aug 1847]
Joshua P of Bucksport ME & Elizabeth S HATCH at Castine ME [22 Apr 1852]
Paulina of Wales ME & Elbridge DIXON at Gardiner ME [4 Nov 1847]
BASSICK Ruby Jane & A R MUDGETT at Prospect ME 5th [15 Jul 1852]
BASTON Charles of Lexington & Mary KNOWLES at New Portland ME [7 August 1851]
Elizabeth & Stephen C MILLS at Norridgewock ME [17 Jun 1852]
Esther A & Seth HOLBROOK of Starks ME at Mercer ME [31 Jul 1851]
BATCHELDER Amaril L of Lisbon ME & John W CROOKER of Brunswick ME at Augusta ME [10 Jan 1850]
Augustin L of Litchfield ME & Mary S EDWARDS at Gardiner ME [21 May 1846]
Benjamin & Elizabeth C WALTON by Rev Geo BATES at the Union Meeting-house at Fayette ME [11 Nov 1843]
Calvin of Belmont ME & Ann PATTERSON at Belfast ME [28 May 1842]
Caroline, d/o Josiah of Hallowell ME, & B B BROWN at Exeter [25 Sept 1841]

BATCHELDER (cont.) Charlotte O, d/o Col J R BACHELDER, of Readfield ME & James BELL Esq of Monson ME by Hon E FULLER at Readfield ME [6 Jun 1837]
Chas G merchant of Hallowell ME & Susan W youngest d/o the late Col Charles CURTIS by Rev Dr GRAY 9th inst at Jamaica Plain NY [25 Dec 1841]
Edward H of Mobile AL & Angelina B CARLTON at Belfast ME [9 Oct 1851]
Elbridge G & Harriet HINKLEY of Vassalboro ME by Robert JACK Esq at Lisbon ME on 26th Feb [11 Mar 1852]
Elizabeth M & Robert ROGERS at Phippsburg ME [13 Aug 1846]
Emily A & Charles L CLEMENT at Hallowell ME [9 Nov 1848]
Fidelia & Timothy BATCHELDER Jr at Phipsburg ME [3 Aug 1848]
Frances C & James COBURN at Portland ME [24 Jul 1845]
Harriet A & Moses M HODSDON at Levant ME [24 May 1849]
James R Col of Readfield ME & Mrs Ann WHITE widow of the late Hon Benjamin WHITE by David WHITE Esq on Sunday last at Monmouth ME [1 Jan 1836]
Josiah O of Hallowell ME & Frances W OSGOOD of London at Pittsfield NH [5 Sept 1844]
Levi L Capt of Phipsburg ME & Nancy G PATERSON at Portland ME [14 Aug 1845]
Mehitable D of Saco ME & Benj H PRESCOTT of Westbrook ME at Saco ME [3 Jun 1836]
Nancy & Samuel SAUNDERS of New Sharon ME at Waterville ME [20 May 1847]
Pamelia C & HARTWELL John at Readfield ME [12 Oct 1848]
Willard & Margaret GOODELL at Prospect ME [15 Aug 1844]
BATES Abby & William FORSYTH at Wilton ME [1 Jun 1848]
Alexander of Richmond ME & Elizabeth (Mrs) HALL at Litchfield ME [28 Dec 1848] & [4 Jan 1849]
Charles A & E Augusta DREW by Rev PEET all of Norridgewock ME at Norridgewock ME [28 May 1846]
Charles A & Margaret d/o Hon D FARNSWORTH at Norridgewock ME [5 Feb 1842]
Constantine 2nd of Waterville ME & Mary E LORD by Rev HAWES 11 Mar at Augusta ME [22 Mar 1849]
Cynthia G & Solomon BATES at Fairfield ME [28 Mar 1850]
Deborah R & Charles S NORCROSS at Waterville ME [12 Feb 1852]
Hamlett editor of the *St Croix Courier* & Martha LANGLEY at Calais ME [31 Oct 1834]
Harriet & Samuel HANSON at Leeds ME on 9th inst [20 Apr 1848]
Henry H & Miranda SPRAGUE both of Greene ME at GREENE on 4th inst [9 Oct 1841]
James L & Frances A OLIVER at W Bath ME [19 Feb 1846]
John Esq of Phillips ME & Margaret DAIN at Bowdoinham ME [29 May 1851]
Lorene A & Benjamin WILLIAMS Esq of Solon ME at Anson ME [25 Apr 1840]
Lucy Ann & Reuben GIBBS Jr at Waterville ME [7 Oct 1847]

BATES (cont.) Lydia C J d/o Hon James BATES of Norridgewock ME & James B FARNSWORTH merchant of Waterville ME on Tues evening last by Rev J PEET at Norridgewock [6 Jun 1840]
Mary Ann & Edward SELDEN at Norridgewock ME [19 Aug 1843]
Mary B & Isaac B TOZIER Thanksgiving evening by Rev S F SMITH at Waterville ME [4 Dec 1841]
Newell H & Frances A LANE at Dexter ME [20 Jan 1848]
Phebe & John McKENNON at Belfast ME [1 May 1851] & [24 Apr 1851]
Sarah T & Daniel M HASKELL at Garland ME [19 Feb 1846]
Solomon W Esq of Norridgewock ME & Elizabeth D DENNIS at Gardiner ME [5 Dec 1844]
Solomon & Cynthia G BATES at Fairfield ME [28 Mar 1850]
William H & Jane BLACKMAN at Eastport ME [9 Jul 1846]
BATTLES George W & Arminta BUCK at Buckfield ME [15 Jan 1852]
BATTIE Angeline S d/o William Esq of Thomaston ME, & John H McCLELLAN Esq of Boston MA at Thomaston ME [17 Sept 1842]
BAXTER Francis W & Lavina HOLLAND both of Dixfield ME by Rev Daniel GOULD on 17th inst at Dixfield ME [20 Mar 1835]
BAYLEY also see **BAILEY**
Jacob & Frances LEE at Lee ME by J B LUDDEN Esq [26 Jun 1851]
BAZIN Joshua W of Boston MA & Frances A SPRINGER at Portland ME [20 Nov 1845]
BEAL/BEALE Charles of Bangor ME & Laura CHANDLER of Minot ME at M [25 Mar 1836]
Daniel B & Susan PITTS at Dover [12 Feb 1842]
George L of Norway ME & Belinda B THOMPSON at Rumford ME [24 Jul 1851]
Isaac of Kirkland ME, formerly of Augusta ME, & Clara A PACKARD at Lowell MA [18 Nov 1847]
Japheth & Rachel THWING at Augusta ME by Rev Stephen ALLEN of Farmington ME [3 Jul 1851]
John D & Mary E POTTLE at Norway ME [1 May 1851]
Margaret & Amos SMALL at Bowdoin ME [23 Jun 1852]
Mary E & Benj WRIGHT both of Greene ME at Webster ME [8 Feb 1849]
Mary L & Hiram GRAY of Benton ME at Brighton ME [9 Oct 1851]
Nathaniel C & Mary ROBBINS at Phillips ME [17 May 1849]
Sarah H & John C BURRILL at Sangerville ME [11 May 1848]
William Jr & Lucinda BACON both of (Winthrop ME) by Rev BAILEY at (Winthrop ME) on 13 Aug [22 Aug 1840]
William of Limerick ME & Catherine PARSONS of Newfield at Limerick ME [18 Jul 1840]
BEALS Arunah & Mary COFFIN d/o James of Leeds ME by Rev S S LEIGHTON at Leeds ME [24 Jul 1845]
Betsey & Benjamin HERSEY at Turner ME [22 Jan 1852]
Elizabeth & Capt David NICHOLS Jr at Searsport ME [20 Mar 1845]
James of Monroe ME & Hannah THOMPSON of Frankfort ME at Prospect ME [11 Jul 1844]
John R of Bath ME & Catharine A VIGOREUX at Gardiner ME [14 Sept 1848]
Joseph of Livermore ME & Catherine BOOTHBY of Turner? 17 Nov at Livermore ME [10 Dec 1842]
Lucinda & John HOSLEY at Livermore ME [30 Nov 1839]

BEALS (cont.) Mary C & William CRANE of Bangor ME at Wiscasset ME [25 Apr 1844]
Mary S & Abram JORDAN at Brunswick ME [23 May 1844]
Melancy L & Calvin RECORD at Turner ME [22 Jan 1852]
BEAN Abigail & Charles W RICHARDSON at Livermore Falls ME [12 Aug 1852]
Albert F of Readfield ME & Ann Jane d/o P H RICE Esq at Monson ME [5 Sept 1844]
Amanda M F & Silas F LEIGHTON at Augusta ME on 3 August by Rev Z THOMPSON [7 August 1851]
Bethiah & Samuel CORSON Jr of Hartland ME at Harmony ME [8 Feb 1844]
Bradford & Louisa Jane COFFIN at Waterboro ME [18 Feb 1847]
Celia & Washington BLAKE of Salem at Readfield ME [22 Feb 1844]
Dolly L & Sylvanus B WYMAN at Livermore ME [29 May 1838]
Eli B of Conway NH & Mary O SPRING at Hiram ME [25 Jun 1846]
Elizabeth J & Samuel A BLODGETT at Belfast ME [6 May 1847]
Emery O Esq Attorney at Law & Elizabeth H CRAIG 8th inst at Readfield ME [17 Oct 1844]
Emily J & Joshua SMITH of Biddeford ME at Brownfield ME [15 Feb 1849]
Eveline M & Sampson A COOLIDGE at Readfield ME [18 Mar 1852]
Frances A & Abigail L TREVETT at Frankfort ME [22 Feb 1844]
Hannah of Prospect & George GILMORE at Belfast ME [12 Dec 1844]
Ira & Florentine A WING both of East Livermore ME at Livermore ME [10 Jun 1847]
Isaac B & Harriet S MANSON at Limington ME [26 Jun 1851]
Isaiah C & Irena CONANT 26 Aug at Jay [26 Aug 1852]
Isreal Jr & Roxana PAINE at Jay ME on Jan 30 [24 Feb 1848]
John O & Almira SINCLAIR at Bangor ME [11 Jul 1844]
John & Sarah BEAN at Etna ME [18 Apr 1834]
Joseph of Washington ME & Emily COOMBS at Whitefield ME [30 Mar 1848]
Josiah Jr & Eunice S LANE both of Brooks ME at Belfast ME [4 Dec 1851]
Josiah & Mrs Zeroah B WOODSOM at Old Town ME [12 Apr 1849]
Laura & Warren STEPHENSON at Belfast ME [17 Oct 1837]
Leonard H & Sarah F MORRILL at Hallowell ME [20 Nov 1851]
Lucinda & Wm H DYER of Salem at Readfield ME [8 Nov 1849]
Lucy of Readfield ME & Barzilla HARRINGTON of China ME by Rev ROBINSON 12th inst at Readfield ME [21 Oct 1843]
Mary R & Samuel Q CURRIER at Mt Vernon ME [26 Oct 1848]
Mary T & Sylvester B KITREDGE at Readfield ME [7 Sept 1839]
Mary (Mrs) & Peter PIERCE 18th inst at Bingham ME [2 Nov 1839]
Rosanna & Elisha H PETTINGILL 26th ult at Livermore Falls ME [9 Oct 1841]
Rosannah & Sylvester GORDON both of Hallowell ME at Readfield ME [13 Sept 1849]
Sarah & John BEAN at Etna ME [18 Apr 1834]
BEARCE Delphina of Canton ME & John W HERRICK of Old Town ME Tues evening 13 Dec by James Monroe HOLLAND Esq at Canton ME [24 Dec 1842]

BEARCE (cont.) Dilana & Albert PRATT at Foxcroft ME [21 May 1846]
    Isaac of Calais ME & Bethsheba LONG at Buckfield ME [17 Apr 1835]
    Mary & Nehemiah HANSON at Readfield ME [29 Jan 1846]
BEARD I W of Brunswick ME & Mary A TODD of Portsmouth NH at Portsmouth NH [23 Sept 1836]
    Mary A & Elias D PIERCE at Brunswick ME [30 Sept 1836]
BEATH Martha L & Thomas L NUDD both of Charleston ME? at East Corinth ME [28 Mar 1850]
BECK Joseph L Capt of Augusta ME & Mary Ann PUTNAM of Hallowell ME 12 Sept by Rev E M TOBIE at Hallowell [19 Sept 1837]
    Mary M & Joshua P BOWLES Mon evening by Rev FULLER at Augusta ME [23 Dec 1843]
    Sylvania & Capt Adam GODFREY at Augusta ME [1 Apr 1843]
    Thomas F & Eliza SMITH at Augusta ME [25 Nov 1836]
BECKET/BECKETT Hepsibeth & Alfred C HILLMAN at Temple ME [10 Jul 1845]
    John & Emma d/o Samuel MANNING Esq 14th inst by Rev W R FRENCH at Lewiston ME [25 Feb 1847]
    Mary & George W ROBINSON at Cushing ME [27 Jan 1848]
    Sarah P & Davis E VARRELL at Lewiston ME [13 Mar 1851]
    Sophia M & Thomas W LOTHROP at Belfast ME [25 Jun 1846]
BECKFORD Augustus T printer & Clara H WING at Bangor ME [14 Jan 1847]
    Coleman F & Mary S GRAY at Lubec ME [11 Jan 1849]
    Harriet of Richmond ME & Isaac SAWYER Jr of Hallowell ME at Augusta ME [19 Sept 1837]
BEDELL William & Sarah STETSON formerly of Dover on 26th ult at New York City [13 Feb 1845]
BEE J M & Martha A FLOWER at Geneva NY [5 Mar 1842]
BEEBE Alfred S of Norwich CT & Sarah A PALMER at Bangor ME [3 Oct 1844]
BEEDE Richard H & Mary BROWN at Levant ME [18 Jan 1840]
BEEDLE Walter & Mary E WYMAN at Richmond ME [15 Mar 1849]
BEEMAN John & Sarah F CARR both of Hallowell ME on 27 Jul by Rev William A DREW at Augusta ME [5 Aug 1852]
    Stephen T of Oxford ME & Aphia BRETT at Paris ME [19 Apr 1849]
BEETLE Richard of Edgartown m Eunice R LAMBERT of Gardiner ME at Boston MA [22 May 1851]
BELCHER Abby D d/o Hon Hiram BELCHER & John L CUTLER Esq by Rev I ROGERS 16th ult at Farmington [2 Sept 1843]
    David P Capt of Camden ME & Abby H THOMAS at Lincolnville ME [9 Sept 1847]
    Drusilla F d/o A BELCHER Esq & Anson STANLEY on Tues last at Winthrop ME [4 Dec 1838]
    Hannibal of Farmington ME & Lucy A BRETT at Strong ME [23 Jan 1845]
    James Rev & Mary Jane HOPKINS at Ellsworth ME [25 Sept 1851]
    Lucy S & Thomas H WELLMAN at Belmont ME [24 Oct 1844]
    Margaret M & Alex A ABBOT at Farmington ME [27 Sept 1849]
    Sarah & Charles A WING by Rev David THURSTON 18th inst at Winthrop ME [27 Nov 1841]
BELL Harriet C & George M ELDER at Portland ME [2 Jan 1845]

BELL (cont.) James Esq of Monson ME & Charlotte O d/o Col J R BACHELDER of Readfield ME by Hon E FULLER at Readfield ME [6 Jun 1837]
    Robert of Washington Co ME & Lucy COMSTOCK at Lubec ME [14 Nov 1844]
    Thomas F & Susan T TRASK by Rev C F ALLEN 18th inst at Augusta ME [29 Nov 1849]
BELLOWS Augusta & B A PERKINS of Bangor ME at Freedom ME [24 May 1849]
BELYEA D Wilmot & Mary A EMERY d/o the late J D EMERY Esq at Augusta ME on 9th Jun 1851 by Rev Mr JUDD [12 Jun 1851]
BEMENT Susan F B & Judson WILLIAMS of Waterville ME at Dexter ME [21 Oct 1847]
BEMIS Catherine M & Charles WOODBURY both of Paris ME at Norway ME [5 Mar 1846]
    Charlotte F & Cyprian BENSON at Paris ME [28 Oct 1843]
    Elvira & Abner MOORE both of Livermore ME by Rev LAURENCE at Sumner ME [17 Aug 1839]
    Mary S & J M HERSEY at Lincoln ME [16 Apr 1846]
BENJAMIN Elmira F & Wm H WALLACE at Waldoboro ME [28 May 1846]
    Ernestine & Thomas O HASKELL at Livermore ME [14 Mar 1844]
    L N Miss & G LAMKIN of Boston MA at Whitefield ME [31 Jan 1850]
    Lucy & Lemuel STANLEY both of Winthrop ME by Rev E ROBINSON 23rd ult at Readfield ME [10 Dec 1842]
    William of Skowhegan ME & Mary CHASE at Bingham ME [19 Aug 1847]
BENNER Absalom & Saloma MINK at North Waldoboro ME on 4th May 1851 by Reuben ORFF Esq [15 May 1851]
    Barbara K & John LASH 2nd at Waldoboro ME [17 Dec 1842]
    Burnham C of Whitefield ME & Frances M TALPEY at Hallowell ME [5 Sept 1844]
    Clarke of Gardiner ME & Julia A THEOBALD at Dresden ME [6 Jan 1848]
    Henry 2d formerly of Pittston ME & Hannah E CROOKER formerly of Bath me at Boston MA [28 Nov 1840]
    Hermon & Louisa K RUSSELL by Reuben ORFF at North Waldoboro ME on 13th inst [24 Feb 1848]
    Leonards & Helen A LOVEJOY at Rockland ME [1 Jul 1852]
    Mary H & George MARDEN on 10 Aug by Wm C CARR Esq at North Palermo ME [19 Aug 1852]
    Nathaniel Dea & Aphia/Apphire F HALEY of Webster ME d/o Hon Dea HALEY 13 Jun at Lisbon ME [1 Jul 1847][29 Jul 1847]
    Oscar E & Julia Ann MINK at North Waldoboro ME on 21 Dec by Reuben ORFF Esq [25 Dec 1851]
    Rebecca & Silas PROCK both of Waldoboro ME at N Waldoboro ME on 14 Sept by Reuben ORFF Esq [25 Sept 1851]
    Sarah A & William PITCHER on 4 Nov by Reuben ORFF Esq at N Waldoboro ME [15 Nov 1849]
    Susan & F A LAMBERT at Waldoboro ME [5 Mar 1846]
BENNET/BENNETT Abel & Lucy Ann FRYE at Belfast ME [19 Apr 1849]
    Angeline & Moses S SMITH at Thomaston ME [10 Aug 1848]
    Charles E formerly of New Gloucester ME & Mary O ODIORNE formerly of Portsmouth NH at Boston MA [8 Feb 1844]

BENNET (cont.) Charlotte L & Arvida BRIGGS at Parkman ME [7 Jun 1849]
Deborah, d/o Nathaniel BENNETT, Esq & Lee MIXER at Norway ME [29 May 1845]
George of Augusta ME & Rachel J HOGAN at Bath ME [11 Nov 1843]
James of Greenwood ME & Polly UPTON at Norway ME [6 Jun 1844]
Lydia Ann & Isaac KNOWLTON of Pembroke ME at Dennyville ME [2 Oct 1851]
Martha L & Ansel SHERY at Starks ME [30 Apr 1842]
Mary A & James A GRAFFOM at Thomaston ME [29 Jul 1833]
Mary C & Franklin J WOODS at (Augusta) ME on 23 Feb [26 Feb 1852]
Mary Jane & George H PHILLIPS at Thomaston ME [9 Mar 1848]
Orinda & Pearley HEATH at Gilead ME [29 Apr 1847]
Samuel of Augusta ME & Sarah LIBBY at Litchfield ME [4 Oct 1849]
William & Mrs Isabella FOSTER at Bath ME [1 May 1835]
Zady Ann & Christopher MOORE at Hallowell ME [16 Jul 1846]
BENNOCK John Esq & Mrs Mary BARTLETT of Orono ME at Bangor ME [28 Aug 1838]
BENSON Ann d/o W S BENSON Esq & George BOWDOIN US Navy at Brooksville ME [21 Jan 1843]
Cyprian & Charlotte F BEMIS at Paris ME [28 Oct 1843]
David ae 54 years & Susan HEWETT of Charlton ae 16 years at Sturbridge MA [30 Jan 1845]
Elizabeth d/o Dr Peleg BENSON & Lloyd THOMAS by Rev Daniel D TAPPEN 27th inst at Winthrop ME [4 Jul 1837]
George D & Susan FRENCH at Saco ME [9 Aug 1849]
Harriet E & Jones PRATT Jr both of Windsor ME on 4 Dec by William PERCIVAL Esq at China ME [13 Dec 1849]
John, M.D., & Achsa Jane d/o Wm MARTIN Esq at Newport [11 Sept 1835]
Mary Ann & George BOWDEN at Brooksville ME [11 Feb 1843]
Mary Ann & Israel A FLETCHER at Hartford ME [12 Jun 1845]
Matthew & Caroline THURSTON of Madison ME at Solon ME [2 Apr 1846]
Ruth B & Benjamin YOUNG Jr both of Hartford ME at Paris ME [31 Jul 1845]
Sarah of Biddeford ME & Euran HOBBS at Waterborough ME [10 Jul 1835]
BENT D Chandler of Manchester NH & Arabella R HOLMES at Paris ME [27 Nov 1851]
John Esq Publisher of the *Eastern Democrat* & Dolly KEYES at Eastport ME [29 Aug 1834]
BERRY Angelina J & Dr T P KNOX at Boston MA [4 Mar 1852]
Arthur Esq of Augusta ME & Mary PARR d/o John TAYLOR Esq of Creniton England at Boston MA [24 Sept 1842]
Benjamin & Rosannah HANSON at Bangor ME [18 Jun 1846]
Charles H & Cynthia J HARRIS at Danville ME [22 Feb 1849]
Eliza J & Jos W ROGERS at Kittery ME [14 August 1851]
Francis E of Topsham ME & Charlotte JONES at Durham ME [30 Mar 1848]
Franklin W of Boston MA & Abigail S MARSHALL at Belfast ME [7 Oct 1847]

BERRY (cont.) Freedom of Cornish ME & Catherine PENDEXTER of Parsonsfield ME at East Parsonsfield ME [13 Mar 1851]
Georgia C & Charles L LOWELL Esq of Rockland ME at Thomaston ME [12 Jun 1851]
Harriet & Capt Sewall L BERRY at Prospect ME [8 Aug 1844]
Helen A & Chas PARKER of Buxton ME at Standish ME [6 Dec 1849]
John D & Mary S BERRY at Fayette ME [5 Apr 1849]
Joshua of New Sharon ME & Cordelia SMITH by Rev J H INGRAHAM 20th inst at Winthrop ME [1 Jun 1839]
Julia S & Josiah G MACY/MARCY of New York at Gardiner ME [16 Jul 1846] & [13 Aug 1846]
Laura A & W H ATKINSON at Wayne ME [24 Dec 1846]
Lucy A & Andrew BABB at Saco ME [5 Jul 1849]
Lydia of Scarborough ME & Cyrus Foss TAPLEY of Wayne ME at Scarborough ME [12 Feb 1836]
Martha & William F SCAMMON at Biddeford ME [31 Jan 1850]
Mary Jane & Hiram SMITH at Gardiner ME [8 Aug 1844]
Mary Jane & Thomas WINSLOW at Bath ME [13 Jan 1848]
Mary S & John D BERRY at Fayette ME [5 Apr 1849]
Mary & James LOVELAND at Brighton ME [29 Apr 1836]
Nahum M BERRY & Mary A SHUTE at Prospect ME [1 Feb 1844]
Olive Caroline & John C MORRILL at Auburn ME [18 Nov 1847]
Phebe C & William HAYMAN of Boston at Belfast ME [24 Oct 1844]
Sarah J of Norway ME & James M ABBOT of Oxford ME at Waterford [1 Feb 1849]
Sewall L Capt & Harriet BERRY at Prospect ME [8 Aug 1844]
Stephen A & Mary L PRATT on 17th inst at Augusta ME [21 Mar 1834]
Stephen & Mary J MORSE at Phipsburg ME [5 Aug 1847]
W M & Betsey A S GODFREY Biddeford ME at Bowdoinham ME [21 Dec 1848]
William G & Mary M JONES at Thomaston ME [15 Jan 1846]
Willis Jr of New Sharon ME & Gratia Ann eldest d/o the late Rev Fifield HOLT at Bloomfield ME [4 Jan 1840]

BESSE Belden & Isabella F HOPKINS at Albion ME [29 Jul 1852]
Ephraim S of Monmouth ME & Julia Ann BESSE of Wayne ME on 19 May by John MAY Esq at Winthrop ME [31 May 1849]
Julia Ann of Wayne ME & Ephraim S BESSE of Monmouth ME on 19 May by John MAY, Esq at Winthrop ME [31 May 1849]
Lucy & Benjamin NORRIS 2nd both of Wayne ME by Isaac BOWLES Esq at Winthrop ME [6 Feb 1838]
Mercy & Charles E SMITH by Ephraim MAXIM Esq at Wayne ME — Extended Notice— [31 Jan 1850]
Patience & Richard M WING of Fayette ME at Wayne ME [8 Jul 1847]

BESSEE Celia & West ROBINSON at Foxcroft ME [1 Nov 1849]
Thomas of Harrison ME & Augusta Ann DOE by Rev S W MORSE at Augusta ME [24 Dec 1846]

BESSICK Susan H & Capt James P RICH of Bucksport ME at Bangor ME [28 Feb 1837]

BESSY William G of Wayne ME & Elizabeth CURRIER at Winthrop ME [9 Dec 1847]

BETANCUE Joseph of Boston MA & Mary E PERCY at Bath ME [30 Oct 1841]

BETTY John W & Eliza HART at Portland ME [23 May 1844]
BEVERAGE Martha W & Charles L ALLEN at Thomaston ME [15 Jan 1846]
  Susan & Theodore H DILLINGHAM of Bangor ME at Camden ME [26 Feb 1842]
BEVERIDGE George & Martha F PIPER at Thomaston ME [22 Jan 1846]
BIBBER Frederick & Zelia Ann HARRINGTON at Eastport ME [21 Jan 1847]
  John & Martha TOOTHAKER both of Harpswell ME by E G BUXTON Esq 9th inst at Yarmouth ME [13 Sept 1849]
  Mary J of Lisbon ME & Seth CROSMAN at Durham ME [2 Aug 1849]
  Myrick & Ann Eliza APPLEBY at Eastport ME [29 Jul 1836]
BICKFORD Aaron & Mary Ann BOUDEN at Norridgewock ME [21 Jan 1843]
  Abigail of Kennebunkport ME & Nathan D CENTER at Saco ME [27 Aug 1846]
  Emily & James P DINSMORE at Skowhegan ME [9 Jan 1845]
  F J (Miss) of Belgrade ME & Mr F B McCLURE at Hallowell ME [27 Mar 1851]
  Frances & Eugene F COLLINS of North Anson ME at Skowhegan ME [25 Apr 1850]
  Hiram & Caroline GULLIVER at Hermon ME [18 Jan 1840]
  James of Gardiner ME & Sally RICHARDSON of Greene ME at Greene ME [9 Oct 1841]
  Leonard P & Vesta J TIBBETTS at Gardiner ME [20 Nov 1845]
BICKMORE Stephen S & A Sarah A PITCHER at Waldoboro ME [2 Mar 1848]
  William of Appleton ME & Abizer Ann NASH of Bremen ME by Waite W KEENE Esq 7th inst at Bremen [27 Jul 1839]
BICKNELL Alfred & Sarah J PILLSBURY on 23 Nov at Augusta ME [9 Dec 1847]
  Deborah T & Holland W NOYES at Augusta ME [9 Oct 1841]
  George & Tabitha RICHMOND by Rev George BATES at Turner ME [15 Jan 1842]
  James A & Octavia W SAMPSON of Bowdoinham ME by W A DREW 15th inst at Bowdoinham [26 Jun 1845]
  James M & Sarah S STEVENS of Northport ME at Belfast ME [2 Oct 1851]
  James & Harriet P MCKEEN both of Belmont ME at Belfast ME [30 May 1837]
  Nancy B & William R GILSON of Abington MA by Rev William A DREW on 26th inst at Augusta ME [29 Jul 1847]
  Nancy & Francis F ALLENWOOD at Belmont ME [12 Aug 1847]
  Sylvia W & Cyrus WOODSUM at Hallowell ME [1 Jan 1846]
BIGELOW Charles & Abigail WESTON both of Bloomfield ME? at Nashua NH [9 Mar 1848]
  Elizabeth & George W TAYLOR at Norridgewock ME [8 May 1845]
  Ephraim & Sarah B FLAGG on Thurs eve last by Rev Arthur DRINKWATER at Bloomfield ME [9 Feb 1839]
  Henry, M.D., of Buxton ME & Matilda Ann POOL d/o Lott POOL Esq at Boston MA on 25th inst [5 Sept 1840]
  Jotham Esq & Mary A JOHNSON at Skowhegan ME [8 Mar 1849]
BIGGER Phebe & John JACOBS by J CURRIER Esq at Mt Vernon ME [3 Apr 1838]

Marriage Notices from the "Maine Farmer"

BILLINGS Amelia O of Northport ME & Henry M COX at Belfast ME [7 Jan 1847]
    Charles W & Ellen HUNTER at Clinton ME [13 Sept 1849]
    Emily C & David W ROWE of Oxford ME at Woodstock ME [21 Aug 1851]
    Mary S & Wm N WOODSUM at Albion ME [4 Jan 1849]
    Miranda T & Eben'r HANDY of Union ME on 26 Sept by Thos BURRILL Esq at Albion ME [7 Oct 1847]
    William B & Miss F E RICHARDSON at Eastport ME [14 Sept 1848]
BILLINGTON Daniel C of Hallowell ME & Mary W NORRIS at Wayne ME [29 Jan 1846]
    Ichabod & Patience FROST at Wayne ME [12 Feb 1836]
    Jane of Winthrop ME & James H MACOMBER of Readfield ME on Thurs eve last by Samuel P BENSON Esq at Winthrop ME [25 Jan 1840]
    Mary & Dwight MINER at Hallowell ME [10 Jan 1850]
BIRD Horace of Watertown MA? & Fanny FISH of Salem MA? at Salem [6 May 1836]
BISBEE/BISBEY Susan H & Henry C GREENLEAF at North Yarmouth ME [3 Feb 1848]
    Thomas J & Silvia STETSON at Gardiner ME [11 Jul 1840]
    Lydia L & Phineas D WEYMOUTH at Biddeford ME [20 Jul 1848]
    America Esq & Mrs Cynthia ROWE of Sumner ME at Paris ME [15 Jan 1846]
    Arvilla S & B J KEEN of Abington MA at Sumner ME [17 Sept 1846]
    George H of Dedham MA & Martha J HERSEY at Fayette ME [14 Jun 1849]
    Hannah & Arthur TULLOCK at Bath ME [4 Sept 1845]
    Harriet N & Charles F TOWER of Roxbury MA at Waterville ME [5 Aug 1847]
    Studley & Amelia J H BOVEY both of Bath ME at Bath [2 Sept 1847]
BISHOP Lucinda G & Mr D D BLUNT at Hallowell ME [11 Jul 1840]
    Cyrus Postmaster & Olive HARRIS by Rev BERNARD at Winthrop ME [27 Feb 1845]
    Drusilla of Winthrop ME & Elijah L TOWNSEND of Danville ME by Rev Asbury CALDWELL of Augusta at Winthrop [9 Sept 1836]
    John & Martha E MAINE at Bath ME [30 Sept 1847]
    John G & Sarah TOWLE both of Augusta ME on 21 Jan by Rev S W FIELD at Hallowell ME [31 Jan 1850]
    Jonathan formerly of Akron OH & Martha SMITH both of Gardiner ME at Gardiner [26 Dec 1844]
    Jonathan G & Margaret W CLARK at Wayne ME [24 Jul 1845]
    Nathan of Fayette ME & Lois W d/o Rev James WILLIAMS at Readfield [25 Apr 1834]
    Ransom & Harriet WOOD 17th inst at Winthrop ME [25 Dec 1838]
    Sarah Ann of Harpswell ME & Joseph GETCHELL at Brunswick ME [18 Dec 1835]
    William of Belfast ME & Mrs Elmira LUCE at Union ME [2 Aug 1849]
    William B of Mt Vernon ME & Roxana ROWE at Belgrade ME [16 Jul 1846]
    William H & Mrs Eunice S FOGG at Bangor ME [27 May 1843]
BISKEY Sarah L & Capt Judson R WASHBURN at Thomaston ME [20 Mar 1845]

BITTUES Elizabeth E & John MANLEY on 24 Jun by Rev JUDD at Augusta ME [1 Jul 1847]
 Mary eldest d/o Arno BITTUES Esq & Sam'l V HOMAN Tues morn by Rev JUDD at Augusta ME [5 Mar 1842]
BIXBY/BIXBEE Amos Esq of Searsport ME & Augusta H CARISLE at Norridgewock ME [6 Nov 1851]
 Ann R & Elias J HALE at Athens ME [6 Jan 1848]
 Cromwell Jr & Catharine WING at Skowhegan ME [26 Oct 1848]
 Sumner & Mrs Sarah CARLISLE of Bingham ME at Norridgewock ME [13 Nov 1838]
BLABUN Joseph E & Martha M SMITH at Phillips ME [21 Jun 1849]
BLACK Catherine N & Wilson COLCORD at Prospect ME [20 Jul 1848]
 Elizabeth & Capt J R HODGKINS at Winthrop ME on 23 Jan [27 Jan 1848]
 F H of Frankfort ME & Abby H ROBINSON at Belfast ME [7 Dec 1848]
 Lavina B & Loring DOUGHTY at Harpswell ME [21 Dec 1848]
 H T Esq & Julia A FULLER of Albion ME on 28 Feb by Rev J SMITH at Palermo ME [15 Mar 1849]
 Henry Esq of Orange Co & widow Eliza GRAY of Green Co d/o Henry BROWN merchant of Bluehill ME by Rev WHITE at New York City [27 Mar 1841]
 James L of Cambridge NH & Lieviatha SCRIBNER of Letter B ME at Letter B [8 Jan 1846]
 Janet C & Wilmont I HUSSEY on 30th ult at Augusta ME [10 Jun 1847]
 Martha Augusta & Rev Thomas B DEAN of Taunton MA by Rev BURGESS on 19th inst at St Mark's Church in Augusta ME [27 Nov 1845]
 Sarah of Brewer & Capt Thomas GOODALE of Bucksport ME at Bangor ME [31 Jul 1845]
 Sarah E & George W SNOW at Augusta ME [20 Nov 1841]
 William M of E Thomaston ME & Mary N MARSHALL of E Machias ME at Thomaston ME [16 Aug 1849]
BLACKBURN Cinthia B & H L CUSHING at Augusta ME [24 Dec 1846]
 Henry L of this city (Augusta) ME & Sarah B SPRAGUE by Talman LOWELL Esq at Phipsburg on Mar 2d [18 Mar 1852]
BLACKER Sarah C of Boston MA & James M HILTON of Augusta ME by Rev Robert BLACKER of Livermore ME at Boston [25 Nov 1847]
BLACKINTON James M & Elizabeth BUTLER at Thomaston ME [6 Jan 1837]
 Sophia & Benj B PALMER both of Thomaston ME at Thomaston [16 Jul 1846]
BLACKISTON Harriet d/o Thomas BLACKISTON sailmaker & T SNOW of Skowhegan ME at Quebec Canada [20 Apr 1839]
BLACKLEY George A & Phillota RUMERY at Lubec ME [22 Jan 1852]
BLACKMAN Hannah E & Shepherd P RANDALL at (Augusta) ME [25 May 1848]
 Jane & Wm H BATES at Eastport ME [9 Jul 1846]
BLACKSTON Hartson of New Sharon ME & Ruth W REED of Wayne ME by Rev Samuel FOGG of Winthrop ME at Wayne ME on the 13th inst [19 Sept 1840]

BLACKSTONE Eliza A & R SHACKLEY of Portland ME at Pownal ME [30 Jan 1845]
Hartson & Cynthia J REED both of New Sharon ME at Farmington ME [10 Jun 1852]
Manassah of New Sharon ME & Phebe FURBUSH of Augusta ME at Belgrade ME [13 Feb 1835]
BLACKWELL Asa & Lucy R WITHEE at Norridgewock ME [17 Apr 1838]
Dennis Col of Fairfield ME & Susan CLARK at Hallowell ME [23 Aug 1849]
Elizabeth & James WOOD 2nd both of Norridgewock ME at Norridgewock [13 Feb 1841]
Emily E & Sylvanus MORSE at Norridgewock ME [3 Jul 1845]
Hannah & Stephen S THAYER at Waterville ME [20 Jan 1848]
Harriet E & Selden WADE both of Norridgewock ME at Skowhegan ME [15 Aug 1844]
Micah A of Madison ME & Eliza A STEWART at Norridgewock ME [19 Nov 1846]
Olive S & Josiah MELCHER of Sandwich MA at Waterville ME [18 Jan 1849]
Sarah J & John P SPEAR at Madison ME [26 Apr 1849]
Sarah & Daniel LORD New Year's Day at West Waterville ME [8 Jan 1846]
BLAGDEN William & Hannah GULLIFER at Skowhegan ME [8 Jan 1839]
BLAGDON Mary Ann & Samuel BLAKE at Wiscasset ME [16 Oct 1845]
BLAGGE Samuel merchant & Eliza A d/o F A BUTMAN Esq by Rev WISWELL 24th inst at Dixmont ME [2 Nov 1839]
BLAIR Benjamin P & Elizabeth P SAVAGE d/o John SAVAGE by Rev J H INGRAHAM at Augusta ME [4 May 1839]
Harriet E & Frederic W LEWIS at Whitefield ME [17 Feb 1848]
Harriet L & Abial LIBBY at Richmond ME [8 Jan 1852]
Harriet & Reed BARTLETT formerly of Eastport ME at Dayton OH [29 May 1845]
Henrietta & Thomas FOSTER both of Dresden ME at Litchfield ME [24 Jun 1847]
J & Miss Bazelice VAILLIEUX at Bloomfield ME? [24 May 1849]
BLAISDEL/BLAISDELL Ann Eliza & Capt Ephraim MYERS at Rockland ME [2 Oct 1851]
Beulah & Ezekiel OLIVER at Phipsburg ME [5 Aug 1847]
Elijah S of Thomaston ME & Sophia A KNOX of Machias ME by Rev J A PERRY on 1st inst [15 Feb 1844]
Elizabeth & Noah WENTWORTH by M A CHANDLER Esq on 12th ult at Rome ME [1 Feb 1849]
Hosea of Sidney ME & Nancy LADD d/o the late John LADD by Rev ROBINSON at Winthrop ME [28 Oct 1843]
Hosea & Lucinda B LADD both of Sidney ME at Sidney [18 Mar 1836]
John & Marietta A POPE at Gardiner ME [22 Nov 1849]
John & Mary G d/o Hon Ebenezer HERRICK at Lewiston ME [28 Jan 1833]
Joseph & Mary R HAYNES at Smithfield ME [24 Sept 1846]
Mary of Hampden ME & Stephen SMITH at Orono (Old Town) ME [7 Sept 1833]
Octavia Ann & Matthew POTTER at Hallowell ME [25 Jun 1846]

BLAISDEL (cont.) Richd S & Mary C AREY at E Thomaston ME [8 Oct 1846]
Richard & Sarah Jane NOWELL at Kennebunkport ME [28 Mar 1850]
Sarah & J BURLEIGH at Thomaston ME [6 Nov 1845]
Wealthy L & James D WALLIS at Phipsburg ME [12 Feb 1846]

BLAKE Augustine Esq & Ann R BARROWS both of Monmouth ME by Rev Jedadiah PRESCOTT at Monmouth ME [16 Mar 1839]
Billings of St Stephens New Brunswick Canada & Nancy MARSHALL on 2 Sept by Rev MILES at Hallowell ME [5 Sept 1834]
Caroline A of Monmouth ME & Oliver H JEWELL of Lincoln ME by David THURSTON Esq at Monmouth ME [12 Mar 1842]
Caroline A & John C TIBBETS at Hallowell ME on 25 Oct [2 Nov 1848]
Christina M of Bangor ME & James L HALLOWELL of Belfast ME at Bangor ME [30 Sept 1847]
Ebenezer C of Augusta ME & Louisa M eldest d/o John LOVERING Esq Sheriff of Aroostook Co ME on 25th ult at Houlton ME [13 May 1843]
Eliza T & Thomas S JACK at Harpswell ME [31 Oct 1844]
Elizabeth C & John ARNO both of Monmouth ME at Litchfield ME [16 Jan 1845]
Emeline & George W ROGERS both of Newfield ME at Bridgton ME [3 Dec 1842]
Eunice M & John BOUTELLE of Hopkinton NH at Corinth ME [18 Oct 1849]
Frances B & Samuel SEYMOUR at Brewer ME [31 Aug 1839]
Greenleaf M & Arabella WILCOX at Monmouth ME [31 Dec 1836]
Harrison Esq of Harrison ME & Susan d/o Dea A CARY of Bridgeton ME at Harrison ME [18 Nov 1836]
Henry M of Monmouth ME & Lydia HORN of Great Falls NH at Great Falls [25 Sept 1835]
Hiram & Nancy CORSON at West Waterville ME [8 Feb 1844]
Increase of Farmington ME & Sarai [sic; see also p. 389 Francis Butler's History of Farmington ME 1885] FARNSWORTH at Norridgewock ME [10 Oct 1844]
Jane of Portland ME & William RANDALL Esq of Topsham ME at Portland ME [25 Nov 1843]
Levi A of Brewer ME & R W JORDAN of Raymond ME on 27 Jan by Rev WRIGHT at Poland ME [13 Feb 1841]
Lucinda & Cyrus WHEELER both of Waterville ME by Wm HAMLEN at Sidney ME [9 Jan 1838]
Martin R of New York & A STORMS at Standish MA [22 Aug 1844]
Mary G & Anthony STAPLES both of Bowdoinham ME at Augusta ME [3 Sept 1846]
Mary S & John I TINKHAM by Rev INGRAHAM of Augusta ME at Winthrop ME [25 Jan 1840]
Octavia M & Augustus CLEAVES of Biddeford ME at Limington ME [8 Oct 1846]
Reuben & Jane NEWBEGIN at Hope ME [14 Aug 1838]
Richard & Elizabeth HORTON at Freedom ME [30 May 1844]
Robert of Salem & Rachel EMERSON at Fayette ME [4 Apr 1850]
Samuel & Mary Ann BLAGDON at Wiscasset ME [16 Oct 1845]
Sophia C & Rev R M SAWYER at Otisfield ME [8 Jan 1852]
Washington of Salem & Celia BEAN at Readfield ME [22 Feb 1844]

BLAKE (cont.) William A Esq of Bangor ME & Frances A CURTIS only d/o Capt Winslow CURTIS of Frankfort ME at Frankfort [9 Jan 1845]
William & Deborah R MOODY at Hope ME [30 Dec 1847]
Wilmont & Mary Ann MUNSEY at Wiscasset ME [8 Jul 1836]
BLANCHARD Abel & Eliza A SAWYER on 1 Mar by M A CHANDLER Esq at Belgrade ME [8 Mar 1849]
Abner J of Boston MA & Mary A LUCE formerly of Readfield ME at Portland ME [4 Mar 1847]
Adeline P & William T HARRIS at North Yarmouth ME [2 May 1834]
Charles of Blanchard ME & Mary J CLEAVELAND at Bloomfield ME [15 Jul 1847]
Christiana d/o Capt S BLANCHARD & Col S R LYMAN Postmaster of Portland ME on Thurs eve by Rev CHICKERING at Portland ME [13 Aug 1842]
Elizabeth E & William T MEADER both of Hallowell ME at Pittston ME [17 Sept 1846]
E F & George S CLARK of Boston at Pittston ME [12 Nov 1846]
Jane of Augusta ME & George PENNEY of Belgrade ME by Silas CARTER at Augusta ME [5 Jun 1838]
Louisa & Alex TROOP 2nd at Pittston ME [25 Jan 1849]
Lovina & Simeon WESTON of Mt Vernon ME at Wilton ME [3 Jun 1847]
Mary H & John W MITCHELL of North Yarmouth ME at Portland ME [8 Feb 1844]
Nancy M & Sumner A PATTEN, M.D., of Shirley ME at Blanchard ME [15 Nov 1849]
Orchilla & Rev Jerome HARRIS, pastor of the Universalist Society of Prospect ME at Prospect ME [1 Jan 1846]
Roxannah & James C TAYLOR at Brunswick ME [19 Sept 1844]
Rufus of Hallowell ME & Mary KINSMAN of Gardiner ME on Thurs eve last by John DUNN Esq at Hallowell ME [20 Mar 1838]
Samuel Capt of Dresden ME & Anjenetta LEWIS at the cross roads at Hallowell ME [7 Sept 1833]
Samuel L & Frances A ROLLINS at Hallowell ME [3 Feb 1848]
Sylvanus J & Belinda DUDLEY of Readfield ME at West Winthrop ME [23 Jun 1852]
Theresa V of Cumberland ME & Hon Thomas DAVEE of Blanchard ME Sherriff of Somerset Co by Rev WESTON on 9th inst at Cumberland ME [16 Oct 1835]
William M/N of Cumberland ME & Priscilla M THOMPSON at Gray ME [24 Apr 1845] & [8 May 1845]
BLATCHFORD E of Augusta ME & Eliza T d/o the late Capt George LANE on 19th inst at Rockport MA [30 Oct 1845]
Joseph Jr & Margaret E TRECARTIN at Eastport ME [7 Mar 1850]
BLETHEN Abraham G & Mary M RUSSELL at Temple ME [4 Apr 1844]
Auvilla & Henry HACKETT of Lewiston ME at Lisbon ME [9 May 1844]
Caroline H & William S HERSEY at Dover ME? [25 Mar 1852]
Cynthia B & Lewis WHITNEY at Durham ME [2 May 1844]
Elizabeth F & George W SANBORN at Swanville ME [28 Jan 1847]
James A & Almeda S THAYER at Foxcroft ME [17 Jun 1852]
Nathaniel W & Marinda WILSON at Belfast ME [30 Sept 1847]
Susan M & John P HOLBROOK at Parkman ME [3 Jun 1852]
BLIN Betsey & Aaron HILTON at Woolwich ME [25 Dec 1835]

BLIN (cont.) David & Harriet YOUNG at Pittston ME [5 Oct 1848]
    Hezekiah & Harriet Newell ALLEY both of Boston MA at Bath ME [13 Aug 1846]
BLISH Harriet E & Noah WOODS Esq of Gardiner ME at Hallowell ME [15 Oct 1846]
    James Capt & Isabella JOSE at Hallowell ME [30 Nov 1833]
    Mary Paulina d/o Capt James BLISH of Hallowell ME & Capt Stacy B LEWIS of Galveston TX at New York City [23 Oct 1845]
    Sarah J & Phineas PRATT at Gardiner ME [27 Apr 1848]
BLISS James S Rev of Ft Wayne IN & Eliza M MERRILL at Portland ME [10 Oct 1844]
    M B of Wilbraham MA & Martha J FULLER of Pittston ME at Dresden ME [28 May 1846]
BLODGETT Elizabeth & John P Rev SKEELE of Hallowell ME at Bucksport ME [20 Feb 1851]
    Mary T d/o Dea Bliss BLODGETT & Rev Enoch POND of Georgetown ME by Rev Dr POND, 25th ult at Bucksport ME [10 Jun 1843]
    Samuel A & Elizabeth J BEAN at Belfast ME [6 May 1847]
BLOOD Arthur M & Mary L SLATTERY at Thomaston ME [26 Feb 1852]
    Ezekiel D & Almira WAUGH at Readfield ME [27 Feb 1841]
    George Capt & Mrs Mary EDGECOMB at Gardiner ME on 8th inst [25 Jan 1849]
    Henry P of Bucksport ME & Eliza WHITE of Orland ME at Atkinson ME [13 May 1847]
    John W of Waldo ME & Julia G METCALF at Camden ME [28 Jan 1847]
    Mary Mrs & Silas C BRYANT at Union ME [24 Apr 1851]
    Mary & Daniel D LAKEMAN of Hallowell ME at Boston MA [4 Apr 1844]
    Oliver & Nancy M JONES at Augusta ME [30 May 1837]
    Rachel (Mrs) & William PARSONS of Sebec ME at Foxcroft ME [15 May 1845]
    William H & Cordelia A GALLOPP at Thomaston ME [8 Oct 1846]
BLOSSOM Alden Gen & Jane WOOD at Turner ME [10 Apr 1851]
    George W of Turner ME & Faustina A B FOGG at Gray ME [29 Nov 1849]
    Noble of Norway ME & Mary Ann BOLSTER at Paris ME [19 Dec 1844]
    Noble & Mrs Eliza TWITCHELL both of Portland ME on Thurs eve by E WILEY at Portland ME [2 Oct 1835]
    Waldo & Susan d/o William CARY Esq at Turner ME [22 May 1835]
BLUE Jacob P Lt & Mary J PRESCOTT by Elder J B PRESCOTT on 1st inst at Monmouth ME [4 Jan 1834]
    John of Monmouth ME & Agnis KEEN of Leeds ME by Rev Jedediah B PRESCOTT at Monmouth ME [15 Feb 1840]
    Mary Jane (Mrs) & Beza L STORER by Rev J PRESCOTT at Monmouth ME [11 Sept 1845]
BLUNT Aaron D & Helen TITCOMB on 25 Jun at Norridgewock ME [8 Jul 1852]
    D D of Norridgewock ME & Lucinda G BISHOP of Mt Vernon ME at Hallowell ME [11 Jul 1840]
    Sarah C & Mr A H WYMAN at Norridgewock ME [1 Jan 1852]
    Thomas J & Nancy STONE at Union ME [20 May 1847]
BOARDMAN Aphia W & Wm P LONGLEY at Norridgewock ME [3 Jan 1850]
    Eliza F & Thomas P WHITE at Hope ME [26 Feb 1852]
    Elmira J & George W GREATEN at Starks ME [26 Jun 1845]

BOARDMAN (cont.) George H of Mercer ME & Ruhamah FRIZZELL at Starks ME [1 Oct 1846]
    Isaac M Capt & Keziah EMERY at Belfast ME [20 Jul 1848]
    John & Martha W BARTLETT at Bangor ME [24 Jan 1834]
    Mary E & Rev Henry DEXTER at Milltown ME [20 Feb 1851]
    Mary E & William S LONGLEY at Norridgewock ME [19 Feb 1852]
    Mary & H B STOYWEL Esq at Farmington ME [9 Oct 1845]
    Mehitable of Bloomfield ME & Levi POWERS of Norridgewock ME at Bloomfield [20 Jan 1837]
    Nancy D H & Sandborn DINSMORE of Norridgewock ME at Bloomfield ME [24 Jul 1845]
    Ruth A & George DYER Jr of Searsmont ME at Belfast ME [27 Mar 1845]
    Samuel M & Amelia H HILL of New Portland ME at Norridgewock ME [22 May 1851]
    Sarah A of Hope ME & Uriah E McINTIRE of Camden ME at Belfast ME [22 Jul 1847]
    Sarah O & Frederick HOYT of Bloomfield ME at Norridgewock ME [7 Feb 1850]
    Seth C Capt & Sarah F CHUTE at Belfast ME [14 Oct 1847]
    Thomas of Frankfort ME & Margaret Ann DOWNS of Swanville ME at Prospect ME [16 Apr 1842]
BOBINSON Margaret L & Geo H KEITH of North Bridgewater MA on 3 Sept by Rev JUDD at Augusta ME [13 Sept 1849]
BODFISH Charles N Gen & Mary Ann WYMAN at Norridgewock ME [13 Nov 1838]
    David P & Delia DAMON at Gardiner ME [5 Sept 1844]
BODGE Almira & Adoniram Judson MACE at Readfield ME [8 Jan 1846]
BODWELL Sarah & Joseph C JAYNE of New Sharon ME at Hallowell ME [18 Nov 1843]
BOGAN John & Mary Jane EDWARDS at Belfast ME [13 May 1852]
BOGS Lucy Ann & Isaac I BURTON at Warren ME [29 Jan 1846]
BOHANAN Margaret H & Henry P WHITNEY at Alexander ME [14 Feb 1850]
BOIES Gilman of Skowhegan ME & Lucy H BOIES at Calais ME [15 Nov 1849]
    Ithamer of Skowhegan ME & Emma ROBINSON of Concord at Bingham ME [1 Jul 1852]
    Lucy H & Gilman BOIES of Skowhegan ME at Calais ME [15 Nov 1849]
BOLAND Ruth A & Ansel LOTHROP of Belfast ME at Damariscotta ME [24 Apr 1845]
BOLDEN Sarah C of Bath ME & George WILLIAMS formerly of Boston MA by Rev ELLINGWOOD on 31st ult at Bath ME [15 Apr 1843]
BOLKCOM Ann Elizabeth & Walter GETCHELL at Waterville ME [7 Dec 1833]
BOLSTER Mary Ann & Noble BLOSSOM of Norway ME at Paris ME [19 Dec 1844]
BOND Alanson & Lucinda KENNEDY at Jefferson ME [19 Mar 1846]
    Alexander K & Zalema JACKSON at Jefferson ME [19 Mar 1846]
    Caroline M youngest d/o the late Thomas BOND Esq & Thomas H SANFORD merchant of Bangor ME by Rev E GILLET, DD on 6th inst at Hallowell ME [26 Sept 1837]

BOND (cont.) Hannah & William YOUNG of Washington ME at Jefferson ME [18 Jan 1840]
  Henry of Nobleboro ME & Eliza A FARNHAM at Sidney ME [1 Aug 1837]
  Henry of Nobleboro ME & Eliza Ann BAKER at Sidney ME [18 Jul 1837]
  Henry & Anna COTTLE of Mt Vernon ME at Boston MA [25 Oct 1849]
  Hollis Esq & Abigail YORK at Brewer ME [13 May 1852]
  Merinda H & John ROGERS of Phipsburg ME at Lewiston ME [21 Jun 1849]
  Philinde & Joseph BREED at Shehoygan Falls WI [20 Jul 1848]
  Samuel J & Emily WRIGHT at Jefferson ME [19 Mar 1846]
BONNER Parmela C & Melvin O REDLIN, Jr at Pittston ME [1 Jul 1847]
BONNEY Andrew H of Phillips ME & Sarah R d/o Daniel MARSTON Esq by Rev EDGECOMB on 1st inst at Mt Vernon ME [4 Jun 1846]
  Apphia R & Elbridge G BRIDGHAM of Paris ME at Turner ME [23 Apr 1846]
  Betsey B & George C COFFIN at Buckfield ME [27 Feb 1841]
  Calvin F of Wayne ME & Mary L LAINE at Hallowell ME [20 Jun 1844]
  Deborah & Charles R JONES at Turner ME [5 Feb 1852]
  I N & Emily STANLEY by Seth MAY Esq on 8th inst at Winthrop ME [20 Jun 1837]
  Isaac N of Monson ME & Lucy H MONROE of Abbot at Abbot ME [13 Jul 1839]
  Mary A & John READ at Turner ME on the 18th ult [8 Jun 1848]
  Rowland B & Jane RECORD both of Minot ME at Buckfield ME [27 Feb 1851]
BONSEY Mercy & Parlin F HILDRETH at Ellsworth ME [12 Sept 1840]
BOOBAR Ezra D & Rebecca A FOSTER both of Milo ME at Foxcroft ME [27 Jul 1839]
BOOBIER William & Philena DONNELL at Bath ME [14 Feb 1850]
BOODY Alvin Esq the Principal of the Academy at Fryeburg ME & Sarah E SMALL of Lewiston ME at Portsmouth NH [11 Mar 1852]
  Henry B & Ann Maria PROCTOR at Westbrook ME [11 Jul 1840]
  Hannah (Mrs) & Joseph W COLE at Saco ME [17 Jun 1847]
  Olive & Benjamin KELLEY both of Orono ME by Myric EMERSON Esq at Orono ME [29 Apr 1843]
BOOKER Charles & Mrs Fanny WHITNEY by John PETTINGILL on 10th inst at Augusta ME [14 Mar 1850]
  Hannah L & Joseph ROWSE at (Augusta) ME [13 Jan 1848]
  Jane H & Addison METCALF of Lisbon ME at Bowdoinham ME [19 Apr 1849]
  Jane of Durham ME & Luther STORER of Bath ME at Durham ME [26 Jun 1838]
  John of Bowdoin ME & Julia Ann BAKER of Litchfield ME at Bath ME [14 May 1846]
  Lydia Ann & Timothy BOOKER at Gardiner ME [29 Apr 1847]
  Mary J & Herrick HUNTINGTON at Gardiner ME [6 Jan 1848]
  Sarah of Gardiner ME & Thomas BOOKER of No 6 ME at Gardiner ME [23 Sept 1847]
  Thomas of No 6 ME & Sarah BOOKER of Gardiner ME at Gardiner ME [23 Sept 1847]
  Timothy & Lydia Ann BOOKER at Gardiner ME [29 Apr 1847]
BOOTH Betsey & Louis BOULANGER at Skowhegan ME [22 Nov 1849]

BOOTHBAY Charles, M.D., & Helen L SWEETSIR at New Gloucester ME [12 Feb 1852]
  Jeremiah F & Nancy P SUTHERLAND both of Biddeford at Saco ME [13 Apr 1848]
  Thaddeus F of Embden ME & Philena FELKER at Concord [1 Jan 1852]
BOOTHBY Alexander Dr & Eliza D GRANT of Bridgton ME at Unity ME [26 Apr 1849]
  Arthur & Rachel C SCAMMON at Saco ME [29 Mar 1849]
  Catherine of Turner? ME & Joseph BEALS of Livermore ME 17 Nov at Livermore [10 Dec 1842]
  Hannah & John H SCRIBNER at Unity ME [21 Jan 1843]
  Ichabod of Livermore ME & Mrs Rebecca JONES at Norway ME [28 Aug 1851]
  Samuel of Turner & Fanny FOSS of Leeds at Leeds ME [10 Dec 1842]
BORLAND Joseph G of Newcastle ME & Abigail d/o Edmund DANA Esq of Wiscasset ME on Tues morn last by Rev MATHER at Wiscasset ME [8 Oct 1842]
  Ruth Ann & Maj Ansel LOTHROP of Belfast ME at Nobleboro ME [8 May 1845]
  Sarah C d/o Capt Samuel & Capt Arthur CHILD at Damariscotta ME [10 Sept 1846]
BORNHEIMER John of Waldoboro ME & Abigail GREENOUGH at Wiscasset ME [25 Jun 1842]
BOSSE Henry O & Almira CROOKER at Oxford ME [14 Aug 1845]
BOSTON Cyrene & Clark MITCHELL both of Avon ME on 6 Dec by Charles J TALBOT Esq at Phillips ME [16 Dec 1847]
  Phebe J & Benjamin F MORSE both of (Augusta) ME on 3 Feb by T SEARLS Esq at Hallowell ME [21 Feb 1850]
BOSWORTH Abel W formerly of Norridgewock ME & Rachel M WEIR at Mobile AL [14 Mar 1844]
  Abigail of Starks ME & Josiah HINKLEY at Mercer ME [20 Jan 1837]
  Anna & Augusta ARNOLD at Bath ME [27 May 1852]
  Lucinda H & Cephas R VAUGHAN at Madison ME [10 Feb 1848]
  Cyrus & Mary A PARKER at Norridgewock ME [18 Feb 1847]
  Warren W of Solon ME & Emeline BURNS at Madison ME [10 Jul 1851]
BOUDEN Mary Ann & Aaron BICKFORD at Norridgewock ME [21 Jan 1843]
BOULANGER Louis & Betsey BOOTH at Skowhegan ME [22 Nov 1849]
BOULTEN Ruth S & William F JOHNSON at Albion ME [25 Nov 1847]
BOULTER Lettice E & Isaac S MORSE at Montville ME on 16th Jun [23 Jun 1852]
BOURK Bernice B & John RAMSEY, publisher of the *Thomaston National Republican* at Bath ME [22 Jul 1833]
BOURN/BOURNE Abby of Sandwich MA & L CLAY Esq of Gardiner ME at New York City [8 Oct 1846]
  Major & Dorcus ROUNDS at Poland ME [29 Aug 1844]
  William Col & Lydia CURTIS at Wells ME [30 Oct 1835]
BOUTELLE Helen R d/o Hon Timothy, & Edwin NOYES Esq Attorney at Law Thurs eve at Waterville ME [21 Aug 1841]
  John of Hopkinton NH & Eunice M BLAKE at Corinth ME [18 Oct 1849]
BOUTELLE Susan W & Benjamin R PAGE Esq of Conway NH at Bloomfield ME [16 Oct 1851]

BOVEY Amelia J H & Studley BISBEE both of Bath ME at Bath [2 Sept 1847]
    Elizabeth A N & Andrew M'FADDEN at Bath ME [11 Mar 1847]
    Samuel C & Mehitable TIBBETTS at Bath ME [28 Jan 1847]
    Sarah F & William H LOVEJOY at Bath ME [4 Dec 1851]
BOWDEN George & Mary Ann BENSON at Brooksville ME [11 Feb 1843]
    Mary & Christopher ERSKINE both of Pittston ME at Augusta ME [11 Dec 1845]
    Sarah & Charles WILLIAMS both of Augusta ME by Charles A RUSS Esq at China ME [14 Jan 1843]
BOWDITCH G of Portland ME & Olive A LIBBY at Limerick ME [21 Sept 1848]
BOWDOIN George of US Navy & Ann d/o Wm S BENSON Esq at Brooksville ME [21 Jan 1843]
BOWEN Isaac Lt of US 1st Artillery, & Catherine CARY at Houlton Aroostook Co ME [10 Apr 1845]
    Mary & Capt William SMALL both of Prospect ME at Belfast ME [7 Jan 1847]
    Rebecca & Elbridge THOMPSON at Bath ME [18 Dec 1845]
BOWKER David & Sylvina Gordon of MT Vernon ME at Readfield ME [30 Aug 1849]
    Joseph & Hannah A LARRABEE at Phipsburg ME [14 Mar 1837]
    Lydia & Dea Stephen MARTIN at Bradford ME [30 Dec 1836]
    Parker H & Charlotte A HUSSEY at Hallowell ME [20 Nov 1851]
    Robert & Martha DUNNING at Brunswick ME [19 Dec 1834]
    Samuel Rev of Union & Elizabeth EATON at Harpswell ME [4 May 1848]
BOWLEN Lorenzo A & Mary K CHASE both of Palermo ME at Montville ME [25 Apr 1850]
BOWLER Charles & Susan A GARDINER of this town (Augusta) ME by Rev Jesse MARTIN at China ME on 14 Jun [29 Jun 1848]
    Mary J & Wm A HAMLIN both of Augusta ME at Sidney ME [22 Mar 1849]
BOWLES Cilenda & Richard F PATTERSON at Belfast ME [8 Nov 1849]
    Elvira H & Mr W H CHASE of Bucksport ME at Rockland ME [8 May 1851]
    Ithamer & Elvira H SPEARS at Thomaston ME [8 Apr 1847]
    Joshua P & Mary M BECK Mon eve by Rev FULLER at Augusta [23 Dec 1843]
    Mary & James W WING both of Winthrop ME at Wayne ME [23 Jul 1846]
    Sophronia (Mrs) & John MORRILL 2nd on 6 Nov at Winthrop ME [13 Nov 1841]
    Thomas S & Eliza d/o Jacob EMMONS Esq on the 23rd by Rev NOTT at Bath ME [5 Feb 1842]
BOWLEY Gideon & Nancy NOYES at Gardiner ME [11 Dec 1845]
    Hannah & John A KING at Skowhegan ME [2 Dec 1843]
    Mary S & Charles LITTLEFIELD at Hartland ME [7 Mar 1850]
BOWMAN Abel & Syrene KNOWLES at Readfield ME [25 Apr 1840]
    Abijah of Topsham ME & Mary B GOWELL at Bowdoin ME [4 Feb 1847]
    Baxter & Caroline E STEWART at Gardiner ME [8 Feb 1844]
    Christiana of Sidney ME & Gustavus MARSHALL of Waterville ME at Hallowell ME [9 Jan 1851]

BOWMAN (cont.) Christopher C & Harriet M STOVER on Tue morn by Rev M FULLER at Augusta ME [16 May 1844]
John & Amelia A CLARK both of Sebasticook ME at Bloomfield ME [27 Jul 1848]
Sarah H of Augusta ME & Dr Thomas SHERMAN of Dresden ME at Augusta ME [23 Nov 1833]
Susan G & James NASH at Gardiner ME [6 Nov 1838]
William J & Olive WADE by J J EVELETH Esq 7th inst at Augusta ME [15 Aug 1844]
BOWMEN Amos of Burnham ME & Dolley DOLIFF of Belmont ME at Burnham ME [8 Jul 1836]
BOWN J T Capt of Bath & Lydia Ann MERRITT of Brunswick ME at New York City [15 Jun 1848]
BOYD Adam J & Mary P WHITE at East Machias ME [26 Aug 1847]
Caroline & Capt Henry TREAT at Frankfort ME [26 Jul 1849]
Eleanor & William BROWN both of Deer Island ME at Eastport ME [15 Jan 1846]
Elizabeth & Wm LEWIS on Sun eve last by Rev Daniel FULLER of Winthrop ME at Wayne ME [9 May 1834]
Lendal G S & Theresa ORNE d/o Hon Nicolas EMERY at Portland ME [11 Sept 1835]
Sarah F & Gilbert C TRUFANT of Bath ME at Wiscasset ME [28 Aug 1835]
Thurston H & Sarah PARSONS at Dover ME/NH? [11 May 1839]
BOYDEN Eliza & George GATES of Nova Scotia Canada at Perry ME? [5 Mar 1846]
BOYINGTON Jane S & Jacob HASKELL of Salem MA at Augusta ME on 2 Feb by Rev Z THOMPSON [13 Feb 1851]
Mary Jane & Charles B BARKER at (Augusta) ME on 1st inst [13 Apr 1848]
BOYNTON A R, M.D., & Mary C HALE of Norridgewock ME at Lowell MA [17 Jan 1850]
Edward Capt of Alna ME & Mary Jane GIVEN at Newcastle ME [6 May 1843]
Gorham L of Bangor ME & Louisa M BASFORD at Dixmont ME [15 May 1835]
Harriet & George CHADBOURN of Gorham ME at Cornish ME [25 Feb 1847]
James L & Adeline SHEPARD by Stewart FOSTER Esq at Hallowell ME [26 Jun 1845]
James L & Mary WILLIAMSON at Hallowell ME [27 Nov 1841]
Mahalia L & Mr J J WILLIAMS at (Augusta) ME on 23d inst [1 Jun 1848]
Martha H & Ashur BURNS at Augusta ME [22 Aug 1840]
Mary D & John INGERSOLL both of Gorham ME at South Windham ME [21 Oct 1847]
Mehitable Ann & Hosea WEST at Hallowell ME [22 Jun 1848]
Stephen & Lydia Ann HAMILTON by Rev W A P DILLINGHAM at (Augusta) ME [6 Jul 1848]
Thurston H & Sarah PARSONS at Dover [27 Apr 1839]
BRACE Mary & Charles WILSON at Bath ME [7 Sept 1833]
BRACKET/BRACKETT Benjamin & Susan TUFTS at New Gloucester ME [9 Aug 1849]

BRACKET (cont.) Caroline & Eleazer EDGECOMB at Belmont ME [18 May 1848]
Edwin C & Sarah A SWETT both of Biddeford ME at Saco ME [26 Jun 1851]
Fanny L & David B SAWYER at Norway ME [8 Aug 1840]
Frances J & Mr Albion K P GRANT at Denmark ME [7 Apr 1848]
Hiram & Mary C FOSTER at No 11 Aroostook County ME [14 Aug 1845]
James H & Deborah R BROWN at China ME [28 Feb 1850]
James & Rebecca RACKLIFF at Thomaston ME [5 Feb 1836]
John & & Hannah N TURNER at Levant ME [21 Aug 1851]
Joshua of Belfast ME & Julia Ann HILL at Lincolnville ME [11 Mar 1847]
Mary Jane & Wm RHOADES of Thomaston ME at Belfast ME [11 Mar 1847]
Mehitable, ae 47, & Wm HARMOND, a Revolutionary soldier, ae 70 at Gorham ME [6 May 1833]
Nancy of Brunswick ME & Willoughby H BAILEY of Harrington ME at Brunswick ME [28 May 1842]

BRADBURY Ammi R Rev of Auburn ME & Caroline L JOHNSON at Farmington ME [14 Mar 1844]
Charles Capt & Nancy M BUTLER at Thomaston ME [22 Oct 1846]
Charles & Mrs Martha RICH at Bloomfield ME [3 Dec 1846]
Edwin of Standish ME & Mary C HOPKINSON at Buxton ME [29 May 1845]
Emily & Francis K SWAN at Calais ME [7 Oct 1843]
Louisa Jane of Chesterville ME & Nathaniel GAGE of New Sharon ME at Farmington ME [7 Jan 1843]
Lucius Esq & Emily GOULD at Eastport ME [21 Jan 1847]
Matilda A only d/o John BRADBURY Esq & J W POTTLE of St Louis at Bangor ME 13th ult [2 Oct 1845]
Matilda F & Joseph HOYT at Wilton ME [26 Dec 1844]
Matthias V & Eunice C WATSON at Parkman ME [9 Jan 1845]
Osgood, Esq formerly of New Gloucester ME & Mary Mourina DINSMOOR at Burlington VT [2 Oct 1845]
Sabrina E of Norway ME & William P STEVENS of Carroll at Norway ME [19 Mar 1846]
Samuel H Rev & Mary E SMALL of Lubec ME at Eastport ME [15 Jan 1846]
Sarah E & Obed C BURGESS by Rev W A DREW at Augusta ME [28 Aug 1842]
Stephen D & Maria S MAYHEW at Dennysville ME [2 Jan 1845]
William of Thomaston ME & Sarah B HARRINGTON at Newcastle ME [19 Sept 1844]

BRADFORD Alice P & Melzar GILBERT at Turner ME [13 Nov 1838]
Flora C & Meritt COOLIDGE of Hallowell ME at Livermore ME [7 Dec 1833]
Joseph C & Elizabeth A CHADSEY at Bath ME [4 Jul 1840]
Joseph H of Lynn ME & Joanna H McINTIRE at New Sharon ME on May 28th [8 Jun 1848]
Louisa & George S MORRILL at Winthrop ME on Dec 5 [14 Dec 1848]
Martha B & Joseph H LOCKE of Boston MA and formerly of Hallowell ME at Livermore ME [25 Sept 1845]

BRADFORD (cont.) Martha B & Joseph M LOCKE of Boston MA at Livermore ME [4 Sept 1845]
Mary E & Noble N MONROE both of Auburn ME at Turner ME [26 Aug 1847]
Mary & Capt Charles B LEMONT at Bath ME [11 Nov 1843]
Osca Miss & Brinsley S KELLEY of Winthrop ME at Turner ME [30 Oct 1851]
Prudence formerly of Turner ME & A A SOULE at Harmony ME [18 Jan 1844]
Prudence D & Capt Alfred A SOULE at Harmony ME [8 Feb 1844]
Roxana & Seth HARRIS Jr at Turner ME [13 Nov 1838]
Zoa Miss & Reuel TOWER at Turner ME [22 Jan 1852]
BRADISH John of Biddeford ME & Mrs Mary CARPENTER at Waterborough ME [7 Oct 1847]
BRADLEY Abigail Mrs ae 19, & Dennis FAIRBANKS of Letter F ME ae 56 at Wakefield [15 Apr 1847]
Asa & Mrs Lovina WORTH by Jonathan MOWER Esq at Vassalboro ME on 25 Jan [12 Feb 1852]
Henry W & Nancy S KINCAID at Hallowell ME [1 Jan 1846]
Jane Augusta & Joseph WILLIAMS both of Harpswell ME at Bath ME [23 Jul 1846]
Phebe & John A TURNER at Vassalboro ME on 14 Oct by Edward GRAY Esq [30 Oct 1851][13 Nov 1851]
Sarah Ann Mrs & Daniel COLE Jr at Saco ME [4 Dec 1835]
Sarah Mrs & Abijah USHER of Hollis ME at Fryeburg ME [27 Nov 1845]
Timothy F of Topsham ME & Eleanor D MORSE at Brunswick ME [9 Nov 1833]
William G of Bradford ME & Phebe E TREWORGY at Bluehill ME [7 Mar 1840]
BRADMAN Sophia Ann & Col Wm ELLINGWOOD of Frankfort ME at Belfast ME [23 Nov 1839]
BRADSTREET Silas of Liberty ME & Clarissa REED at China ME [2 Nov 1848]
William & Julia S TARBOX at Gardiner ME [27 Jan 1848]
Joseph Esq of Gardiner ME & Laura STEVENS of Worcester ME at Worcester [12 Feb 1842]
Thomas F Esq of Jefferson ME & Caroline T WHITAKER at Albion ME [24 Jun 1843]
BRAGDON Hiram H & Caroline A DIMOCK at Limington ME [27 May 1847]
Huldah T & James B MITCHELL at Bath ME [23 Dec 1847]
Martha & Freeman HODGSDON at York ME [22 Apr 1836]
Oliver & Adeline CUTTS both of Monroe ME at Monroe [6 Feb 1845]
BRAGG Albert H & Roxana F FARRINGTON at Vassalboro ME on Feb 2 by John HOMANS Esq [6 Feb 1851]
Alvin of China ME & Sarah F RICHARDSON of Winslow ME at Vassalboro ME [18 Apr 1834]
Ann E & George F RICHARDS of China ME at Vassalboro ME on Mar 2d by John HOMANS Esq [6 Mar 1851]
Charles A & Marcia HUSTON at Dover [20 Mar 1841]
Eliza M & Eliakim AMES of Old Town ME on 9 Aug by William BOWLER Esq at China ME [16 Aug 1849]

BRAGG (cont.) George W & Mrs Sophia RANDALL on 26 Dec at Augusta ME [15 Feb 1844]
George & Christiana G WILSON at Albion ME [9 Sept 1847]
Lucy A & Edward A LAWRENCE at Castine ME [27 Mar 1845]
Lydia of Winslow ME & Capt Geo PILSBURY Jr on 3 Oct at Vassalboro ME [11 Oct 1849]
Lydia F & Gustavus B PAGE of China ME on 26 Aug by John MOWER Esq at East Vassalboro ME [30 Aug 1849]
Martha & Jacob WYMAN on Sun eve by David G ROBINSON Esq at Winslow ME [3 Apr 1845]
Rebecca & John McLANE at Vassalboro ME [29 Jul 1852]
Samuel & Mercy JACOBS at Sidney ME [31 Oct 1840]
Sarah P & Lorenzo FARRINGTON at East Vassalboro ME [30 Aug 1849]
Simon & Martha LYON at (Augusta) ME [25 May 1848]
Washington J, M.D., & Katharine P WOODSUM by Rev Cyril PEARL on 18th inst at Hartford ME [4 Jun 1842]
BRAILEY Eliza W & Joseph HUFF Jr both of Hallowell ME at Gardiner ME [15 Mar 1849]
Jane W & John L PRATT by Kendall WRIGHT Esq at Weld ME [8 Jul 1852]
Patience A & James H WINSLOW at Thomaston ME [14 Nov 1844]
BRAINARD Catharine & Joseph DEEPARR at Bath ME [12 Mar 1846]
Elizabeth of East Winthrop ME & David CARGILL of Hallowell ME on Sunday last by Rev F MERRIAM at the Baptist Meeting House in East Winthrop ME [23 Sept 1843]
Nehemiah S & Sarah G CLARK at New Sharon ME [26 Aug 1843]
Rufus A of Hallowell ME & Rosetta F BRIDGHAM at Paris ME [29 Oct 1846]
Rufus A 2nd & Abigail H SHAW on Sun eve by Rev Franklin MERRIAM on 20th ult at Winthrop ME [12 Jun 1841]
William A & Roxana WEEKS at New Sharon ME [6 May 1847]
BRAINERD Franklin & Clarinda SHEPARD at Readfield ME on Jul 20 by Rev LEWIS [7 Aug 1851]
S A Miss & Dr George FIELD at Northfield MA [11 Mar 1852]
BRALEY Frances W & Thaddeus DAY at Hallowell ME [29 Jan 1846]
BRAMHALL John C & Hannah E ROBINSON at Belfast ME [21 May 1846]
BRAN/BRANN Adelia & A J Mr WRIGHT at Gardiner ME [20 Feb 1851]
Benjamin B & Abigail Matilda WINTERS at Waterville ME [3 Jun 1852]
Catharine of Belgrade ME & Daniel MOSHER by S TITCOMB Jr Esq on 8th inst Augusta ME [16 Sept 1847]
Cyrus & Nancy WYERS at Gardiner ME [16 Oct 1835]
Francis H & Loraina E HOUSE by Rev Mr ALLEN at (Augusta) ME on 30 Apr [11 May 1848]
Hannah & D H KELLY at East Hallowell ME [27 Sept 1849]
Harriet Ann & Henry CANNON of Hallowell ME at Gardiner ME [7 Jun 1849]
Martha A & Henry A ALBEE at Hallowell ME [10 Jun 1852]
Roxanna & S W TOWNSEND at Gardiner ME [26 Apr 1849]
Simon & Mary SOMES at Albion ME [2 Mar 1839]
Susan & Jas W TRASK both of Gardiner ME at East Hallowell ME [27 Sept 1849]
William & Sybil TOWL at Gardiner ME [5 Dec 1844]

Marriage Notices from the "Maine Farmer"

BRANCH Bryant of Belgrade ME & Susan Wade at Smithfield ME [14 Oct 1843]
Hannah F & Henry SIVADIE at Augusta ME [16 Jul 1846]
Helen Z & Geo A NORCROSS on 28 Nov at Augusta ME [9 Dec 1847]
Ira & Mary Jane RICHARDSON by Rev FARMER at Belgrade ME [7 Sept 1833]
Mary C d/o Mr Palmer BRANCH of Augusta ME & John L FERSON at Lowell MA [3 Dec 1846]
William of Waterville ME & Emeline ROWE by Thomas ELDRED Esq on 19th inst at Belgrade ME [30 Oct 1845]
BRANDISH Ann Maria & Dr Alexander PARSONS of Eastport ME at Portland ME [24 Oct 1844]
BRANSCOMB John & Lucy E PARSHLEY at Bath ME [20 May 1836]
BRAWN Jonathan of Bloomfield ME & Mrs Hannah FELKER at Bangor ME [14 Mar 1844]
Nancy Mrs & S B BYRAM at Dover ME [11 Jan 1849]
BRAY Eliphalet D Gen & Caroline CHIPMAN both of Kingfield ME by Charles PIKE Esq on 20th inst at Kingfield ME [5 Dec 1834]
Harrison & Kezia M WEYMOUTH both of Dedham MA at Freeman ME [28 Feb 1850]
Lucia Maria of Skowhegan ME & John SEAVEY Jr of Starks ME at Bloomfield ME [14 Mar 1850]
Lucy Ann & Edward A LAWRENCE at Castine ME [20 Mar 1845]
Washington of Naples ME & Catharine JORDAN at Casco ME [9 Jul 1846]
BRAYTON Samuel B of Cranston RI & Harriet DREW at Newfield ME [23 Apr 1846]
BRAZIER Eunice K & Allen CARVER at Belfast ME [10 Jul 1838]
Nancy & Moses WELLS at Phillips ME [22 Apr 1833]
BREARCLIFFE Catharine of St Andrews New Brunswick Canada & W R SNOW publisher of the *Frontier Journal*, Calais ME at St Andrews [21 Aug 1845]
BRECK Edward Jr of Nobleboro ME & Mary DEARBORN at Vassalboro ME [19 Aug 1847]
BREED Henry N of Lynn MA & Maria N ROBERTS formerly of (Augusta) ME at Danvers MA [20 May 1852]
Joseph & Philinde BOND formerly of Bangor ME at Shehoygan Falls WI [20 Jul 1848]
Rebecca S & John WYER by Edward GRAY Esq at Vassalboro ME [18 Jan 1849]
BREMNER Amy J & Francis M LAMB at Winslow ME on New Year's eve [8 Jan 1852]
BRETT Aphia & Stephen T BEEMAN of Oxford ME at Paris ME [19 Apr 1849]
H A (Mr) of Lewiston ME & Hannah T GIBBS at Bridgewater [20 Nov 1851]
John of Augusta ME & Caroline KIMBALL of Hallowell ME by Geo M WESTON Esq at Augusta ME [3 Apr 1845]
Lucy A & Hannibal BELCHER of Farmington ME at Strong ME [23 Jan 1845]

BRETTUM Francis W d/o William H BRETTUM Esq of Livermore ME & R S MORRISON of Frankfort ME at Livermore ME [4 Dec 1845]

BRETTUN Emily A & Joel A WHITMORE at Livermore ME [12 Oct 1848]
Susan S & L STRICKLAND at Livermore ME [2 Nov 1848]

BREWER Caroline & Smith TINKHAM at Robbinston ME [13 Jul 1848]
J of Charlotte ME & Sarah W LOWETT at Perry ME [12 Jun 1845]
Thomas M Dr of Boston MA one of the editors of the *Atlas* & Sally R COFFIN at Damariscotta ME [7 Jun 1849]

BREWSTER Elitha G & Edwin J DELANO at Rockland ME [3 Jun 1852]
George M of Bridgewater MA & Elvira BUCK at Norway ME [19 Dec 1844]
Henry B of Boston MA publisher of the *Independant Messenger* & Susan O EASTMAN at Fryeburg ME [21 Aug 1835]
Mary Ann & Woster LEIGHTON of Lubec ME at Eastport ME [21 Mar 1850]
Sarah C & Bethuel WASHBURN at Parkman ME [30 Apr 1846]
Sarah K & Hazen B NELSON at Thomaston ME [29 Jan 1846]

BRIARD Julia & Stephen DOE of Windsor ME at Jefferson ME [15 Jul 1847]
Oliver Jr of Boston MA & Helen M CHASE at Waterville ME [10 Sept 1846]

BRIDGE Charles & Nancy AMES at Gardiner ME on 10th inst [28 Dec 1848]
Horatio Esq purser in United States Navy & Charlotte MARSHALL of Boston MA at New York [4 Jun 1846]
Mary P & Edward C LOWE at Brunswick ME [8 May 1845]
William Esq & Mrs Eliza J WILLIAMS at Augusta ME [9 Jan 1841]

BRIDGES Jeremiah P of Lexington MA & Susannah SHAW of Waterville ME at Clinton ME on 26th Mar [10 Apr 1851]
Stephen O & Martha C WENTWORTH of Deer Island ME at Eastport ME [2 Jan 1845]

BRIDGHAM Elbridge G of Paris ME & Apphia R BONNEY at Turner ME [23 Apr 1846]
Everett H of Leeds ME & Sally A WORTHING of China ME at Vassalboro ME [22 Jul 1847]
Maria L & Lucius DRESSER of Turner ME at West Minot ME [7 Sept 1839]
Mary J & Joseph D HAM at Wayne ME [29 Jan 1846]
Persis & Charles A FRENCH at Minot ME [13 Feb 1851]
Rosaltha Mrs & Horatio EASTMAN of Conway NH at Bridgton [25 Oct 1849]
Rosetta F & Rufus A BRAINARD of Hallowell ME at Paris ME [29 Oct 1846]
Valentine R & Mehitable C JOSSELYN at Leeds ME on 1 May 1851 by Rev C FULLER [8 May 1851]
William P, M.D., & Delphina K HAYFORD at Canton ME [23 Apr 1846]

BRIGHT Winslow of Cambridge MA & Martha E NOYES of Brunswick ME at Gardiner ME [26 Nov 1846]

BRIER Mehitable & John ANNIS at Goose River [29 Jan 1852]
Abigail S of Belfast ME & Amos GROUT Jr by Rev S G SARGENT at Belfast ME [25 Jun 1842]

BRIERRY A O Miss & Samuel ODIORNE at Bowdoin ME [19 Oct 1848]

BRIERY Uriah & Rachel GOODWIN both of Gardiner ME at Litchfield ME [17 Sept 1846]

Marriage Notices from the "Maine Farmer"

BRIGGS Arvida & Charlotte L BENNETT at Parkman ME [7 Jun 1849]
    Bartlett & Deborah Jane WOODS both of Belmont ME at Belfast ME [31 Jul 1845]
    Benjamin P & Susan SNELL d/o John E SNELL of Augusta ME at Winthrop ME [23 Nov 1839]
    Caleb of Benton ME & Mrs H BRIGGS at Porter ME (The parties are both heroes of the Revolution, the bridegroom about 80, the bride 75, and this marriage gives her a third husband by the name BRIGGS) [11 Apr 1844]
    Frances Elizabeth & John TURNER Jr by Isaac STRICKLAND Esq at Livermore ME [14 Nov 1837]
    George W & Harriet WING at Brunswick ME [22 Oct 1846]
    Hannah J & Marcellus FLAGG at Belmont ME [8 Apr 1847]
    Henry of Vassalboro ME & Elira M SMITH at Woodstock VT on 30 Dec [16 Jan 1851]
    H Mrs & Caleb BRIGGS of Benton ME at Porter ME [11 Apr 1844] See Caleb)
    Jane T & Aaron HAYDEN Esq of Eastport ME at Robbinston ME [24 Jun 1847]
    Julia Jones & William W HOBBS by Isaac STRICKLAND Esq at Livermore ME [14 Nov 1837]
    Louisa S eldest d/o Dr C BRIGGS & Wheelock CRAIG Rev of New Bedford MA? at Augusta ME by Rev Dr TAPPAN [16 Jan 1851]
    Margaret Elizabeth & Samuel O SMITH at Portland ME [11 Jan 1844]
    Margaret H Benjamin S FARROW at Brunswick ME [25 Feb 1847]
    Mary Ann & Isaac N WADSWORTH at Winthrop ME [10 Feb 1848]
    Mary H & John E ANDREWS of Boston MA at Hampden ME [14 August 1851]
    Mary Jane & Robert B DAVIS at (Augusta) ME on New Year's eve [15 Jan 1852]
    Meriam B of Turner ME & Eben G MARTIN of Poland ME by Ezekiel MARTIN Esq on 29th ult at Turner ME [3 Apr 1835]
    Moses of Winthrop ME & Lucy BURR of Litchfield ME at Litchfield [25 Dec 1838]
    Olive of Greene ME & James MERRILL of Lisbon ME by Alfred PIERCE Esq on 19th ult at Greene [7 Feb 1834]
    Peter Capt & Rebecca A HIGGINS at Bath ME [3 Apr 1845]
    Philena & Jacob ROBBINS at the Friends' Meeting House at Winthrop ME [27 Apr 1839]
    R D (Miss) & William FROST at Auburn ME [2 Jan 1851]
    Surranus & Mary Ann HOBBS at Livermore ME [21 Nov 1844]
    Vashti A & Robert H FOLSOM, by Anson CHURCH Esq on 5th inst at Augusta ME [12 Nov 1846]
    Wealthy S & Timothy B LOVELL at Dover ME [5 Sept 1844]
    William 2nd & Rachel DUNNING at Auburn ME [8 Apr 1843]
    William S of Dover ME & Susan W DAVIS, d/o Asa DAVIS Esq of Hallowell ME on Tues eve last by Rev ADLAM at Hallowell ME [26 Jun 1841]
BRIMIJINE Jesse P & Sarah E PETERS at Bath ME [20 Mar 1845]
    Mary T & Horatio N WINSLOW at Bath ME [28 Feb 1837]
BRITNEY Priscilla & Charles H OLMSTEAD at Calais ME [4 Mar 1847]
BRITT William & Melissa M MANNING at Camden ME [12 Feb 1852]

BRITT (cont.) Catharine H of Shirley ME & William MARBLE of Wilson ME on 22 May at Shirley [18 Jun 1842]
 Charles & Julia KIMBALL of Hallowell ME at Augusta ME [22 Oct 1846]
BROAD Daniel S & Mrs Mary Jane BURRILL at East Eddington ME [21 May 1842]
BROCK Margaret A J & John C VARNEY at Dover ME [8 Feb 1844]
 Jas W & Mary F TOWNS both of Kennebec ME at Augusta ME on 25th Sept by Rev H M BLAKE [16 Oct 1851]
BROCKWAY Henry L & Almira L DORR at Dover ME? [15 May 1851]
BRONSON Frances Swan & Rev Jonathan EDWARDS at (Augusta) ME on 31st Aug [14 Sept 1848]
BROOKING James M Capt of Bath ME & Mrs Cordelia T FOSTER at Bowdoinham ME [8 Apr 1836]
BROOKINGS Gardiner H & Susan J SHAW at Woolwich ME [24 Apr 1851]
 Harriet N & John C BABCOCK at Pittston ME [31 May 1849]
 Samuel H Capt & Paulina A SMITH at Hallowell ME [18 Jul 1844]
BROOKS Erastus, Esq of New York, & Margaret Dawes CRANCH yngst d/o Chief Judge CRANCH at Washington DC [25 Jan 1844]
 J S Rev & Fidelia C COBURN of Bloomfield ME on 5 Oct of Mt Hope Mission School at Waterloo, Canada West [4 Nov 1847]
 John C & Caroline W d/o Albion K PARRIS at Washington DC [3 Jun 1847]
 John C & Martha DERBY at Warren ME [19 Oct 1839]
 Lucy Ann of Eastport ME & Luke BROOKS of Salem MA at Eastport ME [6 Nov 1835]
 Lucy Williams eldst d/o W A BROOKS Esq & Hon Samuel CONY by Rev Dr TAPPAN on 22d inst at Augusta ME [29 Nov 1849]
 Luke of Salem MA & Lucy Ann BROOKS of Eastport ME at Eastport [6 Nov 1835]
 Lydia A & Joseph T DONNELL of Gardiner ME at York ME [14 Aug 1845]
 Lydia of Searsmont ME & John T PRESCOTT of Liberty ME at Montville ME [22 Jan 1846]
 Martha Jane & Amos D CROWLEY at Lewiston ME [4 Mar 1852]
 Mary G & John GOSS Jr at Lewiston ME [22 Jul 1847]
 Mary J & Dr E B BANGS of Saco ME at Limerick ME [18 Mar 1847]
 Sarah J & Albert S GREEN at (Augusta) ME on 21st inst [1 Jun 1848]
 Sylvinia & Simon MORRISON both of Hallowell ME at Augusta ME [22 Oct 1846]
BROUNE Isaac F & Lydia E TABER at E Vassalboro ME on 1st Apr 1851 [1 May 1851]
BROWN Achsa & Freeman CLOUGH at Providence RI on 23d Dec [8 Jan 1852]
 Adaline & Joseph NICKLESS at Augusta ME on Aug 7th [21 Aug 1851]
 Addison, M.D., of Lewiston ME & Harriet SINCLAIR of Monmouth ME at Litchfield ME on 12 Jan [16 Jan 1851]
 Adeline & Capt Samuel PARKER at Bloomfield ME [4 Jan 1840]
 Albert of Sebec ME & Pamelia GAREY at Dover ME [27 Nov 1845]
 Alfred S of Boston MA & Mary A HOOK at Providence RI [4 Apr 1850]
 Angeline S & Jesse C MOWER at St Albans ME [12 Feb 1852]
 Anistatia & Hosea B CUSHING at Bath ME [25 Apr 1850]
 Arthur & Martha J WALCH at Bath ME [11 Jun 1846]

BROWN (cont.) Asa Esq of Buxton ME & Rachel CLEAVES of North Yarmouth ME at N Yarmouth [11 Apr 1834]
   Asenath of China ME & John P McCURDY of Palermo ME at China ME [1 Feb 1849]
   Augustus J & Sarah HILL at Bangor ME [10 Jul 1835]
   Aurelia P & Nathan PARSONS at Atkinson ME [17 Jul 1851]
   B B & Caroline d/o Josiah BATCHELDER of Hallowell ME at Exeter ME [25 Sept 1841]
   Beniah & Margaret BARTLETT at Carmel ME [30 Dec 1847]
   Benjamin Jr & Deborah COLLOMORE at Union ME [7 Mar 1837]
   Bradish B Esq & Harriet M FOX of Dover ME at Monson ME [13 Jul 1848]
   Caroline M & Joseph W B CLEMENT at (Augusta) ME on 1st Jun [10 Jun 1852]
   Charles H & Caroline H AMES at Clinton ME [22 Jan 1842]
   Charles of Carroll & Lydia TURNER at Leeds ME on 5 Oct [16 Oct 1851]
   Charles T & Ann McPHERSON of Bloomfield ME at Skowhegan ME [20 Mar 1845]
   Charles & Ann H SYLVESTER by Stephen STROUT Esq at Freedom ME [18 Nov 1847]
   Charlotte d/o Rev Amaziah BROWN & John SHOREY Jr of Athens ME by Rev TRIPP at Harmony ME [23 Jul 1842]
   Cordelia & Sheldon H GREELEY at Palermo ME [28 Oct 1847]
   Cyrus & Mrs Lucretia MANN by Rev Jotham SEWALL at Fayette ME [24 Jan 1834]
   Daniel 2nd & Mary D STONE at Waterford ME [8 Nov 1849]
   Daniel Hon of Waterford ME & Ann HAMLIN at Paris ME by Rev C B DAVIS [6 Feb 1851]
   Daniel Jr of Dover ME & Lucy W THORNDIKE at Foxcroft ME [1 Feb 1849]
   David Rev formerly of Frankfort ME ae 96 & Dolly DODGE ae 86 after a long and tedious courtship of one week at Bucksport ME [25 Nov 1836]
   Deborah R & James H BRACKETT at China ME [28 Feb 1850]
   Dorcas A & Zebulon CHADBOURN Jr at Oxford ME [28 May 1846]
   Dorcas A & Z CHANDLER Jr at Oxford [14 May 1846]
   Ebenezer Jr & Mary Jane DAVIS at Robbinston ME [11 Sept 1845]
   Ebenezer Jr & Mary Jane SMITH of Calais ME at Robbinston ME [28 Aug 1845]
   Edmund P & Joanna PIERCE of Montville ME at Belfast ME [27 Jun 1844]
   Elisha & Janetter L STEVENS by James MACOMBER Esq at Milo ME [25 May 1848]
   Eliza of Hallowell ME & Frederick MEADY at Tiverton RI [15 Nov 1849]
   Eliza Ann & Loammi B YEATON of Richmond ME at Augusta ME [7 Mar 1844]
   Eliza & Robert LAMBERT at Belfast ME [8 Aug 1844]
   Elizabeth A & Mr J C C WARREN at Waterford ME [31 Aug 1848]
   Elizabeth J of Sidney ME & William H TAYLOR at Augusta ME on Jan 1st by Rev Thomas J DUDLEY [9 Jan 1851]
   Elizabeth & Nathaniel W STETSON at Bath ME [15 Nov 1849]

BROWN (cont.) Franklin & Harriet BROWN both of Benton ME at Albion ME [29 Jul 1852]
  George B of New Sharon ME & Julia GREENWOOD of Farmington ME by Rev Isaac ROGERS at Farmington [7 Oct 1847]
  George G of Sebasticook ME & Caroline H FOX at Skowhegan ME [16 Jan 1845]
  George & Margaret HOFFMAN at Bath ME [15 Jun 1848]
  Hannah of Palermo ME & Gustavus HASKELL by Wm PERCIVAL Esq at China ME [8 Apr 1847]
  Hannah L & Daniel HANSCOM at Gardiner ME [24 Aug 1848]
  Harriet L & Orren W CHAMBERLAIN at Stetson ME [29 Jan 1852]
  Harriet & Franklin BROWN both of Benton ME at Albion ME [29 Jul 1852]
  Hawley D & Ann PIKE on 25 Mar at Augusta ME [5 Apr 1849]
  Henry Y & Emeline B THOMPSON of Dresden ME at Hallowell ME [25 Feb 1847]
  Horace L, M.D., of Dunham Canada East & Lucy W WEBSTER at Augusta ME [29 Feb 1844]
  Ira H & Belzorah TURNER at Palermo ME [30 May 1844]
  J W L & Mrs M E A C P WALDRON formerly of Bath ME at New York ME [19 Nov 1846]
  James B & Philena D SAVAGE both of Norridgewock ME at Bloomfield ME [7 Jun 1849]
  James L Capt & Julia A LEWIS formerly of Vassalboro ME by Rev Mr MEDBURY at Newburyport MA on 24 Oct "With the above notice we received the printer's fair proportion of the bridal loaf for which the parties have our thanks. AT this season of the year every thing is giving away to the SCARLET & YELLOW LEAF hue but we think Miss Julia the fair bride chose quite the pleasantest way to be DONE BROWN" [16 Nov 1848]
  Jane & Capt James ELDRIDGE of Bucksport ME at Orland ME [4 Feb 1833]
  Jerome B W & Abby J RICHARDSON at (Augusta) ME [22 Jun 1848]
  Joel T & Melissa D TRACY at Lewiston ME [14 August 1851]
  John 2nd & Margaret ROBBINS at Rockland ME [1 Jul 1852]
  John Jr & Martha SCHOFFIELD of Livermore ME at Fayette ME [11 Feb 1833]
  John M & Harriet JOHNSON at Belfast ME [18 Dec 1845]
  John O & Lucy HOWE at Hallowell ME [11 Nov 1843]
  John S G & Rebecca HALEY on 23rd ult at Calais ME [10 Jun 1843]
  John T & Sylpha McCURTY by Rev PEET at Gardiner ME [15 Apr 1843]
  John & Mrs Joanna THOMAS at Portland ME [16 May 1844]
  John & Tryphena P SHEPHERD on 30th ult at Brighton ME [20 Feb 1845]
  Joseph A BROWN & Mary E DENNISON at Gardiner ME [23 Dec 1847]
  Joseph C & Almeda B FITZGERALD of Albion ME at Benton ME [11 Mar 1852]
  Joseph D & Mary PINEO both of Campobello at Eastport ME [16 Dec 1843]
  Joseph & Lucy SHATTUCK at Solon ME [22 Jan 1846]
  Joseph & Lydia L KING at Pittston ME [31 May 1849]
  Julia A & Phillip PHILLIPS at Mt Vernon ME on 28th May [1 Jun 1848]

BROWN (cont.) Julia E & F H WEYMOUTH at Gardiner ME [20 Dec 1849]
Lavina M & Newall H LADD at Clinton ME [22 Jan 1842]
Loten L & Laura A KING on Sun eve last by Shepherd LAUGHTON Esq at Pittston ME [18 Dec 1841]
Louisa J & Charles ROBINSON 2nd by Willard HAMMOND Esq at Guilford ME [17 Apr 1838]
Lucinda P & Lafayette HUNTON both of Readfield ME by Rev C FULLER at Wayne ME [15 Mar 1849]
Lydia J & Moses HANSON on Xmas eve by E W KELLEY Esq at Winthrop ME [10 Jan 1850]
Margaret A of Wayne ME & William J W VARNUM of Wayne ME at Leeds ME on Dec 31st by Rev Walter FOSS [9 Jan 1851]
Maria C of Sidney ME & Daniel W GAMMON of Kennebec ME at Augusta ME on Dec 4 by Rev J STEVENS [11 Dec 1851]
Martha J & John STEVENS at Belfast ME [13 Jan 1848]
Martha T & William ELLIS 2nd of Waterville at Clinton ME [21 Dec 1839]
Mary A & Charles S KINCAID at Boston MA on 30 Apr [6 May 1852]
Mary A & Eben P KNOWLES at Hallowell ME [5 Feb 1846]
Mary A & Henry D WAKEFIELD at Gardiner ME [31 May 1849]
Mary A & Isaac T MORRISON of Boothbay ME at Knox ME [26 Dec 1844]
Mary Ann late of Saco ME & Capt Luther PERKINS by Rev F MERRIAM at Winthrop ME [15 Oct 1846]
Mary Elizabeth & Oscar B EDGECOMB at Gardiner ME [26 Aug 1852]
Mary H & Nath'l S PARTRIDGE at Bangor ME [11 Jul 1844]
Mary Jane & David L MORSE at Harmony ME [10 Aug 1848]
Mary Jane & Enoch C FARNHAM of Albion ME by Rev INGRAHAM on 4th inst at Augusta ME [12 Dec 1844]
Mary M & William H HAMLIN at Sweden ME [19 Feb 1852]
Mary Mrs & Arthur McGUIRE at Sebec ME [6 May 1852]
Mary T (Mrs) & Henry M GOODWIN of Plainfield MI at Newport ME? [30 Oct 1841]
Mary & Capt Thomas R PILLSBURY of Thomaston ME at Northport ME [30 Jan 1845]
Mary & Richard H BEEDE at Levant ME [18 Jan 1840]
N C & Mary MORRILL at Belfast ME [1 Jan 1846]
Nancy & Orison MAYO both of Fairfield ME at Bloomfield ME [17 May 1849]
Nathaniel of Vinalhaven ME & Sabra ORN at Thomaston ME [24 Apr 1845]
Olive J BROWN & T S LEWIS of Waterborough at Buxton ME [15 Mar 1849]
Olive & Rufus COFFIN at No 11 Aroostook ME [2 Mar 1848]
Olive & Silas ALLEN at Brunswick ME [3 Aug 1848]
Phebe Y & James DOWNES at Swanville ME on 13 Feb by M H HOLMES Esq [27 Feb 1851]
Phebe (Mrs) & Ephraim BALLARD at Augusta ME [4 Jul 1837]
Rebecca A of Gardiner ME & Thomas B HARLOW of Plymouth MA at Gardiner ME [6 Nov 1845]
Robert & Mary A HALLETT at West Waterville ME [12 Jul 1849]
Royal, of Clinton ME & Charlotte H NEWELL at Winslow ME [17 Jul 1838]

BROWN (cont.) Ruth P & Mr B F JONES at Monmouth ME on 6th Apr 1851 by Rev Walter FOSS [10 Apr 1851] & [17 Apr 1851]
    S Mary of Bath ME & John ELDER Esq of Portland ME at Bath ME [23 Oct 1845]
    Samuel E & Amelia MACE both of Readfield ME at Winthrop ME on 27th Jul [7 August 1851]
    Samuel & Clarissa TOBEN both of Wayne ME at Wayne [23 May 1844]
    Sarah & Caleb KIMBALL at Bath ME [19 Feb 1836]
    Sarah & Erastus BARTLETT at Atkinson ME [17 Jun 1852]
    Sarah & James MAXFIELD at Mt Vernon ME [29 Jun 1848]
    Sophia H d/o G W BROWN Esq merchant & Prof D Talcott [sic] SMITH of the Theological Seminary at Bangor ME [2 May 1840]
    Sophronia D of Belgrade ME & John H DUDLEY of Hallowell ME by Rev MERRIAM at East Winthrop ME [15 Apr 1847]
    Sophronia H of Pittston ME & Nathan LONGFELLOW 2nd of Palermo ME on Thurs eve last by Rev E SCAMMON at Pittston ME [25 Sept 1845]
    Thomas of Baldwin ME & Harriet B PIERCE at the Forks of the Kennebec River ME [27 Jun 1834]
    Thomas Esq of New Harmony LA & Serena MORGRIDGE of Litchfield ME at Litchfield ME [31 Aug 1848]
    Thomas H, M.D., & Juliette HAMMOND at Paris ME [30 Dec 1847]
    Thomas W of Brownfield ME & Clara S LOUGEE at Parsonsfield ME [17 Apr 1851]
    Thomas & Eleanor ALEXANDER at Harpswell ME [5 Aug 1836]
    W M E Esq & Lucy L WHITE at Solon ME [2 Jul 1846]
    William J & Mary A HARRIMAN at Clinton ME [20 Jan 1848]
    William P & Urania H WAKEFIELD at Saco ME [17 Dec 1846]
    William & Eleanor BOYD both of Deer Island ME at Eastport ME [15 Jan 1846]
    William & Hannah GAZELIN on Mon last by Samuel WOOD Esq at Winthrop ME [29 Apr 1836]
    William & Jane Ann DEMUTH at Waldoboro ME [8 Feb 1840]
BROWNELL Nancy T & I J CORBETT on 18 Jun by Rev H M BLAKE at Augusta ME [15 Jul 1852]
BROWNING Sarah & John MCCLURE at Augusta ME [18 Nov 1843]
BRUCE Ruth & Simon FRENCH at Hallowell ME [25 Nov 1836]
BRUMLEY Joseph B of Norwick CT & Vesta I STEVENS at East Thomaston ME [14 Mar 1850]
BRUNN John Jr of Gardiner ME & Mrs Elcy PILLSBURY of Nobleboro ME by Rev E TRASK at Nobleboro ME [25 Dec 1838]
BRYANT Alvin & Martha F HATTSON at Saco ME [4 Apr 1850]
    Cyrus Col of Anson ME & Julia A WILLIAMS at Hartland ME [23 Jan 1841]
    Cyrus F of Fairfield ME & Olive P STURGIS at Vassalboro ME [11 Apr 1844]
    David & Malansa TIMBERLAKE both of Livermore ME at Turner ME [2 Jan 1845]
    G E S & Nancy S DEXTER at Dover ME [21 Nov 1844]
    John C of Montville ME & Emeline J PUTNAM of Searsport ME at Freedom ME [20 Mar 1851]
    John of Hermon ME & Mary Jane D HERSEY at Dexter ME [12 Feb 1846]

Marriage Notices from the "Maine Farmer"

BRYANT (cont.) Judith (Mrs) & Sullivan DOTON of Freedom at Palermo ME [10 May 1849]
  Lovina & Josiah PAINE Jr both of New Portland ME at Anson ME [17 Apr 1838]
  Lucinda C & George MAHONEY at Orneville ME [7 Aug 1845]
  Lydia Mrs & Isaac MANN at Buckfield ME [24 Aug 1848]
  Mary E & Sam'l A McCUTCHEON at West Bath ME [8 Feb 1849]
  Nancy H of Bristol ME & James S COLBY at Boston MA [18 Jul 1844]
  Sarah A & Josiah CLARK at Smithfield ME? [8 Feb 1849]
  Sarah H & Oliver A WEBBER Esq of Vassalboro ME on 6 Feb by Rev Josiah W PEET at Gardiner [8 Feb 1849]
  Sarah & Timothy ROWELL both of Vassalboro ME on 25th ult at Vassalboro ME [11 Nov 1836]
  Silas C & Mrs Mary BLOOD at Union ME [24 Apr 1851]
  Susan & Emerson ROSE at Turner ME [30 Nov 1839]
  William M of Industry ME & Sophronia A FLETCHER of Wilton ME by Elder Nathan MAYHEW at Jay ME on Jun 8th [17 Jun 1852]
BRYATHER Alfred S of Searsport ME & Louisa DYER at Unity ME [8 Apr 1847]
BUBIER Amy & Jackson DAVIS at Lewiston ME [22 Jan 1852]
  Nancy & Charles E BANGS at Auburn ME [14 Feb 1850]
BUBRE John & Mary J WHEELER at Webster ME [15 Apr 1852]
BUCHNAM B F of Lewiston ME & L G TINKHAM of Sidney ME on New Year's by Rev TILLEY at Sidney [7 Jan 1847]
BUCK Arminta & George W BATTLES at Buckfield ME [15 Jan 1852]
  Mary & Orin BARTLETT at Abbott ME [27 Apr 1848]
  Austin & Ann TURNER at Belfast ME [24 Jan 1834]
  Elvira & George M BREWSTER of Bridgewater MA at Norway ME [19 Dec 1844]
  Francis C of Paris ME & S Louisa PRINCE of Buckfield ME at Turner ME [3 Jan 1850]
  Hannah & Edmund ALLEN of Hartford ME at Sumner ME [29 Jan 1846]
  Susan C & Charles W CHADWICK of Gilford NH by Rev W A P DILLINGHAM on 16th inst at Augusta ME [25 Oct 1849]
  William P & Mary A TUBBS of Norway ME at Paris ME [2 Dec 1847]
BUCKER Samuel Capt & Caroline M HEATH at Bath ME [14 Oct 1836]
BUCKHART George ae 90 & Elizabeth GRAYHILL ae 60 at Harlen Co NY [29 Jul 1833]
BUCKMAN Clara A & J G TIBBETTS at Lisbon ME [6 Aug 1846]
BUCKMINSTER Ann M & John WIGGIN of Augusta ME at Saco ME [19 Nov 1846]
BUCKNAM Abba P & George A DOANE of Boston ME at Eastport ME [23 Jul 1846]
  Almira & Capt Alexander PUMROY at Falmouth ME [9 Oct 1835]
  Calvin of Hebron ME & L G TWITCHELL at Paris ME [29 Mar 1849]
  Ellen J & Joseph M LIVERMORE at Eastport ME [18 Mar 1847]
  James M & Caroline P DRINKWATER at North Yarmouth ME [2 Dec 1843]
  William W & Sarah MERRITT at Eastport ME [21 Aug 1845]
BUDGE Margaret E & Valencourt S PALMER both of Levant ME at Bangor ME [1 May 1845]

BUDDINGTON Amy Jane & Capt Samuel WATTS at London England [16 Mar 1848]
BUDLONG Rhodes A & Julia P ROBERTS at Lewiston ME [12 Jun 1851]
BUFFUM Albion K P & Harriet B LAWRENCE at Gardiner ME [26 Jun 1845]
Patience & David WINSLOW of Westbrook ME at Durham ME [13 May 1847]
BUKER Mary F & A W HAMLIN of Gardiner ME at Bowdoin ME [1 Jul 1852]
 Urban of Phillips ME & Alcy M PULCIFER at Weld ME on 20th Mar by Isaac TYLER Esq [27 Mar 1851]
BULFINCH Sophronia & H H Capt LOVELL of Barnstable MA at Waldoboro ME [6 Feb 1851]
BULLARD Pressy & Gascar ROCKO at Bath ME [2 Jan 1845]
BULLOCK Thomas & Mary E ALEXANDER at Northport ME [18 Sept 1851]
BUMP George W & Mary LAUGHLER at Farmington [14 Sept 1848]
BUMPERS Mary Ann of Hebron ME & John W CHASE of Minot ME at Hebron ME [26 Dec 1840]
BUMPUS Elvina S & John E C CUMMINGS at Bath ME [28 Aug 1851]
 Harriet G & Ephraim GODDING at Livermore ME [31 Jan 1850]
 Mary & Russell STOCKWELL at Mexico ME [27 Jun 1840]
BUNKER James G & Joanna H SPRAGUE of Bath ME at Nantucket MA [8 Aug 1840]
 Lucy J & Thomas R MAYO at Bangor ME [20 Jul 1848]
 Joseph Jr & Mary STEVENS at Athens ME [29 Nov 1849]
 Lydia Downes d/o Capt Alexander D BUNKER & David T WARREN formerly of Winthrop ME by Rev EDES at Nantucket MA [28 Sept 1839]
 Rosannah & Farwell W BURGESS at Lewiston ME [11 Jan 1849]
BURBANK Abner Esq & Eliza A HARMON at Limerick ME [2 May 1837]
 Adino J & Clarissa J MURRAY at Auburn ME [6 Sept 1849]
 Alexander Dr of Shelburne & Vesta LOWELL at Lewiston ME [29 Apr 1847]
 Alma E & Mark LOWELL of Lewiston ME at Bethel ME [28 Jan 1847]
 Benjamin F & Eliza J KINCAID both of this city (Augusta) ME by Rev Mr RUST at Portsmouth NH at the Mansion House on 28th April [6 May 1852]
 Eliza & Edward P WESTON principal of Lewiston Falls Academy (later called Edward Little High School of Auburn ME) at Bethel ME [20 Mar 1841]
 Emily & Robert P HERSON at Newfield ME [22 Jun 1848] & [8 Jun 1848]
 Hannah C & Joshua B LOWELL Esq of Farmington ME at Freeman ME [13 Mar 1851]
 James & Jane C AUSTIN by Rev A MOORE on 6th inst at Augusta ME [17 Apr 1845]
 Joseph P of Augusta ME & Eliza J KENNEDY of Whitefield ME at Whitefield ME [21 Jul 1843]
 Moody & Aurilla GREENE by Rev Josiah PEET at Norridgewock ME [28 May 1846]
BURBANKS Johnson Capt & Rachel B CHOATE at Whitefield ME [14 Aug 1835]
BURDIN Caroline & Asa HEATH Jr both of Sidney ME by Rev TAPPAN at Augusta ME [18 Dec 1838]

Marriage Notices from the "Maine Farmer" 55

BURDEN Winslow & Sylvis Mrs REMICK by S TITCOMB Jr at Augusta ME on Dec 3 [14 Dec 1848]

BURGESS Betsey E & Joseph C WEBB at Fairfield ME on Oct 17th [14 Dec 1848]
- Elisha of Vassalboro ME & Mary A ROBINSON at Albion ME on 1 May by T BURRILL Esq [8 May 1851]
- LaFayette M of East Livermore ME & Hannah I GRAVES by Rev C FULLER at Wayne ME [25 Mar 1852]
- widow ae 78, & John WERTZ, a Revolutionary soldier, ae 78, on 30th ult Allentown PA [10 Aug 1833]
- Alexander Rev Rector of St Mark's Church & Mary W d/o Calvin SELDEN Esq of Norridgewock ME by Rev FALES of Brunswick ME at St Marks Church on 17th inst at Augusta ME [25 Sept 1845]
- Bartlett of Wayne ME & Rebekah HAM of Fayette ME at Fayette ME [29 Jan 1839]
- Farwell W & Rosannah BUNKER at Lewiston ME [11 Jan 1849]
- Frances & Roby MARSTON of Wilton ME at Wayne ME [18 Oct 1849]
- Francis I & Orenia S DICKEY of Monroe ME at Hallowell ME [22 Jul 1847]
- Gustavus & Susan N COWAN both of Palermo ME by Clifford S WORTHING Esq at Palermo ME [5 Jun 1845]
- Joseph Jr & Savina M SOUL at Fairfield ME [15 Oct 1842]
- Mary Ann & Joseph COOMBS of Nobleboro ME at Vassalboro ME [14 Oct 1843]
- Mary Jane & John C GASLIN by Samuel P BENSON Esq 22nd ult at Winthrop ME [2 Dec 1836]
- Obed C & Sarah E BRADBURY by Rev W A DREW at Augusta ME [28 Aug 1842]
- Rebecca & William JOY both of Waterville ME on 29 Jan at Waterville ME [5 Feb 1846]
- Samuel Dea of Paris ME & Mrs Lydia LAKE of New Sharon ME by Rev WILLIAMSON at New Sharon ME [18 Apr 1844]
- Saphrona F of Wayne ME & Capt Joseph SMITH of Hallowell ME at Wayne ME [31 Aug 1839]

BURGIN Arthur D & Phebe Jane JACKSON at Belfast ME [16 Mar 1848]
- Lewis & Adeline HAYCOCK at Eastport ME [1 May 1835]

BURK Hannah T of Phipsburg ME & Elisha M OAKES Jr at Gloucester MA [15 Jul 1843]

BURKE James of Bradley ME & Rachel GATCHEL of Charlestown MA by Rev Rufus H STINCHFIELD on 3rd inst at Wayne ME [26 Nov 1842]

BURKETT Henry A & Abby W HEMENWAY both of Camden ME at Belfast ME [5 Nov 1846]
- Rebecca & Watson NOWELL at Winslow ME [19 Aug 1836]

BURKMAR Eliza J & Isaac L DUNTON both of Belfast ME at Montville ME [1 Feb 1849]

BURLEIGH H O (Mr) of Foxcroft ME & Sarah C LORING at Guilford ME [6 Jan 1848]
- A & Miss H G HAYDEN at Waterville ME [13 Jun 1844]
- Ann E & Daniel R WING of Gardiner ME at Fairfield ME [13 Feb 1845]
- G E & John H RICE Esq of Monson ME at Dexter ME [16 Dec 1847]
- J & Sarah BLAISDELL at Thomaston ME [6 Nov 1845]
- Otis F & Harriet N SEVERS at Wayne ME [20 Jun 1840]

BURLEY Nancy S & Jabez YOUNG on 22 May at Lenneus Aroostook Co ME [16 Jul 1842]
Sylvester S & Minerva Ann SAFFORD at Lewiston ME [27 Nov 1851]
BURNHAM Aaron & Alexia STAPLES both of Biddeford ME at Kennebunkport ME [15 Apr 1852]
Alexander & Susan A STAPLES at Biddeford ME [7 Oct 1847]
Alexis of Dixfield ME & Caroline A RANDALL at Wilton ME [19 Oct 1848]
Eliza A & Gilman D LANCY at Exeter ME [29 Apr 1852]
George O & Hannah J HOOPER at Biddeford ME [21 Nov 1844]
Hannah S & Charles HOWE at Cherryfield ME [13 May 1847]
John of Parsonsfield ME & Sally ADAMS at Newfield ME [25 Mar 1847]
Lucy J & Augustus SMITH at Bridgton ME on Jun 15 by Rev Jacob BRAY [10 Jul 1851]
Martha E & J W GOODWIN at Lubec ME [8 Mar 1849]
Mary A & Eben CARVER at Troy ME [29 Jul 1852]
Nelly (Mrs) & Virgil GRISWOLD of Westfield MA at Thomaston ME [28 Sept 1839]
Nicholas R merchant & Almira RUGGLES at Calais ME [11 May 1839]
William Col & Mary SPROWL at Machias ME. The occasion was celebrated by the ringing of bells and the firing of cannon [4 Jul 1834]
William D & Roxana RICHARDS of Saco ME at Biddeford ME [23 Aug 1849]
BURNELL Alfred P & Nancy J BARROWS both of Norway ME at South Paris ME [25 Apr 1844]
BURNES William E & Rachel E FARR at Poland ME [17 Feb 1848]
Martha & William GRAFTON at Thomaston ME [30 Apr 1846]
Mary S & Luther PIERCE of Solon ME at Madison ME [9 Jul 1846]
BURNESS Moody C & Eunice GARDNER at China ME [31 Jul 1835]
BURNHAM Aaron & Alexia STAPLES both of Biddeford ME at Kennebunkport ME [15 Apr 1852]
Alexis of Dixfield ME & Caroline A RANDALL at Wilton ME [19 Oct 1848]
Eliza A & Gilman D LANCY at Exeter ME [29 Apr 1852]
Alexander & Susan A STAPLES at Biddeford ME [7 Oct 1847]
George O & Hannah J HOOPER at Biddeford ME [21 Nov 1844]
Hannah S & Charles HOWE at Cherryfield ME [13 May 1847]
John, of Parsonsfield ME & Sally ADAMS at Newfield ME [25 Mar 1847]
Martha E & J W GOODWIN at Lubec ME [8 Mar 1849]
Mary A & Eben CARVER at Troy ME [29 Jul 1852]
Nelly (Mrs) & Virgil GRISWOLD of Westfield MA at Thomaston ME [28 Sept 1839]
Nicholas R merchant & Almira RUGGLES at Calais ME [11 May 1839]
William Col & Mary SPROWL at Machias ME The occasion was celebrated by the ringing of bells and the firing of cannon [4 Jul 1834]
William D & Roxana RICHARDS of Saco ME at Biddeford ME [23 Aug 1849]
BURNS Ashur & Martha H BOYNTON at Augusta ME [22 Aug 1840]
John W & Eunice S POST at Thomaston ME [6 Jan 1848]
Daniel & Deborah TITCOMB at Hallowell ME [13 Jan 1837]
Joseph W of Hollis ME & Mary E ATKINSON at Buxton ME [15 Jul 1847]
Mary J & George B DAGGETT at Union ME [25 Nov 1847]
William & Huldah LUCE at Union ME [20 Jun 1844]

BURNS (cont.) Wilson C & Susan J LOVETT of Nobleboro ME at Bremen ME [7 Oct 1847]
Emeline & Warren W BOSWORTH of Solon ME at Madison ME [10 Jul 1851]
John 3rd of Madison ME & Gratia Ann WESTON at Bloomfield ME [16 Oct 1851]
William 3rd Capt & Maria L MORTON of Bristol ME at Bremen ME [9 Oct 1851]
BURPEE Eleanor A (Mrs) of Eastport ME & Samuel AVERILL of Northfield at Machias ME [9 Jul 1846]
Hannah S & Charles C TYLER, publisher of the *Eastport Sentinel* at Machias ME [2 May 1844]
Mehitable M & Henry AVERILL of Northfield at Machias Port ME [26 Aug 1847]
BURR Benjamin A printer & Ann LAW at Bangor ME [16 May 1844]
Hiram of Brewer ME & Betsey Lovina JOHNSON of Springfield ME? at Springfield [31 Jul 1838]
Julia Ann & George S MARSTON at Gardiner ME [9 Apr 1842]
Lucy of Litchfield ME & Moses BRIGGS of Winthrop ME at Litchfield ME [25 Dec 1838]
Joseph J of Brewer ME & Lucy P LINCOLN of Searsmont ME at Bangor ME [1 May 1851]
BURRELL H & Lydia H WOODMAN of Norridgewock ME at Fairfield ME [9 Nov 1848]
John printer of Bangor ME & Emily E HOOK at Skowhegan ME [27 Nov 1841]
BURRILL Henry W & Sarah A WEEKS at Corinna ME [20 Apr 1848] & [7 Apr 1848]
John C & Sarah H BEAL at Sangerville ME [11 May 1848]
Almira of Vienna ME & Samuel H CHEEVER at Boston MA [27 May 1836]
Caroline D & Charles WATERMAN at Sangerville ME [15 Aug 1844]
Esther F of Corinna ME & Philander WHITING of Newport ME at Corinna ME [13 Jul 1836]
George & Olive TUPPER at Canaan ME [29 Apr 1836]
John of Boston MA & Rebecca A WHEELER at Worcester MA [21 Mar 1837]
Maria & George SMITH of Bangor ME at Fairfield ME [24 Dec 1846]
Mary & Porter BANKS of Fairfield ME at Canaan ME [29 Aug 1844]
Mary & Thomas H GREELY of Boston MA at Albion ME [14 May 1846]
Mary Jane (Mrs) & Daniel S BROAD at East Eddington ME [21 May 1842]
BURT James of Gardiner ME & Harriet A BARNEY of Waterville ME at Norwick CT [18 May 1848]
Ruth of Turner ME & Elijah HAMLEN at Paris ME [21 Jun 1849]
BURTON Edwin M of Gorham ME & Lucy L FORD formerly of Gray ME at Cincinatti OH [20 Feb 1851]
George R & Lucy E CLARK at Thomaston ME [20 Jul 1848]
Alfred & Elonia HEALEY at Thomaston ME [14 May 1846]
Eliza Ann & Benj P ROBINSON at Cushing ME [14 May 1846]
Isaac I & Lucy Ann BOGS at Warren ME [29 Jan 1846]
John & Nancy WRIGHT at Clinton ME [22 Nov 1849]
BUSH Edward W & Margaret A LEARNED both of Burnham ME at Clinton ME [20 Jan 1848]

BUSH (cont.) John Jr formerly of Vassalboro ME & Harriet M NOYES at Bangor ME [28 Aug 1851]
Theodore A & Clara Browne POOLER on 7th inst at Bloomfield ME [22 Oct 1846]
BUSHEL Amelia & Joshua PECK on 17th ult at Washington ME? [18 Jul 1834-Extended Notice]
BUSHEY Peter & Pauline BAREU of Cornville ME at Madison ME [18 Feb 1847]
BUSWELL Charles H & Irena P PHILBRICK at Exeter ME [8 Apr 1852]
Eleanor & Thomas PAINE at Hallowell ME [4 Mar 1852]
David L & Matilda McADAMS at Dexter ME [21 May 1846]
Joseph P of Solon ME & Julia A TURNER of Norridgewock ME at Skowhegan ME [4 Jan 1844]
BUTLAND Dorothy & Asa C LIVINGSTON at Saco ME [1 Jan 1846]
J M of Hollis ME & Margaret C DAME at Saco ME [29 Sept 1849]
BUTLER Albert B formerly of Hallowell ME & Jennie KNOX at Portland ME [17 Jun 1852]
Alonzo, of Augusta ME & Mary DODGE of New Boston NH at Windsor VT [30 Sept 1847]
Ann J d/o Rev John BUTLER of North Yarmouth ME & Phinehas BARNES of Waterville ME at N Yarmouth ME [29 Aug 1837]
Caroline & Charles W PLAISTED on 1 Jan by Amos S KING Esq at Phillips ME [8 Feb 1849]
Charles W & Rebecca M SAWYER at (Augusta) ME on 6th May [13 May 1852]
Dr Samuel W of Newport ME & Emeline A CACKUS at Farmington ME [8 Apr 1843]
Elizabeth L d/o Rev John BUTLER & George H NASON all formerly from Augusta ME at Greenfield MA [26 Aug 1852]
Elizabeth & James M BLACKINTON at Butler [6 Jan 1837]
Elizabeth & Moses C JUDKINS of Cincinnati OH at Cornville ME [7 Oct 1843]
Esteria & J E FARNAM of Shelbyville KY on 15th inst at North Yarmouth ME [29 Aug 1837]
F G Esq & Julia A WENDALL at Farmington ME [21 Aug 1842]
Gorham & Mrs Catharine PALMER at Thomaston ME [29 Jan 1846]
Hannah & Charles B MUDGET of Hallowell ME at Freeport ME [10 Jul 1845]
Harriet D & John S LEEMAN on 27th inst at Hallowell ME [4 Sept 1845]
Henry & Mary Ann FARNSWORTH at Norridgewock ME [13 Jun 1837]
Joanna & J W WARREN of Newburgh NY at Cornville ME [22 Jul 1847]
John of Thomaston ME & Rachael SPEAR at Warren ME [4 Sept 1845]
Levi & Susan VILES at Norridgewock ME [4 Oct 1849]
Mary D & Robert S PAINE at Cornville ME [17 Feb 1848] & [2 Mar 1848]
Mary Jane & Reuben CUTLER of Strong ME at Farmington ME [1 Jan 1846]
Mary S of Hallowell ME & L T THRELDKELD at Shelbyville KY [12 Aug 1847]
Nancy M & Capt Charles BRADBURY at Thomaston ME [22 Oct 1846]
Rebecca & Eliphaz GAY at Farmington ME [4 May 1848]
Reliance & Ebenezer PINKHAM at Strong ME [29 Jun 1839]

BUTLER (cont.) Rev Nathaniel of Turner ME & Jeannett L EMERY at Paris ME [28 Feb 1850]
    S Louisa & Warren B GILMAN at Farmington ME [26 Feb 1852]
    W S & Emma J CLARK at Lincoln ME [6 May 1847]
BUTMAN Almira C & S G MOORE of Bangor ME at Dixmont ME [25 Jan 1844]
    Eliza A d/o F A BUTMAN Esq & Samuel BLAGGE merchant by Rev WISWELL 24th inst at Dixmont ME [2 Nov 1839]
    Ellen A & George H THAYER at Plymouth ME [16 Mar 1848]
    F A Jr of Bangor ME & Laura M MOORE of Gardiner ME at Dixmont ME [25 Jan 1844]
    Julia E & Capt John T MOORE of Gardiner ME at Dixmont ME [10 Jul 1845]
BUTLER Eliza K Mrs & Robert DOUGHTY at Hallowell ME [18 Dec 1851]
    Henrietta C of Cornville ME & Horatio N KINCAID of Cornville at Cornville ME by Rev PACKARD [6 Feb 1851]
BUTTERFIELD Charles W & Caroline DOE at Milford [1 Feb 1844]
    Edna A & Jason L TAYLOR both of Norridgewock ME at Skowhegan ME [19 Aug 1852]
    Emma H & Chas R MCFADDEN at Vassalboro ME [22 Feb 1849]
    Fanny N & Thomas M TEAGUE at Wilton ME [18 Jun 1846]
    Hannah & Josiah BACON Esq by Elijah WOOD Jr Esq 24th ult at Hartland ME [1 Jan 1836]
    Isaac of Wilton ME & Rebecca GORDON of Mt Vernon ME at Sidney ME [1 Jan 1846]
    John H of Weston ME & Mary G CRABTREE at Topsfield ME on 19th Jul by Dan PINEO Esq [21 Aug 1851]
    John Jr & Mary T FINSON at Hartland ME [24 Jan 1850]
    John of Sumner ME & Martha RICHARDSON of Greenwood ME at Greenwood [21 Mar 1840]
    Joseph & Lucetta HOPKINS at Milford [10 Feb 1848]
    Josiah of Hartland ME & Elizabeth GIVEN at St Albans ME [3 Apr 1851]
    Mary E & Robert DAVIS at Milford [10 Feb 1848]
    Robert Esq of Bowdoinham ME & Nancy T RUSSELL of Brunswick ME at Bath ME [18 Jul 1844]
BUTTS John W & Sarah A PRINCE at New Portland ME [9 May 1844]
BUXTON Edward S & Lydia CHASE on 22 Jan by Rev HOBERT at North Yarmouth ME [6 Feb 1835]
    Mary Steele (Mrs) & Nicholas RIDEOUT Esq at Cumberland ME [21 Mar 1844]
BUZWELL Abigail of Wales ME & Capt Cyrus FLAGG of Topsham ME at Winthrop ME [6 Mar 1845]
    John & Eleanor B SMITH at Hallowell ME [16 Nov 1839]
BUZZELL Clarrinda & Colwell L COUILLARD at Bangor ME [14 Mar 1844]
    Elizabeth of Lowell & David F ROLFE of Limington ME at Lowell MA [10 Dec 1846]
    Emeline of Vassalboro ME & Alden LEWIS at Whitefield [1 Jul 1852]
    Hiram W & Sarah E ELDRIDGE both of Skowhegan ME at Bloomfield ME [24 May 1849]
    James F & Lydia POTTER at Bloomfield ME [28 Aug 1851]
    Prescilla & Benj B WILSON of Topsham ME at Winthrop ME [1 Jan 1846]

BYRAM Huldah Allen of East Bridgewater & Asa MILLET, M.D., of Mattapoiset on Sabbath morning 5th inst at the Unitarian meeting house, by Rev LORD, of Plymouth at East Bri MA [23 Dec 1843]
 James R & Mrs Eunice B WALTON by Rev M HOWARD at Gardiner ME [17 Sept 1842]
 S B & Mrs Nancy BRAWN at Dover [11 Jan 1849]

- C -

CABLES Capt John F CABLES of Cohasset MA & Priscilla E GRANT at East Thomaston ME [14 Mar 1850]
CACKUS Emeline A & Dr Samuel W BUTLER of Newport at Farmington ME? [8 Apr 1843]
CAFFREY Ellen & Ira H LOW at Waterville ME [11 Feb 1847]
 William A & Mary WHITE at Waterville ME [16 Dec 1847]
CAIN Clarinda N & Chandler PHILBRICK at Windsor ME [1 Jun 1848]
 John B of Clinton ME & Emily E CHASE at Fairfield ME [27 Sept 1849]
CALDEN Washburn & Relief S JEWELL at Bath ME [28 Nov 1844]
CALDER Henry & Sarah J SMALL both of Campobello at Eastport ME [2 Jan 1841]
CALDERWOOD Irvine of Knox ME & Emily Jane LEVEBSELLER by Reuben ORFF Esq at North Waldo' ME on 21st inst [30 Mar 1848]
 Nelson of Washington & Mrs Margaret NOYES at Jefferson ME [14 Sept 1848]
 Lydia & Levi IRISH at Waldo Plantation ME [19 Dec 1844]
CALDWELL Rev Asbury, of the (Methodist) Maine Annual Conference, of Winthrop ME & Olive E MERRILL at Kennebunkport ME [22 Jul 1836]
 Caroline W & R R ROBINSON at Portland ME [28 Aug 1838]
 Merritt, principal of the Maine Wesleyan Seminary, & Rosamond CUSHMAN at New Gloucester ME [4 Mar 1833]
 Richard B of Wiscasset ME, publisher of the *Lincoln Republican*, & Ellsie Ann GOULD by Rev FREEMAN of Augusta ME on 17th inst at Pittston ME [5 Sept 1841]
 William & Abigail, d/o the late Daniel STONE Esq at Augusta ME [2 Jan 1838]
 William H of Rumford ME & Elizabeth McALLISTER at Canton ME [4 Jul 1844]
CALER Eliza Ann & Lewis BARTON at Centreville [3 Aug 1848]
CALHOUN A P s/o Hon J C CALHOUN & Eugenia CAMPBELL d/o Col I I CAMPBELL at Columbia SC [4 Feb 1833]
CALKIN M of the Sandwich Islands (Hawaiian Islands USA) & Eveline JOHNSON formerly of Winthrop ME Sun eve last by Rev THURSTON at Hallowell ME [28 Oct 1842]
CALL James H & Sarah W HUNTER at Hallowell ME [9 May 1844]
 Sarah E & Capt Wm S BALLARD at Gardiner ME [19 Sept 1844]
CALPH Sophia M & Arthur HEAL at Belmont ME [13 Mar 1845]
CAME Mark R of Oldtown ME & Sarah M HOBSON at Standish ME [2 May 1844]
CAMPBELL A W of South Carolina & Irene MERRILL of Maine at Clinton LA [12 Mar 1846]

CAMPBELL (cont.) Abner P of Bowdoin ME & Olive S CURTIS by Rev Walter FOSS at Leeds ME [21 Mar 1850]
   Achsah R & Thomas H WIGGINS at Bowdoinham ME [15 Jun 1848]
   Alfred of Newcastle ME & Agnes C GIVEN at Brunswick ME [4 Dec 1835]
   Andrew of Brunswick ME & Sarah WING of Wayne ME by Moses WING Esq at Wayne [29 Jun 1839]
   Charles & Eliza R COLE at Frankfort ME [7 Oct 1847]
   Dorcas A & Heman R POLAND both of Gardiner ME at Hallowell ME [8 Aug 1844]
   Emeline & John E GOODWIN at Gardiner ME [7 Dec 1848]
   Emma B & Sylvester GORDEN at Chelsea [12 Jun 1851]
   Eugenia d/o Col I I CAMPBELL & A P CALHOUN s/o Hon J C CALHOUN at Columbia SC [4 Feb 1833]
   H H Dr & Julia A TOBEY both of Fairfield ME at Waterville ME [17 Jul 1851]
   Hiram & Mary B ELLIOT at Bath ME [9 Apr 1846]
   Jane C m Rufus L PALMER of Alna ME at New Castle ME [22 May 1851]
   John B & Mrs Margaret W NORTON at Montville ME [20 May 1847]
   Merrill & Elizabeth MOORISON both of Gardiner ME by Rev H M BLAKE at (Augusta) ME on 3d Mar [18 Mar 1852]
   Morrill & Rachel SHAW at Bath ME [2 Mar 1848]
   Nancy A & John Q ADAMS at Cherryfield ME [27 May 1843]
   Nancy & Sewall W TAPLEY at Frankfort ME [8 Apr 1847]
   Otis W & Sarah M DAVIS both of Foxcroft ME at Dover ME [20 Feb 1851]
   Phebe & David CARVER at Paris ME [6 May 1847]
   Rachel M (Mrs) & George COLLINS of Solon ME at Harmony ME [8 Feb 1844]
   Robert & Emeline D PARKER at Frankfort ME [22 Feb 1844]
   Rosana & Charles REED at Jay ME [29 Oct 1846]
   Salome M & Abraham C PERCY at Phipsburg ME [28 Mar 1850]
   Sarah A & Arad H HALL both of Newcastle ME 21 Feb by Rev Geo S G SPENCE at Augusta ME [7 Mar 1850]
   Sarah (Mrs) & Sullivan WARREN of Parkman ME at Sangerville ME [20 Mar 1841]
   Wm & Polly HEWETT both of Livermore ME at Turner ME [14 Feb 1850]
CANADA Julia & Simon/Simeon H LOWELL at Waterville ME [4 & 11 Apr 1840]
CANNON Ebenezer of Hallowell ME & Hannah L LORD at Gardiner ME [7 Dec 1848]
   Henry of Hallowell ME & Harriet Ann BRANN at Gardiner ME [7 Jun 1849]
CAPEN Sarah M & Eben S WELCH of Monmouth ME at Gardiner ME [3 Jun 1847]
   Susan E & Hiram LAWRENCE at Gardiner ME [9 Jan 1851]
CARD Elizabeth & John PARKER at Brunswick ME [21 Oct 1836]
   George W & Nancy CARD at Woolwich ME [6 Jun 1837]
   Joel Jr & Rebecca A HALL both of Bowdoinham ME by Elder C QUINNAM at Litchfield ME [8 Jul 1847]
   John W S of Woolwich ME & Isabel B WHITE at Dresden ME [1 Nov 1849]
   Mary E of Bowdoin ME & Wm H MORRISON at Bath ME [2 Aug 1849]
   Nancy & George W CARD at Woolwich ME [6 Jun 1837]

CARDIFF Ellen & D C M'CARTY at Portland ME [19 Aug 1836]
CARELTON Sophrona, d/o Ebenezer CARELTON, & Amos STETSON of Wayne ME at Winthrop ME [2 May 1844]
CAREY Charles C & Elizabeth RICHARDS both of Camden ME at Lincolnville ME [10 Feb 1848]
   Ebenezer & Hannah DAVIS of North Salem MA after a tedious courtship of one hour at Minot ME [2 Jan 1835]
   Mary Ann & Rev Daniel KENDRICK of Dennis MA at Brunswick ME [27 Feb 1841]
CARGILL David of Hallowell ME & Elizabeth BRAINARD of East Winthrop ME on Sunday last by Rev F MERRIAM at the Baptist Meeting House at East Winthrop ME [23 Sept 1843]
   Sarah D (Mrs) & Dr C A JORDAN at Bangor ME [26 Jun 1845]
CARLE Enoch of Sangerville ME & Lydia Ann CLOUGH by Rev Caleb MUGFORD at Readfield ME [19 Jul 1849]
   Mary Ann of Camden ME & Capt John CROCKETT at Thomaston ME [14 Sept 1839]
CARLETON - see CARLTON
CARLISLE Augusta H & Amos BIXBY Esq of Searsport ME at Norridgewock ME [6 Nov 1851]
   Capt John D of Richmond ME & Mary E LIBBY of Portland ME at Providence RI [7 Mar 1850]
   Sarah (Mrs) of Bingham ME & Sumner BIXBEE at Norridgewock ME [13 Nov 1838]
CARLTON Angelina B & Edward H BATCHELDER of Mobile AL at Belfast ME [9 Oct 1851]
   Benj M & Elizabeth H GETCHELL, both of Vassalboro ME on 8th inst at Augusta ME [31 Dec 1842]
   Charles B & Mary C SHAW, of Wiscasset ME at Whitefield ME [5 Apr 1849]
   Cynthia of Gardiner & Henry LOVEJOY of Sidney ME by Rev THURSTON at Gardiner ME [21 Mar 1844]
   D R of Belfast ME & S A HUNT at Liberty ME [22 Jul 1847]
   Elizabeth H & Nathn'l P DOLE of Alna ME at Vassalboro ME [27 Mar 1841]
   John W Capt of Belfast ME & Frances A EVERETT at Montville ME [12 Feb 1852]
   Margaret J & George A ROLLINS 17 Oct by Rev Albert COLE at Vassalboro ME [13 Dec 1849]
   Samuel C of Phillips ME & Julia A THOMPSON of Farmington ME at Farmington ME [12 Nov 1842]
   Samuel & Harriet N EASTMAN at Camden ME [5 Aug 1847]
   Susan M & Wm H HUNT of Montville ME at Belfast ME [12 Jul 1849]
   Warren & Eliza TRASK at Alna ME [5 Feb 1842]
   William of Troy ME & Sarah TORREY of Plymouth ME at Dixmont ME [7 Oct 1847]
CARNEY Abigail & Sumner MYERS at Dresden ME [4 Oct 1849]
   Thomas J Rev of Wayne ME & Julia A FLETCHER at Boston MA [10 May 1849]
CARPENTER D Esq & Frances G MOSHIER at Sacarappa [1 Jul 1847]
   George F & Olivett NEWCOMB at Eastport ME [5 Mar 1846]

CARPENTER (cont.) Hannah & Joseph WARMELL of Boston MA at Eastport ME [27 Feb 1845]
Mary (Mrs) & John BRADISH of Biddeford ME at Waterborough ME [7 Oct 1847]
Newell of Charlestown MA & Mary E MAXFIELD formerly of Skowhegan ME at Oxford MA [25 Mar 1847]
Ruth H & Thos VOSE of Robbinston ME at Milltown ME [3 Jan 1850]
Sarah A & Dr Hiram HILL of Augusta ME by Rev COLE at Hallowell ME [8 Aug 1837]
Simon of Waterboro ME & Dorcas CHADBOURNE at Limerick ME [6 Mar 1851]
Susan P & Benj C SEWALL of Bath ME at Foxcroft ME [14 Nov 1844]

CARR Abigail W & Capt Salathiel C NICKERSON of Belfast ME by Rev FESSENDEN at East Thomaston ME [1 Jun 1839]
Albert C & Mary A WASSON both of Readfield ME at E Windsor ME on May 6 by Rev S POWERS [3 Jul 1851]
Daniel of Mt Vernon ME & Ruth Ann SEAVEY at Vienna ME [26 Oct 1839]
Daniel & Louisa S ADAMS at Portland ME [31 Jul 1835]
Frances J & Charles A LOVERING of Augusta ME at Hallowell ME [25 Mar 1847]
Frances & Albert J LONGFELLOW of Augusta ME on 25 Dec by Rev Wm A DREW at Hallowell ME [3 Jan 1850]
George W formerly of Belfast ME & Emeline M SUMMERS at New York ME [28 Aug 1838]
Helen A d/o Dea Danl CARR of Winthrop ME & Benjamin SMITH principal of Litchfield Academy at Winthrop on 20th Feb 1851 by Rev Daniel THURSTON [27 Feb 1851]
Lemont P & Miranda TITCOMB at Bowdoin ME [28 Oct 1847]
Martha of Bowdoinham ME & David WAIT at Bowdoin ME [18 Apr 1837]
Mary A & John S GORDON at Vienna ME on Mar 18th [8 Apr 1852]
Octavia & William T SNOW of Belfast ME at Hallowell ME [18 Jun 1846]
Reuben of Pittsfield ME & Caroline COWIN at Palmyra ME [19 Dec 1844]
Richard L & Lucinda L PERRY at Burnham ME [28 May 1842]
Ruth C & Col Andrew MARSTERS by Rev Eli THURSTON at Hallowell ME [29 Jan 1842]
Samuel & Harriet C HAWKES at Minot ME [28 Dec 1848]
Sarah B d/o Dea Danl CARR of Winthrop ME & Henry WOODWARD at Winthrop on 20th Feb 1851 by Rev Daniel THURSTON [27 Feb 1851]
Sarah F & John BEEMAN both of Hallowell ME on 27 Jul by Rev William A DREW at Augusta ME [5 Aug 1852]

CARROL Rebecca & Capt Saml TOLMAN at W Camden ME [27 Sept 1849]
CARROLL Ann & Cyrus LORD at Lewiston ME [19 Aug 1852]
CARSLEY Hiram of Lynn MA & Mercy A HOWARD by Rev John ALLEN at Augusta ME [10 May 1849]
Julia A & Albert O CLOUGH, printer, at Saco ME [26 Jun 1845]
CARSON Tryphosa & George ALEXANDER at Belfast ME [18 Jun 1846]
CARTER Adeline J formerly of Lowell & Wm JAQUES of the Ten Hills Farm of Charlestown MA by Rev T ADAMS at Vassalboro ME [13 Apr 1839]
Alice A & Rev Mark GOULD at Bethel ME [19 Feb 1852]
Briggs T MD & Margaret J WEEKS at Jefferson ME [3 Sept 1846]

CARTER (cont.) Emery & Eliza J NICKERSON of Swanville ME at Frankfort ME [22 Jan 1842]
    Geo G of Portland ME & Mary A FALES at Thomaston ME [14 Mar 1850]
    Henry L of Augusta ME & Abagail MATHEWS of Hallowell at Hallowell ME [21 Sept 1833]
    James & Mary J SWASEY at Bucksport ME [22 Jan 1846]
    Jerusha (white lady) & Matthias SKEETUP (colored gentleman) both of Carthage ME at Weld ME [21 Mar 1844]
    John S, printer, & Charlotte MATHEWS d/o John MATHEWS by Rev C GARDNER at Waterville ME [13 Jun 1844]
    John & Mary JOHNSON at Hallowell ME [26 Sept 1834]
    Joseph C Capt, of the brig *Diana*, of Boston & Hannah T LORD of Hallowell ME 24 Nov by Rev DIELL at Oahu Sandwich Islands (Hawaii Island USA) [13 Jun 1834]
    Mary C & G R SULLIVAN at Brookline MA [20 Jul 1848]
    Mary Jane & John A DIXON at Kittery ME [29 Mar 1849]
    Pamelia W of Parkman ME & Rev William BAILEY of Buxton ME at Parkman [16 May 1840]
    Ruby A & David W MOREY of Belmont ME at Montville ME [3 Apr 1851]
    Sewall P of Belfast ME & Ellen G KIMBALL at Gardiner ME [7 Oct 1847]
    Tryphena M & Levi M WEBBER at Etna on New Year's Day [8 Jan 1852]

CARVELLE - see CARVILLE

CARVER Allen & Eunice K BRAZIER at Belfast ME [10 Jul 1838]
    David & Phebe CAMPBELL at Paris ME [6 May 1847]
    Eben & Mary A BURNHAM at Troy ME [29 Jul 1852]
    Capt James N & Lydia C WENTWORTH of Belfast ME at Searsport ME [8 May 1845]
    Maj John of Leeds ME & Mrs Martha SMITH of Akron OH at Gardiner ME [8 Aug 1844]
    Lorenzo & Catharine WILLIS at Thomaston ME [2 Dec 1847]
    Nathan Jr of Livermore ME & Hannah G WINTER at Wilton ME [30 Apr 1846]
    Ruth d/o John CARVER Esq & Samuel P TRUE by Elder W FOSS at Leeds ME [27 Nov 1841]

CARVEY Isaac & Deborah NORTON at Lincolnville ME [19 Oct 1839]

CARVILLE Elmira D & Sewall N GOSS at Lewiston ME [19 Aug 1852]
    Ezra R of Lewiston ME & Dorcas Ann JORDAN at Webster ME on Jun 22nd by Jesse DAVIS Esq [3 Jul 1851]
    Harriet & Elisha HANSON at Lewiston ME [16 Oct 1845]
    Milton of Lewiston ME & Lucy L McKENNEY at Greene ME [30 Mar 1848] & [13 Apr 1848]
    Miss E & Samuel A MERRILL of Lawrence MA at Lewiston ME [11 Apr 1850]

CARY Catharine & Lt Isaac BOWEN, US 1st Artillery, at Houlton Aroostook Co ME [10 Apr 1845]
    Franklin L of Gardiner ME & Mary A BANGS at Sidney ME [3 Dec 1846]
    Simeon Esq of Hallowell ME & Eunice BANKS at Boston MA [1 Jan 1846]
    Susan, d/o William CARY Esq, & Waldo BLOSSOM by Isaac CROSS Esq at Turner ME [22 May 1835]
    Susan, d/o Dea A CARY of Bridgton ME & Harrison BLAKE Esq of Harrison ME at Harrison ME [18 Nov 1836]

CASCOM Mr E H of Southampton MA & Mrs Sarah A MORRIL at Biddeford ME [10 Apr 1845]
CASE Ann S & Ephraim GAY at East Thomaston ME [8 Oct 1846]
    Elisha S & Joanna JUDKINS at East Readfield ME [1 Jul 1847] he Esq [15 Jul 1847]
    Isaac of Thomaston & Mary A HALL at Belfast ME [19 Jul 1849]
    John S & Lucy C WHITE at Rockland ME [19 Aug 1852]
    Nancy B & Nathaniel C WESTON of Hallowell ME 21st inst by Rev John ALLEN at Readfield ME [30 Dec 1847]
    Rosalinda & Capt Peter MANTER of Tisbury MA at Farmington ME [23 Jul 1846]
    Thomas H & Harriet COGGINS at Lubec ME [22 Feb 1849]
CASEY Nancy M & Wm L JOHNSON 25th ult at Carmel ME [18 Jan 1840]
CASNER Silas N & Miss Elizabeth FYLER at Waldoboro ME [31 Aug 1848]
CASS Ann Cornelia & Nathan P WOODS of Bloomfield ME at Cornville ME [17 Jul 1851]
CASWELL Almon & Joanna K WILLIAMS at Mercer ME on 10th Jun [23 Jun 1852]
    Catharine B & Isaac M GRANT at Thomaston ME [23 Oct 1845]
    Francis B of Harrison ME & Eunice M RUSSELL at Bethel ME [6 Sept 1849]
    Mary P & Jonathan C PHILLIPS at Turner ME [19 Dec 1837]
    Rosilla & Henry HASKELL at Otisfield ME [21 Mar 1850]
CATE Albion of Dresden ME & Martha FOYE at Wiscasset ME [29 Nov 1849]
CATES Comfort & Rev B F SPRAGUE at Thorndike ME [1 Aug 1840]
    Harriet M & Dr Joseph N SMITH of Mt Vernon ME at Thorndike ME [28 Mar 1844]
    Jonathan & Mrs Eunice FLY on 25 Nov at Hallowell ME [6 Dec 1849]
CAVERLY Mary F & Ware L FOLSOM at Stetson ME [29 Jan 1852]
CENTER Nathan D & Abigail BICKFORD of Kennebunkport ME at Saco ME [27 Aug 1846]
CHADBORNE/CHADBOURNE Caroline of Lyman ME & Wm G CHADBOURNE Esq of Westbrook ME at Lyman ME [25 Dec 1845]
    Dorcas & Simon CARPENTER of Waterboro ME at Limerick ME [6 Mar 1851]
    Emily & David HOBART of Acton MA at East Madison ME [19 Nov 1846]
    George of Gorham ME & Harriet BOYNTON at Cornish ME [25 Feb 1847]
    Hannah & Enos P SMALL at Saco ME [12 Apr 1849]
    Isaiah Jr & Irene LEIGHTON at Harmony ME [15 Jan 1846]
    James & Mary GRAVES at Vassalboro ME [28 Jan 1843]
    Nathaniel of Sanford ME & Mrs Lydia GOOCH of Alfred ME at Alfred ME [1 May 1838]
    Rosamond of Harmony ME & John PEASE of Wellington ME at Harmony ME [2 Nov 1839]
    Susannah H & Mr EATON at Newburyport MA [27 May 1852]
    William G Esq of Westbrook ME & Caroline CHADBOURNE of Lyman ME at Lyman ME [25 Dec 1845]
    Z Jr & Miss Dorcas A BROWN at Oxford ME [28 May 1846]
CHADSEY Elizabeth A & Joseph C BRADFORD at Bath ME [4 Jul 1840]
CHADWICK Augustus J & Jane O HILTON on Sunday eve by Rev WILLIAMS at Augusta ME [31 Jul 1845]

CHADWICK (cont.) Charles W of Gilford NH & Susan C BUCK by Rev W A P DILLINGHAM on 16th inst at Augusta ME [25 Oct 1849]
David E & Elizabeth J ALLEN at Lewiston ME [23 Jun 1852]
CHAFFEE Maria W & Ira A SALMON of Portland ME at Vassalboro ME [6 Mar 1851]
CHALLIES Elizabeth A & Gilmore EMERY at Newfield ME [25 Mar 1847]
CHALMERS Rev Milton & Lucetta STRATTON at Albion ME [25 Jun 1846]
Sybil of Albion ME & John WHITCOMB of Waldo Plantation ME at Albion ME [2 Apr 1842]
CHAMBERLAIN/CHAMBERLIN Abigail & Benjamin S PHILBRICK of Mt Vernon ME at Foxcroft ME [29 Feb 1840]
Calvin Esq of Foxcroft ME & Lavina PHILBROOK at Mt Vernon ME [13 Nov 1838]
Calvin Esq of Foxcroft ME & Mary R CONVERSE at Charlton MA [1 Apr 1847]
Charles H Senior Editor of the Bath *Tribune* & Susan G WILSON at Livermore ME [8 Jun 1848]
Chester of Foxcroft ME & Laura Ann J WARREN at Sangerville ME [27 Apr 1839]
Eliza W & James WHITTIER of Old Town ME at Bradford ME [16 Dec 1847]
Elizabeth of Henriville & David OWEN of Bath ME (formerly of Montgomery, AL), at Henriville, Lower Canada [21 May 1842]
George & Hannah BACHELER, at Fayette ME [23 Sept 1843]
Hannah F & Daniel D CROCKER Esq of Calais ME at Foxcroft ME [17 Jan 1850]
Henry M of Auburn ME & Martha Ann SOPER of Gray ME on Thanksgiving evening, by Chas MEGQUIER Esq at Gray ME [30 Dec 1843]
Isabel & Nathaniel REYNOLDS both of Sidney ME on 29 Nov at East Boston MA [24 Jan 1850]
John H & Mary E ROUNDEY at Benton ME [19 Feb 1852]
Joseph of Clinton ME & Mary Ann CHAMBERLIN at Hallowell ME [20 Jun 1834]
Mary Ann & Joseph CHAMBERLIN of Clinton ME at Hallowell ME [20 Jun 1834]
Nancy (Mrs) of Unity ME & Zebulon MURCH of Foxcroft ME at Foxcroft ME [16 May 1844]
Nathaniel Jr & Lucy PLUMMER at Dover NH [3 Jun 1852]
Orren W & Harriet L BROWN at Stetson ME [29 Jan 1852]
Reuel of Augusta ME & Jane NICKLESS of Vassalboro ME at Sidney ME [10 Jul 1845]
CHANDLER Aaron of Jay ME & Mary Ann DAVIS at Farmington ME [18 Sept 1845]
Alanson M of Minot ME & Harriet MANN of Paris ME at Paris ME [27 Jul 1839]
Capt Joseph & Mary OAKES both of North Yarmouth ME at New York [1 Aug 1844]
Cyntha A of Foxcroft ME & Charles H SANFORD of Sebec ME at Augusta ME [10 Jul 1845]

CHANDLER (cont.) Cyrus C formerly of Winthrop ME & Mary Jane KEEN at East Thomaston ME [3 Sept 1846]
 Cyrus of Bridgewater Plt ME? & Rosetta J PRAY at Livermore ME [16 Apr 1846]
 Daniel F & Emily J STURTEVANT on Wed eve by Rev CLEAVELAND at Winthrop ME [26 Dec 1840]
 Elias B of Waterville ME & Caroline M GOODWIN at St Albans ME [22 Feb 1849]
 Elvina Z of Winthrop ME & B C WING of Bangor ME by Rev B F ROBBINS at Winthrop ME [21 May 1846]
 Frances L & George G FULLER at Saco ME [4 Jun 1851]
 George L & Mary H FOSTER late of Alna ME by Rev STOW at the Federal Street Church at Boston MA [30 Jul 1842]
 Harrison & Susan B HOLMES by Rev THURSTON at Winthrop ME extended notice [31 Jan 1850]
 Heather Ann, d/o Alfred CHANDLER, & William GOWER of Industry ME by Rev RANDALL at Winthrop ME [16 Jul 1842]
 Isaac H & Caroline Elizabeth d/o Earl SHAW Esq at Boston MA [9 Dec 1843]
 Jesse & Mary WRIGHT both of Farmington ME at Temple ME [11 Mar 1852]
 Joanna of Foxcroft ME & Enoch P GOODWIN of Sebec ME at Foxcroft [2 Jul 1842]
 Joseph of Wayne ME & Susan M C STEARNS of Dracutt MA on 7th inst at Dracutt [17 Jul 1845]
 Laura of Minot ME & Charles BEALE of Bangor ME at Minot [25 Mar 1836]
 Lucilla T of Winthrop ME & A S C STRICKLAND Esq of Wilton ME on Tues morn last by Rev THURSTON at Winthrop ME [11 Nov 1836]
 Lucy & Bailey JACOBS of Abbot ME at Wayne ME [17 Oct 1844]
 M A of Augusta ME & Sarah Jane TINKHAM of Wiscasset ME by Rev Seneca WHITE at Wiscasset ME [10 Oct 1834]
 Margaret Melvina, d/o Enos CHANDLER, & Silas T FLOYD on 27 Nov by Rev B F ROBBINS all of Winthrop ME at Winthrop ME [3 Dec 1846]
 Martha Jane & Francis COBB at Thomaston ME [26 Oct 1839]
 Mary A & S I LOVEJOY both of Thomaston ME at Thomaston ME [13 Feb 1841]
 Mary Jane of Wayne ME & Stedman KENDALL at Wayne [13 Apr 1839]
 Mary Lindy, d/o Enos CHANDLER, & Rev B F ROBBINS all of Winthrop ME on 30 Oct by Rev F FOSTER at Winthrop ME [7 Nov 1844]
 Miss E R & Adoniram J MACE of Readfield ME at Winthrop ME on 20th Feb by John MAY Esq [6 Mar 1851]
 Miss L G & Josiah WRIGHT (Jr) at Foxcroft ME [23 Nov 1848]
 Nancy T m A A Mr MANWELL both of Winthrop ME at Dover NH on 21st ult [4 Jun 1851]
 Peleg W Esq of Boston MA & Martha Ann BUSH d/o Professor CLEAVELAND of Bowdoin College at Brunswick ME [19 Dec 1837]
 Salina (Mrs) of Auburn ME & Benjamin CONANT at Turner ME [4 Apr 1850]
 Sarah F & Benjamin H CLEAVES at Saco ME [19 Mar 1846]

CHANDLER (cont.) Sarah Mariah & Rev Ariel CHUTE of Oxford ME at Bangor ME [13 May 1836]
 Sarah P W & Wm A RUTHERFORD of Boston MA on Sun eve last by Rev JUDD at the residence of Mrs Gen CHANDLER at Augusta ME [21 Feb 1850]
 Susan O & George P GIVEN at Brunswick ME [7 Jan 1847]
 Vesta & Solon G WALKER at Paris ME [18 Jul 1840]
 Zebulon Jr & Dorcas A BROWN at Oxford ME [14 May 1846]

CHANEY B G & M SYLVESTER both of Hallowell ME by Rev BRAGDON at Hallowell ME [26 Jun 1841]
 John P & Caroline NORRIS at Solon ME [27 Dec 1849]
 Jotham & Abigail L ROBERTS both of South Berwick ME at Kittery ME [21 Mar 1837]
 Rev S Freeman of Buxton ME & Abby D JOHNSON at Farmington ME [21 Aug 1842]
 Susan of Whitefield ME & Samuel LINSCOTT of Damariscotta ME at East Pittston ME [1 Feb 1849]
 William & Dorcas TURNER by James MERRILL Esq at Whitefield ME [8 Oct 1842]

CHAPLIN/CHAPIN Edwin of Belchertown MA & Catharine S WOOD at Camden ME [22 Oct 1842]

CHAPLES Benjamin A & Nancy WHITHAM at Thomaston ME [23 Dec 1847]
 David & Susan D GIBBS at Glenburn ME [23 Jul 1846]
 Richard J & Laurietta A MAYO at Otisfield ME [15 Feb 1849]

CHAPMAN C W Esq of New York, (Foreign Agent of the Southampton Bachelor Society and last but one of its members) & Susan AMES of Belchertown at Belchertown [4 Sept 1838]
 Calatia & Charles G AVERAL both of Damariscotta ME at Wiscasset ME [20 Mar 1851]
 Charles P & Harriet N MARCH on 28 Dec by L C SMITH Esq at Starks ME [4 Jan 1849]
 D W & Mary A HASKELL by Wm PERCIVAL Esq at China ME [4 Feb 1847]
 Harriet of Gilead ME & Brown THURSTON of Portland ME on 19th ult by Rev David THURSTON of Winthrop ME at Gilead [13 Aug 1842]
 Henry & Mrs Angeline AUSTIN at Nobleboro ME [4 Feb 1843]
 Isaac & Hannah WALKER at Saco ME [16 Jan 1838]
 Joseph Jr & Abby SIDELINGER both of Nobleboro ME at Thomaston ME [11 Mar 1847]
 Julia A & Mr A T STOCKING at North Searsport ME [21 Sept 1848]
 Lucinda & Martin L CHAPMAN by Rev E TRASK at Nobleboro ME [25 Dec 1838]
 Martha J & Augustus N COWAN at Bath ME [5 Feb 1852]
 Martha T of Starks ME & Sylvanus B WALTON of Mercer ME at Smithfield ME [11 Nov 1843]
 Martin L & Lucinda CHAPMAN by Rev E TRASK at Nobleboro ME [25 Dec 1838]
 Mary C & Abernethy GROVER at Bethel ME [17 Feb 1848]
 Milton W of Bethel ME & Mary YATES at Paris ME [10 Jun 1847]
 N S Mr & Mary P COTTERELL of Northport ME at Belfast ME [12 Nov 1846]

CHAPMAN (cont.) Rebecca of Mercer ME & Nathan SEGARS of Durham ME on 3 Jul at Augusta ME [15 Jul 1852]
Royal L of Nobleboro ME & Elizabeth E MARR of Alna ME at Belfast ME [11 Jun 1846]
Salome B & Ira C KIMBALL at Bethel ME [13 Apr 1848]
W H Mr of (Augusta) ME & Serena SEWALL by O W WASHBURN Esq at China ME on 8th inst [25 May 1848]
CHAPPLES William A of Thomaston ME & Mary C HYLER at Cushing ME [31 Oct 1844]
CHASE Abijah B Esq of Sebec ME & Mary E KIDDER at Dover ME [11 May 1848]
Alexander H of Bangor ME & Jane G FARRAR of Harmony ME at Bangor ME [25 Dec 1838]
Alice A & Rev Abraham R LUNT of Freeport ME at Brunswick ME [22 Aug 1844]
Arthur L & Lucy GRAHAM at Lowell MA [5 Aug 1847]
Calvin S & Martha Jane ANDREWS at Pleasant Ridge ME [13 Dec 1849]
Capt Amos T & Sophronia WEBSTER both of Portland ME at New Gloucester ME [4 Sept 1838]
Caroline M, d/o Joseph CHASE Esq, & John M CUSHING at Sebec ME [19 Sept 1844]
Clarissa J & Asa MCMARLAND proprietor of the *New Hampshire Statesman* at Meredith NH [26 Jun 1845]
Cynthia, d/o Israel CHASE Esq, & Dr William B SMALL of Wilton ME on 24 Aug by Rev HOUGHTON at Fayette ME. The guests manifested fine glee on the occasion, promoted by the accelerating qualities of pure cold water, without the aid of wine. [12 Sept 1834]
David & Sally Maria LAMPHER at Sebec ME [14 Mar 1850]
Deborah & John W TODD at Bangor ME [26 Aug 1843]
Dr Rufus M of Fairfield ME & Ann Elizabeth POPE at Windsor ME [23 Sept 1843]
Elias & Laura CLIFFORD at Paris ME [23 May 1840]
Elizabeth L of Winslow ME & Jefferson TAYLOR of Vassalboro ME by Amos STICKNEY Esq at Vassalboro [8 Aug 1837]
Ellen, d/o the late Stephen CHASE of Fryeburg ME, & Charles H TAYLOR of Clark County VA at Fryeburg ME [27 Aug 1846]
Emeline of Augusta & Noah W CROSS of Gardiner ME on Sun morn last by Rev N W WILLIAMS at Augusta ME [30 Oct 1845]
Emily E & John B CAIN of Clinton ME at Fairfield ME [27 Sept 1849]
Frances & Leonard D SHEPLEY at Portland ME [17 May 1849]
G W formerly of Haverhill MA & Frances A DYER at New Sharon ME [17 Jan 1850]
George M Esq & Harriet G NORWOOD at Camden ME [22 Jul 1836]
Hall Dr of Waterville ME & Sarah Richardson TIBBETS at Topsham ME [19 Sept 1844]
Helen M & Oliver BRIARD JR of Boston MA at Waterville ME [10 Sept 1846]
Henrietta A & Dr Edwin P SNOW of Atkinson ME at Sebec ME [28 Mar 1850]
Hiram & Sarah D TITCOMB at Anson ME [22 Feb 1844]

CHASE (cont.) J G of Springfield MA & Sarah C S G THORNTON at Saco ME [14 May 1846]
James T & Almira E PARKER at Livermore ME [26 Oct 1848]
John JR & Susan A DAVIS at Unity ME [5 Mar 1846]
John W of Minot ME & Mary Ann BUMPERS of Hebron ME at Hebron [26 Dec 1840]
John W & Eunice G ROGERS at Stetson ME [31 Aug 1839]
Lizzie A of Farmington ME & Mr M S M TAYLOR Esq of Montpelier VT at Farmington Falls ME [24 Jul 1851]
Lowell G & Sophia G BALCH d/o H G BALCH Esq at Lubec ME [10 Oct 1840]
Lucinda & Richard SAVAGE at Wiscasset ME [6 May 1847]
Lucy & George HATCH at Richmond ME [8 Aug 1844]
Lydia & Edward S BUXTON on 22 Jan by Rev HOBERT at North Yarmouth ME [6 Feb 1835]
Marshall D of Harrison & Flora A FAIRBANKS at Waterford ME [29 Apr 1852]
Martha T & Wm T JOHNSON of Augusta at Portland ME [12 Dec 1837]
Mary A of Fairfield ME & Ashur SAVAGE of Waterville ME at Skowhegan ME [16 Jan 1851]
Mary Ann of Norridgewock ME & Alonzo HAMILTON of Saco ME at Norridgewock ME [4 Jan 1840]
Mary E & John W DOUGHLASS at Hallowell ME [12 Oct 1848]
Mary K & Lorenzo A BOWLEN both of Palermo ME at Montville ME [25 Apr 1850]
Mary & Wm BENJAMIN of Skowhegan ME at Bingham ME [19 Aug 1847]
Mr F A & Rachel L STURTEVANT at Fayette ME [27 Apr 1848]
Mr M & Eliza TILTON at Livermore ME [14 Nov 1840]
Mr W H of Bucksport ME & Elvira H BOWLES at Rockland [8 May 1851]
Nathaniel Colonel of Turner ME & Mrs Hannah W HAYFORD at Augusta ME [21 Jul 1843]
Nathaniel of Sidney ME & Abba GOULD of New Sharon ME at Boston MA on 23 Dec by Rev Theodore PARKER [2 Jan 1851]
Oliver of Monroe ME & Lavina C ELLIS of Waldo ME at Belfast ME [13 Jun 1844]
Persis E & Moses MAYO of Milo ME at Kilmarnock ME [4 Sept 1851]
Rev Seth B of Paris ME & Mary E HOLMES of Peru ME at Monmouth ME [4 Mar 1847]
Sarah E & John H COOK at Augusta ME [20 Apr 1839]
Solomon & Nancy H STEPHENS at Paris ME [11 Apr 1837]
Solon & Ann PHILLIPS at Turner ME [23 Oct 1845]
Sparrow & Olive RIDEOUT of Brunswick ME at Topsham ME [8 Jul 1843]
Stephen J & Miss C E KIMBALL of Athens ME at Andover MA [13 Jan 1848]
Stephen L & Flora D GASLIN at (Augusta) ME [25 May 1848]
Valeria A of Minot ME & Samuel STETSON of Danville ME at Hebron ME [16 Apr 1846]
William & Lucy P FULLER at Augusta ME [19 Dec 1840]
CHEEVER Betsey J & Reuben G W DODGE at Blue Hill ME [23 Sept 1847]
Samuel H & Almira BURRILL of Vienna ME at Boston MA [27 May 1836]
CHENEREY George W & Caroline SPRAGUE at Gardiner ME [2 Oct 1845]

Marriage Notices from the "Maine Farmer"

CHENERY Catharine M & Moses DOLE at Westbrook ME [24 Jun 1836]
CHENEY George H of Newport NH & Sarah D DAVIS of Winthrop ME Tues morn last by Rev David THURSTON at Winthrop ME [5 Aug 1833]
CHESLEY Justina C & Rev John R GREENOUGH JR, Pastor of the Baptist Church in Old Town ME at Bangor ME [7 Oct 1847]
  Thomas H of Boston MA & Mrs Emily HEATH 5 Feb by Rev A BURGESS at Augusta ME [14 Feb 1850]
CHICK Benjamin of Madrid ME & VAIELETTA TRACY at Farmington ME [6 Jan 1848]
  Esther A & Edwin W WEDGEWOOD Esq at Cornish ME [17 Apr 1851]
  Jane H & Thomas S JACKSON Thanksgiving evening by Rev ROBINSON at Winthrop ME [16 Dec 1843]
  Mary (Mrs) & Joseph O ALLEN both of Litchfield ME at Monmouth ME [21 Mar 1844]
  Nathan & Elizabeth C FLANDERS of Buxton ME at Limerick ME [10 Jun 1847]
  Sophia & Samuel THOMPSON at Topsham ME [11 Jan 1844]
  Thaddeus A formerly of Bangor ME & Martha Augusta BARTON 10 Sept at Augusta ME [20 Sept 1849]
  Thomas M & Charlotte W Hilton at Wiscasset ME [19 Nov 1846]
  William Esq & Jane RECORDS formerly of Buckfield ME at Amherst MA? [7 Jan 1847]
  William H & Ruth A HINKLEY at Litchfield ME [24 Feb 1848]
CHILD/CHILDS Abby & Warren A AMES at Farmington ME [24 May 1849]
  Albion K P Dr of Jay ME & Lucy A KYES at Wilton ME [13 Dec 1849]
  Ann Eliza eldest d/o James L CHILD Esq of Augusta ME & Lt Robert M A WALWRIGHT of the US Army (ordnance corps) now in command at US Arsenal in Augusta ME of the city of Washington DC? at Augusta ME by Rev Dr TAPPAN [9 Sept 1843]
  Arthur Captain & Sarah C d/o Captain Samuel BORLAND at Damariscotta ME [10 Sept 1846]
  Edwin B & Melissa M DAVIS at Canton ME [3 Jun 1847]
  Emeline & Alpheus DODGE of Wiscasset ME at Hallowell [2 May 1834]
  James & Mary RACKLIFF both of Muscle Ridge Plantation ME? at St George ME [18 Jun 1846]
  John H & Naomi S HILTON 27 Jun at Norridgewock ME [12 Jul 1849]
  Lydia L of Canton & H T PETERSON of East Livermore ME at Jay ME [19 Jul 1849]
  Lyman of Jay ME & Nancy ADAMS of Madison ME at Embden ME [10 Jan 1850]
  Martha Ann & Joseph STILL of Wiscasset ME at Hallowell [5 Jun 1835]
  Sarah R, eldest d/o Greenwood C CHILD Esq, & Wm L WALKER Esq of Newport ME by Rev JUDD 25th ult at Augusta ME [15 Aug 1844]
CHIPMAN Caroline & Gemeral Eliphalet D BRAY both of Kingfield ME by Charles PIKE Esq 20th inst at Kingfield ME [5 Dec 1834]
  Cyrus M & Hepsebah MANN 31 Jan at Greene ME [27 Feb 1838]
  Eleazer M of Salem & Abigail M MANSFIELD of Bath ME at Athol MA [12 Mar 1846]
  Joshua & Mrs Polly LARRABEE at New Portland ME [29 Nov 1849]
  Sarah C of Portland ME & Lorenzo MERRILL of New Gloucester ME at Portland [7 Dec 1833]

CHISAM Samuel of Alna ME & Arletta MYERS at Pittston ME [18 Dec 1845]
CHISM Susan & Joseph HURLEY at Alna ME [28 Feb 1834]
CHOAT Betsey & Alfred SHELDON of Waldo Plantation ME at Montville ME [28 May 1842]
CHOATE Clarissa & Elbridge CHOATE by Wm PERCIVAL Esq at China ME [1 Jul 1847]
  Elbridge & Clarissa CHOATE, same as above
  Rachel B & Capt Johnson BURBANKS at Whitefield ME [14 Aug 1835]
CHURCH Abigail & Ira MERROW at Hartland ME [17 Aug 1848] & [3 Aug 1848]
CHURCH Albert Rev of the Maine (Methodist) Annual Conference, & Philena d/o John PATTEE Esq of Searsmont ME at Searsmont [4 Jul 1837]
  Geo G Capt of Gardiner ME & Mrs Elizabeth TURNER of St Anns Jamaica at New York City [31 Jan 1850]
  Hiram & Elvira DOBLE at Avon ME [26 Jul 1849]
  John & Mrs Elizabeth BARTON of Mercer ME at Farmington ME [25 Dec 1845]
  Joseph of Phillips ME & Martha MOORS of Madrid ME 25 Mar by Hon John L BLAKE at Phillips ME [22 Apr 1843]
CHURCHILL/CHURCHELL Edgar M of Augusta ME & Catharine BAKER at Woolwich ME [28 Jan 1833]
  Emily A & Daniel H PEASLEE at Danville ME [8 Mar 1849]
  James of New Portland ME & Clarissa THOMPSON of Embden ME at Solon ME [14 Jan 1847]
  Joseph W & Mary DOANE at Raymond ME [16 Aug 1849]
  Lucinda & John SAVAGE 3rd inst at Augusta ME [21 Oct 1847]
  Lucy Ann B & Augustus V WASHBURN at Buckfield ME [13 Feb 1851]
  Mary C & Albert THOMAS of Hallowell ME on 6th inst at Augusta ME [14 Jun 1849]
  Nathan & Harriet THOMAS both of Buckfield ME at Buckfield [17 Jul 1845]
  Paulina C & Lewis WARD at Augusta ME on 19th Aug by Asaph R NICHOLS Esq [28 Aug 1851]
CHUTE Ariel Rev of Oxford ME & Sarah Mariah CHANDLER at Bangor ME [13 May 1836]
  Sarah F & Capt Seth C BOARDMAN at Belfast ME [14 Oct 1847]
  Serene N. d/o Curtis CHUTE, late of Cumberland ME, both of Carthage ME by Elder MAYO at Carthage [30 Dec 1843]
CILLEY George A of (Augusta) ME & Charlotte D MARSHALL of Charlestown MA at Providence RI on 9th Jan [9 Mar 1848]
CLAFLIN Mr W M of Danvers MA & Harriet SMITH at Gardiner ME [1 Apr 1852]
CLAPHAM Charles G & Roxana WARD at China ME [1 Aug 1834]
CLAPP Charles B & Mercy P d/o Hon Edward SWAN at Gardiner ME [3 Oct 1844]
  David of Nobleboro ME & Mary S WILDER at Wiscasset ME [14 Nov 1844]
  Nancy E & Josephus NASH of Portland ME at Bath ME [11 Oct 1849]
  Stephen & Maria SWEAT both of Brownville ME at Maxfield ME [27 Aug 1846]
CLAREY ALLEN Esq & Margaret J DEE both of Georgetown ME at Phipsburg ME [6 Mar 1845]

Marriage Notices from the "Maine Farmer"

CLARK/CLARKE Aaron & Josephine HOWE both of Deer Isle ME at Eastport ME [28 Jan 1847]
Abigail B & William W THOMPSON at Jay ME [3 Apr 1841]
Albert H & Eliza A WORTH at China ME [11 Feb 1847]
Almira M (Mrs) & Moses SHORT at Bangor ME [12 Jun 1845]
Amanda L & Thomas R KINGSBERRY Esq of Bradford ME at Atkinson ME [17 Jun 1847]
Amanda of Moultonboro NH & Rev John SIMPSON of the Maine (Methodist) Annual Conference at Moultonboro NH [6 Jul 1839]
Amelia A & John BOWMAN at Bloomfield ME [27 Jul 1848]
Angeline & Thomas LILLY at (Augusta) ME on Sunday evening last [9 Mar 1848]
Arthur C & Mrs L A PETTINGILL by John A PETTINGILL Esq at (Augusta) ME [16 Nov 1848]
B F & Betsey LIBBY at Belfast ME [29 Mar 1849]
Bunker & Abigail GREENWOOD at Farmington ME [13 Dec 1849]
Caroline F & Capt Robert H McKOWN at Bath ME [21 Nov 1834]
Charlotte A & George S PETERS at Providence RI [12 Oct 1848]
Charlotte G & Roby K LINNELL of Belgrade ME at Augusta ME [18 Feb 1833]
Cordelia & Henry STERLING at Atkinson ME [24 Apr 1845]
D P of Unity ME & Lucy E WARREN at Freedom ME [12 Aug 1852]
Delia A & John C TALLMAN at Bath ME [9 Sept 1847]
Drusilla & John GOULDING at Perry ME [12 Feb 1836]
E M & Hannah M d/o A M SHAW at Winthrop ME [11 Dec 1838]
Edwin W & Caroline E STARBIRD of Foxcroft ME at Atkinson ME [11 Mar 1852]
Elvina B & Emery D CLARK both of China ME at Augusta ME on Dec 21st by Asaph R NICHOLS Esq [25 Dec 1851]
Emery D & Elvina B CLARK both of China at Augusta ME on Dec 21st by Asaph R NICHOLS Esq [25 Dec 1851]
Emma J & W S BUTLER at Lincoln ME [6 May 1847]
Eve R, d/o Elisha CLARK Esq, & Joseph W STUART of Belgrade ME at China ME [22 Oct 1846]
Eveline A & George H PARSHLEY at Bath ME [11 Nov 1847]
Everline & John C TUCKER at Palermo ME [27 Jul 1848]
Frances M & Daniel C BARKER at Portland ME [12 Jun 1845]
G W of Cahawba AL & Mary E RUSS at Belfast ME [14 Aug 1838]
George S of Boston MA & E F BLANCHARD at Pittston ME [12 Nov 1846]
Hannah G & Charles C EMERY at Sangerville ME [25 May 1848]
Hannah M & J W TAYLOR at Sidney ME [10 Jul 1845]
Harriet A & B R LEAVITT at Hallowell ME [15 Jul 1847]
Harriet J & Zacheus JOHNSON 18 Jul by Rev H M BLAKE at Augusta ME [29 Jul 1852]
Harriet & J E HARRIMAN at Frankfort ME [30 May 1844]
Henry W & Emeline WILLIAMS at Augusta ME [11 Jul 1844]
Hezekiah Crockett & Sylva Stevens RAWSON at Paris ME [9 May 1837]
Horatio & Lucinda McLAUGHLIN of Anson ME by Mr Winslow at New Portland ME [8 Jun 1848]
Isaac Jr, Captain, & Mary HUTCHINSON at Belfast ME [6 May 1847]
James & Mary Ann MOODY at Vassalboro ME [10 Dec 1846]

CLARK (cont.) Jane Helen & Eleazer C GETCHELL at Sebasticook ME [31 Dec 1842]
Joan H CLARK (Mrs) & Walden S PARKS at Skowhegan ME [22 Jul 1847]
John M of Sidney ME & Olive WRIGHT of Livermore ME at Livermore [25 Apr 1844]
John S & Frances M H WHITTIER of Vassalboro ME at Sebasticook ME [4 Feb 1847]
John W & Mary N WILSON both of Hallowell ME at Bingham ME [1 Jun 1848]
Jonathan of Tewksbury MA & Persis WHITTIER formerly of Winthrop ME at Methuen MA [4 Feb 1843]
Joseph K of Wiscasset ME & Lucretia G FULLER, d/o the late Judge FULLER of Augusta ME at Boston MA on 27th ult [10 Jan 1850]
Joseph & Sarah L McCAUSLAND at Augusta ME [22 Oct 1846]
Josiah & Sarah A BRYANT at Smithfield ME [8 Feb 1849]
Judson G of Portland ME & Zilphina N FOSSET at Bath ME [8 Apr 1847]
Julia A & Jon B MORRELL both of China ME at Vassalboro [8 Feb 1844]
Julia Ann & Albion JONES both of Nobleboro ME at Gardiner ME [23 Sept 1847]
Levi of Sebec & Ruth WITHAM of Milo ME at Milo ME [24 Sept 1846]
Lovina P & Chester S SMITH 22 Apr by Rev JUDD at Augusta ME [3 May 1849]
Lucinda & David ORR 2nd at Harpswell ME [1 Apr 1843]
Lucretia & George H DUNN by Rev NORRIS at Hallowell [10 Jun 1833]
Lucy E & George R BURTON at Thomaston ME [20 Jul 1848]
Lucy & Amos NOURSE MD of Hallowell ME at Boston MA [30 Sept 1836]
Margaret W & Jonathan G BISHOP at Wayne ME [24 Jul 1845]
Mary Abba & D P HATCH at Lewiston ME [3 Jan 1850]
Mary Ann & Peasly PLUMMER of Palermo ME at Washington ME [2 Dec 1843]
Mary Jane & Adam L NORCROSS on Sun morn last at Hallowell ME [16 May 1834]
Mary N & George W FRENCH of Hallowell at Gardiner ME [13 Nov 1845]
Mary N & Simon JOHNSON at Hallowell ME [18 Dec 1851]
Mary of Pembroke ME? & John GREEN at Dennysville ME [2 Jan 1845]
Mary Sand & Wm PINKHAM at Lincoln ME [6 & 13 Sept 1849]
Mary W & James O JAQUES of Gardiner ME at Tewksbury MA [25 Nov 1847]
Miss A F & Joseph STEVENS at New Portland ME [8 Jun 1848]
Miss M & J W VIDETTO at Stetson ME [27 Jul 1848]
N of Gardiner ME & Maria A G T HOLBROOK at Hallowell [31 Aug 1848]
Nancy A & Capt John A SPEAR at East Thomaston ME [3 Aug 1848]
Nancy & N (Nathaniel) L INGERSOLL, Colonel at Danville ME [23 Jan 1838]
Philotia & Capt Joshua COGGINS at Lubec ME [23 Dec 1847]
Randall B & Mary Jane DOWNS at Eastport ME [20 May 1847]
Rev Sumner of Unity ME & Frances LANE at Searsport ME [20 Mar 1845]
Sarah D B of Boston MA & Col John McCLINTOCK of Boothbay ME at Boston MA [19 Oct 1839]
Sarah G & Nehemiah S BRAINARD at New Sharon ME [26 Aug 1843]
Sarah Jane & John S CRAIG at (Augusta) ME on 3 Apr [13 Apr 1848]

CLARK (cont.) Sarah L & Adrah HATCH of Bristol ME at Newcastle ME [18 Feb 1847]
    Sarah P & John B WING Esq of Letter D Plantation ME at Fort Fairfield ME at Sangerville ME [8 Apr 1843]
    Sarah & John W HASKELL both of Thomaston ME [13 Feb 1841]
    Sophia A & Horace SILSBY of Blue Hill ME at Brewer ME [3 Jan 1850]
    Stephen S, assistant editor *New York Express*, & C A ILSLEY, at Westbrook ME [6 May 1847]
    Susan & Col Dennis BLACKWELL of Fairfield ME on 5 Aug at Hallowell ME [23 Aug 1849]
    Thomas Jr of Boston MA & Arvesta H LEWIS at Waterville ME [15 Jan 1852]
    William H & Mary E FRENCH at Belfast ME [20 Jul 1848]
    Wm M & Mrs Sabra DEARBORN at Hallowell ME [24 Sept 1846]
CLARRY Martha G of Wilton ME & Wm W MOWER at Jay ME [19 Aug 1847]
    William & Mary Ann TRASK at Hallowell ME [23 Apr 1846]
CLARY Cordelia & Joseph IRISH at Union ME [16 Nov 1839]
    Louisa & Manley ELLIS of Prospect ME at Brooks ME [19 Jun 1835]
    Louisa of Brooks ME & Stephen H KNIGHT of Boston ME at New York ME [11 Mar 1847]
    Nathan G & Ann J WEBB of Warren ME at Wilton ME [17 Jun 1847]
CLAY Eliza & Nath'l EMERY at Buxton ME [23 Aug 1849]
    Francis A & Matilda M GREAR at Augusta ME by Rev Z THOMPSON [16 Oct 1851]
    James C & Lucinda M COSS both of Gardiner ME at Hallowell ME [7 Jan 1847]
    John Randolph, Secretary of the Legation of the United States at St Petersburgh (Russia), & Jane Tucker MacKnight CRAWFORD, d/o Wm CRAWFORD Esq of Edinburgh 18 Jun at Venice [7 Aug 1845]
    L Esq of Gardiner ME & Abby BOURNE of Sandwich MA at New York City [8 Oct 1846]
    Olive B d/o Richard CLAY & L I MACOMBER at Gardiner ME [21 Dec 1833]
    Ruth & Mr S N McFARLAND at Bluehill ME [25 Dec 1851]
CLAYS Henry of Camden & Miss MELVIN at Waldoboro ME [15 Oct 1842]
CLAYTON William of Dixfield ME & Sarah A WAIT of Jay ME by Rev A SANDERSON 10th inst at Jay [25 Jun 1842]
CLEAVELAND - see BUSH, CHANDLER
    Amanda M & W C KENT at Brewer ME [6 Jul 1848]
    Benjamin JR & Octava WENTWORTH at Embden ME [19 Aug 1843]
    Dinsmore of Madison ME & Eliza P BARNARD at Bloomfield ME [15 Jul 1847]
    Elizabeth A & Dr George WOODHOUSE of Meredith NH at Brunswick ME [25 Nov 1847]
    Ellen M & John H NYE at Fairfield ME [27 Nov 1851]
    Jefferson of Embden ME & Susan Ann WASSON of Anson ME at Norridgewock ME [18 Apr 1837]
    Martha Ann Bush, d/o Prof CLEAVELAND of Bowdoin College (Brunswick ME), & Peleg W CHANDLER Esq of Boston MA at Brunswick ME [19 Dec 1837]

CLARK (cont.) Mary J & Charles BLANCHARD of Blanchard ME at Bloomfield ME [15 Jul 1847]
 Rosannah & George W DURRILL at Bloomfield ME [7 Oct 1843]
 W S of Burlington NJ & Mary Ann DWINEL 4th inst at Bangor ME [17 Sept 1842]

CLEAVES Augustus of Biddeford ME & Octavia M BLAKE at Limington ME [8 Oct 1846]
 Benjamin H & Sarah F CHANDLER at Saco ME [19 Mar 1846]
 Charles of Abbot & Nancy ELLIOT Mrs at Kilmarnock ME [25 Sept 1851]
 Daniel Esq of Biddeford ME & Hannah M TUCKER at Saco ME [25 Sept 1835]
 Eliza & Jonas TAYLOR at Kennebunk ME [1 Jan 1836]
 Jane & Sylvanus HATCH by J B SWANSON Esq at Windsor ME [14 Feb 1837]
 Mary & Edward H STAPLES both of Biddeford ME at Saco ME [26 Feb 1846]
 Nancy & William S RING at Gardiner ME [22 Nov 1849]
 Rachel of North Yarmouth ME & Asa BROWN Esq of Buxton ME at N Yarmouth ME [11 Apr 1834]
 Stephen & Lydia LARRABEE at Prospect ME [17 Jun 1836]
 William W & Hannah TILTON of London NH by Chandler Eastman Esq at Exeter [4 Sept 1835]

CLEMENT/CLEMENTS Charles L & Emily A BACHELDER at Hallowell ME [9 Nov 1848]
 Joseph W B of Franklin NH & Caroline M BROWN by Rev A DALTON at (Augusta) ME on 1st Jun [10 Jun 1852]
 Nancy & Loren W JUDKINS at Belgrade ME on Oct 1 [12 Oct 1848]
 Phebe A & Samuel G ROSS at Biddeford ME [5 Aug 1852]
 Thomas R of Montville ME & Marcia M MARDEN by D Blin FULLER Esq at Albion ME [27 Jul 1848]

CLIFFORD Abigail & Jacob HEATH by J B SWANTON at Windsor ME [14 Feb 1837]
 Albert & Hannah LANDERS of Woodstock ME at Paris ME [17 Jul 1841]
 Andrew J & Phebe TREAT both of Prospect ME at Belfast ME [4 Dec 1851]
 Clarimond & Alvan S THAYER both of Paris ME at Paris [17 Sept 1846]
 Clarissa Jane & Capt Gustavus A SWASEY, master of ship *Empire*, 16th inst by Rev J T GILMAN at Bath ME [3 Dec 1842]
 Clementina E & Capt Abiel W SHERMAN both of Edgecomb ME at Boston MA [11 Nov 1843]
 Elizabeth N & James I PLUMMER both of Augusta ME Sun eve last by D G ROBINSON Esq at Winslow [11 Dec 1845]
 Hannah & Sherburne HEATH at Windsor ME [20 Jun 1837]
 John H & Helen M SMITH at Belfast ME [4 Apr 1840]
 John N & Clymentia GLIDDEN 4th inst at Augusta ME [14 Oct 1847]
 John of Patricktown Plt ME & Jane SHEA at Georgetown ME [27 May 1852]
 Laura & Elias CHASE at Paris ME [23 May 1840]
 Mary & Isaac HEATH by J B SWANTON Esq at Windsor ME [14 Feb 1837]

CLIFFORD (cont.) Mr D J & Margaret M KINGSBURY both of Bath ME at Exeter NH [15 Apr 1852]
  S Melvina & Henry D FRENCE at Fayette ME on 20 Apr [6 May 1852]
  Timothy & Sarah PINGREE by S BEAN Esq at Lee [9 Mar 1848]
CLOSE Arabella B & J W EMERY printer at Bangor ME [8 Jul 1847]
CLOUDMAN Elizabeth Ann & Geo W FULLERTON by Rev WEBBER at Bangor ME [23 Jul 1842]
  Maria F & Moses A YOUNG both of Norway ME at South Paris ME [22 Jan 1846]
CLOUGH Albert O printer & Julia A CARSLEY at Saco ME [26 Jun 1845]
  Alvira & Dimond HUBBARD at Topsham ME [27 Apr 1848]
  Caroline & Capt Wm WALKER at Bluehill ME [29 Jul 1836]
  Freeman & Achsa BROWN at Providence RI on 23d Dec [8 Jan 1852]
  Harriet B & Samuel P FOWLER both of Boxford MA at Readfield ME [9 Dec 1847]
  Horace & Rhoda A DUNLAP at Parsonfield ME [5 Nov 1846]
  Ira & Mary J VINING by D B SWANTON Esq at Windsor ME [14 Feb 1837]
  James of Readfield ME & Sarah DUDLEY of Mt Vernon ME 10th inst by Dudley FOGG Esq at Mt Vernon [20 Feb 1835]
  Jeremiah Jr of Lewiston ME & Sarah A WIGHT by Rev Benjamin FOSTER at Monmouth ME [20 Jan 1848]
  Jeremiah of Topsham ME & Mrs Elizabeth QUIMBY at Westbrook ME [24 Oct 1844]
  Joseph & Ellcetee V PARTRIDGE at Prospect ME [8 Aug 1844]
  Joseph & Mary B RIDEOUT at Westbrook ME [31 Jul 1835]
  Lydia Ann & Enoch CARLE of Sangerville ME by Rev Caleb MUGFORD at Readfield ME [19 Jul 1849] Extended Notice
  Mary A & Capt David MARSTON of Fairhaven MA 9 Aug at Monmouth ME [3 Sept 1846]
  Nancy & Daniel Guilford at Saco ME [17 Jun 1852]
  Rhoda P d/o Elijah CLOUGH Esq of Mt Vernon ME, & Sewall N WATSON of Fayette ME on 7 Jul by Rev A DRINKWATER at Readfield ME [5 Aug 1847]
CLOUSE Angelica & Gardner LIGHT of Worcester MA at Union ME [30 Apr 1846]
  Horatio N & Mary F HARRIS at Union ME [13 Nov 1851]
CLUFF Samuel & Emma Jane PRATT at Saco ME [26 Feb 1852]
  Heber & Betsey SEAVEY at Kennebunkport ME [8 Apr 1836]
COAKLEY John & Lydia S STETSON at Bath ME [6 Nov 1845]
COBB Amasa & Betsey TARBELL of Vassalboro ME at Norridgewock ME [20 Mar 1835]
  Ambrose S & Vesta Jane DUNBAR at Warren ME [13 Mar 1841]
  Anson B of Biddeford ME & Lydia T SINNOT of Saco ME at Saco [30 Oct 1845]
  Augusta & Wm SANFORD of Bath ME at Minot ME [19 Mar 1846]
  Betsey & David LOVEITT at Cape Elizabeth ME [6 May 1836]
  Charles F Esq of New Gloucester ME & Keziah CORSON of Bangor ME at Bangor ME [9 Jan 1845]
  Elizabeth A & Orin B CROOKER at Norway ME [25 Apr 1844]
  Francis & Martha Jane CHANDLER at Thomaston ME [26 Oct 1839]

COBB (cont.) Hester Ann & Henry DAY Sunday eve 22nd ult by Oakes HOWARD Esq at Winthrop ME [22 May 1838]
  Isaac of Abbot ME & Mary AUSTIN of Parkman ME [16 Nov 1833]
  Isabel & Freeman ROYAL at Bangor ME [15 Aug 1844]
  Josiah C of Falmouth ME & Mary P SAWYER of Westbrook ME at Cumberland ME [15 Jan 1846]
  Lewis & Jerusha L SNELL at Winthrop ME [23 Nov 1839]
  Lorain of Winthrop ME & Martha SHAW of Turner ME 28 May at Turner ME [17 Jun 1843]
  Loring & Mary E LACROIS by Oaks HOWARD Esq at Winthrop ME [28 May 1846]
  Love Mrs & Cyrus HEWES both of Hermon at Hermon ME [22 May 1845]
  Luther & Rachel HOWARD Sun last by Rev J B PRESCOT at Winthrop ME extended notice [8 Jan 1836]
  Lydia P & John C LUNT of Oxford ME at Otisfield ME [16 May 1844]
  Miles S of Searsmont ME & Hannah VAUGHN of Union ME at Union [3 Apr 1835]
  Otis C of Minot ME & Lucy W CORSON at Bangor ME [18 Mar 1847]
  Rachel & Nelson VALENTINE at Poland ME [25 Jun 1846]
  Rufus A of New Gloucester ME & Esther WORMWOOD of Kennebunk ME at Kennebunk [19 Feb 1836]
  Samuel & Sarah CRAFFAM both of Cape Elizabeth ME at Cape Elizabeth [10 Oct 1837]
  Stephen of Chelsea ME & Susan A FARNHAM by Edward GRAY Esq at Vassalboro ME on 26th May [10 Jun 1852]
  Stephen & Mrs Priscilla SWAN at Bangor ME [1 Aug 1844]
  William A B & Nancy W PALMER at Dover NH [18 Mar 1847]
COBBETT Cordelia & Reuben M'KENNY at Brunswick ME [19 Dec 1834]
COBLEIGH Daniel of Roxborough MA? & Anna PERKINS at Biddeford ME [4 Mar 1852]
COBURN Betsey of Turner ME & Hathill ROE of Sumner ME at Turner ME [4 Apr 1837]
  C A & Ami McKISSICK by S P SHAW Esq at Parkman ME [16 Dec 1847]
  Deacon of Parkman & Elvira JACKSON at Sangerville ME [11 Jun 1846]
  Eleazer & Eleanor EMERY at Bloomfield ME [1 May 1845]
  Fidelia C of Bloomfield ME & Rev J S BROOKS on 5 Oct at Waterloo, Canada West, Mt Hope Mission School [4 Nov 1847]
  James & Frances C BATCHELDER at Portland ME [24 Jul 1845]
  John C of Pittston ME & Margaret E STINSON of Arrowsic ME at Georgetown ME [5 Aug 1847]
  Justus & Mary VOCE at Bath ME [4 Sept 1845]
  Silas & Laura FORBES at No 11 Aroostook Co ME [18 Feb 1847]
  Simeon of Monmouth ME & Diantha L ELLIS of Lowell MA at Monmouth ME [24 Jun 1847]
  William of New Sharon ME & Elizabeth BAILEY at Farmington ME [16 Jan 1851]
COCHRAN Abigail & Abram COCHRAN of New Boston NH at Wiscasset ME [11 Feb 1847]
  Abram & Abigail COCHRAN same as above
  Capt F & Eliza A TRIPP both of Searsport ME at Frankfort [25 Sept 1851]
  Jane M & Theodore THUNDERER at Shirley ME [11 Jul 1844]

COCHRAN (cont.) John C Hon m Susan M SNOWMAN at Rockland ME on May 8th [22 May 1851]
    Martha A & John C FLINT at Bangor ME [6 Nov 1845]
    Mary Jane & Isaac MESERVEY both of Orono ME at Bangor ME [2 Jan 1845]
    Miss M J & Timothy WALL at Ellsworth ME [3 Aug 1848]
    Sarah B d/o Jonathan COCHRAN, & Wm R SMITH publisher of the *Augusta Age* at Bangor ME [7 Jan 1843]
CODDING James D of Exeter NH & Elizabeth W PRESCOTT at Newport [4 May 1848]
CODDINGTON Angeline & Horace C DWINEL formerly of Farmington ME on 18 Mar by Wm CROSON Esq at Warren County OH [8 Jun 1839]
CODMAN Randolph A L Esq & Caroline PORTER at Portland ME [13 Nov 1838]
COFFEE Michael & Maria PERKINS of Hartland ME at Palmyra ME [18 May 1848]
COFFIN Albarona F & John ANDERSON of Limington ME at Limerick ME [22 Apr 1847]
    Alonzo K & Catharine F DUNHAM at No 11 Aroostook Co ME [28 Jan 1847]
    Artemas W of Freedom ME & Mariby SCRIBNER at Unity ME [26 Dec 1837]
    Daniel & Sarah L COLLINS at Norway ME [20 Mar 1845]
    David N B of Boston & Sarah J HAYWARD of (Augusta) ME at Lowell MA [22 Jan 1852]
    Frances & Ellis TITFORD at Topsham ME [10 Sept 1846]
    George C & Betsey B BONNEY at Buckfield ME [27 Feb 1841]
    Isaac H & Mary T FOOTE at Wiscasset ME [8 May 1851]
    Isaiah D of Edgartown MA & Henrietta GILPATRICK at Hallowell ME [16 Oct 1851]
    Louisa Jane & Bradford BEAN at Waterboro ME [18 Feb 1847]
    Louisa of No 11 R5 (now Ashland) Aroostook County ME & Benj N SYLVESTER of No 12 R6 ME by Wm GARDINER Esq at No 11 Aroostook Co ME [23 Sept 1847]
    Lucretia B & Rev James A MILLIKEN at Columbia ME? on 28th ult [24 Oct 1840]
    Lucy E & Eben BANGS at Sweden ME [19 Feb 1852]
    Lucy Elizabeth only d/o Capt John COFFIN of Newburyport MA, & Henry W PAINE Attorney at Law of Hallowell 1 May Mon eve by Rev Thomas B FOX at Newburyport MA [9 May 1837]
    Mary d/o James COFFIN of Leeds ME & Arunah BEALS by Rev S S LEIGHTON at Leeds [24 Jul 1845]
    Nathan of Leeds & Aurelia GOTT of Wayne ME at Turner ME [23 Oct 1845]
    Rufus & Olive BROWN at No 11 Aroostook Co ME [2 Mar 1848]
    Sally R & Dr Thomas M BREWER of Boston MA one of the editors of the *Atlas* at Damariscotta [7 Jun 1849]
    Sophronia B & Elliot WALKER Esq of Corinna ME at Waterville ME [19 Aug 1852]
    Susan & Towns ROACH of Bangor ME at Frankfort ME [30 Oct 1838]
    William & Mary HOLBROOK at Harpswell ME [21 Sept 1848]

COFFREN Charlotte C & Wm H KENT of Mt Vernon ME at Vienna ME [18 Nov 1847]
COFREN Fidelia of Boston MA & Wm W LOWELL of Dover ME at Bangor ME [13 Jun 1844]
    James W of the firm of Cofren & Blatchford of Augusta ME, & H Frances MAYHEW 17 Nov by Rev J S THURSTON at Mercer ME [11 Dec 1845]
    Thomas J of New Sharon ME, formerly of Vienna ME, & Ruth H KIMBALL on 25 Dec by Rev EDGECOMB at Vienna ME [22 Jan 1846]
COGAN Jane & Henry LYNCH 11 Jul by Rev PUTNAM at Augusta ME [15 Jul 1852]
COGGINS Harriet & Thomas H CASE at Lubec ME [22 Feb 1849]
    Joshua Capt & Philotia CLARK at Lubec ME [23 Dec 1847]
COLBATH William O of Exeter ME & Phebe M PIPER of Stetson at Stetson ME [9 May 1837]
COLBOURN Capt Eben of Castine ME & Abigail D DONNELL at Bath ME [4 Jul 1840]
COLBURN Alfred of (Augusta) ME & Maria Ann SOUTHWICK Jacob S Esq at Vassalboro ME [6 Jan 1848]
    Anna & Mr J T HINKLEY of Bluehill ME at Orono ME [13 Nov 1851]
    John Jr & Susan SPRINGER both of Augusta ME at Hallowell ME [19 Feb 1846]
    Joseph F & Margaret A SOPER at Pittston ME [10 Aug 1848]
    Maria & Carlton HOUDLETTE of Richmond ME at Pittston ME [11 Oct 1849]
    Rebecca A F & Sylvanus KNOWLTON at Mercer ME [28 Jun 1849]
    Silas & Ann Maria GAUBERT both of Richmond ME on 2 Dec at Richmond [11 Dec 1845]
COLBY Adalaide & Frederick W LIBBY at East Thomaston ME [6 Sept 1849]
    Alex & Abigail ROBINSON by Rev J STEVENS at (Augusta) ME [8 Jan 1852]
    Amos Jr & Nancy KILBRITH both of Gray ME on 29th inst by Rev F MERRIAM of Winthrop ME at Hallowell ME [5 Jun 1845]
    Charlotte & Hiram DENNIS at Moscow ME [6 May 1847]
    Ebenezer Jr of Webster ME & Mary Ann GAGE at Clinton ME [20 Jun 1844]
    Edward Capt & Augusta JORDAN at Bath ME [1 Feb 1844]
    Ellen & Oliver C TOZIER at Waterville ME [16 Jan 1851]
    Emeline P & Tilen GOULD both of Woolwich ME at Wiscasset ME [15 Apr 1843]
    Henry of Wiscasset ME & Mary A COLBY at Westport ME [9 Apr 1846]
    James S & Nancy H BRYANT of Bristol ME at Boston MA [18 Jul 1844]
    John & Susan HEATH at Patricktown Plantation ME [3 Jul 1835]
    M C & Oliver STOVER of Harpswell ME at Webster ME [25 Nov 1847]
    Marshall B of Concord NH & Dolly M ABBOT at Rumford ME [1 Feb 1849]
    Mary A & Henry COLBY of Wiscasset ME at Westport ME [9 Apr 1846]
    Mary A & Walter B GETCHELL both of Waterville ME at New York [6 Aug 1846]
    William ae 17 & Mary A DODGE ae 13 at Liberty ME [7 Aug 1835]
COLCORD Amanda M & William L YOUNG at Prospect ME [10 Oct 1844]

COLCORD (cont.) George H & Mary Josephine PHILBRICK both of Foxcroft ME at Dover ME [26 Aug 1847]
   John W Principal of the Hancock Seminary NH & Martha O COLCORD at Portland ME [16 May 1844]
      Martha O & John W COLCORD same as above
      Mary L & Rev Woodman H WATSON of Holden MA at Hallowell ME [5 Aug 1843]
      Wilson of Searsport ME & Catherine N BLACK at Prospect ME [20 Jul 1848]

COLE Abiah & William B ROYAL at Paris ME [25 Feb 1847]
   Albert A & M HUTCHINS at Brighton ME [30 Jan 1851]
   Allen P of Bangor ME & Hannah M KENNISON 12th inst by Rev Arthur DRINKWATER at Fayette ME [21 Oct 1847]
   Allen P of Winthrop ME & Mary F PROCTOR d/o Dea Uriah PROCTOR of Hartford ME by Rev W FOSS at Hartford [2 Sept 1843]
   Amanda C & Wm ALLEN preceptor of Thornton Academy at Saco ME [6 Mar 1845]
   Ann Elizabeth & Nahum THURSTON Jr 6 Oct by Rev HAWES at Union ME [28 Oct 1847]
   Betsey & Zenas POOL at Greenwood ME? [12 Nov 1846]
   Daniel Jr & Mrs Sarah Ann BRADLEY at Saco ME [4 Dec 1835]
   Eliza R & Charles CAMPBELL at Frankfort ME [7 Oct 1847]
   George W & Marandia COOPER at Paris ME [31 Jul 1838]
   Ivory of Brownfield ME & Rachel HALL at Norway ME [27 Nov 1851]
   Jeremiah & Anna BAILEY of Auburn ME at Lewiston ME [24 May 1849]
   Joseph W & Mrs Hannah BOODY at Saco ME [17 Jun 1847]
   Julia Ann & Dickerson LEWIS Capt both of Hallowell ME at Augusta ME [13 Jan 1837]
   Lucy Ann & George WINSLOW of Nobleboro ME at Waldoboro ME [4 Nov 1847]
   Lydia E d/o the late Wm COLE Esq. & Joseph WILLIS all of Buckfield ME on 26th ult at Buckfield [9 Oct 1841]
   Mrs Eliza D & Hon Harrison LOWELL at Biddeford ME [7 Dec 1848]
   Richard L & Sarah L DAVIS at Paris ME [8 Jan 1852]
   S W of Cornish ME, Editor of the *Yankee Farmer* & Martha S d/o Greeley HANNAFORD at Cape Elizabeth ME [4 Dec 1835]
   Sarah E & Dr Henry L NICHOLS 7th inst by Rev JUDD at Augusta ME [16 Sept 1847]
   Sarah E & Paul H PEASE 19th inst by Rev Asahel MOORE at Augusta ME [26 Dec 1844]
   Thomas P & Ruth E OVERLOCK both of Waldoboro ME at Warren ME [29 Jan 1846]

COLEMAN Asiel & Mary SPENCER both of Skowhegan ME at Solon ME [8 Jun 1848]
   Sarah & Franklin PRAY at Brunswick ME [30 Mar 1848]
   Hannah & Clement HUTCHINS both of Kennebunkport ME at Saco ME [30 Apr 1846]

COLESEN Isaac & Elizabeth A KERR both of Deer Isle ME at Eastport ME [16 Dec 1843]

COLKET Hiram of Hallowell ME & Julia Ann PRESCOTT at Readfield ME [15 Apr 1836]

COLLAMORE Susan Jane & Levi F DEAN Capt at Lincolnville ME [5 Aug 1852]
William & Susan DAVIS at Bremen ME [20 Apr 1848]
COLLER Sarah S & John W HINKLEY at Bath ME [28 Nov 1840]
COLLEY Elizabeth T & Alexander T PREBLE at Gardiner ME [1 Jan 1846]
James & Mrs Olive STOWELL at Gray ME [11 Dec 1845]
Moses of Gray ME & Harriet E PORTER at Portland ME [11 Mar 1847]
COLLINS Albert J & Elmacia D KINCAID both of Cornville ME at South Solon ME [18 Apr 1850]
Almira of Lynn & James M HOOD of Boston MA at Gardiner ME [14 Nov 1844]
Anne & Horatio KING publisher of the *Jeffersonian* at Portland ME [12 Jun 1835]
Charles & Eliza TARBOX at Gardiner ME [7 Nov 1844]
D Capt formerly of Portland ME & Elizabeth M ANDERSON at Collinsville IL [2 Apr 1846]
Eliza & Charles HINKLEY of Cambridge MA at New Gloucester ME [27 Feb 1845]
Eugene F of North Anson ME & Frances BICKFORD at Skowhegan ME [25 Apr 1850]
Eunice H & William ROYAL at Gardiner ME [25 Feb 1847]
George B & Fidelia LOVEJOY of Salem ME at Phillips ME [18 Mar 1847]
George of Solon ME & Mrs Rachel M CAMPBELL at Harmony ME [8 Feb 1844]
George W & Elizabeth F GREENE at St Albans ME [16 Apr 1846]
James F of Anson ME & Betsey WOOD of Mercer ME at Mercer [6 Nov 1838]
James H of Salem ME & Elmira KINNEY at Farmington ME [13 Nov 1851]
James H & Melinda SPRAGUE of Phillips ME by Joshua T EATON Esq at Strong ME [14 Sept 1848]
John of Kennebec ME & Emily WINSLOW of Falmouth ME at Portland ME [11 Sept 1851]
Maria & Sewall LIBBY at Gardiner ME [1 Jul 1847]
Martha of Bingham ME & Isiah WESTON of Cornville ME at Bingham [19 Feb 1846]
Mary A & Alfred MERRILL at Portland ME [3 Oct 1840]
Otis F of St Albans ME & Sarah MERRYFIELD at Gardiner ME [11 Nov 1843]
Samuel of Winthrop ME & Clarissa FRENCH of Gardiner ME at Gardiner [21 Feb 1837]
Sarah L & Daniel COFFIN at Norway ME [20 Mar 1845]
Thomas & Betsey CROMETT formerly of Augusta ME at Jackson Jackson County OH [22 Nov 1849]
Waldo Capt & Abigail D SHORT at Bangor ME [20 Aug 1846]
COLLOMORE Deborah & Benjamin BROWN Jr at Union ME [7 Mar 1837]
COLLUM Hannah W & Avery C BARTLETT at Ellsworth ME [4 Dec 1851]
COLMAN George & Lorentha PEAVEY at Augusta ME on 12 Feb by Rev C F ALLEN [20 Feb 1851]
Mary Ann of Windsor ME & Daniel C GARDNER of Vassalboro ME 10th inst by Rev T J SWEAT [21 Jan 1847]
Sarah & Franklin PRAY at Brunswick ME [2 Mar 1848]

COLMAN (cont.) Susannah R & C M HATHAWAY of Augusta ME on 23 Jun by Rev BRAY at Vassalboro ME [12 Aug 1852]
COLSON Alvin & Sarah Ann NUTT on 9 Nov by Levi DUNBAR Esq at Etna ME [15 Nov 1849]
 James M & Rebecca STORER 10th inst at Gardiner ME [30 Dec 1847]
 Phebe A & John TYLER at Frankfort ME [27 May 1852]
 Reuben & Esther JENKINS at Monroe ME [24 Apr 1851]
COLTON N H Capt formerly of Hartford CT & Harriet A LEACH of Castine ME at Bangor ME [29 Feb 1844]
COMSTOCK Louisa & Amos STORER of Robbinston ME at Lubec ME [15 Jul 1847]
 Lucy & Robert BELL of Trescott at Lubec ME [14 Nov 1844]
CONANT Ann M & Henry A PENNY at Portsmouth NH [27 May 1852]
 Benjamin & Mrs Salina CHANDLER of Auburn ME at Turner ME [4 Apr 1850]
 Irena & Isiah C BEAN on 26 Aug at Jay ME [26 Aug 1852]
 Lucy A & Arnold PEASE of Wilton ME at Temple ME [22 Nov 1849]
 Mark P & Martha Ann HARMON at Brunswick ME [6 Dec 1849]
 Mrs Maria & Mr F T PHELPS at Camden ME [29 Jan 1852]
 Oliver J & Nancy P AMES at Thomaston ME [6 Jan 1848]
 Thomas of Peru ME & Rosilla C LEIGHTON at Augusta ME on 25th Oct by Asaph R NICHOLS [30 Oct 1851]
CONDON Frances E & Lewis RICHARDSON at Thomaston ME [14 Jan 1847] & Frances R & Lewis RICHARDSON Senior Publisher of the *Lime Rock Gazette* at East Thomaston ME [4 Feb 1847]
 Joseph & Rosanna H PIERCE at Brunswick ME [21 Sept 1848]
 Thomas J & Sarah C FURBUSH by George P BROWN Esq at Dixmont ME [15 Feb 1840]
CONE Julia A F of Columbus NH & Benj W DONNEL of Alna ME at Skowhegan ME [8 Mar 1849]
 Samuel & Clorinda AUSTIN both of Skowhegan ME at Canaan ME [20 Sept 1849]
CONNER Elizabeth F & Samuel RICE of Farmington ME at Gardiner ME [21 Mar 1850]
 John W & Lucretia M HUNT at Sebasticook ME [20 Sept 1849]
 Jonathan & Mary J ROGERS at Windsor ME [1 Jun 1848]
 Julia & William H FERRIS of South Berwick ME 16 Jun by Rev ALLEN at Augusta ME [26 Jul 1849]
 Mary Ann & Hiram ROLLINS by Rev MORSE at Augusta [17 Jun 1847]
 Mary Mrs of Augusta ME & Isiah J WHITMAN Esq on 1 Jan by Elder A KAVANAGH at Dover NH [11 Apr 1850]
 Mary O & Martin DOWLING 3rd inst at Augusta ME [14 Oct 1847]
 Priscilla of New Sharon ME & Isaac N WHITTIER of Vienna ME at Vienna ME [2 Mar 1839]
CONNOR Hannah of Unity ME & Nathan H GETCHEL of Pittsfield ME by Rev S S WHITE at Unity ME [2 Apr 1842]
 John & Mary PITTS at Fairfield ME [21 May 1846]
 Rosamond & George R PORTER of Freeport ME at New Sharon ME [27 Jun 1844]
CONVERS Nathan of Bath ME & Miss McFADDEN at Nobleboro ME [3 Jul 1838]

CONVERSE Mary R & Calvin CHAMBERLAIN Esq of Foxcroft ME at Charlton MA [1 Apr 1847]
CONY Daniel & Mary, d/o Capt Samuel GILL, Tues eve last by Rev John H INGRAHAM at Augusta ME [8 Oct 1842]
   Ellen M & Samuel McDEVITT 7th inst at Augusta ME [30 Aug 1849]
   Hon Samuel & Lucy Williams BROOKS eldest d/o W A BROOKS Esq 22nd inst by Rev Dr TAPPAN at Augusta MA [29 Nov 1849]
   Martha C/H & Stephen H NICHOLS/NICHOLAS at Strong ME [22/8 Jun 1848]
   Olive S & John H PACKARD at (Augusta) ME on 17th Oct [26 Oct 1848]
   Philena S & Samuel D WORTHLEY at Strong ME [20 May 1847]
   Robert R & Sarah A KIMBALL at Gardiner ME [4 Nov 1847]
   Samuel Esq of Orono ME & Mary H SEWALL at Farmington ME [9 Nov 1833]
COOK Adeline B & Reuel CROWELL at Canaan ME [23 Oct 1845]
   Adrich B & Julia KNIGHTS at Brunswick ME [13 Feb 1845]
   Albert of Vassalboro ME & Eliza F THOMAS at Sidney ME on 7th Sept by the Rev Wm TILLEY [18 Sept 1851]
   Betsey Mrs & Wm DANLEY at Rumford ME [27 Jun 1840]
   Charles M of Bath ME & Emily F MARBLE at Hallowell ME [16 Nov 1848]
   Daniel M & Mary HOLDEN both of Casco ME at Casco [2 Apr 1846]
   Delilah M & Hon Levi JOHNSON both of Canaan ME at Skowhegan ME [30 Sept 1836]
   E & Sewall LOVELL of Abbot ME at Palmyra ME [27 May 1847]
   Fuller G & Charlotte A STEVENS at Waterville ME [19 Jun 1838]
   Harriet F & Alfred H PREBLE at Madison ME [8 Jan 1846]
   James Capt & Mrs Nancy LEACH at Orland ME [14 Oct 1847]
   John H & Frances A WHITNEY at Hallowell ME [16 Sept 1847]
   John H & Sarah E CHASE at Augusta ME [20 Apr 1839]
   Louisa & Hiram KINCAID Sat eve last by J L VARNEY Esq at Augusta ME [30 Oct 1845]
   Martha & Edward L PRATT at Vassalboro ME on 12th inst [21 Dec 1848]
   Newell & Asenath LINSCOTT at Jefferson ME [1 Jan 1852]
   Oliver P & Harriet N SMITH at Sidney ME [28 Mar 1844]
   Sophronia & Hiram WARES at Pittston ME [3 Jul 1851]
   Sybil B & Samuel C BAKER at Lewiston ME [26 Feb 1852]
   William of Vassalboro ME & Hannah MORRISON of Albion 8th inst by S BURRILL Esq at Albion ME [12 Nov 1846]
COOKSON Mr A 2d of Freedom ME & Caroline JOHNSON at Belfast ME [24 Aug 1848]
COOLBROTH Mary J & Albert TUKEY at Portland ME [14 Aug 1835]
COOLEY Benjamin & Lydia R TOWNES both of Bingham ME at Solon ME [15 Aug 1844]
   Henry S General formerly of Augusta ME & Helen M REED at Quincy IL [16 Oct 1845]
   Mary Ann & Wm H LANSING both of West Troy NY on 7 Nov 1837 at West Troy NY [29 Feb 1840]
   W & Mary SMALL at Thomaston ME [6 Nov 1845]
COOLIDGE Caroline & David E FIFIELD at Dexter ME [30 Apr 1846]
   Charles P & Margaret A FLETCHER by Rev INGRAHAM at Augusta ME [21 Sept 1839]

Marriage Notices from the "Maine Farmer"

COOLIDGE (cont.) E of Solon & Mary E POLLARD of Cornville ME at Cornville ME [17 Jul 1845]
    Lucy & Clarendon WATERS at Livermore ME [24 Jul 1835]
    Meritt of Hallowell ME & Flora C BRADFORD at Livermore ME [7 Dec 1833]
    Sampson A & Eveline M BEAN at Readfield ME [18 Mar 1852]
    Susan & Pulaski McCRILLIS at Dexter ME [12 Feb 1846]
    Winthrop of Livermore ME & Deborah SANBORN at Boston MA [10 Apr 1851]

COOMBS Abby F & Abel HOMSTED at Winthrop ME on 20 May [27 May 1852]
    Abner Jr & Augusta A PARTRIDGE both of Augusta ME at Hallowell ME [28 Feb 1850]
    Ann J & Reuel STICKNEY of Windsor ME at Whitefield ME [15 Apr 1847]
    Archibald & Harriet KELLOCH both of Thomaston ME [10 Aug 1839]
    Charlotte & Franklin MAGOON at Durham ME [20 Apr 1848]
    Diana & John A WADE at Lincolnville ME [16 Jul 1842]
    Emily & Joseph BEAN at Whitefield ME [30 Mar 1848]
    Hannah L of Bowdoinham ME & Robert BARNES of Hartland ME at Topsham ME [30 Sept 1843]
    Henry B & Hannah S LINN at Windsor ME [27 Apr 1848]
    Hezekiah P Esq Publisher of the *Thomaston Recorder* & Lucinda SPOFFARD at Thomaston ME [21 Aug 1842]
    Joseph of Nobleboro ME & Mary Ann BURGESS at Vassalboro ME [14 Oct 1843]
    Joshua of Augusta ME & Isabella F McCORRISON at Bath ME [26 Feb 1846]
    Lucretia M & Mr A Judson MACOMBER at Belfast ME [16 Mar 1848]
    Lucy Jane & Robert E REDMAN at Brooksville ME [16 Oct 1845]
    Lydia A & Hiram G PENNIMAN Capt at East Thomaston ME [9 Aug 1849]
    Lydia Mrs & Levi C RANDALL at Lewiston ME [10 Jul 1845]
    Robert of Bowdoin ME & Elizabeth R GRANT of Richmond ME at Richmond [17 Oct 1844]
    Thomas H of Bradford ME & Martha P BARTON at Sebasticook ME [9 Mar 1848]
    Thomas T of New Gloucester ME & Abigail B JONES at Canton ME [13 Nov 1851]
    Watson F & Mary H SARGENT both of Brewer ME at Bangor ME [8 Apr 1843]
    William B & Celia F WEBBER by Rev L WENTWORTH at China ME on 3d March [11 Mar 1852]

COOPER Adeline & John T WHITMORE of Bowdoinham ME at Pittston ME [22 May 1845]
    Charles Esq of Bangor ME & Emeline Matilda COOPER of Pittston ME at Pittston [9 Jan 1841]
    Emeline Matilda & Charles COOPER same as above
    Marandia & Geo W COLE at Paris ME [31 Jul 1838]
    Nancy & Ephraim WILLET of Damariscotta ME at Hallowell ME [20 Nov 1851]
    William W Dr of Henderson County KY & Frances A TUTTLE of Canaan ME at Bracken County OH [21 Jan 1847]

COPELAND Ann of Dexter & David STOCKBRIDGE at Corinth ME [19 Jun 1845]
Celia & Daniel LARA at Turner ME [19 Jul 1849]
Hannah B of Corinna ME & Wm A LUCE at Exeter ME [8 Feb 1840]
Lawrence of Bridgewater MA & Mary L SNELL d/o John E SNELL of Winthrop ME by Rev Sumner ELLIS at Boston " ... the receipt of not a slice but a whole bridal loaf ... This makes the sixth good wife and true that ... SNELL has furnished as many thrifty young men from his domestic fold - Mary is the last of the flock ... sorry to lose her from Maine ... we rejoice she goes back to the Pilgrims ..." [19 Feb 1852]
Lucy Ann m Jacob PEASLEE Esq both of Pittston ME at Boston MA [29 May 1851]
Mr S O of West Bridgewater MA & Susan E DULON of Boston MA at Augusta ME on 3 Mar 1851 by Rev INGRAHAM [6 Mar 1851]
Priscilla S & Joseph RANDALL at Warren ME [4 Mar 1847]
Sarah & James SWETT at Hampden ME [10 Jul 1835]
COPP Jane B & Henry STEVENS of Hallowell ME on 23 Sept at Augusta ME [4 Oct 1849]
CORBETT Abel P & Lydia TRACY at Farmington ME [19 Jul 1849]
Horace L & Mary E STROUT at Durham NH [11 Jun 1846]
I J & Nancy T BROWNELL 18 Jun by Rev H M BLAKE at Augusta ME [15 Jul 1852]
Isaac J of Brunswick ME & Rhoda Ann WASHBURN at Gardiner ME [24 Oct 1844]
Martha & George McLURE of Solon ME at Farmington ME [24 Oct 1844]
Peter & Nancy ADAMS 12th inst by John A WOODS Esq at Farmington ME [28 Mar 1840]
William R & Betsey ROBBINS at Brunswick ME [6 Aug 1846]
CORDIS Samuel & Mary WOOD Tues eve last by Rev David THURSTON at Winthrop ME [10 Oct 1834]
CORDWELL Lydia C & David SANBORN Capt of Norway ME at Paris ME [15 Apr 1847]
COREY Lucy M & Rev Jos RICKER of Belfast ME at Brookline MA [31 May 1849]
CORLISH Lucinda ae 20 & Thomas LOWELL ae 70 at Dixmont ME [21 Sept 1833]
CORLISS Edwin & Catharine ADLAR at Eastport ME [16 Aug 1849]
Lucy of North Yarmouth ME & Rev Geo W QUINBY Pastor of the Universalist Societies of Livermore and Winthrop ME on 25 Dec by Rev Charles C BURR of Hallowell ME at North Yarmouth ME [2 Jan 1838]
CORNFORTH Aurilla P & Benjamin F MANTER at Industry ME [3 Jul 1851]
George & Rebecca MANTER at Industry ME [1 Jan 1846]
John & Susan HUBBARD at West Waterville ME [8 Feb 1844]
CORNISH Daniel G & Amelia STARBIRD both of Bowdoinham ME at Litchfield ME [4 May 1848]
Humphrey & M HATCH at Thomaston ME [5 Feb 1846]
John & Elizabeth REED at Bath ME [12 Feb 1846]
CORSON Elisha C of Winthrop ME & Lucy T CRAM at Hampton Falls NH [21 Nov 1837]

CORSON (cont.) Keziah of Bangor ME & Charles F COBB Esq of New Gloucester ME at Bangor ME [9 Jan 1845]
  Lucy & Otis C COBB of Minot ME at Bangor ME [18 Mar 1847]
  Mary Jane & Joseph HOOK Jr of Skowhegan ME at Canaan ME [25 Apr 1840]
  Nancy & Hiram BLAKE at West Waterville ME [8 Feb 1844]
  Samuel Jr of Hartland ME & Bethiah BEAN at Harmony ME [8 Feb 1844]
CORY Susannah G of Brookline MA & Gilbert PULLEN of Augusta ME at Brookline MA [30 May 1840]
COSS Lucinda M & James C CLAY both of Gardiner ME at Hallowell ME [7 jan 1847]
COSTELOW Susan H & George SAVAGE at Woolwich ME [20 Feb 1851]
  Benjamin of Gardiner ME & Jerusha THOMAS at Bowdoin ME [29 Oct 1846]
COTHREN William Esq of Farmington ME & Hannah M PEABODY of Gorham ME at Lewiston ME [17 Apr 1851]
COTTER Joseph of Boston & Henrietta KELSEY at Nobleboro ME [28 Feb 1834]
  Simon H & Sally C HOWE at Nobleboro ME [16 Oct 1845]
COTTERELL Mary P of Northport ME & N S CHAPMAN at Belfast ME [12 Nov 1846]
COTTLE Betsey of Industry ME & Capt Reuben HILL at New Portland ME [22 Feb 1844]
  Catharine & Bartlett GOULD at Augusta ME [22 Aug 1840]
  Lovina of Augusta ME & Emery KNOWLES of Readfield ME on 17 Oct at Sidney ME [1 Nov 1849]
  Mary Anna of Mt Vernon ME & Henry BOND at Boston MA [25 Oct 1849]
  Nancy E & James WALKER of Alna ME at East Mt Vernon ME [24 Aug 1839]
  Sophia of Phillips ME & Moses MORRISON of Madrid ME at Avon ME [15 May 1838]
COTTON Chloe & Benjamin KIRKPATRICK at Hope ME [22 Jun 1848]
  George & Nancy D CURTIS at Bath ME [17 Jul 1838]
  John H & Christina H COX at Auburn ME [21 Aug 1851]
  Mr H Q of Bath & Miss M E W THOMPSON of Thomaston at West Camden ME [24 Aug 1848]
COTTRELL/COTTRILL Ellen & Thomas MASON Esq of Bangor ME at Newcastle ME [15 Oct 1846]
  Martin L Capt & Eliza M KNOWLTON both of Northport ME at Belfast ME [18 Jun 1846]
  Mary Ann Mrs & Axel HAYFORD both of Belfast at Belfast ME [6 Feb 1845]
  Mary R & Wm H FROHOCK both of Northport ME at Belfast ME [15 Oct 1846]
  Sarah P Mrs & John P BAGLEY Capt at Belfast ME [10 Oct 1844]
COUCH Helen & Geo S SYLVESTER at Hallowell ME [4 Feb 1847]
  Mary Jane Amarose WHITNEY at Augusta ME [30 Aug 1849]
COUILLARD Colwell L & Clarrinda BUZZELL at Bangor ME [14 Mar 1844]
  Elijah printer & Lydia J LOWELL at Bangor ME [6 Nov 1845]
  Zilpha Mrs & Charles PALMER Esq of Belfast at Frankfort ME [9 Sept 1847

COULBORN Serecta A of Pittston ME & Freeman PLUMMER of Manchester IA at Hallowell ME [26 Mar 1846]
COULLARD Hephzibah of Chesterville ME & Isaac MASON at Vienna ME [18 Mar 1847]
COUNCE Emily S & Elisha LINNELL both of Thomaston ME at New York [30 Sept 1847]
COURIER Harriet & Albion P ARNOLD at Readfield ME [20 Jun 1834]
COURSER E & Mary A HILL at Wilton ME [6 Sept 1849]
COUSINS John & Sylvia M HALEY at Hollis ME [6 Jun 1844]
   Joseph & Sarah L WORKS at Guilford ME? [3 Apr 1851]
   Samuel F & Rhoda H STEVENS at Abbot ME [10 Dec 1846]
   Sarah E & Justus C HERSEY of Dexter ME at Abbot ME [17 Jan 1850]
COVAL Mary C & Henry WHITING at Fairfield ME [11 Jan 1844]
COVEL C of Bath & Mary O ELDER of Portland ME at Portland [11 Dec 1841]
COVIL Hiram of Pittston ME & Mary Jane RICHARDSON of Whitefield ME at Alna ME [16 Jan 1845]
COWAN/COWEN Augustus N & Martha J CHAPMAN at Bath ME [5 Feb 1852]
   Caroline A & Charles WOODMAN at Sidney ME [23 Sept 1843]
   Francis H & Martha N EMERY at Bangor ME [2 Jan 1845]
   John H & Mary DOE of Burnham ME at Clinton ME [7 Nov 1840]
   Susan N & Gustavus BURGESS both of Palermo ME by Clifford S WORTHING Esq at Palermo [5 Jun 1845] see COWENS below
   Turner of Lisbon ME & Adriana GREEN at Brunswick ME [27 Mar 1845]
COWDEN Charlotte M d/o Joseph COWDEN Esq US Consul at Glasgow, (Scotland?) & Wm SANFORD merchant of Bangor ME at Bucksport ME [1 Oct 1846]
COWE Alfred H ae 18 & Mrs Mehitable THOMPSON ae 68 at Ogdensburg NY [20 Aug 1846]
COWENS Susan N & Gustavus BURGESS of China ME at Palermo ME [23 Aug 1845]
COWIN Caroline & Reuben CARR of Pittsfield ME at Palmyra ME [19 Dec 1844]
COWING Dolly Mrs & Joseph WOODWARD of Lisbon ME at Lewiston ME [18 Feb 1847]
COX Albina S & John ALEXANDER of Litchfield ME by Rev GRANT at Bowdoin ME [28 Jan 1843]
   Antoinette & D M TRUE at Searsmont ME [5 Jul 1849]
   Christina H & John H COTTON at Auburn ME [21 Aug 1851]
   Elisha & Irene HARDING at Bath ME [31 Oct 1840]
   Elizabeth C & A SPENCER at Auburn ME [18 Jan 1849]
   Esther & Stillman MASON at Parkman ME [21 Nov 1837]
   G L & Frances A SMILEY at Hallowell ME [21 Aug 1841]
   Harriet A & Benj R ROBINSON of East Bridgewater MA at Brunswick ME [23 Aug 1849]
   Henry M & Amelia O BILLINGS of Northport ME at Belfast ME [7 Jan 1847]
   Hester Ann of Hallowell ME & George W HOWLAND of Fairhaven MA at Hallowell ME [30 Oct 1838]

COX (cont.) Hiram C of Bristol ME & Hannah P HUSTON of Eastport ME at Thomaston ME [10 Jul 1845]
Jane G of Bristol ME & Rufus Adams of Chelmsford MA at Boston MA [27 Aug 1846]
Lydia Ann of Bowdoin ME & David CURTIS at Webster ME [9 Sept 1847]
Martha Mrs of Hallowell ME & Rev Obed WILSON of Bingham Thurs eve last by Rev WEBBER at Hallowell ME [7 Mar 1837]
Mary D & Dr Elisha J FORD at Gardiner ME [23 Nov 1839]
Mary J & John DILLON at Eastport ME [12 Jul 1849]
Mrs Mary & Benjamin BARSTOW at Gardiner ME [23 Nov 1848]
Rev Daniel of the Maine Annual Conference of the Methodist E Church & Mary B MARSTON by Rev J SPAULDING at Bath ME [17 Jun 1833]
Sarah H m J G FLETCHER of Boston ME at Pittston ME [4 Jun 1851]
Susan Z d/o John COX Esq. & George Henry PREBLE Esq USN at Portland ME [4 Dec 1845]
William P of Hartford ME & Louisa P DYER at Buckfield ME [20 Mar 1845]

COY Granville of Winthrop ME & Adaline E KIMBALL by Ammi WEST Esq at Greene ME [30 Dec 1847]
Julia P & Chas KEMPTON of Sidney ME on 28th inst at Augusta ME [8 Feb 1849]
Louisa J & David MARSHALL of Foxcroft ME at Sangerville ME [4 Dec 1851]
Lovisa L of Winthrop ME & Lightbourn N FITZ formerly of Bath ME on Sun eve last by Rev ROBINSON at Winthrop ME [6 May 1843]

COZZENS William W of Bangor ME & Mrs M TWITCHELL at Waterville ME [7 Jun 1849]

CRABTREE Mary G & John H BUTTERFIELD of Weston ME at Topsfield ME on 19th Jul by Dan PINEO Esq [21 Aug 1851]

CRAFFAM - see GRAFFAM
Sarah & Samuel COBB both of Cape Elizabeth at Cape Elizabeth ME [10 Oct 1837]

CRAFTS Amasa Esq of Wilton ME & Mary J HENRY at Bloomfield ME [23 Nov 1848]
Mary Augusta & Dea Jonas PHINNEY both of Jay ME on 3rd inst by Rev Walter FOSS at Leeds ME [14 Oct 1847]

CRAIG Caroline & Mr A F SHERBURN at Readfield ME [28 Sept 1848]
Charles P & Diana W LADD at Philips ME [12 Mar 1842]
Edwin & Elizabeth HAMLEN at Augusta ME [2 Jan 1838]
Elizabeth H & Emery O BEAN Esq Attorney at Law 8th inst at Readfield ME [17 Oct 1844]
George D of Readfield ME & Mary Angeline LOVEJOY at East Boston MA [18 Mar 1852]
John S & Sarah Jane CLARK at (Augusta) ME on 3 Apr [13 Apr 1848]
Nancy M & Alfred OLIVER at Augusta ME [29 Oct 1846]
Wheelock Rev of New Bedford MA & Louisa S BRIGGS eldest d/o Dr C BRIGGS at Augusta ME by Rev Dr TAPPAN [16 Jan 1851]

CRAINE Mrs D W & Deacon Orin TINKHAM at Fayette ME [13 Jul 1848]

CRAM Calvin H Esq merchant & Mary D WARREN 10th inst at Portland ME [21 Sept 1839]

CRAM (cont.) Emeline O of East Livermore ME & Theodore M RICHARDSON of Weld ME by Rev Walter FOSS at Leeds ME [26 Aug 1852]
  Frederick & Isabella CRAM at Montville ME [25 May 1839]
  Isabella & Frederick CRAM at Montville ME [25 May 1839]
  John P of Bangor ME & Annis C RANLETT at Hallowell ME [28 Oct 1847]
  Lucy T & Elisha C CORSON of Winthrop ME at Hampton Falls NH [21 Nov 1837]
  Lydia & Samuel VARIEL at Mt Vernon ME on 8th inst [19 Oct 1848]
  Mary E & Manley FRIZZELL of Starks ME at New Sharon ME [1 Oct 1846]
  Sewall & Mrs Annourill R C STONE at Wilton ME [13 Jun 1844]
CRANCH Margaret Dawes of Washington DC youngest d/o Chief Judge CRANCH, & Erastus BROOKS Esq of New York at Washington DC [25 Jan 1844]
CRANDLEMIRE Benjamin & Judith PARKER at Lee [30 Apr 1846]
CRANE Dulcina M & Luther D EMERSON by Rev DRINKWATER at Fayette ME [12 Aug 1852]
  Eliza J of Warren ME & Josiah MAXCY of Gardiner ME at Lynn MA [11 Dec 1851]
  William of Bangor ME & Mary C BOALS at Wiscasset ME [25 Apr 1844]
CRASH George & Eleanor HOWES at Bath ME [4 Jul 1840]
  James P & Martha A LOMBARD both of Windham ME at Westbrook ME [21 May 1846]
  Samuel V & Elizabeth A HOXIE at Saco ME [4 Mar 1852]
CRAWFORD Fanny & E C SNELL of Winthrop ME at Sidney ME [12 Mar 1846]
  Jane Tucker MacKnight d/o Wm CRAWFORD Esq of Edinburgh, & John Randolph CLAY Secretary of the Legation of the United States at St Petersburgh (Russia) on 18 Jun at Venice [7 Aug 1845]
  William J & Elizabeth JEWETT at Bath ME [19 Dec 1834]
CREAMER Solomon & Margaret WEAVER at Waldoboro ME [26 Feb 1846]
CREASY Benjamin B & Phebe W GILMAN both of Mt Vernon ME on 21 Nov by G A BENSON Esq at Winthrop ME [22 Nov 1849]
CREECH James C Capt & Eleanor S MEANS at Freeport ME [1 Aug 1844]
CREFTS Zibeon & Miranda NOYES at Auburn ME [29 Mar 1849]
CREWS William Esq of South Bend IA [sic; editors think the paper meant Indiana] & Emily WHITE of Augusta ME at Manchester NH on 18 Oct by Rev Mr CLARKE [30 Oct 1851]
CRIPS Moses & Hannah J ROBERTS of Topsham ME at Brunswick ME [19 Sept 1844]
CROCKER Catharine Mrs & Dea Thomas DECKER at Boothbay ME [23 Jan 1838]
  Daniel D Esq of Calais ME & Hannah F CHAMBERLAIN at Foxcroft ME [17 Jan 1850]
  E G of Dixmont ME & Clarissa HILLMAN of Troy ME at Troy [3 Jul 1845]
  Samuel & Caroline DUDLEY at Pittston ME [1 Jul 1847]
  Thomas Esq & Almira DAVIS formerly of Methuen MA at Paris [10 Oct 1844]
CROCKETT/CROCKET Abigail D & Jonathan G TOWN at Norway ME [19 Mar 1846]

Marriage Notices from the "Maine Farmer"

CROCKETT (cont.) Americus of Abbot ME & Sylvia BALLOU of Turner ME at Turner [1 Feb 1840]
Benjamin & Eliza F McALLISTER at Paris ME [28 Feb 1850]
Capt Columbus of Abbot ME & Deborah W THOMPSON at New Sharon ME [16 Apr 1846]
Clarissa & William GOFF at Sumner ME [20 Mar 1841]
Cyprian C & Margaret JORDAN at Webster ME on 28 Oct by Jesse DAVIS Esq [6 Nov 1851]
Eliza W of Rockland ME & George L SMITH at Bath ME [31 Jul 1851]
Ephraim S of Norway ME & D PENLEY at Danville ME [25 Apr 1844]
Francina G & Salmon TOWNSEND Jr of Turner ME at Greene ME [12 Mar 1846]
George Esq of Stetson ME & Mary S MOOER at Wilton ME [25 Jan 1840]
Hannah & Samuel D LEMAN at Abbot ME [8 Feb 1844]
John Capt & Mary Ann CARLE of Camden ME at Thomaston ME [14 Sept 1839]
Joshua B of Paris ME & Esther J FROST at Norway ME [19 Apr 1849]
Joshua B & Columbia CURTIS at Oxford/Paris ME [9 May 1844]
Lorenzo D & Sarah B THAYER at Lowell MA [11 Oct 1849]
Mary d/o David CROCKETT member of Congress from Tennesee, & Dr Wm McNEILL 12th ult at Columbia TN [24 Jan 1834]
Nancy H & Hiram B WILLIAMS of Belfast ME at Thomaston ME [27 Nov 1845]
Ruth & Ford GAY at Knox ME [23 Nov 1848]
Typhena [*sic*; spelled "Tryphena" in *Maine Freewill Baptist Repository*, issue 16 June 1849] & Curtis SHAW both of Standish ME at Windham ME [24 May 1849]
William W of Norway ME & Lydia STETSON at West Sumner ME [29 Nov 1849]

CROMMETT/CROMETT Betsey formerly of Augusta ME & Thomas COLLINS at Jackson Jackson County OH [22 Nov 1849]
James R of Sebec ME & Betsey TURNER of Foxcroft ME at Bangor ME [19 Dec 1844]
Mary E & George F HOWARD at Dexter ME [12 Feb 1852]

CROMWELL Almyra of Norridgewock ME & Orrin FARNHAM of Vassalboro ME at Lawrence MA on May 12 [12 Jun 1851]
Amasa of Mercer ME & Isabel POMROY of Starks ME at Smithfield ME [3 Dec 1846]
Oliver & Margaret STOYELL at Mercer ME [11 Jun 1846]

CROOKER Almira & Henry O BOSSE at Oxford ME [14 Aug 1845]
Hannah E & Henry BENNER at Boston MA [28 Nov 1840]
Isaac Jr of Bath ME & Eveline GREENLOW at Phipsburg ME [29 Apr 1852]
Jane M & Wm DAVIS at Lisbon ME [11 Jan 1844]
John W of Brunswick ME & Amaril L BATCHELDER of Lisbon ME at Augusta ME [10 Jan 1850]
Malvina & Silas STUDLEY of Boston MA at Bath ME [19 Feb 1846]
Mark H of Bristol ME & Mary DODGE on Thurs morn last at Hallowell ME [5 Sept 1834]
Orin B & Elizabeth A COBB at Norway ME [25 Apr 1844]
Timothy S & Lydia A WINSLOW at Bath ME [9 Jul 1846]

CROOT Richard & Maria WALLACE both of Bloomfield ME at Skowhegan ME [8 May 1845]
CROSBY Abel C of Milford NH & Joann TRUFANT of Winthrop ME on Thanksgiving evening by Rev THURSTON at Winthrop ME [26 Nov 1842]
   Caroline J & Samuel AYER of Embden at Waterville ME [22 Feb 1840]
   Charlotte C & W S PEABODY at Bangor ME [13 Jun 1844]
   Eliza Ann of Readfield ME & John E VARNEY of Augusta ME by Wm C FULLER Esq at Readfield ME [25 Mar 1843]
   George A & Lucy Jane JOY on 27 Jun by Asaph R NICHOLS Esq at Augusta ME [1 Jul 1852]
   Hanford & Miriam A ROBINSON at Montville ME [1 Apr 1852]
   J S of Bangor ME & Mrs Mary E ROWELL of Hampden ME on 9th inst at Hampden [25 Sept 1838]
   Josiah Esq & Mary FOSS at Dexter ME [15 Mar 1849]
   Josiah & Merinda Jane SWEET both of Arrowsic Sagadahoc Co ME at Wiscasset ME [22 Feb 1844]
   Lemuel of Phillips ME & Thirza C PORTER of Strong ME on 30 Mar by Rev Dexter WATERMAN at Strong ME [22 Apr 1843]
   Lt Thompson H of the US Army & Lydia C MILLS both of Norridgewock ME by Rev Henry BACON at Providence RI on 12th inst [30 Nov 1848]
   Martha C of Madison ME & John W WHITAKER at Belfast ME [8 Jan 1846]
   Martha & James ATKINSON at Chesterville ME [16 Mar 1839]
   Mary B Mrs & Lemuel PREBLE of Woolwich ME at Phippsburg ME [7 Jan 1847]
   Mary E of Readfield ME & Lewis MOODY of Pittston ME at Readfield ME [25 Mar 1843]
   Sarah G of Plymouth ME & Ebenezer JORDAN of Marion OH at Norridgewock ME [3 Sept 1846]
   Sarah J d/o Luther CROSBY Esq & Henry LANCASTER at Albion ME on May 29th by O W WASHBURN Esq [12 Jun 1851]
CROSMAN Sarah B & Thomas D WARD at China ME [30 Sept 1836]
   Seth & Mary J BIBBER of Lisbon ME at Durham ME [2 Aug 1849]
CROSS Amherst S Dr of Hallowell ME & Mary KEZER of Winthrop ME at Winthrop [1 Feb 1849]
   Caroline & Samuel FOSTER at Norway ME [3 Jun 1852]
   Caroline & Wm LOVEJOY of Vassalboro ME at Augusta ME [15 Oct 1846]
   Emeline P & Wellington CROWELL of China ME by Rev B F SHAW at Vassalboro ME [6 Dec 1849]
   Hannah H of Augusta ME & Samuel WINTER Jr of Pittston ME at China ME [25 Nov 1843]
   Isabella A & James H HAM at Hallowell ME [2 Jan 1835]
   Louisa J & Barek HATCH both of Belmont ME at Belfast ME [30 May 1844]
   Lydia & Amasa FITCH at Gardiner ME [8 Jan 1839]
   Margaret E F T of Belmont ME & Abiel C MOREY of Searsmont ME at Belfast ME [3 Oct 1844]
   Mary J Mrs & Jos R WELLS at Gardiner ME [25 Jan 1849]
   Mary O & Sylvanus S MOORE of Katahdin Iron Works at Foxcroft ME [22 Jul 1852]

CROSS (cont.) Mary W & David MILLER on Sun morn last by Rev J H INGRAHAM at Augusta ME [22 Oct 1842]

Mary & Albert T ELLIS at Belfast ME [16 Sept 1843]

Mary & Isaac JACKSON at Belmont ME [26 Dec 1837]

Nancy T & Bancroft W THOMAS of Ellsworth ME at Bluehill ME [11 Jan 1849]

Nancy & Michael DELAITTRE at Sebec ME [15 Aug 1844]

Noah W of Gardiner ME & Emeline CHASE of Augusta ME on Sun morn last by Rev N W WILLIAMS at Augusta ME [30 Oct 1845]

Sarah A & Geo F GODFREY on 15 Aug by Rev DALTON at Augusta ME [26 Aug 1852]

Sarah J m Wm D RANKINS at Augusta ME on May 25 by Asaph NICHOLS Esq [29 May 1851]

Sophia & Benjamin F GAZELIN at (Augusta) ME on Sept 25th [5 Oct 1848]

Submittance & Elezer WHITCOMB at Belmont ME [26 Aug 1836]

William L & Caroline W SAFFORD by Rev Mr MORRILL at Vassalboro ME on 8th instant [20 Apr 1848]

William of Vassalboro ME & Mrs Clarissa FOSTER at Windsor ME on 14th Sept by Rev Thomas J DUDLEY of (Augusta ME) [30 Oct 1851]

CROSSMAN Charles H of Gardiner ME & Mary T WITHAM of Phillips ME on 9th inst by Lot M MORRILL Esq at Augusta ME [14 Jun 1849]

Irene E of Greene ME & Charles W OLIVER of Worcester at Cambridge MA [11 Jan 1840]

James F of Windsor ME & Abigail PRATT of Windsor ME by Wm PERCIVAL Esq at China ME [4 May 1848]

Jesse & Esther B STONE at Belfast ME [3 Aug 1848]

Joseph of Norridgewock ME & Winneford PETERS at Fairfield ME [12 Apr 1849]

CROSWELL Mary G of Farmington ME, d/o T CROSWELL Esq & John T GOWER of Makawao (Hawaii Islands), he late of New Sharon ME at Honolulu Sandwich Islands (Hawaii Islands) on May 2 [17 Jul 1851]

Samuel of Mercer ME & Ruhamah ROBBINS at Norridgewock ME [2 May 1840]

Thomas MD of Weld ME & Henrietta OWEN of Brunswick ME on 6th inst by Rev T A ADAMS at Brunswick ME [24 Sept 1842]

CROUCH Lodonia & Demerrick SPEAR at East Thomaston ME [13 Sept 1849]

CROWELL Angeline S & Chandler G HAMLIN both of Gardiner ME at Hallowell ME [11 Oct 1849]

Augustus & Hannah Maria PERLEY at Vassalboro ME [10 Dec 1846]

Betsey & Arba PENNEY at Waterville ME [27 Jun 1834]

Clarissa of Waterville ME & Sullivan HOLMAN Dr of Canaan ME at Fairfield ME [28 Oct 1836]

E G merchant of Canaan ME & Sally EATON d/o Benj EATON Esq at Canaan ME [3 Aug 1841]

Elijah S of Jefferson ME & Mary Ann KENNEDY of Waldoboro ME at Jefferson ME [2 Sept 1836]

Laura A of China ME & Robert H G HUBBARD of Bath ME on 3 Aug by Daniel C STANWOOD Esq City Clerk at Augusta ME [12 Aug 1852]

CROWELL (cont.) Lydia A & Charles C STONE at Augusta ME on 28 Sept by S TITCOMB Esq [2 Oct 1851]
Maria Louisa & Moses WELLS at Augusta ME [4 Jul 1837]
Martha S of Dexter ME & Wm C D PAGE of Newburyport MA 6th inst by Rev KALLOCH at Augusta ME [18 Jan 1849]
Mehitable & William PHILLIPS Capt at Hampden ME [14 Aug 1841]
Miller & Sarah B SHAW by Rev W A DREW at Augusta ME [27 Nov 1838]
Nathan of Sidney ME & Mrs Abigail HERRIN at Skowhegan ME [18 Feb 1847]
Reuel & Adeline B COOK at Canaan ME [23 Oct 1845]
Sarah G & Jeremiah PAGE at Dexter ME [23 Nov 1839]
Solomon of Palmyra, Wayne Co, NY & Louisa D C MANLEY at Canadaigua NY [18 Jan 1844]
Wellington of China ME & Emeline P CROSS by Rev B F SHAW at Vassalboro ME [6 Dec 1849]
CROWLEY Amos D & Martha Jane BROOKS at Lewiston ME [4 Mar 1852]
CRUMPTON Lucinda A of Industry ME & John RECORD of Phillips ME at Farmington ME [18 Jan 1849]
CUMMINGS Asa of Sidney ME & Eliza TILLSON at Readfield ME [29 Apr 1833]
Benjamin C & Almira TWITCHELL at Paris ME [18 Dec 1835]
Charles of Solon ME & Jane WHITNEY at Hallowell ME [31 May 1849]
Elizabeth & Albert SMITH at Augusta ME [9 Jan 1851]
Enos of Sidney ME & Emeline ROGERS of Belgrade ME on 31 Oct by Rev Walter FOSS at Leeds [29 Nov 1849]
Francis of Albany ME? & Hepzibah HOLT at Bethel ME [4 Jun 1851]
Hannah E & Hiram BASS of Freeport ME at Farmington ME [27 Jun 1844]
Harriet M & Charles SAUNDERS at Augusta ME on 1 May 1851 by Elder Thomas J DUDLEY [8 May 1851]
Horace & Emeline H ALBY of Bethel ME at Oxford ME [26 Dec 1844]
John E C & Elvina S BUMPUS at Bath ME [28 Aug 1851]
John of Freedom ME & Mary E WHITE at Readfield ME [21 Feb 1850]
Julia A & Isaac McFARLAND at Waterville ME [7 Dec 1848]
Larned of Sumner ME & Nancy WHITE at Dixfield ME [6 Jun 1837]
Lucy A & Silenus U HAWKS at Paris ME [25 Mar 1852]
Lucy D & Luther W KEEN at Augusta ME [28 May 1846]
Luther C & of Eddington ME & Sarah A BAILEY at Milford ME [1 Nov 1849]
Nancy B & Mr E H G MARSHALL at Norway ME [31 Aug 1848]
Rev Joseph of Amenia Seminary NY & Deborah S HASKELL at Litchfield ME [28 Aug 1842]
Roxana & Chas L ELDER both of Lewiston ME at Norway ME [27 Dec 1849]
Russell A of Winthrop ME & Catharine H AMES at Hallowell ME [18 Apr 1850]
Simon H Col & Sibell A JACKSON at Paris ME [22 Jan 1846]
Susan of Hallowell ME & Jacob B TRUE at Augusta ME on 19 Nov by Rev J STEVENS [27 Nov 1851]
Zilphia H & John H MORRILL Capt of Bangor ME at Augusta ME [25 Feb 1847]

CUMNER John C of Tory NY & Sylvinia R WHITE of East Readfield ME at New York City on 17 Aug [4 Sept 1851]
CUMSTON Nancy & Wm MOULTON Esq of Portland ME at Monmouth ME [25 Nov 1836]
CUNNINGHAM Abigail Mrs & Wm F DAVIS of Whitefield ME at Palermo ME [25 Jun 1846]
- Alexander Capt & Nancy Ann SEVEY both of Wiscasset ME at Dresden ME [7 Feb 1850]
- Ebenezer & Rosella I HOLMES both of Swanville ME at Belfast ME [30 Sept 1847]
- Elizabeth a smiling lass of 60 & William FLY a youthful swain of 80 on 3rd inst by E CUNNINGHAM Esq at Edgecomb ME [17 Jun 1833]
- Elizabeth & John W SWAZEY Esq both of Bucksport ME at Providence RI on 3 inst (Apr 3) 1851 [24 Apr 1851]
- James H & Elizabeth A LITTLE at Pittston ME [27 Jun 1844]
- James O & Lucetta A WILSON by Rev W FROTHINGHAM at Belfast ME [3 Dec 1842]
- Mary & Adam K KIDD both of Madison ME at Skowhegan ME [3 Jan 1850]
- Philena L & Josiah H EMERSON at Belfast ME [19 Sept 1844]
- Rachel & David KINCAID both of Madison ME at Bingham ME [4 Jun 1846]
- Ruth N & Mr R H SMART at Searsport ME [1 Apr 1852]

CURRIER Abby P & George W WHITE of Montville ME at Hallowell ME [18 Jul 1844]
- Arminda & Ensign FRYE on 22nd ult at Skowhegan ME [15 Feb 1840]
- E G & Mary MORRILL of Augusta ME by Rev A P HILLMAN at Winthrop ME [29 Jan 1839]
- Elizabeth & Wm G BESSEY of Wayne ME at Winthrop ME [9 Dec 1847]
- George of Lynn MA & Sarah WOODMAN of Searsmont ME at Searsmont ME [10 Jul 1845]
- Isaac C & Elizabeth V JACKSON at Minot ME [21 Jan 1847]
- J S Mr & Miss S E DUNN Rev John ALLEN at Mt Vernon ME on 6th inst [16 Mar 1848]
- John Col & Mary WILLIAMS 2nd inst at Readfield ME [14 Dec 1839]
- Julia D of Greenville ME & R G DENNETT at Wilson ME [4 Feb 1847]
- Martha & John SIDES Esq at Waldoboro ME [22 Apr 1852]
- Mary Ann of Winthrop ME & Matthias SMITH of Readfield ME at Wayne ME [8 Jul 1847]
- Mary E & Samuel FAUNCE at Wayne ME [5 Mar 1846]
- Mary Jane & William MORSE Jr at West Gardiner ME [21 Aug 1835]
- Mary S & John CUSHMAN at Portland ME [20 May 1836]
- Noah Jr & Delia C MORTON both of Boston formerly of Winthrop ME at New York [29 Jun 1848]
- Samuel Q of Boston MA & Mary R BEAN d/o John BEAN Esq by Elder James PEARL at Mt Vernon ME [26 Oct 1848]
- Sarah & Gustavus MORRIL at Winthrop ME [16 Jan 1838]
- Sarah & Thomas STEVENS at Anson ME [14 Jan 1847]
- Sarah & Henry BAKER at Winthrop ME [4 Nov 1847]
- Susan Mrs of Hallowell ME & Joseph LOCKE Gen of Bloomfield ME on 21 Jan at Augusta ME [29 Jan 1846]

CURRIER (cont.) Thomas Esq of Skowhegan ME & Mary TOWLE of Farmington ME by Rev S B WITHERELL at Avon ME [27 Mar 1838]
 Violetta S & Samuel P GROW at Vassalboro ME [30 Mar 1848]
 William H & Lucy E MITCHELL at Kennebunk ME [28 Feb 1837]
 William P & Harriet JOHNSON on Fri eve last at Hallowell ME [21 Mar 1834]
CURRY Julia F & Albert J WILLIAMS at Eastport ME [2 Mar 1848]
CURTIS Adeline of Leeds ME & James D GILBERT of Turner ME at Leeds ME [19 Nov 1846]
 Albert Capt of Brunswick ME & Alice D SCOLFIELD at Harpswell ME [10 Apr 1841]
 Alexander B & Almira T MARSHALL at Swanville ME [28 Jan 1847]
 Almira of Frankfort ME & Reuben S SMART at Swanville ME [17 Oct 1837]
 Ansel M & Mary Jane MILLIKEN at Portland ME [8 Feb 1844]
 Bailey & Prudence B FREEMAN at Brunswick ME [25 Jan 1840]
 Charity of Webster ME & Daniel ALLEN grandson of Capt Elijah ALLEN who remarried on this same day, at Bowdoin ME [14 Nov 1844]
 Charles S & Amanda F HAM 25th inst at Hallowell ME [2 Jan 1835]
 Columbia & Joshua B CROCKETT at Oxford ME [9 May 1844]
 David & Lydia Ann COX of Bowdoin ME at Webster ME [9 Sept 1847]
 David H & Rachel T MERRIAM at Bowdoin ME [18 Mar 1847]
 Edmund of Woodstock ME & Irene D YOUNG at Greenwood ME [26 Feb 1846]
 Florentine & Robert CURTIS at Freeport ME [19 Feb 1836]
 Frances A only d/o Capt Winslow CURTIS of Frankfort ME, & William A BLAKE Esq of Bangor ME at Frankfort ME [9 Jan 1845]
 Hannah L of Richmond ME & Elias H LAWRENCE of Gardiner ME at Bowdoinham ME [11 Jan 1849]
 Jenette G of Richmond ME & John DRAKE of China ME on 13 Jan by Pardon TINKHAM Esq at Albion ME [17 Jan 1850]
 Jesse of Boston MA & Alice P FURBUSH of Wells ME at Boston [28 Nov 1844]
 Joel of Bowdoinham ME & Sophia SPOFFORD at Webster ME [26 Dec 1844]
 John of Hallowell ME & Matilda TAPLEY at Litchfield ME [18 Apr 1834]
 John Jr of Minot ME & Elizabeth G JEPSON at Lewiston ME [15 Nov 1849]
 Joseph H & Harriet N KINKSBURY both of Biddeford ME at Saco ME [28 Feb 1837]
 Joseph P of Topsham ME & Mary B PETTINGILL at Wayne ME [9 Dec 1847]
 Joshua of Bowdoinham ME & Sophia B PURRINGTON of Bath ME by Rev STEARNS at Bath [27 Jul 1839]
 Kingsbury of Paris ME & S J YOUNG of Greenwood ME at Norway ME [8 Jan 1846]
 Leonard & Charlotte KNOWLES at Bluehill ME [29 Jul 1836]
 Louisa & A B ADAMS by Wm R HERSEY Esq at Lincoln ME [16 Apr 1846]
 Lydia & Daniel MOORES at Frankfort ME [10 Oct 1840]
 Lydia & Samuel TRACE 18 Oct by Milo WALTON Esq at Amity ME [3 Dec 1846]

CURTIS (cont.) Lydia & William BOURN Col at Wells ME [30 Oct 1835]
   Margaret & Oliver H P GREENLIEF by Hartley KIMBALL Esq at Mercer ME [25 May 1839]
   Mary d/o James CURTIS Esq of Camden ME & Capt James STACKPOLE by Rev CHAPMAN at Camden ME [4 May 1839]
   Mary & Llewellyn MOORE at Dexter ME [20 Jun 1844]
   Mary A & John FROST at Gardiner ME [26 Apr 1849]
   Moses & Mary SEKINS at Swanville ME [28 Jan 1847]
   Nancy D & George COTTON at Bath ME [17 Jul 1838]
   Olive S & Abner P CAMPBELL of Bowdoin ME by Rev Walter FOSS at Leeds ME [21 Mar 1850]
   Otis of Dixfield ME & Mary FLETCHER at Wilton ME [14 Dec 1839]
   Robert & Florentine CURTIS at Freeport ME [19 Feb 1836]
   Rosann [see p. 164, Elder's *History of Lewiston ME*, 1989] eldest d/o the late Peleg CURTIS Esq, & Washington GARCELON Esq by Rev NORTON at Harpswell ME [27 Nov 1838]
   Sophia & Caleb SUMMER 25th inst by Mr PIERCE at Leeds ME [2 Jan 1835]
   Stephen H & Mary L LANCASTER both of Bowdoinham ME at Gardiner ME [22 Nov 1849]
   Susan B of Bath ME & Geo D FOLSOM of Bucksport ME at New York ME [10 Sept 1846]
   Susan W youngest d/o the late Col Charles CURTIS, & Chas G BATCHELDER merchant of Hallowell ME by Rev Dr GRAY on 9th inst at Jamaca Plain [25 Dec 1841]
   Theodore S of Portland & Esther MOORE at Brunswick ME [10 Sept 1846]
   Thomas M of Freeport ME & Anstress M WOODSIDE at Brunswick ME [7 Jan 1847]
   William & Tamar McINTIRE at Bath ME [25 Apr 1837]

CURTISS Catharine & David GORHAM Capt after a long and tedious courtship of twenty years--but at last! by Rev SHEPHERD at Stratford Extended Notice [26 Sept 1837]

CUSHING Andre of Bangor ME & Delia RICH at Frankfort ME [12 Feb 1846]
   Ann Maria & Samuel D FOGG Capt Wed eve by Rev David THURSTON at Winthrop ME [6 Jun 1840]
   Elizabeth & John S KIDDER both of Madison ME at Bloomfield ME [4 Mar 1847]
   H L & Cinthia B BLACKBURN at Augusta ME [24 Dec 1846]
   Hiram of Weymouth MA & Mary Frances ROBINSON of Vassalboro ME on 17th inst at Vassalboro ME [30 Apr 1842]
   Hiram & Harriet B IRVING at Augusta ME [10 Sept 1846]
   Horatio Esq of Skowhegan ME & Martha A WHEELER at Waterville ME [2 Sept 1847]
   Hosea B & Anistatia BROWN at Bath ME [25 Apr 1850]
   James & Rachel SPRAGUE d/o Nathaniel SPRAGUE all of Phipsburg ME at Phipsburg ME [10 Sept 1842]
   James O & Clementine B WOODCOCK at Thomaston ME [1 Jan 1846]
   John M & Caroline M CHASE d/o Joseph CHASE Esq at Sebec ME [19 Sept 1844]
   Louisa & William H GILMAN at Phipsburg ME [11 Dec 1845]

CUSHING (cont.) Lucy T of Winthrop ME & Elisha ATKINSON of New Sharon ME on Weds last by Rev THURSTON at Winthrop [6 Feb 1835]
Luther & Abigail FROST at Bloomfield ME [16 Jan 1851] & [6 Feb 1851]
McCobb & Mary M WHITTIER of Readfield ME by Loring CUSHING Esq at Augusta ME [1 May 1845]
Philena & James MALCOLM at Phipsburg ME [30 Jul 1846]
Robert T & Sarah C PAINE at Thomaston ME [6 Jan 1837]
Sarah Winslow Mrs & Ralph C JOHNSON Esq of Belfast ME at Camden ME [14 Dec 1839]

CUSHMAN Alden of Oxford ME & Susan R GETCHELL at Wayne ME by Rev C FULLER [2 Oct 1851]
David N of Norway ME & Eliza Ann LUFKIN at Pownal ME [8 Nov 1849]
Emma L & Samuel W REYNOLDS of Philadelphia PA at Portland ME [24 Sept 1846]
George W Gen & Mary FRENCH both of Woodstock ME at Paris ME [29 Jul 1843]
Gustavus G Esq of Bangor ME & Harriet HOSFORD at Thetford VT [27 Mar 1845]
Harriet O of Brunswick ME & Daniel E PENDEXTER of Bartlett NH at New Gloucester ME [24 Dec 1846]
J B D & E P PIERCE of Houlton ME at Bangor ME [11 Mar 1847]
J S Dr of New Gloucester ME & Sarah M BAKER at Portland ME [19 Nov 1846]
Jacob of Hallowell ME & Sophia at Waldoboro ME [19 Dec 1837]
Jeannette A & Joshua R HAMMOND of Crystal Plantation ME at Woodstock ME [19 Jul 1849]
Job of Waterford ME & Eliza HARRIS at Gray ME [21 Mar 1850]
John & Mary S CURRIER at Portland ME [20 May 1836]
Lucy & William STEWART at Lewiston ME [6 Feb 1851]
Mary Ann & Josiah JORDAN at Monson ME [14 & 21 Nov 1840]
Mary Jane & Capt A S DALY at Thompson CT [27 Jul 1848]
Mary Jane & Eldridge LERMOND Capt both of Warren ME at Thomaston ME [29 Aug 1844]
Rosamond & Merritt CALDWELL principal of the Maine Wesleyan Seminary at New Gloucester ME [4 Mar 1833]
Rufus & Sarah Ann OWEN at Portland ME [5 Dec 1844]
Sarah W & Benjamin TARBOX at Phillips ME [13 May 1847]
Sophia & Jacob CUSHMAN of Hallowell ME at Waldoboro ME [19 Dec 1837]
Susan of Monson ME & Wm PRATT 2nd of Foxcroft ME at Monson ME [8 Apr 1843]
Sylvina & Benjamin STEVENS Jr at Portland ME [23 Jan 1845]
William M & Mary E HOBBS at Norway ME [22 Mar 1849]

CUTLER Elbridge G Rev of Belfast ME & Clara A ABBOTT by Rev I ROGERS at Belfast [10 Jun 1843] & Clara A ABBOTT d/o Jacob on 21st inst by Rev Isaac ROGERS at Farmington [3 Jun 1843]
Hannah M & Philip S PAGE of Boston MA at Farmington ME [29 Jul 1843]
John L Esq & Abby D d/o Hon Hiram BELCHER on 16th ult by Rev I ROGERS at Farmington ME [2 Sept 1843]

Marriage Notices from the "Maine Farmer"

CUTLER (cont.) John L Esq of Farmington ME & Zilpha Ingraham WILLIAMS d/o Hon Reul WILLIAMS by Rev Mr JUDD at (Augusta) ME on 18th Oct [26 Oct 1848]
    Mary Jane & Capt Alex B MUNROE at Bristol ME [26 Feb 1852]
    Matilda A & Augustus PRESCOTT at Lewiston ME [11 Mar 1852]
    Nathan Hon of Farmington ME & Mrs Harriet WELD at Brunswick ME [19 Jun 1838]
    Reuben of Strong ME & Mary Jane BUTLER at Farmington ME [1 Jan 1846]
    Ruth of Industry ME & James B WOOD at Norridgewock ME [2 Oct 1845]
    Sarah A & John MORRISON at Thomaston ME [6 Nov 1845]
    Velina & Joseph WORCESTER at Thomaston ME [19 Aug 1836]
CUTTER Abraham L of Boston MA & Harriet H SEWALL at Bath ME [14 Nov 1844]
    Benjamin O of Sebec ME & Bertha TOWNE at Dover ME [15 Aug 1844]
    Charlotte & Ephraim LIBBY at Pownal ME [2 May 1844]
    Cyrus & Mary DAY only d/o Daniel DAY Esq at Nobleboro ME [4 Feb 1833]
    Susan T & Samuel ADLAM at Newport RI on 3 Jun [24 Jun 1852]
CUTTING Anna D & Josiah D FRISBY at Phipsburg ME [11 Oct 1849]
    William H of Phillips ME & Sally E PULCIFER at Weld ME by I TYLOR Esq [3 Apr 1851]
CUTTS Adeline & Oliver BRAGDON both of Monroe ME at Monroe [6 Feb 1845]
    Elisha & Eliza Jane LINCOLN by J H MACOMBER Esq at Milo ME on 27 Aug [14 Sept 1848]
    Frances A & Eben GIVEN at Milo ME [25 May 1848]

- D -

DABNEY Mr S W of Fayal Azores & Harriet W WEBSTER d/o Dr J W WEBSTER at Cambridge MA [17 Apr 1851]
DACY Sophia & Joshua S WHITMAN both of Greenwood ME at Norway ME [19 Mar 1846]
DAGGETT Dennis of Phillips & Mary WRIGHT at Guilford ME [6 Mar 1845]
    Elizabeth S & Proctor J GILBERT at Kennebec ME [4 Sept 1851]
    George B & Mary J BURNS at Union ME [25 Nov 1847]
    Jonathan C & Abigail MARSH at East Sangerville ME [18 Nov 1843]
    Mary & Rev Joseph C ASPENWALL of the Maine (Methodist) Conference at Bangor ME [2 May 1837]
    Samuel & Mrs Mary STETSON at Union ME [9 Feb 1839]
    Susan Ann of Leeds ME ae 25 & Master David HARDY of Wilton ME ae 13 years at Leeds [13 Mar 1838]
    William H of Portsmouth VA & Hannah E JUDKINS of Augusta ME at New York City [18 Nov 1847]
DAGLE Miles & Lucretia JACKMAN of Sangerville ME at Dexter ME [15 Apr 1847]
DAILEY/DAILY/DALY A S Capt of (Augusta) ME & Mary Jane CUSHMAN of Dracut MA at Thompson CT [27 Jul 1848]
    Daniel C Monmouth ME & Esther HATCH of Greene ME at Leeds ME [21 Dec 1848]

DAILEY (cont.) Elijah S & Mary Ann TABER both of Augusta ME at Vassalboro ME [22 Mar 1849]
    Mary Jane & Royal THOMAS Jr at Searsmont ME [11 July 1844]
    Orinda & Thomas B GROSS 21st ult at Camden ME [2 Sept 1836]
    Rebecca & Geo F DUDLEY of Milford by Hon C HOLLAND at Canton ME [10 Jan 1850]
    Roana S & James WING Capt at Wayne ME [6 Feb 1838]
    Z S Capt & Catharine P SANFORD at Augusta ME [4 Feb 1843]
DAIN James & Harriet RANDALL of Lewiston ME at Durham ME [21 May 1846]
    Margaret m John BATES Esq of Phillips ME at Bowdoinham ME [29 May 1851]
DAKIN Daniel & Hannah DOWNING both of Bangor ME at Kirkland ME [13 Jan 1848]
DALLIFF Sewall & Betsey WILLEY on 4 July at Augusta ME [22 July 1847]
DALY - see DAILEY
DAME Margaret C & J M BUTLAND of Hollis ME at Saco ME [20 Sept 1849]
    Miss C J & Mr G HACKETT at Parsonsfield ME [14 Sept 1848]
    Sarah M m James A WINN of Great Falls NH at Farmington [29 May 1851]
DAMON Delia & David P BODFISH at Gardiner ME [5 Sept 1844]
    Jane T of Lynn MA & Rev Giles BAILEY Pastor of the Universalist Society of Winthrop ME by Rev L WILLIS at Lynn MA [6 June 1840]
    Lydia R & Thorndike ALLEN Jr at Stetson ME [20 May 1847]
    Sarah & Henry M HEWES Esq publisher of the *Thomaston Republican* and the *Temperance Advocate* at Wiscasset ME [30 May 1834]
DAMREN Joel T & Mrs Mary J ABBOT by Isaiah ROLLINS Esq at Belgrade ME on 14th inst [30 Mar 1848]
    Samuel of Boston & Olive JORDAN at Danville ME [4 Dec 1851]
    Eleanor W, d/o W DAMREN, & Cyrus GUILD Jr of Winthrop ME at Belgrade ME [27 Feb 1841]
    Lydia Y & A N LORD both of Belgrade ME at B [8 May 1835]
DANA Abigail d/o Edmund DANA Esq of Wiscasset ME & Joseph G BORLAND of Newcastle ME on Tues morn last by Rev MATHER at Wiscasset ME [8 Oct 1842]
    Amos W of Boston & Eduah L BARTELS at Portland ME [8 Feb 1844]
    Catharine P d/o Hon Judah DANA, & Henry B OSGOOD Esq at Fryeburg ME [30 May 1840]
    Edward Jr & Ardelia L WARNER at Augusta ME [17 Dec 1846]
    John W Esq & Caroline P FOWLER at Portland ME [7 June 1849]
DANE Francis B Esq of Troy NY & Miria B NASON at Livermore ME [8 July 1847]
    John & Abigail ODLIN both of Fayette ME by Rev E ROBINSON at Fayette [12 Aug 1843]
DANFORTH Aaron B & Mary T WILLIAMSON at Augusta ME on 23 Jan by Asaph R NICHOLS Esq [30 Jan 1851]
    Charles Esq Attorney at Law of Gardiner ME & Julia S DINSMORE at Norridgewock [23 Jan 1845]
    Isaac H & Elizabeth A PETERS at Brunswick ME [8 Jan 1852]

DANFORTH (cont.) Mary C of Winthrop ME & David McLELLAN of San Francisco CA proprietor of Maine Hotel at New York City at Trinity Church on Aug 31st by Rev Dr HOBART [18 Sept 1851]
    Mary O Mrs & Luther WEST at Belfast ME [9 Apr 1846]
    Milo M & Rhoda Ann HILTON of Starks ME at Madison ME [8 June 1848]
    Newland & Cordelia FULLER at Lagrange ME [22 Jan 1839]
    Sarah E of Winthrop & Charles D ELMES of Taunton MA Sun eve last by Rev Giles BAILEY at Winthrop ME [20 Nov 1841]
    Sarah E & Clark P TRUE at Norway ME [15 Jan 1852]
    Stillman A & Margaret S PLUMMER at Charlestown [8 Mar 1849]
DANIELS Elizabeth A d/o Ebenezer DANIELS of Portland ME & Horatio HILL of Bangor ME on 29 Nov Tues by Rev SADDLER at Portland [10 Dec 1842]
    Harvey M ae 17 & Margaret MOON ae 14 at Woodford VT both of the children must have been Moon Struck [31 Oct 1837]
    Mary Jane & Edward HAMLIN at Portland ME [10 Oct 1837]
DANLEY William & Betsey COOK Mrs at Rumford ME [27 June 1840]
DARLING Samuel & Susan FLAGG at Auburn ME [20 Mar 1851]
DARRAH Sarah & Frederick DYER at Oldtown ME [30 May 1844]
DASHIEL Louisa C Mrs of Boston MA & Lewellyn J MORSE at Bangor ME [26 Aug 1843]
DAVEE Hon Thomas of Blanchard Sheriff of Somerset Co ME & Theresa V BLANCHARD of Cumberland ME on 9th inst by Rev WESTON at Cumberland ME [16 Oct 1835]
DAVENPORT Almira & Samuel INGRAHAM Capt at Augusta ME [13 Feb 1835]
    Benjamin H & Margaret A HASKETH at Hallowell ME [20 May 1843]
    Betsey C Mrs of Hallowell ME & Jarvis M NORCROSS of Augusta ME at Hallowell ME [20 Mar 1841]
    Charles & Catherine T DUNCAN at Bath ME [18 Nov 1836]
    Cyrus & Lucy T ALLEN of Turner ME by Rev C FULLER at Wayne ME [6 Sept 1849]
    Emeline A & William H PRESCOTT at Chelsea ME? [1 Apr 1852]
    John M & Emeline WHITE at Hallowell ME [9 May 1844]
    Julia O of Wayne ME & Albion HOOD of Turner ME at Wayne ME [15 Mar 1840]
    Mary Jane of Hallowell ME & David PAGE of Fairfield ME at Hallowell ME [13 Nov 1838]
    Sophia S of Augusta ME & William DAY of West Jefferson ME at Hallowell ME [1 Jan 1846]
    William H of Hallowell ME & Mary A LORD at Litchfield ME [30 July 1846]
DAVIDSON Mary L & J Henry PULLEN at Monson ME [31 Dec 1842]
    Nancy of Lubec ME & William MOFFIT at East Machias ME [13 Aug 1846]
    Park & Edith TUCKER of Robinson ME at Calais ME [2 July 1846]
DAVIS A G & Julia FREEMAN at Hallowell ME [21 Feb 1850]
    Aaron of Chelsea & Abby C GRAY of Hallowell at Augusta ME on Jan 20th by Rev Z THOMPSON [6 Feb 1851]
    Abby L of St Louis MO? & Wildes T THOMPSON Capt of New York formerly of Bath ME at New Orleans LA? [20 Aug 1846]

DAVIS (cont.) Abigail H Mrs & James T NICHOLS formerly of Buxton ME at Saco ME [9 Apr 1846]
 Abigail of Brooks ME & Charles H THOMPSON of Frankfort ME at Belfast ME [24 Jan 1834]
 Abigail & Chas MARSTON at Bath ME [19 Dec 1834]
 Achsah A & Sumner R JOHNSON of Milwaukee WI at Strong ME [2 Sept 1847]
 Almira formerly of Methuen MA & Thomas CROCKER Esq at Paris ME [10 Oct 1844]
 Alonzo & Julia A SARGENT at Sidney ME [25 Jan 1849]
 Amos Esq of Bangor ME & Miss C S WELD at Brunswick ME [2 Nov 1848]
 Ann Caroline & Manley EAMES at Farmington ME [10 Oct 1840]
 Ann & John DOLLOFF Jr at Readfield ME [7 Dec 1848]
 Azelia & David S SANBORN on 21 June at Webster ME [28 June 1849]
 Betsey Jane & Alexander STINSON at Auburn ME [12 Aug 1852]
 Betsey L & Robert NEWBEGIN of Falmouth ME on 1 Aug by Rev Z THOMPSON at Augusta ME [5 Aug 1852]
 Betsey Mrs m Elkanah McLELLAN of Gardiner ME at Farmington ME [22 May 1851]
 Calvin H of Canterbury NH & Ann P MATHEWS of Waterville ME at Lake Village NH [28 Aug 1851]
 Charles C & Mary FOSSETT at Strong ME [29 Feb 1840]
 Charles T & Sarah L STROUT at Portland ME [24 Apr 1845]
 Charles & Elvira STANFORD at Gardiner ME [2 Jan 1851]
 Charlotte & Reuben HARDING of Phillips ME at Hallowell ME [20 Sept 1849]
 Chloe Ann & Sidney MASON at Fairfield ME [15 May 1851]
 Daniel & Martha J SOPER of Livermore ME at Turner ME [18 Jan 1849]
 David Esq of Edgarton MA & Octavia J BACKUS of Farmington ME at New York [20 Mar 1845]
 David of Ottoway IL & Ruth PARKER at New Portland ME [7 Oct 1847]
 Edward & Abigail P STAPLE at Wellington Piscataquis Co ME [23 June 1852]
 Eliza A & John P MERRILL at Biddeford ME [26 Aug 1847]
 Eliza C & John B WATTS of Thomaston ME at Boston MA [25 Sept 1851]
 Eliza & Merritt SANDERS of Brewer ME at Sangarville ME [25 Dec 1845]
 Elizabeth E & Jonas HASTINGS of Northborough MA at Mount Vernon ME [17 Oct 1834]
 Elizabeth & Calvin ROBINSON at Union ME [3 Feb 1848]
 Elizabeth & Robert FOSSETT both of Strong ME at Farmington ME [6 Nov 1851]
 Emeline & Reuben WHITEHOUSE at Wellington ME [23 June 1852]
 Esther & John H FOGG of Brooks ME at Belfast ME [10 Oct 1844]
 Evander L & Mary A WING both of Belgrade ME at Sidney ME on 23 Oct [13 Nov 1851]
 Flora & Joseph WINSLOW of Portland ME at Hallowell ME [28 Nov 1844]
 Frances Ann & James HALL Capt of Augusta ME at Bath ME [15 Aug 1834]
 Frances M & Benjamin M HUNT at Lubec ME [16 Apr 1846]
 Francis Esq & Julia A ELLIS Thanksgiving evening at Augusta ME [9 Dec 1836]

DAVIS (cont.) Franklin A of Sidney ME & Charlotte S LEWIS at Waterville ME [18 Jan 1849]
   Hannah of North Salem MA & Ebenezer CAREY after a tedious courtship of one hour at Minot ME [2 Jan 1834]
   Harrison N & Emma GREENLIEF at New Portland ME [9 July 1846]
   Horace of Ellsworth ME & Susan KEYES at Orland ME [14 Oct 1847]
   Jackson & Amy BUBIER at Lewiston ME [22 Jan 1852]
   James Jr & Delilah GRIFFIN at Augusta ME [23 Sept 1843]
   Jesse of Webster ME & Mary Ann WOODBURY at Litchfield ME [20 Mar 1845]
   John A & Sarah J SPAULDING at Palmyra ME [3 Apr 1851]
   John C & Ann M WIGGIN at Lewiston ME [8 Feb 1849]
   John H & Almira MERRILL at Bangor ME [12 June 1845]
   John L of Lisbon ME & Abigail JORDAN at Lewiston ME [25 Mar 1847]
   John P Esq & Leonice M HORR both of Bridgton ME at Portland ME [28 Aug 1845]
   John T formerly of Biddeford ME & Sarah GREENWOOD formerly of Weston ME at Milton/Milltown ME? [23 Apr 1842]
   Jonas of Raymond & Elizabeth OSGOOD at Durham ME [18 Apr 1850]
   Jones S & Susan A ROGERS at Belfast ME [6 Jul 1848]
   Leroy W Capt of New Bedford MA & Sarah G BYRAM of Guilford ME at Guilford [8 Jan 1846]
   Lorenzo M & Susan J EMERY of Fairfield ME at Waterville ME [18 Dec 1851]
   Louisa M Mrs & Eben WOODBURY at Houlton ME [16 Sept 1843]
   Lydia of Industry & Philander WEEKS of Farmington ME at Industry ME [7 Jan 1843]
   Martha J & Charles B HUNTER of Topsham ME at Hallowell ME [10 Jan 1850]
   Mary Ann & Aaron CHANDLER of Jay ME at Farmington ME [18 Sept 1845]
   Mary Ann & John WOOSTER Capt at Lubec ME [19 Feb 1846]
   Mary Jane & Ebenezer BROWN Jr at Robbinstown ME [11 Sept 1845]
   Mary & Edward PINE Capt at Phipsburg ME [8 Aug 1844]
   Mary & Joseph WRIGHT of Monmouth ME at Lewiston ME [10 Jan 1850]
   Mary & Simeon HUNT at Auburn ME [4 Jan 1844]
   Mary & Wm A NICHOLS 25 Nov at Augusta ME [9 Dec 1847]
   Matilda & Franklin WAKEFIELD at China ME on 22 Feb [11 Mar 1852]
   Mehitable W & Sam'l P KIMBALL 26th ult at Hallowell ME [4 Nov 1843]
   Melissa M & Edwin B CHILD at Canton ME [3 June 1847]
   Mercy & Joel Foster at Buckfield ME [12 Mar 1846]
   Moses & Sophrona MASON of Augusta ME by S FOSTER Esq at Hallowell ME [15 Aug 1840]
   Nancy P & Isaac SYLVESTER of Freeport ME at Westbrook ME [29 May 1845]
   Nancy P & John WYMAN at Bangor ME [11 July 1844]
   Nathan & Caroline NICHOLS at Augusta ME [22 Apr 1847]
   Olive H & Noah GRANT at Kittery ME [3 Aug 1848]
   Orrin G & Caroline C GILMAN at Corinth [11 July 1844]
   Phebe Jane & Eben T MATHEWS at Elliotsville [22 Jan 1852]
   Rhoda of Bowdoin & Gordon G DREW of Boston at Boston MA [23 Oct 1841]

DAVIS (cont.) Robert B of Sidney ME & Mary Jane BRIGGS at (Augusta) ME on New Year's Eve [15 Jan 1852]
    Robert Jr & Mary E BUTTERFIELD at Milford [10 Feb 1848]
    Robert M & Ann MASON at Fairfield ME [4 Oct 1849]
    Robinson A & Abigail J BAKER at Farmington ME [9 Mar 1848]
    Sarah C & Artemas FOSTER at Machias ME [27 Jul 1848]
    Sarah D of Winthrop ME & George H CHENEY of Newport NH Tues morn last by Rev David THURSTON at Winthrop ME [5 Aug 1833]
    Sarah L & Richard L COLE at Paris ME [8 Jan 1852]
    Sarah M d/o Joshua DAVIS Dr of Sidney ME & Daniel EDGERLY Esq at Mobile AL [18 July 1844]
    Sarah M & Otis W CAMPBELL both of Foxcroft ME at Dover ME [20 Feb 1851]
    Sarah S & Abiel ABBOTT Esq at Farmington ME [23 Oct 1845]
    Sarah W & Edward B SWAN at Gardiner ME [8 Feb 1840]
    Sarah & William TOLMAN at Thomaston ME [10 Oct 1844]
    Sophia S & Edwin ELLIS Dr at Farmington ME [9 Dec 1847]
    Statira & Josiah H SHEPARD at Union ME [4 Jan 1849]
    Susan A & John CHASE Jr at Unity ME [5 Mar 1846]
    Susan M & Isaac E RICHARDSON of New Gloucester ME at Pownal ME [30 Jan 1845]
    Susan W d/o Asa DAVIS Esq of Hallowell ME & Wm S BRIGGS of Dover ME Tues eve last by Rev ADLAM at Hallowell ME [26 June 1841]
    Susan & Israel PROCTOR of Kennebunkport ME at Biddeford ME [2 Apr 1846]
    Susan & William COLLAMORE at Bremen ME [20 Apr 1848]
    Sylvanus & Eliza J HASEY at Albion ME [15 Feb 1849]
    Talbot C & Louisa B DOCKHAM of Tuftonboro NH at Augusta ME [24 June 1847]
    Theodore S of Brownville, Piscataquis Co ME & Mary T S SWEAT at Maxfield, Penobscot Co ME [5 Dec 1844]
    Thomas C & Betsey A GASLIN by A R NICHOLS Esq at (Augusta) ME on 14th inst [18 May 1848]
    Thomas J (printer) & Cornelia HARMON both of Saco ME by Rev S WATERHOUSE at Scarboro' on 22d Feb [4 Mar 1852]
    Thomas & Rachel A SOPER of Livermore ME by Job PRINCE Esq at Turner ME [11 May 1848]
    William F of Whitefield ME & Mrs Abigail CUNNINGHAM at Palermo ME [25 June 1846]
    William L of Poland ME & Ann GREENHALGH of Gardiner ME at Gardiner [18 Dec 1845]
    William & Jane M CROOKER at Lisbon ME [11 Jan 1844]
    William & Martha Ann MASON at Belfast ME [21 Mar 1850]
    Zebulon & Mary Jane HATCH at Thomaston ME [4 Mar 1847]

DAVISON Charles Henry s/o James D of Ruchill, Lanark, Co., Scotland & Louisa Mathda WESTON d/o Hon Nathan WESTON of (Augusta) ME by Recorder TILTON at New York City on 2d June [10 June 1852]

DAWES/DAWS Caroline W & A WATERHOUSE of Durham ME at New Gloucester ME [19 Dec 1844]
    Ezra H & Annis RIDEOUT at Litchfield ME [17 June 1847]
    Frances L & Ashur FLETCHER both of Bloomfield ME at Thompson CT [18 Nov 1847]

DAWES (cont.) John & Elizabeth GOTT both of Mt Desert ME at East Black Island [27 Jul 1848]
Martha & Amos GARLAND at Bloomfield ME [27 Nov 1851]
Olive & Wm H TOOTHAKER both of Richmond at Bowdoin ME [10 June 1847] DAY
Abby L & Edward T SWAIN at Hallowell ME [1 Feb 1844]
Abner of Bangor ME & Lydia H GOVER of Monmouth ME at Monmouth ME [13 Nov 1841]
Charlotte of Durham ME & Elisha LUNT at Brunswick ME [25 Nov 1847]
Clarissa & Samuel M PARCHER of Winthrop ME on 30 Sept at Leeds ME [11 Oct 1849]
Daniel of Nobleboro ME & Mary EAMES at Jefferson ME [18 Jan 1840]
David S of Orient ME & Emily RUSSELL by Milo WALTON at Amity ME [3 Dec 1846]
Elizabeth Jane & Ambrose POTTER at Augusta ME [30 Aug 1849]
Emerson O & Sarah FLETCHER both of Jarvis Gore ME at Eddington ME [21 Oct 1847]
Francis J of Hallowell ME & Mary L WEYMOUTH of Gardiner ME at Providence RI [18 Dec 1851]
Hannah S & Hezekiah SMILY of Hallowell ME at Augusta ME [23 July 1846]
Harriot L & Rowland FREEMAN of Milo ME by Rev Robert LOW at Hallowell ME [28 Mar 1834]
Henry & Hester Ann COBB Sun eve 22nd ult by Oakes HOWARD Esq at Winthrop ME [22 May 1838]
John M & Susan E MOWER both of Wilton ME at Jay ME [19 Aug 1847]
Judith B of Leeds & Henry A TORSEY of Winthrop ME at Leeds ME [13 Feb 1838]
Julia Ann & Isaac HOPKINS of Brunswick ME at Durham ME [30 Dec 1836]
Martha K & Leverett LORD Monday 22nd inst by Rev COLE at Hallowell ME [4 Dec 1841]
Mary only d/o Daniel DAY & Cyrus CUTTER at Nobleboro ME [4 Feb 1833]
Mary & William A STEVENS of Hallowell ME at Gardiner ME [17 May 1849]
Olive E & Albert J BARRETT at Dover [7 Apr 1848]
Phillip W & Laura A D HASKELL by James B HASKELL Esq at China ME [29 Jan 1852]
Thaddeus H & Frances W BRALEY at Hallowell ME [29 Jan 1846]
William of West Jefferson ME & Mrs Sophia S DAVENPORT of Augusta ME at Hallowell ME [1 Jan 1846]
William Rev of Woolwich ME & Henrietta H MORSE at Bath ME [4 Jul 1840]

DAYTON Sarah & James JEWELL 13th inst at Bath ME [29 May 1841]

DEAL Catharine & Asa BARNES both of Waldoboro ME at Nobleboro ME [23 Dec 1836]

DEALAND Mary Ann & George W ANTHONY at Hallowell ME [5 Mar 1846]

DEALY Owen of Winthrop ME & Helen FURLONG by Rev RYAN at Jefferson ME [15 Feb 1844]

DEAN Abigail B of Temple ME & Thomas W JEPSON of China ME at Friends Meeting House at Wilton ME [14 Nov 1844]

DEAN (cont.) Delphus & Ephraim J ULMER at Rockland ME [27 Mar 1851]
Esther A & Isaac TUCKER Jr of Buckfield ME at Paris ME [19 July 1849]
Harriet & James W ORMSBEE at Thomaston ME [23 Dec 1847]
Levi F Capt & Susan Jane COLLAMORE at Lincolnville ME [5 Aug 1852]
Rebecca of Barnard ME & Andrews G MOOR of Sebec ME at Dover ME? [15 May 1851]
Thomas B Rev of Taunton MA & Martha Augusta BLACK on 19th inst by Rev BURGESS at St Marks Church in Augusta ME [27 Nov 1845]

DEARBORN Ann C ae 30 & Ezekiel ANDREWS ae 18 at Corinna ME [11 Apr 1844]
Calvin & Miss Louis ATKINS Mon eve 31 July by Rev FOSTER at Winthrop ME [5 Aug 1843]
Eliza of Portland ME & Rev Orange SCOTT Presiding Elder on Providence District New England Conference Mon last by Rev C BAKER at Portland ME [9 Ovt 1835]
Harriet & David STANLEY Esq 29th ult by Rev David THURSTON at Winthrop ME [6 Jan 1837]
Howard & Hannah B WELLS at Hallowell ME [30 Aug 1849]
John O & Eliza A HANSCOM both of Readfield ME at Augusta ME on 30 Aug by Lot M MERRILL Esq [18 Sept 1851]
John & Mary Jane MERRILL at Augusta ME [29 Oct 1846]
Mary Ann & J Young SCAMMON Esq Counselor at Law of Chicago IL Thurs eve 10th inst by Rev WORCESTER at Bath ME [22 Aug 1837]
Mary J & Jeremiah BAKER Jr of Yarmouth ME at Biddeford ME [31 Jan 1850]
Mary Jane & Isaac SHERMON by Anson CHURCH Esq at Augusta ME [29 Oct 1846]
Mary Jane & Joseph A GRIFFIN at Hallowell ME on 12th June [23 June 1852]
Mary & Edward BRECK Jr of Nobleboro ME at Vassalboro ME [19 Aug 1847]
Sabra Mrs & Wm M CLARK at Hallowell ME [24 Sept 1846]
William F & Elvira WALKER Mrs at Monmouth ME [18 July 1837]

DEARING Rev John & Sarah B KENDALL at Bath ME [4 Jul 1840]

DEARTH Mr L L & Elizabeth C FLANDERS at Sangerville ME [11 May 1848]

DeBECK John of Eddington ME & Harriet EUSTIS of Prospect ME at Prospect [24 Oct 1840]

DECKER Esther & John L STANLEY both of Winthrop ME at Wayne ME [27 Mar 1845]
Henry W & Elizabeth S LOCKE Wed eve last by Rev COLE at Hallowell ME [18 Apr 1837]
Mary of Gardiner & Isaac C WELCOMBE of Hallowell ME at Gardiner ME [15 Jan 1846]
Melinda M & Samuel W HATCH A B both of Bowdoinham ME at Providence RI [16 Aug 1849]
Thomas Dea & Catherine CROCKER Mrs at Boothbay ME [23 Jan 1838]

DeCOSTER Harriet A & Leander S SWAN at Paris ME [5 Feb 1852]

DECRENEY F A of Portland & Frances J LIBBY of Brunswick ME at Portland ME [14 Jan 1847]

DECKROW Harriet & T S KEENE at Freedom ME? [6 Nov 1845]

DeCROW A A of Freedom ME & Theopilus SPAULDING at Belfast ME [22 Jan 1846]

DeCROW (cont.) Azubah A of Freedom ME & Thomas R SHUTE Capt at Belfast ME [14 Oct 1847]
  Olivia & Mark HALL of Thorndike ME at Lincolnville ME [26 Dec 1837]
DEE Margaret J & Allen CLAREY Esq both of Georgetown ME at Phipsburg ME [6 Mar 1845]
DEEPARR Joseph & Catharine BRAINARD at Bath ME [12 Mar 1846]
DEERING Esther & Mary J PRATT at Paris ME [10 Oct 1840]
  J F & Dorcas Ann TOWNSEND at Saco ME [20 Jul 1848]
DEERING Elizabeth H & W R PORTER at South Paris ME [4 June 1846]
  Harriet of Bath ME & Ezekiel T WEBB of Woolwich ME by Rev John DEERING at Bath [16 Jan 1841]
  Sarah J & Geo F SKINNER at Corinth ME [29 July 1852]
  Stephen & Caroline F POTTER at Augusta ME [20 June 1840]
  William of Paris ME & Abigail R BARBOUR at Gray ME [22 Nov 1849]
  William Jr & Lydia A GOULD at Saco ME [24 July 1838]
DeFRATUS Manuel & Ann Maria HUTCHEE both of West Gardiner ME by Rev GRANT at Litchfield ME [30 Oct 1845]
DeLAINE David I of Calais ME & Jane C HUSTON of Portland ME at Portland ME [12 Sept 1840]
DeLAITTRE Michael & Nancy CROSS at Sebec ME [15 Aug 1844]
DeLANO Edwin J & Elitha G BREWSTER at Rockland ME [3 June 1852]
  Matilda S of Sidney ME & Theodore W LONGLEY of Sidney at Augusta ME on 31 Dec by Rev C F ALLEN [9 Jan 1851]
  Phebe E & Dr Joseph P SMALL at Rumford ME on 11th inst [20 May 1852]
DELANO Alice R Mrs d/o late Benjamin RIGGS Esq. & Sewall WATSON Esq of Augusta ME at Georgetown ME [24 Dec 1846]
  Ira B Capt of Bath & Jane P ROGERS at Topsham ME [12 Oct 1839]
  Lorenzo Esq formerly of Maine & Eliza STINNETT Mrs a native of Cherokee at Park Hill Cherokee Nation [27 Feb 1845]
DELANY Francis of Brunswick ME & Mary SHERIDEN Mrs by Rev DREW at Augusta ME [4 Feb 1847]
DeLESDERNIER Francis W of Calais ME & Sophia B THORNBURN at New York [20 Nov 1835]
DeLUE Tobias & Laura E HANNAH at Calais ME [30 Oct 1841]
DeMERITT Eben & Martha KENNEY at Liberty ME [25 Mar 1833]
DEMPSEY Hugh of Waterville ME & Maria WHEELER d/o Heber WHEELER Esq at Norridgewock ME [23 Sept 1847]
DeMUTH Catherine & Martin B HARRIMAN at Waldoboro ME [5 Feb 1842]
  Jane Ann & William BROWN at Waldoboro ME [8 Feb 1840]
  Mary E & Lewis WINCHINBAUCH at Waldoboro ME [3 May 1849]
  Susan & James HARRIMAN at Waldoboro ME [12 Feb 1846]
DENACO William & Deborah NORTON at Thomaston ME [15 Aug 1844]
DENNEN Stephen M of North Wayne ME & Martha S SANDERSON Thanksgiving Day by Rev TILTON at New Sharon ME [20 Dec 1849]
DENNESS Hannah E of Hallowell ME & Harrison G O WASHBURN of Belfast ME at Hallowell [7 Nov 1834]
DENNETT Eliza J & Wm W HATCH Capt at Castine ME [21 Nov 1844]
  John & Sophia STEVENSON at Saco ME [11 July 1844]
  R G & Julia D CURRIER of Greenville ME at Wilson ME [4 Feb 1847]
DENNIS Julia C & Mr D D GARLAND at Hallowell ME [30 Mar 1848]

DENNIS Abigail Mrs & Samuel GREY by Charles A RUSS Esq at China ME [13 Apr 1839]
    Elizabeth D & Soloman W BATES Esq of Norridgewock ME at Gardiner ME [5 Dec 1844]
    Hiram & Charlotte COLBY at Moscow ME [6 May 1847]
    Lewis & T SANBORN at Charleston ME? [13 May 1843]
    Mary Ann & Orman FOLSOM of Corinth ME at Charleston ME? [13 May 1843]
    Mary C of Passadumkeag ME & Ira H HASKELL at Lincoln ME [21 Jan 1847]
    Selah G & Bethia THORNDIKE at Thomaston ME [5 Aug 1847]
DENNISON Almira & Lorenzo D WYATT Sun eve last at Brunswick ME [4 Mar 1836]
    Benjamin G & Susan TOWNS at Brunswick ME [6 Nov 1838]
    Emma E & Charles E OWEN both of Brunswick ME at Freeport ME [14 Oct 1847]
    Julia C & Algernon W HINKSON at Brunswick ME [25 Feb 1847]
    Mary E & Joseph A BROWN at Gardiner ME [23 Dec 1847]
DENNY Mary of Worcester & Hon N P DENNY of Leicester at Albany [7 Aug 1845]
    Hon N P & Mary DENNEY same as above
DENSMORE Cynthia V of Auburn ME & Henry S NEWMAN 3rd inst by Rev JONES at Auburn [7 May 1842]
DERBY Martha & John C BROOKS at Warren ME [19 Oct 1839]
DEROUT Sarah P Mrs of Winthrop ME & Alexander WING of Peru ME on 6 Jan by Thomas PHILLIPS Esq at Winthrop [7 Feb 1834]
DESHON Elijah & Matilda Y JACKSON at Jefferson ME [16 Feb 1839]
DeVEREUX
    Ralph Jr & Hester Ann HARRIMAN at Prospect ME [10 Sept 1846]
DeWOLF Nancy Mrs & Joseph MACOMBER at Bath ME [5 Mar 1842]
DEXTER Betsey of Winthrop ME & Isaac RICH 2nd of Harpswell ME by Rev John ALLEN at Winthrop ME [3 Apr 1838]
    Caroline R Mrs & Dr John MASON 2nd inst by Prof SMITH at Bangor ME [23 Dec 1847]
    Henry Rev & Mary E BOARDMAN at Milltown ME [20 Feb 1851]
    Isaac of Wayne ME & Susan METCALF 19th inst by Rev THURSTON at Winthrop ME [28 Nov 1834]
    Louisa & David RICH Capt of Harpswell ME at Wayne ME [20 Feb 1835]
    Nancy S & G E S BRYANT at Dover ME [21 Nov 1844]
    Stephen T of Boston MA & Betsey R FROST of Wayne ME on 26th inst by Rev Robert C STARR at Wayne [6 May 1843]
    William C & Sarah Jane LONGFELLOW at Newport ME [16 Jan 1838]
DIBELL Edward of Bath & Emeline P MILLS by Rev A DALTON of (Augusta) ME at Belgrade ME [10 June 1852]
DICKENSON - see DICKINSON
    G Esq Attorney at Law of West Prospect ME & Ellen GETCHELL at Waterville ME [7 Mar 1841]
    Joseph Jr & Lydia NASON at Wiscasset ME [17 Dec 1846]
DICKERMAN George H of Stoughton MA & S A P SAWTELLE at Sidney ME [15 July 1847]

DICKERSON Julia & Ira TRAFTON of Gardiner ME at Georgetown ME [24 Sept 1846]
DICKEY John J & Charlotte A KELLEY at Phillips ME on 25th Feb 1851 by Hon J A LINSCOTT [6 Mar 1851]
   Orenia S of Monroe ME & Francis I BURGESS at Hallowell ME [22 July 1847]
DICKINSON - see DICKENSON
   Hannah & Francis FAIRSERVICE of Alna ME at Wiscasset ME [10 Oct 1844]
DICKSON Charles of Clinton ME & Mary ELLIOT at Canaan ME [17 Jul 1851]
DIGGINS James N of Wayne ME & Lucinda L YOUNG at East Livermore ME [1 May 1845]
DIKE Samuel F Rev of Bath ME & Miriam d/o Rev Thomas WORCESTER morning of 10th inst at Boston [23 Apr 1842]
DILL Eben M of Webster ME & Susan B WRIGHT at Lewiston ME [28 Oct 1847]
   James of Phillips ME & Nancy NESBIT Mrs at Letter E ME [12 Aug 1847]
   Orren & Laura M WAKEFIELD at Gardiner ME [26 Feb 1846]
DILLINGHAM Enos C of Dixfield ME & Castella JONES at Canton ME [27 Jul 1848]
   Joseph Capt & Marcia MITCHELL at Freeport ME [26 June 1835]
   Ruth H & Nathaniel R FREEMAN formerly of Norridgewock ME at Sandwich MA [3 Oct 1844]
   Theodore H of Bangor ME & Susan BEVERAGE at Camden ME [26 Feb 1842]
   W A P Pastor of the Universalist Church in Augusta ME & Caroline P TOWNSEND 21 Oct by Rev William A DREW at Sidney ME [4 Nov 1847]
DILLON John & Mary J COX at Eastport ME [12 July 1849]
DIMMOCK Nancy W d/o Dr Henry DIMMOCK of Limington ME & Henry P PRATT senior Publisher of the *National Republican* at Saco ME [3 June 1833]
   William of Limington ME & Jane SWETT at Hollis ME [17 Dec 1846]
DIMOCK Caroline A & Hiram H BRAGDON at Limington ME [27 May 1847]
DINGLEY Daniel & Frances E HAYDEN at Winslow ME [15 Jan 1852]
   Elizabeth d/o Amaso DINGLEY Esq of Winslow ME, & William MATHEWS Esq Editor of the *Gardiner Blade* 14th inst at Winslow ME [30 Oct 1845]
   Elizabeth W & David W STANDISH at Bath [11 July 1834]
   Harvey E of Providence RI & Harriet B ROSS of Augusta ME on Thurs last by Rev A MOORE at Augusta [7 Aug 1845]
   Mary Helen, eldest d/o Charles DINGLEY Esq formerly of Hallowell ME, & George H GOSSIP Esq 24th inst at New York City [6 Mar 1841]
   Sarah & James HUNTER at Bowdoinham ME [7 Nov 1840]
   William B & Eunice LIBBY at Richmond ME [4 Oct 1849]
DINSMOOR Mary Mourira & Osgood BRADBURY Esq formerly of New Gloucester ME at Burlington VT [2 Oct 1845]
DINSLOW Emma J G & Smith MAXCY at Gardiner ME [10 June 1852]
DINSMORE Abner of Bingham ME & Julia A GETCHELL at Anson ME [14 Nov 1844]

DINSMORE (cont.) Asa Esq & Nancy MYERS at Nobleboro ME [2 Sept 1836]
   Betsey S of Bloomfield ME & Isaac FLETCHER Esq of Sidney ME at Bloomfield ME [14 Dec 1833]
   Bounds C & Susan A SAWYER both of China ME at China [1 Feb 1849]
   Calvin C of Glenburn ME & Adeline A PULLEN of Exeter ME at Levant ME [16 Jan 1851]
   Cephas & Sally HILTON at North Anson ME [9 Apr 1846]
   Curran & Henrietta M KENDALL at Skowhegan ME [2 Nov 1839]
   Cynthia P & James M DINSMORE at Bath ME [20 Jan 1848]
   Gustavus S of Dixmont ME & Nancy F SAVAGE by Rev Z Thompson at (Augusta) ME on 1st Mar [18 Mar 1852]
   Harriet A of Richmond ME & Benj F STETSON of Bath ME at Gardiner ME [3 Jan 1850]
   James M of Richmond ME & Cynthia P DINSMORE of Richmond ME at Bath ME [20 Jan 1848]
   James P & Emily BICKFORD at Skowhegan ME [9 Jan 1845]
   Julia S & Charles Danforth Esq attorney at Law of Gardiner ME at Norridgewock ME [23 Jan 1845]
   Lucy & Rev Eusebius HEALD of Atkinson ME at Norridgewock ME [7 Jan 1847]
   Lydia & Paul STOVER Capt of Harpswell ME at Anson ME [14 Nov 1844]
   Mary L of Cape Elizabeth & Ebenezer ARMSTRONG of Portland ME at Cape Elizabeth ME [23 May 1844]
   Mary Mrs m Charles R NASH both of Harrington ME at Addison ME [29 May 1851]
   Nahum & Sarah A TRECARTIN at Eastport ME [25 Apr 1844]
   Olive & William B SNOW both of Madison ME at Bloomfield ME on 19th June by Rev Mr HATHAWAY [26 June 1851]
   Sanborn & Sarah J LONGLEY at Norridgewock ME [2 May 1840]
   Sandborn of Norridgewock ME & Nancy D H BOARDMAN at Bloomfield ME [24 July 1845]
   Sarah V & Mr M HARRIS at North Auburn ME [17 Aug 1848]
   Sarah & William VARNUM at Anson ME [29 July 1833]
   Susan H & Amos HEALD of Bingham ME at Anson ME [10 Apr 1851]
DIX Mary Adelaide & John H WILLIAMS at Portland ME [29 Aug 1840]
DIXBY Luther Jr & Arletta H d/o Jessy ROWELL Esq Postmaster of Jefferson ME by Rev STREETER at Boston MA [22 June 1839]
DIXON Clarissa & Mr H G GREELY at Clinton ME [20 Jan 1848]
   Elbridge & Paulina BASSETT of Wales ME at Gardiner ME [4 Nov 1847]
   Elizabeth & Edward RYONSON of Brunswick ME at Wales ME [12 June 1835]
   John A & Mary Jane CARTER at Kittery ME [29 Mar 1849]
   Louisa & John P ABBOT at Gardiner ME [24 Jan 1850]
DOAN Lucy Ann & Charles Libby at Pownal ME [27 Jul 1848]
DOANE George A of Boston MA & Abba P BUCKNAM at Eastport ME [23 July 1846]
   John H & Caroline W ELDRIDGE of Brewer ME at East Orrington ME [15 July 1847]
   Lucy Ann & Charles LIBBY at North Pownal ME [4 Sept 1845]
   Mary & Jos W CHURCHILL at Raymond ME [16 Aug 1849] DOAR
   Lucy Ann & Simeon RIDER at Belfast ME [21 Aug 1845]

DOBBINS Maria H of Falmouth ME & S Jewett of Portland at Portland ME [6 Feb 1845]
DOBLE Arabella of Sumner ME & Augustus PHELPS of Paris ME at Buckfield ME [29 Mar 1849]
  Elvira & Hiram CHURCH at Avon ME [26 July 1849]
DOCKENDORFF Margaret & Abner KEENE by J B SWANTON Esq at Windsor Kennebec Co ME [14 Feb 1837]
DOCKHAM Henry & Julia S MELLUS at Thomaston ME [24 Aug 1848]
DOCKHAM Louisa B of Tuftonboro NH & Talbot C DAVIS at Augusta ME [24 June 1847]
DODD Richard C of Winthrop ME & Elizabeth WYMAN of New Sharon ME on Sunday last by Samuel WYMAN Esq at New Sharon ME [22 May 1835]
DODGE Almira & Edwin LORD Capt of Ellsworth ME at Bluehill ME [26 Aug 1847]
  Alpheus of Wiscasset ME & Emeline CHILDS at Hallowell ME [2 May 1834]
  Archibald S of Burnham ME & Rosanna MITCHELL at Troy ME [22 June 1848]
  Benjamin F & Jane R PHILBRICK at Skowhegan ME [10 Dec 1846]
  Dolly ae 86 & David BROWN Rev formerly of Frankfort ME ae 96 after a long and tedious courtship of one week at Bucksport ME [25 Nov 1836]
  Ebenezer of Edgecomb ME & Emeline K AVERILL of Alna ME at New Castle ME [27 May 1852]
  Elbridge H & Lucy M SPAULDING at Thomaston ME [20 Jul 1848]
  Hannah of Thomaston ME & Sumner ALLEN at Montville ME [25 May 1839]
  Harriet M T & Cyrus ROWE senior Publisher of the *Republican Journal* at Bluehill ME [22 July 1847]
  James H & Judith B LEAR at Belfast ME [13 May 1852]
  John N late of Fayette ME & Melissa PECK of Clinton ME at Worthington OH [23 Nov 1839]
  John Rev, Pastor of the Congregational Church in Waldoboro ME & Ann J GODFREY at Bangor ME [30 Apr 1842]
  John W of Skowhegan ME & Mary L GILMAN at Augusta ME [16 Nov 1839]
  Marietta M of Wiscasset ME & Ebenezer TRASK Capt of Edgecomb ME on 2nd inst at Wiscasset ME [15 Apr 1843]
  Mary A ae 13 & William COLBY ae 17 at Liberty ME [7 Aug 1835]
  Mary of New Boston NH & Alonzo BUTLER of Augusta ME at Windsor VT [30 Sept 1847]
  Mary & Mark H CROOKER of Bristol ME on Thurs morn last at Hallowell ME [5 Sept 1834]
  Reuben G W & Betsey J CHEEVER at Bluehill ME [23 Sept 1847]
  Rulof & Sarah E BAILEY at Portland ME [2 May 1837]
  William W of New Boston NH? & Martha Ann SMITH of Cornville ME at Windsor VT [30 Sept 1847]
DOE Adaline P & Samuel K WORTH by Jon MOWER Esq at Vassalboro ME [26 July 1849]
  Augusta Ann & Thomas BESSEE of Harrison ME by Rev S W MORSE at Augusta ME [24 Dec 1846]

DOE (cont.) Caroline & Charles W BUTTERFIELD at Milford ME [1 Feb 1844]
    Emeline E of Hebron ME & John C HUTCHINSON of Buckfield ME at Paris ME [11 Feb 1847]
    Emma J & Martin C ROGERS at Belfast ME [11 July 1844]
    George W & Elizabeth PERKINS by Rev Mr Allen at (Augusta) ME on 25 Oct [9 Nov 1848]
    Harris & Fancina NEAL at China ME [30 May 1844]
    Harrison of Windsor ME & Ann Maria JACKSON at China ME [15 Apr 1847]
    Harrison & Lydia Ann HARRIMAN d/o Rev Jesse HARRIMAN all of Windsor at Windsor ME? [4 July 1837]
    Ira W & Dorothy A DYER at Saco ME [15 May 1845]
    Mary & John H COWEN at Clinton ME [7 Nov 1840]
    Nancy J of Limerick ME & Zacheus WILSON of Parsonsfield ME at East Parsonsfield ME [13 Mar 1851]
    Sarah & John FREEMAN at Vassalboro ME [24 June 1833]
    Sophia M & Geo C SIMMONS at Fairfield ME [8 Mar 1849]
    Stephen of Windsor ME & Julia BRIARD at Jefferson ME [15 July 1847]

DOLBIER Mary C & Charles R K PORTER of New Portland ME on 4 July by E F PILLSBURY Esq at Kingfield ME [22 July 1846] DOLE
    Caroline P & Albert NOYES at Bangor ME [25 Apr 1840] & [5 Dec 1840]
    Daniel D Rev of Bloomfield (Skowhegan) ME & Emily H BALLARD at Gardiner ME [10 Oct 1840]
    Moses & Catharine M CHENERY at Westbrook ME [24 June 1836]
    Nancy G & John H TITCOMB at Hallowell ME [5 Sept 1840]
    Nathaniel P of Alna ME & Elizabeth H CARLTON at Vassalboro ME [27 Mar 1841]

DOLIFF Dolley of Belmont ME & Amos BOWMEN of Burnham ME at Burnham [8 July 1836]

DOLLEY Laura Jane F & Loammi B THOMPSON of Jay ME at Weld ME [21 Oct 1847]

DOLLOFF Emma & Samuel TORN both of Paris ME at Paris ME [17 Aug 1839]
    John Jr & Ann DAVIS d/o Samuel DAVIS Esq both of Mt Vernon ME by Daniel CRAIG Esq at Readfield ME [7 Dec 1848]

DONLEY Sophronia O of Sumner ME & Samuel THOMAS of Buckfield ME [9 Apr 1842]

DONNELL Abigail D & Capt Eben COLBOURN at Bath ME [4 Jul 1840]
    Asa S of Waterville ME & Eliza A HATCH of Litchfield ME at Augusta ME on 17 Nov by Rev J STEVENS [20 Nov 1851]
    Benjamin W of Alna ME & Julia A F CONE of Columbus NH at Skowhegan ME [8 Mar 1849]
    Benjamin & Mary E EDES at Bath ME [13 May 1836]
    Elice & William LINCH by Rev GILMAN at Bath ME [2 Jan 1841]
    Frances J & B Franklin FIELD at Gardiner ME [25 Apr 1850]
    John & Mary MARRIOTT at Bath ME [30 Jan 1845]
    Joseph T of Gardiner ME & Lydia A BROOKS at York ME [14 Aug 1845]
    Jotham MD of Houlton ME & Maria E MITCHELL at Bangor ME [31 Aug 1848]
    Kingsbury & Mary HARRIS at Webster ME on 15 Oct by Jesse DAVIS Esq [23 Oct 1851]

DINSMORE (cont.) Mary J of Harpswell ME & Moses L BARSTOW of Brunswick ME at Durham ME [23 Apr 1846]
  Oliver of Buxton ME & Nancy MOSHER of Temple ME at Readfield ME [18 Feb 1847]
  Philena & Wm BOOBIER at Bath ME [14 Feb 1850]
  Rachael & Noah M GOULD of Lincolnville ME at Searsmont ME [4 Feb 1833] & [18 Feb 1833]
  Rachel T & Ephraim H RUSSEL Capt by Rev STEARNS at Bath ME [4 Feb 1833]
  William M of Beverly MA & Mary M HODGDON at Bath ME [21 Aug 1842]
  William S & Sarah Jane BAILEY at Bath ME [5 Dec 1844]
DOOLITTLE Ira R & Betsey M HILTON of Starks ME on 20 Mar by Rev Calvin GARDNER at Waterville ME [19 Apr 1849]
DORMAN Eunice & Peter FOLSOM by Dudley FOGG Esq at Mt Vernon ME [3 Apr 1838]
  Mariette d/o Hon Orrin DORMAN of Lower Canada, & Dr David G ROBINSON, M.D., of Monmouth ME on 22 Dec at North Troy VT [7 Jan 1843]
DOROTHY Isaac C & Ruth PARKER at Skowhegan ME [21 Mar 1850]
DOORE Lois & Bradbury TEWSBURY at Atkinson ME [11 May 1848]
DORR Almira L & Henry L BROCKWAY at Dover ME? [15 May 1851]
  Edmund & Harriet M PISH at Lincoln ME [1 Apr 1847]
  Martha & E F PIERCE both of Skowhegan ME at Bloomfield ME [28 Mar 1837]
  Mary E & William A TREAT at Brewer ME [25 Dec 1851]
  Sarah Mrs & Wm REMICK of Elliot ME at North Berwick ME [19 Mar 1846]
  Sarah & M B RICH of Bucksport ME at Frankfort ME [28 Mar 1837]
  William S & Mary S LOWELL both of Bucksport ME at Frankfort ME [28 Jan 1847]
DOTEN Melvina of Knox ME & Thomas PEARSONS of Belmont ME at Waldo ME [12 Nov 1846]
  Sullivan of Freedom ME & Mrs Judith BRYANT at Palermo ME [10 May 1849]
DOUGHTY David of Cumberland ME & Almira WALLACE at Phipsburg ME [15 Jan 1836] Julia Ann ae 15 & Master Rufus SMITH ae 14 at Brunswick ME [7 Nov 1837]
  Loring & Lavina B BLACK at Harpswell ME [21 Dec 1848]
  Robert & Eliza K BUTLER Mrs at Hallowell ME [18 Dec 1851]
  William H & Rachel GRAFFAM both of Fairfield ME at Waterville ME [15 June 1848]
DOUGLASS - DOUGHLASS, DOUGLAS
  Abner & Elmira DOUGLASS at Gardiner ME [13 Nov 1851]
  Alfred & Frances E NASH both of West Gardiner ME at Hallowell ME [27 Feb 1845]
  Charles & Harriet A NEAL at Hallowell ME [28 Dec 1848]
  Eleazer C & Maria J SPEAR at Gardiner ME [2 Jan 1851]
  Elmira & Abner DOUGLASS at Gardiner ME [13 Nov 1851]
  Hannah & John ROLLINS of Union ME at Augusta ME [29 Oct 1846]
  Harriet J & John C GARET at Dover ME? [22 Jan 1852]
  Joanna S & John E ROLFE by Nathan ABBOT Esq at Rumford ME [11 May 1839]

DOUGLASS (cont.) John W & Mary E CHASE at Hallowell ME [12 Oct 1848]
   John & Rhoana R NICKERSON at Topsham ME [17 June 1836]
   John & Sarah JONES at St Albans ME [5 Nov 1846]
   Mary A P & Henry ARTHUR at Hallowell ME [15 Feb 1849]
   Mary R Mrs & Thomas LUCE of Hampden ME at Belfast ME [25 July 1844]
   Mary & Eli D BASSET at Gardiner ME [19 Aug 1847]
   Olive & Charles A FISHER at Whitefield ME [1 Jan 1852]
   Rhoda C & John TARR at Brunswick ME [27 Feb 1845]
   Sarah B & Moses TUSHNOE at Hallowell ME [1 Jan 1846]
   Susan J of Dorcester MA & Robert PATTERSON at Hope ME [17 Oct 1837]
   Susan Mrs of Boston MA & Isaac LANE of Hollis ME Thurs morn last by Rev Dr SHARP at Boston MA [21 Jan 1833]
DOW Aaron Dr of Kingsbury & Liberty S d/o the late Abraham MOORE Esq of Abbot ME at Abbot [17 July 1845]
   Abigail S Mrs & Robert MORRISON at Sebec ME [13 Jan 1848]
   Absalom S & Loranah S DREW at New Limerick ME [6 May 1852]
   Catharine & Ebenezer MUSEY by Rev MATHER at Wiscasset ME [8 Oct 1842]
   Charles R & Lucy E SKILLIN by Rev ALLEN at North Yarmouth ME on 20 Mar [15 Apr 1852]
   Daniel & Mary R MERITHEW at Belmont ME [13 Mar 1845]
   David & Sarah A EDGECOMB at Bath ME [5 Feb 1846]
   Edwin & Adeline S ATTWOOD of New Gloucester ME at Poland ME [16 May 1844]
   G S C of the firm of Dow and Lyon, & Elizabeth C d/o Samuel SYLVESTER Esq all of Bangor ME Thurs eve 7th inst by Rev POMROY at Bangor [16 Dec 1843]
   George F & Mary F STAPLES at Biddeford ME [12 Apr 1849]
   Hannah & Alexander ERSKINE at Whitefield ME [3 July 1835]
   Helen S & Amasa TRACY at Thompson CT [2 Mar 1848]
   John of Lyman & Abba YOUNG of Hollis ME at Biddeford ME [4 Mar 1852]
   Josiah F of Lynn MA & Sarah J BARKER of Cornish ME at Cornish [15 Oct 1846]
   Martha Ann & David HORN at Athens ME [27 Jan 1848]
   Mary Jane & Ephraim F WELLMAN both of Strong ME at Farmington ME [5 Mar 1846]
   Moses G of Norway ME & Ellen M LOWELL at Portland ME [20 June 1844]
   Thirsa L & Josiah F PRESCOTT 3rd inst at Phillips ME [13 Feb 1838]
   Thomas Capt & Sally ROLLINS at Pittston ME [16 Nov 1833]
   Walter & Frances Ann MACONIC at Alna ME [3 Jul 1851]
   William H of Waterville ME & Delia WILLIAMS at Bath ME [20 June 1834]
   William N of China ME & Sarah WELLMAN by Samuel PATTERSON Esq at Strong ME [18 Mar 1833]
   William of Boston MA & Sophia A SMITH at Waterville ME [29 June 1848]
DOWLING Martin & Mary O CONNER 3rd inst at Augusta ME [14 Oct 1847]
DOWNE Mary Ann E & John G SOMES both of Bangor ME at Dutton ME [13 Mar 1835]

DOWNES James & Phebe Y BROWN at Swanville ME on 13 Feb by M H HOMLES Esq [27 Feb 1851]
    Lorinda & John H MERRILL at Levant ME [28 Oct 1847]
    Samuel W of Orland ME & Irene HANCOCK of Boston at Boston [27 Nov 1835]
DOWNING Amos of Winthrop ME & Lucy W ORCUTT 14th inst by Rev BRAGDON at Brunswick ME [26 June 1838]
    Hannah & Daniel DAKIN at Kirkland ME [13 Jan 1848]
    James R & Diana LITTLEFIELD both of Cambridge ME at Harmony ME [15 Jan 1846]
DOWNS Albert J & Abigail HEYWOOD both of Mercer ME on 1 Oct at Mercer [4 Dec 1845]
    Joseph & Ann E WIGGIN at Albion ME [17 Sept 1846]
    Lewis W & Mary E WHEELDEN at Orrington ME [11 Nov 1847]
    Margaret Ann of Swanville ME & Thos BOARDMAN of Frankfort ME at Prospect ME [16 Apr 1842]
    Mary Jane & Randall B CLARK at Eastport ME [20 May 1847]
    William of Orono ME & Semantha G LAMBERT at Dover ME? [17 Jan 1850]
DOWSE Mary L & Joseph A MAYNARD of Waterville ME at Winslow ME [28 Aug 1845]
DOYAL Hugh of Trescott & Irene HUCKINS at Lubec ME [21 Jan 1847]
DOYEA John & Elizabeth FONTJAMI at Bath ME [16 Jan 1841]
DOYLE Eliza J & Thaddeus S SAUNDERS at Orland ME [21 Sept 1848]
    Elizabeth A & Michael HOULEHAN at Augusta ME on 23d inst (23 Aug) by Rev Mr O'REILLY [28 Aug 1851]
    Isaac & Diana T DWIGHT at Bangor ME [1 Aug 1844]
    Patric & Sally YOUNG after a courtship of 25 years at Newcastle ME [11 Jan 1844]
DRAKE Adeline W & Phineas H SAWYER at Elliotsville ME [3 Apr 1851]
    Dianna & John E SAWYER at Elliotsville [26 June 1835]
    Harriet M & Rufus H GRAY at Milo ME on 9 Nov [16 Nov 1848]
    John of China & Jennette G CURTIS of Richmond ME on 13 Jan by Pardon TINKHAM Esq at Albion [17 Jan 1850]
    Lydia M Mrs & Francis A TUCKER at Guilford ME [3 June 1852]
    Martha & Asa SYLVESTER of Plymouth ME at Albion ME [1 Mar 1849]
    Mary & Lucius L GILBERT at Parkman ME [11 Feb 1847]
    Relief & Capt William GRAY at Thomaston ME [12 Sept 1840]
    Velina V & Francis B HOWARD of Brownfield ME at Milo ME on 7 Mar by James H MACOMBER Esq [20 Mar 1851]
DRESSER Elijah A & Nancy DYER at Turner ME [15 Apr 1847]
    Elijah H & Nancy FRENCH by Job PRINCE Esq at Turner ME [29 Apr 1847]
    Lucius of Turner ME & Maria L BRIDGHAM at West Minot ME [7 Sept 1839]
    Martha K & Capt Cyrus K WOOD at Turner ME [9 Mar 1848]
    Matilda Ann & Samuel D GAREY at Saco ME [21 May 1846]
    Richard of Pownal ME & Mary A HAMMOND at New Gloucester ME [29 Apr 1847]
DREW Alvin P Capt & Mary M SHAW at Bath ME [8 Jan 1846]
    Charles C & Mercyette YOUNG of Winthrop ME at Lowell on 28 Dec [16 Jan 1851]

DREW (cont.) E Augusta & Charles A BATES by Rev PEET all of Norridgwock ME at Norridgwock ME [28 May 1846]
Esther & Aaron B FOX at Athens ME [27 Jan 1848]
George E of San Francisco CA & Harriet T HASKELL of Topsham ME at California [19 Aug 1852]
Gordon G of Boston MA & Rhoda DAVIS of Bowdoin ME at Boston MA [23 Oct 1841]
Harriet of Readfield ME & Stephen REED of Woolwich ME 29 Nov by Rev F MERRIAM of Winthrop at East Readfield ME [3 Dec 1842]
Harriet & Samuel B BRAYTON of Cranston RI at Newfield [23 Apr 1846]
Henry P of Brunswick ME & Harriet HALL of Portland ME at Portland [21 Nov 1837]
Loranah S & Absalom S DOW at New Limerick ME [6 May 1852]
Theresa M, eldest d/o Rev W A DREW, & Enoch SAMPSON Esq merchant of Bowdoinham ME on Sun last at Universalist Church by Rev W A DREW at Augusta ME [13 June 1844]
Thomas L of Glenburn ME & Harriet N EVERETT of New Portland ME at New Portland [14 May 1846]

DRINKWATER Alice J & Charles H PAINE foreman of the *Gazette* office 12 Aug by Rev W O THOMAS at Rockland ME [26 Aug 1852]
Angeline & Charles RICHARDS at Northport ME [28 Jan 1847]
Arthur F Esq of Bluehill ME & Susan B BARSTOW adopted d/o Isaac BACKUS Esq at Canterbury CT [23 Sept 1847]
Caroline P & James M BUCKNAM at North Yarmouth ME [2 Dec 1843]
Joseph S & Mary E ALEXANDER at Topsham ME [6 May 1843]
Thomas E Capt of Belfast ME & Sarah P WHITE at Biddeford ME [15 Jan 1846]

DROUGHT Sarah of Jay ME & Joseph OAKMAN Capt of Hallowell ME by Aaron HOLMES Esq at Jay [5 Nov 1842]

DRUMMOND Harriet T & Josiah C HUTCHINSON on 4 Jan by A COLE Esq at Winslow ME [22 Mar 1849]
James Rev of Lewiston Falls ME & Esther A SWEET of Dedham MA at Dedham [2 July 1842]
James & Rebecca MORSE at Phipsburg ME [26 Aug 1836]
Maria L of Bangor ME & Albert G PAGE at Bath ME [20 Mar 1845]
William & Mary G STOCKBRIDGE at Bath ME [9 Nov 1848]

DRURY Drusilla & Isaac S TOWNSEND of Wilton ME at Jay ME [11 Feb 1843]

DUDLEY A S Rev & Lydia F MANLEY at Norridgewock ME [7 Dec 1839]
Belinda & Sylvanus J BLANCHARD at West Winthrop ME [23 June 1852]
Caroline & Samuel CROCKER at Pittston ME [1 July 1847]
Charles & Hannah YOUNG both of Readfield ME at Livermore Falls ME [19 Dec 1844]
David of Aroostook No 11 ME & Ellen M MEIGS at China ME [23 Sept 1847]
Eben F & Louisa A STOWE both of Augusta ME at Hallowell ME [25 Dec 1851]
George F of Milford & Rebecca DAILEY by Hon C HOLLAND at Canton ME [10 Jan 1850]
Henry of Mt Vernon ME & Mary Whittier by Josiah WHITTIER Esq at Readfield ME [18 July 1834]

DUDLEY (cont.) James H Esq of Boston MA & Mrs Elizabeth C HOLT of Saco ME at Dover [28 Jan 1847]
Jane W of China & Erastus TOBY of Patricktown Plantation ME at China ME [11 Nov 1836]
John C m Mehitable DUDLEY at Readfield ME on May 22 by Rev MUGFORD [29 May 1851]
John H of Hallowell ME & Sophronia D BROWN of Belgrade ME by Rev MERRIAM at East Winthrop ME [15 Apr 1847]
Mary E of Augusta ME & Cornelius ADLE of Readfield ME at Hallowell ME [9 Oct 1845]
Mehitable m John C DUDLEY at Readfield ME on May 22 by Rev MUGFORD [29 May 1851]
Melissa A & Amos SMITH at Milford [5 Feb 1852]
Nancy A & James STURGIS at China ME on 7th June [29 June 1848]
Prudence & Wm MOORE of Dixmont ME at East Readfield ME [24 Aug 1839]
Sarah of Mt Vernon ME & James CLOUGH of Readfield ME on 10th inst by Dudley FOGG Esq at Mt Vernon [20 Feb 1835]
Sarah & Wm H SHAW of Edmunds (New Brunswick Canada?) at Dennysville Washington Co ME [20 Sept 1849]
Sibyl & Charles PULLEN at China ME [13 May 1836]
William K & Sarah W WHITTIER on 4th inst by Daniel CRAIG Esq at Readfield ME [11 Dec 1845]

DULON Susan E of Boston MA & Mr S O COPELAND of West Bridgewater MA at Augusta ME on 3 Mar 1851 by Rev INGRAHAM [6 Mar 1851]

DULY Palmer & Frances J WYMAN at Phipsburg ME [11 Jan 1844]

DUNBAR Jesse of Palermo ME & Ruth AMES at Jefferson ME [10 Jan 1850]
Lydia M & William R ROIX at Belfast ME [7 Jan 1847]
Mary Ann of Newport & Joseph B HOSKENS Capt of Portland ME at Newport [23 Mar 1839]
Mary J & Henry T RIVERS at Thomaston ME [11 Sept 1851]
Olive Ann & John S NEWCOMB at Warren ME [13 Mar 1841]
Otis H of Waterville ME & Mary TALBOT of Winslow ME on 22nd ult by Rev JEWETT at Winslow ME [12 Feb 1836] Vesta Jane & Ambrose S COBB at Warren ME [13 Mar 1841]

DUNCAB John 2d & Susan LIBBY of Northport at Lincolnville ME [13 May 1852]

DUNCAN Catharine T & Charles DAVENPORT at Bath ME [18 Nov 1836]
William H Capt & Abigail P MAGOUN at Bath ME [17 Oct 1844]

DUNHAM Albion K P of Paris ME & Catherine STONE at Waterford ME [1 Oct 1846]
Andrew E & Amanda M HAWES of Hallowell ME at Bath ME [26 Apr 1849]
Catharine F & Alonzo K COFFIN at No 11 Aroostook Co ME [28 Jan 1847]
Daniel J & Emily SNOW at Brunswick ME [14 Jan 1846]
Eliza L & James MERRILL at Paris ME [8 Apr 1852]
John W of Portland ME & Mary A R FULLER at East Livermore ME [5 Oct 1848]
Lucy L & Orson LEADBETTER at Leeds ME by Rev C FULLER [8 May 1851]

DUNHAM (cont.) Martha Ann & Daniel WHALEN on th 24th by Rev J T GILMAN at Bath ME [5 Feb 1842]
    Rebecca R & Arthur W GILES Capt of Gardiner ME at Brunswick ME [24 June 1843]
    Rufus & Emeline STEVENS at Westbrook ME [9 May 1837]
    Sam'l W DUNHAM & Rachel E ANDREWS of Woodstock ME at Paris ME [22 Mar 1849]
    Sibil of the Society of Friends & Joseph ESTES of Vassalboro ME at Leeds ME [9 May 1837]

DUNLAP Hannah & Capt Joseph ADAMS at Brunswick ME [19 Sept 1840]
    Loyal of Vassalboro ME & Harriet N THOMS. at Augusta ME [17 Sept 1846]
    Martha of Brunswick ME & Hiram WHITEHOUSE of Unity ME on 29th ult at Brunswick ME [8 Jan 1836]
    Nahum of Lewiston ME & Nancy F SMALL at Lisbon ME [14 Mar 1844]
    Rhoda A & Horace CLOUGH at Parsonfield ME [5 Nov 1846]
    Richard T Gen & Harriet TITCOMB d/o Rev Benj TITCOMB on 29th ult at Brunswick ME [8 Jan 1836]

DUNN Elbridge G & Sarah H MERROW at Poland ME [11 Jan 1849]
    Emily E & Wm C HINKLEY Wed eve last by Rev DWIGHT all of Portland ME at Portland [16 Oct 1838]
    George H & Lucretia CLARK by Rev NORRIS at Hallowell ME [10 June 1833]
    James Jr & Ruth H STROUT at Poland ME [4 Apr 1837]
    John Jr of Hallowell ME & Elizabeth HASKELL Mrs by Daniel T PIKE Esq at Augusta ME [10 July 1838]
    Jonah & Anna ATWOOD Mrs at Mt Vernon ME [5 Mar 1846]
    Julia A d/o John DUNN Esq, & Charles PINCIN of Gardiner ME on 28th ult at Hallowell ME [6 Feb 1841]
    Louisa A of Poland ME & Johnson SMITH of Gray at Gray ME [14 May 1846]
    Lucy Ann d/o John DUNN Esq, & Elbridge G WILSON of Gardiner ME at Hallowell ME [27 Nov 1835]
    Mary Jane of Belgrade ME & Charles Coburn PRESCOTT of Winthrop ME on 20th inst by Rev F MERRIAM of Winthrop ME at Belgrade ME [27 Feb 1845]
    S E Miss & Mr J S CURRIER at Mt Vernon ME on 6th inst [16 Mar 1848]
    Thomas W of Thomaston ME & Eliza Ann GILES at St George ME [22 Apr 1847]

DUNNELL Achsah H & George KNOX Rev Pastor of the Baptist Church in Topsham ME at Buxton ME [29 Jan 1842]

DUNNELLS John E MD of Waterborough ME & Mary E RUSSELL at Newfield ME [27 Mar 1845]

DUNNING Anna & Abiel GOODRICH Capt both of Harpswell ME by Rev William HARLOW at Harpswell ME [11 Mar 1833]
    Benjamin Capt & Martha Jane PENNELL at Brunswick ME [4 Feb 1843]
    Elijah & Harriet A DUTTON at Norway ME [21 June 1849]
    Irene & Israel B NORCROSS Capt of Bangor ME at Charleston [4 Feb 1847]
    J F of Boston & Joanna S LEMONT at Brunswick ME [29 Oct 1846]
    Jane & David S PERKINS at Brunswick ME [28 Oct 1836]
    Martha & Robert BOWKER at Brunswick ME [19 Dec 1834]

DUNNING (cont.) Mary & Joseph SESSIONS at Brunswick ME [2 Nov 1833]
Rachel & Wm BRIGGS 2nd at Auburn ME [8 Apr 1843]
DUNSMORE James A & Almira MOSHER at Temple ME [20 June 1837]
Martha of Temple ME & Charles RIPLEY of Farmington ME [20 June 1837]
DUNTON Abigail & Leonard HEATH both of Whitefield ME at Augusta ME on 1 Dec by Rev J STEVENS [4 Dec 1851]
Joshua of Athens ME & Mary Ann BARKER at Cornville ME [27 Feb 1851]
Isaac L & Eliza J BURKMAR both of Belfast ME at Montville ME [1 Feb 1849]
Israel & Catharine JONES on 21 Mar at Augusta ME [1 Apr 1847]
Silas W of Milbury MA & Olivia L GUILD of Augusta ME on 23 Aug at Thompson CT [17 Sept 1846]
DUPUY Catherine J of New York & Rufus M'LELLAN Gen of Matagorda TX 12th ult by Rev J CLAPP at New Orleans LA? [18 July 1837]
DURANT William Editor of the *Chronicle* & Elizabeth Jane HOOPER at St John New Brunswick Canada [8 Jan 1846]
DURELL Abigail of Saco ME & Rufus B KENDRICK at Saco ME [1 Jan 1846]
Henry of Boston & Nancy MIZER at Paris ME [19 Aug 1836]
DUREN Alexander R & Mary E NASON at Augusta ME [16 Nov 1839]
Charles Rev of Sangerville ME & Serena M'KEEN at Belfast ME [2 Oct 1841]
E F of Bangor ME & Mary C HYDE of Portland ME at Portland [17 June 1836]
Mathew M Jr & Ripsey Ann MILLER at Bangor ME [22 May 1845]
Sarah & Nathaniel HAINES at Augusta ME [15 Aug 1837]
DURFEE Hannah d/o Benj DURFEE, hero of the Revolution, & Sheffel WEAVER Capt, a pensioner of the Revolution at Fall River [14 Mar 1834]
DURGAN John Capt & Margaret MERRYMAN at Harpswell ME [29 May 1835]
DURGIN Charles S of Solon & Susan A GORDON Sunday 4th inst by Rev WARREN at Augusta ME [15 Feb 1844]
Ephraim & Martha A WELCH at Limerick ME [13 Jan 1848]
Jeremiah & Sarah A STURTEVANT Mrs at Limerick ME [7 Mar 1850]
Lydia A & Samuel T MAXWELL at Parsonsfield ME [27 Jan 1848]
Rebecca E & Isaac D WHITE at Parsonsfield ME [27 Jan 1848]
Selome A & Orin WALKER at Stoneham ME [27 Jul 1848]
William N & Caroline E SAUNDERS of Swanville ME at Belfast ME [1 Jan 1852]
DURRILL George W & Rosannah CLEAVELAND at Bloomfield ME [7 Oct 1843]
DUSTEN Lanee of Eastport ME & Nelson MOREY of Deer Isle ME at Eastport ME [13 Feb 1845]
DUSTIN Robert Jr & Emily WINSLOW on 17 Dec by John MARBLE Esq at Vassalboro ME [27 Dec 1849]
DUSTON James S & Olivia S THOMPSON at Bath ME [30 Sept 1847]
Jesse Capt & Isabella S THOMPSON Mrs at Bath [22 Apr 1847]
DUTTON Harriet A & Elijah DUNNING at Norway ME [21 June 1849]

DUTTON (cont.) Jesse Esq of Ellsworth ME & Elizabeth W LEACH at Hallowell ME [28 Nov 1840]
   John L & Rebecca WAIT Hallowell ME at (Augusta) ME [4 May 1848]
   Lorenzo D of Livermore ME & Eunice MORRISON at Fayette ME [21 Oct 1843]
   Lucretia C & Jonathan B PINKHAM Sunday last by J J EVELETH Esq at Augusta ME [3 Sept 1846]
   Mason W of Phillips ME & Eliza J MAYO at Freeman ME on 3 Apr 1851 by Lemuel CROSBY Esq [10 Apr 1851]
   Melvina & Isaac EASTMAN of Liberty ME on 8 July by John MARBLE Esq at Vassalboro ME [12 July 1849]
   Nathaniel C & Betsey SHAW by L CUSHING Esq at Augusta ME [11 Apr 1844]
   Robert merchant & Julia d/o John GODFREY Esq at Bangor ME [12 June 1841]
   Sarah W & Smith BAKER of Bingham ME at New Sharon ME [12 Nov 1846]
   William H of Bangor ME & Sarah E TORRY at Belfast ME [6 Jul 1848]
DWIGHT Diana T & Isaac DOYLE at Bangor ME [1 Aug 1844]
   Mary Fannie & Cyrus RICHMOND of San Francisco CA at Hallowell ME [9 Jan 1851]
DWINAL Harriet E & Augustine HEARSEY at Foxcroft ME [23 May 1844]
   Lydia & Joseph KILLGORE of Topsham ME at Lisbon ME [14 Mar 1850]
   Sarah & Daniel SMITH at Lisbon ME [12 Oct 1848]
DWINEL Horace C formerly of Farmington ME & Angeline CODDINGTON on 18 Mar by Wm CROSON Esq at Warren County OH [8 June 1839]
   Mary Ann & W S CLEVELAND of Burlington NJ 4th inst at Bangor ME [17 Sept 1842]
DYER Ann M & Thomas H LADD at Hallowell ME [28 Dec 1848]
   C W & Harriet SOULE on 27 Feb by Rev J T HAWES at New Sharon ME [8 Mar 1849]
   Caska & Ebenezer AREY at Thomaston ME [27 Apr 1848]
   Dorothy A & Ira W DOE at Saco ME Extended Notice [15 May 1845]
   Eliza B & Phineas B HAMMOND both of Sidney ME at Augusta ME [14 Oct 1843]
   Elizabeth Ann & Dudley PIKE at Saco ME [24 Sept 1846]
   Elizabeth K & Albert H HODGMAN of Camden ME at Searsmont ME [5 Mar 1846]
   Emeline & James R FOGG at Prospect ME [24 Aug 1848]
   Ezra F of Baldwin ME & Ann Maria MCKENNEY of Scarborough ME at Saco ME [30 Apr 1846]
   Frances A & G W CHASE formerly of Haverhill MA at New Sharon ME [17 Jan 1850]
   Frederick & Sarah DARRAH at Oldtown ME [30 May 1844]
   George Jr of Searsmont ME & Ruth A BOARDMAN at Belfast ME [27 Mar 1845]
   Isaac of Skowhegan ME & Lydia F EMERY at Bloomfield ME [17 Jul 1851]
   John B & Martha J MOSHER at Augusta ME on 27 Aug by Rev Z THOMPSON [4 Sept 1851]
   John DYER Capt of New York & Lucy M PECK at Belfast ME [22 June 1839]

DYER (cont.) John & Betsey B GOODRIDGE at Industry ME [8 Oct 1842]
Joseph M of Bangor & Eliza M PENNELL at Portland ME [2 May 1844]
Louisa P & William P COX of Hartford ME at Buckfield ME [20 Mar 1845]
Louisa & Alfred S BRYATHER of Searsport ME at Unity ME [8 Apr 1847]
Margaret A & Mr J Q A SARGENT at Brunswick ME [15 June 1848]
Martha S & Joseph JORDAN at New Sharon ME [25 Jul 1840]
Martha & Willard J HEMENWAY at Searsmont ME [14 May 1846]
Nancy & Elijah A DRESSER at Turner ME [15 Apr 1847]
Nathaniel & Harriet L MARTIN at Poland ME [27 Mar 1851]
Olive & Samuel TARBOX at Biddeford ME [4 Mar 1852]
Parmenas Dr & Hannah W BAKER at New Sharon ME [2 Dec 1847]
Rachel H & Joshua N BANGS at Pownal ME [27 Mar 1845]
Richard & Caroline VINING at Durham ME [2 May 1844]
Sarah D & William HEATH at Brunswick ME [26 Dec 1844]
Sarah of Portland & Thomas W NEWMAN of Brunswick ME by Rev DWIGHT at Portland ME [22 May 1838]
Selden & Mary Jane ROSS both of Sidney ME at Sidney ME [20 Feb 1845]
William H of Salem & Lucinda BEAN at Readfield ME [8 Nov 1849]

- E -

EAMES Ann Mary & Timothy B PERRY at Bath ME [21 Sept 1848]
Anna F & Daniel FLINT of Albany at Newry [18 Apr 1850]
Frank P & Abby P HOWES at Belfast ME [2 Aug 1849]
Jane of Appleton ME & Job INGRAHAM 2nd at Camden ME [15 Apr 1847]
Manley Esq of Dover & Ann Caroline DAVIS at Farmington ME [10 Oct 1840]
Mary & Daniel DAY of Nobleboro ME at Jefferson ME [18 Jan 1840]
Nancy & Edward JONES at Jefferson ME [6 Jun 1837]
Phineas & Philena N THOMPSON at Embden ME [27 Dec 1849]
EARL Benjamin & Hannah SEVERANCE at Bangor ME [16 Oct 1845]
Henry of Boston MA & Mary Ann HARRIS at Windsor ME? [28 Sept 1839]
EARLE Elizabeth & Franklin GRANT at South Berwick ME [30 Apr 1840]
George Maj of Brunswick ME & Mary Ann TIBBETS of Lisbon ME by Rev WHEELER at Topsham ME [3 Jun 1843]
Mary S of Brunswick ME & Bryce M PATTEN Esq director of the Kentucky Institute for the blind at Clifton KY [14 Aug 1851]
EASTERBROOK Arria & Charles J NOYES by Rev ADAMS at Brunswick ME [5 Aug 1836]
Sally & Daniel VINING at Calais ME [14 Mar 1837]
EASTMAN Caleb & Mary ORBITON Mrs at Fayette ME [25 Sept 1845]
Cassandana m John A MORRILL Esq at Limerick ME [29 May 1851]
David L Esq formerly of VT & Nancy C KIDDER of Skowhegan ME at St Charles ILL [26 Jun 1851]
George of Vassalboro ME & Mary E HUFF at Wilton ME [15 Jul 1852]
Harriet N & Samuel CARLTON at Camden ME [5 Aug 1847]
Hon B D & Nancy F WHITNEY at Limestone River Pt Aroostook Co ME [7 Mar 1850]

EASTMAN (cont.) Horatio of Conway NH & Rosaltha BRIDGHAM Mrs at Bridgton ME [25 Oct 1849]
    Isaac of Liberty ME & Melvina DUTTON 8 Jul by John MARBLE Esq at Vassalboro ME [12 Jul 1849]
    J R of Buxton ME & Eliza Ann QUINBY of Westbrook ME at Portland ME [7 Jun 1849]
    Lydia Mrs & John B NASON of Bethel ME at Waterford ME [2 Aug1849] & [9 Aug 1849]
    Nancy & Joseph IRISH Esq at Haverhill MA on Jun 17 by Rev Henry PLUMMER [3 Jul 1851]
    Susan D & Albion P WHITNEY at Limestone River Pt Aroostook Co ME [7 Mar 1850]
    Susan O & Henry B BREWSTER of Boston publisher of the *Independent Messenger* at Fryeburg ME [21 Aug 1835]
    Susan of Bradford ME & Jewitt SANBORN at Charleston ME [13 May 1843]
    Susan & Israel WITHAM at East Thomaston ME [23 Apr 1846]
    Violet of Vassalboro ME & Jesse T STEVENS of Cambridgeport MA at Fairfield ME [15 Jan 1846]
EASTY Aaron of East Winthrop ME & Sarah TIBBETS of Belgrade ME on Sunday 15th inst by David FULLER Esq at Readfield [21 Aug 1841]
EATON Amanda J of Bowdoinham ME & Samuel C MORSE of Freeport ME at Brunswick ME [11 Feb 1847]
    Ann L of Brunswick ME & Harrison HUBBARD of East Cambridge MA by Rev J HAWKES at Bowdoinham ME [22 Oct 1846]
    Antoinette & Edwin L SNOW at Thomaston ME [26 Jun 1838]
    Catherine & Charles E RUNDLET of Gardiner ME at Dorchester MA [15 May 1835]
    Clarissa M & Jonathan STICKNEY Esq at Perry ME [25 Feb 1843]
    Eliab L of Farmington ME & Julia W HACKETT at New Vineyard ME [6 Mar 1851]
    Elizabeth J of Hermon ME & Elisha PETTINGILL of Sangerville ME at Bangor ME [22 May 1845]
    Elizabeth & Rev Samuel BOWKER at Harpswell ME [4 May 1848]
    Humphrey M & Melissa WHITE at Dixfield ME [4 Jul 1840]
    Joanna & Jeremiah FRIEND at Sedgwick ME [29 Jul 1836]
    Joseph V of South Reading MA & Ellen Frances UPTON by Rev Mr JACQUES at Winthrop ME [29 Apr 1852]
    John 2nd & Ann PIERCE both of Brunswick ME at Brunswick ME [20 Nov 1845]
    Joshua T Esq & Christania P NORTON by Samuel EASTMAN Esq at Strong ME [18 Feb 1847]
    Louisa d/o Amherst EATON Esq & Mr S Harris AUSTIN at Boston MA on 22 Oct [6 Nov 1851]
    Marietta B & Robert W SAVAGE at Fairfield ME [8 Jan 1852]
    Mr of Wells & Susannah H CHADBORNE of Vassalboro ME at Newburyport MA [27 May 1852]
    Oscar Capt & Mary STANDISH at Warren ME [13 Mar 1841]
    Sally d/o Benj EATON Esq, & E G CROWELL merchant of Canaan ME at Canaan ME [3 Aug 1841]
    Sewall & Eliza A FOSS at Brunswick ME [29 Jan 1852]
    Sewall & Elizabeth K PORTER at Mt Vernon ME [26 Jun 1845]

EATON (cont.) Tamar of Norridgewock ME & Burnham C GREELEY at (Augusta) ME on Jun 29 by S WILLIAMSON Eld [10 Jul 1851]

EDDARD - see ELDRED

EDDY Temperance B & Noah BARKER Esq of Exeter ME at Corinth ME [18 Jan 1840]
    W R of Skowhegan ME & Lydia M WALKER at Madison ME [30 Apr 1846]
    William H of Boston ME & Caroline N WILLIS of Strong ME at Strong [18 Dec 1845]

EDES Almira & Reuben BARTOL at Portland ME [15 Feb 1844]
    Dorcas W & John W KELEY at Dover ME [8 Apr 1852]
    Mary E & Benjamin DONNELL at Bath ME [13 May 1836]
    Sarah of Portland ME & Simon B PRESCOTT of Winthrop ME 24th ult by Rev KENT at Freeport ME [1 Jan 1836]

EDGAR David & Elizabeth HURLBERT at Eastport ME [25 Sept 1851]

EDGECOMB Abigail S & Geo W WADLEIGH at Parsonfield ME [7 Oct 1847]
    Abigail & William J FULLERTON of Woolwich ME at Bath ME [7 Jan 1847]
    Arthur & Sarah Ann MOSELY of Bowdoin ME at Topsham ME [11 Jan 1844]
    Benjamin Jr of Livermore ME & Rosalinda L FOSS of East Livermore ME by Walter FOSS at Leeds ME [27 Jan 1848]
    Catharine & George VAUGHN at Bath ME [24 Jul 1845]
    Elbridge G MD & Julia F HOWARD both of Turner ME at Livermore ME [21 Jun 1849]
    Eleazer & Caroline BRACKETT of Belfast ME at Belmont ME [18 May 1848]
    Loring of Poland ME & Lucy E ROBBINS at Buckfield ME [22 Feb 1844]
    Mary Mrs & George BLOOD Capt 8th inst at Gardiner ME [25 Jan 1849]
    Mary & Benjamin A SAWTELLE of Limerick ME at Limington ME [4 Sept 1851]
    Olive Mrs & Clement MESERVEY of Hallowell ME 19th inst at Webster ME [29 Jan 1846]
    Oscar B & Mary Elizabeth BROWN at Gardiner ME [26 Aug 1852]
    Rachel & Eliphalet PRAY at Gardiner ME [21 Mar 1844]
    Robert & Mary Ann BAILEY both of Litchfield ME by Elder Wm O GRANT at Litchfield ME [21 Mar 1840]
    Sarah A & David DOW at Bath ME [5 Feb 1846]
    William of Hollis ME & Elizabeth R USHER of Limerick ME at Limington ME [21 Sept 1848]

EDGERLY Daniel Esq & Sarah M d/o Dr Joshua DAVIS of Sidney ME at Mobile AL [18 Jul 1844]

EDGERLEY Horace & Urana B SWAN at Paris ME [10 May 1849]
    Loring G of Sangerville ME & Sarah E SPRAGUE at Dexter ME [10 May 1849]

EDMUNDS Charles C merchant of Belfast ME & Marianna NEWELL of Winslow ME by Rev G GARDINER at Waterville [15 Feb 1840]
    Philip D of Lowell & Susan Harriet WILLIS at Framingham MA [13 Jun 1840]
    Thomas S of Lowell & Harriet Susan WILLIS at Framingham MA [13 Jun 1840]

EDWARD William & Eliza B LENNELL 5th inst by Sam'l FESSENDEN Esq at the Portland Jail [27 May 1843]

EDWARDS Clark S & Maria A MASON at Bethel ME [3 Jan 1850]
  Eliza J of Otisfield ME & Eleazer D MARSHALL at Paris ME [8 Nov 1849]
  Elizabeth of Belfast ME & George KNIGHTS Capt of Northport ME at Belfast ME [15 Apr 1836]
  Harriet S & Andrew L ALLEN at Belfast ME [6 Jul 1848]
  Mary Jane & John BOGAN at Belfast ME [13 May 1852]
  Mary S & Augustin L BATCHELDER of Litchfield ME at Gardiner ME [21 May 1846]
  Newton Esq of Boston MA & Mary Sawtelle WILLIAMS d/o Hon Daniel WILLIAMS of this town (Augusta) by Rev Mr BURGESS at St Mark's Church (Augusta) on 30th Aug [14 Sept 1848]
  Oliver S & Ellen MARSTON at Gardiner [24 Jun 1847]
  Rev Jonathan of Andover MA & Frances Swan BRONSON d/o Hon David BRONSON of (Augusta) by Rev Dr TAPPAN at (Augusta) on 31st Aug [14 Sept 1848]

EELLS Dr N A & Celia MATHEWS at Lincoln ME [20 Mar 1851]
  Israel & Rhoda A JORDAN Mrs at Freeport ME [4 Apr 1850]
  Lorenzo & Dorothy L RICE at Guilford ME [29 Apr 1852]

EGAN Charlotte S Mrs & Warren WILLIAMSON Col of Gardiner ME at Pittston ME [24 Dec 1846]
  John & Hannah KEEFE at Augusta ME [15 Jul 1852]

ELA Jacob Jr of Starks ME & Susannah R GILMAN at Hallowell ME [12 Jul 1849]
  Rachel D & Asa WAUGH at Starks ME [22 Nov 1849]
  Richard of Washington City & Lucia KING at Saco ME [15 Aug 1844]

ELAY Robert D & Harriet R GREENLEAF at Abbot ME [14 Oct 1847]

ELDEN Edward T of Waterville ME & Mary E TOBEY at Fairfield ME [22 Nov 1849]
  Jones R & Caroline R FAIRFIELD on 1 Jan by Rev SHELDON at Waterville ME [9 Jan 1845]
  Perley G & Eliza D LARRABEE at Bradford ME [12 Feb 1842]

ELDER Alvah of New Portland ME & Caroline A GALE on 7th inst by Rev JUDD at Augusta ME [17 May 1849]
  Catherine G of New Portland ME & Warren HILL at New Portland ME [25 Dec 1841]
  Charles L & Roxana CUMMINGS both of Lewiston ME at Norway ME [27 Dec 1849]
  Frances M & L D WILKINSON Esq at Saco ME [12 Apr 1849]
  George M & Harriet C BELL at Portland ME [2 Jan 1845]
  Isaiah & L K FULLER Mrs of Portland ME at Guilford ME [12 Jul 1849]
  John Esq of Portland ME & S Mary BROWN of Bath ME at Bath [23 Oct 1845]
  Lois G of Albion ME & Sullivan B PRIEST of Vassalboro ME at China ME [30 Apr 1846]
  Mary Ann & Leonard MOORES Jr both of Gardiner ME 12 Sept at Augusta ME [16 Sept 1847]
  Mary O of Portland ME & C COVEL of Bath at Portland ME [11 Dec 1841]
  Morrell of Gray ME & Susan VARNEY at Windham ME [18 Jun 1846]
  Peter P of New Portland ME & Catherine FELKER at Concord ME [19 Jun 1845]
  William & Laura A PEABODY Sun eve last by Rev E ROBINSON at Winthrop ME [25 Jul 1844]

Marriage Notices from the "Maine Farmer"   125

ELDRED Susan & Benjamin S JONES by H STEVENS Esq at Pittston ME (N.B. this newspaper reported "EDDARD", but the *Vital Records of Pittston ME*, printed in 1911 by the MHS, p218, states: Susan "ELDRED" m 16 Sept 1835 Benjamin JONES) [2 Oct 1835]

ELDRIDGE Caroline W of Brewer ME & John H DOANE at East Orrington ME [15 Jul 1847]
  Daniel L & Mary EMERY Mrs at Biddeford ME [25 Dec 1845]
  James Capt of Bucksport ME & Jane BROWN at Orland ME [4 Feb 1833]
  Lucy A & George F PIERCE Capt at Orrington ME [11 Nov 1847]
  Rebecca & Michael KEATON at Belfast ME [10 Jul 1838]
  Sarah E & Hiram BUZZELL both of Skowhegan ME at Bloomfield ME [24 May 1849]

ELLERY William Capt & Lucy PARKHURST at Dixmont ME [30 Apr 1846]

ELLINGWOOD Edward of Frankfort ME & Mary MORRISON at Monroe ME [27 Nov 1851]
  John & Comfort MORRILL at Frankfort ME [26 Oct 1839]
  Joseph & Byance HARTFORD both of Swanville ME at Belfast ME [5 Mar 1846]
  Lydia & George WHITE at Frankfort ME [22 Jun 1848]
  Sarah & Mr M S STAPLES at Frankfort ME [22 Jun 1848]
  William Col of Frankfort ME & Sophia Ann BRADMAN at Belfast ME [23 Nov 1839]

ELLIOT/ELLIOTT Benjamin of New Portland & Martha STEWART/STEWARD at New Vineyard [16 Oct 1845] & [26 Jun 1845] [*sic*]
  Betsey M & Wm M MORSE Capt both of Raymond ME at Rumford ME [12 Nov 1842]
  Drussillia of Mercer ME & Nathaniel LADD at Abbot ME [19 Sept 1844]
  Harriet S & Parker M REED at Phipsburg ME [14 May 1846]
  Hazen B & Eunice B GARY by Solomon HEALD Esq at Lovell ME on 16th inst [26 Oct 1848]
  Hiram F Esq & Clara S HOCKEY at Freedom ME [6 Nov 1845]
  Isaac S & Nancy T AREY at Belfast ME [12 Aug 1852]
  James of Corinna ME & M McINTIRE at Bloomfield ME [27 May 1847]
  James of Kilmarnock ME & Emily A KNIGHT at Sebec ME [31 Jul 1851]
  John E & Delphina P TOWLE at Levant ME [24 May 1849]
  Louisa J & D Blin FULLER at Portsmouth NH at the Rockingham House [25 Mar 1852]
  Lydia H & William ROGERS at Bath ME [2 Jul 1846]
  Margaret & Ammi M WHITE of Springfield MA at Bath ME [5 Nov 1846]
  Mary A of Levant ME & Mr A HANSON of Bangor ME at Augusta ME [2 Jan 1851]
  Mary B & Hiram CAMPBELL at Bath ME [9 Apr 1846]
  Mary & Charles DICKSON of Clinton ME at Canaan ME [17 Jul 1851]
  Mrs Almira & John STEWARD at New Portland ME [17 Feb 1848]
  Nancy Mrs & Charles CLEAVES of Abbot at Kilmarnock ME [25 Sept 1851]
  Nancy & Daniel HAINES at Hallowell ME [27 Jul 1848]
  S W Dr of Dover ME & Susan E PAUL of Hallowell ME at Gardiner ME [4 Dec 1841]

ELLIS Albert T & Mary CROSS at Belfast ME [16 Sept 1843]
  Catharine & Henry P PENCE 16 Oct at Lubec ME [6 Nov 1845]

ELLIS (cont.) Charles B of Winslow ME & Melvina S HUTCHINSON by Rev S F WETHERBEE at Corinna ME on 2d inst [30 Mar 1848]
Diantha L of Lowell MA & Simeon COBURN of Monmouth ME at Mon [24 Jun 1847]
E A & Mr W M LADD at Sidney ME [21 Sept 1848]
E H of Waldo ME & Sarah A WALKER of Belfast ME by Rev D FORBES at Waldo [25 Jun 1842]
Edwin Dr & Sophia S DAVIS at Farmington ME [9 Dec 1847]
Elizabeth & Walter GIFFORD at Sidney ME [23 Apr 1846]
Frederick & Serene N CHUTE late of Cumberland ME both of Carthage ME by Elder MAYO at Carthage [30 Dec 1843]
Hadassah C of Wilton ME & John KELSEY Capt of Canton ME at Jay ME [25 Jun 1846]
Harriet & Franklin A HEWINS Mon eve last at Augusta ME [18 Apr 1844]
Hollis & Ruth C FLETCHER at South Prospect ME [23 Sept 1847]
James F & Flavilla KINCAID both of Oldtown ME at Passadumkeag ME [5 Jul 1849]
John of Smithfield ME & Louisa F WORKS at Mercer ME [19 Aug 1843]
Joshua Jr of Fairfield ME & Mary Ann HAMILTON at Waterville ME [1 Jul 1843]
Julia A & Frances DAVIS Esq Thanksgiving evening at Augusta ME [9 Dec 1836]
Lavina C of Waldo ME & Oliver CHASE of Monroe ME at Belfast ME [13 Jun 1844]
M L & Henry E BAILEY at Farmington ME [2 Nov 1848]
Manley of Prospect ME & Louisa CLARY at Brooks ME [19 Jun 1835]
Maria D & Jos E JOY of Portsmouth NH at Fairfield ME [3 May 1849]
Nehemiah of Augusta ME & Almira LOVEJOY of Sidney ME at Sidney [31 Oct 1834]
Reuben N & Eliza STOVER at Bluehill ME [16 Apr 1842]
Seth N Capt of Harwich MA & Ann B MATHEWS of Prospect ME at Belfast ME [19 Sept 1844]
Stephen Jr Capt & Nancy TREAT at Prospect ME [20 Apr 1848]
Thomas B Jr of Saco ME & Hester Ann EMERY of Biddeford ME at Saco ME [27 Aug 1846]
Thomas & Rosanna McCONNELL at Calais ME [30 Apr 1846]
Timothy R & Sarah H TOWNSEND at Sidney ME [10 Apr 1841]
William 2nd of Waterville ME & Martha T BROWN at Clinton ME [21 Dec 1839]
William B & Mary Ann ROBINSON both of Sidney ME at Waterville ME [6 Dec 1849]
ELLISON William & Sidney F MURPHY all of Calais ME on the 25th at Calais ME [10 Jun 1843]
ELLNER Orrilla J & John KEEN Jr at Leeds ME [13 Mar 1851]
ELLSWORTH Sarah & Obed W RUSSELL of Phillips ME at Avon ME [17 May 1849]
ELMES Carlton D & Mary FREEMAN at Hallowell ME [21 Oct 1843]
Carlton D & Mary PEASLEY at Hallowell ME [21 May 1846]
Charles D of Taunton MA & Sarah E DANFORTH of Winthrop ME on Sun eve last by Rev Giles BAILEY at Winthrop ME [20 Nov 1841]
ELWELL/ELLWELL Benjamin of Westbrook ME & Lavina ALLEN of Gray ME at Windham ME [10 Aug 1848]

ELWELL (cont.) Betsey & Ezra HALL Capt at Belfast ME [4 Dec 1851]
   Betsey & Marquis PARKER at Buxton ME [4 Sept 1851]
   Dolly P & Henry G POTE Capt at Northport ME [11 Feb 1847]
   James W of New York & Olive P ROBINSON at Bath ME [25 Jul 1844]
   Melvin C & Eliza J MOODY at Gardiner ME [3 Jul 1851]
   William of Skowhegan ME & Sarah G GEORGE of Athens ME at Athens [6 Jun 1840]
ELY Sarah S & Justus L PASCO of Lowell at Wilbraham MA [5 Feb 1846]
EMERSON Sabrina D of Hallowell ME & George H GETCHELL at Augusta ME on 31st Aug by Asaph R NICHOLS Esq [4 Sept 1851]
EMERSON Charles K & Charlotte A EMERSON at Hallowell ME [15 Jan 1846]
   Charlotte A & Charles K EMERSON same as above
   Daniel W of Palmyra ME & Mary A HUSSEY of Sanford ME at Portsmouth NH [5 Aug 1852]
   Josiah H & Philena L CUNNINGHAM at Belfast ME [19 Sept 1844]
   Isaac C & Sarah ROBINSON at Hallowell ME [18 Jun 1846]
   Luther D & Dulcina M CRANE by Rev DRINKWATER at Fayette ME [12 Aug 1852]
   Mary & George W PRESSEY at Waterville ME [4 Apr 1844]
   Mary C & Abraham PETTINGILL Col at Hampden ME [2 Apr 1846]
   Nathan Dr of Oakland ME & E Augusta ROBINSON at Portland ME [14 Oct 1847]
   Orrin & Louisa THING Sun last by Rev Calvin GARDNER of Waterville ME at Hallowell ME [8 May 1838]
   Rachael & Robert BLAKE of Salem at Fayette ME [4 Apr 1850]
   Sarah Elizabeth & S C HOLMAN of Boston MA 11 Mar by Rev JUDD at Augusta ME [22 Mar 1849]
   Sarah T & Samuel FOOTE both of Bath ME at Lisbon ME [9 Sept 1836]
   Walter Capt & M A SNOW at Bucksport ME [11 Oct 1849]
EMERY Adeline & Geo MORANG at Eastport ME [8 Nov 1849]
   Almira & George ROBINSON at Augusta ME [28 Sept 1833]
   Asa of Bloomfield ME & Miriam M PERKINS of South Paris ME at Skowhegan ME [19 Dec 1844]
   Barker Capt & Elizabeth MILLER 12th inst by Rev TAPPAN at Hampden ME [29 Apr 1843]
   Bosette M of Poland ME & Daniel M WIGHT of Letter B ME on 17th ult by John J BRAGG Esq at Letter B ME [29 Jul 1843]
   Calvin & Rebecca GRANT both of South Berwick ME at Dover ME/NH? [10 Jul 1851]
   Charles C of Waterville ME & Hannah G CLARK at Sangerville ME [25 May 1848]
   Diana ae 16 & Robert TRIPP ae 18 at Harmony ME [8 Feb 1844]
   Edwin T & Susan M PERRY at Thomaston ME [4 Mar 1847]
   Eleanor & Eleazer COBURN at Bloomfield ME [1 May 1845]
   Gilmore & Elizabeth A CHALLIES at Newfield ME [25 Mar 1847]
   Harriet C & William A ABBOT Capt of Ellsworth ME on 24 Sept by Rev STONE at Biddeford [9 Oct 1845]
   Harriet & Josiah B FIELD at Bloomfield ME [29 Jul 1847]
   Hester Ann of Biddeford ME & Thomas B ELLIS Jr of Saco ME at Saco [27 Aug 1846]
   Hiram & Harriet G GODFREY at Orono ME [29 Feb 1844]

EMERY (cont.) Horace & Elizabeth B WILLIAMS both of Athens ME at Skowhegan ME [29 Jun 1848]
    J W printer & Arabella B CLOSE at Bangor ME [8 Jul 1847]
    James & Nancy HALL at Augusta ME [28 Dec 1839]
    Jeannett L & Nathaniel BUTLER Rev of Turner ME at Paris ME [28 Feb 1850]
    Joshua T of Portland ME & Sarah MOORE of Standish ME at Standish [30 Sept 1847]
    Keziah & Capt Isaac M BOARDMAN at Belfast ME [20 Jul 1848]
    Lydia F & Isaac DYER of Skowhegan ME at Bloomfield ME [17 Jul 1851]
    Martha N & Francis H COWAN at Bangor ME [2 Jan 1845]
    Mary A d/o the late J D EMERY Esq & Mr D Wilmot BELYEA at Augusta ME on 9th Jun 1851 by Rev Mr JUDD [12 Jun 1851]
    Mary Ann & Thomas AGRY at Fairfield ME [20 Dec 1849]
    Mary D & Phineas HANSON by Rev BAILEY at Buxton ME [30 Apr 1842]
    Mary Mrs & Daniel L ELDRIDGE at Biddeford ME [25 Dec 1845]
    Mrs Abigail & Nathan D RICE Esq of Union ME at Augusta ME on 7 May 1851 by Rev Mr JUDD [22 May 1851]
    Nath'l & Eliza CLAY at Buxton ME [23 Aug 1849]
    Reuben & Mahala SIMPSON at Winslow ME [25 Apr 1840]
    S M & Ruth SPENCER at Bangor ME [4 Mar 1833]
    Sarah Elizabeth & S C HOLMAN of Boston MA on 11 Mar by Rev JUDD at Augusta ME [22 Mar 1849]
    Susan A & Richmond L WILLIAMS both of Athens ME at Skowhegan ME [4 Feb 1847]
    Susan J of Fairfield ME & Lorenzo M DAVIS at Waterville ME [18 Dec 1851]
    Susan & William S BADGER on 30 Nov by Rev S JUDD at Augusta ME [10 Dec 1846]
    Theresa Orne d/o Hon Nicholas EMERY, & Lendal G S BOYD at Portland ME [11 Sept 1835]
    William H & Mary GIFFORD 10th inst by Rev J C STOCKBRIDGE at Fairfield ME [4 Mar 1847]

EMMONS Ann Maria S & Robert FOLLINSBEE of Portland ME at Georgetown ME [3 Apr 1845]
    Delia d/o Williams EMMONS Esq of Hallowell ME & Benjamin TAPPAN Rev of Hampden ME by Rev TAPPAN of Augusta ME at Hallowell ME [18 Sept 1838]
    Eliza d/o Jacob EMMONS Esq. & Thomas S BOWLES 23 Jan by Rev NOTT at Bath ME [5 Feb 1842]
    Joseph 3rd & Betsey ROBERTS at Lyman [1 Jul 1852]

ERSKINE Mary T & William M FLINT at Sangerville ME [8 Apr 1852]

ERSKIN John E of Bristol ME & Olive STINSON of Topsham ME on 9th ult at New York [6 May 1843]

ERSKINE Alexander & Hannah DOW at Whitefield ME [3 Jul 1835]
    Christopher & Mary BOWDEN both of Pittston ME at Augusta ME [11 Dec 1845]
    Eliza A & James PEACOCK at Gardiner ME [25 Oct 1849]
    Lucy Mrs of Palermo ME & Jon WINSLOW Esq at Albion ME [4 Apr 1850]
    Mary J of Bristol ME & L P LAMBART of North Yarmouth ME at Bristol ME [11 Dec 1845]

ESTERBROOK/ESTABROOK David N of Oldtown ME & Mary A MORTON at Windsor ME [2 Sept 1847]
    Frances Ann & Albert G TENNY of Baltimore MD?/OH? at Brunswick ME [9 Sept 1836]
    George M & Eliza R PAGE at Oldtown ME [4 Nov 1847]
    James K & Lois Ann OWEN at Brunswick ME [31 Oct 1844]
ESTY Abby D & Dr Joseph MERRILL at Gardiner ME [19 Oct 1848]
ESTERS Charles & Maria B GREELY both of Augusta 28th ult by William PERCIVAL Esq at China [1 Feb 1849]
ESTES Elvina A & George W HASKELL of Kennebec (now Manchester) ME at China ME by J D ESTES Esq [3 Jul 1851]
    Thomas & Mrs Sophronia STEVENS both of Exeter ME at Stetson ME [8 Jun 1848]
    Abigail & Daniel R WING of Monmouth ME on 3rd inst by Rev N GUNNISON at Vassalboro ME [14 Mar 1850]
    Elsa & Joseph FOGG of Harrison ME at Bethel ME [14 Jun 1849]
    James Capt & Mary YORK both of Bethel ME at Bethel [23 Nov 1839]
    John & Elizabeth L KENNEDY at China ME [14 Dec 1833]
    Joseph of Vassalboro ME & Sibil DUNHAM of the Society of Friends at Leeds ME [9 May 1837]
    Mary Ann & David J C FOSS at Portland ME [7 Aug 1845]
    Olive & Edwin E JASPER of Minot ME at Lewiston ME [19 Aug 1847]
    Sarah of Raymond ME & Obadiah GOULD of Raymond ME at China ME [11 Nov 1836]
ESTIS Jonathan & Sarah RODGERS at Corinna ME [11 Apr 1844]
ESTY George H & Lucinda A SHOREY both of Waterville ME at Augusta ME [18 Nov 1843]
    J W & Abigail, d/o Rev S FOGG, both of Winthrop ME Sun eve last by Rev MERRIAM at Winthrop ME [31 Jul 1845]
EUSTIS Esther & David HALE Dr of Livermore ME at Jay ME [30 Sept 1843]
    Harriet & John DeBECK at Prospect ME [24 Oct 1840]
    Solon & Lovey JOHNSON Mrs of Frankfort ME at Belfast ME [18 Feb 1847]
EVANS/EVENS Alexander & Elizabeth H FOSTER of Skowhegan ME at East Abbington MA [25 Sept 1845]
    Amy & Thomas LANCASTER both of Albion ME by Rev Wm BOWLER at China ME [11 Nov 1836]
    Benj D & Sarah H GOODWIN at St Albans ME [25 Apr 1837]
    Catherine & William STACY at Bath ME [2 Jan 1845]
    Charles A & Eleanora W THACHER of Saco ME at Concord NH [5 Nov 1847]
    Ellen L & Folliot T LALLY at Gardiner ME [26 Oct 1848]
    Lydia & George W FORD at Wayne ME by Rev C FULLER [2 Oct 1851]
    Robert & Margaret KNIGHT at Portland ME [11 Mar 1836]
EVELETH Benjamin F & Harriet STONE at Gardiner ME [2 Dec 1847]
    John H of Augusta ME & Martha d/o Hon Silas HOLMAN at Bolton [27 Nov 1835]
    Sarah B Mrs & Samuel A MORSE of Machias ME at Minudia NS [18 Jul 1844]
    Silas & Mary KIRK 20 Jul at Monson ME [5 Sept 1844]
EVERETT Frances A & Capt John W CARLTON at Montville ME [12 Feb 1852]

EVERETT (cont.) Harriet N of New Portland ME & Thomas L DREW of Glenburn ME at New Portland ME [14 May 1846]
John & Ellen KEAN at Bath ME [10 Oct 1844]
EWER Eliza J & Peter LAZO at Brownville ME [10 Feb 1848]
EWERS John A of Hallowell ME & Abigail LAKEMAN of Boston MA second d/o John LAKEMAN of Hallowell ME at New York [5 Jun 1841]

- F -

FABYAN S Capt editor of the *Lawrence Vanguard* & Mary S HOWES d/o Edward HOWES of Gardiner ME at Boston MA [12 Oct 1848]
FAIRBANKS Charles H printer formerly of Winthrop ME & Adelia C AILES of Philadelphia PA on 2 Jun at Philadelphia [10 Jul 1845]
Cyrus C of Winthrop ME & Sarah Norris PILLSBURY by David THURSTON at Hallowell ME on 15 Jan [22 Jan 1852]
Daniel A & Elizabeth WAUGH by Rev THURSTON at Winthrop ME [7 May 1846]
Dennis of Letter F ME ae 56 & Abigail BRADLEY Mrs ae 19 at Wakefield NH? [15 Apr 1847]
Eliza Ann d/o Enos FAIRBANKS of Winthrop ME, & Alexander HATCH Dr of Augusta ME on Tues last by Rev DREW at Winthrop ME [2 Jan 1838]
Flora A & Marshall D CHASE at Waterford ME [29 Apr 1852]
Franklin T formerly of this town (Winthrop ME) & Susan STEWART of Farmington ME by Rev ROGERS at Farmington ME [11 Jun 1842]
George G preceptor of Hebron Academy (of Hebron Oxford Co ME) & Caroline M MARROW by David THURSTON at Monmouth ME [25 May 1848]
George S & Caroline MOODY at Monmouth ME [22 Jun 1839]
H W of Farmington ME & M Caroline LADD of Hallowell ME Wed morn last by Rev Eli THURSTON at Hallowell ME [15 Jun 1839]
Hannah, d/o Dennis FAIRBANKS Esq of Presque Isle Plantation Aroostook Co ME, & Orrin WHITNEY of Letter D Plantation Aroostook Co ME 7 Nov by John B WING Esq at Presque Isle Plantation ME [1 Jan 1842]
Henry of Monmouth ME & Pamelia WEBB of Portland ME at Portland [19 Oct 1833]
John L Dr formerly of Winthrop ME & Mary E RICHARDSON at Monmouth ME [4 Feb 1843]
Joseph Esq of Farmington ME & Martha SAMPSON at Temple ME [27 Nov 1851]
Leonard O formerly of Winthrop ME & Mary D THOMPSON formerly of Turner ME at Nashua Village NH [12 Oct 1833]
Levi Jr & Mary Jane MOODY at Monmouth ME [22 Jun 1839]
Lucy M of Parkman OH & Daniel H MANSFIELD Rev at Thomaston ME [19 Jun 1845]
Mary Elizabeth & Ezra MITCHELL of Wayne ME at Mt Vernon ME [20 Nov 1851]
Oran & Sybil G FAIRBANKS at Monmouth ME [14 Dec 1839]
Sarah F & James M HOLLAND Esq of Canton ME Thurs 1 Sept by Rev D THURSTON [3 Sept 1842]

FAIRBANKS (cont.) Sarah & Benjamin AYER of Freedom ME on 13 Apr by Rev Daniel FULLER at Winthrop ME [9 May 1834]
Sybil G & Oran FAIRBANKS at Monmouth ME [14 Dec 1839]
Thaddeus H & Mary E PILLSBURY 31st ult at Hallowell ME [11 Sept 1845]

FAIRFIELD Caroline R & Jones R ELDEN on 1 Jan by Rev SHELDON at Waterville ME [9 Jan 1845]
Edward & Mary D ROGERS at Topsham ME [6 Nov 1838]
George A & Eliza WARREN at Skowhegan ME [24 Oct 1837]
Henry A of Andover MA & Margaret S HEATH of Bath ME at Bath [1 Jul 1836]
Paulina & Allen MARDEN at China ME [22 Apr 1836]

FAIRBROTHER R J Miss & Mr M MULRAY at Norridgewock ME [9 Nov 1848]

FAIRSERVICE Frances of Alna ME & Hannah DICKINSON at Wiscasset ME [10 Oct 1844]

FALES Albert C & Lucinda GATES at Thomaston ME [23 Dec 1836]
Almira H & William M VANSTONE at Thomaston ME [5 Aug 1847]
Ann & Joseph ULMER at Thomaston ME [3 Oct 1837]
Benjamin W of Thomaston ME & Mrs Hannah McKELLAR of St George ME at Thomaston ME [17 Oct 1840]
Mary A & Geo G CARTER of Portland ME at Thomaston [14 Mar 1850]
Mary Ann & Thomas ROSE at Thomaston ME [23 Oct 1841]
Orrin Capt & Clementine B WEBB at Thomaston ME [8 Jul 1847]
Penelope G & Hon Edward ROBINSON at Thomaston ME [2 Jul 1846]
Sarah V & Seth P SHAW Jr of Rockland ME at Thomaston [20 Nov 1851]
Sarah & Charles LORING merchant at Thomaston ME [29 Jul 1833]
Thomas F Rev of Brunswick ME & Margaret P NELSON at Portland ME [29 Apr 1847]

FARGO Sarah C & Austin HOBART at South Solon ME [8 May 1851]

FARLEY Susan & Samuel D PORTER of Rochester NY at Waldoboro ME [15 Aug 1834]

FARMER Abby H & Alpheus E GUILD of Augusta ME on 27 Jun by Rev HACKETT at Temple ME [8 Jul 1852]
Whitney of Hallowell ME & Martha Ann WETHERBY of Charlestown MA at Gardiner ME [5 Mar 1846]

FARNAHAM Jane D of Jefferson ME & William S NORCROSS 22nd ult by Rev WHITEHOUSE at Jefferson ME [4 Jan 1844]

FARNAM J E of Shelbyville KY & Esteria BUTLER 15th inst at North Yarmouth ME [29 Aug 1837]

FARNHAM Ann & Obed W HAYNES of Edinburgh at Passadumkeag ME [5 Sept 1841]
Eliza A & Henry BOND of Nobleboro ME at Sidney ME [1 Aug 1837]
Eliza W & Nelson THAYER at Sidney ME [11 Jan 1844]
Enoch C of Albion ME & Mary Jane BROWN 4th inst by Rev INGRAHAM at Augusta ME [12 Dec 1844]
Esther & Manly PRESSY at Waterville ME [23 Oct 1851]
Levi O of Sangerville ME & Abigail N RAND at Bucksport [11 Jul 1837]
Love W & Samuel W FARNHAM at Lewiston ME [19 Dec 1844]
Maria A of Cazenovia NY & Charles SEVERANCE formerly of Augusta ME at Buffalo NY [18 Jul 1837]

FARNHAM (cont.) Martha & George HIGGINS of Belmont ME at Jefferson ME [24 Apr 1845]
    Orrin Capt of Portland ME & Catharine A GRANT at Gardiner ME [2 Dec 1836]
    Orrin of Vassalboro ME & Almyra CROMWELL of Norridgewock ME at Lawrence MA on May 12 [12 Jun 1851]
    Samuel S & Mehitable TAYLOR both of Augusta ME at Windsor ME [25 Sept 1841]
    Samuel W & Love W FARNHAM at Lewiston ME [19 Dec 1844]
    Susan A & Stephen COBB at Vassalboro ME on 26th May [10 Jun 1852]
    Susan O & John OSBORN Jr at Dover ME? [20 May 1847]
    Thomas Jr of Bath ME & Elizabeth J WEEKS at Hallowell ME [15 Mar 1849]

FARNSWORTH Charles H Dr of Bridgton ME & Lois S NELSON at Jay ME [19 Jul 1849]
    George Maj of Norridgewock ME & Susan FARNSWORTH at Lisbon ME [29 Oct 1846]
    Harriet M & M C RICHARDSON Dr of Hallowell ME at Bridgton ME [17 Sept 1846]
    Hon Drummond of Norridgewock ME & Julia A WHITMORE of West Cambridge MA at New York NY [18 Jun 1846]
    James B merchant of Waterville ME & Lydia C J BATES d/o Hon James BATES of Norridgewock ME on Tues eve last by Rev J PEET at Norridgewock ME [6 Jun 1840]
    Josiah of Lisbon ME & Caroline JORDAN at Webster ME on 27 Oct [9 Nov 1848]
    Margaret d/o Hon D FARNSWORTH, & Charles A BATES at Norridgewock ME [5 Feb 1842]
    Mary Ann & Henry BUTLER at Norridgewock ME [13 Jun 1837]
    Sarai & Increase BLAKE of Farmington ME at Norridgewock ME [10 Oct 1844]
    Susan & Geo FARNSWORTH Maj of Norridgewock ME at Lisbon ME [29 Oct 1846]

FARNUM Martha Ann & Josiah F TEMPLE of Montville ME at Knox ME [23 Jan 1851]
    Daniel & W VIRGIN of Rumford ME at Rumford ME [18 Mar 1833]
    Simon H & Mary Jane McRILLIS at Rumford ME [29 May 1841]

FARR Cynthia & Levi JONES at Friends meeting house in Hallowell ME [25 Apr 1840] & [5 Dec 1840]
    G W Dr of Lewiston ME & Hannah ALLEY at Lynn MA [28 Dec 1848]
    Rachel E & William E BURNES at Poland ME [17 Feb 1848]

FARRAR Catharine of Searsmont ME & Capt Isaac WATTS at Waldoboro ME [21 May 1846]
    David & Phebe FLYNT Mrs at Gardiner ME [19 Sept 1844]
    Deborah & John W RUSSELL at Gardiner ME [2 Oct 1845]
    Jane G of Harmony ME & Alexander H CHASE of Bangor ME at Bangor ME [25 Dec 1838]
    Isaac Esq of Bangor ME & Caroline W FULLER at Augusta ME [19 Jun 1835]

FARRELL Hannah M & Newall STURTEVANT merchant of Nantucket MA Sun eve 19th inst by Rev WEBBER at Hallowell ME [28 Nov 1837]

FARRELL (cont.) Harriet & Albert J WEBB of Winthrop ME at Washington DC [17 Dec 1846]
Sarah Ann & Jonas ROBESON of New Orleans at Hallowell ME [30 Sept 1843]

FARREN - FARRIN - see FERRIN
Almira D of Topsham & Capt Nathaniel SNOW at Bath ME [23 Jan 1845]
George H of Richmond ME & Lorinda MANN at Webster ME [15/29 Apr 1852]
Joseph W & Emeline NEWELL at Bath ME [29 Apr 1847]
Sophronia & Ephraim LARABEE at Brunswick ME [31 Jan 1834]
William J & Ann E THURLOW at Litchfield ME [31 Aug 1848]

FARRINGTON Allen P & Maria S ULMER at Thomaston ME [23 Sept 1847]
Ebenezer Jr & Mary M SCOFIELD both of Livermore ME at Fayette ME [29 Jan 1839]
Ira P & Harriet E HAYES at Oxford ME [24 Jan 1850]
Laura & Joseph I JOHNSON at Augusta ME on Dec 17th by Rev Z THOMPSON [2 Jan 1851]
Lorenzo & Sarah P BRAGG at East Vassalboro ME [30 Aug 1849]
Mary J & J Warren MYRICK of Lawrence MA on 7 Mar by Elder S S NASON at Troy ME [14 Mar 1850]
Roxana F & Albert H BRAGG at Vassalboro ME on Feb 2 by John HOMANS Esq [6 Feb 1851]
Sylvia Jane & Milton ROBINSON at Oxford ME [10 Dec 1846]

FARROW Benjamin S & Margaret H BRIGGS at Brunswick ME [25 Feb 1847]
Elisha & Caroline YOUNG of Gouldsboro ME at Steuben ME [28 Jan 1847]
Nathan & Caroline A PATTERSON of Belfast ME at Northport ME [12 Aug 1852]
Sarah & Watson HINDS both of Belfast ME by Rev S G SARGEANT at Belfast ME [11 Mar 1843]

FARWELL Julia & Benjamin C JOY at Winthrop ME [18 Apr 1844]

FASSETT Francis H & Mima Ann WELCH at Bath ME [26 Aug 1847]
Henry Jr & Amanda PEASE at Union ME [18 Apr 1844]
John & Mary MITCHELL Mrs at Bath ME [22 Apr 1847]

FAUGHT Luther R of Sidney ME & Mary J STAPLES at Belgrade ME [19 Aug 1852]
Theodore of Sidney ME & Sarah GLITTEN of Vassalboro ME at Hallowell ME [30 Oct 1845]

FAULKNER Jane & S STEVENS at Fort Kent Aroostook Co ME [11 Mar 1847]

FAUNCE Samuel & Mary E CURRIER at Wayne ME [5 Mar 1846]

FAWETT John & Mary ANDERSON at Robbinstown ME [17 Apr 1835]

FAYETTE Louisa J & George H KIMBALL at Jersey City [29 Jan 1852]

FELKER Catharine Jane & Rev Abiel WOOD Jr, Pastor of the Baptist Church in Wiscasset ME at Wiscasset ME [8 Aug 1834]
Catherine & Peter P ELDER of New Portland ME at Concord ME [19 Jun 1845]
Daniel of Embden ME & Martha F GARDINER of Palermo ME at Albion ME [18 Jan 1844]
Ezra D & Jane E SMITH of Windham ME at Portland ME [29 May 1845]

FELKER (cont.) Hannah Mrs & Jonathan BRAWN of Bloomfield ME at Bangor ME [14 Mar 1844]
    Olive E & John W LAWSON at Prospect ME [28 Dec 1833]
    Philena & Thaddeus F BOOTHBAY at Concord ME? [1 Jan 1852]
FELLOWS Clarinda S of Fayette ME m Benjamin H MORRILL at E Livermore ME [4 Jun 1851]
    Emily M & Zina H GREENWOOD both of Augusta ME on 8 Nov at Hallowell ME [29 Nov 1849]
    Hannah L & John MAULL at Augusta ME [19 Jun 1838]
    Nathan P of Fayette ME m Julia A FRENCH at Chesterville ME [22 May 1851]
FELT Elvina L & Edward WELCH Jr at Hallowell ME [27 Nov 1845]
    Lucy S of Greenwood ME & Abner C LIBBY of Limerick ME at Buxton ME [6 Dec 1849]
    Mehitable P & John HATHAWAY of Paris ME at Woodstock ME [6 Feb 1851]
FENLEY Levi W & Maria MANN at Portland ME [28 Nov 1844]
FENNEL Julia A Mrs & Lewis E BAILEY at Gardiner ME [6 Jan 1848]
FERGUSON Hannah & Geo HEMMENWAY of Searsmont ME at Belfast ME [11 May 1839]
FERMAGE William & Mrs Charlotte HASTINGS at Bath ME [14 Nov 1834]
FERNALD Anthony H & Dolly H FURLONG at Portland ME [2 Apr 1846]
    Mary Ann Mrs & George HALL at Kennebunkport ME [1 May 1838]
    Mary Jane & Benjamin FLETCHER at Kittery ME [23 Mar 1839]
    Sarah & Thomas B WENTWORTH both of Parsonfield ME at Limerick ME [14 Feb 1850]
FERNE Peter & Rosanna STUREVANT at Foxcroft ME [28 Sept 1848]
FERRIN Charles D & Mary SAVAGE at Norridgewock ME [17 Apr 1838]
FERRIS William H of South Berwick ME & Julia CONNER on 16 Jun by Rev ALLEN at Augusta ME [26 Jul 1849]
FERSON John L & Mary C d/o Palmer BRANCH of Augusta ME at Lowell MA [3 Dec 1846]
FEW Joseph & Susan S FOY both of Gardiner ME at New York NY [4 Sept 1845]
FICKETT Daniel of Harrington Washington Co ME & Cynthia S WING at Bangor Penobscot Co ME [3 Apr 1845]
    Levi of Raymond ME & Sarah FICKETT of Cape Elizabeth ME at Cape Elizabeth [10 Oct 1837]
    Moses 2nd & Sarah SAWYER [note paper stated "Moses FICRETT"] at Millbridge ME? [17 Aug 1848]
    Sarah & Levi FICKETT same as above
FIELD B Franklin & Frances J DONNELL at Gardiner ME [25 Apr 1850]
    Charles of Lisbon ME & Emma WOTTON at Bath ME [4 Dec 1851]
    Charles of (Augusta) ME & Mary C FOLSOM at Starks ME [19 Oct 1848]
    Eliza A & Franklin WILSON at (Augusta) ME on 18th inst [27 Jan 1848]
    George Dr & Miss S A BRAINERD of China ME at Northfield MA [11 Mar 1852]
    Harriet P & John WINNETT of Randolph MA at Gardiner ME [8 Jul 1847]
    Jonathan of Buxton ME & Nancy ROBERTS at Waterboro ME [13 May 1847]
    Josiah B & Harriet EMERY at Bloomfield ME [29 Jul 1847]

FIELD (cont.) Rachel & Nathan PERRY at Waterville ME [8 Mar 1849]
   Thomas of Brewer ME & Mrs Emma HUNTRESS of Bangor ME at Brewer ME [5 Mar 1842]
   Zibeon & Mrs Eliza B WHITMAN of Dedham MA at Chesterville ME [16 Mar 1848]
FIELDS Catharine & Enos C ULMER by J H BECKETT Esq at Thomaston ME [15 Jul 1836]
   Charles of Freeport ME & Ruth A RICE of Scarborough ME at Portland ME [3 Apr 1845]
FIFIELD Benj H of Readfield ME & Lovina B HALL at Belgrade ME [10 May 1849]
   Daniel C & Zillah A THEFETHEN both of Bangor ME at Corinna ME [20 Jan 1848]
   David E & Caroline COOLIDGE at Dexter ME [30 Apr 1846]
   Joanna M & Levi HOYT 2d both of Readfield ME at Augusta ME on 4th Sept by Rev H M BLAKE [18 Sept 1851]
   Leah & Gideon STETSON at Lincoln ME [2 Sept 1847]
FILES Elisha & Althea MOULTON at Thorndike ME [21 May 1846]
   Patience & Gershom SKILLINGS both of Gorham ME on 12th by Jeremiah PARKER Esq at Gorham ME [29 Apr 1843]
   Winthrop P & Ann LOMBARD at Gorham ME [16 May 1837]
FILLEBROWN James S of Readfield ME & Anna L LADD at Farmington ME [18 Oct 1849]
   Marinda d/o James FILLEBROWN Esq. & John LAMBERT Esq at Readfield ME [30 Oct 1838]
   Sarah M & Willard HOPKINS at Winthrop ME on Mar 12th [20 Mar 1851]
FINAL William & Sarah Jane GOULD both of Old Town ME by Rev N W SHELDON at Vassalboro ME [30 Mar 1848]
FINCH Miranda & Dr William TREAT formerly of Gardiner ME at Buffalo NY [24 Jul 1851]
   W H & Louisa MARSH at Eastport ME [11 Nov 1847]
FINNEY Samuel G of Baltimore ME & Eunice P NEAL of Charlestown ME at Burlington IA [2 Dec 1843]
FINSON Mary T & John BUTTERFIELD Jr at Hartland ME [24 Jan 1850]
FIRBUSH Keziah H & Samuel HEWEY Capt of Webster ME at Topsham ME [8 Aug 1844]
FISH E Mr & Fidelia MORRISON at Starks ME on 4th Jul [10 Aug 1848]
   Fanny of Salem MA? & Horace BIRD of Watertown MA at Salem Extended Notice [6 May 1836]
   Samuel of Liberty ME & Louisa McGLOTHLIN of Eaton NH at Salem MA [11 Jan 1840]
   Sarah I & Mr A P POWERS of Bloomfield ME at Hartland ME [6 Nov 1851]
FISHER Addison of Hopkinton MA & Martha MOULTON at York ME [13 Jun 1844]
   Charles A of Alna ME & Olive DOUGLASS at Whitefield ME [1 Jan 1852]
   Diantha E & William PEACOCK at Litchfield ME [17 Sept 1842]
   Eliza A & Elias W WILLIAMSON on 3 Nov by Rev C F ALLEN at Augusta ME [15 Nov 1849]
   Foster & Susan B GATES at Robbinston ME [26 Feb 1846]
   Harriet S & Jesse G SPRAGUE of Charlotte ME at Calais ME [22 Oct 1846]

FISHER (cont.) James J of Bath ME & Sarah A GREENLEAF at Wiscasset ME [14 Nov 1844]
    Levi of Charlotte ME & Susan S WATERMAN at Belfast ME [5 Dec 1844]
    Lucy Mrs of Litchfield ME & Richard M PINKHAM of Hallowell ME at Litchfield ME [18 Dec 1845]
    Martha A H & Samuel G GLIDDEN Capt both of Newcastle ME at Providence RI [26 Jul 1849]
    Robert & Betsey I GRANT of Norridgewock ME by Francis DAVIS Esq at (Augusta) ME on 22d May [27 May 1852]
    W H Mr of Bremen ME & Mary A WESTON of Augusta ME at Boothby ME [11 Sept 1851]

FISK/FISKE George D of Sacramento City CA & Elizabeth C LORING at Boston MA on 12th Jul by Rev Dr ADAMS [7 August 1851]
    H Clauson of Willimantic CT & P Avadna PERRY on 16 Jan by Edward BLAKE Esq at Augusta ME [31 Jan 1850]
    John O Rev of Bath ME & Mary A TAPPAN at (Augusta) ME on 19th inst [28 Sept 1848]
    Lucy A & William SHEAF of Portland ME at Ellsworth ME [9 Sept 1847]
    Mary W of Fayette ME & Stephen TAFT of Wayne on 13th inst by R C STARR at Wayne ME [19 Nov 1842]
    Mr FISK of Leeds ME & Eliza KIMBALL d/o Heber KIMBALL Esq of Turner ME on Sun eve last by Edward BLAKE Esq at Hartford ME [7 Mar 1837]
    Phebe A & James E HAMLEN on 11 Jul at Augusta ME [22 Jul 1847]

FITCH Amasa & Lydia CROSS at Gardiner ME [8 Jan 1839]
    Maria & Edward WEEKS at Vassalboro ME [18 Jul 1840]

FITTS Andrew J of Southampton NH & Eliza A PILSBURY at Newport ME? [1 Oct 1846]
    Lydia & William D SEWALL Jr at Bath ME [17 Apr 1851]
    Sarah & Henry TALMAN at Bath ME [7 Sept 1833]

FITZ Lightbourn N formerly of Bath ME & Lovisa L COY of Winthrop ME on Sun eve last by Rev ROBINSON at Winthrop [6 May 1843]

FITZGERALD Almeda B & Joseph C BROWN at Benton ME [11 Mar 1852]
    Henry & Ann M SKINNER at Camden ME [22 Jul 1847]
    Paulina of York ME & Wm ADAMS of Canaan at York ME [23 Oct 1845]

FLAGG Cyrus Capt of Topsham ME & Abigail BUZWELL of Wales ME at Winthrop ME [6 Mar 1845]
    Ednah & Jas MITCHELL both of Auburn ME at Danville ME [5 Jul 1849]
    Eliza M & Benj F MUDGETT Esq at Hampden ME [20 Aug 1846]
    Eliza & Offin P GETCHELL both of Waterville ME at Sebasticook ME [31 Jan 1850]
    James & Mary Jane KIMBALL both of Augusta ME Sun morn last by Rev Thos ADAMS at Augusta ME [18 Sept 1841]
    John P & Mary MERRICK 23rd ult at Hallowell ME [4 Nov 1843]
    John S & Mehitable SHAW at Clinton ME [11 Mar 1852]
    Marcellus & Hannah J BRIGGS at Belmont ME [18 Apr 1847]
    Martha A & Joshua WHITE at Auburn ME [23 Oct 1851]
    Sarah B & Ephraim BIGELOW Thurs eve last by Rev Arthur DRINKWATER at Bloomfield ME [9 Feb 1839]
    Susan & Samuel DARLING at Auburn ME [20 Mar 1851]

FLANDERS Benjamin of Waldoboro ME & Harriet MESERVEY of Jefferson ME at N Waldoboro ME on 12 Jan by Reuben ORFF Esq [16 Jan 1851]

FLANDERS (cont.) Elizabeth C of Buxton ME & Nathan CHICK at Limerick ME [10 Jun 1847]
    Elizabeth C & Mr L L DEARTH at Sangerville ME [11 May 1848]
    Henry T & Esther KELLEY by Daniel EVANS Jr at Mayfield ME [16 Jul 1842]
    Martha & Hiram KALER at Waldoboro ME [30 Sept 1847]
    Mehitable & Asa H SAWTELLE of Corinna ME at Garland ME [11 Apr 1840]
    Rebecca C & Darius McCRILLIS at Cornville ME [17 Jun 1847]
    Thomas Jr of Cornville ME & Salina MALBON of Skowhegan ME at Skowhegan [17 Aug 1839]
    William Jr & Elmira MORRISON at Solon ME [12 Mar 1846]
    William & Harriet ACHORN by Reuben ORFF at Waldoboro ME on 4th inst [13 Apr 1848] & [4 May 1848]

FLETCHER Amy P & Geo A MANNING 17th inst by Anson Church Esq at Augusta ME [25 Oct 1849]
    Asa S & R Amanda FLETCHER at Wilton ME [26 Feb 1846]
    Ashur & Frances L DAWES both of Bloomfield ME at Thompson CT [18 Nov 1847]
    Benjamin & Mary Jane FERNALD at Kittery ME [23 Mar 1839]
    Charlotte & Timothy MOORE at Wilton ME [6 Jun 1837]
    Isaac Esq of Sidney ME & Betsey S DINSMORE of Bloomfield ME at Bloomfield [14 Dec 1833]
    Israel A & Mary Ann BENSON at Hartford ME [12 Jun 1845]
    J G of Boston MA m Sarah H COX at Pittston ME [4 Jun 1851]
    Julia A & Thos J CARNEY Rev of Wayne ME at Boston MA [10 May 1849]
    Julia A & Wallace McFARLAND at Bloomfield ME [7 Apr 1848]
    Margaret A & Charles P COOLIDGE by Rev INGRAHAM at Augusta ME [21 Sept 1839]
    Mary & Edward J PEET both of Norridgewock ME at New York City NY on Jul 9 by Rev George B CHEEVER [24 Jul 1851]
    Mary & Otis CURTIS of Dixfield ME at Wilton ME [14 Dec 1839]
    Mary Ann & James A GOODWIN of Gardiner ME at Boston MA [23 Jan 1851]
    Mary Ann & Sam'l ROBINSON at Mt Vernon ME [2 Jan 1835]
    Oliver F & Emily HATHAWAY both of Wilton ME at Jay ME [17 Jun 1852]
    Omes of Augusta ME & Ruth BARTLETT at Searsmont ME [28 May 1842]
    R Amanda & Asa S FLETCHER at Wilton ME [26 Feb 1846]
    Ruth C & Hollis ELLIS at South Prospect ME [23 Sept 1847]
    S S of New Bedford MA & Caroline A PARTRIDGE at Orland ME [15 Aug 1844]
    Sarah & Emerson O DAY both of Jarvis GORE ME at Eddington ME [21 Oct 1847]
    Sophronia A & William M BRYANT at Jay ME on Jun 8th [17 Jun 1852]

FLINT Alden of Montville ME & Marcia Ann WESTON at Madison ME [25 Apr 1844]
    Charlotte & Cyrus WOODMAN of Wisconsin on 5 Jan at Tremont IL [19 Feb 1842]
    Clarissa N of Bath ME & Shaw NORRIS of Edgartown MA at Bath ME [12 Aug 1836]
    Daniel of Albany ME & Anna F EAMES at Newry ME [18 Apr 1850]
    Harriet & James F TARBOX at Thomaston ME [14 Oct 1847]

FLINT (cont.) James A of #11 Aroostook Co ME & Lydia G PARKER of Patten ME by S BEAN Esq at Lee ME on 27th Feb [9 Mar 1848]
 John C & Martha A COCHREN at Bangor ME [6 Nov 1845]
 John E & Emeline M D HOLMES at Thomaston ME [14 Oct 1847]
 John P & Mary E HIGGINS at Bath ME [27 May 1836]
 Sarah & Dr Sumner GOULD at North Anson ME [5 Oct 1848]
 William M & Mary T ERSKINE at Sanderville ME [8 Apr 1852]
FLITNER Eli & Mary GOODWIN at Pittston ME [10 Apr 1851]
FLOOD Bythena & Asa PRATT of Sebasticook ME at Clinton ME [8 Jan 1846]
 Ebenezer T & Louisa LEATHERS at Biddeford ME [8 Apr 1852]
 Eliza & D L Mr HUNTER both of Clinton ME at Canaan ME [31 Jul 1851]
 Sarah Ann & Daniel PLUMMER at (Augusta) ME on 9th Jun [17 Jun 1852]
FLOWER Martha A & J M BEE at Geneva NY [5 Mar 1842]
FLOYD Alfred & Mary F HAINS at Biddeford ME [7 May 1846]
 Silas T & Margaret Melvina d/o Enos CHANDLER all of Winthrop ME on 27 Nov by Rev B F ROBBINS at Winthrop [3 Dec 1846]
FLY Alden of Damariscotta ME & Sarah E YEATON at Chelsea ME [4 Mar 1852]
 Eunice Mrs & Jona CATES 25 Nov at Hallowell ME [6 Dec 1849]
 Franklin & Sarah MARSTON 29th ult by Rev A MOORE at Augusta ME [17 Jul 1845]
 Orrin & Amelia BARTLETT at Augusta ME on 7th Jan by Rev Z THOMPSON [23 Jan 1851]
 William a youthful swain of 80 & Elizabeth CUNNINGHAM a smiling lass of 60y on 3rd inst by E CUNNINGHAM Esq at Edgcomb ME [17 Jun 1833]
 William Prof of Mathematics U S Navy & Mary E PERKINS at Topsham ME [18 Jul 1844]
FLYNT Josiah of Farmington ME & Frances T PAUL of Anson ME at Hallowell ME [25 Jul 1840]
 Phebe Mrs & David FARRAR at Gardiner ME [19 Sept 1844]
FOGG Abigail d/o Rev S FOGG, & J W ESTY both of Winthrop ME on Sun eve last by Rev MERRIAM at Winthrop ME [31 Jul 1845]
 Caroline H & John R WYMAN at Fairfield ME [2 Aug 1849]
 Catharine C eldest d/o of Rev S FOGG, & Marcellus HOUGHTON Lieut on Thanksgiving even by Rev S FOGG at Winthrop ME [4 Dec 1841]
 Elijah & Mrs Charity POLLARD both of Wales ME at Gardiner ME [27 Mar 1851]
 Eunice S Mrs & William H BISHOP at Bangor ME [27 May 1843]
 Ezekiel K & ELiza A JENNINGS at Industry ME [20 Nov 1851]
 Faustina A B & George W BLOSSOM of Turner ME at Gray ME [29 Nov 1849]
 G G Miss & David N MOULTON of Lewiston ME at Greene ME [13 Mar 1851]
 James R of Brooks ME & Emeline DYER of Phillips ME at Prospect ME [24 Aug 1848]
 John B & Lucy A KING of Winthrop ME at Monmouth ME [29 Oct 1846]
 John H of Brooks ME & Esther DAVIS at Belfast ME [10 Oct 1844]
 Joseph of Harrison ME & Elsa ESTES at Bethel ME [14 Jun 1849]

Marriage Notices from the "Maine Farmer"

FOGG (cont.) Josiah N of Readfield ME & Hannah W SHAW by Rev FILES at Winthrop ME [22 Jun 1839]
    Lucady & Wingate TITCOMB at Parsonfield ME [17 Apr 1835]
    Mary A & Robert C THOMSON at Hampton NH [3 Jun 1852]
    Mary Ann & Elias T MILLIKEN of Boston MA at Saco ME [1 Feb 1844]
    Moses & Louisa RICHARDSON both of Winthrop ME Thursday 1st inst by Rev Wm A DREW at Augusta ME [9 Oct 1835]
    Nathan & Sarah G IRELAND at Sebec ME [13 Jan 1848]
    Rachel L of Bath ME & Peter H TRASK Bath ME at Boston MA [23 Jan 1851]
    Samuel D Capt & Ann Maria CUSHING Wednesday eve by Rev David THURSTON at Winthrop ME [6 Jun 1840]
    Samuel of Greene ME & Abigail C BAILEY of Minot ME by Rev D T STEVENS at Minot [4 May 1839]
    Samuel of Readfield ME & Mary Ann STEVENS of Monmouth ME at Winthrop ME [25 Jun 1846]
    Simon Jr & Hannah W KENNISTON at Houlton Aroostook Co ME [4 Apr 1834]
FOLGER Francis M & Eliza J KEATON at Augusta ME [25 Sept 1851]
FOGLER Lucy T & Robert PAUL at Thomaston ME [15 Oct 1846]
FOLLANSBEE Joshua of the US Army & Louisa A SEWELL, d/o Daniel SEWELL Esq of Farmington ME at Washington City DC [13 May 1843]
    Prescott of Waterville ME & Mary Ann LOW at Fairfield ME [1 Feb 1844]
FOLLET Abigail & John P SUTHERLAND on Sunday eve 18th inst by Oliver FOSTER Esq at Winthrop ME [23 May 1834]
    Mary of Winthrop ME & John LADD of Vienna ME by Elias WHITING Esq at Winthrop ME [30 Sept 1836]
FOLLETT Cyrus H of Wellington ME & Demaress HERRINGTON at Parkman ME [9 Nov 1839]
FOLLEY Robert & Mary Ann TURNER by Rev John H INGRAHAM at (Augusta) ME on 16th May [27 May 1852]
FOLLINSBEE Robert of Portland ME & Ann Maria S EMMONS at Georgetown ME [3 Apr 1845]
FOLSOM Abigail B & William S WOODBURY on Mon eve last at Monmouth ME [11 Nov 1843]
    Albert & Rachel Ann WHARFF at Augusta ME [22 Oct 1846]
    Cyrus H & Elizabeth ALLEN by John CURRIER Esq at Mt Vernon ME [1 Aug 1840]
    DeWitt C & & Lucy J WESTCOTT both of Bucksport ME at Providence RI [6 Nov 1851]
    Eliza J & John ATHEARN at Starks ME on 6th Apr [13 Apr 1848]
    Elizabeth & Benjamin P THOMPSON at Pittston ME [6 Jul 1848]
    Florila D of West Waterville ME & Joseph D GILMAN at Norridgewock ME [22 Apr 1847]
    George D of Bucksport ME & Susan B CURTIS of Bath ME at New York NY [10 Sept 1846]
    Harriet A & John O GILMAN by David WHITE Esq at Monmouth ME [27 Mar 1835]
    John B & Ann F KENNEY both of Dover ME at Foxcroft ME [20 Feb 1851]
    Joshua of Fairfield & Martha J SMITH at Waterville ME [27 Jun 1837]
    Lucinda S of Industry ME & Harlow KNIGHT of Bingham ME at Starks ME [7 May 1846]

FOLSOM (cont.) Martha J of Winthrop ME & Addison G PACKARD of Buckfield ME at Readfield ME on Oct 31st [6 Feb 1851]
Mary C & Charles FIELD at Starks ME [19 Oct 1848]
Mehitabel B & Isaac GETCHELL both of Winthrop ME by James R MARSTON at Mt Vernon ME [13 Sept 1849]
Orman of Corinth ME & Mary Ann DENNIS at Charleston ME [13 May 1843]
Peter Maj & Cordelia SOULE at Harmony ME [8 Feb 1844]
Peter & Eunice DORMAN by Dudley FOGG Esq at Mt Vernon ME [3 Apr 1838]
Robert H & Vashti A BRIGGS on 5th inst by Anson CHURCH Esq at Augusta ME [12 Nov 1846]
Ware L & Mary F CAVERLY at Stetson ME [29 Jan 1852]
Wyatt H & Rebecca B RING at Orono ME [14 Nov 1844]

FONTAN Francis & Joanna ADAMS by D T PIKE Esq at Augusta ME [13 Dec 1849]

FONTJAMI Elizabeth & John DOYEA at Bath ME [16 Jan 1841]
Mary & George SIMPSON at Bath ME [16 Jan 1841]

FOOTE Anna B youngest d/o Hon Erastus FOOTE, & J AVERILL Capt of San Francisco CA 4 Jul by Rev U BALKAM at Wiscasset ME [15 Jul 1852]
Benj F & Hannah E RIDEOUT at Bath ME [15 Feb 1849]
Erastus Jr & Sarah P WOOD at Wiscasset ME [8 Jul 1847]
Mary T & Isaac H COFFIN at Wiscasset ME [8 May 1851]
Samuel & Sarah T EMERSON both of Bath ME at Lisbon ME [9 Sept 1836]
Susan J & David H TRUFANT of New Orleans at Bath ME [13 Aug 1846]

FORBES Adelaide & Hart E WARING Rev, Missionary for Java at New York NY [25 Apr 1837]
Emily & Nathan HATHAWAY of Boston MA at Paris ME [14 Jan 1847]
Ephraim Rev & Mrs Azabah GOVE at Edgecomb ME [1 May 1835]
Henry H & Sophia C TAPLEY at Belfast ME [20 Feb 1845]
Laura & Silas COBURN at No 11 Aroostook ME [18 Feb 1847]

FORD Angelone & Albert A MYRICK at Lewiston ME [23 Jun 1852]
B F of Mayfield ME & Deborah Ann WARD at Brighton ME [8 May 1851]
Elisha J Dr & Mary D COX at Gardiner ME [23 Nov 1839]
Eliza J & E L GOWEN at Farmington ME [9 Oct 1845]
George W & Lydia EVANS at Wayne ME by Rev C FULLER [2 Oct 1851]
Henry of Farmington ME & Abigail H ROBINSON at Mt Vernon ME [17 Oct 1834]
J R of Eastport ME & Mary HUDDLESTON at Lubec ME [11 Dec 1845]
Lucy L formerly of Gray ME & Edwin M BURTON of Gorham ME at Cincinnati OH [20 Feb 1851]
Sarah A & Am M GREELY 16 Jun at China ME [1 Jul 1852]
Sybil M & Robert M MORRISON of Farmington ME at East Livermore ME [17 Jan 1850]

FORSYTH William of Lowell MA? & Abby BATES at Wilton ME [1 Jun 1848]

FORSAITH Jonathan W merchant of Brunswick ME & Sarah C HUNTER of Topsham ME at Topsham ME [21 Feb 1834]

FOSS Alpheus L of Leeds ME & Abigail J HALL of Lowell MA at Boston MA [4 Mar 1843]

Marriage Notices from the "Maine Farmer" 141

FOSS (cont.) Augustus B of Lowell MA & Parthenia WHITNEY at Freedom ME [8 Jul 1847]
    Columbia d/o the late Mr FOSS of Livermore ME, & Samuel B MORRISON, M.D., of Parkman ME at Livermore ME [22 Jan 1839]
    David J C & Mary Ann ESTES at Portland ME [7 Aug 1845]
    Eliza A & Sewall EATON at Brunswick ME [29 Jan 1852]
    Emery of Wayne ME & Sarah E FOSS by Rev Walter FOSS at Leeds ME on 4th Mar [11 Mar 1852]
    Fanny of Leeds ME & Samuel BOOTHBY of Turner ME at Leeds ME [10 Dec 1842]
    Ira H & Sarah A TUFTS at Saco ME [5 Jul 1849]
    James O & Ann M RANDALL at Lewiston ME [27 Jan 1848]
    James printer of Biddeford ME & Frences JORDAN at Portland ME [21 Jan 1847]
    Jane H & Andrew R TIBBETTS at Saco ME [11 Nov 1847]
    Jedidiah & George HARMON by Rev Walter FOSS at Leeds ME [15 May 1835]
    Jeremiah Jr & Elizabeth N HANKERSON both of Wayne ME on Sun last by Rev Daniel FULLER at Winthrop ME [23 May 1834]
    Maria C & Joseph M GORDAN at Biddeford ME [20 Jul 1848]
    Mary Ann & Luther C SARGENT at Brewer ME [6 Jan 1848]
    Mary Ann & Valmore STURTEVANT both of Wayne ME at Fayette ME [8 May 1851]
    Mary & Josiah CROSBY Esq at Dexter ME [15 Mar 1849]
    Olive L Mrs of Milo ME & Abner K HURD of Unity ME at Foxcroft ME [12 Feb 1846]
    Rosalinda L & Benjamin EDGECOMB at Leeds ME [27 Jan 1848]
    Sally of Leeds ME & Benaiah H TAYLOR of Farmington ME at Leeds ME [23 Jan 1841]
    Sarah E & Emery FOSS at Leeds ME on 4th Mar [11 Mar 1852]
    Sarah J & Summer I PRATT of Corinna ME at St Albans ME [4 Jun 1851]
    Sophia & Dr James SAWYER of Saco ME at Limington ME [3 Jun 1847]
    William H & Lauriett M FURLONG at Biddeford ME [13 Sept 1849]
FOSSETT George M & Sarah TOWNSEND at Union ME [11 Jul 1844]
    Mary & Charles C DAVIS at Strong ME [29 Feb 1840]
    Robert & Elizabeth DAVIS both of Strong ME at Farmington ME [6 Nov 1851]
    Zilphina N & Judson G CLARK of Portland ME at Bath ME [8 Apr 1847]
FOSTER Abby A & W H GILMAN 24 Jun by Rev D THURSTON at Winthrop ME [28 Jun 1849]
    Artemas of East Machias ME & Sarah C DAVIS of Wesley ME at Machias ME [27 Jul 1848]
    Benjamin T & Susan M HARRINGTON at Thomaston ME [30 Sept 1847]
    Charles Hubbard & Elizabeth AMES by John MAY Esq at Winthrop ME on 17th Jun [23 Jun 1852]
    Charles O & Angelia A PARLIN at East Winthrop ME [4 Oct 1849]
    Charles of Boston MA & Caroline B LOWELL at East Machias ME [5 Jul 1849]
    Charles S of Monroe WI formerly of Winthrop ME & Mary McCOOL at Freeport IL [7 Feb 1850]
    Charles & Sally BAIRD at Canton ME [3 Jun 1847]

FOSTER (cont.) Clarissa H & Elijah GROVER Esq of Wesley ME at Skowhegan ME [4 Oct 1849]
Clarissa Mrs & William CROSS of Vassalboro ME at Windsor ME on 14th Sept by Rev Thomas J DUDLEY of (Augusta ME) [30 Oct 1851]
Columbus Esq & Mary E WHEELER at La Grange ME [17 Jan 1850]
Cordelia T Mrs & James M BROOKING Capt of Bath ME at Bowdoinham ME [8 Apr 1836]
Ebenezer & Mary Jane SPROWL at Montville ME [13 Nov 1845]
Elizabeth H of Skowhegan ME & Alexander EVANS at East Abbington MA [25 Sept 1845]
Emeline & John FROST at Norway ME [28 May 1846]
Eveline M & George A LONGFELLOW of Winthrop ME by Rev MUGFORD at Hallowell ME [4 Dec 1841]
Franklin of Hallowell ME & Margaret K LORD of Augusta ME by Rev William A DREW at Augusta ME [5 Mar 1842]
Hannah N d/o Oliver FOSTER Esq of Winthrop ME, & N R PIKE of Hallowell ME by Rev F MERRIAM on Sun eve at Winthrop ME [11 Sept 1845]
Hermon N & Eliza MOORE at Argyle ME [12 Apr 1849]
Isabella Mrs & William BENNETT at Bath ME [1 May 1835]
J B editor of *Zion's Advocate* of Portland ME & Ann Doe ROBINSON at Waterville ME [17 Jun 1852]
J B of Brewer ME & Susan L ROWELL at Frankfort ME [12 Aug 1847]
Jane of Brunswick ME & Humphrey AUBENS at Bath ME [22 Jan 1836]
Joel & Mercy DAVIS at Buckfield ME [12 Mar 1846]
John M of Bangor ME & Mrs Cynthia SPAULDING at Thomaston ME [14 Nov 1844]
Juliana C & Job A SPENCER at Gray ME [7 Dec 1848]
Leonard of Leeds ME & Rosilla A WILLIAMS at Turner ME [19 Jun 1838]
Lydia H & George W WENTWORTH at Winthrop ME [24 Aug 1848]
Lydia & Levi WARD at (Augusta) ME [16 Mar 1848]
Maria C & Marshall MORSE at Gray ME [27 Sept 1849]
Martha F M & James G WEST at Belfast ME [27 May 1852]
Mary C & Hiram BRACKETT at No 11 Aroostook County ME [14 Aug 1845]
Mary E & Charles H HAYDEN at Eastport ME [26 Aug 1847]
Mary H late of Alna ME & George L CHANDLER by Rev STOW at the Federal Street Church at Boston MA [30 Jul 1842]
Nancy d/o Nathaniel FOSTER Esq. & Edwin F QUINBY Rev at North Yarmouth ME [21 Jan 1843]
Olive & Dr Ebenezer GRANT of Palermo ME at Albion ME [20 Jun 1834]
Rebecca A & Ezra D BOOBAR both of Milo ME at Foxcroft ME [27 Jul 1839]
Samuel Vassalboro ME & Mary C FRYE at Salem ME?MA? [2 Mar 1848]
Samuel & Caroline CROSS of Bethel ME at Norway ME [3 Jun 1852]
Sarah & B F (Mr) UPTON of Bath ME at Topsham ME [24 Jul 1851]
Sophia G & Wm C TALBOT of East Machias ME at Eastport ME [4 Jun 1846]
Stephen & Diadamia JOHNSON Mrs by Levi FAIRBANKS Esq at Monmouth ME [13 Mar 1835]
Susan F & Franklin PARTRIDGE at Sacarappa ME [1 Jul 1847]

FOSTER (cont.) Thomas & Henrietta BLAIR both of Dresden ME at Litchfield ME [24 Jun 1847]
    Uriah of Clinton ME & Elizabeth S WARE of Augusta ME on 27th ult by Rev MORSE at Augusta ME [4 Jun 1846]
    Warren & Ervilla GILBERT on 2nd inst at Leeds ME [4 Jan 1834]

FOUNTAIN Rhoda M & Wm H HOPKINS of Hallowell ME at Bristol ME [1 Apr 1847]
    Sarah S & Henry H TEEL at St George ME [4 Dec 1845]

FOWLE Caroline M & Ferdinand S RICHARDS on Thurs eve last by Charles C BURR at Hallowell ME [14 Aug 1838]

FOWLER Asahel of Boston MA & Caroline Matilda JOHNSON of Waterville ME at Boston MA [11 Apr 1840]
    B D of Pittsfield ME & Betsey SCRIBNER at Unity ME [16 Mar 1848]
    Caroline P & John W DANA Esq at Portland ME [7 Jun 1849]
    Elizabeth L & Albert TOBEY at Fairfield ME [17 Jan 1850]
    George W of Saco ME & Mary M RICH at East Eddington ME [5 Feb 1852]
    Hannah D & Israel J PERRY Jr of East Thomaston ME at Salem ME [22 Aug 1844]
    James Jr of Unity ME & C STACKPOLE d/o W STACKPOLE by Rev S S NASON at Albion ME [7 Feb 1850]
    N L & Mary M FURBER both of Fairfield ME at Waterville ME [4 Feb 1847]
    Olive & Reuben PRATT at Foxcroft ME [26 Jul 1849]
    Samuel P & Harriet B CLOUGH both of Boxford MA at Readfield ME [9 Dec 1847]
    Thomas L & Betsey L SEAVEY at Saco ME [20 Nov 1835]
    William P & Fanny W RUSSEL at Augusta ME [12 & 19 Dec 1837]

FOX Aaron B & Esther DREW at Athens ME [27 Jan 1848]
    Abby B & Bradbury R MALBON at Skowhegan ME [6 Dec 1849]
    Caroline H & George G BROWN of Sebasticook ME at Skowhegan ME [16 Jan 1845]
    Harriet M & Bradish B BROWN at Monson ME [13 Jul 1848]

FOY/FOYE Elizabeth B & William G RICKER at Gardiner ME [7 Nov 1844]
    James of Gardiner ME & Harriet STICKNEY of (Augusta) ME at Newport ME on 28 Apr [20 May 1852]
    John & Harriet ALBEE by Rev A P HILLMAN at Wiscasset ME [5 Feb 1842]
    Martha & Albion CATE of Dresden ME at Wiscasset ME [29 Nov 1849]
    Mary & Everett ANDREWS at Gardiner ME [21 Mar 1850]
    Susan S & Joseph FEW both of Gardiner ME at New York NY [4 Sept 1845]
    William E & Caroline T GRIFFIN of Gardiner ME [d/o Reuben & Fanny GRIFFEN] [N.B. These were all of American-Black Ancestry] at Augusta ME on 24 Sept by Rev J STEVENS [2 Oct 1851]

FRANCIS Isabel E & William B HASELINE at Boston MA [29 Jun 1848]
    C L of Norway ME & Priscilla H WHITAKER at Houlton ME [6 Sept 1849]
    Elbridge of Turner ME & Cynthia D MILLETT by Rev Walter FOSS at Leeds ME [11 Jan 1849]
    Eunice S of Turner ME & Benj F JONES at Livermore ME [1 Mar 1849]
    Oren & Mrs Sarah P TRYON by Rev M FULLER at Hallowell ME [1 May 1845]

FRANKLIN John Sir of England, the Arctic Explorer, & Ann PORDEN. She was born 1795, widowed in 1847(?), and had knowledge of Greek and other languages [4 Mar 1852]
    Louisa of Peru ME & Winfield S SHACKLEY of Canton ME at Hartford ME [4 Dec 1845]

FRASER John S & Orinda M MOSHER d/o Stephen MOSHER of Hallowell ME at New York City [15 Aug 1840]

FRATERS Manuel D & Ann Maria HUTCHEE both of West Gardiner ME by Rev GRANT at Litchfield ME [30 Oct 1845]

FREEMAN Elizabeth Hassam eldest d/o Rev F FREEMAN of Sandwich MA, & Dr I SNELL Jr of Augusta ME by Rev Frederick FREEMAN at Sandwich MA [22 Jul 1847]
    Frances S & Dr Tristram READMAN at Cherryfield ME [24 Jan 1834]
    George M & Martha L SIMPSON at York ME [16 Jan 1838]
    John A & Minervas S SMALL at Windham ME [27 Jan 1848]
    John & Sarah DOE at Vassalboro ME [24 Jun 1833]
    Joseph of Strong ME & Sarah H SMITH at Harrison ME [5 Feb 1846]
    Julia & A G DAVIS at Hallowell ME [21 Feb 1850]
    Lois of Leeds ME & Isaac PLUMER of Wales ME on New Years evening by Joel SMALL Esq at Wales ME [15 Jan 1839]
    Mary & Carlton D ELMES at Hallowell ME [21 Oct 1843]
    Morton Capt of Middlebury MA & Louisa JENNINGS by Rev Walter FOSS at Wayne ME [18 Mar 1836]
    Nathaniel R formerly of Norridgewock ME & Ruth H DILLINGHAM at Sandwich MA [3 Oct 1844]
    Phylander & Esther REDING at South Berwick ME [11 Apr 1850]
    Prudence B & Bailey CURTIS at Brunswick ME [25 Jan 1840]
    Rowland of Milo ME & Harriot L DAY by Rev Robert LOW at Hallowell ME [28 Mar 1834]
    Statira of Bowdoin ME & Richard R GAURON of Brunswick ME at Bath ME [1 Apr 1847]

FRENCE Henry D & S Melvina CLIFFORD by Joseph GERRY at Fayette ME on 20 Apr [6 May 1852]

FRENCH Adaline & George W HALL of Brighton ME at Solon ME [13 Mar 1845]
    Adeline of Lincolnville ME & Luther HAYDEN of East Thomaston ME on 5th inst at Lincolnville ME [25 Jun 1842]
    Augustus C & Harriet S HALE of Exeter ME at Milo ME [31 Dec 1842]
    Augustus S Esq & Caroline M WHITNEY both of Dexter ME by Rev W S CILLEY at Dexter ME on 14th inst [30 Mar 1848]
    Augustus S & Sarah Arabella WHITE at Dexter ME [7 Nov 1844]
    Barnabas & Esther AUSTIN at China ME [4 Jan 1834]
    Charles A & Persis BRIDGHAM at Minot ME [13 Feb 1851]
    Clarissa of Gardiner ME & Samuel COLLINS of Winthrop ME at Gardiner ME [21 Feb 1837]
    David Capt of Mt Vernon ME & Polly WOOD at New Sharon ME [8 Jul 1833]
    David & Matilda KENNON at Brunswick ME [31 Oct 1844]
    George W of Hallowell ME & Mary N CLARK at Gardiner ME [13 Nov 1845]
    Hannah J of Cornville ME & John G REED of Madison ME at Solon ME [30 Jan 1851]

FRENCH (cont.) Hannah Jane of Cornville ME & John G REED of Madison ME at Solon ME [13 Feb 1851]
Isaac & Adaline B RAWSON at Waldoboro ME [12 Feb 1846]
James of Bangor ME & Ann Maria RICE at Union ME [30 Dec 1847]
Jane & John ROBBINS at Belfast ME [21 Aug 1845]
John S & Julia A GORDON at Livermore ME [31 Oct 1840]
Julia A m Nathan P FELLOWS of Fayette ME at Chesterville ME [22 May 1851]
Loring & Hannah AVERILL at Saco ME [17 Sept 1846]
Martha Ann & Clark KNIGHT of Boston MA at Norway ME [4 Sept 1845]
Mary E & William H CLARK at Belfast ME [20 Jul 1848]
Mary & Church P LEAVETT by Rev George BATES at Turner ME [2 Dec 1836]
Mary & Geo W CUSHMAN Gen both of Woodstock ME at Paris ME [29 Jul 1843]
Moses of Solon ME & Sarah F KIDDER at Norridgewock ME [16 Oct 1845]
Nahum C & Mary Jane HIGGINS by Rev BUXTON at Albion ME [1 Nov 1849]
Nancy & Elijah H DRESSER by Job PRINCE Esq at Turner ME [29 Apr 1847]
Olive H & Isaac M HOBART at Oldtown ME [5 Feb 1852]
Sarah S & John S KIMBALL of Bangor ME at Garland ME [23 Dec 1836]
Simon & Ruth BRUCE at Hallowell ME [25 Nov 1836]
Susan & George D BENSON at Saco ME [9 Aug 1849]
Theodore of Thomaston ME & Sarah L ULRICK at Portland ME [23 Oct 1845]
William W & Sophia A OTIS by J TRENCH Esq at Norridgewock ME [12 Aug 1847]
William & Martha NORTON at Madison ME [8 Oct 1846]

FRETHY Adelade & Elias WEBBER at Hallowell ME [18 Dec 1851]

FRIEND Jeremiah & Joanna EATON at Sedgewick ME [29 Jul 1836]
John S & Rebecca SAVAGE at Bluehill ME [19 Aug 1847]
Nathaniel a Revolutionary Soldier aged 81 & Mrs Mary SMITH, To the bride no doubt that "One Friend old is worth a hundred new" at Beverly MA [1 May 1845]

FRINGENI Mr M & Miss R N WOOD at Windham ME [10 Aug 1848]

FRISBEE Sands & Sarah KIMBALL at Belfast ME [7 Jan 1847]

FRISBY Josiah D & Anna D CUTTING at Phipsburg ME [11 Oct 1849]

FRIZZELL Manley of Starks ME & Mary E CRAM at New Sharon ME [1 Oct 1846]
Mary W & Andrew PINKHAM at Starks ME [17 Jan 1850]
Ruhamah & George H BOARDMAN of Mercer ME at Starks ME [1 Oct 1846]

FROHOCK Huldah & Peter TOWER Jr at Belmont ME [26 Dec 1837]
John R & Francina H RHOADS both of Northport ME at Belfast ME [14 August 1851]
Julia A & Joseph PRESCOTT at Belmont ME [30 Jan 1845]
William H & Mary R COTTRELL both of Newport ME at Belfast ME [15 Oct 1846]

FROST Abigail P & Luther CUSHING at Bloomfield ME [6 Feb 1851] & [16 Jan 1851]

FROST (cont.) Allen & Nancy HERSOM at Belgrade ME [6 Feb 1841]
    Betsey R of Wayne ME & Stephen T DEXTER of Boston MA on 26th inst by Rev Rob't C STARR at Wayne ME [6 May 1843]
    Betsey & Otis KEAG (KEAY?) at Albion ME [15 Jun 1839]
    Elizabeth & Harlow MORSE at Litchfield ME [2 Mar 1839]
    Elizabeth & Theopilus WATERHOUSE Jr of Standish ME at Gorham ME [13 Mar 1845]
    Esther & Joshua B CROCKETT of Paris ME at Norway ME [19 Apr 1849]
    Eunice A & Jacob H SWAN of Denmark ME at Norway ME [12 Dec 1844]
    Henry D & & Ann MURRAY at Readfield ME on 1st Jun by Hon Edward FULLER [12 Jun 1851]
    I Jr & Deborah C NICHOLS at Monmouth ME [27 Mar 1841]
    John & Emeline FOSTER at Norway ME [28 May 1846]
    John & Jane GRAHAM at Eliot ME [30 Oct 1835]
    John & Mary A CURTIS at Gardiner ME [26 Apr 1849]
    John & Mrs Eliza SANBORN at Canaan ME [22 Feb 1849]
    Joseph & Sarah SNOW at Ellsworth ME [1 Apr 1833]
    Joshua & Adeline JOHNSON at Belgrade ME [8 May 1835]
    Lucrenta D & Joshua E JOHNSON at Eastport ME [22 Jan 1852]
    Lydia & Fines HODGDON at Litchfield ME [12 Oct 1848]
    Martha of Cornville ME & Fuller GRAVES of Vassalboro ME at Cornville ME [28 Jan 1843]
    Mary D & Asa THAYER of Norway ME at Bethel ME [1 May 1851]
    Mary E & John W Mitchell at Litchfield ME [31 Aug 1848]
    Melancy B & Benjamin F LAMPSON of Boston MA at Wayne ME by Rev C FULLER [2 Oct 1851]
    Moses Jr & Nancy RICHARDSON 4th inst by Rev D THURSTON at Monmouth ME [14 Oct 1843]
    Mrs Anna & Jeremiah HOBBS at Norway ME [13 Jan 1848]
    Nathaniel B of Wayne ME & Julia MACUMBER of Winthrop ME on 24th ult by Elder STARR at Winthrop ME [6 Mar 1841]
    Octavia d/o Wm FROST Esq, & James McKEEN, M.D., at Topsham ME [4 Jul 1834]
    Patience & Ichabod BILLINGTON at Wayne ME [12 Feb 1836]
    Samuel A & Susan A WING she is 14 years old at Winthrop ME [15 May 1851]
    Sarah of Topsham ME & Israel PUTNAM, M.D., of Bath ME at Topsham ME [31 Jan 1834]
    Sumner of Albany ME & Mrs Eliza FULLER of Norway ME at Norway ME [25 Sept 1845]
    William Maj of Topsham ME & Phebe C GREELY at Bangor ME [21 Nov 1840] & [14 Nov 1840]
    William & Miss R D BRIGGS at Auburn ME [2 Jan 1851]
FRUNG Valentine of Monmouth ME & Sarah PETERSON of Winthrop ME at Augusta ME by Rev E B WEBB [4 Sept 1851]
FRYE/FRY Ensign & Amanda CURRIER 22nd ult at Skowhegan ME [15 Feb 1840]
    Hannah S & Hartwell O WARD on Christmas eve by Rev B F SHAW at China MA [10 Jan 1850] Extended Notice [3 Jan 1850]
    Harriet & Benjamin B Alexander at North Haven Knox Co ME [20 Jul 1848]
    Jesse H & Lucy F BANNAN at Belfast ME [27 May 1843]

FRYE (cont.) Lucy Ann & Abel BENNETT at Belfast ME [19 Apr 1849]
  Mary C & Samuel FOSTER at Salem [2 Mar 1848]
FULLER Albert & Mary F PEARSONS at Bloomfield ME [29 Jan 1852]
  Alden of Minot ME & Sarah A H WALKER at Paris ME [2 Aug 1849]
  Asa C Capt & Mary Jane SNOW at Thomaston ME [16 Jul 1846]
  Benjamin C & Eliza Ann C HOOPER both of Portland ME at New York NY [6 Mar 1845]
  Betsey & Alvardo HAYFORD at Canton ME [19 Dec 1837]
  Caleb Rev & Elizabeth R SWIFT at Wayne ME [8 Jan 1846]
  Caroline S & Edwin ROSE at Thomaston ME [24 Oct 1834]
  Caroline W & Isaac FARRAR Esq of Bangor ME at Augusta ME [19 Jun 1835]
  Catherine M Mrs d/o Hon Nathan WESTON, & Ira WADLEIGH Esq of Oldtown ME on Christmas evening by Rev BURGESS at St Mark's Church at Augusta ME [2 Jan 1845]
  Catherine & John T TOWLE at Hallowell ME [16 Oct 1851]
  Charles P & Abigail SWIFT at Oxford ME [21 May 1842]
  Cordelia & Newland DANFORTH at Lagrange ME [22 Jan 1839]
  D Blin Esq of Albion ME & Louisa J ELLIOT of Knox ME by Rev PEABODY at Portsmouth NH at the Rockingham House [25 Mar 1852]
  David H & Esther A HILDRETH at Gardiner ME [22 Mar 1849]
  Delia J & Sam'l S ROGERS on 1 Jan by Rev C F ALLEN at Augusta ME [10 Jan 1850]
  Eliza Mrs of Norway ME & Sumner FROST of Albany ME at Norway ME [25 Sept 1845]
  Erastus of (Augusta) ME & Elizabeth MERRY by Rev Mr FOGG at Woolwich ME [1 Jan 1852]
  Frances W & Woodbury STINCHFIELD at Wayne ME by Rev C FULLER [2 Oct 1851]
  George G & Frances L CHANDLER at Saco ME [4 Jun 1851]
  George W & Martha NOYES at Jay ME [9 May 1837]
  Gerry of Nashville TN & Abba WHELPLEY at Eastport ME [27 Mar 1845]
  Harriet & Oliver STONE both of this town (Winthrop ME) on Mon last by Rev Wm A DREW at Augusta ME [19 Oct 1833]
  Haskell & Sarenia HATCH on 10 Jul by S SEARS Esq at Lagrange ME [30 Jul 1842]
  Henry W Jr Esq of Augusta ME & Mary Stover GODDARD d/o Nathaniel GODDARD Esq of Boston MA at Boston MA [27 Nov 1835]
  Henry W of Bangor ME & Sarah R LADD on Sat morn last by Rev Alexander BURGESS at St Marks Church at Augusta ME [5 Aug 1852]
  Isaac M of Jay & Mary J LYFORD at Livermore Falls ME [13 Apr 1848]
  J of Fairfield ME & Deborah ROGERS of Augusta ME at Augusta ME [9 Jan 1841]
  Jane C & Richmond B KEEN at Paris ME [7 Nov 1840]
  John D & Charlotte REED of Hermon ME at Carmel ME [20 Jul 1848]
  Jonathan H of Freedom ME & Mary A BAKER at Albion ME [4 Apr 1840]
  Joshua E & Sarah N d/o George ROBINSON Capt on 4th inst at Thomaston ME [21 Feb 1841]
  Julia A of Albion ME & H T BLACK Esq on 28 Feb by Rev J SMITH at Palermo ME [15 Mar 1849]
  L K Mrs of Portland ME & Isiah ELDER at Guilford ME [12 Jul 1849]

FULLER (cont.) Louisa & John WINSLOW on 18 May by Rev BARNARD at Winthrop ME [5 Jun 1845]
    Lucretia G d/o the late Judge FULLER of Augusta ME, & Joseph K CLARK of Wiscasset ME on 27th ult at Boston MA [10 Jan 1850]
    Lucy P & William CHASE at Augusta ME [19 Dec 1840]
    Lucy & William C STINSON at Pittsfield ME [2 Sept 1847]
    Margaret J MILDREDGE Mrs of Scarborough ME & Edward HATCH of Acton ME at Roxbory MA [22 May 1845]
    Martha J of Pittston ME & M B BLISS of Wilbraham MA at Dresden ME [28 May 1846]
    Mary A R & John W DUNHAM at East Livermore ME [5 Oct 1848]
    Mary S & John T SPOFFARD Capt at Thomaston ME [14 Oct 1847]
    Miles & Lydia B HEAL at Lincolnville ME [20 May 1847]
    Nancy Mrs & Frederick LACROIS both of Winthrop ME on 25th ult by Elder Jedediah B PRESCOTT at Monmouth ME [4 Jan 1834]
    Samuel Jr & E J SIDELINGER both of Union ME at Warren ME [30 May 1844]
    Sarah A of Pittston ME & Capt Ira MAXCY at Gardiner ME [7 Jun 1849]
    Sarah M & Charles F WHITING at East Winthrop ME [19 Feb 1852]
    Sewall of Waterville ME & Hannah HUNTINGTON at Gardiner ME [22 May 1851]
    Susan A & James B HYLER of Thomaston ME at South Thomaston ME [27 Mar 1851]
FULLERTON George W & Elizabeth Ann CLOUDMAN by Rev WEBBER at Bangor ME [23 Jul 1842]
    Martha Ann & Gideon G STINSON at Woolwich ME [19 Dec 1840]
    William J of Woolwich ME & Abigail EDGECOMB at Bath ME [7 Jan 1847]
FULMER Jacob K Rev of Bucksport ME & Eliza Ann HOPKINS at Hampden ME [15 Jul 1836]
FULMUR Eliza Ann Mrs d/o Capt Isaac HOPKINS of Hampden ME, & Rufus L HINCKLEY Dr of Boston MA on 30th ult by John WILLIAMS Esq of Bangor ME at Hampden ME [9 Dec 1843]
FULTON Dan & Priscinda MERROW at Bowdoinham ME [21 Jan 1847]
    S A Miss & William J WILLIAMS at Bowdoinham ME [9 Nov 1848]
FURBER Charlotte M & H G O WASHBURN at Belfast ME [3 Oct 1844]
    Mary M & N L FOWLER both of Fairfield ME at Waterville ME [4 Feb 1847]
    S W of Hampden ME & Lucy A METCALF at Milo ME [8 Jun 1848]
    Theodore & Sarah H W HEALD at Milo ME [18 Nov 1843]
FURBISH Lydia W & Albert P POWELL at Hallowell ME [1 Jan 1846]
    Olive & Joshua RAMSDELL at Kennebunk ME [28 Aug 1835]
FURBUSH - see FIRBUSH
    Alice P of Wells ME & Jesse CURTIS of Boston MA at Boston MA [28 Nov 1844]
    Charity & Wm H TUTTLE of Freeman ME at North Anson ME [15 Mar 1849]
    Eliza Ann & Alfred HAMILTON of Woolwich ME by Samuel MOODY Esq at Lisbon ME [8 Feb 1840]
    Harriet & Francis A WALDRON of Portland ME at Brunswick ME [30 Jul 1846]

FURBUSH (cont.) Harriet C & George W GRANT of Newburyport MA at Hallowell ME [18 Oct 1849]
Phebe of Augusta ME & Manassah BLACKSTONE of New Sharon ME at Belgrade ME [13 Feb 1835]
Sarah C & Thomas J CONDON by George P BROWN Esq at Dixmont ME [15 Feb 1840]

FYLER Martha M & Dean PRAY at Augusta ME on 6 Oct by Rev Mr WEBB [16 Oct 1851]
Elizabeth Miss & Silas N CASNER at Waldoboro ME [31 Aug 1848]

- G -

GAGE Caroline & Wm MEANS by A R NICHOLS Esq at Augusta ME [21 Oct 1847]
Elivina H & C F STEVENS at West Waterville ME [5 Oct 1848]
Elizabeth B & Ebenezer WYMAN at Newport ME [14 May 1842]
Frederick & Sarah J HOLBROOK both of Strong ME at Farmington ME [23 Jan 1845]
Irene B & Samuel WARREN at Waterford ME [22 Jan 1846]
Mary Ann & Ebenezer COLBY Jr of Webster ME at Clinton ME [20 Jun 1844]
Mary C E & John E SOPER at Dixmont ME [9 Nov 1848]
Nathaniel of New Sharon ME & Louisa Jane BRADBURY of Chesterville ME at Farmington ME [7 Jan 1843]

GAHAN Mary & Samuel SMALL Jr at Phipsburg ME [12 Apr 1849]

GALE Caroline A & Alvah ELDER of New Portland ME on 7th inst by Rev JUDD at Augusta ME [17 May 1849]
Hannah N & Benjah THOMPSON at (Augusta) ME [18 May 1848]
John & Selena A SWIFT both of Monmouth ME on 13th inst by Rev S HINKLEY at Monmouth ME [17 Jun 1843]

GALEN Knowles of Dresden ME & Mary E HOLBROOK of Bath ME at Phippsburg ME [7 Jan 1847]

GALLISON Mary W & Erastus O PENDLETON at Northport ME [28 Feb 1837]

GALLOPP Cordelia A & Wm H BLOOD at Thomaston ME [8 Oct 1846]

GALUSHA Florilla & Amanda ROBINSON at Augusta ME [15 Mar 1849]

GAMMON Abial O of Naples ME & Susan D STINSON at Arrowsic ME [28 Jun 1849]
D M & Ann M LUNT at Litchfield ME [22 Nov 1849]
Daniel W of Kennebec ME & Maria C BROWN of Sidney ME at Augusta ME on Dec 4 by Rev J STEVENS [11 Dec 1851]
Ezekiel D & Hannah J BARNES at Portland ME [22 Jan 1846]
William G & Martha L HOWARD at Canton ME [6 May 1852]

GANNETT Rev GANNETT of West Gardiner ME & Miss SHAW of Boston MA at Hallowell ME [28 Oct 1847]

GARCELON Alonzo, M.D., of Lewiston ME & Augusta Ann WALDRON of Dover NH at Great Falls NH [25 Sept 1841]
Clarissa J & Stephen Robinson SKINNER at Lewiston ME [18 Jan 1849] & [25 Jan 1849]
Horatio G of Brunswick ME & Eliza A SOULE of Danville ME at Lewiston Falls ME [24 Dec 1846]

GARCELON (cont.) Washington Esq & Rosau eldest d/o of the late Peleg CURTIS Esq by Rev NORTON at Harpswell ME [27 Nov 1838]

GARDINER - GARDNER
- Alexander & Mrs Nancy M Mrs YOUNG both of Augusta ME at China ME on Sunday last by Eld William BOWLER [20 Feb 1851]
- Almira H & Elisha PIERCE both of Bangor ME at Bangor [12 Feb 1846]
- Britannia & Samuel THOMAS both of Buckfield ME by Rev W A DREW at Augusta ME [14 Mar 1844]
- Caroline & Franklin HATHAWAY at Hallowell ME [1 Jul 1847]
- Daniel C of Vassalboro ME & Mary Ann COLMAN of Windsor ME on Sun eve 10th inst by Rev T J SWEAT [21 Jan 1847]
- Delia Tudor d/o R H GARDINER Esq & George JONES Jr of Savannah GA at Gardiner ME [10 Oct 1834]
- Eunice & Moody C BURNESS at China ME [31 Jul 1835]
- Frederic Rev of Saco ME & Caroline V VAUGHAN at Gardiner ME [3 Sept 1846]
- Frederick & Lovinia SMART by Oliver PRESCOTT Esq at (Augusta) ME on 4th inst [13 Jan 1848]
- Harriet d/o Robert H GARDINER, & Richard SULLIVAN Esq of New York NY at Gardiner ME [24 Sept 1846]
- Hartwell Capt of Vassalboro ME & Elvira TURNER d/o Rev Richard TURNER of Windsor ME at Windsor ME [4 Jul 1837]
- Henry D Capt of Nantucket & Caroline B TURNER at Whitefield ME [28 Jan 1847]
- Jacob Jr & Mrs Eliza ANDERSON at Cornville ME by Elder RUSSELL [12 Jun 1851]
- Joseph & Orinda SIMPSON both of Eastport ME at St Andrews New Brunswick Canada [21 Aug 1851]
- L & Wm HARKNESS both of Camden ME at Camden [17 Jul 1845]
- Levi F of Bloomfield ME & Sarah C GREENE of Norridgewock ME by Thomas C JONES Esq at Norr [3 Dec 1846]
- Louisa J & David WILBER at Pembroke ME [22 Jan 1852]
- Martha F of Palermo ME & Daniel FELKER of Embden ME at Albion ME [18 Jan 1844]
- Mary Ann Mrs & Asborough WARNER on 25th ult by Rev A MOORE at Augusta ME [12 Dec 1844]
- Robert H Jr of Gardiner ME & S FENWICK d/o the late Noble W JONES Esq of Savannah GA 28 Jun by Rev VINTON at Newport RI [9 Jul 1842]
- Susan A & Charles BOWLER at China ME on 14 Jun [29 Jun 1848]
- Thomas J of Providence RI & Mary A NELSON d/o Jacob NELSON of Wayne ME 12 Apr at Pensacola West Florida [6 Jun 1840]
- William & Eliza A HAMMELL Thanksgiving evening by Rev BABCOCK at Gardiner ME [18 Dec 1841]

GARLAND Amos & Martha DAWES at Bloomfield ME [27 Nov 1851]
- D D of Boston MA & Julia C DENNIS at Hallowell ME [30 Mar 1848]
- John L & Clarissa P RAWSON at Paris ME [1 Jan 1846]
- Seth & Martha Ann WARE both of Augusta ME on 24 Nov by Rev ALLEN at Farmington ME [6 Dec 1849]
- Seth & Mary B HORN both of Augusta ME at Hallowell ME [16 Jul 1846]

GAREY Charles A & Harriet O HANDY of Garland ME at Exeter ME [18 Sept 1851]

GAREY (cont.) John C & Harriet J DOUGLASS at Dover ME [22 Jan 1852]
   Pamelia & Albert BROWN of Sebec ME at Dover ME [27 Nov 1845]
   Samuel D & Matilda Ann DRESSER at Saco ME [21 May 1846]
GARY Eunice B & Hazen B ELLIOTT at Lovell ME on 16th inst [26 Oct 1848]
GASLIN Betsey A & Thomas C DAVIS at (Augusta) ME on 14th inst [18 May 1848]
   Flora D & Stephen L CHASE at (Augusta) ME [25 May 1848]
   John C & Mary Jane BURGESS 22nd ult by Samuel P BENSON Esq at Winthrop ME [2 Dec 1836]
   Roxana & Elijah H MORSE of Mohawk NY at Vassalboro ME [28 Aug 1842]
   Sarah N of Readfield ME & Alden NORRIS of Livermore ME by Elder MORRILL at Livermore ME [25 Mar 1843]
GATCHELL - see GETCHELL
   John W & Sarah ANDREWS both of Waldo ME on 25th ult at Augusta ME [16 Jan 1845]
   Rachel of Charlestown MA & James BURKE of Bradley ME on 3rd inst by Rufus H STINCHFIELD at Wayne ME [26 Nov 1842]
GATCOMB Mary Mrs & Mr YOUNG at Grand Menan (Island in the Bay of Fundy, Canada) [11 Feb 1847]
GATES Betsey Mrs & Robert LOUD Capt at Bristol ME [29 Feb 1844]
   Emily B m Samuel A MACOMBER of Abbot ME at Monson ME [29 May 1851]
   George H & Eliza L PACKARD at Monson ME [10 Dec 1846]
   George of Nova Scotia Canada & Eliza BOYDEN at Perry ME [5 Mar 1846]
   Louisa Jane & Albert ROBERTSON at Monson ME? [5 Jun 1845]
   Lucinda & Albert C FALES at Thomaston ME [23 Dec 1836]
   Samuel D of Bangor ME & Mary E PRINCE at Portland ME [22 May 1845]
   Susan B & Foster FISHER at Robbinston ME [26 Feb 1846]
GAUBERT Alonzo & Sarah E SAFFORD by Rev S ALLEN at (Augusta) ME on Sept 28th [5 Oct 1848]
   Ann Maria & Silas COLBURN both of Richmond ME on 2 Dec at Richmond ME [11 Dec 1845]
GAULT Hannah S & Daniel BAILEY by Jere BURGIN Esq at Eastport ME [6 Feb 1845]
GAURON Richard R of Brunswick ME & Statira FREEMAN of Bowdoin ME at Bath ME [1 Apr 1847]
GAY A W & Sarah T GOODING at Waldo ME [28 Jan 1847]
   Anna N Mrs & Frederic BALLARD at Farmington ME [14 Nov 1844]
   Charles of Gardiner ME & Martha W d/o Geo W PERKINS Esq by Rev HOWARD at Augusta ME [23 Dec 1843]
   Eliphaz & Rebecca BUTLER at Farmington ME [4 May 1848]
   Ephraim & Ann S CASE at East Thomaston ME [8 Oct 1846]
   Fisher & Lenora D HEWETT at Thomaston ME [29 Jan 1846]
   Ford of Waldo ME & Ruth CROCKETT at Knox ME [23 Nov 1848]
   Joanna Mrs & John S STETSON at Union ME [9 Feb 1839]
   Lucretia & John SNOW at Bath ME [12 Feb 1846]
   Mark & Sarah M GILES at Cushing ME [31 Oct 1844]
   Martin Gay, M.D., of Boston MA & Eleanor ALLEN at Gardiner ME [31 Oct 1844]
   Oliver & Frances SPEAR at Rockland ME [25 Sept 1851]

GAY (cont.) William Esq & Rhoda HARDY at Strong ME [20 May 1847]
William & Catharine WILLIAMS at Augusta ME [4 Apr 1840]
GAZELIN Benjamin F & Sophia CROSS of Vassalboro ME by Rev Mr ALLEN at (Augusta) ME on Sept 25th [5 Oct 1848]
Hannah & William BROWN Mon last by Samuel WOOD Esq at Winthrop ME [29 Apr 1836]
GENTHNER Betha S & Robinson L HALER at Waldoboro ME on 26th inst [30 Mar 1848]
GEORGE Eunice of Leeds ME & David O NELSON of Mercer ME formerly of Winthrop ME on Mon last at Turner ME [19 Jun 1841]
Jacob H of Prospect ME & Lucy E WISE at Belfast ME [1 Jul 1852]
Samuel P of Bowdoinham ME & Harriet Ann PURRINGTON at Embden ME [9 Mar 1848]
Sarah G of Athens ME & William ELLWELL of Skowhegan ME at Athens ME [6 Jun 1840]
GERALD Joseph of York ME & Tabitha ADAMS of Canaan ME by Elder E LEWIS at Clinton ME [8 Aug 1840]
GETCHELL - see GATCHELL
Anna E of Vassalboro ME & L M LELAND of Augusta ME at Vassalboro ME on Dec 9th [25 Dec 1851]
Caroline A & John E NPYES at Portsmouth NH on 2 Jan [29 Jan 1852]
George H & Sabrina D EMERSON of Hallowell ME at Augusta ME on 31st Aug by Asaph R NICHOLS Esq [4 Sept 1851]
Joseph of Etna ME & Hannah NORTON at Palermo ME [31 Oct 1840]
Roxana & Amos BARRY at East Machias ME [1 Jun 1848]
Susan R & Alden CUSHMAN of Oxford ME at Wayne ME by Rev C FULLER [2 Oct 1851]
Thomas A of Camden ME & Clarissa M STINSON at Deer Isle ME by Rev Jonathan ADAMS [14 August 1851]
GEDFREY Ann J & John DODGE Rev Pastor of the Congregational Church in Waldoboro ME at Bangor ME [30 Apr 1842]
GEE Joseph F & Isabella BARTLETT both of Wayne ME at Mt Vernon ME [17 May 1849]
GELASPIE Margaret & Robert HASTY at Baring Washington Co ME [25 Dec 1845]
GENTHNER Harriet E & E T HARVEY Esq of Atkinson ME at Parkman ME [12 Apr 1849]
GERREL Samuel of Orono ME & Mary Ann C WORTH at Corinth ME [12 Oct 1833]
GERRISH E P & Julia A W SCOTT at Portland ME [16 May 1844]
Mary Jane of Lebanon ME/NH? & Sylvanus HATCH of Great Falls NH at Lebanon [3 Dec 1842]
GERRY Hon Elbridge of Waterford ME & Anna St Clair JENNESS on 22 Nov at Portsmouth NH [6 Dec 1849]
GERTS Ann M d/o the late Capt Martin GERTS of Portland ME, & John H RILEY of Boston MA on Tues eve by Rev FARRINGTON at Portland ME [11 Mar 1843]
GETCHELL Andrew T of Litchfield ME & Mary RICE at Hallowell ME [5 Aug 1843]
Arthur L & Frances E LEEMAN on 28 Jan by A R NICHOLS Esq at Augusta ME [31 Jan 1850]

GETCHELL (cont.) Asa & Lucretia G LITTLEFIELD at Winslow ME [21 Feb 1850]
- Charlotte & Amaziah TONNEY of Carmel ME at Belfast ME [25 Apr 1850]
- Christopher & Emma MOOAR at Lewiston ME [3 May 1849]
- Eleazer C & Jane Helen CLARK at Sebasticook ME [31 Dec 1842]
- Elizabeth H & Benj M CARLTON both of Vassalboro ME on 8th inst at Augusta ME [31 Dec 1842]
- Elizabeth M & G M SILSBY at Hallowell ME [25 Mar 1847]
- Ellen & J G DICKENSON Esq Attorney at Law of West Prospect ME at Waterville ME [7 Mar 1840]
- Emma C & Wm H HUMPHREY of North Yarmouth ME at Waterville ME [22 Jul 1852]
- Harriet & Tufton SIMPSON both of Winslow ME by Rev GARDNER at Waterville ME [12 Aug 1843]
- Isaac & Mehitable B FOLSOM both of Winthrop ME by James R MARSTON Esq at Mt Vernon ME [13 Sept 1849]
- James & Cornelia TUCKER at Bath ME [27 May 1836]
- James & Melvira RIDEOUT at Richmond ME [8 Aug 1844]
- Joseph & Sarah Ann BISHOP of Harpswell ME at Brunswick ME [18 Dec 1835]
- Julia A & Abner DINSMORE of Bingham ME at Anson ME [14 Nov 1844]
- Margaret Ann & Ellis SYLVESTER Capt at Phipsburg ME [4 Jun 1846]
- Nathan H of Pittsfield ME & Hannah CONNOR of Unity ME by Rev S S WHITE at Unity [2 Apr 1842]
- Offin P & Eliza FLAGG both of Waterville ME at Sebasticook ME [31 Jan 1850]
- Sarah A & Eleazer HAWES both of Northport ME at Belfast ME [2 Apr 1846]
- Walter B & Mary A COLBY both of Waterville ME at New York NY [6 Aug 1846[
- Walter & Ann Elizabeth BOLKCOM at Waterville ME [7 Dec 1833]
- William of Sidney ME & Vesta PIERCE at Augusta ME [9 May 1837]

GIBBS Albion P of Livermore ME & Mary T HOWARD on Sunday last by Rev ROBINSON at Winthrop ME [30 Dec 1843]
- Ann C of Livermore ME & Capt Lawson L WATTS at Hallowell ME [5 Sept 1844]
- Elizabeth of Livermore ME & E N SHAW of China ME at Hallowell ME [31 Jan 1850]
- Hannah of Canton ME & Isaac NOYES of Minot ME on Sunday last by Rev Reuben MILNER at Canton ME [20 Mar 1835]
- Hannah T & Mr H A BRETT of Lewiston ME at Bridgewater MA? [20 Nov 1851]
- James & Mary Jane KALER at Waldoboro ME [12 Feb 1846]
- John T Editor of the *Dover Gazette* & Mrs Ann T MARCH at Dover NH [9 May 1844]
- John & Eliza THWING at Wiscasset ME [30 Sept 1847]
- Phebe Jane & Elisha PERRY both of Chesterville ME at Fayette ME by H B LOVEJOY Esq [1 May 1851]
- Reuben Jr & Lucy Ann BATES at Waterville ME [7 Oct 1847]
- Sarah Ann of Livermore ME & A S SAWTELL of the firm of SAWTELL and MASON of Hallowell ME on Sunday last at Livermore [20 Mar 1838]
- Susan D & David CHAPLIN at Glenburn ME [23 Jul 1846]

GIBSON H F of Brownfield ME & Harrison G O MORTON of Winthrop ME on 4 May by Rev Abner DAVIS at Brownfield ME [19 Jun 1841]
  Rebecca G d/o Hon S GIBSON of Denmark ME, & Jesse HOWE, M.D., of Lee ME? at Norway ME [28 Oct 1843]
  Samuel & Joanna WOODMAN at Fairfield ME [21 Feb 1850]
  Zachariah 2nd of Brownfield ME & Mary F MORTON of Winthrop ME on 5th inst by Rev David THURSTON at Winthrop ME [13 Nov 1835]
GIDDINGS A R Esq & Deborah TARBOX at Danville ME [11 Apr 1850]
GIFFORD Emily & Daniel AYER of Vassalboro ME on 23 Jan by D Blin FULLER Esq at Albion ME [7 Feb 1850]
  Jacob & Sarah SHOREY both of Sidney ME at Waterville ME [4 Sept 1845]
  Joseph 2nd & Matilda LAWRENCE at Fairfield ME [21 Feb 1850]
  Mary & William H EMERY on 10th inst by Rev J C STOCKBRIDGE at Fairfield ME [4 March 1847]
  Walter & Elizabeth ELLIS at Sidney ME [23 Apr 1846]
GILBERT Aurelia J & John G PHINNEY at Hallowell ME on 22 Oct [2 Nov 1848]
  Betsey & Alfred JEWELL of Winthrop ME at Wayne ME [18 Oct 1849]
  Caleb of Turner ME & Eliza RUSSELL of Phipsburg ME at Phipsburg [18 Nov 1836]
  Caleb S of Leeds ME & Louisa TORSEY of Winthrop ME at Winthrop [6 Feb 1838]
  Charles G & Sarah STORER at Hallowell ME [4 Jun 1846]
  Corolus & Olive R GILBERT at Turner ME [19 Jul 1849]
  Ervilla & Warren FOSTER 2nd inst at Leeds ME [4 Jan 1834]
  James D of Turner ME & Adeline CURTIS of Leeds ME at Leeds [19 Nov 1846]
  Lucius L & Mary DRAKE at Parkman ME [11 Feb 1847]
  Lydia J of Leeds ME & William J HARMON at Brunswick ME [10 Dec 1846]
  Marinda J & John H HANSOM both of Leeds ME at Winthrop ME by S P BROWN Esq [27 Mar 1851]
  Melzar & Alice P BRADFORD at Turner ME [13 Nov 1838]
  Merriam C of Greene ME & Abraham C TOOTHAKER at Brunswick ME [4 Feb 1847]
  Olive R & Corolus GILBERT at Turner ME [19 Jul 1849]
  Proctor J & Elizabeth S DAGGETT at Kennebec ME [4 Sept 1851]
  Sarah S & Joshua C HANKS of Lynn MA at Hallowell ME [8 Nov 1849]
  Washington of Saco ME & Jane BADGER at Brunswick ME [27 Jun 1844]
GILBRETH Benjamin H & Emily J STINCHFIELD at Farmington ME [12 Mar 1842]
  Martha Ann & Elisha H GLIDDEN of Freedom ME at Belfast ME [18 Jun 1846]
  Parthenia F & Marcus P HOWE of Camden ME at Farmington ME [15 Oct 1842]
GILCHREST Betsey & Owen LONG at St George ME [7 Mar 1840]
  Rufus Capt & Angelia WHEELER at Thomaston ME [11 Jul 1844]
GILE Jeremiah & Abigail KIMBALL at Alfred ME [29 Mar 1849]
  William N & Mrs Hannah PHILBRICK by E CLOUGH Esq at Mt Vernon ME on 19th inst [7 Apr 1848]

Marriage Notices from the "Maine Farmer" 155

GILES Arthur W Capt of Gardiner ME & Rebecca R DUNHAM at Brunswick ME [24 Jun 1843]
  Charles publisher of the *Waldo Signal* & Eunice B SALMON at Belfast ME on 17th ult (17 Aug) by Rev William FROTHINGHAM [9 Sept 1843]
  Charles & Eunice B SALMOND at Belfast ME [2 Sept 1843]
  Eliza Ann & Thomas W DUNN of Thomaston ME at St George ME [22 Apr 1847]
  Priscilla & Newell WILSON at Ellsworth ME [4 Dec 1851]
  Sarah M Mrs & Mark GAY at Cushing ME [31 Oct 1844]
GILL Mary d/o Samuel GILL Capt, & Daniel CONY Tues eve last by Rev John H INGRAHAM at Augusta ME [8 Oct 1842]
  Samuel Jr Capt & Hannah WHITNEY by Rev DREW at Augusta ME [27 May 1847]
GILLET E d/o Rev E GILLET of Hallowell ME, & William H PEARCE at Natchez MS [28 Mar 1837]
GILLEY Joseph & Hannah HILTON on 24th inst by Anson CHURCH Esq at Augusta ME [28 Oct 1847]
GILLIGAN Ellen of Eastport ME & James MURPHY of East Machias ME at Eastport ME [13 Feb 1845]
GILLPATRICK Olive & Joseph PERRY Capt both of Gardiner ME at Gorham ME [4 Dec 1845]
GILMAN A H & Sarah G NEAL at Skowhegan ME [12 Dec 1840]
  Allen of Monmouth ME & Mary ROBIE by Rev Dr TAPPAN at Hallowell ME [3 Oct 1844]
  Caroline C & Orrin G DAVIS at Corinth ME [11 Jul 1844]
  Charles R of Monmouth ME & Mary J MARSTON at Gardiner ME [27 Nov 1845]
  Dudley & Hannah M SEWALL at Bath ME [18 Oct 1849]
  Gideon & Harriet K SAWYER by Rev Dr GILLETT at (Augusta) ME [6 Jan 1848]
  John O & Harriet A FOLSOM by David White Esq at Monmouth ME [27 Mar 1835]
  John T Dr of Portland ME & Helen Augusta, d/o Reuel WILLIAMS at Augusta ME [5 Sept 1837]
  Joseph D & Florila D FOLSOM of West Waterville ME at Norridgewock ME [22 Apr 1847]
  Maria C & Charles M ROBERTS of Gardiner ME at Monmouth ME [15 Apr 1847]
  Mary Emeline & Charles E KIMBALL at Hallowell ME [27 Mar 1851]
  Mary L & John W DODGE of Skowhegan ME at Augusta ME [16 Nov 1839]
  Mary S & Joshua WELLS Jr at Mt Vernon ME [15 Jan 1836]
  Milton M formerly of Hallowell ME & Amelia RUNNELS at New York ME [24 Apr 1845]
  Phebe W & Benj B CREASY both of Mt Vernon ME on 21 Nov by G A BENSON Esq at Winthrop ME [22 Nov 1849]
  Sarah Ann & Samuel K PORTER Dr at Mercer ME [28 Feb 1850]
  Sarah & Peleg WILCOX at Monmouth ME [3 Jun 1843]
  Stephen of Sangerville ME & Lydia McLOUD at Dover ME [25 Mar 1852]
  Susannah R & Jacob ELA Jr of Starks ME at Hallowell ME [12 Jul 1849]
  W H & Abby A FOSTER on 24 Jun by Rev D THURSTON at Winthrop ME [28 Jun 1849]

GILMAN (cont.) Warren B of Mercer ME & S Louisa BUTLER at Farmington ME [26 Feb 1852]
William H & Louisa CUSHING at Phipsburg ME [11 Dec 1845] William H & Lydia M WYMAN at Phipsburg ME [20 Nov 1851]
William S of Liberty ME & Sarah L NORRIS of Boston MA on Thurs last by Rev THURSTON at Winthrop ME [1 Apr 1836]
William S W & Harriet Maria MERROW at Augusta ME on 18 Oct by Rev Zenas THOMPSON [23 Oct 1851]

GILMAR Amelia M d/o David GILMAR Esq formerly of Montgomery AL, & Charles A SEWALL merchant of Shreveport formerly of Hallowell ME on 22 Feb at Hickory Hill Parish of Caddo LA [10 Apr 1838]

GILMORE Delia T & Seth W JENNINGS of North Wayne ME by CHASE Esq at Turner ME Extended Notice [9 Aug 1849]
George & Hannah BEAN of Prospect ME at Belfast ME [12 Dec 1844]
John Col & Mrs Eliza HOWARD by Rev STARR at Leeds ME [19 Jun 1841]
Lucy A & Capt Robert O PATTERSON at Belfast ME [19 Mar 1846]
Sarah J & James W WHITE at Belfast ME [23 Dec 1847]
Simeon of Turner ME & Esther ADAMS at Norridgewock ME [25 Mar 1847]

GILPATRICK Albion K P of Webster ME & Olive C ALLEN of Freeport ME at Brunswick ME [25 Feb 1843]
Augusta S & George S HOLT at Topsham ME [28 Oct 1847]
Eliza & Thomas T STIMSON at Limerick ME [3 Jul 1847]
Henrietta & Isaiah D COFFIN of Edgartown MA at Hallowell ME [16 Oct 1851]
James & Mary HARMON at Saco ME [3 Jun 1847]
Maria of Biddeford ME & Noah J SANBORN of Tamworth NH at Saco ME [12 Aug 1852]
Samuel B Capt & Margaret J GOVE of Limington ME at Biddeford ME [5 Aug 1852]
Samuel Col & Eliza A ALLEN at Limerick ME [20 Feb 1851]

GILSON Charles A of Portland ME & Abgie L MEGQUIRE d/o Dr T L M at Winthrop ME on 11 Apr [22 Apr 1852]
William R of Abington MA & Nancy B BICKNELL on 26th inst by Rev William A DREW at Augusta ME [29 Jul 1847]

GINN John O & Mary A ROBINSON at Belmont ME [5 Jul 1849]

GIVEN Agnes C & Alfred CAMPBELL of Newcastle ME at Brunswick ME [4 Dec 1835]
Agnes R & Syvanus HALL at Lewiston ME [30 Mar 1848]
David T & Cynthia TAYLOR on 24th ult at Brunswick ME [3 Jun 1836]
Eben & Frances A CUTTS at Milo ME [25 May 1848]
Elizabeth & Josiah BUTTERFIELD of Hartland ME at St Albans ME [3 Apr 1851]
George P & Susan O CHANDLER at Brunswick ME [7 Jan 1847]
Harriet N & Charles S PENNELL at Brunswick ME [25 Apr 1840] & [5 Dec 1840]
John A of Brunswick ME & Isabella H SPEAR at Bowdoinham ME [5 Nov 1846]
Mary Jane & Edward BOYNTON Capt of Alna ME at Newcastle ME [6 May 1843]
Mehitable C & David S STANWOOD at Brunswick ME [24 Sept 1846]

Marriage Notices from the "Maine Farmer"

GIVEN (cont.) Rebecca Jane of Topsham ME & Dwinal POWERS of Dresden ME at Bowdoinham ME [23 Jan 1841]

GLASPHY Mary & Thomas KELLY at Hallowell ME [6 Sept 1849]

GLASS Laura A Mrs of Turner ME & Daniel WESTON of Livermore ME on 9 Oct by E MARTIN Esq at Turner ME [17 Oct 1834]

Moses of Woolwich ME & Mercy WAKEFIELD at Gardiner ME [22 Nov 1849]

Sarah J & Elisha JAMES at Gardiner ME [1 Jan 1852]

GLAZIER F Jr & Emma J G SWAN at Gardiner ME [5 Apr 1849]

GLEASON Elijah Jr & Pamelia J HALLETT at Waterville ME [18 Mar 1852]

Flora & Wyman RICHARDSON at West Waterville ME [1 Jan 1846]

GLIDDEN Barker B of Belfast ME & Julia S PARKER at (Augusta) ME on 25th Dec [1 Jan 1852]

Caroline A Mrs & Capt Thos J HENRY at Bath ME [7 Jun 1849]

Clymentia & John N CLIFFORD on 4th inst at Augusta ME [14 Oct 1847]

David S of Bremen ME & Catharine W REED at Nobleboro ME [14 Jan 1847]

Elisha H of Freedom ME & Martha Ann GILBRETH at Belfast ME [18 Jun 1846]

Isaac C of Alna ME & Harriet N PALMER at Hallowell ME [8 Jan 1852]

John A & Emma J BAKER both of Gardiner ME at Hallowell ME [10 Jan 1850]

Margaret of Newcastle ME & Josiah HODGKINS of Jefferson ME at Newcastle ME [23 May 1844]

Orville & Miss Hannah T PEARL at Orneville (formerly Milton, then Almond) Piscataquis Co ME [31 Aug 1848]

Samuel G Capt & Martha A H FISHER both of Newcastle ME at Providence RI [26 Jul 1849]

Vesta Volutia & Thomas KENNEDY Jr both of Alna ME at Fayette ME [31 Jul 1845]

GLINES Clarissa & David KNAPP Esq at Rumford ME [14 Dec 1833]

GLITTEN Sarah of Vassalboro ME & Theodore FAUGHT of Sidney ME at Hallowell ME [30 Oct 1845]

GLOVER Aurelia H & Washington WRIGHT at Minot ME [4 May 1839]

George W & Philena HARTFORD both of Camden ME at Rockland ME [19 Aug 1852]

GLYNN Matthias & Hannah Everett LORD adopted d/o Andrew H LORD Esq by Rev THURSTON at Winthrop ME [21 May 1846]

GODDARD Abigail of Brunswick ME & Jordan ALEXANDER at Topsham ME [24 Sept 1846]

Eliza & Jacob SAMPSON at Hallowell ME [18 Dec 1845]

Ephraim F & Mary S S HUTCHINGS of Rumford ME at Andover ME [3 Oct 1840]

Mary Stover d/o Nathaniel GODDARD Esq of Boston MA, & Henry W FULLER Jr Esq of Augusta ME at Boston MA [27 Nov 1835]

Reuben H & Jane S HOWARD at Litchfield ME [31 Dec 1842]

Thatcher & Mary Ann KIMBALL both of Rumford ME by P C VIRGIN Esq at Rumford [6 Mar 1835]

GODDING Ephraim & Harriet G BUMPUS at Livermore ME [31 Jan 1850]

Sarah T & A W GAY at Waldo ME [28 Jan 1847]

GODFREY Adams Capt & Sylvinia BECK at Augusta ME [1 Apr 1843]

GODFREY (cont.) Adeline & John HITCHBORN at Orono ME [29 Feb 1844]
Betsey A S & W M BERRY at Bowdoinham ME [21 Dec 1848]
Charlotte J & Thomas RICE at Bangor ME [1 Jun 1848]
Elmira B & Jonathan HARRIMAN Capt of Bucksport ME at Orrington ME [7 Oct 1847]
Emeline & William Henry ROBINSON at (Augusta) ME [26 Oct 1848]
George F & Sarah A CROSS on 15 Aug by Rev DALTON at Augusta ME [26 Aug 1852]
Harriet G & Hiram EMERY at Orono ME [29 Feb 1844]
Julia d/o John GODFREY Esq. & Robert DUTTON merchant at Bangor ME [12 Jun 1841]
Priscilla A & James B N GOULD of Kennebunk ME at Augusta ME [5 Jun 1835]
William & Charity AUBENS at Bath ME [1 Apr 1847]

GODING Affa Jane & Surranus MERRILL by Isaac STRICKLAND Esq at Livermore ME [14 Nov 1837]
Esther S & Edward D NUTTING at Gardiner ME [26 Apr 1849]
Nancy C of Livermore ME & Ira REYNOLDS of Canton ME by Ruel WASHBURN Esq at Livermore ME [27 Feb 1835]
Nathaniel & Rachel H MOTHERWELL both of Gardiner ME at Windsor ME [9 Sept 1847]

GOFF Julia A & A K P WELCH of Monmouth ME at Auburn ME [12 Mar 1846]
Sewall of Auburn ME & Sarah HAM at Lewiston ME [20 Mar 1845]
William & Clarissa CROCKET at Sumner ME [20 Mar 1841]

GOLDER Dorcas & William S ROGERS of Saco ME at Lewiston ME [4 Oct 1849]

GOLDES Joseph & Mary Jane WING on 30th ult at Augusta ME [10 Dec 1846]

GOLDFUS Martha Mrs & Lucius B ROBERTSON of New Sharon ME at Jay ME [19 Dec 1844]

GOLDSMITH Catherine & Levi JENNINGS of Boston MA on 19th inst by Moses SPRINGER Esq at Gardiner ME [31 Oct 1837]
Hannah of Phillips ME & Daniel HOLT by I TYLER Esq at Weld ME [1 Nov 1849]
Mehitable & John ROBERTS on 19th inst by Moses SPRINGER Esq at Gardiner ME [31 Oct 1837]

GOLDTHWAITE Daniel S of (Augusta) ME & Mary Jane PHILBRICK of (Augusta) ME at Lowell MA [16 Mar 1848]
Edward C & Parthena B WARE both of Augusta ME on 18 Jan by Rev A MOORE at Winslow ME [5 Feb 1846]
Sarah & James MAXWELL at Portland ME [8 Jul 1843]

GOOCH Lydia Mrs of Alfred ME & Nathaniel CHADBOURNE of Sanford ME at Alfred ME [1 May 1838]
Warwick & Mary H WENTWORTH at Kennebunk ME [5 Feb 1852]

GOOD Miss M Elizabeth & Andrew I LYNN at Hallowell ME [15 Jan 1852]

GOODALE David Henry merchant of Hallowell ME & Eliza PHILBROOK of Winthrop ME on Thurs eve last by Rev Daniel D TAPPEN at Winthrop ME [12 Dec 1837]
Elizabeth Mrs & Bartholomew NASON Esq of Augusta ME at Hallowell ME [29 Apr 1833]

GOODALE (cont.) Sarah L & Burnham WARDWELL at Bangor ME [27 Jul 1848]
Thomas Capt of Bucksport ME & Sarah BLACK of Brewer ME at Bangor ME [31 Jul 1845]
GOODELL James & Mrs Abigail MILLER both of Northport ME at Belfast ME [18 Sept 1845]
Margaret & Willard BACHELDER at Prospect ME [15 Aug 1844]
GOODENOUGH Mr J N of Boston MA & Maria WILLIAMS of Strong ME at Farmington ME [23 Oct 1851]
GOODENOW Daniel Hon of Alfred ME & Mrs Catherine P OSGOOD of Fryeburg ME at Portland ME [24 Aug 1848]
Valeria of Alfred ME & Daniel P STONE of Boston MA at Alfred ME [22 Aug 1837]
William Esq & Eliza QUINCY at Portland ME [26 Jun 1835]
GOODING Hannah & Edward P THOMPSON at Pownal ME [22 Feb 1844]
Insign & Josephine STEVENS at Livermore ME [7 May 1846]
William H of Portland ME & Susan P MERRILL at Lisbon ME [3 Oct 1844]
GOODNO David H Dr of Hallowell ME & Elizabeth PIDGE on 21st inst at Providence RI [31 May 1849]
GOODNOW John Esq of Hiram ME & Sarah P d/o John W APPLETON Esq at Portland ME [30 Jan 1845]
GOODRICH Abiel Capt & Anna DUNNING both of Harpswell ME by Rev William HARLOW at Harpswell ME [11 Mar 1833]
Josiah H & Nancy C STEVENS at Moscow ME [25 Apr 1850]
GOODRIDGE Asa & Clarissa RICKER at Smithfield ME [24 Jan 1850]
Betsey B & John DYER at Industry ME [8 Oct 1842]
GOODSPEED Caroline A & Clement F MOODY on 27 Jun by Rev L WENTWORTH at China ME [8 Jul 1852]
GOODWIN Abigail A & Robert S STARBIRD at Gardiner ME [4 May 1848]
Alvin B & Mrs Arabella C KIMBALL at Rumford ME [24 Jul 1851]
Benjamin F & Emeline C MORRISON at Gardiner ME [4 May 1848]
Caroline M & Elias B CHANDLER of Waterville ME at St Albans ME [22 Feb 1849]
Daniel Hon & Julia MERRILL of Portland ME at Detroit MI [31 Jul 1845]
Eliza H & Henry B McCOBB Esq at Saco ME [14 Jun 1849]
Elizabeth A & Orlanda LUQUES at Saco ME [6 May 1847]
Enoch P of Sebec ME & Joanna CHANDLER of Foxcroft ME at Foxcroft [2 Jul 1842]
George W Capt & Sarah J PENNELL of Dover ME at Foxcroft [1 Mar 1849]
Harriet & Edward SEABURY at North Yarmouth ME [13 Jul 1848]
Helen L & Samuel M'LELLAN of Bath ME at Dresden ME [1 Oct 1846]
Henry M of Plainfield MI & Mrs Mary T BROWN at Newport ME? [30 Oct 1841]
J H & Sally ATKINSON at Montville ME [16 Feb 1839]
J W & Martha E BURNHAM at Lubec ME [8 Mar 1849]
James A of Gardiner ME & Mary Ann FLETCHER at Boston MA [23 Jan 1851]
Joanna of Litchfield ME & George S RICHARDSON at Gardiner ME [23 Dec 1847]
John E & Emeline CAMPBELL at Gardiner ME [7 Dec 1848]
John E & Mary E KEIN at Hallowell ME [26 Aug 1843]

GOODWIN (cont.) John J of Avon ME & Hildo B SPRAGUE at Phillips ME [23 Jul 1846]
John & Hannah A GRASON at Lubec ME [17 Jun 1847]
Josiah of Waterville ME & Mary Jane WHITE of Readfield ME at Portsmouth NH [20 May 1852]
Margaret O & Thomas J TWYCROSS 2nd inst by Rev DONNELS at Dresden ME [18 Jul 1844]
Mary & Eli Flitner at Pittston ME [10 Apr 1851]
Rachel & Bryant RICHARDSON at Canaan ME [6 Jun 1837]
Rachel & Uriah BRIERY both of Gardiner ME at Litchfield ME [17 Sept 1846]
S B & Harriet PAINE by Rev MORSE at Augusta ME [26 Nov 1846]
Samuel of Dresden ME & Harriet BARKER at Wayne ME [10 Sept 1846]
Sarah H & Benj D EVANS at St Albans ME [25 Apr 1837]
T D of Pittston ME & Louisa J JEWELL of Winthrop ME at East Winthrop ME [13 Nov 1845]
Thomas & Mary A KNOX at Gardiner ME [14 May 1846]
GOOGINS William of Waterboro ME & Martha A SMITH at Hollis ME [6 May 1847]
GOOKIN Mary O & Samuel D SMITH at Dover NH [26 Feb 1852]
GORDON - GORDAN - GORDEN - GORDIN
Agnes H of Pittston ME & A Patten THOMPSON of Gardiner ME at Augusta ME on 26 Jul by Rev Z THOMPSON [7 Aug 1851]
Charles H & Amanda A ROWELL of Newport ME? by Asaph R NICHOLS Esq at (Augusta) ME on 6th Mar [11 Mar 1852]
Charles W of Hallowell & Mahala L JACOBS at China ME [11 Apr 1850]
Daniel W & Susan A GORDON at Augusta ME [4 Mar 1847]
Dorotha J of Readfield ME & Horatio S RANDALL at Fayette ME [16 Apr 1846]
Evelina E & James PICKERING at Sullivan ME [6 Jul 1848]
Hannah E & James E MERRILL at Readfield ME [4 May 1848]
Henry F & Nancy R RYANT at Hallowell ME [14 Feb 1850]
Henry & Emily SAFFORD at Fayette ME [16 Nov 1848]
Herrick W of Augusta ME & Harriet HODGDON 17th inst at Portsmouth NH [26 Jul 1849]
John S & Mary A CARR by Rev J EDGCOMB at Vienna ME on Mar 18th [8 Apr 1852]
Jonathan R of New Sharon ME & Joanna C SHAW at Norridgewock ME [7 Dec 1839]
Joseph M of Franklin ME & Maria C FOSS at Biddeford ME [20 Jul 1848]
Julia A & John S FRENCH at Livermore ME [31 Oct 1840]
Mary Ann & Josiah W TUCKER of Mercer ME at Vienna ME [28 Feb 1850]
Miles of Weld ME & Betsey JUDKINS at Phillips ME [11 Feb 1843]
Rebecca of Mt Vernon ME & Isaac BUTTERFIELD of Wilton ME at Sidney ME [1 Jan 1846]
Roseline & David KIMBALL of Mercer ME at Vienna ME [28 Feb 1850]
Seth of Biddeford ME & Betsey A PERKINS of Kennebunk ME at Biddeford ME [13 Apr 1848]
Susan A & Charles S DURGIN of Solon ME on Sunday 4th inst by Rev WARREN at Augusta ME [15 Feb 1844]
Susan A & Daniel W GORDON at Augusta [4 Mar 1847]

GORDON (cont.) Sylvester & Emma B CAMPBELL at Chelsea ME? [12 Jun 1851]
  Sylvester & Rosannah BEAN both of Hallowell ME at Readfield ME [13 Sept 1849]
  Sylvina of Mt Vernon ME & David BOWKER at Readfield ME [30 Aug 1849]

GORHAM David Capt & Catharine CURTISS after a long and tedious courtship of twenty years but at last by Rev SHEPHERD at Stratford Extended Notice [26 Sept 1837]
  George W & Elizabeth F LANGLEY at Bangor ME [16 May 1837]
  Isaac B of Lancaster NH & Louisa P YOUNG at Norway ME [10 Oct 1840]
  Olive J & Capt James ATKINS both of Hallowell ME on 19th ult by Rev D FORBES at Hallowell ME [8 Jun 1839]

GOSS Cyrus of Foxcroft ME & Mrs Arabel TUTTLE on 28 Mar at Garland ME [14 May 1842]
  Dexter of Danville ME & Eunice Maria WILSON at Lewiston ME [4 Jan 1844]
  Frances M & Wentworth HOLT of Hermon ME at Levant ME [21 Aug 1851]
  John Jr & Mary G BROOKS at Lewiston ME [22 Jul 1847]
  Mary J & Jeremiah PARKER of Yarmouth ME at Danville ME [7 Mar 1850]
  Sewall N & Elmira D CARVILLE at Lewiston ME [19 Aug 1852]

GOSSIP George H Esq & Mary Helen eldest d/o Charles DINGLEY Esq formerly of Hallowell ME on 24th inst at New York City [6 Mar 1841]

GOTT Alfreda of Wayne ME & Otis HOWARD of Winthrop ME on Sun eve last by Elder ROBINSON at Readfield ME [1 Jul 1843]
  Aurelia of Wayne ME & Nathan COFFIN of Leeds ME at Turner ME [23 Oct 1845]
  Elizabeth & John DAWS at East Black Island ME [27 Jul 1848]

GOUD Susan & & William WADLEY on 31 Oct at Belgrade ME [20 Nov 1845]

GOULD Abba of New Sharon ME & Nathaniel CHASE of Sidney ME at Boston MA on 23 Dec by Rev Theodore PARKER [2 Jan 1851]
  Amanda P & Ezra D HANSCOMB at Biddeford ME [18 Feb 1847]
  Ann C Mrs & Samuel STONE of Woburn ME at Augusta [18 Nov 1843]
  Bartlett of Pittston ME & Catharine COTTLE d/o John COTTLE of Windsor ME at Augusta ME [22 Aug 1840]
  Betsey & Silas SEVERY of Dixfield ME at Carthage ME [9 May 1837]
  Caroline R & W W RICE of Hampden ME at Norridgewock ME [18 Jan 1849]
  Daniel Jr & Mrs Hannah JONES at Hope ME [3 Jun 1847]
  David & Elsey GROVER both of Calais ME at Calais [14 Sept 1839]
  Edwin D of Sangerville ME & Nancy R LANE of Dexter ME at Exeter ME [29 Jul 1852]
  Elisha D of Winthrop ME & Susan E GOULD of Leeds ME at Leeds [22 Aug 1837]
  Ellsie Ann & Richard B CALDWELL of Wiscasset ME publisher of the *Lincoln Republican* on 17th inst by Rev FREEMAN of Augusta ME at Pittston ME [5 Sept 1841]
  Elvira A & Stephen NORTON at Mt Vernon ME on New Years's night [8 Jan 1852]

GOULD (cont.) Emily & Lucius BRADBURY Esq at Eastport ME [21 Jan 1847]
    Erastus E publisher of the *Portland Transcript* & Mary E RANDALL at Portland ME [16 Nov 1848]
    Eunice & Barnabas HOWARD at Leeds ME [25 Apr 1834]
    Frances N & Uriah Esq REED at E Livermore ME [24 Feb 1848]
    G W of Farmington ME & Florinda W SOPER at Hanson MA [15 Oct 1846]
    George of Dixmont ME & Catharine R SWEETSIR of Newburgh ME at Newburgh [8 Jul 1843]
    George T & Eliza Ann LAPHAM at Auburn ME [17 Feb 1848]
    H Wethering Dr of Boston MA & Elizabeth ILLSLEY at Danville ME [28 Mar 1850]
    Harrison & Nancy LANE at Leeds ME [19 Jun 1838]
    Harrison & Sarah STINCHFIELD at Leeds ME [14 Oct 1847]
    Horace K of Bangor ME & Sarah Annette KELSEY of Augusta ME at Hartford CT [17 Dec 1846]
    Horace of Winthrop ME & Mrs Charlotte A GRAY of Boston MA on 17 Dec by Rev DAVIS at Litchfield ME [4 Jan 1849]
    James B N of Kennebunk ME & Priscilla A GODFREY at Augusta ME [5 Jun 1835]
    Lucy A & Charles F STAPLES at Biddeford ME [13 Sept 1849]
    Lydia A & William DEERING Jr at Saco ME [24 Jul 1838]
    Lydia Mrs & Sam'l HUNNEWELL Capt at Solon ME [16 Aug 1849]
    Mark Rev of Andover & Alice A CARTER at Bethel ME [19 Feb 1852]
    Noah M of Lincolnville ME & Rachael DONNELL at Searsmont ME [4 Feb 1833]
    Obadiah of Raymond ME & Sarah ESTES of Raymond ME at China ME [11 Nov 1836]
    Roxy Ann & Alonzo M PROCTOR of New Sharon ME at Farmington ME [29 Oct 1846]
    Sarah E d/o Joshua GOULD Esq, & James RICE of Union ME at Norridgewock ME [24 Jul 1841]
    Sarah Jane & William FINAL at Vassalboro ME [30 Mar 1848]
    Sumner Dr of Madison ME & Sarah FLINT at North Anson ME [5 Oct 1848]
    Susan E of Leeds ME & Elisha D GOULD of Winthrop ME at Leeds ME [22 Aug 1837]
    Tilden & Emeline P COLBY both of Woolwich ME at Wiscasset ME [15 Apr 1843]
    W A & Hannah R MAHURIN both of Smith ME at Norridgewock ME [30 Nov 1848]
    William of Concord ME? & Clarissa JEWETT at South Solon ME [14 Jan 1847]
    William & Lucy LAWRENCE by Rev CLAPP at Pittston ME [3 Jul 1838]
GOULDING John & Drusilla CLARK at Perry ME [12 Feb 1836]
    Joseph G of Wayne ME & Frances P HUBBARD of Waterville ME at Waterville ME [11 Jul 1840]
GOULDSMITH Lucy of Phillips ME & Capt David B HAWES at Hallowell ME [6 Sept 1849]
GOVE Azabah Mrs & Rev Ephraim FORBES at Edgecomb ME [1 May 1835]
    Delia & Alexander MONTARE at Bath ME [31 Oct 1844]

GOVE (cont.) Evelina H & Frederic D SEWALL Esq at Bath ME [22 Nov 1849]
Johnson of Readfield ME & Lucinda ATKINS d/o Rev Charles ATKINS of Mt Vernon ME at Mt Vernon ME [13 Mar 1838]
Lydia H of Monmouth ME & Abner DAY of Bangor ME on 3 Nov by Rev Isaac DOWNING at Monmouth ME [13 Nov 1841]
Margaret J of Limington ME & Capt Samuel B GILPATRICK at Biddeford ME [5 Aug 1852]
Moses J of Readfield ME & Lucinda ATKINS d/o Rev Charles ATKINS by Rev C ATKINS at Mt Vernon ME [3 Apr 1838]
Ruth P & John U BARROWS by Rev J B PRESCOTT at Monmouth ME [23 Jan 1841]
Samuel M & Sarah GREELY d/o Henry GREELY Esq by Dudley MOODY Esq at the meeting house at Kent's Hill (Readfield) ME [1 Aug 1840]
GOWELL Charles & Emerline McALLISTER at Sumner ME [20 Mar 1841]
Mary B & Abijah BOWMAN of Topsham ME at Bowdoin ME [4 Feb 1847]
GOWEN Charles of Sanford ME & Maria ROBINSON of Newburyport MA on 3rd inst at Newburyport MA [17 Jul 1845]
E L & Eliza J FORD at Farmington ME [9 Oct 1845]
Elizabeth W of Kennebunk ME & Haven SARGEANT of Boston MA at Kennebunk ME [23 May 1844]
GOWER Charles W of Greenville ME & Clarissa J HAWES of Vassalboro ME on 21st inst by Rev ADAMS of Augusta at Vassalboro [30 Jan 1841]
George D of New Sharon ME & Ellen MANSFIELD at Hampden ME [25 Apr 1850]
John T of Makawao & Mary G CROSWELL of Farmington ME by T CROSWELL Esq he late of New Sharon ME at Honolulu Sandwich Islands on May 2 [17 Jul 1851]
Mary d/o John GOWER Esq, & Rev D B RANDALL of the Maine (Methodist) Conference at Industry ME [18 May 1839]
William of Industry ME & Hesther Ann CHANDLER d/o Alfred CHANDLER by Rev RANDALL at (Winthrop ME) [16 Jul 1842]
GOWIN Abigail & Vose REYNOLDS at Winslow ME [24 May 1849]
GOWN Erasmus K a soldier of the Revolution aged 82 & Theresa W SWENEY aged 22 at Montville ME [12 Oct 1833]
GRAFFAM - see CRAFFAM
GRAFFAM James A & Mary A BENNET at Thomaston ME [29 Jul 1833]
M Ann & Otis A WRIGHT of Webster ME at Lewiston ME [20 Dec 1849]
Rachel & William H DOUGHTY at Waterville ME [15 Jun 1848]
GRAFTON William & Martha BURNES at Thomaston ME [30 Apr 1846]
GRAHAM Elcy of Milton Plantation Oxford Co ME & Moses P KIMBALL of Lowell MA at Rumford ME [30 Sept 1847]
Jane & John FROST at Eliot ME [30 Oct 1835]
John C & Susan M WOOD at Rumford ME [4 May 1848]
Lucy & Arthur L CHASE at Lowell MA [5 Aug 1847]
GRANCE Mary Mrs of Freeport ME aged 75 & Capt Elijah ALLEN aged 78 at Bowdoin ME [14 Nov 1844]
GRANDIN David Seabury Dr late of New York, & Mrs Jane Maria LANE formerly Miss LEE of Brunswick ME on the 21st by Rev ADAMS at Brunswick ME [3 Oct 1837]

GRANGER Abraham H Rev of Warren ME & Frances M KIMBALL at Waterville ME [9 Dec 1843]

GRANT Abigail & Luther JESSYLN both of Frankfort ME at Troy ME [26 Oct 1839]

    Albion K P & Frances J BRACKETT at Denmark ME [7 Apr 1848]

    Almira R & Abraham F PREBLE of Bowdoinham ME at Richmond ME [26 Apr 1849]

    Annett M & Thomas P SHUTE at Prospect ME [13 Jun 1844]

    Betsey I & Robert FISHER at (Augusta) ME on 22d May [27 May 1852]

    Catharine A & Capt Orrin FARNHAM of Portland ME at Gardiner ME [2 Dec 1836]

    Clementine C & Capt William R HEAGAN at North Prospect ME [15 Apr 1852]

    Ebenezer Dr of Palermo ME & Olive FOSTER at Albion ME [20 Jun 1834]

    Ebenezer of Saco ME & Nancy STEVENS at Buxton ME [11 Mar 1847]

    Eliza D of Bridgton ME & Alex BOOTHBY Dr at Unity ME [26 Apr 1849]

    Elizabeth L & Henry WASHBURN Jr at Gardiner ME [25 Feb 1843]

    Elizabeth R of Richmond ME & Robert COOMBS of Bowdoin ME at Richmond ME [17 Oct 1844]

    Ellen & Hon John OTIS at Hallowell ME on 21st Aug [31 Aug 1848]

    Esther & Capt Franklin HARRIMAN at Prospect ME [1 Feb 1849]

    Franklin & Elizabeth EARLE at South Berwick ME [30 Apr 1846]

    George W of Newburyport MA & Harriet C FURBUSH at Hallowell ME [18 Oct 1849]

    George W & Harriet M STINSON 1st inst at Prospect ME [15 Jan 1842]

    Isaac M & Catharine B CASWELL at Thomaston ME [23 Oct 1845]

    Jefferson of Frankfort ME & Emeline PLUMMER at Newburyport MA [19 Dec 1840]

    Lewis of Biddeford & Augusta A ROLLINS at Saco ME [21 Dec 1848]

    M & Sarah LOVEJOY by John HAM Esq at Sidney ME [22 Oct 1842]

    Maria L & Wilson HEATH at (Augusta) ME [27 Apr 1848]

    Mark & Abigail STEVENS of Lebanon ME? at South Berwick ME [24 Jul 1838]

    Mary E & Ivory LITTLEFIELD of Kennebunk ME at Portsmouth NH [9 Oct 1851]

    Mary E & Loring W ROGERS at Orrington ME [3 Feb 1848]

    Mary & Barker A NEAL of Wiscasset ME at Gardiner ME [17 Apr 1851]

    Nancy C & Thomas W ROBERTS of Howland ME at Brewer ME [20 Feb 1845]

    Noah & Olive H DAVIS of Newburyport MA at Kittery ME [3 Aug 1848]

    Olivia Buckminster d/o Samuel C GRANT Esq. & George BACON of Boston MA at Hallowell ME [9 Oct 1845]

    Priscilla E & John F CABLES Capt of Cohasset MA at East Thomaston ME [14 Mar 1850]

    Rebecca & Calvin EMERY both of S Berwick ME at Dover ME [10 Jul 1851]

    Sarah E & Enoch LEATHERS at Hermon ME [11 Sept 1851]

    Thirsa H & Ira PLUMMER at Sebasticook ME [7 Apr 1848]

    William B Jr of Gardiner ME & Catharine BABSON of Wiscasset ME at Wiscasset ME [6 Nov 1841]

GRANT (cont.) William S of Gardiner ME & Betsey L JOSSELYN d/o Alvah JOSSELYN Esq by Rev Mr BURGESS at (Augusta) ME on Monday evening at St Mark's Church [27 Jan 1848]

GRASON Hannah A & John GOODWIN at Lubec ME [17 Jun 1847]

GRAVES Fuller of Vassalboro ME & Martha FROST of Cornville ME at Cornville [28 Jan 1843]
- Hannah I & LaFayette M BURGESS at Wayne ME [25 Mar 1852]
- Isaac of Topsham ME & Rebecca PRINCE at Brunswick ME [23 Apr 1846]
- John of S Thomaston ME & Mrs Lydia SMITH at Thomaston ME [10 Jul 1851]
- Mary & James CHADBOURN at Vassalboro ME [28 Jan 1843]
- Osgood & Eliza J RIDLEY by Rev C FULLER at Wayne ME [3 Feb 1848]
- Perley G & Mercy WILLIAMS at Thomaston ME [5 Jun 1845]
- Rachel Amelia & Capt Jacob TOMPKINS at Bangor ME [19 Aug 1847]

GRAY Abby C of Hallowell ME & Aaron DAVIS of Chelsea ME at Augusta ME on Jan 20th by Rev Z THOMPSON [6 Feb 1851]
- Abigail & Jonathan J HARDY both of Plymouth ME by William H NASON Esq at Plymouth ME [13 Mar 1838]
- Albert & Mary D MAGOON at Sangerville ME [4 Apr 1840]
- Alexander of Woolwich ME & Martha SHAW on 25th ult by Rev MORSE at Winthrop ME [9 Dec 1847]
- Almira of Orono ME & Hiram W JEWELL of Lincoln ME at Bangor ME [18 Mar 1836]
- Andrew aged 18 & H HOWARD aged 19 at Brooksville ME [11 Feb 1843]
- Arthur of Naples ME & Margaret WYER at Harpswell ME [5 Apr 1849]
- Caroline & John McMULLEN at Thomaston ME [5 Feb 1846]
- Charlotte A Mrs of Boston ME & Horace GOULD of Winthrop ME on 17 Dec by Rev DAVIS at Litchfield ME [4 Jan 1849]
- Cornelia A & Orrington LUNT Esq at Bowdoinham ME [29 Jan 1842]
- Cyrus H & Hannah E AVERY of Vienna ME at Readfield ME [11 Apr 1840]
- Eliza widow of Green Co d/o Henry BROWN merchant of Bluehill ME, & Henry BLACK Esq of Orange Co by Rev WHITE at New York City [27 Mar 1841]
- Ellen & Joseph C HAWES at North Anson ME [27 Jul 1848]
- Harriet of Starks ME & Winthrop NORTON Jr at Norridgewock ME [9 May 1844]
- Hiram of Benton ME & Mary L BEAL at Brighton ME [9 Oct 1851]
- James W & Sarah E HAM at Whitefield ME [30 Mar 1848]
- John of South Berwick ME & Temperance WINN at York ME [29 Jul 1847]
- Joshua R of Dorchester MA & Almira C MITCHELL at Vassalboro ME by Rev Mr BRAY [16 Oct 1851]
- Luther & Harriet A ALLEN on 9 Dec by Elder N F NASON at Plymouth ME [27 Dec 1849]
- Mary S & Coleman F BECKFORD at Lubec ME [11 Jan 1849]
- Moses Esq & Nancy J PAGE of Hallowell ME d/o late Moses B GILMAN at Chicago IL on 23 Dec [23 Jan 1851]
- Nancy P of Bowdoinham ME & G H LOWELL of Gardiner ME at Waldoboro ME [19 Feb 1846]
- Nancy & Samuel LEWIS at Hallowell ME [7 Dec 1848]
- Olivia & Sullivan ANDREWS at Paris ME [23 May 1840]

GRAY (cont.) Rufus H of LaGRANGE ME & Harriet M DRAKE by J H MACOMBER Esq at Milo ME on 9 Nov [16 Nov 1848]
  Samuel of China ME & Eliza M KIMBAL of Windsor ME at Windsor [7 Mar 1844]
  Samuel T of Waldoboro ME & Nancy HUTCHINSON at Vassalboro ME [22 Apr 1847]
  William Capt & Relief DRAKE at Thomaston ME [12 Sept 1840]
GRAYHILL Elizabeth aged 60 & George BUCKHART aged 90 at Harlen Co NY [29 Jul 1833]
GREAR Matilda M & Francis A CLAY at Augusta ME by Rev Z THOMPSON [16 Oct 1851]
GREATON Rebecca W & Enoch L GREENLEAF at Starks ME [12 Jun 1851]
GREATEN George W & Elmira J BOARDMAN at Starks ME [26 Jun 1845]
GREELEY A M & Sarah A FORD on 16 Jun at China ME [1 Jul 1852]
  Allen Rev of Turner ME & Susan SWALLOW at North Yarmouth ME [26 Mar 1846]
  Betsey M & John D SOULE both of Palermo ME by C H SPRING Esq at Montville ME [5 Feb 1839]
  Burnham C & Tamar EATON of Norridgewock ME at (Augusta) ME on Jun 29 by S WILLIAMSON Eld [10 Jul 1851]
  Hannah M Mrs & Sulvanus LAUGHTON at Hallowell ME [29 Oct 1846]
  James & Sarah J RAND of Swanville ME at Searsport ME [31 Aug 1848]
  John P of Bangor ME & Julia A BARTLETT at Camden ME [8 May 1845]
  John W & Martha BARTLETT by Rev Theodore HILL at Mt Vernon ME [21 Feb 1850]
  Laura Ann & Thos WINTER at Gardiner ME [8 Aug 1844]
  Maria B & Charles ESTERS both of Augusta ME on 28th ult by William PERCIVAL Esq at China ME [1 Feb 1849]
  Maria G of Palermo ME & Ambrose SPARROWK of Augusta ME by Joseph GREELEY Esq at China ME [9 Jan 1845]
  Mary Ann & Seth T PARSONS at Smithfield ME [26 Oct 1848]
  Mr H G & Clarissa DIXON at Clinton ME [20 Jan 1848]
  Octavia & Francis KINSMAN both of Augusta ME at Providence RI on Aug 8th [21 Aug 1851]
  Phebe C & Maj William FROST at Bangor ME [21 Nov 1840] & [14 Nov 1840]
  Sarah & Samuel M GOVE at the meeting house at Kent's Hill (Readfield) ME [1 Aug 1840]
  Sheldon H & Cordelia BROWN at Palermo ME [28 Oct 1847]
  Thomas H of Boston MA & Mary BURRILL at Albion ME [14 May 1846]
GREEN/GREENE Abby A & Jonathan HILL at Bath ME [25 Feb 1847]
  Adriana & Turner COWEN of Lisbon ME at Brunswick ME [27 Mar 1845]
  Albert S & Sarah J BROOKS at (Augusta) ME on 21st instant [1 Jun 1848]
  Aurilla & Moody BURBANK by Rev Josiah PEET at Norridgewock ME [28 May 1846]
  Caroline F d/o Hon Nathaniel GREENE of Topsham ME, & Thomas W NEWMAN printer of the *Advocate of Freedom*, Hallowell ME on 23rd inst by Rev T N LORD at Thomaston ME [27 Feb 1841]
  Daniel aged 83 & Mrs Mary TRASK aged 64 both of Augusta ME at Hallowell ME [23 Oct 1845]

GREEN (cont.) Elizabeth F & George W COLLINS at St Albans ME [16 Apr 1846]
 Frances Ann d/o Henry GREEN formerly of Portland ME, & Charles V SMITH on 10th inst by Rev THURSTON of Winthrop ME at Augusta ME [21 Oct 1843]
 Hannah & Jeremiah THORN on 18 Oct by O A WEBBER Esq at Vassalboro ME [4 Nov 1847]
 Harriet N & Zebulon REED at Bath ME [16 Jul 1846]
 John & Mary CLARK of Pembroke ME at Dennysville ME [2 Jan 1845]
 John & Sarah J NORWOOD at West Camden ME [13 Sept 1849]
 Joseph B & Maria H MILLS both of Providence RI by Rev Charles WILLETT at Thompson CT on 10 Oct [31 Aug 1848]
 Joseph & Mary Jane WILSON at Belfast ME [30 Aug 1849]
 Levi B of Brunswick ME & Eleanor S WAIRE of Gardiner ME at Gardiner ME [24 Jun 1833]
 Lucinda & Robert PLUMMER at Biddeford ME [21 Dec 1848]
 Lucy A & James H ANDREWS both of Eastport ME at Perry ME [9 Dec 1836]
 Margaret G & Daniel ROLLINS at Camden ME [13 May 1852]
 Martha K of Wilton ME & Sylvanus B PHILBRICK of Chesterville ME at Farmington ME [13 Nov 1851]
 Mary H & F A PIKE Esq at Calais ME [8 Oct 1846]
 Mary S of Augusta ME & Edmund HANSCOM of Lowell MA on 22 Oct in Trinity Church by Rev John L WATSON at Boston MA [7 Nov 1844]
 Nath'l C & Keziah Ann WYMAN at Lexington ME [4 Jan 1849]
 Noah & Sarah Jane ROWE both of Smithfield ME at Hallowell ME [30 Oct 1845]
 Sarah C of Norridgewock ME & Levi F GARDNER of Bloomfield ME by Thomas C JONES Esq at Norridgewock ME [3 Dec 1846]
 Sarah F & Oliver T SMALL of Windsor ME on Sun eve last by Rev WILLIAMS at Augusta ME [15 Aug 1844]
 Susannah & Hon Thomas RICE on 16th at Winslow ME [5 Mar 1842]
 Timothy M of Naples ME & E A RICHARDSON at Gilead ME [19 Apr 1849]

GREENHALGH Ann of Gardiner ME & William L DAVIS of Poland ME at Gardiner ME [18 Dec 1845]

GREENLAW Ruth & William HASTINGS Esq at Bristol ME [30 May 1837]

GREENLEAF Adaline B Mrs & Capt James AULD at Westport ME [7 Jan 1847]
 Emma & Harrison N DAVIS at New Portland ME [9 Jul 1846]
 Emmy & Lyman WING of Monmouth ME by Jonathan G HUNTON Esq at Readfield ME [5 Oct 1833]
 Enoch L & Rebecca W GREATON at Starks ME [12 Jun 1851]
 Gardiner of Anson ME & Hannah A PINKHAM by Rev Mr GOLDTHWAIT at Vassalboro ME on 17 Nov [20 Jan 1848]
 Harriet R & Robert D ELAY at Abbot ME [14 Oct 1847]
 Henry C & Susan H BISBEE at North Yarmouth ME [3 Feb 1848]
 Joseph & Irene HOOK at Skowhegan ME [21 May 1846]
 Lydia A of Starks ME & John B MAXFIELD by M LITTLEFIELD Esq at Skowhegan ME [22 Jul 1852]
 Mary A & Lewis E WRIGHT of Woolwich ME at Westport ME [26 Mar 1846]

GREENLEAF (cont.) Moses Esq of Williamsburg ME & Martha d/o Col J LEE of Milo ME at Bucksport ME [22 Jan 1839]
 Oliver H P & Margaret CURTIS—also Spencer PRESSEY & Harriet MERRIL—John W LINNELL & Rebecca WHITCOMB all of Mercer by Hartley KIMBALL Esq at Mercer ME [25 May 1839]
 Reuben & Rosina LEEMAN at Augusta ME [25 Apr 1837]
 Sarah A & James J FISHER of Bath ME at Wiscasset ME [14 Nov 1844]
 Sarah & Andrew R NEWELL at New Sharon ME [25 Jul 1840]
 Susan B & Capt John McNEAR of Wiscasset ME at Westport ME [2 Dec 1843]
 Susan & B Y HOLBROOK Capt at Wiscasset ME [16 Oct 1845]

GREENLOW Arletta & John HASTINGS at Bristol ME [4 Oct 1849]
 Eveline & Isaac CROOKER at Phipsburg ME [29 Apr 1852]
 Hannah of Georgetown ME & Thomas OLIVER of Phipsburg ME by Andrew REED Esq at Phipsburg ME [16 Oct 1838]

GREENOUGH Abigail & John BORNHEIMER of Waldoboro ME at Wiscasset ME [25 Jun 1842]
 Catharine W & Peter P PARSONS of Farmington ME at New Sharon ME [12 Nov 1846]
 John R Jr Rev Pastor of the Baptist Church in Oldtown ME & Justina C CHESLEY at Bangor ME [7 Oct 1847]

GREENWOOD Abigail & Bunker CLARK at Farmington ME [13 Dec 1849]
 Alanson A of Augusta ME & Eliza Ann NESS d/o Capt Ranlett N of Searsmont ME at Vassalboro ME on Feb 15 [27 Feb 1851]
 Julia of Farmington ME & George B BROWN of New Sharon ME by Rev Isaac ROGERS at Farmington ME [7 Oct 1847]
 Julia & Cephas MOONY of Concord NH at Clinton ME [14 Oct 1847]
 Noah C & Susan E TARBOX at New Gloucester ME [3 Jul 1845]
 Philomelia & Edwin E WILDER of Bridgton ME at Farmington ME [5 Aug 1847]
 Samuel W & Lorann QUIMBY at Greene ME [25 Jan 1849]
 Sarah formerly of Weston ME & John T DAVIS formerly of Biddeford ME at Milton ME [23 Apr 1842]
 Veris & Ellen WILKINS at Greene ME [25 Jan 1849]
 Zina H & Emily M FELLOWS both of Augusta ME on 8 Nov at Hallowell ME [29 Nov 1849]

GREER Albert & Louisa Ann RICHARDS at Belmont ME [28 Mar 1850]

GREGG Charles & Catharine ORR of Brunswick ME at Andover ME [11 Sept 1851]

GREGORY Caroline C & James MORTON at Thomaston ME [9 Mar 1848]

GREY Samuel & Mrs Abigail DENNIS by Charles A RUSS Esq at China ME [13 Apr 1839]

GRIDLEY Charles H of Boston MA & Mary Bertha MORRISON at Dresden ME [28 Jan 1847]

GRIFFIN Caroline T of Gardiner ME [d/o Reuben & Fanny GRIFFEN] & William E FOY [N.B. these two were of American-Black Ancestry] at Augusta ME on 24 Sept by Rev J STEVENS [2 Oct 1851]
 Delilah & James DAVIS Jr at Augusta ME [23 Sept 1843]
 Eliphaz D & Martha Ann ROGERS at Freeport ME [24 Oct 1844]
 Eliza G & Isaiah STETSON of Bangor ME at Brunswick ME [11 Sept 1851]

GRIFFIN (cont.) Elizabeth & William T PLAISTED of Danville ME at Greene ME [23 Jul 1846]
George & Sarah C TUFT at Boston MA [28 Sept 1833]
Isaac Jr of Minot ME & Sarah E LEMONT of Greene ME at Greene [24 Jul 1841]
James S of Windsor ME & Sarah E PLUMMER at Freeport ME [11 Jul 1844]
Joseph A of Boston MA & Mary Jane DEARBORN at Hallowell ME on 12th Jun [23 Jun 1852]
Samuel D & Olive SMITH on Thurs 27th ult by Rev A MOORE at Augusta ME [6 Mar 1845]
GRIFFITH Lotan of Hallowell ME & Clarrissa LANE of Augusta ME by Silas CARTER at Augusta ME [5 Jun 1838]
William A & Mrs Mary SAMPSON both of Winthrop ME on 30 Dec by John HEARSEY Esq at Canton Point ME [4 Jan 1840]
GRIGGS Charles & Eliza HARRIS at Oldtown ME [25 Jul 1844]
GRINNELL Cornelia & N P WILLIS Esq of New York NY at New Bedford [22 Oct 1846]
William of Exeter ME? & Martha IRISH of Union ME at Union [22 Jan 1839]
GRISWOLD Virgil of Westfield MA & Mrs Nelly BURNHAM at Thomaston ME [28 Sept 1839]
GROSS Caroline & John SIDELENGER of Nobleboro ME at Waldoboro ME [14 Mar 1844]
Gilbert & Abigail O STEVENS at Hallowell ME [4 Dec 1845]
Thomas B & Orinda DAILEY on 21st ult at Camden ME [2 Sept 1836]
GROTON Ellen E K & Hon P O J SMITH at Portsmouth NH [15 Jan 1852]
GROUSE Elizabeth & George WEBSTER of Bath ME at Brunswick ME [18 Sept 1845]
William & Mary PIERCE of Monmouth ME by Rev THURSTON at Winthrop ME [15 Jun 1839]
GROUT Amos Jr & Abigail S BRIER of Belfast ME by Rev S G SARGENT at Belfast ME [25 Jun 1842]
GROVE Eleanor Mrs & Joshua YOUNG Esq of Mercer ME on 19th inst at Wiscasset ME [22 Nov 1849]
GROVER Abernethy Esq & Mary C CHAPMAN at Bethel ME [17 Feb 1848]
Andrew & Mary A RAYNES at Auburn ME [21 Oct 1847]
Elbridge J & Mercy L HOPKINS at Brunswick ME [8 Oct 1846]
Elijah Esq of Wesley ME & Clarissa H FOSTER at Skowhegan ME [4 Oct 1849]
Elsey & David GOULD both of Calais ME at Calais ME [14 Sept 1839]
Hannah & Daniel TARR of Webster ME at Bowdoin ME [1 Feb 1849]
Lovis & Elmore SCRIBNER at Letter B ME [8 Jan 1846]
Lucy Ann of Sidney ME & Worcester N HALE of West Waterville ME on New Year's Day at Sidney [8 Jan 1846]
Samuel M Esq of Guilford ME & Frances PULLEN at Levant ME [22 Jul 1852]
GROVES Mary of Litchfield ME d/o David GROVES Esq & William H POTTER of Wales ME late from California at Augusta ME on 24 (Apr) 1851 by Rev W A DREW [1 May 1851]

GROVES (cont.) Nancy A & Barnabas B RUSSELL of Madison ME at Skowhegan ME [9 Apr 1846]

GROW Samuel P & Violetta S CURRIER d/o Charles CURRIER Esq by Rev N W SHELDON at Vassalboro ME [30 Mar 1848]

GROWS James & Assenath WORRY at Bath ME [17 May 1849]

GUBTEL Elijah & Harriet SHUMAN by J H BECKETT Esq at Union ME [15 Jul 1836]

GUFF Hiram H of Hallowell ME & Melissa WHITNEY at Cabotville MA [28 Oct 1847]

GUILD Alpheus E of Augusta ME & Abby H FARMER on 27 Jun by Rev HACKETT at Temple ME [8 Jul 1852]

Cyrus Jr of Winthrop ME & Eleanor W d/o W DAMREN at Belgrade ME [27 Feb 1841]

Lucy B & Freeman BARKER on 16 Dec by Rev DILLINGHAM at Augusta ME [23 Dec 1847]

Maria D & Thomas LOVEJOY of Farmington ME on 18th inst by Rev N W WILLIAMS at Augusta ME [27 Jun 1844]

Olivia L of Augusta ME & Silas W DUNTON of Milbury MA 23 Aug at Thompson CT [17 Sept 1846]

Samuel of Augusta ME & Eliza E LYON at Readfield ME [11 Apr 1844]

Samuel E & Mary F ROWE of Lowell MA at Strong ME [5 Aug 1847]

GUILE James W of Lowell MA & Mary B HERSEY at Hallowell ME [16 Jul 1846]

GUILFORD Daniel & Nancy CLOUGH at Saco ME [17 Jun 1852]

GULLIFER Hannah & William BLAGDEN at Skowhegan ME [8 Jan 1839]

GULLIVER Caroline & Hiram BICKFORD at Hermon ME [18 Jan 1840]

GUPPY Sarah F & Parker L WILSON at Corinth ME [6 Feb 1851]

GUPTILL David L & Abigail A d/o Stephen WINSLOW on Sun last at the Methodist Chapel by Rev FULLER at Augusta ME [10 Apr 1838]

Nancy & Sherman SMITH of Steuben at Gouldsboro ME [24 Jun 1847]

Philetia C of Thomaston ME & Winchester L RICE of Camden ME at Thomaston ME [22 Oct 1846]

GURNEY Rebecca C & Wm B UPTON at Norway ME [25 Oct 1849]

GUSHEE Rebecca D & Thaddeus E RIPLET of Hope ME at Appleton ME [7 May 1846]

GUY Ann Mrs & David HOWCROFT at Dover ME [13 Jul 1848]

- *H* -

HACKER Isaac & Miss Jane M ALLEN at Brunswick ME on the 19th inst [29 Aug 1834]

Rachel & Benjamin F ATKINSON at Brunswick ME [19 Jun 1845]

HACKETT Ezekiel & Miss Charlotte THOMPSON at Phillips ME [5 Dec 1834]

G & Miss C J DAME both of Jackson NH at Parsonsfield ME [14 Sept 1848]

Henry of Lewiston ME & Auvilla BLETHEN at Lisbon ME [9 May 1844]

John & Susan HOWARD at Brooksville ME [29 Apr 1836]

Joseph L & Miss Deborah RIDGEWAY at New Vineyard ME [15 May 1845]

Julia W & Eliab L EATON of Farmington ME at New Vineyard ME [6 Mar 1851]

Marriage Notices from the "Maine Farmer"

HADLOCK Joseph of Falmouth ME & Maria WASHBURN at Paris ME [19 Nov 1846]
  Smith formerly of Mt Desert ME & Sarah SKILLINGS at Bangs Island ME [5 Aug 1843]
HAGGETT Henry F & Miss Paulina S WADE at Norridgewock ME [14 Jan 1847]
HAGAN Rosilla & John WILSON of Freedom ME at Anson ME [1 Nov 1849]
HAGER James Esq & Henrietta LILLY at Richmond ME [28 Dec 1848]
HAHN Levi M of Boston MA & Betsey TINKHAM by Rev Mr THURSTON at (Winthrop) ME [19 Sept 1840]
  Betsey T Mrs & Oakes HOWARD Esq at Winthrop ME (see p 429 of Stackpole's *History of Winthrop ME*) [8 May 1851]
HAINES/HAINS Charles of Biddeford ME & Frances HAYES of North Yarmouth ME at Dover NH [5 Feb 1852]
  Charles of Readfield ME & Eliza A LOW of Kennebec (now Manchester) ME by Rev S POWERS at Winthrop ME on 21st Mar [25 Mar 1852]
  Columbus Esq of East Livermore ME & Anne P TOWNSEND at Sidney ME [9 Dec 1847]
  Content W & John MAY Esq at Winthrop ME on Sat evening last by Elder ROBINSON [21 Jul 1843]
  Daniel of Parkman ME & Nancy ELLIOTT of (Augusta) ME at Hallowell ME [27 Jul 1848]
  Elmira & Hiram BARTON of Wayne ME at Readfield ME [25 Jun 1846]
  Lydia A of Saco ME & Loren J MILLIKEN at Buxton ME [17 Dec 1846]
  Mary C & Ezra KEMPTON of Phillips ME at Lake Settlement ME [28 Mar 1844]
  Mary F & Alfred FLOYD at Biddeford ME [7 May 1846]
  Mary G of Dorchester MA & William H HARLOW of Roxbury, formerly of ME [10 Jul 1838]
  Nathaniel & Sarah DUREN at Augusta ME [15 Aug 1837]
  Rufus R & Elizabeth F MARSTON at Bath ME [18 Sept 1851]
  S L Esq & Miss A W TALLALEE at Bangor ME [27 May 1847]
  Samuel Capt of New York NY & Abbe M LEWIS at Waterville ME [8 Jan 1852]
  Sarah J & Benjamin F PEASE at Hallowell ME [14 Sept 1848]
  Silas A B Esq of Green Bay WI & Harriet C NEIL of Skowhegan ME at Lynn MA [10 Jul 1851]
HALE Abby formerly of (Augusta) ME & Jos NUDD of Waterville ME at Newburyport MA on 10 Apr 1851 [8 May 1851]
  Anna M & George H NIEBUHR of Bath ME at Portland ME [31 Oct 1844]
  Calvin G of Norridgewock ME & Cordelia A MACOMBER at Winthrop ME on Jul 12 [23 Jul 1846]
  David Dr of Livermore ME & Esther EUSTIS at Jay ME [30 Sept 1843]
  Elias J of Foxcroft ME & Ann R BIXBY at Athens ME [6 Jan 1848]
  Harriet S of Exeter ME & Augustus C FRENCH at Milo ME [31 Dec 1842]
  Ira L & Miss Ann E RICHARDSON at Brunswick ME [11 Nov 1847]
  Mary C of Norridgewock ME at Lowell MA & A R BOYNTON, M.D., [17 Jan 1850]
  Mary J & Albert W PAINE at Foxcroft ME [18 Jul 1840]
  Nathaniel & Mary WHITNEY at Bridgton ME [16 Apr 1846]
  Roswell, formerly of this town (Winthrop ME) & Mrs Hannah, wid/o the late Harrison HOLTON of Houlton ME on 2d Mar [19 Mar 1842]

HALE (cont.) Susan, d/o the late Capt Abel COFFIN, & Ephraim A HYDE, M.D., of Freeport ME at Newburyport MA on 5th inst [21 Jan 1843]
Worcester N of West Waterville ME at Sidney ME on New Years's Day [8 Jan 1846]

HALER Robinson L & Betha S GENTHNER by Reuben ORFF Esq at Waldoboro ME on 26th inst [30 Mar 1848]

HALEY Abby A & Andrew J WOODMAN of Saco ME at Cornish ME [13 Feb 1851]
Aphia F of Webster ME, d/o Hon Deacon HALEY, & Deacon Nathaniel BENNER at Lisbon ME on 13th Jun [1 Jul 1847]
George W & Susan A MITCHELL at Bath ME [2 Sept 1847]
James Esq of Frankfort ME & Julia Ann HALEY at Hampden ME [19 Mar 1846]
Joel & Phebe Ann HASKELL both of Portland ME at Durham ME on 20th inst [2 Jul 1842]
John R of Augusta ME & Philomela R, d/o Rev Henry KENDALL of Topsham ME [28 Dec 1839]
Joseph Jr & Eliza HATCH at Hollis ME [2 Nov 1833]
Julia Ann & James HALEY at Hamden ME [19 Mar 1846]
Olive W & Paul HUSSEY at Biddeford ME [5 Feb 1852]
Rebecca & John S G BROWN at Calais ME on 23d ult [10 Jun 1843]
Sarah S of Bath ME & James M SOULE of Chelsea ME at Bath ME [20 Feb 1845]
Susan F of Webster & John YEATON of Stafford NH at Dorchester MA [18 Dec 1845]
Sylvia M & John COUSIND at Hollis ME [6 Jun 1844]

HALL A W Miss & William F WENTWORTH at Lebanon ME [27 Jul 1848]
Abigail J of Lowell & Alpheus L FOSS of Leeds ME at Boston MA [4 Mar 1843]
Alanson & Angeline STARKS of Monmouth ME [26 Jun 1841]
Amanda of Topsham ME & Thomas E NOYES, printer at Brunswick ME [12 Jun 1838]
Andrew J of Buckfield ME & Mary HOOPER at Paris ME [23 Jan 1851]
Ann Elizabeth & Silas S LOW of Bangor ME at Thomaston ME [1 Apr 1843]
Ann Maria & Mr L S ADAMS at Litchfield ME on 30th ult [19 Oct 1848]
Arad H & Sarah A CAMPBELL both of Newcastle ME at Augusta ME on 21 Feb by Rev George S G SPENCER [7 Mar 1850]
Caroline O Mrs & Lot WIGGIN at Limerick ME [23 Nov 1848]
Charles & Caroline PAGE at Wayne ME [23 May 1844]
Clara B & John W INGRAHAM of Montville ME at Knox ME [22 Feb 1844]
Dorcas A & James M HALL at Bowdoinham ME on Jul 4th by Elder C QUINNAM [8 Jul 1847]
E Wallis of Boston MA & Apphia A BADGER at Kittery ME [3 Aug 1848]
Elizabeth B & Orren TUBBS at Mechanic Falls ME [23 Nov 1848]
Elizabeth Mrs & Alexander BATES of Richmond ME at Litchfield ME [4 Jan 1849]
Elizabeth (Mrs) & Alexander BATES at Litchfield ME [28 Dec 1848]
Ezra Capt & Betsey ELWELL at Belfast ME [4 Dec 1851]
George of Portland ME & Rebecca W THATCHER at Saco ME [20 Aug 1846]

HALL (cont.) George S & Ann Augusta, eldest d/o A R NICHOLS Esq at Augusta ME on 5th Apr by Rev Mr JUDD [16 Apr 1846]
George W of Brighton ME & Adaline FRENCH at Solon ME [13 Mar 1845]
George & Mrs Mary Ann FERNALD at Kennebunkport ME [1 May 1838]
Gertrude A & Newell ALLEN late of Foxcroft ME at Parma Centre NY [21 Mar 1844]
Harriet of Portland ME & Henry P DREW of Brunswick ME at Portland ME [21 Nov 1837]
Horatio of Brunswick ME & Rebecca ROGERS of Phipsburg ME by Andrew REED Esq [16 Oct 1838]
Ira H of Athens ME & Betsey C WESTON at Norridgewock ME [7 Dec 1848]
Isaac S & Apphia C ASHFORD at Windsor ME [8 Jul 1852]
J Henry Rev of Paris KY & Wealthy Frances PETTINGILL of Winthrop ME by Rev Dr EDGAR of Nashville TN at "Gothic Chapel" of the Mammoth Cave of Kentucky on Apr 26th [20 May 1852]
James Capt of Augusta ME & Francis Ann DAVIS at Bath ME [15 Aug 1834]
James M & Dorcas A HALL at Bowdoinham ME on 4th Jul by Elder C QUINNAM [8 Jul 1847]
James N Jr & Miss Mary C AMES at Belfast ME [3 Sept 1846]
James N & Emily Jane PURINGTON at Portland ME [4 Jul 1834]
John G & Mrs Augusta ROBBINS at China ME by James B HASKELL [20 Sept 1849]
John S & Rosanna A MURRAY at Norridgewock ME [8 Feb 1849]
John & Lydia Ann KINCAID at Bath ME [28 Mar 1850]
Joseph B of Presque Isle Aroostook Co ME & Francis K NEWELL at Sangerville ME [4 Mar 1847]
Joseph H & Mary F SAVAGE at Augusta ME on Sunday evening last by Rev C FULLER [19 Nov 1842]
Julia A & Ansel G TAYLOR at Presque Isle Aroostook Co ME [13 Jan 1848]
Livermore R & Mary A MILLER of Lowell MA at Rumford ME [28 Jan 1847]
Louisa D & Stephen N HALL of Brunswick ME at Bowdoin ME [11 Jun 1846]
Lovina B & Benjamin H FIFIELD of Readfield ME at Belgrade ME [10 May 1849]
Lydia Ann & George HOBBS at Saco ME [8 Apr 1847]
Lydia & Franklin TWITCHELL at Paris ME [8 Apr 1852]
Lydia & John Holbrook Jr at Norridgewock ME [5 Dec 1844]
Marcella M of Presque Isle Aroostook Co ME & Mr Joseph W HINES of Boston MA by Rev J G MERRILL [9 Sept 1847]
Margaret & Capt Stephen L HARRIS at North Yarmouth ME [9 Jul 1846]
Mark of Throndike ME & Olivia DeCROW at Lincolnville ME [26 Dec 1837]
Mary A & Isaac CASE of Thomaston ME at Belfast ME [19 Jul 1849]
Mary E & George W SUTHERLAND at Saco MA [5 Jul 1849]
Mary E & Joel W THOMAS both of Rockland ME? at Salem [10 Jul 1851]
Nancy & James EMERY at Augusta ME [28 Dec 1839]
Octavia F & Charles S WEEKS of Vassalboro ME at China ME [10 Apr 1851]

HALL (cont.) Rachel & Ivory COLE of Brownfield ME at Norway ME [27 Nov 1851]
- Rebecca A & Joel CARD Jr at Litchfield ME both of Bowdoinham ME [8 Jul 1847]
- Rhoda of North Berwick ME & Joseph W MITCHFIELD at Medford MA [8 Feb 1844]
- Samuel P & Miss Abigail B TREWORGY at Ellsworth ME [28 Dec 1839]
- Shelton L Esq & Elizabeth P APPLETON of Rockford IL at Portland ME [18 Sept 1845]
- Stephen N of Brunswick ME & Louisa D HALL at Bowdoin ME [11 Jun 1846]
- Stephen of Norway ME & Miss Sarah T MAYO of Brownville ME at Vassalboro ME [1 Mar 1849]
- Stephen (43y) & Lydia KELLY (age 77y) at North Yarmouth ME on the town farm, by a vote of the town [9 Dec 1836]
- Susannah & William HALL of Athens ME at Hartland ME [3 Apr 1851]
- Syvanus & Agnes R GIVEN at Lewiston ME [30 Mar 1848]
- Theodata L & Thomas SMITH of Hallowell ME [22 Aug 1844]
- William M of Gorham ME & Ann E REED of Westbrook ME [2 May 1844]
- William of Athens ME & Susannah HALL at Hartland ME [3 Apr 1851]

HALLETT/HALLET Adaline & William MILLS at Belgrade ME [20 Jan 1848]
- Augustus & Miss Helen MacGRATH at West Waterville ME [30 Jul 1846]
- Caroline & Jason STEVENS of Augusta ME at West Waterville ME on the 16th inst by S KIMBALL Esq [20 Dec 1849]
- Climena & William W WOODBURY, principal of the Augusta High School at Augusta ME [27 Nov 1841]
- Harriet A, d/o the late Elisha HALLETT Esq. Seth C WHITEHOUSE at Augusta ME by the Rev Mr WEBB [26 Aug 1852]
- Jonathan of West Waterville ME & Miss Sophia P WINGATE at Hallowell ME [14 Feb 1850]
- Mary A & Robert BROWN at West Waterville ME [12 Jul 1849]
- Nathan C of (Augusta) ME & Clara A RICHARDSON by Joseph CUMMINGS Esq at Belgrade ME [17 Aug 1848]
- Pamelia J & Elijah GLEASON at Waterville ME [18 Mar 1852]
- Sarah E d/o Watson F HALLETT Esq & Charles H MULLIKEN at Augusta ME on Dec 3rd by Rev WEBB [18 Dec 1851]
- Watson Esq of Augusta ME & Miss Priscilla PURINTON at Topsham ME [3 Jun 1836]

HALLOWELL Caleb & Emeline JONES at Windsor ME [3 Jul 1851]
- James L of Belfast ME & Christina M BLAKE of Bangor ME at Bangor [30 Sept 1847]
- [Lady] sis/o the late Mr HALLOWELL & Samuel VAUGHAN an English merchant in London [see story about the VAUGHAN family] at Hook part of Hallowell ME "some four or five years before the close of the eighteenth century" (1795-1796) [30 Oct 1851]
- Lucy P & Ora C WYMAN at Windsor ME [7 Mar 1844]
- Sarah M & Josiah PLUMMER at Whitefield ME on Aug on 17th [24 Aug 1848]

HAM Albert N & Mary Ann d/o Major L M JUDKINS at Augusta ME [4 Dec 1841]
- Amanda F & Charles S CURTIS at Hallowell ME on the 25th inst [2 Jan 1835]

HAM (cont.) James H & Miss Isabella A CROSS at Hallowell ME [2 Jan 1835]
- Jane & Willard WALKER at Bath ME [24 Oct 1834]
- John Edward & Julia A JOHNSON at Augusta ME [9 Dec 1843]
- John of Limerick ME & Mary R LANE at Waterboro ME [14 August 1851]
- Joseph D & Mary J BRIGHAM at Wayne ME [29 Jan 1846]
- Rebekah & Bartlett BURGESS of Wayne ME of Fayette ME [29 Jan 1839]
- Sarah E & James W GRAY at Whitefield ME [30 Mar 1848]
- Sarah & Sewall GOFF of Auburn ME at Lewiston ME [20 Mar 1845]

HAMBLEN
- Wellington B & Miss Philena P ROBINSON at Sidney ME on 12th inst [23 Oct 1845]

HAMBLET Phebe & John MOORE Jr at Solon ME [2 Jan 1851]

HAMBLIN Lucy Jane & Rev Hollis RUSSELL at Andover MA/ME? [5 Oct 1848]

HAMILTON Alfred of Woolwich ME & Eliza Ann FURBUCH at Lisbon ME by Samuel MOODY Esq [8 Feb 1840]
- Alonzo of Saco ME & Miss Mary Ann CHASE of Norridgewock ME [4 Jan 1840]
- Charles of Worcester MA & Miss Jane INGHAM at Bath ME [23 Aug 1849]
- George S, formerly of Barre MA & Mary J INGHAM formerly of Mt Vernon ME at Augusta ME on Thursday evening last by Rev William A DREW [12 Dec 1844]
- George & Jane TOURTLOTTE at Ellsworth ME [4 Dec 1851]
- Hannah & John W RUSSELL at Vassalboro ME on 17th Aug by Rev L WENTWORTH [28 Aug 1851]
- James Jr of Elmira, Chemung Co, NY & Sarah Jane WRIGHT of Lewiston ME at Lewiston ME [30 Sept 1847]
- Lucinda of Webster ME & Leander M MACOMBER of Monmouth ME at Wales ME [25 Mar 1847]
- Lydia Ann & Stephen BOYNTON at (Augusta) ME [6 Jul 1848]
- M A of Vassalboro ME & Joseph S SMITH of Hallowell ME at Augusta ME on May 13th by Rev W A P DILLINGHAM [24 May 1849]
- Margaret Ewing & John McNEIL at Augusta ME [2 Jan 1838]
- Mary Ann & Joshua ELLIS Jr of Fairfield ME at Waterville ME [1 Jul 1843]
- Rebecca & Simeon FURBUSH of Webster ME at Monmouth ME [28 Aug 1845]
- Robney L & Miss Harriet E JONES at Belfast ME [12 Jul 1849]
- Solomon & Lydia LEMFEST at Swanville ME [19 Mar 1846]
- Uriah & Mary MOODY at Bath ME [11 Jul 1834]

HAMLEN/HAMLIN A W of Gardiner ME & Mary F BUKER at Bowdoin ME [1 Jul 1852]
- Almira & Marcus V REYNOLDS at Augusta ME [5 Dec 1837]
- Ann & Daniel Hon BROWN of Waterford ME at Paris ME by Rev C B DAVIS [6 Feb 1851]
- Chandler G & Angeline S CROWELL both of Gardiner ME at Hallowell ME [11 Oct 1849]
- Charles H of Augusta ME & Sarah E PALMER d/o Barnabas P Esq at Kennebunk ME on May 1st by Rev SWAN [15 May 1851]
- Edward & Mary Jane DANIELS at Portland ME [10 Oct 1837]

HAMBLEN (cont.) Elijah & Ruth BURT of Turner ME at Paris ME [21 Jun 1849]
    Elizabeth & Edwin CRAIG at Augusta ME [2 Jan 1838]
    Henry C of Augusta ME & Miss Abby L HOBART at Hingham MA [26 Dec 1840]
    James E & Phebe A FISK at Augusta ME on 11 Jul [22 Jul 1847]
    Jane F & Luther M WILLIAMS at Vassalboro ME [28 Mar 1834]
    Julian & Mr E A NASON at Augusta ME on Tuesday evening last by Rev Benjamin TAPPAN [12 Jun 1838]
    Melinda C & Edmund C WARREN at Winslow ME [16 Nov 1848]
    Sarah C of Hampden ME & Andrew T WINGATE of Boston MA at New York NY [16 Oct 1845]
    T A & Fanny WELLINGTON at Albion ME on Jan 2 [23 Jan 1851]
    William A & Mary J BOWLER both of Augusta ME at Sidney ME [22 Mar 1849]
    William H & Mary M BROWN of Lovell ME at Sweden ME [19 Feb 1852]
HAMLET Laura Jane of Brownville ME & William R PERHAM of Williamsburg ME at Milo ME [31 Jul 1851]
HAMMELL Eliza A & William GARDINER at Gardiner ME on Thanksgiving by Rev Mr BABCOCK [18 Dec 1841]
HAMMOND Azel of Peru ME & Sarah MAXIM at Wayne ME on 4th Mar [22 Apr 1852]
    Betsey M & Abner PIPER of Templeton MA at Sidney ME [2 Sept 1847]
    Cordelia A & Samuel P PRAY of Monson ME at Guilford ME [10 Oct 1844]
    J P Rev of Bangor ME & Nannie PAGE at Alexandria VA [30 Dec 1847]
    Jairus K & Eliza HOOPER at Paris ME [15 Mar 1849]
    Joshua R of Crystal Plt (Aroostook Co) ME & Jennette A CUSHMAN at Woodstock ME [19 Jul 1849]
    Juliette & Thomas H BROWN, M.D., at Paris ME [30 Dec 1847]
    Mary A & Richard DRESSER at New Gloucester ME [29 Apr 1847]
    Nancy & Enoch LITTLEFIELD at Brunswick ME [13 May 1852]
    Phineas B & Miss Eliza B DYER both of Sidney ME at Augusta ME [14 Oct 1843]
HAMMONS Hiram & Miss Rhoda ARNOLD at Dixmont ME [7 Jan 1847]
HAMOR Cornelius T & Sally HOPKINS at Eden ME [18 Dec 1835]
HANCHE Abraham & Margaret HART at Bath ME [21 Mar 1844]
HANCOCK Irene of Boston MA & Samuel W DOWNES of Orland ME at Boston MA [27 Nov 1835]
    Rachel & James W HARMON at Falmouth ME [3 Dec 1842]
HANDY Ebenezer of Union ME & Miranda T BILLINGS at Albion ME on 26th Sept by Thomas BURRILL Esq [7 Oct 1847]
    Elizabeth of Wayne ME & Thomas B SWIFT of Fayette ME [23 May 1844]
    Harriet O of Garland ME & Charles A GAREY at Exeter ME [18 Sept 1851]
    Martha Ann & John PALMER both of Hallowell ME at Gardiner ME [24 Oct 1834]
    Pauline B & George SHAW at Albion ME [8 Jun 1839]
    Prudence of Wayne ME & Sylvanus PRATT of Berlin ME at Wayne ME on 16th ult by Isaac BOWLES Esq of this town (Winthrop) ME [9 Jan 1835]
    Robert G & Mary E AMES at Hallowell ME on 21st by Rev Mr BUTLER [1 Jan 1842]

Marriage Notices from the "Maine Farmer" 177

HANDY (cont.) William Capt of Standish MA & Mary VICKEY by Rev J PEET at Norridgewock ME [5 Oct 1848]
HANKERSON John Jr of Madrid ME & Margaret B RUSSEL at Carthage ME by H STORER Esq [14 Dec 1839]
    Marinda & William TARBOX Esq of Phillips ME at Madrid ME [11 Feb 1847]
HANKS Joshua C of Lynn MA & Miss Sarah S GILBERT at Hallowell ME [8 Nov 1849]
HANNAFORD Corydon C & Mrs Huldah E TITUS both of Monmouth ME by Rev D B RANDALL [3 Apr 1841]
    Martha S, d/o Greely HANNAFORD, & Mr S W COLE of Cornish ME, Editor of the *Yankee Farmer* at Cape Elizabeth ME [4 Dec 1835]
HANNAH Laura E & Tobias DELUE at Calais ME [30 Oct 1841]
HANNIE Francis Maj of Arkansas & Wealthy B J RANDALL at Bath ME [25 Jun 1846]
HANNIFORD Thomas J & Lydia Jane TRASK at Wiscasset ME [13 May 1847]
HANNOR Sarah of Eden ME & Capt Edward HODGKINS Capt of Hancock ME at Eden ME by Lenord J THOMAS [12 Feb 1842]
HANSCOM Daniel of Hallowell ME & Hannah L BROWN at Gardiner ME [24 Aug 1848]
    Eliza A & John O DEARBORN both of Readfield ME at Augusta ME on 30 Aug by Lot M MERRILL Esq [18 Sept 1851]
    Emily L & Samuel WEYMOUTH at (Augusta) ME [20 May 1852]
    Julia Ann & Mr C W HILTON at (Augusta) ME [29 Apr 1852]
    Edmund of Lowell MA & Mary S GREEN of Augusta ME at Boston MA on 22d Oct in Trinity Church by Rev John L WATSON [7 Nov 1844]
    Jonathan of Jay ME & Lydia LAKE of Wilton ME at East Dixfield ME [25 Dec 1845]
    Martha of Hallowell ME & Walter W PHILBRICK Esq at Augusta ME by J J EVELETH [28 May 1846]
    Moses Jr of Waterville ME & Artie RICHARDSON of Lowell MA at Nashua NH [3 Sept 1846]
    Samuel Jr & Miss Margaret J MARSHALL at Berwick ME [29 Mar 1849]
    Sarah E of New Gloucester ME & Horace B STANCLIFT of Saco ME [1 Feb 1849]
    Sarah J & Nelson L LAWRENCE at East Machias ME [18 Nov 1847]
    Washington & Rectina B JUDKINS at Winthrop ME on 29 May by Rev F FOSTER [5 Jun 1845]
HANSCOMB Alpheus A, publisher of the *Maine Democrat* & Miss Mary MILLIKEN at Saco ME [7 Oct 1843]
    Ezra D & Miss Amanda P GOULD at Biddeford ME [18 Feb 1847]
HANSOM A of Bangor ME & Mary A ELLIOT of Levant ME at Augusta ME [2 Jan 1851]
    Abigail & John W TAYLOR at Lyman ME [8 Mar 1849]
    Abner & Miss Rebecca L NASH at Sidney ME [11 Feb 1847]
    Andrew & Nancy SMALL at China ME [26 Feb 1846]
    David of Orono ME & Lucy Ann RICE of the former place at Buxton ME [26 Aug 1836]
    Elisha & Harriet CARVILL at Lewiston ME [16 Oct 1845]
    Hannah & Paul KNIGHT at Scarborough ME [29 May 1835]

HANSOM (cont.) J W & Miss Elizabeth Ann PIKE at Atkinson ME [14 Jun 1849]
- John H & Marinda J GILBERT both of Leeds ME at Winthrop ME by S P BROWN Esq [27 Mar 1851]
- John W & Miss Mary A PERKINS at Biddeford ME [1 Feb 1844]
- John & Betsey Ann REACH at Bath ME [15 May 1845]
- John & Catharine TURNER of Perkins ME at Bath ME [25 Jan 1849]
- Mary A & Samuel R ALLEN at Smithfield ME [5 Apr 1849]
- Mary & James SMALL at China ME [26 Feb 1846]
- Moses of Windham ME & Miss Betsey WATERHOUSE of Westbrook ME at Westbrook [24 Jun 1836]
- Moses & Miss Lydia J BROWN at Winthrop ME on Christmas Eve by E W KELLEY Esq [10 Jan 1850]
- Narcissa & Arnold S RICHMOND of Hallowell ME at Buxton ME on Sunday eve on 16th inst [1 Jan 1839]
- Nathaniel of Buxton ME & Mary L WOODMAN of Hollis ME by Rev Mr SEAVEY at Hollis ME [11 Jul 1840]
- Nehemiah & Mary BEARCE at Readfield ME [29 Jan 1846]
- Noah of Portland ME & Mary C WINSLOW at Windham ME [25 Nov 1847]
- Phineas & Mary D EMERY at Buxton ME by Rev Mr BAILEY [30 Apr 1842]
- Rosannah & Benjamin BERRY at Bangor ME [18 Jun 1846]
- Royal B & Miss Ann PIKE at Saco ME [4 Dec 1845]
- Samuel of Mt Vernon ME & Harriet BATES at Leeds ME on 9th inst [20 Apr 1848]
- Sarah Mrs & Nathaniel LUFKIN at North Yarmouth ME by Rev C HOBART [19 Mar 1842]
- Sylvia, d/o Mr Noyes SMITH of Mt Vernon ME, & Nathaniel REMICK of Augusta ME at Mt Vernon ME on 2d inst by Samuel TITCOMB Jr Esq [9 Jan 1845]
- V C & Miss Eliza LOWELL at Windham ME [1 Apr 1836]
- W K A & Ellen H BARNEY, d/o Hon Charles BARNEY at Atkinson ME on Jan 13th by E F HAMMOND Esq [8 Feb 1849]

HAPGOOD Margaret M & Enoch C MOODY at Augusta ME on 21st by Rev Mr DREW [28 Jan 1847]
- Nancy L of Waterford ME & Gustavus A STEWARD of Anson ME at Waterville ME [11 Apr 1844]

HARADEN Caroline S & Enoch S HILTON of Unity ME at Belfast ME [21 May 1846]

HARBACH Catherine P & Nathaniel HATCH at Camden ME [1 Apr 1852]

HARDEN Abigail W & Daniel HUTCHASON at Bangor ME [11 Jul 1844]
- John F Capt & Sarah Jane PILLSBURY at Rockland ME [25 Dec 1851]

HARDING Abijah S & Miss Maria JOHNSON both of Hampden ME at Bangor ME [24 Jul 1835]
- Agnes & Josepph McDONALD Esq at Windham ME both of Gorham ME [26 Mar 1846]
- Edward of New Orleans & Miss Louisa H McLELLAN at Bath ME [25 Sept 1841]
- Harriet of Haverhill MA & John H HARRIS of Bath ME printer and publisher of the *Maine Inquirer* [5 Aug 1833]
- Irene & Elisha COX at Bath ME [31 Oct 1840]
- Jedediah & Dorcas TAILOR at New Sharon ME [18 Sept 1835]

HARDING (cont.) Nehemiah & Mrs Mary W LARRABEE at Bath ME [25 Nov 1843]
  Reuben of Phillips ME & Miss Charlotte DAVIS at Hallowell ME [20 Sept 1849]
  Richard Capt of Truro MA & Frances E MITCHELL at North Yarmouth ME [18 Sept 1846]
HARDISON Dorcas Jane & Jonas McDUFFIE both of South Berwick ME at Elliot ME [1 Aug 1844]
HARDY Caleb of Fryeburg ME & Laura Ann SAWTELLE at Turner ME [4 Apr 1837]
  Daniel of Boston MA & Ann T SIMONTON at Portland ME [7 Nov 1844]
  David of Wilton ME (age 13y) & Miss Susan Ann DAGGETT of Leeds ME (25 yrs) at Leeds [13 Mar 1838]
  Jonathan J & Abigail GRAY both of Plymouth ME at Plymouth by William H NASON Esq [13 Mar 1838]
  Jonathan S of Starks ME & Miss Almira WOOD at Norridgewock ME [23 Jul 1842]
  Josiah S & Sarah H MERRITT at Bath ME [6 Nov 1835]
  Mary Ann & William H TOWLE at Winthrop ME on Monday evening last by Rev CALDWELL [27 Feb 1835]
  Olive & Asa TOWNSEND of Wilton ME at Carthage ME [9 May 1837]
  Rhoda & William GAY at Strong ME [20 May 1847]
  William A of Boston MA & Angeria HENDERSON of Richmond ME at Cambridge MA [30 Sept 1847]
  Weston & Miss Maria H ARNOLD both of Bremen ME at Thomaston ME [5 Feb 1846]
HARE Julia & David P RING at Eastport ME [19 Feb 1846]
HARKNESS William & Miss L GARDNER both of Camden ME [17 Jul 1845]
HARLOW Clarissa & John F RUSS at Strong ME [13 Jun 1844]
  George W Esq, editor of the *Attala (Mississippi) Gazette* and formerly of Augusta ME, & Miss Elizabeth J HIGHT of Louisville at Louisville KY [7 Oct 1843]
  Jane & Horatio THOMPSON at Minot ME [19 Dec 1837]
  Lenora J & William MORGAN of Dexter ME at Sangerville ME [15 Apr 1847]
  Louisa of Peru at Canton ME [14 Feb 1850]
  Maria L Mrs & Jarvis C WARDWELL at Roxbury MA [29 Jan 1852]
  Sylvina & Samuel P NILES at Minot ME [19 Dec 1837]
  Thomas B of Plymouth MA & Rebecca A BROWN of Gardiner ME [6 Nov 1845]
  William H of Roxbury, formerly of Maine & Mary G HAINES of Dorchester MA [10 Jul 1838]
  William of Minot ME & Stilla B JONES of Turner ME at Turner by Ezekiel MARTIN Esq [23 Oct 1835]
HARMON Catherine H & Samuel B PHILPOT of Limerick ME at Buxton ME [15 Jul 1847]
  Charles & Saloma MANSON at Saco ME [29 Jul 1847]
  Cornelia & Thomas J DAVIS at Scarboro ME on 22d Feb [4 Mar 1852]
  Daniel B & Miss Rebecca NUTTING at Brunswick ME [13 Aug 1846]
  Daniel H of Gorham ME & Sarah P LEGROW at Windham ME [28 Dec 1848]
  Eliza A & Abner BURBANK Esq at Limerick ME [2 May 1837]

HARLOW (cont.) Elizabeth & Mr H M HILL at Providence RI on 27 Apr [13 May 1852]
George W of Boston (printer) & Miss Isabella K TILDEN of Belfast ME at Belfast on Thursday last [10 Jun 1843]
George & Jedidiah FOSS at Leeds ME by Rev Walter FOSS [15 May 1835]
James W & Rachel HANCOCK at Falmouth ME [3 Dec 1842]
Martha Ann & Mark P CONANT at Brunswick ME [6 Dec 1849]
Mary Ann & Aaron S HUBBARD of Thorndike ME at Harrison ME [23 Jan 1845]
Mary & James GILPATRICK at Saco ME [3 Jun 1847]
Priscilla & Hiram STEVENS at Fayette ME [6 Apr 1839]
Sarah G & Joseph SMITH of Marshfield ME at East Machias ME [26 Aug 1847]
William J & Lydia J GILBERT of Leeds ME at Brunswick ME [10 Dec 1846]

HARMOND William, a AmRev age 70y, & Miss Mehitable BRACKETT age 47y at Gorham ME [6 May 1833]

HARNDEN William P & Betsey THOMPSON at Farmington ME [11 Jan 1849]

HARRIMAN Drusilla & Thomas MASON at Orland ME [22 Apr 1847]
Franklin Capt & Miss Esther GRANT at Prospect ME [1 Feb 1849]
Hester Ann & Ralph DEVEREUX Jr at Prospect ME [10 Sept 1846]
J E & Harriet CLARK at Frankfort ME [30 May 1844]
James & Susan DEMUTH at Waldoboro ME [12 Feb 1846]
Jonathan Capt of Bucksport ME & Miss Elmira B GODFREY at Orrington ME [7 Oct 1847]
Lydia Ann, d/o Rev Jesse HARRIMAN, & Mr Harrison DOE both of Windsor ME at Windsor [4 Jul 1837]
Martin B & Miss Catherine DEMUTH at Waldoboro ME [5 Feb 1842]
Mary A & William J BROWN at Clinton ME [20 Jan 1848]
William of Montville ME & Sarah A PARSONS of Roxbury VT at Lowell MA [10 Dec 1846]
William of Sebec ME & Miss Hannah PRATT at Foxcroft ME [27 Mar 1845]

HARRINGTON Allen & Lucinda B SPEAR at Thomaston ME [6 Nov 1845]
Barzilla of China ME & Lucy BEAN of Readfield ME [21 Oct 1843]
Eliza A & Benjamin K MITCHELL at Gardiner ME [11 Jan 1849]
George of Roxbury MA & Amelia L SIMMONS of Eastport ME at Boston MA [24 Jul 1838]
Hannah G of Camden ME & Nathaniel PILLSBURY of E Thomaston ME [29 May 1841]
Hezekiah Capt & Miss Margaret McINTIRE of Phipsburgh ME at Georgetown ME [4 Sept 1845]
Sarah B & William BRADBURY of Thomaston ME at Newcastle ME [19 Sept 1844]
Sarah G & Joseph HENDERSON of St George ME at Thomaston ME [12 Nov 1842]
Susan M & Benjamin T FOSTER at Thomaston ME [30 Sept 1847]
Zelia Ann & Frederick BIBBER at Eastport ME [21 Jan 1847]

HARRIS Ann B & Gideon F STETSON at Eastport ME [11 Jun 1846]
Asenath B & Dennis HIGGINS at North Yarmouth ME [25 Jul 1834]
Cynthia J & Charles H BERRY at Danville ME [22 Feb 1849]

HARRIS (cont.) Eliza & Charles GRIGGS at Oldtown ME [25 Jul 1844]
    Eliza & Job CUSHMAN of Waterford at Gray ME [21 Mar 1850]
    Elizabeth & Capt James MATTHEWS at Deer Isle ME [15 Jul 1843]
    Jacob S & Louisa M RANDALL at (Augusta) ME on 16th inst [7 Dec 1848]
    Jacob S & Lousa M ROLLINS by Asaph R Nichols Esq at (Augusta) ME on 16th inst [30 Nov 1848]
    Jerome Rev, pastor of the Universalist Society of Prospect ME & Miss Orchilla BLANCHARD at Prospect ME [1 Jan 1846]
    John H of Bath, printer/publisher of the *Maine Inquirer* & Miss Harriet HARDING of Haverhill MA [5 Aug 1833]
    Julia M & William W INGALLS at Mercer ME on 2nd inst [20 Apr 1848] & [18 May 1848]
    Lorenzo D & Ellen LOWE at Eastport ME [15 May 1845]
    Lucy Frances & Henry Orville LEONARD of Worcester MA at Winthrop ME on Oct 6th by Rev Mr THURSTON [31 Oct 1844]
    M & Sarah V DINSMORE at North Auburn ME [17 Aug 1848]
    Martin 2d of Turner ME & Betsey MASON at Buckfield ME [26 Dec 1844]
    Mary Ann & Henry EARL of Boston MA at Windsor ME [28 Sept 1839]
    Mary D & Joseph S STODDARD at Brunswick ME on the 18th inst by Rev Benjamin TITCOMB [29 Jan 1836]
    Mary F & Horatio N CLOUSE at Union ME [13 Nov 1851]
    Mary & Kingsbury DONNELL at Webster ME on 15 Oct by Jesse DAVIS Esq [23 Oct 1851]
    Moses & Hannah PALMER at Pittston ME [5 Feb 1836]
    Nathan C, M.D., of Addison ME & Miss Harriet Ann WOODBURY at Minot ME [4 Sept 1845]
    Olive & Cyrus BISHOP PM at Winthrop ME by Rev Mr BARNARD [27 Feb 1845]
    Seth Jr & Miss Roxana BRADFORD at Turner ME [13 Nov 1838]
    Stephen L & Miss Margaret HALL of Litchfield ME at North Yarmouth ME [9 Jul 1846]
    William T & Adeline P BLANCHARD at North Yarmouth ME [2 May 1834]
    William & Miss Ann MASON at Eastport ME [6 Feb 1846]

HART Chester of St George ME & Miss Rosana THOMPSON of Thomaston ME at Thomaston ME [23 Dec 1836]
    Eliza & John W BETTY at Portland ME [23 May 1844]
    Margaret & Abraham HANCHE at Bath ME [21 Mar 1844]
    Mary & Levi RODRING at Bath ME [29 Aug 1844]
    Mary M & Edward LANGLEY at Bath ME [14 Oct 1847]

HARTFORD Byance & Joseph ELLINWOOD at Belfast ME both of Swanville ME at Belfast ME [5 Mar 1846]
    James & Louisa A HICKS both of Harrison ME at Waterford ME [19 Nov 1846]
    John H & Julia E SMITH at Augusta ME on Monday morning last by Rev William A DREW [1 Jul 1847]
    Loring & Miss Emeline AVERY at Georgetown ME [5 Nov 1846]
    P M & Mr G W KINCAID at Hiram ME [6 May 1852]
    Philena & George W GLOVER at Rockland ME both of Camden ME [19 Aug 1852]

HARTSHORN Margaret S & Albion K WENTWORTH at Belfast ME [27 Nov 1851]

HARTHORN Keturah S Mrs & Capt Albion WALL at St George ME [6 Mar 1838]
HARTWELL John, M.D., of (Augusta) ME & Pamelia C BACHELDER d/o Col James R B by Rev Mr FULLER at Readfield ME [12 Oct 1848]
George of Lincoln MA & Margaret R REDMAN at Brooksville ME [15 Jul 1847]
HARVELL Harriet & Leander TAYLOR at Solon ME both of Madison ME [27 Aug 1846]
HARVEY E T Esq of Atkinson ME & Miss Harriet E GENTHNER at Parkman ME [12 Apr 1849]
Flora B of Harmony ME & John F PRAY at Augusta ME on 19th Jan by Rev George S G SPENCER [21 Feb 1850]
Florentine C & Francis B KEEN at Letter D Plt (Aroostook Co) ME both of Presque Isle ME [25 Feb 1847]
HASELINE William B of Gardiner ME & Isabel E FRANCIS at Boston MA [29 Jun 1848]
HASEY Eliza J & Sylvanus DAVIS at Albion ME [15 Feb 1849]
William of Albion ME & Betsey TURNER of Bangor ME at Augusta ME on Dec 19th [2 Jan 1851]
HASKELL Abner of Bangor ME & Axie RACLIFF at Unity ME [19 Jun 1835]
Abner & Mrs Martha LYON at Augusta ME on 5th Jun by Elder J D WEST [8 Jul 1852]
Albert & Elizabeth A LANCASTER at China ME by James B HASKELL Esq [2 Dec 1847]
Alfred & Elizabeth OWEN at Portland ME [2 Jan 1845]
Betsey Jane & Elijah ROBERTS at China ME [10 Jan 1850]
C NILES of Newburyport MA & Harriet WOODS of Bloomfield ME [16 May 1844]
Calvin L & Polly Jane KENNEDY at Jefferson ME [10 Jul 1851]
Caroline E & Capt Frederick P SPOFFORD at Deer Isle ME [29 May 1845]
Caroline & George WEEKS, merchant at Jefferson ME [7 Mar 1837]
Daniel M & Sarah T BATES at Garland ME [19 Feb 1846]
Deborah S & Rev Joseph CUMMINGS of Amenia Seminary NY at Litchfield ME [28 Aug 1842]
Eliza C & Capt John B RICHARDSON at Deer Isle ME [5 Dec 1844]
Elizabeth & John DUNN Jr of Hallowell ME at Augusta ME by Daniel T PIKE Esq [10 Jul 1838]
Elizabeth & Oliver HOWARD at Deer Isle ME [8 Apr 1847]
Erances [sic] & Horace P HUBBARD at Topsham ME [13 Jun 1844]
Erastus of (Augusta) ME & Mary C WILLIAMS by Rev Mr FESSENDEN at East Thomaston ME on 18th inst [25 May 1848]
George W of Kennebec ME & Elvina A ESTES at China ME by J D ESTES Esq [3 Jul 1851]
Gustavus & Hannah BROWN of Palermo ME at China by William PERCIVAL Esq [8 Apr 1847]
H D & Miss Nancy B MARSTON at Livermore ME [18 Jan 1844]
Harriet T of Topsham ME & George E DREW of San Francisco CA [19 Aug 1852]
Henry & Rosilla CASWELL at Otisfield ME [21 Mar 1850]
Ira H & Mary C DENNIS of Passadumkeag ME at Lincoln ME [21 Jan 1847]
Isaac & Jane ROBINSON at Brunswick ME [27 Aug 1846]

HASKELL (cont.) J L & Lydia HASKELL of Poland ME at New Gloucester ME [1 Apr 1847]
  Jacob of Salem MA & Jane S BOYINGTON at Augusta ME on 2 Feb by Rev Z THOMPSON [13 Feb 1851]
  John W & Sarah CLARK both of Thomaston ME [13 Feb 1841]
  Laura A D & Phillip W DAY at China ME [29 Jan 1852]
  Levi & Mary TINKHAM at Winthrop ME on Thursday evening last by Rev David THURSTON [28 Dec 1833]
  Lucy A & Cyrus T ARNOLD at Farmington ME [3 Oct 1844]
  Lydia of Poland ME & Mr J L HASKELL at New Gloucester ME [1 Apr 1847]
  Mary A & Mr D W CHAPMAN at China ME by William PERCIVAL Esq [4 Feb 1847]
  Mary A & Stephen E WITHAM at Monmouth ME [4 Jul 1840]
  Mary Ann of Gardiner ME & James WOODBURY of Litchfield ME at Gardiner ME by Rev G BAILEY of (Winthrop) ME [20 Mar 1841]
  Mary Ann & George STEVENS at Bluehill ME [12 Aug 1847]
  Mary Ann & Washington PATTERSON at Belfast ME [5 Dec 1844]
  Mary H & Mr J F RUSSELL at East Livermore ME [18 Jan 1849]
  Medafer of Bangor ME merchant & Caroline THORNDIKE at Camden ME [26 Dec 1834]
  Melissa D & David W Capt PINKHAM of Bath ME at Lowell MA on 9th Jan by Rev TWOMBLY [23 Jan 1851]
  Nahum Esq editor of the *Vermont Mercury* of Woodstock VT, & Mrs Paulina R NEIL of Skowhegan ME [25 Jun 1846]
  Nancy M & Wilson HERSEY at Hallowell ME [6 Jan 1848]
  Orin & Miss Asenath WASHBURN at Livermore ME by Aaron BARTON Esq [7 Aug 1838]
  Ruth W & William TRAFTON Esq of Shapleigh ME at Livermore ME [3 Jul 1841]
  Samuel & Adaline KALER at Union ME [16 Nov 1839]
  Sarah of Livermore ME & E H W SMITH of Augusta ME [11 Sept 1835]
  Sarah & Joseph R SAWYER at Levant ME [18 Jan 1840]
  Sophia J of Palmyra ME & James S NORRIS at St Crois Co WI [12 Mar 1846]
  Susan H & Jacob T LEWIS at Steuben ME [11 Jan 1844]
  Thomas O & Ernestine BENJAMIN at Livermore ME [14 Mar 1844]
  William of Auburn ME & Miss Charity VARNEY at Windham ME [16 Apr 1846]
HASKETH Margaret A & Benjamin H DAVENPORT [20 May 1843]
HASKINS Phebe Ann & Joel HALEY at Durham ME on 20th inst both of Portland ME [2 Jul 1842]
HASSELL Jason & Elizabeth TOWNE at Sebec ME [21 Jan 1847]
HASTINGS Charlotte & William FERMAGE at Bath ME [14 Nov 1834]
  John & Miss Arletta GREENLOW at Bristol ME [4 Oct 1849]
  Jonas of Northborough MA & Elizabeth E DAVIS at Mount Vernon ME [17 Oct 1834]
  Joseph of Stow ME & Mary PATTEE of Searsmont ME [5 Dec 1837]
  Luke & Mary Ann MARSH both of Bangor ME at Hampden ME [29 Jul 1852]
  O'Neil R of Bethel ME & Mary Ann SMALL at Newry ME [8 May 1845]
  Sarah J & Albert H SMALL of Newry ME at Bethel ME [6 May 1847]

HASTINGS (cont.) William Esq & Ruth GREENLAW at Bristol ME [30 May 1837]
HASTY George W & Rebecca WILSON at Baring Washington Co ME [25 Dec 1845]
    Harriet N of Westbrook ME & Joel N MOODY of Monmouth ME [5 Feb 1839]
    Robert & Miss Margaret CELASPIE at Baring Washington Co ME [25 Dec 1845]
HATCH Abby & Benjamin ADAMS at Gray ME [12 Sept 1844]
    Abigail, d/o Dr Alexander HATCH, & Mr Peter ROLLINS, merchant of Vassalboro ME at Augusta ME by Rev William A DREW [31 Jul 1838]
    Adrah of Bristol & Sarah L CLARK at Newcastle ME [18 Feb 1847]
    Alexander Dr of Augusta ME & Eliza, d/o Enos FAIRBANKS of Winthrop ME at Winthrop ME on Tues last by Rev Mr DREW [2 Jan 1838]
    Barak & Louisa J CROSS at Belfast ME both of Belmont ME [30 May 1844]
    Caroline & Edward S NORTON at Gardiner ME [18 Jul 1840]
    D P & Mary Abba CLARK at Lewiston ME [3 Jan 1850]
    E K Capt & Miss Margaret K J PATTERSON at Dresden ME [19 Feb 1846]
    Edward of Acton ME & Mrs Margaret J Mildredge FULLER of Scarboro' ME at Roxbury MA [22 May 1845]
    Eliza A of Litchfield ME & Asa S DONNELL of Waterville ME at Augusta ME on 17 Nov by Rev J STEVENS [20 Nov 1851]
    Eliza & Joseph HALEY Jr at Hollis ME both of Hollis [2 Nov 1833]
    Elizabeth S & Joshua P BASSETT at Castine ME [22 Apr 1852]
    Esther & Daniel C DALY at Leeds ME [21 Dec 1848]
    Eunice & Milton PATTERSON at Belfast ME [25 Dec 1835]
    Frances P & Charles T PLIMPTON of Boston MA at Bath ME [23 Jan 1845]
    George & Lucy CHASE at Richmond ME [8 Aug 1844]
    Harriet E & Peter M VIGOREAU of Gardiner ME at Bath ME [14 Jan 1847]
    Harriet P & Capt John WEBB at Dresden ME [4 Jan 1849]
    Jesse A 2d of Greene ME & Elizabeth A NEALE at Litchfield ME [21 Jun 1849]
    Leonard Capt & Miss Delia Ann P LORING at North Yarmouth ME [30 Sept 1847]
    Lydia Jane & James PATTERSON at Portland ME [5 Dec 1844]
    Margaret & Hiram L WING at Bath ME [15 Nov 1849]
    Mary Jane & Zebulon DAVIS at Thomaston ME [4 Mar 1847]
    Miss M & Mr Humphret CORNISH at Thomaston ME [5 Feb 1846]
    Moses C & Martha J PISHON at Augusta ME [10 Jun 1847]
    Nancy of Lewiston ME & George PROCTOR Jr at Lisbon ME [17 Dec 1846]
    Nathaniel Jr of Westbrook ME & Catherine P HARBACH at Camden ME [1 Apr 1852]
    Phebe & Simon STEVEN at Eastport ME [26 Mar 1842]
    Samuel W HATCH AB & Miss Melinda M DECKER both of Bowdoinham ME at Providence RI [16 Aug 1849]
    Sarenia & Haskell FULLER at LaGrange ME on 10th Jul by S SEARS Esq [30 Jul 1842]

HATCH (cont.) Sylvanus of Great Falls NH & Mary Jane GERRISH of Lewiston ME at Lebanon ME?/NH? [3 Dec 1842]
    Sylvanus & Jane CLEAVES at Windsor ME by J B SWANTON Esq [14 Feb 1837]
    Thomas & Miss Julia Ann SINCKLEY at Hallowell ME on 6th inst by Elder H ALBEE [19 Jun 1845]
    William B Capt of Pembroke ME & Mrs Naomi REYNOLDS at Eastport ME [23 Dec 1847]
    William L & Harriet M TRUSSELL at Thomaston ME [26 Feb 1852]
    William W & Eliza J DENNETT at Castine ME [21 Nov 1844]
    William & Mrs Charlotte G SMITH at Belfast ME [15 Nov 1849]
HATHAWAY C M Mr of Augusta ME & Susannah R COLMAN at Vassalboro ME on 23d Jun by Rev Mr BRAY [12 Aug 1852]
    Edward & Priscilla WHITNEY at Frankfort ME [14 Mar 1837]
    Emily & Oliver F FLETCHER at Jay ME [17 Jun 1852]
    Franklin & Caroline GARDNER at Hallowell ME [1 Jul 1847]
    John of Paris ME & Mehitable P FELT at Woodstock ME [6 Feb 1851]
    Nathan of Boston MA & Emily FORBES at Paris ME [14 Jan 1847]
HATHORN Paul D & Loanthe WAYNE at Milford ME [13 Jan 1848]
    Zenus F of Solon ME & Elvira MORSE at Norridgewock ME [7 Apr 1848]
HATHORNE Mary of Woolwich ME & Rev Edward R WARREN of New Castle at Bath ME [11 Dec 1835]
HATTER Anthony of Strawsburg [sic] France & Abby B WHITE of Windsor ME at Boston MA [5 Aug 1843]
HATTSON Martha F & Alvin BRYANT at Saco ME [4 Apr 1850]
HAUGHTON Francis C of Lewiston ME & Emeline PULSIFER of Auburn ME at Lowell MA on Jan 11th by Rev EDDY [23 Jan 1851]
HAUGTON Lewis W, M.D., of Waterford ME & Miss Esther T WESTON at Otisfield ME [29 Jan 1842]
HAUPT Julia A & Charles A STORER at Providence RI both of Waldoboro ME [20 Sept 1849]
HAVENER Aldana C & Samuel A SLEEPER at Rockland ME [26 Jun 1851]
HAVENER Robert R of Frankfort ME & Miss Sarah F LINDSEY at Thomaston ME [20 May 1847]
HAVEY Nathan of Boston MA & Eveline B SHAW at (Augusta) ME [27 Jan 1848]
HAWES Amanda M of Hallowell ME at Bath ME [26 Apr 1849]
    Benjamin S 2d & Rachael STORER at Weld ME [4 Apr 1844]
    Betsey of Weld ME & Azel E HOUGHTON at Weld ME [20 Feb 1845]
    Clarissa J of Vassalboro ME & Charles W GOWER of Greenville ME at Vassalboro ME on 21st inst by Rev Mr Mr ADAMS of Augusta ME [30 Jan 1841]
    David B Capt & Lucy GOULDSMITH of Phillips ME at Hallowell ME [6 Sept 1849]
    Eleazer & Sarah A GETCHELL of Northport NE at Belfast ME [2 Apr 1846]
    Hanson & Abigail W POST at East Thomaston ME [26 Mar 1846]
    Joseph C & ELLEN GRAY at North Anson ME [27 Jul 1848]
    Lydia A & David T JONES at Weld ME on 1st Jun [15 Jun 1848]
    Mary A of Newton MA & Joseph WILLIAMS of Winthrop ME at Boston MA on Sept 6th by Rev Mr Driver [17 Sept 1842]

HAWES (cont.) Melvina L & Mr S R PARLIN of Norwich CT at Weld ME on 20 Mar by Rev J B WHEELWRIGHT [27 Mar 1851]
 Orick of Aroostook Co ME & Susan HORN at Vassalboro ME [4 Feb 1843]
 Otis of Vassalboro ME & Almira S RANDALL at Topsham ME [29 Jun 1839]
 Silas & Margaret HILLS at Union ME [28 Sept 1848]
 Temperance of Vassalboro ME & Samuel HOMANS Esq on 29th inst by Rev A MOORE [6 Feb 1845]

HAWKES/HAWKS Emeline C & James MYERS of Brandon Mississippi & Miss Emeline C HAWKES at Hallowell ME on Wednesday evening last by Rev Mr WEBBER [22 Aug 1837]
 Harriet C & Samuel CARR at Minot ME [28 Dec 1848]
 Julia A & Samuel A LAUGHTON at Hallowell ME [10 Jan 1850]
 Sarah Mrs & William MORMAN (each ae 75y) at Warren ME [6 May 1833]
 Silenus U of Minot ME & Lucy A CUMMINGS at Paris ME [25 Mar 1852]

HAWKINS Washington of York ME & Miss Manetta SCHANKS at Eastport ME [28 May 1846]

HAYCOCK Adeline & Lewis BURGIN at Eastport ME [1 May 1835]

HAYDEN Aaron Esq of Eastport ME & Jane T BRIGGS at Robbinston ME [24 Jun 1847]
 Charles H & Mary E FOSTER at Eastport ME [26 Aug 1847]
 Frances E & Daniel DINGLEY at Winslow ME [15 Jan 1852]
 H G & Mr A BURLEIGH at Waterville ME [13 Jun 1844]
 Luther of East Thomaston ME & Adeline FRENCH of Lincolnville ME [25 Jun 1842]
 Mary J & Isaac HOLBROOK of Phipsburg ME at Bath ME [10 Jan 1850]
 Sarah & Samuel S PARKER at Waterville ME [24 Apr 1845]
 Susan L & Francis NELSON of Richmond VA at Eastport ME [14 Aug 1835]

HAYES Charles E & Lucinda A ADAMS at Kittery ME [27 Mar 1845]
 Charles of Industry ME & Ann E BALDWIN at New Sharon ME [31 May 1849]
 Eliza of Industry ME & Enoch WESTON of Madison ME at Industry ME [2 Oct 1845]
 Frances & Charles HAINS at Dover NH [5 Feb 1852]
 Gustavus & Sarah C SHAW both of Industry ME at Industry ME [20 Jun 1844]
 Harriet E & Ira P FARRINGTON at Oxford ME [24 Jan 1850]
 Hezekiah of Poland ME & Miss Sarah Jane RAND of Minot ME at Minot [4 Apr 1837]
 Martha Ann & William W RITCHIE at Frankfort ME on 4 May [10 Jun 1843]
 Phebe W & Edward E RICHARDSON of Dracut MA at Limington ME [18 Apr 1850]

HAYFORD Alvardo & Betsey FULLER at Canton ME [19 Dec 1837]
 Axel & Mrs Mary Ann COTTRELL both of Belfast ME [6 Feb 1845]
 Delphina K & William P BRIDGHAM, M.D., at Canton ME [23 Apr 1846]
 Eliza & Andrew BARROWS at Canton ME [25 Nov 1836]
 Hannah W Mrs & Col Nathaniel CHASE of Turner ME at Augusta ME [21 Jul 1843]
 Roulana & Sewall PATTERSON at Belfast ME [1 Jan 1846]

HAYMAN William of Boston MA & Miss Phebe C BERRY at Belfast ME [24 Oct 1844]

HAYNES Ann L & William C AUMOCK at Saco ME [20 Jul 1848]
   Jacob of Industry ME & Mrs Mary P WESTON at Madison ME [12 Sept 1844]
   Martha Ann & Norman S WILLIAMS both of Monson ME [13 Jun 1844]
   Mary R & Joseph BLAISDELL at Smithfield ME [24 Sept 1846]
   Mr (printer) and editor of the *Democrat* & Miss Susan PALMER at Bangor ME [10 Apr 1845]
   Nancy C & Asa S TOWNSEND of Sidney ME at Hallowell ME on 1 Jan by Rev W A P DILLINGHAM [7 Feb 1850]
   Obed W of Edinburgh & Ann FARNHAM at Passadumkeag ME [5 Sept 1841]
   Sarah R & Obed W PIERCE of Lexington ME at Smithfield ME [28 Aug 1845]

HAYS Joanna of Oxford ME & Joshua H THAXTER of Portland ME at Oxford ME [5 Jun 1841]

HAYWARD Charles Esq, mayor of that city (Bangor) ME & Amanda M LESLIE at Bangor ME [3 Jun 1847]
   Henry of Hallowell ME & Eunice SNELL of Winthrop ME "this is the sixth dau of Mr SNELL that has been taken from the ample farm-house within a few years ... there is one of the same sort left ..." at Winthrop ME by Rev Mr ELLIOT [27 Feb 1851]
   Mary B & Joseph L SMILEY at Sidney ME by Rev William TILLY [5 Jun 1845]
   Sarah J & David N B COFFIN at Lowell MA [22 Jan 1852]

HAYWOOD Emily & Mr Stephen ANDREWS of Waterville ME at Winthrop ME [9 Nov 1833]
   Sarah Frances of Waterville ME & Hugh O'DONNELL of Hallowell ME at Lynn MA on 8th Aug [28 Aug 1851]

HAZARD Samuel L of Boston ME & Miss Oliva B WOODMAN of Wilton ME at Wilton ME by A S C STRICKLAND Esq on Sunday evening on 9th Feb [14 Mar 1840]

HAZEN Edmund & Miss Sarah R NESS at Brunswick ME [28 May 1846]
   Martin O of Nashua NH & Martha SEARLE of Skowhegan ME at Lawrence MA [18 Dec 1851]

HEAD Aroline E & Horace WELT at Waldoboro ME by Newall W LUDWIG [21 Sept 1839]

HEAGAN William R Capt & Clementine C GRANT at North Prospect ME [15 Apr 1852]
   Richard P & Matilda POLAND at Prospect ME [1 Apr 1852]

HEAL Arthur & Miss Sophia M CALPH at Belmont ME [13 Mar 1845]
   Franklin & Mary MOODY at Belmont ME [15 Apr 1836]
   Lydia B & Miles FULLER at Lincolnville ME [20 May 1847]
   Martha & Samuel OGIER of Camden ME at Searsmont ME [27 Dec 1849]

HEALD Amos of Bingham ME & Susan H DINSMORE at Anson ME [10 Apr 1851]
   Benjamin & Eleanor F McDANIELS by Solomon HEALD Esq at Lovell ME on 9th inst [21 Dec 1848]
   Ellen H of Calais ME & Rev C D A JOHNSON of the Maine (Methodist) Annual Conference at China ME [23 Jan 1845]

HEALD (cont.) Eusebius Rev of Atkinson ME & Lucy DINSMORE at Norridgewock ME [7 Jan 1847]
    Rosina & Hosea SULLIVAN of Frankfort ME at Camden ME [12 Jul 1849]
    Sarah H W & Theodore FURBER at Milo ME [18 Nov 1843]
    Thomas H & Mary A ROGERS at Anson ME [11 Apr 1840]
    Wellington & Eliza Ann HUSSEY of Fairfield ME at Norridgewock ME [7 Jan 1847]

HEALEY Dodge Capt & Charlotte A WITCHELL at Thomaston ME [11 Jul 1844]
    Elonia & Alfred BURTON at Thomaston ME [14 May 1846]

HEALY Aaron of New York NY & Elizabeth WESTON, d/o Stephen WESTON at Skowhegan ME [17 Oct 1844]
    Edward Capt & Sarah SPEAR, youngest d/o Elkanah Esq at Thomaston ME [19 Sept 1844]
    P W & Mr J S WOODBURY of Portland ME at Thomaston ME [28 Aug 1845]

HEARD Robert H & Miss Ruth ROWELL at Thomaston ME [8 Jan 1846]

HEARSEY Augustine & Harriet E DWINAL at Foxcroft ME [23 May 1844]

HEATH A M C, editor of the *Coldwater Fountain* [later called the *Maine Journal*], & Sarah H PHILBROOK both of Gardiner ME at Augusta ME on Aug 3rd at the residence of Frederic ABORN by Rev Mr HYDE of Gardiner [5 Aug 1852]
    Asa Jr & Miss Caroline BURDIN both of Sidney ME at Augusta ME by Rev Mr TAPPAN [18 Dec 1838]
    Caroline M & Capt Samuel BUCKER at Bath ME [14 Oct 1836]
    Catharine Mrs & Thomas SEABURY Esq of Parkman ME at Mt Vernon ME [8 Feb 1849]
    Emily Mrs & Thomas H CHESLEY of Boston MA at Augusta ME on Feb 5 by Rev A BURGESS [14 Feb 1850]
    Isaac & Mary CLIFFORD at Windsor ME by J B SWANTON Esq [14 Feb 1837]
    Jacob & Abigail CLIFFORD at Windsor ME by J B SWANTON Esq [14 Feb 1837]
    Joel H & Mary HEATH both of Brownville ME at Milo ME [31 Jul 1851]
    Jonathan M & Miss Olive WATERHOUSE at Monmouth ME [14 Dec 1839]
    Joseph of Hallowell ME & Mary JEWEL at China ME on 11 Apr by William PERCIVAL Esq [25 Apr 1850]
    Leonard & Abigail DUNTON both of Whitefield ME at Augusta ME on 1 Dec by Rev J STEVENS [4 Dec 1851]
    Margaret S of Bath ME & Henry A FAIRFIELD of Andover MA [1 Jul 1836]
    Mary & Benjamin WILBUR at Strong ME [21 Jan 1833]
    Mary & Joel H HEATH both of Brownville ME at Milo ME [31 Jul 1851]
    Mildred A & James H McFARLAND at North Hancock ME [29 Apr 1852]
    Otis S & Mrs Elizabeth PARTRIDGE both of Jefferson ME at Patricktown ME on Oct 11th by Thomas BRAN Esq [25 Oct 1849]
    Pearley & Orinda BENNETT at Gilead ME [29 Apr 1847]
    Randolph & Emily WOODWARD at Augusta ME on Thursday evening last by Rev C FULLER [31 Dec 1842]
    Seneca W & Nancy Jane SILSBY at Bath ME [26 Oct 1848]
    Sherburne & Hannah CLIFFORD at Windsor ME [20 Jun 1837]
    Simeon A & Mary Ann ROSS at Bangor ME [24 Apr 1845]

HEATH (cont.) Susan & John COLBY at Patricktown Plt ME [3 Jul 1835]
 William & Sarah D DYER at Brunswick ME [26 Dec 1844]
 Wilson of Hallowell ME & Maria L GRANT of Norridgewock ME at (Augusta) ME [27 Apr 1848]
HEDGE Henry & Miss Alathea WEEKS at Vassalboro ME [8 Nov 1849
HEDGEWOOD William & Miss A M WHARFF by Rev J T BARTLETT at Lewiston ME on 1st Jan [5 Feb 1852]
HEMENWAY Aaron & Silstina TOLMAN at Camden ME [11 Dec 1851] [4 Dec 1851]
 Abby W & Henry A BURKETT at Belfast ME both of Camden ME [5 Nov 1846]
 George of Searsmont ME & Miss Hannah FERGUSON at Belfast ME [11 May 1839]
 Willard J & Miss Martha DYER at Searsmont ME [14 May 1846]
HEMINGWAY/HEMINWAY Cynthia Mrs & Samuel WEBB Esq at Brunswick ME [1 Feb 1849]
 Mary & Robert PIERPONT at Rumford ME [4 Feb 1833]
HEMLEN Timothy & Fannie WELLINGTON at Albion ME [30 Jan 1851]
HENAKY Catherine & Capt Thomas T TATE at Thomaston ME [14 Oct 1847]
HENDERSON Alice & Augustus MORSE at Thomaston ME [1 Aug 1844]
 Angeria of Richmond ME & William A HARDY of Boston MA at Cambridge [30 Sept 1847]
 James Capt & Jane SINGER at Thomaston ME [23 Oct 1841]
 Joseph of St George ME & Miss Sarah G HARRINGTON at Thomaston ME [12 Nov 1842]
 Mary J & Capt William SUMNER at Richmond [17 Feb 1848]
 Thomas Jr of Webster ME & Mary E JONES of Freeman ME at Kingfield ME on 20 Oct by E P PILLSBURY Esq [30 Oct 1851]
HENINGER Henry (age 104y) & Miss Eliza A PECK (age 83y) at Marion Co (Mississippi) [16 Oct 1835]
HENLE Julius & Mary WINN of Waterville ME at Albany NY [30 Jan 1851]
HENRY Mary B & Jacob WILSON at Litchfield ME on 26th Aug [14 Sept 1848]
 Mary J & Amasa CRAFTS at Bloomfield ME [23 Nov 1848]
 John A Rev of Skowhegan ME & Miss Hannah P LOMBARD at Augusta ME [1 Oct 1842]
 Mary F F & J PARKER at Bath ME [26 Dec 1844]
 Thomas J Capt & Mrs Caroline A GLIDDEN at Bath ME [7 Jun 1849]
HENSON Sarah E & Frederick E SHAW at Bangor ME [25 Mar 1852]
HERBERT George W & Miss Clarinda PATRIDGE at Bucksport ME [12 Aug 1843]
HERBET Henry W of England & Sarah d/o John BARKER Esq at Bangor ME [11 Jan 1840]
HERRICK Adeline & Josiah RANLETT at Thomaston ME [18 Feb 1847]
 Amos of Sedgwick ME & Sarah H SPOFFORD at Deer Island ME [14 Nov 1844]
 Anson, publisher of the *Maine Free Press* & Miss Lydia WOOD at Wiscasset ME [27 May 1833]
 Daniel of Gardiner ME & Miss Emily HERRICK of North Yarmouth ME [30 Dec 1836]

HERRICK (cont.) Emily & Daniel HERRICK of Gardiner ME at North Yarmouth ME [30 Dec 1836]
Everlina & Daniel L WEYMOUTH of Topsham ME at Lisbon ME [12 Aug 1836]
John W of Old Town ME & Delphina BEARCE of Canton ME on Tuesday eve 13 Dec by John W HERRICK Esq [24 Dec 1842]
Lydia P & Robert SMILEY at Gardiner ME [7 Feb 1850]
Mary C & Isaac N BARTON at Alfred ME [7 Oct 1847]
Mary G, d/o Hon Ebenezer HERRICK, & John BLAISDELL at Lewiston ME [28 Jan 1833]
Sarah W & James NEWELL at Harmony ME [10 Aug 1848]
Sarah & John H KANNAN at Saco ME [12 Mar 1846]
William Capt & Sophronia ROBBINS at Tremont (formerly Mansel, part of Mt Desert) Hancock Co ME [5 Feb 1852]
HERRIN Abigail & Nathan CROWELL of Sidney ME at Skowhegan ME [18 Feb 1847]
Louisa & Daniel S WALKER at Knox ME [23 Jan 1851]
HERRING Joanna A & Dexter S BAILEY of Foxcroft ME at Guilford ME [3 Jan 1850]
Julia of Winnebago Co IL & Frederick KNOX, formerly of Norway ME at Sugar River Precinct IL [24 Apr 1845]
HERRINGTON Demaress & Cyrus H FOLLETT of Wellington ME at Parkman ME [9 Nov 1839]
HERSEY Almy & John TAYER at Foxcroft ME [1 Jul 1847]
Benjamin of Danville ME & Betsey BEALS at Turner ME [22 Jan 1852]
Cornelius & Nancy STURGIS of Vassalboro ME at Boston ME [31 Oct 1840]
Cyrus & Phila SHAW at Auburn ME [15 Jan 1846]
Edward & Ann REYNOLDS both of Gardiner ME at Hallowell ME [20 Nov 1851]
Hiram B of Number 4, Aroostook County ME & Miss Harriet THAYER at Foxcroft ME [9 Apr 1842]
J M & Mary S BEMIS at Lincoln ME [16 Apr 1846]
James Capt of Sumner ME & Miss Louisa d/o Capt John BARRETT of Sumner ME [23 Mar 1839]
Justus C of Dexter ME & Miss Sarah E COUSINS at Abbot ME [17 Jan 1850]
Martha J & George BISBEE of Dedham MA at Fayette ME [14 Jun 1849]
Mary B & James W GUILE of Lowell MA at Hallowell ME [16 Jul 1846]
Mary Jane D & John BRYANT of Herman ME at Dexter ME [12 Feb 1846]
William H & Lucy WINSLOW both of Winthrop ME at E Windsor ME on Jun 25 by Rev S POWERS [3 Jul 1851]
William S of New Bedford MA & Caroline H BLETHEN of Foxcroft ME at Dover ME [25 Mar 1852]
Wilson Weymouth MA & Nancy M HASKELL at Hallowell ME [6 Jan 1848]
HERSON Nancy & Allen FROST at Belgrade ME [6 Feb 1841]
Robert P & Emily BURBANK both of Acton ME at Newfield ME [8 Jun 1848] & [22 Jun 1848]
HERVEY Lucinda & James M NILES at Brunswick ME [30 Jul 1846]
Mary C & David INGALLS of Bath ME at Newburyport MA [29 May 1845]

HESCOCK James M of Wilton ME & Miss Leonora PARKER at Jay ME [8 Nov 1849]
HESSEY Wentworth D of Sangerville ME & Miss Mary E STACKPOLE at South Berwick ME [22 May 1845]
HEWES Cyrus & Mrs COBB both of Hermon ME [22 May 1845]
    Henry M Esq, publisher of the *Thomaston Republican* and the *Temperance Advocate* at Wiscasset & Miss Sarah DAMON [30 May 1834]
    Julius Jr & Mary KIMBALL both of Hermon ME at Levant ME [4 Jul 1844]
    Virgil H of Augusta ME & Mrs Eliza McLANE formerly of Boston MA at Gardiner ME [15 Jun 1839]
HEWETT Ebenezer (age 78y) & Miss Sarah HEWETT (age 17y) at Brunswick Co NJ [6 May 1833]
    Lenora D & Fisher GAY at Thomaston ME [29 Jan 1846]
    Polly & William CAMPBELL at Turner ME both of Livermore ME [14 Feb 1850]
    Sarah (age 17y) & Ebenezer HEWETT (age 78y) at Brunswick Co NJ [6 May 1833]
HEWEY Francis C of Andover ME & Mary A WILBER at Phillips ME [4 Oct 1849]
    Samuel Capt of Webster ME & Keziah H FIRBUSH at Topsham ME [8 Aug 1844]
HEWINS Franklin A of Augusta ME & Miss Eliza Jane RIGGS at Georgetown ME [10 Jun 1847]
    Franklin A & Harriet ELLIS at Augusta ME on Monday evening last [18 Apr 1844]
    Nancy D & James J JONES at Kennebec ME [15 May 1851]
HEWITT Albion E & Rebecca W WILEY at Thomaston ME [12 Apr 1849]
    Charles H & Tryphena SHERBURN at Prospect ME [15 Jul 1852]
    Julia & Samuel of Winthrop at Livermore ME [24 Jul 1845]
HEYWARD Olive M & John S PIKE at Mercer ME [24 Oct 1840]
HEYWOOD Ann & Charles JOY at Sebasticook ME [9 Nov 1848]
    Abigail & Albert J DOWNS at Mercer ME [4 Dec 1845]
    Caroline & Amos HODSON of Clinton ME on 30 Jan [5 Feb 1846]
HIBBARD Isaac L of Farmington ME & Mary G SARGENT of Methuen MA [10 Jun 1843]
HICKS John & Caroline WRENN at Gardiner ME on 16 Jan [30 Jan 1851]
    Levi J & Julia B YOUNG at Augusta ME [14 Oct 1843]
    Louisa A & James HARTFORD at Waterford ME both of Harrison ME [19 Nov 1846]
HIGGINS Abbion R P of Thomaston ME & Lurania R BANGS at New Sharon ME [26 Nov 1846]
    Ambrose & Phebe REMICK at Eden ME [29 Jan 1839]
    Caroline S & Thomas M L PARKER of Lisbon ME at Topsham ME [11 Nov 1847]
    Cyrus Jr Capt & Miss Sarah M SMITH of Eastport ME at Hampden ME [20 Mar 1845]
    Dennis & Miss Asenath B HARRIS at North Yarmouth ME [25 Jul 1834]
    Elbridge of Richmond ME & Miss Mary Jane LIVERMORE at Brunswick ME [25 Feb 1847]

HIGGINS (cont.) Eliza Ann W & David W TINKHAM at Hallowell ME [4 Mar 1836]
George of Belmont ME & Miss Martha FARNHAM at Jefferson ME [24 Apr 1845]
Hannah E & Mr J B S HOLBROOK at Bath ME [16 Aug 1849]
Henry & Esther W VARNUM at Richmond ME [23 Sept 1847]
Jane G of Hampden ME & James H STUART of Vassalboro ME at Hampden ME [14 Mar 1837]
Jane H of Hampden ME & R S TORRY at Dixmont ME [4 Mar 1843]
John C of Fayette ME & Sarah C STEWARD at Skowhegan ME [6 Nov 1851]
John W of Belmont ME & Eliza H SNOW at Lincolnville ME [20 Apr 1848]
Joseph C Capt & Hannah NICKERSON at Bucksport ME [20 Aug 1846]
Lydia A & Samuel R WATERHOUSE at Litchfield ME [20 Jan 1848]
Lydia D of Bath ME & Luther M OLIVER of Phipsburg ME at Bath ME [23 Oct 1845]
Martha Jane & Calvin TAYLOR at Sebasticook ME [7 Jun 1849]
Mary Ann & John WOODARD of Lisbon ME at Topsham ME [3 May 1849]
Mary B & Elbridge G WALDEN at Hampden ME [30 Oct 1838]
Mary E & John P FLINT at Bath ME [27 May 1836]
Mary Jane & Nahum C FRENCH at Albion ME by Rev BUXTON [1 Nov 1849]
Mary L of Spring Hill, Frederickton New Brunswick Canada & William E SARGISSON (formerly of England) at LaGrange ME by T H BATES [30 Jul 1842]
Micah of Portland ME & Mary Ann WHITNEY at Lewiston ME [11 Jun 1846]
Rebecca A & Capt Peter BRIGGS at Bath ME [3 Apr 1845]
Sarah of Pittsfield & Richard WOOD at Winslow ME [26 Aug 1847]
Sarah & David MITCHELL Esq of Temple ME at Farmington ME [7 Mar 1837]
Solomon T & Miss Mercey E REED at Bath ME [19 Apr 1849]
Stephen & Miss Eliza WHITE at Augusta ME on 4 Jul by Thomas J DUDLEY Esq [8 Jul 1852]
Susan & William PARDY at Bath ME [8 Nov 1849]
HIGHT B M of Bloomfield ME & Martha HILTON at Anson ME [7 Apr 1848]
Cordelia F & Joseph L LOTHROP at Norridgewock ME [5 Oct 1848]
Elizabeth J of Louisville & George W HARLOW Esq, editor of the *Attala [Mississippi] Gazette*, and formerly of Augusta ME at Louisville KY [7 Oct 1843]
Hannah & Charles YALLALEE, a printer of Bangor ME at Norridgewock ME [6 Aug 1846]
Helen & Lyman PERRY at Bloomfield ME [31 May 1849]
Mary Ann & Stephen L TOBEY at Athens ME [29 Nov 1849]
R S & Emeline S BARKER both of Athens ME at Skowhegan ME [29 Jun 1848]
HILBORN Esther of Oxford ME & Joseph S ROUNDS at Norway ME [30 Apr 1846]
HILDRETH Esther A & David H FULLER at Gardiner ME [22 Mar 1849]
Mary E & Asa LIBBY at Gardiner ME [9 Jan 1851]
Parlin F & Mercy BONSEY at Ellsworth ME [12 Sept 1840]

Marriage Notices from the "Maine Farmer"

HILL A M & Zelinda HODGES [30 Jul 1846]
    Abagail & Joseph R NELSON at Bangor ME on the 9th inst [18 Jul 1840]
    Amelia H of New Portland ME & Samuel M BOARDMAN at Norridgewock ME [22 May 1851]
    Betsey D & Charles RIDEOUT at Bath ME [30 Mar 1848]
    Caleb & Almira KNOWNLTON at Danville ME [4 Jan 1849]
    Caroline P & John ALLEN of Alfred ME at Lyman ME [1 Jul 1852]
    D N & Sophia Ann TOTMAN both of Bath ME [11 Dec 1845]
    Deborah A & Joseph M MORSE of Carthage ME at Wilton ME [6 Sept 1849]
    Eliza C & William C BANKS at Bangor ME [6 Jan 1848]
    Eliza L W & Silas W TURNER at Norridgewock ME [23 Jul 1842]
    Elizabeth C & Alvan TRASK at Bangor ME [4 Jul 1840]
    Elizabeth D & Samuel Col MERRILL of Tamworth NH at Buxton ME [6 Feb 1851]
    Elizabeth & Knowlton PENNY of Augusta ME at Readfield ME on 26th ult by Eliab LYON [18 Apr 1840]
    Elizabeth & Lewis BARKER of Stetson ME at Exeter ME [13 Aug 1846]
    Francis E, M.D., of Biddeford ME & Nancy T LITTLEFIELD of Saco ME at Providence RI on Jan 1st [16 Jan 1851]
    Francis W & Sarah Ann TRUE at Exeter ME [23 Jan 1845]
    Frederick T of Lyman ME & Miss Lydia S LUNT of Kennebunk ME [4 Dec 1845]
    H M Mr & Elizabeth HARMON both of Gardiner ME at Providence RI on 27 Apr [13 May 1852]
    Hiram of Augusta ME & Sarah A CARPENTER at Hallowell ME on Wednesday evening last by Rev Mr COLE [8 Aug 1837]
    Hiratio of Bangor ME & Elizabeth A d/o Mr Ebenezer DANIELS of Portland ME at Portland on Thuesday on 29 Nov by Rev Mr SADDLER [10 Dec 1842]
    Ichabod of Saco ME & Mrs Mary SMITH of Kennebunkport ME at Biddeford ME [28 May 1846]
    James P & Emeline P SIMPSON of Winslow ME at Waterville ME [1 Mar 1849]
    James W & Helen JEWETT formerly of Norridgewock ME at Bangor ME [27 Jun 1844]
    Jeremiah Jr of Smithfield ME & Ellen POOLER of Bloomfield ME at Skowhegan ME [16 Jan 1851]
    John S & Hellen A SMALL by Rev Luther WISWALL at Thorndike ME on Apr 4th [15 Apr 1852]
    Jonathan & Abby A GREEN at Bath ME [25 Feb 1847]
    Julia Ann & Joshua BRACKETT of Belfast ME at Lincolnville ME [11 Mar 1847]
    Keziah & Henry NOBLE of Norway ME at Paris ME [30 Apr 1846]
    Martha & John BARKER Jr at Bangor ME [10 Jul 1835]
    Mary A & E COURSER at Wilton ME [6 Sept 1849]
    Mary A & Joseph W KIDDER at Skowhegan ME [3 Jan 1850]
    Mary H & W H C STEARNS at Sullivan ME [2 Jul 1846]
    Nathaniel Jr & Emily TOTMAN both of Bath ME at Bath ME [20 Jan 1848]
    O A Mr of North Yarmouth ME & Mary S SMALL at Limington ME [14 Sept 1848]

HILL (cont.) Olive R & Solomon LOW at Norridgewock ME [26 Feb 1836]
Randall L & Miss Esther ROSS at Skowhegan ME [15 Feb 1840]
Reuben Capt & Miss Betsey COTTLE of Industry ME at New Portland ME [22 Feb 1844]
Sarah A & Eli LITTLEFIELD at Biddeford ME [10 Jul 1851]
Sarah A & Newman T WHITTIER of Rome ME at (Augusta) ME on 25th Sept by Rev William A DREW [27 Sept 1849]
Sarah & Augustus J BROWN at Bangor ME [10 Jul 1835]
Sarah & Harvey RAMSDELL at this town (Winthrop ME) on Sept 14th by Rev F MERRIAM [24 Sept 1842]
Stephen of Baltimore MD & Elizabeth SEWALL at Bath ME [23 Aug 1849]
Warren & Miss Catherine G ELDER at New Portland ME [24 Dec 1841]
William Jr Capt & Harriet A HOOPER at Biddeford ME [5 Oct 1848]
HILLARD Mary W & Mr P H HOLMES at Washington DC on 31 Jan [19 Feb 1852]
HILLBORN Elliot S of New York & Sarah Jane ROBBINS at Paris ME [27 Jun 1844]
HILLMAN Alfred C & Miss Hepsibeth BECKET at Temple ME [10 Jul 1845]
Clarissa of Troy ME & Mr E G CROOKER of Dixmont ME at Troy ME [3 Jul 1845]
Rosanna S & John A WELCH at Albany NY [24 Aug 1848]
HILLS Benjamin B & Miss Amelina H OXTON at Union ME [29 Mar 1849]
Israel R & Saline ROBBINS of Appleton ME at Union ME [13 Nov 1851]
Lucina & John PATTERSON of Warren ME at Cushing ME [3 Oct 1844]
Margaret & Silas HAWES at Union ME [28 Sept 1848]
HILTON Aaron & Betsey BLIN at Woolwich ME [25 Dec 1835]
Betsey M of Starks ME & Ira R DOOLITTLE at Waterville ME on 20 Mar by Rev Calvin GARDNER [19 Apr 1849]
C W Mr & Julia Ann HANSCOM by John PETTINGILL Esq at (Augusta) ME [29 Apr 1852]
Caroline of Winthrop ME & Elijah PAGE of Livermore ME at Winthrop ME by Seth MAY Esq [11 Apr 1837]
Catherine of Winthrop ME & Elijah PAGE of Livermore ME at Winthrop ME on 25 Jan by William C FULLER Esq [6 Feb 1835]
Charles E & Miss Priscilla L TODD at Hallowell ME on 22d ult [4 Nov 1843]
Charlotte W & Thomas M CHICK at Wiscasset ME [19 Nov 1846]
E Addison Mr of Norridgewock ME & Eliza MILLS of Belgrade ME by Rev Mr GARDNER at Waterville ME [25 May 1848]
Enoch C of Unity ME & Carline S HARADEN at Belfast ME [21 May 1846]
Hannah & Joseph GILLEY at Augusta ME on 24th inst by Anson CHURCH [28 Oct 1847]
Isaac W & Lucinda S REED at Augusta ME by Rev Mr FULLER [7 Mar 1844]
James M of Augusta ME & Sarah C BLACKER of Boston at Boston MA [25 Nov 1847]
James M of Starks ME & Mrs Lois H PIERCE at New Portland ME [7 Feb 1850]
Jane O & Augustus J CHADWICK at Augusta ME on Sunday eve by Rev Mr WILLIAMS [31 Jul 1845]
Jarvis of Starks & Miss Betsey H MANTOR of Industry ME at North Anson ME [29 Nov 1849]

Marriage Notices from the "Maine Farmer"

HILTON (cont.) John & Sarah WHEELER d/o Heber WHEELER Esq at Norridgewock ME on 27 Jun [15 Jul 1852]
  Julia & William TAYLOR at Wiscasset ME [17 Dec 1842]
  Louisa & John JONES at Augusta ME [7 Sept 1833]
  Martha & Anthony C ASHFORD at Windsor ME on 15 Jun by A COOMBS Esq [8 Jul 1852]
  Martha & Mr B M HIGHT at Anson ME [7 Apr 1848]
  Mary E & Isaac McCAUSLAND at Hallowell ME [10 Dec 1846]
  Mary & William WILLIAMS at Windsor ME [4 Jul 1837]
  Nancy of Solon ME (age 50y) & Isaac PATTEN of Bloomfield ME (age 69y) at Solon on 23 Jun by William VARNUM Esq [1 Jul 1843]
  Naomi S & John H CHILDS at Norridgewock ME on 27 Jun [12 Jul 1849]
  Pamelia Mrs & Daniel PUTNAM Esq at Belfast ME [3 Jun 1847]
  Rhoda Ann & Milo M DANFORTH at Madison ME [8 Jun 1848]
  Ruth A & Charles G ANDREWS at Corinna ME [28 Jan 1847]
  Sally & Cephas DINSMORE at North Anson ME [9 Apr 1846]
  Semantha & Loring B JONES at Norridgewock ME [27 Jun 1844]
  Sylva Mrs & Mr Barton TURNER at Wiscasset ME [25 Feb 1843]
  William B & Rhoda LITTLE both of Bremen ME by Elder MERRIAM at Searsmont ME on 16 Oct [2 Nov 1848]
HINCKLEY/HINKLEY Ann R & Crosby MAYO at Carmel ME [30 Dec 1847]
  Barney & Malvina WHEELER d/o William L W both formerly of Bangor ME at San Francisco CA on 5 Nov [15 Jan 1852]
  Caroline W & Albert MARSH at Hallowell ME [15 Jan 1846]
  Charles of Cambridge MA & Eliza COLLINS at New Gloucester ME [27 Feb 1845]
  Cynthia A & Timothy M SANBORN at Monroe ME [14 August 1851]
  Daniel of Livermore ME & Miss Elvira PACKARD at Augusta ME on 15 Dec by Rev Mr DILLINGHAM [27 Dec 1849]
  David & Miss Mary SARGEANT at Gardiner ME by Rev A C ADAMS [28 Mar 1840]
  Elizabeth P & David STEARNS at Monroe ME [23 May 1840]
  Ephraim (age 30) & Miss Jane HUMPHREYS (age 55y) after a tedious courtship of 12 hours on Plt Number 1 ME [22 Apr 1833]
  Eunice D of Guilford ME & William H WAKEFIELD at Sangerville ME [25 Apr 1850]
  Gideon of Lisbon ME & Bethiah F PETTENGILL at Livermore ME [8 Aug 1844]
  Hannibal C & Sarah F RICHARDS at Hallowell ME [28 Dec 1839]
  Harriet & Elbridge G BACHELDER at Lisbon ME on 26 Feb [11 Mar 1852]
  Hiram & Miss Mary A TOBEY both of this town (Augusta) ME at Hallowell ME by Rev S W FIELD [9 Aug 1849]
  J T Mr of Bluehill ME & Anna COLBURN at Orono ME [13 Nov 1851]
  J W Dr of East Boston MA & Nancy D WASGATT at Mt Desert ME [29 Apr 1852]
  Jacob S & Miss Angelina PRESSLEY at Eastport ME [15 Mar 1849]
  James W of Greenville ME & Mary J LADD of Starks ME at Madison ME [7 Feb 1850]
  John W of Georgetown ME & Sarah S COLLER of Bath ME at Bath [28 Nov 1840]

HINCKLEY (cont.) Josiah & Miss Abigail BOSWORTH of Starks ME at Mercer ME [20 Jan 1837]
Nancy N & Caleb WILLARD of New Sharon ME at Mercer ME [18 Apr 1837]
Nancy P & Caleb WILBUR of New Sharon ME at Mercer ME [20 Jan 1837]
Nathaniel Esq of Barnstable MA & Ann Judson PAGE of New Sharon ME at Boston MA [25 Dec 1851]
Nicholas Capt & Belinda ROWELL by Rev Isaac LORD at Monmouth ME [20 May 1852]
Ransom of Bradley ME & Miss Catherine ALLEN at Frankfort ME [12 Feb 1846]
Richard F & Sarah E RUSH at Bath ME [3 Jul 1851]
Roxanna & Capt Cyrus WOOD at New Sharon ME [24 Aug 1839]
Rufus L Dr of Boston MA & Mrs Eliza Ann FULMUR, d/o Capt Isaac HOPKINS of Hampden ME, at Hampden ME on 30th ult by John WILLIAMS Esq of Bangor ME [9 Dec 1843]
Ruth A & William H CHICK at Litchfield ME [24 Feb 1848]
Seth Esq & Miss Rosannah STEVENS of New Sharon ME at Mercer ME [20 Jan 1837]
Seth Esq & Miss Roxana STEVENS of Orono ME at Mercer ME [18 Apr 1837]
William C & Emily E DUNN all of Portland ME at Portland ME on Wed eve last by Rev Mr DWIGHT [16 Oct 1838]
William of Monroe ME & Almira MASON of Prospect ME at Belfast ME [22 Jan 1836]

HINDS Asher Esq of Clinton ME & Mrs Lucy H LUNT of Bath ME [4 Feb 1833]
Ashur & Rebecca S JUNKINS both of Township Number 6, 9th Range ME at Dover ME [1 Feb 1849]
Crosby Esq of Clinton ME & Isabella W SHEPHERD at Waterville ME [19 Jun 1841]
E W Mr of Kingfield ME & Sarah J SPRAGUE at Farmington ME [23 Oct 1851]
Emma & Capt Joseph ADDITON of Wilton ME at Livermore ME on May day by Rev G W QUINBY [11 May 1839]
Juliana & Salathiel TILTON at Livermore ME [5 Oct 1839]
Lucy V & William ROBBINS of Boston MA at Pittston ME [17 Sept 1846]
Maria of Livermore ME & Nathan SAWTELLE of Turner ME [4 Apr 1837]
Ruby & Crosby BARTON Esq of Sinney (Sidney) ME at Sebasticook ME [4 Feb 1843]
Samuel H of Kingfield ME & Miss Priscilla AYER at Embden ME [8 Oct 1846]

HINES Joseph W of Boston MA & Marcella M HALL of Presque Isle ME on 29 Aug by Rev J G MERRILL [9 Sept 1847]

HINGS George & Rachel WOOD at St Louis KY [14 Aug 1845]

HINKSON Algernon W & Miss Julia C DENNISON at Brunswick ME [25 Feb 1847]
Judith & Charles MORSE of Milton Plt Oxford Co ME at Rumford ME on 30 Dec by A H ABBOTT Esq [23 Jan 1851]

HINTON Elizabeth & John MARSHALL at Augusta ME [30 May 1837]

HISCOCK Eliza Ann, d/o Col William HISCOCK, & George TUKEY at Nobleboro ME by Rev Mr Scammon [25 Dec 1838]

Marriage Notices from the "Maine Farmer"

HISCOCK (cont.) Lucy & Samuel SPEAR at Dixfield ME [16 Sept 1847]
    Roan & Willard SEVERY at Dixfield ME [18 Jun 1846]
HITCHBORN John & Adeline GODFREY at Orono ME [29 Feb 1844]
HITCHCOCK Enos Esq of Strong ME & Abby READ at Farmington ME [13 Dec 1849]
    Jane A & W H WALDRON of Lewiston ME at Boston MA [31 May 1849]
HITCHINGS Jonas B & Isabel E WILLIAMS at Harmony ME [7 Mar 1850]
HOBART Abby L of Hingham MA & Henry C HAMLEN of Augusta ME at Hingham MA [26 Dec 1840]
    Austin & Sarah C FARGO at South Solon ME [8 May 1851]
    Caroline & William H MORTON at Hingham MA on 19th inst [26 Oct 1848]
    Clementine & Enoch at Solon ME [6 Aug 1846]
    David of Acton MA & Miss Emily CHADBURN at East Madison ME [19 Nov 1846]
    Enoch Augustus of Boston MA & Sarah Caroline NICHOLS d/o Asaph R NICHOLS Esq at Augusta on 20 Mar [28 Mar 1850]
    Isaac Esq of Edmunds & Julia T JONES d/o the late JONES of North Yarmouth ME at Portland ME [12 Sept 1844]
    Isaac M & Olive H FRENCH at Oldtown ME [5 Feb 1852]
    Walter & Miss Catherine R PAUL at Solon ME [30 Apr 1846]
HOBBS Elizabeth & Daniel L STACY at Berwick ME [21 Jan 1847]
    Emily J & Joseph A THOMAS at East Livermore ME [16 Jan 1845]
    Euran & Miss Sarah BENSON of Biddeford ME at Waterboro ME [10 Jul 1835]
    George & Lydia Ann HALL at Saco ME [8 Apr 1847]
    Henry & Mrs Fanny ROGERS at Augusta ME [29 May 1838]
    Jeremiah Jr & Mrs Anna FROST at Norway ME [13 Jan 1848]
    Lewis of Livermore ME & Miss Margaret SETHERS of Hallowell ME at (Hallowell) ME on Sunday evening 22d inst by Rev E M TABIE [31 Oct 1837]
    Maria Archibald, d/o George HOBBS Esq at Eastport ME, & Peter SCOTT Esq, Lieut in the British Navy [8 Apr 1847]
    Mary Ann & Surranus BRIGGS at Livermore ME [21 Nov 1844]
    Mary E & William G ROGERS of Brownville ME at Milo ME [31 Jul 1851]
    Mary E & William M CUSHMAN at Norway ME [22 Mar 1849]
    Minerva Ann & & Luther HUTCHINS of Chelsea MA at Norway ME [6 Mar 1845]
    Nancy M & Isaac MALOON of Temple ME at Farmington ME [11 Jul 1844]
    Samuel of Livermore ME & Laura Ann JONES at Turner ME [11 May 1839]
    William W & Miss Julia Jones BRIGGS at Livermore ME by Isaac STRICKLAND Esq [14 Nov 1837]
HOBSON Sarah M & Mark R CAME at Standish ME [2 May 1844]
HOCH Calvin of Thomaston ME & Harriet A SCHWARTZ at Waldoboro ME [12 Dec 1837]
HOCKEY Clara S & Hiram F ELLIOTT Esq at Freedom ME [6 Nov 1845]
HODGDON Almira D Mrs & Ezakiel H HODGDON at Limerick ME [2 Jul 1846]
    E G of Clinton ME & Miss Rosina KIDDER at Albion ME [4 Jan 1849]
    Ezakiel H & Mrs Almira D HODGDON at Limerick ME [2 Jul 1846]

HODGDON (cont.) Fanny A & William McNELLY Jr at Benton ME [13 Nov 1851]
    Fines of Lebanon ME & Lydia FROST at Litchfield ME [12 Oct 1848]
    Harriet N & James LEADBETTER at Palmyra ME [21 Oct 1847]
    Harriet & Herrick W GORDON of Augusta ME at Portsmouth NH on 17th inst [26 Jul 1849]
    Harriet & John TUTTLE at Saco ME [23 Aug 1849]
    Mary M HODGDON & William M DONNELL of Beverly MA at Bath ME [21 Aug 1842]
    Matilda Jane & Capt Samuel M REED at Boothbay ME [3 Apr 1845]
    Phebe Ann of Westport ME & Lorenzo LAWRENCE at Bath ME [16 Sept 1847]
    Samuel Jr & Sarah HODGE at Gardiner ME [17 May 1849]
    William & Sarah B ARRAS at Bath ME [23 Apr 1846]
HODGE Charles E & Zelinda W PINKHAM both of this town (Hallowell ME) at Hallowell by Rev TOBIE [13 Feb 1838]
    David at age 102y and two months & Miss Elizabeth RAILY age 40y both of Columbia Co GA, Mr H was at Braddock's defeat, serving throughout the whole period of the American Revolutionary War. He was married in GA by John McGEHEE [1 Jul 1836]
    Sarah Jr & Sarah HODGE at Gardiner ME [17 May 1849]
HODGES Caroline & Capt George AGRY both of Hallowell ME at New York on 8th inst [25 Sept 1841]
    George & Mrs Sarah M WASS at Hallowell ME [15 Jan 1842]
    Joseph Jr & Miss Abigail ROBERTSON at Belmont ME [15 Aug 1844]
    Zelinda & Mr A M HILL at Hallowell ME [30 Jul 1846]
HODGKINS Ai B [sic] & Harriet N MERROW of Auburn ME at Lewiston ME [30 Jan 1851]
    Caroline & Ephraim B WEEKS at Jefferson ME [3/17 Apr 1851]
    Edward A & Sarah E ROWE at Bath ME on 6th inst by P PALMER [5 Feb 1842]
    Edward of Hancock ME & Mrs Sarah HANNOR of Eden at Eden ME by Lenord J THOMAS Esq [12 Feb 1842]
    J R Capt of Gardiner ME & Elizabeth BLACK of Winthrop ME by Rev B F ROBBINS at Winthrop ME on 23 Jan [27 Jan 1848]
    Josiah of Jefferson ME & Margaret GLIDDEN of New Castle ME at New Castle [23 May 1844]
    Matthew & Elizabeth STEWART at Augusta ME [11 Feb 1847]
    Sarah J & John C JONES at Litchfield ME [20 Jul 1848]
    William E & Nancy D THOMAS at Bath ME [13 Aug 1846]
    William & Joanna P ROBINSON at Thomaston ME [16 Jul 1846]
    William & Miss Jane PIERCE at Augusta ME on the 20th inst by William WOART Esq [23 Sept 1847]
HODGMAN Albert H of Camden ME & Miss Elizabeth K DYER at Searsmont ME [5 Mar 1846]
HODSDON Susan L & Charles H PERRIGO at Milo ME [25 May 1848]
HODGSDON Freeman & Miss Martha BRADGON at York ME [22 Apr 1836]
    Mary & Capt Samuel YORK of Falmouth ME at Turner ME [6 Apr 1839]
    Moses M & Harriet A BATCHELDER at Levant ME [24 May 1849]
    Rachel J & Capt Lewis N WEST at Pownal ME [24 May 1849]
    Vira of Jay ME & Capt John ADAMS of Madison ME at North Anson ME [10 Jan 1850]

Marriage Notices from the "Maine Farmer"

HODSON Amos of Clinton ME & Mrs Caroline HEYWOOD of Winthrop ME at Clinton ME on 30 Jan [5 Feb 1846]
   Asa of Somersworth NH & Nancy McKENNEY of Hollis ME at Saco ME [4 Dec 1845]
HOFFMAN Margaret & George BROWN at Bath ME [15 Jun 1848]
HOGAN Nicholas L & Miss Jane H STINSON at Arrowic ME [26 Aug 1847]
   Rachel J & George BENNETT of Augusta ME at Bath ME [11 Nov 1843]
HOIT Elizabeth C of Saco ME & James H DUDLEY Esq of Boston MA at Dover ME [28 Jan 1847]
HOLBROOK Abigail W & Alfred VILES Jr at Mercer ME both of Starks ME [18 Feb 1847]
   B Y Capt & Susan GREENLIEF at Wiscasset ME [16 Oct 1845]
   Clarissa & Orville W TINKHAM of Norridgewock ME at Bloomfield ME [21 Jun 1849]
   Harriet E of Starks ME & Simeon C HOLBROOK at Mercer ME on the 26th ult [12 Nov 1846]
   Isaac of Phipsburg ME & Mary J HAYDEN at Bath ME [10 Jan 1850]
   J B S & Hannah E HIGGINS at Bath ME [16 Aug 1849]
   John Jr & Lydia HALL at Norridgewock ME [5 Dec 1844]
   John Jr & Sarah Jane SALLY at North Anson ME [15 Jul 1852]
   John P & Susan M BLETHEN at Parkman ME [3 Jun 1852]
   Maria A G T & N CLARK at Hallowell ME [31 Aug 1848]
   Mary E of Bath ME & Mr Knowles GALEN of Dresden ME at Phippsburg ME [7 Jan 1847]
   Mary & William COFFIN at Harpswell ME [21 Sept 1848]
   Sarah J & Frederick GAGE both of Strong ME at Farmington ME [23 Jan 1845]
   Seth of Starks ME & Esther A BASTON at Mercer ME [31 Jul 1851]
   Simeon C & Harriet E HOLBROOK of Starks ME at Mercer ME on the 26th ult [12 Nov 1846]
   Thomas K Capt & Melissa ROBINSON at Rockland ME [31 Jul 1851]
HOLCOMB Jonas G & Parmelia R PRESCOTT at Augusta ME [19 Jun 1838]
HOLDEN Mary & Daniel M COOK at Casco ME [2 Apr 1846]
   Otis & Margaret RAY at Moose River ME [25 Jan 1849]
   Samuel Jr & Annis HUGHEY at Moose River ME [4 Jun 1851]
HOLLAND Amanda B & Nathaniel T SHAW of Buckfield ME at Livermore ME [27 Sept 1849]
   Cordelia & Samuel F TUTTLE of Portland ME at Belfast ME [7 Sept 1833]
   Hannah & Joseph W SYLVESTER at Hallowell ME on Sunday last by Rev Mr CROSS [29 May 1838]
   James L & Anna HUNTINGTON at Pittston ME both of Hallowell ME [18 Mar 1847]
   James M Esq of Canton ME & Miss Sarah F FAIRBANKS of (Winthrop ME) at Winthrop by Rev David THURSTON on Thurs morn 1 Sept [3 Sept 1842]
   Lavina & Francis W BAXTER borth of Dixfield ME on the 17th inst by Rev Daniel GOULD [20 Mar 1835]
   Maria J & Isaac T SAVAGE at Waterville ME [30 Oct 1851]
   Rebecca J & Jeremiah WEBBER at Lewiston ME [21 Jun 1849]
   Richard & Mary Jane SWIFT at Brunswick ME on the 22d inst by Rev George LAMB [21 Jan 1833]

HOLLOM Elizabeth & John C BAILEY of Maxfield ME at Sebec ME [21 Aug 1851]
HOLMAN Angeline & Gilman STORER at Dixfield ME [25 Mar 1852]
    Cordelia & Greenleaf G RICHARDS at Wayne ME [22 Apr 1852]
    Eliza & Rand WHITE at Dixfield ME [6 Sept 1849]
    Emeline K & Samuel C WILDER at Temple ME [22 Jul 1852]
    Franklin & Vesta G NEWTON at Dixfield ME [2 Aug 1849]
    Gustavus of Weld ME & Miss Hannah SANBORN at Strong ME [14 Oct 1847]
    Margaret & Mr T G WORMWOOD at Phipsburg ME [22 Apr 1852]
    Martha, d/o Hon Silas HOLMAN, & John H EVELETH of Augusta ME at Bolton MA [27 Nov 1835]
    S C of Boston MA & Sarah Elizabeth EMERY at Augusta ME on 11 Mar by Rev Mr JUDD [22 Mar 1849]
    Sullivan Dr of Canaan ME & Clarissa CROWELL of Waterville ME at Fairfield ME [28 Oct 1836]
HOLMES Allyn & Miss Hannah J SAWYER at Gardiner ME on 28 Jan by Rev Mr CLAPP [27 Feb 1838]
    Almira & Jona A PERKINS at Smithfield ME [24 Sept 1846]
    Alonzo S & Mrs H W BARSTOW at Bath ME [27 Jul 1848]
    Arabella R & D Chandler BENT of Manchester NH at Paris ME [27 Nov 1851]
    Arlitta M & Capt John G BARSTOW at Newcastle ME [3 Sept 1842]
    Caleb B, merchant & Lucy B PRIOR at Bangor ME [22 Jun 1839]
    Emeline, M.D., & John E FLINT at Thomaston ME [14 Oct 1847]
    Hannah S & William C RAMSEY at East Thomaston ME [30 Oct 1835]
    Isaac of Augusta ME & Sopronia JOSSELYN of Hampden ME on 25 Jul by Rev MITCHELL [5 Aug 1847]
    Jerusha & Thomas TASH at Foxcroft ME [24 Feb 1848]
    John Hon of Alfred ME & Mrs Caroline F SWAN youngest d/o the late Gen Henry KNOX at Thomaston ME [15 Aug 1837]
    Joseph & Miss Betsey JONES both of Winthrop ME at Augusta ME [5 Feb 1839]
    Julia A of Bangor ME & Ashford BAKER of Weymouth MA at Turner ME [30 Nov 1839]
    Mary E of Peru ME & Rev Seth B CHASE of Paris ME at Monmouth ME [4 Mar 1847]
    N W of Dixmont ME & Miss Mary E REED at Albion ME [12 Feb 1846]
    P H of Winthrop ME & Mary W HILLARD formerly of Lawrence MA by Rev BROWN at Washington DC on 31 Jan [19 Feb 1852]
    Rosella I & Ebenezer CUNNINGHAM at Belfast ME both of Swanville ME [30 Sept 1847]
    Susan B & Harrison CHANDLER at Winthrop ME by Rev Mr THURSTON [31 Jan 1850]
    W B Esq of Alfred ME & Phebe W LITTLE at Castine ME [25 Mar 1836]
HOLT Daniel & Hannah GOLDSMITH of Phillips ME at Weld ME by I TYLER Esq [1 Nov 1849]
    Diantha L & Albert J SMALL at Norway ME [27 Dec 1849]
    George S & Augusta S GILPATRICK at Topsham ME [28 Oct 1847]
    Gratia Ann eldest d/o late Rev Fifield HOLT, & William BERRY Jr of New Sharon ME at Bloomfield ME [4 Jan 1840]
    Hepzibah & Francis CUMMINGS of Albany ME at Bethel ME [4 Jun 1851]

HOLT (cont.) Isaac Capt of Clinton ME & Olive RAND by Elder LEWIS at Canaan ME on 22d April [29 Apr 1852]
    Jonah Esq & Miss Almira M WILCOX at Bluehill ME [29 Mar 1849]
    Lucinda & Ira WALDRON at Sebasticook ME [8 Mar 1849]
    Lydia A & George TUFTS at Norway ME [20 Jun 1844]
    Lydia of Winthrop ME & John F STEVENS of Andover MA at Winthrop ME on Thursday evening last by the Rev Mr FULLER [28 Sept 1833]
    Philanda & Cyrus WALDRON at Sebasticook ME on 26 Oct [8 Nov 1849]
    Wentworth of Hermon ME & Frances M GOSS at Levant ME [21 Aug 1851]
HOLTON John A Maj & Vilena STEVENS formerly of Maine at Quincy IL [11 Sept 1845]
HOLWAY Isaac & Susan R PINKHAM both of Sidney ME at Waterville ME on 30 May by Joseph MARSTON Esq [19 Jun 1845]
    Seth & Thankful SMITH at Fairfield ME [21 Jan 1833]
HOLYOKE Caleb of Brewer ME & Abby Y PARKER at Hampden ME [7 Jan 1843]
HOMAN Samuel V & Mary eldest d/o Arno BITTUES Esq at Augusta ME on Thurs morning by Rev Mr JUDD [5 Mar 1842]
HOMANS Caroline A & Howard PETTINGILL at (Augusta) ME [7 Dec 1848]
    Samuel Esq of this town ME & Temperance HAWES of Vassalboro ME on 29th inst by Rev A MOORE [6 Feb 1845]
HOMER Mary L of Portland ME & Luther P WINSLOW at Portland ME [2 May 1844]
    Zenas & Cynthia H d/o Col S LAKE at Bucksport ME [17 Aug 1839]
HOMSTED Abel Jr of Skowhegan ME & Abby F COOMBS of Readfield ME by Rev P JAQUES at Winthrop ME on 20 May [27 May 1852]
HOOD Albion of Turner ME & Miss Julia O DAVENPORT of Wayne ME at Wayne [15 Mar 1849]
    Almira & Luther W KIMBALL at Gardiner ME [22 Apr 1852]
    James M of Boston MA & Almire COLLINS of Lynn MA at Gardiner ME [14 Nov 1844]
HOOKE Mary L & Mr D Henrie PRIME at Cambridge MA [1 Apr 1852]
HOOK Emily E & John BURRELL, printer at Skowhegan ME [27 Nov 1841]
    Irene & Joseph GREENLIEF at Skowhegan ME [21 May 1846]
    Joseph Jr of Skowhegan ME & Mary Jane CORSON at Canaan ME [25 Apr 1840]
    Josiah S & Miss Maria L JEROME at Bangor ME [6 Feb 1845]
    Mary A & Alfred S BROWN of Boston MA at Providence RI [4 Apr 1850]
    Sarah M & David H LIBBY at Belfast ME [5 Apr 1849]
HOOKER George W & Eliza A BALLENTINE both of Augusta ME at Sidney ME [3 Apr 1851]
HOOLE Mary A & Henry B at Portland ME [23 Sept 1836]
HOOPER Edwards H C of Biddeford ME & Miss Elizabeth WHITE at Hallowell ME [19 Aug 1847]
    Eleanor Jane of Deer Island ME & George TRECARTIN both of Deer Island Washington Co ME at St Andrews New Brunswick Canada [21 Aug 1851]
    Eliza Ann C & Benjamin C FULLER at New York both of Portland ME [6 Mar 1845]
    Eliza & Jairus K HAMMOND at Paris ME [15 Mar 1849]

HOOPER (cont.) Elizabeth Jane & William DURANT, editor of the *Chronicle* at St John New Brunswick Canada [8 Jan 1846]
    Hannah J & George O BURNHAM at Biddeford ME [21 Nov 1844]
    Harriet A & Capt William HILL at Biddeford ME [5 Oct 1848]
    Joseph C Dr of Frankfort ME & Helen M WALLINGFORD of Kennebunk ME at Bangor ME [25 Sept 1845]
    Mary & Andrew J HALL of Buckfield ME at Paris ME [23 Jan 1851]
    Sarah L of Bangor ME & Harrison G PRESCOTT ME [6 Feb 1845]
HOOTON Susan & John LIPSCOTT at Portland ME [23 May 1844]
HOPKINS see FULMER
    Albert Prof of Williams College, Williamston MA & Miss Louisa S eldest d/o the late Dr PAYSON at Portland ME [11 Sept 1841]
    Catharine & William TAPLEY at Gardiner ME [22 Jan 1846]
    Dorcas & Elias BANKS at Portland ME [19 Jun 1845]
    Eliphalet S of Rumford ME & Mary Ann NICKERSON at New Portland ME [25 Apr 1840]
    Eliphalet S Rev of Rumford ME & Mary Ann NICKERSON at New Portland ME [28 Nov 1840] & [5 Dec 1840]
    Eliza Ann of Hampden ME & Rev Jacob K FULMER of Bucksport ME at Hampden ME [15 Jul 1836]
    George B & Nancy LORD at Ellsworth ME [12 Dec 1840]
    George & Sarah M RICH at Eden ME [26 Dec 1834]
    Isaac of Brunswick ME & Julia Ann DAY at Durham ME [30 Dec 1836]
    Isabella F & Belden BESSE at Albion ME [29 Jul 1852]
    J R, editor of the *Mattanawcook Observer* at Lincoln ME & Miss E NUTE [1 Apr 1847]
    Joseph & Miss Hannah S PHILBRICK at Mt Vernon ME by Arthur DRINKWATER [4 Jan 1834]
    Lovine formerly of Peru ME & Samuel W LIBBY of Litchfield ME at Winthrop ME [12 Dec 1844]
    Lucetta & Joseph BUTTERFIELD at Milford ME [10 Feb 1848]
    Mark R Rev of Old Town ME & Miss Caroline W PATTEN at Skowhegan ME [12 Apr 1849]
    Mary Jane & Rev James BELCHER at Ellsworth ME [25 Sept 1851]
    Mercy L & Elbridge J GROVER at Brunswick ME [8 Oct 1846]
    Randal of this town (Augusta) ME & Miss Olive M SARGENT at Milbridge ME [1 Mar 1849]
    Richard of Hallowell ME of Hallowell & Rachal PINKHAM of Litchfield ME [21 Mar 1840]
    Robert T & Susanna B KING at Winthrop ME [24 Feb 1848] & [10 Feb 1848]
    Sally & Cornelius T HAMOR at Eben ME [18 Dec 1835]
    Sarah A & Marshall P MARTIN of Portland ME at New Sharon ME [11 Feb 1847]
    William of Vinalhaven ME & Lucinda E TYLER at China ME on 17th Jan by William PERCIVAL Esq [24 Jan 1850]
    Willard & Sarah M FILLEBROWN at Winthrop ME on Mar 12th [20 Mar 1851]
    William H of Hallowell ME & Rhoda M FOUNTAIN at Bristol ME [1 Apr 1847]
    William of Trenton ME & Ann LALAND at Eden ME [23 Jan 1841]

HOPKINSON A J & Miss Caroline WOODWARD at Whitefield ME [19 Apr 1849]
  Mary C & Edwin BRADBURY of Standish ME at Buxton ME [29 May 1845]
HORN David Jr & Martha Ann DOW at Athens ME [27 Jan 1848]
  Lydia of Great Falls NH & Henry M BLAKE of Monmouth ME at Great Falls NH [25 Sept 1835]
  Maria & Oscar H PALMER at Augusta ME on 27 Sept by Rev J STEVENS [2 Oct 1851]
  Mary B & Seth GARLAND both of Augusta ME at Hallowell ME [16 Jul 1846]
  Ruth & Walter ABBOTT at Bath ME [15 May 1845]
  Sophronia L & Anderson PARKER of Corinth ME at Ripley ME [25 Sept 1838]
  Susan & Orick HAWES of Aroostook Co ME at Vassalboro ME [4 Feb 1843]
HORR Elizabeth B & Orrin TUBBS at Mechanic Falls ME [14 Dec 1848]
  John H & Almira B AYER at Saco ME [10 Sept 1846]
  Leonice M & John P DAVIS Esq at Portland ME both of Bridgton ME [28 Aug 1845]
HORTON Elizabeth & Richard BLAKE at Freedom ME [30 May 1844]
HOSFORD Harriet & Gustavus G CUSHMAN Esq of Bangor ME at Thetford (Orange Co VT?) [27 Mar 1845]
HOSKENS Joseph B of Portland ME & Miss Mary Ann DUNBAR of Newport ME [23 Mar 1839]
HOSKINS Tryphosa & Jonas P WYMAN at Bangor ME [25 Dec 1851]
  William B & Miss Maria MILES both of Calais ME at St Stephens New Brunswick Canada [13 Jul 1839]
HOSLEY Caroline & Solomon H ALDEN at Livermore ME [30 Nov 1839]
  John & Miss Lucinda BEALS at Livermore ME [30 Nov 1839]
HOSMER Harriet L & George F AYERS of E Thomaston ME at Camden ME [28 Jun 1849]
HOTCHKISS Edward Rev of the Maine (Methodist) Conference & Olive Amanda SAWYER of (Wayne NY) at Wayne on 3 Mar [23 Mar 1839]
HOUDLETT Lovis of Dresden ME & Mrs Rachel SMITH at Augusta ME on 9th inst by Rev Mr INGRAHAM [16 Jan 1845]
HOUDLETTE Carlton of Richmond ME & Maria COLBURN at Pittston ME [11 Oct 1849]
HOUGH Mary & Increase ROBINSON at Fairfield ME [11 Mar 1833]
HOUGHTON Azel E & Betsey HAWES of Weld ME [20 Feb 1845]
  Daniel & Sophia PARLIN at Weld ME on 12 Apr by I PARLINS Esq [26 Apr 1849]
  Eunice & James D TOWN at Gardiner ME [17 Sept 1842]
  Helen M & Dexter D SMITH at Gardiner ME on 19 Sept [21 Dec 1848]
  John R of Boston MA & Anne S d/o Nathaniel BADGER Esq of Brunswick ME [2 Sept 1843]
  Malvina, only d/o late Rev Josiah HOUGHTON of Winthrop ME, & Charles H NOURSE of Bolton MA at this town (Winthrop) ME on 17th inst by Rev Mr MERRIAM [22 Oct 1842]
  Marcellus Lieut & Miss Catherine C eldest d/o Rev S FOGG at Winthrop ME by Rev S FOGG on Thanksgiving evening [4 Dec 1841]

HOUGHTON (cont.) Ruth S & Capt Horatio G RUSS at Paris ME [23 May 1840]

HOULEHAN Michael & Elizabeth A DOYLE at Augusta ME on 23d inst (23 Aug) by Rev Mr O'REILLY [28 Aug 1851]

HOULTON Eunice & Charles JOHNSON at Kittery ME [23 Mar 1839]
    Hannah Mrs widow of the late Harrison HOULTON, & Mr Roswell HALE formerly of (Winthrop ME) on 2 Mar at Houlton Aroostook Co ME [19 Mar 1842]
    Julia, d/o J HOULTON Esq, & William HUSSEY of Bangor ME at Houlton Washington Co (now in Aroostook Co ME) [8 Jul 1833]
    Williard Esq & Miss Mary A WHITE at Houlton Aroostook Co ME [22 Apr 1843]

HOUSE Allen Jr & Miss Roxana F WING at Wayne ME [13 Mar 1835]
    David & Mrs Nabby TORRY both of Turner ME at Buckfield ME [3 Apr 1851]
    Isaiah C & Mary D WEST at Farmington ME [7 Dec 1839]
    Leilles & James NICHOLESS at East Livermore ME on 27th ult by Columbus HAINES Esq [4 Jan 1844]
    Loraina E & Francis H BRANN at (Augusta) ME on 30 Apr [11 May 1848]
    Sylvanus H & Drusilla A KING both of Monmouth ME at Hallowell ME [11 May 1848]

HOUSTON Benjamin of Gardiner ME & Miss Elizabeth A HOUSTON at Waterville ME [17 Apr 1845]
    Elizabeth & Benjamin HOUSTON of Gardiner ME at Waterville ME [17 Apr 1845]
    Joseph & Mrs Echsa WALKER at Dover ME [5 Sept 1844]

HOVEY Bernard K & Miss Angeline NORTON at Farmington ME [20 Nov 1838]
    Henry B Esq formerly of (Augusta) ME & Mrs Martha MORRISON at East Boston ME on 6th Dec [24 Jan 1850]
    John N of Hallowell ME & Caroline WADE at (Augusta) ME [24 Feb 1848]
    Lewis P & Abby C PEARSONS at Hallowell ME [27 Jun 1844]
    Lewis P & Miss Catharine PREBLE both of Hallowell ME at Hallowell ME on Sept 7 by Rev E M TOBIE [19 Sept 1837]
    Sarah E & John H JARVIS Jr of Ellsworth ME at Waldoboro ME [23 Sept 1836]

HOWARD Abigail of Phillips ME & Thomas WHITE Esq at Winthrop ME on 7th inst by Rev David THURSTON [11 Mar 1847]
    Alvan G & Amanda M RICKER at Foxcroft ME [29 Apr 1852]
    Asa S of Rumford ME & Betsey S ROBERTS of Hanover ME [30 Sept 1847]
    Barnabus & Eunice GOULD at Leeds ME [25 Apr 1834]
    Caroline M d/o Mr Dean HOWARD of Winthrop ME, & Jacob TILTON at Mt Vernon ME on Thursday the 11th inst by Rev David THURSTON [20 Nov 1841]
    Charles B of Livermore ME & Miss Elizabeth Ann WAUGH at Readfield ME [22 Jan 1842]
    Charles P & Mrs Mary YORK at Waterford ME [13 May 1852]
    Daniel & Miss Phebe MAXIM both of this town (Winthrop) ME at Gardiner ME on 26th ult by Rev Mr SANBORN [4 Dec 1835]
    Eliza Ann & Daniel WHITE at Vassalboro ME [29 Feb 1844]

HOWARD (cont.) Eliza J & Moses H RIPLEY at (Winthrop) ME on Tuesday evening last by Rev David THURSTON [16 Nov 1833]
Eliza Mrs & Col John GILMORE at Leeds ME by the Rev Mr STARR [19 Jun 1841]
Elizabeth & Arthur ANDREWS at Warren ME [13 Mar 1841]
Fanny & Luther REED of Augusta ME at Sidney ME [7 Dec 1839]
Francis B of Brownfield ME & Velina V DRAKE at Milo ME on 7 Mar by James H MACOMBER Esq [20 Mar 1851]
G W & Miss Mary Ann MUNROE at Brooksville ME [29 Apr 1836]
George F of Lancaster MA & MAry E CROMMETT of Corinna ME at Dexter ME [12 Feb 1852]
H Miss (age 19y) & Andrew GRAY (age 18y) at Brooksville ME [11 Feb 1843]
Harriet Newell & Rev R E TAYLOR at Vassalboro ME on 13th inst [29 Aug 1840]
Harvey & Miss Sarah B VALENTINE at Bangor ME [4 Sept 1845]
Jane S & Reuben H GODDARD at Litchfield ME [31 Dec 1842]
John & Sobrina WINSLOW at Phillips ME [22 Apr 1833]
Joseph & Abby S PERKINS both of this town (Augusta) ME by Rev Mr MASON at Williamsburg Long Island on 18th inst [2 Nov 1848]
Julia F & Elbridge G EDGECOMB, M.D., at Livermore ME both of Turner ME [21 Jun 1849]
Lucy A & Mr M P WOODCOOK at Searsmont ME [17 Apr 1851]
Lydia & Orren WATERMAN at Winthrop ME by Rev Mr BAILEY [11 Jun 1842]
Martha L & William G GAMMON at Canton ME [6 May 1852]
Mary L & Philip TURNER at Leeds ME [18 Jul 1834]
Mary T & Albion P GIBBS at Winthrop ME on Sunday last by Rev Mr ROBINSON [30 Dec 1843]
Mercy A & Hiram CARSLEY of Lynn MA at (Augusta) ME by Rev John ALLEN [10 May 1849]
Oakes Esq & Mrs Betsey T HAHN at Winthrop ME [8 May 1851]
Oliver & Miss Elizabeth HASKELL at Deer Isle ME [8 Apr 1847]
Otis of Winthrop ME & Alfred GOTT of Wayne ME at Readfield ME on Sunday last by Elder ROBINSON [1 Jul 1843]
Rachel & Luther COBB at (Winthrop) ME on Sunday last by Rev J B PRESCOT [8 Jan 1836]
Susan & John HACKET at Brooksville ME [29 Apr 1836]
Warren of Wilton ME & Miss Hannah M LARRABEE at Mt Vernon ME [18 Apr 1850]
William H & Martha D PICKETT at Portland ME [30 Jan 1845]
HOWCROFT David & Mrs Ann GUY at Dover ME [13 Jul 1848]
HOWE Adaline & Charles R LAWRENCE at (Augusta) ME on Sunday last [29 Jun 1848]
Charles & Miss Hannah S BURNHAM at Cherryfield ME [13 May 1847]
George T Capt & Charlotte J ALLEN at Greene ME [14 Dec 1848]
Henry of Paris ME & Miss Lucy C NEWBERT at Dedham MA [25 Mar 1847]
Jesse, M.D., of Lee & Rebecca G d/o Hon S GIBSON of Denmark ME at Norway ME [28 Oct 1843]
Josephine & Aaron CLARK both of Deer Island Washington Co ME at Eastport ME [28 Jan 1847]

HOWE (cont.) Lucy S & Mr Oren WHITMAN at Turner ME on 29 Nov by Rev Mr BATES [24 Dec 1842]
    Lucy & John O BROWN at Hallowell ME [11 Nov 1843]
    Marcus P of Camden ME & Miss Parthenian F GILBRETH at Farmington ME [15 Oct 1842]
    Nahum B Capt & Miss Sarah P UNDERWOOD at Readfield ME [15 Aug 1837]
    Rebecca W of Castine ME & Capt Samuel WHITNEY of New Orleans at Lincolnville ME [5 Dec 1844]
    Sally C & Simon H COTTER at Nobleboro ME [16 Oct 1845]
HOWELL John Elder & Miss Lucinda S ARMSTRONG at Readfield ME [9 Jul 1846]
HOWES Abby P & Franks P EAMES at Belfast ME [2 Aug 1849]
    Eleanor & George CRASH at Bath ME [4 Jul 1840]
    Louisa & Thomas WEYMAN of China ME at Vassalboro ME [27 Feb 1838]
    Mary S & Capt S FABYAN at Boston ME [12 Oct 1848]
    S A & Miss Jane S YOUNG at Belfast ME [5 Nov 1946]
    Sarah H & James SHANNON at Boston MA [12 Oct 1848]
    Susan S & Thomas B RIDLEY at New Sharon ME [12 Nov 1846]
HOWLAND Ann C & Charles PETTENGILL at Brunswick ME [30 Sept 1843]
    George W of Fairhaven MA & Hester Ann COX at Hallowell ME [30 Oct 1838]
HOXIE Caroline W & David S MOORES of Readfield ME at Sidney ME on 19th inst by Joshua DAVIS Esq [26 Dec 1844]
    Caroline & Ira L MacKAY at Fairfield ME [11 Oct 1849]
    Elizabeth A & Samuel V CRASH at Saco ME [4 Mar 1852]
    George F of Newburgh ME & Miss Olive PATTEN at Hermon ME [14 Jan 1847]
    Henry H of (Augusta) ME & Caroline B LANCASTER at Bath ME on Dec 16th [1 Jan 1852]
    Jessemine & Ezra PURINGTON at Sidney ME on 13 Jan [24 Jan 1850]
    Levi & Lydia A MASON at Fairfield ME [23 Aug 1849]
    Orrin & Sarah Jane ALLEN at Fairfield ME [1 Jul 1847]
    Ruth J & Joseph S NYE at Fairfield ME [14 Sept 1848]
    Silas E & Miss Eliza A SHERMAN at Sidney ME [27 Feb 1838]
HOYT Dorothy N & Gerdner J TAFT of Millbury MA at Farmington ME [20 Dec 1849]
    Dorothy N & Ira W SMITH of Milbury MA at New Portland ME [22 Nov 1849]
    Frederick of Bloomfield ME & Miss Sarah O BOARDMAN at Norridgewock ME [7 Feb 1850]
    Joseph & Matilda F BRADBURY at Wilton ME [26 Dec 1844]
    Levi 2d & Joanna M FIFELD both of Readfield ME at Augusta ME on 4th Sept by Rev H M BLAKE [18 Sept 1851]
    Martha & Mark G WALKER at Weld ME [10 Jun 1852] & [3 Jun 1852]
    Mary & William PARKER at Berlin ME [4 Apr 1837]
    Thomas C & Abby C WEEKS both of (Augusta) ME at Jefferson ME on 30 Dec [8 Jan 1852]
    William & Sarah Jane KNOWLES at East Readfield ME [4 Jun 1846]
HUBBARD Aaron S of Thorndike ME & Miss Mary Ann HARMON at Harrison ME [23 Jan 1845]

HUBBARD (cont.) Augustus & Mehitable B PRAY at Sanford ME both of Shapleigh ME [29 Jul 1847]
    Dimond & Alvira CLOUGH at Topsham ME [27 Apr 1848]
    Eliza C & Robert P STROUT at Brunswick ME [15 Oct 1846]
    Frances P & Joseph G GOULDING at Waterville ME [11 Jul 1840]
    Harrison of East Cambridge MA & Miss Ann L EASTON of Bowdoinham ME by the Rev J HAWKES [22 Oct 1846]
    Horace P of Brunswick ME & Frances J HASKELL at Topsham ME [13 Jun 1844]
    Margaret & Gustavus B VARNEY at Gardiner ME [16 Jan 1851]
    Mary E & Peleg H TRACY at Palmyra ME [13 Jan 1848] & [20 Jan 1848]
    Nancy & Alpheus MEAD at Boston MA [13 Apr 1848]
    Robert H G of Bath ME & Miss Laura A CROWELL of China ME at Augusta ME on 3rd by Daniel S STANWOOD Esq City Clerk [12 Aug 1852]
    Sarah A & James O McINTIRE Esq at Cornish ME [19 Mar 1846]
    Susan & John CORNFORTH at West Waterville ME [8 Feb 1844]
HUCKINS Irene & Hugh DOYAL of Trescott ME at Lubec ME [21 Jan 1847]
HUDDLESON Margaret & George SAUNDERS of Trescott ME at Lubec ME [21 Jan 1847]
HUDDLESTON Mary & J R FORD of Eastport ME at Lubec ME [11 Dec 1845]
HUDLON Henry & Emily F MARTIN at Gulford ME [11 Apr 1850]
HUFF Ambrose & Mary JONES of Turner ME at Cooper ME [9 May 1844]
    Joseph Jr & Miss Eliza W BRAILEY both of Hallowell ME at Gardiner ME [15 Mar 1849]
    Mary E & George EASTMAN of Vasslboro ME at Wilton ME [15 Jul 1852]
    Mary Jane & James T BAILEY at Hallowell ME [20 May 1847]
HUGHEY Annis & Samuel HOLDEN Jr at Moose River ME [4 Jun 1851]
HUGHES Maria Louisa of Frankfort KY & Charles T MANN formerly of Hallowell ME at Yazoo City MS [26 Jun 1851]
    William H & Mary WENTWORTH both of Winslow ME at Waterville ME [12 Aug 1847]
HUME Sophia B & Walter H WETHERBEE at Augusta ME on 16th ult by A R NICHOLAS Esq [10 Jun 1847]
HUMPHREY Betsey A & Michael L WHITNEY at North Yarmouth ME [13 Jan 1848]
    Fortina & Walcott RICHARDSON of Livermore ME at Jay ME [19 Jul 1849]
    Henry P & Miss Augusta M WESTON at Portland ME both of Gray ME [23 Jan 1845]
    Mary C & Asa MITCHELL at North Yarmouth ME [15 May 1838]
    William H of North Yarmouth ME & Emma C GETCHELL at Waterville ME [22 Jul 1852]
HUMPHREYS Annie E & John H KIMBALL Esq of Bath ME at Brunswick ME [13 Nov 1851]
    Jane (age 55y) & Ephraim HINKLEY (age 30y) after a tedious courtship of 12 hours at Plantation # 1 ME [22 Apr 1833]
HUNNEWELL Andrew & Miss Mary Jane SMITH at Solon ME [24 Jul 1845]
    Samuel Capt & Mrs Lydia GOULD at Solon ME [16 Aug 1849]
    William T & Elizabeth ROBBINS at Solon ME [16 Jan 1851]

HUNT Ann S & William PERKINS at (Augusta) ME on New Year's Day [8 Jan 1852]
    Ann & Nathaniel STIMPSON of Bath ME at Berwick ME [20 Sept 1849]
    Benjamin M & Frances M DAVIS at Lubec ME [16 Apr 1846]
    Clarisa & Henry M PRESCOTT at Brunswick ME [28 Dec 1833]
    George W H & Miss Mary A C PRESCOTT at Readfield ME [9 Dec 1847]
    James L & Winaford J HUNT of Georgetown ME at Bath ME [20 Apr 1848]
    Jane W, d/o Mr William HUNT, & Joseph ANTHONY at Augusta ME on Thursday evening last by Rev Mr TAPPAN [17 Oct 1844]
    Jane & Joel ADAMS both of Readfield ME at Readfield by Rev Mr WEBBER [24 Jan 1834]
    Jeremiah Jr & Salome G WOODSIDE at Brunswick ME [1 Apr 1843]
    Lorana & Capt Hiram KNOWLTON at Montville ME [7 Mar 1837]
    Lucretia M & John W CONNER at Sebasticook ME [20 Sept 1849]
    Lucy H & Asher HINDS Esq of Clinton ME at Bath ME [4 Feb 1833]
    Mary Elizabeth & Benjamin D AUSTIN at Augusta ME [18 Feb 1847]
    Merrill & Miss Mary JOY at Readfield ME on 19th inst by the Rev David THURSTON of (Winthrop) ME [29 Jan 1836]
    Persis & Mr M ROLLINS of Appleton ME at Hallowell ME [11 Nov 1847]
    S A & D R CARLTON of Belfast ME at Liberty ME [22 Jul 1847]
    Simeon & Miss Mary DAVIS at Auburn ME [4 Jan 1844]
    William H of Montville ME & Susan M CARLTON at Belfast ME [12 Jul 1849]
    William H & Mrs Deborah STAPLES at Township # 3, East Branch ME [20 May 1843]
    William of Pittston ME & Martha D LAMB at Hallowell ME [29 Apr 1847]
    Winaford J & James L HUNT at Bath ME [20 Apr 1848]
HUNTER Charles B of Topsham ME & Martha J DAVIS at Hallowell ME [10 Jan 1850]
    D L Mr & Eliza FLOOD both of Clinton ME at Canaan ME [31 Jul 1851]
    Elizabeth & Ira WHIDDEN at Clinton ME by Samuel HAINS Esq [5 Mar 1842]
    Ellen & Charles W BILLINGS at Clinton ME [13 Sept 1849]
    George of Clinton ME & Louisa J SHOREY at Oldtown ME [21 Oct 1847]
    James of Pittsfield ME & Sarah DINGLEY at Bowdoinham ME [7 Nov 1840]
    Lithgow (age 89y) & Miss Nancy WORK (age 18y) at Topsham ME [26 Nov 1846]
    Mary A & James E ROWELL at the Forks ME [27 Sept 1849]
    Mary A & Joshua T RANDALL at Readfield ME [4 Apr 1844]
    Rachel A & Jermy [sic] M PORTER at Strong ME [18 Dec 1845]
    Sarah C of Topsham ME & Jonathan W FORSITH, merchant of Brunswick ME at Topsham ME [21 Feb 1834]
    Sarah W & James H CALL at Hallowell ME [9 May 1844]
    Statira P & John MATHEWS Jr of Waterville ME at Clinton ME [25 Mar 1847]
HUNTING J Hobart & Miss Sarah ROBBINS at Guilford ME [24 Sept 1846]
    John of Corinth ME (age 63y) & Miss Sarah ROLLINS (age 23y) at Freedom ME [14 Aug 1841]
HUNTINGTON Anna & James L HOLLAND both Hallowell ME at Pittston ME [18 Mar 1847]

HUNTINGTON (cont.) Benjamin G & Mrs Lucinda SMITH at Augusta ME on 14th ult [1 Apr 1847]
C J, recently of Brookfield MA, & Rev Thomas SIMONS, American Missionary at Maukmein Burmah [14 Mar 1834]
Hannah & Sewall FULLER of Waterville ME at Gardiner ME [22 May 1851]
Herrick & Mary J BOOKER at Gardiner ME [6 Jan 1848]
Judith & Alvan MAYO both of Hallowell ME at Augusta ME on 11th inst by Rev Mr FULLER [22 Aug 1844]
Levi & Miss Phebe WINSLOW by Arthur PLUMER Esq at Gardiner ME [4 Feb 1833]
Uriel F & Sarah MOULTON of Topsham ME at Bowdoinham ME [26 Mar 1842]
Wallace of Windham CT & Cynthia WARD at Brunswick ME [19 Nov 1846]

HUNTON Alice & Obed WING Jr at Livermore ME on the 1st inst by Lewis HUNTON Esq [9 Jan 1835]
James & Irene MORTON at Windsor ME by J B SWANTON Esq [14 Feb 1837]
Lafayette & Miss Lucinda P BROWN both of Readfield ME [15 Mar 1849]
Mary Ann & Joshua T RANDALL of Bloomfield ME at Readfield ME [21 Mar 1844]

HUNTRESS Emma & Thomas FIELD of Brewer ME [5 Mar 1842]

HURD Abner K of Unity ME & Mrs Olive L FOSS of Milo ME at Foxcroft ME [12 Feb 1846]
Daniel L & Miss Laura Ann WEBSTER at Augusta ME on 15th inst [25 Sept 1845]

HURLBERT Elizabeth & David EDGAR at Eastport ME [25 Sept 1851]
Lewis J of Gardiner ME & Caroline LEEMAN of Gardiner ME at Augusta ME on 31 Dec [9 Jan 1851]

HURLEY Joseph & Susan CHISM at Alna ME [28 Feb 1834]

HUSSEY Ann & Samuel S MORSE at Fairfield ME [9 May 1844]
Charlotte A & George H NYE at Hallowell ME [11 Dec 1851]
Charlotte A & Parker H BOWKER at Hallowell ME [20 Nov 1851]
Drusilla & Franklin PULLEN at Waterville ME by Rev Samuel LEWIS [19 Oct 1839]
Eben & Mrs Frances T SMITH at (Augusta) ME on 13th Jan [29 Jan 1852]
Eliza Ann & Wellington HEALD at Norridgewock ME [7 Jan 1847]
Frances & Josiah LIBBY at Turner ME on 13 Apr by C T RICHARDSON Esq [6 May 1843]
George B & Betsey TAYLOR at China ME [30 Dec 1847]
Martha & Horatio BACHE at Biddeford ME [27 Jul 1848]
Mary A of Sanford ME & Daniel W EMERSON of Palmyra ME at Portsmouth NH [5 Aug 1852]
Mary L of Readfield ME & James B MURCH Esq of Unity ME [14 Feb 1837]
Mr B S of Limerick ME & Lavina T MILLER at Sanford ME [24 Apr 1851]
Nancy C & Everett W PATRIDGE at Jefferson ME [9 Oct 1845]
Oliver C of Nantucket MA & Miss Elizabeth B PINKHAM at Sidney ME [5 Feb 1846]
Paul & Olive W HALEY at Biddeford ME [5 Feb 1852]

HUSSEY (cont.) Reuben Dr of Athens ME & Rebecca R WYMAN of Brighton ME at Ripley ME [30 Mar 1848]
Ruth & Elijah & Miss Ruth HUSSEY at China ME [17 Jun 1847]
Ruth & Peter W MORRILL at Portland ME at the Friends meeting house [21 Aug 1838]
Sarah H of Dover NH & John M WEBSTER at Augusta ME [10 Apr 1841]
Stephen of Dover ME & Miss Abigail P WILEY of Newburgh ME at Dixmont ME [5 Nov 1846]
William Jr & Harriet LANE both of Dover ME at Atkinson ME [11 Dec 1851]
William of Bangor ME & Miss Julia d/o J HOULTON Esq at Houlton Washington Co (Now in Aroostook Co ME) [8 Jul 1833]
William & Eunice B MITCHELL at Wiscasset ME [13 Jun 1844]
Wilmot I & Miss Janet C BLACK at Augusta ME [10 Jun 1847]

HUSTON Betsey & Warren P KENDALL both of Unity ME at Knox ME [18 Sept 1851]
Hannah P & Hiram C COX of Bristol ME at Thomaston ME [10 Jul 1845]
Jane C & David I DELAINE at Portland ME [12 Sept 1840]
Joseph T, Preceptor of Bath Academy & Miss Lucy A THOMPSON at Bath ME [19 Dec 1834]
Marcia & Charles A BRAGG at Dover ME [20 Mar 1841]

HUTCHASON Daniel & Abigail W HARDEN at Bangor ME [11 Jul 1844]

HUTCHES Ann Maria & Manuel D FRATERS both of West Gardiner ME at Litchfield ME [30 Oct 1845]

HUTCHINGS/HUTCHINS Clements & Miss Hannah COLEMAN both of Kennebunkport ME at Saco ME [30 Apr 1846]
Dolly d/o Ezra HUTCHINGS, & Richard PORTER Esq at Bangor ME [27 Jun 1840]
Hannah E & Reuel W LORD at Hallowell ME [1 Mar 1849]
Hannah & James A REED at Gardiner ME [11 Nov 1843]
John S of Cambridge MA & Miss Phebe S ROWE of Portland ME at South Paris ME [23 Sept 1847]
Luther of Chelsea ME & Miss Minerva Ann HOBBS at Norway ME [6 Mar 1845]
M & Albert A COLE at Brighton ME [30 Jan 1851]
Mary S S & Ephraim F GODDARD at Andover ME [3 Oct 1840]
Matilda & Paul TOWLE of Exeter ME at Atkinson ME [17 Jul 1845]
Nathaniel & Mary D JONES at Monmouth ME at Monmouth ME by Elder William O GRANT [17 Jul 1838]
Sarah Ann & George STACY of Bath ME at Phippsburg ME [7 Jan 1847]
Sarah E & Paul WILD at East Winthrop ME by Rev F MERRIAM [16 Jul 1846]

HUTCHINSON Caroline & Jacob MUDGETT at Hallowell ME [7 Oct 1847]
E B of Natick MA & Miss Martha A NEAL at Pittston ME [1 Nov 1849]
Ebenezer S of Albany & Miss Betsy F PINGREE at Norway ME [26 Jun 1845]
Edward B & Miss Caroline E JONES at Saco ME both of Lowell MA [3 Sept 1846]
Experience & Elijah L NORCROSS Esq of Garland ME at Monmouth ME on 29th ult [21 Feb 1837]
George L & Miss Caroline TYLER at Gardiner ME [3 Dec 1846]
Harriet L & Charles R MOORE at Pittston ME [10 Feb 1848]

Marriage Notices from the "Maine Farmer"

HUTCHINSON (cont.) Henry & Harriet S BAKER all of Portland ME at Portland ME [13 Feb 1845]
   Horace & Gustava ALDEN at Turner ME [18 Jan 1840]
   John C of Buckfield ME & Emeline E DOE of Hebron ME at Paris ME [11 Feb 1847]
   Josiah C & Miss Harriet T DRUMMOND at Winslow ME on 4 Jan by A COLE Esq [22 Mar 1849]
   Julia T & George WARREN at Gardiner ME [25 Mar 1836]
   Martha C of Readfield ME & Moody E THURLO of Calais ME at Mt Vernon ME [27 May 1836]
   Martha Jane & Elijah PINKHAM at Hallowell ME [10 Feb 1848]
   Mary Jane of Fayette ME & Rev Frederic Augustus WADLEIGH at Augusta ME [14 Oct 1843]
   Mary & Capt Isaac CLARK Jr at Belfast ME [6 May 1847]
   Melvina S & Charles B ELLIS at Corinna ME on 2d inst [30 Mar 1848]
   Nancy & Samuel T GRAY of Waldoboro ME at Vassalboro ME [22 Apr 1847]
   Ruth B & Sylvester KIDDER at Dixfield ME [11 Jun 1842]
   Shepard of Gardiner ME & Sabry RICHARDSON at Litchfield ME [1 Feb 1844]
   Sumner & Miss Frances A C SAWYER [8 Jul 1847]
   Theophilus & Laura PORTER of Mt Vernon ME at Readfield ME [9 Dec 1847]
HYDE Abby Ann & Rev George F MAGOUN at Bath ME [16 Sept 1847]
   Almira M T & Theodore S TREVETT at Bath ME [27 May 1847]
   Ephraim A, M.D., of Freeport ME & Miss Susan HALE d/o the late Capt Abel COFFIN of Newburyport MA on 5th inst [21 Jan 1843]
   Henry M & Miss Amelia H JEROME at Bangor ME [6 Feb 1845]
   Mary C of Portland ME & Mr E F DUREN of Bangor ME at Portland ME [17 Jun 1836]
   William L Rev of Gardiner ME & Frances E RICE at Wiscasset ME [20 May 1852]
   Zina Esq of Bath ME & Eleanor M LITTLE at Boston MA [2 May 1840]
HYLER James B of Thomaston ME & Susan A FULLER at South Thomaston ME [27 Mar 1851]
   Hannah E & Oliver J ROBINSON at Cushing ME [1 Jan 1846]
   Lydia M HYLER at Cushing ME [4 Jul 1844]
   Mary C & William A CHAPPLES of Thomaston ME at Cushing ME [31 Oct 1844]
   Permelia & Warren PRIEST at Cushing ME [21 Aug 1845]

INGALLS William W & Julia M HARRIS by Rev Mr NICKERSON at Mercer ME on 2nd inst [20 Apr 1848] & [18 May 1848]
IRELAND Sarah G & Nathan FOGG at Sebec ME [13 Jan 1848]
INGALLS Mary A & Elbridge W MARKS of Penobscot ME at Bluehill ME [17 Apr 1851]
INGERSOLL Hannah & Rufus E MITCHELL both of Gorham ME at Windham ME [13 Mar 1851]

IRISH Joseph Esq & Nancy EASTMAN at Haverhill MA on 17 Jun by Rev Henry PLUMMER [3 Jul 1851]
 Oliver W & Sarah W SMITH at Milo ME on 11 Oct by James H MACOMBER Esq [23 Oct 1851]
IRVING Margaret of Georgetown ME & Lyman Oliver of Phipsburg ME at Bath ME [15 May 1851]
ILSLEY C A & Stephen S CLARK, assistant editor *NY Express* at Westbrook ME [6 May 1847]
 Elizabeth & Dr H Wethering GOULD of Boston MA at Danville ME [28 Mar 1850]
INGALLS Adaline of Mercer ME & William LANCASTER at New Sharon ME [27 Sept 1849]
 David of Bath ME & Mary C HERVEY at Newburyport MA [29 May 1845]
 Henry Esq & Susan JOHNSTON at Wiscasset ME [29 Nov 1849]
 John D of Charlestown MA & Phebe ORCUTT of Bluehill ME at Boston MA [26 Nov 1846]
 Samuel M of Mt Vernon ME & Silvina P WING at Wayne ME by Alonzo WING Esq [28 Dec 1833]
INGERSOLL John & Mary D BOYNTON both of Gorham ME at South Windham ME [21 Oct 1847]
 N L Col & Nancy CLARK at Danville ME [23 Jan 1838]
INGHAM Jane & Charles HAMILTON of Worcester MA at Bath ME [23 Aug 1849]
 Mary J formerly of Mt Vernon ME & George S HAMILTON formerly of Barre MA at Augusta ME on Thurs evening last by Rev William A DREW [12 Dec 1844]
INGRAHAM Job 2d & Jane EAMES of Appleton ME at Camden ME [16 Apr 1847]
 John W of Montville ME & Clara B HALL at Knox ME [22 Feb 1844]
 Marcia P C, d/o Rev J W INGRAHAM, & G W LADD of Bangor ME at Augusta ME on 9th inst at St Mark's church [21 Oct 1843]
 Mark L & Julia A SNOW all of Thomaston ME at Thomaston ME [8 Jan 1846]
 Samuel Capt Almira DAVENPORT at Augusta ME [13 Feb 1835]
INNES Robert & Hannah SMALL at Bath ME [16 Jul 1846]
IRISH Emily D & Charles B ATWOOD at Buckfield ME [2 Sept 1847]
 Joseph & Cordelia CLARY at Union ME [16 Nov 1839]
 Levi & Lydia CALDERWOOD at Waldo Plantation ME [19 Dec 1844]
 Martha of Union ME & William GRINNELL of Exeter ME at Union ME [22 Jan 1839]
IRVING Harriet B & Hiram CUSHING at Augusta ME [10 Sept 1846]

- J -

JACK Bernice P of Litchfield ME & Maj Thomas M RICHARDSON of Monmouth ME [13 Jun 1844]
 Thomas S & Eliza T BLAKE at Harpswell ME [31 Oct 1844]
 Zebulon Esq & Sarah Jane PREBLE at Bowdoinham ME [10 Jul 1851]
JACKINS Charles & Nancy NILES at Gardiner ME [1 Apr 1843]
 Thomas B & Hannah WAIT at Gardiner ME [21 Feb 1850]
JACKMAN James M & Martha Jane RUNLET at Solon ME [13 Mar 1845]

JACKMAN (cont.) Lucretia of Sangerville ME & Miles DAGLE at Dexter ME [15 Apr 1847]

JACKSON Altea & Amasa JACKSON at Belmont ME [26 Apr 1849]
- Amasa & Altea JACKSON at Belmont ME [26 Apr 1849]
- Ann Maria & Harrison DOE of Windsor ME at China ME [15 Apr 1847]
- C B of Sangerville ME & Catherine F LAUGHTON at Harmony ME [24 Apr 1851]
- Charles G of (Winthrop) ME & Martha B KIMBALL at Turner ME [28 Nov 1840]
- E M Rev of the New England (Methodist) Conference & Abba E McLELLAN at Gorham ME [5 Jun 1845]
- Elijah Jr & Miss H E LORD at Pittston ME [15 Jun 1848]
- Eliza S & John MAXWELL at Winthrop ME by Rev Daniel FULLER [22 Aug 1834]
- Elizabeth V & Isaac C CURRIER at Minot ME [21 Jan 1847]
- Elvira & Deacon COBURN of Parkman ME at Sangerville ME [11 Jun 1846]
- Emily R of Winthrop ME & Roger LAPHAM of Pittston ME [2 Apr 1846]
- George W & Mary JAMESON of Palermo ME at Jefferson ME [14 Sept 1848]
- Isaac & Mary CROSS at Belmont ME [26 Dec 1837]
- James H & Mary W STONE at Paris ME [22 Feb 1844]
- James W & Clarinda KENNEDY at Jefferson ME [19 Mar 1846]
- John & Susan W SMITH at Hampden ME [20 Nov 1851]
- Joseph of Boston MA & Ellen M MACOMBER at Monmouth ME by the Rev Mr DAY [24 Jan 1850]
- Lemuel 2d & Olive JASPER at Lewiston ME [2 Oct 1851]
- M E & Mr John W WHITTEMORE at Montville ME [29 Jul 1852]
- Marcus Q of Liberty ME & Flora B McLANAHAN at Chelsea ME [8 Apr 1852]
- Matilda Y & Elijah DESHON at Jefferson ME [16 Feb 1839]
- Olive F & Micajah C STROUT at Gorham ME [11 Jul 1840]
- Orrington & Lucinda JONES at Jefferson ME [14 Sept 1848]
- Phebe Jane & Arthur D BURGIN at Belfast ME [16 Mar 1848]
- Phebe & John YALE at Winthrop ME [2 May 1844]
- Rebecca H & Amos H WALL of Bath ME at Phipsburg ME [30 Jul 1846]
- Robert L & Nancy RICHMOND at Winthrop ME on Mon morning last by the Rev David THURSTON [22 Jul 1833]
- Robert & Miss Drusilla MARR at Bath ME [31 Jan 1850]
- Samuel of Winthrop ME & Julia HEWITT at Livermore ME [24 Jul 1845]
- Samuel W Esq & Lorenda RICHARDSON at Jefferson ME [18 Jan 1840]
- Sibell A & Col Simon H CUMMINGS at Paris ME [22 Jan 1846]
- Sylvia & Henry A SHERMON at North Belmont ME [19 Aug 1843]
- Thomas S & Jane H CHICK at Winthrop ME on Thanksgiving evening by Rev Mr ROBINSON [16 Dec 1843]
- William of Walpole MA & Susan PINKHAM at Strong ME [18 Sept 1845]
- William & Louisa WARD at Augusta ME on 31 Dec by Rev Z THOMPSON [9 Jan 1851]
- William & Mrs Sarah JORDAN at Thomaston ME [16 Mar 1839]
- Zalema & Alexander K BOND at Jefferson ME [19 Mar 1846]

JACOBS Bailey of Abbot ME & Lucy CHANDLER at Wayne ME [17 Oct 1844]

JACOBS (cont.) John 2d & Parinthia A WING both of Mt Vernon ME at Readfield ME by Rev Benjamin P REED [9 Dec 1847]
    John & Phebe BIGGER at Mt Vernon ME by J CURRIER Esq [3 Apr 1838]
    Julia A & John S RICKER at Providence RI [14 Sept 1848]
    Lucy Ann & Nathan NASON at Sidney ME by William HAMLEN Esq [16 May 1837]
    Lydia S, d/o Edward F Esq & Rev H W MORSE, pastor of the Universalist Society in Exeter NH at Scituate MA [6 Jul 1839]
    Mahala L & Charles W GORDON of Hallowell ME at China ME [11 Apr 1850]
    Mary & Benjamin KING both of Winthrop ME at East Winthrop ME on 13 Aug by Rev S POWERS [21 Aug 1851]
    Mary & John B STAIN at Mt Vernon ME [7 Dec 1848]
    Mary & Joseph A KELLY at Avon ME [4 May 1848]
    Mercy & Samuel BRAGG at Sidney ME [31 Oct 1840]
    Olive L & Charles MOORE of Waterville ME at Pittsfield ME [24 Jun 1843]
    Samuel H & Ann WYMAN at Fairfield ME [25 Apr 1850]
JAMES Elisha Jr & Sarah J GLASS at Gardiner ME [1 Jan 1852]
JAMESON Alvah Col & Celia A PERKINS at Topsham ME [6 Jul 1848]
JAMESON James Capt of Bath ME & Charity MUSTARD at Topsham ME by Rev T N LORD [27 Nov 1838]
    John & Lydia Jane PACKARD at Hope ME [27 Nov 1851]
    Mariah R & William MONROE at Thomaston ME [3 Oct 1844]
    Mary & George W JACKSON at Jefferson ME [14 Sept 1848]
    Samuel & Harriet W MUSTARD at Topsham ME [21 Nov 1837]
JAQUES James O of Gardiner ME & Mary W CLARK at Tewksbury MA [25 Nov 1847]
    William of the "Ten Hills Farm" of Charleston MA & Adeline J CARTER formerly of Lowell MA at Vassalboro ME by Rev T ADAMS [13 Apr 1839]
JARVIS Abigail & John T STONE at Gardiner ME [18 Jun 1846]
    John H Jr of Ellsworth ME & Sarah E HOVEY at Waldoboro ME [23 Sept 1836]
JASPER Edwin E of Minot ME & Olive ESTES at Lewiston ME [19 Aug 1847]
    Olive & Lemuel JACKSON 2d at Lewiston ME [2 Oct 1851]
JAYNE Joseph C of New Sharon ME & Sarah BODWELL at Hallowell ME [18 Nov 1843]
JECK Samuel W & Elizabeth B LIBBY [21 Mar 1850]
JEFFERS John of Starks ME & Ann D RYANT at Farmington ME [14 Sept 1848]
JELLESON Abel H & Betsey H ROBERTS at Saco ME [10 Sept 1846]
JENINGS Samuel M of Wayne ME & Mary LOBDELL of Portland ME at Portland on 15th inst by Rev W PIERCE [2 Apr 1842]
JENKINS Augusta A & John A PERKINS at Augusta ME [8 Jan 1846]
    Esther & Reuben COLSON at Monroe ME [24 Apr 1851]
    William A of Lee & Mary AUSTIN at Great Falls NH [25 Feb 1843]
JENKS Edward A a proprietor of the *Manchester American* & Harriet S STINCKEY of Waterville ME at Concord NH [3 Jun 1852]
    Henry E Capt & Mrs Thankful WAKEFIELD at Bath ME [21 Sept 1833]

JENNES Sarah of Readfield ME & George RUTTERFIELD of Farmington ME at Winthrop ME [14 Nov 1844]
JENNESS Anna St Clair & Hon Elbridge GERRY of Waterford ME at Portsmouth NH [6 Dec 1849]
JENNINGS Eliza A & Ezekiel K FOGG at Industry ME [20 Nov 1851]
   Eliza A & Josiah B ADDITION at Leeds on 5 May [13 May 1852]
   Levi of Boston MA & Catherine GOLDSMITH at Gardiner ME on the 19th inst by Moses SPRINGER Esq [31 Oct 1837]
   Louisa & Capt Morton FREEMAN of Middlebury MA at Wayne ME by Rev Walter FOSS [18 Mar 1836]
   Seth W of North Wayne ME & Delia GILMORE at Turner ME by Mr CHASE Esq [9 Aug 1849]
JENNIS James & Mary T PERLY at Winthrop ME [4 Jul 1844]
JEPSON Elizabeth G & John CURTIS Jr of Minot ME at Lewiston ME [15 Nov 1849]
   Thomas W & Abigail B DEAN of Temple ME at Wilton ME at Friends meeting house [14 Nov 1844]
JEROME Amelia H & Henry M HYDE at Bangor ME [6 Feb 1845]
   Maria L & Josiah S HOOK at Bangor ME [6 Feb 1845]
JESSYLN Luther & Abigail GRANT at Troy ME both of Frankfort ME [26 Oct 1839]
JEWELL Alfred of Winthrop ME & Betsey GILBERT at Wayne ME [18 Oct 1849]
   Gould of Brunswick ME & Elizabeth F ALEXANDER of Topsham ME [16 Apr 1842]
   Hiram W of Lincoln ME & Almira GRAY of Orono ME at Bangor ME [18 Mar 1836]
   James & Sarah DAYTON at Bath ME on 13th inst [29 May 1841]
   Louisa J of Winthrop ME & Mr T D GOODWIN of Pittston ME at East Winthrop ME [13 Nov 1845]
   Mary & Joseph HEATH of Hallowell ME at China ME on 11 Apr by William PERCIVAL Esq [25 Apr 1850]
   Oliver H of Lincoln ME & Caroline A BLAKE of the former place (Monmouth) at Monmouth by David THURSTON Esq [12 Mar 1842]
   R W & L M WHITE both of Bath at Bath ME [2 Oct 1845]
   Relief S & Washburn CALDEN at Bath ME [28 Nov 1844]
   Sarah at Athens ME & Daniel ROBERTS at Solon ME [23 Jul 1846]
   William & Almira LANDERKIN of Gardiner ME at Litchfield ME [6 May 1847]
JEWETT Amanda formerly of Bloomfield ME & Herbert TRULL of Tewksbury MA [30 May 1840]
   Bryce & Rachel WILSON of Skowhegan ME at Unity ME [2 Oct 1851]
   Charles & Mary C PULLEN at Dexter ME [15 Apr 1847]
   Clarissa & William GOULD of Concord ME at South Solon ME [14 Jan 1847]
   Elizabeth & Peleg S ROBINSON at Gardiner ME [2 Dec 1847]
   Elizabeth & William J CRAWFORD at Bath ME [19 Dec 1834]
   Eunice & Edward RICHARDS at Portland ME [6 Nov 1835]
   George W of Sidney ME & Mary Ann MOODY at Readfield ME by Rev N ALLEN [28 Aug 1841]
   Helen & James W HILL both formerly of Norridgewock ME at Bangor ME [27 Jun 1844]

JEWETT (cont.) Joshua & Miss Jane O'HARA at Norridgewock ME [15 Apr 1847]
    Lovina, d/o Deacon Nathan JEWETT, of Solon ME, & Quincy P WOOD of Anson ME at Solon ME on Thurs last by Rev Mr LORING [13 Mar 1838]
    Mary E & Edward MERRILL at Swanville ME [4 Jun 1851]
    S of Portland ME & Maria H DOBBINS of Falmouth ME [6 Feb 1845]
    Samuel Esq of Gardiner ME & Mrs Abagail STEVENS of Litchfield ME [18 Mar 1833]
    William K & Margaret J ALLEN of Augusta ME at Portland ME [24 Oct 1844]
    William & Rosilla A SMITH at Madison ME [7 Oct 1847]
JOCE William M of Readfield ME & Lucy SEDGLEY at (Winthrop) ME by Rev Mr Robinson [9 Sept 1843]
JOHNSON - see JONES
JOHNSON Abby D & Rev S Freeman CHANEY of Buxton ME at Farmington ME [21 Aug 1842]
    Adeline T & Thomas C NOBLE at Farmington ME [29 May 1835]
    Adeline & Joshua FROST at Belgrade ME [8 May 1835]
    Ann E & Daniel STONE at Wiscasset ME [7 Oct 1843]
    Barbara & John STEVENS of Belfast ME at Bremen ME [30 Aug 1849]
    Bathshebe & John W PIPER of Gardiner ME [10 May 1849]
    Betsey Lovina & Hiram BURR of Brewer ME at Springfield ME [31 Jul 1838]
    C D A of Maine (Methodist) Annual Conference & Ellen H HEALD of Calais ME at China ME [23 Jan 1845]
    Caroline L & Rev Ammi R BRADBURY of Auburn ME at Farmington ME [14 Mar 1844]
    Caroline Matilda of Waterville ME at Boston MA & Asahel FOWLER of Boston MA [11 Apr 1840]
    Caroline & Mr A COOKSON at Belfast ME [24 Aug 1848]
    Charles & Eunice HOULTON at Kittery ME [23 Mar 1839]
    Cyrus P of Lowell MA & Emily SMALL at South Thomaston ME [25 Apr 1850]
    Daniel Jr of Litchfield ME & Miss Lucy PALMER at Pittston ME [1 Jul 1847]
    Daniel & Nancy MARR at Topsham ME [10 Aug 1848]
    Deborah & William LOWELL at Winthrop ME on Thanksgiving evening by Rev David THURSTON [4 Dec 1841]
    Delia E & Mr William ROBERTS at Bath ME [15 Jan 1846]
    Diadamia & Stephen FOSTER at Monmouth ME by Levi FAIRBANKS Esq [13 Mar 1836]
    Edward R Esq & Clarissa OSGOOD at Bangor ME [30 May 1837]
    Eliza & Capt John WIATT at Gardiner ME [28 Oct 1847]
    Elizabeth & Thomas PARKER at Eastport ME [26 Dec 1834]
    Eveline formerly of Winthrop ME & Mr M CALKIN of Sandwich Island at Hallowell ME by Rev Mr THURSTON on Sunday evening last [28 Oct 1842]
    G W of Gardiner ME & Miss Rebecca J THOMPSON of Farmington ME at Farmington by E C ROLFE [2 Jul 1846]
    Hannah M & Benjamin WHITTIER of Monroe ME at Farmington ME [13 Jun 1844]

JOHNSON (cont.) Harriet & John M BROEN at Belfast ME [18 Dec 1845]
    Harriet & William P CURRIER at Hallowell ME on Friday evening last [21 Mar 1834]
    J F & Miss M E RUSSELL at Pittston ME [3 Feb 1848]
    James B & Lucy RICHARDSON at Monmouth ME [13 Mar 1835]
    James & Mary OVER at Thomaston ME [24 Sept 1846]
    Jane Philena & David MILIKIN at Saco ME [25 Apr 1844]
    John Rev & Arethusa Anna STEVENS at Eastport, ME under appointment as missionary to China ME [17 Jun 1847]
    Joseph I & Laura FARRINGTON at Augusta ME on Dec 17th by Rev Z THOMPSON [2 Jan 1851]
    Joshua E & Lucrenta D FROST at Eastport ME [22 Jan 1852]
    Judith A & John Edward HAM at Augusta ME [9 Dec 1843]
    Judith F, d/o Phillip C JOHNSON Esq, & Hiram JONES at Augusta ME [9 Jan 1841]
    Julia A & Levi RARIDAN at Pittston ME [7 Nov 1844]
    Levi of Carmel ME & Zoe W SPRATT of Etna ME at Dixmont ME [24 Jun 1847]
    Levi & Delilah M COOK at Skowhegan ME [30 Sept 1836]
    Lovey Mrs & Solon EUSTIS at Belfast ME [18 Feb 1847]
    Lucy R & JAmes H ALLEY of Winslow ME at Albion ME on 11 Mar by P TINKHAM Esq [20 Mar 1851]
    Maria & Abijah S HARDING at Bangor ME both of Hampden ME [24 Jul 1835]
    Mark & Sarah SIMMONS at Hallowell ME [7 Feb 1834]
    Mary A & Jotham BIGELOW Esq at Skowhegan ME [8 Mar 1849]
    Mary A & William F LIBBY of Portland ME at New Gloucester ME [23 May 1844]
    Mary J of Farmington ME & Thomas L NAY of Bangor ME at Farmington ME on Tues the 11th inst by Rev Isaac ROGERS [22 Jan 1842]
    Mary & John CARTER at Hallowell ME [26 Sept 1834]
    Oliver & Betsey THOMPSON at Wiscasset ME [16 Nov 1833]
    Paul & Mrs McGUIRE of Lubec ME at Eastport ME [6 Mar 1845]
    Philomela of Winthrop ME & Samuel ADAMS of Hallowell ME at Winthrop ME on Sunday last at the Congregational Meeting House [20 Jul 1839]
    Rachel H of Freedom ME & Thomas BAKER of Albion ME at Thorndike ME [18 Oct 1849]
    Ralph C Esq of Belfast ME & Mrs Sarah Winslow CUSHING at Camden ME [14 Dec 1839]
    Rebecca of Richmond ME & William THOMAS at Gardiner ME [16 Jan 1846]
    Sally of Exeter ME (age 40y) & Meshech PRESCOT of Lisbon ME (age 67y) at Corinna ME [11 Apr 1844]
    Samuel formerly of Winthrop ME & Miss Mary Elizabeth MOULTON formerly of MA at Cincinnati OH on 3rd inst by Rev J A GURLEY [25 Jan 1844]
    Samuel W & Sarah MARSH at Hallowell ME [16 May 1844]
    Sarah E & Jeremiah YOUNG at Vassalboro ME on 30 Sept by J MARTIN Esq [9 Oct 1851]
    Shepherd H & Miss Irene PACKARD at Camden ME [8 Oct 1846]

JOHNSON (cont.) Simon of Hallowell ME & Eliza S MELVIN of Readfield ME at Readfield ME on Weds evening last by Rev George WEBBER [12 Jun 1838]
 Simon & Mary N CLARKE at Hallowell ME [18 Dec 1851]
 Sophia of Monmouth ME & Mr Greenleaf SMITH at Winthrop ME [8 Jan 1836]
 Sumner R of Milwaukee WI & Miss Achsah A DAVIS at Strong ME [2 Sept 1847]
 Veranus Capt & Mrs Julia PAUL at East Thomaston ME [24 Aug 1848]
 William Capt & Hannah M TOBEY at Machiasport ME [19 Jul 1849]
 William F & Ruth S BOULTEN of Waterville ME at Albion ME [25 Nov 1847]
 William H & Miss Jane PARKER at Gorham ME [23 Jan 1845]
 William H & Miss Susan H TWOMBLY at Hallowell ME [27 Sept 1849]
 William L & Nancy M CASEY at Carmel ME on 25th ult [18 Jan 1840]
 William T of Augusta ME & Martha T CHASE at Portland ME [12 Dec 1837]
 Zacheus & Harriet J CLARK at Augusta ME on 18th Jul by the Rev H M BLAKE [29 Jul 1852]
JOHNSTON D of New Orleans & Miss S F PERKINS at Castine ME [14 Sept 1848]
 Hugh & Mrs Bridget SWEENEY at Belfast ME [15 Apr 1852]
 S W of Bremen ME & Hannah M LINCOLN at Wiscasset ME [26 Mar 1846]
 Susan & Henry INGALLS at Wiscasset ME [29 Nov 1849]
JOICE Olive & William Parsons at Richmond ME [10 Feb 1848]
JONES Abigail B & Thomas T COOMBS of New Gloucester ME at Canton ME [13 Nov 1851]
 Abigail & Ezra S SMITH both of Hallowell ME at Augusta ME by Rev C FULLER [21 Nov 1844]
 Adeline & Joseph W LOVEJOY at Dixfield ME [8 Jul 1843]
 Albion & Julia Ann CLARK both of Nobleboro ME at Gardiner ME [23 Sept 1847]
 Alexander & Elizabeth Ann PARRITT at Eastport ME [27 Jun 1844]
 Alvah & Elizabeth D PRATT at Skowhegan ME [1 Jul 1852]
 Amanda M & David L M SALTMARSH at Weld ME [3 Oct 1840]
 Amanda M & Vance MERRILL at Turner ME [23 Oct 1851]
 Amanda & Mr McLELLAN at Litchfield ME [23 May 1837]
 Ambrose of Bristol ME & Abby ROBINSON at Mountville ME [1 Apr 1852]
 Araminta P & John C MERRILL at Paris ME [9 Mar 1848]
 Aroline [sic] E & Andrew LIBBEY both of Union ME at Searsmont ME [18 Jun 1846]
 Austen & Miss Pumpkin JONES at Mobile AL [14 Mar 1834]
 Austin & Henrietta F SHORT at Bangor ME [15 Aug 1844]
 B F & Ruth P BROWN at Monmouth ME on 6th Apr 1851 by Rev Walter FOSS [10/17 Apr 1851]
 Benjamin F & Eunice S FRANCIS of Turner ME at Livermore ME [1 Mar 1849]
 Benjamin of Gardiner ME & Mary Jane TOWLE at Dixmont ME [21 Mar 1850]
 Benjamin S & Frances L PARMENTER of Boston MA at Pittston ME [23 Nov 1848]

JONES (cont.) Benjamin S & Susan EDDARD at Pittston ME by R STEVENS Esq [2 Oct 1835]
- Bethiah of Brooksville ME & Benjamin H MERRIMAN at Castine ME [19 Jun 1845]
- Betsey & Henry T PRIME at Gardiner ME [25 Dec 1835]
- Betsey & Jacob RUSSELL at Weld ME [28 Dec 1848]
- Betsey & Joseph HOLMES at Augusta ME [5 Feb 1839]
- Betsey & Moses BAILEY at Friends meeting house in Winthrop ME [25 Apr 1840] & [5 Dec 1840]
- Boynton of Lisbon ME & Sabra JONES of Readfield ME [21 Dec 1839]
- Caroline E & Edward B HUTCHINSON both of Lowell MA at Saco ME [3 Sept 1846]
- Castella & Enos C DILLINGHAM at Canton ME [27 Jul 1848]
- Catharine W of Washington ME & David TURNER at Palermo ME [11 Jun 1846]
- Catharine & Israel DUNTON at Augusta ME on Mar 21 [1 Apr 1847]
- Charles Livermore & Elizabeth JONES at Leeds ME [21 Dec 1848]
- Charles R & Debrorah BONNEY at Turner ME [5 Feb 1852]
- Charles W Esq & Mrs Julia Octavia PAGE at St Mark's Church in Augusta ME on Sunday Evening by Rev Mr BURGESS [7 Aug 1845]
- Charlotte N Mrs & Reuben H YEATON at Mercer ME on 21 Mar [20 May 1852]
- Charlotte & Francis E BERRY at Durham ME [30 Mar 1848]
- Cyrus of China ME & Lois A PURINGTON at Vassalboro ME on 27 Sept by Howard G ABBOTT Esq [11 Oct 1849]
- David T & Lydia A HAWES by Ira PARLIN Esq at Weld ME on 1 Jun [15 Jun 1848]
- Delia & Augustus A WARREN at Kittery ME [4 Sept 1851]
- Dorothy G & Daniel RING at Belfast ME [13 Jun 1844]
- Edward & Nancy EAMES at Jefferson ME [6 Jun 1837]
- Elizabeth C & Mr F A MAYHEW at Foxcroft ME [11 Jan 1849]
- Elizabeth & Charles JONES at Leeds ME [21 Dec 1848]
- Emeline T of Pittston ME & Charles M WEBBER of Gardiner ME at New York City [28 Oct 1847]
- Emeline & Caleb HALLOWELL at Windsor ME [3 Jul 1851]
- Emily J & W S KYLE of Peru ME at Pownal ME [2 Aug 1849]
- Europe & Oppha B MERRILL both of Turner ME at Turner ME on 29th Sept by Ezekiel MARTIN [5 Oct 1833]
- Everet & Sally G WHITMAN at Turner ME [13 Nov 1835]
- George Jr of Savannah GA & Delia TUDOR d/o R H GARDINER Esq at Gardiner ME [10 Oct 1834]
- Hannah Mrs & Daniel GOULD Jr at Hope ME [3 Jun 1847]
- Harriet A & Mr J S ADAMS at Chelsea ME [25 Dec 1851]
- Harriet E & Robney L HAMILTON at Belfast ME [12 Jul 1849]
- Harriet & Seth ANDREWS at Warren ME [28 Jun 1849]
- Hiram & Miss Judith F & d/o Phillip C JOHNSON Esq at Augusta ME [9 Jan 1841]
- Ivory & Miss Charlotte N LITTLEFIELD at Bangor ME [13 May 1836]
- James J & Nancy D HEWINS at Kennebec ME [15 May 1851]
- John C & Sarah J HODGKINS at Litchfield ME [20 Jul 1848]
- John Capt & Miss Elizabeth LYON of Readfield ME [2 Jan 1838]
- John & Louisa HILTON at Augusta ME [7 Sept 1833]

JONES (cont.) Joshua Pittston ME & Susan K TRASK at Jefferson ME [2 Mar 1848]
 Judith, formerly of Norridgewock ME, & Stedman BARRY of Springfield MA at Lowell MA [10 Dec 1846]
 Judith F d/o P C JOHNSON Esq formerly of (Augusta ME) & James G WILSON Esq of Hastings NY at New York City [16 Oct 1851]
 Julia T, d/o the late Dr David JONES of North Yarmouth ME, & Isaac HOBART Esq of Edmonds at Portland [12 Sept 1844]
 Laura Ann & Samuel HOBBS of Livermore ME at Turner ME [11 May 1839]
 Leonard C & Harriet S WINSLOW at Hallowell ME [4 Dec 1851]
 Levi & Cynthia FARR at the Friends meeting house in Hallowell ME [5 Dec 1840] & [25 Apr 1840]
 Lorenzo of Wilton ME & Arabella B NEWMAN at Dixfield ME [9 Mar 1848]
 Loring B & Semantha HILTON at Norridgewock ME [27 Jun 1844]
 Lucinda & Orrington JACKSON at Jefferson ME [14 Sept 1848]
 Maria & Benjamin TURNER of Patricktown Plt ME at Washington ME [11 Mar 1847]
 Martha L of Winthrop ME & George M PULLEN of Gardiner ME at East Winthrop ME [7 Oct 1847]
 Martha & David P SANBORN at Weld ME on 11 Apr by I PARLIN Esq [26 Apr 1849]
 Mary Ann & James AXTELL at Augusta ME [30 Jan 1838]
 Mary D & Nathaniel HUTCHINS at Monmouth ME by Elder William O GRANT [17 Jul 1838]
 Mary E of Freeman ME & Thomas HENDERSON Jr of Webster ME at Kingfield ME on 20 Oct by E P PILLSBURY Esq [30 Oct 1851]
 Mary E & Nathaniel SMALL at Augusta ME by Rev Mr MORSE [26 Nov 1846]
 Mary M & William C BERRY at Thomaston ME [15 Jan 1846]
 Mary of Turner ME & Ambrose HUFF at Cooper ME [9 May 1844]
 Nancy M & Oliver BLOOD at Augusta ME [30 May 1837]
 Olive & James STARR Esq of Jay ME at Turner ME [2 Sept 1843]
 Owen & Janette THOMAS at Williamsburg Piscataquis Co ME [11 Oct 1849]
 Peleg T Esq & Miss Lydia H WHITTIER at Lincoln ME [6 May 1847]
 Pumpkin & Ausen JONES at Mobile AL? [14 Mar 1834]
 Rebecca & Ichabod BOOTHBY of Livermore ME at Norway ME [28 Aug 1851]
 Reuben & Lydia R PARLIN by Isaac TYLER Esq at Weld ME on 25th ult [15 Jun 1848]
 S Fenwick, d/o the late Noble W JONES Esq of Savannah GA, & Robert H GARDINER Jr of Gardiner ME at Newport RI on 28 Jun by Rev VINTON [9 Jul 1842]
 Sabra & Boynton JONES of Lisbon ME at Readfield ME [21 Dec 1839]
 Sarah & John DOUGLASS at St Albans ME [5 Nov 1846]
 Silas B & Sarah P WOODBURY of Lancaster PA at Bangor ME [3 Feb 1848]
 Simeon H & Elizabeth H STONE at Sweden ME [22 May 1845]
 Sophia D & Charles M BAILEY at Winthrop ME at Friends meeting house [14 Nov 1844]

KEENE (cont.) Luther W & Miss Lucy D CUMMINGS at Augusta ME by Rev William A DREW [21 May 1846]
 Marinda & Joel WHITE at Winthrop ME [2 Mar 1848]
 Mary Jane & Cyrus C CHANDLER formerly of Winthrop ME at East Thomaston ME [3 Sept 1846]
 Mary P & James PACKARD at Greenwood ME [13 Apr 1848]
 Richmond B of Sumner ME & Jane C FULLER at Paris ME [7 Nov 1840]
 Seneca W & Mary Ann MORTON at Bremen ME [21 Jan 1833]
 Sophia & Samuel SNOW at (Augusta) ME on 6th Apr [15 Apr 1852]
 T S & Miss Harriet DECKROW at Freedom ME [6 Nov 1845]
KEIN Mary E & John F GOODWIN at Hallowell ME [26 Aug 1843]
KEITH David K & Mary P BARNES at Thomaston ME [13 Nov 1845]
 George H of North Bridgewater MA & Margaret ROBINSON at Augusta ME on 3rd Sept by Rev Mr JUDD [13 Sept 1849]
 Mary Ann & James S NASH at Minot ME [3 Oct 1840]
 Mary & Capt Hugh PEABODY at Thomaston ME [10 Aug 1833]
 Samuel S Jr & Lucy MAria SEEKENS of Swanville ME at Brooks ME [1 Feb 1849]
KEIZER Francis C & Nancy OVERLOCK at North Waldoboro ME on 27th Nov by Reuben ORFF Esq [4 Dec 1851]
KELLEY - KELEY - KELLY
 Amos & Lydia J MERRILL at Gardiner ME [26 Apr 1849]
 Benjamin & Olive BOODY both of Orono ME by Myric EMERSON Esq [29 Apr 1843]
 Brinsley S of Winthrop ME & Osca BRADFORD at Turner ME [30 Oct 1851]
 Charlotte A & John J DICKEY at Phillips ME on 25th Feb 1851 by Hon J A LINSCOTT [6 Mar 1851]
 Cyrus K MD of St Johnsbury & Mary McCLARA WRIGHT at Bethel ME [19 June 1845]
 D H & Hannah BRANN at East Hallowell ME [27 Sept 1849]
 Daniel C & Martha J PERRY at Gardiner ME [22 Feb 1849]
 Esther & Henry T FLANDERS at Mayfield ME by Daniel EVANS Jr [16 Jul 1842]
 John W & Dorcas W EDES both of Guilford ME at Dover ME [8 Apr 1852]
 Joseph A of Phillips ME & Mary JACOBS at Avon ME [4 May 1848]
 Lydia (age 77y & Stephen HALL (age 44y) "at the town farm in North Yarmouth ME, according to an unanimous vote of the town, passed at the Sept meeting" [9 Dec 1836]
 Mary P of Sidney ME & Edward S UPHAM of Gardiner ME at Sidney ME on 27 Feb 1851 [6 Mar 1851]
 Nancy J & Peter WALKER Esq of Brighton Somerset Co ME at Mayfield Somerset Co ME [30 Oct 1851]
 Thomas & Mary GLASPHY at Hallowell ME [6 Sept 1849]
 Thomas & Mary Jane MUSTARD at Phipsburg ME [14 Jan 1847]
 Webster Esq, counsellor at law of Frankfort ME & Lucilla S PIERCE, d/o the late Waldo PIERCE Esq of Frankfort at Boston on 24th ult by Rev Mr ROGERS [3 Sept 1842]
KELLOCH Harriet & Archibald COOMBS at Thomaston ME [10 Aug 1839]
 James S & Emeline McKELLAR at Thomaston ME [22 Oct 1846]
KELLOCK James O & Lucy THOMAS at Waldo ME [11 Feb 1847]

KELSEY Henrietta & Joseph COTTER of Boston MA at Nobleboro ME [28 Feb 1834]
   John Capt of Canton ME & Mrs Hadassah C ELLIS of Wilton ME at Jay ME [25 June 1846]
   Sarah Annette of Augusta ME & Horace K GOULD of Bangor ME at Hartford CT [17 Dec 1846]
   Susan W & Orrin WALTZE at (Augusta) ME on 26 Sept 26 [5 Oct 1848]
KEMPTON Charles of Sidney ME & Julia P COY at Augusta ME on 28th inst [8 Feb 1849]
   Ezra Jr of Phillips ME & Mary C HAINS at Lake Settlement [28 Mar 1844]
KENDALL Abigail & Benjamin I SMART at Freedom ME [24 Apr 1838]
   Franklin B & ANN E PAINE at Phipsburg ME [2 Sept 1847]
   George & Mrs Mary NORTON at Livermore ME [24 Jul 1835]
   Henrietta M & Curran DINSMORE at Skowhegan ME [2 Nov 1839]
   Henry G of Canaan ME & Sarah MANSON of Clinton ME at Gardiner ME [21 Oct 1847]
   Hepsibeth & William WITHAM at Lyman ME [9 Jul 1846]
   Mary Y & Rev Cyrus SCAMMON at Pitston ME on 27th inst by Rev Mr ROBINSON [4 Jul 1837]
   Philomela R, d/o Rev Henry KENDALL of Topsham ME, & Dr John R HALEY of Augusta ME [28 Dec 1839]
   Samuel of Mount Vernon ME & Martha M MORSE at Augusta ME on 4th inst by J W PATTERSON Esq [8 Oct 1846]
   Samuel P & Mehitable W DAVIS at Hallowell [4 Nov 1843]
   Sarah B & Rev John DEARING at Bath ME [4 Jul 1840]
   Sarah & Thomas P LEIGHTON at Perry ME [27 Jul 1848]
   Stedman of this town (Winthrop ME) & Mary Jane CHANDLER at Wayne [13 Apr 1839]
   Warren P & Betsey HUSTON both of Unity ME at Knox ME [18 Sept 1851]
KENDRICK Daniel Rev of Dennis MA & Mary Ann CAREY at Brunswick ME [27 Feb 1841]
   Harriet D & Samuel S SMITH, printer at Bangor ME [28 Oct 1836]
   Joseph Jr & Caroline E PIKE at Bangor ME [19 Aug 1836]
   Rufus B & Abigail DURELL at Saco ME [1 Jan 1846]
KENISTON Sophia & David PERRY of Fitzwilliam at Gardiner ME [20 May 1847]
KENNEDY Clarinda & James W JACKSON at Jefferson ME [19 Mar 1846]
   Eliza J & Joseph P BURBANK at Whitefield ME [21 Jul 1843]
   Elizabeth L & John ESTES at China ME [14 Dec 1833]
   Julia & Isaac McLURE both of Hallowell ME at Augusta ME on the 18th inst by Benjamin A G FULLER [25 Jun 1846]
   Lucinda & Alanson at Jefferson ME [19 Mar 1846]
   Mary Ann of Waldoboro ME & Elijah S CROWELL of Jefferson ME at Jefferson [2 Sept 1836]
   Michael Jr of Troy VT & Amanda M WEBBER d/o Oliver A WEBBER Esq "We don't exactly like to have the Vermonters carry our Kennebec girls out of the State and away off beyond the Green Mountains but if they will go God bless them and Vermont too." at Vassalboro' ME on 7 Apr 1851 by Rev Dr TAPPAN of Augusta ME [10 Apr 1851]
   Polly Jane & Calvin L HASKELL at Jefferson ME [10 Jul 1851]
   Thomas Jr & Miss Vesta Volutia GLIDDEN at Fayette ME [31 Jul 1845]

JONES (cont.) Stilla B of Turner ME & William HARLOW of Minot ME at Turner ME by Ezekiel MARTIN Esq [23 Oct 1835]
    Susan E m Albert A MITCHELL at Canton ME [22 May 1851]
    Thaddeus B Capt of Bangor ME & Harriet J WINSLOW at Westbrook ME [4 Nov 1843]
    Valona & Joseph L MARSHALL at Hebron ME [4 Jun 1851]
    William H of Saco ME & Almira J ADAMS at Lewiston ME [18 Jan 1849]
    Zoa M & William O PARLIN at Weld ME [15 Jan 1852]

JORDAN Abigail & John L DAVIS of Lisbon ME at Lewiston ME [25 Mar 1847]
    Abram & Mary S BEALS at Brunswick ME [23 May 1844]
    Affiah & Lucius L LOTHROP at Webster ME on 4 May 1851 by Jesse DAVIS Esq [15 May 1851]
    Ann Maria & Ichabod KENT at Ellsworth ME [7 Mar 1840]
    Apphia of the former place & John RAND of Bangor ME at Cape Elizabeth ME [6 May 1836]
    Augusta & Capt Edward COLBY at Bath ME [1 Feb 1844]
    C A Dr & Mrs Sarah D CARGILL at Bangor ME [26 Jun 1845]
    Caroline B & Mr T J WHITEHEAD at Oxford ME [20 Apr 1848]
    Caroline & Josiah FARNSWORTH at Webster ME on 27 Oct [9 Nov 1848]
    Catherine & Washington BRAY of Naples at Casco ME [9 Jul 1846]
    Clement Jr of Portland ME & Charlotte W KNIGHT at Durham ME [20 Apr 1848]
    Dorcas Ann & Ezra R CARVILLE of Lewiston ME at Webster ME on Jun 22nd by Jesse DAVIS Esq [3 Jul 1851]
    Dyer P & Miss Mary A WHITTAKER at Ellsworth ME [27 March 1841]
    Ebenezer of Marion Iowa & Sarah G CROSBY of Plymouth ME at Norridgewock ME [3 Sept 1846]
    Eliza Ann & Isaac G JORDAN at Webster ME on 3 Dec [14 Dec 1848]
    Elizabeth & Capt William LARKIN at Eastport ME [27 Jul 1848]
    Eunice & Peter L TAMAZO at Bath ME [29 Apr 1847]
    Frances & James FOSS, printer of Biddeford ME at Portland ME [21 Jan 1847]
    Francis C of Brunswick ME & Lydia H LEMONT at Bath ME [7 Nov 1844]
    Francis M of Danville ME & Perthena A RICKER of Greene ME at Auburn ME [30 Jan 1851]
    Hannah of Bridgton ME & Archibald THOMPSON of Boston MA at Boston [16 Jul 1842]
    Harriet F & George P WENTWORTH at Augusta ME on 19 Sept by Rev J STEVENS [25 Sept 1851]
    Harriet of Etna ME & Granville WALL of Monroe ME by J C FRIENDS Esq [5 Feb 1839]
    Harriet & Edward B WOOD at Freeport ME [21 Jan 1847]
    Henry Capt & Miss Harriet G THOMAS at New York NY [1 Nov 1849]
    Isaac G & Eliza Ann JORDAN by Jesse DAVIS Esq at Webster ME on Dec 3 [14 Dec 1848]
    Israel of Casco ME & Cynthia BRAY d/o Gen WOODMAN of Naples ME on 23rd inst [4 Mar 1847]
    James P of Danville ME & Eunice NEWBEGIN at Poland ME [17 Aug 1848]
    Jane & James SMALL at Portland ME [31 Oct 1844]
    Joseph W & Roxana BARSTOW at Brewer ME [23 Dec 1836]

JORDAN (cont.) Joseph & Martha S DYER both of Mercer ME at New Sharon ME [25 Jul 1840]
   Josiah, M.D., & Mary Ann CUSHMAN at Monson ME? [14 Nov 1840] & [21 Nov 1840]
   Julia Ann & Ivory LORD at Gardiner ME [13 May 1833]
   L of Lisbon ME & Elizabeth C WATTS at Wales ME [10 Aug 1848]
   Lawrence of Saco ME & Mary RICE at Wiscasset ME [21 Dec 1839]
   Lucy & William LUNT at Gardiner ME [23 Sept 1836]
   Margaret & Cyprian C CROCKETT at Webster ME on 28 Oct by Jesse DAVIS Esq [6 Nov 1851]
   Mary A of Albany ME & George W STONE at Waterford ME [8 Mar 1849]
   Moses & Lucretia WITHAM at Kingfield ME by Rev J TRUE [30 Mar 1839]
   Nancy of Webster ME & Page PINGREE of Denmark ME at Lewiston ME [23 Jan 1851]
   Nathaniel & Masiah TITCOMB at North Yarmouth ME [7 Mar 1837]
   O W & Margaret ROBINSON at Thomaston ME [20 Nov 1845]
   Olive & Samuel DAMREN of Boston MA at Danville ME [4 Dec 1851]
   R W of Raymond ME & Mr Levi A BLAKE of Brewer ME at Poland ME on Jan 27th by Rev Mr WRIGHT [13 Feb 1841]
   Rhoda A & Israel EELLS at Freeport ME [4 Apr 1850]
   Robert of Ipswich MA & Martha F PERLEY by Mr MORSE at Winthrop ME [16 Nov 1848]
   Sarah Mrs & William JACKSON at Thomaston ME [16 Mar 1839]
   Susan P & Gardiner WINSLOW at Thomaston ME [14 Nov 1844]
   William H & Caroline KEEN both of Oxford ME at Paris ME [26 Jun 1851]
   Zachariah & Sabrina PAGE at Parsonsfield ME both of Parsonsfield ME [16 May 1840]
JORDEN Calvin P & Miss Mary E ANDERSON at Ellsworth ME [9 Jul 1846]
JOSE Isabella & Capt James BLISH at Hallowell ME [30 Nov 1833]
JOSS Sarah H & William PORTER of Mt Vernon ME at Readfield ME [9 Dec 1847]
JOSSELYN Betsey L & William S GRANT at (Augusta) ME on Mon evening at St Mark's Church [27 Jan 1848]
   Eliza L & George W RICKER both of Augusta ME at Lynn MA on 4 Mar [13 Mar 1851]
   Mary F of Augusta ME & John H LYNDE of Augusta ME at Norridgewock ME on Sunday morning 9 Feb by Rev Josiah PEET [13 Feb 1851]
   Mary Jane & Francis M WATSON of Bath ME [2 May 1837]
   Mehitable C & Valentine R BRIDGHAM at Leeds ME on 1 May 1851 by Rev C FULLER [8 May 1851]
   S Caroline & George D STANLEY at New York City on 11th Feb [19 Feb 1852]
   Sopronia of Hampden ME & Isaac HOLMES of Augusta ME at Hampden ME on 25 Jul by Rev Mr MITCHELL [5 Aug 1847]
JOURDAN Elizabeth & Elisha THURLOW at Litchfield ME [18 Jul 1837]
JOY Benjamin A & Miss Adaline STUBBS at Winthrop ME on Mon evening last by John MAY Esq [11 Apr 1834]
   Benjamin C & Julia FARWELL at Winthrop ME [18 Apr 1844]
   Charles of Clinton ME & Ann HEYWOOD at Sebasticook ME [9 Nov 1848]
   Delia & Allen L TRUFANT at Winthrop ME by Rev Mr BATES [7 May 1846]
   Emery F of Winthrop ME & Adeline ROBBINS at Union ME [14 Jun 1849]

JOY (cont.) Fanny & Isaac TOWNSEND Jr at Belfast ME [22 Jan 1846]
  Hannah & Oren H STANLEY at Winthrop ME on 20 Jan by Rev F FOSTER [25 Jan 1844]
  Harford of Detroit MI & Miss Sarah WOODS at Hallowell ME [21 Feb 1837]
  Harrison & Mary E BALLENTINE at Waterville ME [14 Mar 1844]
  Joseph E of Portsmouth NH & Maria D ELLIS at Fairfield ME [3 May 1849]
  Lucy Jane & George A CROSBY at Augusta ME on 27 Jun by Asaph R NICHOLS Esq [1 Jul 1852]
  Mary & Merrill HUNT at Readfield ME on 19th inst by Rev David THURSTON of Winthrop [29 Jan 1836]
  Pamelia P & Loring G SAMPSON at Winthrop ME by Rev F FOSTER [13 Jun 1844]
  Sabrina & Gorham A LUCE on Wed morning by Rev David THURSTON [22 Jul 1833]
  William of Orono ME & Dorcas ALLEN at Bangor ME on 4th inst [17 Dec 1842]
  William & Rebecca BURGESS both of Waterville ME on 29 Jan [5 Feb 1846]
JUDD Apphia P d/o Syvester JUDD, & Joseph H WILLIAMS Esq of Augusta ME at Northampton MA [9 Oct 1842]
  Sylvester Rev & Jane Elizabeth, d/o Hon Ruel WILLIAMS at Augusta ME on 31st ult by Rev John INGRAHAM [11 Sept 1841]
JUDKINS Alice K/R & Columbia NYE of Fairfield ME at Bloomfield ME [7 August 1851] & [24 Jul 1851]
  Alvin of North Yarmouth ME & Laura MOODY of Auburn ME at Danville ME [6 Jul 1848]
  Amanda Augusta & Edward J WHITE Jr at Monmouth ME [8 Feb 1844]
  Betsey & Miles GORDON of Weld ME at Phillips ME [11 Feb 1843]
  Clara A & Danville A ARNOLD at (Augusta) ME on 1st Jan by Rev W A DREW [10 Jan 1850]
  E J & George McGAFFEY at Mt Vernon ME on 20th Oct [28 Oct 1847]
  Hannah E of Augusta ME & William H DAGGETT of Portland VA at New York City [18 Nov 1847]
  Harriet & Joshua B RICHARDSON at Norway ME [28 Jan 1847]
  Joanna & Elisha S CASE at East Readfield ME [1 Jul 1847][15 Jul 1847]
  Loren W & Nancy CLEMENTS both of (Augusta) ME by Ariel HINKLEY Esq at Belgrade ME on 1 Oct [12 Oct 1848]
  Mary Ann, d/o Major L M, & Albert N HAM at Augusta ME [4 Dec 1841]
  Moses C of Cincinnnati OH & Elizabeth BUTLER at Cornville ME [7 Oct 1843]
  Rebecca S & Ashur HINDS both of Township #6 ME at Dover ME [1 Feb 1849]
  Rectina B & Washington HANSCOM at Winthrop ME on 29th May by Rev F FOSTER [5 Jun 1845]
JUMPER Mary A & Maj Amaziah SAWTELLE of Bangor ME at Dexter ME [10 Oct 1844]

- K -

KALER Adeline & Samuel at Union ME [16 Nov 1839]
    Clarissa & Dr Franklin L ROBINSON of Jefferson ME [5 Mar 1842]
    Hiram & Martha FLANDERS at Waldoboro ME [30 Sept 1847]
    Louisa J & Mr E A MILLER of Bremen ME at Waldoboro ME [1 Feb 1849]
    Margaret & Cyrus LEVENSALER at Waldoboro ME [12 Feb 1846]
    Mary C & Asa W WINSLOW at Waldoboro ME [11 Nov 1847]
    Mary Jane & James GIBBS at Waterboro ME [12 Feb 1846]
KALLOCH Hannah L & George W MACOMBER of Augusta ME at Warren ME on 24th Oct by Rev I KALLOCH [1 Nov 1849]
    Lory A & Eliza THORNDIKE at Warren ME [12 Mar 1846]
KALLOCK Horace & Phebe S SWALLOW at Belfast ME [9 May 1844]
KANADY Hiram of Avon & Maria KANADY at Farmington ME [26 Nov 1846]
    Maria & Hiram KANADY at Farmington ME [26 Nov 1846]
KANNAN John H & Sarah HERRICK at Saco ME [12 Mar 1846]
KASSON Mary Ann & Mr Chauncey STRONG at Bethlem CT "By this connection, he became son of his sister, brother to his uncle, nephew to his brother, and cousin to his nephew. She became sister to her mother, daughter to her brother, sister to her aunt, aunt to her cousin, niece to her brother, and cousin to her niece." [24 June 1833]
KEAN Norris of Oldtown ME & Sarah A NYE at Skowhegan ME [10 Feb 1848]
KEAG Otis & Miss Betsey FROST at Albion ME [15 June 1839]
KEAN Ellen & John EVERETT at Bath ME [10 Oct 1844]
    Mercy Ann & William S NEWBURY of Vinalhaven ME at Montville ME [26 Dec 1837]
KEATON Michael & Rebecca ELDRIDGE at Belfast ME [10 Jul 1838]
KEATING Mary E & Jacques LETERONEAU at Fayette ME by H LOVEJOY Esq [6 Mar 1851]
    Thomas & Amelia WHITEHOUSE of Smithfield ME at Augusta ME on 5 Jan by Rev Z THOMPSON [23 Jan 1851]
KEATON Eliza J & Francis M FOLGER at Augusta ME [25 Sept 1851]
    Izetta & Alton SOULE at Augusta ME on 19 Jan 1851 by Asaph R NICHOLS Esq [23 Jan 1851]
KEEFE Hannah & John EGAN at Augusta ME [15 Jul 1852]
KEENE/KEEN Abner & Margaret DOCKENDORFF at Windsor ME by J B SWANTON [14 Feb 1837]
    Agnis of Leeds ME & John BLUE of Monmouth ME at Monmouth by Rev Jedediah B PRESCOTT [15 Feb 1840]
    B J of ABINGTON MA & Arvilla S BISBEE at Sumner ME [17 Sept 1846]
    Caroline & William H JORDAN both of Oxford ME at Paris ME [26 June 1851]
    Charles H & Eliza SANBORN of Waldo ME at Belfast ME [27 Apr 1848]
    Charles & Nancy YOUNG at Augusta ME on 24th June [5 Jul 1849]
    Ephraim C & Mary E ROWE at Brooks ME [12 Feb 1836]
    Eveline R & John R LIBBY of Monmouth ME at Leeds ME [13 Sept 1849]
    Francis B & Florentine C HARVEY both of Presque Isle Aroostook Co ME at Letter D Plantation ME [25 Feb 1847]
    John Jr & Orrilla J ELLNER at Leeds ME [13 Mar 1851]

KEENE (cont.) Luther W & Miss Lucy D CUMMINGS at Augusta ME by Rev William A DREW [21 May 1846]
    Marinda & Joel WHITE at Winthrop ME [2 Mar 1848]
    Mary Jane & Cyrus C CHANDLER formerly of Winthrop ME at East Thomaston ME [3 Sept 1846]
    Mary P & James PACKARD at Greenwood ME [13 Apr 1848]
    Richmond B of Sumner ME & Jane C FULLER at Paris ME [7 Nov 1840]
    Seneca W & Mary Ann MORTON at Bremen ME [21 Jan 1833]
    Sophia & Samuel SNOW at (Augusta) ME on 6th Apr [15 Apr 1852]
    T S & Miss Harriet DECKROW at Freedom ME [6 Nov 1845]
KEIN Mary E & John E GOODWIN at Hallowell ME [26 Aug 1843]
KEITH David K & Mary P BARNES at Thomaston ME [13 Nov 1845]
    George H of North Bridgewater MA & Margaret ROBINSON at Augusta ME on 3rd Sept by Rev Mr JUDD [13 Sept 1849]
    Mary Ann & James S NASH at Minot ME [3 Oct 1840]
    Mary & Capt Hugh PEABODY at Thomaston ME [10 Aug 1833]
    Samuel S Jr & Lucy MAria SEEKENS of Swanville ME at Brooks ME [1 Feb 1849]
KEIZER Francis C & Nancy OVERLOCK at North Waldoboro ME on 27th Nov by Reuben ORFF Esq [4 Dec 1851]
KELLEY - KELEY - KELLY
    Amos & Lydia J MERRILL at Gardiner ME [26 Apr 1849]
    Benjamin & Olive BOODY both of Orono ME by Myric EMERSON Esq [29 Apr 1843]
    Brinsley S of Winthrop ME & Osca BRADFORD at Turner ME [30 Oct 1851]
    Charlotte A & John J DICKEY at Phillips ME on 25th Feb 1851 by Hon J A LINSCOTT [6 Mar 1851]
    Cyrus K MD of St Johnsbury & Mary McCLARA WRIGHT at Bethel ME [19 June 1845]
    D H & Hannah BRANN at East Hallowell ME [27 Sept 1849]
    Daniel C & Martha J PERRY at Gardiner ME [22 Feb 1849]
    Esther & Henry T FLANDERS at Mayfield ME by Daniel EVANS Jr [16 Jul 1842]
    John W & Dorcas W EDES both of Guilford ME at Dover ME [8 Apr 1852]
    Joseph A of Phillips ME & Mary JACOBS at Avon ME [4 May 1848]
    Lydia (age 77y & Stephen HALL (age 44y) "at the town farm in North Yarmouth ME, according to an unanimous vote of the town, passed at the Sept meeting" [9 Dec 1836]
    Mary P of Sidney ME & Edward S UPHAM of Gardiner ME at Sidney ME on 27 Feb 1851 [6 Mar 1851]
    Nancy J & Peter WALKER Esq of Brighton Somerset Co ME at Mayfield Somerset Co ME [30 Oct 1851]
    Thomas & Mary GLASPHY at Hallowell ME [6 Sept 1849]
    Thomas & Mary Jane MUSTARD at Phipsburg ME [14 Jan 1847]
    Webster Esq, counsellor at law of Frankfort ME & Lucilla S PIERCE, d/o the late Waldo PIERCE Esq of Frankfort at Boston on 24th ult by Rev Mr ROGERS [3 Sept 1842]
KELLOCH Harriet & Archibald COOMBS at Thomaston ME [10 Aug 1839]
    James S & Emeline McKELLAR at Thomaston ME [22 Oct 1846]
KELLOCK James O & Lucy THOMAS at Waldo ME [11 Feb 1847]

KELSEY Henrietta & Joseph COTTER of Boston MA at Nobleboro ME [28 Feb 1834]
  John Capt of Canton ME & Mrs Hadassah C ELLIS of Wilton ME at Jay ME [25 June 1846]
  Sarah Annette of Augusta ME & Horace K GOULD of Bangor ME at Hartford CT [17 Dec 1846]
  Susan W & Orrin WALTZE at (Augusta) ME on 26 Sept 26 [5 Oct 1848]
KEMPTON Charles of Sidney ME & Julia P COY at Augusta ME on 28th inst [8 Feb 1849]
  Ezra Jr of Phillips ME & Mary C HAINS at Lake Settlement [28 Mar 1844]
KENDALL Abigail & Benjamin I SMART at Freedom ME [24 Apr 1838]
  Franklin B & ANN E PAINE at Phipsburg ME [2 Sept 1847]
  George & Mrs Mary NORTON at Livermore ME [24 Jul 1835]
  Henrietta M & Curran DINSMORE at Skowhegan ME [2 Nov 1839]
  Henry G of Canaan ME & Sarah MANSON of Clinton ME at Gardiner ME [21 Oct 1847]
  Hepsibeth & William WITHAM at Lyman ME [9 Jul 1846]
  Mary Y & Rev Cyrus SCAMMON at Pitston ME on 27th inst by Rev Mr ROBINSON [4 Jul 1837]
  Philomela R, d/o Rev Henry KENDALL of Topsham ME, & Dr John R HALEY of Augusta ME [28 Dec 1839]
  Samuel of Mount Vernon ME & Martha M MORSE at Augusta ME on 4th inst by J W PATTERSON Esq [8 Oct 1846]
  Samuel P & Mehitable W DAVIS at Hallowell [4 Nov 1843]
  Sarah B & Rev John DEARING at Bath ME [4 Jul 1840]
  Sarah & Thomas P LEIGHTON at Perry ME [27 Jul 1848]
  Stedman of this town (Winthrop ME) & Mary Jane CHANDLER at Wayne [13 Apr 1839]
  Warren P & Betsey HUSTON both of Unity ME at Knox ME [18 Sept 1851]
KENDRICK Daniel Rev of Dennis MA & Mary Ann CAREY at Brunswick ME [27 Feb 1841]
  Harriet D & Samuel S SMITH, printer at Bangor ME [28 Oct 1836]
  Joseph Jr & Caroline E PIKE at Bangor ME [19 Aug 1836]
  Rufus B & Abigail DURELL at Saco ME [1 Jan 1846]
KENISTON Sophia & David PERRY of Fitzwilliam at Gardiner ME [20 May 1847]
KENNEDY Clarinda & James W JACKSON at Jefferson ME [19 Mar 1846]
  Eliza J & Joseph P BURBANK at Whitefield ME [21 Jul 1843]
  Elizabeth L & John ESTES at China ME [14 Dec 1833]
  Julia & Isaac McLURE both of Hallowell ME at Augusta ME on the 18th inst by Benjamin A G FULLER [25 Jun 1846]
  Lucinda & Alanson at Jefferson ME [19 Mar 1846]
  Mary Ann of Waldoboro ME & Elijah S CROWELL of Jefferson ME at Jefferson [2 Sept 1836]
  Michael Jr of Troy VT & Amanda M WEBBER d/o Oliver A WEBBER Esq "We don't exactly like to have the Vermonters carry our Kennebec girls out of the State and away off beyond the Green Mountains but if they will go God bless them and Vermont too." at Vassalboro' ME on 7 Apr 1851 by Rev Dr TAPPAN of Augusta ME [10 Apr 1851]
  Polly Jane & Calvin L HASKELL at Jefferson ME [10 Jul 1851]
  Thomas Jr & Miss Vesta Volutia GLIDDEN at Fayette ME [31 Jul 1845]

KENNEDY (cont.) William R & Julia E MARSON of Pittston ME at Augusta ME on 25 Feb by Rev JUDD [13 Mar 1851]

KENNEY Ann F & John B FOLSOM both of Dover ME at Foxcroft ME [20 Feb 1851]

   Caroline G of Sidney ME & Benjamin Franklin STONE at Gardiner ME [10 Apr 1851]

   Darby & Margaret WILSON at Dixfield ME [7 Mar 1850]

   Frances A & Thomas MASON at Westbrook ME [18 June 1846]

   Joshua & Lucretia H SMITH at Brewer ME [14 Sept 1839]

   Martha & Austin AVERILL at Newcastle ME [22 Apr 1852]

   Martha & Eben DEMERITT at Liberty ME [25 Mar 1833]

   Norris of South Manchester CT & Ann LORD at West Gardiner ME [11 Sept 1851]

KENNISON Amenda M & William T WADLIN at Biddeford ME [27 Jul 1848]

   Andrew & Miss Rosanna SAMPSON at Temple ME [21 May 1846]

   Hannah M & Allen P COLE of Bangor ME at Fayette ME on 12th inst by Rev Arthur DRINKWATER [21 Oct 1847]

   Samuel & Sophia MILLS at Milo ME [19 Jul 1849]

   Sarah & Chase PAGE at Milo ME [19 Jul 1849]

KENNISTON Hannah W & Simon FOGG Jr at Houlton Aroostook Co ME [4 Apr 1834]

KENNON Matilda & David FRENCH at Brunswick ME [31 Oct 1844]

KENSELL Laura ANN & Richard H PINKHAM of Boston MA at Augusta ME [18 Nov 1847]

KENSINGTON Julia & Freeman TROTT at Gardiner ME [1 Jan 1846]

KENT Charles & Hannah D THING at Mt Vernon ME by Rev Walter SARGENT [10 Sept 1842]

   Charlotte & George RUDGE at Rio de Janeiro [11 Mar 1852]

   Ichabod & Ann Maria JORDAN At Ellsworth ME [7 Mar 1840]

   Mary A OF Bangor ME & Reuben R ROLLINS of Augusta ME at Bangor ME on 26th ult [4 Nov 1843]

   W C & Amanda M CLEAVELAND at Brewer ME [6 Jul 1848]

   William H of Mt Vernon ME & Charlotte C COFFREN at Vienna ME [18 Nov 1847]

KERR Elizabeth A & Isaac COLESEN both of Deer Island Washington Co ME at Eastport ME [16 Dec 1843] KERSHNER

   Catherine & Edwin KINCAID at Flagstaff ME [18 May 1848]

KEYES Dolly & John BENT Esq, publisher of the *Eastern Democrat*, at Eastport ME [29 Aug 1834]

   Josiah & Miss Rachel PARKER both of Rumford ME by P C VIRGIN Esq [6 Mar 1835]

   Oliver & Mary B K NORRIS at Livermore ME on the 1st inst by Lewis HUNTON Esq [21 Mar 1834]

   Susan & Horace DAVIS at Orland ME [14 Oct 1847]

KEZER Mary & Dr Amherst S CROSS of Hallowell ME at Winthrop ME [1 Feb 1849]

KIDD Adam K & Mary CUNNINGHAM at Skowhegan ME both of Madison ME [3 Jan 1850]

KIDDER Eliza G & Sumner H STANLEY of Winthrop ME at Norridgewock ME [9 Jul 1846]

KIDDER (cont.) John S & Miss Elizabeth CUSHING both of Madison ME at Bloomfield ME [4 Mar 1847]
Joseph T formerly of Norridgewock ME & Pamelia LOCKE at West Cambridge MA [11 Nov 1847]
Joseph W & Mary A HILL at Skowhegan ME [3 Jan 1850]
Joseph W & Sarah YORK at Skowhegan ME by M Littlefield Esq [10 Jul 1851]
Llewellyn Esq & Mehitable M ROBINSON at Skowhegan ME [12 Dec 1840]
Mary E & Abijah B CHASE at Dover ME [11 May 1848]
Nancy C of Skowhegan ME & David L EASTMAN Esq formerly of VT at St Charles IL [26 June 1851]
Rosina & Mr E G HODGDON of Clinton ME at Albion ME [4 Jan 1849]
Sarah F & Moses FRENCH of Solon ME at Norridgewock ME [16 Oct 1845]
Sarah W & George PAGE at Augusta ME at St Mark's Church on Monday last by Rev A BURGESS [26 Aug 1847]
Sylvester & Ruth B HUTCHINSON at Dixfield ME [11 June 1842]
Tyler & Louisa A MORROW at Dixfield ME [13 May 1847]
KIFF Jane & John WHITNEY at Belmont ME [7 Aug 1835]
KILBRITH Nancy & Amos COLBY Jr both of Gray ME at Hallowell ME on 29th inst by Rev F MERRIAM of Winthrop ME [5 June 1845]
Sullivan of Hartford ME & Sarah E WADSWORTH at the Cross Roads in Hallowell ME [27 June 1844]
KILBOURNE H E Miss & Dr Sylvester OAKES at Wilton ME [1 June 1848]
KILBOURN Rhoda of Harrison ME & Jonathan PEABODY of Gilead Oxford Co ME at Bridgton ME [15 Feb 1849]
KILBURN Elvira & Reuben RICH at Bucksport ME [23 Mar 1839]
Paron C of Bucksport ME & Eliza G TREAT at Frankfort ME [23 Mar 1839]
KILGORE Julia Ann & William H TAYLOR at Norridgewock ME [15 Jul 1847]
KILLGORE Joseph of Topsham ME & Miss Lydia DWINAL at Lisbon ME [14 Mar 1850]
KILLMAN Thomas F & Clara E MUDGET at Prospect ME [30 May 1844]
KILLSA Mary Ann & Edward B LERMOND at Thomaston ME [24 Oct 1834]
KILMAN Richard & Miss Diadama RICHARDS at Prospect ME [22 Jan 1842]
KIMBALL A S Mr of New Portland ME & Miss S W LOVEJOY at Fayette ME [28 Sept 1848]
Abigail & Jermiah GILE at Alfred York Co ME [29 Mar 1849]
Adaline E & Granville COY of Winthrop ME at Greene ME by Ammi WEST Esq [30 Dec 1847]
Alice C & John A MESERVE at Rockland ME [26 Feb 1852]
Arabella C Mrs & Alvin B GOODWIN at Rumford ME [24 July 1851]
Benjamin F & Silome T BARTLETT both of New Portland ME at North Anson ME [7 Mar 1850]
C E Miss & Stephen J CHASE at Andover MA [13 Jan 1848]
Caleb & Sarah BROWN at Bath ME [19 Feb 1836]
Caroline F of Turner ME & Milton WELCH of Monmouth ME at Livermore ME [23 Sept 1847]

KIMBALL (cont.) Caroline of Foxcroft ME & Hiram C PRATT of Abbot ME at Sebec ME [21 Jan 1847]
Caroline of Hallowell ME & John BRETT of Augusta ME at Augusta on 25th by George M WESTON Esq [3 Apr 1845]
Charles E & Mary Emeline GILMAN at Hallowell ME [27 Mar 1851]
Charles P of Norway ME & Mary E PORTER at Camden ME [12 Jul 1849]
Charlotte & Walter MASON Jr at Bethel ME [13 Jan 1837]
David of Mercer ME & Miss Roseline GORDEN at Vienna ME [28 Feb 1850]
Eliza, d/o Heber KIMBALL Esq of Turner ME & Mr FISK of Leeds ME at Hartford ME on Sunday last by Edward BLAKE Esq [7 Mar 1837]
Eliza M & Samuel GRAY of China ME at Windsor ME [7 Mar 1844]
Eliza N & Albert PRIDE at Skowhegan ME [26 Sept 1837]
Elizabeth D & Elijah BARTER both of Hallowell ME at Augusta ME on 7th inst by Rev William A DREW [16 Sept 1847]
Ellen G & Sewall P CARTER of Belfast ME at Gardiner ME [7 Oct 1847]
Ezra Dr of Milo ME & Mrs Adeline QWEN at Vassalboro ME [9 Jul 1842]
Frances M & Miss Frances M KIMBALL at Waterville ME [9 Dec 1843]
George F of Norway ME & Lucretia J MORTON at Paris ME [21 Aug 1851]
George H of Gardiner ME & Louisa J FAYETTE at Jersey City [29 Jan 1852]
Ira C & Salome B CHAPMAN at Bethel ME [13 Apr 1848]
Isabella C & Charles H MILLER at Belfast ME [22 Jan 1846]
Jane & George H LOMBARD at Biddeford ME [26 Feb 1852]
Jedediah A & Mary H KITTSTON at Bridgton ME [28 Jan 1847]
John H Esq of Bath ME & Annie E HUMPHREYS at Brunswick ME [13 Nov 1851]
John S of Bangor ME & Sarah S FRENCH at Garland ME [23 Dec 1836]
Joseph D of Orono ME & Pheba A ROBINSON of Monmouth ME at Monmouth [27 Mar 1835]
Julia A, d/o Artemas KIMALL, & Samuel TICOMB Jr Esq at Augusta ME on Thursday last by Rev Mr JUDD [27 Feb 1845]
Julia A & Charles G TWING at China ME [25 Dec 1851]
Julia A & Dr Frederic P THEOPALD at Gardiner ME [26 Oct 1848]
Julia of Hallowell ME & Charles BRITT at Augusta ME [22 Oct 1846]
Lucy C, youngest d/o the late James KIMBALL Esq of Newburyport MA, & Alfred REDINGTON Esq of Augusta ME, Adjutant General of this state at Bath ME on 5th inst [26 Nov 1846]
Luther W & Almira HOOD at Gardiner ME [22 Apr 1852]
Maria & William BARNES at Greene ME [19 Mar 1846]
Mark D of Hollis ME & Esther C SANBORN of Norway ME at Paris ME [10 Aug 1848]
Martha B & Charles G JACKSON at Turner ME [28 Nov 1840]
Martha & John O'DONNELL at Hallowell ME [26 Nov 1846]
Mary Ann & Thatcher GOODARD at Rumford ME both of Rumford [6 Mar 1835]
Mary E & Capt Samuel W KIMBALL at Hallowell ME [4 June 1846]
Mary Jane & James FLAGG both of Augusta ME at Augusta on Sunday morning last by Rev Thomas ADAMS [18 Sept 1841]
Mary & Julius HEWES Jr at Levant ME both of Herman ME [4 Jul 1844]
Moses P of Lowell MA & Elcy GRAHAM of Milton Plantation Oxford Co ME at Rumford Oxford Co ME [30 Sept 1847]

KIMBALL (cont.) Moses S of Bethel Oxford Co ME & Catherine YOUNG of Greenwood Oxford Co ME at Norway Oxford Co ME [19 Dec 1844]
Nancy C & Israel D RUSSELL of Roxbury MA at Hallowell ME [9 Dec 1847]
Ruth H & Thomas J COFREN of New Sharon ME formerly of Vienna ME on 25 Dec by Rev Mr EDGECOMB [22 Jan 1846]
Samuel W Capt & Miss Mary E KIMBALL at Hallowell ME [4 June 1846]
Samuel & Nancy Ann STUART at Belgrade ME [15 Jan 1846]
Sarah A & Robert R CONY at Gardiner ME [4 Nov 1847]
Sarah E of Winthrop ME & Thomas L STANTON of Monmouth ME on 12th inst by Elder J J PRESCOTT [16 Oct 1845]
Sarah & Sands FRISBEE at Belfast ME [7 Jan 1847]
Susan & Albert G McLAIN at Seasmont ME by Cyrus KELLAR Esq [3 Aug 1839]
William R Esq of Canton ME & Miss Frances F, d/o late Capt Samuel RAWSON of Paris ME at New York on 20th ult [9 Jul 1842]

KINCAID Charles S of this city (Augusta) ME & Mary A BROWN d/o Benjamin BROWN of Birmingham England by Rev Mr CLINCH at Boston MA on 30 Apr [6 May 1852]
David & Rachel CUNNINGHAM both of Madison ME at Bingham ME [4 June 1846]
Edwin & Catherine KERSHNER at Flagstaff ME [18 May 1848] Eliza J & Benjamin F BURBANK at Portsmouth NH at the Mansion House on 28th April [6 May 1852]
Elmacia D & Albert J COLLINS at South Solon ME both of Cornville ME [18 Apr 1850]
Flavilla & James F ELLIS both of Oldtown ME at Passadumkeag ME [5 Jul 1849]
G W Mr & Miss P M HARTFORD at Hiram ME [6 May 1852]
Hiram & Louisa COOK at Augusta ME on Sat evening last by J L VARNEY Esq [30 Oct 1845]
Horatio N of Cornville ME & Henrietta C BUTLER of Cornville ME at Cornville by Rev PACKARD [6 Feb 1851]
Lydia Ann & John HALL at Bath ME [28 Mar 1850]
Marica Cony d/o Alexander KINCAID, & William H NORCROSS at Augusta ME on 17th inst [25 Feb 1847]
Nancy S & Henry W BRADLEY at Hallowell ME [1 Jan 1846]
Rachel & Samuel MUNCEY at Wiscasset ME [4 Feb 1833]
Robert L of Whitefield ME & Rachel WEEKS of Alna ME at Hallowell ME [1 Mar 1849]

KING Albion K P & Helen J SWAIN at Skowhegan ME [6 Nov 1851]
B F of Winthrop ME & Ann C WING [24 Dec 1846]
Benjamin & Mary JACOBS both of Winthrop ME at East Winthrop ME on 13 Aug by Rev S POWERS [21 Aug 1851]
Drusilla A & Sylvanus H HOUSE at Hallowell ME [11 May 1848]
Horatio, publisher of the *Jeffersonian* & Miss Anne COLLINS at Portland ME [12 June 1835]
Isaac N & Miss Lovinia THOMAS at Winthrop ME by Rev D THURSTON [16 Jul 1846]
James of Bloomfield ME & Mrs Pamelia C SMITH at Skowhegan ME [18 Apr 1850]
Jarius K & Jane S SHAW at Paris ME [30 Jan 1838]

KING (cont.) Jason of Monmouth ME & Mrs Clarissa ALLEN formerly of Winthrop ME at Newport RI on the 4th inst [14 Nov 1840]
    John A & Hannah BOWLEY at Skowhegan ME [2 Dec 1843]
    Laura A & Loten L BROWN at Pittston ME on Sunday evening last by Shepherd LAUGHTON [18 Dec 1841]
    Lucia & Richard ELA of Washington City at Saco ME [15 Aug 1844]
    Lucy A of Winthrop ME & John B FOGG at Monmouth ME [29 Oct 1846]
    Lydia L & Joseph BROWN at Pittston ME [31 May 1849]
    Malinda A & Robert J LOWGER at Hallowell ME [16 Mar 1848]
    Mary E & David D THOMPSON at Hallowell ME [22 Aug 1840]
    Newton & Lavinia THOMAS at Winthrop ME [16 Jul 1846]
    Pamelia M & George S STEVENS of Dover ME?/NH? on 13th at Monmouth ME [8 Jul 1852]
    Sabra C & Jason WING both Wayne ME at Winthrop ME on Wednesday last by Rev J H INGRAHAM [14 Nov 1837]
    Susanna B/Susannah B & Robert T HOPKINS/HOPSKINS at Winthrop ME [24 Feb 1848] & on 3rd Feb [10 Feb 1848]
    William H of Monmouth ME & Jane H STEARNS at Lowell MA [18 May 1848]
    William of Ripley ME & Abigail MARR of this town (Augusta) ME at Litchfield ME [26 Nov 1846]
    William S & Lucy Ann SNELL at Hallowell ME [3 May 1849]
KINGSBERRY Thomas R Esq of Bradford ME & Amanda L CLARK at Atkinson ME [17 June 1847]
KINGSBURY John R Capt of Bradford ME & Hannah WHITNEY at Dexter ME [11 Apr 1850]
    Margaret M & Mr D J CLIFFORD at Exeter NH [15 Apr 1852]
KINGSLEY Harriet Jane & William G BAGER of Bangor ME [21 Nov 1844]
    Isaac & Huldah POLLARD at Augusta ME [5 Aug 1833]
KINISTON Ezekiel of Liberty ME & Miss Caroline H LINSCOTT at Windsor ME [12 Sept 1837]
KINKSBURY Harriet N & Joseph H CURTIS at Saco ME both of Biddeford ME [28 Feb 1837]
KINNEY Elmira & James H COLLINS of Salem ME at Farmington ME [13 Nov 1851]
KINNEY Abigail & William BALDWIN of Livermore ME at Westbrook ME [11 Feb 1833]
    Johannah & Dwight MINOR at Hallowell ME [24 Apr 1835]
KINSLEY George H & Eunice S MERRILL at Sidney ME [1 Apr 1852]
    KINSMAN
    Francis & Octavia GREELEY both of Augusta ME at Providence RI on Aug 8th [21 Aug 1851]
    Mary & Rufus BLANCHARD of this town (Hallowell) ME at Hallowell on Thursday evening last by John DUNN Esq [20 Mar 1838]
KIRK Mary & Silas EVELETH at Monson ME on 20th Jul [5 Sept 1844]
KIRKPATRICK Benjamin & Chloe COTTON at Hope ME [22 June 1848]
KITREDGE Sylvester B & Mary T BEAN at Readfield ME [7 Sept 1839]
KITTREDGE/KITTRIDGE Albana & C W RICH Esq at Milo ME [1 Apr 1847]
    C F Capt of Paris ME & Miss Phebe KNAPP at Rumford ME [27 Nov 1845]

KITTREDGE (cont.) George B of Readfield ME & Miss Mercey SAVAGE at Augusta ME on Sunday morning last by Rev Mr INGRAHAM [26 Aug 1847]
    Mary E & Henry B UPHAM of Trenton MI at Dexter ME [12 June 1851]
    Mary S & Nathan P ROWELL at Weld ME by Rev J B WHEELWRIGHT [18 Dec 1851]
KITTSTON Mary H & Jedediah A KIMBALL at Bridgton ME [28 Jan 1847]
KNAPP Daniel S of Lynn MA & Betsey C MERRILL of New Sharon ME at Farmington ME on 14th inst [28 Sept 1848]
    Anthony E & Margaret MILLER at Portland ME [6 Mar 1838]
    Asa of Leeds ME & Miss S B THOMPSON at Kingfield ME [30 Dec 1847]
    David Esq & Clarissa GLINES at Rumford ME [14 Dec 1833]
    Mary Jane & Jacob SHAW of Lowell MA [25 Nov 1847]
    Phebe & Capt C F KITTREDGE at Rumford ME [27 Nov 1845]
    William G & Cynthia A RIPLEY at Leeds ME by Rev Walter FOSS [19 Nov 1846]
KNIGHT Caroline & Capt E N WITHERLY at Lincolnville ME [23 Oct 1841]
    Charlotte W & Clement JORDAN at Durham ME [20 Apr 1848]
    Clark of Boston MA & Martha Ann FRENCH at Norway ME [4 Sept 1845]
    Cordelia & Elijah ADAMS at Portland ME [13 Mar 1845]
    Emily A & James ELLIOT of Kilmarnock ME at Sebec ME [31 July 1851]
    Emily J & Nathaniel N SKILLIN at Biddeford ME [3 Aug 1848]
    Harlow of Bingham ME & Lucinda S FOLSOM at Starks ME [7 May 1846]
    Harriet E F & Benjamin PATCH at Otisfield ME [7 May 1846]
    Margaret & Robert EVENS at Portland ME [11 Mar 1836]
    Paul & Hannah HANSON at Scarborough ME [29 May 1835]
    Stephen H of Boston MA & Miss Louisa CLARY of BROOKS at New York NY [11 Mar 1847]
    Stephen & Sarah A YORK at Bingham ME [15 May 1845]
    Susan & James L WEBB at Deer Isle ME [16 Jul 1843]
    W Arnold of New York City & Emma A WENHENBURG of (Augusta) ME at Portsmouth NH on 6th Mar [18 Mar 1852]
    William & Sarah LEBARRON at Norway ME [23 Jan 1845]
KNIGHTS George Capt of Northport ME & Miss Elizabeth EDWARDS of Belfast ME at Belfast [15 Apr 1836]
    Julia & Adrich B COOK at Brunswick ME [13 Feb 1845]
    William & Miriam WALKER at Brunswick ME [22 Aug 1834]
KNOLTON John C of Montville ME & Sarah A WEBB of China ME at China [26 Nov 1842]
KNOWLAND Elethusa & William POTE of New Gloucester ME at Sidney ME [9 Oct 1851]
KNOWLES Amos P & Lucy E YOUNG at Lincolnville ME [14 August 1851]
    Catherine S & Capt Elisha K PENDLETON at Belfast ME [13 Feb 1841]
    Charlotte & Leonard CURTIS at Bluehill ME [29 Jul 1836] Eben P & Mary A BROWN at Hallowell ME [5 Feb 1846]
    Emery of Readfield ME & Miss Lovina COTTLE of Augusta ME at Sidney ME on 17 Oct [1 Nov 1949]
    George H & Elizabeth P NEAL at Hallowell ME [31 Jan 1850]
    John of Fayette ME & Rosilla RICHARDS at Chesterville ME [4 Feb 1843]
    Mary Ann & Owen WENTWORTH of Kennebunk ME at Corinna ME [1 Nov 1849]

KNOWLES (cont.) Mary & Charles BASTON of Lexington Somerset Co ME at New Portland Somerset Co ME [7 August 1851]
 Rhoda & James MINOT at Sidney ME on 28 June [13 Jul 1848]
 Sarah Jane & William HOYT at East Readfield ME by Rev L PACKARD [4 June 1846]
 Stephen S of Augusta ME & Mary Ann SMILEY at Sidney ME [24 May 1849]
 Susan & Deacon Isaac KNOX at Clinton ME [26 Aug 1847]
 Syrene & Abel BOWMAN at Readfield ME [25 Apr 1840]
KNOWLTON Almira & Caleb HILL at Danville ME [4 Jan 1849]
 Catharine Elizabeth & Samuel WARREN at Chesterville ME [17 Aug 1848]
 Clarissa & Robert B LANPHER at Sangerville ME [27 Apr 1848]
 Eliza A d/o David KNOWLTON, & Benjamin A SWAN, printer at Augusta ME on 16th inst by the Rev Mr Morse [20 May 1847]
 Eliza M & Capt Martin L COTTRELL both of Northport ME at Belfast ME [18 June 1846]
 Fessenden & Ellen SPEAR at Auburn ME [25 Oct 1849]
 Hiram Capt & Lorana HUNT at Montville ME [7 Mar 1837]
 Isaac of Pembroke ME & Lydia Ann BENNETT at Dennyville ME [2 Oct 1851]
 John W & Almira F AMES at Belfast ME both of Swanville ME [29 May 1845]
 Joseph of Farmington ME age 18y & Sarah H PRATT of New Vineyard ME age 15y at New Vineyard [18 Mar 1847]
 Joshua & Belinda PILSBURY at Farmington ME [13 June 1844]
 Mary Jane of Swanville ME & Jeremiah SMALL at Waldo ME [20 Nov 1845]
 Sarah & John R ADAMS at Farmington ME [20 Dec 1849]
 Sylvanus & Rebecca A F COLBURN at Mercer ME [28 June 1849]
 William G & Nancy W SWEETSER at Bath ME [15 Nov 1849]
KNOX Albion P & Susanna S WYMAN at Peru ME on 7 Dec by Jonas GREENE Esq [18 Dec 1851]
 Ellen S & Charles O WILSON at Portland ME [27 Mar 1845]
 Frederick, formerly of Norway ME & Julia HERRING of Winnebago Co IL at Sugar River Precinct IL [24 Apr 1845]
 George Rev, pastor of the Baptist Church in Topsham ME & Achsah H DUNNELL at Buxton ME [29 Jan 1842]
 George & Sarah BARRON at Topsham ME [11 Mar 1847]
 Isaac Deacon & Susan KNOWLES at Clinton ME [26 Aug 1847]
 Jennie & Albert B BUTLER at Portland ME [17 June 1852]
 Mary A & Thomas GOODWIN at Gardiner ME [14 May 1846]
 Sophia A of Machias ME & Mr Elijah S BLAISDELL of Thomaston ME at Machias ME on 1st inst by Rev J A PERRY [15 Feb 1844]
 Supply G & Betsey A SESSION at Biddeford ME [14 Sept 1848]
 T P Dr of Hyannis MA & Angelina J BERRY of Belfast ME at Boston MA [4 Mar 1852]
KUHN Boyd of Waldoboro ME & Hannah R PERCIVAL at China ME on 22 June by Rev L WENTWORTH [26 June 1851]
KYES Lucy A & Dr A K P CHILDS of Jay ME at Wilton ME [13 Dec 1849]
KYLE W S of Peru ME & Miss Emily J JONES at Pownal ME [2 Aug 1849]

- L -

LABAREE [sic] Ruth Ann & William H MANNING at Whitefield ME [3 May 1849]
LABREE Mary E & William LINCOLN of Corinna ME [19 Apr 1849]
LACROIS Emeline B & George C WHITNEY by the Rev William A DREW both of this town (Winthrop) ME at Augusta ME [17 Aug 1833]
    Frederick & Mrs Nancy FULLER at Monmouth ME on the 25th ult by Elder Jedediah B PRESCOTT both of this town (Winthrop) ME [4 Jan 1834]
    Frederick & Mrs Mary S SHAW by Benjamin LOMBARD Esq at Wayne ME on the 10th inst both of Winthrop ME [21 Feb 1841]
    Mary E & Loring COBB at Winthrop ME by Oaks HOWARD Esq [28 May 1846]
LADD Alfred of New York formerly of (Augusta) ME & Fannie W WALKER d/o Dr Wiliam J WALKER at Boston MA [15 June 1848]
    Anna L & James S FILLEBROWN of Readfield ME at Farmington ME [18 Oct 1849]
    Aurelia F & John A ROLLINS at Belfast ME [30 Oct 1835]
    C N of Hallowell ME & Harriet N PATTERSON at Edgecomb ME [6 Nov 1841]
    Cyrus K of Brewer ME, a merchant, & Mary R PHILLIPS of Bangor ME at Brewer ME by Rev Mr CAVERNO [16 Dec 1843]
    Diana W & Charles P CRAIG at Phillips ME [12 Mar 1842]
    Ellen S & Henry H WELLES of Wyolusing PA, she was the d/o Gen S G LADD [18 Oct 1849]
    G W of Bangor ME & Marcia P C d/o Rev J H INGRAHAM at Augusta ME on 9th inst at St Mark's Church by Rev Mr FREEMAN [21 Oct 1843]
    Harriet N of Edgecomb ME & William LOWELL of Wiscasset ME [8 Nov 1849]
    James T & Catherine ORR both of Garland ME at Dexter ME [27 Feb 1851]
    John of this town (Hallowell) ME & Sarah Jane NOURSE of Bangor ME on Thurs last at Bangor ME [5 Sept 1837]
    John of Vienna ME & Mary FOLLET of (Winthrop) ME by Elias WHITING Esq [30 Sept 1836]
    Julia Maria d/o Gen S G LADD of Farmington ME & Lewis H TITCOMB of (Augusta ME) on 6th inst by Rev Isaac ROGERS [8 Oct 1846]
    Louisa J & Mr S P WITHAM at Gardiner ME [12 June 1851]
    Lucinda B & Hosea BLAISDELL both of Sidney ME at Sidney [18 Mar 1836]
    M Caroline of Hallowell ME & H W Fairbank of Farmington ME at Hallowell ME on Weds morning last by Rev Eli THURSTON [15 June 1839]
    Mary J of Starks ME & James W HINKLEY of Greenville ME at Madison ME [7 Feb 1850]
    Nancy, wid/o John LADD, & Nehemiah PIERCE Esq of Monmouth ME at Winthrop ME [25 Jan 1844]
    Nancy d/o the late John LADD, & Hosea BLAISDELL of Sidney ME at Winthrop ME by Rev Mr ROBINSON [28 Oct 1843]
    Nathaniel & Drussillia ELLIOT of Mercer ME at Abbott ME [19 Sept 1844]

Marriage Notices from the "Maine Farmer" 235

LADD (cont.) Newall H & Lavina M BROWN at Clinton ME [22 Jan 1842]
 Sarah R & Henry W FULLER of Bangor ME at Augusta ME at St Mark's Church on Sat morning last by Rev Alexander BURGESS [5 Aug 1852]
 Sarah S & Lyman MOORE at (Augusta) ME on Mar 4th [11 Mar 1852]
 Thomas H & Ann M DYER at Hallowell ME [28 Dec 1848]
 W M of Winthrop ME & Miss E A ELLIS at Sidney ME [21 Sept 1848]
LAINE Mary L & Calvin F BONNEY of Wayne ME at Hallowell ME [20 Jun 1844]
LAIR Emely & Jeremiah MITCHEL both of Washington ME by Rev BARRY at Vassalborough ME on 30 ult [30 Oct 1838]
LAKE Caroline Amelia & Henry P TURNER both of Bucksport ME at Ellsworth ME [25 Dec 1851]
 Cynthia H d/o Col S LAKE & Zenas HOMER at Bucksport ME [17 Aug 1839]
 Lucy Ann & Daniel C LUCE at New Sharon ME on the 1st inst [17 Oct 1840]
 Lydia of New Sharon ME & Dea Samuel BURGESS of Paris ME by Rev WILLIAMSON at New Sharon ME [18 Apr 1844]
 Lydia of Wilton ME & Jona HANSCOM of Jay ME in E Dixfield ME [25 Dec 1845]
LAKEMAN Abigail of Boston MA, 2nd d/o John LAKEMAN, of Hallowell ME & John A EWERS of Hallowell ME at New York NY [5 June 1841]
 Daniel D of Hallowell ME & Mary BLOOD at Boston MA [4 Apr 1844]
 Mary L & William O TOMPKINS of Boston MA at Hallowell ME [21 Oct 1847]
LAKEN Harriet & Isaiah SMITH at Charlotte ME [14 June 1849]
 John & Abigail F PIERCE at Etna ME [6 Jul 1839]
LALAND Ann & William HOPKINS of Trenton ME at Eden ME [23 Jan 1841]
LALLY Folliot T Major of Portland ME & Ellen L EVANS d/o Hon George EVANS by Bishop BURGESS at Gardiner ME [26 Oct 1848]
LAMB Abby & Stephen RICHARDS at Rockville CT [14 Dec 1848]
 Cornelia Ann & Nicholas LYON at Winooski by Rev Mr FOREST [5 June 1838]
 Francis M & Amy J BREMNER by Rev A PALMER at Winslow ME on New Year's Eve [8 Jan 1852]
 Luther Dr & Oliver WINTER at Carthage ME [12 Nov 1846]
 Martha D & William HUNT of Pittston ME at Hallowell ME [29 Apr 1847]
 Mary S of Worcester MA & Joseph LYON at Worcester on 21st by Rev Mr PEABODY "And the lion shall lie down with the lamb" [22 May 1838]
 Samuel D of Brunswick ME & Ruth Ann H MAYO at Hallowell ME [7 Dec 1848]
LAMBERT/LAMBART Abel M of Strong ME & Ann H PERRY of Camden ME [8 Mar 1849]
 Eunice R of Gardiner ME m Richard BEETLE of Edgartown MA at Boston MA [22 May 1851]
 Ferdinand & Marietta M, d/o Horatio G ALLEN Esq of Bath ME [12 Feb 1842]
 George & Almira McLARREN at Eastport ME [9 Oct 1845]
 James Jr & Alice SPARKS at Brunswick ME [8 Oct 1846]
 John Esq & Marinda, d/o James FILLEBROWN Esq [30 Oct 1838]
 L B of North Yarmouth ME & Mary J ERSKINE of Bristol ME [11 Dec 1845]

LAMBERT (cont.) Mary & Col John ROWELL of Jay ME at Readfield ME on the 15th inst [27 May 1847]
    Robert & Eliza BROWN at Belfast ME [8 Aug 1844]
    Sarah H & Isaac AMES at Skowhegan ME [29 Jul 1852]
    Semantha G & William DOWNS of Orono ME at Dover ME [17 Jan 1850]
LAMKIN G of Boston MA & Miss L N BENJAMIN at Whitefield ME [31 Jan 1850]
    Simeon S & Mary A WARNER at Jay ME on Mar 20th [8 Apr 1852]
LAMPHER Arthur C of Bucksport ME & Louisa C STEPHENSON at Belfast ME [20 Mar 1851]
    Sally Maria & David CHASE at Sebec ME [14 Mar 1850]
LAMPSON Benjamin F of Boston MA & Melancy B FROST at Wayne ME by Rev C FULLER [2 Oct 1851]
LANCASTER Caroline B & Henry H HOXIE at Bath ME on Dec 16th [1 Jan 1852]
    Elizabeth A & Albert HASKELL at China ME, by James B HASKELL Esq [2 Dec 1847]
    George W & Anne M PERKINS at (Augusta) ME by Rev Mr WILLIAMS [24 Dec 1846]
    Harriet N& Steven L REESE at Augusta ME on Sunday morning the 6th inst at the State Street Chapel [17 Oct 1844]
    Henry & Sarah J CROSBY d/o Luther CROSBY Esq at Albion ME on May 29th by O W WASBURN Esq [12 June 1851]
    John M & Mrs Catherine NEILLY at Lee on the 22d Jul by J B LUDDEN Esq [5 Aug 1852]
    Levi P & Hannah I NOWELL of Winslow ME at Albion ME [1 Aug 1834]
    Maria L & Woodin NORRIS at (Augusta) ME on 29th ult by Rev W A DREW [10 Dec 1846]
    Mary L & Stephen H CURTIS both of Bowdoin ME at Gardiner ME [22 Nov 1849]
    Mary of Winthrop ME & Robert T PAINE of Skowhegan ME (extended notice) [1 Jan 1839]
    Sarah & Benjamin THOMAS both of Maxfield ME [6 Mar 1845]
    Sewall Esq of Augusta ME & Adeline E SYMONDS of Boxford MA at Boxford MA [23 Sept 1836]
    Sewall Esq & Rebecca SIMONDS at Augusta ME by J R ABBOT Esq [25 Feb 1847]
    Thomas & Amy EVENS both of Albion ME at China ME by Rev William BOWLER [11 Nov 1836]
    William & Adaline INGALLS of Mercer ME at New Sharon ME [27 Sept 1849]
LANCY Gilman D & Eliza A BURNHAM at Exeter ME [29 Apr 1852]
LANDER Warren & Tryphena B PIKERING at Brighton, Somerset Co, ME [29 Apr 1836]
    William & Joann ROWE of East Pond Plantation ME at Fairfield ME [13 June 1837]
LANDERKIN Almira of Gardiner ME & William JEWELL at Litchfield ME [6 May 1847]
    Phebe & William Eugene WALKER of Portland ME at Gardiner ME [18 Apr 1850]
LANDERS Hannah of Woodstock ME & Albert CLIFFORD at Paris ME [17 Jul 1841]

LANE Barbour & Louisa MERRILL at Augusta ME on the 22d inst by Rev Asahel MOORE [26 Dec 1844]
Betsey & Lewis MONK Jr at Paris ME [28 Feb 1837]
Clarrissa of Augusta ME & Lotan GRIFFITH of Hallowell ME at Augusta ME by Silas CARTER [5 June 1838]
Edwin A & Ellen St CLAIR at Auburn ME [30 Jan 1851]
Eliza T, d/o the late Capt George LANE, & E BLATCHFORD of Augusta ME at Rockport MA on the 19th inst [30 Oct 1845]
Eunice S & Josiah BEAN Jr both of Brooks ME at Belfast ME [4 Dec 1851]
Fanny & Robert THOMPSON at Fayette ME [26 Sept 1840]
Frances A & Newell H BATES at Dexter ME [20 Jan 1848]
Frances & Rev Sumner CLARK of Unity ME at Searsport ME [20 Mar 1845]
George & Gracia McCRILLIS at Bloomfield ME [8 May 1851]
Harriet & William HUSSEY Jr both of Dover at Atkinson ME [11 Dec 1851]
Isaac of Hollis ME & Mrs Susan DOUGLASS of Boston MA at Boston on Thurs morning last by Rev Dr SHARP [21 Jan 1833]
James Jr of Fayette ME & Louisa WYMAN at Livermore Falls ME [6 May 1843]
Jane Maria (formerly Miss LEE of Brunswick) ME & Dr David Seabury GRANDIN formerly of New York at Brunswick ME on the 21st by Rev Mr ADAMS [3 Oct 1837]
Joseph & Sarah WITHAM at Poland ME [26 Mar 1846]
Marshall & Mary A UNDERWOOD both of Fayette ME at Chesterville ME by Rev J H CONANT [6 Mar 1851]
Martha & Capt Charles ORCUTT both of Northport ME at Belfast ME [13 Feb 1845]
Mary Almira & David WILKINS Jr at Sangerville ME both of Parkman ME [24 Jul 1845]
Mary R & John HAM of Limerick ME at Waterboro ME [14 August 1851]
Nancy of Calais ME & Daniel SHERMAN at Calais ME [4 Mar 1836]
Nancy R of Dexter ME & Edwin L GOULD of Sangerville ME [29 Jul 1852]
Nancy & Harrison GOULD at Leeds ME [19 June 1838]
Orson ae 21y & Betsey BACON ae 43y at Anson ME on 14th inst by John LEATHHEAD Esq [26 Feb 1836]
Otis & Eunice F MERRILL of Saco ME at Biddeford ME [14 June 1849]
Rachel & James C WARREN Esq of Detroit ME at Webster ME [8 Feb 1849]
LANG Theodate & Charles LOWELL at Saco ME [10 Aug 1848]
LANGDON Sarah & Levi WEBBER at Ellsworth ME [12 Sept 1840]
LANPHER Robert B & Clarissa KNOWLTON at Sangerville ME [27 Apr 1848]
LANGLEY Edward & Mary M HART at Bath ME [14 Oct 1847]
Elizabeth F & George W GORHAM at Bangor ME [16 May 1837]
Joseph L Esq & Mary A LANGLEY at Durham NH after an engagement of five minutes [6 Feb 1845]
Martha & Hamlette BATES, editor of the *St Croix Courier*, at Calais ME [31 Oct 1834]
Mary A & Joseph L LANGLEY Esq [6 Feb 1845]
LANNAN Joel S & Sarah RICHMOND at Turner ME [12 Sept 1834]

LANSING William H & Mary Ann COOLEY both of West Troy NY on 7 Nov 1837 [29 Feb 1840]
LAPHAM Eliza Ann & George T GOULD at Auburn ME [17 Feb 1848]
  Roger of Pittston ME m Emily R JACKSON of Winthrop ME [2 Apr 1846]
LARA Daniel & Celia COPELAND at Turner ME [19 Jul 1849]
LARGE Rebecca T & James F WEEKS, printer, formerly of Augusta ME at Davertown OH [1 May 1838]
LARKIN William Capt & Elizabeth JORDAN at Eastport ME [27 Jul 1848]
LARRABEE Ann & William MARDEN at East Thomaston ME [9 Aug 1849]
  Benjamin 2d & Angeline TRUE at Portland ME [8 Feb 1844]
  Benjamin Capt & Angeline TRUE at Portland ME [15 Feb 1844]
  Daniel M of Wales ME & Sarah RANKINS at Monmouth ME on 7 Feb by John SAFFORD Esq [1 Mar 1849]
  Eliza D & Perley G ELDEN at Bradford ME [12 Feb 1842]
  Ephraim & Sophronia FARRIN at Brunswick ME [31 Jan 1834]
  Hannah A & Joseph BOWKER at Phipsburg ME [14 Mar 1837]
  Hannah M & Warren HOWARD of Wilton ME at Mt Vernon ME [18 Apr 1850]
  John formerly of Mt Vernon ME & Rachel WADE at Greenbush WI [25 Dec 1851]
  Lydia & Stephen CLEAVES at Prospect ME [17 June 1836]
  Mary W & Capt Nehemiah HARDING at Bath ME [25 Nov 1843]
  Otis & Sarah Jane ACHORN at Thomaston ME [22 Mar 1849]
  Polly & Joshua CHIPMAN at New Portland ME [29 Nov 1849]
  Solomon & Nancy STEVENS at Thomaston ME [24 Aug 1848]
LARSOETL [sic] Hannah & John WHITTEN at Burnham ME [8 Jul 1836]
LARY Emma & Jeremiah RIDLON at Saco ME [19 Aug 1847]
LASH John 2d & Barbara K at Waldoboro ME [17 Dec 1842]
  Mary Ann & Charles WELD 2d at Waldoboro ME [19 Dec 1837]
LASLEY Eliza & Patrick WHALEN both of Deer Island (part of Harrington Washington Co) ME at Eastport [2 Jan 1841]
LASSAR Lucy & John PLANT at Bath ME [28 Nov 1844]
LASSEL James M & Mary F WOODBRIDGE both of Norway ME at Cambridge MA [2 Jan 1845]
LATER Ann Jane & Henry McKOWN of Fairfield ME at Skowhegan ME [17 Jul 1851]
LATHAN Artemas, formerly of Gray ME, & Mary D WHITE at Greenfield Penobscot Co ME [27 June 1844]
  Woodward W & Elvira MORSE at Norway ME [30 Mar 1839]
LATHROP Ansel Maj of Belfast Waldo Co ME & Ruth Ann BORLAND [8 May 1845]
LAUGHLER Caroline & Bowman PALMER of Readfield ME at Hallowell ME [4 Apr 1844]
  Catherine F & Mr C B JACKSON of Sangerville ME at Harmony ME [24 Apr 1851]
  Mary & George W BUMP at Farmington ME [14 Sept 1848]
  Samuel A & Julia A HAWKINS at Hallowell ME [10 Jan 1850]
  Sarah E & Charles W MARBLE at Harmony ME [30 Nov 1848]
  Stephen W & Eveline S ARNOLD at Appleton ME [24 June 1847]
  Susan A & Charles H WESTON at Norridgewock ME [7 Dec 1848]
  Sylvanus & Hannah M GREELEY at Hallowell ME [29 Oct 1846]

LAUGHLER (cont.) W P of Auburn ME & Elizabeth F PRENTISS at Cornville ME [6 Mar 1851]
LAW Aaron of Boston MA & Louisa SCHWARTZ of Waldoboro ME at Indian Head, Nashville NH [18 Oct 1849]
 Ann & Benjamin A BURR, printer, at Bangor ME [16 May 1844]
 Benjamin L Jr of Union ME & Mary C WEAVER of Washington ME at N Waldoboro ME on 4 Dec by Reuben ORFF Esq [11 Dec 1851]
LAWRENCE Charles R of Brunswick ME & Adaline HOWE by Rev Dr TAPPAN at (Augusta) ME on Sunday last [29 June 1848]
 Dolly M & James TARBOX Jr at Gardiner ME [22 Feb 1849]
 Drusila & Franklin McGOWN of Boston MA at Gardiner ME [29 Jan 1846]
 Edward A & Lucy A BRAGG at Castine ME [27 Mar 1845]
 Edward A & Lucy Ann BRAY at Castine ME [20 Mar 1845]
 Edward & Sally PIKE at Lubec ME [28 Aug 1835]
 Elias H of Gardiner ME & Hannah L CURTIS of Richmond ME at Bowdoinham ME [11 Jan 1849]
 Farnsworth & Malinda B LAWRENCE at Bangor ME [15 Jul 1843]
 Harriet B & Albion K P BUFFUM at Gardiner ME [26 June 1845]
 Hiram & Susan E CAPEN at Gardiner ME [9 Jan 1851]
 Jane & Mr C W SAMPSON at Temple ME on 13th inst by Rev S HACKETT [6 June 1840]
 Lorenzo & Phebe Ann HODGDON of Westport ME at Bath ME [16 Sept 1847]
 Louisa & Charles E TOBEY at Fairfield ME [6 Feb 1838]
 Lucy & William GOULD at Pittston ME by Mr CLAPP [3 Jul 1838]
 Matilda & Joseph GIFFORD 2d at Fairfield ME [21 Feb 1850]
 Nelson L & Sarah J HANSON at East Machias ME [18 Nov 1847]
 Sarah & Selden TAYLOR of Sebasticook ME at Skowhegan ME [13 Mar 1851]
 Sophronia C & Dr William WENTWORTH at Cornville ME [28 Mar 1837]
LAWRY Eleanor & Jesse THOMAS at Friendship ME [19 Dec 1840]
LAWSON Laurette & Peter P PEABODY at Starks Centre ME [16 Mar 1848]
LAZO Peter & Eliza J EWER at Brownville ME [10 Feb 1848]
LAWSON Eliza W & Rev Cyrus TIBBETTS of Hampton Falls NH at Augusta ME [24 June 1847]
 John W & Olive E FELKER at Prospect ME [28 Dec 1833]
LEACH Charles N Capt of Portland ME & Eunice M WALKER at North Yarmouth ME [2 Jan 1845]
 Elizabeth W & Jesse DUTTON at Hallowell ME [28 Nov 1840]
 Harriet A of Castine ME & Capt N H COLTON, formerly of Hartford CT at Bangor ME [29 Feb 1844]
 Mary Ann & Jotham S VILES at (Augusta) ME on 1st Oct [12 Oct 1848]
 Nancy & Capt James COOK at Orland ME [14 Oct 1847]
LEADBETTER James & Harriet N HODGDON at Palmyra ME [21 Oct 1847]
 Laura A & Mr H F WINGATE at Hallowell ME [10 Dec 1846]
 Orson & Lucy L DUNHAM at Leeds ME by Rev C FULLER [8 May 1851]
LEAR Judith B & James H DODGE at Belfast ME [13 May 1852]
LEARNED Margaret A & Edward W BUSH at Clinton ME [20 Jan 1848]
LEARD James & Ruth ALIFF both of Gardiner ME at Hallowell ME [9 Aug 1849]

LEATHERS Enoch & Sarah E GRANT at Hermon ME [11 Sept 1851]
  Louisa & Ebenezer T FLOOD at Biddeford ME [8 Apr 1852]
  Stephen S of Brooks ME & Catherine M WATTS at Knox ME [27 May 1852]
  Jonathan & Stiley WOOD, "A clergyman, in Lowell MA, says the *Dedham Patriot* lately turned WOOD into LEATHER, as appears by the notice, on Thanksgiving day by Rev Mr THURSTON. So they are both Leather now, and we supposed he is to be the upper leather, though if she is to be reckoned the sole leather we hope she is not to be hammered [9 Jan 1838]

LEAVETT/LEAVITT Asa of Turner ME & Amelia POLLARD at Livermore ME [24 May 1849]
  B R & Harriet A CLARKE at Hallowell ME [15 Jul 1847]
  Charles P & Mary FRENCH at Turner ME by Rev George BATES [2 Dec 1836]
  Clarissa & Caleb W ALLEN of Somerville MA at Bath ME [18 Jul 1844]
  Elihu of Newry ME & Maria A SARGENT of Riley Plt ME at Bethel ME [13 Jul 1848]
  George S of Chelmsford MA m Charlotte E PAINE at Winslow ME [4 June 1851]
  Hiram H of Dexter ME & Hannah W WOOD of Winthrop ME at Winthrop on 12th June by Rev Mr Thurston [5 Sept 1844]
  Lucy B & Mr I M SHERMAN at (Augusta) ME [26 Oct 1848]
  Mary & Nathaniel ROBINSON at Mt Vernon ME [27 Nov 1846]
  Olive & Hon Job PRINCE on 28th ult at Turner ME [9 Jan 1845]
  Rhoda & James SEDGELEY Jr at Winthrop ME on 14th inst by Rev Mr MORSE [23 Dec 1847]
  Seth & Ann LIBBY at Gray ME by Ephraim LAWRENCE Esq [2 Oct 1835]

LEBARRON Sarah & William KNIGHT [23 Jan 1845]

LEE see LANE, GRANDIN

LEE Frances & Jacob BAYLEY at Lee by J B LUDDEN Esq [26 June 1851]
  John J & Maria B SWAZEY at Bucksport ME [26 Aug 1847]
  Laura P & Freeman ROLLINS at Lee by J B LUDDEN Esq [26 June 1851]
  Martha, d/o Col J LEE of Milo ME, & Moses GREENLEAF Esq of Williamsburg ME at Bucksport ME [22 Jan 1839]
  Mary E & Stillman THORP at Brunswick ME [9 Nov 1833]
  Sarah E & Francis T SARGENT of New York at Hallowell ME [23 Oct 1851]
  William & Sarah TILTON at Lee by J H PERKINS Esq on 18 July [5 Aug 1852]

LEEDS Ann Elizabeth & Horace WATERS of Augusta ME at Brookline MA [30 May 1840]

LEEMAN Caroline of Gardiner ME & Lewis J HURLBERT of Gardiner ME at Augusta ME on 31 Dec [9 Jan 1851]
  Frances E & Arthur L GETCHELL at Augusta ME by A R NICHOLS Esq on 28 Jan [31 Jan 1850]
  John A & Susan L MAGOON both of Litchfield ME in Fayette ME [14 Aug 1845]
  John S & Harriet D BUTLER in Hallowell ME on 27th inst [4 Sept 1845]
  Rosina & Reuben GREENLEAF in Augusta ME [25 Apr 1837]
  William of Wiscassett ME & Lucretia ALLEN of Alexandria DC by Rev JOHNSTON at Alexandria DC [16 Jan 1841]

LEGROW Asa Col & Mary Ann Morrell at Windham ME by Elias BAKER Esq on 3rd inst [16 Apr 1842]
    Sarah P & Daniel H HARMON at Windham ME [28 Dec 1848]
LEIGH R W Capt & Caroline Tapley in Hallowell ME [22 Oct 1846]
LEIGHTON Abijah & Lydia E PHELPS at Eastport ME [27 Jul 1848]
    Daniel M & Nancy MORRISON at Calais ME [29 Aug 1834]
    Gilbert M Capt of Steuben ME & Mary S WHITNEY at Freeman ME [18 May 1848]
    Irene & Isaiah CHADBOURN Jr in Harmony ME [15 Jan 1846]
    J Jr & Martha PACKARD both of Vassalboro ME by Rev Mr MORSE at Winthrop ME [27 Jan 1848]
    Joanna & William ADAMS at Steuben ME by Samuel MOORE Esq all of Steuben ME [12 Feb 1842]
    Jonathan & Elizabeth LITTLEFIELD by Rev Obid WILSON all of Skowhegan ME [23 Mar 1839]
    Laura Ann & Nathaniel NASON at Augusta ME by L CUSHING Esq [21 Nov 1844]
    Leonard of Portland ME & Caroline P TRUNDY at Wiscasset ME [6 Jul 1848]
    Lucinda & Phillip RUSSELL by Rev THOMPSON in Falmouth ME [29 Apr 1843]
    Lydia & Mr C G STAPLES at Biddeford ME [22 June 1848]
    Maria & Bryce M STEWARD at Solon ME [13 Feb 1851][30 Jan 1851]
    Mary E & James N WADE at Augusta ME [15 Jan 1846]
    Mary & John WITHAM at Washington ME [11 Mar 1847]
    Priscilla & Wm ATWATER in Steuben ME [2 May 1837]
    Rosilla C & Thomas CONANT of Peru ME at Augusta ME on 25th Oct by Asaph R NICHOLS [30 Oct 1851]
    Sarah Jane & Warner R LEIGHTON by Dr Ira THING at Mt Vernon ME on Mar 3rd [14 Mar 1850]
    Silas F & Amanda M F BEAN at Augusta ME on 3 August by Rev Z THOMPSON [7 August 1851]
    Thomas P & Sarah KENDALL at Perry ME [27 Jul 1848]
    Warner R and Saran Jane LEIGHTON by Dr Ira Thing at Mt Vernon ME on Mar 3rd [14 Mar 1850]
    Woster of Lubec ME & Mary Ann BREWSTER at Eastport ME [21 Mar 1850]
    --- & Nathaniel ROBINSON at Mt Vernon ME [6 Jun 1837]
LELAND L M of Augusta ME & Anna E GETCHELL of Vassalboro ME at Vassalboro on 9 Dec [25 Dec 1851]
LEMAN Samuel D & Hannah CROCKETT at Abbot ME [8 Feb 1844]
LEMFEST Lydia & Solomon HAMILTON at Swanville ME [19 Mar 1846]
LEMONT Charles B & Mary BRADFORD at Bath ME [11 Nov 1843]
    Charles D Capt of Bath ME & Joanna SEWALL at Hallowell ME on Thurs Morning last by Rev E THURSTON [31 Jul 1838]
    David & Lavinia C WYLIE at Bath ME [13 Nov 1851]
    Isaac Jr of Bath ME & Harriet N PRESCOTT in Portland ME [23 Sept 1847]
    Joanna S & J F DUNNING of Boston ME at Brunswick ME [29 Oct 1846]
    Julia Ann & Elijah LOW of Bangor ME at Bath ME [4 Apr 1834]
    Lydia H & Francis C JORDAN of Brunswick ME at Bath ME [7 Nov 1844]
    Sarah E & Isaac GRIFFIN Jr of Minot ME at Greene ME [24 July 1841]

LEMONT (cont.) Silas S of Gardiner ME & Phebe A TOOTHAKER at Litchfield ME [15 Apr 1847]
LENNAN Joel S of Hallowell ME & Sarah RICHMOND at Turner ME on Sun Aug 31 [5 Sept 1834]
 Lucy F & Amasa RING at Richmond ME [10 Sept 1846]
LENNELL Eliza B & William EDWARD in the Portland ME jail on 6th inst by Sam'l FESSENDEN Esq [27 May 1843]
LEONARD Daniel W of Knox ME & Mary Ann RANDOLPH of Monroe ME at Montville ME [24 Apr 1845]
 Frances Amelia d/o Silas L & William P RATHBONE Esq of Providence RI at Augusta ME on 12th inst by Rev JUDD [20 Dec 1849]
 Henry Orville of Worcester MA & Lucy Francis HARRIS of Winthrop ME on 6 Oct by Rev THURSTON [31 Oct 1844]
 Joseph B of Boston MA & Charlotte Ann MORSE at Bath ME [20 Aug 1846]
 L W Rev of Dublin NH & Mrs Elizabeth D SMITH at Exeter NH [10 Apr 1851]
 Silas Esq & Emeline M d/o late Levi ROGERS on Mon eve last at Augusta ME [4 Jan 1840]
LEPLAIN Drusilla A & Leander H ROSS of Phippsburg ME at Gardiner ME [1 Nov 1849]
LERMAN Ansel & Mary A Maxey at Searsmont ME [19 Sept 1844]
LERMOND Charles & Rebecca MORTON at Warren ME [25 Dec 1841]
 Edward B & Mary Ann KILLSA at Thomaston ME [24 Oct 1834]
 Eldridge Capt & Mary Jane CUSHMAN both of Warren ME at Thomaston ME [29 Aug 1844]
 George W & Ann YOUNG at Thomaston ME [8 May 1845]
 Maria of Warren ME & Capt William WELLSBY at Thomaston ME [20 Feb 1845]
LESLIE Amanda M & Hon Mayor Charles HAYWARD Esq of Bangor at Bangor [3 June 1847]
LESSNER Catharine & Joseph U SHATTUCK at Thomaston ME [19 Aug 1847]
LETERONEAU Jacques & Mary E KEATING at Fayette ME by H LOVEJOY Esq [6 Mar 1851]
LEVEBSELLER Emily Jane & Irvine CALDERWOOD at North Waldo' ME on 21st inst [30 Mar 1848]
LEVENSALER Cyrus & Margaret KALER at Waldoboro ME [12 Feb 1846]
LEWIS Abbe M & Capt Samuel HAINES at Waterville ME [8 Jan 1852]
 Alden & Emeline BUZZELL of Vassalboro ME at Whitefield ME [1 July 1852]
 Alvin B & Caroline PARKER at Waterville ME [3 June 1847]
 Anjenetta & Capt Samuel BLANCHARD of Dresden ME in Hallowell ME at the Cross Roads in Hallowell [7 Sept 1833]
 Arvesta H & Thomas CLARK at Waterville ME [15 Jan 1852]
 Charlotte S & Franklin A DAVIS of Sidney ME at Waterville ME [18 Jan 1849]
 Dickerson Capt & Julia Ann COLE both of Hallowell ME at Augusta ME [13 Jan 1837]
 Frederic W & Harriet E BLAIR at Whitefield ME [17 Feb 1848]
 Hannah E & Augustus L SCAMMON at Biddeford ME [3 Aug 1848]

LEWIS (cont.) Helena & Charles LITTLEFIELD at Brunswick ME [14 Sept 1848]
    Isaiah & Susannah WELLS at Bristol ME [8 Apr 1847]
    Jacob T & Susan H HASKELL at Steuben ME [11 Jan 1844]
    Joseph C & Mary S LEWIS at Cherryfield ME [27 May 1843]
    Julia A & Capt James L BROWN at Newburyport MA on 24 Oct "With the above notice we received the printer's fair proportion of the bridal loaf for which the parties have our thanks. At this season of the year every thing is giving away to the SCARLET & YELLOW LEAF hue but we think Miss Julia the fair bride chose quite the pleasantest way to be DONE BROWN" [16 Nov 1848]
    Maria & John Mariner at Brunswick ME [18 Dec 1835]
    Mary Ann & Seth MAXIM 2nd both of Wayne ME on Sunday last by Rev FULLER of Winthrop ME [28 Mar 1834]
    Mary S & Joseph C LEWIS at Cherryfield ME [27 May 1843]
    Samuel H P of Portland ME & Dolly S LUNT of Bowdoinham ME by Orrington LUNT Esq at Bowdoinham ME on Sun Morning last [16 Oct 1838]
    Samuel of West Gorham ME & Nancy GRAY at Hallowell ME [7 Dec 1848]
    Sarah B & Capt Gustavus O WEST of Hallowell ME at Vassalboro ME [8 Apr 1833]
    Stacy B Capt of Galveston TX & Mary Paulina d/o Capt James BLISH of Hallowell ME at New York City NY [23 Oct 1845]
    Susan A & Joseph E STEVENS in West Waterville ME [11 Sept 1845]
    Sylvia of Buckfield ME & Stephen D PRATT by John DENNETT Esq at Paris ME [13 Feb 1845]
    T S of Waterborough ME & Olive J BROWN at Buxton ME [15 Mar 1849]
    William M of Skowhegan ME & M F MORRILL at Farmington ME [28 May 1846]
    William & Elizabeth BOYD at Wayne ME on Sun eve last by Rev Daniel FULLER of Winthrop ME [9 May 1834]

LIBBY - LIBBEY Abial, M.D., & Harriet L BLAIR at Richmond ME [8 Jan 1852]
    Abigail & Isaac S LUNT both of Gray ME at North Yarmouth ME by E G BUXTON Esq on 10th inst [14 Oct 1847]
    Abner C of Limerick ME & Lucy S FELT of Greenwood ME at Buxton ME [6 Dec 1849]
    Andrew & Aroline [sic] E JONES both of Union ME at Searsmont ME [18 June 1846]
    Ann & Seth LEAVIT at Gray ME by Ephraim LAWRENCE Esq [2 Oct 1835]
    Asa D & Clementine A STICKNEY both of (Augusta) ME at Hallowell ME on 8th Apr [18 Apr 1850]
    Asa & Mary E HILDRETH at Gardiner ME [9 Jan 1851]
    Betsey V & Isaac LIBBY both of Paris ME at Mechanic Falls ME [9 Aug 1849]
    Betsey & Mr B F CLARK at Belfast ME [29 Mar 1849]
    Bradbury & Nancy B WEEKS both of (Augusta ME) at Sidney ME on 19th inst [26 Nov 1846]
    Caroline M & Jason PLUMMER both of Gorham ME at Windham ME [7 May 1846]

LIBBY (cont.) Charles J of Cornville ME & Martha Ann ATWOOD of Skowhegan ME at Showhegan [3 Oct 1840]
    Charles & Lucy Ann DOAN of Durham ME at Pownal ME [27 Jul 1848]
    Charles & Lucy Ann DOANE at North Pownal ME [4 Sept 1845]
    David H & Sarah M HOOK at Belfast ME [5 Apr 1849]
    Eliza of Pownal ME & William TUFTS of New Gloucester ME at Pownal ME [17 June 1836]
    Elizabeth A & Joseph SIPHERS at Gardiner ME [10 May 1849]
    Elizabeth B & Samuel W JACK at Richmond ME [21 Mar 1850]
    Elizabeth T of Belgrade ME & Howard M SAWTELLE of Sidney ME at Waterville ME [27 June 1844]
    Ephraim & Charlotte CUTTER at Pownal ME [2 May 1844]
    Eunice & William B DINGLEY at Richmond ME [4 Oct 1849]
    Frances J of Brunswick ME & Mr F A DeCRENEY of Portland ME at Portland ME [14 Jan 1847]
    Frances Mrs & Robert PIKE at Eastport ME [23 Dec 1847]
    Franklin & Ellen M STURGIS at Vassalboro ME on 25th inst [30 Dec 1847]
    Frederick W & Adalaide COLBY at East Thomaston ME [6 Sept 1849]
    Hanson of Lowell MA & Elizabeth SHERMAN at Monson MA?/ME? [17 June 1847]
    Isaac & Betsey V LIBBY both of Paris ME at Mechanic Falls ME [9 Aug 1849]
    John R of Monmouth ME & Eveline R KEENE at Leeds ME [13 Sept 1849]
    Josiah & Frances HUSSEY at Turner ME on 13 Apr by C T RICHARDSON Esq [6 May 1843]
    Lee of Turner ME & Sarah C RICHARDS of East Livermore ME by Rev C FULLER at Wayne ME on 4th Apr [22 Apr 1852]
    Margaret & William MURROW at Gardiner ME [30 Nov 1833]
    Mary E of Portland ME & Capt John D CARLISLE of Richmond ME at Providence RI [7 Mar 1850]
    Mary & Major PLAISTED at Gorham ME [28 June 1849]
    Noah S & Hannah S RICHARDSON at Litchfield ME [21 May 1846]
    Olive A & Abner TUTTLE Jr all North Yarmouth ME on 7th inst by E G BUXTON Esq [19 Mar 1842]
    Olive A & Mr G BOWDITCH at Limerick ME [21 Sept 1848]
    R W & Betsey PHILLIPS both of Avon ME at Phillips ME [29 Nov 1849]
    Samuel W of Litchfield ME & Lovina HOPKINS formerly of Peru ME at Winthrop ME [12 Dec 1844]
    Sarah of Corinna ME & Benjamin W SHAW of Garland ME at Corinna ME [4 Mar 1843]
    Sarah & Samuel BENNETT of this town (Augusta) ME at Litchfield ME [4 Oct 1849]
    Sewall & Maria COLLINS at Gardiner ME [1 Jul 1847]
    Shirley & Mary A MITCHELL at Gardiner ME [18 Dec 1845]
    Susan & Capt John DUNCAB at Lincolnville ME [13 May 1852]
    William F of Portland ME & Mary A JOHNSON at New Gloucester ME [23 May 1844]
    William T of Lowell MA & Martha K ADAMS at Buxton ME [24 Sept 1846]
LIGHT Ann M & William VINAL at Hope ME on May 18 [29 May 1851]
    Gardner of Worcester MA & Angelica CLOUSE at Union ME [30 Apr 1846]
LILLY Henrietta & James HAGER Esq at Richmond ME [28 Dec 1848]

LILLY (cont.) Thomas & Angeline CLARK by Rev Mr ALLEN at (Augusta) ME on Sunday evening last [9 Mar 1848]
    Victoria of Dresden ME & B F WHITE of Gardiner ME at Dresden [25 Sept 1845]

LIMIKEN David & Rachael R WHEELER both of St George ME at Thomaston ME [23 Jan 1845]

LINCH William & Elice DONNELL at Bath ME by Rev Mr GILMAN [2 Jan 1841]

LINCOLN Angeline & Mellen ROBINSON at Litchfield ME [26 Oct 1839]
    Caroline T of Searsmont ME & William G LINSCOTT of Orono ME at Searsmont ME [26 Aug 1836]
    Eben Jr & Eliza A YOUNG at Bath ME [8 Apr 1836]
    Edward Capt & Roxy SMITH at Nobleboro ME [29 May 1838]
    Eliza Jane & Elisha CUTTS at Milo ME on 27 Aug [14 Sept 1848]
    Elizabeth B & George F TALBOT Esq of East Machias ME at Dennysville ME [13 Nov 1851]
    Emeline B & Asa WALKER Esq, editor of the *Bangor Gazette*, at Bangor ME [20 Aug 1846]
    Hannah M & Mr S W JOHNSTON of Bremen ME at Wiscasset ME [26 Mar 1846]
    Helen M & Capt William A MATTHEWS Jr at Eastport ME [18 Apr 1850]
    Jesse of Eastham MA & Hannah WOODARD of Bowdoin ME at Topsham ME [20 Apr 1848]
    Joshua & Martha AUSTIN at Newcastle ME [15 Oct 1846]
    Lucy P of Searsmont ME & Joseph J BURR of Brewer ME at Bangor ME [1 May 1851]
    M E Miss & John G RICHARDSON at Brunswick ME [1 June 1848]
    William of Corinna ME & Mary E LABREE at Dexter ME [19 Apr 1849]

LINDSAY Martha J O & Stephen M STURTEVANT at Milo ME on Aug 6th [17 Aug 1848]

LINDSEY Jeremiah & Caroline PIERCE at Prospect ME [9 Feb 1839]
    Novella & James MOULTON of Wayne ME at Leeds ME on 10th inst [14 Oct 1847]
    Sarah F & Robert R HAVENER of Frankfort ME at Thomaston ME [20 May 1847]

LINKFIELD Benjamin & Augusta STINCHFIELD at Skowhegan ME [5 Apr 1849]

LINN Hannah S & Henry B COOMBS at Windsor ME [27 Apr 1848]
    David Jr & Mrs Betsey WHITE at this city (Augusta) ME on 4th Apr by Anson CHURCH Esq [11 Apr 1850]

LINNEKIN Mary E F & Charles MURRAY of Boothbay ME at Belfast ME [21 Mar 1850]

LINNELL Elisha & Emily S COUNCE both of Thomaston ME at New York NY [30 Sept 1847]
    John W & Rebecca WHITCOMB all of Mercer ME by Hartley KIMBALL Esq [25 May 1839]
    Roby K of Belgrade ME & Charlotte G CLARK at Augusta ME [18 Feb 1833]

LINSCOTT Asenath & Newell COOK at Jefferson ME [1 Jan 1852]
    A & Rebecca SNOW at Harpswell ME [10 Aug 1848]

LINSCOTT (cont.) Caroline H of Windsor ME & Ezekiel KINISTON of Liberty ME [12 Sept 1837]
  Isaac Capt & Mary WOODWARD at Brunswick ME [10 Sept 1846]
  Samuel of Damariscotta ME & Susan CHANEY of Whitefield ME at East Pittston ME [1 Feb 1849]
  William G of Orono ME & Caroline T LINCOLN of Searsmont ME [26 Aug 1836]
LINSCOTTE Eliza J & Nathaniel STANWOOD at Brunswick ME [23 Dec 1847]
LIPSCOTT John & Susan HOOTON at Portland ME [23 May 1844]
LITCHFIELD Electro A & Herman MERO at Union ME [24 Dec 1846]
  Horace & Hannah E NEWCOMB at Bath ME [23 Apr 1846]
  Lewis K of Rollinsford NH & Sarah B PAGE of Winthrop ME at Salmon Falls NH [7 August 1851]
  Nelson P B of Lewiston ME & Maria RINES of Skowhegan ME at Bloomfield ME [18 Nov 1847]
LITTLE Augusta P, d/o Doty LITTLE Esq, & Woodbridge ODLIN Esq of Exeter NH at Castine ME [24 Oct 1844]
  Eleanor M & Zina HYDE Esq of Bath ME at Boston MA [2 May 1840]
  Elizabeth A & James H CUNNINGHAM at Pittston ME [27 June 1844]
  Elizabeth M T & George H AMBROSE at Lewiston Falls ME [28 Oct 1847]
  Elizabeth R & Charles M NORTON at Bath ME [10 June 1847]
  Lucy T, d/o Doty LITTLE Esq, & Rev A A PHELPHS of Boston MA at Castine ME [24 Oct 1844]
  Phebe W & W B HOLMS Esq of Alfred ME at Castine ME [25 Mar 1836]
  Rachel Ann & Reed NICHOLS at Bath ME [5 Feb 1846]
  Rhoda & William B HILTON at Searsmont ME on 16 Oct [2 Nov 1848]
  Thomas B Esq of Lewiston Falls ME & Mrs Fanny B TOWNE at Bethel ME [16 Jan 1845]
  Thomas Esq & Elizabeth L SPRINGER at Augusta ME [13 Nov 1845]
  William S & Lousa H PERRY by Rev E B WEBB at (Augusta) ME on 21st Mar [1 Apr 1852]
LITTLEFIELD Ann E & Daniel ALLEN at Monmouth ME [18 Jul 1837]
  Caroline P of Providence RI & Clement WEBSTER Jr, editor of the *County Herald* at Saco ME on 15th inst by Mr Norton [25 May 1839]
  Charles of Providence RI & Helena LEWIS at Brunswick ME [14 Sept 1848]
  Charles & Mary S BOWLEY at Hartland ME [7 Mar 1850]
  Charles & Rebecca P TUPPER at Belgrade ME [23 Feb 1844]
  Charlotte N & Ivory JONES at Bangor ME [13 May 1836]
  Diana & James R DOWNING both of Cambridge ME at Harmony ME [15 Jan 1846]
  Diantha, d/o the late A Z LITTLEFIELD of Skowhegan ME, & George W TYLER at Sheboygan Wisconsin [4 Mar 1847]
  Eli & Sarah A HILL at Biddeford ME [10 Jul 1851]
  Elias & Elbridge PLUMMER at Saco ME [1 Aug 1844]
  Eliza E & Albion K P MACE both of Readfield ME at Belgrade ME on 1st of Feb by M A CHANDLER Esq [13 Feb 1851]
  Elizabeth W & Thomas WHITTEN of Augusta ME at Hallowell ME [22 Feb 1840]
  Elizabeth & Jonathan LEIGHTON at Skowhegan ME by Rev Obid WILSON [23 Mar 1839]

LITTLEFIELD (cont.) Enoch Esq of Auburn ME & Nancy HAMMOND at Brunswick ME [13 May 1852]
Frederic of Wells ME & Mary A MARTIN at Augusta ME on 18th Aug [28 Aug 1851]
Hannah & Malachi NICKERSON Jr at Belfast ME [21 May 1842]
Ivory of Kennebunk ME & Mary E GRANT at Portsmouth NH [9 Oct 1851]
Joseph & Sylvinia Ann TRACE at Durham ME [20 Apr 1848]
Kingman & Christiana STARBIRD at Hartland ME [3 Apr 1851]
Lucretia G & Asa GETCHELL at Winslow ME [21 Feb 1850]
Mary Ann of Brunswick ME & Francis W SHAW of Bloomfield ME at Skowhegan ME [28 Nov 1837]
Mary C & Erastus W BAILEY at Foxcroft ME [6 May 1852]
Nancy T of Saco ME & Francis E HILL, M.D., of Biddeford ME at Providence RI on Jan 1st [16 Jan 1851]
Nathaniel & Olive E PITTS at Hallowell ME [19 Feb 1846]
Sarah & Charles C WEBBER at Kennebunk ME both of York ME [10 Oct 1837]
Thomas Col of Auburn ME & Lowny READ of Sangerville ME [4 Mar 1843]
Walter R & Mary E ADAMS [19 Sept 1844]
William B & Mrs Eunice NORCROSS at Hallowell ME by Rev E THURSTON [3 Apr 1845]
LIVERMORE Joseph M & Ellen J BUCKNAM at Eastport ME [18 Mar 1847]
Mary Jane & Elbridge HIGGINS of Richmond ME at Brunswick ME [25 Feb 1847]
LOBDELL Mary of Portland ME & Samuel M JENINGS of Wayne ME at Portland ME on 15th inst by Rev W PIERCE [2 Apr 1842]
LIVINGSTON Asa C & Dorothy BUTLAND at Saco ME [1 Jan 1846]
LOCKE Arthur D & Louisa NORCROSS at Augusta ME on Jan 23 [6 Feb 1851]
Christina R & Henry S PARKER of Belfast ME at Mt Vernon ME on 29 Dec by Rev EDGECOMB [2 Jan 1851]
Daniel P & Nancy MOSHIER both of Augusta ME on 13th inst at Belgrade ME by J DAVIES Esq [25 Feb 1847]
Elbridge W of New Gloucester ME m Elizabeth A WHITING, recently Principal of one of the Public Schools in Winthrop ME, & d/o Calvin WHITING Esq at Portland ME by Rev C C BURR [16 May 1840]
Elizabeth S & Henry W DECKER at Hallowell ME on Weds evening last by Rev Mr COLE [18 Apr 1837]
Hosea B of Hallowell ME & Elizabeth W PILLSBURY d/o William at Augusta ME on Weds last by Rev William A DREW [19 Sept 1844]
Joseph Gen of Bloomfield ME & Susan CURRIER of Hallowell ME at Augusta ME on Jan 21 [29 Jan 1846]
Joseph H of Boston MA formerly of Hallowell ME & Martha B BRADFORD at Livermore ME [25 Sept 1845] & [4 Sept 1845]
Mary S & Samuel WOODS at (Augusta) ME on 29 Feb [11 Mar 1852]
Nancy & Jacob B WILBUR at Newcastle ME [13 May 1852]
Pamelia & Joseph T KIDDER formerly of Norridgewock ME at West Cambridge MA [11 Nov 1847]
Simon J & Lydia A TIBBETTS at Saco ME [3 June 1847]
Thomas S of Temple ME & Experience B ADAMS of Farmington ME at Temple ME [22 July 1852]

LOCKE (cont.) Timothy H of Saco ME & Elizabeth L NOBLE of Parsonsfield ME at Newfield ME [8 Feb 1844]
LOGAN John W & Margaret SARGENT both of Searsport ME at Belfast ME [24 June 1847]
LOMBARD Ann & Winthrop P FILES at Gorham ME [16 May 1837]
    Diana & Philander MORTON of Hallowell ME by Rev David THURSTON at Readfield ME [24 Oct 1834]
    George H of Saco ME & Jane KIMBALL of Denmark ME at Biddeford ME [26 Feb 1852]
    Hannah P of Augusta ME & Rev John A HENRY of Skowhegan ME at Augusta ME [1 Oct 1842]
    Isaac & Bethena S MERRILL at Auburn ME [12 Feb 1852]
    Joseph & Almira SMITH at Thomaston ME [18 June 1846]
    Martha A & James P CRASH both of Windham ME at Westbrook ME [21 May 1846]?
    Mary Ann & Eri WILLIS at Augusta ME [12 Sept 1837]
    Rosilla & Edwin BARRETT at Weld ME [17 June 1852]
    Roxana B & David G PLUMMER of Portland ME at Readfield ME on 11th inst [19 March 1846]
    William H & Sarah J MILLS Belgrade ME at (Augusta) ME on Nov 24 [7 Dec 1848]
LONG Bethsheba & Isaac BEARCE of Calais ME at Buckfield ME [17 Apr 1835]
    Mary Jane & Newell WEEKS at Abbot ME [28 Jan 1847]
    Owen & Betsey GILCHREST at St George ME [7 Mar 1840]
    Sylvanus H & Eliza J WORMELL at Thomaston ME [4 May 1848]
LONGFELLOW Albert G of Augusta ME & Frances CARR at Hallowell ME on Dec 25 by Rev Wm A DREW [3 Jan 1850]
    Alex W & Elizabeth C PORTER at Westbrook ME [21 Aug 1851]
    Anne Sophia & Rev Uriah BALKAM at (Augusta) ME at the residence of her step-father Hon Asa REDINGTON [1 Apr 1852]
    Elizabeth in Hallowell ME & Sherburne SLEEPER of Belfast ME on Thurs last by Rev Jonathan COLE [11 Apr 1837]
    George A of Winthrop ME & Eveline M FOSTER at Hallowell ME by Rev MUGFORD [4 Dec 1841]
    Laura L & David S LYON at (Augusta) ME on 1st inst [10 Feb 1848]
    Nathan 2nd of Palermo ME & Sophronia H BROWN of Pittston ME on Thurs eve last by Rev E SEAMMON [25 Sept 1845]
    Sarah Jane & William C DEXTER at Newport ME [16 Jan 1838]
LONGLEY Charles W of Sidney ME & Elizabeth A SWIFT of Wareham MA in Fall River MA [15 Oct 1846]
    Eunice H & George L D BARTON printer both of Paris ME at Boston MA [2 Oct 1851]
    Judith B & Warren RUSSELL both of Madison ME at Skowhegan ME [29 Nov 1849]
    Mary M & Thomas SPRAGUE at Bath ME [31 July 1851]
    Melita of Sidney ME & Hiram SOULE of Waterville ME at Sidney ME [9 Jan 1838]
    Robbins & Elizabeth MONROE at Waterford ME [29 Nov 1849]
    Rufus H of Kingfield ME & Catherine C WILSON at Augusta ME [22 Aug 1834]
    Sarah J & Sanborn DINSMORE at Norridgewock ME [2 May 1840]

LONGLEY (cont.) Theodore W of Sidney ME & Matilda S DELANO of Sidney ME at Augusta ME on 31 Dec by Rev C F ALLEN [9 Jan 1851]
  William P & Aphia W BOARDMAN at Norridgewock ME [3 Jan 1850]
  William S & Mary E BOARDMAN at Norridgewock ME [19 Feb 1852]
LOOK John J & Susan L WENDELL at Farmington ME [10 May 1849]
LOOMIS Alvan of Hallowell ME & Sarah J MARTIN [8 Apr 1847]
  Caroline E & Thomas J SMITH at Hallowell ME [20 Nov 1841]
LOPANS Eliza W & Capt Sullivan WEBSTER at Boston MA [8 Aug 1840]
LORD A N & Lydia Y DAMREN all of Belgrade ME [8 May 1835]
  Abigail & Sewall C WHITTIER at Mt Vernon ME on 10 inst [16 Nov 1839]
  Alvah of Athens ME & Louisa WALKER of Solon ME [27 Aug 1846]?
  Ann & Norris KENNEY of South Manchester CT at West Gardiner ME [11 Sept 1851]
  Augustine of Hallowell ME & Mehitable MELVIN at Auburn NH [6 Aug 1846]
  Cyrus & Ann CARROLL at Lewiston ME [19 Aug 1852]
  Daniel & Sarah BLACKWELL at West Waterville ME on New Year's Day [8 Jan 1846]
  Edwin Capt of Ellsworth ME & Almira DODGE at Bluehill ME [26 August 1847]
  Elbridge G & Charlotte WRIGHT at Bangor ME on 20th ult [12 Oct 1839]
  Elizabeth G & Gideon BARKER at China ME on 30 Jul [3 Aug 1848]
  Eunice H & Allen D NILES at Hallowell ME on 12th inst by Rev C FULLER [19 June 1845]
  Eunice & Charles LOTHROP by Rev W A Drew at Augusta ME [12 June 1838]
  George & Sarah F THRASHER at Portland ME [20 May 1836]
  H E Miss & Elijah JACKSON at Pittston ME [15 June 1848]
  Hannah Everett adopted d/o Andrew H LORD Esq & Matthias GLYNN at Winthrop ME by Rev THURSTON [21 May 1846]
  Hannah L & Ebenezer CANNON at Gardiner ME [7 Dec 1848]
  Hannah T of Hallowell ME & Capt Joseph C CARTER of the brig *Diana* at Oahu Sandwich Islands on Nov 24 1833 by Rev DIELL [13 June 1834]
  Ivory & Julia Ann JORDAN at Gardiner ME [13 May 1833]
  James H K & Ann R RICH at Bath ME [22 July 1836]
  John 3rd & Catharine P WEEKS at Parsonsfield ME [March 11 1847]
  John F of Kennebunkport ME & C O WENTWORTH at Kennebunk ME [25 Dec 1845]
  John of Limington ME & Abigail MASON at Porter ME [29 Jan 1846]
  Joseph D & Sarah H TODD at Hallowell ME on Thurs eve last by Rev COLE [9 mar 1839]
  Leverett & Martha K DAY at Hallowell ME on Mon 22 inst by Rev COLE [4 Dec 1841]
  Margaret K of Augusta ME & Franklin FOSTER of Hallowell ME by Rev William A DREW at Augusta ME [5 Mar 1842]
  Mark Jr & Sarah Jane MAHONEY at Augusta ME on 22 Dec [2 Jan 1851]
  Martha C & Isaac C WATERHOUSE at Hallowell ME [13 Feb 1851]
  Mary A & William H DAVENPORT of Hallowell ME in Litchfield ME [30 July 1846]
  Mary E & Constantine BATES 2nd in Augusta ME on 11 March by Rev H HAWES [22 Mar 1849]

LORD (cont.) Mathew of Bridgeport CT & Jane SCOFIELD of Wilton ME at NY on Apr 5 [8 May 1835]
    Nancy & George B HOPKINS at Ellsworth ME [12 Dec 1840]
    Reuel W & Hannah E HUTCHINS at Hallowell ME [1 Mar 1849]
    Sarah M & Henry K BAKER editor of the *Free Press and Advocate* at Hallowell ME [11 Dec 1835]
    Susan D & Capt Charles THOMPSON at Kennebunkport ME [3 Apr 1838]
    Thomas N & Mary E TUPPER in Hallowell ME on 3rd inst by Rev THURSTON both of Winthrop ME [18 Sept 1835]

LORING Almira & Isaac NASH of Calais ME in Perry ME [24 Dec 1846]
    Asa T & Adelia PATTEN in Phippsburg ME by Rev Asa T LORING Pastor of Congregational Church [10 Apr 1845]
    Charles merchant & Sarah FALES in Thomaston ME [29 July 1833]
    Delia Ann P & Capt Leonard HATCH in North Yarmouth ME [30 Sept 1847]
    Elizabeth C & George D FISKE of Sacramento City CA at Boston MA on 12th Jul by Rev Dr ADAMS [7 August 1851]
    George A of Richmond ME & Sarah S WYMAN of Boothbay ME in Lexington ME [4 Jan 1849]
    Hannah & Dennis PAGE in Pownal ME [22 Feb 1844]
    James B & Jane RICHARDSON in St George ME [7 Mar 1840]
    Richmond Jr Capt & Sarah RING at North Yarmouth ME [2 May 1834]
    Sarah C & Mr H O BURLEIGH at Guilford ME [6 Jan 1848]

LOTHROP Ansel of Belfast ME & Ruth A BOLAND in Damariscotta ME [24 Apr 1845]
    Benjamin of Canton ME & Abigail WHITNEY at Lisbon ME [7 Mar 1834]
    Betsey & Capt Joshua TURNER at Leeds ME on Wed 28th inst [26 Oct 1833]
    Charles & Eunice Augusta LORD at Augusta ME by Rev W A DREW [12 June 1838]
    David F of Leeds ME & Caroline S MORSE in Lisbon ME [17 Dec 1846]
    Joseph L of Mt Vernon ME & Cordelia F HIGHT at Norridgewock ME [5 Oct 1848]
    Lucius L & Affiah JORDAN at Webster ME on 4 May 1851 by Jesse Davis Esq [15 May 1851]
    Solomon L & Hannah TURNER in Leeds ME [2 May 1840]
    Thomas W & Sophia M BECKETT in Belfast ME [25 June 1846]

LOUGEE Clara S & Thomas W BROWN of Brownfield ME at Parsonsfield ME [17 Apr 1851]

LOUD Robert Capt & Betsey GATES in Bristol ME [29 Feb 1844]
    William M & Lucy Ann STANTIALL at Richmond ME [22 Mar 1849]

LOUIS Albion K & Caroline B TRULL at Bath ME [5 July 1849]

LOVEITT David & Betsey COBB at Cape Elizabeth ME [6 May 1836]

LOVEJOY Almira & Nehemiah ELLIS of Augusta ME at Sidney ME [31 Oct 1834]
    Ann & Wallace McKENNEY at Augusta ME [15 Aug 1840]
    Anna L T & Edwin E UPHAM of Readfield ME on 14th inst by Rev Wm TILLY at Sidney ME [21 May 1846]
    Edwin P & Elvina ROBBINS at East Thomaston ME [7 Aug 1838]
    Fidelia of Salem ME & George B COLLINS at Phillips ME [18 Mar 1847]
    Helen A & Leonards BENNER at Rockland ME [1 Jul 1852]

LOVEJOY (cont.) Henry of Sidney ME & Cynthia CARLTON of Gardiner ME by Rev THURSTON [21 Mar 1844]
Hiram of Greenwood ME & Elizabeth P WITT at Norway ME [23 Jan 1845]
John of W Newbury MA m Fanny L SMILEY at Sidney ME on May 21 by Rev William TILLEY [29 May 1851]
Joseph W & Adeline JONES at Dixfield ME [8 Jul 1843]
Maria F & H G O MORRISON Esq at Fayette ME [16 Oct 1841]
Mary Angeline & George D CRAIG at East Boston MA [18 Mar 1852]
Mary Ann & John F NUTE at Sebec ME [17 Jan 1850]
S I & Mary A CHANDLER both of Thomaston ME [13 Feb 1841]
S W Miss & Mr A S KIMBALL at Fayette ME [28 Sept 1848]
Sarah & M GRANT at Sidney ME by John HAM Esq [22 Oct 1842]
Sewell C & Pamelia PAGE at Sidney ME [5 Feb 1846]
V R of Gardiner ME & Abigail WHARF at Litchfield ME [21 Jan 1833]
Van Rensselaer of Gardiner ME & Rosanna BABB at Boston MA [8 Feb 1849]
William H & Sarah F BOVEY at Bath ME [4 Dec 1851]
William of Vassalboro ME & Caroline CROSS at Augusta ME [15 Oct 1846]

LOVELAND James & Mary BERRY at Brighton ME [29 Apr 1836

LOVELL Deelsa & James M MOORE both of Gardiner ME at Vienna ME on Dec 2 by T C NORRIS Esq [11 Dec 1851]
H H Capt of Barnstable MA & Sophronia BULFINCH at Waldoboro ME [6 Feb 1851]
Jesse B & Rebecca OLIVER at Phipsburg ME [10 Sept 1846]
Sewell of Abbot & E COOK at Palmyra ME [27 May 1847]

LOVERING Charles A of Augusta ME & Frances J CARR at Hallowell ME [25 Mar 1847]
John & Priscilla C WOOD d/o Dea Enoch W in Winthrop ME by Rev Josiah HOUGHTON on Apr 2nd [10 Apr 1835]
Louisa eld d/o John L Esq sheriff of Aroostook Co ME & Ebenezer C BLAKE of Augusta ME at Houlton Aroostook Co ME on 25 ult [13 May 1843]

LOVETT Joseph of Kirkland ME & Paulenah RIDLEY of Wayne ME [15 Mar 1849]
Margaret E & Gerry AVERILL at Portland ME [25 Apr 1844]
Susan J of Nobleboro ME & Wilson C BURNS at Bremen ME [7 Oct 1847]

LOVITT Emily E & David MOORE at Pittston ME [5 Jan 1849]

LOW Elijah of Bangor ME & Julia Ann LEMONT at Bath ME [4 Apr 1834]
Eliza A & Charles HAINS at Winthrop ME on 21st Mar [25 Mar 1852]
Ephraim Jr of Mercer ME & Hannah OSBORN of Rome ME at Smithfield ME [26 Nov 1846]
George H of North Yarmouth ME & Abigail WINSLOW of Cumberland ME [15 Apr 1836]
Greenfield & Mrs Harriet BACON at Lincoln ME [3 Aug 1848]
Greenlief S of Vassalboro ME & Ann R SMILEY at Sidney ME [28 Mar 1844]
Ira H & Ellen CAFFREY at Waterville ME [11 Feb 1847]
Laura S & Richard STEWART 2nd of Gardiner ME at Winthrop ME on 12 inst [26 Sept 1837]
Martha E & Calvin PERCY of Boston MA at Bath ME [30 Oct 1841]

LOW (cont.) Nehemiah of Berwick ME & Sarah E ROBERTS at Somersworth NH [20 Aug 1846]
 Silas S of Bangor ME & Ann Elizabeth HALL at Thomaston ME [1 Apr 1843]
 Soloman & Olive R HILL at Norridgewock ME [26 Feb 1836]
LOWE Edward C & Mary P BRIDGE at Brunswick ME [8 May 1845]
 Ellen & Lorenzo D HARRIS at Eastport ME [15 May 1845]
LOWELL A Esq of East Machias ME & Louisa PRESCOTT at Farmington ME [19 Nov 1850]
 Albert Maj of Concord ME? & Abba REED of Madison ME at Fairfield ME [21 Feb 1850]
 Araline & Sidney LUDDEN of Lincoln ME at Lee ME by Shepherd BEAN Esq [5 Aug 1852]
 Caroline B & Chas FOSTER of Boston ME at East Machias ME [5 July 1849]
 Charles L Esq of Rockland ME & Georgia C BERRY at Thomaston ME [12 June 1851]
 Charles & Theodate LANG [note paper reported groom as "Caarles" at Saco ME [10 Aug 1848]
 Eliza & V C HANSON at Windham ME [1 Apr 1836]
 Elizabeth ae 17 & Daniel RANDALL ae 50 at Ripley ME after a courtship of 24 hrs [29 July 1833]
 Elizabeth & Gen Henry SEWALL at Augusta ME [14 Sept 1833]
 Ellen M & Moses G DOW of Norway ME at Portland ME [20 Jun 1844]
 G H of Gardiner ME & Nancy P GRAY of Bowdoinham ME at Waldoboro ME [19 Feb 1846]
 Harrison Hon & Mrs Eliza D COLE at Biddeford ME [7 Dec 1848]
 Jane & Heman WHIPPLE at Solon ME [13 Jul 1848]
 John C & Celina SMITH at Bath ME [28 Aug 1845]
 Joshua B Esq of Farmington ME & Hannah C BURBANK at Freeman ME [13 Mar 1851]
 Lois H of Farmington ME & Martin K BAILEY of Cohasset ME at Farmington ME [17 July 1841]
 Louisa of Saco ME & Capt Thomas B WILLETT of Brunswick ME at Saco ME [14 Jan 1847]
 Lydia J & Elijah COUILLARD, printer at Bangor ME [6 Nov 1845]
 Mark of Lewiston ME & Alma E BURBANK at Bethel ME [28 Jan 1847]
 Mary S & William S DORR both of Bucksport ME at Frankfort ME [28 Jan 1847]
 Miriam & Edmond W SHAW of Portland ME at Minot ME [5 Feb 1839]
 Nathaniel H of Windham ME & Mary P ALLEN of Augusta ME at Augusta ME [13 Nov 1845]
 Reuben H & Nancy A MORGAN at East Thomaston ME [13 Apr 1848]
 Simeon H & Julia CANIDA at Waterville ME [4 Apr 1840]
 Simon H & Julia CANADA at Waterville ME [11 Apr 1840]
 Thomas ae 70 & Lucinda CORLISH ae 20 at Dixmont ME [20 Sept 1833]
 Thomas & Dorcas MERRILL at Saco ME [26 Feb 1852]
 Timothy B & Wealthy S BRIGGS at Dover ME [5 Sept 1844]
 Vesta & Dr Alexander BURBANK of Shelburne (MA? VT? NH?) at Lewiston ME [29 Apr 1847]
 William of Wiscassett ME & Harriet N LADD of Edgecomb ME at Baltimore MD [8 Nov 1849]

LOWELL (cont.) William W of Dover ME & Fidelia COFREN of Boston MA at Bangor ME [13 June 1844]
    William & Deborah JOHNSON at Winthrop ME on Thanksgiving Evening by Rev David THURSTON [4 Dec 1841]
LOWETT Sarah W & J BREWER of Charlotte ME at Perry ME [12 June 1845]
LOWGER Robert J & Malinda A KING at Hallowell ME [16 Mar 1848]
LOYD Eleanor & William BROWN both of Deer Island (part of Harrington Washington Co ME) at Eastport ME [22 Jan 1846]
LUCE Alonzo A of Wayne ME & Almira McNEAR of Boston MA at Wayne ME on Dec 2 by Rev B H STINCHFIELD [9 Dec 1843]
    Caroline of Winthrop ME & Nathaniel T TALBOT Esq of Camden ME at the Congregational meeting house in Winthrop ME on Sun last by Rev David THURSTON [23 Sept 1843]
    Charlotte L & William K STORY at Readfield ME [14 June 1849]
    Cordelia C & James J PRESCOTT at Readfield ME [9 Dec 1847]
    Daniel C & Lucy Ann LAKE at New Sharon ME on the 1st inst [17 Oct 1840]
    Emily A & Isaiah RICHARDS at New Vineyard ME [27 Apr 1848]
    Gorham A & Sabrina JOY on Wed morning by Rev David THURSTON [22 July 1833]
    Huldah & William BURNS at Union ME [20 June 1844]
    Leonard of Industry & E N SPRAGUE at Farmington ME [14 Nov 1844]
    Mary A formerly of Readfield ME & Abner J BLANCHARD of Boston MA at Portland ME [4 Mar 1847]
    Mary & Job MORSE at New Sharon ME [10 Feb 1848]
    Orin & Elenor C ROWELL in Livermore ME [5 Dec 1837]
    Philena & Sanborn L VILES of Industry ME at North Anson ME [15 Jul 1852]
    Thomas of Hampden ME & Mary R DOUGLAS at Belfast ME [25 Jul 1844]
    Thomas W of New Vineyard ME & Mary A STAPLE at Temple ME [22 July 1852]
    William A & Hannah B COPELAND of Corinna ME in Exeter ME [8 Feb 1840]
LUCY Elmira & William BISHOP of Belfast ME at Union ME [2 Aug 1849]
LUDDEN Sidney of Lincoln ME & Araline LOWELL at Lee ME on July 25 by Shepherd BEAN Esq [5 Aug 1852]
LUDWIG Joseph & Sabra MOODY at Waldoboro ME [27 Nov 1838]
LUDWIN Joseph W of Camden ME & Catharine S POST at Thomaston ME [22 Oct 1842]
LUFKIN Eliza Ann & David N CUSHMAN of Norway ME at Pownal ME [8 Nov 1849]
    Jacob of Phillips ME & Clarissa MOULTON of Madrid ME by Joseph DOW Esq at Phillips ME [7 Jan 1847]
    Jacob of Rumford ME & Lucy ADAMS at Farmington ME [11 Dec 1851]
    Moses & Hannah VIRGIN at Rumford ME [18 Mar 1833]
    Naomi & Nathan WITHAM in Chesterville ME [7 Mar 1837]
    Nathaniel & Sarah HANSON by Rev C HOBART at North Yarmouth ME [19 Mar 1842]

LUMBARD Eliza H & William OLIVER both of Belgrade ME by J SPRINGER Esq at Augusta ME [21 Mar 1844]

LUNT Abraham R Rev of Freeport ME & Alice A CHASE in Brunswick ME [22 Aug 1844]

    Almira L & James T AUSTIN at Brunswick ME [6 Dec 1849]

    Ann M & D M GAMMON at Litchfield ME [22 Nov 1849]

    Caroline M & Dr George F MELLEN at Saco ME on Apr 6th [15 Apr 1852]

    Dolly S of Bowdoinham ME & Samuel H P LEWIS of Portland ME on Sun Morning last in Bowdoinham ME by Orrington LUNT Esq [16 Oct 1838]

    Elisha & Charlotte DAY of Durham ME at Brunswick ME [25 Nov 1847]

    Hannah G & George READ at Bangor ME [1 Oct 1842]

    Isaac S & Abigail LIBBEY both of Gray ME at Yarmouth ME on 10 inst by E G BUXTON Esq [14 Oct 1847]

    James Capt of Freeport ME & Hester A MORSE at Brunswick ME [30 Sept 1847]

    John C of Oxford ME & Lydia P COBB at Otisfield ME [16 May 1844]

    John & Angeline WITHAM at Bangor ME [28 Jan 1847]

    Lydia S of Kennebunk ME & Frederick T HILL of Lyman ME at Kennebunk ME [4 Dec 1845]

    M A d/o Johnson LUNT Esq & Jarvis WILLIAMS of Biddeford ME by Rev JUDD at Augusta ME on Mon Morning last [16 Jan 1845]

    Orrington Esq & Cornelia A GRAY in Bowdoinham ME [29 Jan 1842]

    Rosanna M d/o Wm M REED Esq of Boothbay ME & Edmund PEARSON merchant of Waterville ME at Boothbay ME on 23nd inst by Rev David CUSHMAN [27 Feb 1841]

    Sarah E of Calais ME & William WELLS at Belfast ME [30 Jan 1845]

    William & Lucy JORDAN at Gardiner ME [23 Sept 1836]

LUQUES Orlando & Elizabeth A GOODWIN at Saco ME [6 May 1847]

LYDSTONE Nancy & Hiram SHOREY Esq at Litchfield ME [28 Nov 1844]

LYFORD Aaron S & Harriet L PHILBRICK at Mt Vernon ME on 7th inst by Rev INGRAHAM [27 Nov 1838]

    J Stone & Olive B PATTEN d/o Capt Rob't P of Frankfort ME in Wilton ME on 14th inst by Rev PERHAM [31 Dec 1842]

    Mary J & Isaac M FULLER at Livermore Falls ME [13 Apr 1848]

    Oliver S & Irene MORSE at Livermore ME [10 June 1847]

    Samuel L of Livermore ME & Sarah W ADDISON at Dexter ME [13 July 1839]

    Sarah & Eben PARKER of Foxcroft ME at Sebec ME [22 May 1851]

LYMAN S R Col P M of Portland ME & Christiana BLANCHARD d/o Capt S B at Portland ME on Thurs by Rev CHICKERING [13 Aug 1842]

LYNCH Henry & Jane COGAN at Augusta ME on July 11 by Rev PUTNAM [15 July 1852]

    Ruth Ann of Bath ME & Isaac PREBLE of Bowdoinham ME at New York NY [25 Jan 1840]

LYNDE Frances T & Marshall SPAULDING Esq at Norridgewock ME on 9th inst [30 Nov 1848]

    John H of Augusta ME & Mary F JOSSELYN of Augusta ME at Norridgewock ME on Sunday Morning Feb 9th by Rev Josiah PEET [13 Feb 1851]

LYNN Andrew I & Miss M Elizabeth GOOD at Hallowell ME [15 Jan 1852]

LYNN (cont.) David S of Readfield ME & Laura L LONGFELLOW at (Augusta) ME on 1st inst [10 Feb 1848]
Eliza E & Samuel GOULD of Augusta ME at Readfield ME [11 Apr 1844]
Elizabeth of Readfield ME & Capt John JONES at Hallowell ME [2 Jan 1838]
Joseph of Holden & Mary S LAMB of Worcester MA by Rev PEABODY at Worcester on 21st ult [22 May 1838]
Martha & Abner HASKELL by Eld J D WEST at Augusta ME on June 5 [8 July 1852]
Martha & Simon BRAGG at (Augusta) ME [25 May 1848]
Mary Ann & William MILLIKEN Esq of Burnham ME at Gardiner ME [11 Jan 1849]
Nicholas & Cornelia Ann LAMB by Rev FOREST at Winooski VT? [5 June 1838]
Tabor & Sylvia E SANFORD by Rev N GUNNISON at Augusta ME on Oct 29 [7 Nov 1844]
William H of Readfield ME & Maria L SANDFORD at Augusta ME on 29 ult by Rev N GUNNISON [16 May 1844]

- M -

MacDONALD Alexander & Mary H ORMSBY of (Augusta) ME by Rev E H CHAPIN at New York City on 31st Jul [14 Sept 1848]
MacDONALD - see also McDONALD
MACE Adoniram J of Readfield ME & Miss E R CHANDLER at Winthrop ME on 20th Feb by John MAY Esq [6 Mar 1851]
Adoniram Judson & Almira BODGE at Readfield ME [8 Jan 1846]
Albion K P & Eliza E LITTLEFIELD ME both of Readfield ME at Belgrade ME on 1st of Feb by M A CHANDLER Esq [13 Feb 1851]
Amelia & Samuel E BROWN both of Readfield ME at Winthrop ME on 27th Jul [7 August 1851]
William & Abby WADSWORTH of Winthrop ME at Winthrop ME on 29th Feb by Rev MERRIAM [11 Mar 1843]
MacGRATH Ira L & Caroline HOXIE at Fairfield ME [11 Oct 1849]
MACOMBER/MACUMBER A Judson & Lucretia M COOMBS at Belfast ME [16 Mar 1848]
Asa A of Dover ME & Mary T WATSON at Harmony ME by Elder BAILEY of Cornville Somerset Co ME [18 Apr 1844]
Cordelia A & Calvin G HALE of Norridgewock ME at Winthrop ME on 12 Jul [23 Jul 1846]
Ellen M & Joseph JACKSON of Boston MA at Monmouth ME by the Rev DAY [24 Jan 1850]
Elvira H of Readfield ME & Giles STRAW of Garland ME at Readfield ME on Weds evening last by Samuel P BENSON Esq [25 Jan 1840]
George W of (Augusta) ME & Hannah L KALLOCH at Warren ME on 24th Oct by Rev I KALLOCH [1 Nov 1849]
James H of Readfield ME & Jane BILLINGTON of Winthrop ME at Winthrop on Thurs evening last by Samuel P BENSON Esq [25 Jan 1840]
John A & Caroline A WESTON at Durham ME [11 Jun 1846]
Joseph & Mrs Nancy DeWOLF at Bath ME [5 Mar 1842]

MACOMBER (cont.) Julia of (Winthrop ME) & Nathaniel B FROST of Wayne ME [6 Mar 1841]
    L I Mr & Olive B d/o Richard CLAY at Gardiner ME [21 Dec 1833]
    Leander M of Monmouth ME & Lucinda HAMILTON of Webster ME [25 Mar 1847]
    O T of Concordia Parish LA to Deborah R ALEXANDER at Farmington ME [2 Sept 1843]
    Olive & Mr N B NORTON at Gardiner ME [4 Dec 1845]
    Samuel A of Abbot ME & Emily B GATES at Monson ME [29 May 1851]
    William A & Sarah P BALLARD both of Monmouth ME at Hallowell ME [31 Jan 1850]
MACONIC Frances Ann & Walter DOW at Alna ME [3 Jul 1851]
MACY Josiah G of New York NY & Julia S BERRY at Gardiner ME [16 Jul 1846]
MADDOCKS Elizabeth H at Belfast ME & Josiah G MADDOCKS at Hallowell ME [26 Aug 1852]
    Isabel & Lemuel SMITH at Ellsworth ME [23 Sept 1847]
    Joseph G & Elizabeth H MADDOCKS of Belfast ME at Hallowell ME [26 Aug 1852]
MADDOX Eleazer & Maria METCALF at Appleton ME [14 Mar 1844]
    Nathaniel Jr & Jane H TRIPP both of Appleton ME at Belfast ME [10 Aug 1839]
MAGNA John & Harriet MAXIM at Wayne ME on 20th April [8 May 1851]
MAGOON Franklin & Charlotte COOMBS at Durham ME [20 Apr 1848]
    Mary D & Albert GRAY at Sangerville ME [4 Apr 1840]
    Susan L & John A LEEMAN both of Litchfield ME at Fayette ME [14 Aug 1845]
MAGOUN Abigail P & Capt William H DUNCAN at Bath ME [17 Oct 1844]
    George F & Abby Ann HYDE at Bath ME [16 Sept 1847]
MAHLMAN William & Louisa PHELPS at Lubec ME [13 May 1847]
MAHONEY Frances E & Capt Mark WELCH at Northport ME [14 Jan 1847]
    George & Lucinda C BRYANT at Orneville Piscataquis Co ME [7 Aug 1845]
    Sarah Jane & Mark LORD Jr at Augusta ME on 22 Dec [2 Jan 1851]
MAHURIN Hannah R & W A GOULD at Norridgewock ME [30 Nov 1848]
MAIN/MAINE Mary E & Timothy of Brunswick ME at Bath ME [25 Mar 1847]
    Martha E & John BISHOP at Bath ME [30 Sept 1847]
MAINES Lydia R & David WYMAN Jr at Brighton ME [20 Mar 1851]
MAINS Sebeus C Esq of Little Falls NY & Julia O STEVENS of Pittston ME [30 Sept 1843]
MALBAN Nancy H & George W ROBINSON at Skowhegan ME [2 Dec 1847]
MALBON Bradbury R & Abby B FOX at Skowhegan ME [6 Dec 1849]
    Gardiner & Elizabeth ROBINSON at Skowhegan ME [11 Mar 1847]
    Mary H of Skowhegan ME & Moses B MERRILL at Boston MA [11 Feb 1847]
    Salina of Skowhegan ME & Thomas FLANDERS Jr of Cornville ME at Skowhegan ME [17 Aug 1839]
MALCOM James & Philena CUSHING at Phipsburg ME [30 Jul 1846]
MALCOMB Hiram & Sarah PERCY at Phipsburg ME [22 Apr 1836]

MALOON Isaac of Temple ME & Nancy M HOBBS at Farmington ME [11 Jul 1844]
Mary & Isaac BARKER at Belfast ME [19 Oct 1839]
MANLEY Amasa W & Martha J NASON both of (Augusta) ME by Rev Mr GARDNER at Waterville ME [19 Oct 1848]
James S of Norridgewock ME & Caroline SEAWALL d/o Charles S by Rev Benj TAPPAN at Augusta ME [7 Dec 1839]
John & Elizabeth E BITTUES by Rev JUDD on 24 Jun at Augusta ME [1 Jul 1847]
Louisa D C formerly of (Augusta ME) & Solomon CROWELL of Palmyra Wayne Co NY at Canadaigua NY [18 Jan 1844]
Lydia F & Rev A S DUDLEY at Norridgewock ME [7 Dec 1839]
MANN Abigail S & Almond PEABODY at Hampden ME [19 Aug 1836]
Ariel W of Boston MA & Harriet C SANFORD at Hallowell ME [20 Jun 1844]
Charles T formerly of Hallowell ME & Maria Louisa HUGHES of Frankfort KY at Yazoo City MS [26 Jun 1851]
Eunice & Andrew STEELE of Castine ME at Brewer ME [16 Dec 1847]
Harriet of Paris ME & Alanson M CHANDLER of Minot ME at Paris ME [27 Jul 1839]
Hepsebah & Cyrus M CHAPMAN on 31 Jan at Greene ME [27 Feb 1838]
Horace Hon Secretary of the Board of Education & Mary T PEABODY at Boston MA [27 May 1843]
Isaac & Mrs Lydia BRYANT both of Paris ME at Buckfield ME [24 Aug 1848]
Lorinda & George H FARREN at Webster ME [15 Apr 1852] & [29 Apr 1852]
Lucretia & Cyrus BROWN by Rev Jotham SEAWALL at Fayette ME [24 Jan 1834]
Maria & Levi W FENLEY at Portland ME [28 Nov 1844]
William of Slatersville RI & Sarah B METCALF by Rev D THURSTON at Winthrop ME [19 Jul 1849]
MANNERS Mary & William WING at Augusta ME on Feb 16th 1851 [27 Feb 1851]
MANNING Emma d/o Samuel M Esq at Lewiston ME on 14th inst & John BECKETT by Rev W R FRENCH [25 Feb 1847]
George A & Amy P FLETCHER at Augusta ME by Anson CHURCH Esq [25 Oct 1849]
Henry, see Menry
Jane Q & Charles H REYNOLDS at Lewiston ME [25 Mar 1847]
Louisa R & Stuart J PARK of Gardiner ME at Lynn MA [10 Jul 1851]
Melissa M & William BRITT at Camden ME [12 Feb 1852]
Menry ([sic] should be "Henry", see page 437, *Early Families of Newfield, ME* by Ruth Ayers) & Lydia THOMPSON at Newfield ME [1 Feb 1844]
R H merchant of New York NY & Sarah P SWAN only d/o Francis S Esq by Rev Mr KEELER at Calais ME [21 Nov 1840]
Timothy D & Orrinda P WALKER at Thomaston ME [10 Oct 1844]
William Dr & Nancy S ATKINSON at South Berwick ME [20 Jul 1848]
William H & Ruth Ann LABAREE at Whitefield ME [3 May 1849]
MANSFIELD Abigail M of Bath ME & Eleazer M CHIPMAN of Salem in Athol MA [12 Mar 1846]

MANSFIELD (cont.) Daniel H Rev & Lucy M FAIRBANKS of Parkman OH at Thomaston ME [19 Jun 1845]
Ebenezer B of Camden ME & Priscilla B R MANSFIELD of Hope ME at Hope on 13th inst [25 Jul 1837]
Ellen & George D GOWER of New Sharon ME at Hampden CT [25 Apr 1850]
Julia A of Foxcroft ME & Ephraim TURNER of Milo ME [16 Sept 1843]
Mary Jane & Thomas G MARSTON of Nobleboro ME at Washington ME [13 Jun 1844]
Priscilla B R & Ebenezer B MANSFIELD of Camden ME at Hope ME by Rev JONES [25 Jul 1837]

MANSON Harriet S & Isaac B BEAN at Limington ME [26 Jun 1851]
Salmona & Charles HARMON at Saco ME [29 Jul 1847]
Sarah E of Clinton ME & Henry G KENDALL of Canaan ME at Gardiner ME [21 Oct 1847]

MANTER Benjamin F & Aurilla P CORNFORTH at Industry ME [3 Jul 1851]
Peter Capt of Tisbury MA & Rosalinda CASE at Farmington ME [23 Jul 1846]
Rebecca & George CORNFORTH at Industry ME [1 Jan 1846]

MANTOR Betsey H of Industry ME & Jarvis HILTON of Starks ME at North Anson ME [29 Nov 1849]

MANWELL A A Mr & Nancy T CHANDLER both of Winthrop ME at Dover NH on 21st ult [4 Jun 1851]

MARBLE Charles W & Sarah E LAUGHTON at Harmony ME [30 Nov 1848]
Emily F & Charles M COOK at Hallowell ME [16 Nov 1848]
Horace D & Roxana T WOODMAN at Wilton ME [30 Aug 1849]
William of Wilson (surrender of organization in 1849, area divided to Greenville, Shirley & Elliotsville) Piscataquis Co ME & Catharine H BRITT of Shirley ME at Shirley on 22nd of May [18 Jun 1842]

MARCH Ann T Mrs & John T GIBBS editor of the *Dover Gazzette* at Dover NH [9 May 1844]
Caroline & Waldo A PERKINS at Nashua NH on the 11th inst [25 May 1848]
George & Augusta ME A PALMER at Rockland ME [6 Feb 1851]
Harriet N & Chas P CHAPMAN at Starks ME on 28 Dec by L G SMITH Esq [4 Jan 1849]

MARCY Josiah G of New York & Julia S Berry at Gardiner ME [13 Aug 1846]

MARDEN Allen & Paulina FAIRFIELD at China ME [22 Apr 1836]
George & Mary H BENNER at North Palermo ME on 10 Aug by Wm C CARR Esq [19 Aug 1852]
John A & Amanda D WENTWORTH at Bangor ME by George W SNOW Esq [2 Dec 1847]
Marcia M & Thomas R CLEMENTS at Albion ME [27 Jul 1848]
Mary E of Boston MA & Horace STARBIRD at Livermore ME [27 Nov 1851]
Stephen P of West Cambridge MA & Julia A AVERY at Whitefield ME on 23 Sept [27 Sept 1849]
William & Ann LARRABEE at East Thomaston ME [9 Aug 1849]

MAREAN Charles & Louisa MAREAN both of Standish ME at Raymond ME [8 Jul 1847]

MAREAN (cont.) Louisa & Charles MAREAN both of Standish ME at Raymond ME [8 Jul 1847]
MARKS Elbridge W of Penobscot ME & Mary A INGALLS at Bluehill ME [17 Apr 1851]
MARINER John & Maria LEWIS at Brunswick ME [Dec 18 1835]
   Malvina M & Capt John TOOTHAKER at Belfast ME [1 Jul 1852]
MARR Abigail of Augusta ME & William KING of Ripley ME at Litchfield ME [26 Nov 1846]
   Anne Maria & Mr H NORTON at China ME by W PERCIVAL Esq [9 Jan 1851]
   Catharine & Col Henry MARR of Wales ME at Webster ME [16 Dec 1847]
   Dennis of Gardiner ME & Philena BAILEY at Augusta ME [20 Nov 1841]
   Drusilla & Robert JACKSON at Bath ME [31 Jan 1850]
   Elizabeth E of Alna ME & Royal L CHAPMAN of Nobleboro ME at Belfast ME [11 Jul 1846]
   Elizabeth & David SAVAGE at Washington ME [31 Mar 1847]
   Henry Col of Wales ME & Catharine MARR at Webster ME [16 Dec 1847]
   John & Ann MILLER at Cape Elizabeth ME [23 May 1844]
   John & Diana STROUT by Joel SMALL Esq at Wales ME [13 Aug 1846]
   Mary Jane & Warren PIERCE Esq of Boothbay ME at Georgetown ME [13 Mar 1841]
   Nancy & Daniel JOHNSON at Topsham ME [10 Aug 1848]
   Sophia E & Ebenezer S ALLEN at Bath ME [17 Feb 1848]
   William M & Ruth M MAY by Rev David THURSTON at Winthrop ME on Mon eve last [24 Jun 1836]
MARRINER Jedediah & Eliza Ann WOODSIDE both of Brunswick ME at Bath ME [28 Nov 1843]
   Paulina S & Daniel T PURRINGTON at Brunswick ME [7 May 1846]
MARRIOT Elizabeth & William T MARROW [5 Dec 1844]
   Fanny & William POLDEN at Bath ME [15 Jul 1847]
   Mary & John DONNELL at Bath ME [30 Jan 1845]
MARROW see MERROW
MARROW Abigail & Isaac RICHARDS of Monmouth ME at Winthrop ME on Aug 25 by Francis FULLER Esq [6 Sept 1849]
   Caroline M & George G FAIRBANKS at Monmouth ME [25 May 1848]
   Ebenezer & Harriet WADSWORTH at Winthrop ME on Sun morning last by Rev INGRAHAM [8 May 1838]
   William T & Elizabeth MARRIOT at Bath ME [5 Dec 1844]
MARS James F & Lucy TOWNSEND at Brunswick ME [28 Mar 1837]
MARSH Abigail S & Rev Daniel Dana TAPPAN of Winthrop ME at Newburyport MA [25 Jul 1837]
   Abigail & Jonathan C DAGGETT at E Sangerville ME [18 Nov 1843]
   Albert & Caroline W HINKLEY at Hallowell ME [15 Jan 1846]
   James D & Apphia RICKER at Bath ME [10 Aug 1848]
   Louisa & W H FINCH at Eastport ME [11 Nov 1847]
   Mary Ann & Luke HASTINGS both of Bangor ME at Hampden ME [29 Jul 1852]
   Sarah & Samuel W JOHNSON at Hallowell ME [16 May 1844]
MARSHALL Abigail S & Franklin W BERRY of Boston ME at Belfast ME [7 Oct 1847]
   Almira T & Alexander B CURTIS at Swanville ME [28 Jan 1847]

MARSHALL (cont.) Charlotte D & George A CILLEY at Providence RI on 9th Jan [9 Mar 1848]
 Charlotte of Boston MA & Horatio BRIDGE Esq purser United States Navy at New York NY [4 Jun 1846]
 David of Foxcroft ME & Louisa J COY at Sangerville ME [4 Dec 1851]
 E H G of Paris ME & Nancy B CUMMINGS at Norway ME [31 Aug 1848]
 Eleazer D & Eliza J EDWARDS of Otisfield ME at Paris ME [8 Nov 1849]
 Gustavus of Waterville ME & Christiana BOWMAN of Sidney ME at Hallowell ME [9 Jan 1851]
 Harrison & Margaret Ann TOZER at Waterville ME [26 Dec 1840]
 John H & Martha A BANKS at Augusta ME [12 Jul 1849]
 John & Elizabeth HINTON at Augusta ME [30 May 1837]
 Joseph L & Valona JONES at Hebron ME [4 Jun 1851]
 Margaret J & Samuel HANSCOM Jr at Berwick ME [29 Mar 1849]
 Mary N of E Machias ME & William M BLACK of E Thomaston ME at Thomaston ME [10 Aug 1849]
 Nancy & Billings BLAKE of St Stevens New Brunswick Canada at Thomaston ME by Rev MILES at Hallowell ME on 2 Sept [5 Sept 1834]
 Susan Ann of Augusta ME & Joseph McCAUSLAND of Hallowell ME at Thompson CT on Sept 6 [11 Sept 1845]

MARSTERS Andrew Col & Ruth E CARR at Hallowell ME by Rev Eli THURSTON [29 Jan 1842]

MARSON Julia E of Pittston ME & William R KENNEDY at Augusta ME on Feb 25th by Rev JUDD [13 Mar 1851]

MARSTON Abel G of Andover & Ann Matilda WEST at Holmes [14 Jan 1847]
 Benjamin F & Hannah W at Monmouth ME [10 Apr 1841]
 Benjamin of Waterville ME & Sarah A SMITH at Norway ME on 29th ult [20 Apr 1848]
 Chris & Abigail DAVIS at Bath ME [19 Dec 1834]
 David Capt of Fairhaven MA & Mary A CLOUGH at Monmouth ME on Aug 9 [3 Sept 1846]
 Dulcenia D & Amasa MILES of Freeman ME at Farmington ME [11 Jan 1844]
 Eben & Eleanor SMITH at Norway ME [28 Mar 1850]
 Eliza R of Winthrop ME & John TIMLIN of Portland ME at Hallowell ME on 22nd inst by Stewart FOSTER Esq [5 Jun 1845]
 Eliza & Oliver MARSTON at Waterville ME [14 Oct 1843]
 Elizabeth F & Rufus R HAINES at Bath ME [18 Sept 1851]
 Elizabeth J & Simeon POTTER at Gardiner ME [15 Mar 1849]
 Elizabeth M & Charles K MATHEWS at Waterville ME [2 Mar 1848]
 Ellen & Oliver S EDWARDS at Gardiner ME [24 Jun 1847]
 George S & Julia Ann BURR at Gardiner ME [9 Apr 1842]
 Hannah W & Benjamin MARSTON at Monmouth ME [10 Apr 1841]
 Harriet S & George W STICKNEY at Waterville ME [25 May 1848]
 Lucy A & Edwin A MORSE at Bath ME [18 Jul 1844]
 Martha & David G PRIDE at Waterford ME [3 Jun 1852]
 Mary B & Rev Daniel COX of the Maine (Methodist) Annual Conf at Bath ME by Rev J SPAULDING [17 Jun 1845]

MARSTON (cont.) Mary J & Charles R GILMAN of Monmouth ME at Gardiner ME [27 Nov 1845]
Nancy B & H D HASKELL at Livermore ME [18 Jan 1844]
Nancy & Capt Benjamin STINSIN of Bowdoinham ME at Bath ME [7 Aug 1835]
Oliver & Mrs Eliza MARSTON at Waterville ME [14 Oct 1843]
Rachel J & Isaac R RUNNELLS at Lexington [20 Jan 1848]
Roby of Wilton ME & Frances BURGESS at Wayne ME [18 Oct 1849]
Sarah R d/o Daniel M Esq & Andrew H BONNEY of Phillips ME at Mt Vernon ME on 1st inst by Reve EDGECOMB [4 Jun 1846]
Sarah & Franklin FLY at Augusta ME on 29th ult by Rev A MOORE [17 Jul 1845]
Stephen of Mt Vernon ME & Susan E only d/o Samuel WYMAN Esq of New Sharon ME at New Sharon on Tues Sept 29 by Rev J T HAWES [15 Oct 1846]
Thomas G of Nobleboro ME & Mary Jane MANSFIELD at Washington ME [13 Jun 1844]
William H & Octavia PATTEE at Bath ME [2 Jul 1846]
William P & Emeline A RUSSELL at Bath ME [11 Apr 1850]
MARTIN Achsa Jane d/o Wm M Esq & John BENSON M D of at Newport ME [11 Sept 1835]
Clarissa M & Henry W OWEN of Wayne ME at Augusta ME [1 Jul 1833]
Eben G of Poland ME & Meriam BRIGGS of Turner ME at Turner ME on 29th ult by Ezekial MARTIN Esq [3 Apr 1835]
Eliza J & Franklin E OSBORN of Charlestown MA at Augusta ME on 16th Aug by Rev Mr WEBB [28 Aug 1851]
Emily F & Henry HUDLON Esq at Guilford ME [11 Apr 1850]
George W & Olifve RAFFORD at No 11 5th Range Aroostook Co ME on Aug 19 by Edward F GARLAND Esq [13 Sept 1849]
Harriet L & Nathaniel DYER at Poland ME [27 Mar 1851]
Harriet S & Edward PAGE at Bangor ME [26 Jun 1845]
Isabella & Abel WALKER at Lincolnville ME [25 Mar 1836]
John M & Elizabeth A WILLETT at Bristol ME [20 Apr 1848]
John & Anvella ABBOT at Rumford ME by P C VIRGIN Esq all of Rumford ME [6 Mar 1835]
Joshua & Sussannah TRASK at Hallowell ME [4 Feb 1843]
Lydia O & David PARKER at Guilford ME [6 Jan 1848]
Marcia & Dr E L SYLVESTER at East Turner ME [27 Jan 1848]
Marshall P of Portland ME & Sarah HOPKINS at New Sharon ME [11 Feb 1847]
Mary A & Frederic LITTLEFIELD of Wells ME at Augusta ME on 18th Aug [28 Aug 1851]
Mary of Rumford & Phineas STERNS of Bethel ME at Rumford ME by B BARTLETT Esq [6 Mar 1835]
Sarah J & Alvan LOOMIS of Hallowell ME at Winthrop ME [8 Apr 1847]
Seth of New Gloucester ME & Mary MORSE of Winthrop ME on Feb 26 by Rev BARNARD [6 Mar 1845]
Seth of Upper Gloucester ME & Octavia H ROBBINS of Winthrop ME at Winthrop by Rev THURSTON [24 Dec 1842]
Stephen Dea & Lydia BOWKER at Bradford ME [30 Dec 1836]
Thomas H & Mary Ann SMITH at Bangor ME [4 Apr 1837]

MARWICK Albert of Portland ME & Caroline L BAILEY at Pittston ME [2 Oct 1845]
MASON Abigail & John LORD of Limington ME at Porter ME [29 Jan 1846]
    Albert J & Abby ABBOTT at S Berwick ME [27 Jun 1844]
    Almira of Prospect ME & William HINKLEY of Munroe ME at Belfast ME [22 Jan 1836]
    Andrew G of (Augusta) ME & Hannah A MORE by Rev Walter FOSS at Leeds ME [13 Jul 1848]
    Ann & Robert M DAVIS at Fairfield ME [4 Oct 1839]
    Betsey & Martin HARRIS 2nd of Turner ME at Buckfield ME [26 Dec 1844]
    Charlotte & Alonzo PENNEY at Hallowell ME [23 Nov 1833]
    Eliza Ann & Wm HARRIS at Eastport ME [6 Feb 1845]
    G W & Sarah W ALLEN (Augusta) ME at Hallowell ME on 11th inst [21 Dec 1848]
    H E W & Levi WHITNEY at Milltown, both of that place [20 Feb 1849]
    H & Harriet SAUNDERS at Orland ME [21 Sept 1848]
    Hannah C of Augusta ME & James C RUNNELS at Hallowell ME on May 17 by Rev FOSTER [29 May 1851]
    Ira & Mary E TRULL at Bath ME [5 Jul 1849]
    Isaac of Biddeford ME & Frances SMILEY at Augusta ME by JJ Eveleth Esq on 23rd inst [30 Apr 1846]
    Isaac & Hepzibah COULLARD of Chesterville ME at Vienna ME [18 Mar 1847]
    Jeremiah M of Limington ME & Martha WOODMAN at Buxton ME [23 Aug 1849]
    John B of Bethel ME & Mrs Lydia EASTMAN at Waterford ME [9 Aug 1849]
    John Dr & Mrs Caroline R DEXTER at Bangor ME on 2nd inst by Prof SMITH [23 Dec 1847]
    Lydia A & Levi HOXIE at Fairfeild ME [23 Aug 1849]
    Maria A & Clark S EDWARDS at Bethel ME [3 Jan 1850]
    Martha Ann & William DAVIS at Belfast ME [21 March 1850]
    Mary J Mrs & Ambrose H ROBINSON at Rockland ME [1 Jan 1852]
    Mary & Capt David STURGIS Jr of Norridgewock ME at Pittston ME by Rev Darius FORBES of Hallowell [14 Dec 1839]
    Samuel of Augusta ME & Diantha THOMPSON of Bangor ME at Bangor ME [1 Feb 1849]
    Sidney & Chloe Ann DAVIS at Fairfield ME [15 May 1851]
    Sophrona & Moses DAVIS at Hallowell ME [15 Aug 1840]
    Stillman & Esther COX at Parkman ME [21 Nov 1837]
    Thomas Esq of Bangor ME & Ellen COTTRILL at Newcastle ME [15 Oct 1846]
    Thomas & Drusilla HARRIMAN at Orland ME [22 Apr 1847]
    Thomas & Frances A KENNEY at Westbrook ME [18 Jun 1846]
    Walter Jr & Charlotte KIMBALL at Bethel ME [13 Jan 1837]
MASTER William A & Elizabeth D SMILEY at Hallowell ME on Weds morning 12th Nov by Rev J P STEELE [20 Nov 1851]
MASTERS Jerusha A & Thomas McHENRY of St John New Brunswick Canada at Bath ME [19 Feb 1842]

MASTERS (cont.) Sarah E & Alonzo A MELVIN of Boston ME at Hallowell ME [20 May 1847]
MASTIN Benjamin & Melinda RIDEOUTY both (Augusta ME) at Rome ME on the 3rd inst by James L VARNEY Esq [12 Dec 1844]
MATHEWS Abigail of Hallowell ME & Henry L CARTER of Augusta ME [21 Sept 1833]
   Ann B of Prospect ME & Capt Seth N ELLIS of Harwich MA at Belfast ME [19 Sept 1844]
   Ann P of Waterville ME & Calvin H DAVIS of Canterbury NH at Lake Village NH [28 Aug 1851]
   Arvilla S & Thomas N PURINGTON at Bath ME [15 Feb 1849]
   Celia & Dr N A EELLS at Lincoln ME [20 Mar 1851]
   Charles K & Elizabeth M MARSTON at Waterville ME [2 Mar 1848]
   Charlotte d/o John M & John S CARTER, printer, at Waterville ME by Rev C GARDNER [13 Jun 1844]
   Eben T & Phebe Jane DAVIS at Elliotsville ME [22 Jan 1852]
   Ebenezer & Mrs Electa PENDEXTER at Sebasticook ME [27 Dec 1849]
   Eliza A L of Sidney ME & William F ROBIE of Readfield ME at Augusta ME 21 Dec by Lot MERRILL Esq [4 Jan 1849]
   John Jr of Waterville ME & Statira P HUNTER at Clinton ME [25 Mar 1847]
   Roxana S & Carlos E NELSON of Winslow ME at Sebasticook ME [30 Aug 1849]
   Susan & William Francis Y SIMMONS [24 Apr 1835]
   William Esq & Elizabeth d/o Amasa DINGLEY Esq on 14th inst at Winslow ME by Rev C GARDINER [30 Oct 1845]
MATTHEWS Elijah & Hannah WINSLOW at Hallowell ME [23 Dec 1843]
   James Capt & Elizabeth HARRIS at Deer Isle ME [15 Jul 1843]
   Jonathan Capt of Monson ME & Mrs Eunice SOULE at Shirley ME [19 Aug 1852]
   William A Jr Capt & Helen M LINCOLN at Eastport ME [18 Apr 1850]
MAULL John & Hannah L FELLOWS at Augusta ME [19 Jun 1838]
MAURAN Mary T of Warren RI & Rev John C STOCKBRIDGE of Waterville ME [5 Dec 1844]
MAXCY Ira Capt & Sarah A FULLER of Pittston ME at Gardiner ME [7 Jun 1849]
   Josiah of Gardiner ME & Eliza J CRANE of Warren ME at Lynn MA [11 Dec 1851]
   Lydia A & Joseph R WHITTIER Jr at (Augusta) ME on the 19th inst by Rev A KALLOCH [23 Aug 1849]
   Smith & Emma J G DINSLOW of Richmond at Gardiner ME [10 Jun 1852]
MAXEY Elizabeth R & Daniel SHOREY at (Augusta) ME on Sunday evening last [12 Oct 1848]
   Mary A & Ansel LERMAN at Searsmont ME [19 Sept 1844]
MAXFIELD James & Sarah BROWN at Mt Vernon ME [29 Jun 1848]
   John B & Lydia A GREENLEAF of Starks ME at Skowhegan ME by M LITTLEFIELD Esq [22 Jul 1852]
   Mary E formerly of Skowhegan ME & Newell CARPENTER of Charlestown MA at Oxford MA [25 Mar 1847]
   Mary P & William STEVENS of Gardiner ME at China ME [2 Dec 1847]

MAXIM Aurilla & Jeremiah TAYLOR at Lewiston ME [2 Jan 1851]
   Betsey B & Orrin TAYLOR both of Fairfield ME at Dover NH [23 Aug 1849]
   Harriet & John MAGNA at Wayne ME on 20th April [8 May 1851]
   Mary W & Gardner PERKINS of East Livermore ME on 30 Nov at Wayne ME by Elder B L LOMBARD [6 Dec 1849]
   Phebe & Daniel HOWARD both of (Winthrop) ME at Gardiner ME on 26th ult by Rev Mr SANBORN [4 Dec 1835]
   Sarah & Azel HAMMOND at Wayne ME on 4th Mar [22 Apr 1852]
   Seth 2d & Mary Ann LEWIS both of Wayne ME on Sunday last by Rev Mr FULLER of (Winthrop) ME [28 Mar 1834]
   Sullivan & Clarissa A SINKLER at Palmyra ME [21 Jan 1833]
MAXWELL Daniel of Windham & Abby MOOAR at Lewiston ME [3 May 1849]
   James & Sarah (GOLDTHWAIT) at Portland ME [8 Jul 1843]
   John & Eliza S JACKSON at Winthrop ME by Rev Daniel FULLER [22 Aug 1834]
   Martha & William M SAUNDERS of Augusta ME at Wales ME [9 Jan 1841]
   Mary A & Alvan BACON MD at Worcester MA of Biddeford ME [20 Dec 1849]
   Samuel T & Lydia A DURGIN at Parsonsfield ME [27 Jan 1848]
MAY Eunice & David RAND at New Gloucester ME [4 Apr 1837]
   John Esq & Mrs Content W HAINES at Winthrop ME on Saturday evening last by Elder ROBINSON [21 Jul 1843]
   Ruth M & William M MARR by Rev David THURSTON on Monday evening at Winthrop ME [24 Jun 1836]
MAYALL John & Susan ADAMS at Skowhegan ME [19 Aug 1843]
MAYBERRY Martha B & Francis H WHITMAN of Norway ME at Otisfield ME [7 Nov 1844]
MAYBURY Mary & Joseph ROBERTS at Solon ME [29 Apr 1836]
MAYERS Abial & Ella BAILEY at Bath ME [20 Jun 1844]
   Winter & Mrs Martha A WHALAND at Bath ME [17 Feb 1848]
MAYHEW F A & Elizabeth C JONES at Foxcroft ME [11 Jan 1849]
   Frances H & James W COFREN of the firm of COFREN & BLATCHFORD of Augusta ME at Mercer ME on 17 Nov by Rev J S THURSTON [11 Dec 1845]
   Maria S & Stephen D BRADBURY at Dennysville ME [2 Jan 1845]
   Martha J & George W PATTERSON at Belfast ME [19 Feb 1852]
MAYNARD C D Jr of (Augusta ME) & Frances M SMELLEGE at Portland ME [3 Sept 1846]
   George S & Martha E WHITE at Gardiner ME [28 Feb 1850]
   Hosea B & Louisa NYE at Fairfield ME [21 Jan 1847]
   Joseph A of Waterville ME & Mary L DOWSE at Winslow ME [28 Aug 1845]
   Levi P of Fairfield ME & Lorana W ORR at Bowdoinham ME [25 Jul 1840]
MAYO Eliza J & Mason W DUTTON of Phillips ME at Freeman ME on 3 Apr 1851 by Lemuel CROSBY Esq [10 Apr 1851]
   Moses of Milo ME & Persis E CHASE at Kilmarnock ME [4 Sept 1851]
   Mr J B of Dover & Eliza SPRAGUE at Pembroke [21 Sept 1848]

MAYO (cont.) Ruth Ann H & Samuel D LAMB at Hallowell ME [7 Dec 1848]
Thomas R of Amherst & Lucy J BUNKER of Brewer ME at Bangor ME [20 Jul 1848]
Alvan & Judith HUNTINGTON both of Hallowell ME at Augusta ME on 11th inst by Rev FULLER [22 Aug 1844]
Crosby & Ann R HINKLEY at Carmel ME [30 Dec 1847]
Elizabeth R & Capt W S SMITH at Frankfort ME [28 Mar 1837]
Laurietta A & Richard J CHAPLIN at Otisfield ME [15 Feb 1849]
Orison & Nancy BROWN both of Fairfield ME at Bloomfield ME [17 May 1849]
Randall & Ursula WEDGEWOOD at Brownville ME [11 Oct 1849]
Sarah T & Stephen HALL of Norway ME at Vassalboro ME [1 Mar 1849]
Susan Emma & George W WEEKS of Boston MA at Hallowell ME [27 Nov 1845]

McADAMS Mary J & Thomas S WETHERBEE at Dexter ME [22 Jan 1846]
Matilda & David L BUSWELL at Dexter ME [21 May 1846]

McALISTER/McALLISTER Benjamin G & Nancy STILES at Stoneham Oxford Co ME [5 Aug 1852]
Charlotte Ann & Rev Asahel Moore, of the Maine (Methodist) Annual Conference [11 Jul 1837]
Edwin & Sarah THOMPSON at Thomaston ME [31 Aug 1848]
Eliza F & Benjamin CROCKETT at Paris ME [28 Feb 1850]
Emerline & Charles GOWELL at Sumner ME [20 Mar 1841]
Mary Jane & William M MONROE at Rockland ME [11 Sept 1851]
Mary & Elbridge G STARBIRD at Dover ME? [25 Dec 1845]

McCABE Lorenzo D of Athens OH & Martha E d/o Daniel SEWALL of Farmington ME at Washington DC [28 Aug 1845]

McCALLISTER Elizabeth & William H CALDWELL of Rumford ME at Canton ME [4 Jul 1844]

McCARTY D C & Ellen CARDIFF at Portland ME [19 Aug 1836]

McCAUSLAND Charles W & Margaret WARE at Gardiner ME [22 Mar 1849]
Gideon C & Miss Eliza C PAUL both of Hallowell ME at Thompson CT on Nov 9th [23 Nov 1848]
Isaac & Mary E HILTON at Hallowell ME [10 Dec 1846]
Joseph of Hallowell ME & Susan Ann MARSHALL of Augusta ME at Thompson CT on Sept 6th [11 Sept 1845]
Mary B & James NASH at Gardiner ME [22 Mar 1849]
Sarah L & Joseph CLARK at Augusta ME [22 Oct 1846]
W W of Bath ME & Caroline B MOORE at Pittston ME [12 Feb 1852]

McCLELLAN Emily, d/o Judah McCLELLAN Esq, & Abraham SANBORN Esq of Levant ME at Bloomfield ME [21 Feb 1834]
John H Esq of Boston MA & Angeline S BATTIE d/o William BATTIE Esq of Thomaston ME [17 Sept 1842]
John of Skowhegan ME & Lydia G REDINGTON at Waterville ME [16 Jan 1851]
Theodore S Esq & Mary Jane OWEN at Brunswick ME [31 Dec 1842]

McCLINTOCH John Col of Boothbay ME & Sarah D B CLARK of Boston MA at Boston MA [19 Oct 1839]

McCLINTOOK John Capt of Bristol ME & Mary B d/o Capt SHAW at (Winthrop) ME on 26 Sept by Rev Franklin MERRIAM [16 Oct 1841]

McCLOUD Curtis of Boston MA & Miss Sarah G SMITH at Wiscasset ME [13 Jun 1834]
McCLUER J S of Lawrence MA & Miss S B WHEELER at Farmington ME [11 Sept 1851]
McCLURE F B & Miss F J BICKFORD of Belgrade ME at Hallowell ME [27 Mar 1851]
 John & Sarah BROWNING at Augusta ME [18 Nov 1843]
 Jonathan S & Ann J ROSS both of Hallowell ME at Jay ME by J M FOLLETT on 26 ult [7 Jan 1847]
 William Capt & Martha L ROLLINS both of Bowdoinham ME at Providence RI [4 Sept 1851]
McCOBB Arthur & Nancy RUST of Belfast ME at Boothbay ME [1 Apr 1852]
 Henry B Esq & Eliza H GOODWIN at Saco ME [14 Jun 1849]
 Julia & Mark BARKER Esq of Exeter ME at Orrington ME [28 Jun 1849]
 Lydia & William R NEWTON at Bath ME [20 May 1836]
 Parker Jr Esq & Eliza Greenleaf BALCH of Haverhill MA [25 Apr 1844]
McCOMB William of Foxcroft ME & Louisa J RICH at East Eddington ME [27 Jul 1848]
McCONNELL Rosanna & Thomas ELLIS at Calais ME [30 Apr 1846]
McCORD Sarah F Mrs & Ansyl G WATSON at (Augusta) ME on Jul 7 by Frances DAVIS Esq [10 Jul 1851]
McCORRISON Isabella F & Joshua COOMBS of Augusta ME at Bath ME [26 Feb 1846]
McCRILLIS Elizabeth H of Bloomfield ME & James N RUSSELL of Hartland ME at Skowhegan ME [20 Feb 1851]
 Gracia & George LANE at Bloomfield ME [8 May 1851]
 Darius & Rebecca C FLANDERS at Cornville ME [17 Jun 1847]
 J H Capt & Miss Phebe G RODGERS at Belfast ME [22 Jan 1836]
 Martha Jane of Cornville ME & William Q WHEELER of Norridgewock ME at Skowhegan ME [10 Jun 1847]
 Pulaski & Susan COOLIDGE at Dexter ME [12 Feb 1846]
McCUCHEN Samuel of Waltham MA & Hannah T SPRINGER at Bath ME [11 Apr 1837]
McCULLY John & Diantha J THOMAS at Farmington ME [13 May 1847]
McCURDY James Capt & Mary POOR at Eastport ME [23 Jul 1846]
 John P of Palermo ME & Asenath BROWN of China ME at China [1 Feb 1849]
McCURTY Sylpha & John T BROWN at Gardiner ME by Rev Mr PEET [15 Apr 1843]
McCUTCHEON Samuel A & Mary E BRYANT at West Bath ME [8 Feb 1849]
McDEVITT Samuel & Miss Ellen M CONY at (Augusta) ME on 7th inst [30 Aug 1849]
McDANIELS Eleanor F & Benjamin HEALD at Lovell ME on 9th inst [21 Dec 1848]
McDONALD Catherine Ann & James ROSS at Calais ME [2 May 1844]
 Daniel & Martha AKNOS at Eastport ME [8 Nov 1849]
 Joseph Esq & Agnes HARDING both of Gorham ME at Windham ME [26 Mar 1846]
 Lydia Emery & Hon Isaac REED at Bangor ME [3 Jun 1852]
 Nancy M & Elder John B WESTON at Skowhegan ME [29 Mar 1849]

McDUFFIE Daniel & Mary Jane STANLEY at (Winthrop) ME on Weds evening last, by Rev David THURSTON [26 Oct 1833]

John & Abigail TROTT both of (Winthrop) ME by Mr THURSTON at (Winthrop) ME on Monday last [15 Aug 1840]

Jonas & Dorcas Jane HARDISON both of South Berwick ME at Elliot ME [1 Aug 1844]

McFADDEN Alexander Capt & Susan J BAILEY at Wiscasset ME [20 Feb 1845]

Andrew & Elizabeth A N BOVEY at Bath ME [11 Mar 1847]

Charles R & Emma H BUTTERFIELD at Vassalboro ME [22 Feb 1849]

Charles & Calista RAWSEN at Paris ME [1 Jul 1847]

E W Esq & Zilpha BAKER of Bingham ME at Embden ME [8 Apr 1843]

George W Capt & Sarah A PARRITT both of Lubec ME at Eastport ME [2 Aug 1849]

Miss & Nathan CONVERS of Bath ME at Nobleboro ME [3 Jul 1838]

McFARLAND Aaron P Esq of Montville ME & Rosetta A WALKER at Liberty ME [17 Aug 1848]

David & Martha A STROUT both of Wales ME at Augusta ME [15 Jan 1846]

Isaac & Julia A CUMMINGS of Winthrop ME at Waterville ME [7 Dec 1848]

James H & Mildred A HEATH at North Hancock ME [29 Apr 1852]

Mary Elizabeth, eldest d/o William McFARLAND, & Henry B PEARSON Esq of Philadelphia PA [26 Dec 1840]

S N & Ruth CLAY at Bluehill ME [25 Dec 1851]

Stutley S & Mary Jane MILLER both of (Augusta ME) at Augusta ME [26 Dec 1844]

Wallace of Hopkinton MA & Julia A FLETCHER at Bloomfield ME [7 Apr 1848]

McGAFFEY George & Miss E J JUDKINS at Mt Vernon ME on 20th Oct [28 Oct 1847]

McGLOTHLIN Louisa of Eaton NH & Samuel FISH of Liberty ME at Salem MA [11 Jan 1840]

McGOUN Hannah & John C ROSS at Camden ME [8 Aug 1844]

McGOWN Franklin of Boston MA & Drusila LAWRENCE at Gardiner ME [29 Jan 1846]

McGRATH Bernard B of Pittston ME & Catharine McGRATH at Whitefield ME [28 Jan 1847]

Helen & Augustus HALLETT at West Waterville ME [13 Aug 1846]

McGREGOR Stephen & Miriam C MORTON at Lubec ME [21 Jan 1847]

McGUIRE Arthur of Milo ME & Mrs Mary BROWN at Sebec ME [6 May 1852]

Mrs of Lubec ME & Paul JOHNSON at Eastport ME [6 Mar 1845]

McHENRY Thomas of St John New Brunswick Canada & Jerusha A MASTER at Bath ME [19 Feb 1842]

McINTIRE Benjamin G & Lydia W TAYLOR at Norridgewock ME [8 May 1844]

Clarinda & James B WHEELER at Bloomfield ME [29 Jun 1848]

Eliza A & Albert H PARKS at Norridgewock ME [21 Jan 1847]

Francis H of Winthrop ME & Frances A WHEELOCK of Readfield ME at Newburyport MA [8 Jan 1852]

McINTIRE (cont.) James O Esq & Sarah A HUBBARD at Cornish ME [19 Mar 1846]
  Joanna H & Joseph H BRADFORD at New Sharon ME on May 28th [8 Jun 1848]
  Lorenzo of Norridgewock ME & Clarissa WESTON at Bloomfield ME [27 Dec 1849]
  M Miss & James ELLIOTT of Corinna ME at Bloomfield ME [27 May 1847]
  Margaret of Phipsburgh ME & Capt Hezekiah HARRINGTON at Georgetown ME [4 Sept 1845]
  Mary F of Boston MA & Henry S RICH of Bangor ME at New York NY [23 Oct 1845]
  Susan & John WESTON at Bloomfield ME [18 Dec 1851]
  Tamas & William CURTIS at Bath ME [25 Apr 1837]
  Uriah E of Camden ME & Sarah A BOARDMAN of Hope ME at Belfast ME [22 Jul 1847]

McINTOSH John & Abigail WADE at Belfast ME [11 Feb 1847]
  W C & Miss Lucretia WALSH at Thomaston ME [22 Oct 1846]

McKACHNIE Charlotte L & Henry A SHOREY at Auburn ME [23 Jun 1852]

McKEEN Harriet P & James BICKNELL both of Belmont ME [30 May 1837]
  James MD & Miss Octavia d/o William FROST Esq at Topsham ME [4 Jul 1834]
  Serena & Rev Charles DUREN of Sangerville ME at Belfast ME [2 Oct 1841]

McKELLAR Hannah Mrs & Benjamin W FALES at Thomaston ME [17 Oct 1840]

McKELLAR Emeline & Capt James S KELLOCH at Thomaston ME [22 Oct 1846]

McKENNA Mary F & Mr N WITHAM of Oldtown ME at Levant ME [3 May 1849]

McKENNAN John of Deer Isle ME & Frances SHAW at Thomaston ME [5 Feb 1846]

McKENNEY Ann Maria of Scarborough ME & Ezra F DYER of Baldwin ME at Saco ME [30 Apr 1846]
  Clarissa G & Isaac WHITE at West Bath ME [26 Mar 1846]
  John & Margaret NUTE at Wiscasset ME [15 Apr 1843]
  Julia A of Gray & Gustavus A SMITH of Passadumkeag ME at Milford ME [22 Jan 1846]
  Lucy L & Milton CARVILL at Greene ME [30 Mar 1848] & [13 Apr 1848]
  Mary A & Thomas SAVAGE [6 Aug 1846]
  Nancy of Hollis ME & Asa HODSON of Somersworth NH at Saco ME [4 Dec 1845]
  Reuben & Cordelia COBBETT at Brunswick ME [19 Dec 1834]
  Sarah & James MESERVE at Portland ME [20 May 1836]
  Sophronia & Amos SMILEY at Bath ME [18 Oct 1849]
  Wallace & Ann LOVEJOY at Augusta ME [15 Aug 1840]

McKENNON John & Phebe BATES at Belfast ME [1 May 1851] & [24 Apr 1851]

McKINNE Patrick & LOVINA NEWTON at Moose River ME [17 Feb 1848]

McKINNEY Charles O & Susan STARKEY at Unity ME [11 Apr 1850]

McKISSICK Ami & Miss C A COBURN at Parkman ME by S P SHAW Esq [16 Dec 1847]
McKOWN Henry of Fairfield ME & Ann Jane LATER at Skowhegan ME [17 Jul 1851]
 Robert H Capt & Caroline F CLARK [21 Nov 1834]
McLAIN Albert G & Susan KIMBALL by Cyrus KELLAR Esq at Searsmont ME [3 Aug 1839]
McLANAHAN Flora B & Marcus Q JACKSON at Chelsea ME? [8 Apr 1852]
McLANE Eliza Mrs formerly of Boston MA & Virgil H HEWES of Augusta ME at Gardiner ME [15 Jun 1839]
 John & Rebecca BRAGG at Vassalboro ME [29 Jul 1852]
McLARREN Almira & George LAMBERT at Eastport ME [9 Oct 1845]
McLAUGHIN David P & Susanna E PIPER both of Madison ME at Mayfield Somerset Co ME [25 Apr 1844]
 Jane & Abram MORRISON of Carmel ME at Albion ME [15 Jul 1847]
McLAUGHLIN Abba W & Mr J P BARTLETT at New Portland ME [29 Apr 1852]
 Lucinda & Horatio CLARK at New Portland ME [8 Jun 1848]
 Lucy Ann, formerly of Portland ME & Henry WIGAND of Cleveland OH at New York City NY on Jul 16th [6 Aug 1846]
 Rebecca of Industry & William S STEWARD of Gardiner ME [28 Aug 1845]
McLELLAN Abba E & Rev E M JACKSON of the Methodist Episcopal Conference at Gorham ME [5 Jun 1845]
 Adeline D & Joseph H ALLEN at Bath ME [28 Oct 1847]
 Caroline W & Alpheus S PACKARD of Rhetoric in Bowdoin College at Portland ME [3 Oct 1844]
 David of San Francisco CA proprietor of Maine Hotel & Mary C DANFORTH of Winthrop ME at New York City at Trinity Church on Aug 31st by Rev Dr HOBART [18 Sept 1851]
 Elkanah of Gardiner ME & Betsey DAVIS Mrs at Farmington ME [22 May 1851]
 Eunice & Rev Clarke PERRY at Gorham ME [26 Sept 1840]
 James S of Richmond ME & Ann F STEVENS at Roxbury MA [5 Nov 1846]
 Louisa H & Edward HARDING of New Orleans [25 Sept 1841]
 Mr & Amanda JONES at Litchfield ME [23 May 1837]
 Rufus Gen of Matagorda TX & Catherine J DUPUY of New York at New Orleans LA on 12th ult by Rev J CLAPP [18 Jul 1837]
 Samuel E & Sarah E BABB at Saccarappa ME [4 Jun 1846]
 Samuel of Bath ME & Helen L GOODWIN at Dresden ME [1 Oct 1846]
 Sarah B of Gardiner ME & Greenleaf S ROGERS of Augusta ME at Gardiner ME on Monday morning last by Rev Mr CLAPP [6 Jun 1834]
 Sarah B & Capt Samuel SNOW at Bath ME [31 Oct 1844]
McLEAD Alexander of Stanford Upper Canada (of steamer *Caroline Celebrity*) & Miss Helen NORMAN, eldest d/o Capt MOR(i)SON of Stanford [23 Apr 1842]
McLOUD Lydia & Stephen GILMAN at Dover [25 Mar 1852]
McLURE George of Solon ME & Miss Martha CORBETT at Farmington ME [24 Oct 1844]

McLURE (cont.) Isaac & Julia KENNEDY both of Hallowell ME at Augusta ME on the 18th inst by Benjamin A G FULLER Esq [25 Jun 1846]
    James H & Emily A NASON at Palmyra ME on 25 Oct by Elder N F NASON [27 Dec 1849]
McMANNUS William & Jane MERRYMAN at Brunswick ME [5 Dec 1840] & [25 Apr 1840]
McMANUS Nancy & Robert STANWOOD at Brunswick ME [16 Sept 1836]
    Robert Capt of Portland ME & Priscilla PURRINGTON at Topsham ME [28 Sept 1839]
    Robert Capt of Brunswick ME & Mary PURINGTON at Topsham ME [1 Oct 1846]
McMARLAND Asa, Proprietor of the New Hampshire Statesman & Clarissa J CHASE at Meredith NH [26 Jun 1845]
McMASTERS James Capt & Ellen VALENTINE at Eastport ME [14 May 1846]
    Ellen Maria & Thomas J STREET at Bath ME on Thursday evening by the Rev Mr STEARNS [23 Oct 1838]
McMULLEN John & Caroline GRAY at Thomaston ME [5 Feb 1846]
McNEAR Almira of Boston MA & Alonzo A LUCE of Wayne ME [9 Dec 1843]
    John Capt of Wiscasset ME & Susan B GREENLEAF at Westport ME [2 Dec 1843] McNEIL
    John & Mrs Margaret Ewing HAMILTON at Augusta MA [2 Jan 1838]
    William Doctor & Miss Mary CROCKETT d/o David CROCKETT, member of Congress from Tennessee "Go ahead!" in Columbia TN [24 Jan 1834]
McNELLEY Arthur of Clinton ME & Amanda L REED at Benton ME [13 Feb 1851]
McNELLY William Jr & Fanny A HODGDON at Benton ME [13 Nov 1851]
McPASKIEL Andrew & Sarah E BARTLETT both of Warren ME at Thomaston ME [10 Oct 1844]
M'COOL Mary & Charles S FOSTER of Monroe WI, formerly of Winthrop at Freeport IL [7 Feb 1850]
McPHERSON Ann of Bloomfield ME & Charles T BROWN at Skowhegan ME [20 Mar 1845]
McPHETERS Elizabeth & Samuel SMITH at Bangor ME [30 Oct 1845]
    Rebecca & Daniel B BANE at Bangor ME [30 Oct 1845]
    Sarah A & Joel M YORK Esq at Bangor ME [14 Aug 1841]
McQUESTEN Frances P & Charles T WHITTIER at Bangor ME [16 May 1844]
McQUILLAN Martha P & Henry WILLIAMS at Portland ME [12 Apr 1849]
McRIFLES Joseph P & Sophia W SMITH at Milburn ME [25 Apr 1834]
McRILLIS Mary Jane & Simon H FARNUM at Rumford ME [29 May 1841]
    Sarah J & Col E H SCRIBNER of Waterville ME at Great Falls NH [9 Sept 1847]
MEAD Alpheus & Nancy HUBBARD of Fayette ME at Boston MA [13 Apr 1848]
MEADER Susan L & William M PHILLIPS at Waterville ME [6 Jun 1844]
    William T & Elizabeth E BLANCHARD both of Hallowell ME at Pittston ME [17 Sept 1846]
MEADY Alex & Mrs Louisa N PLUMMER at Hallowell ME [12 Oct 1848]
    Frederick & Eliza BROWN of Hallowell ME at Tiverton RI [15 Nov 1849]

MEANS Eleanor S & Capt James C CREECH at Freeport ME [1 Aug 1844]
  William P M & Sarah H SNELL d/o the late Dr I SNELL by Rev Dr TAPPAN at (Augusta) ME [20 Jul 1848]
  William & Miss Caroline GAGE at Augusta ME by A R Nichols Esq [21 Oct 1847]
MECRACKEN Jane & Alexander ADAMS at Eastport ME [29 Jul 1836]
MEGQUIETER Benjamin C & Charlotte MERRILL at Poland ME on Thanksgiving evening by Rev Thomas WILLIAMS [18 Dec 1841]
MEGQUIRE Abgie L & Charles A GILSON at Winthrop ME on 11 Apr [22 Apr 1852]
MEGUIRE Huldah & Benjamin G ANGOVE both of Sebec ME at Foxcroft ME [4 Sept 1851]
  Mary D & Asa B ANGOVE both of Sebec ME at Foxcroft ME [4 Sept 1851]
MEIGS Ellen M & David DUDLEY of No 11 Aroostook Co, ME at China ME [23 Sept 1847]
  Eunice & John C PERLEY at Vassalboro ME [16 Mar 1848]
MELCHER I H & Miss Marie MORSE at Brunswick ME [3 May 1849]
  Josiah of Sandwich MA & Olive S BLACKWELL at Waterville ME [18 Jan 1849]
MELLEN George F Dr of Yazoo MS & Caroline M LUNT d/o Johnson LUNT by Rev Edward S DWIGHT at Saco ME on Apr 6th [15 Apr 1852]
  George L of Paris ME & Nancy N WING at Portland ME [22 Jul 1852]
MELLUS Julia S & Henry DOCKHAM at Thomaston ME [24 Aug 1848]
  Mary & John WARREN at Hallowell ME [24 Aug 1833]
MELVIN Alonzo A & Sarah E MASTER at Hallowell ME [20 May 1847]
  Benjamin F of Hope ME & Susan WHITTEN of Montville ME at Freedom ME [27 May 1847]
  Eliza S of Readfield ME & Simon JOHNSON of Hallowell ME at Readfield ME on Weds evening last by Rev George WEBBER [12 Jun 1838]
  Mehitable & Augustine LORD of Hallowell ME at Auburn NH [6 Aug 1846]
  Miss & Henry CLAYS of Camden ME at Waldoboro ME [15 Oct 1842]
  Sarah & Henry SMITH at Hallowell ME [10 Jun 1852]
  Sophia C & Bradbury H THOMAS at Readfield ME on Tuesday last by Rev Mr WEBBER of Hallowell ME [5 Jun 1838]
MERNSEY Sarah of Augusta ME & John PERKINS of Readfield ME at Readfield ME by Daniel CRAIG [10 Apr 1838]
MERO Herman & Electro A LITCHFIELD at Union ME [24 Dec 1846]
  Sarah F of Union ME & Elijah V ANDERSON at Warren ME [29 Jul 1852]
MERRIAM Franklin Rev of Winthrop ME & Miss Eunice C, d/o Edmund WARD of China ME on the 15th inst by Rev B F SHAW [18 Sept 1845]
  Rachael T & David H CURTIS at Bowdoin ME [18 Mar 1847]
  Sarah C & Lebbeas OAKS at Garland ME [1 Feb 1844]
MERRICK Mary & John P FLAGG at Hallowell ME on 23d ult [4 Nov 1843]
  Maryman & Lorenzo A PARKHURST both of Etna ME on 1st inst by Edward SMART Esq [14 Jan 1843]
  Thomas B of Philadelphia PA & Elizabeth M WHITE at Hallowell ME by Rev Mr COLE [21 Dec 1839]

MERRILL Abram of Windsor ME & Deborah NEAL of China ME by William PERCIVAL 2d Esq [3 Dec 1846]
Albert N & Freelove WYMAN [15 Feb 1849]
Alfred printer of Portland ME & Mary A COLLINS formerly of Boston MA at Portland ME [3 Oct 1840]
Almira S & Jonas C TEBBETS at Saco ME [17 Sept 1846]
Almira & John H DAVIS at Bangor ME [12 Jun 1845]
Alvan & Hannah TYLER at Windsor ME [15 Feb 1849]
Amos & Elmira A NICHOLS at (Augusta) ME on 13th inst [27 Jan 1848]
Augusta J & Ichabod B TRACY at (Augusta) ME on 3d Jan [8 Jan 1852]
Bethena S & Isaac LOMBARD at Auburn ME [12 Feb 1852]
Betsey C & Daniel S KNAPP at Farmington ME on 14th inst [28 Sept 1848]
Catharine & Lewis G TRAFTON at Biddeford ME [13 Sept 1849]
Chandler R & Hannah THOMPSON both of Frankfort ME at Belfast ME [15 Jul 1843]
Charlotte & Benjamin MEGQUIETER at Poland ME on Thanksgiving evening by Rev Thomas WILLIAMS [18 Dec 1841]
David W of New Gloucester ME & Pamelia SOULE at Lewiston ME [19 Dec 1844]
Dorcas & Thomas LOWELL at Saco ME [26 Feb 1852]
Edward & Mary E JEWETT at Swanville ME [4 Jun 1851]
Elias T of Parkman & Mary A SPRAGUE at Greene ME [18 Mar 1852]
Elias W of Webster ME & Sarah Ann TITCOMB at North Yarmouth ME [12 Dec 1840]
Eliza M & Rev James S BLISS of Fort Wayne Indiana at Portland ME [10 Oct 1844]
Elizabeth & Mr E PAGE at (Augusta) ME on 30 Apr [11 May 1848]
Eunice F of Saco ME & Otis LANE at Biddeford ME [14 Jun 1849]
Eunice S & George H KINSLEY at Sidney ME [1 Apr 1852]
Harriet T & George W TUFTS of Danvers MA at Levant ME [21 May 1846]
Harriet & Benjamin ADAMS Jr at (Hallowell) ME on the 25th ult by Elder INGRAHAM [8 May 1838]
Harriet & Spencer PRESSEY at Mercer ME by Hartley KIMBALL Esq [25 May 1839]
Horatio of Columbia CT & Sarah WHITMAN of Turner ME [1 Feb 1849]
Irene of Maine & Mr A W CAMPBELL of South Carolina at Clinton LA [12 Mar 1846]
J W of Manchester NH & Sarah SMITH at Lewiston ME [24 Apr 1851]
James E of Turner ME & Hannah E GORDON at Readfield ME [4 May 1848]
James of Lisbon ME & Olive BRIGGS of Greene ME at Greene ME on the 19th ult by Alfred PIERCE Esq [7 Feb 1834]
James & Eliza L DUNHAM at Paris ME [8 Apr 1852]
John C & Araminta P JONES both of Andover ME at Paris ME [9 Mar 1848]
John Dr & Miss Paulina SAWTELLE at Norridgewock ME [13 Nov 1838]
John H & Lorinda DOWNES at Levant ME [28 Oct 1847]
John P & Miss Eliza A DAVIS at Biddeford ME [26 Aug 1847]
Joseph Dr & Abby D ESTY at Gardiner ME [19 Oct 1848]
Joseph E & Mary J WHITEHOUSE at Paris ME [27 Jan 1848]

MERRILL (cont.) Julia of Portland ME & Hon Daniel GOODWIN at Detroit MI [31 Jul 1845]
    Juliette & Lemuel A STILSON at Waterville ME [5 Nov 1846]
    Lorenzo of New Gloucester ME & Sarah C CHIPMAN of Portland ME [7 Dec 1833]
    Louisa & Barbour LANE at Augusta ME on the 22d inst by Rev Asahel MOORE [26 Dec 1844]
    Lydia J & Amos KELLEY at Gardiner ME [26 Apr 1849]
    Mary A & Mr Woodbury L STATON at Oxford ME [18 Feb 1847]
    Mary Jane & John DEARBORN at Augusta ME [29 Oct 1846]
    Moses B & Mary H MALBON of Skowhegan ME at Boston MA [11 Feb 1847]
    Nancy & Moses MOODY at Salisbury MA [26 Jun 1841]
    Nathan of Pittsfield ME & Betsey WRIGHT at Greene ME [9 Apr 1846]
    Noah of Skowhegan ME & Paulina WALKER at Anson ME [30 Jan 1851]
    Olive E & Rev Asbury CALDWELL of the Maine (Methodist) Annual Conference of (Winthrop) ME at Kennebunkport ME [22 Jul 1836]
    Orpha B & Europe JONES at Turner ME on 29th Sept by Ezekiel MARTIN [5 Oct 1833]
    Philena F & Thomas ALLARD at Lewiston ME [2 Jan 1851]
    Samuel A of Lawrence MA & Miss E CARVELLE at Lewiston ME [11 Apr 1850]
    Samuel Col of Tamworth NH & Elizabeth D HILL at Buxton ME [6 Feb 1851]
    Silas of Saco & Abigail SAWYER at Portland ME [26 Dec 1844]
    Surranus & Affa Jane GODING at Livermore ME by Isaac STRICKLAND [14 Nov 1837]
    Susan P & William H GOODING of Portland ME at Lisbon ME [3 Oct 1844]
    Susan & Rufus PATTEN at Topsham ME [15 May 1835]
    Theodore D & Emily E WAITE eldest d/o Silas L WAITE Esq at Sidney ME on 31st Aug by Rev Mr JUDD [4 Sept 1851]
    Thomas of Smithfield ME & Louisa BARNES of Hartland ME at Waterville ME [23 Oct 1851] & at West Waterville ME [9 Oct 1851]
    Vance & Amanda M JONES at Turner ME [23 Oct 1851]

MERRIMAN Benjamin H & Bethiah JONES of Brooksville ME at Castine ME [19 Jun 1845]
    Isabella A & Adoniram J POTTER at Bath ME [18 May 1848]
    Jacob A & Susan S BAKER at Portland ME [5 Aug 1833]

MERRIT John & Joanna TOOTHAKER at Brunswick ME [8 Oct 1846]

MERITHEW Mary R & Daniel DOW at Belmont ME [13 Mar 1845]

MERRITT Lydia Ann & Capt J T BOWN at New York City [15 Jun 1848]
    Sarah & William W BUCKNAM at Eastport ME [21 Aug 1845]
    Sarah H & Josiah S HARDY [6 Nov 1835]

MERROW see MARROW
    Harriet Maria & William S W GILMAN at Augusta ME on 18 Oct by Rev Zenas THOMPSON [23 Oct 1851]
    Harriet N of Auburn ME & Ai B (Brooks; see page 217, Elder's *History of Lewiston ME*) HODGKINS at Lewiston ME [30 Jan 1851]
    Hartford of Cannan ME & Zenobia d/o Daniel WELLS Esq of Clinton ME at Skowhegan ME [7 Oct 1847]

MERROW (cont.) Hiram & Jane ROYAL at Minot ME [12 Dec 1840]
    Ira of Clinton ME & Abigail CHURCH at Hartland ME [17 Aug 1848] & [3 Aug 1848]
    James H & Susan M REYNOLDS at (Augusta) ME on 16th Nov [23 Nov 1848]
    Maj Josiah M & Elinor PURRINGTON at Bowdoinham ME [5 Feb 1846]
    Priscinda & Dan FULTON at Bowdoinham ME [21 Jan 1847]
    Sarah H & Elbridge G DUNN at Poland ME [11 Jan 1849]
    Sophia & Charles H RAY at Auburn ME [22 Apr 1852]
MERRY Elizabeth & Erastus FULLER at Woolwich ME [1 Jan 1852]
    John C & Abigail C I WALDRON at Eastport ME [23 Jul 1846]
MERRYFIELD Sarah & Otis F COLLINS of St Albans ME at Gardiner ME [11 Nov 1843]
    William Jr of Solon ME & Patience OTIS at Fairfield ME [22 May 1845]
MERRYMAN Jane & William McMANNUS at Brunswick ME [25 Apr 1840] & [5 Dec 1840]
    Lydia S & Capt Norton STOVER at Harpswell ME [31 Oct 1844]
    Margaret & Capt John DURGAN at Harpswell ME [29 May 1835]
    Martha & Capt Charles C SNOW at Brunswick ME [18 May 1848] & [4 May 1848]
    W & Miss Catherine PARKER at Brunswick ME [27 Nov 1838]
MESERVE James & Sarah McKENNEY at Portland ME [20 May 1836]
    John A Esq & Alice C KIMBALL at Rockland ME [26 Feb 1852]
MESERVEY Clement of Hallowell ME & Olive EDGECOMB at Webster ME on 19th inst [29 Jan 1846]
    Harriet of Jefferson ME & Benjamin FLANDERS of Waldoboro ME at N Waldoboro ME on 12 Jan by Reuben ORFF Esq [16 Jan 1851]
    Isaac & Mary Jane COCHRAN both of Orono ME at Bangor ME [2 Jan 1845]
METCALF Addison of Lisbon ME & Jane H BOOKER at Bowdoinham ME [19 Apr 1849]
    Gorham & Emma WATTS at Hallowell ME [18 Nov 1847]
    Julia G & John W BLOOD of Waldo ME at Camden ME [28 Jan 1847]
    Lucy A & Mr S W FURBER at Milo ME [8 Jun 1848]
    Maria & Eleazer MADOX at Appleton ME [14 Mar 1844]
    Sarah B & William MANN of Slatersville RI at Winthrop ME by Rev D THURSTON [19 Jul 1849]
    Susan & Isaac DEXTER of Wayne ME at (Winthrop) ME by Rev Mr THURSTON [28 Nov 1834]
MICHAELS Mary Mrs & Nehemiah SMART at Belfast ME [1 Apr 1847]
MILD Charles & Mary Francis SMITH by Hiram ROSE Esq at Newport ME [18 May 1848]
MILES Maria & William B HOSKINS both of Calais ME at St Stephens, New Brunswick Canada [13 Jul 1839]
    Mary E Mrs & Reuben BARTON at (Augusta) ME on 11th inst [19 Oct 1848]
MILLAY Philip E & Amanda M ROLLINS at Lynn MA both of Pittston ME at Lynn MA [17 May 1849]
MILLER Abby S & B W NORRIS of Skowhegan ME at Farmington ME [30 Jan 1851]
    Abigail E Mrs & George G MITCHELL at Thomaston ME [13 Nov 1845]

MILLER (cont.) Abigail & James GOODELL both of Northport ME at Belfast ME [18 Sept 1845]
    Ann & John MARR at Cape Elizabeth ME [23 May 1844]
    Betsey Ann Mrs & Nathaniel TOBY at North Waldoboro ME on 27 Dec [8 Jan 1852]
    Charles H & Isabella C KIMBALL at Belfast ME [22 Jan 1846]
    David & Mary W CROSS at Augusta ME on Sunday morning last Rev J H INGRAHAM [22 Oct 1842]
    E A of Bremen ME & Miss Louisa J KALER of Waldoboro ME [1 Feb 1849]
    Elizabeth & Capt Barker EMERY at Hamden ME on 12th inst by Rev Mr TAPPAN [29 Apr 1843]
    Harriet & Capt George SNOW at Thomaston ME [11 Jul 1844]
    Jane N Mrs & George WILKINS Esq of Brownville ME at Hampden ME [6 March 1845]
    John B of Albany ME & Miss Temperance A WARDWELL at Otisfield ME [7 Jan 1847]
    Lavina T & Mr B S HUSSEY of Limerick ME at Sanford ME [24 Apr 1851]
    Livona & Benjamin SHAW both of Sidney ME at Augusta ME [9 Mar 1839]
    Margaret & Anthony E KNAPP at Portland ME [6 Mar 1838]
    Mary A of Lowell MA & Livermore R HALL at Rumford ME [28 Jan 1847]
    Mary F & Capt Richard H WADE of Dresden ME at Wiscasset ME [2 Nov 1833]
    Mary Jane & Frances M ROLLINS Jr of Vassalboro ME [24 Jun 1847]
    Mary Jane & Stutley S McFARLAND both of (Augusta ME) at Augusta [26 Dec 1844]
    Peter & Maria STEVENS at Hallowell ME [25 Apr 1850]
    Ripsey Ann & Mathew M Jr at Bangor ME [22 May 1845]
    Sophia L & Capt Charles WHITNEY 2d at Hampden ME [19 Aug 1843]
    William W of Cushing ME & Margaret A WATTON at Waldoboro ME [18 Jul 1844]

MILLETT Asa MD of Mattapoiset Rochester Co MA & Huldah Allen BYRAM of East Bridgewater MA on Sabbath Morning 5th inst at the Unitarian meeting house by Rev Mr LORD of Plymouth [23 Dec 1843]
    Catharine of Leeds ME & Rev Wilson C RIDER of Wayne ME [15 Jun 1839]
    Cynthia D & Elbridge of Turner ME at Leeds ME by Rev Walter FOSS [11 Jan 1849]
    Francis D of Leeds ME & Lucinda PHILLIPS at Auburn ME [8 Apr 1852]
    Mrs ae 78y & Mr Josiah TILSON ae 78y at Hartford ME [28 May 1846]
    Polly of Leeds & Francis SAFFORD of Turner at Winthrop ME by Elder Haze [2 Dec 1836]

MILLIKEN see LIMIKEN and WHEELER
    Charles of Gardiner ME & Rebecca S BANGS at Sidney ME [3 Dec 1846]
    Charlotte & Samuel R BAKER both of Saco ME at Charlestown MA [11 Sept 1851]
    David & Jane Philena JOHNSON at Saco ME [25 Apr 1844]
    Elias T of Boston ME & Mary Ann FOGG at Saco ME [1 Feb 1844]
    Eunice & Samuel P SIAS of Roxbury MA at Saco ME [19 Feb 1846]

MILLIKEN (cont.) James A Rev & Lucretia B COFFIN only d/o Col B C at Columbia ME on 28th ult [24 Oct 1840]
  Loren J & Lydia A HAINES of Saco ME at Buxton ME [17 Dec 1846]
  Mary Jane & Ansel M CURTIS at Portland ME [8 Feb 1844]
  Mary & Alpheus A HANSCOMB, publisher of the *Maine Democrat*, at Saco ME [7 Oct 1843]
  William Esq of Burnham ME & Mary Ann LYON at Gardiner ME [11 Jan 1849]
MILLIONS Eunice B of this city (Hallowell) ME & Capt Silvanus PRINCE of North Yarmouth ME at Portland ME [6 Mar 1838]
MILLS Eliza & Mr E Addison HILTON at Waterville ME [25 May 1848]
  Emeline P & Edward DIBELL at Belgrade ME [10 Jun 1852]
  Jacob Jr & Harriet ROSS d/o the late William ROSS at Portland ME [4 Apr 1834]
  John & Caroline SMITH both of Belgrade ME [7 Nov 1834]
  Lydia Ann of Monson & Francis E WHITCOMB at Boston MA [30 May 1844]
  Lydia C & Lieut Thompson H CROSBY at Providence RI on 12th inst [30 Nov 1848]
  Maria H & Joseph B GREENE at Thompson CT on 10 Oct [31 Aug 1848]
  Prudentia F & Franklin M WOODARD at Newport [2 Apr 1846]
  R M Ellen MORRILL by Lot M MORRILL at Readfield ME [16 Nov 1848]
  Richard & Lucretia A TOZIER at Waterville ME [1 Jun 1848]
  Rozilla Mrs & Capt Stephen M PRATT of New Vineyard ME at New Portland ME [31 Jul 1851]
  Sarah J & William H LOMBARD at (Augusta) ME on Nov 24 [7 Dec 1848]
  Sophia & Samuel KENNISON at Milo ME [19 Jul 1849]
  Stephen C & Elizabeth BASTON at Norridgewock ME [17 Jun 1852]
  Thomas of Gardiner ME & Sarah J POTTLE at Pittston ME [22 Nov 1849]
  William & Adaline HALLETT at Belgrade ME [20 Jan 1848]
MILTON Charles G of Belgrade ME & Martha P d/o David ROBINSON Esq of Sidney ME on 19th ult [10 Jul 1845]
MINER Dwight & Mary BILLINGTON at Hallowell ME [10 Jan 1850]
MINIX Margaret & John PETERS at Bath ME [31 Oct 1844]
MINK Charles C & Clarissa K MINK at Waldoboro ME [6 Jan 1837]
  Julia Ann & Oscar E BENNER at North Waldoboro ME on 21 Dec by Reuben ORFF Esq [25 Dec 1851]
  Mary Jane & Samuel M WALTER at North Waldoboro ME on 5 Jul by Reuben ORFF Esq [12 Jul 1849]
  Saloma & Absalom BENNER at North Waldoboro ME on 4th May 1851 by Reuben ORFF Esq [15 May 1851]
  Sophronia & John G BARNARD at North Waldoboro ME by Reuben ORFF Esq [25 Dec 1851] MINOR
  Dwight & Johannah KINNEY at Hallowell ME [24 Apr 1835]
MINOT James Jr of Belgrade ME & Rhoda KNOWLES of Readfield ME by Rev A W CUMMINGS at Sidney ME on 28th Jun [13 Jul 1848]
MIRICK Augustus D of Camden ME & Sarah C STETSON at Thomaston ME [31 Oct 1844]
MITCHELL Abigail C of Lowell MA & Charles A THOMS of Leeds ME by Walter FOSS [8 Jan 1846]
  Albert A & Susan E JONES at Canton ME [22 May 1851]

MITCHELL (cont.) Almira C & Joshua R GRAY of Dorchester MA at Vassalboro ME by Rev Mr BRAY [16 Oct 1851]
   Almira E & Lloyd O ROBBINS at Chesterville ME [22 March 1849]
   Anna B & Elisha WINTER at Carthage ME? [10 Jun 1852] & [17 Jun 1852]
   Asa & Mary C HUMPHREY at North Yarmouth ME [15 May 1838]
   Benjamin K & Eliza A BARRINGTON at Gardiner ME [11 Jan 1849]
   Benjamin P & Mary ROBERTS at East Thomaston ME [27 Sept 1849]
   Charlotte A & Capt Dodge HEALEY at Thomaston ME [11 Jul 1844]
   Clark & Cyrene BOSTON both of Avon ME at Phillips ME on 6th Dec by Charles J TALBOT Esq [16 Dec 1847]
   Daniel & Hannah P WELD formerly of Bloomfield ME at Dover ME [6 Nov 1838]
   David Esq of Temple ME & Sarah HIGGINS at Farmington ME [7 Mar 1837]
   David & Belinda R ANDERSON at Freedom ME [3 Apr 1851]
   Edward H of Maumee City OH & Frances A PAGE at Bath ME [12 Jun 1851]
   Eunice B & William HUSSEY at Wiscasset ME [13 Jun 1844]
   Ezra of Wayne ME & Mary Elizabeth FAIRBANKS at Mt Vernon ME [20 Nov 1851]
   Frances E & Capt Richard HARDING of Truro MA at North Yarmouth ME [18 Sept 1846]
   Franklin B & Mary J PAGE at Phillips ME [26 Jul 1849]
   George G & Mrs Abigail E MILLER at Thomaston ME [13 Nov 1845]
   Hiram C & Joanna BAIRD at Canton ME [23 Oct 1851]
   James B & Huldah T BRAGDON at Bath ME [23 Dec 1847]
   James & Ednah FLAGG both of Auburn ME at Danville ME [5 Jul 1849]
   James & Mary Jane OWEN at Bath ME [3 May 1849]
   Jane W & George R RUSSELL on 25th ult at Bangor ME [4 Nov 1843]
   Jeremiah of Cumberland ME & Mary PAINE of Pownal ME [25 Jul 1834]
   Jeremiah & Emely LAIR both of Washington ME on 30th ult [30 Oct 1838]
   John W of Lewiston ME & Mary E FROST at Litchfield ME [31 Aug 1848]
   John W of North Yarmouth ME & Mary H BLANCHARD [8 Feb 1844]
   Joseph W formerly of Bath ME & Mrs Rhoda HALL of North Berwick ME at Medford MA [8 Feb 1844]
   Jotham W & Lovina WOODS at Bloomfield ME [21 Mar 1850]
   Lucretia D & John O SPRAGUE at Thomaston ME [9 Jul 1846]
   Lucy E & William H CURRIER at Kennebunk ME [28 Feb 1837]
   Lydia Jane of Mercer ME & Henry G SMITH at Hallowell ME [6 Mar 1851]
   Marcia & Capt Joseph DILLINGHAM at Freeport ME [26 Jun 1835]
   Margaret P & Abraham T MOSES at Bath ME [28 Nov 1840]
   Maria E & Jotham DONNELL at Bangor ME [31 Aug 1848]
   Maria Mrs & Thomas ROGERS at Eastport ME [29 Apr 1847]
   Mary A & Shirley LIBBEY at Gardiner ME [18 Dec 1845]
   Mary M & George VINAL at Dover ME? [22 Jun 1848]
   Mary & John FASSET at Bath ME [22 Apr 1847]
   Narcissa B & Rev Joseph SHERMAN, Professor in Jackson College at Portland ME [3 Oct 1837]

MITCHELL (cont.) Olive of Washington ME & Richard PEEVY of Liberty ME at Vassalboro ME [30 Oct 1838]
   Rachel E & Alfred MORSE of Lubec ME at Bradford ME [14 Jan 1847]
   Rhoda of Carthage ME & Albert WINGATE of Hallowell ME at Carthage ME by Rev R MOORE [9 Jul 1842]
   Rosanna & Archibald S DODGE at Troy ME [22 Jun 1848]
   Rufus E & Hannah INGERSOLL both of Gorham ME at Windham ME [13 Mar 1851]
   Sarah S of Avon ME & Emory PLAISTED [4 Oct 1849]
   Sarah & Ebenezer YOUNG at Thomaston ME [4 May 1839]
   Susan A & Dr George W HALEY at Bath ME [2 Sept 1847]
   Thomas G & Laura Ann PACKARD at Auburn ME [18 Feb 1847]
MIXER Lee & Deborah BENNETT d/o Nathaniel BENNETT Esq at Norway ME [29 May 1845]
MIZER Nancy & Henry DURELL of Boston MA at Paris ME [19 Aug 1836]
MOFFITT Caleb G & Louisa M NORCROSS at Livermore ME [29 May 1845]
   William & Nancy DAVIDSON of Lubec ME at East Machias ME [13 Aug 1846]
MONK Elias & Eliza TURNER at Buckfield ME [13 Mar 1845]
   George W & Mary B ABBOTT at Albion ME by D B FULLER Esq [24 Jul 1851]
   Harriet & Charles RECORDS Jr of Poland ME at Buckfield ME [26 Dec 1844]
   Lewis Jr & Betsey LANE at Paris ME [28 Feb 1837]
   Simeon & Mary A ROWE of Minot ME at Mechanic Falls (part of Minot & Poland ME, until 1893; see *Maine Public Laws & Resolves*, Chapter 550) [25 Oct 1849]
MONROE Barnabas H & Sarah Jane PALMER at West Camden ME [16 Aug 1849]
   Charles & Adeline A SMITH at Portland ME [31 Jan 1834]
   Elizabeth & Robbins LONGLEY at Waterford ME [29 Nov 1849]
   Lucy H & Isaac N BONNEY of Monson ME at Abbot ME [13 Jul 1839]
   Noble N & Mary E BRADFORD both of Auburn ME at Turner ME [26 Aug 1847]
   William M & Mary Jane McALISTER at Rockland ME [11 Sept 1851]
   William & Mariah R JAMESON at Thomaston ME [3 Oct 1844]
MONSON Angelina & Elisha P PARHER of Chesterville ME at Farmington ME [29 Jun 1839]
   Joseph H & Ann E SLADE both of Hallowell ME at Augusta ME [23 Sept 1843]
MONTAIR Mary Mrs & Peter TAMAZO at Bath ME [12 Jul 1849]
MONTARE Alexander & Delia GOVE at Bath ME [31 Oct 1844]
MONTGOMERY Angeline R of Cushing ME & Elisha THURSTON, A.B., Principal of the Charleston Academy [2 Sept 1843]
MOOAR Abby & Daniel MAXWELL of Windham ME [3 May 1849]
   Emma & Christopher GETCHELL at Lewiston ME [3 May 1849]
MOODY Caroline & George S FAIRBANKS at Monmouth ME [22 Jun 1839]
   Clement F & Caroline A GOODSPEED at China ME on 27 Jun by Rev L WENTWORTH [8 Jul 1852]
   Cynthia M & Samuel STEVENS at Fort Kent Aroostook Co ME [8 Jun 1848]

MOODY (cont.) Deborah R & William BLAKE at Hope ME [30 Dec 1847]
Eldon D & Sophia WELCH at Monmouth ME [3 Jun 1843]
Eliza J & Melvin C ELWELL at Gardiner ME [3 Jul 1851]
Enoch C & Margaret M HAPGOOD at Augusta ME on 21st by Rev Mr DREW [28 Jan 1847]
Esther A & George F YOUNG at Pittston ME [7 Dec 1848]
Hannah S & George A OSBORN of Danvers MA at Augusta ME on 20th inst by Rev Dr TAPPAN [27 Jun 1844]
James & Esther A WALLACE at Lincolnville ME [13 May 1852]
Joel N of Monmouth ME & Harriet N HASTY of Westbrook ME [5 Feb 1839]
Laura & Alvin JUDKINS at Danville ME [6 Jul 1848]
Lewis of Pittston ME & Mary E CROSBY of Readfield ME [25 March 1843]
Lydia M & Lot SAMPSON of Hartford ME at Peru ME [10 Jun 1847]
Mary Ann & George W JEWETT of Sidney ME at Readfield ME by Rev N ALLEN [28 Aug 1841]
Mary Ann & James CLARK at Vassalboro ME [10 Dec 1846]
Mary B & Nathan S MORSE at Paris ME [26 Apr 1849]
Mary Jane & Levi FAIRBANKS Jr at Monmouth ME [22 Jun 1839]
Mary & Franklin HEAL at Belmont ME [15 Apr 1836]
Mary & Uriah HAMILTON at Bath ME [11 Jul 1834]
Moses & Nancy MERRILL at Salisbury MA [26 Jun 1841]
Richard C & Hannah F WELMAN at Pittston ME [28 Aug 1851]
Sabra & Joseph LUDWIG at Waldoboro ME [27 Nov 1838]
Samuel L of Webster ME & Miss Apphia G SPOFFORD of Greene ME at Leeds ME on 4th Jul by Josiah DAY 2d [26 Jul 1849]
Seth & Mercy E PEAVY at Windsor ME [29 Jan 1852]
Solomon of Nobleboro ME & Susan MOODY of Wiscassett ME at Waldoboro ME [25 Dec 1841]
Susan of Wiscassett ME & Solomon MOODY of Nobleboro ME [25 Dec 1841]

MOOER Mary S & George CROCKET Esq of Stetson ME at Wilton ME [25 Jan 1840]

MOOERS Sarah of Whitefield ME & Daniel SAVAGE of (Augusta) ME [16 Oct 1845]
William & Sarah SMITH at Pittston ME [10 Apr 1851]

MOON Cephas of Concord NH & Julia GREENWOOD at Clinton ME [14 Oct 1847]
Lucinda & Moses N BAKER at Hancock ME [22 Apr 1852]
Margaret ae 14y & Harvey M DANIEL ae 17y at Woodford VT "Both these children must have been moon struck." [31 Oct 1837]

MOOR Andrews G of Sebec ME & Rebecca DEAN of Barnard ME at Dover ME? [15 May 1851]
Charles of Clinton ME & Ann Priest at Waterville ME [20 May 1843]

MOORE Abner & Elvira BENIS both Livermore ME at Sumner ME by Rev Mr LAURENCE [17 Aug 1839]
Albion K formerly of Skowhegan ME & Elizabeth SERGENT at Savanvah GA [2 Jan 1845]
Albion & Elizabeth WORTHING at Orono ME [25 Oct 1849]
Alice A & Andrew P SPEAR at Madison ME on 24 Oct [16 Nov 1848]

MOORE (cont.) Alice & Allen WITHAM at Gardiner ME [29 Feb 1844]
Asahel Rev of Maine (Methodist) Annual Conference & Charlotte Ann McALLISTER at St Stephens New Brunswick Canada [11 Jul 1837]
Bethsheba of Orono ME & George M WESTON Esq of Augusta ME [30 May 1844]
Caroline B & Mr W W McCAUSLAND at Pittston ME [12 Feb 1852]
Charles of Waterville ME & Olive L JACOBS at Pittsfield ME [24 Jun 1843]
Charles R & Harriet L HUTCHINSON at Pittston ME [10 Feb 1848]
Charles & Mrs Priscilla ROLLINS at Gardiner ME [15 Mar 1849]
Christopher & Zady Ann BENNETT at Hallowell ME [16 Jul 1846]
Cyrus & Almira NUTTING at Madison ME [15 Oct 1846]
Daniel of Munroe ME & Lydia CURTIS of Swanville ME at Frankfort ME [10 Oct 1840]
David & Emily E LOVITT at Pittston ME [25 Jan 1849]
Edwin of Whitefield ME & Rebecca A TURNER of China ME at China [11 Mar 1852]
Eliza & Hermon N FOSTER at Argyle ME [12 Apr 1849]
Esther & Theodore S CURTIS of Portland ME at Brunswick ME [10 Sept 1846]
Henry & Catherine A VAN HORN at Eastport ME [31 Jul 1851]
James M & Deelsa LOVELL both of Gardiner ME at Vienna ME on Dec 2 by T C NORRIS Esq [11 Dec 1851]
John Jr & Phebe HAMBLET at Solon ME [2 Jan 1851]
John T Capt at Dixmont ME of Gardiner ME & Julia E BUTMAN [10 Jul 1845]
Laura M of Gardiner ME & F A BUTMAN Jr of Bangor ME at Dixmont ME [25 Jan 1844]
Liberty S, d/o the late Abraham MOORE Esq of Abbot ME, & Dr Aaron DOW of Kingsbury Piscataquis Co ME at Abbot ME [17 Jul 1845]
Llewellyn & Mary CURTIS at Dexter ME [20 Jun 1844]
Lucy W & Mr D P TIFFANY at Sidney ME [6 May 1843]
Lyman & Sarah S LADD both of Gardiner ME by Asaph R NICHOLS Esq at (Augusta) ME on Mar 4th [11 Mar 1852]
Maria I & Henry P NASON at Waterville ME [26 Jun 1851]
Maria & William BALKAM at Thomaston ME [28 Mar 1850]
Martha & Josiah ROGERS Jr of Bow NH at Concord NH [4 Feb 1833]
Mary E, d/o late Capt John MOORE, & Rev John ORR of Gouverneur NY at Christ Church at Gardiner ME on 13th ult by Rev W R BABCOCK [5 Nov 1842]
Mary & Josiah T WHITNEY at Moose River ME [4 Jun 1851]
Mary S & George CROCKET Esq of Stetson ME at Wilton ME [1 Feb 1840]
Phebe Mrs & Maj James ULMER of Thomaston ME at Union ME [27 May 1847]
S G of Bangor ME & Almira C BUTMAN at Dixmont ME [25 Jan 1844]
Salina both Hartland ME & Francis T SWIFT at St Albans ME [4 Apr 1850]
Sarah G & Josiah S WITHEREL at Abbot ME [1 Aug 1834]
Sarah of Standish ME & Joshua T EMERY of Portland ME at St Albans ME [30 Sept 1847]

MOORE (cont.) Sarah & James WHORFF at Madison ME [17 May 1849]
Sophronia M & John O SMITH at Gardiner ME [23 Nov 1848]
Sylvanus S of Katahdin Iron Works ME & Mary O CROSS at Foxcroft ME [22 Jul 1852]
Thankful S of Gardiner ME & Thomas M PEAKER of Tisbury MA at Cambridge [22 May 1851]
Timothy & Charlotte FLETCHER at Wilton ME [6 Jun 1837]
William Esq of Moble & Almeday WYMAN at Skowhegan ME [9 May 1837]
William H & Mary Jane WILSHIRE both of Orono ME at Bangor ME [18 Jul 1844]
William of Dixmont ME & Prudence DUDLEY at East Readfield ME [24 Aug 1839]
Zavilla & Henry WHELPLEY of Eastport ME [21 Mar 1844]

MOORES Abner J & Lydia J at Gardiner ME [14 Mar 1850]
David S of Readfield ME & Caroline W HOWIE of Sidney ME on 19th inst by Joshua DAVIS Esq [26 Dec 1844]
Leonard Jr & Mary Ann ELDER both of Gardiner ME at Augusta ME on 12 Sept [16 Sept 1847]
N of Vienna ME & Martha W PORTER at New Sharon ME [5 Feb 1846]
Robert B & Maria Antoinette TRUE at Mercer ME [27 Feb 1845]
Sarah C, d/o Sailing Master R W MOORES USN, & Lewis M STILLMAN at Mercer ME on the 3rd inst by the Rev Oren SILES [28 Nov 1844]

MOORISON Elizabeth & Merrill CAMBPELL at (Augusta) ME on 3d Mar [18 Mar 1852]

MOORS Martha of Madrid ME & Joseph CHURCH of Phillips ME at Phillips on 25 Mar by Hon John L BLAKE [22 Apr 1843]

MORANG George & Adeline EMERY at Eastport ME [8 Nov 1849]

MORE Hannah A & Andrew G MASON at Leeds ME [13 Jul 1848]
Ira & Arvilla Amanda PULLEN at China ME on 21 Mar by J GREELY Esq [3 May 1849]

MOREY Abiel C of Searsmont ME & Margaret E F T CROSS of Belmont ME [3 Oct 1844]
Albert G of Belmont ME & Maria SMITH at Belfast ME [28 May 1846]
David W of Belmont ME & Ruby A CARTER at Montville ME [3 Apr 1851]
Jane & William K STAPLES at Oxford ME [3 Aug 1848]
Nelson of Deer Isle ME & Lanee DUSTEN of Eastport ME [13 Feb 1845]

MORGAN Eleanor & Richard STOKES at Hallowell ME [13 Nov 1841]
Francis B Esq & Miss Serena REDMAN at Brooksville ME by Hon John R REDMAN [23 Oct 1838]
Little T of Thomaston ME & Lydia B PIERCE at Boston MA [22 Apr 1847]
Nancy A & Reuben H LOWELL at East Thomaston ME [13 Apr 1848]
William of Dexter ME & Lenora J HARLOW at Sangerville ME [15 Apr 1847]
Zaccheus R & Miss Ann Myra WEST at Winthrop ME on Sunday last by Mr CALDWELL [12 Jun 1835]

MORMAN William & Mrs Sarah HAWKES at Warren ME, each 75y of age [6 May 1833]

MORGRIDGE Serena & Thomas BROWN at Litchfield ME [31 Aug 1848]

MORRELL Alexander H of Litchfield ME & Eliza J SEAVEY of Hallowell ME at Litchfield ME [10 Jul 1845]

MORRELL (cont.) Alice Mrs of East Livermore ME & Capt Joseph WHARFF of Gardiner ME at Wayne ME on 10th March [28 Mar 1850]
 Benjamin C & Philena W SPRINGER at Richmond ME [17 Feb 1848]
 Benjamin H & Clarinda S FELLOWS of Fayette ME at E Livermore ME [4 Jun 1851]
 Comfort & John ELLINGWOOD at Frankfort ME [26 Oct 1839]
 Ellen & R M MILLS at Readfield ME [16 Nov 1848]
 Emeline & Charles PARE of Quincy MA at Belgrade ME [12 Nov 1846]
 Emily D & Sewall B PAGE at Winthrop ME on Monday evening last by Samuel P BENSON Esq [17 Jul 1843]
 George S & Louisa BRADFORD Rev B F ROBBINS at Winthrop ME on Dec 5 [14 Dec 1848]
 Gustavus & Sarah CURRIER at Winthrop ME [16 Jan 1838]
 Hannah Jane & Capt N T SMITH at Brownville ME [15 Aug 1844]
 Harriet & William RICKER at Dexter ME [24 Oct 1840]
 Henry F & Sally F SMITH at Brownville ME [15 Aug 1844]
 Horatio & Hannah M SHAW at Palmyra ME [7 Jan 1847]
 Jane Mrs of (Winthrop ME) & John SAVAGE of Augusta ME at Augusta on Monday last by Rev Mr FULLER [9 Dec 1843]
 Jedediah H of Williamsburg ME & Ellen Mariah M RICHARDSON of Brownville ME on 1 Jun [24 Jun 1836]
 John 2d of Lowell MA & Melvina STEVENS of Winthrop ME by Rev W A DREW at (Augusta) ME on 7th Sept [28 Sept 1848]
 John 2d & Mrs Sophronia BOWLES at (Winthrop) ME on 6 Nov [13 Nov 1841]
 John A Esq & Cassandana EASTMAN at Limerick ME [29 May 1851]
 John C & Olive Caroline BERRY at Auburn ME [18 Nov 1847]
 John H Capt of Bangor ME & Zilphia H CUMMINGS at Augusta ME [25 Feb 1847]
 Jonathan B & Julia A CLARK both of China ME at Vassalboro ME [8 Feb 1844]
 Lewis C & Lydia M WATERHOUSE at Poland ME [19 Apr 1849]
 Lot M Esq of Readfield ME & Charlotte H VANCE of (Augusta) ME at New York NY [5 Dec 1844]
 Mary Ann & Col Asa LEGROW at Windham ME on 3rd inst by Elias BAKER Esq [16 Apr 1842]
 Mary Jane & Samuel W BARKER of Pittston ME at Hallowell ME on Weds evening last [6 Mar 1845]
 Mary of Augusta ME & Mr E G CURRIER at Winthrop ME by Rev A P HILLMAN [29 Jan 1839]
 Mary of Hallowell ME & Cornelius ALLEN at Augusta ME by Rev William A DREW [21 Nov 1834]
 Mary & Mr N C BROWN at Belfast ME [1 Jan 1846]
 Miss M F & William M LEWIS at Farmington ME [28 May 1846]
 Nancy A & Benjamin F BAKER Esq of Norridgewock ME at Athens ME [1 May 1851]
 Peter W & Ruth HUSSEY at Portland ME at Friends meeting house [21 Aug 1838]
 Sarah A & F H CASCOM of Southampton MA at Biddeford ME [10 Apr 1845]
 Sarah F & Leonard H BEAN at Hallowell ME [20 Nov 1851]

MORRELL (cont.) Shepherd of Orneville Piscataquis Co ME & Clarinda V WOODBURY at Bradford Penobscot Co ME [5 Aug 1847]
    Sherburne of Winthrop ME & Harriet M STEVENS of Fayette ME at Fayette on 3rd inst by Rev L C STEVENS [16 May 1840]
    Susanna & Ephraim SEVERANCE of Bangor ME at Belfast ME [3 Jul 1838]

MORRIS Elizabeth & Rev George W ADAMS of Newfield ME at Limerick ME [10 Oct 1837]

MORRISON Abram of Carmel ME & Jane McLAUGHLIN at Albion ME [15 Jul 1847]
    Asenath M & William STEVENS at Ellsworth ME [7 Apr 1848]
    Catherine F both of Wayne ME & Sumner C MOULTON, merchant at Wayne ME on 19th inst by Rev E Robinson of (Winthrop ME) [28 Jan 1843]
    Catherine & Elijah WILLIAMS at Portland ME [23 Jan 1845]
    Charity & William WHITNEY at West Bath ME [15 Feb 1849]
    Darillus & Harriet P WHITTIMORE at Livermore ME [13 Jun 1840]
    Elbridge G of Canaan ME & Malvina A SAWTELLE at Sidney ME on 3d Nov by Rev GARDNER [18 Nov 1847]
    Elmira & William FLANDERS Jr at Solon ME [12 Mar 1846]
    Emeline C & Benjamin F GOODWIN at Gardiner ME [4 May 1848]
    Eunice & Lorenzo D DUTTON of Livermore ME at Fayette ME [21 Oct 1843]
    Fidelia & Mr E FISH at Starks ME on 4th Jul [10 Aug 1848]
    H G O Esq of Sebec ME & Maria F LOVEJOY at Fayette ME [16 Oct 1841]
    Hannah of Albion ME & William COOK of Vassalboro ME at Albion ME on 8th inst by S BURRILL Esq [12 Nov 1846]
    Isaac T of Boothbay ME & Mary A BROWN [26 Dec 1844]
    John & Sarah A CUTLER at Thomaston ME [6 Nov 1845]
    Julia Ann & George WHIBLEY all of East Madison ME at Solon ME [12 Mar 1846]
    Martha Mrs & Henry B HOVEY Esq formerly of (Augusta) ME at East Boston ME on 6th Dec [24 Jan 1850]
    Mary Bertha & Charles H GRIDLEY of Boston MA at Dresden ME [28 Jan 1847]
    Mary E & Palmer WALLIS at Phipsburgh ME [5 Mar 1846]
    Mary & Edward ELLINGWOOD of Frankfort ME at Monroe ME [27 Nov 1851]
    Moses of Madrid ME & Sophia COTTLE of Phillips ME at Avon ME [15 May 1838]
    Nancy & Daniel M LEIGHTON at Calais ME [29 Aug 1834]
    R S of Frankfort ME & Frances W d/o William H BRETTUM of Livermore ME [4 Dec 1845]
    Robert FOGG & Mrs Abigail S DOW at Sebec ME [13 Jan 1848]
    Robert M of Farmington ME & Miss Sybil M FORD at East Livermore ME [17 Jan 1850]
    Samuel B MD of Parkman ME & Miss Columbia, d/o the late Mr FOSS of Livermore ME [22 Jan 1839]
    Simon & Sylvinia BROOKS both of Hallowell ME at Augusta ME [22 Oct 1846]

MORRISON (cont.) Susan of Boothbay ME & Jeremiah NORTON at Bath ME [28 Nov 1844]

MORRISSA William H & Mary E CARD of Bowdoin ME at Bath ME [2 Aug 1849]

MORROW Louisa A & Tyler KIDDER at Dixfield ME [13 May 1847]

MORSE Abel M of Starks ME & Mary BAKER at New Sharon ME by Rev C SCAMMAN [23 Oct 1841]

Alfred of Lubec ME & Rachel E MITCHELL at Bradford ME [14 Jan 1847]

Augustus & Alice HENDERSON at Thomaston ME [1 Aug 1844]

Benjamin F & Phebe J BOSTON both of this (Augusta) ME at Hallowell ME on 3d Feb by T SEARLS Esq [21 Feb 1850]

Caroline S & David F LOTHROP of Leeds ME at Lisbon ME [17 Dec 1846]

Charles of Milton Plt Oxford Co ME & Judith HINKSON at Rumford ME on 30 Dec by A H ABBOTT Esq [23 Jan 1851]

Charlotte Ann & Joseph B LEONARD of Boston MA at Bath ME [20 Aug 1846]

David L of Waterville ME & Mary Jane BROWN at Harmony ME [10 Aug 1848]

Edward P Esq & Martha A MORSE at Wiscasset ME [2 Jul 1846]

Edwin A & Lucy A MARSTON at Bath ME [18 Jul 1844]

Eleanor D & Timothy R BRADLEY of Topsham ME at Brunswick ME [9 Nov 1833]

Elias A of Taunton MA & Mary Ann SMALL at Jay ME [8 Apr 1833]

Elijah H of Mohawk NY & Roxana GASLIN at Vassalboro ME [28 Aug 1842]

Elijah of Bremen ME & Caroline NASH of Nobleboro ME at Thomaston ME [9 Oct 1845]

Elijah of Jay ME & Lavina SILVER at Rumford ME [6 Apr 1839]

Elivira & Zenus F HATHORN at Norridgewock ME [7 Apr 1848]

Elizabeth A Mrs & Prescot L PIKE at Oxford ME both of Norway ME [28 Oct 1843]

Ellen & Mr N B SHEPARD of Lowell MA at Bloomfield ME [1 Nov 1849]

Elvira & Woodward W LATHAM at Norway ME [30 Mar 1839]

Emeline & Swanton RANKS at Bath ME [10 Jan 1850]

George W & Mary H RICE at Union ME [24 Oct 1840]

H W Rev, pastor of the Universalist Society in Exeter NH & Lydia A JACOBS, d/o Edward F JACOBS Esq [6 Jul 1839]

Hannah F of Portland ME & Benjamin SWETT of Bangor ME at Gray ME [4 Mar 1836]

Harlow & Elizabeth FROST at Litchfield ME [2 Mar 1839]

Henrietta H & Rev William DAY at Bath ME [4 Jul 1840]

Hester A & Capt James LUNT of Freeport ME at Brunswick ME [30 Sept 1847]

Hiram & Delia E STANTIAL at Hallowell ME [4 Jun 1851]

Irene & Oliver S LYFORD at Livermore ME [10 Jun 1847]

Isaac S & Lettice E BOULTER both of Knox ME by I C HALL Esq at Montville ME on 16th Jun [23 Jun 1852]

J Parker & Mary F F HENRY at Bath ME [26 Dec 1844]

James G & Susan WILSON both of Troy ME at Belfast ME [18 Jun 1846]

MORSE (cont.) James Jr & Abby NICHOLS of S Thomaston ME at Rockland ME [4 Dec 1851]
James T Capt & Margaret W SEWALL at Phipsburg ME [8 Nov 1849]
Job Deacon of Farmington ME & Mary LUCE at New Sharon ME [10 Feb 1848]
Joseph M of Carthage ME & Deborah A HILL at Wilton ME [6 Sept 1849]
Leander & Sarah J SWIFT at Belmont ME [3 Apr 1851]
Lewellyn J & Mrs Louisa C BASHIEL of Boston MA at Bangor ME [26 Aug 1843]
Lucinda S of Norway ME & Charles A SCOTT of Dixfield ME at Bethel ME [9 Aug 1849]
Lucy H & Horatio WILBUR at Livermore ME [16 Apr 1846]
Marie & Mr I H MELCHER at Brunswick ME [3 May 1849]
Marshall & Maria C FOSTER at Gary ME [27 Sept 1849]
Martha A & Edward P MORSE Esq both of Union ME at Wiscasset ME [2 Jul 1846]
Martha Ann T & Mark L SYLVESTER Esq of Lincolnville ME at Phipsburg ME [3 Dec 1846]
Martha M & Samuel KENDALL of Mt Vernon ME at Augusta ME on 4th inst by J W PATTERSON Esq [8 Oct 1846]
Martha & Ichabod A PETTINGILL of Monmouth ME at Winthrop ME on 22d Feb by Rev Mr MORSE [1 Mar 1849]
Mary B & Hon S M POND of Buckport ME at New York NY [23 Oct 1845]
Mary E & Elias W SHAW of China ME at Hallowell ME on 2d inst [11 Sept 1845]
Mary J of Norway & John WOODMAN of Norway ME at Providence RI [16 Jan 1851]
Mary J & Stephen BERRY at Phipsburg ME [5 Aug 1847]
Mary Jane & Sewall MORSE at Phipsburg ME [16 Jan 1841]
Mary of Winthrop ME & Seth MARTIN of New Gloucester ME at Winthrop ME on 26th Feb by Rev Mr BARNARD [6 Mar 1845]
Merriam & Gilbert ALLEN of Fayette ME at Carthage ME [6 Nov 1851]
Nancy & Mr Boyd SIDELINGER at Friendship ME [19 Aug 1852]
Nathan S & Mary B MOODY at Paris ME [26 Apr 1849]
Rebecca & James DRUMMOND at Phipsburg ME [26 Aug 1836]
Roxana of East Dixfield ME & Daniel SAFFORD Jr of Fayette ME at Livermore ME [20 Dec 1849]
S O of Charlestown & Rosanna WIXSON formerly of Augusta ME at South Andover MA [28 May 1846]
Samuel A of Machias ME & Mrs Sarah B EVELETH at Minudia Nova Scotia Canada [18 Jul 1844]
Samuel B of Wilton ME & Catherine W PATTERSON at Augusta ME [24 Aug 1839]
Samuel C of Freeport ME & Amanda J EATON of Bowdoinham ME at Brunswick ME [11 Feb 1847]
Samuel S & Ann HUSSEY at Fairfield ME [9 May 1844]
Scott of Bath ME & Pauline WEEKS at Phipsburg ME [25 Apr 1844]
Seretha D & Mr E Whitman SWETT at Livermore ME [24 Jun 1847]
Sewall & Mary Jane MORSE at Phippsburg ME [16 Jan 1841]
Susan & William H BARNARD at Waldoboro ME [23 Jan 1838]
Sylvanus & Emily E BLACKWELL at Norridgewock ME [3 Jul 1845]

MORSE (cont.) W H & Sarah E BARTON d/o Dea Gideon BARTON at Windsor ME on Jun 29 by Rev William BOWLER [3 Jul 1851]
   William Jr & Mary Jane CURRIER at West Gardiner ME [21 Aug 1835]
   William M Capt & Betsey M ELLIOT both of Raymond ME [12 Nov 1842]

MORTEN Peleg & Mary H PRATT at Windsor ME by J B SWANTON Esq [19 Sept 1837]

MORTON Albert of Thomaston ME & Harriet W WIGGIN of Brooks ME at Belfast [18 Dec 1845]
   Angeline & Samuel N TUFTS at (Winthrop) ME [18 Dec 1838]
   Benjamin T of New Vineyard ME & Hannah THOMAS at New Portland ME [10 Jun 1843]
   Betsey & Miles PRATT at Windsor ME by J B SWANTON [30 May 1834]
   Cephias of Winthrop ME & Sarah Jane SMART at Vienna ME [25 May 1848]
   Clarissa J Jason S TAYLOR at Norridgewock ME [26 Apr 1849]
   Cornelius B & Mrs Eliza A TOWLE at Augusta ME on Monday by the Rev Mr JUDD [27 May 1843]
   Delia C & Noah CURRIER at New York NY [29 Jun 1848]
   Hallet W of Boston formerly of Winthrop ME & Lavina S ROBINSON at Lowell MA by Rev C H SMITH [3 Jul 1845]
   Harrison G O of Winthrop ME & Miss H F GIBSON of Brownfield ME on 4 May by Rev Abner DAVIS [19 Jun 1841]
   Irene & James HUNTON at Windsor ME by J B SWANTON Esq [14 Feb 1837]
   James & Caroline C GREGORY at Thomaston ME [9 Mar 1848]
   Lucretia J & George F KIMBALL of Norway ME at Paris ME [21 Aug 1851]
   Maria L of Bristol ME & Capt William BURNS 3rd at Bremen ME [9 Oct 1851]
   Martha Ann & David AVERILL at Portland ME [13 Mar 1845]
   Martha B & Albert B STEVENS of Windham ME at Saccarappa ME [4 Jun 1846]
   Mary A & David N ESTERBROOK of Oldtown ME at Windsor ME [2 Sept 1847]
   Mary Ann & Seneca W KEENE at Bremen ME [21 Jan 1833]
   Mary F & Zachariah GIBSON 2d of Brownfield ME at (Winthrop) ME on the 5th inst by Rev David THURSTON [13 Nov 1835]
   Miriam C & Stephen McGREGOR at Lubec ME [21 Jan 1847]
   Philander, merchant of (Hallowell) ME & Sarah C WOOD, d/o Elijah WOOD Esq of Winthrop ME at Winthrop on Weds last by Rev D D TAPPAN [24 Oct 1837]
   Philander of Hallowell ME & Diana LOMBARD at Readfield ME on Tuesday last by Rev David THURSTON [24 Oct 1834]
   Rebecca & Charles LERMOND at Warren ME [25 Dec 1841]
   Samuel & Lucy Ann WILDER at Wiscasset ME [27 Mar 1845]
   Sarah & Mr J W ARCHER at Lincoln ME [1 Apr 1847]
   William H of (Augusta) ME & Caroline HOBART d/o Samuel HOBART Esq at Hingham MA on 19th inst [26 Oct 1848]

MOSELY Elisha H & S A A L SAMPSON at New Gloucester ME [17 Jun 1847]
   Emily & Abraham TARR at Etna ME [8 Jun 1848]

MOSELY (cont.) Mary & Edward TETFORD of Topsham ME at Bowdoin ME [31 Oct 1844]
Sarah Ann of Bowdoin ME & Arthur EDGECOMB at Topsham ME [11 Jan 1844]
MOSES Abraham T of Waldoboro ME & Margaret P MITCHELL of Bath ME at Bath [28 Nov 1840]
Harriet & Rufus H WOOD at Bath ME [31 Aug 1848]
James S & Adeline C ROWE at Bangor ME [12 Mar 1842]
Silas of Scarborough ME & Mary Ann ABBOT at Portland ME [21 Jan 1847]
MOSHER Almira & James A DUNSMORE at Temple ME [20 Jun 1837]
Daniel & Catherine BRAN of Belgrade ME at Augusta ME on 8th inst by S TITCOMB Esq [16 Sept 1847]
Elizabeth D & Thomas WHITE both of Augusta ME at Providence RI on 19th Sept [2 Oct 1851]
Martha J & John B DYER at Augusta ME on 27 Aug by Rev Z THOMPSON [4 Sept 1851]
Mary G & Capt Joseph ALEXANDER of Brunswick ME at Gorham ME [12 Jun 1845]
Nancy of Temple ME & Oliver DONNEL of Buxton ME at Readfield ME [18 Feb 1847]
Orinda M & John S FRASER at New York City NY [15 Aug 1840]
MOSHIER Frances G & D CARPENTER Esq at Sacarapa ME [1 Jul 1847]
Nancy & Daniel P LOCKE both of Augusta ME at Belgrade ME on 13th inst by J DAVIES Esq [25 Feb 1847]
MOSIER Olive S & Benjamin TOMPKINS both of Unity ME at Montville ME [3 Jan 1850]
MOSTMAN William Capt of Hope ME & Mrs Sybil PARKER at Belfast ME [28 May 1842]
MOTHERWELL Mehitable & Elias TAYLOR at Windsor ME [30 Mar 1848]
Rachel H & Nathaniel GODING both of Gardiner ME at Windsor ME [9 Sept 1847]
MOTT Adam & Aunt TUTTLE of Freeman ME at Temple ME "Their entire weight is said to be 580 lbs - the gentleman weighing 340 & the lady 240 lbs" [18 May 1848]
Mary, d/o Adam MOTT of Wilton ME, & Levi WING of Greene ME, at the Friends meeting house in Wilton [19 Dec 1840]
MOULTON Althea & Elisha FILES at Thorndike ME [21 May 1846]
Clarissa of Madrid ME & Jacob LUFKIN of Phillips ME by Joseph DOW Esq [7 Jan 1847]
David N of Lewiston ME & Miss G G FOGG at Greene ME [13 Mar 1851]
Dennis & Miss Rosanna PICKARD both of Madrid ME at Phillips ME by Joseph DOW Esq [7 Jan 1847]
George B of Gardiner ME & Mary BARKER of Pittston ME by Rev A BURGESS at (Augusta) ME at St Mark's Church [6 Jan 1848]
James of Wayne ME & Novella LINDSEY at Leeds ME on 10th inst [14 Oct 1847]
Martha & Addison FISHER of Hopkinton MA at York ME [13 Jun 1844]
Mary Elizabeth formerly of Massachusetts & Samuel JOHNSON formerly of Winthrop ME at Cincinnati OH on the 3rd inst by Rev J A CURLEY [25 Jan 1844]

MOULTON (cont.) Mary F & George F at Parsonsfield ME [28 Mar 1844]
  Oliver & Catherine SHAW of Weymouth MA at Pittston ME [11 Jan 1849]
  Sarah of Topsham ME & Uriel F HUNTINGTON at Bowdoinham ME [26 Mar 1842]
  Sumner C, merchant, & Catherine F MORRISON both of Wayne ME at Wayne ME on 19th inst by Rev E ROBINSON of (Winthrop ME) [28 Jan 1843]
  William Esq of Portland ME & Nancy CUMSTON at Monmouth ME [25 Nov 1836]
MOWER Duane & Cynthia ALLEN at Greene ME [23 Jun 1852]
  Harrison G O of Turner ME & Delora SYLVESTER by Elder David NUTTER at Livermore ME on 18th Jan [5 Feb 1852]
  Jesse C & Angeline S BROWN at St Albans ME [12 Feb 1852]
  Susan E & John M DAY both of Wilton ME at Jay ME [19 Aug 1847]
  William W & Martha G CLARRY of Wilton ME at Jay ME [19 Aug 1847]
MUDGETT A R & Ruby Jane BASSICK at Prospect ME on the 5th [15 Jul 1852]
  Benjamin F Esq & Eliza M FLAGG at Hampden ME [20 Aug 1846]
  Charles B of Hallowell ME & Hannah BUTLER at Freeport ME [10 Jul 1845]
  Clara E & Thomas F KILLMAN at Prospect ME [30 May 1844]
  Clarrissa & William PATTERSON at Northport ME [5 Sept 1840]
  Jacob & Mrs Catherine HUTCHINSON at Hallowell ME [7 Oct 1847]
MULLIKEN Charles H & Sarah E HALLETT d/o Watson F HALLETT Esq at Augusta ME on Dec 3rd by Rev WEBB [18 Dec 1851]
  George S Esq Attorney at Law of (Augusta) ME & Maria H OWEN at Brunswick ME on 30 May [15 Jun 1848]
MULRAY M of Skowhegan ME & Miss R J FAIRBROTHER at Norridgewock ME [9 Nov 1848]
MUNCEY Samuel 2nd & Rachel KINCAID at Wiscassett ME [4 Feb 1833]
MUNROE Alex B Capt Jr of Bristol ME & Mary Jane CUTLER of Rockland ME at Bristol ME [26 Feb 1852]
  Mary Ann & G W HOWARD at Brooksville ME [29 Apr 1836]
  Sarah M & Capt Harris ROBINSON at Thomaston ME [31 Jul 1845]
MUNSEY Rebecca W & Mr F C PULLEN at Waterville ME [8 May 1851]
  Mary Ann & Wilmot BLAKE at Wiscasset ME [8 Jul 1836]
MURCH Ebenezer Jr of Plymouth ME & Nancy W WINSLOW at Dixmont ME [27 Nov 1851]
  James & Eliza A PERKINS at Frankfort ME [8 Apr 1847]
  James B Esq of Unity ME & Mary L HUSSEY of Readfield ME at Readfield by Hon E FULLER [14 Feb 1837]
  Zebulon of Foxcroft ME & Mrs Nancy CHAMBERLAIN of Unity ME at Foxcroft ME [16 May 1844]
MURPHEY Eliza A & John C PARSHLEY at Bath ME [10 Aug 1848]
MURPHY James of East Machias ME & Ellen GILLIGAN at Eastport ME [13 Feb 1845]
  Maria & Jeremy WYMAN at Jefferson ME [5 Jun 1835]
  Mary & James POTTOR of Whitefield ME at Wiscasset ME [25 Jan 1844]
  Sally Y & Timothy PLUMMER both of Whitefield ME at Windsor ME [8 Apr 1847]
  Samuel & Hannah F SIAS at Oldtown ME [18 Jun 1846]

MURPHY (cont.) Sidney F & William ELLISON at Calais ME on the 25th [10 Jun 1843]
 Susan & Rev Giles BAILEY, pastor of the Universalist Church in Brunswick ME at Alstead NH [6 Feb 1845]
MURRAY Amaziah D & Nancy S WYMAN both of Bloomfield ME at Bloomfield [29 Jul 1847]
 Ann & Henry D FROST & at Readfield ME on 1st Jun by Hon Edward FULLER [12 Jun 1851]
 Charles of Boothbay ME & Mary E F LINNEKIN at Belfast ME [21 Mar 1850]
 Clarissa J & Adino J BURBANK at Auburn ME [6 Sept 1849]
 Eliza Mrs & Eben BAILEY at (Augusta) ME on 25 Mar [8 Apr 1852]
 Rosanna A & John S HALL at Norridgewock ME [8 Feb 1849]
MURROW William & Margaret LIBBEY at Gardiner ME [30 Nov 1833]
MUSEY Ebenezer & Catherine DOW at Wiscasset ME by Rev Mr MATHER [8 Oct 1842]
MUSTARD Charity of Topsham ME & Capt James JAMESON of Bath ME [27 Nov 1838]
 Harriet W & Samuel JAMESON at Topsham ME [21 Nov 1837]
 Mary Jane & Thomas KELLEY at Phipsburg ME [14 Jan 1847]
MUZZY Jonas & Nancy F RICHARDSON at Gardiner ME [25 Apr 1840]
MYERS Ephraim Capt & Ann Eliza BLAISDELL at Rockland ME [2 Oct 1851]
 Arletta & Samuel CHISAM of Alna ME at Pittston ME [18 Dec 1845]
 James of Brandon MS & Miss Emeline C HAWKES at Hallowell ME on Weds evening last by Rev Mr WEBBER [22 Aug 1837]
 Nancy & Asa DINSMORE Esq at Nobleboro ME [2 Sept 1836]
 Sumner & Mrs Abigail CARNEY at Dresden ME [4 Oct 1849]
MYRICK see MIRICK
 Albert A & Angelone FORD at Lewiston ME [23 Jun 1852]
 Francis & Mary PLANT at Bath ME [4 Jan 1849]
 J Warren of Lawrence MA & Mary J FARRINGTON at Troy ME on Mar 7th by Elder S S NASON [14 Mar 1850]
 Julia A & Horatio TUTHILL of Providence RI at Kennebec ME on 31st Mar by I N WADSWORTH Esq [24 Apr 1851]
 Melinda M of Bangor ME & Menander PEARSON at Portland ME [22 Apr 1847]

- N -

NASH Abizer Ann of Bremen ME & William BICKMORE of Appleton ME at Bremen ME by Waite W KEENE Esq on 7th inst [27 July 1839]
 Andrew L E, M.D., of Sweden ME & Rebecca STONE at Waterford ME [5 Feb 1852]
 Caroline of Nobleboro ME & Elijah MORSE of Bremen ME at Thomaston ME [9 Oct 1845]
 Charles R & Mrs Mary DINSMORE both of Harrington Washington Co ME at Addison Washington Co ME [29 May 1851]
 Christiana of Readfield ME & Isaac NORCROSS of Lowell MA at Boston ME on July 4 [16 Jul 1846]
 Clorinda C & Nathaniel N WASS at Addision Point ME [14 Oct 1847]

NASH (cont.) Frances E & Alfred DOUGLASS both of West Gardiner ME at Hallowell ME [27 Feb 1845]
   Isaac of Calais ME & Almira LORING at Perry ME [24 Dec 1846]
   J H of Fall River MA & Margaret J ANDERSON at Webster ME [16 Sept 1847]
   James S & Mary Ann KEITH at Minot ME [3 Oct 1840]
   James & Mary B McCausland at Gardiner ME [22 Mar 1849]
   James & Susan G BOWMAN at Gardiner ME [9 Nov 1838]
   Joseph & Catherine H ROBINSON both of Sidney ME by Rev William WARD at Belgrade ME on 13th Dec [28 Dec 1848]
   Josephus of Portland ME & Nancy E CLAPP at Bath ME [11 Oct 1849]
   Martha P & William W WEST of Belfast ME at Portland ME [19 Dec 1844]
   Rebecba [sic] L & Abner HANSON at Sidney ME [11 Feb 1847]

NASON B of Bethel ME & Lydia EASTMAN (see John B MASON) at Waterford ME [2 Aug 1849]
   Bartholomew Esq of Augusta ME & Mrs Elizabeth GOODALE at Hallowell ME [29 Apr 1833]
   E A & Miss Julian HAMLEN at Augusta ME on Tues eve last by Rev Benj TAPPAN [12 Jun 1838]
   Elias C of Augusta ME & Maria W BALCH at Boston MA on Feb 21 [7 Mar 1850]
   Eliza & Job L WHITE at Wiscasset ME [25 Jun 1842]
   Emily A & James B McLURE at Palmyra ME on Oct 25 by Eld N F NASON [27 Dec 1849]
   George H & Elizabeth L BUTLER d/o Rev John Ball formerly of Augusta ME at Greenfield MA [26 Aug 1852]
   Henry P & Maria I MOORE at Waterville ME [26 Jun 1851]
   Jacob & Hannah E WITHAM at Biddeford ME [13 Apr 1848]
   Lydia & Joseph DICKENSON Jr at Wiscasset ME [17 Dec 1846]
   Maria P & Oliver S SANFORD of Boston MA at Hallowell ME on 4th inst by Rev E THURSTON [12 Jun 1845]
   Martha J & Amasa W MANLEY at Waterville ME [19 Oct 1848]
   Mary E & Alexander R DUREN at Augusta ME [16 Nov 1839]
   Miria B & Francis B DANE Esq of Troy NY at Livermore ME [8 Jul 1847]
   Nathan & Lucy Ann JACOBS at Sidney ME by William HAMLEN Esq [16 May 1837]
   Nathaniel & Laura Ann LEIGHTON at Augusta ME by L CUSHING Esq [21 Nov 1844]
   Olive late of Albion ME & Jacob L WIGGIN at China ME by Rev H PROCTOR [11 Sept 1841]
   Rufus & Nancy STILSON at Waterville ME [4 Oct 1849]
   Sarah & David R PRESSAN of Avon ME at Temple ME on 11 Sept [25 Sept 1851]
   William & Mary A WINGATE at Hallowell ME on Tues last by Rev B TAPPAN [19 Sept 1837]

NAY John S of Palmyra ME & Sophronia P ROBINSON of Cornville ME at Skowhegan ME [27 Mar 1851]
   Thomas L of Bangor ME & Mary J JOHNSON of Farmington ME at F on Tues 11th inst by Rev Isaac ROGERS [22 Jan 1842]

NEAL Barker A of Wiscasset ME & Mary GRANT at Gardiner ME [17 Apr 1851]

NEAL (cont.) Deborah of China ME & Abram MERRILL of Windsor ME by William PERCIVAL 2nd Esq [3 Dec 1846]
    Elizabeth P & George H KNOWLES at Hallowell ME [31 Jan 1850]
    Ellen & James E YEATON of Richmond at Hallowell ME [25 Dec 1845]
    Eunice P of Charleston ME & Samuel G FINNEY of Baltimore MD at Burlington IA [2 Dec 1843]
    Fancina & Harris DOE at China ME [30 May 1844]
    Harriet A & Charles DOUGLASS at Hallowell ME [28 Dec 1848]
    John & Sarah R VICKERY both of Belmont ME at Montville ME 7 May 1846]
    Martha A & E B HUTCHINSON of Natick MA at Pittston ME [1 Nov 1849]
    Miriam Mrs of Gardiner ME & Joshua WALKER at Litchfield ME [15 Aug 1837]
    Sarah G & A H GILMAN at Skowhegan ME [12 Dec 1840]
NEALE Elizabeth A & Jesse A HATCH 2nd of Greene ME at Litchfield ME [21 Jun 1849]
NEALLEY Edward S J Esq Attorney at Law & Lucy C d/o Hon Hezekiah PRINCE at Thomaston ME on Tues 5th inst [15 Jul 1836]
NEALLY G C Esq & Jane M WHITE of Portland ME at Monroe ME [28 Oct 1842]
NEIL Elizabeth L & George F TALBOT Esq of Machias ME at Skowhegan ME [6 Jun 1844]
    Harriet C of Skowhegan ME & Silas A B HAINES of Green Bay WI he an Esq at Lynn MA [10 Jul 1851]
    Paulina R Mrs & Nahum HASKELL Esq, Editor of *Vermont Mercury*, Woodstock at Skowhegan ME [25 Jun 1846]
NEILLY Catherine Mrs & John M LANCASTER at Lee July 22nd by J B LUDDEN Esq [5 Aug 1852]
NELSON Abby A & Charles WARREN at Winthrop ME [1 Jul 1847]
    Abigail R & Jeremiah STINCHFIELD of Danville ME at New Gloucester ME [22 Jul 1852]
    Addison & Mary Ann NELSON both of Oxford ME at Mechanic Falls ME [14 Jun 1849]
    Carlos E of Winslow ME & Roxana S MATHEWS at Sebasticock ME [30 Aug 1849]
    Caroline & Eliakim NORTON at Wayne ME [10 Oct 1840]
    Clarinda & William BARNEY at Atkinson ME [16 Sept 1843]
    David O of Mercer ME formerly of Winthrop ME & Eunice GEORGE of Leeds ME at Turner ME on Mon last [19 Jun 1841]
    Hazen B & Sarah K BREWSTER at Thomaston ME [29 Jan 1846]
    John & Sarah REYNOLDS at Hallowell ME [30 Jul 1846]
    Joseph R of (Winthrop) ME & Abagail HILL d/o David HILL of Bangor ME by Rev Mr MALTHY at Bangor ME on the 9th inst [18 Jul 1840]
    Lois S & Dr Charles H FARNSWORTH of Bridgton ME at Jay ME [19 Jul 1849]
    Margaret P & Rev Thomas F FALES of Brunswick ME at Portland ME [29 Apr 1847]
    Martha J & Cyrus B SWIFT at Winthrop ME on Sunday evening on 14th May by Rev F FOSTER [20 May 1843]
    Mary A, d/o Jacob NELSON of Wayne ME, & Mr Thomas J GARDINER of Providence RI at Pensacola West Florida on 12th Apr [6 Jun 1840]

NELSON (cont.) Mary Ann & Addison NELSON both of Oxford ME at Mechanics Falls ME [14 Jun 1849]
 Mary Jane, d/o Isaac NELSON, of (Winthrop ME), & William NOYES of Hallowell ME, publisher of the *Chronicle* on 10th Oct at (Winthrop) [16 Oct 1838]
 S M of China ME & Margaret E PORTER of Oldtown ME at Augusta ME on 2 Oct by Asaph R NICHOLS Esq [16 Oct 1851]
 Sarah of Winthrop ME & Samuel WOOD of Wilton ME at Readfield ME [2 Mar 1839]
 William Francis Rev of Richmond VA & Susan L HAYDEN at Eastport ME [14 Aug 1835]
NESBIT Nancy Mrs & James DILL of Phillips ME at Letter E ME [12 Aug 1847]
NESS Eliza Ann d/o Capt Ranlett N of Searsmont ME & Alanson A GREENWOOD of Augusta ME at Vassalboro ME on Feb 15 [27 Feb 1851]
 Sarah R & Edmund HAZEN at Brunswick ME [28 May 1846]
NEVENS Eunice S & Aaron OSGOOD at Lewiston ME [3 Feb 1848]
 William W & Mary BAILEY at Sweden ME [19 Feb 1852]
NEWBEGIN Eunice & James P JORDAN at Poland ME [17 Aug 1848]
 Jane & Reuben BLAKE at Hope ME [14 Aug 1838]
 Robert of Falmouth ME & Betsey L DAVIS at Augusta ME on 1st Aug by the Rev Z THOMPSON [5 Aug 1852]
NEWBERT Lucy C & Henry HOWE of Paris ME at Dedham [25 Mar 1847]
NEWBURY William S of Vinalhaven ME & Mercey Ann KEAN at Montville ME [26 Dec 1837]
NEWCOMB Hannah E & Horace LITCHFIELD at Bath ME [23 Apr 1846]
 John S & Olive Ann DUNBAR at Warren ME [13 March 1841]
 Martha A & Hiram WHITE at Gardiner ME [16 Jan 1845]
 Olivett & George F CARPENTER at Eastport ME [5 Mar 1846]
 William of Milo ME & Nancy WATSON of Dover ME at Foxcroft ME [8 Jan 1852]
NEWDISK W D & Eliza Jane SHAY at Arrowsic ME [17 Sept 1846]
NEWELL Andrew R & Sarah GREENLEAF of Mercer ME at New Sharon ME [25 Jul 1840]
 Charlotte H & Royal BROWN of Clinton ME at Winslow ME [17 Jul 1838]
 Emeline & Joseph W FARRIN at Bath ME [29 Apr 1847]
 Francis C & S S STEVENS of Belfast ME at Winslow ME [22 Oct 1842]
 Francis K & Joseph B HALL of Presque Isle Aroostook Co ME at Sangerville ME [4 Mar 1847]
 James Jr of Durham ME & Sarah W HERRICK at Harmony ME [10 Aug 1848]
 Lorenzo D & Miss C P WETHERN at New Portland ME [25 Dec 1841]
 Marianna of Winslow ME & Charles C EDMUNDS, merchant of Belfast ME at Waterville ME by Rev C GARDINER [15 Feb 1840]
 Salina A & Henry A TURNER at Whitefield ME on 23d Aug by Hiram GLIDDEN Esq [27 Sept 1849]
NEWHALL Jonathan Esq of Washington ME & Margaret YEATS of Winthrop ME at Waldoborough ME on Thurs morning last [9 May 1840]
 Orsons D of Paris ME & Miss S N NUTTER of Portsmouth NH at Boston MA [6 Feb 1845]

NEWHALL (cont.) Samuel M of Paris ME & Louisa J SHACKLEY of Norway ME [1 Oct 1842]

NEWMAN Arabella B & Lorenzo JONES at Dixfield ME [9 Mar 1848]
  Harriet Ann & Silas L WEBB at Winthrop ME on Weds evening on 22 Jan by David THURSTON [6 Feb 1845]
  Henry S of (Winthrop ME) & Cynthia V DENSMORE of Auburn ME at Auburn on the 3rd inst by Rev Mr JONES [7 May 1842]
  Jacob & Lucinda RICHARDSON of Reading MA at Dixfield ME [11 Oct 1849]
  Mary Ann & George R WELD of Livermore ME at Dixfield ME [14 Jan 1847]
  Thomas W, printer of the *Advocate of Freedom*, Hallowell ME, & Miss Caroline F GREENE, d/o Hon Nathaniel GREENE of Topsham ME [27 Feb 1841]
  Thomas W of Brunswick ME & Sarah DYER of Portland ME at Portland ME by Rev Mr DWIGHT [22 May 1838]

NEWTON Lovina & Patrick McKINNE at Moose River ME [17 Feb 1848]
  Vesta G & Franklin HOLMAN at Dixfield ME [2 Aug 1849]
  William R & Lydia McCOBB at Bath ME [20 May 1836]

NICHERSON Warren Esq of Orrington ME & Mrs Nancy PARKER of Gorham ME at Gorham by Cyril PEARL [27 Jun 1840]

NICHOLAS - NICHLESS - NICKOLESS - NICKLESS
  James & Leilles HOUSE at East Livermore ME on 27th ult by Columbus HAINES Esq [4 Jan 1844]
  Jane of Vassalboro ME & Reuel CHAMBERLAIN of Augusta ME at Sidney ME [10 Jul 1845]
  Joseph & Adaline BROWN at Augusta ME on Aug 7th [21 Aug 1851]
  Stephen H of Carlisle MA & Martha H CONY at Strong ME [8 Jun 1848]

NICHOLS A D (Dr) & Kate H ACHORN both Rockland ME at Albany NY [19 Aug 1852]
  Abby of S Thomaston ME & James MORSE Jr at Rockland ME [4 Dec 1851]
  Alice P & Mr J J ATWOOD of Greenville ME at Abbot ME [30 Dec 1847] & [20 Jan 1848]
  Ann Augusta, eldest d/o A R NICHOLS Esq, & George S HALL at Augusta ME on 5 April by Rev Mr JUDD [16 Apr 1846]
  Caroline & Nathan DAVIS at Augusta ME [22 Apr 1847]
  David Jr Capt & Elizabeth BEALS at Searsport ME [20 Mar 1845]
  Deborah C & Mr I FROST Jr at Monmouth ME [27 Mar 1841]
  Elmira A & Amos MERRILL at (Augusta) ME on 13th inst [27 Jan 1848]
  George W, printer, of Thomaston ME, & Miss Susan G TREADWELL at Salem MA [14 Nov 1834]
  George W, Sr Editor & Proprietor of the *Lincoln Patriot*, & Penelope P WINSLOW at Marshfield MA [6 Nov 1838]
  Hannah formerly of Bristol ME & Samuel REDINGTON Esq of Vassalboro ME at Hampden ME [23 Feb 1839]
  Henry L & Miss Sarah E COLE at Augusta ME on 7th inst by Rev Mr JUDD [16 Sept 1847]
  James H Capt & Mrs Elizabeth J RUSSELL at Bath ME [16 Jul 1846]
  James T formerly of Buxton ME & Mrs Abigail H DAVIS at Saco ME [9 Apr 1846]
  Julia A & Samuel AYER at Pittston ME [23 Dec 1847]

NICHOLS (cont.) Octavia & Asel STANLEY at Wiscasset ME [19 Sept 1834]
    Reed & Rachel Ann LITTLE at Bath ME [5 Feb 1846]
    Sarah Caroline, d/o Asaph R NICHOLS Esq, & Enoch Augustus HOBART of Boston MA at this city (Augusta) on 20th Mar [28 Mar 1850]
    Stephen H of Carlisle MA & Martha C CONY at Strong ME [22 Jun 1848]
    William A & Mary DAVIS at Augusta ME on 25th Nov [9 Dec 1847]
NICKERSON Benjamin L of Prospect & Lucy A NICKERSON at Belfast ME [4 Sept 1851]
    Bethiah S & Darius ALDEN of Augusta ME at Strong ME [20 Nov 1839]
    Elijah & Nancy WENTWORTH at Webster ME [9 Jan 1851]
    Eliza J & Emery CARTER of Swanville ME at Frankfort ME [22 Jan 1842]
    Hannah K & Capt Joseph C HIGGINS at Bucksport ME [20 Aug 1846]
    Jedidah & James S F SMITH of Monmouth ME at Mercer ME [27 Mar 1845]
    Lucy A & Benjamin L NICKERSON of Prospect ME at Belfast ME [4 Sept 1851]
    Malachi Jr & Hannah LITTLEFIELD at Belfast ME [21 May 1842]
    Mary Ann & Rev Eliphalet S HOPKINS at New Portland ME [28 Nov 1840] & [5 Dec 1840]
    Mary Ann & Rev Eliphalet S HOPKINS of Rumford ME at New Portland ME [25 Apr 1840]
    Mary E of Belfast ME & Dr Samuel M SMITH of Prospect ME at Belfast [15 Apr 1836]
    Rhoana R & John DOUGLAS at Topsham ME [17 Jun 1836]
    S H Esq of Swanville ME & Miss A P STOWERS of Prospect ME at Prospect [3 Jul 1845]
    Salathiel C Capt of Belfast ME & Abigail W CARR at East Thomaston ME by the Rev Mr FESSENDEN [1 Jun 1839]
    Sarah H & Capt Amasa BARTLETT Jr of Orrington ME at Skowhegan ME [30 Nov 1848] & [15 Feb 1849]
    Seth Jr & Flavilla W PRIEST at Vassalboro ME [14 Dec 1839]
    Theopilus of Brewer ME & Lydia F SMITH at Belfast ME [7 Aug 1845]
NICKLES Timothy & Hester Ann YOUNG at Wayne ME both of Fayette ME [25 Feb 1847]
NIEBUHR George H of Bath ME & Anna M HALO at Portland ME [31 Oct 1844]
NILES Allen D & Eunice H LORD at Hallowell ME on 12th inst by Rev C FULLER [19 Jun 1846]
    Amasa of Freeman ME & Dulcentia N MARSTON at Farmington ME [11 Jan 1844]
    James M & Lucinda HERVEY [30 Jul 1846]
    Jeremiah A & Jane THORN at Webster ME [5 Apr 1849]
    Joseph of Lisbon ME & Nancy TRASK at Leeds ME by Rev Walter FOSS [19 Feb 1846]
    Nancy & Nancy NILES at Gardiner ME [1 Apr 1843]
    Samuel P & Sylvia HARLOW at Minot ME [19 Dec 1837]
NOBLE Elizabeth L & Timothy H LOCKE of Saco ME at Newfield ME [8 Feb 1844]
    Hannah E of New Sharon ME & Mr Elijah TOBY at Farmington Falls ME [29 Apr 1847]
    Henry of Norway ME & Keziah HILL at Paris ME [30 Apr 1846]
    Olive & James M PAINE at Norway ME [17 Aug 1848]

NOBLE (cont.) Thomas C & Adeline T JOHNSON at Farmington ME [29 May 1835]
NODDING Benjamin & Ann WHALEN both of West Isles at Eastport ME [19 Dec 1844]
NORCROSS Adan L & Mary Jane CLARK at Hallowell ME on Sunday morning last [16 May 1834]
    Adna L of (Augusta ME) & Mrs Sarah C SMITH at New York City on 14th ult [2 Oct 1845]
    Angeline & Joseph TILTON at Farmington ME [13 Mar 1845]
    Charles S of Danville ME & Deborah R BATES at Waterville ME [12 Feb 1852]
    E L & Miss Ann E WOODBRIDGE at Hallowell ME [10 Dec 1846]
    Elijah L Esq of Garland ME & Mrs Experience HUTCHINSON of Winthrop ME at Monmouth on 29th ult [21 Feb 1837]
    Eunice Mrs & William B LITTLEFIELD at Hallowell ME by Rev E THURSTON [3 Apr 1845]
    Ezra H of Winthrop ME & Miss Locinda W TOZIER of Monmouth ME at Augusta ME on 1st Feb [19 Feb 1842]
    George A & Helen Z BRANCH at Augusta ME on 28th Nov [9 Dec 1847]
    Henry & Mrs Susan P PETTENGILL at Augusta ME [29 Oct 1846]
    Isaac of Lowell MA & Christiana NASH of Readfield ME at Boston MA on 4th Jul [16 Jul 1846]
    Israel B Capt of Bangor ME & Irene DUNNING at Charleston [4 Feb 1847]
    Jarvis M of Augusta ME & Mrs Betsey C DAVENPORT of Hallowell ME [20 Mar 1841]
    Julia A of Hallowell ME & William WYMAN at Augusta ME [15 Aug 1834]
    Louisa M & Caleb G MOFFITT at Livermore ME [29 May 1845]
    Louisa & Arthur D LOCKE at Augusta ME on Jan 23 [6 Feb 1851]
    Marion W & Franklin TOZIER of Waterville ME at Hallowell ME [23 Dec 1843]
    Mary E & William N SOULE of Boston MA at Augusta ME on Thurs the 15th inst [30 Oct 1845]
    William H & Miss Maricia Cony d/o Alexander KINCAID at Augusta ME on 17th inst [25 Feb 1847]
    William S of (Augusta ME) & Miss Jane D FARNAHAM of Jefferson on 22d ult by Rev Mr WHITEHOUSE [4 Jan 1844]
NORMAN Helen, eldest d/o Capt MOR(i)SON of Stanford Upper Canada & Alexander McLEAD (of Steamer *Caroline Celebrity*) [23 Apr 1842]
NORRIS Alden of Livermore ME & Miss Sarah N CASLIN of Readfield ME at Livermore ME [25 Mar 1843]
    B W of Skowhegan ME & Abby S MILLER at Farmington ME [30 Jan 1851]
    Benjamin 2d & Lucy BESSE both of Wayne ME at Winthrop ME by Isaac BOWLES Esq [5 Feb 1838]
    Caroline & John P CHANEY at Solon ME [27 Dec 1849]
    Harriet N & William WING at Wayne ME on 30th Apr by Rev Mr MILLETT [29 May 1845]
    Ichabod C of Livermore ME & Armida F WOOD of (Winthrop ME) at Winthrop by Rev Thurston [23 Jan 1841]
    James S & Sophia J HASKELL of Palmyra ME at St Croix Co, Wisconsin [12 Mar 1846]
    L G & Mary Ann SMITH of Wayne ME at Winthrop ME [14 Jan 1847]

NORRIS (cont.) Mary A C & Arthur SPRING at Monmouth ME [6 Mar 1838]
    Mary B K & Oliver KEYES at Livermore ME on the 1st inst at Lewiston ME by Mr HUNTON Esq [21 Mar 1834]
    Mary J & James H THORN at Winthrop ME [7 Dec 1848]
    Mary W & Daniel C BILLINTON of Hallowell ME at Wayne ME [29 Jan 1846]
    Perlando O of Fayette ME & Mrs Lucy K SMITH at Wayne ME [24 Apr 1836]
    Sarah L & William S GILMAN of Liberty ME at Winthrop ME on Thurs last by Rev Mr Thurston [1 Apr 1836]
    Susan C & Charles M SCAMMON at Pittston ME [24 Aug 1848]
    Woodin & Maria L LANCASTER at Augusta ME on 29th ult by Rev W A DREW [10 Dec 1846]

NORTH Mary Catherine, eldest d/o Col W A S NORTH, & Daniel C WESTON Esq of Augusta ME at D(?)anbesburg NY on the 4th inst by Rev Mr THOMAS [22 Oct 1842]

NORTHY Mary E & Edwin SARGENT of Lawrence MA at Pittston ME [11 Jan 1849]

NORTON Angeline & Bernard K HOVEY at Farmington ME [20 Nov 1838]
    Charles M & Miss Elizabeth R at Bath ME [10 Jun 1847]
    Christania P & Joshua T EATON Esq at Strong ME by Samuel EASTMAN Esq [18 Feb 1847]
    David Jr & Lydia Jane NORTON at Montville ME [28 Mar 1844]
    Deborah & Isaac CARVEY at Lincolnville ME [19 Oct 1839]
    Deborah & William DENACO at Thomaston ME [15 Aug 1844]
    E S & Robert F NORTON at Farmington ME [23 Nov 1848]
    Edward P of Madison ME & Hannah M TODD [11 Jul 1834]
    Edward S & Caroline HATCH at Gardiner ME [18 Jul 1840]
    Edwin A of Portland ME & Abigail BABSON at Wiscasset ME [16 Nov 1833]
    Edwin & Amanda E at Farmington ME [3 Apr 1841]
    Eliakim of Avon ME & Caroline NELSON d/o Jacob NELSON of Wayne ME by Rev G BAILEY at Wayne ME [10 Oct 1840]
    Eliza W & John R WHITTEN at Skowhegan ME [17 Jun 1852]
    H & Anne Maria MARR at China by W PERCIVAL Esq [9 Jan 1851]
    Hannah & Joseph GETCHELL at Palermo ME [31 Oct 1840]
    James & Esther A WILDES at Bath ME [27 Aug 1846]
    Jeremiah R of Strong ME & Keziah M VINING of Avon ME [3 Apr 1841]
    Jeremiah & Amanda F STEVENS at Strong ME [11 Jun 1846]
    Jeremiah & Susan MORRISON of Boothbay ME at Bath ME [28 Nov 1844]
    Lydia Jane & David NORTON Jr at Montville ME [29 Mar 1844]
    Margaret W Mrs & John B CAMPBELL at Montville ME [20 May 1847 & 3 Jun 1847]
    Martha & William FRENCH at Madison ME [8 Oct 1846]
    Mary E & Edwin Plummer, editor of the *Norway Advertiser*, & Mary E NORTON at Portland ME [28 Jan 1847]
    Mary & George KENDALL at New Vineyard ME [20 May 1843]
    Milford P Esq of Bangor ME & Mary A d/o Edward RUSSELL [15 Jul 1833]
    N B & Olive MACOMBER at Gardiner ME [4 Dec 1845]
    Rebecca & Capt Thomas SNOWBALL at Bluehill ME [3 Aug 1848]

NORTON (cont.) Robert F & E S NORTON at Farmington ME [23 Nov 1848]
 Ruth & William TOBEY at Norridgewock ME [14 Sept 1833]
 Stephen of East Readfield ME & Elvira A GOULD by Rev J BILLINGS at Mt Vernon ME on New Years's night [8 Jan 1852]
 Thomas F & Susan AMES at Farmington ME [11 Apr 1850]
 Warren & Elmina ROBBINS at Phillips ME [16 May 1837]
 Wilson P & Mary E PARKER at Farmington ME [9 Oct 1851]
 Winthrop Jr & Harriet GRAY of Starks ME at Norridgewock ME [9 MAy 1844]

NORWOOD Harriet G & George M CHASE Esq at Camden ME [22 Jul 1836]
 John W & Lucy C SHERMAN at Thomaston ME [1 Jul 1847]
 Sarah J & John GREENE at West Camden ME [13 Sept 1849]

NOTT Elizabeth & Martha Ann SCAMMON at Saco ME [15 Oct 1846]
 Handel G & Louisa SMITH at Bath ME [12 Feb 1846]
 Theodore of Winthrop ME & Caroline WALKER at East Dixfield ME [25 Sept 1845]

NOUGH Catharine Smion [sic] Paul & Simon Lewis Tgoosath OTTUTOSON, "The happy couple belong to the St Francis tribe of Indians" [26 Feb 1846]

NOURSE Amos, M.D.,of Hallowell ME & Lucy CLARK at Boston MA [30 Sept 1836]
 Charles H of Bolton MA & Malvina, only d/o the late Rev Josiah HOUGHTON of Winthrop ME at (Winthrop ME) on 17th inst by Rev Mr MERRIAM [22 Oct 1842]
 Sarah Jane of Bangor ME & John LADD of (Hallowell) ME on Thurs last [5 Sept 1837]

NOWELL Cyrus & Mary E TINKHAM at Calais ME [26 Sept 1840]
 Hannah I of Winslow ME & Levi P LANCASTER at Albion ME [1 Aug 1834]
 Sarah Jane & Richard BLAISDEL at Kennebunkport ME [28 Mar 1850]
 Simon of Fairfield ME & Miss H Augusta WEEKS at Waterville ME [11 Oct 1849]
 Watson & Rebecca BURKETT at Winslow ME [19 Aug 1836]

NOYES Albert & Caroline P DOLE at Bangor ME [5 Dec 1840]
 Albert & Caroline P DOLE at Bangor ME [25 Apr 1840]
 Ann Maria & William PALMER Esq, publisher of the *Gardiner Spectator* at Brunswick ME on Thurs evening on 28 Oct by Rev Mr HOWARD [6 Nov 1841]
 Augusta M & Capt Joseph G STOVER both of Bucksport ME at New York NY [16 Jul 1842]
 Benjamin of Falmouth ME & Eliza A L ALLEN of Poland ME on 21st ult [15 Jan 1842]
 Charles J & Arria EASTERBROOK at Brunswick ME by Rev Mr ADAMS [5 Aug 1836]
 Edwin Esq attorney at law & Miss Helen R BOUTELLE, d/o of Hon Timothy BOUTELLE at Waterville on Thurs evening by Rev S F SMITH [21 Aug 1841]
 Ellen N & Robert P POTE at Belfast ME [25 Jul 1840]
 Elizabeth A of Monmouth ME & Joseph H SMITH of Augusta ME [19 Jun 1841]
 Hannah & Capt John SOUTHARD at Jefferson ME [14 Sept 1848]

NOYES (cont.) Harriet M & John BUSH Jr formerly of Vassalboro ME at Bangor ME [28 Aug 1851]
Holland W & Miss Deborah T BICKNELL at Augusta ME [9 Oct 1841]
Isaac of Minot ME & Hannah GIBBS of Canton ME on Sunday last by Rev Reuben MILNER [20 Mar 1835]
Isaac & Miss Betsey WALKER at Livermore ME [27 Apr 1839]
Jane, youngest d/o the William D CHASE of Portland ME, & Octavus L WRIGHT of Brewer ME at Parkman ME [3 Jun 1843]
John E of Gardiner ME & Caroline A GETCHELL d/o Arthur GETCHELL of (Augusta) ME at Portsmouth ME on 2 Jan [29 Jan 1852]
Joseph C of Eastport ME & Helen M ALLING of Salisbury CT at Washington City [24 Jul 1838]
Margaret & John VINAL at Jefferson ME [3 Sept 1846]
Margaret Mrs & Nelson CALDERWOOD at Jefferson ME [14 Sept 1848]
Martha & Charles H WINSLOW at Pittston ME [21 Feb 1837]
Martha & George W FULLER at Jay ME [9 May 1847]
Martha E of Brunswick ME & Winslow BRIGHT of Cambridge MA at Gardiner ME [26 Nov 1846]
Mary Ann Keating & John T WINSLOW of Westbrook ME [11 Jan 1844]
Miranda & Zibeon CRAFTS at Auburn ME [29 Mar 1849]
Nancy & Gideon BOWLEY at Gardiner ME [11 Dec 1845]
Thomas E, printer of Ellsworth ME & Amanda HALL of Topsham ME at Brunswick ME [12 Jun 1838]
William of Hallowell ME, Publisher of the *Chronicle* & Mary Jane d/o Isaac NELSON of Winthrop ME on 10 Oct [16 Oct 1838]
William & Margaret ALIFF at Gardiner ME [21 Aug 1845]
NUDD Jos of Waterville ME & Abby HALE formerly of (Augusta) ME at Newburyport MA on 10 Apr 1851 [8 May 1851]
Mary Ann D & Mr J C BARTLETT both of Waterville ME at Providence RI on 3 Sept by Rev J HOBART [18 Sept 1851]
Thomas L & Martha L BEATH both of Charleston ME at East Corinth ME [28 Mar 1850]
NUTE Ann E & Mr J R HOPKINS, editor of the *Mattanawcook Observer* at Lincoln ME [1 Apr 1847]
John F & Mary Ann LOVEJOY at Sebec ME [17 Jan 1850]
Margaret & John McKENNEY at Wiscasset ME [15 Apr 1843]
NUTT Sarah Ann & Alvin COLSON at Atna ME on 9th Nov by Levi DUNBAR Esq [15 Nov 1849]
NUTTER Mary E & Andrew J BAILEY at Wiscasset ME [3 Feb 1848]
S N of Portsmouth NH & Orson D NEWHALL of Paris ME at Boston MA [6 Feb 1845]
NUTTING Almira & Cyrus MOORE at Madison ME [15 Oct 1846]
Edward D & Esther S GODING at Gardiner ME [26 Apr 1849]
Georgianna & Caleb W WILEY at Calais ME [25 Jun 1846]
Prescott & Sarah ROGERS at Norridgewock ME [28 Mar 1844]
Rebecca & Daniel B HARMON at Brunswick ME [13 Aug 1846]
Seviah & Zachariah W NUTTING at Norridgewock ME [15 Jan 1846]
Warren of Augusta ME & Sarah SALLEY of Embden ME at Augusta ME [15 May 1838]
Zachariah W & Seviah NUTTING at Norridgewock ME [15 Jan 1846]
NYE Columbia of Fairfield ME & Alice K JUNKINS at Bloomfield ME [7 August 1851] & Alice R JUNKINS at Bloomfield ME [24 Jul 1851]

NYE (cont.) George H & Charlotte A HUSSEY at Hallowell ME [11 Dec 1851]
   John H & Ellen M CLEVELAND at Fairfield ME [27 Nov 1851]
   Joseph S & Ruth J HOXIE at Fairfield ME [14 Sept 1848]
   Sarah A & Norris KEAN at Skowhegan [10 Feb 1848]
   H R Rev of Bangor ME & Harriet A P WELCH at Lowell ME [28 Aug 1845]
   Joseph F of Fairfield ME & Mary A BANKS at Augusta ME on 11th inst by Rev S ALLEN [23 Sept 1847]
   Louisa & Hosea B MAYNARD at Fairfield ME [21 Jan 1847]
   Ruth & Miles G PRATT at Lincoln ME [6 May 1847]

- O -

OAK Lorenzo & Mrs Flavis H WEBB at Garland ME [12 Sept 1844]
OAKES Elisha M Jr & Miss Hannah T BURK of Phipsburg ME at Gloucester ME [15 Jul 1843]
   Marinda M & Daniel PLUMMER at Sangerville ME [23 Oct 1845]
   Mary & Capt Joseph CHANDLER at New York NY [1 Aug 1844]
   Sylvester Dr of Danville ME & Miss H E KILBOURNE at Wilton ME [1 Jun 1848]
OAKMAN Capt Joseph of Hallowell ME & Sarah DROUGHT of Jay ME at Jay by Aaron HOLMES Esq [5 Nov 1842]
OAKS Lebbeas & Sarah C MERRIAM at Garland ME [1 Feb 1844]
OBEAR Lendall W & Edna STANLEY at Sedwick ME by Rowland CARLTON Esq [23 Oct 1838]
O'BRIEN Hannah of Brunswick ME & Joseph O'BRIEN of Philadelphia PA at Brunswick ME [5 Aug 1836]
   Joseph of Philadelphia PA & Hannah O'BRIEN of Brunswick ME at Brunswick ME [5 Aug 1836]
O'CONNER - see CONNER, DOWLING
O'DONNELL Hugh of Hallowell ME & Sarah Frances HAYWOOD of Waterville ME at Lynn MA on 8th Aug [28 Aug 1851]
   John & Miss Martha KIMBALL at Hallowell ME [26 Nov 1846]
ODELL Jacob & Frances A WINCHESTER at Eastport ME [25 Sept 1835]
ODIORNE Mary Jane & True W TOWNSEND at Gardiner ME [3 Feb 1848]
   Mary O formerly of Portsmouth NH & Charles E BENNETT formerly of New Gloucester ME at Boston MA [8 Feb 1844]
   Samuel Jr of Litchfield ME & Miss A O BRIERRY at Bowdoin ME [19 Oct 1848]
ODLIN Abigail & John DAME both of Fayette ME at Fayette by Rev E ROBINSON [12 Aug 1843]
   Woodbridge of Exeter NH & Augusta P LITTLE d/o Doty LITTLE Esq at Castine ME [24 Oct 1844]
OGIER Lewis of Camden ME ae 84y & Betsey M YOUNG ae 74y at Lincolnville ME [4 Jul 1844]
   Samuel of Camden ME & Martha HEAL at Searsmont ME [27 Dec 1849]
O'HARA Charles W of Worcester MA & Irene E CROSSMAN of Greene ME at Cambridge MA [11 Jan 1840]
   Ezekiel & Buelah BLAISDELL at Phipsburg ME [5 Aug 1847]
   Frances A & James L BATES at West Bath ME [19 Feb 1846]
   Luther M of Phipsburg ME & Lydia D HIGGINS of Bath ME [23 Oct 1845]
   Mary Jane & Joshua JEWETT at Norridgewock ME [15 Apr 1847]

O'HARA (cont.) Oliver & Nancy M CRAIG at Augusta ME [29 Oct 1846]
  Rebecca P & Jesse B LOVELL at Phipsburg ME [10 Sept 1846]
  Thomas H & Augusta A PATTEN at Phipsburg ME [14 Jan 1847]
  Thomas of Phipsburg ME & Hannah GREENLOW of Georgetown ME at Phipsburg ME by Andrew REED Esq [16 Oct 1838]
  William & Eliza H LUMBARD both of Belgrade ME at Augusta ME by J SPRINGER Esq [21 Mar 1844]
OLIVER Alden S & Eliza Jane SMALL at Phipsburg ME [2 Oct 1851]
  Lyman of Phipsburg ME & Margaret IRVING of Georgetown ME at Bath ME [15 May 1851]
  Thomas Esq & Alice H WYLIE at Winnegance [21 Aug 1851]
OLMSTEAD Charels H & Priscilla BRITNEY at Calais ME [4 Mar 1847]
ORBITON Mary Mrs & Caleb EASTMAN at Fayette ME [25 Sept 1845]
ORCUTT Charels & Martha LANE both of Northport ME at Belfast ME [13 Feb 1845]
  Lucy W & Amos DOWNING of Winthrop ME at Brunswick ME on the 14th inst by Rev Mr BRAGDON [26 Jun 1838]
  Phebe of Bluehill ME & John D INGALLS of Charlestown at Boston MA [26 Nov 1846]
ORDWAY Caleb F & Clariss M STARRETT at Orono ME [22 Feb 1849]
  Lydia M & Mr T M POWER at Dexter ME [7 Apr 1848]
  Norway Esq & Olive G ROBBINS [26 Aug 1852]
ORFF Clarissa & Chamberlain SIMMONS at Waldoboro ME [8 Feb 1840]
ORMSBEE James W & Harriet DEAN at Thomaston ME [23 Dec 1847]
ORMSBY D V B & Miss L'Orient P SMILEY both of Augusta ME at Thompson CT [26 Aug 1843]
  Mary H & Alexander MacDONALD at New York City on 31st Jul [14 Sept 1848]
  Ruth P & Eli J WING of Chesterville ME at Augusta ME on 17th inst by Rev J W SAWYER [25 Nov 1847]
ORN Sabra & Nathaniel BROWN of Vinalhaven ME at Thomaston ME [24 Apr 1845]
ORNE Jacob C & Miss Abigail OSYER at Bremen ME on the 29th inst by W W KEENE Esq [11 Dec 1838]
  Sarah G of Cambridgeport MA & Charles A PAGE of Hallowell ME at Thompson ME [10 Dec 1846]
ORR Abigail & William A SYLVESTER at Harpswell ME [31 Oct 1844]
  Catharine of Brunswick ME & Charles GREGG at Andover [11 Sept 1851]
  Catherine & James T LADD both of Garland ME at Dexter ME [27 Feb 1851]
  David 2nd & Lucinda CLARK at Harpswell ME [1 Apr 1843]
  Elizabeth, d/o the late Hon Benjamin ORR of Brunswick ME, & John A POOR Esq at Bangor ME on 21st inst [30 Nov 1839]
  Irene & Sewall REED of Topsham ME at Bowdoinham ME [3 Sept 1846]
  John Rev of Gouverneur NY & Mary E d/o late Capt John MOORE at Christ Church at Gardiner ME on 13th ult by Rev W R BABCOCK [5 Nov 1842]
  Lorana W & Levi P MAYNARD at Bowdoinham ME [25 Jul 1840]
  M K Mrs & Rufus K PAGE Esq of Hallowell ME at Medford MA [26 Nov 1846]

ORR (cont.) Margaret C d/o the late Hon Benjamin ORR of Brunswick ME, & Col Alfred J STONE of Brunswick ME at Bangor ME [14 Mar 1840]
    Maria & Harrison G OTIS at Topsham ME [5 Nov 1846]

OSBORN Franklin E of Charlestown MA & Eliza J MARTIN at Augusta ME on 16th Aug by Rev Mr WEBB [28 Aug 1851]
    Hannah of Rome ME & Ephraim LOW Jr of Mercer ME at Smithfield ME [26 Nov 1846]
    Harriet L & Francis H SLEEPER of Boston MA [3 Dec 1846]
    Harriet S of (Belfast) ME & Edward BAKER of (Hallowell) ME at Belfast [8 Aug 1837]
    John Jr & Susan O FARNHAM at Dover ME? [20 May 1847]
    Susan B & Cyrus S WATSON at Williams College Grant, Aroostook Co ME [28 Oct 1847]

OSBORNE Amanda Malvina & Ira SCARLE at Madison ME [16 May 1834]
    Ellen & John WILLIAMS of Calais ME at Eastport ME [5 Oct 1839]
    George A of Danvers MA & Hannah S MOODY at Augusta ME on 20th inst by Rev Dr TAPPAN [27 Jun 1844]

OSGOOD Aaron of Durham ME & Eunice S NEVENS at Lewiston ME [3 Feb 1848]
    Catherine P Mrs & Hon Daniel GOODENOW at Portland ME [24 Aug 1848]
    Charles & Lucy A WOODCOOK at Gardiner ME [12 Apr 1849]
    Clarissa & Edward R JOHNSON Esq at Bangor ME [30 May 1837]
    Elizabeth & Jonas DAVIS of Raymond ME at Durham ME [18 Apr 1850]
    Frances W of London & Josiah O BATCHELDER of Hallowell ME at Pittsfield NH [5 Sept 1844]
    H P Rev of North Auburn ME & Abigail W SOULE at Turner ME [30 Mar 1848]
    Henry B Esq & Catharine P DANA d/o Hon Judah DANA at Fryeburg ME [30 May 1840]
    Hudson & Eliza Ann SMART at Prospect ME [13 Feb 1835]
    Lemuel S & Mrs Phebe OSGOOD at Bluehill ME [17 Jun 1847]
    Lucia of Osgood of Palermo ME & Hon Parker SHELDON of Gardiner ME at Dorchester MA [18 Nov 1847]
    Phebe & Lemuel S OSGOOD at Bluehill ME [17 Jun 1847]
    Rosanna G of Exeter ME & William THOMPSON Esq, publisher of *Democrat* at Bangor ME [30 Apr 1846]

OSMAR Joseph B & Lydia P WHITNEY of Dover ME at Foxcroft ME [15 Aug 1844]

OSYER Abigail & Jacob C ORNE at Bremen ME on the 29th inst by W W KEENE Esq [11 Dec 1838]
    Harrison G & Maria ORR at Topsham ME [5 Nov 1846]
    Martha Jane, d/o Oliver OTIS Esq of Hallowell ME, & Mr C Henry STRICKLAND of Wilton ME at Hallowell ME [1 Jan 1842]
    Patience & William MERRYFIELD Jr of Solon ME at Fairfield ME [22 May 1845]
    Sophia A & William W FRENCH at Norridgewock ME by J TRENCH Esq [12 Aug 1847]

OTIS Hon John & Ellen GRANT d/o Capt S C GRANT at Hallowell ME on 21st Aug [31 Aug 1848]

OTTUTOSON Simon Lewis Togoosath & Catherine Simon Paul NOUGH at Alfred ME "The happy couple belong to the St Francis tribe of Indians." [26 Feb 1846]
OVER Mary & James JOHNSON at Thomaston ME [24 Sept 1846]
OVERLOCK Lucinda & Edward ULMER at Rockland ME [7 Aug 1851]
    Nancy & Francis C KEIZER at North Waldoboro ME on 27th Nov by Reuben ORFF Esq [4 Dec 1851]
    Mary Mrs & Nathan REED at Waldoboro ME [27 Nov 1838]
    Ruth E & Thomas P COLE both of Waldoboro' at Warren ME [29 Jan 1846]
OWEN Adeline & Ezra KIMBALL of Milo ME at Vassalboro ME [9 Jul 1842]
    Benjamin & Nancy M AUBINS at Bath ME [26 Sept 1840]
    Charles E & Emma E DENNISON both of Brunswick ME at Freeport ME [14 Oct 1847]
    Daniel M of Saco ME & Jane WOODMAN at Hollis ME on 16th inst [28 Oct 1842]
    David of Bath ME (formerly of Montgomery AL) & Elizabeth CHAMBERLAIN of Henriville at Henriville LC [21 May 1842]
    Elizabeth & Alfred HASKELL at Portland ME [2 Jan 1845]
    Hannah J of Topsham ME & John ROGERS of Brunswick ME at Topsham ME by George ROGERS Esq [15 Jul 1833]
    Henrietta of Brunswick ME & Thomas CROSWELL, M.D., of Weld ME at Brunswick ME on 6th inst [24 Sept 1842]
    Henry W of Wayne ME & Clarissa M MARTIN at Augusta ME [1 Jul 1833]
    Jane M & John Poleresozky/DePoleresozky of Dresden ME at Wayne ME [26 Jul 1849]
    Julia & Thomas PENNEL at Brunswick ME both of Portland ME [20 Nov 1845]
    Lois Ann & James K ESTABROOK at Brunswick ME [31 Oct 1844]
    Maria H & George S MULLIKEN at Brunswick ME on 30 May [15 Jun 1848]
    Mary Jane & James MITCHELL at Bath ME [3 May 1849]
    Mary Jane & Theodore S McCLELLAN Esq at Brunswick ME [31 Dec 1842]
    Mary & Capt John SMITH at Bowdoin ME [20 Nov 1845]
    Rachael of Wayne ME & Mr Aaron TOWLE of the firm of CARR & TOWLE of Winthrop ME [20 Nov 1838]
    Robert M & Cordelia L STONE at Brunswick ME [25 Jan 1849]
    Roxana & Alphonso P RICHMOND at Leeds ME [24 Feb 1848]
    Sarah Ann & Rufus CUSHMAN at Portland ME [5 Dec 1844]
OXTON Amelia H & Benjamin B HILLS at Union ME [29 Mar 1849]

- P -

PACKARD Addison G of Buckfield ME & Martha J FOLSOM of Winthrop ME at Readfield ME on Oct 31st [6 Feb 1851]
    Alpheus S, Professor of Rhetoric in Bowdoin ME & Mrs Caroline W McLELLAN at Portland ME [3 Oct 1844]
    Ann & Isaac T BABBET of Oakham MA at Winthrop ME [12 Jun 1838]
    Clara A & Isaac BEALE of Kirkland ME, formerly of Augusta, at Lowell [18 Nov 1847]

PACKARD (cont.) Cyrus A & Sarah B PACKARD at Blanchard ME [11 May 1848]
   Eliphalet & Ann d/o Benjamin PERKINS in Winthrop ME on 20th ult, by Rev J INGRAHAM [1 Apr 1836]
   Eliza L & George H GATES at Monson [10 Dec 1846]
   Elvira & Daniel HINKLEY of Livermore ME at Augusta ME on 5th Dec [27 Dec 1849]
   Emeline, d/o Deacon PACKARD, & Merriam HORACE PARLIN Esq at East Winthrop ME on 14th inst [23 Dec 1843]
   Henry & Caroline A WAUGH at East Winthrop ME on Monday evening last by Rev F MERRIAM [4 Jun 1846]
   Irene & Shepherd H JOHNSON at Camden ME [8 Oct 1846]
   James & Mary P KEEN at Greenwood ME [13 Apr 1848]
   John H & Olive S CONY d/o Capt John CONY by Rev Mr DILLINGHAM at (Augusta) ME on 17th Oct [26 Oct 1848]
   Laura Ann & Rev Thomas G MITCHELL at Auburn ME [18 Feb 1847]
   Lydia Jane & John JAMESON at Hope ME [27 Nov 1851]
   Martha & Mr J LEIGHTON at Winthrop ME [27 Jan 1848]
   Miss H A & Lewis SHERBURNE at Turner ME [23 Nov 1848]
   Sarah B & Cyrus A PACKARD at Blanchard ME [11 May 1848]
   Sybil & Samuel RICHARDS at Augusta ME on Thanksgiving morning by Rev Mr INGRAHAM [18 Dec 1838]

PAGE Addison of Hartford CT & Sophronia PAGE of (Winthrop ME) at Winthrop on Tues morning last by Samuel P BENSON Esq [26 Sept 1834]
   Albert G & Maria L DRUMMOND of Bangor ME at Bath ME [20 Mar 1845]
   Alvah & Harriet A SHUTE at Belfast ME by Rev A PINGREE [11 Mar 1843]
   Ann Judson of New Sharon ME & Nathaniel HINCKLEY Esq of Barnstable MA at Boston MA [25 Dec 1851]
   Benjamin R Esq of Conway NH & Susan W BOUTELLE at Bloomfield ME [16 Oct 1851]
   Caroline & Charles HALL at Wayne ME [23 May 1844]
   Charles A of Hallowell ME & Sarah G ORNE of Cambridgeport MA [10 Dec 1846]
   Charles of Quincy MA & Emeline MORRILL at Belgrade ME [12 Nov 1846]
   Chase & Sarah KENNISON at Milo ME [19 Jul 1849]
   David of Fairfield ME & Mary Jane DAVENPORT of Hallowell ME [13 Nov 1838]
   Delia & Jacob SMART at Searsport ME [27 Nov 1851]
   Dennis & Hannah LORING at Pownal ME [22 Feb 1844]
   E Jr & Elizabeth MERRILL at (Augusta) ME on 30 Apr [11 May 1848]
   Edward & Harriet S MARTIN at Bangor ME [26 Jun 1845]
   Elijah of Livermore ME & Caroline HILTON of Winthrop ME at Winthrop by Seth MAY Esq [11 Apr 1837]
   Elijah of Livermore ME & Catherine HILTON of Winthrop ME at Winthrop on Jan 25th by William C FULLER Esq [6 Feb 1835]
   Eliza R & George M ESTABROOK at Oldtown ME [4 Nov 1847]
   Ellen S & Parker E WILDES at Dorchester MA on 22d Oct [9 Nov 1848]
   Flavius J of Winthrop ME & Bethiah ADDITON at Dexter ME [12 Jun 1841]

PAGE (cont.) Frances A & Edward H MITCHELL of Maumee City OH at Bath ME [12 Jun 1851]
  George R of Belgrade ME & Harriet E d/o the late Judge THATCHER of Bingham ME at Greene ME by Rev Mr SYKES [13 Nov 1841]
  George & Sarah W KIDDER at Augusta ME at St Mark's Church on Monday last by Rev A BURGESS [26 Aug 1847]
  Gustavus B of China ME & Lydia F BRAGG at East Vassalboro ME on Aug 26th by John MOWER Esq [30 Aug 1849]
  Hannah & Horatio N PAGE at Winthrop ME [24 Oct 1837]
  Harriet Y & Niven C ROBINSON at Cushing ME [20 Nov 1845]
  Horatio N of Norridgewock ME & Miss Hannah PAGE at Winthrop ME [24 Oct 1837]
  Isaac W of Norridgewock ME & Dolly PARKMAN at Solon ME [11 Jul 1844]
  Jeremiah & Sarah G CROWELL at Dexter ME [23 Nov 1839]
  Julia A & James STANLEY Esq of Farmington ME at Hallowell ME [2 Oct 1841]
  Julia Octavia & Charles W JONES Esq at St Mark's Church in Augusta ME on Sunday evening by Rev Mr BURGESS [7 Aug 1845]
  Lucinda H & Charles K TURNER both of Norridgewock ME at Skowhegan ME [4 Jun 1846]
  Lucretia M & Jonathan P ROGERS, Counsellor at Law of Bangor ME at Hallowell ME [10 Aug 1833]
  Mary J & Franklin B MITCHELL at Phillips ME [26 Jul 1849]
  Mary of Winthrop ME & Silas ALDEN at Jay ME [15 May 1851]
  Nancy J of Hallowell ME d/o late Moses B GILMAN & Moses GRAY Esq at Chicago IL on 23 Dec [23 Jan 1851]
  Nannie & Rev J P HAMMOND at Alexandria VA [30 Dec 1847]
  Pamelia & Sewall C LOVEJOY at Sidney ME [5 Feb 1846]
  Philip S of Boston MA & Hannah M CUTLER at Farmington ME [29 Jul 1843]
  Rebecca M, d/o the late Dr William PAGE, & Owen WOODSIDE at Brunswick ME [21 Dec 1833]
  Rufus K Esq of Hallowell ME & Mrs M K ORR at Medford [26 Nov 1846]
  Sabrina & Zachariah JORDAN both of that town at Parsonsfield ME [16 May 1840]
  Sarah B of Winthrop ME & Lewis K LITCHFIELD of Rollinsford NH at Salmon Falls NH [7 August 1851]
  Sewall B & Emily D MORRILL at Winthrop ME on Monday evening last by Samuel P BENSON [17 Jun 1843]
  Sophronia & Addison PAGE of Hartford CT at Winthrop ME on Tues morning [26 Sept 1834]
  Susan C & Ephraim G WILLARD both of Brownville ME at Brownville ME on 16th inst by E A JENKS Esq [25 May 1839]
  Susan G & James B ALLEN at Monroe ME [27 May 1852]
  William C D of Newburyport MA & Martha S CROWELL of Dexter ME by Rev Mr KALLOCH [18 Jan 1849]
  William P of Sidney ME & Huldah ALLEN at Augusta ME on 15th Feb [1 Mar 1849]
  William R & Eliza AUSTIN at Belgrade ME [14 Dec 1833]
PAINE Achsah & Samuel C PRATT at Augusta ME [11 Jul 1834]

PAINE (cont.) Albert W Esq of Bangor ME & Mary J HALE d/o Capt J HALE of Foxcroft (now Dover-Foxcroft) ME at Foxcroft ME [18 Jul 1840]
Ann E & Franklin B KENDALL at Phipsburg ME [2 Sept 1847]
Ann R & Moses T RICE of New Orleans LA at Eastport ME [7 August 1851]
Charles H, foreman of the *Gazette* office & Alice J DRINKWATER at Rockland ME on 12th Aug by Rev W O Thomas [26 Aug 1852]
Charlotte E & George S LEAVITT of Chelmsford MA at Winslow ME [4 Jun 1851]
Daniel & Elizabeth REDLAND at Thomaston ME [13 Nov 1845]
Edward A & Silby STRATTON at Winslow ME [21 Dec 1848]
Edward Capt & Mary DAVIS at Phipsburg ME [8 Aug 1844]
Edward & Frances A BAKER at Eastport ME [15 Jan 1846]
Harriet & Mr S B GOODWIN at Augusta ME by Rev Mr MORSE [26 Nov 1846]
Henry M & Elizabeth J RICH by Rev Joseph GERRY at Jay ME on Apr 4th [6 May 1852]
Henry W Esq attorney at law of (Hallowell) ME & Lucy Elizabeth only d/o Capt John COFFIN of (Hallowell) at Newburyport MA on Monday evening May 1 by Rev Thomas B FOX [9 May 1837]
James M of Waterford ME & Olive NOBLE at Norway ME [17 Aug 1848]
James & Miss Salome SKILLIN of Pownal ME at Durham ME [15 Jul 1843]
Josiah Jr & Lovina BRYANT of New Portland ME at Anson ME [17 Apr 1838]
Louisa D & Franklin B WHITTEMORE at Jay ME [1 Nov 1849]
Mary of Pownal ME & Jeremiah MITCHELL of Cumberland ME [25 Jul 1834]
Moses L of Jay ME & Lucia Elvira AMES at Chesterville ME [4 Apr 1850]
Nicholas E Esq of Sanford ME & Abby Mary d/o the late Capt Oakman SPRAGUE of Bath ME at South Berwick ME [8 Aug 1834]
Rebecca S & Josiah ROBINSON at Cornville ME [18 Mar 1852]
Robert S of Skowhegan ME & Mary D BUTLER at Cornville ME [2 Mar 1848] & [17 Feb 1848]
Robert T of Skowheagan ME & Mary LANCASTER at Augusta ME on Christmas Morning [1 Jan 1839]
Roxana & Israel BEAN Jr at Jay ME on Jan 30 [24 Feb 1848]
Sarah C & Percival, M.D., at Anson ME [9 Aug 1849]
Sarah C & Robert T CUSHING at Thomaston ME [6 Jan 1837]
Sarah W of Bangor ME & Joseph P STINCHFIELD at Dover ME [25 Jun 1846]
Thomas of Starks ME & Eleanor BUSWELL at Hallowell ME [4 Mar 1852]
PALL Harriet N & Moses O STILES of Haverhill MA [16 Dec 1847]
PALMER Augusta A & George MARCH at Rockland ME [6 Feb 1851]
Augustus & Mary E SANFORD [18 Jun 1846]
Benjamin B & Sophia BLACKINTON all of Thomaston ME [16 Jul 1846]
Bowman of Readfield ME & Caroline LAUGHTON at Hallowell ME [4 Apr 1844]
Catharine Mrs & Gorham BUTLER at Thomaston ME [29 Jan 1846]
Charles Esq of Belfast ME & Mrs Zilpha COUILLARD at Frankfort ME [9 Sept 1847]

PALMER (cont.) Charlotte R & Dr Charles SNELL of Bangor ME at Waterville ME on 2d inst by Rev Mr SMITH [12 Feb 1836]
  Gorham & Caroline STEVENS at East Winthrop ME [20 May 1847]
  Hannah L S & David S STINSON of Bath ME at Hallowell ME [27 Jun 1840]
  Hannah & Moses HARRIS at Pittston ME [5 Feb 1836]
  Harriet N & Isaac C GLIDDEN at Hallowell ME [8 Jan 1852]
  John & Martha Ann HANDY both of Hallowell ME at Gardiner ME [24 Oct 1834]
  Lucy & Daniel JONSON Jr of Litchfield ME at Pittston ME [1 Jul 1847]
  Mary Ann W & James C PULLEN at Barnard ME [21 Jan 1847]
  Mary F & John BRAY, printer at Bangor ME by Mr John S SAYWARD all of Bangor ME [11 Dec 1841]
  Monroe of Waterville ME & Augusta G POMROY [24 Jan 1850]
  Nancy W & William A B COBB at Dover ME [18 Mar 1847]
  Oscar H & Maria HORN at Augusta ME on 27 Sept by Rev J STEVENS [2 Oct 1851]
  Rufus L of Alna ME & Jane C CAMPBELL at New Castle ME [22 May 1851]
  Samuel & Mary REED at Windsor ME by J B SWANTON Esq [14 Feb 1837]
  Sarah A & Alfred S BEEBE of Norwich CT at Bangor ME [3 Oct 1844]
  Sarah E d/o Barnabas P Esq & Charles H HAMLEN of Augusta ME at Kennebunk ME on May 1st by Rev SWAN [15 May 1851]
  Sarah Jane & Barnabas H MONROE at West Camden ME [16 Aug 1849]
  Susan & Mr HAYNES (printer) and editor of the *Democrat* at Bangor ME [10 Apr 1845}
  Tristram D of Bangor ME & Cynthia W SHEDD of Madaceunk ME? at Herman ME [22 Aug 1844]
  Valencourt S & Margaret E BUDGE both of Levant ME at Bangor ME [1 May 1845]
  Washington & Eliza A STEWART at Pittston ME [7 Nov 1844]
  William Esq, publisher of the *Gardiner Spectator*, & Miss Ann Maria NOYES at Brunswick ME on Thurs evening on 28th Oct by Rev Mr HOWARD [6 Nov 1841]
PARCHER Elisha P of Chesterville ME & Miss Angelina MONSON at Farmington ME [29 Jun 1839]
  Samuel M of Winthrop ME & Clarissa DAY at Leeds ME on 30 Sept [11 Oct 1849]
PARDEE Myron Esq of Oswego NY & Caroline A WEBBER at Augusta ME at St Mark's Church by Rev Mr BURGESS [19 Aug 1847]
PARDY William & Miss Susan HIGGINS at Bath ME [8 Nov 1849]
PARIS Lydia W & Thomas J of Phipsburgh ME at Bath ME [26 Dec 1844]
PARK Elisha & Betsey WALTON at Chesterville ME [27 Nov 1845]
  Sarah H & Capt Charles PENDLETON at Prospect ME [14 Mar 1837]
  Stuart J of Gardiner ME & Louisa R MANNING at Lynn MA [10 Jul 1851]
  William of Boston MA & Arabella SWEETLAND of Hallowell ME at Charlestown MA [28 Jan 1847]
PARKARD Lucinda K of (Augusta) ME & Susan J WYMAN d/o Ezekiel WYMAN by Rev PARKARD at China [29 Apr 1852]

PARKER Abby W & Albert F ADAMS of Skowhegan ME at Waterville ME [20 Mar 1851]
  Abby Y & Caleb of Brewer ME at Hampden ME [7 Jan 1843]
  Almira E & James T CHASE at Livermore ME [26 Oct 1848]
  Anderson of Corinth ME & Sophronia L HORN at Ripley ME on 10th inst [25 Sept 1838]
  Augusta & Horatio C SPRAGUE at Dexter ME [20 Jan 1848]
  Benjamin & Judith WHITCOMB both of Bloomfield ME at Skowhegan ME [28 Nov 1837]
  Caroline & Alvin B LEWIS at Waterville ME [3 Jun 1847]
  Catherine & W MERRYMAN at Brunswick ME [27 Nov 1838]
  Charles of Buxton ME & Helen A BERRY at Standish ME [6 Dec 1849]
  Christiana W & Samuel E RAND at Stoneham ME? [5 Aug 1852]
  David of Corinth ME & Lydia O MARTIN at Guilford ME [6 Jan 1848]
  Eben of Foxcroft ME & Sarah LYFORD at Sebec ME [22 May 1851]
  Emeline D & Robert CAMPBELL at Frankfort ME [22 Feb 1844]
  Harriet A & Henry L K WIGGINS, M.D., at Greene ME [19 Aug 1847]
  Harriet B & Jacob A SMITH, one of the proprietors of the *Bangor Whig* [16 Sept 1836]
  Henry S of Belfast ME & Christina R LOCKE at Mt Vernon ME on 29 Dec by Rev EDGECOMB [2 Jan 1851]
  Jacob S & Ruth PARKER at Durham ME [24 Feb 1848]
  Jane D of Madrid ME & William H SKILLINS at Farmington ME [7 May 1846]
  Jane & William H JONSON at Gorham ME [23 Jan 1845]
  Jeremiah of Yarmouth ME & Mary J GOSS at Danville ME [7 Mar 1850]
  John & Elizabeth CARD at Brunswick ME [21 Oct 1836]
  Jonas of Norridgewock ME & Hannah VARNEY at Bloomfield ME [4 Dec 1851]
  Judith & Benjamin CRANDLEMIRE at Lee ME? [30 Apr 1846]
  Julia S & Barker B GLIDDEN at (Augusta) ME on 25th Dec [1 Jan 1852]
  Leonora & James M HESCOCK of Wilton ME at Jay ME [8 Nov 1849]
  Lydia G & James A FLINT at Lee ME on 27th Feb [9 Mar 1848]
  Marquis & Betsey ELWELL at Buxton ME [4 Sept 1851]
  Mary A & Cyrus BOSWORTH at Norridgewock ME [18 Feb 1847]
  Mary E & Wilson P NORTON at Farmington ME [9 Oct 1851]
  Nancy of Gorham ME & Warren NICHERSON Esq at Gorham ME [27 Jun 1840]
  Olive & Noah ROBINSON at Waterborough ME [31 Jul 1845]
  Orren & Mary PETERSON of Lisbon ME at Augusta ME [22 Jan 1846]
  Rachel & Josiah KEYES at Rumford ME by P C VIRGIN Esq [6 Mar 1835]
  Ruth T of Skowhegan ME & John P VARNEY of Fairfield ME at Skowhegan ME by Moses LITTLEFIELD [9 Oct 1845]
  Ruth & David DAVIS of Ottoway IL at New Portland ME [7 Oct 1847]
  Ruth & Isaac C DOROTHY at Skowhegan ME [21 Mar 1850]
  Ruth & Jacob S PARKER at Durham ME [24 Feb 1848]
  Samuel Capt & Adeline BROWN at Bloomfield ME [4 Jan 1840]
  Samuel of Fayette ME & Flavilla SMITH at Livermore ME [20 Dec 1849]
  Samuel S & Sarah HAYDEN at Waterville ME [24 Apr 1845]
  Sybil & Capt William MOSTMAN at Belfast ME [28 May 1842]
  Thomas M L & Caroline S HIGGINS at Topsham ME [11 Nov 1847]
  Thomas & Elizabeth JOHNSON at Eastport ME [26 Dec 1834]

PARKER (cont.) William & Mary HOYT at Berlin ME [4 Apr 1837]
    Worster of Castine ME & Miss Wealthy Ann, eldest d/o Rev Professor Pond at Bangor ME [4 Mar 1833]
PARKHURST Annette E & William A PARSONS at Norway ME [24 Jan 1850]
    Eleanor F, d/o Eleanor F PARKHURST, & Ansel PERKINS at Unity ME on New Year's Day by Jona H FULLER Esq [3 Jan 1850]
    John L & Almira R SPENCER both of Unity ME at Freedom ME [6 Mar 1851]
    Lorenzo A & Maryman MERRICK both of Etna ME on the 1st inst by Edward SMART Esq [14 Jan 1843]
    Lucy & Capt Willaim ELLERY at Dixmont ME [30 Apr 1846]
    Mary & Charles TAYLOR of Albion ME at Unity ME [27 Mar 1851]
PARKMAN Dolly & Isaac W PAGE at Solon ME [11 Jul 1844]
    Mary A & John S WEBB at Skowhegan ME [9 Aug 1849]
PARKS Albert H & Eliza A McINTIRE at Norridgewock ME [21 Jan 1847]
    Walden S & Mrs Joan H CLARK at Skowhegan ME [22 Jul 1847]
    William Esq of Ionia MI & Wealthy THOMPSON of Bath ME at Waconsta MI [8 Feb 1844]
PARLIN Amos F of Milburn ME & Climena STEWARD [21 Nov 1834]
    Angelia A & Charles C FOSTER at East Winthrop ME [4 Oct 1849]
    Augustus of Winthrop ME & Elizabeth A WHITING at Union ME [27 Jun 1844]
    Climena M & John T PIKE Esq at Winthrop ME on 6 Dec by Rev Mr MERRIAM [11 Dec 1841]
    Dorcas Mrs & Ebenezer WHITNEY of Phillips ME at Jay ME [11 Feb 1843]
    Harrison & Urania d/o Capt Jonathan WHITNEY at Winthrop ME on Thurs evening on 31 Dec by Rev Franklin MERRIAM [9 Jan 1841]
    Horace Esq & Emeline d/o Deacon PACKARD at East Winthrop ME on 14th inst by Rev Mr MERRIAM [23 Dec 1843]
    Lydia R & Reuben JONES at Weld ME on 25th ult [15 Jun 1848]
    S R of Norwich CT & Melvina L HAWES at Weld ME on 20 Mar by Rev J B WHEELWRIGHT [27 Mar 1851]
    Sophia & Daniel HOUGHTON at Weld ME on 12th Apr [26 Apr 1849]
    William O & Zoa M JONES at Weld ME [15 Jan 1852]
PARMENTER Frances L & Benjamin S JONES at Pittston ME [23 Nov 1848]
    Columbus G & Harriet E WORTHEN at China ME both of China [26 Nov 1842]
PARR Mary & Arthur BERRY Esq of Augusta ME & Miss Mary PARR d/o John TAYLOR Esq of Creniton England at Boston MA [24 Sept 1842]
PARRIS Caroline W d/o A K PARRIS, & John C BROOKS of Portland ME at Washington ME [3 Jun 1847]
PARRITT Elizabeth & Alexander JONES at Eastport ME [27 Jun 1844]
    Sarah A & Capt George W McFADDEN at Eastport ME both of Lubec ME [2 Aug 1849]
PARSHLEY Charles & Mary Jane YORK of Exeter NH at Brunswick ME [8 Oct 1846]
    Emily J & Albion P SWANTON at Sangerville ME [27 Apr 1848]
    George H & Eveline A CLERK at Bath ME [11 Nov 1847]
    John C of New Orleans & Eliza A MURPHEY at Bath ME [10 Aug 1848]
    John C & Lucy Jane TIGHE at Bath ME on Sunday morning last [27 Jun 1840]

PARSHLEY (cont.) Lucy E & John BRANSCOMB at Bath ME [20 May 1836]
PARSONS Alexander (Dr) of Eastport ME & Ann Maria BRANDISH at Portland ME [24 Oct 1844]
   Catherine & William BEAL at Limerick ME [18 Jul 1840]
   Jefferson & Betsey K TAYLOR both of Augusta ME at Hallowell ME [25 Mar 1847]
   Nathan & Aurelia P BROWN at Atkinson ME [17 Jul 1851]
   Peter P of Farmington ME & Catherine W GREENOUGH at New Sharon ME [12 Nov 1846]
   Richard & Huldah PLUMMER at Portland ME [2 May 1844]
   Sarah A Roxbury VT & William HARRIMAN of Montville ME [10 Dec 1846]
   Sarah & Thurston H BOYNTON at Dover ME [27 Apr 1839]
   Seth T & Mary Ann GREELEY at Smithfield ME [26 Oct 1848]
   Solomon of Danville ME & Olive STURTIVANT at Hebron ME [1 Jul 1852]
   Sophia d/o Capt Jotham P of Bangor ME & Samuel P BAKER, cashier of Mariners Bank of Wiscasset ME, at Bangor ME [5 Feb 1836]
   William A & Annette E PARKHURST at Norway ME [24 Jan 1850]
   William H & Sarah M PRESTON [20 Jun 1844]
   William Jr & Mrs Mary SMITH at Bath ME [29 Aug 1837]
   William of Litchfield ME & Olive JOICE at Richmond ME [10 Feb 1848]
   William of Sebec ME & Mrs Rachel BLOOD at Foxcroft ME [15 May 1845]
PARTRIDGE Augusta A & Abner COOMBS Jr at Hallowell ME both of Augusta ME [28 Feb 1850]
   Caroline A & S S FLETCHER of New Bedford MA at Orland ME [15 Aug 1844]
   Charles H of Gardiner ME & Bridget WESTON at Madison ME [3 Aug 1841]
   Elizabeth Mrs & Otis S HEATH both of Jefferson ME at Patricktown Plantation ME by Thomas BRAN Esq on Oct 11 [25 Oct 1849]
   Ellcetee V PARTRIDGE & Joseph CLOUGH at Prospect ME [8 Aug 1844]
   Franklin & Susan F FOSTER at Sacarappa ME [1 Jul 1847]
   Hannah of Gardiner ME & William J PLUMMER of Skowhegan ME at Hallowell ME [17 Oct 1837]
   Joseph R & Julia A PARTRIDGE at (Augusta) ME [13 Jan 1848]
   Julia A & Joseph R PARTRIDGE at (Augusta) ME [13 Jan 1848]
   Lucy G & Albion G ACHORN at Thomaston ME [5 Mar 1846]
   Mary R & Hannibal SMITH at Paris ME [7 Nov 1837]
   Nathaniel S & Mary H BROWN at Bangor ME [11 Jul 1844]
   Thomas & Sarah W PRATT at Vassalboro ME by Rev E R WARREN [11 Nov 1836]
PASCO Justus L of Lowell MA? & Sarah S ELY at Wilbraham MA [5 Feb 1846]
PATCH Benjamin & Harriet E F KNIGHT at Otisfield ME [7 May 1846]
PATERSON Nancy G & Capt Levi BATCHELDER of Phipsburg ME at Portland ME [14 Aug 1845
PATRIDGE Clarinda of Orland ME & George W HERBERT at Bucksport ME [9 Oct 1845]
   Everett W & Nancy C HUSSEY at Jefferson ME [9 Oct 1845]
PATTEE Andrew J of Fryeburg ME & Abigail M STONE of Waterford ME at Waterford [14 Mar 1850]

PATTEE (cont.) Mary of Searsmont ME & Rev Joseph HASTINGS at Searsmont ME [5 Dec 1837]
  Octavia E & Mr William H MARSTON at Bath ME [2 Jul 1846]
  Philena, d/o John PATTEE Esq, of Searsmont ME & Rev Albert CHURCH of the Maine (Methodist) Annual Conference [4 Jul 1837]

PATTEN Adelia & Rev Asa T LORING, pastor of Congregational Church in P at Phipsburg ME [10 Apr 1845]
  Alfred Capt of Bowdoinham ME & Maria RUSS of Monson MA [24 Jul 1835]
  Augusta A & Thomas H OLIVER at Phipsburg ME [14 Jan 1847]
  Bryce M Esq director of the Kentucky Institute for the Blind & Mary S EARLE of Brunswick ME at Clifton KY [14 August 1851]
  Caroline W & Rev Mark R HOPKINS of Old Town ME at Skowhegan ME [12 Apr 1849]
  Frances A & Capt Andrew PERCY both of Phipsburg ME at Providence RI [2 Sept 1847]
  Harriet T & Jarvis SLADE of Boston MA at Bath ME [10 Oct 1844]
  Isaac of Bloomfield ME ae 69 & Miss Nancy HILTON ae 50 of Solon ME by William VARNUM Esq on June 23rd at Solon ME [1 Jul 1843]
  Jane F & Joseph F SAUNDERS of Palermo ME at China ME [18 Apr 1834]
  Lincoln Capt of Topsham ME & Mrs Mary E WHITNEY at Bowdoinham ME [17 Jul 1851]
  Mary & Bradbury ROBINSON Jr at Bloomfield ME [1 Apr 1843]
  Mathew Capt & Mrs Susan SUMNER of Bowdoinham ME at Topsham ME [5 Dec 1837]
  Olive B d/o Capt Rob't P of Frankfort ME & J Stone LYFORD at Wilton ME on 14th inst by Rev PERHAM [31 Dec 1842]
  Olive & George F HOXIE of Newburgh ME at Hermon ME [14 Jan 1847]
  Rufus & Susan MERRILL at Topsham ME [15 May 1835]
  Sarah E & Daniel C PRESCOTT at Thomaston ME [29 Apr 1847]
  Sumner A (MD) of Shirley ME & Nancy M BLANCHARD at Blanchard ME [15 Nov 1849]

PATTERSON Ann & Calvin BATCHELDER of Belmont ME at Belfast ME [28 May 1842]
  Caroline A of Belfast ME & Nathan FARROW at Northport ME [12 Aug 1852]
  Catherine W & Samuel B MORSE of Wilton ME at Augusta ME [24 Aug 1839]
  David S & Anna P WARD of China ME at Vassalboro ME on 5 Oct by Edward GRAY Esq [16 Oct 1851]
  Ephraim Q of Bangor ME & Aroline [sic] P VIVUAN of Vassalboro ME at Salem [31 Jul 1851]
  George W & Martha J MAYHEW at Belfast ME [19 Feb 1852]
  Harriet N & C N LADD of Hallowell ME at Edgecomb ME [6 Nov 1841]
  Isaac of Limerick ME & Mary BAKER at Cornish ME [18 Feb 1847]
  James B of Waldo Plantation ME & Abigail PERKINS at Belfast ME [27 Feb 1845]
  James & Lydia Jane HATCH at Portland ME [5 Dec 1844]
  John of Industry ME & Veronica U M ROCHE formerly of Boston MA at Mt Vernon, Posey Co IN on Nov 25 [1 Feb 1840]
  John of Warren & Lucina HILLS at Cushing ME [3 Oct 1844]

PATTERSON (cont.) Margaret K J & Capt E K HATCH at Dresden ME [19 Feb 1846]
    Milton & Eunice HATCH at Belfast ME [25 Dec 1835]
    Nathaniel Esq & Mary E WHITTIER at Belfast ME [27 May 1852]
    Otis Capt & Lucy Ann GILMORE at Belfast ME [12 Mar 1846]
    Rachel & Theophilus STANLEY at Hampden ME [13 May 1833]
    Richard F & Cilenda BOWLES at Belfast ME [8 Nov 1849]
    Robert O Capt & Lucy A GILMORE at Belfast ME [19 Mar 1846]
    Robert & Susan J DOUGLAS of Dorchester MA at Hope ME [17 Oct 1837]
    Sarah & Emerson SAWYER at Bangor ME [19 Nov 1842]
    Sewall & Rouland HAYFORD at Belfast ME [1 Jan 1846]
    Washington & Mary Ann HASKELL at Belfast ME [5 Dec 1844]
    William of Belfast ME & Clarrissa MUDGET at Northport ME [5 Sept 1840]

PAUL Catherine R & Walter ROBERT at Solon ME [30 Apr 1846]
    Eliza C Miss & Gideon C McCAUSLAND at Thompson CT on Nov 9th [23 Nov 1848]
    Frances T & Josiah FLYNT at Hallowell ME [25 Jul 1840]
    Joseph & Lydia J ALLEN at E Thomaston ME [25 Oct 1849]
    Julia Mrs & Capt Veranus JOHNSON at East Thomaston ME [24 Aug 1848]
    Mary & Henry YORK at South Thomaston ME [16 Aug 1849]
    Robert & Lucy T FOGLER at Thomaston ME [15 Oct 1846]
    Susan E & Dr S W ELLIOT of Dover ME of Hallowell ME at Gardiner ME [4 Dec 1841]
    Sylvester & Esther P WARREN both of Westbrook ME at Biddeford ME [20 Jul 1848]
    Theodore & Louisa J PIKE at Auburn ME [4 Mar 1852]
    Thomas S & Martha A RUSSELL at Hallowell ME [21 Dec 1848]
    V B & Ann E SANBORN both of Waldo ME at Knox ME [20 Mar 1851]
    William & Clarinda THURSTON at Peru ME [23 May 1840]

PAYNE Lycurgus V & Lydia B PENDLETON of Northport ME at Belfast ME [19 Dec 1844]

PAYSON Elizabeth & Rev George L PRENTISS of New Bedford MA at Portland ME [1 May 1845]
    Louisa S eld d/o late Dr P & Prof Albert HOPKINS of Williams College, Williamstown MA at Portland ME [11 Sept 1841]

PEABODY Almond & Abigail S MANN at Hampden ME [19 Aug 1836]
    Hannah M of Gorham ME & William COTHREN Esq of Farmington ME at Lewiston ME [17 Apr 1851]
    Hugh Capt & Mary KEITH at Thomaston ME [10 Aug 1833]
    Jesse & Elizabeth ROSE d/o late Hon Daniel R at Thomaston ME [27 Jun 1840]
    Jonathan of Gilead ME & Rhoda KILBOURN of Harrison ME at Bridgeton ME [15 Feb 1849]
    Laura A & William ELDER at Winthrop ME on Sun eve last by Rev ROBINSON [25 Jul 1843]
    Mary T & Hon Horace MANN Secretary of the Board of Education at Boston MA [27 May 1843]
    Peter P & Laurette LAWSON at Starks Centre ME [16 Mar 1848]
    W S & Charlotte C CROSBY at Bangor ME [13 Jun 1844]

PEACOCK Abba Jane & William S WARD at Richmond ME [5 Mar 1846]

PEACOCK (cont.) James & Eliza A ERSKINE at Gardiner ME [25 Oct 1849]
 Lavina & Samuel WEEKS at Gardiner ME [4 Feb 1833]
 Lucy J & David M STEVENS at Gardiner ME [14 May 1846]
 William & Diantha FISHER at Litchfield ME [17 Sept 1842]
PEAKER Thomas M of Tisbury & Thankful S MOORE of Gardiner ME at Cambridge ME [22 May 1851]
PEARCE William H & E GILLET d/o Rev E G of Hallowell ME at Natchez MS [28 Mar 1837]
PEARL Hannah T Miss & Orville GLIDDEN at Orneville ME [31 Aug 1848]
PEARSON Albert (Dr) & Adeline BAKER at Albion ME [24 Jun 1843]
 Ann M & Rev Enoch POND D D Prof of Theological Institute at Bangor ME [20 Jul 1839]
 Edmund Jr Esq & Laura L PERRIMAN at Machias ME [5 Feb 1852]
 Edmund merchant of Waterville ME & Mrs Rosanna M LUNT d/o Wm REED Esq of Boothbay at Boothbay ME on 23rd inst by Rev David CUSHMAN [27 Feb 1841]
 Henry B Esq of Philadelphia PA & Mary Elizabeth Eld d/o William McFARLAND at Waterville ME [26 Dec 1840]
 Menander & Melinda M MYRICK both of Bangor ME at Portland ME [22 Apr 1847]
 Sumner C of Belmont ME & Julia A WHEELER at Boston MA [25 Sept 1851]
PEARSONS Abby C & Lewis P HOVEY at Hallowell ME [27 Jun 1844]
 Mary F & Mr Albert FULLER at Bloomfield ME [29 Jan 1852]
 Thomas of Belmont ME & Melvina DOTEN of Knox ME at Waldo ME [12 Dec 1846]
PEASE Amanda & Henry FASSET Jr at Union ME [16 Apr 1846]
 Arnold of Wilton ME & Lucy A CONANT at Temple ME [22 Nov 1849]
 Benjamin F & Sarah J HAINES at Hallowell ME [14 Sept 1848]
 John of Wellington ME & Rosamond CHADBOURN of Harmony ME at Harmony ME [2 Nov 1839]
 Mercy D of Hope ME & Rev John N RINES at Lincolnville ME [25 Jul 1834]
 Paul H & Sarah E COLE at Augusta ME on 19th inst by Rev Asahel MOORE [26 Dec 1844]
PEASLEE D B of Pittston ME & Mary J PEASLEE at Hallowell ME [5 Apr 1849]
 Daniel H & Emily A CHURCHILL at Danville ME [8 Mar 1849]
 George L (Dr) of Wilton ME & Susan M ANDREWS at Rumford ME [5 Apr 1849]
 Jacob Esq & Lucy Ann COPELAND both of Pittston ME at Boston MA [29 May 1851]
 Mary J & D B PEASLEE of Pittston ME at Hallowell ME [5 Apr 1849]
PEAVEY Lorentha & George COLMAN at Augusta ME on 12 Feb by Rev C F ALLEN [20 Feb 1851]
PEASLEY Mary PEASLEY & Carlton D ELMES at Hallowell ME [21 May 1846]
PECK Eliza A ae 83 & Henry MENINGER ae 104 at Marion Co MS [16 Oct 1835]
 Joshua & Amelia BUSHEL at Washington ME on 17th ult [18 Jul 1843]
 Lucy M & Capt John DYER of New York at Belfast ME [22 Jun 1839]

PECK (cont.) Melissa of Clinton ME & John N DODGE late of Fayette ME at Worthington OH [23 Nov 1839]

PEAVY Mercy E & Seth MOODY at Windsor ME [29 Jan 1852]

Rachel & Eben REED at Windsor ME [29 Jan 1852]

PEDER Mrs Ann & George N WOOD at (Augusta) ME on 9th June [17 Jun 1852]

PEET Edward J & Mary Fletcher both of Norridgewock ME at New York City NY on July 9 by Rev George B CHEEVER [24 Jul 1851]

PEIRCE Susan D & Samuel D THURSTON at Waterville ME [1 Jun 1848]

PEEVY Richard of Liberty ME & Olive MITCHELL of Washington ME at Vassalboro ME [30 Oct 1838]

PENCE Henry P & Catherine ELLIS at Lubec ME on 16 October [6 Nov 1845]

PENDEXTER Catherine of Parsonsfield ME & Freedom BERRY of Cornish ME at East Parsonsfield ME [13 Mar 1851]

Daniel E of Bartlett NH at New Gloucester ME & Harriet O CUSHMAN of Brunswick ME [24 Dec 1846]

Edmund & Sarah H REED both of Glenburn ME at Bangor ME [29 Aug 1844]

Electa Mrs & Ebenezer MATHEWS at Sebasticook ME [27 Dec 1849]

PENDLETON B E of Belfast ME & A A TRISKEY at Saco ME [3 Jul 1845]

Charles Capt & Sarah PARK at Prospect ME [14 Mar 1837]

Elisha K & Catherine S KNOWLES at Belfast ME [13 Feb 1841]

Erastus O & Mary W CALLISTON at Northport ME [28 Feb 1837]

Grace A & Otis D WILSON at Belmont ME [13 May 1852]

Harriet Maria & Jos TREAT 2nd at Camden ME [21 Jun 1849]

Isaac Capt & Catherine THORNDIKE at Camden ME [22 Apr 1852]

Lucinda C & Abram WENTWORTH both of Searsport ME at Waldo ME [23 May 1846]

Lydia B of Northport ME & Lycurgus V PAYNE at Belfast ME [19 Dec 1844]

Lydia of Calais ME & Silas BAILEY of Topsfield ME at Eastport ME [14 Aug 1845]

Rosetta L & John B STINSON at Prospect ME [9 Sept 1847]

PENLEY Sarah D & Ephraim S CROCKETT at Danville ME [25 Apr 1844]

PENNELL Charles S & Cornelia P ADAMS at Brunswick ME [30 Jan 1845]

Charles S & Harriet N GIVEN at Brunswick ME [25 Apr 1840] & [5 Dec 1840]

Clement Jr & Sara SAWYER at Portland ME [11 Jan 1844]

Eliza M & Joseph M DYER of Bangor ME at Portland ME [2 May 1844]

Lewis of Brunswick ME & Esther SLOCOMB of RI at Evansville IN [31 Jul 1838]

Martha Jane & Capt Benjamin DUNNING at Brunswick ME [4 Feb 1843]

Robert 2nd of Brunswick ME & Caroline SOULE at Freeport ME [4 Feb 1843]

Sarah J of Dover ME & Capt Geo W GOODWIN at Foxcroft ME [1 Mar 1849]

Thomas & Julia OWEN both of Brunswick ME at Brunswick ME [20 Nov 1845]

PENNIMAN Hiram G Capt & Lydia A COOMBS at E Thomaston ME [9 Aug 1849]

PENNY/PENNEY Arba & Betsey CROWELL at Waterville ME [27 Jun 1834]

PENNY (cont.) Edward W & Elizabeth D STONE at Worcester MA both parties are deaf mute former inmates of the Hartford Asylum for the Deaf and Dumb (Mutes) [23 May 1837]
   George of Belgrade ME & Jane BLANCHARD of Augusta ME at Augusta ME [5 Jun 1838]
   Henry A of Waterville ME & Ann M CONANT of Topsham ME at Portsmouth NH [27 May 1852]
   Jane Mrs of Belgrade ME & Simon ROBBINS of Rome ME at W Sidney ME [22 Mar 1849]
   Knowlton of Augusta ME & Elizabeth HILL at Readfield ME on 26th ult by Elia LYON Jr Esq [18/25 Apr 1840]
PEPPER Rosanna & Peter AVERY at Bath ME [30 Jul 1848]
PERCIVAL Hannah R & Boyd KUHN of Waldoboro ME at China ME on 22 June by Rev L WENTWORTH [26 Jun 1851]
   Philander S & Bethiah K WESTON both of Augusta ME at Augusta on Tues last by Rev BURGESS [30 Sept 1847]
PERCY Abraham C & Salome M CAMPBELL at Phipsburg ME [28 Mar 1850]
   Andrew T Capt & Frances S PATTEN both of Phipsburg ME at Providence RI [2 Sept 1847]
   Calvin of Boston MA & Sarah LOW at Bath ME [30 Oct 1841]
   Mary E & Joseph BETANCUE of Boston MA at Bath ME [30 Oct 1841]
   Sarah & Hiram MALCOMB at Phipsburg ME [22 Apr 1836]
   William G of Phipsburg ME & Minerva WHITMORE at Bowdoinham ME [16 Sept 1847]
PERHAM Emily a & Sylvester WALKER both of Wilton ME at Jay ME by M STONE Jr Esq [19 Aug 1852]
   John Rev of Madison ME & Mrs Lucilla STRICKLAND at Wilton ME [5 Dec 1844]
   William R of Williamsburg ME & Laura Jane HAMLET of Brownville ME at Milo ME [31 Jul 1851]
PERKINS Abby S & Joseph HOWARD at Williamsburg Long Island on 18th inst [2 Nov 1848]
   Abigail M & James B PATTERSON of Waldo Plantation ME at Belfast ME [27 Feb 1845]
   Alvin T & Eliza Ann SAVELS at Gardiner ME [4 Mar 1833]
   Ann d/o Benjamin P & Eliphalet PACKARD at Winthrop ME on 20th ult by Rev J INGRAHAM [1 Apr 1836]
   Anna & Daniel COBLEIGH at Biddeford ME [4 Mar 1852]
   Anne M & George W LANCASTER at Augusta ME by Rev WILLIAMS [24 Dec 1846]
   Ansel & Eleanor F PARKHURST d/o H P at Unity ME on New Year's Day by Jona H FULLER Esq [3 Jan 1850]
   Augustine & Ruth W SPRINGER at Waterville ME [11 Apr 1837]
   B A of Bangor ME & Augusta BELLOWS at Freedom ME [24 May 1849]
   Betsey A & Seth GORDON at Biddeford ME [13 Apr 1848]
   Bradbury & Sarah G WALKER at Cornville ME [20 Feb 1851]
   Celia A & Col Alvah JAMESON at Topsham ME [6 Jul 1848]
   Daniel B & Sarah ALBEE at Boston MA [11 Jul 1837]
   Daniel Dea of Frankfort ME & Nancy VINAL at Dixmont ME [30 Mar 1848]
   David S & Jane DUNNING at Brunswick ME [28 Oct 1836]
   Eliza A & James MURCH at Frankfort ME [8 Apr 1847]

PERKINS (cont.) Eliza Ann & Benjamin Franklin WING in (Winthrop ME) on Sunday evening 24 Apr by Rev David THURSTON [7 May 1842]
    Elizabeth & George W DOE at (Augusta) ME on 25 Oct [9 Nov 1848]
    Eunice C & Gilbert A WOODWARD at Winthrop ME on 1st inst [13 Jul 1848]
    Gardner of E Livermore ME & Mary W MAXIM at Wayne ME on Nov 30 by Eld B L LOMBARD [6 Dec 1849]
    Harriet of Bridgton & James AYRES at Salem MA [21 Jan 1847]
    James & Elvira F WADE at Augusta ME on Nov 25 by J J EVELETH Esq [2 Dec 1847]
    John A & Augusta A JENKINS at Augusta ME [8 Jan 1846]
    John of Readfield ME & Sarah MERNSEY of Augusta ME at Readfield by Daniel CRAIG Esq [10 Apr 1838]
    John & Martha PINKHAM of Boothbay ME at Georgetown ME [3 Oct 1844]
    Jonathan A & Almira HOLMES at Smithfield ME [24 Sept 1846]
    Jotham S & Mary WRIGHT at Newcastle ME [17 May 1849]
    Laura & Ebenezer B SIBLEY at Augusta ME [28 Nov 1841]
    Lavinia & Seth SCAMMON of Saco ME at Kennebunkport ME [3 Jul 1841]
    Livonia & Benjamin RUST at Augusta ME [3 Jun 1833]
    Luther Capt & Mary Ann BROWN late of Saco ME at Winthrop ME by Rev F MERRIAM [15 Oct 1846]
    Marcia & Thomas T WASHBURN Esq of Orono ME at Bridgewater [22 Jul 1836]
    Margaret & Jeremiah SWEETSER at Hermon ME [20 Apr 1848] & [7 Apr 1848]
    Maria & Michael COFFEE at Palmyra ME [18 May 1848]
    Martha W d/o George W PERKINS Esq & Charles GAY of Gardiner ME at Augusta ME by Rev HOWARD [23 Dec 1843]
    Mary A & John W HANSON at Biddeford ME [1 Feb 1844]
    Mary E & William FLY Prof of Mathematics US Navy at Topsham ME [18 Jul 1844]
    Miriam M of South Paris ME & Asa EMERY of Bloomfield ME at Skowhegan ME [19 Dec 1844]
    Nathaniel of Augusta ME & Rachel V SHAW of Sidney ME by L CUSHING Esq at Sidney ME [16 May 1844]
    Richard F Esq of Augusta ME & Emeline P AVERY at Hallowell ME by Rev COLE [23 Dec 1843]
    Richard Jr & Louisa YORK at Ellsworth ME [11 Nov 1847]
    S F Miss & Mr D JOHNSTON at Castine ME [14 Sept 1848]
    Spencer of Old Town ME & Martha J WILLIAMS of Orrington ME at Bangor ME [12 Apr 1849]
    Stephen & Mrs Miranda STONE at Kennebunkport ME [25 Dec 1845]
    Waldo A of (Augusta) ME & Caroline MARCH at Nashua NH on the 11th inst [25 May 1848]
    William of Gardiner ME & Ann S HUNT d/o William H of (Augusta) ME by Rev Mr WEBB at (Augusta) on New Year's Day [8 Jan 1852]
PERLEY John C & Eunice MEIGS at Vassalboro ME [16 Mar 1848]
    Martha F & Robert JORDAN at Winthrop ME [16 Nov 1848]
    Hannah Maria & Augustus CROWELL at Vassalboro ME [10 Dec 1846]

PERLEY (cont.) Francis Capt of Winthrop ME & Mrs Sarah ADAMS at Augusta ME on Mar 8 by Rev A DREW [22 Mar 1849]
PERLY Mary T & James JENNIS at Winthrop ME [4 Jul 1844]
PERRIGO Charles H & Susan L HODSDON at Milo ME [25 May 1848]
PERRIMAN Laura L & Edmund PEARSON at Machias ME [5 Feb 1852]
PERRY Angeline & Alexander C THAYER at Paris ME [29 Jan 1842]
   Ann H of Camden ME & Abel M LAMBERT of Strong ME at Farmington ME [8 Mar 1849]
   Clarke Rev of Standish ME & Eunice McLELLAN at Gorham ME [26 Sept 1840]
   David of Fitzwilliam NH & Sophia KENISTON at Gardiner ME [20 May 1847]
   Elisha & Phebe Jane GIBBS both of Chesterville ME at Fayette ME by H B LOVEJOY Esq [1 May 1851]
   George W & Hannah A PHINNEY at Augusta ME on New Year's Day by Rev W A DREW [4 Jan 1844]
   Henry of Richmond ME & Sarah WING of Litchfield ME at Gardiner ME [21 Mar 1850]
   Isabella H d/o John P Esq & Horace WILLIAMS at Stillwater ME [11 Jul 1834]
   Israel J Jr of E Thomaston ME & Hannah D FOWLER at Salem [22 August 1844]
   John W of Brunswick ME & Laura B SMITH d/o John SMITH Esq of Readfield ME by Rev BAILEY of (Winthrop) ME at Readfield ME [29 Aug 1840]
   Joseph Capt & Olive GILLPATRICK both of Gardiner ME at Gorham ME [4 Dec 1845]
   Lincoln of Gardiner ME & Mary L REED at Dresden ME [22 Feb 1849]
   Louisa H & William S LITTLE at (Augusta) ME on 21st Mar [1 Apr 1852]
   Lowly Ann & Alvin SHERMAN at Appleton ME [8 Jul 1847]
   Lucinda L & Richard L CARR at Burnham ME [28 May 1842]
   Lydia B & Lewis S PICKETT at (Augusta) ME at the Universalist Chapel on Sunday afternoon [2 Nov 1848]
   Lyman & Helen HIGHT at Bloomfield ME [31 May 1849]
   Martha B & Capt F W TALBOT of Portland ME at Phipsburg ME [18 Jun 1846]
   Martha J & Daniel C KELLEY at Gardiner ME [22 Feb 1849]
   Mary E & James WARE at (Augusta) ME on 23d May [3 Jun 1852]
   Nathan & Rachel FIELD at Waterville ME [8 Mar 1849]
   P Avadna & H Clauson FISKE of Willamantic CT at Augusta ME on Jan 16 by Alanson STARKS Esq [31 Jan 1850]
   Ruhama Ann & Abraham W ALLEN at Minot ME [20 Jan 1837]
   Susan M & Edwin T EMERY at Thomaston ME [4 Mar 1847]
   Timothy B of Phipsburg ME & Ann Mary EAMES at Bath ME [21 Sept 1848]
PETERS Elizabeth A & Isaac H DANFORTH at Brunswick ME [8 Jan 1852]
   George S Esq of Ellsworth ME & Charlotte A CLARK of Hallowell ME at Providence RI [12 Oct 1848]
   John & Margaret MINIX at Bath ME [31 Oct 1844]
   Matilda of Brunswick ME & William SEWALL of Brunswick ME at Augusta ME on 2 Jan by George MULLIKEN Esq [23 Jan 1851]
   Sarah E & Jesse P BRIMIJINE at Bath ME [20 Mar 1845]

PETERS (cont.) Winneford & Joseph CROSSMAN of Norridgewock ME at Fairfield ME [12 Apr 1849]
PETERSON H T of E Livermore ME & Lydia L CHILDS of Canton ME at Jay ME [19 Jul 1849]
   Mary of Lisbon ME & Orren PARKER at Augusta ME [22 Jan 1846]
   Sarah of Winthrop ME & Valentine FRUNG of Monmouth ME at Augusta ME by Rev E B WEBB [4 Sept 1851]
PETTINGILL Abraham Col & Mary C EMERSON at Hampden ME [2 Apr 1846]
   Bethiah F & Maj Gideon HINKLEY of Lisbon ME at Livermore ME [8 Aug 1844]
   Charles & Ann C HOWLAND at Brunswick ME [30 Sept 1843]
   E F of Fayette ME & S B WALTON at E Livermore ME [8 Aug 1844]
   Elisha H & Rosanna BEAN at Livermore Falls ME on 26th ult [9 Oct 1841]
   Elisha of Sangerville ME & Elizabeth J EATON of Hermon ME at Bangor ME [22 May 1845]
   Henry A of Augusta ME & Lavinia B STICKNEY at Eastport ME [1 May 1838]
   Howard & Caroline A HOMANS by Rev DR TAPPAN at (Augusta) ME [7 Dec 1848]
   Ichabod A of Monmouth ME & Martha MORSE at Winthrop ME on Feb 22 by Rev MORSE [1 Mar 1849]
   L A Mrs & Arthur C CLARK at (Augusta) ME [16 Nov 1848]
   Mansfield H & Elizabeth C YOUNG at Augusta ME on 1st inst [9 Jan 1845]
   Mary B & Joseph P CURTIS of Topsham ME at Wayne ME [9 Dec 1847]
   Rachel of Bath ME & John STREET of Portland ME at Phipsburg ME [14 Nov 1834]
   Sarah Jackson & Dr Horatio Gates ALLEN of Winthrop ME at Bath ME [26 Oct 1833]
   Susan P Mrs & Henry NORCROSS at Augusta ME [29 Oct 1846]
   Wealthy Frances & Rev J Henry HALL at "Gothic Chapel" of the Mammoth Cave of Kentucky on Apr 26th [20 May 1852]
PHELPS A A Rev of Boston MA & Lucy T LITTLE d/o Doty L Esq at Castine ME [24 Oct 24 1844]
   Augustus of Paris ME & Arabella DOBLE of Sumner ME at Buckfield ME [29 Mar 1849]
   F T & Mrs Maria CONANT at Camden ME [29 Jan 1852]
   Louisa M & Jacob WELLMAN at New York [20 Jul 1848]
   Louisa & William MAHLMAN at Lubec ME [13 May 1847]
   Lydia E & Abijah LEIGHTON at Eastport ME [27 Jul 1848]
PHILBRICK Benjamin 2nd of Mt Vernon ME & Nancy SANBORN at Vienna ME [6 Jun 1837]
   Benjamin S of Mt Vernon ME & Abagail CHAMBERLAIN at Foxcroft ME [29 Feb 1840]
   Betsey & Joel WILLIAMS at Skowhegan ME [9 Jan 1838]
   Chandler of Jefferson ME & Clarinda N CAIN at Windsor ME [1 Jun 1848]
   Ellen A & Robert B TUTTLE at Skowhegan ME [20 Apr 1839]
   Hannah Mrs & William N GILE at Vernon (Mt Vernon ME)? on 19th inst [7 Apr 1848]

PHILBRICK (cont.) Hannah S & Joseph HOPKINS at Mt Vernon ME by Eld Arthur DRINKWATER [4 Jan 1834]
 Harriet L & Aaron S LYFORD at Mt Vernon ME on 7th inst by Rev INGRAHAM [27 Nov 1838]
 Irena P & Charles H BUSWELL at Exeter ME? [8 Apr 1852]
 Jane R & Benjamin F DODGE at Skowhegan ME [10 Dec 1846]
 Johnson of China ME & Ellen C Randall at Augusta ME by Rev W A DREW [13 Jan 1844]
 Mary Jane & Daniel S GOLDTHWAITE at Lowell MA [16 Mar 1848]
 Mary Josephine & George H COLCORD both of Foxcroft ME at Dover ME [26 Aug 1847]
 Sarah & Samuel D ARNOLD at Skowhegan ME [8 Jan 1839]
 Sylvanus B of Chesterville ME & Martha K GREEN of Wilton ME at Farmington ME [13 Nov 1851]
 Walter W & Mrs Wealthy RICKER at Augusta ME on Sunday morning by Rev C FULLER [16 Jul 1844]
 Walter W Esq & Mrs Martha HANSCOM of Hallowell ME at Augusta ME by J J Eveleth Esq [23 May 1846]

PHILBROOK Alden W & Mary W WHITTEN at Augusta ME [14 May 1846]
 Charles & Elizabeth d/o Rev D THURSTON of Winthrop ME at Winthrop ME at the Congregational meeting house on Thurs evening last, by Rev Mr THURSTON [22 Jun 1839]
 Eliza of Winthrop ME & David Henry GOODALE, merchant of (Hallowell) on Thurs evening last by Rev Daniel D TAPPAN [12 Dec 1837]
 Lavina & Calvin CHAMBERLAIN Esq of Foxcroft ME at Mt Vernon ME [13 Nov 1838]
 Moses of Levant ME & Mary THOMAS at Winthrop ME on Tues Eve last by Rev David THURSTON [21 Dec 1833]
 Orra A Mrs & Frederick ABORN at Augusta ME on Jan 5 by Rev C F ALLEN [17 Jan 1850]
 Sarah H & A M C HEATH, editor of the *Fountain and Journal*, both of Gardiner ME at the residence of Frederick ABORN in Augusta ME on Aug 3rd by Rev HYDE of Gardiner ME [5 Aug 1852]

PHILLIPS Ann & Solon CHASE at Turner ME [23 Oct 1845]
 Betsey & R W LIBBY both of Avon ME at Phillips ME [29 Nov 1849]
 Calvin S Esq & Mary H SCAMMON at Rockland ME [11 Sept 1851]
 Caroline M & Silas REDINGTON at Waterville ME [28 Mar 1844]
 Charles R of Waterville ME & Cathelina E PRAY of Monmouth ME by Rev Dr GILLETT at Hallowell on 1st June [15 Jun 1848]
 Cyrene & Sylvester SILVERY at Eastport ME [14 Sept 1848]
 G Alfred of Waterville ME & Marcia H TUCKER of Fairfield ME at Providence RI [26 Jun 1851]
 George H & Mary Jane BENNETT at Thomaston ME [9 Mar 1848]
 Jonathan C & Mary P CASWELL at Turner ME [19 Dec 1837]
 Lucinda & Francis D MILLETT at Auburn ME [8 Apr 1852]
 Mary R of Bangor ME & Cyrus K LADD of Brewer ME, merchant by Rev CAVERNO [16 Dec 1843]
 Phillip Esq of Turner ME & Julia A BROWN by Elder James PEARLE at Mt Vernon ME on 28th May [1 Jun 1848]
 William Capt & Mehitable CROWELL at Hampden ME [14 Aug 1841]
 William M & Susan L MEADER at Waterville ME [6 Jun 1844]

PHILPOT Lucinda & Hannah M SAWTELLE at Limerick ME [20 Jul 1848]

Marriage Notices from the "Maine Farmer" 319

PHILPOT (cont.) Samuel B of Limerick ME & Catherine H HARMON at Buxton ME [15 Jul 1847]
PHINNEY Hannah A & George W PERRY at Augusta ME on New Year's Eve by Rev W A DREW [4 Jan 1844]
    John G of (Augusta) ME & Aurelia J GILBERT by Rev William A DREW at Hallowell ME on 22 Oct [2 Nov 1848]
    Jonas Dea & Mary Augusta CRAFTS both of Jay ME at Leeds ME on 3rd inst by Rev Walter FOSS [14 Oct 1847]
PHIPPS Martin W of Holliston & Amelia H ROBINSON of Paris ME at Albany [26 Feb 1846]
PHOENIX Sarah & Jordan S W STUBBS at Pownal ME [7 Nov 1844]
PICKARD Rosanna & Dennis MOULTON both of Madrid ME at Phillips ME by Joseph DOW Esq [7 Jan 1847]
PICKERING James & Evelina E GORDON of Franklin ME at Sullivan ME [6 Jul 1848]
    Tryphena B & Warren LANDER at Brighton in Somerset Co ME [29 Apr 1836]
PICKETT
    Lewis S & Lydia B PERRY by Rev Mr DILLINGHAM at (Augusta) ME at the Universalist Chapel on Sunday afternoon [2 Nov 1848]
    Martha D & William H HOWARD at Portland ME [30 Jan 1845]
PIDGE Elizabeth & David H GOODNO of Hallowell ME at Providence RI on 21st inst [31 May 1849]
PIERCE Abigail F & John LAKEN at Etna ME [6 Jul 1839]
    Almira & Miles C WILLIAMS at Readfield ME [1 Aug 1840]
    Ann & John EATON 2nd both of Brunswick ME [20 Nov 1845]
    Caroline & Jeremiah LINDSEY at Prospect ME [9 Feb 1830]
    Catherine & Rev William R BABCOCK at Newport RI [14 Nov 1840]
    Clarissa W of Wales ME & William L SMALL of Pownal ME at Monmouth ME [24 Jun 1847]
    David Y of Bowdoin ME & Caroline C WARREN eldest d/o Col H I W of Pownal ME on 24th inst by Rev Jabez WOODMAN [2 Jan 1841]
    David Y (MD) & Cornelia B WARREN both of Pownal ME at New Gloucester ME [31 May 1849]
    E F & Martha DORR both of Skowhegan ME at Bloomfield ME [5 Apr 1849]
    E J Miss & Capt Jeremiah R POPE at Falmouth ME [17 Aug 1848]
    E P of Houlton Aroostook Co ME & Miss J B D CUSHMAN at Bangor ME [11 Mar 1847]
    Eleanor & Joseph STUDLEY both of Windsor ME at Augusta ME [23 Nov 1833] & at Vassalborough [30 Nov 1833]
    Elias D & Mary A BEARD at Brunswick ME [30 Sept 1836]
    Elisha & Almira H GARDINER all of Bangor ME [12 Feb 1846]
    Eliza T of Belfast ME & Capt James AREY at Frankfort ME [22 Jan 1846]
    George F & Lucy A ELDRIDGE at Orrington ME [11 Nov 1847]
    Harriet B & Thomas BROWN of Baldwin ME at the Forks of the Kennebec ME [27 Jun 1834]
    Jane M & Rev Richard B THURSTON of Waterville at Friendship PA [1 Jul 1847]
    Jane & William HODGKINS at Augusta ME on 20th inst by Wm WOART Esq [23 Sept 1847]

PIERCE (cont.) Joanna of Montville ME & Edmund P BROWN at Belfast ME [27 Jun 1844]
  John M of Greenfield & Mrs Mary D RICKER d/o George RICKER of Lynn MA at Hartford CT [25 May 1848]
  Lois H & James M HILTON of Starks ME at New Portland ME by Rev MOORE [7 Feb 1850]
  Lucilla S d/o late Waldo P Esq of Frankfort ME & Webster KELLEY Esq councillor at law of Frankfort ME at Boston MA on 24th ult [3 Sept 1842]
  Luther of Solon & Mary S BURNES at Madison ME [9 Jul 1846]
  Lydia B & Little T MORGAN of Thomaston ME at Boston MA [22 Apr 1847]
  M E Miss & Mark TRAFTON at Townsend [1 Jun 1848]
  Mary & William GROUSE at Winthrop ME by Rev THURSTON [15 Jun 1839]
  Nehemiah Esq of Monmouth ME & Mrs Nancy wid/o late John LADD at Winthrop ME [25 Jan 1844]
  Obed W of Lexington ME & Sarah B HAYNES [23 Aug 1845]
  Peter & Mrs Mary BEAN at Bingham ME on 18th inst [2 Nov 1839]
  Rosanna H & Joseph CONDON at Brunswick ME [21 Sept 1848]
  Thomas Capt & Jane WEBBER both of Bristol ME at Boothbay ME [15 Jan 1842]
  Vesta & William GETCHELL of Sidney ME at Augusta ME [9 May 1837]
  W D Capt & Emma A VARNEY of Thomaston ME at E Thomaston ME [28 Jun 1849]
  Warren Esq of Boothbay ME & Mary Jane MARR at Georgetown ME [13 Mar 1841]
  William T of Windsor ME & Lucy Ann BABCOCK at Augusta ME [7 Dec 1839]
PIERPONT Robert of Livermore ME & Mary HEMINWAY at Rumford ME [4 Feb 1833]
PIGGOT Elenor Mrs & Randle WHITE at Portland ME [16 May 1844]
PIKE Ann & Hawley BROWN at Augusta ME on Mar 25 [5 Apr 1836]
  Ann & Royal B HANSON at Saco ME [4 Dec 1845]
  Caroline E & Joseph KENDRICK Jr at Bangor ME [19 Aug 1836]
  Catharine B & Lloyd T PULLEN at Kingfield ME [27 Sept 1849]
  Dudley & Elizabeth Ann DYER at Saco ME [24 Sept 1846]
  Elizabeth Ann & J W HANSON at Atkinson ME [14 Jun 1849]
  F A Esq & Mary H GREEN at Calais ME [8 Oct 1846]
  Irena & Francis ABBOTT at Cornish ME on Oct 12 by Rev N HOBART [15 Nov 1849]
  John S & Olive M HEYWARD at Mercer ME [24 Oct 1840]
  John T attorney at law of Augusta ME & Climena M PARLIN of Winthrop ME at Winthrop on Dec 6 by Rev MERRIAM [11 Dec 1841]
  Louisa J & Theodore PAUL at Auburn ME [4 Mar 1852]
  Lydia S formerly of Bridgton ME & Edmund TRAFTON 2nd of Cornish ME at Portland ME [4 Jun 1846]
  N R of Hallowell ME & Hannah H FOSTER d/o Oliver F Esq of Winthrop ME at Winthrop on Sunday Eve last by Rev F MERRIAM [11 Sept 1845]
  Prescot L & Mrs Elizabeth A MORSE both of Norway ME at Oxford ME [23 Oct 1843]

PIKE (cont.) Richard Rev of Dorchester MA & Frances WEST d/o late Col A W ATHERTON at Portland ME on Weds eve by Rev Dr NICKELS [11 Mar 1843]
 Robert & Mrs Frances LIBBY at Eastport ME [23 Dec 1847]
 Sally & Edward LAWRENCE at Lubec ME [28 Aug 1835]
 Susan & I E ADDAMS of Boston MA at Saco ME [9 Apr 1846]
PILLSBURY/PILSBURY Belinda Mrs of Hallowell ME & Joshua KNOWLTON at Farmington ME [11 Jul 1844] & [13 Jun 1844]
 Elcy of Noblboro' ME & John BRUN Jr of Gardiner ME by Rev E TRASK at Nobleboro ME [25 Dec 1838]
 Eliza A & Andrew J FITTS of Southampton NH at Newport [1 Oct 1846]
 Elizabeth W d/o Wm P & Moses B LOCKE of Hallowell ME at Augusta ME on Weds last by Rev WM A DREW [19 Sept 1844]
 Emeline D of Northport ME & George W PILLSBURY of Thomaston ME at Belfast ME [24 Apr 1836]
 George Jr Capt at Vassalboro ME & Lydia BRAGG of Winslow ME [11 Oct 1849]
 George W of Thomaston ME & Emeline D PILLSBURY of Northport ME at Belfast ME [24 Apr 1836]
 Mary E & Thaddeus FAIRBANKS at Hallowell ME on 31st ult [11 Sept 1845]
 Nancy M & Elbridge C PITCHER both of Northport ME at Belfast ME by Rev McKEEN [11 Mar 1836]
 Nathaniel of E Thomaston ME & Hannah G HARRINGTON of Camden ME at Camden [29 May 1841]
 Sarah J & Alfred BICKNELL at Augusta ME on Nov 23 [9 Dec 1847]
 Sarah Jane & Capt John F HARDEN at Rockland ME [25 Dec 1851]
 Sarah Norris & Cyrus C FAIRBANKS at Hallowell ME on 15 Jan [22 Jan 1852]
 Thomas R Capt of Thomaston ME & Mary BROWN at Northport ME [30 Jan 1845]
 Tristam & Adelia B RIDLON both of Portland ME [9 Oct 1845]
PINCIN Charles of Gardiner ME & Julia A DUNN d/o John D Esq at Hallowell ME [6 Feb 1841]
PINEO Mary & Joseph D BROWN both of Campobello (New Brunswick Canada) at Eastport ME [16 Dec 1843]
PINGREE Betsy F & Ebenezer HUTCHINSON of Albany at Norway ME [26 Jun 1845]
 Page of Denmark ME & Nancy JORDAN of Webster ME at Lewiston ME [23 Jan 1851]
 Sarah & Timothy CLIFFORD at Lee [9 Mar 1848]
PINKHAM Andrew & Mary W FRIZZELL at Starks ME [17 Jan 1850]
 David W Capt of Bath ME & Melissa D HASKELL at Lowell MA on 9th Jan by Rev TWOMBLY [23 Jan 1851]
 E E & Ann M WADSWORTH at Hallowell ME [15 Mar 1849]
 Ebenezer & Reliance BUTLER at Strong ME [29 Jun 1839]
 Elijah & Martha Jane HUTCHINSON at Hallowell ME [10 Feb 1848]
 Elizabeth B & Oliver C HUSSEY of Nantucket MA at Sidney ME [5 Feb 1846]
 Hannah A & Gardiner GREENLIEF at Vassalboro ME on 17 Nov [20 Jan 1848]

PINKHAM (cont.) Jonathan B & Lucretia DUTTON at Augusta ME on Sunday last by J J EVELETH Esq [3 Sept 1846]
  Martha of Boothbay ME & John PERKINS at Georgetown ME [3 Oct 1844]
  Nathan of N Bridgewater MA & Sarah Ann REYNOLDS of Sidney ME at S by Rev TILLY [14 May 1846]
  Nicholas of Turner ME & Melvira WENTWORTH at Auburn ME [20 Feb 1851]
  Rachel of Litchfield ME & Richard HOSKINS of Hallowell ME by Eld Wm O GRANT at L [21 Mar 1840]
  Richard H of Boston MA & Laura Ann KENSELL at Augusta ME [18 Nov 1847]
  Richard M of Hallowell ME & Mrs Lucy FISHER of Litchfield ME [18? Dec 1845]
  Sarah B & Franklin POWERS of Bath ME at Augusta ME on Nov 25th by A R NICHOLS Esq [6 Dec 1849]
  Susan R & Isaac HOLWAY both of Sidney ME at Waterville ME on May 30th by Joseph MARSTON Esq [18 Jun 1845]
  Susan & William JACKSON of Walpole MA at Strong ME [18 Sept 1845]
  William & Mary Sand CLARK at Lincoln ME [6 Sept 1849]
  Zelinda W & Charles E HODGE both of Hallowell ME by Rev TOBIE at Hallowell ME [13 Feb 1838]

PIPER Abner of Templeton MA & Betsey M HAMMOND at Sidney ME [2 Sept 1847]
  F J Capt & Lydia A SWAN at Camden ME [23 Oct 1845]
  John W of Gardiner ME & Bathsheba JOHNSON at Richmond ME [10 May 1849]
  Jonathan of Madison ME & Rebecca WESRON at Bloomfield ME [24 Jun 1847]
  Martha F & George BEVERIDGE at Thomaston ME [22 Jan 1846]
  Phebe M of Stetson ME & William O COLBATH of Exeter ME at Stetson ME [9 May 1837]
  Sarah of Winthrop ME & Amos ADAMS of Belgrade ME at Gardiner ME [8 Jul 1833]
  Susanna E & David P MCLAUGHIN both of Madison ME at Mayfield ME? [25 Apr 1844]

PISH Harriet M & Edmund DORR at Lincoln ME [1 Apr 1847]

PISHON Abby S & Dr Octavus WRIGHT at Clinton ME [29 Oct 1846]
  Caroline & Charles W STONE at Augusta ME on Mon Eve last by Rev F FREEMAN [14 Jan 1843]
  Martha J & Moses C HATCH at Augusta ME on 30th ult [10 Jun 1847]

PITCHER Charlotte & William H VOSE at Belfast ME [24 Jun 1843]
  Elbridge G & Nancy M PILLSBURY both of Northport ME at Belfast ME by Rev McKEEN [11 Mar 1836]
  Nancy A & William A WHITE at Belfast ME [19 Mar 1846]
  Sarah A A & Stephen S BICKMORE at Waldoboro ME [2 Mar 1848]
  William & Sarah A BENNER at N Waldoboro' ME on Nov 4 by Reuben ORFF Esq [15 Nov 1849]

PITTS Abner & Lydia L SIMMONS at Gardiner ME [15 May 1851]
  Mary & John CONNOR at Fairfield ME [21 May 1846]
  Olive R & Nathaniel LITTLEFIELD at Hallowell ME [19 Feb 1846]
  Orin & Martha W THOMAS at New Portland ME [20 Sept 1849]

PITTS (cont.) Susan & Daniel B BEAL at Dover ME [12 Feb 1842]
PLACE Mary of Saco ME & John G T RICHARDSON of Dover NH? at Portsmouth NH [2 Aug 1844]
PLAISTED Charles W & Caroline BUTLER at Phillips ME on Jan 1 by Amos S KING Esq [8 Feb 1849]
   Emory & Sarah S MITCHELL of Avon ME at Phillips ME [4 Oct 1849]
   Ira & Olive C ROBBINS at Phillips ME [5 Mar 1842]
   Major Mr & Mary LIBBY at Gorham ME [28 Jun 1849]
   William T of Danville ME & Elizabeth GRIFFIN at Greene ME [23 Jul 1846]
   William T of Lewiston Falls (Auburn-Danville) ME & Elizabeth GRIFFIN at Greene ME [6 Aug 1846]
PLANT John & Lucy LASSER at Bath ME [28 Nov 1844]
   Mary & Francis MYRICK at Bath ME [4 Jan 1849]
PLIMPTON Charles T of Boston MA & Frances P HATCH [23 Jan 1845]
PLUMER/PLUMMER Charles & Phebe S G YOUNG at Belfast ME [26 Dec 1844]
   Daniel L & Harriet S WITHAM at China ME [8 Feb 1840]
   Daniel & Marinda M OAKES at Sangerville ME [23 Oct 1845]
   Daniel & Sarah Ann FLOOD by D C STANWOOD City Clerk at (Augusta) ME on 9th June [17 Jun 1852]
   David G of Portland ME & Roxana B LOMBARD at Readfield ME on 11th inst [19 Mar 1846]
   Edwin, editor of the *Norway Advertiser* & Mary E NORTON at Portland [28 Jan 1847]
   Elbridge & Eliza LITTLEFIELD at Saco ME [1 Aug 1844]
   Elizabeth & Charles SAWYER at Augusta ME [23 Jan 1838]
   Emeline & Jefferson GRANT of Frankfort ME at Newburyport MA [19 Dec 1840]
   Freeman of Manchester LA & Mrs Serecta A COULBORN of Pittston ME [26 Mar 1846]
   Huldah & Richard PARSONS at Portland ME [2 May 1844]
   Ira & Thirsa H GRANT at Sebasticook ME [7 Apr 1848]
   Isaac of Wales ME & Lois FREEMAN of Leeds ME at Wales on New Year's Evening by Joel SMALL [15 Jan 1839]
   James I & Elizabeth N CLIFFORD both of Augusta ME at Winslow ME on Sun eve last by D G ROBINSON Esq [11 Dec 1845]
   Jason & Caroline M LIBBY both of Gorham ME at Windham ME [7 May 1846]
   Joseph A of Alna ME & Martha Ann WOODBRIDGE at Newcastle ME [13 Dec 1849]
   Josiah 3rd & Sarah M HALLOWELL by Jason M CARLETON Esq at Whitefield ME on Aug on 17th [24 Aug 1848]
   Louisa N Mrs & Alex MEADY at Hallowell ME [12 Oct 1848]
   Lucy & Nathaniel CHAMBERLIN at Dover ME? [3 Jun 1852]
   Margaret S & Stillman A DANFORTH at Charlestown ME? [8 Mar 1849]
   Martin K & Martha SAWYER at Bloomfield ME [17 Jun 1847]
   Naoma & Samuel A TODD at Alna ME [28 Feb 1834]
   Peasly of Palermo ME & Mary Ann CLARK at Washington ME [2 Dec 1843]
   Robert & Lucinda GREENE at Biddeford ME [21 Dec 1848]
   Sarah E & James S GRIFFIN of Windsor ME at Freeport ME [11 Jul 1844]

PLUMER (cont.) Timothy & Sally Y MURPHY both of Whitefield ME at Windsor ME [8 Apr 1847]
William J of Skowhegan ME & Hannah PARTRIDGE of Gardiner ME at Hallowell ME [17 Oct 1837]
William S & Sibyl STEARNS at Monroe ME [23 May 1840]
Wilmot W of Addison ME & Jane H WARD at Cherryfield ME [29 Jul 1852]

POLAND Matilda & Richard P HEAGAN at Prospect ME [1 Apr 1852]

POLAND Heman R & Dorcas A CAMPBELL both of Gardiner ME at Hallowell ME [8 Aug 1844]

POLDEN William & Fanny MARRIOTT at Bath ME [15 Jul 1847]

POLERESCZKY John of Dresden ME & Jane M OWEN at Wayne ME [26 Jul 1849]

POLLARD Amelia & Asa LEAVITT at Livermore ME [24 May 1849]
Charity Mrs & Elijah FOGG both of Wales ME at Gardiner ME [27 Mar 1851]
Huldah & Isaac KINGSLEY at Augusta ME [5 August 1833]
John M & Julia A STETSON of Brunswick ME at Topsham ME [6 May 1843]
Luther C & Sally B STINCHFIELD by J H MACOMBER Esq at Milo ME on 2d Nov [9 Nov 1848]
Mary E & E COOLIDGE of Solon ME at Cornville ME [17 Jul 1845]
Thomas L & Mary R BALLARD at Augusta ME on Jan 16 by Rev JUDD [24 Jan 1850]

POLLEY Jerusha of Bangor ME & Abraham PREBLE Esq of Bowdoinham ME at Topsham ME [17 May 1849]

POMROY Augusta G & Monroe PALMER of Waterville ME at Brattleboro VT [24 Jan 1850]
Isabel & Amasa CROMWELL of Mercer ME at Smithfield ME [3 Dec 1846]
John & Esther ST CLAIR at Bangor ME [15 August 1844]

POND Caroline of Bangor ME & Charles PROCTOR, M.D., of Rowley MA at Bangor ME [4 Dec 1838]
Daniel of Paris ME & Rebecca PRINCE of Bucksfield ME at B [6 Jul 1839]
Enoch Rev DD Prof in the Theological Institute & Ann M PEARSON at Bangor ME [20 Jul 1839]
Enoch of Georgetown ME & Mary T BLODGETT d/o Dea Bliss B at Bucksport ME on 25th ult by Rev Enoch POND [10 Jun 1843]
H A d/o Col Asa P of Ellsworth & Harrison TWEED Esq of Calais ME at Ellsworth ME [17 Sept 1842]
S M Hon of Bucksport ME & Mrs Mary B MORSE at New York NY [23 Oct 1845]
Wealthy Ann eld d/o Rev Prof POND & Rev Worster PARKER of Castine ME at Bangor ME [4 Mar 1833]

POOL/POOLE Eben Capt & H Florinda PRATT at Bangor ME [27 May 1843]
Hannah M & Henry S SMALL at Portland ME [17 Feb 1848]
Matilda Ann & Henry BIGELOW at Boston MA on 25th inst [5 Sept 1840]
N C & Catharine WEYMOUTH at Abbot ME [26 Mar 1846]
Thomas R Capt of (Augusta) ME & Susanna S PRESCOTT of Readfield at Readfield on 18th inst by Rev Mr POOLE of Whitefield [30 Jan 1845]
William Rev of Whitefield ME & Harriett NEWELL d/o the late Rev William ALLEN at Jefferson ME [5 August 1836]

POOL (cont.) Zenas & Betsey COLE at Greenwood ME [12 Nov 1846]
POOLER Ellen of Bloomfield ME & Jeremiah HILL Jr of Smithfield ME at Skowhegan ME [16 Jan 1851]
    Clara Browne & Theodore A BUSH at Bloomfield ME [22 Oct 1846]
POOR Elbridge & Susan STEVENS both of Andover ME [7 Feb 1834]
    Henry & Margaret L WYER at Portland ME by Rev Dr TYLER [11 Mar 1833]
    John of Newburyport MA & Nancy TITCOMB of Cumberland ME both deaf and dumb (mute) at Falmouth ME [30 Sept 1843]
    John A Esq & Elizabeth d/o late Hon Benjamin ORR of Brunswick ME at Bangor ME on 21st inst [30 Nov 1839]
    Mary & Capt James McCURDY at Eastport ME [23 Jul 1846]
POPE Ann Elizabeth & Dr Rufus M CHASE of Fairfield ME at Windsor ME [23 Sept 1843]
    Jeremiah R Capt & Miss E J PIERCE at Falmouth ME [17 Aug 1848]
    Marietta A & John BLAISDELL at Gardiner ME [22 Nov 1849]
    Mary Eliza d/o Capt J P USN & Maj F O WYSE of United States Army at Augusta ME on Tues morn July 6 by Rev PUTNAM [15 Jul 1852]
PORDEN Ann & Sir John FRANKLIN, she had knowledge of Greek and other languages [4 Mar 1852]
PORTER C G Rev of Bangor ME & Ann M SMITH at Bath ME [17 May 1849]
    Caroline & Randolph A L CODMAN Esq at Portland ME [13 Nov 1838]
    Charles RK of New Portland ME & Mary C DOLBIER at Kingfield ME on July 4 by E F PILLSBURY Esq [22 Jul 1852]
    Elizabeth C & Alex W LONGFELLOW at Westbrook ME [21 Aug 1851]
    Elizabeth K & Sewall EATON at Mt Vernon ME [26 Jun 1845]
    Eunice H & Dr Edmund RUSSELL at Strong ME [27 Jan 1848]
    George R of Freeport ME & Rosamond CONNOR at New Sharon ME [27 Jun 1844]
    Hannah D & David H STUBBS at Franklin ME [12 Feb 1852]
    Hannah & Capt Elbridge G WRIGHT at Mt Vernon ME by Dudley FOGG Esq [25 Apr 1840]
    Harriet E & Moses COLLEY of Gray ME at Portland ME [11 Mar 1847]
    Jerry M & Rachel A HUNTER at Strong ME [18 Dec 1845]
    Laura of Mt Vernon ME & Theophilus HUTCHINSON at Readfield ME [9 Dec 1847]
    Margaret E of Oldtown ME & Mr S M NELSON of China ME at Augusta ME on 2 Oct by Asaph R NICHOLS Esq [16 Oct 1851]
    Martha W & N MOORES of Vienna ME at New Sharon ME [5 Feb 1846]
    Mary A & William WOODS of Calais ME at Lubec ME [14 Nov 1844]
    Mary E & Charles P KIMBALL of Norway ME at Camden ME [12 Jul 1849]
    Rachel L & Thomas WITT of Norway ME at Paris ME [18 Dec 1845]
    Richard Esq & Dolly d/o Ezra HUTCHINGS at Bangor ME [27 Jun 1840]
    Samuel D of Rochester NY & Susan FARLEY at Waldoboro ME [15 Aug 1834]
    Samuel K Dr & Sarah Ann GILMAN at Mercer ME [28 Feb 1850]
    Sarah & Horace A ANDREWS at Augusta ME [18 Jul 1837]
    Thirza C of Strong ME & Lemuel CROSBY of Phillips ME at Strong ME on Mar 30 by Rev Dexter WATERMAN [22 Apr 1843]
    Thomas & Mary AUSTIN at China ME [26 Feb 1846]
    W R & Elizabeth H DEERING at South Paris ME [4 Jun 1846]
    William H & Emeline PRATT at Paris ME [11 Dec 1845]

PORTER (cont.) William of Mt Vernon ME & Sarah H JOSS at Readfield ME [9 Dec 1847]
PORTERFIELD Jane & William WILSON at Bristol ME [25 Feb 1847]
POST Abigail W & Mr Hanson HAWES at E Thomaston ME [26 Mar 1846]
    Catherine S & Joseph LUDWIN of Camden ME at Thomaston ME [22 Oct 1842]
    Enoch of S Thomaston ME & Hannah F SUMNER at Union ME [6 Feb 1851]
    Eunice S & John W BURNS at Thomaston ME [6 Jan 1848]
POTE Caroline A & Mr Sharon E BANKS at Belfast ME [5 Feb 1846]
    Henry G Capt & Dolly P ELWELL at Northport ME [11 Feb 1847]
    Robert P & Ellen N NOYES at Belfast ME [25 Jul 1840]
    William of New Gloucester ME & Elethusa KNOWLAND at Sidney ME [9 Oct 1851]
    William & Sarah THURSTON at Belfast ME [30 Jan 1845]
POTTER Abigail & Elisha SMALL at Bowdoinham ME [25 Sept 1851]
    Adoniram J & Isabella A MERRIMAN at Bath ME [18 May 1848]
    Ambrose & Elizabeth Jane DAY at Augusta ME [30 Aug 1849]
    Caroline F & Stephen DEERING at Augusta ME [20 Jun 1840]
    Fergus & Elizabeth APPLEBY at Eastport ME [11 Nov 1847]
    George F & Emmie T ROBINSON at Augusta ME on Thurs morning last by Rev JUDD [5 Aug 1852]
    Hennetta & Arthur L WILSON at Topsham ME [7 Nov 1840]
    Lucy W & William B STEARNS at Portsmouth NH [19 Feb 1852]
    Lydia & James F BUZZELL at Bloomfield ME [28 Aug 1851]
    Mary E & George RICH 2nd both of Waterville ME at Hallowell ME [20 Nov 1851]
    Mary E & John M ROBERTS both of West Gardiner ME at Gardiner ME [13 Mar 1851]
    Matthew & Octavia Ann BLAISDELL at Hallowell ME [25 Jun 1846]
    Simeon & Elizabeth J MARSTON at Gardiner ME [15 Mar 1849]
    William H of Wales (ME) late from Califorina & Mary GROVES of Litchfield ME d/o David GROVES Esq at Augusta ME on 24 (Apr) 1851 by Rev W A DREW [1 May 1851]
POTTLE J W of St Louis MO & Matilda only d/o John BRADBURY Esq at Bangor ME on 13th ult [2 Oct 1845]
    Mary E & John D BEAL at Norway ME [1 May 1851]
    Sarah J & Thomas MILLS of Gardiner ME at Pittston ME [22 Nov 1849]
POTTOR James of Whitefield ME & Mary MURPHY at Wiscasset ME [25 Jan 1844]
POWELL Albert P of Boston ME & Lydia W FURBISH at Hallowell ME [1 Jan 1846]
POWER T M of Orono & Lydia M ORDWAY of Newport ME at Dexter ME [7 Apr 1848]
POWERS A P of Bloomfield ME & Sarah I FISH at Hartland ME [6 Nov 1851]
    Dwinal of Dresden ME & Rebecca Jane GIVEN of Topsham ME at Bowdoinham ME [23 Jan 2841]
    Franklin of Bath ME & Sarah B PINKHAM at Augusta ME by A R NICHOLS Esq on Nov 25 [6 Dec 1849]
    Levi of Norridgewock ME & Mehitable BOARDMAN of Bloomfield ME [20 Jan 1837]
    Mary & Henry SWAIN at Brunswick ME [13 May 1847]

Marriage Notices from the "Maine Farmer" 327

POWERS (cont.) Nathan H & Amanda W SMITH at Sedgewick ME on Feb 20 by E PINKHAM [9 Mar 1839]
Reed W of Brunswick ME & Amanda M ALLEN at Bowdoin ME [13 Jan 1848]

PRATT Abigail & James F CROSSMAN at China ME [4 May 1848]
Albert & Dilana BEARCE at Foxcroft ME [21 May 1846]
Asa of Sebasticook ME & Bythena FLOOD at Clinton ME [8 Jan 1846]
Charles of Newport ME & Olive A STURTEVANT at Dexter ME [20 Jan 1848]
Cynthia & Roswell B PRATT at Foxcroft ME [23 May 1844]
Edward L & Martha COOK by Edward GRAY Esq at Vassalboro ME on 12th inst [21 Dec 1848]
Elizabeth D & Alvah JONES at Skowhegan ME [1 Jul 1852]
Emeline & William H PORTER at Paris ME [11 Dec 1845]
Emma Jane & Samuel CLUFF at Saco ME [26 Feb 1852]
Frances B & Alfred R TRUE at N Yarmouth ME [7 Nov 1837]
George of Medford MA & Lydia A WHITNEY at Belmont ME [14 Aug 1851]
H Florinda & Capt Eben POOL at Bangor ME [27 May 1843]
Hannah C & John C WARREN at Paris ME [17 Sept 1846]
Hannah & William HARRIMAN of Sebec ME at Foxcroft ME [27 Mar 1845]
Henry P, senior publisher of the *National Republican*, & Nancy W DIMMOCK d/o Dr Henry D of Limington ME at Saco ME [3 Jun 1833]
Hiram C of Abbot ME & Caroline KIMBALL of Foxcroft ME at Sebec ME [21 Jan 1847]
Huldah E & Paul W WHITEHOUSE at (Augusta) ME on Monday last [12 Oct 1848]
John L & Jane W BRAILEY at Weld ME by Kendall WRIGHT Esq [8 Jul 1852]
Jones Jr & Harriet BENSON both of Windsor ME at China ME on Dec 4 by William PERCIVAL Esq [13 Dec 1849]
Julia A & Levi M STEWART at Newport ME [4 Apr 1850]
Mary H & Peleg MORTEN at Windsor ME by J B SWANTON Esq [19 Sept 1837]
Mary J & Esther DEERING at Paris ME [10 Oct 1840]
Mary J & John W SEARS at E Livermore ME [6 Dec 1849]
Mary Jane, d/o Benjamin P Esq, of N Yarmouth ME & B F SHAW, principal of Vassalboro Academy, at N Yarmouth ME on Thanksgiving eve [11 Dec 1841]
Mary Jane & John N WOOD at Augusta ME on 4th inst by Rev W A P DILLINGHAM [13 Sept 1849]
Mary L & Stephen A BERRY at Augusta ME on 17th inst [21 Mar 1834]
Miles G & Ruth NYE at Lincoln ME [6 May 1847]
Miles & Betsey MORTON at Windsor ME by J B SWANTON [30 May 1834]
Phineas Esq & Sarah J BLISH of Hallowell ME at Gardiner ME [27 Apr 1848]
Rachel A & W T RICHARDSON at Augusta ME on 31st ult [21 Jun 1849]
Rachel Ann & John WHITE at Weld ME [18 Jan 1844]
Reuben & Olive FOWLER at Foxcroft ME [26 Jul 1849]
Roswell B & Cynthia PRATT at Foxcroft ME [23 May 1844]
Samuel C & Achsah PAINE at Augusta ME [11 Jul 1834]
Sarah H of New Vineyard ME ae 15 & Joseph KNOWLTON ae 18 of Farmington ME at New Vineyard ME [18 Mar 1847]

PRATT (cont.) Sarah W & Thomas PARTRIDGE at Vassalboro ME by Rev E R WARREN [11 Nov 1836]
  Stephen D & Sylvia LEWIS of Buckfield ME at Paris ME by John DENNET Esq [13 Feb 1845]
  Stephen M Capt of New Vineyard ME & Mrs Rozilla MILLS at New Portland ME [31 Jul 1851]
  Summer I of Corinna ME & Sarah J FOSS at St Albans ME [4 Jun 1851]
  Sylvanus of Avon ME & Sarah Ann AMES of Avon by Joseph DOW Esq at Phillips ME on Feb 15th [2 Mar 1848]
  Sylvanus of Berlin ME & Prudence HANDY of Wayne ME at Wayne on 16th ult by Isaac BOWLES Esq of Winthrop ME [9 Jan 1835]
  William 2nd of Foxcroft ME & Susan CUSHMAN of Monson ME at Monson [8 Apr 1843]

PRAY Almon C & Harriet M TURNER at Auburn ME [1 Feb 1849]
  Cathelina E & Charles R PHILLIPS at Hallowell ME on 1st June [15 Jun 1848]
  Dean of Augusta ME & Elizabeth SMITH of Hallowell ME on Mon last [29 May 1838]
  Dean & Martha M FYLER at Augusta ME on 6 Oct by Rev Mr WEBB [16 Oct 1851]
  Eliphlet & Rachel EDGECOMB at Gardiner ME [21 Mar 1844]
  Franklin & Sarah COLEMAN at Brunswick ME [30 Mar 1848] & [2 Mar 1848]
  John, printer, & Mary F PALMER all of Bangor ME by John S SAYWARD [11 Dec 1841]
  John/Joshua F & Flora B HARVEY of Harmony ME at Augusta ME on Jan 19 by Rev George S G SPENCE [21 Feb 1850] & [28 Feb 1850]
  Mehitable B & Augustus HUBBARD both of Shapleigh ME at Sanford ME [29 Jul 1847]
  Peter Jr & Laura Ann PRIEST at Vassalboro ME [11 Nov 1836]
  Rosetta J & Cyrus CHANDLER of Bridgewater Pt at Livermore ME [16 Apr 1846]
  Samuel P of Monson ME & Cordelia A HAMMOND of Foxcroft ME at Guilford ME [10 Oct 1844]

PREBLE Abraham Esq of Bowdoinham ME & Jerusha POLLEY of Bangor ME at Topsham ME [17 May 1849]
  Abraham F of Bowdoinham ME & Almira R GRANT at Richmond ME at Richmond [26 Apr 1849]
  Abraham T & Elizabeth COLLEY at Gardiner ME [1 Jan 1846]
  Alfred H & Harriet F COOK at Madison ME [8 Jan 1846]
  Catharine & Lewis P HOVEY both of Hallowell ME at H on Sept 7 by Rev E M TOBIE [19 Sept 1837]
  Elizabeth & George BAKER at Newcastle ME [6 Nov 1845]
  Emeline & Manuel S WOOD of Vassalboro ME at Winslow ME [18 Jun 1846]
  George Henry Esq of United States Navy & Susan Z COX d/o John C Esq at Portland ME [4 Dec 1845]
  Harriet & Jacob RICHARDS at Hallowell ME [21 Jul 1843]
  Isaac of Bowdoinham ME & Ruth Ann LYNCH of Bath ME at New York [25 Jan 1840]
  Joseph J & Jane TROTT of Woolwich ME at Richmond ME [15 Nov 1849]

PREBLE (cont.) Lemuel of Woolwich ME & Mrs Mary B CROSBY at Phippsburg ME [7 Jan 1847]
 Sarah Jane & Zebulon JACK Esq at Bowdoinham ME [10 Jul 1851]
 Serena Mrs & Solomon A WHEELER at Winslow ME [16 Nov 1848]

PRENTISS Elizabeth F & Mr W P LAUGHTON of Auburn ME at Cornville ME [6 Mar 1851]
 George L Rev of New Bedford MA & Elizabeth PAYSON at Portland ME [1 May 1845]
 Sargent S Hon of Vicksburg MS & Mary Jane WILLIAMS of Natchez at Natchez [23 Apr 1842]

PRESCOTT Amory & Hannah SEARLE d/o Samuel S Esq at Madison ME [21 Feb 1834]
 Augustus & Matilda A CUTLER of Turner ME at Lewiston ME [11 Mar 1852]
 Benjamin H of Westbrook ME & Mehitable D BATCHELDER of Saco ME [3 Jun 1836]
 Charles Coburn of Winthrop ME & Mary Jane DUNN of Belgrade ME at B on 20th inst by Rev F MERRIAM of Winthrop ME [27 Feb 1845]
 Daniel C & Sarah E PATTEN at Thomaston ME [29 Apr 1847]
 Edward Jr & Rosannah RICHARDS of Lincolnville ME at Boston MA [30 Sept 1847]
 Elizabeth W & James D CODDING at Newport ME [4 May 1848]
 Franklin & Mary Jane WARE at Augusta ME on 13th inst [26 Mar 1846]
 G G of Boston MA & Miss E E SCAMMON at Waterville ME [24 Feb 1848]
 Harriet N & Isaac LEMONT Jr of Bath ME at Portland ME [23 Sept 1847]
 Harrison G of Exeter ME & Sarah L HOOPER of Bangor ME at B [6 Feb 1845]
 Henry M & Clarisa HUNT at Brunswick ME [28 Dec 1833]
 James J & Cordelia C LUCE at Readfield ME [9 Dec 1847]
 John of Readfield ME & Emeline E SANFORD at Augusta ME [22 Feb 1840]
 John T of Liberty ME & Lydia BROOKS of Searsmont ME at Montville ME [22 Jan 1846]
 Jonathan Jr of Easton MA & Harriet A TRAFTON at Gardiner ME [4 Nov 1847]
 Joseph & Julia A FROHOCK at Belmont ME [30 Jan 1845]
 Josiah F & Thirsa L DOW at Phillips ME on 3rd inst [13 Feb 1838]
 Julia Ann & Hiram COLKET of Hallowell ME at Readfield ME [15 Apr 1836]
 Louisa & A LOWELL Esq of E Machias ME at Farmington ME [19 Nov 1846]
 Lucinda P of Winthrop ME & E Copeland SNELL at W by Oakes HOWARD Esq [15 Jan 1839]
 Mary A C & George W H HUNT at Readfield ME [9 Dec 1847]
 Mary J & Lt Jacob P BLUE by Eld J B PRESCOTT at Monmouth ME on 1st inst [4 Jan 1834]
 Meshach of Lisbon ME ae 67 & Sally JOHNSON of Exeter ME ae 40 at Corinna ME [11 Apr 1844]
 Olive S & Hiram S YOUNG of Fayette ME at Vienna ME [5 Apr 1849]
 Parker C Esq & Mrs Sarah H PRESCOTT at Newport ME [20 Mar 1841]
 Parmelia R & Jonas G HOLCOMB at Augusta ME [19 Jun 1838]
 Sarah H Mrs & Parker C PRESCOTT Esq at Newport ME [20 Mar 1841]

PRESCOTT (cont.) Simon B of Winthrop ME & Sarah EDES of Portland ME at Freeport ME on 24th ult by Rev KENT [1 Jan 1836]
    Susanna S of Readfield ME & Capt Thomas R POOLE of (Augusta ME) at Readfield ME on 18th inst by Rev POOLE of Whitefield ME [30 Jan 1845]
    William H of Hallowell ME & Emeline A DAVENPORT at Chelsea ME [1 Apr 1852]
PRESSAN David R of Avon ME & Sarah NASON at Temple ME on 11 Sept [25 Sept 1851]
PRESSY/PRESSEY George W & Mary EMERSON at Waterville ME [4 Apr 1844]
    Manly & Esther FARNHAM at Waterville ME [23 Oct 1851]
    Spencer & Harriet MERRIL at Mercer ME [25 May 1839]
PRESSLEY Angelina & Jacob S HINKLEY at Eastport ME [15 Mar 1849]
PRESSY Experience B Mrs & Lemuel ADAMS of Farmington ME at Mercer ME [27 Jun 1844]
PRESTON Sarah M & William H PARSONS at Bangor ME [20 Jun 1844]
PRIDE Albert & Eliza N KIMBALL at Skowhegan ME [26 Sept 1837]
    David G & Martha MARSTON of Norway ME at Waterford ME [3 Jun 1852]
PRIEST Ann & Charles MOOR of Clinton ME at Waterville ME [20 May 1843]
    Falvilla W & Seth NICKERSON Jr of Swanville ME at Vassalboro ME [14 Dec 1839]
    Laura Ann & Peter PRAY Jr at Vassalboro ME [11 Nov 1836]
    Sullivan B of Vassalboro ME & Lois G ELDER of Albion ME at China ME [30 Apr 1846]
    Warren & Permelia HYLER at Cushing ME [21 Aug 1845]
    William B of Vassalboro ME & Hannah TAYLOR of China ME at C [Feb 25 1843]
PRIME D Henrie printer of the *Belfast Signal* & Mary L HOOKE at Cambridge MA [1 Apr 1852]
    Henry T & Betsey JONES at Gardiner ME [25 Dec 1835]
PRINCE Christopher & Marion WEBB at Thomaston ME [14 May 1846]
    Job Hon & Olive LEAVETT both of Turner ME at T on 28th ult [9 Jan 1845]
    Lewis W of Industry ME & Mary E UMBERHIND at Richmond ME [18 Mar 1847]
    Lucy C d/o Hon Hezekiah P. & Edward S J NEALLY Esq attorney at law at Thomaston ME on Tues 5th inst [15 Jul 1836]
    Mary E & Samuel D GATES of Bangor ME at Portland ME [22 May 1845]
    Nancy P youngest d/o late Hon Hezekiah P & Rev Lorenzo B ALLEN, pastor of the First Baptist Church all of Thomaston ME at Thomaston on Weds eve Oct 19 by Rev Jacob WASHBURN [28 Oct 1842]
    Rebecca of Bucksfield ME & Daniel POND of Paris ME at Bucksfield ME [6 Jul 1839]
    Rebecca & Isaac GRAVES of Topsham ME at Brunswick ME [23 Apr 1846]
    S Louisa of Buckfield ME & Francis C BUCK of Paris ME at Turner ME by Job PRINCE Esq [3 Jan 1850]
    Sarah A & John W BUTTS at New Portland ME [9 May 1844]

PRINCE (cont.) Silvanus Capt of N Yarmouth ME & Eunice B MILLIONS of Hallowell ME at Portland ME [6 Mar 1838]
PRIOR Lucy B & Caleb B HOLMES, merchant, at Bangor ME [22 Jun 1839]
PROCK Silas & Rebecca BENNER both of Waldoboro ME at N Waldoboro on 14 Sept by Reuben ORFF Esq [25 Sept 1851]
PROCTOR Abigail & Charles ROBERTS at Bath ME [5 Mar 1846]
    Alonzo M of New Sharon ME & Roxy Ann GOULD at Farmington ME [29 Oct 1846]
    Ann Maria & Henry B BOODY at Westbrook ME [11 Jul 1840]
    Charles (Dr) of Rowley MA & Caroline POND of Bangor ME [4 Dec 1838]
    Deacon Uriah of Canton ME & Betsey A SMITH of Fayette ME at East Livermore ME on June 8th by Aaron BARTON Esq [26 Jun 1851]
    George Jr & Nancy HATCH of Lewiston ME at Lisbon ME [17 Dec 1846]
    Israel of Kennebunkport ME & Susan DAVIS at Biddeford ME [2 Apr 1846]
    Martha J & Ephraim J ULMER at Thomaston ME [27 May 1847]
    Mary F d/o Dea Uriah P of Hartford ME & Allen P COLE of Winthrop ME by Rev W FOSS at H [2 Sept 1843]
PROVINS Ann M & Charles Frederick SWAN at Augusta ME on Thurs eve last by Rev Dr TAPPAN [4 Nov 1847]
PUGSLEY Mary & Richard T SKOFIELD at Saco ME [18 May 1848]
PULCIFER Alcy M & Urban BUKER of Phillips ME at Weld ME on 20th Mar by Isaac TYLER Esq [27 Mar 1851]
    Sally E & William H CUTTING of Phillips ME at Weld ME by I TYLOR Esq [3 Apr 1851]
PULLEN Adeline A of Exeter ME & Calvin C DINSMORE of Glenburn ME at Levant ME [16 Jan 1851]
    Arvilla Amanda & Ira MORE at China ME on Mar 21 by J GREELY Esq [3 May 1849]
    Charles & Sibyl DUDLEY at China ME [13 May 1836]
    F C & Rebecca W MUNSEY at Waterville ME [8 May 1851]
    Frances & Samuel M GROVER Esq of Guilford ME at Levant ME [22 Jul 1852]
    Franklin & Drusilla HUSSEY at Waterville ME by Rev Samuel LEWIS [19 Oct 1839]
    George M of Gardiner ME & Martha L JONES of Winthrop ME at E Winthrop ME [7 Oct 1847]
    Gilbert of Augusta ME & Susannah G CORY of Brookline MA at Brookline MA [30 May 1840]
    J Henry & Mary L DAVIDSON at Monson ME? [31 Dec 1842]
    James C & Mary Ann W PALMER at Barnard ME [21 Jan 1847]
    Julia A & Amos F WETHERN at Kingfield ME [4 May 1848]
    Lloyd T & Catharine B PIKE at Kingfield ME [27 Sept 1849]
    Mary C & Charles JEWETT at Dexter ME [15 Apr 1847]
    Sumner B of Livermore ME & Alvira WHITING on 19th inst by Rev HOUGHTON [28 Nov 1834]
    Thomas S of Winthrop ME & Hariet BAILEY of Greene ME at Greene ME [20 May 1836]
PUMROY Alexander Capt & Almira BUCKMAN at Falmouth ME [9 Oct 1835]
PURINGTON - PURINTON - PURRINGTON
    Daniel T & Paulina S MARRINER at Brunswick ME [7 May 1846]

PURINGTON (cont.) Elinor & Maj Josiah M MERROW PM at Bowdoinham ME [19 Feb 1846][5 Feb 1846]
Emily Jane & James N HALL at Portland ME [4 Jul 1834]
Ezra of Bowdoin ME & Jessamine HOXIE at Sidney ME [24 Jan 1850]
Harriet Ann & Samuel P GEORGE at Embden ME [9 Mar 1848]
J F of Bowdoin ME & Abby E RIDLON at Monmouth ME [27 Jul 1848]
Lois A & Cyrus JONES of China ME at Vassalboro ME by Howard G ABBOT Esq [11 Oct 1849]
Mary of Dover ME & Leonard ROBINSON of Foxcroft ME at Bloomfield ME [22 Jun 1839]
Mary & Capt Robert McMANUS of Brunswick ME at Topsham ME [1 Oct 1846]
Miriam of Topsham ME & Rev William SEWALL at Topsham ME [27 Jun 1840]
Priscilla & Capt Robert Mc MANUS of Portland ME at Topsham ME [28 Sept 1839]
Priscilla & Watson F HALLET Esq of Augusta ME at Topsham ME [3 Jun 1836]
Sophia B of Bath ME & Joshua CURTIS of Bowdoinham ME at Bath ME by Rev STEARNS [27 Jul 1839]
Thankful & Capt Timothy R STINSON at Bowdoinham ME [27 Jul 1848]
Thomas N & Arvilla S MATHEWS at Bath ME [15 Feb 1849]
William Dea ae 54 & Sylvia WOODWORTH ae 17 at Bowdoinham ME [21 Dec 1833]
Z S of Gardiner ME & Clarinda WELLS at Georgetown MA [6 Dec 1849]

PUSHARD Lucy & Hiram ALBEE at Wiscasset ME [25 Feb 1847]

PUSHAW Lucinda & Abraham TOURTILOTTE JR at Ellsworth ME [28 Dec 1839]

PULSIFER Emeline of Auburn ME & Francis C HAUGHTON of Lewiston ME at Lowell MA on Jan 11th by Rev EDDY [23 Jan 1851]
Josiah D & Helen A WOODBURY at Minot ME [8 Jun 1848]

PUTNAM Daniel Esq & Mrs Pamelia HILTON at Belfast ME [3 Jun 1847]
Emeline J of Searsport ME & John C BRYANT of Montville ME at Freedom ME [20 Mar 1851]
George W Capt of Boston MA & Susan E THOMPSON of York ME at York ME [30 Sept 1847]
Isreal (MD) of Bath ME & Sarah FROST of Topsham ME at Topsham ME [31 Jan 1834]
Mary Ann of Hallowell ME & Capt Joseph L BECK of Augusta ME at Hallowell ME by Rev E M TOBIE [19 Sept 1837]

QUIMBY Albus K & Mary Ellen THOMS [sic] at Augusta ME on July 3rd by Rev A DALTON [15 Jul 1852]
Elizabeth Mrs & Jeremiah CLOUGH at Westbrook ME [24 Oct 1844]
Lorann & Samuel W GREENWOOD at Greene ME [25 Jan 1849]

QUINBY Edwin F Rev & Nancy FOSTER d/o Nathaniel F Esq at N Yarmouth ME [21 Jan 1843]
Eliza Ann of Westbrook ME & J R EASTMAN of Buxton ME at Portland ME [7 Jun 1849]
George W Rev, pastor of the Universalist Societies of Livermore ME and Winthrop ME & Lucy CORLISS of N Yarmouth ME at North Yarmouth ME on Christmas Day Dec 25 by Rev Charles C BURR of Hallowell ME [2 Jan 1838]

Marriage Notices from the "Maine Farmer"

QUINBY (cont.) Moses E of Newburyport MA & Deborah P RICKER of Wales ME at Augusta ME on 12 th inst by Rev William DREW [2 Sept 1847]
QUINCY Eliza & William GOODENOW Esq at Portland ME [26 Jun 1835]
  Sabre T & Gideon TIRRELL of Clarkville NH at Farmington ME? [2 Apr 1846]
QUINNAM Jacob B & Caroline THOMPSON at Wiscasset ME [9 Sept 1847]
QUINT Joan G of Topsham ME & Rev Walter T SARGENT pastor of the Baptist Church in Bowdoinham ME by Rev C C CONE [3 Jul 1841]

- *R* -

RACKLEY Louisa Jane & Bryant ROBINSON at Greene ME [19 Jun 1838]
RACLIFF Axie & Abner HASKELL of Bangor ME at Unity ME [19 Jun 1835]
  Fanny O & Albert G WHEELER of Farmington ME at Industry ME [3 Jul 1841]
RACKLIFF Ezekiel & Mary WAUGH at Starks ME [2 Jul 1846]
  Mary & James CHILD both of Muscle Ridge Plantation ME at St George ME [18 Jun 1846]
  Rebecca & James BRACKETT at Thomaston ME [5 Feb 1836]
RAFFORD Olive & George W MARTIN at No 11, 5th Range, Aroostook Co, ME on Aug 19 by Edmund F GARLAND Esq [13 Sept 1849]
RAFTER Daniel of Jefferson ME & Martha Antenetter ANDREWS at Warren ME [13 Mar 1841]
  Eliza C & Isaac G VANNAH both of Gardiner ME at Whitefield ME [8 Feb 1849]
RAILY Elizabeth ae 40y & David HODGE ae 102y 2m both of Columbia Co GA. He was at Braddock's defeat and served throughout the whole period of the Revolutionary War. They were married by John McGEHEE Esq at GA [1 Jul 1836]
RAMFORD John of Fayette ME & Relief WHITTIER at Readfield ME [24 Apr 1845]
RAMSDELL Harvey & Sarah HILL by Rev F MERRIAM in (Winthrop ME) on 14 Sept [24 Sept 1842]
  Joshua & Olive FURBISH at Kennebunk ME [28 Aug 1835]
  Mary E & Daniel H ROBBINS at China ME on 13th ult [17 Feb 1848]
RAMSEY John, publisher of the *Thomaston National Republican* & Bernice B BOURK at Bath ME [22 Jul 1833]
  John M & Cyenne STEVENS of Barnard VT at Skowhegan ME [21 Oct 1836]
  William C & Hannah S HOLMES at E Thomaston ME [30 Oct 1835]
RANA Sarah H & Stephen AUSPLUND of Prospect ME at Thorndike ME [12 Aug 1852]
RAND Abigail N & Levi O FARNUM of Sangerville ME at Bucksport ME [11 Jul 1837]
  David C & Mary T ROLLINS both of Hallowell ME at Livermore Falls ME [9 Sept 1847]
  David & Mrs Eunice MAY at New Gloucester ME [4 Apr 1837]
  George F & Mary F MOULTON at Parsonsfield ME [28 Mar 1844]
  John of Bangor ME & Apphia JORDAN of Cape Elizabeth ME [6 May 1836]

RAND (cont.) Marshall H & Mrs Emeline L SMITH at Frankfort ME of 18th inst by S H NICKERSON Esq [2 Apr 1842]
  Nancy & Horace B BARSTOW at Bangor ME [20 Nov 1835]
  Olive & Capt Isaac HOLT at Canaan ME on 22d April [29 Apr 1852]
  Samuel E & Christiana W PARKER at Stoneham ME [5 Aug 1852]
  Sarah J & James GREELY at Searsport ME [31 Aug 1848]
  Sarah Jane of Minot & Hezekiah HAYES of Poland ME at Minot ME [4 Apr 1837]

RANDALL Almira S & Otis HAWES at Topsham ME [20 Jun 1839]
  Ann M & James O FOSS at Lewiston ME [27 Jan 1848]
  Caroline A & Alexis BURNHAM at Wilton ME [19 Oct 1848]
  Clementine B & William M ROBINSON both of Vassalboro ME at China ME on 5th inst by A H ABBOE Esq [9 May 1840]
  D B Rev of Maine (Methodist) Conference & Mary GOWER d/o John G Esq at Industry ME [18 May 1839]
  Daniel ae 50 & Elizabeth LOWELL ae 17 after a courtship of 24 hours at Ripley ME (Believe it or not) [29 Jul 1833]
  Ellen C & Johnson PHILBRICK of China ME at Augusta ME by Rev W A DREW [18 Jan 1844]
  Harriet of Lewiston ME & James DAIN at Durham ME [21 May 1846]
  Helen J & Edwin SAWTELLE of Livermore ME at Dixfield ME [13 Dec 1849]
  Horatio S & Dorotha J GORDON of Readfield ME at Fayette ME [16 Apr 16 1846]
  Isaac H & Mrs Sophrona P ROBERTS at Vassalboro ME [10 Oct 1840]
  Isaiah Jr & Mercy H TOWNSEND at Saco ME [25 Dec 1845]
  Joseph & Priscilla S COPELAND at Warren ME [4 Mar 1847]
  Joshua T of Bloomfield ME & Mary Ann HUNTON at Readfield ME [21 Mar 1844] & [4 Apr 1844]
  Levi C & Mrs Lydia COOMBS at Lewiston ME [10 Jul 1845]
  Louisa M & Jacob S HARRIS at (Augusta) ME on 16th inst [7 Dec 1848]
  Mary E & Erastus E GOULD at Portland ME [16 Nov 1848]
  Reuben P & Abigail SMITH at Augusta ME on 12th inst by Rev S ALLEN [23 Sept 1847]
  Shepherd P & Hannah E BLACKMAN at (Augusta) ME [25 May 1848]
  Sophia Mrs & George W BRAGG at Augusta ME on Dec 26 [15 Feb 1844]
  Susan & Elbridge G REED at Vassalboro ME [16 Sept 1843]
  Theodosia W & Jacob TRUE of Sangerville ME at Wellington ME on 2nd inst by B BURSLEY Esq [18 Jun 1842]
  Wealthy B J & Maj Francis HANNIE of Arkansas at Bath ME [25 Jun 1846]
  William Esq of Topsham ME & Jane BLAKE of Portland ME at Portland [25 Nov 1843]
  William G of Auburn ME & Pamelia A STETSON at Lewiston ME [28 Nov 1844]

RANDELL Andrew H & Mary RICHARDSON at Brooks ME [15 Aug 1844]

RANDLETT Mary H of Alna ME & Maj John SMITH Jr of Readfield ME at Alna [2 Jan 1838]

RANDOLPH Mary Ann D of Monroe ME & Daniel W LEONARD of Knox ME at Montville ME [24 Apr 1845]

RANGELY John of Farmington ME & Mary C youngest d/o Ebenezer WEBSTER Esq of Portland ME in Portland ME on Weds eve last by Rev CHICKERING [16 Oct 1838]

RANGERLY James Jr & Harriet WARE at Farmington ME by Robert GOODENOW Esq [16 Jan 1838]

RANKIN Robert & Abby B WARDWELL of Thomaston ME at Richmond VA [19 Feb 1846]

C F of Brownville ME & Betsey RICHARDSON at Atkinson ME [28 Sept 1848]

RANKINS Sarah & Capt Daniel M LARBREE of Wales ME at Monmouth ME Feb 7 by John SAFFORD Esq [1 Mar 1849]

Thomas J & Mary E STEVENS at Augusta ME on Apr 5th by John A PETTINGILL Esq [18 Apr 1850]

William D & Sarah J CROSS at Augusta ME on May 25 by Asaph NICHOLS Esq [29 May 1851]

RANKS Swanton & Emeline MORSE at Bath ME [10 Jan 1850]

RANLETT Annis C & John P CRAM of Bangor ME at Hallowell ME [28 Oct 1847]

Josiah & Adeline HERRICK at Thomas [Feb 18 1847]

RARIDAN Levi & Julia A JOHNSON at Pittston ME [7 Nov 1844]

RATHBONE William P Esq of Providence RI & Frances Amelia LEONARD d/o Silas L Esq at Augusta ME on 12th inst by Rev JUDD [20 Dec 1849]

RAWSEN Calista & Charles McFADDEN at Paris ME [1 Jul 1847]

RAWSON Adaline B & Ixaac FRENCH at Waldoboro ME [12 Feb 1846]

Clarissa P & John L GARLAND at Paris ME [1 Jan 1846]

Frances F d/o the late Capt Samuel R of Paris ME & William R KIMBALL Esq of Canton at New York on 29th ult [9 May 1837]

Linda M & Samuel D WEEKS at Paris ME [22 May 1851]

Sylva Stevens & Hezekiah Crockett CLARK at Paris ME [9 May 1837]

RAY Charles H & Sophia MERROW at Auburn ME [22 Apr 1852]

Margaret & Otis HOLDEN at Moose River ME [25 Jan 1847]

RAYNES Mary A & Andrew GROVER at Auburn ME [21 Oct 1847]

REA Lavinia & Capt Paul SAWYER of Isleboro ME at Castine ME [7 Jun 1849]

READ Abby & Enos HITCHCOCK Esq of Strong ME at Farmington ME [13 Dec 1849]

George & Hannah G LUNT at Bangor ME [1 Oct 1842]

John civil engineer of Winthrop ME & Mary A BONNEY by Rev Mr BUTLER at Turner ME on the 18th ult [8 Jun 1848]

Lowny of Sangerville ME & Col Thomas LITTLEFIELD of Auburn ME at Sangerville ME [4 Mar 1843]

Sarah C d/o late Hon John R of Strong ME & Moses STEVENS, junior publisher of *The Blade* at Augusta ME [3 Oct 1844]

READMAN Tristram (Dr) & Frances S FREEMAN at Cherryfield ME [24 Jan 1834]

RECORD Calvin Esq of Lewiston ME & Melancy L BEALS at Turner ME [22 Jan 1852]

Charles Jr of Poland ME & Harriet MONK at Buckfield ME [26 Dec 1844]

Emery T & Comfort C SMITH at Buckfield ME [13 Feb 1851]

Huldah M & Rufus ROGERS at Dover ME [12 Aug 1852]

RECORD (cont.) Jane formerly of Buckfield ME & William CHICK Esq at Amherst ME [7 Jan 1847]
    Jane & Rowland B BONNEY both of Minot ME at Buckfield ME [27 Feb 1851]
    John of Phillips ME & Lucinda A CRUMPTON of Industry ME at Farmington ME [18 Jan 1849]
REDING Esther & Phylander FREEMAN at South Berwick ME [11 Apr 1850]
REDINGTON Alfred Col & Elizabeth WILLIAMS at Augusta ME [13 Jan 1837]
    Alfred Esq, Adj General of the state, of Augusta ME & Lucy C youngest d/o the late James KIMBALL Esq of Newburyport MA at Bath 5th inst [26 Nov 1846]
    Asa (see - LONGFELLOW & BALKAM) [1 Apr 1852]
    Caroline & Hon Isaac of Waldoboro ME at Augusta ME [6 Nov 1841]
    Lydia G & John McCLELLAN of Skowhegan ME at Waterville ME [16 Jan 1851]
    Samuel REDINGTON Esq of Vassalboro ME & Mrs Hannah NICHOLS formerly of Bristol ME at Hampden ME [23 Feb 1839]
    Silas & Caroline M PHILLIPS at Waterville ME [28 Mar 1844]
REDLAND Elizabeth & Daniel PAINE at Thomaston ME [13 Nov 1845]
REDLIN Melvin O Jr & Parmela C BONNER at Pittston ME [1 Jul 1847]
REDMAN Emily S & Cyrus ROBERTS at Brooksville ME [16 Oct 1845]
    Margaret R & George HARTWELL of Lincoln MA at Brooksville ME [15 Jul 1847]
    Robert E & Lucy Jane COOMBS at Brooksville ME [16 Oct 1845]
    Serena & Francis B MORGAN Esq at Brooksville ME by Hon John R REDMAN [23 Oct 1838]
REDMOND Peter & Nancy B L WHITNEY at Moose River ME [25 Jan 1849]
REED Abba of Madison ME & & Maj Albert LOWELL at Fairfield ME [21 Feb 1850]
    Amanda L & Arthur McNELLEY of Clinton ME at Benton ME [13 Feb 1851]
    Ann E of Westbrook ME & William M HALL of Gorham ME at Westbrook ME [2 May 1844]
    Catharine W & David S GLIDDEN of Bremen ME at Nobleboro ME [14 Jan 1847]
    Charles & Rosanna CAMPBELL at Jay ME [29 Oct 1846]
    Charlotte H & John BARWISE of Garland ME at Skowhegan ME [4 Oct 1849]
    Charlotte & John D FULLER at Carmel ME [20 Jul 1848]
    Clarissa & Silas BRADSTREET at China ME [2 Nov 1848]
    Cynthia J & Hartson BLACKSTONE at Farmington ME [10 Jun 1852]
    Drusilla & George A BANCROFT of Readfield ME at Albion ME [25 Nov 1847]
    Eben & Rachel PEAVY by Stephen F PIERCE Esq at Windsor ME [29 Jan 1852]
    Elbridge G & Susan RANDALL at Vassalboro ME [16 Sept 1843]
    Eliza A d/o John R & David E TOWLE at Augusta ME [16 May 1834]
        Eliza & Isaac Abbot at Sebasticook ME on Oct 6 by James W NORTH Esq [19 Nov 1842]
    Elizabeth & John CORNISH at Bath ME [12 Feb 1846]
    Emily T & Edward P Capt STINSON at Bath ME [2 Mar 1848]

REED (cont.) F & Sarah A WEEKS at Bath ME [13 Nov 1851]
    Francis & Mercy E WEBSTER in Bath ME [23 Jul 1846]
    Harvey of Livermore ME & Adeline RICHARDS of Winthrop ME on Sun Morning last by E R WARREN [22 Jun 1839]
    Helen M & Gen Henry S COOLEY formerly of Augusta ME at Quincy, IL [16 Oct 1845]
    Henrietta & Rev S W TAYLOR at East Cambridge MA 17 June [23 Jun 1852]
    Hosea B, printer of Augusta ME & Martha A WARREN at Standish ME on Mar 25 by James FOSS Esq [4 Apr 1850]
    Isaac Hon of Waldoboro ME & Caroline REDINGTON at Augusta ME [6 Nov 1841]
    Isaac Hon of Waldoboro ME & Lydia Emery McDONALD at Bangor ME [3 Jun 1852]
    James A & Hannah HUTCHINGS at Gardiner ME [11 Nov 1843]
    John G of Madison ME & Hannah J FRENCH of Cornville ME at Solon ME [30 Jan 1851]
    John G of Madison ME & Hannah Jane FRENCH of Cornville ME at Solon ME [13 Feb 1851]
    Josiah W ae 42 & Lucinda WARNER ae 12 1/2 at Rowe (Rome) ME [6 May 1833]
    Lucinda S & Isaac W HILTON at Augusta ME by Rev FULLER [7 Mar 1844]
    Lucy H of Dresden ME & Cyrus YEATON of Pittston ME at Dresden ME [8 Jan 1846]
    Luther of Augusta ME & Fanny HOWARD at Sidney ME [7 Dec 1839]
    Mary L & Lincoln PERRY of Gardiner ME at Dresden ME [22 Feb 1849]
    Mary & Samuel PALMER at Windsor ME by J B SWANTON Esq [14 Feb 1837]
    Mercy E & Solomon T HIGGINS at Bath ME [19 Apr 1849]
    Nancy P of Skowhegan ME & Thomas BARWISE at Kenduskeag ME [22 Jul 1852]
    Nathan & Mrs Mary OVERLOCK in Waldoboro ME [27 Nov 1838]
    Parker M & Harriet S ELLIOT at Phipsburg ME [14 May 1846]
    Rev A W of Stetson ME & A BARTON at Albion ME [23 Jan 1851]
    Ruth W & Hartson BLACKSTON at Wayne ME on the 13th inst [19 Sept 1840]
    Samuel M Capt & Matilda Jane HODGDON at Boothbay ME [3 Apr 1845]
    Sarah E d/o John R Esq of Augusta ME & Harrison BAKER of Bangor ME at Augusta ME on 26th inst by Rev William A DREW [28 May 1846]
    Sarah H & Edmund PENDEXTER both of Glenburn ME at Bangor ME [29 Aug 1844]
    Sarah Jane & Eben F RUSSELL at New Sharon ME [12 Nov 1846]
    Sewall of Topsham ME & Irena ORR at Bowdoinham ME [3 Sept 1846]
    Stephen of Woolwich ME & Harriet DREW of Readfield ME at E Readfield ME on Nov 29 by Rev F MERRIAM of Winthrop ME [3 Dec 1842]
    Susan J & George WINN both of Benton ME at Lowell MA [4 Dec 1851]
    Uriah Esq of Danville ME & Frances N GOULD by Lewis HUNTON Esq at E Livermore ME [24 Feb 1848]
    Waterman & Emily THURSTIN in Windsor ME [4 Jul 1837]

REED (cont.) William F M of Hampden ME & Sophia S TOWN at Augusta ME [22 Apr 1847]
    Zebulon & Harriet N GREENE at Bath ME [16 Jul 1846]
REESE Stephen L & Harriet N LANCASTER at Augusta ME on Sunday Morning the 6th inst at the State St Chapel by Rev S ADLUM [17 Oct 1844]
REGAN John & Sarah WILSON of Plennfield New Brunswick Canada [12 Sept 1844]
REID Bradford Y & Fraziette C STEVENS at Vassalboro ME on Sept 26 [7 Oct 1847]
REMICK Enoch & Clementine HOBART at Solon ME [6 August 1846]
    John & Jane BARTON at N Anson ME [1 Mar 1849]
    Nathaniel of Augusta ME & Mrs Sylvia HANSON d/o Noyes SMITH of Mt Vernon ME on 2d inst by Samuel TITCOMB JR Esq [9 Jan 1845] & [16 Jan 1845]
    Phebe & Ambrose HIGGINS at Eden ME [29 Jan 1839]
    Sylvis Mrs & Winslow BURDEN at Augusta ME on Dec 3 [14 Dec 1848]
    W of Eliot ME & Mrs Sarah DORR at N Berwick ME [19 Mar 1846]
RENDELL Caroline J & Harrison STEELE at Prospect ME [29 Mar 1849]
REYNOLDS Ann & Edward HERSEY both of Gardiner ME at Hallowell ME [20 Nov 1851]
    Charles H & Jane Q MANNING at Lewiston ME [25 Mar 1847]
    Ira of Canton ME & Nancy C GODING of Livermore ME by Ruel WASHBURN Esq [27 Feb 1835]
    Jonathan E & Dorcas S SQUIRE of Madison ME at Sidney ME [23 Apr 1846]
    Marcus V of Sidney ME & Almira HAMLEN at Augusta ME [5 Dec 1837]
    Mary P & Erastus TORRY at Bangor ME [2 Oct 1835]
    Naomi Mrs & Capt William B HATCH of Pembroke ME at Eastport ME [23 Dec 1847]
    Nathaniel & Isabel CHAMBERLAIN both of Sidney ME at E Boston MA [24 Jan 1850]
    Samuel W of Philadelphia PA & Emma CUSHMAN at Portland ME [24 Sept 1846]
    Samuel & Sophronia ROBERTS at Lubec ME [5 Jul 1849]
    Sarah Ann of Sidney ME & Nathan PINKHAM of N Bridgewater MA at Sidney ME by Rev TILLY [14 May 1846]
    Sarah Jane & Barzilla D WOOD at Sidney ME [8 May 1851]
    Sarah Jane & Whitman B THAYER of Sidney ME at Augusta ME [23 Aug 1849]
    Sarah & John NELSON at Hallowell ME [30 Jul 1846]
    Susan M & James H MERROW at (Augusta) ME on 16th Nov [23 Nov 1848]
    Susan P & William ROBBINS of Augusta ME at Sidney ME [14 Mar 1840]
    Vose & Abigail GOWIN at Winslow ME [24 May 1849]
    William of Sidney ME & Mary Elizabeth SPINNEY at Phipsburg ME on Nov 12 by Rev STAPLES [22 Nov 1849]
RHOADS Francina H & John R FROHOCK both of Northport ME at Belfast ME [14 August 1851]
RHINES Mary & Charles STILKEY at Augusta ME by Caleb FULLER [12 August 1843]

RHOADES Sarah M & J A SMITH, M.D., of Vassalboro ME at Providence RI on Jul 4 [29 Jul 1852]
William of Thomaston ME & Mary Jane BRACKET at Belfast ME [11 Mar 1847]

RICE Dorothy L & Lorenzo EELS at Guilford ME [29 Apr 1852]
Frances E & Rev William L HYDE at Wiscasset ME [20 May 1852]
Frederick B & Rebecca A SUMNER both of Camden ME at Goose River ME [4 Mar 1852]
Mary H & George W MORSE at Union ME [24 Oct 1840]
Mehitable & Samuel TIBBETTS at Hallowell ME [5 Dec 1840]
Moses T of New Orleans LA & Ann R PAINE at Eastport ME [7 Aug 1851]
Nathan D Esq of Union ME & Mrs Abigail EMERY at Augusta ME on 7 May 1851 by Rev Mr JUDD [22 May 1851]
R D Esq & Mrs Almira E ROBINSON of Augusta ME at Augusta ME [28 Nov 1840]
Richard & Lucretia A TOZIER at Waterville ME [8 Jun 1848]
Thomas & Charlotte J GODFREY of Taunton MA at Bangor ME [1 Jun 1848]

RICH Ann Jane d/o P H Esq & Albert F BEAN at Monson ME [5 Sept 1844]
Ann Maria & James FRENCH of Bangor ME at Union ME [Dec 30 1847]
Ann R & James H K LORD at Bath ME [22 Jul 1836]
C W Esq & Albana KITTREDGE at Milo ME [1 Apr 1847]
Cyrus C & Emily WADE at Union ME on Oct 17 [Oct 26 1839]
David Capt of Harpswell ME & Louisa DEXTER at Wayne ME [20 Feb 1835]
Delia & Andre CUSHING of Bangor ME at Frankfort ME [12 Feb 1846]
Edward & Eliza SPARROW at Hampden ME [21 Jan 1833]
Elizabeth J & Henry M PAINE at Jay ME on Apr 4th [6 May 1852]
Eveline & Simeon SAVAGE of Lowell MA at Union ME [3 Dec 1846]
George 2nd & Mary E POTTER both of Waterville ME at Hallowell ME [20 Nov 1851]
Henry S of Bangor ME & Mary F McINTIRE of Boston MA at New York NY [23 Oct 1845]
Isaac 2nd of Harpswell ME & Betsey DEXTER of Winthrop ME by Rev John ALLEN at Winthrop ME [[3 Apr 1838]
James of Bowdoinham ME & Mrs Cassenmark ROGERS at Topsham ME [24 Dec 1846]
James of Union ME & Sarah E GOULD d/o Joshua G Esq at Norridgewock ME [24 Jul 1841]
James P Capt of Bucksport ME & Susan H BESSICK at Bangor ME [28 Feb 1837]
John H Esq of Monson ME & G E BURLEIGH in Dexter ME [16 Dec 1847]
John H & B ANDREWS of Gardiner ME at Hallowell ME [12 Dec 1844]
Louisa J & William McCOMB at East Eddington ME [27 Jul 1848]
Lucy Ann of Buxton ME & David HANSON of Orono ME at Buxton ME [26 Aug 1836]
M B of Bucksport ME & Sarah DORR at Frankfort ME [28 Mar 1837]
Maria of Hallowell ME & Octavius WRIGHT of Lewiston ME at Augusta ME [27 Jun 1837]
Martha Mrs & Charles BRADBURY at Bloomfield ME [3 Dec 1846]
Mary M & George W FOWLER at East Eddington ME [5 Feb 1852]

RICH (cont.) Mary & Andrew T GETCHELL of Litchfield ME at Hallowell ME [5 Aug 1843]
 Mary & Lawrence JORDAN of Saco ME at Wiscasset ME [21 Dec 1843]
 Mary & Robert WATERMAN of Belfast ME at Brooks ME [13 May 1847]
 Mehitable d/o John R & Samuel TIBBETS of Monmouth ME at Hallowell ME [25 Apr 1840]
 Reuben of Otisfield ME & Leafy WHITNEY d/o Daniel W of same place in Oxford ME by Rev Dan PERRY [10 Jun 1833]
 Reuben & Elvira KILBURN at Bucksport ME [23 Mar 1839]
 Richard Capt & Mrs Alice J ATHERN at Bath ME [14 Nov 1834]
 Rozilla & John A TINKHAM at Monmouth ME on Thanksgiving Evening by Eld J PRESCOTT [7 Dec 1839]
 Ruth A of Scarboro ME & Charles FIELDS of Freeport ME at Portland ME [3 Apr 1845]
 Samuel of Farmington ME & Elizabeth F CONNOR at Gardiner ME [21 Mar 1850]
 Sarah M & George HOPKINS at Eden ME [26 Dec 1834]
 Thomas Hon & Susannah GREENE at Winslow ME on 16th [5 Mar 1842]
 W W of Hampden ME & Caroline R GOULD at Norridgewock ME [18 Jan 1849]
 William Jr of Augusta ME & Sarah A ROBINSON at Bath ME [20 Feb 1845]
 Winchester L of Camden ME & Phileta C GUPTILL of Thomaston ME [22 Oct 1846]

RICHARDS Adeline of Winthrop ME & Harvey REED of Livermore ME on Sun morning last at Winthrop ME by Rev E R WARREN [22 Jun 1839]
 Ann of Winthrop ME & Theodore Trevett of Bath ME at E Winthrop [15 Nov 1845]
 Charles & Angeline at Northport ME [28 Jan 1847]
 Cordelia & Amos WYMAN of Hallowell ME at Winthrop ME [14 Oct 1847]
 Diadama & Richard KILMAN at Prospect ME [22 Jan 1842]
 Edward & Eunice JEWETT at Portland ME [6 Nov 1835]
 Eliza & George RICHARDS at Belfast ME [25 Mar 1833]
 Elizabeth & Charles C CAREY at Lincolnville ME [10 Feb 1848]
 Farnham & Mary WADSWORTH at Lincolnville ME [9 May 1844]
 Ferdinand S & Caroline M FOWLE at Hallowell ME on Thurs eve last by Rev Charles C BURR [14 Aug 1838]
 George F of China ME & Ann E BRAGG at Vassalboro ME on Mar 2d by John HOMANS Esq [6 Mar 1851]
 George & Eliza RICHARDS at Belfast ME [25 Mar 1833]
 Greenleaf G & Cordelia HOLMAN at Wayne ME [22 Apr 1852]
 Isaac of Monmouth ME & Abigail MARROW at Winthrop ME by Francis FULLER Esq on Aug 25 [6 Sept 1849]
 Isaiah of Strong ME & Emily A LUCE at New Vineyard ME [27 Apr 1848]
 Jacob & Abigail SMITH at Hallowell ME [1 Jan 1846]
 Jacob & Harriet PREBLE at Hallowell ME [21 Jul 1843]
 Joseph & Agnes C SALMOND at Belfast ME [8 Aug 1844]
 Levi of East Livermore ME & Orlaney WRIGHT of Lowell MA at Nashville NH [3 Aug 1848] & on 25th Apr [6 Jul 1848]
 Louisa Ann & Albert GREER at Belmont ME [28 Mar 1850]
 Nancy W & David B SILSBY of Lewiston ME at Ellsworth ME [6 Nov 1851]

RICHARDS (cont.) Rosannah of Lincolnville ME & Edward PRESCOTT Jr at Boston MA [30 Sept 1847]
Rosilla & John KNOWLES of Fayette ME at Chesterville ME [4 Feb 1843]
Roxana of Saco ME & William D BURNAM at Biddeford ME [23 Aug 1849]
Samuel & Sybil PACKARD both of Winthrop ME in Augusta ME on Thanksgiving morning [18 Dec 1838]
Sarah C & Lee LIBBY at Wayne ME on 4th Apr [22 Apr 1852]
Sarah F & Hannibal C HINKLEY at Hallowell ME [28 Dec 1839]
Sarah & Abel STEVENS of Fayette ME at E Winthrop ME [14 Feb 1850]
Sophronia & David STURDIVANT at Parkman ME [21 Nov 1837]
Stephen formerly of (Augusta) ME & Abby LAMB at Rockville CT [14 Dec 1848]
Susan E & Charles ALLEN at Boston MA [3 Aug 1848]
William & Cornelia M WALTER at Boston MA [7 Oct 1847]
Wilson of Liberty ME & Helen WATERMAN of Appleton ME at S Montville ME on Jan 27 [7 Feb 1850]

RICHARDSON Abby J & Jerome B W BROWN at (Augusta) ME [22 Jun 1848]
Ann E & Ira L HALE at Brunswick ME [11 Nov 1847]
Artie of Lowell MA & Moses HANSCOM Jr of Waterville ME at Nashua NH [3 Sept 1846]
Aurelia & Benjamin F BARTLETT both of N P at North Anson ME [9 Apr 1846]
Betsey & Mr C F RANKIN at Atkinson ME [28 Sept 1848]
Bryant & Rachel GOODWIN at Canaan ME [6 Jun 1837]
Calvin A & Lucy ATKINS both of Winthrop ME at Livermore ME by Rev G W QUINBY [20 Jul 1839]
Charles C & Margaret WILLIAMS at Bath ME [22 Jan 1836]
Charles W & Abigail BEAN at Livermore Falls ME [12 Aug 1852]
Clara A & Nathan C HALLETT at Belgrade ME [17 Aug 1848]
Dorcas & Sullivan WASHBURN of Gardiner ME at Litchfield ME [21 Aug 1842]
E A & Timothy M GREEN of Naples ME at Gilead ME [19 Apr 1849]
Eben of New Portland ME & Abby E A SMITH at Pittston ME [17 Jul 1845]
Edward E of Dracut MA & Phebe W HAYES at Limington ME [18 Apr 1850]
Ellen Mariah M of Brownville ME & Jedidiah MORRILL of Williamsburg ME at Brownville ME on June 1 [24 Jun 1836]
Elvira of Readfield ME & William A SMITH at Augusta ME [Jun 18 1846]
Ezra B & Amanda B WILSON at Hallowell ME [2 Aug 1849]
F E & William B BILLINGS at Eastport ME [14 Sept 1848]
Franklin & Louisa BAILEY both of Pittston ME at Hallowell ME [18 Oct 1849]
George S & Joanna GOODWIN of Litchfield ME at Gardiner ME [25 Dec 1847]
Hannah S & Noah S LIBBY at Litchfield ME [21 May 1846]
Isaac E of New Gloucester ME & Susan M DAVIS at Pownal ME [30 Jan 1845]
Isaac JR & Caroline SANBORN at Gorham ME [5 Aug 1852]
Jane & James B LORING at St George ME [7 Mar 1840]
Jenette G & Erastus F WEEKS at Jefferson ME [3 Sept 1846]

RICHARDSON (cont.) John B Capt & Eliza C HASKELL at Deer Isle ME [5 Dec 1844]
    John G T of Dover NH? & Mary PLACE of Saco ME at Portsmouth NH [22 Aug 1844]
    John G & Miss M E LINCOLN at Brunswick ME [1 Jun 1848]
    Joshua B & Harriet JUDKINS at Norway ME [28 Jan 1847]
    Lewis, senior publisher of the *Lime Rock Gazette*, & Frances R CONDON at E Thomaston ME [4 Feb 1847]
    Lewis & Frances E CONDON at Thomaston ME [14 Jan 1847]
    Lorenda & Samuel W JACKSON Esq at Jefferson ME [18 Jan 1840]
    Louisa & Moses FOGG both of Winthrop ME at Augusta ME on Thurs the 1st inst by William A DREW [9 Oct 1835]
    Lucinda of Reading MA & Jacob NEWMAN at Dixfield ME [11 Oct 1849]
    Lucy & James B JOHNSON at Monmouth ME [13 Mar 1835]
    M C (Dr) of Hallowell ME & Harriet M FARNSWORTH at Bridgton ME [17 Sept 1846]
    M C (Dr) & Mary S WINGATE at Hallowell ME [20 Sept 1849]
    Martha Ann of Toronto, Upper Canada & William H ALLEN principal of the Augusta High School at Toronto, Upper Canada [14 Oct 1836]
    Martha of Greenwood ME & John BUTTERFIELD of Sumner ME [21 Mar 1840]
    Mary E & Dr John L FAIRBANKS formerly of Winthrop ME at Monmouth ME [4 Feb 1843]
    Mary Jane of Whitefield ME & Hiram COVIL of Pittston ME at Alna ME [16 Jan 1845]
    Mary Jane & Ira BRANCH at Belgrade ME by Rev FARMER [7 Sept 1833]
    Nancy F & Jonas MUZZY at Gardiner ME [25 Apr 1840]
    Nancy & Moses FROST Jr at Monmouth ME on 4th inst by Rev D THURSTON [14 Oct 1843]
    Priam & Abigail WALKER at Litchfield ME [16 Nov 1839]
    Sabry & Shepard HUTCHINSON of Gardiner ME at Litchfield ME [1 Feb 1844]
    Sally of Greene & James BICKFORD of Gardiner ME at Greene ME [9 Oct 1841]
    Sarah F of Winslow ME & Alvin BRAGG of China ME at Vassalboro ME [18 Apr 1854]
    Theodore M of Weld ME & Emeline O CRAM of E Livermore ME at Leeds ME by Rev Walter FOSS [26 Aug 1852]
    Theodore of Phillips ME & Elizabeth A WHITE d/o Henry WHITE both of Mt Vernon ME by Daniel CRAIG Esq at Readfield [7 Dec 1848]
    Thomas M Maj of Monmouth ME & Bernice P JACK of Litchfield ME at Litchfield ME on May 12 [13 Jun 1849]
    W T & Rachel A PRATT at Augusta ME on 31st ult [21 Jun 1849]
    Walcott of Livermore ME & Fortina HUMPHREY at Jay ME [19 Jul 1849]
    Wyman & Flora GLEASON at W Waterville ME [1 Jan 1846]
RICHERSON Mary & Andrew H RANDELL at Brooks ME [15 Aug 1844]
RICHMOND Alphonso P of Turner ME & Roxana OWEN by Rev Walter FOSS at Leeds ME [24 Feb 1848]
    Arnold S of Hallowell & Narcissa HANSON of Buxton ME at Buxton Sun eve 16th inst [1 JAn 1839]
    Cyrus of San Francisco CA & Mary Fannie DWIGHT at Hallowell ME [9 Jan 1851]

Marriage Notices from the "Maine Farmer" 343

RICHMOND (cont.) Nancy & Robert L JACKSON at Winthrop ME on Mon morning last by Rev David THURSTON [22 Jul 1833]
    Sarah & Joel S LENNAN of Hallowell ME at Turner ME on Sun Aug 31 [5 Sept 1834]
    Tabitha & George BICKNELL at Turner ME by Rev George BATES [15 Jan 1842]

RICKER Amanda M & Alvan G HOWARD at Foxcroft ME [29 Apr 1852]
    Apphia & James D MARSH at Bath ME [10 Aug 1848]
    Clarissa & Asa GOODRIDGE at Smithfield ME [24 Jan 1850]
    Deborah P & Moses E QUINBY of Newburyport MA at Augusta ME on 12th inst by Rev William DREW [2 Sept 1847]
    Elizabeth & Asa B ROBINSON at Bath ME [17 Jul 1855]
    George W & Eliza L JOSSELYN both of Augusta ME at Lynn MA on 4th Mar [13 Mar 1851]
    John S of Bangor ME & Julia A JACOBS at Providence RI [14 Sept 1848]
    Joseph Rev of Belfast ME & Lucy M COREY at Brookline MA [31 May 1849]
    Mary Alice & Oliver THOMPSON at China ME [9 Dec 1836]
    Mary D Mrs & John M PIERCE at Hartford CT [25 May 1848]
    Mary Mrs & Eben'r WHITEN at Waterboro Center ME [6 Sept 1849]
    Perthena A of Greene ME & Francis M JORDAN of Danville ME at Auburn ME [30 Jan 1851]
    Wealthy Mrs & Walter W PHILBRICK at Augusta ME on Sunday Morning by Rev C FULLER [18 Jul 1844]
    William G & Elizabeth B FOY at Gardiner ME [7 Nov 1844]
    William of Topsham ME & Harriet MORRILL of Dexter ME at Dexter [24 Oct 1840]

RIDEOUT Annis & Ezra H DAWES at Litchfield ME [17 Jun 1847]
    Benjamin & Prudence RIDEOUT at Brunswick ME [28 Sept 1839]
    Charles & Betsey D HILL at Bath ME [30 Mar 1848]
    Cordelia & Capt Benj F SANDFORD of Topsham ME at Bowdoinham ME [26 Mar 1842]
    Hannah E & Benjamin F FOOTE at Bath ME [15 Feb 1849]
    Mary B & Joseph CLOUGH at Westbrook ME [31 Jul 1835]
    Melinda & Benjamin MASTIN at Rome ME by James L VARNEY on 3rd inst [12 Dec 1844]
    Melvira & James GETCHELL at Richmond ME [8 Aug 1844]
    Nicholas Esq & Mrs Mary STEELE of Buxton ME at Cumberland ME [21 Mar 1844]
    Olive of Brunswick ME & Sparrow CHASE at Topsham ME [8 Jul 1843]
    Prudence & Benjamin RIDEOUT at Brunswick ME [28 Sept 1839]

RIDER Simeon & Lucy Ann DEAR at Belfast ME [21 Aug 1845]
    Thomas J & Jane SMITH at Thomaston ME [5 Feb 1836]
    Wilson C Rev of Wayne ME & Catharine MILLET of Leeds ME at Leeds ME [15 Jun 1839]

RIDGEWAY Deborah & Capt Joseph L HACKETT at New Vineyard ME [15 May 1845]

RIDGELY Thomas B & Susan S HOWES at New Sharon ME [12 Nov 1846]

RIDLEY Alexander & Rachel J ADERTON at Bowdoinham ME [25 Sept 1851]
    Eliza J & Osgood GRAVES at Wayne ME [3 Feb 1848]

RIDLEY (cont.) Paulenah of Wayne ME & Joseph LOVETT of Kirkland ME at Wayne ME [15 Mar 1847]
Susan J & William F WEBB of Prospect ME at Monroe ME [30 Sept 1847]
RIDLON Abby E & J F PURRINGTON at Monmouth ME [27 Jul 1848]
Adelia B & Tristam PILLSBURY both of Portland ME [9 Oct 1845]
Jeremiah & Emma LARY at Saco ME [19 Aug 1847]
Joseph Jr of Georgetown ME & Sarah E USHER [10 Apr 1845]
RIDOUT Johnson Jr & Elizabeth D WHITMORE at Bath ME [11 Dec 1845]
RIGBY George of Auburn ME & Dorcas Jane ALDRICH of Auburn ME by Rev Walter FOSS at Webster on June 6th [17 Jun 1852]
RIGGS Eliza Jane & Franklin A HEWINS of Augusta ME at Georgetown ME [10 Jun 1847]
John A & S A Maria WHITE at Georgetown ME [28 Jun 1849]
RILEY John H of Boston MA & Ann M GERTS d/o late Capt Martin G at Portland ME on Tues eve by the Rv FARRINGTON [11 Mar 1843]
RINES John N Rev & Mercy D PEASE of Hope ME in Lincolnville ME [25 Jul 1847]
William of Westport ME & Roxana TIBBETTS [1 May 1845]
RING Amasa S & Lucy F LENNAN at Richmond ME [10 Sept 1846]
Charles L of Lubec ME & Margaret E RUGGLES of Calais ME [6 Nov 1845]
Clement P & Lucy AMES at Lewiston ME [6 Dec 1849]
Daniel & Dorothy G JONES at Belfast ME [13 Jun 1844]
David P & Julia HARE at Eastport ME [19 Feb 1846]
Joann L & Joseph TITCOMB at N Yarmouth ME [30 Dec 1836]
Rebecca B & Wyatt H FOLSOM at Orono ME [14 Nov 1844]
Sarah Mrs & Capt Richmond LORING Jr at N Yarmouth ME [2 May 1834]
Sarah of Litchfield ME & Henry PERRY of Richmond ME at Gardiner ME [21 Mar 1850]
William S & Nancy CLEAVES at Gardiner ME [22 Nov 1849]
RINGGOLD T L Lt USA & Susan BROWN only d/o late Hon A P UPSHUR at Northampton Co VA [27 Aug 27 1846]
RIPLEY Charles of Farmington ME & Martha DINSMORE of Temple ME [20 Jun 1837]
Cynthia A & William G KNAPP at Leeds ME by Rev Walter FOSS [19 Nov 1846]
Damaris of Appleton ME & George WHITE of Hermon ME at Union ME [25 Jan 1849]
Edwin H of Bath ME & Julia M WHITE at Hallowell ME by Rev George SHEPPARD [11 Mar 1836]
Hosea of Boston MA & Julia STURGIS at Vassalboro ME [9 Jul 1846]
John & Mrs Mary S C SYLVESTER at Bath ME [11 Mar 1847]
John S & Adeline B TIBBETS at Augusta ME by Asaph B NICHOLS Esq [10 Dec 1846]
Moses H & Eliza J HOWARD in Winthrop ME on Tues eve last by Rev David THURSTON [16 Nov 1833]
Thaddeus E of Hope ME & Rebecca D GUSHEE at Appleton ME [7 May 1846]
RITCHIE William W & Martha Ann HAYES at Frankfort ME on May 4 [10 Jun 1843]
RIVORS Hannah & Richard RIVORS at St George ME [6 Mar 1845]

RIVERS Henry T & Mary J DUNBAR at Thomaston ME [11 Sept 1851]
ROACH Betsy Ann & John HANSON at Bath ME [15 May 1845]
    Jane & Edward B RUSSEL of Salem MA at Bath ME on 30 ult [Dec 17 1842]
    Towns of Bangor ME & Susan COFFIN at Frankfort ME [30 Oct 1838]
ROAK William D & Ann S WAGG at Durham ME [15 Jul 1843]
ROBB Ann C & William G TURNER both of Leeds ME on 26th ult [25 Dec 1835]
ROBBINS Adelia H & Charles SHERER at Thomaston ME [15 Oct 1846]
    Adeline & Emery F JOY of Winthrop ME at Union ME [14 Jun 1849]
    Augusta Mrs & John G HALL at China ME by James B HASKELL [20 Sept 1849]
    B F Rev & Mary LINDY d/o Enos CHANDLER all of Winthrop ME on Oct 30 by Rev F FOSTER [7 Nov 1844]
    Betsy & William R CORBERR at Brunswick ME [6 Aug 1846]
    Charlotte of Turner ME & Hiram WARREN of Minot ME [28 Oct 1836]
    Daniel H of Vassalboro ME & Mary E RAMSDELL by William PERCIVAL Esq at China on 13th ult [17 Feb 1848]
    Delphina S & Charles J TALBOT at Phillips ME on Mar 23 by Archibald TALBOT Esq [22 Apr 1843]
    Elizabeth & Samuel ROBBINS at Tremont ME [5 Feb 1852]
    Elizabeth & William T HUNNEWELL at Solon ME [16 Jan 1851]
    Elmina & Warren NORTON at Phillips ME [16 May 1837]
    Elvina & Edwin P LOVEJOY at E Thomaston ME [7 August 1838]
    Jacob & Philena BRIGGS at Friends Meeting House in Winthrop ME [27 Apr 1839]
    Jerusha W, printeress, & Otis WILLIAMS, printer, all of Winthrop ME on Thanksgiving Day eve by Rev B F ROBBINS [2 Dec 1847]
    John & Jane FRENCH at Belfast ME [21 Aug 1845]
    Joseph T & Mary Jane SARGENT both of Exeter ME [13 Feb 1845]
    Lloyd C/O & Almira E MITCHELL at Chesterville ME [22 Mar 1849]
    Lucy E & Loring EDGECOMB of Poland ME at Buckfield ME [22 Feb 1844]
    Margaret & John BROWN 2nd at Rockland ME [1 Jul 1852]
    Mary & Nathaniel C BEAL at Phillips ME [17 May 1849]
    Octavia H of (Winthrop ME) & Seth MARTIN of Upper Gloucester (New Gloucester ME) [24 Dec 1842]
    Olive C & Ira PLAISTED at Phillips ME [5 Mar 1842]
    Olive G & George J ORDWAY Esq at Norway ME [26 August 1852]
    Oliver & Esther STARR of E Thomaston ME at Thomaston ME [27 Sept 1849]
    Orphea Ann & Justin THOMAS of Hartford ME at Winthrop ME [17 Apr 1845]
    Rev A B of Muscatine Iowa & Mary S ARNOLD at Monmouth ME [9 Oct 1851]
    Ruhamah & Samuel CROSWELL of Mercer ME at Norridgewock ME [2 May 1840]
    Saline of Appleton ME & Israel R HILLS at Union ME [13 Nov 1851]
    Samuel & Elizabeth ROBBINS at Tremont [5 Feb 1852]
    Sarah Jane & Elliot S HILLBORN of New York NY at Paris ME [27 Jan 1844]
    Sarah & J Hobart HUNTING at Guilford ME [24 Sept 1846]

ROBBINS (cont.) Simon of Rome ME & Mrs Jane PENNEY of Belgrade ME at W Sidney ME [22 Mar 1849]
   Sophronia & Capt William HERRICK at Tremont [5 Feb 1852]
   William of Augusta ME & Sarah P REYNOLDS of Sidney ME at Sidney [14 Mar 1840]
   William of Boston MA & Lucy V HINDS at Pittston ME [17 Sept 1846]
   Zilpha S & William H WIGGIN of Lowell MA at Phillips ME on Dec 30 by Hon J A LINSCOTT [4 Jan 1849]

ROBERTS Abigail L & Jotham CHANEY both of S Berwick ME at Kittery ME [21 Mar 1837]
   Benjamin & Maria B BARTON at Waldoboro ME [8 Feb 1840]
   Betsey H & Abel H JELLESON at Saco ME [10 Sept 1846]
   Betsey S of Hanover ME & Asa HOWARD Esq of Rumford ME at Rumford [30 Sept 1847]
   Betsey & Dr Eben STONE at Westbrook ME [17 Aug 1848]
   Betsey & Joseph EMMONS 3d at Lyman [1 Jul 1852]
   Charles M of Gardiner ME & Maria C GILMAN at Monmouth ME [15 Apr 1847]
   Charles & Abigail PROCTOR at Bath ME [5 Mar 1846]
   Cyrus & Emily S REDMAN at Brooksville ME [16 Oct 1845]
   Daniel & Sarah JEWELL of Athens ME at Solon ME [23 Jul 1846]
   Darius L of Brooksville ME & Lydia M TIBBETTS at Sedgwick Bay ME [27 Jul 1848]
   Elijah Jr & Betsey Jane HASKELL at China ME [10 Jan 1850]
   Elizabeth C & Milton ROBERTS at Brooks ME [19 Aug 1843]
   George T & Mary TITCOMB at Kennebunk ME [23 Mar 1839]
   Hannah J of Topsham ME & Moses CRIPS at Brunswick ME [19 Sept 1844]
   Harriet M of Alfred ME & Bartholemew WENTWORTH of S Berwick ME [1 May 1838]
   Isabella & Capt Alfred WEST at Wiscasset ME [17 Jul 1845]
   John M & Mary E POTTER both of West Gardiner ME at Gardiner ME [13 Mar 1851]
   John & Mehitable GOLDSMITH at Gardiner ME on 19th inst by Moses SPRINGER Esq [31 Oct 1837]
   Joseph & Mary MAYBURY at Solon ME [29 Apr 1836]
   Julia P & Rhodes A BUDLONG at Lewiston ME [12 Jun 1851]
   Maria N & Henry N BREED at Danvers MA [20 May 1852]
   Mary & Benj P MITCHELL at E Thomaston ME [27 Sept 1849]
   Mary & Samuel ROBERTS Jr of Lyman at Waterboro ME [24 Apr 1851]
   Milton & Elizabeth C ROBERTS at Brooks ME [19 Aug 1843]
   Nancy & Jonathan FIELD of Buxton ME at Waterboro ME [13 May 1847]
   Noah & Lorena VEAZIE at Isleboro ME [20 Jul 1848]
   Samuel Jr of Lyman & Mary ROBERTS at Waterboro ME [24 Apr 1851]
   Samuel & Alice ALLEN at Rome ME [11 Feb 1843]
   Sarah E & Nehemiah LOW of Berwick ME at Somersworth ME [20 Aug 1846]
   Sophrona P Mrs & Isaac H RANDALL at Vassalboro ME [10 Oct 1840]
   Sophronia & Samuel REYNOLDS at Lubec ME [5 Jul 1849]
   Thomas W of Howland ME & Nancy C GRANT at Brewer ME [20 Feb 1845]
   W & Mrs Delia E JOHNSON at Bath ME [15 Jan 1846]

ROBERTSON Abigail & Joseph HODGES Jr at Belmont ME [15 Aug 1844]
    Albert & Louisa Jane GATES at Monson ME [5 Jun 1845]
    John of Manchester England, manufacturer, & Rebecca WILLIAMS of Boston MA at New York [24 Aug 1833]
    Lucius B of New Sharon ME & Mrs Martha GOLDFUS at Jay ME [19 Dec 1844]
    William Jr & E G RUSSELL both of Moscow ME at Bingham ME [22 Nov 1849]
ROBESON Jonas of N Orleans & Sarah Ann FARRELL at Hallowell ME [30 Sept 1843]
ROBIE Mary & Allen GILMAN of Monmouth ME at Hallowell ME by Rev DR TAPPAN [3 Oct 1844]
    William F of Readfield ME & Eliza A L MATHEWS of Sidney ME at Augusta ME on Dec 21st by Lot M MORRILL Esq [4 Jan 1849]
ROBINSON (see BOBINSON)
    Abby H & F H BLACK at Belfast ME [7 Dec 1848]
    Abby & Ambrose JONES at Mountville ME [1 Apr 1852]
    Abigail H & Henry FORD of Farmington ME at Mt Vernon ME [17 Oct 1834]
    Abigail & Alex COLBY at (Augusta) ME [8 Jan 1852]
    Almeda & Allen TUTTLE of Buckfield ME at Sumner ME on Feb 9 by Z ROBINSON Esq [21 Feb 1850]
    Almira E Mrs & R D RICE at Augusta ME [28 Nov 1840]
    Amanda & Mr Florilla GALUSHA at Augusta ME [15 Mar 1849]
    Ambrose H & Mrs Mary J MASON at Rockland ME [1 Jan 1852]
    Amelia H of Paris ME & Martin W PHIPPS of Holliston at Albany [26 Feb 1846]
    Ann Doe & Mr J B FOSTER at Waterville ME [17 Jun 1852]
    Ardra ROBINSON of Sidney ME & Thomas H at Augusta ME [27 Dec 1849]
    Asa B & Elizabeth RICKER at Bath ME [17 Jul 1835]
    Augusta E & Dr Nathan EMERSON of Orland ME at Portland ME [14 Oct 1847]
    Benj P ROBINSON & Eliza Ann BURTON at Cushing ME [14 May 1846]
    Benjamin R of E Bridgewater MA & Harriet A COX at Brunswick ME [23 Aug 1849]
    Benjamin & Sarah E WASHBURN at Thomaston ME [2 Jan 1845]
    Bradbury Jr & Mary PATTEN at Bloomfield ME [1 Apr 1843]
    Bryant & Louisa Jane RACKLEY at Greene ME [19 Jun 1838]
    Calvin & Elizabeth DAVIS at Union ME [3 Feb 1848]
    Catherine H & Joseph NASH at Belgrade ME on 13th Dec [28 Dec 1848]
    Celia C & William E TURNER at Dover ME [28 Sept 1848]
    Charles 2d & Louisa J BROWN at Guilford ME by William HAMMOND Esq [17 Apr 1838]
    David G, M.D., of Monmouth ME & Mariette DORMAN d/o Hon Orrin D of Lower Canada at N Troy VT on Dec 22 [7 Jan 1843]
    Edward Hon & Penelope G FALES at Thomaston ME [2 Jul 1846]
    Elijah D & Celinda N ROWE at Lewiston ME [15 Jan 1836]
    Elizabeth & Gardiner MALBON at Skowhegan ME [11 Mar 1847]
    Emma J & Henry P Rev TORSEY A M at Hallowell ME, she was Preceptress of same [28 Dec 1848]

ROBINSON (cont.) Emma of Concord ME & Ithammer BOIES of Skowhegan ME at Bingham ME [1 Jul 1852]
    Emmie T & George F POTTER at Augusta ME on Thurs morning last by Rev JUDD [5 Aug 1852]
    Esther A & Benj A SMITH at Hallowell ME on Aug 19 by Rev W A P DILLINGHAM [13 Sept 1849]
    Franklin L MD of Jefferson ME & Clarissa KALER at Waldoboro ME [5 Mar 1842]
    George W & Mary BECKETT at Cushing ME [27 Jan 1848]
    George W & Nancy H MALBAN at Skowhegan ME [2 Dec 1847]
    George & Almira EMERY at Augusta ME [28 Sept 1833]
    Hannah E & John C BRAMHALL at Belfast ME [21 May 1846]
    Harriet B & Capt John O RONEY at Thomaston ME [27 Aug 1846]
    Harriet M & Cyrus THORP of Wiscasset ME at Alna ME [9 Oct 1851]
    Harris Capt & Sarah M MUNROE at Thomaston ME [31 Jul 1845]
    Increase & Mary HOUGH at Fairfield ME [11 Mar 1833]
    J F & Mary J SWIFT both of Gardiner ME at Hallowell ME [2 Nov 1848]
    James 2d of Brentwood NH & Lucinda ROBINSON at Mt Vernon ME [17 Oct 1834]
    James & Charlotte YEATON of Northport ME at Belfast ME [16 Sept 1843]
    James & Lydia HYLER at Cushing ME [4 Jul 1844]
    Jane & Isaac HASKELL at Brunswick ME [27 Aug 1846]
    Joanna P & William HODGKINS at Thomaston ME [16 Jul 1846]
    Joseph of Webster ME & Sarah H SWETT at Readfield ME [9 Dec 1847]
    Josiah Esq & Rebeca S PAINE at Cornville ME [18 Mar 1852]
    Lavina S & Hallet W MORTON of Boston MA, formerly of Winthrop ME at Lowell MA by Rev G H SMITH [3 Jul 1845]
    Leonard of Foxcroft ME & Mary PURINGTON of Dover ME at Bloomfield ME [22 Jun 1839]
    Lucinda & James ROBINSON 2d of Brentwood NH at Mt Vernon ME [17 Oct 1834]
    Lydia F of Dover ME & Sherman STONE of Ripley ME at Dover ME by Rev Nat'l ROBINSON [12 Feb 1842]
    Lydia & Elisha BARROWS both of (Augusta) at Augusta ME on 5th ult by Rev E FREEMAN [7 May 1846]
    Margaret & O W JORDAN at Thomaston ME [20 Nov 1845]
    Maria & Charles GOWEN of Sanford ME at Newburyport MA 3rd inst [17 Jul 1845]
    Martha P d/o David R Esq of Sidney ME & Charles G MILTON of Belgrade ME at Sidney ME on 19th ult [19 Jul 1845]
    Mary A & Elisha BURGESS of Vassalboro ME at Albion ME on 1 May by T BURRILL Esq [8 May 1851]
    Mary A & John O GINN at Belmont ME [5 Jul 1849]
    Mary Ann & William G ELLIS both of Sidney ME at Waterville ME [6 Dec 1849]
    Mary C & Royal WRIGHT at Newcastle ME [27 Nov 1845]
    Mary Frances & Hiram CUSHING of Weymouth MA on 17th inst at Vassalboro ME [30 Apr 1842]
    Mary P d/o Capt William R & Charles J WINGATE at Augusta ME [30 Nov 1833]
    Mehitable M & Llewellyn KIDDER Esq at Skowhegan ME [12 Dec 1840]

ROBINSON (cont.) Melissa & Thomas K HOLBROOK Capt at Rockland ME [31 Jul 1851]
   Mellen & Angeline LINCOLN at Litchfield ME [26 Oct 1839]
   Milton & Sylvia Jane FARRINGTON at Oxford ME [10 Dec 1846]
   Miriam A & Hanford CROSBY at Mountville ME [1 Apr 1852]
   Nancy J H & Benjamin SAWYER of Bangor ME at Thomaston ME [16 Sept 1836]
   Nathaniel & Mary LEAVITT at Mt Vernon ME [27 Nov 1845]
   Nathaniel & Miss LEIGHTON at Mt Vernon ME [6 Jun 1837]
   Niven C & Harriet Y PAGE at Cushing ME [20 Nov 1845]
   Noah & Olive PARKER at Waterborough ME [31 Jul 1845]
   Olive P & James W ELWELL of New York at Bath ME [25 Jul 1844]
   Oliver J & Hannah E HYLER at Cushing ME [1 Jan 1846]
   Peleg S & Elizabeth JEWETT at Gardiner ME [2 Dec 1847]
   Pheba A of Monmouth ME & Joseph D KIMBALL of Orono ME at Monmouth ME [27 Mar 1835]
   Philena P & Wellington B HAMBLEN at Sidney ME on 12 inst [23 Oct 1845]
   R R & Caroline W CALDWELL at Portland ME [28 Aug 1838]
   Richard Jr & Mary WENTWORTH at Thomaston ME [12 Sept 1840]
   Samuel Capt & Mrs Elizabeth WILLIAMS at Oxford ME [15 Jan 1836]
   Samuel & Mary Ann FLETCHER at Mt Vernon ME [2 Jan 1835]
   Sarah A & William RICE Jr of Augusta ME at Bath ME [20 Feb 1845]
   Sarah E & Ira THING at Mt Vernon ME [26 Jul 1849]
   Sarah E & William H STACEY of Hallowell ME at Litchfield ME [30 Sept 1836]
   Sarah Mrs & John WOODS of Bloomfield ME at Cambridge ME [14 Feb 1850]
   Sarah N d/o Capt George R & Joshua E FULLER at Thomaston ME on 4th inst [21 Feb 1841]
   Sarah & Isaac C EMERSON at Hallowell ME [18 Jun 1846]
   Sarah & Joseph L MITCHELL at Gardiner ME [16 Jul 1846]
   Sophronia P of Cornville ME & John S NAY of Palmyra ME at Skowhegan ME [27 Mar 1851]
   Wealthy M & Capt Wildes T THOMPSON of Brunswick ME at Bath ME [19 Sept 1834]
   West & Celia BESSEE at Foxcroft ME [1 Nov 1849]
   William C & Susan H STEVENS at Bangor ME [26 Mar 1842] & on 26 inst by John SAYWARD Esq all of that place [2 Apr 1842]
   William Henry & Emeline GODFREY by Rev Mr KALLOCH at (Augusta) ME [26 Oct 1848]
   William M & Clementine B RANDALL both of Vassalboro ME at China ME on 5th inst by A H ABBOT Esq [9 May 1840]
   William S & Eunice SAMPSON of Winthrop ME at Hallowell ME [12 Nov 1846]

ROCHE Veronica U M formerly of Boston MA & John PATTERSON of Industry ME at Mt Vernon Posey Co, IN on Nov 25 [1 Feb 1840]

ROCKO Gaskar & Pressy BULLARD at Bath ME [2 Jan 1845]

ROCKWOOD Darius of Belgrade ME & Susan AVERY of Pittston ME by Asaph NICHOLS Esq at Augusta ME [4 Jun 1846]
   Sarah E & Charles SWIFT of Gardiner ME at Augusta ME [30 Dec 1847]

RODGERS Eunice of Cornwallis Nova Scotia Canada & Jas THORPE at Eastport ME [12 Sept 1844]
    Phebe G & Capt J H McCRILLIS at Belfast ME [22 Jan 1836]
    Sarah & Jonathan ESTIS at Corinna ME [11 Apr 1844]
    Susan & Seth SUMNER at Bowdoinham ME [14 Aug 1835]
RODRING Levi & Mary HART at Bath ME [29 Aug 1844]
ROE Hathill of Sumner ME & Betsey COBURN of Turner ME [4 Apr 1837]
ROGERS Caroline A & Benjamin SARGENT at Belfast ME [21 Oct 1847]
    Cassendmark Mrs & James RICH of Bowdoinham ME at Topsham ME [24 Dec 1846]
    Deborah of Augusta ME & J FULLER of Fairfield ME at Augusta ME [9 Jan 1841]
    Emeline M d/o late Levi R & Silas LEONARD Esq at Augusta ME on Mon eve last [4 Jan 1840]
    Emeline of Belgrade ME & Enos CUMMINGS of Sidney ME by Rev Walter FOSS at Leeds ME on Oct 31 [29 Nov 1849]
    Emily A of Brownville ME & Theodore TREADWELL of Frankfort ME at Atkinson ME [17 Jul 1851]
    Eunice G & John W CHASE at Stetson ME [31 Aug 1839]
    Eunice of Newburg ME & Francis F TINKHAM of Albion ME at Dixmont ME by A T C DODGE Esq [21 Mar 1850]
    Fanny Mrs & Henry HOBBS at Augusta ME on Sun eve last [29 May 1838]
    Frances & Joseph BAKER Esq at Augusta ME [20 Nov 1841]
    George W & Emeline BLAKE both of Newfield ME at Bridgeton ME [3 Dec 1842]
    Greenleaf of Augusta ME & Sarah B McLELLAN of Gardiner ME at Gardiner by Rev CLAPP on Mon morning last [6 Jun 1834]
    Harriet N & Peleg SPRAGUE at Bath ME [29 Feb 1844]
    Jane P & Capt Ira DELANO of Bath ME at Topsham ME [12 Oct 1839]
    John of Brunswick ME & Hannah J OWEN of Topsham ME at Topsham by George ROGERS Esq [15 Jul 1833]
    John of Phipsburg ME & Merinda H BOND at Lewiston ME [21 Jun 1849]
    Jonathan P Esq of Bangor ME & Lucretia M PAGE at Hallowell ME [10 Aug 1833]
    Jos W & Eliza J BERRY at Kittery ME [14 Aug 1851]
    Josiah Jr of Bow NH & Martha MOORE at Concord NH [4 Feb 1833]
    Loring W & Mary E GRANT at Orrington ME [3 Feb 1848]
    Martha Ann & Eliphaz D GRIFFIN at Freeport ME [24 Oct 1844]
    Martha H F & Simon N TAYLOR at Norridgewock ME [25 Nov 1847]
    Martha & Richard ADAMS at Topsham ME [4 Jan 1849]
    Martha & Simon TAYLOR at Norridgewock ME [11 Nov 1847]
    Martin C & Emma J DOE at Belfast ME [11 Jul 1844]
    Mary A & Thomas H HEALD at Anson ME [11 Apr 1840]
    Mary D & Edward FAIRFIELD at Topsham ME [6 Nov 1838]
    Mary J & Jonathan CONNER at Windsor ME [1 Jun 1848]
    Myra E & Capt John P BAGLEY at Belfast ME [23 Dec 1847]
    N B Rev of Hallowell ME & Miss Lydia G BAILEY at Hopkinton NH [25 Oct 1849]
    Rebecca of Phipsburg ME by Andrew REED Esq [16 Oct 1838]
    Robert & Miss Elizabeth M BATCHELDER at Phippsburg ME [13 Aug 1846]

ROGERS (cont.) Rufus & Huldah M RECORD at Dover ME? [12 Aug 1852]
    Samuel S & Delia J FULLER at Augusta ME on 1 Jan by Rev C F ALLEN [10 Jan 1850]
    Sarah & Prescott NUTTING at Norridgewock ME [28 Mar 1844]
    Susan A & Jones S DAVIS at Belfast ME [6 Jul 1848]
    Thomas & Mrs Maria MITCHELL at Eastport ME [29 Apr 1847]
    William G of Brownville ME & Mary E HOBBS at Milo ME [31 Jul 1851]
    William J Capt & Frances A WEST at Belfast ME [8 Feb 1849]
    William S of Saco ME & Dorcas GOLDER at Lewiston ME [4 Oct 1849]
    William & Lydia H ELLIOT at Bath ME [2 Jul 1846]
ROIX William R & Lydia M DUNBAR at Belfast ME [7 Jan 1847]
ROKES Samuel & Lucy WOTTON both of Warren ME at Waldoborough ME [14 Mar 1844]
ROLF Enoch C of Farmington Falls ME & Emeline SMALL of former place (Rumford ME?) at Rumford by Dr Simeon FULLER [8 Jun 1839]
ROLFE Betsey C & Peter TRASK of Mexico ME at Rumford ME [6 Jun 1844]
    David F of Limington ME & Elizabeth BUZZELL of Lowell at Lowell MA [10 Dec 1846]
    John E & Miss Joanna S DOUGLASS at Rumford ME by Nathan ABBOTT Esq [11 May 1839]
ROLLE Ellen & Solomon YOUNG at Falmouth ME [11 Jan 1844]
ROLLIN Ichabod Jr & Sarah WATSON at Parkman ME [9 Jan 1845]
    Joan H & Samuel A WATSON at Parkman ME [9 Jan 1845]
ROLLINS Augusta A & Lewis GRANT at Saco ME [21 Dec 1848]
    Daniel Jr & Margaret G GREEN at Camden ME [13 May 1852]
    Frances A & Samuel L BLANCHARD at Hallowell ME [3 Feb 1848]
    Freeman & Laura P LEE at Lee ME by J B LUDDEN Esq [26 Jun 1851]
    Lousa M & Jacob S HARRIS at (Augusta) ME on 16th inst [30 Nov 1848]
    Martha L & Capt William McCLURE both of Bowdoinham ME at Providence RI [4 Sept 1851]
    Mary E & Joshua P SIMONTON at Camden ME [4 Mar 1852]
    Amanda M & Philip E MILLAY both of Pittston ME at Lynn MA [17 May 1849]
    Evelina F & Harrison A SMITH Esq at Vassalboro ME [10 Jun 1833]
    Francis M of Vassalboro ME & Miss Mary Jane MILLER at Augusta ME [24 Jun 1847]
    George A Margaret J CARLTON at Vassalboro ME on 17th Oct by Rev Albert COLE [13 Dec 1849]
    Hiram & Mary Ann CONNER at Augusta ME by Rev Mr MORSE [17 Jun 1847]
    John of Union & Hannah DOUGLASS at Augusta ME [29 Oct 1846]
    John A of Vassalboro ME & Aurelia F LADD at Belfast ME [6 Nov 1835]
    Lucy Ann & Rev Mr WEBBER at Hallowell ME on Tues evening last by Rev Mr WEBBER [17 Apr 1838]
    M of Appleton ME & Persis HUNT at Hallowell ME [11 Nov 1847]
    Mary T & David C RAND at Livermore ME both of Hallowell ME [9 Sept 1847]
    Peter, merchant of Vassalboro ME & Abigail d/o Dr Alexander HATCH at Augusta ME by Rev William A DREW [31 Jul 1838]
    Priscilla & Charles MOORE at Gardiner ME [15 Mar 1849]
    Reuben R of Augusta ME & Miss Mary A KENT of Bangor ME at Bangor on 26th ult [4 Nov 1843]

ROLLINS (cont.) Sally & Capt Thomas DOW at Pittston ME [16 Nov 1833]
   Samuel S of Great Falls NH & Sarah Ann THOMS of Ossipee NH [20 Feb 1845]
   Sarah (age 23y) & Deacon John HUTING of Corinth ME (age 63 yrs) at Freedom ME [14 Aug 1841]
   Sarah P & William L WITHAM at Gardiner ME [9 Apr 1846]
   Timothy E of Camden NJ & Miss Caroline S WATSON of Dover ME at Dover [3 Jul 1845]

RONEY John O Capt & Harriet B ROBINSON at Thomaston ME [27 Aug 1846]

ROOCH Royal & Lois H WHITCOMB at Moscow ME [21 May 1846]
   Royal & Mrs Sylvia WHITCOMB of Hampden ME at Moscow ME by J D HILL Esq [11 Nov 1847]

ROSE Edwin & Miss Caroline S FULLER at Thomaston ME [24 Oct 1834]
   Elizabeth, d/o the late Hon Daniel ROSE at Thomaston ME, & Jesse PEABODY [27 Jun 1840]
   Emerson & Miss Susan BRYANT at Turner ME [30 Nov 1839]
   Thomas & Mary Ann FALES at Thomaston ME [23 Oct 1841]

ROSS Ann J & Jonathan S McCLURE at Jay ME by Rev J M FOLLETT on 26th ult [7 Jan 1847]
   Daniel B & Eliza E WALES of Saco ME at Biddeford ME [5 Jul 1849]
   Esther & Randall L HILL at Skowhegan ME [15 Feb 1840]
   Harriet, d/o of the late M William ROSS, & Jacob MILLS Jr [4 Apr 1834]
   Harriet B of Augusta ME & Harvey E DINGLEY at Augusta ME on Thurs last by Rev A MOORE [7 Aug 1845]
   James & Catherine Ann McDONALD at Calais ME [2 May 1844]
   John C & Hannah McGOUN at Camden ME [8 Aug 1844]
   Leander H of Phipsburg ME & Drusilla A LAPLAIN at Gardiner ME [1 Nov 1849]
   Margerie & Hiram STEWART at Bath ME [9 Sept 1836]
   Maria & Jordan F STINSON of Albion ME at Newport ME [21 May 1846]
   Mary Ann & Simeon A HEATH at Bangor ME [24 Apr 1845]
   Mary J & Leander WEEKS at Jefferson ME on 17th inst [28 Jan 1847]
   Mary Jane & Selden DYER at Sidney ME [20 Feb 1845]
   Samuel G & Phebe A CLEMENT at Biddeford ME [5 Aug 1852]
   Susan & William SWAIN at Skowhegan ME [1 Jan 1846]

ROUNDEY Mary E & John H CHAMBERLAIN at Benton ME [19 Feb 1852]

ROUNDS Dorcas & Major BOURNE at Poland ME [29 Aug 1844]
   Joseph S & Mrs Esther HILBORN of Oxford ME at Norway ME [30 Apr 1846]

ROWE Adeline C & Adeline C ROWE at Bangor ME [12 Mar 1842]
   Amanda P & William S WHITMAN at China ME [8 Jul 1847]
   Celinda N & Elijah D ROBINSON at Lewiston ME [15 Jan 1836]
   Cynthia Mrs & America BISBEE Esq at Paris ME [15 Jan 1846]
   Cyrus, senior publisher of the *Republican Journal* & Harriet M T DODGE at Bluehill ME [22 Jul 1847]
   David W of Oxford ME & Emily C BILLINGS at Woodstock ME [21 Aug 1851]
   Emeline & Mr William BRANCH of Waterville ME at Belgrade ME on 19th inst by Thomas ELDRED Esq [30 Oct 1845]
   Frances E R & Thomas H WHITE both Readfield ME by Asaph R NICHOLS Esq at Augusta ME on Jan 1st [10 Jan 1850]

ROWE (cont.) Joann of East Pond Plantation ME & William LANDER at Fairfield ME [13 Jun 1837]
    Mary A & Simeon MONK all of Minot ME at Mechanic Falls (Poland-Minot) ME [25 Oct 1849]
    Mary E & Ephraim C KEENE at Brooks ME [12 Feb 1836]
    Mary F of Lowell MA & Samuel GUILD at Strong ME [5 Aug 1847]
    Phebe S of Portland ME & John S HUTCHINS of Cambridge MA at S Paris ME [23 Sept 1847]
    Roxana & William B BISHOP of Mt Vernon ME at Belgrade ME [16 Jul 1846]
    S P of Greenwood ME & Elvira STEVENS of Norway ME at Norway ME [6 Feb 1845]
    Samuel & Rheasylvia A TUTTLE at Palmyra ME [27 Mar 1851]
    Sarah E & Edward A HODFKINS at Bath ME on 6th inst by R PALMER [5 Feb 1842]
    Sarah Jane & Noah GREEN both of Smithfield ME at Hallowell ME [30 Oct 1845]

ROWELL Aaron & Mary P TAPLEY at Frankfort ME [28 Jan 1847]
    Amanda A & Charles H GORDON at (Augusta) ME on 6th Mar [11 Mar 1852]
    Arletta H d/o Jessy R Esq, P M of Jefferson ME & Luther DIXBY Jr at Boston MA by Rev STREETER [22 Jun 1839]
    Belinda & Capt Nicholas HINKLEY at Monmouth ME [20 May 1852]
    Elenor C & Orin LUCE at Livermore ME [5 Dec 1837]
    Eliphalet, printer & Ellen F SMITH youngest d/o Capt Samuel S at Hallowell ME [12 Dec 1844]
    George & Charlotte WENTWORTH of Brighton ME at Solon ME [13 Feb 1851]
    Isaac & Margaret W ADAMS at Litchfield ME [14 May 1846]
    James E & Mary A HUNTER at the Forks ME [27 Sept 1849]
    John Col of Jay ME & Mary LAMBERT at Readfield ME on 15th inst [27 May 1847]
    Lucy & Charles SHAW at Augusta ME by Rev SAWYER [27 May 1847]
    Mary E Mrs of Hampden ME & J S CROSBY of Bangor ME at H on 9th inst [25 Sept 1838]
    Nathan P & Mary S KITTREDGE at Weld ME by Rev J B WHEELWRIGHT [18 Dec 1851]
    Ruth & Robert H HEARD at Thomaston ME [8 Jan 1846]
    Susan L & J B FOSTER of Brewer ME at Frankfort ME [12 Aug 1847]
    Timothy & Sarah BRYANT both of Vassalboro ME at Vassalboro on 25th ult [11 Nov 1836]
    Washington Esq & Mary SMITH at Madison ME [18 May 1839]

ROWSE Edward Jr & Charlotte W SWAN d/o Benjamin S Esq at Augusta ME [21 Sept 1839]
    John B formerly of (Augusta ME) at North Hamilton Co OH & Margaret SILVER of North Bend [1 Jan 1846]
    Joseph & Hannah L BOOKER by Rev A BURGESS at (Augusta) ME [13 Jan 1848]

ROYAL Freeman & Isabel COBB at Bangor ME [15 Aug 1844]
    Jane & Hiram MERROW at Minot ME [12 Dec 1840]
    William & Eunice H COLLINS at Gardiner ME [25 Feb 1847]
    William B & Abiah COLE at Paris ME [25 Feb 1847]

RUDGE George Jr (of the house of Maxwell WRIGHT) & Charlotte KENT d/o Hon Edward KENT the American Consul of Bangor ME at Rio de Janeiro [11 Mar 1852]

RUGGLES Almira & Nicholas R BURNHAM at Calais ME [11 May 1839]
    Margaret E & Charles L RING of Lubec ME at Calais ME [6 Nov 1845]

RUMERY Phillota & George A BLACKLEY at Lubec ME [22 Jan 1852]

RUNDLET Charles E of Gardiner ME & Catherine EATON at Dorchester MA [15 May 1835]
    Martha Jane & James M JACKMAN at Solon ME [13 Mar 1845]

RUNNELLS Isaac R & Rachel J MARSTON both of Hallowell ME at Lexington [20 Jan 1848]

RUNNELS Amelia & Milton M GILMAN formerly of Hallowell ME at New York NY [24 Apr 1845]
    James C & Hannah C MASON of Augusta at Hallowell ME on May 17 by Rev FOSTER [29 May 1851]

RUSH Sarah E & Richard F HINKLEY at Bath ME [3 Jul 1851]
    Sylvanus & Harriet E BARTER [23 Dec 1847]

RUSS Horatio G Capt & Ruth S HOUGHTON at Paris ME [23 May 1840]
    John F of Salem ME & Clarissa HARLOW at Strong ME [13 Jun 1844]
    Maria of Monson & Capt Alfred PATTEN of Bowdoinham ME at Monson MA [24 Jul 1835]
    Martha Ann of New Sharon ME & Ira THING of Mt Vernon ME at New Sharon [18 Sept 1838]
    Mary E & G W CLARK of Cahawba AL at Belfast ME [14 Aug 1838]

RUSSELL/RUSSEL Abigail Mrs of Starks ME & James J ADAMS of Anson ME at Norridgewock ME [23 Nov 1839]
    Barnabas B of Madison ME & Nancy A GROVES at Skowhegan ME [9 Apr 1846]
    Deborah L Mrs & Daniel ADAMS of Norridgewock ME at Madison ME [6 Dec 1849]
    E G at Bingham ME & William ROBERTSON Jr both of Moscow ME [22 Nov 1849]
    Eben F & Sarah Jane REED at New Sharon ME [12 Nov 1846]
    Edmund Dr & Eunice H PORTER at Strong ME [27 Jan 1848]
    Edward B of Salem MA & Jane ROACH at Bath ME on 30th ult [17 Dec 1842]
    Eliza & Caleb GILBERT of Turner ME at Phipsburg ME [18 Nov 1836]
    Elizabeth J Mrs & Capt James H NICHOLS at Bath ME [16 Jul 1846]
    Emeline A & William P MARSTON at Bath ME [11 Apr 1850]
    Emily & David S DAY of Orient ME at Amity ME by Milo WATSON [3 Dec 1846]
    Ephraim H Capt & Rachel T DONNELL at Bath ME by Rev STEARNS [4 Feb 1833]
    Eunice M & Francis B CASWELL of Harrison ME at Bethel ME [6 Sept 1849]
    Fanny F & Henry A WYMAN Esq of Skowhegan ME at New Sharon ME [7 Jun 1849]
    Fanny W & William P FOWLER at Augusta ME [12 & 19 Dec 1837]
    George R & Jane W MITCHELL at Bangor ME on 25th ult [4 Nov 1843]
    Hollis Rev of Schoolcraft MI formerly of Bingham ME & Lucy Jane HAMBLIN of Tewksbury MA at Andover [5 Oct 1848]

Marriage Notices from the "Maine Farmer"

RUSSELL (cont.) Israel D of Roxbury MA & Nancy C KIMBALL at Hallowell ME [9 Dec 1847]
    J F of Hallowell ME & Mary H HASKELL at E Livermore ME [18 Jan 1849]
    J J of Barring & Mary SARGENT at N Yarmouth ME [14 Oct 1836]
    Jacob & Betsey JONES at Weld ME [28 Dec 1848]
    James N of Hartland ME & Elizabeth H McCRILLIS of Bloomfield ME at Skowhegan ME [20 Feb 1851]
    John W & Deborah FARRAR at Gardiner ME [2 Oct 1845]
    John W & Hannah HAMILTON at Vassalboro ME on 17th Aug by Rev L WENTWORTH [28 Aug 1851]
    Joseph Rev & Elizabeth H AMES both of Farmington ME at Strong ME [15 Feb 1849]
    Louisa K & Hermon BENNER at North Waldoboro ME on 13th inst [24 Feb 1848]
    M E Miss & Mr J F JOHNSON at Pittston ME [3 Feb 1848]
    Margaret B & John HANKERSON Jr Madrid ME at Carthage ME by H STORER Esq [14 Dec 1839]
    Martha A & Thomas S PAUL at Hallowell ME [21 Dec 1848]
    Mary E & John E DUNNELS, M.D., of Waterborough ME at Newfield ME [27 Mar 1845]
    Mary M & Abraham G BLETHEN at Temple ME [4 Apr 1844]
    Mary S d/o Edward R & Milford P NORTON Esq of Bangor ME at N Yarmouth ME by Rev Mr NICHOLS [15 Jul 1833]
    Nancy T Mrs of Brunswick ME & Robert BUTTERFIELD Esq of Bowdoinham ME at Bath ME [18 Jul 1844]
    Obed W of Phillips ME & Sarah ELLSWORTH at Avon ME [17 May 1849]
    Osgood of Dublin NH & Amelia A SINCLAIR at Ellsworth ME [23 Sept 1847]
    Perkins of Readfield ME & Elizabeth A SHAW of Winthrop ME by Rev Mr MORSE at Readfield ME on 3d inst [19 Oct 1848]
    Philip & Lucinda LEIGHTON at Falmouth ME by Rev THOMPSON [29 Apr 1843]
    Rebecca & John WATSON at Hallowell ME by Rev FULLER [27 Mar 1845]
    Warren & Judith B LONGLEY both of Madison ME at Skowhegan ME [29 Nov 1849]

RUST Benjamin & Livonia PERKINS at Augusta ME [3 Jun 1849]
    Burtha E & John B WALKER, M.D., at Washington ME [28 Jun 1849]
    Nancy & Arthur McCOBB at Boothbay ME [1 Apr 1852]

RUTTERFIELD George of Farmington ME & Sarah JAMES of Readfield ME at Winthrop ME [14 Nov 1844]

RUTHERFORD William A of Boston MA & Sarah P W CHANDLER in Augusta ME on Sun Eve last by Rev JUDD at the residence of Mrs Gen CHANDLER [21 Feb 1850]

RYAN William at Belmont ME & Sarah E WHITCOMB both of Waldo ME [25 Feb 1847]

RYANT Ann D & John JEFFERS at Farmington ME [14 Sept 1848]
    Nancy R & Henry F GORDON at Hallowell ME [14 Feb 1850]

RYONSON Edward of Brunswick ME & Elizabeth DIXON at Wales ME [12 Jun 1835]

- S -

SAFFORD Caroline W & William L CROSS at Vassalboro ME on 8th inst [20 Apr 1848]
    Charles W of (Winthrop ME) & Mary G d/o Paul STICKNEY Esq at Hallowell on Sept 25 [15 Oct 1842]
    Daniel Jr of Fayette ME & Roxana MORSE of E Dixfield ME at Livermore ME [20 Dec 1849]
    Emily & Henry GORDON at Fayette ME [16 Nov 1848]
    Francis of Turner ME & Polly Millett of Leeds ME at Winthrop ME by Eld HAZE [2 Dec 1836]
    Louisa & John SHAW at Augusta ME [4 Apr 1840]
    Minerva Ann & Sylvester S BURLEY at Lewiston ME [27 Nov 1851]
    Sarah E & Alonzo GAUBERT at (Augusta) ME on Sept 28th [5 Oct 1848]
SAGER William F of Gardiner ME & Eliza S RICHARDS at Hallowell ME [17 Aug 1833]
SALLEY Sarah of Embden ME & Warren NUTTING of Augusta ME at Embden ME [15 May 1838]
SALLY Sarah Jane & John HOLBROOK Jr at N Anson ME [15 Jul 1852]
SALMON Eunice B & Charles GILES publisher of the *Waldo Signal* at Belfast ME on 17th ult (17 Aug) by Rev William FROTHINGHAM [9 Sept 1843]
    Ira A of Portland ME & Maria W CHAFFEE at Vassalboro ME [6 Mar 1851]
SALMOND Agnes C & Joseph RICHARDS at Belfast ME [8 Aug 1844]
    Eunice B & Charles GILES at Belfast ME [2 Sept 1843]
SALTMARSH David L M & Amanda M JONES at Weld ME [3 Oct 1840]
SAMPSON Abel of Temple ME & Zeruah F STEWART of Farmington ME at Farmington ME [7 May 1842]
    C W & Jane LAWRENCE both of Temple ME at Temple ME on 13th inst by Rev S HACKETT [6 Jun 1840]
    Emily P & Lewis M WORK at Topsham ME [28 Oct 1847]
    Enoch Esq, merchant of Bowdoinham ME & M Theresa DREW eld d/o Rev W A DREW at Augusta ME on Sun last at the Universalist Church by Rev W A DREW [13 Jun 1844]
    Eunice of Winthrop ME & William S ROBINSON at Hallowell ME [12 Nov 1846]
    Harriet G & Matthew P SPEAR Esq at Bowdoinham ME [1 Jul 1833]
    Jacob & Eliza GODDARD at Hallowell ME [18 Dec 1845]
    Loring G & Pamelia P JOY at Winthrop ME by Rev F FOSTER [13 Jun 1844]
    Lot of Hartford ME & Lydia M MOODY at Peru ME [10 Jun 1847]
    Lucy W & Ezekiel H ALEXANDER at Vinalhaven ME [22 Jan 1846]
    Martha & Joseph FAIRBANKS Esq of Farmington ME at Temple ME [27 Nov 1851]
    Mary Mrs & William A GRIFFITH both of Winthrop ME at Canton Point ME on Dec 30 by John HEARSEY Esq [4 Jan 1840]
    Octavia W of Bowdoinham ME & James A BICKNELL of (Augusta ME) at Bowdoinham ME on 15th inst by W A DREW [26 Jun 1845]
    Rosanna & Andrew KENNISON at Temple ME [21 May 1846]
    Rufus A & Maria G WHITE at Topsham ME [2 Oct 1851]

SAMPSON (cont.) S A A L at New Gloucester ME & Elisha H MOSELY [17 Jun 1847]
    William A & Elizabeth G WINGATE both of Hallowell at Hallowell [11 May 1848]
SANBORN Abraham Esq of Levant ME attorney at law & Emily McCLELLAN d/o Judah M Esq at Bloomfield ME [21 Feb 1834]
    Abraham Esq of Waterville ME & Maria SAWTELLE at Norridgewock ME [5 Oct 1839]
    Ann E & Mr V B PAUL both of Waldo ME at Knox ME [20 Mar 1851]
    Caroline & Isaac RICHARDSON Jr at Gorham ME [5 Aug 1852]
    Catherine B & James VICKERY at Belfast ME [3 Oct 1840]
    Daniel Capt & Mrs Lucy ULMER at Thomaston ME [28 Oct 1847]
    David Capt of Norway ME & Lydia C CORDWELL at Paris ME [15 Apr 1847]
    David P & Martha JONES at Weld ME on Apr 11 by I PARLIN Esq [26 Apr 1849]
    David S & Azelia DAVIS at Webster ME on June 21 [28 Jun 1849]
    Deborah & Winthrop COOLIDGE of Livermore ME at Boston MA [10 Apr 1851]
    Eliza Mrs & John FROST at Canaan ME [22 Feb 1849]
    Eliza & Charles H KEEN at Belfast ME [27 Apr 1848]
    Esther C & Mark D KIMBALL at Paris ME [10 Aug 1848]
    George W & Elizabeth F BLETHEN at Swanville ME [28 Jan 1847]
    Hannah & Gustavus HOLMAN of Weld ME at Strong ME [14 Oct 1847]
    Jewitt & Susan EASTMAN of Bradford ME at Charleston ME [13 May 1843]
    Mary A of Lowell ME & William F ABBOT of Belfast ME at Knox ME [29 Jul 1847]
    Mary S & Peter C THOMAS at Weld ME [3 Oct 1840]
    Nancy & Benjamin PHILBRICK 2nd of Mt Vernon ME at Vienna ME [6 Jun 1837]
    Noah J of Tamworth NH & Maria GILPATRICK of Biddeford ME at Saco ME [12 Aug 1852]
    Phebe & Jerome STEVENSON at Belfast ME [25 Jul 1840] & [8 Aug 1840]
    Reuben & Mary E SMITH both of Biddeford ME at Kennebunkport ME [20 Jul 1848]
    T Miss & Lewis DENNIS at Charleston ME [13 May 1843]
    Timothy M & Cynthia A HINCKLEY at Monroe ME [14 Aug 1851]
SANDER William A of Wisconsin Territory & Harriet N SPAULDING of Norridgewock ME at Albany NY [29 Aug 1844]
    Merritt of Brewer ME & Eliza DAVIS at Sangerville ME [25 Dec 1845]
SANDERSON Martha S & Stephen M DENNAN at New Sharon ME on Thanksgiving Day by Rev TILTON of N Wayne [20 Dec 1849]
SANDFORD Benjamin F Capt of Topsham ME & Cordelia RIDEOUT at Bowdoinham ME [26 Mar 1842]
    Maria L & William H LYON of Readfield ME at Augusta ME on 39th ult by Rev N GUNNISON [16 May 1844]
SANFORD Catharine & Capt Z S DALY at Augusta ME [4 Feb 1843]
    Charles H of Sebec ME & Cyntha A CHANDLER of Foxcroft ME at Augusta ME [10 Jul 1845]
    Emeline E & John PRESCOTT of Readfield ME at Augusta ME [22 Feb 1840]

SANFORD (cont.) Emily & Levi L YOUNG both of Augusta ME at Belgrade ME on 10th inst [15 Oct 1846]
Harriet C & Ariel W MANN of Boston MA at Hallowell ME [20 Jun 1844]
M Caroline eld d/o Philo S Esq of W & Rev Eli THURSTON of Hallowell ME at Wrentham MA on 20th inst by Rev FISK [3 Jul 1838]
Mary E & August PALMER at Bath ME [18 Jun 1846]
Oliver S of Boston MA & Maria P NASON at Hallowell ME on 4th inst by Rev E THURSTON [12 Jun 1845]
Samuel W & Lucy H TROWBRIDGE at Bath ME [25 Mar 1847]
Sylvia E & Tabor LYON at Augusta ME on Oct 29 by Rev N GUNNISTON [7 Nov 1844]
Thomas B Capt of New York & E P TAYLOR at Bangor ME [18 Jun 1846]
Thomas H, merchant of Bangor ME & Caroline M BOND youngest d/o late Thomas B Esq in (Hallowell? ME) on 6th inst by Rev E GILLET DD [26 Sept 1837]
William Jr of Bath ME & Augusta COBB at Minot ME [19 Mar 1846]
William, merchant of Bangor ME & Charlotte M COWDEN d/o Joseph C Esq US Consul at Glasgow Scotland at Bucksport ME [1 Oct 1846]

SARGENT/SARGEANT Benjamin E of Bangor ME & Hannah T SAVAGE at Augusta ME on Thurs morning last by Rev WILLIAMS [27 Aug 1846]
Benjamin & Caroline ROGERS at Belfast ME [21 Oct 1847]
Edwin of Lawrence MA & Mary E NORTHY at Pittston ME [11 Jan 1849]
Francis T of New York & Sarah E LEE at Hallowell ME [23 Oct 1851]
Harriet of Canaan ME & Phillip THAYER of Waterville ME at Clinton ME [1 Jul 1847]
Haven B of Boston MA & Elizabeth W GOWEN of Kennebunk ME at Kennebunk [23 May 1844]
J A & Maria WHITING at Portland ME [9 May 1844]
J Q A of Manchester NH & Margaret A DYER at Brunswick ME [15 Jun 1848]
Julia A & Alonzo DAVIS at Sidney ME [25 Jan 1849]
Luther C & Mary Ann FOSS at Brewer ME [6 Jan 1848]
Lydia of Wilton ME & Hubbard WILSON of Hookset NH at Wilton ME? [12 Nov 1842]
Margaret S & John W LOGAN both of Searsport ME at Belfast ME [24 Jun 1847]
Maria A & Elihu LEAVETT at Bethel ME [13 Jul 1848]
Mary G of Methuen MA & Isaac L HIBBARD of Farmington ME? [10 Jun 1843]
Mary H & Watson F COOMBS both of Brewer ME at Bangor ME [8 Apr 1843]
Mary Jane & Joseph T ROBBINS both of Exeter ME at Exeter ME [13 Feb 1845]
Mary & David HINKLEY at Gardiner ME by Rev A C ADAMS [28 Mar 1840]
Mary & David HINKLEY at Gardiner ME [4 Apr 1840]
Mary & J J RUSSELL of Barring at N Yarmouth ME [14 Oct 1836]
Olive M & Randal HOPKINS of Augusta ME at Milbridge ME [1 Mar 1849]
Walter T Rev, pastor of the Baptist Church in Bowdoinham ME, & Joan G QUINT of Topsham ME at Topsham by Rev C C CONE [3 Jul 1841]

SARGISSON William E, formerly of England & Mary L HIGGINS of Spring Hill, Frederickton New Brunswick Canada by T H BATES [30 Jul 1842]

SAUNDERS Caroline E & William N DURHAM at Belfast ME [1 Jan 1852]
    Charles & Harriet M CUMMINGS at Augusta ME on 1 May 1851 by Elder Thomas J DUDLEY [8 May 1851]
    George of T & Margaret HUDDLESTON at Lubec ME [21 Jan 1847]
    Harriet & Mr H MASON at Orland ME [21 Sept 1848]
    Jemima & Phineas AMES at Dover ME? [Aug 15 1844]
    Joseph F of Palermo ME & Jane F PATTEN at China ME [18 Apr 1834]
    Mary E & Lyman TRASK of Belgrade ME at China ME [29 Jul 1847]
    Samuel of New Sharon ME & Nancy BACHELDER at Waterville ME [20 May 1847]
    T O & Glimena WADE at Waterville ME [22 Feb 1849]
    Thaddeus S & Eliza J DOYLE Belfast ME at Orland ME [21 Sept 1848]
    William M of Augusta ME & Martha MAXWELL at Wales ME [9 Jan 1841]

SAVAGE Ashur of Waterville ME & Mary A CHASE of Fairfield ME at Skowhegan ME [16 Jan 1851]
    Betsey Ann & John SMART at Vassalboro ME [6 May 1852]
    Charles Jr & Thankful SAVAGE at Augusta ME on 16th inst by Rev DREW [27 Jun 1844]
    Daniel of (Augusta ME) & Sarah MOOERS of Whitefield ME at Whitefield ME [16 Oct 1845]
    David & Elizabeth MARR at Washington ME [11 Mar 1847]
    Elizabeth P d/o John S & Benjamin P BLAIR at Augusta ME by Rev J H INGRAHAM [4 May 1839]
    George & Susan H COSTELOW at Woolwich ME [20 Feb 1851]
    Hannah T & Benjamin E SARGENT of Bangor ME at Augusta ME on Thurs morning last by Rev WILLIAMS [27 Aug 1846]
    Isaac T & Maria J HOLLAND at Waterville ME [30 Oct 1851]
    John of Augusta ME & Mrs Jane MORRILL of (Winthrop ME) at Augusta on Mon last by Rev FULLER [9 Dec 1843]
    John & Lucinda CHURCHILL at Augusta ME on 3rd inst [21 Oct 1847]
    Josephine L & J Varney STANWOOD at Jefferson ME [18 Oct 1849]
    Lucy Ann & Gorham D SIMMONS formerly of Hallowell ME at Bangor ME on New Years Eve [16 Jan 1845]
    Mary d/o John S of Jay ME & (Ezra TUTTLE of Georgetown MA at Charlestown MA, m int 11 Feb 1842, see "Vital Records of Charlestown MA" p. 674, *NEHGS* 1984) [16 Apr 1842]
    Mary F & Joseph H HALL at Augusta ME on Sun Eve last by Rev C FULLER [19 Nov 1842]
    Mary & Charles D FERRIN at Norridgewock ME [17 Apr 1838]
    Mercy & George KITTREDGE of Readfield ME at Augusta ME on Sun morning last by Rev INGRAHAM [26 Aug 1847]
    Nancy F & Gustavus S DINSMORE at (Augusta) ME on 1st Mar [18 Mar 1852]
    Philena D & James B BROWN at Bloomfield ME both of Norridgewock ME [7 Jun 1849]
    Rebecca & John S FRIEND at Bluehill ME [19 Aug 1847]
    Richard & Lucinda CHASE at Wiscasset ME [6 May 1847]
    Robert W & Marietta B EATON at Fairfield ME [8 Jan 1852]
    Sophilia Mrs & James ALLEN at Bath ME [19 Dec 1834]

SAVAGE (cont.) Thankful & Charles Jr at Augusta ME on 16th inst by Rev DREW [27 Jun 1844]
 Thomas & Mary A McKENNEY at Bath ME [6 Aug 1846]
SAVELS Eliza Ann & Alvin T PERKINS at Gardiner ME [4 Mar 1847]
SAWIN Henry & Mary POWERS at Brunswick ME [13 May 1847]
SAWTELLE/SAWTELL A S, of the firm of SAWTELL & MASON of Hallowell ME & Sarah Ann GIBBS of Livermore ME at Livermore ME on Sun afternoon last [20 Mar 1838]
 Almeda S & Amos TRASK at Waterville ME on 26th May at the Rev Mr WESTON's [10 Jun 1852]
 Amaziah Maj of Bangor ME & Mary JUMPER at Dexter ME [10 Oct 1844]
 Asa H of Corinna ME & Mehitable FLANDERS at Garland ME [11 Apr 1840]
 Benjamin A of Limerick ME & Mary EDGECOMB at Limington ME [4 Sept 1851]
 Charles K & Paulina C BANGS at Sidney ME [19 Feb 1846]
 Deborah E & James E SPRINGER at Augusta ME [29 Jul 1847]
 Edwin of Livermore ME & Helen J RANDALL at Dixfield ME [13 Dec 1849]
 Hannah M & Lucinda PHILPOT at Limerick ME [20 Jul 1848]
 Hannibal M formerly of Cornish ME & Susan M TABOR of Fairhaven MA at Augusta ME on Thur morning last by Rev N W WILLIAMS [18 Dec 1845]
 Harriet & Elisha WOODSUM of Mercer at Sidney ME [25 Sept 1845]
 Howard M of Sidney ME & Elizabeth T LIBBEY of Belgrade ME at Waterville ME [27 Jun 1844]
 Laura Ann & Caleb HARDY of Fryburg ME at Turner ME [4 Apr 1837]
 Malvina A & Elbridge G MORRISON of Canaan ME at Sidney ME on Nov 3d by Rev C GARDINER [18 Nov 1847]
 Maria & Abraham SANBORN Esq of Waterville ME at Norridgewock ME [5 Oct 1839]
 Nathan of Turner ME & Maria HINDS of Livermore ME at Livermore ME [4 Apr 1837]
 Paulina & Dr John MERRILL at Norridgewock ME [13 Nov 1838]
 S A P & George H DICKERMAN of Stoughton MA at Sidney ME [15 Jul 1847]
 Zypporah B & James F SPRINGER at Augusta ME on July 18 by L CUSHING Esq [19 Aug 1847]
SAWYER Abigail & Silas MERRILL of Saco ME at Portland ME [26 Dec 1844]
 Augustus D of Vassalboro ME & Harriet SMITH at Hallowell ME [22 Feb 1840]
 Benjamin W of Bangor ME & Nancy J H ROBINSON at Thomaston ME [16 Sept 1836]
 Charles & Elizabeth PLUMMER at Augusta ME [23 Jan 1838]
 Cordelia A & George TITCOMB of Portland ME at Saco ME [18 Feb 1847]
 David B of Norway ME & Fanny L BRACKETT of Harrison ME at Norway ME [8 Aug 1840]
 Eliza A & Abel BLANCHARD at Belgrade ME on Mar 1 by M A CHANDLER Esq [8 Mar 1849]
 Eliza B & Benjamin ADAMS Esq at New Portland ME [16 Aug 1849]
 Eliza J of Vinalhaven ME & Capt William YEATON Jr in Northport ME [11 Feb 1847]

SAWYER (cont.) Emerson of Hampden ME & Sarah PATTERSON at Bangor ME [19 Nov 1842]
    Emily J & Eleazer SNELL at Starks ME on Jan 13 [6 Feb 1851] & [6 Mar 1851]
    Frances A C & Sumner HUTCHINSON at Atkinson ME [8 Jul 1847]
    Hannah J & Allyn HOLMES at Gardiner ME on Jan 28 by Rev CLAPP [27 Feb 1838]
    Harlow H & Margaret Ann ATWOOD at North Wayne ME on Sun Sept 26 by Rev C FULLER [7 Oct 1847]
    Harriet K & Gideon GILMAN at (Augusta) ME [6 Jan 1848]
    Harriet N & Rufus P WILBUR at Portland ME [12 Aug 1836]
    Isaac Jr of Hallowell ME & Harriet BECKFORD of Richmond at Augusta ME [19 Sept 1837]
    Isaac & Salome THOMPSON at Limerick ME [16 Jul 1846]
    James Dr of Saco ME & Sophia FOSS at Limington ME [3 Jun 1847]
    James Elder of Saco ME & Mrs Eliza ATKINSON of Buxton ME at Saco ME [15 May 1851]
    John E & Dianna DRAKE at Elliotsville ME [26 Jun 1835]
    Joseph R & Sarah HASKELL at Levant ME [18 Jan 1840]
    Lydia & Elishia BARKER at Norridgewock ME [27 Apr 1848]
    Martha at Bloomfield ME & Martin K PLUMMER [17 Jun 1847]
    Martha & Solomon ADAMS Jr of Farmington ME at Wilton ME [19 Sept 1844]
    Mary P of Westbrook ME & Josiah COBB of Falmouth ME at Cumberland ME [15 Jan 1846]
    Olive Amanda of Wayne NY & Rev Edward HOTCHKISS of the Methodist E Conference at W [23 Mar 1839]
    Paul Capt of Isleboro ME & Lavinia REA at Castine ME [7 Jun 1849]
    Phineas H & Adeline W DRAKE at Elliotsville ME? [3 Apr 1851]
    R M Rev, Pastor of the Congregational Church of Winthrop ME & Sophia C BLAKE at Otisfield [8 Jan 1852]
    Rebecca M & Charles W BUTLER at (Augusta) ME on 6th May [13 May 1852]
    Sarah E & Clement PANNELL Jr at Portland ME [11 Jan 1844]
    Sarah & James SMITH of Boothbay ME at Wiscasset ME [20 Mar 1851]
    Sarah & Moses FICKETT at Millbridge ME? [17 Aug 1848]
    Susan A & Bounds C DINSMORE both of China ME at China [1 Feb 1849]
    Truman H & Elizabeth M ANDERSON at Norridgewock ME [27 Jan 1848]

SCALES Enoch Col & Octavia WOODMAN at Wilton ME [30 Aug 1849]
    George W & Sarah J SOULE at Waterville ME [2 Aug 1849]

SCAMMON Augustus L of Saco ME & Hannah E LEWIS of Kennebunk ME at Biddeford ME [3 Aug 1848]
    Charles M & Susan C NORRIS at Pittston ME [24 Aug 1848]
    Cyrus Rev & Mary Y KENDALL at Pittston ME on 27th inst by Rev ROBINSON [4 Jul 1837]
    E E Miss & Mr G G PRESCOTT at Waterville ME [24 Feb 1848]
    Franklin & Harriet AGRY at Hallowell ME [21 Sept 1833]
    J Young Esq, counselor at law of Chicago, IL & Mary Ann DEARBORN at Bath ME on Thurs eve 10th inst by Rev WORCESTER [22 Aug 1837]
    John Q Esq & Julia A A CUTTS at Saco ME [3 Jul 1845]
    Martha Ann & Eliphalet NOTT at Saco ME [15 Oct 1846]

SCAMMON (cont.) Mary A & Joseph THOMAS of Eden ME at Franklin ME [23 Jan 1841]
    Mary H & Calvin S PHILLIPS Esq at Rockland ME [11 Sept 1851]
    Rachel C & Arthur BOOTHBY at Saco ME [29 Mar 1849]
    Seth of Saco ME & Lavinia PERKINS at Kennebunkport ME [3 Jul 1841]
    William F & Martha BARRY at Biddeford ME [31 Jan 1850]
SCHANKS Manetta & Washington HAWKINS of York ME at Eastport ME [28 May 1846]
SCHOFFIELD Martha of Livermore ME & John BROWN Jr at Fayette ME [11 Feb 1833]
SCHWARTZ Harriet A & Calvin HOCH of Thomaston ME at Waldoboro ME [12 Dec 1837]
    John F & Mary Jane ACORN at North Waldoboro ME [15 May 1851]
    Louisa of Waldoboro ME & Aaron LAW of Boston at Indian Head, Nashville NH [18 Oct 1849]
SCOFIELD Jane of Wilton ME? & Mathew LORD of Bridgeport at New York on Apr 5 [8 May 1835]
    Mary M & Ebenezer FARRINGTON Jr both of Livermore ME at Fayette ME [29 Jan 1839]
    Alice D & Capt Albert CURTIS of Brunswick ME at Harpswell ME [10 Apr 1841]
SCOTT Charles A of Dixfield ME & Lucinda S MORSE of Norway ME at Bethel ME [9 Aug 1849]
    Julia A W & E P GERRISH at Portland ME [16 May 1844]
    Mary J & Hiram AVERILL at Readfield ME [15 Feb 1849]
    Orange Rev, presiding eld at Providence Dist, New England (Methodist?) Conf & Eliza DEARBORN of Portland ME at Portland on Mon last by Rev C BAKER [9 Oct 1835]
    Peter Astle, LT in the British Navy & Maria ARCHIBALD d/o George HOBBS Esq at Eastport ME [8 Apr 1847]
    Sarah Maria & John WARE Esq of Athens ME at Wayne ME [22 Jan 1842]
SCRIBNER Albert L & Sabrina M THOMPSON both of Unity ME at Thorndike ME [2 Oct 1851]
    Betsey & Mr B D FOWLER at Unity ME [16 Mar 1848]
    E H Col of Waterville ME & Sarah J M'CRILLIS at Great Falls NH [9 Sept 1847]
    Elmore & Lovis GROVER at Letter B ME [8 Jan 1846]
    John H & Hannah BOOTHBY at Unity ME [21 Jan 1843]
    Lieviatha of Letter B ME & James L BLACK of Cambridge NH at Letter B [8 Jan 1846]
    Mariby & Artemas W COFFIN of Freedom ME at Unity ME [26 Dec 1837]
    Virgil & Isadore R ALLEN both of Readfield ME at Hallowell ME [28 Sept 1848]
SCRUTON Michael H of Augusta ME & Lydia AUSTIN at Belgrade ME on 21st ult [2 Oct 1845]
SEABURY Edward & Harriet GOODWIN at North Yarmouth ME [13 Jul 1848]
    Thomas Esq of Parkman ME & Mrs Catherine HEATH at Mt Vernon ME [8 Feb 1849]
SEARLE Hannah, d/o Samuel S Esq, & Amory PRESCOTT at Madison ME [21 Feb 1834]

Marriage Notices from the "Maine Farmer"

SEARLE (cont.) Ira & Amanda Malvina OSBORNE at Madison ME [16 May 1834]
    Martha of Skowhegan ME & Martin O HAZEN of Nashua NH at Lawrence MA [18 Dec 1851]
SEARS John W & Mary J PRATT at E Livermore ME [6 Dec 1849]
    Mary K & Samuel M VEAZIE at Rockland ME [1 Jan 1852]
    Moses B & Deborah THOMAS both of Winthrop ME at Wayne ME by Rev ROBINSON [9 Nov 1833]
    Wm H & Rhoda WYMAN of Fayette ME [21 Dec 1839]
SEAVEY Ansel of Starks ME & Zenette S YOUNG of Fayette ME at Wayne ME by N B FROST Esq [25 Feb 1847]
    Betsey & Heber CLOUGH at Kennebunkport ME [8 Apr 1836]
    Betsey L & Thomas L FOWLER at Saco ME [20 Nov 1835]
    Eliza J of Hallowell ME & Alexander MORRILL of Litchfield ME at Litchfield [10 Jul 1845]
    John Jr of Starks ME & Lucia Maria BRAY of Skowhegan ME at Bloomfield ME [14 Mar 1850]
    Ruth Ann at Vienna ME & Daniel CARR of Mt Vernon ME [26 Oct 1839]
    Clarissa & James SPENCER both of Starks ME at Anson ME by William VARNUM Esq [5 Dec 1834]
SEDGELEY/SEDGLEY James Jr & Rhoda LEAVITT at Winthrop ME on 14th inst by Rev MORSE [Dec 23 1847]
    Lucy & William M JOCE of Readfield ME at (Winthrop) ME by Rev Mr ROBINSON [9 Sept 1843]
SEEKINS Emily L & Charles BAILEY at Windsor ME [21 Sept 1848]
    Lucy Maria of Swanville ME & Samuel S KEITH Jr of Brooks ME [1 Feb 1849]
    Margaret of Windsor ME & James WARD of Vassalboro ME at Windsor [19 Sept 1837]
SEGARS Nathan of Durham ME & Rebecca CHAPMAN of Mercer ME at Augusta ME on July 3rd [15 Jul 1852]
SEKINS Mary & Moses CURTIS at Swanville ME [28 Jan 1847]
SELDEN Edward & Mary Ann BATES at Norridgewock ME [19 Aug 1843]
    Mary W, d/o Calvin S Esq of Norridgewock ME & Rev Alexander BURGESS, rector of said church at Augusta ME on the 17th inst at St Mark's Church by Rev FALES of Brunswick ME [25 Sept 1845]
SENTER Frederick A Capt, master of the brig *Porto Rico*, & Jane H BARTER at Hallowell ME by Rev DREW [13 Nov 1845]
SERGENT Elizabeth & Albion K MOORE Esq, formerly of Skowhegan ME, at Savannah GA [2 Jan 1845]
SESSION Betsey A & Supply G KNOX at Biddeford ME [14 Sept 1848]
SESSIONS Joseph & Mary DUNNING at Brunswick ME [2 Nov 1833]
SETHERS Margaret of Hallowell ME & Lewis HOBBS of Livermore ME at Hallowell ME on Sunday eve 22nd inst by Rev E M TOBIE [31 Oct 1837]
SEVERANCE Anna & Columbus ARNOLD both of (Augusta ME) at Skowhegan ME [24 Jul 1845]
    Charles formerly of Augusta ME & Maria A FARNUM of Cazenovia NY at Buffalo NY [18 Jul 1837]
    Ephraim of Bangor ME & Susanna MORRILL at Belfast ME [3 Jul 1838]

SEVERANCE (cont.) Hannah & Benjamin EARL at Bangor ME [16 Oct 1845]
SEVERS Harriet N & Otis F BURLEIGH at Wayne ME [20 Jun 1840]
SEVERY Silas of Dixfield ME & Betsey GOULD at Carthage ME [9 May 1837]
    Willard & Roan HISCOCK at Dixfield ME [18 Jun 1846]
SEVEY Nancy Ann & Capt Alex CUNNINGHAM both of Wiscasset ME at Dresden ME [7 Feb 1850]
SEWALL/SEWELL B Dr of Somerville MA & Hannah W SHEPPARD at Wiscasset ME [5 Jun 1845]
    Benjamin C of Bath ME & Susan P CARPENTER at Foxcroft ME [14 Nov 1844]
    Caleb B & Catharine S TURNER formerly of Livermore ME at Quincy IL [11 Sept 1845]
    Caroline A & George T SOULE at Farmington ME [21 Jun 1849]
    Caroline d/o Charles S & James S MANLEY of Norridgewock ME at Augusta ME on Weds morning last by Rev Benjamin TAPPAN [7 Dec 1839]
    Catharine R & Enoch H TIBBETS at Hampden ME [22 Feb 1849]
    Charles A, merchant of Shreveport, and formerly of Hallowell ME & Amelia M d/o David GILMAR Esq, formerly of Montgomery AL at Hickory Hill, Parish of Caddo, LA on the 22nd of Feb [10 Apr 1838]
    David & Louisa A STEPHENS at Sumner ME on 22nd inst [18 Apr 1840]
    Elizabeth & Stephen HILL of Baltimore MD [23 Aug 1849]
    Frances E & John STEWART of Brunswick ME at China ME on 30th March [10 Apr 1851]
    Frances & John STEWART of Bath ME at Augusta ME [24 Apr 1851]
    Frederick D Esq & Evelina H GOVE at Bath ME [22 Nov 1849]
    Hannah M & Dudley GILMAN at Bath ME [18 Oct 1849]
    Harriet H & Abraham L CUTTER of Boston MA at Bath ME [14 Nov 1844]
    Henry Gen & Elizabeth LOWELL at Augusta ME [14 Sept 1833]
    Henry & Harriet V SMITH at Augusta ME on 3d inst by Rev BURGESS [11 Nov 1847]
    Joanna & Capt Charles D LEMONT of Bath at Hallowell ME on Thurs morning last by Rev E THURSTON [31 Jul 1838]
    Louisa A Esq of Farmington ME & Joshua FOLLANSBEE of the US Army at Washington City [13 May 1843]
    Lucy P & Ezekiel H WELCH at Bath ME [10 Jan 1850
    Margaret W & Capt James T MORSE at Phipsburg ME [8 Nov 1849]
    Martha E d/o Daniel S of Farmington ME & Prof Lorenzo D McCABE of Athens OH at Washington DC [28 Aug 1845]
    Mary H & Samuel CONY Esq of Orono ME at Farmington ME [9 NOv 1833]
    Matilda B & Albion P SNOW at Winthrop ME [3 Jun 1852]
    Samuel M of Sangerville ME & Hannah C TRUFANT at Winthrop ME on 16th Oct by Rev P JAQUES [30 Oct 1851]
    Serena & Mr W H CHAPMAN at China ME on 8th inst [25 May 1848]
    Thomas Rev s/o Prof Thomas S of Washington DC & Julia E WATERS d/o F G W Esq of Bath ME at Baltimore MD on 19th inst by Rev Dr DORSEY [28 Nov 1844]
    William D Jr & Lydia FITTS at Bath ME [17 Apr 1851]

SEWALL (cont.) William of Brunswick ME & Matilda PETERS of Brunswick ME at Augusta ME on 2 Jan by George MULLIKEN Esq [23 Jan 1851]
  William Rev & Miriam PURRINGTON of Topsham ME at Topsham ME [27 Jun 1840]
SEYMOUR Samuel & Frances B BLAKE at Brewer ME [31 Aug 1839]
SHACKFORD Samuel & Mary M TINKHAM at Eastport ME [7 Aug 1851]
SHANNON James of Louisville KY & Sarah H HOWES at Boston MA [12 Oct 1848]
SHARKLEY Ebenezer & Harriet SHIRLAND at Winslow ME [11 May 1848]
SHACKLEY Louisa J of Norway ME & Samuel M NEWHALL of Paris ME at Norway ME [1 Oct 1842]
  R of Portland ME & Eliza BLACKSTONE at Pownal ME [30 Jan 1845]
  Winfield S of Canton ME & Louisa FRANKLIN of Peru ME at Hartford ME [4 Dec 1845]
SHALLON Edward ae 15 & Susan STEVENS ae 13 at Keesville NY [10 Apr 1835]
SHANNON Samuel T & Martha A P STEVENS at Saco ME [6 Nov 1845]
SHATTUCK Joseph U & Catharine LESSNER at Thomaston ME [19 Aug 1847]
  Lucy & Joseph BROWN at Solon ME [22 Jan 1846]
SHAW Abigail H & Rufus BRAINARD 2nd at Winthrop ME on Sunday evening 20th ult by Rev Franklin MERRIAM [12 Jun 1841]
  B F, principal of Vassalboro Academy & Mary Jane PRATT d/o Benjamin P Esq of North Yarmouth ME at North Yarmouth on Thanksgiving eve [11 Dec 1841]
  Benjamin W of Garland ME & Sarah LIBBEY at Corinna ME [4 Mar 1843]
  Benjamin & Livona MILLER both of Sidney ME at Augusta ME [9 Mar 1839]
  Betsey & Nathaniel DUTTON at Augusta ME by L CUSHING Esq [11 Apr 1844]
  Caroline Elizabeth d/o Earl S Esq & Isaac H CHANDLER at Boston MA [9 Dec 1843]
  Catharine of Weymouth MA & Oliver MOULTON at Pittston ME [11 Jan 1849]
  Charles & Lucy ROWELL by Rev SAWYER at Augusta ME [27 May 1847]
  Charlotte A formerly of Norridgewock ME & Z Eugene STONE formerly of Paris ME at Lowell MA [11 Feb 1847]
  Curtis & Typhena CROCKETT both of Standish ME at Windham ME [24 May 1849]
  Cyrus H of China ME & Mary Ann YOUNG at Thomaston ME [22 Jan 1852]
  Daniel P Esq of Sanford ME & Sarah Elizabeth WAKEFIELD at Kennebunkport ME [9 Oct 1851]
  Daniel W & Helen L TARBLE at Levant ME [22 Jul 1852]
  Diana E & Dr Samuel TEWKSBURY of Frankfort ME at Oxford ME [20 Jun 1844]
  E N of China & Elizabeth GIBBS of Livermore ME at Hallowell ME [31 Jan 1850]
  Ebenezer of China ME & Mrs Mary H WHITTING of Charleston MA at Boston MA [27 may 1843]
  Edmond W of Portland ME & Miriam LOWELL at Minot ME [5 Feb 1839]

SHAW (cont.) Elias W of China ME & Mary E MORSE at Hallowell ME on 2d inst [11 Sept 1845]
Elizabeth A & Perkins RUSSELL at Readfield ME on 3d inst [19 Oct 1848]
Elizabeth & Edward P WELTS at Bloomfield ME [10 Jun 1852]
Emily N of Industry ME & Manchester F WAUGH of Mercer ME at Industry ME at the meeting house on 16th ult by Rev John PERHAM [20 Jun 1844]
Evebline B & Nathan HAVEY at (Augusta) ME [27 Jan 1848]
Frances & John McKENNAN of Deer Isle ME at Thomaston ME [5 Feb 1846]
Francis E & Mrs Velona WHITMAN of Auburn ME by John E BRIGGS Esq [5 Jun 1845] & [19 Jun 1845]
Frederick E Esq of Orland ME & Sarah E HENSON formerly assistant teacher in Foxcroft Academy (Dover-Foxcroft ME) at Bangor ME [25 Mar 1852]
George W of Cincinnati OH & Sarah E ARNOLD of Mercer ME at Norridgewock ME [15 May 1838]
George & Pauline B HANDY at Albion ME [8 Jun 1839]
Hannah M d/o A M S & E M CLARK at Winthrop ME [11 Dec 1838]
Hannah M & Horatio MORRILL at Palmyra ME [7 Jan 1847]
Hannah W & Josiah N FOGG of Readfield ME at Winthrop ME by Rev FILES [22 Jun 1839]
Jacob of Lowell MA & Mary Jane KNAPP at Leeds ME [25 Nov 1847]
Jane S & Jarius KING at Paris ME [30 Jan 1848]
Joanna C & Jonathan R GORDON of New Sharon ME at Norridgewock ME [7 Dec 1839]
John W & Mary H SMITH at Woolwich ME [25 Apr 1837]
John & Louisa SAFFORD at Augusta ME [4 Apr 1840]
John & Ruth S STETSON at Bath ME [13 May 1836]
Joseph A & Caroline S WEBBER by Asaph R NICHOLS Esq at Augusta ME on 17th inst [21 Sept 1848]
Julia Ann B & Mason P RICHARDS both of Nashua and formerly of Winthrop at Nashua NH on Mar 4 by Rev RICHARDS [6 Mar 1841]
Martha of Turner ME & Lorain COBB of Winthrop ME at Turner ME on May 28 [17 Jun 1843]
Martha & Alexander GRAY of Woolwich ME at Winthrop ME on 25th ult by Rev MORSE [9 Dec 1847]
Mary B d/o Capt S & Capt John McCLINTOCK of Bristol at Winthrop ME on Sept 26 by Rev Franklin MERRIAM [16 Oct 1841]
Mary C of Wiscasset ME & Charles B CARLETON at Whitefield ME [5 Apr 1849]
Mary M & Capt Alvin P DREW at Bath ME [8 Jan 1846]
Mary Mrs of Sebec ME & Daniel AMES of Sangerville ME at Swanville ME [26 Dec 1837]
Mary S Mrs & Frederick LACROIS both of Winthrop ME at Wayne ME on 10th inst by Benjamin LOMBARD Esq [21 Feb 1841]
Mehitable & John S FLAGG at Clinton ME [11 Mar 1852]
Miss of Boston MA & Rev GANNETT of West Gardiner ME at Hallowell ME [28 Aug 1847]
Nathaniel T of Buckfield ME & Amanda B HOLLAND at Livermore ME [27 Sept 1849]

SHAW (cont.) Parker D of Brunswick ME & Lydia W VARNEY at China ME on Oct 14th by William PERCIVAL Esq [18 Oct 1849]
    Phila & Cyrus HERSEY at Auburn ME [15 Jan 1846]
    Rachel V of Sidney ME & Nathaniel PERKINS of Augusta ME at Sidney ME by L CUSHING Esq [16 May 1844]
    Rachel & Morrill CAMPBELL at Bath ME [2 Mar 1848]
    Sabra W of Boston MA & David F WAUGH of Mercer ME at Norridgewock ME [4 Oct 1849]
    Sarah A & Peter ARMSTRONG at Phipsburg ME [23 Jun 1852]
    Sarah B & Miller CROWELL at Augusta ME by Rev W A DREW [27 Nov 1838]
    Sarah C & Gustavus HAYES both of Industry ME at Industry ME [20 Jun 1849]
    Sarah & Amasa WOOD at Winthrop ME on Thurs morning last by Elder HOUGHTON [Dec 28 1833]
    Seth P Jr of Rockland ME & Sarah V FALES at Thomaston ME [20 Nov 1851]
    Susan J & Gardiner H BROOKINGS at Woolwich ME [24 Apr 1851]
    Susannah of Waterville ME & Jeremiah P BRIDGES of Lexington MA at Clinton ME on 26th Mar [10 Apr 1851]
    William H of Edmunds & Sarah DUDLEY at Dennysville ME [20 Sept 1849]
SHAY Elisa Jane & W D NEWDISK at Arrowsic ME [17 Sept 1846]
SHEA Jane & John CLIFFORD at Georgetown ME [27 May 1852]
    Mary R & John AVERY at Phipsburg ME [22 Apr 1852]
    Nathan of Georgetown ME & Susan SHEA at Pittston ME [11 Apr 1840]
SHEAF William of Portland ME & Lucy A FISK at Ellsworth ME [9 Sept 1847]
SHEDD Cynthia W of Madaceunk ME? & Tristram D PALMER of Bangor ME at Hermon ME [22 Aug 1844]
SHELDON Alfred of Waldo Plantation ME & Betsey CHOAT at Montville ME [28 May 1842]
    Parker Hon of Gardiner ME & Lucia OSGOOD of Palermo ME at Dorcester MA [18 Nov 1847]
SHEPARD - SHEPHERD - SHEPHARD
    Adeline & James L BOYNTON at Hallowell ME by Stewart FOSTER Esq [26 Jun 1845]
    Amasa of Jefferson ME & Eloisa G ARNOLD of Hope ME at Whitefield ME [14 Mar 1840]
    Clarinda & Franklin BRAINERD at Readfield ME on July 20 by Rev LEWIS [7 Aug 1851]
    Isabella W & Crosby HINDS Esq of Clinton ME at Waterville ME [19 Jun 1841]
    Josiah H & Statira DAVIS at Union ME [4 Jan 1849]
    Lorenzo H D & Sarah H TUCK at Biddeford ME [27 Jul 1848]
    N B of Lowell MA & Ellen MORSE at Bloomfield ME [1 Nov 1849]
    Noah E Esq of Union ME & Jane Ann BARNARD of Waldoboro ME at N Waldoboro on Dec 10th by Rev H W LATHAM [18 Dec 1851]
    Tryphena P & John BROWN at Bridgton ME 30th ult [20 Feb 1845]
SHEPLEY A N C & William H SMITH at Saco ME [22 Jun 1848]
    Emily E & George BARSTOW of Hillsborough NH at Saco ME [20 Jun 1844]

SHEPLEY (cont.) Leonard D at Portland ME & Frances CHASE [17 May 1849]
SHEPPARD Hannah W & B SEWALL, M.D., of Somerville MA at Wiscasset ME [5 Jun 1845]
SHERBURN/SHERBURNE A F & Caroline CRAIG at Readfield ME [28 Sept 1848]
   Abby R of Augusta ME & Joel B BARTLETT of Kennebec ME at Hallowell ME [16 Oct 1851]
   Cyrus S & Rebecca A STINSON at Prospect ME on 6th [15 Jul 1852]
   Lewis of Oxford ME & Miss H A PACKARD of Buckfield ME at Turner ME [23 Nov 1848]
   Tryphena & Charles H HEWITT at Prospect ME on July 4 [15 Jul 1852]
SHERER Charles & Adelia H ROBBINS at Thomaston ME [15 Oct 1846]
SHERIDAN Mary Mrs & Francis DELANY of Brunswick ME at Augusta ME by Rev DREW [4 Feb 1847]
SHERMAN A M & Mr J THOMPSON at East Thomaston ME [13 Apr 1848]
   Abiel W Capt at Boston MA & Clementina E CLIFFORD both of Edgecomb ME on [Nov 11 1843]
   Alpheus of Thomaston ME & Mary E WHITCOMB at Yarmouth ME [25 Sept 1851]
   Alvin & Lowly Ann PERRY at Appleton ME [8 Jul 1847]
   Daniel of Perry & Mrs Nancy LANE of Calais ME at Calais ME [4 Mar 1836]
   Eliza A & Silas E HOXIE at Sidney ME [27 Feb 1838]
   Elizabeth & Hanson LIBBY of Lowell at Monson ME [17 Jun 1847]
   I M & Lucy B LEAVITT by Elder FREEMAN at (Augusta) ME [26 Oct 1848]
   Isaac & Mary Jane DEARBORN at Augusta ME by Anson CHURCH Esq [29 Oct 1846]
   Joseph Rev, professor in Jackson College, Columbia TN & Narcissa B MITCHELL at Portland ME [3 Oct 1837]
   Lucy C & John NORWOOD at Thomaston ME [Jul 1 1847]
   Sarah H Mrs of Augusta ME & Edmund J BAKER Esq of Dorchester MA at Springfield MA [16 Sept 1847]
   Thomas Dr of Dresden ME & Sarah H BOWMAN of Augusta ME at Augusta [23 Nov 1833]
SHERMON Henry A & Sylvia JACKSON at North Belmont ME [19 Aug 1843]
SHERY Ansel & Martha L BENNET at Starks ME [30 Apr 1842]
SHILLING David & Mary WAIT at Columbus OH [1 Jul 1836]
    In these hard times our creditors will say,
    To wait with us they no longer are willing;
    But here's a tender-hearted lady gay,
    Who, by her a-Waiting, got an honest Shilling.
SHIRLAND Harriet & Ebenezer SHARKLEY at Winslow ME [11 May 1848]
SHIRTLIFF - see SHURLIFF
   Silvin & Lois TIMBERLAKE at Livermore ME on 5th inst by Maj Isaac STRICKLAND [13 Nov 1835]
SHOREY Ancel & Mary E WOODSUM at Waterville ME [5 Aug 1847]
   Daniel Jr & Elizabeth R MAXEY by Rev Mr KALLOCH at (Augusta) ME on Sunday evening last [12 Oct 1848]
   Daniel of S Berwick ME & Charlotte YOUNG at York ME [20 Aug 1846]

Marriage Notices from the "Maine Farmer"

SHOREY (cont.) Henry A & Charlotte L McKACHNIE both of Waterville at Auburn ME [23 Jun 1852]
    Hiram Esq & Nancy LYDSTONE at Litchfield ME [28 Nov 1844]
    John Jr of Athens ME & Charlotte BROWN d/o Rev Amaziah B at Harmony ME by Rev TRIPP [23 Jul 1842]
    Louisa J & George HUNTER of Clinton ME at Oldtown ME [21 Oct 1847]
    Lucinda A & George H ESTY both of Waterville ME at Augusta ME [18 Nov 1843]
    Sarah & Jacob GIFFORD both of Sidney ME at Waterville ME [4 Sept 1845]
    Sophia Jane & Josiah TILTON at Monmouth ME by J M HEATH Esq [13 Dec 1849]
SHORT Abigail D & Capt Waldo COLLINS at Bangor ME [20 Aug 1846]
    Henrietta F & Austin JONES at Bangor ME [15 Aug 1844]
    Moses & Mrs Almira M CLARK at Bangor ME [12 Jun 1845]
SHUMAN Mary A & Hiram TEAGUE at Waldoboro ME [5 Sept 1840]
SHUMAN Harriet & Elijan GUBTEL at Union ME by J H BECKETT Esq [15 Jul 1836]
    Joseph & Almira WALTER at Waldoboro ME by Reuben ORFF Esq [23 Dec 1847]
    Solomon & Dorothy WELT at Waldoboro ME [25 Dec 1835]
SHURLIFF -see **SHIRTLIFF**
    Maria A & Calvin W WHITMAN of Hebron ME at Livermore ME [27 Nov 1851]
SHUTE Harriet A & Alvah PAGE at Belfast ME by Rev A PINGREE [11 Mar 1843]
    Mary A & Nahum M BERRY at Prospect ME [1 Feb 1844]
    Sewall & Bethana STONE at Prospect ME [13 Jun 1844]
    Thomas P & Annett M GRANT at Prospect ME [13 Jun 1844]
    Thomas R Capt & Azubah A DeCROW of Freedom ME at Belfast ME [14 Oct 1847]
SIAS Hannah F & Samuel MURPHY at Oldtown ME [18 Jun 1846]
    Samuel P of Roxbury MA & Eunice MILLIKEN at Saco ME [19 Feb 1846]
SIBLEY Ebenezer B & Laura PERKINS at Augusta ME [28 Nov 1837]
    Persis youngest d/o William S Esq & Hon Charles ANDREWS Speaker of the House of Representatives at Freedom ME on 22nd ult by Rev John TRUE [9 Jul 1842]
SIDELENGER Abby & Joseph CHAPMAN Jr both of Nobleboro ME at Thomaston ME [11 Mar 1847]
    Boyd of Waldoboro ME & Nancy MORSE at Friendship ME [19 Aug 1852]
    E J & Samuel FULLER Jr both of Union at Warren ME [30 May 1844]
    John of Nobleboro & Caroline GROSS at Waldoboro ME [14 Mar 1844]
    Josiah & Sarah ACHORN all of W at Waldoboro ME [26 Feb 1846]
SIDELINKER Franklin & Christiana SMITH at Dover ME [25 Apr 1850]
SIDES John Esq & Martha CURRIER at Waldoboro ME [22 Apr 1852]
SIEGARS Frederick & Maria E SIEGARS at South Dresden ME [8 Jan 1852]
    Maria E & Frederick SIEGARS at South Dresden ME [8 Jan 1852]
SILSBY David B of Lewiston ME & Nancy W RICHARDS at Ellsworth ME [6 Nov 1851]
    Nancy Jane & Seneca W HEATH at Bath ME [26 Oct 1848]
    G M & Elizabeth M GETCHELL at Hallowell ME [25 Mar 1847]

SILSBY (cont.) Horace of Bluehill ME & Sophia A CLARKE at Brewer ME [3 Jan 1850]
SILVER Lavina & Elijah MORSE of Jay ME at Rumford ME [6 Apr 1839]
  Margaret of North Bend & John B ROWSE formerly of (Winthrop ME) at N Hamilton Co OH [1 Jan 1846]
SILVERY Sylvester & Cyrene PHILLIPS at Eastport ME [14 Sept 1848]
SIMMONS Lydia L & Abner PITTS at Gardiner ME [15 May 1851]
SIMMONS Amelia L of Eastport ME & George HARRINGTON of Roxbury MA at Boston MA [24 Jul 1838]
  Chamberlain & Clarissa ORFF at Waldoboro ME [8 Feb 1840]
  George C & Sophia M DOE at Fairfield ME [8 Mar 1849]
  Gorham D formerly of Hallowell ME & Lucy Ann SAVAGE at Bangor ME on New Years Eve [16 Jan 1845]
  Harvey B & Jane SUMNER of Union ME at Warren ME [29 Jul 1852]
  Sarah & Mark JOHNSON at Hallowell ME [7 Feb 1834]
  Willard S & Charlotte TITCOMB at N Yarmouth ME [2 May 1834]
  William Francis Y & Susan MATHEWS at Camden ME [24 Apr 1835]
SIMONDS Rebecca & Sewall LANCASTER Esq at Augusta ME by J R ABBOT Esq [25 Feb 1847]
SIMONS Thomas Rev American Missionary & C J HUNTINGDON recently of Brookfield MA at Maulmein, Burma [14 Mar 1834]
SIMONTON Ann T & Daniel HARDY of Boston MA at Portland ME [7 Nov 1844]
  Eliza A & Robert WHITE of Belfast ME at Camden ME [23 Oct 1845]
  Joshua P & Mary E ROLLINS at Camden ME [4 Mar 1852]
SIMPSON Clarissa & Joseph SPAULDING Jr of Dixmont ME in Plymouth ME on the 17th inst by Jesse ROBINSON Esq of Dixmont ME [30 Jan 1838]
  Emeline P of Winslow ME & James P HILL at Waterville ME [1 Mar 1849]
  George & Mary FONTJAMI at Bath ME [16 Jan 1841]
  John Rev. of the Maine (Methodist?) Annual Conference & Amanda CLARK of Moultonboro NH at Moultonboro NH [6 Jul 1839]
  Mahala & Reuben EMERY at Winslow ME [25 Apr 1840]
  Martha L & George M FREEMAN at York ME [16 Jan 1838]
  Mary D & Joseph WINE at Bath ME [15 Apr 1852]
  Orinda & Joseph GARDNER both of Eastport ME at St Andrews New Brunswick Canada [21 Aug 1851]
  Samuel of Alna ME & Dorinda WATSON of Fayette ME at Fayette by Rev P POND [3 Jul 1841]
  Sarah & Dennis THURSTON at Avon ME [29 Nov 1849]
  Thomas Jr & Harriet SNOW at Brunswick ME [1 Feb 1844]
  Tufton & Harriet GETCHELL both of Winslow ME at Waterville ME by the Rev GARDNER [12 Aug 1843]
SINCLAIR Almira & John O BEAN at Bangor ME [11 Jul 1844]
  Amelia A & Osgood RUSSELL of Dublin NH at Ellsworth ME [23 Sept 1847]
  Hannah & Ezra WHITMAN at Winthrop ME on Sat eve Dec 31 by Rev David THURSTON [13 Jan 1837]
  Harriet of Monmouth & Addison BROWN, M.D., of Lewiston ME at Litchfield ME on 12 Jan [16 Jan 1851]
  Lucinda & William WEBB at Bath ME [31 Jul 1835]

Marriage Notices from the "Maine Farmer" 371

SINGER Mary Jane of T & Capt James HENDERSON at Thomaston ME [23 Oct 1841]
SINGLETON John H of Thomaston ME & Angelica B WESTON at Warren ME [16 Aug 1849]
SINKLER Benjamin of Levant ME & Mrs Susanna ATKINSON of Corinna ME at Newport ME [13 Jul 1839]
    Clarissa A & Sullivan MAXIM at Palmyra ME [21 Jan 1833]
SINKLEY Julia Ann & Thomas HATCH at Hallowell ME on 6th inst by Eld H ALBEE [19 Jun 1845]
SINNOTT Lydia T of S & Anson B COBB of Biddeford ME at Saco ME [30 Oct 1845]
    Martha & David WOODMAN at Saco ME [15 Mar 1849]
SIPHERS Joseph & Elizabeth A LIBBY at Gardiner ME [10 May 1849]
SIVADIE Henry & Hannah F BRANCH at Augusta ME [16 Jul 1846]
SKEELE John P Rev of Hallowell ME & Elizabeth BLODGETT at Bucksport ME [20 Feb 1851]
SKEETUP Matthias ("a colored [Black] gentleman") & Jerusha CARTER (white lady) both of Carthage ME at Weld ME [21 Mar 1844]
SKILLIN Lucy E & Charles R DOW at North Yarmouth ME on 20 Mar [15 Apr 1852]
    Nathaniel N & Emily J KNIGHT at Biddeford ME [3 Aug 1848]
    Roseann & Edward M YATES of the *Ellsworth Herald* office at Ellsworth ME on Jun 19 [1 Jul 1852]
    Salome & James PAINE both of Pownal ME at Durham ME [15 Jul 1843]
SKILLINGS Gershom & Patience FILES all of Gorham ME at Gorham on 12th by Jeremiah PARKER Esq [29 Apr 1843]
    Hannah & Charles C WILCOX of New Vineyard ME at Strong ME [17 Jan 1850]
    Sarah & Smith HADLOCK formerly of Mt Desert ME on Bangs Island ME 17th ult [5 Aug 1843]
SKILLINS William H Jane D PARKER both of Madrid ME at Farmington ME [7 May 1846]
SKINNER Ann M & Henry FITZGERALD at Camden ME [22 Jul 1847]
    George F & Sarah J DEERING at Corinth ME [29 Jul 1852]
    Stephen R & Clarissa J GARCELON at Lewiston ME [18 Jan 1849]
SKOFIELD
    Richard T of East Livermore ME & Mary PUGSLEY at Saco ME [18 May 1848]
SLADE Ann E & Joseph MONSON both of Hallowell ME at Augusta ME [23 Sept 1843]
    Jarvis of Boston MA & Harriet T PATTEN at Bath ME [10 Oct 1844]
SLATTERY Mary L & Arthur M BLOOD at Thomaston ME [26 Feb 1852]
SLEEPER Francis H of Boston MA & Harriet L OSBORN at Belfast ME [3 Dec 1846]
    Samuel A & Aldana C HAVENER at Rockland ME [26 Jun 1851]
    Sarah E & Oliver SWETLAND at Thomaston ME [14 Jan 1847]
    Sherburne of Belfast ME & Elizabeth LONGFELLOW at Hallowell ME on Thurs last by Rev Jonathan COLE [11 Apr 1837]
SLOAN Martha Mary & Alvan E SMALL, druggist of Saco ME, at Bath ME [8 Aug 1834]

SLOCOMB Esther of RI & Lewis PENNEL of Brunswick ME at Evansville IN [31 Jul 1838]
SLOPER Susan M & Volney A SPRAGUE Esq of Corinna ME at Waterville ME [22 Feb 1849]
SMALL Albert H of Newry ME & Sarah J HASTINGS at Bethel ME [6 May 1847]
  Albert J & Diantha L HOLT at Norway ME [27 Dec 1849]
  Alvan E, druggist of Saco ME & Martha Mary SLOAN at Bath ME [8 Aug 1834]
  Amos & Margaret BEAL of Bowdoinham ME at Bowdoin ME [23 Jun 1852]
  Charity Mrs & Samuel WILLIAMS of Bowdoin ME at Topsham ME [17 Jul 1851]
  Charles & Esther J WELCH at Chelsea ME [12 Jun 1851]
  Elisha & Abigail POTTER at Bowdoinham ME [25 Sept 1851]
  Eliza Jane & Alden S OLIVER at Phipsburg ME [2 Oct 1851]
  Elizabeth M & Ansel G TRASK both of Westbrook ME at Gorham ME [23 May 1837]
  Emeline of (Rumford?) ME & Dr Enoch C ROLF of Farmington ME at Rumford ME [8 Jun 1839]
  Emily & Cyrus P JOHNSON of Lowell MA at South Thomaston ME [25 Apr 1850]
  Enos P at Saco ME & Hannah CHADBOURNE at Saco ME [12 Apr 1849]
  George ae 80 & Dorcas BARTON ae 55 after a courtship of one hour at Raymond ME on Aug 26 [18 Sept 1841]
  Hannah & Robert INNES at Bath ME [16 Jul 1846]
  Hellen A & John S HILL at Thorndike ME on Apr 4th [15 Apr 1852]
  Henry S & Hannah M POOLE at Portland ME [17 Feb 1848]
  James & Jane JORDAN at Portland ME [31 Oct 1844]
  James & Mary HANSON at China ME [26 Feb 1846]
  Jeremiah & Mary Jane KNOWLTON of Swanville ME at Waldo ME [20 Nov 1845]
  Joseph P Dr & Phebe E DELANO of Milton Plt ME by Rev B CHASE at Rumford ME on 11th inst [20 May 1852]
  Lydia & John C WING at Brunswick ME [18 Mar 1847]
  Mary Ann & Charles H BARKER, M.D., of Buxton Centre ME at Cornish ME [21 Jan 1847]
  Mary Ann & Elias A MORSE of Taunton MA at Jay ME [8 Apr 1833]
  Mary Ann & O'Neil R HASTINGS of Bethel ME at Newry ME [8 May 1845]
  Mary E of Lubec ME & Rev Samuel H BRADBURY at Eastport ME [15 Jan 1846]
  Mary G & George A TOZIER at Troy ME [19 Feb 1852]
  Mary S & Mr O A HILL at Limington ME [14 Sept 1848]
  Mary & Capt G W STURTEVANT at Richmond ME [26 Apr 1849]
  Mary & W COOLEY at Thomaston ME [6 Nov 1845]
  Minervas S & John A FREEMAN at Windham ME [27 Jan 1848]
  Nancy F & Nahum DUNLAP of Lewiston ME at Lisbon ME [14 Mar 1844]
  Nancy & Andrew HANSON at China ME [26 Feb 1846]
  Nathaniel & Mary E JONES at Augusta ME by Rev MORSE [26 Nov 1846]
  Oliver T of Windsor ME & Sarah F GREENE at Augusta ME on Sun eve last by Rev WILLIAMS [15 Aug 1844]
  Samuel Jr & Mary GAHAN at Phipsburg ME [12 Apr 1849]

SMALL (cont.) Sarah E & Alvin BOODY at Portsmouth NH [11 Mar 1852]
    Sarah J & Henry CALDER both of Campobello, Bay of Fundy, Canada at Eastport ME [2 Jan 1841]
    William B, M.D., of Wilton ME & Cynthia CHASE d/o Israel C Esq at Fayette ME on Aug 24 by Rev HOUGHTON [12 Sept 1834]
    William Capt & Mary BOWEN both of Prospect ME at Belfast ME [7 Jan 1847]
    William Jr & Eunice M THATCHER by E G BUXTON at North Yarmouth ME [7 Apr 1848]
    William L of Pownal ME & Clarissa W PIERCE of Wales ME at Monmouth ME [24 Jun 1847]

SMART Benjamin I & Abigail KENDALL at Freedom ME [24 Apr 1838]
    E K Col at Camden ME & Sarah R THAYER d/o Hon J T [20 Nov 1845]
    Eliza Ann & Hudson OSGOOD at Prospect ME [13 Feb 1835]
    Hannah J & Edward S STEVENS both of Swanville ME at Belfast ME [12 Jun 1841]
    Jacob & Delia PAGE at Searsport ME [27 Nov 1851]
    John & Betsey Ann SAVAGE at Vassalboro ME [6 May 1852]
    Lovinia & Frederick GARDNER at (Augusta) ME on 4th inst [13 Jan 1848]
    Nehemiah & Mrs Mary MICHAELS at Belfast ME [1 Apr 1847]
    R H of Prospect & Ruth N CUNNINGHAM of Swanville ME at Searsport ME [1 Apr 1852]
    Reuben S & Almira CURTIS of Frankfort ME at Swanville ME [17 Oct 1837]
    Sarah Jane & Cephias MORTON at Vienna ME [25 May 1848]

SMELLAGE Frances M & C D MAYNARD Jr of (Augusta ME) at Portland [3 Sept 1846]

SMILEY Amos & Sophronia M'KENNEY at Bath ME [18 Oct 1849]
    Ann R & Greenlief S LOW of Vassalboro ME at Sidney ME [28 Mar 1844]
    Bethuel of Gardiner ME & Abigail M SWAIN at Skowhegan ME [8 Mar 1849]
    Elizabeth D & William A MASTER at Hallowell ME on Weds morning 12th Nov by Rev J P STEELE [20 Nov 1851]
    Emily E & John B WEEKS of Vassalboro ME at Sidney ME [9 Dec 1847]
    Fanny L & John LOVEJOY of W Newbury MA at Sidney ME on May 21 by Rev William TILLEY [29 May 1851]
    Frances A & G L COX at Hallowell ME [21 Aug 1841]
    Frances & Isaac MASON of Biddeford ME at Augusta ME on 23rd inst by J J EVELETH Esq [30 Apr 1846]
    Hezekiah of Hallowell ME & Hannah S DAY at Augusta ME [23 Jul 1846]
    Joseph L & Mary B HAYWARD at Sidney ME by Rev William TILLY [5 Jun 1845]
    L'Orient P & Mr D V B ORMSBY both of Augusta ME at Thompson CT [26 Aug 1843]
    Mary Ann & Stephen S KNOWLES of Augusta ME at Sidney ME [24 May 1849]
    Orseamus & Julia C STOWELL at Paris ME [20 Sept 1839]
    Robert & Lydia P HERRICK at Gardiner ME [7 Feb 1850]
    Sarah M & Capt William WASS at Hallowell ME [8 Aug 1840]

SMITH Abby E A & Eben RICHARDSON of New Portland ME at Pittston ME [17 Jul 1845]

SMITH (cont.) Abigail & Jacob RICHARDS at Hallowell ME [1 Jan 1846]
 Abigail & Reuben P RANDALL at Augusta ME on 12th inst by Rev S ALLEN [23 Sept 1847]
 Addy & Levi S VARNEY at Bloomfield ME [6 May 1852]
 Adeline A & Charles MONROE at Portland ME [31 Jan 1834]
 Albert & Elizabeth CUMMONGS at Augusta ME [9 Jan 1851]
 Albert M & Roxanna B WAUGH at Thomaston ME [14 May 1846]
 Almira A & Joseph LOMBARD at Thomaston ME [18 Jun 1846]
 Amanda W & Nathan H POWERS by Mr PINKHAM at Sedgwick ME [9 Mar 1839]
 Amos 2d of Bradley ME & Melissa A DUDLEY at Milford ME [5 Feb 1852]
 Ann M & Rev C G PORTER at Bath ME [17 May 1849]
 Augustus & Lucy J BURNHAM at Bridgton on Jun 15 by Rev Jacob BRAY [10 Jul 1851]
 Benjamin A & Esther A ROBINSON at Hallowell ME on Aug 19th by Rev W A P DILLINGHAM [13 Sept 1849]
 Benjamin principal of Litchfield Academy & Helen A CARR d/o Deacon Daniel CARR of Winthrop ME at Winthrop ME on 20th Feb 1851 by Rev Daniel THURSTON [27 Feb 1851]
 Bethia & Nathaniel BAIRNEE at St Albans ME [16 Jan 1838]
 Betsey A of Fayette ME & Decon Uriah PROCTOR of Canton ME at East Livermore ME on June 8th by Aaron BARTON Esq [26 Jun 1851]
 C A & Rev George S WOODWARD at (Augusta) ME on 30 Oct [9 Nov 1848]
 C E & Sidney P THOMPSON of Troy NY at Waterville ME [29 Jun 1848]
 Caleb & Miss Fanny WINSLOW at Livermore ME [10 Jan 1850]
 Caroline formerly of Harrison ME & Isaiah WYMAN Jr formerly of Phipsburg ME at Boston MA on 23rd ult by Rev J V HIMES [15 Jan 1842]
 Caroline & John MILLS both of Belgrade ME [7 Nov 1834]
 Celina P & John C LOWELL at Bath ME [28 Aug 1845]
 Charles E & Miss Mercy BEASE at Wayne ME by Ephraim MAXIM Esq [31 Jan 1850]
 Charles V & Frances Ann d/o Henry GREEN formerly of Portland ME at Augusta ME on 10th by Rev Mr THURSTON of Winthrop ME [21 Oct 1843]
 Charlotte G & William HATCH at Belfast ME [15 Nov 1849]
 Chester S & Lovina P CLARK at (Augusta) ME on Apr 22d by Rev Mr JUDD [3 May 1849]
 Christiana & Franklin SIDELINKER at Dover ME? [25 Apr 1850]
 Clarissa Ann & Edmund AMES at Norway ME [11 Feb 1847]
 Comfort C & Emery T RECORD at Buckfield ME [13 Feb 1851]
 Cordelia & Joshua BERRY of New Sharon ME at Winthrop ME on the 20th inst by Rev J H INGRAHAM [1 Jun 1839]
 Corrussan D & George W WYMAN of Bridgton ME at Biddeford ME [5 Aug 1852]
 Daniel Talcott Prof & Sophia H d/o G W BROWN Esq merchant [2 May 1840]
 Daniel & Sarah DWINAL at Lisbon ME [12 Oct 1848]
 Dexter D Francestown NH & Helen M HOUGHTON L H GREEN Esq at Gardiner ME on Sept 19th [21 Dec 1848]
 Diana S & Amos D TARR at Lewiston ME [10 May 1849]

SMITH (cont.) Dianthe & Josiah TILTON at Monmouth ME [18 Jan 1840]
    Dorcas Mrs & David WILSON at Edgecomb ME [14 Mar 1837]
    E H W of Augusta ME & Sarah HASKELL of Livermore ME [11 Sept 1835]
    Edmund J of Hallowell ME & Miss Sarah A AMES of Jefferson ME at Augusta ME on Thanksgiving day morning by the Rev Mr JUDD [9 Dec 1847]
    Eleanor B & John BUZWELL at Hallowell ME [16 Nov 1839]
    Eleanor & Eben MARSTON at Norway ME [28 Mar 1850]
    Elira M & Henry BRIGGS of Vassalboro ME at Woodstock VT on 30 Dec [16 Jan 1851]
    Eliza Ann & Peter H ALBEE at Hallowell ME [29 Jun 1848]
    Eliza & Thomas F BECK at Augusta ME [25 Nov 1836]
    Elizabeth D Mrs & Rev L W LEONARD of Dublin NH at Exeter NH [10 Apr 1851]
    Elizabeth of Hallowell ME & Dean PRAY of Augusta ME on Monday last [29 May 1838]
    Elizabeth S & Capt Calvin BALLARD of Gardiner ME at Hallowell ME on Sunday eve last [21 Aug 1838]
    Elizabeth & Edward B THORNE of Augusta ME at Hallowell ME on 14th inst [25 Jul 1844]
    Ellen C T of Richmond ME & Capt William H STURTEVANT of Bowdoinham ME [2 Oct 1845] & [16 Oct 1845]
    Ellen F, youngest d/o Capt Samuel SMITH at Hallowell ME & Eliphalet ROWELL at Hallowell ME [12 Dec 1844]
    Emeline L & Marshall H RAND at Frankfort ME on 18th inst by S H NICKERSON Esq [2 Apr 1842]
    Emily & Edward COSTELOW of Gardiner ME at Readfield ME on 11th Jul by Rev Benjamin P REED [5 Aug 1847]
    Ezra S & Abigail JONES both Hallowell ME at Augusta ME by Rev C FULLER [21 Nov 1844]
    Flavilla & Samuel PARKER of Fayette ME at Livermore ME [20 Dec 1849]
    Frances T Mrs & Eben HUSSEY at (Augusta) ME on 13th Jan [29 Jan 1852]
    George L & Eliza W CROCKETT of Rockland ME at Bath ME [31 Jul 1851]
    George of Bangor ME & Maria BURRILL at Fairfield ME [24 Dec 1846]
    Gilman of Augusta ME & Miss Sarah C d/o Samuel SMITH of Farmington ME at Hallowell ME [7 Sept 1839]
    Glorvina & J King STINCHFIELD at New York City [17 Jun 1852]
    Greenleaf & Miss Sophia JOHNSON of Monmouth ME at Winthrop ME on Nov 29th [8 Jan 1836]
    Gustavus A of Passadumkeag ME & Julia A McKENNEY of Gray ME at Milford ME [22 Jan 1846]
    Hannibal & Miss Mary R PARTRIDGE at Paris ME [7 Nov 1837]
    Harriet N & Oliver P COOK at Sidney ME [28 Mar 1844]
    Harriet V & Henry SEWALL at Augusta ME on 3rd inst by Rev Mr BURGESS [11 Nov 1847]
    Harriet & Augustus D SAWYER at Hallowell ME [22 Feb 1840]
    Harriet & Mr W M CLAFLIN at Gardiner ME [1 Apr 1852]
    Harrison A Esq & Miss Evelina F ROLLINS at Vassalboro ME [10 Jun 1833]
    Helen M & John H CLIFFORD at Belfast ME [4 Apr 1840]

SMITH (cont.) Henry B of Searsport ME & Miss Anna E STILSON at Waterville ME [19 Aug 1847]
    Henry B & Miss Mary A HOOLE at Portland ME [23 Sept 1836]
    Henry G & Lydia Jane MITCHELL of Mercer ME at Hallowell ME [6 Mar 1851]
    Henry of Readfield ME & Sarah MELVIN at Hallowell ME [10 Jun 1852]
    Henry & Frances E SPRAGUE at Farmington ME [30 Nov 1848]
    Hiram & Mary Jane BERRY [8 Aug 1844]
    Hon P O J of Westbrook ME & Ellen E K GROTON d/o Hon Nathaniel G of Bath ME at Portsmouth NH [15 Jan 1852]
    Howard of Litchfield ME & Lucy Ann WENTWORTH at Webster ME [18 Mar 1852]
    Ira W of Milbury MA & Miss Dorothy N HOYT at New Portland ME [22 Nov 1849]
    Isaiah & Miss Harriet LAKEN at Charlotte ME [14 Jun 1849]
    Ivory G of Gardiner ME & Charlotte SPEAR at Hallowell ME on Tues eve 18th ult by Allen RICE Esq [6 Mar 1845]
    J A, M.D., of Vassalboro ME & Sarah M RHOADS at Providence RI on Jul 4th [29 Jul 1852]
    J M & Sarah E WALKER Anson at Norridgewock ME [7 Dec 1848]
    Jacob A, one of the proprietors of the *Bangor Whig*, & Mrs Harriet B PARKER at Reading MA [16 Sept 1836]
    James S F of Monmouth ME & Miss Jedidah NICKERSON at Mercer ME [27 Mar 1845]
    James & Sarah SAWYER of Boothbay ME at Wiscasset ME [20 Mar 1851]
    Jane E of Windham ME & Ezra D FELKER at Portland ME [29 May 1845]
    Jane M & David S SPRINGER at Litchfield ME [25 Jul 1844]
    Jane & Thomas J RIDER at Thomaston ME [5 Feb 1836]
    Joanna H & Grosvenor ALDRICH of Uxbridge MA at Farmington ME [13 Sept 1849]
    John Capt & Mary OWEN both of Bowdoin ME [20 Nov 1845]
    John Esq & Susan D SWIFT at Lewiston ME [13 Jan 1848]
    John Jr of Readfield ME & Miss Mary H RANDLETT of Alna ME at Alna [2 Jan 1838]
    John O & Sophronia M MOORE at Gardiner ME [23 Nov 1848]
    John & Miss Emeline E TWIGGS both of Hermon ME at Bangor ME [13 May 1847]
    Johnson of Gray ME & Louisa A DUNN of Poland ME [14 May 1846]
    Jonathan B of Wilton ME & Philena WELCH by Rev Mr MORSE at Winthrop ME [30 Mar 1848]
    Joseph Capt of Hallowell ME & Miss Saphrona F BURGESS of Wayne ME [31 Aug 1839]
    Joseph H of Augusta ME & Miss Elizabeth A NOYES of Monmouth ME [19 Jun 1841]
    Joseph N of Mt Vernon ME & Harriet N CATES at Thorndike ME [28 Mar 1844]
    Joseph of Marshfield ME?/MA? & Miss Sarah G HARMON at East Machias ME [26 Aug 1847]
    Joseph S of Hallowell ME & Miss M A HAMILTON of Vassalboro ME at Augusta ME on 13th May by Rev W A P DILLINGHAM [24 May 1849]
    Joshua of Biddeford ME & Miss Emily J BEAN at Brownfield ME [15 Feb 1849]

SMITH (cont.) Julia E & John H HARTFORD at Augusta ME on Monday morning last by Rev William A DREW [1 Jul 1847]
   Laura B & John W PERRY at Readfield ME [29 Aug 1840]
   Lemuel & Miss Isabel MADDOCKS at Ellsworth ME [23 Sept 1847]
   Leonard P & Miss Agnes AUSTIN both of Canton ME on 2d inst by Rev George W QUINBY [25 May 1839]
   Lucinda Mrs & Benjamin G HUNTINGTON at Augusta ME on 14th ult [1 Apr 1847]
   Lucretia H & Joshua KENNEY at Brewer ME [14 Sept 1839]
   Lucy K & Perlando O NORRIS of Fayette ME at Wayne ME [24 Apr 1838]
   Lydia F & Theopilus NICKERSON of Brewer ME at Belfast ME [14 Aug 1845]
   Lydia Mrs & John GRAVES of S Thomaston ME at Thomaston ME [10 Jul 1851]
   Lydia S of Lisbon ME & Annanium J DYER at Topsham ME [4 Apr 1840]
   Maria P & James C WICKER of Utica NY at Hallowell ME [27 May 1847]
   Maria & Albert G MOREY of Belmont ME at Belfast ME [28 May 1846]
   Martha A & William GOOGINS of Waterboro ME at Hollis ME [6 May 1847]
   Martha Ann of Cornville ME & William W DODGE of New Boston at Windsor VT [30 Sept 1847]
   Martha J & Joshua FOLSOM of Fairfield ME at Waterville ME [27 Jun 1837]
   Martha M & Joseph E BLABUN at Phillips ME [21 Jun 1849]
   Martha Mrs late of Akron OH & Maj John CARVER of Leeds ME at Gardiner ME [8 Aug 1844]
   Martha & Jonathan BISHOP late of Akron OH at Gardiner ME [26 Dec 1844]
   Martin & Miss Caroline O STICKENY at Hallowell ME [20 Mar 1841]
   Mary A & B F WALKER at Livermore ME [18 Jan 1844]
   Mary Ann of Hallowell ME & John F WADE at Augusta ME by J J EVELETH Esq [4 Apr 1844]
   Mary Ann & L G NORRIS both of Wayne ME [14 Jan 1847]
   Mary Ann & Rufus WARD of Wellington ME? at Brighton ME? [27 May 1847]
   Mary Ann & Thomas H MARTIN at Bangor ME [4 Apr 1837]
   Mary E & Reuben SANBON at Kennebunkport ME [20 Jul 1848]
   Mary Francis & Charles MILD at Newport ME? [18 May 1848]
   Mary H & John W SHAW at Woolwich ME [25 Apr 1837]
   Mary Jane of Calais ME & Ebenezer BROWN Jr at Robbinson ME [28 Ebenezer [28 Aug 1845]
   Mary Jane & Andrew HUNNEWELL at Solon ME [24 Jul 1845]
   Mary L & Rev J L STEVENS, pastor of the Universalist Church in New Sharon ME at Hallowell ME on 10th inst by Rev William A DREW [22 May 1845]
   Mary Mrs of Kennebunkport ME & Ichabod HILL of Saco ME at Biddeford ME [28 May 1846]
   Mary Mrs & Nathaniel FRIEND, a Revolutionary soldier ae 81y at Beverley, "To the bride no doubt that: One Friend old is worth a hundred new" [1 May 1845]
   Mary Mrs & William PARSONS at Bath ME [29 Aug 1837]
   Mary & Washington ROWELL Esq at Madison ME [18 May 1839]

SMITH (cont.) Matthias of Readfield ME & Miss Mary Ann CURRIER of Winthrop ME at Wayne ME [8 Jul 1847]
  Mehitable E & George WAIRE at Gardiner ME [17 Apr 1845]
  Mercey L & Daniel G ANDREWS at Thomaston ME [7 Aug 1845]
  Mila Frances & Charles R WHIDDEN Esq at Calais ME [28 Aug 1845]
  Moses S & Angeline BENNETT at Thomaston ME [10 Aug 1848]
  N T Capt & Hannah Jane MORRELL at Brownville ME [15 Aug 1844]
  Newton & Miss Betsey H TOWN both of Norway ME at Boston MA [4 Dec 1845]
  Obed W & Mrs Sophrinia SMITH at Skowhegan ME [18 Apr 1850]
  Olive A & Warren TAYLOR at Augusta ME on 21st inst by John A PETTINGILL Esq [31 May 1849]
  Olive S & Thomas STICKNEY of Carthage ME at Wilton ME [30 Apr 1846]
  Olive & Samuel D GRIFFIN at Augusta ME on Thurs 27th ult by Rev A MOORE [6 Mar 1845]
  Pamelia C & James KING of Bloomfield ME at Skowhegan ME [18 Apr 1850]
  Paulina A & Capt Samuel H BROOKINGS at Hallowell ME [18 Jul 1844]
  Rachel Mrs & Lovis HOUDLETT of Dresden ME at Augusta ME on 9th inst by Mr INGRAHAM [16 Jan 1845]
  Rosilla A & William JEWETT at Madison ME [7 Oct 1847]
  Roxy & Capt Edward LINCOLN at Nobleboro ME [29 May 1838]
  Rufus (ae 14) & Julia Ann DOUGHTY (ae 15y) at Brunswick ME [7 Nov 1837]
  Sabrina H, d/o Rev James SMITH, & Thomas A ANDERSON at Fayette ME on Jul 1st by Rev James SMITH [19 Jul 1849]
  Sally F & Hanry F at Brownville ME [15 Aug 1844]
  Samuel D & Mary O GOOKIN both of Hollis ME at Dover NH [26 Feb 1852]
  Samuel M Dr of Prospect ME & Mary E NICKERSON of Belfast ME at Belfast [15 Apr 1836]
  Samuel O & Margaret Elizabeth BRIGGS at Portland ME [11 Jan 1844]
  Samuel S, printer & Miss Harriet D KENDRICK at Bangor ME [28 Oct 1836]
  Samuel & Eliza BALLARD both of Sidney ME at Chelsea ME [20 May 1852]
  Samuel & Elizabeth McPHETERS at Bangor ME [30 Oct 1845]
  Sarah A & Benjamin MARSTON at Norway ME on 29th ult [20 Apr 1848]
  Sarah C, d/o Samuel SMITH of Farmington ME, & Gilman SMITH of Augusta ME [7 Sept 1839]
  Sarah C Mrs & Adna L NORCROSS at New York NY on 14th ult [2 Oct 1845]
  Sarah G & Curtis McCLOUD of Boston MA at Wiscasset ME [13 Jun 1854]
  Sarah H & Joseph FREEMAN of Strong ME at Harrison ME [5 Feb 1846]
  Sarah J & Thomas J TREASWELL at East Orrington ME both of Brewer Village ME [22 Apr 1847]
  Sarah Louisa & Rev Handel G NOTT at Bath ME [12 Feb 1846]
  Sarah M of Eastport ME & Capt Cyrus HIGGINS Jr at Hampden ME [20 Mar 1845]
  Sarah W & David W STORER at Bath ME [3 Sept 1846]

SMITH (cont.) Sarah W & Oliver W IRISH at Milo ME on 11 Oct by James H MACOMBER Esq [23 Oct 1851]
    Sarah & Benjamin WATSON at Lowell MA [18 May 1848]
    Sarah & Henry M WAKEFIELD at Gardiner ME [1 Nov 1849]
    Sarah & Mr J W MERRILL of Manchester NH at Lewiston ME [24 Apr 1851]
    Sarah & William MOOERS at Pittston ME [10 Apr 1851]
    Sherman of Steuben ME & Nancy GUPTILL at Gouldsboro ME [24 Jun 1847]
    Solomon & Miss Joana A WAKEFIELD at Gardiner ME [27 May 1833]
    Sophia A & William DOW at Waterville ME [29 Jun 1848]
    Sophia W & Joseph P McRIFLES at Milburn ME [25 Apr 1834]
    Sophronia & Obed W SMITH at Skowhegan ME [18 Apr 1850]
    Stephen & Mary BLAISDELL of Hampden ME at Orono (Old Town) ME [7 Sept 1833]
    Stevens & Mrs Abigail DENNIS at Hallowell ME on 4th inst by Rev S ADLAM [17 Apr 1845]
    Susan W & John JACKSON at Hampden ME [20 Nov 1851]
    Susan & Gideon SPEARIN at Lincoln ME [18 Nov 1847]
    Sylvia Ann, d/o Noyes SMITH, & Nathaniel REMICK of Augusta ME at Mt Vernon ME [16 Jan 1845]
    Thankful & Seth HOLWAY at Fairfield ME [21 Jan 1833]
    Thomas J & Miss Caroline E LOOMIS at Hallowell ME [20 Nov 1841]
    Thomas of Hallowell ME & Miss Theodata L HALL at Gardiner ME [22 Aug 1844]
    Thomas & Miss Lucy WARNER at Augusta ME [15 Aug 1837]
    W S Capt & Miss Elizabeth R MAYO of Boston MA at Frankfort ME [28 Mar 1837]
    William A SMITH & Elvira RICHARDS of Readfield ME at Augusta ME [18 Jun 1846]
    William H & Cordelia WRIGHT at Hallowell ME [4 Sept 1845]
    William H & Miss A N C SHEPLEY at Saco ME [22 Jun 1848]
    William R, publisher of *Augusta Age*, & Sarah B d/o Mr Jonathan COCHRAN at Bangor ME [7 Jan 1843]
    William & Miss Lucy Ann ROLLINS at Hallowell ME on Tues evening last by Rev Mr WEBSTER [17 Apr 1838]
SMYTH Amy & Josiah WARD at Brunswick ME [10 Apr 1851]
SNELL Abby A (d/o John) & Amos WHEELER of Sidney ME at Winthrop ME [24 Jun 1847]
    Ann A (oldest d/o John) E SNELL of Augusta ME, & Lewis WOOD by Rev Mr QUINBY [23 Nov 1839]
    Charles Dr of Bangor ME & Charlotte R PALMER of Waterville ME at Waterville on 2nd inst by Mr SMITH [12 Feb 1836]
    Diana & Caleb TRUE of Industry ME [17 Jul 1838]
    E C Major of Winthrop ME & Fanny CRAWFORD at Sidney ME [12 Mar 1846]
    E Copeland & Lucinda P RESCOTT of (Winthrop ME) at Winthrop by Oakes HOWARD Esq [15 Jan 1839]
    Eleazer & Emily J SAWYER at Starks ME on Jan 13 [6 Feb 1851] & [6 Mar 1851]

SNELL (cont.) Eunice of Winthrop ME "this is the sixth ([sic]; 7th surviving and youngest; see page 593 Stackpole's *History of Winthrop ME*) dau of Mr John E SNELL that has been taken from the ample farm-house within a few years...there is one of the same sort left...." & Henry HAYWARD of Hallowell ME at Winthrop ME by Rev Mr ELLIOT [27 Feb 1851]
    Henrietta & Peter C WARDWELL of Otisfield ME [7 Jan 1847]
    I Jr of Augusta ME & Miss Elizabeth HASSAM, eldest d/o Rev F FREEMAN of Sandwich MA by Rev Frederick FREEMAN [22 Jul 1847]
    James M of Starks ME & Lenora S TRUE at Industry ME [1 Jan 1846]
    Jerusha Loring (4th dau/o John) & Lewis COBB at Winthrop ME [23 Nov 1839]
    Lucy Ann & William S KING at Hallowell ME [3 May 1849]
    Mary L & Lawrence COPELAND at Boston MA "... the receipt of not a slice but a whole bridal loaf sent us...This makes the sixth ([sic]; should state 7th: she was the sixth surviving daughter, see page 593, Stackpoles History of Winthrop) good wife and true that our neighbor SNELL has furnished as many thrifty young men from his domestic fold within a few years -Mary is the last of the flock...." [19 Feb 1852]
    Sarah H & William P M MEANS at (Augusta) ME [20 Jul 1848]
    Sirmantha (2nd dau/o John E SNELL) & Joseph WOOD at Winthrop ME on Sunday evening last by Rev Mr Ingraham [30 Sept 1836]
    Susan, d/o John E SNELL of Augusta ME, & Benjamin P BRIGGS at Winthrop ME [23 Nov 1839]
SNIPE Eveline A of Phipsburg ME & Stephen M TARBOX at Georgetown ME [1 Feb 1849]
SNOW Albion P of Brunswick ME & Matilda B SEWALL by Rev Mr SAWYER at Winthrop ME [3 Jun 1852]
    Charles C Capt & Martha MERRYMAN at Brunswick ME [18 May 1848] & [4 May 1848]
    Deborah & Jordan WOODWARD at Brunswick ME [28 Feb 1834]
    Edwin L & Antoinette EATON at Thomaston ME [26 Jun 1838]
    Edwin P of Atkinston ME & Miss Henrietta A CHASE at Sebec ME [28 Mar 1850]
    Eliza H & John W HIGGINS at Lincolnville ME [20 Apr 1848]
    Elvira P & Joshua K THORNDIKE at Thomaston ME [8 Jan 1846]
    Emily & Daniel J DUNHAM at Brunswick ME [14 Jan 1847]
    George Capt & Harriet MILLER at Thomaston ME [11 Jul 1844]
    George W & Sarah E BLAKE at Augusta ME [20 Nov 1841]
    Harriet & John H THOMPSON at Topsham ME [24 Dec 1846]
    Harriet & Thomas SIMPSON at Brunswick ME [1 Feb 1844]
    John & Lucretia GAY at Bath ME [12 Feb 1846]
    Julia A & Mark L INGRAHAM at Thomaston ME of Thomaston ME [8 Jan 1846]
    Lydia J & Capt Crawford A STOVER at Rockland ME [7 Aug 1851]
    M A Miss & Capt Walter EMERSON at Bucksport ME [11 Oct 1849]
    Mary Jane & Asa C FULLER Capt at Thomaston ME [16 Jul 1846]
    Nathaniel Capt & Almira D FARREN of Topsham ME at Bath ME [23 Jan 1845]
    Rebecca & Mr A LINSCOTT at Harpswell ME [10 Aug 1848]
    Samuel Capt & Sarah B McLELLAN at Bath ME [31 Oct 1844]

SNOW (cont.) Samuel & Sophia KEENE by Rev H M BLAKE at (Augusta) ME on 6th Apr [15 Apr 1852]
    Sarah & Joseph FROST at Ellsworth ME [1 Apr 1833]
    T of Skowhegan ME & Harriet d/o Thomas BLACKISTON, sailmaker at Quebec Canada [20 Apr 1839]
    Thankful & Cyrus AUSTIN at Belgrade ME on 18th inst [21 Sept 1848]
    Thomas Capt of Brunswick ME & Miss M L WATTS at Hallowell ME [21 Oct 1847]
    W R, publisher of the *Frontier Journal* of Calais ME & Catherine BEARCLIFFE of St Andrews New Brunswick Canada at St Andrews [21 Aug 1845]
    William B & Olive DINSMORE both of Madison ME at Bloomfield ME on 19th June by Rev Mr HATHAWAY [26 Jun 1851]
    William Dr of Fairfield ME & Miss Hester Ann WENTWORTH at Readfield ME [29 Apr 1847]
    William T of Belfast ME & Miss Octavia CARR at Hallowell ME [18 Jun 1846]
SNOWBALL Capt Thomas & Rebecca NORTON at Bluehill ME [3 Aug 1848]
SNOWDEAL Elmira & Mr F H BARTLETT at Thomaston ME [24 Aug 1848]
SNOWMAN James & Julia STORER of Weld ME at Weld by J TYLER Esq [20 Feb 1845]
    Susan M & John C COCHRAN Hon at Rockland ME on May 8th [22 May 1851]
SOIETT Julia & Edward YOUNG at Bath ME [18 May 1848]
SOLITUDE Andrew & Mary Ann SWEET at Warren PA on 12th ult "Solitude Sweetened" [26 Aug 1843]
SOMES John G & Miss Mary Ann E DOWNS at Dutton ME all of Bangor ME [13 Mar 1835]
    Mary & Simon BRAWN at Albion ME [2 Mar 1839]
SOPER Florinda W & G W GOULD of Farmington ME at Hanson MA [15 Oct 1846]
    John E of Plymouth ME & Mary C E GAGE at Dixmont ME [9 Nov 1848]
    Margaret A & Joseph F COLBURN at Pittston ME [10 Aug 1848]
    Martha Ann of Gray ME & Henry M CHAMBERLIN of Auburn ME at Gray ME on Thanksgiving evening by Charles MEGQUIER Esq [30 Dec 1843]
    Martha J of Livermore ME & Daniel DAVIS at Turner ME [18 Jan 1849]
    Rachel A & Thomas DAVIS at Turner ME [11 May 1848]
SOUL - SOULE
    Abigail W & Rev H P OSGOOD at Turner ME [30 Mar 1848]
    Alfred A Capt & Miss Prudence D BRADFORD at Harmony ME of Turner ME [18 Jan 1844]
    Alton & Izetta KEATON at Augusta ME on 19 Jan 1851 by Asaph R NICHOLS Esq [23 Jan 1851]
    Angerone M & James M WEST of Waterville ME [17 Jul 1838]
    Caroline & Robert PENNELL 2nd at Freeport ME [4 Feb 1843]
    Cordelia & Maj Peter FOLSOM at Harmony ME [8 Feb 1844]
    Elisha D & Lydia J WING at Skowhegan ME by M LITTLEFIELD [15 Jul 1852]
    Eliza A of Danville ME & Horatio G GARCELON of Brunswick ME at Lewiston Falls ME [24 Dec 1846]

SOUL (cont.) Eunice Mrs & Capt Jonathan MATTHEWS of Monson ME at Shirley ME [19 Aug 1852]
George T & Miss Caroline A SEWALL at Farmington ME [21 Jun 1849]
Harriet & Mr C W DYER at New Sharon ME on 27th Feb by Rev J T HAWES [8 Mar 1849]
Hiram of Waterville ME & Melita LONGLEY at Sidney ME [9 Jan 1838]
James M of Chelsea ME & Sarah S HALEY of Bath ME at Bath [20 Feb 1845]
John D & Miss Betsey M GREELEY both of Palermo ME at Montville ME by C H SPRING Esq [5 Feb 1839]
Mary Ann & Frances at Portland ME [8 Feb 1844]
Nathan A Rev & Miss Almira TIMBERLAKE at Livermore ME [30 Jul 1846]
Norman of Dexter ME & Nancy J WHITE at St Albans ME [14 Aug 1845]
Pameline Mrs & David W MERRILL of New Gloucester ME at Lewiston ME [19 Dec 1844]
Rachel & Gustavus G WILSON at Norridgewock ME [27 Apr 1848]
Robert T Capt of Bath ME & Miss Isabella WADE at Freeport ME [29 May 1845]
Sarah J & George W SCALES at Waterville ME [2 Aug 1849]
Sarah W & James BAILEY at Woolwich ME [13 Jul 1848]
Savina M & Joseph BURGESS at Fairfield ME [15 Oct 1842]
William N of Boston MA & Miss Mary E NORCROSS at Augusta ME on Thurs the 15th inst by Rev Mr WILLIAMS [30 Oct 1845]

SOUTHARD - SOUTHWARD
Cordelia & Horace WOOD at Waterville ME [3 Jun 1852]
John Capt of Richmond ME & Hannah NOYES at Jefferson ME [14 Sept 1848]
Margaret J & Gilmore C BARTLETT at Augusta ME on Dec 1st by Asaph R NICHOLS Esq [13 Dec 1849]

SOUTHWICK Maria Ann & Alfred COLBURN at Vassalboro ME [6 Jan 1848]

SPAULDING Abel W & Miss Cynthia WALKER at Embden ME [5 Feb 1846]
Cynthia Mrs & John M FOSTER at Thomaston ME [14 Nov 1844]
Data A & George H STINEFORD at Foxcroft ME both of Dover ME [12 Aug 1852]
Harriet N of Norridgework ME & William A SANDERS of Wisconsin Territory at Albany NY [29 Aug 1844]
Joseph Jr of Dixmont ME & Miss Clarissa SIMPSON of Plymouth at Plymouth ME on 17th inst by Jesse ROBINSON Esq of Dixmont ME [30 Jan 1838]
Lucy M & Elbridge H DODGE at Thomaston ME [20 Jul 1848]
Maria N of South Thomaston ME & Capt Nathan WILLIAMS at East Thomaston ME [28 Jun 1849]
Marshall Esq & Frances T LYNDE d/o Dr John S LYNDE by Rev Josiah PEET at Norridgewock ME on 9th inst [30 Nov 1848]
Sarah J & John A DAVIS at Palmyra ME [3 Apr 1851]
Theophilus & Miss A A DECROW of Freedom ME at Belfast ME [22 Jan 1846]
Timothy C & Helena WELLS at Embden ME [15 May 1845]

SPARKS Alice & James LAMBERT Jr at Brunswick ME [8 Oct 1846]

SPARROW Eliza & Edward RICE [21 Jan 1833]

SPARROW (cont.) Ambrose of Augusta ME & Miss Maria G GREELEY of Palermo ME at China ME by Joseph GREELEY Esq [9 Jan 1845]
SPEAR Alexander 2d of Warren ME & Miss Rosanna STUDLEY at Waldoboro ME [4 Nov 1847]
- Andrew P & Alice A MOORE by Rev Mr PERHAM at Madison ME on 24 Oct [16 Nov 1848]
- Charles of Bangor ME & Mary F WEEKS at Portland ME [21 Nov 1844]
- Charlotte & Ivory G SMITH of Gardiner ME at Hallowell ME on Thurs eve on 18th ult by Allen RICE Esq [6 Mar 1845]
- Demerrick & Lodonia CROUCH at East Thomaston ME [13 Sept 1849]
- Ellen & Fessenden KNOWLTON at Auburn ME [25 Oct 1849]
- Frances & Oliver GAY at Rockland ME [25 Sept 1851]
- Isabella H & John A GIVEN of Brunswick ME at Bowdoinham ME [5 Nov 1846]
- John A Capt & Nancy A CLARK at East Thomaston ME [3 Aug 1848]
- John P & Miss Sarah J BLACKWELL at Madison ME [26 Apr 1849]
- Lucinda B & Allen HARRINGTON at Thomaston ME [6 Nov 1845]
- Maria J & Eleazer C DOUGLAS at Gardiner ME [2 Jan 1851]
- Matthew P Esq & Harriet G SAMPSON at Bowdoinham ME [1 Jul 1833]
- Rachael & John BUTLER of Thomaston ME at Warren ME [4 Sept 1845]
- Samuel & Miss Lucy HISCOCK at Dixfield ME [16 Sept 1847]
- Sarah, youngest d/o Elkananh SPEAR Esq, & Capt Edward HEALY at Thomaston ME [19 Sept 1844]

SPEARIN Gideon & Susan SMITH at Lincoln ME [18 Nov 1847]
SPEARS Elvira H & Ithamer BOWLES at Thomaston ME [8 Apr 1847]
SPENCE Margaret of St Stephens New Brunswick Canada & William YOUNG at Calais ME [21 Aug 1845]
SPENCER A & Elizabeth C COX at Auburn ME [18 Jan 1849]
- Almira R both of Unity ME & John L PARKHURST at Freedom ME [6 Mar 1851]
- Daniel W of Berwick ME & Miss Sophia TUTTLE at Somersworth NH [30 Sept 1847]
- James & Clarissa SEAVY both of Starks ME at Anson ME by William VARNUM Esq [5 Dec 1834]
- Job A & Juliana C FOSTER of New Gloucester ME at Gray ME [7 Dec 1848]
- Louisa B & Greenlief F WOODS at Waldo ME [25 Oct 1849]
- Mary & Asiel COLEMAN at Solon ME [8 Jun 1848]
- Ruth & Mr S M EMERY at Bangor ME [4 Mar 1833]

SPINNEY Ellether & Charles BANKS at Bath ME [26 Feb 1836]
- Eveline M & John THAYER both of Sidney ME at Augusta ME on 2 Mar by Rev Z THOMPSON [20 Mar 1851]
- Mary Elizabeth & William REYNOLDS of Sidney ME at Phipsburg ME on 12th Nov by the Rev Mr STAPLES [22 Nov 1849]

SOFFORD John T Capt & Mary S FULLER at Thomaston ME [14 Oct 1847]
SPOFFORD Frederick P Capt & Miss Caroline E HASKELL at Deer Isle ME [29 May 1845]
- Lucinda & Hezekieh P COOMBS Esq, publisher of the *Thomaston Recorder* at Thomaston ME [21 Aug 1842]
- Sarah & Aaron STEVENS at Greene ME [1 Apr 1847]

SPOFFORD (cont.) Sarah H & Dr Amos HERRICK of Sedgwick ME at Deer Island ME [14 Nov 1844]
Sophia & Joel CURTIS of Bowdoinham ME at Webster ME [26 Dec 1844]
SPOLET Augusta & Mary Jane STANWOOD at Brunswick ME [9 Apr 1842]
SPRADFORD Charles & Lucy WHITMAN at Skowhegan ME [23 Jan 1845]
SPRAGUE Abby Mary, d/o the late Capt Oakman SPRAGUE of Bath ME, & Nicholas E PAINES Esq of Sanford ME at South Berwick ME [8 Aug 1834]
B F Rev of the Maine Methodist Conference & Comfort CATES at Thorndike ME [1 Aug 1840]
C L & Jane Isabella ARCHABLE at Bath ME [22 Jul 1836]
Caroline, d/o Nathaniel SPRAGUE, & James D SPRAGUE at Phipsburg ME on 20th ult by Samuel L ROGER Esq [10 Sept 1842]
Caroline & George W CHENERY at Gardiner ME [2 Oct 1845]
E N Mrs & Leonard LUCE at Farmington ME [14 Nov 1844]
Eliza & Mr J B MAYO at Pembroke ME [21 Sept 1848]
Frances E & Henry SMITH at Farmington ME [30 Nov 1848]
Hildo [sic] B & John J GOODWIN of Avon ME at Phillips ME [23 Jul 1846]
Horatio C & Augusta PARKER at Dexter ME [20 Jan 1848]
James D & Miss Caroline SPRAGUE, d/o Mr Nathaniel SPRAGUE at Philpsburg ME on 20th ult by Samuel L ROGERS Esq [10 Sept 1842]
James T Capt & Miss Harriet F WEBB all of Thomaston ME [30 Sept 1847]
Jesse G of Charlotte ME & Miss Harriet S FISHER at Calais ME [22 Oct 1846]
Joanna H & James G BUNKER at Nantucket MA [8 Aug 1840]
John O & Lucretia D MITCHELL at Thomaston ME [9 Jul 1846]
Joseph & Miss Ann Whitten at Bangor ME [14 Mar 1834]
Mary A & Elias T MERRILL at Greene ME [18 Mar 1852]
Melinda & James H COLLINS at Strong ME [14 Sept 1848]
Mirinda & Henry H BATES both of Greene ME [9 Oct 1841]
Peleg & Harriet N ROGERS at Bath ME [29 Feb 1844]
Rachel, d/o Nathaniel SPRAGUE, & James CUSHING at Phipsburg ME [10 Sept 1842]
Ruth F & Robert P WHITNEY at Topsham ME [25 Jun 1846]
Sarah B & Henry L BLACKBURN at Phipsburg ME on Mar 2d [18 Mar 1852]
Sarah E & Loring G EDGERLEY of Sangerville ME at Dexter ME [10 May 1849]
Sarah J & Mr E W HINDS of Kingfield ME at Farmington ME [23 Oct 1851]
Sarah M & Leonard C STETSON at Thomaston ME [17 Oct 1840]
Sarah & Hiram ARMSTRONG at Richmond ME [8 Aug 1844]
Thomas & Mary M LONGLEY at Bath ME [31 Jul 1851]
Volney A Esq of Corinna ME & Susan M SLOOPER at Waterville ME [22 Feb 1849]
SPRATT Zoe W & Levi JOHNSON of Carmel ME at Dixmont ME [24 Jun 1847]
SPRING Arthur & Mary A C NORRIS at Monmouth ME [6 Mar 1838]
Mary O & Eli B BEAN of Conway NH at Hiram ME [25 Jun 1846]
SPRINGER David S & Miss Jane W SMITH [25 Jul 1844]

SPRINGER (cont.) Elizabeth L & Thomas LITTLE at Augusta ME [13 Nov 1845]
  Frances A & Joshua W BAZIN of Boston MA at Portland ME [20 Nov 1845]
  Hannah T & Samuel McCUCHEN of Waltham MA [11 Apr 1837]
  James E & Deborah E SAWTELLE at Augusta ME [29 Jul 1847]
  James F & Zypporah B SAWTELLE at Augusta ME on 18th Jul by L CUSHING Esq [19 Aug 1847]
  Jane & Thomas WARD of Freeport ME at Brunswick ME [8 Mar 1849]
  Nancy & Joseph WORK at Bath ME [25 Dec 1838]
  Philena W & Benjamin C MORRILL at Richmond ME [17 Feb 1848]
  Ruth W & Augustine PERKINS at Waterville ME [11 Apr 1837]
  Susan & John COLBURN Jr at Hallowell ME both of Augusta ME [19 Feb 1846]
  Thomas H & Miss Ardra ROBINSON at Augusta ME of Sidney ME [27 Dec 1849]

SPOFFORD Apphia G of Greene ME & Samuel L MOODY of Webster ME at Leeds ME on 4th of July by Josiah DAY 2d Esq [26 Jul 1849]

SPROWL Mary & Col William BURHAM at Machias ME "the occasion was celebrated by the ringing of bells and firing of a cannon" [4 Jul 1834]
  Mary Jane & Ebenezer FOSTER at Montville ME [11 Nov 1845]
  William Jr of Waldoboro ME & Miss Catherine WEBB at Warren ME [12 Dec 1837]

SQUIRE Dorcas S of Madison ME & Johathan E REYNOLDS at Sidney ME [23 Apr 1846]

STACKPOLE Brian & Pamelia STEVENS at Augusta ME on Apr 2 by Alanson STARKS Esq [5 Jun 1845]
  C Miss, d/o William STACKPOLE at Albion ME by Rev S S NASON [7 Feb 1850]
  E of Houlton ME & Miss Mary A WELLINGTON at Albion ME [6 May 1836]
  James Capt & Miss Mary CURTIS d/o James CURTIS of Camden ME at Camden ME by Rev Mr CHAPMAN [4 May 1859]
  Lucy & Richard D STARR at Thomaston ME [14 May 1846]
  Maria & Horatio G TILTON at Portsmouth NH [18 Mar 1852]
  Mary E & Mr D WENTWORTH HESSEY of Sangerville ME at South Berwick ME [22 May 1845]

STACY Daniel L & Miss Elizabeth Ann HOBBS at Berwick ME [21 Jan 1847]
  George of Bath ME & Miss Sarah Ann HUTCHINS at Phippsburg ME [7 Jan 1847]
  William & Catherine EVANS at Bath ME [2 Jan 1845]
  William H of Hallowell ME & Sarah E ROBINSON of Litchfield ME [30 Sept 1836]

STAFFORD Jane P & Jefferson C THOMPSON at Greene ME [25 Jan 1849]
  Joseph C of Boston MA & Miss Maria R WHITNEY [31 Oct 1844]

STAIN Joanna & William L UPHAM at Hallowell ME [11 May 1848]
  John B & Mary JACOBS d/o Jesse E JACOBS by James R MARSTON Esq at Mt Vernon ME [7 Dec 1848]

STANCLIFT Horace B of Saco ME & Miss Sarah E HANSON of New Gloucester ME at Saco ME [1 Feb 1849]

STANDISH David W & Elizabeth W DINGLEY at Bath ME [11 Jul 1834]
  Mary W & Capt Oscar EATON at Warren ME [13 Mar 1841]

STANFORD Elvira & Charles DAVIS at Gardiner ME [2 Jan 1851]
STANLEY Anson & Miss Drusilla F d/o A BELCHER Esq at Winthrop ME on Tues last [4 Dec 1838]
    Asel of Vassalboro ME & Annette WARD at China ME on 19th Mar by Rev B F SHAW [3 Apr 1851]
    Asel & Miss Octavia NICHOLS at Wiscasset ME [19 Sept 1834]
    Clark of Waterville ME & Miss Mary T WARREN at Ellsworth ME [29 Jan 1839]
    David Esq & Miss Harriet DEARBORN at Winthrop ME on 29th ult by Rev David THURSTON [6 Jan 1837]
    Edna & Lendall W OBEAR at Sedwick ME by Rowland CARLTON Esq [23 Oct 1838]
    Emely & Mr I N BONNEY at Winthrop ME on 8th inst by Seth MAY Esq [20 Jun 1837]
    George D & S Caroline JOSSELYN both of (Augusta) ME by Rev E H CHAPIN at New York City on 11th Feb [19 Feb 1852]
    Henry A & Miss Elizabeth S BAMSFORD at East Winthrop ME [20 May 1847]
    James Esq of Farmington ME & Julia A PAGE at Hallowell ME [2 Oct 1841]
    John L & Miss Esther DECKER both of Winthrop ME at Wayne ME [27 May 1845]
    Lemuel & Mrs Lucy BENJAMIN both of Winthrop ME at Readfield ME on 23rd ult by Rev E ROBINSON [10 Dec 1842]
    Mary Jane & Daniel McDUFFIE at Winthrop ME on Weds evening last by David THURSTON [26 Oct 1833]
    Oren H & Miss Hannah JOY at Winthrop ME on 20 Jan by Rev F FOSTER [25 Jan 1844]
    Sumner H of Winthrop ME & Eliza G KIDDER at Norridgewock ME [9 Jul 1846]
    Theophilus & Rachel PATTERSON at Hampden ME [13 May 1833]
STANTIAL Delia E & Hiram MORSE at Hallowell ME [4 Jun 1851]
    Lucy Ann & William M LOUD at Richmond ME [22 Mar 1849]
STANTON Thomas L of Monmouth ME & Sarah E KIMBALL of Winthrop ME at Monmouth ME on 12th inst by Elder J J PRESCOTT [16 Oct 1845]
    Woodbury L & Miss Mary A MERRILL at Oxford ME [18 Feb 1847]
STANWOOD Emily & David S STINSON of Lewiston ME at Augusta ME on Thanksgiving eve by Rev WEBB [11 Dec 1851]
    Daniel C of Augusta ME & Miss Mary Augusta WEBSTER of Salem MA [18 Nov 1836]
    David S & Mehitible C GIVEN at Brunswick ME [24 Sept 1846]
    J Varney & L Josephine SAVAGE at Jefferson ME [18 Oct 1849]
    Mary Jane & Augustus SPOLET at Brunswick ME [9 Apr 1842]
    Nathaniel & Eliza J LINSCOTTE at Brunswick ME [23 Dec 1847]
    Robert & Nancy McMANUS at Brunswick ME [16 Sept 1836]
STAPLE Abigail P & Edward DAVIS at Wellington ME [23 Jun 1852]
    Mary A & Thomas W LUCE of New Vineyard ME at Temple ME [22 Jul 1852]
STAPLES Alexia & Aaron BURNHAM at Kennebunkport ME [15 Apr 1852]
    Anthony & Miss Mary G BLAKE both of Bowdoinham ME at Augusta ME [3 Sept 1846]
    C G & Lydia LEIGHTON at Biddeford ME [22 Jun 1848]

STAPLES (cont.) Charles F & Miss Lucy A GOULD at Biddeford ME [13 Sept 1849]
   Deborah Mrs & William H HUNT at Township No 3, East Branch ME [20 May 1843]
   Edward H & Mary CLEAVES both of Biddeford ME at Saco ME [26 Feb 1846]
   J K L of Gardiner ME & Miss Abba TRUE at Montville ME [12 Jul 1849]
   M S of Swanville ME & Sarah ELLINGWOOD at Frankfort ME [22 Jun 1848]
   Mary B & Mark E STATON at Freeport ME [8 Apr 1852]
   Mary F & George F DOW at Biddeford ME [12 Apr 1849]
   Mary J & Luther R FAUGHT of Sidney ME at Belgrade ME [19 Aug 1852]
   Mary & Edward B WAKEFIELD at Biddeford ME [9 Apr 1846]
   Priscilla & William H WELCH of Bradford ME at Lisbon ME [23 Aug 1849]
   Susan A & Alexander BURHAM at Biddeford ME [7 Oct 1847]
   William K & Jane MOREY at Oxford ME [3 Aug 1848]
STARBIRD Amelia & Daniel G CORNISH at Litchfield ME [4 May 1848]
   Caroline E & Edwin W CLARK at Atkinson ME [11 Mar 1852]
   Christiana & Kingman LITTLEFIELD at Hartland ME [3 Apr 1851]
   Durinda S & Nathan ADAMS 2d at Bowdoin ME [12 Jun 1851]
   Elbridge G & Miss Mary McALLISTER at Dover ME [25 Dec 1845]
   Horace & Mary E MARDEN of Boston MA at Livermore ME [27 Nov 1851]
   Robert S & Abigail A GOODWIN at Gardiner ME [4 May 1848]
STARKEY Susan & Mr Charles O McKINNEY at Unity ME [11 Apr 1850]
STARLING William H & Elizabeth ALBEE both of Monhegan ME at Damariscotta ME [19 Feb 1852]
STARKS Alanson Esq of (Augusta) ME at Monmouth ME [24 Dec 1846]
   Angeline of Monmouth ME & Alanson HALL at Monmouth ME [26 Jun 1841]
STARR Esther of East Thomaston ME & Oliver ROBBINS at Thomaston ME [27 Sept 1849]
   James Esq of Jay ME & Miss Olive JONES at Turner ME [2 Sept 1843]
   Richard D & Miss Lucy STACKPOLE at Thomaston ME [14 May 1846]
STARRETT Cephas & Mary TOLMAN at Thomaston ME [30 May 1837]
   Clarissa M & Caleb F ORDWAY at Orono ME [22 Feb 1849]
   George & Miss Anna E BABCOOK both of Augusta ME at Providence RI on 27th ult [10 May 1849]
STATON Mark E of Poland ME & Mary B STAPLES at Freeport ME [8 Apr 1852]
St CLAIR Ellen & Edwin A LANE at Auburn ME [30 Jan 1851]
   Esther & John POMROY at Bangor ME [15 Aug 1844]
STEARNS Cordelia H & Hiram C STILKEY at (Augusta) ME [20 Jul 1848]
   David & Elizabeth P HINCKLEY at Monroe ME [23 May 1840]
   Jane H & William H KING at Lowell MA [18 May 1848]
   John G & Julia C d/o J C WASHBURN Esq at Calais ME [26 Dec 1840]
   Phineas of Bethel ME & Mary MARTIN of Rumford ME at Rumford by B BARTLETT Esq [6 Mar 1835]
   Sibyl & William S PLUMMER at Monroe ME [23 May 1840]
   Susan M C of Dracutt MA on 7th inst & Joseph CHANDLER [17 Jul 1845]
   W H C of Calais ME & Miss Mary H HILL at Sullivan ME [2 Jul 1846]

STEARNS (cont.) William B & Lucy W POTTER both of Bath ME at Portsmouth NH [19 Feb 1852]

STEDMAN E M of Winthrop ME & Miss Ann L WHITNEY at Canton ME [23 Apr 1846]

Olive B & Henry G WILLIAMS at Sindey ME on 29th ult by Rev John ALLEN [14 Jun 1849]

STEELE Andrew of Castine ME & Eunice MANN at Brewer ME [16 Dec 1847]

Harrison & Caroline J RENDELL at Prospect ME [29 Mar 1849]

STEPHENS Nancy H & Solomon CHASE at Paris ME [11 Apr 1837]

STEPHENSON Alfred J & Miss Abby J WADE both of Sanderville ME by Rev Charles DUREN at Sangerville [26 Feb 1842]

Louisa C & Arthur C LAMPHER of Bucksport ME at Belfast ME [20 Mar 1851]

Warren & Laura BEAN at Belfast ME [17 Oct 1837]

STERLING Henry & Miss Cordelia CLARK at Atkinson ME [24 Apr 1845]

STERRY Sophia A & Harrison WAUGH at Starks ME on 29th Mar [13 Apr 1848]

STETSON Amos of Wayne ME & Sophrona d/o Ebenezer CARELTON at Winthrop ME [2 May 1844]

Benjamin F of Bath ME & Miss Harriet A DINSMORE of Richmond ME at Gardiner ME [3 Jan 1850]

Benjamin L of North Wayne ME & Miss Orrilla WILLIAMS at Winthrop ME by Rev C FULLER [6 Sept 1849]

Charles P & Miss Sarah APPERBY at Brunswick ME [30 Dec 1843]

Gideon F & Miss Ann B HARRIS at Eastport ME [11 Jun 1846]

Gideon & Miss Leah FIFIELD at Lincoln ME [2 Sept 1847]

Gilbert & Nancy C WILBER at Phillips ME [30 Dec 1847]

Isaiah of Bangor ME & Eliza G GRIFFIN at Brunswick ME [11 Sept 1851]

John S & Mrs Joanna GAY at Union ME [9 Feb 1839]

Julia A of Brunswick ME & John M POLLARD at Topsham ME [6 May 1843]

Leonard C & Sarah M SPRAGUE both of Thomaston ME at Thomaston [17 Oct 1840]

Lydia S & John COAKLEY at Bath ME [6 Nov 1845]

Lydia & William W CROCKETT of Norway ME at West Sumner ME [29 Nov 1849]

Mary F & David T STINSON at Bath ME [8 Jan 1846]

Mary Mrs & Samuel DAGGET at Union ME [9 Feb 1839]

Nathaniel W & Elizabeth BROWN at Bath ME [15 Nov 1849]

Oakman S of Bath ME & Miss Harriet N SWEETSER at Cumberland ME [7 Jan 1847]

Pamelia A & William G RANDALL of Auburn ME at Lewiston ME [28 Nov 1844]

Ruth S & John SHAW at Bath ME [13 May 1836]

Samuel of Danville ME & Miss Valeria A CHASE of Minot ME at Hebron ME [16 Apr 1846]

Sarah C & Augustus D MIRICK of Camden ME at Thomaston ME [31 Oct 1844]

Sarah formerly of Dover ME & William BEDELL at New York NY on the 26th ult [13 Feb 1845]

Silvia & Thomas J BISBEE at Gardiner ME [11 Jul 1840]

Marriage Notices from the "Maine Farmer" 389

STEVENS Aaron & Sarah SPOFFORD at Greene ME [1 Apr 1847]
   Abel of Fayette ME & Miss Sarah RICHARD at East Winthrop ME [14 Feb 1850]
   Abigail O & Gilbert GROSS at Hallowell ME [4 Dec 1845]
   Abigail of Lebanon ME at South Berwick ME [24 Jul 1838]
   Abigail of Litchfield ME & Samuel JEWETT Esq of Gardiner ME [18 Mar 1833]
   Albert B of Windham ME & Martha B MORTON of Gorham ME at Saccarappa ME [4 Jun 1846]
   Amanda F & Jeremiah NORTON at Strong ME [11 Jun 1846]
   Ann F & James S McLELLAN of Richmond ME at Roxbury MA [5 Nov 1846]
   Arethusa Anna & Rev John JOHNSON (under appointment as missionary to China) at Eastport ME [17 Jun 1847]
   Augusta Ann & James P WHITTIER at Dover ME [30 Jul 1846]
   B B of Unity ME & Annie C AYER at Freedom ME [3 May 1849]
   Benjamin Jr & Miss Sylvina CUSHMAN at Portland ME [23 Jan 1845]
   C F & Elivina H GAGE at West Waterville ME [5 Oct 1848]
   Caroline & Gorham PALMER at East Winthrop ME [20 May 1847]
   Ceyenne of Barnard VT & John M RAMSEY at Skowhegan ME [21 Oct 1836]
   David M & Lucy J PEACOCK at Gardiner ME [14 May 1846]
   Ebenezer F of Madison ME & Philena WARD of Madison at N Anson ME [28 Dec 1848]
   Edward S & Hannah J SMART both of Swanville ME at Belfast ME [12 Jun 1841]
   Elbridge H of (Winthrop ME) & Rebecca P WOODBURY of Monmouth ME at Monmouth on 14th inst by Rev Mr ROBINSON [24 Sept 1842]
   Elvira of Norway ME & S P ROWE of Greenwood ME [6 Feb 1845]
   Emeline & Rufus DUNHAM at Westbrook ME [9 May 1837]
   Fraziette C & Bradford Y REID at Vassalboro ME [7 Oct 1847]
   George Esq & Miss Mary Ann HASKELL at Bluehill ME [12 Aug 1847]
   George S of Dover ME & Pamelia M KING at Monmouth ME on 13 Jun by Rev J PRESCOTT [8 Jul 1852]
   George W of Pittston ME & Lenora V BAILEY at Gardiner ME [12 Nov 1846]
   Hannah M of Pittston ME & Rev William S BARTLET of Little Falls NY at Gardiner ME at Christ Church Weds 9th inst by Rev William R BABCOCK [19 Jun 1841]
   Harriet M of Fayette ME & Sherburne MORRILL of Winthrop ME at Fayette ME on 3rd inst by Rev L C STEVENS [16 May 1840]
   Henry of Dresden ME & Sophronia WHITE at Winthrop ME [5 Oct 1848]
   Henry of Hallowell ME & Jane B COPP at Augusta ME [4 Oct 1849]
   Hepsey D & Joseph L STEVENS at Gouldsboro ME [21 Oct 1847]
   Hiram & Priscilla HARMON at Fayette ME [6 Apr 1839]
   J L Rev, pastor of the Universalist Church in New Sharon ME & Miss Mary L SMITH at Hallowell ME on 10th inst by Rev William A DREW [22 May 1845]
   Janetter L & Elisha BROWN at Milo ME [25 May 1848]
   Jason of Augusta ME & Miss Caroline HALLETT at West Waterville ME on the 16th inst by S KIMBALL Esq [20 Dec 1849]

STEVENS (cont.) Jesse T of Cambridgeport MA & Miss Violet EASTMAN of Vassalboro ME at Fairfield ME [15 Jan 1846]
- Joanna & Michael WOODWARD at Gardiner ME [28 Jun 1849]
- John Elder of Bath ME & Miss Agnes AMES at Gardiner ME [3 Jun 1847]
- John F of Andover MA & Lydia HOLT of (Winthrop ME) at Winthrop on Thurs evening last by the Rev FULLER [28 Sept 1833]
- John Jr & Martha J BROWN both of Swanville ME at Belfast ME [13 Jan 1848]
- John of Belfast ME & Barbara JOHNSON at Bremen ME [30 Aug 1849]
- Joseph E & Susan A LEWIS at West Waterville ME [11 Sept 1845]
- Joseph L & Hepsey D STEVENS at Gouldsboro ME [21 Oct 1847]
- Joseph of Winthrop ME & Miss A F CLARK by Rev Mr WINSLOW at New Portland ME [8 Jun 1848]
- Josephine & Insign GOODING at Livermore ME [7 May 1846]
- Julia O of Pittston ME & Sebeus C MAINS Esq counsellor at law of Little Falls NY at Gardiner ME [30 Sept 1843]
- L C of Waldoboro ME & Miss Caroline TUCK at Fayette ME on June 20th by Rev A DRINKWATER [8 Jul 1852]
- Laura of Worcester MA & Joseph BRADSTREET Esq at Worcester MA [12 Feb 1842]
- Louisa A & David SEWALL at Sumner ME on 2d inst [18 Apr 1840]
- Luther C Rev of Richmond Village ME & Miss Sarah BANKS at Hartford ME [27 Jun 1834]
- Margaret S & Albion WEBB at Montville ME [19 Feb 1852]
- Maria & Peter MILLER at Hallowell ME [25 Apr 1850]
- Martha A P & Samuel T SHANNON at Saco ME [6 Nov 1845]
- Mary Ann of Monmouth ME & Samuel FOGG of Readfield ME at Winthrop ME [25 Jun 1846]
- Mary E & Thomas J RANKINS at this city (Augusta) ME on Apr 5th by John A PETTINGILL Esq [18 Apr 1850]
- Mary & Joseph BUNKER Jr at Athens ME [29 Nov 1849]
- Melvina & John Morrell at (Augusta) ME on 7th Sept [28 Sept 1848]
- Moses Jr, publisher of the *Blade* & Miss Sarah C READ d/o the late Hon READ of Strong ME at Augusta ME [3 Oct 1844]
- Nancy C & Josiah H GOODRICH at Moscow ME [25 Apr 1850]
- Nancy & Ebenezer of Saco ME at Buxton ME [11 Mar 1847]
- Nancy & Solomon LARRABEE at Thomaston ME [24 Aug 1848]
- Pamelia & Brian STACKPOLE at Augusta ME on Apr 2 by Alanson STARKS Esq [5 Jun 1845]
- Rhoda H & Samuel F COUSINS at Abbot ME [10 Dec 1846]
- Rosannah of New Sharon ME & Seth HINCKLEY at Mercer ME [20 Jan 1837]
- Roxana of Orono ME & Seth HINCKLEY at Mercer ME [18 Apr 1837]
- S S of Belfast ME & Miss Francis C NEWELL at Winslow ME [22 Oct 1842]
- S & Jane FAULKNER at Fort Kent Aroostook Co ME [11 Mar 1847]
- Samuel & Cynthia M MOODY at Fort Kent Aroostook Co ME [8 Jun 1848]
- Sarah H & William C ROBINSON at Bangor ME [26 Mar 1842] & on 26th inst by John S SAYWARD Esq [2 Apr 1842]
- Sarah S of Northport ME & James M BICKNELL at Belfast ME [2 Oct 1851]

STEVENS (cont.) Simon & Miss Phebe HATCH at Eastport ME [26 Mar 1842]
    Sophronia Mrs & Thomas ESTES at Stetson ME [8 Jun 1848]
    Susan & Elbridge POOR at Andover ME [7 Feb 1834]
    Susan (ae 13y) & Edward SHALLON (ae 15) at Keesville NY [10 Apr 1835]
    Thomas & Miss Sarah CURRIER at Anson ME [14 Jan 1847]
    Vester L Joseph B BRUMLEY of Norwich CT at East Thomaston ME [14 Mar 1850]
    Vilena formerly of Maine & Maj John A HOLTON at Quincy IL [11 Sept 1845]
    William A of Hallowell ME & Miss Mary DAY at Gardiner ME [17 May 1849]
    William of Gardiner ME & Miss Mary P MAXFIELD at China ME [2 Dec 1847]
    William P of Carroll & Miss Sabrina E BRADBURY of Norway ME at Norway [19 Mar 1846]
    William & Asenath M MORRISON at Ellsworth ME [7 Apr 1848]
STEVENSON Jerome & Phebe SANBORN both of Waldo Plt ME at Belfast ME [8 Aug 1840] & [25 Jul 1840]
    Sophia & John DENNETT at Saco ME [11 Jul 1844]
STEWARD Bryce M Mr & Maria LEIGHTON at Solon ME [13 Feb 1851] & [30 Jan 1851]
    Caroline E & Baxter BOWMAN at Gardiner ME [8 Feb 1844]
    Climena & Amos F PARLIN at Anson ME [21 Nov 1834]
    Gustavus A of Anson ME & Nancy L HAPGOOD of Waterford ME at Waterville ME [11 Apr 1844]
    John of New Vineyard ME & Mrs Almira ELLIOT at New Portland ME [17 Feb 1848]
    Marcellus & Hannah WILLIAMS both of Anson ME at Skowhegan ME [18 Jul 1844]
    Martha J & Benjamin R ELLIOT of New Portland ME at New Vineyard ME [26 Jun 1845]
    Sarah C & John C HIGGINS of Fayette ME at Skowhegan ME [6 Nov 1851]
    William S of Gardiner ME & Miss Rebecca McLAUGHLIN of Industry ME at Hallowell ME [28 Aug 1845]
STEWART Eliza A & Micah A BLACKWELL at Norridgewock ME [19 Nov 1846]
    Eliza A & Washington PALMER at Pittston ME [7 Nov 1844]
    Elizabeth & Matthew HODGINS at Augusta ME [11 Feb 1847]
    Esther Ann & Samuel S STEWART at Lewiston ME [10 Jan 1850]
    Hiram & Miss Margerie ROSS at Bath ME [9 Sept 1836]
    John of Bath ME & Frances SEWALL at Augusta ME [24 Apr 1851]
    John of Brunswick ME & Frances E SEWELL at China ME on 30th March [10 Apr 1851]
    Levi M & Miss Julia PRATT at Newport ME [4 Apr 1850]
    Martha & Benjamin ELLIOT of New Portland ME at New Vineyard ME [16 Oct 1845]
    Mary Ann & Leander YOUNG at Warren ME [3 Feb 1848]
    Richard 2d of Gardiner ME & Miss Laura S LOW at Winthrop ME on 12th inst [26 Sept 1837]
    Samuel S & Miss Esther Ann STEWART at Lewiston ME [10 Jan 1850]

STEWART (cont.) Sarah C & Maj Isaac N TUCKER at Gardiner ME [29 Jan 1836]
   Susan of Farmington ME & Franklin T FAIRBANKS, formerly of (Winthrop) at Farmington ME by Rev Mr ROGERS [11 Jun 1842]
   Wallis of China ME & Elizabeth TAYLOR at Windsor ME by Charles A RUSS Esq [10 Apr 1838]
   William & Lucy CUSHMAN at Lewiston ME [6 Feb 1851]
   Zeruah F & Abel SAMPSON of Temple ME at Farmington ME [7 May 1842]

STICKNEY Caroline O & Martin SMITH at Hallowell ME [20 Mar 1841]
   Clementine A & Asa D LIBBY at Hallowell ME on Apr 8th both of Augusta ME [18 Apr 1850]
   George W & Harriet S MARSTON at Waterville ME [25 May 1848]
   Harriet S & Edward A JENKS at Concord NH [3 Jun 1852]
   Harriet & James FOYE at Newport on 28 Apr [20 May 1852]
   Jonathan Esq & Miss Clarissa M EATON at Perry ME [25 Feb 1843]
   Lavinia B & Henry A PETTENGILL at Eastport ME [1 May 1838]
   Mary G d/o Paul STICKNEY Esq, & Charles W SAFFORD at Hallowell ME on Sept 25th [15 Oct 1842]
   Reuel of Windsor ME & Ann J COOMBS at Whitefield ME [15 Apr 1847]
   Thomas of Carthage ME & Olive S SMITH of Wilton ME [30 Apr 1846]

STILES Moses O of Haverhill MA & Miss Harriet N PALL at Albion ME [16 Dec 1847]
   Nancy & Benjamin McALLISTER at Stoneham ME [5 Aug 1852]

STILKEY Hiram C & Cordelia H STEARNS both of Bath ME by Rev Mr ALLEN at (Augusta) ME [20 Jul 1848]
   Charles & Miss Mary RHINES at Augusta ME [12 Aug 1843]

STILL Joseph of Wiscasset ME & Martha Ann CHILDS at Hallowell ME [5 Jun 1835]

STILLMAN Lewis M Esq of Hartford CT & Miss Sarah C, d/o Sailing Master F W MOORES USN at Mercer ME on the 3d inst by Rev Oren SIKES [28 Nov 1844]

STILSON Anna E & Henry S SMITH of Searsport ME at Waterville ME [19 Aug 1847]
   Lemuel A & Miss Juliette MERRILL at Waterville ME [5 Nov 1846]
   Nancy A & Rufus NASON at Waterville ME [4 Oct 1849]

STIMPSON Josiah & Martha C STROUT at Biddeford ME [30 Sept 1847]
   Nathaniel of Bath ME & Ann HUNT at Berwick ME [20 Sept 1849]

STIMSON Thomas T & Eliza GILPATRICK at Limerick ME [8 Jul 1847]
   Timothy R Capt & Thankful PURRINGTON at Bowdoinham ME [27 Jul 1848]

STINSON Clarissa M & Thomas A GETCHELL of Camden ME at Deer Isle by Rev Jonathan ADAMS [14 Aug 1851]
   David S of Lewiston ME & Emily STANWOOD at Augusta ME on Thanksgiving eve by Rev WEBB [11 Dec 1851]
   Edward P Capt of Woolwich ME & Emily T REED at Bath ME [2 Mar 1848]
   Thos T & Ruby WIGGINS by David G ROBINSON Esq at Albion ME on 21 Nov [30 Nov 1848]

STINCHFIELD Abigail C & John VOSE both of Winthrop ME at Wayne ME [24 Dec 1846]

STINCHFIELD (cont.) Augusta & Benjamin LINKFIELD at Skowhegan ME [5 Apr 1849]
    Charles B of St Albans ME & Abigail WOOD d/o Elijah W Esq at Winthrop ME on Thurs last by Rev THURSTON [23 Nov 1839]
    Emily J & Benjamin H GILBRETH at Farmington ME [12 Mar 1842]
    J King, M.D., of Elmira NY & Glorvina SMITH of Wayne ME at New York City [17 Jun 1852]
    Jeremiah of Danville ME & Abigail R NELSON at New Gloucester ME [22 Jul 1852]
    Joseph P & Sarah W PAINE both of Bangor ME at Dover ME [25 Jun 1846]
    Olive M & Lucius WOODMAN of New Gloucester ME at Danville ME [1 Aug 1844]
    Sally B & Luther C POLLARD at Milo ME on 2d Nov [9 Nov 1848]
    Sarah & Harrison GOULD at Leeds ME [14 Oct 1847]
    Woodbury & Frances W FULLER at Wayne ME by Rev C FULLER [2 Oct 1851]
STINEFORD George H & Dana A SPAULDING both of Dover ME at Foxcroft ME [12 Aug 1852]
STINNET Eliza Mrs a native of Cherokee & Lorenzo DeLANO Esq formerly of ME at Parkhill, Cherokee Nation [27 Feb 1845]
STINSON Alexander & Betsey Jane DAVIS at Auburn ME [12 Aug 1852]
    Avery & Betsy THURLOW at Deer Isle ME by Joseph STINSON Esq [21 Oct 1836]
    Benjamin Capt of Bowdoinham ME & Nancy MARSTON at Bath ME [7 Aug 1835]
    David S of Bath ME & Hannah L S PALMER at Hallowell ME [27 Jun 1840]
    David T & Mary F STETSON at Bath ME [8 Jan 1846]
    Gideon G & Martha Ann FULLERTON at Woolwich ME [19 Dec 1840]
    Harriet M & George W GRANT at Prospect ME on 1st inst [15 Jan 1842]
    Jane H & Nicholas L HOGAN at Arrowsic ME [26 Aug 1847]
    John B & Rosetta L PENDLETON at Prospect ME [9 Sept 1847]
    Jordan F of Albion ME & Maria ROSS at Newport ME [21 May 1846]
    Margaret E of Arrowsic ME & John C COBURN of Pittston ME at Georgetown ME [5 Aug 1847]
    Olive of Topsham ME & John E ERSKIN of Bristol ME at New York 9th ult [6 May 1843]
    Rebecca A & Cyrus S SHERBURN at Prospect ME on 6th [15 Jul 1852]
    Susan D & Abial O GAMMON of Naples ME at Arrowsic ME [28 Jun 1849]
    William C & Lucy FULLER at Pittsfield ME [2 Sept 1847]
STOCKBRIDGE David at Corinth ME & Ann COPELAND of Dexter ME [19 Jun 1845]
    John C Rev of Waterville ME & Mary T MAURAN of Warren at Warren RI [5 Dec 1844]
    Mary G & William DRUMMOND at Bath ME [9 Nov 1848]
    Sarah H & Merrill THOMAS both of Byron ME at Byron on Nov 29 by John REED Esq [18 Dec 1838]
STOCK Henrietta & Mr J ASIEL at New York City on Apr 27th [11 May 1848]
STOCKIN Miss & Thomas C WOOD at N Yarmouth ME [1 Aug 1837]

STOCKIN (cont.) Louisa of Monmouth ME & Edward STORER of N Yarmouth ME at Monmouth ME on 10th inst by Rev PRESCOTT [16 Oct 1841]
 Lucretia & Beza L STORER both of Monmouth ME at Wayne ME on Sun last by George SMITH Esq [23 Oct 1835]
STOCKING A T of Garland ME & Julia A CHAPMAN of Liberty ME at North Searsport ME [21 Sept 1848]
STOCKWELL Russell & Mary BUMPUS at Mexico ME [27 Jun 1840]
STODDARD Joseph S & Mary D HARRIS at Brunswick ME on 18th inst by Rev Benjamin TITCOMB [29 Jan 1836]
STODDER Deborah M only d/o E C S Esq late of Nashville TN & J W WINSLOW Esq of Readfield at Readfield ME on Oct 30 by Rev F MERRIAM of Winthrop [4 Nov 1843]
STOKES Richard & Eleanor MORGAN at Hallowell ME [13 Nov 1841]
STONE Abigail d/o the late Daniel S Esq & William CALDWELL at Augusta ME [2 Jan 1838]
 Abigail M of Waterford ME & Andrew J PATTE of Fryeburg ME at Waterford [14 Mar 1850]
 Alfred J Col of Brunswick ME & Margaret C ORR d/o the late Hon Benjamin O of Brunswick ME at Bangor ME [14 Mar 1840]
 Annourill R C Mrs & Sewall CRAM at Wilton ME [13 Jun 1844]
 Benjamin Franklin & Caroline G KENNEY of Sidney ME at Gardiner ME [10 Apr 1851]
 Bethana & Sewall SHUTE at Prospect ME [1 Feb 1844]
 C Rev of Fairfield ME & Frances SYLVESTER at Jay ME [24 Jul 1851] & [7 Aug 1851]
 Catharine & Albion K P DUNHAM of Paris ME at Waterford ME [1 Oct 1846]
 Charles C & Lydia A CROWELL at Augusta ME on 28 Sept by S TITCOMB Esq [2 Oct 1851]
 Charles W & Caroline PISHON at Augusta ME on Mon eve last by Rev F FREEMAN [14 Jan 1843]
 Cordelia L & Robert M OWEN at Brunswick ME [25 Jan 1849]
 Daniel P of Boston MA & Valeria GOODENOW of Alfred ME at Alfred [22 Aug 1837]
 Daniel & Ann E JOHNSON at Wiscasset ME [7 Oct 1843]
 Eben Dr & Betsey ROBERTS at Westbrook ME [17 Aug 1848]
 Elizabeth D & Edward W PENNEY at Worcester MA both parties being deaf and mute and formerly inmates at the Hartford Asylum for the Deaf and Dumb [23 May 1837]
 Elizabeth H & Simeon H JONES at Sweden ME [22 May 1845]
 Esther B & Jesse CROSSMAN at Belfast ME [3 Aug 1848]
 George W at Waterford ME & Mary A JORDAN of Albany [8 Mar 1849]
 Harriet & Benjamin F EVELETH at Gardiner ME [2 Dec 1847]
 James of Gardiner ME & Delia Ann THEOBALD at Dresden ME [5 Nov 1842]
 James P Rev of St Johnsbury VT & Mrs Nancy K TOBIN at Belfast ME [25 Oct 1849]
 John T & Abigail JARVIS at Gardiner ME [18 Jun 1846]
 Mary D & Daniel BROWN 2d at Waterford ME [8 Nov 1849]
 Mary W & James H JACKSON at Paris ME [22 Feb 1844]
 Miranda Mrs & Stephen PERKINS at Kennebunkport ME [25 Dec 1845]

Marriage Notices from the "Maine Farmer"   395

STONE (cont.) Nancy & Thomas J BLUNT at Union ME [20 May 1847]
    Oliver STONE & Harriet FULLER both of (Winthrop ME) at Augusta ME on Mon last by Rev William A DREW [19 Oct 1833]
    Phebe G & Noah F WEEKS at Hallowell ME [25 Apr 1850]
    Rebecca & Andrew L E NASH at Waterford ME [5 Feb 1852]
    Samuel of Woburn MA & Mrs Ann GOULD at Augusta ME [18 Nov 1843]
    Sherman of Ripley ME & Lydia F ROBINSON of Dover ME at Dover ME by Rev Nathaniel ROBINSON [12 Feb 1842]
    Susan Jane Mrs & William WALKER at Thorndike ME [25 Feb 1847]
    Z Eugene formerly of Paris ME & Charlotte SHAW formerly of Norridgewock ME at Lowell MA [11 Feb 1847]
STORER Amos of Robbinston ME & Louisa COMSTOCK at Lubec ME [15 Jul 1847]
    Beza L & Lucretia STOCKIN both of Monmouth ME at Wayne ME on Sun last by George SMITH Esq [23 Oct 1835]
    Beza L & Mrs Mary Jane BLUE at Monmouth ME by Rev J PRESCOT [11 Sept 1845]
    Charles A & Julia A HAUPT both of Waldoboro ME at Providence [20 Sept 1849]
    David W & Sarah W SMITH at Bath ME [3 Sept 1846]
    Edward of N Yarmouth ME & Louisa STOCKIN of Monmouth ME at Monmouth on 10th inst by Rev PRESCOTT [16 Oct 1841]
    Gilman of Carthage & Angeline HOLMAN at Dixfield [25 Mar 1852]
    Horace P of Portland ME & Mary T BARKER at Limerick ME [13 May 1847]
    Julia of Weld ME & James SNOWMAN at Weld ME by J TYLER Esq at Weld [20 Feb 1845]
    Luther of Bath ME & Jane BOOKER of Durham ME at Durham [26 Jun 1838]
    Maria H & James P WHEELER at Eastport ME [1 Apr 1836]
    Rachael & Benjamin S HAWES 2d at Weld ME [4 Apr 1844]
    Rebecca & James M COLSON at Gardiner ME on 10th inst [30 Dec 1847]
    Sarah & Charles G GILBERT at Hallowell ME [4 Jun 1846]
STORMS A & Martin BLAKE of New York at Standish MA [22 Aug 1844]
STORRER John & Rooxby [sic] WOLTZE at Waldoboro ME [6 Jan 1837]
STORY William K & Charlotte L LUCE at Readfield ME [14 Jun 1849]
STOUT Julia & George C WAITE at Washington NJ on 27th ult [10 Feb 1848]
STOVER Crawford A Capt & Lydia J SNOW at Rockland ME [7 Aug 1851]
    Eliza & M Reuben N ELLIS at Bluehill ME [16 Apr 1842]
    Harriet M & Christopher C BOWMAN at Augusta ME on Tues morning by Rev M FULLER [16 May 1844]
    John P of St George ME & Elmira B WALL at Thomaston ME [16 Mar 1848]
    Joseph G Capt & Augusta M NOYES both of Bucksport ME at New York [16 Jul 1842]
    Mary E & Henry TAPLEY Jr at York ME [16 Apr 1846]
    Norton Capt & Lydia S MERRYMAN at Harpswell ME [31 October 1844]
    Oliver of Harpswell ME & M C COLBY at Webster ME [25 Nov 1847]
    Paul Capt of Harpswell ME & Lydia DINSMORE at Anson ME [14 Nov 1844]
STOWELL Julia C & Orseamus SMILEY at Paris ME [20 Sept 1849]

STOWELL (cont.) Olive Mrs & James COLBY at Gray ME [11 Dec 1845]
STOWE Louisa A & Eben F DUDLEY both of Augusta ME at Hallowell ME [25 Dec 1851]
STOWERS A P of Prospect ME & S H NICKERSON Esq of Swanville ME at Prospect [3 Jul 1845]
STOYELL Margaret & Oliver CROMWELL at Mercer ME [11 Jun 1846]
STOYWELL H B Esq & Mary BOARDMAN at Framington [9 Oct 1845]
STRATTON Silby & Edward A PAINE at Winslow ME [21 Dec 1848]
STRATTON Lois M of Albion ME & Capt Samuel BADGER of Kittery ME at Newcastle ME [1 Mar 1849]
   Lucetta & Rev Milton CHALMERS at Albion ME [25 Jun 1846]
STRAW Giles & Elvira H MACUMBER of Readfield ME at Readfield ME on Weds eve last by Samuel P BENSON Esq of Winthrop ME [25 Jan 1840]
STREET John of Portland ME & Rachel PETTENGILL of Bath ME at Phipsburg ME [14 Nov 1834]
   Thomas J & Ellen Maria McMORRISON at Bath ME on Thurs eve by Rev STEARNS [23 Oct 1838]
STRICKLAND A S C Esq of Wilton ME & Lucilla T CHANDLER of Winthrop ME on Tues morning last by Rev THURSTON [11 Nov 1836]
   C Henry of Wilton ME & Martha Jane d/o Oliver O Esq at Hallowell ME [1 Jan 1842]
   Jane C & Alonzo WASHBURN at Livermore ME [25 Apr 1850]
   L Esq of Bangor ME & Susan S BRETTUN at Livermore ME [2 Nov 1848]
   Lucilla Mrs & Rev John PERHAM of Madison ME at Wilton ME [5 Dec 1844]
   S T Gen of Bangor ME & Ruth W BACON at Buxton ME [7 May 1846]
STRONG Chauncey & Mary Ann KASSON at Bethlehem CT [24 Jun 1833]
STROUT Diana & John MARR at Wales ME by Joel SMALL Esq [13 Aug 1846]
   Louisa & Moses SYLVESTER at South Freedom ME [3 Oct 1840]
   Martha A & David McFARLAND both of Wales ME at Augusta ME [15 Jan 1846]
   Martha C & Josiah STIMPSON at Biddeford ME [30 Sept 1847]
   Mary E & Horace L CORBETT at Durham ME [11 Jun 1846]
   Micajah C of Limington ME & Olive F JACKSON of Gorham ME at Gorham ME [11 Jul 1840]
   Rebecca & Harvey S WILSON at Bradford ME [2 Jul 1846]
   Robert P & Eliza C HEBBARD at Brunswick ME [15 Oct 1846]
   Ruth H & James DUNN Jr at Poland ME [4 Apr 1837]
   Sarah L & Charles T DAVIS at Portland ME [24 Apr 1845]
STUART Joseph W of Belgrade ME & Eva R CLARK d/o Elisha C Esq at China ME [22 Oct 1846]
   George & Cementha WING at Vassalboro ME [26 Feb 1836]
   James H of Vassalboro ME & Jane G HIGGINS of Hampden ME at Hampden [14 Mar 1837]
   Mary G of Augusta ME & Charles W ATKINS of Mt Vernon ME at Readfield ME [24 Jun 1847]
   Nancy Ann & Samuel KIMBALL at Belgrade ME [15 Jan 1846]
STUBBS Adaline & Benjamin A JOY at Winthrop ME on Mon Eve last by John MAY Esq [11 Apr 1834]

STUBBS (cont.) David H & Hannah D PORTER at Franklin ME? [12 Feb 1852]
    Jordan S W & Sarah PHOENIX at Pownal ME [7 Nov 1844]
STUDLEY Joseph & Eleanor PIERCE both of Windsor ME at Augusta ME [23 Nov 1833] & [30 Nov 1833]
    Robert & Mary Jane ALLEN d/o Rev John A at China ME [16 May 1834]
    Rosanna & Alexander SPEAR 2d of Warren ME at Waldoboro ME [4 Nov 1847]
    Silas of Boston MA & Malvina CROOKER at Bath ME [19 Feb 1846]
STURGESS Ambrose H of Cherryfield ME & Fanny W TIBBETS at Columbia ME [30 Sept 1847]
STURGIS David Capt & Mrs Betsey TAYLOR at Norridgewock ME [24 Apr 1845]
    David Jr of Norridgewock ME & Mary MASON at Pittston ME by Rev Darius FORBES of Hallowell ME [14 Dec 1839]
    Ellen M & Franklin LIBBY at Vassalboro ME on 25th inst [30 Dec 1847]
    James of Vassalboro ME & Nancy A DUDLEY by Rev William BOWLER at China on 7th June [29 Jun 1848]
    Julia & Hosea RIPLEY of Boston MA at Vassalboro ME [9 Jul 1846]
    Nancy & Cornelius HERSEY at Boston MA [31 Oct 1840]
    Olive P & Cyrus F BRYANT of Fairfield ME at Vassalboro ME [11 Apr 1844]
STURTIVANT - STURTEVANT - STUREVANT - STURDEVANT
    David & Sophronia RICHARDS at Parkman ME [21 Nov 1837]
    Dorcas Mrs & John WOODMAN at Winslow ME [25 Oct 1849]
    Emily J & Daniel F CHANDLER at Winthrop ME on Weds eve last by Rev CLEAVELAND [26 Dec 1840]
    G W Capt & Mary SMALL at Richmond ME [26 Apr 1849]
    Joseph Dr of Mechanic Falls ME & Harriet BARTELS at Portland ME [19 Apr 1849]
    Leonard of New Orleans MA? & Mary V WHEELOCK of Readfield ME [16 Jul 1842]
    Newall, merchant, of Nantucket MA & Hannah M FARRELL at Hallowell ME on Sun eve 19th inst by Rev WEBBER [28 Nov 1837]
    Olive A & Charles PRATT at Dexter ME [20 Jan 1848]
    Olive & Solomon PARSONS of Danville ME at Hebron ME [1 Jul 1852]
    Rachel d/o Ephraim S Esq of Cumberland ME & Rev Steven ALLEN of NY at Cumberland [21 Aug 1838]
    Rachel L & Mr F A CHASE at Fayette ME [27 Apr 1848]
    Rosanna & Peter FERNE at Foxcroft ME [28 Sept 1848]
    Sarah A Mrs & Jeremiah DURGIN at Limerick ME [7 Mar 1850]
    Stephen M of Boston MA & Martha J O LINDSAY by James H MACOMBER Esq at Milo ME on Aug 6th [17 Aug 1848]
    Valmore & Mary Ann FOSS both of Wayne ME at Fayette ME [8 May 1851]
    William H Capt of Bowdoinham ME & Ellen C T SMITH of Richmond ME at Richmond [2 Oct 1845]
SULLIVAN G R of Frankfort ME & Mary C CARTER at Brookline MA [20 Jul 1848]
    Hosea of Frankfort ME & Rosina HEALD at Camden ME [12 Jul 1849]
    Richard Esq of New York & Harriet GARDINER d/o Robert H G Esq at Gardiner ME [24 Sept 1846]

SUMMER Caleb & Sophia CURTIN at Leeds ME on 25th inst by Mr PIERCE [2 Jan 1835]
SUMMERS Emeline M & George W CARR formerly of Belfast ME at New York [28 Aug 1838]
SUMNER Hannah F & Enoch POST of S Thomaston ME at Union ME [6 Feb 1851]
   Jane R of Union ME & Harvey B SIMMONS at Warren ME [29 Jul 1852]
   Rebecca A & Frederick B RICE at Goose River ME? [4 Mar 1852]
   Seth & Susan RODGERS at Bowdoinham ME [14 Aug 1835]
   Susan Mrs of Bowdoinham ME & Capt Mathew PATTEN at Topsham ME [5 Dec 1837]
   William Capt of Alna ME & Mary J HENDERSON at Richmond ME [17 Feb 1848]
SUTHERLAND George W & Mary E HALL at Saco ME [5 Jul 1849]
   John P & Abigail FOLLET at Winthrop ME on Sun Eve the 18th inst by Oliver FOSTER Esq [23 May 1834]
   Nancy P & Jeremiah F BOOTHBAY at Saco ME [13 Apr 1848]
SWAIN Abigail M & Bethuel SMILEY of Gardiner ME at Skowhegan ME [8 Mar 1849]
   Achsah C & Mr J Gancelo WING both of Chesterville ME at Farmington ME [17 Jan 1850]
   Edward T & Abby L DAY at Hallowell ME [1 Feb 1844]
   Helen J & Albion K P KING at Skowhegan ME [6 Nov 1851]
   William & Adaline WORTHLEY [2 Dec 1847]
   William & Susan ROSS at Skowhegan ME [1 Jan 1846]
SWALLOW Phebe S & Horace KALLOCK at Belfast ME [9 May 1844]
   Susan & Rev Allen GREELEY of Turner ME at N Yarmouth ME [26 Mar 1846]
SWAN Asa & Harriet N WINSLOW at Bath ME [2 Mar 1848]
   Benjamin A, printer, & Eliza A KNOWLTON d/o David K at Augusta ME on 16th inst by Rev MORSE [20 May 1847]
   Caroline F Mrs, youngest d/o late Gen Henry KNOX & Hon John HOLMES of Alfred ME at Thomaston ME [15 Aug 1837]
   Charles Frederick & Ann M PROVINS at Augusta ME on Thurs eve last by Rev Dr TAPPAN [4 Nov 1847]
   Charlotte W d/o Benjamin S Esq & Edward ROWSE Jr at Augusta ME [21 Sept 1839]
   Edward B & Sarah W DAVIS at Gardiner ME [8 Feb 1840]
   Emeline N & Samuel WEBBER at Gardiner ME [Aug 12 1847]
   Emma J G & F GLAZIER Jr at Gardiner ME [5 Apr 1849]
   Fenno B & Mary M YOUNG of Palermo ME at Gardiner ME [10 Jul 1851]
   Francis K & Emily BRADBURY at Calais ME [7 Oct 1843]
   Francis W of Bloomfield ME & Mary Ann LITTLEFIELD of Brunswick ME at Skowhegan ME [28 Nov 1837]
   Jacob H of Denmark ME & Eunice A FROST at Norway ME [12 Dec 1844]
   Leander S & Harriet A DECOSTER at Paris ME [5 Feb 1852]
   Lydia A & Capt F J PIPER at Camden ME [23 Oct 1845]
   Mary E & J Prescott WYMAN at Augusta ME on Thurs last by Rev B TAPPAN [13 Nov 1838]
   Mercy P d/o Hon Edward S & Charles B CLAPP at Gardiner ME [3 Oct 1844]
   Priscilla Mrs & Stephen COBB at Bangor ME [1 Aug 1844]

SWAN (cont.) Sarah P & R H MANNING at Calais ME [21 Nov 1840]
 Urana B & Horace EDGERLEY at Paris ME [10 May 1849]
SWANTON Albion P of Bangor ME & Emily J PARSHLEY at Sangerville ME [27 Apr 1848]
SWASEY/SWAZEY Gustavus A Capt, master of the *Empire*, & Clarissa Jane CLIFFORD at Bath ME on 16th inst by Rev J T GILMAN [3 Dec 1842]
 Henry S Jr of Bangor ME & Mary L BANN at New Orleans LA [11 Apr 1837]
 John W Esq & Elizabeth CUNNINGHAM both of Bucksport ME at Providence RI on 3 inst (Apr 3) 1851 [24 Apr 1851]
 Maria B & John J LEE at Bucksport ME [26 Aug 1847]
 Mary J & James CARTER at Bucksport ME [22 Jan 1846]
SWEAT Maria & Stephen CLAPP both of Brownfield ME at Maxfield ME [27 Aug 1846]
 Maria T S & Theodore S DAVIS of Brownfield ME at Maxfield ME [5 Dec 1844]
SWEENEY Mrs Bridget & Hugh Johnston at Belfast ME [15 Apr 1852]
SWEET Benjamin D & Eliza Ann AUSTIN at Farmington ME [18 Nov 1843]
 Esther A of Dedham & Rev James DRUMMOND of Lewiston Falls ME at Dedham MA [2 Jul 1842]
 Mary Ann & Abraham SOLITUDE at Warren PA on 12th ult (Dr Holmes remarked Solitude Sweetened)[26 Aug 1843]
 Mary E & Alexander M WAITE at Westbrook ME [11 Jul 1840]
 Merinda Jane & Josiah CROSBY both of Arrowsic ME at Wiscasset ME [22 Feb 1844]
SWEETLAND Arabella of Hallowell ME & William PARK of Boston MA at Charlestown MA [28 Jan 1847]
SWEETSER/SWEETSIR Catharine R of Newburgh ME & George GOULD of Dixmont ME at Newburg ME [8 Jul 1843]
 Harriet N & Oakman S STETSON of Bath ME at Cumberland ME [7 Jan 1847] SWEETSIR [21 Jan 1847]
 Helen L & Charles BOOTHBAY at New Gloucester ME [12 Feb 1852]
 Jeremiah of Newburgh ME & Margaret PERKINS at Hermon ME [7 Apr 1848] & [20 Apr 1848]
 Nancy W & William G KNOWLTON at Bath ME [15 Nov 1849]
SWENEY Theresa W ae 22 & Erasmus K GOWN a revolutionary soldier ae 82 at Montville ME [12 Oct 1833]
SWETLAND Oliver & Sarah E SLEEPER at Thomaston ME [14 Jan 1846]
SWETT Benjamin Capt of Bangor ME & Hannah F MORSE of Portland ME at Gray ME [4 Mar 1836]
 E Whitman & Serentha D MORSE at Livermore ME [24 Jun 1847]
 James & Sarah COPELAND at Hamden ME [10 Jul 1835]
 Jane & William DIMMOCK of Limington ME at Hollis ME [17 Dec 1846]
 Sarah A both of Biddeford ME & Edwin C BRACKETT at Saco ME [26 Jun 1851]
 Sarah H & Joseph ROBINSON of Webster ME at Readfield ME [9 Dec 1847]
SWIFT Abigail & Charles P FULLER at Oxford ME [21 May 1842]
 Charles of Gardiner ME & Sarah E ROCKWOOD at Augusta ME [30 Dec 1847]

SWIFT (cont.) Cordelia & Algernon S WRIGHT of Lawrence MA at Wayne ME by Rev C FULLER [18 Oct 1849]
   Cyrus B & Martha J NELSON both of Wayne ME at Winthrop ME on Sun eve May 14 by Rev F FOSTER [20 May 1843]
   Elizabeth A of Wareham MA & Charles W LONGLEY of Sidney ME at Fall River MA [15 Oct 1846]
   Elizabeth R & Rev Caleb FULLER at Wayne ME [8 Jan 1846 &][22 Jan 1846]
   Francis T & Salina MOORE both of Hartland ME at St Albans ME [4 Apr 1850]
   Lyman & Maria THOMAS at Thomaston ME [14 Aug 1851] & [31 Jul 1851]
   Mary B of Norridgewock ME & Charles WYMAN at Bloomfield ME [27 Dec 1849]
   Mary J & Mr J F ROBINSON at Hallowell ME [2 Nov 1848]
   Mary Jane & Richard HOLLAND at Brunswick ME on 22nd inst by Rev George LAMB [21 Jan 1833]
   Sarah J & Leander MORSE at Belmont ME [3 Apr 1851]
   Selena A & John GALE all of Monmouth ME at Monmouth on 13th inst by Rev S HINKLEY [17 Jun 1843]
   Susan D & John SMITH at Lewiston ME [13 Jan 1848]
   Thomas B of Fayette ME & Elizabeth HANDY of Wayne ME at W [23 May 1844]
   Triphena A & Jonathan T TRASK both of Hallowell ME at Mt Vernon ME on Jan 20th by L VEAZIE Esq [7 Feb 1850]

SYLVESTER Ann H & Charles BROWN at Freedom by Stephen STROUT Esq [18 Nov 1847]
   Asa of Plymouth ME & Martha DRAKE at Albion ME [1 Mar 1849]
   Benj N of No 12 R 6 ME & Louisa COFFIN of No 11 R 5 at No 11 Aroostook Co ME by William GARDINER Esq [23 Sept 1847]
   Charles C & Hannah SYLVESTER both of Leeds ME by Rev C FULLER at Wayne ME on 14th Mar [25 Mar 1852]
   Delora & Harrison G O MOWER at Livermore ME on 18th Jan [5 Feb 1852]
   E L Dr of Greene ME & Marcia MARTIN at East Turner ME [27 Jan 1848]
   Elizabeth C d/o Samuel S Esq & G S C DOW (firm of DOW & LYON) all of Bangor ME at Bangor ME on Thurs eve 7th inst by Rev POMPOY [16 Dec 1843]
   Ellis Capt & Margaret Ann GETCHELL at Phipsburg ME [4 Jun 1846]
   Frances & Rev C STONE of Fairfield ME at Jay ME [24 Jul 1851] & [7 Aug 1851]
   George S & Helen COUCH at Hallowell ME [4 Feb 1847]
   Hannah & Charles C SYLVESTER at Wayne ME on 14th Mar [25 Mar 1852]
   Hervey Jr & Zoa TAYLOR at Buckfield ME on 9th inst by Elder Robert HAZE [14 Mar 1850]
   Isaac of Freeport & Nancy P DAVID at Westbrook ME [29 May 1845]
   Joseph ae 82 & Mrs Thankful YOUNG ae 69 at Freeport ME [12 Jun 1845]
   Joseph W & Hannah HOLLAND at Hallowell ME on Sun last by Rev CROSS [29 May 1838]
   Judith of Freedom ME & Daniel YOUNG at Waldoboro ME [5 Mar 1846]

SYLVESTER (cont.) M & B G CHANEY both of Hallowell ME at H by Rev BRAGDON [26 Jun 1841]
 Mark L Esq of Lincolnville ME & Martha Ann T MORSE at Phipsburg ME [3 Dec 1846]
 Marlboro Capt of Portland ME & Mary Ann WILSON at Hallowell ME on 11th inst [18 Sept 1845]
 Mary S C Mrs & John RIPLEY at Bath ME [11 Mar 1847]
 Moses & Louisa STROUT at South Freedom ME [3 Oct 1840]
 Phebe of Norridgewock ME & Daniel WHITE of Orono ME at Norridgewock ME [21 Mar 1834]
 Rosalinda & Amos THOMS both of Leeds ME at Wayne ME [29 Jan 1846]
 William A & Abigail ORR at Harpswell ME [31 Oct 1844]
SYMONDS Adeline E & Sewall LANCASTER Esq at Boxford MA [23 Sept 1836]

- 7 -

TABER Lydia E & Isaac F BROUNE at East Vassalboro ME on 1st Apr 1851 [1 May 1851]
TABER Mary Ann & Elijah S DALY at Vassalboro ME both of this town (Augusta) ME [22 Mar 1849]
 Susan M of Fairhaven MA & Hannibal M SAWTELL formerly of Cornish ME at Augusta ME on Thurs morn by Rev N W WILLIAMS [18 Dec 1845]
TAFT Gardner J of Millbury MA & Dorothy N HOYT at Farmington ME? [20 Dec 1849]
 Stephen of Wayne ME & Mary W FISK of Fayette ME at Wayne ME on 13th inst by R C STARR [19 Nov 1842]
TAILOR Dorcas & Jedediah HARDING at New Sharon ME [18 Sept 1835]
TALBOT Charles J & Delphinia S ROBBINS at Phillips ME on 23 Mar by Archibald TALBOT Esq [22 Apr 1843]
 Emeline C & Capt Joseph M WING at Bangor ME formerly of Portland ME [22 Apr 1836]
 F W Capt of Portland ME & Martha B PERRY at Phipsburg ME [18 Jun 1846]
 George F Esq of East Machias ME & Elizabeth B LINCOLN at Dennysville ME [13 Nov 1851]
 George F Esq of Machias ME & Elizabeth NEIL at Skowhegan ME [6 Jun 1844]
 Mary of Winslow ME & Otis H DUNBAR of Waterville ME at Winslow ME on the 22d ult by Rev Mr JEWETT [12 Feb 1836]
 Nathaniel T Esq of Camden ME & Caroline LUCE of this town (Winthrop ME) at the Congregational Meeting House in Winthrop ME on Sunday last by Rev David THURSTON [23 Sept 1843]
 William C of East Machias ME & Sophia G FOSTER [4 Jun 1846]
TALLMAN Henry & Sarah FITTS at Bath ME [7 Sept 1833]
 John C & Delia A CLARK at Bath ME [9 Sept 1847]
 Redford Capt & Nancy Ann ALLEN at Richmond ME on 6th inst [7 Oct 1844]
TAMAZO Peter L & Eunice JORDAN at Bath ME [29 Apr 1847]
TAPLEY Caroline M & Capt R W LEIGH at Hallowell ME [22 Oct 1846]

TAPLEY (cont.) Cyrus Foss of Wayne ME & Lydia BERRY at Scarborough ME [12 Feb 1836]
 Frances M & Burnham C BENNER of Whitefield ME at Hallowell ME [5 Sept 1844]
 Henry Jr & Mary E STOVER at York ME [16 Apr 1846]
 Mary P & Aaron ROWELL at Frankfort ME [28 Jan 1847]
 Matilda & John CURTIS of Hallowell ME at Litchfield ME [18 Apr 1834]
 Sewall W & Nancy CAMPBELL at Frankfort ME [8 Apr 1847]
 Sophia C & Henry H FORBES at Belfast ME [20 Feb 1845]
 William & Catherine HOPKINS at Gardiner ME [22 Jan 1846]
TAPPAN Benjamin of Hampden ME & Delia d/o William EMMONS Esq of (Hallowell) at Hallowell on Weds morning last by the Rev Mr TAPPAN of Augusta ME [18 Sept 1838]
 Daniel Dana Rev of Winthrop ME & Abigail MARCH at Newburyport MA [25 Jul 1837]
 Edward (ae 15y) & Harriet ALLEN (ae 11y) at Hemstead Harbor Long Island NY? [4 Sept 1838]
 Mary A & Rev John O FISK at (Augusta) ME on 19th inst [28 Sept 1848]
TARBELL Betsey of Vassalboro ME & Amasa COBB at Norridgewock ME [20 Mar 1835]
TARBLE Helen L & Daniel W SHAW at Levant ME [22 Jul 1852]
TARBOX Benjamin & Sarah W CUSHMAN at Phillips ME [13 May 1847]
 Daniel Jr of Phillips ME & Hannah P TAYLOR of Jay ME at Jay ME on Mar 21 by Rev Dexter WATERMAN [22 Apr 1843]
 Deborah & A R GIDDINGS Esq at Danville ME [11 Apr 1850]
 Eliza & Charles COLLINS at Gardiner ME [7 Nov 1844]
 James F & Miss Harriet FLINT at Thomaston ME [14 Oct 1847]
 James Jr & Dolly M LAWRENCE at Gardiner ME [22 Feb 1849]
 John Capt & Miss Lydia F BARTON eldest d/o Asa BARTON Esq at Garland ME [4 Jun 1842]
 Julia S & William BRADSTREET at Gardiner ME [27 Jan 1848]
 Samuel 3rd & Olive DYER at Biddeford ME [4 Mar 1852]
 Stephen M of Westport ME & Eveline A SNIP of Phipsburg ME at Georgetown ME [1 Feb 1849]
 Susan E & Noah C GREENWOOD at New Gloucester ME [3 Jul 1845]
 Valentine C of Ellsworth ME? & Lavina TIBBETTS of Brownville ME? at Providence RI [24 Jul 1851]
 William Esq of Phillips ME & Marinda HANKERSON at Madrid ME [11 Feb 1847]
TARR Abraham Jr & Emily MOSELY at Etna ME [8 Jun 1848]
 Amos D & Diana S SMITH at Lewiston ME [10 May 1849]
 Daniel of Webster ME & Hannah GROVER at Bowdoin ME [1 Feb 1849]
 John & Rhoda C DOUGLASS at Brunswick ME [27 Feb 1845]
TASH Thomas & Jerusha HOLMES at Foxcroft ME [24 Feb 1848]
TATE Thomas T Capt & Mrs Catherine HENSKY at Thomaston ME [14 Oct 1847]
TAYLOR Amasa Jr of China ME & Miss Martha W WHITEHOUSE at Vassalboro ME by Rev Mr YOUNG [16 Jan 1845]
 Ann & Mr C B THOMAS at Chester MA on 18th Nov [15 Jan 1852]
 Ansel G of Jackson Plt "Dead River" ME & Julia A HALL at Presque Isle Aroostook Co ME [13 Jan 1848]

TAYLOR (cont.) Augustus & Eleanor WILSHIRE of Palmyra ME at (Augusta) ME on July 8 by Rev FOSTER [17 Jul 1851]
Benaiah H of Farmington ME & Sally FOSS of Leeds ME [23 Jan 1841]
Betsey K & Jefferson PARSONS both of Augusta ME at Hallowell ME [25 Mar 1847]
Betsey Mrs & Capt David STURGIS at Norridgewock ME [24 Apr 1845]
Betsey & George B HUSSEY at China ME [30 Dec 1847]
Calvin & Martha Jane HIGGINS at Sebasticook ME [7 Jun 1849]
Charles H of Clark Co VA & Ellen CHASE d/o the late Stephen CHASE of Fryeburg ME [27 Aug 1846]
Charles of Albion ME & Mary PARKHURST at Unity ME [27 Mar 1851]
Cynthia & David T GIVEN at Brunswick ME on 24th ult [3 Jun 1836]
David & Fanny TAYLOR at Augusta ME [18 Dec 1845]
Dorcas & Jedediah HARDING at New Sharon ME [2 Oct 1835]
E P & Capt Thomas B SANFORD at Bangor ME [18 Jun 1846]
Eben of Herman ME & Zeruiah S WOODSUM at Albion ME [15 Mar 1849]
Elias & Mehitable MOTHERWELL at Windsor ME [30 Mar 1848]
Elizabeth & Wallis STEWART of China ME at Windsor ME by Charles A RUSS Esq [10 Apr 1838]
Fanny & David TAYLOR at Augusta ME [18 Dec 1845]
George W & Elizabeth BIGELOW at Norridgewock ME [8 May 1845]
Hannah of China ME & William B PRIEST of Vassalboro ME at China ME [25 Feb 1843]
Hannah P & Daniel TARBOX Jr at Jay ME on 21 Mar by Rev Dexter WATERMAN [22 Apr 1843]
Harrison & Esther F THOMS at Augusta ME [26 Mar 1846]
J W & Hannah M CLARK both of (Augusta) ME at Sidney ME [10 Jul 1845]
James C & Roxannah BLANCHARD at Brunswick ME [19 Sept 1844]
Janas & Eliza CLEAVES at Kennebunk ME [1 Jan 1836]
Jane & George WILLISTON at Brunswick ME [21 Dec 1833]
Jason L & Edna A BUTTERFIELD at Skowhegan ME both of Norridgewock ME [19 Aug 1852]
Jason S & Clarissa J MORTON at Norridgewock ME [26 Apr 1849]
Jefferson of Vassalboro ME & Elizabeth L CHASE of Winslow ME at Vassalboro ME by Amos STICKNEY Esq [8 Aug 1837]
Jeremiah & Aurilla MAXIM at Lewiston ME [2 Jan 1851]
John W & Abigail HANSON at Lyman ME [8 Mar 1849]
Leander & Harriet HARVELL both of Madison ME at Solon ME [27 Aug 1846]
Lydia W & Benjamin G McINTIRE at Norridgewock ME [9 May 1844]
M S M Esq of Montpelier VT & Lizzie A CHASE of Farmington ME at Farmington Falls ME [24 Jul 1851]
Martha Jane & Owen B TAYLOR both Norridgewock ME at Bloomfield ME [21 Jun 1849]
Mary Parr, d/o John TAYLOR Esq of Creniton England at Boston MA, & Arthur BERRY Esq of Augusta ME [24 Sept 1842]
Mehitable & Samuel S FARNHAM at Windsor ME [25 Sept 1841]
Orrin & Miss Betsey B MAXIM both of Fairfield ME at Dover NH [23 Aug 1849]

TAYLOR (cont.) Owen B & Martha Jane TAYLOR both of Norridgewock ME at Bloomfield ME [21 Jun 1849]
    R E Rev of Carbondale PA & Harriet Newell HOWARD d/o Daniel HOWARD Esq of (Augusta) ME by Rev Dr TAPPAN of Augusta ME at Vassalboro ME on 13th inst [29 Aug 1840]
    S W Rev, Pastor of the Baptist Church in Hallowell ME & Henrietta REED at East Cambridge MA 17 June [23 Jun 1852]
    Selden of Sebasticook ME & Sarah LAWRENCE at Skowhegan ME [13 Mar 1851]
    Simon N & Martha H F ROGERS at Norridgewock ME [25 Nov 1847]
    Simon & Martha ROGERS at Norridgewock ME [11 Nov 1847]
    Warren & Olive A SMITH at Augusta ME on 21st inst by John A PETTINGILL Esq [31 May 1849]
    William H & Elizabeth J BROWN of Sidney at Augusta ME on Jan 1st by Rev Thomas J DUDLEY [9 Jan 1851]
    William H & Julia Ann KILGORE at Norridgewock ME [15 Jul 1847]
    William & Julia HILTON at Wiscasset ME [17 Dec 1842]
    Zoa & Hervey SYLVESTER Jr at Buckfield ME on 9th inst by Elder Robert HAZE [14 Mar 1850]

TEAGUE Hiram & Mary A SHUMAN at Waldoboro ME [5 Sept 1840]
    Mary L of Newcastle ME & Addison AUSTIN of Waldoboro ME at Providence [25 Sept 1851]
    Thomas M & Fanny N BUTTERFIELD at Wilton ME [18 Jun 1846]

TEBBETS - See TIBBETTS

TEEL Henry H & Sarah S FOUNTAIN at St George ME [4 Dec 1845]

TEMPLE Josiah F of Montville ME & Martha Ann FARNUM at Knox ME [23 Jan 1851]

TENNEY -TENNY Albert G of Baltimore MD & Frances Ann ESTABROOK at Brunswick ME [9 Sept 1836]
    Alonzo & Miss Charlotte MASON at Hallowell ME [23 Nov 1833]
    Alonzo & Miss Sarah O WHITE at Hallowell ME on 2d inst [18 Apr 1840]
    E J Mr of Taunton MA & Delany S WILBUR at East Livermore ME [29 Jun 1848]
    Eliza A & James William of Winthrop ME at Raymond ME [25 Jan 1844]
    Thomas B & Miss E WHITE at Palmyra ME [1 May 1851]

TETFORD Edward of Topsham ME & Mary MOSELY at Bowdoin ME [31 Oct 1844]

TEWSBURY Bradbury & Lois DOORE at Atkinson ME [11 May 1848]

TEWKSBURY Samuel H Dr of Frankfort ME & Diana E SHAW at Oxford ME [20 Jun 1844]

THATCHER - THACHER
    Eunice M & William SMALL at North Yarmouth ME [7 Apr 1848]
    Eleanora W & Charles A EVANS at Concord NH [5 Nov 1846]
    Harriet E, d/o late Judge THATCHER of Bingham ME & George R PAGE of Belgrade ME at Greene ME by Rev Mr SYKES [13 Nov 1841]
    Rebecca W & George HALL of Portland ME at Saco ME [20 Aug 1846]

THAXTER Joshua H of Portland ME & Joanna HAYS of Oxford ME at Oxford [5 Jun 1841]

THAYER Almeda S & James A BLETHEN at Foxcroft ME [17 Jun 1852]
    Alexander C & Angeline PERRY at Paris ME [29 Jan 1842]
    Alvan S & Clarimond CLIFFORD all of Paris ME [17 Sept 1846]

THAYER (cont.) Asa of Norway ME & Mary D FROST at Bethel ME [1 May 1851]
George H of Waterville ME & ELLEN A BUTMAN at Plymouth ME [16 Mar 1848]
Harriet & Hiram B HERSEY of No 4, Aroostook Co ME at Foxcroft ME [9 Apr 1842]
Horace C & Betsey N WHITEHOUSE both of Augusta ME at Thompson CT on 26th ult [11 Nov 1847]
John & Almy HERSEY at Foxcroft ME [1 Jul 1847]
John & Eveline M SPINNEY both of Sidney ME at Augusta ME on 2 Mar by Rev Z THOMPSON [20 Mar 1851]
Martha C & Charles T WHITNEY of Plymouth ME at Waterville ME [3 May 1849]
Nelson & Eliza W FARNHAM at Sidney ME [11 Jan 1844]
Philip of Waterville ME & Harriet SARGENT of Canaan ME at Clinton ME [1 Jul 1847]
Sarah B & Lorenzo D CROCKETT at Lowell [11 Oct 1849]
Sarah R, d/o Hon J THAYER, & Col E K SMART at Camden ME [20 Nov 1845]
Stephen S & Hannah BLACKWELL at Waterville ME [20 Jan 1848]
Whitman B of Sidney ME & Sarah Jane REYNOLDS at Augusta ME [23 Aug 1849]

THEFETHEN Zillah A & Daniel C FIFIELD at Corinna ME [20 Jan 1848]

THEOBALD Delia Ann & James STONE of Gardiner ME at Dresden ME [5 Nov 1842]
Frederic P Dr & Julia A KIMBALL d/o Capt N KIMBALL by Bishop BURGESS at Gardiner ME [26 Oct 1848]
Julia A & Clarke BENNER at Dresden ME [6 Jan 1848]

THING Hannah D & Charles KENT at Mt Vernon ME by Rev Walter SARGENT [10 Sept 1842]
Ira of Mt Vernon ME & Martha Ann RUSS of New Sharon ME [18 Sept 1838]
Ira & Sarah E ROBINSON at Mt Vernon ME [26 Jul 1849]
Louisa & Orrin EMERSON at Hallowell ME on Sunday last by Rev Calvin GARDNER of Waterville ME [8 May 1838]

THOITS Elbridge & Julia A BAKER at N Yarmouth ME [14 Dec 1848]
Oren & Miss Jennett TRUE at Pownal ME [6 May 1847]

THOMAS Abby H & Capt David P BELCHER of Camden ME at Lincolnville ME [9 Sept 1847]
Albert of Hallowell ME & Mary C CHURCHILL at Augusta ME on 6th inst [14 Jun 1849]
Bancroft W of Ellsworth ME & Nancy T CROSS at Bluehill ME [11 Jan 1849]
Benjamin & Sarah LANCASTER at Howland ME both of Maxfield ME [6 Mar 1845]
Bradbury H & Sophia C MELVIN at Readfield ME on Tues evening last by Rev Mr WEBBER of Hallowell ME [5 Jun 1838]
C B of Standish ME & Ann TAYLOR at Chester MA on 18th Nov [15 Jan 1852]
Charles H of this town (Augusta) ME & Eulalia L VINING of Windsor ME by Eben MEIGS Esq at China ME on 22 Oct [2 Nov 1848]

THOMAS (cont.) Charles L, merchant of Tremont IL & formerly of Winthrop ME, & Miss Emmeline G WARREN d/o Edmund WARREN of New York City on Sunday evening the 4th inst by Rev Dr HAWKES [16 Dec 1836]
  Deborah & Moses B SEARS both of Winthrop ME at Wayne ME by Rev ROBINSON [9 Nov 1833]
  Diantha J & John McCULLY [13 May 1847]
  Elias/Elisha of Rumford ME & Sally D WELLS at Vienna ME [8 Feb 1844] & [18 Jan 1844]
  Eliza F & Albert COOK of Vassalboro ME at Sidney ME on 7th Sept by the Rev William TILLEY [18 Sept 1851]
  George & Temperance P ALLEN at Belmont ME [22 Feb 1849]
  Hannah & Benjamin T MORTON of New Vineyard ME at New Portland ME [10 Jun 1843]
  Harriet G & Capt Henry JORDAN both of Brunswick ME at New York NY [1 Nov 1849]
  Harriet & Nathan CHURCHILL at Buckfield ME [17 Jul 1845]
  James & Paulina WYER at Harpswell ME [24 Jun 1843]
  Jenette & Owen JONES at Williamsburg ME [11 Oct 1849]
  Jerusha & Benjamin COSTELLOW of Gardiner ME [29 Oct 1846]
  Jesse & Eleanor LAWRY at Friendship ME [19 Dec 1840]
  Joanna Mrs & John BROWN at Portland ME [16 May 1844]
  Joel W & Mary E HALL both of Rockland at Salem [10 Jul 1851]
  Joseph A of Abbot ME & Emily J HOBBS at East Livermore ME [16 Jan 1845]
  Joseph of Eden & Mary A SCAMMON at Franklin ME [23 Jan 1841]
  Justin of Hartford ME & Orphea Ann ROBBINS at Winthrop ME [17 Apr 1845]
  Lavinia & Newton KING at Winthrop ME [16 Jul 1846]
  Lloyd & Elizabeth, d/o Dr Peleg BENSON at Winthrop ME on 27th inst by Daniel D TAPPAN [4 Jul 1837]
  Lois M & William J THOMAS at Belfast ME [13 May 1852]
  Lovinia & Isaac N KING at Winthrop ME by Rev D THURSTON [16 Jul 1846]
  Lucy & James O KELLOCK at Waldo [11 Feb 1847]
  Maria & Lyman SWIFT at Thomaston ME [14 Aug 1851] & [31 Jul 1851]
  Martha W & Orin PITTS at New Portland ME [20 Sept 1849]
  Mary & Moses PHILBROOK of Levant ME at Winthrop ME on Tues evening last by Rev David THURSTON [21 Dec 1833]
  Merrill & Sarah H STOCKBRIDGE both of Byron ME at Byron on 29 Nov by John REED Esq [18 Dec 1838]
  Nancy D & William E HODGKINS at Bath ME [13 Aug 1846]
  Peter C of Byron ME & Mary S SANBORN at Weld ME [3 Oct 1840]
  Robert & Maria TOLMAN at Thomaston ME [15 Aug 1840]
  Royal Jr & Mary Jane DAILY at Searsmont ME [11 Jul 1844]
  Samuel of Buckfield ME & Sophronia O DONLEY of Sumner ME [9 Apr 1842]
  Samuel & Britannia GARDNER both of Buckfield ME at Augusta ME [14 Mar 1844]
  William J & Lois M THOMAS of Palmyra ME at Belfast ME [13 May 1852]
  William & Rebecca JOHNSON of Richmond ME at Gardiner ME [16 Jan 1845]

THOMPSON - THOMSON
A Patten of Gardiner ME & Agnes H GORDON of Pittston ME at Augusta ME on 26 July by Rev Z THOMPSON [7 Aug 1851]
Archibald of Boston MA & Hannah JORDAN of Bridgton ME at Boston MA [16 Jul 1842]
Belinda B & George L BEAL of Norway ME at Rumford ME [24 Jul 1851]
Beniah of New Portland ME & Hannah N GALE at (Augusta) ME [18 May 1848]
Benjamin P & Elizabeth FOLSOM at Pittston ME [6 Jul 1848]
Betsey & Aaron TOLMAN at Industry ME [8 Oct 1842]
Betsey & Oliver JOHNSON at Wiscasset ME [16 Nov 1833]
Betsey & William P HARNDEN at Farmington ME [11 Jan 1849]
Caroline & Jacob B QUINNAM at Wiscasset ME [9 Sept 1847]
Clarissa of Embden & James CHURCHILL of New Portland ME [14 Jan 1847]
Charles Capt & Susan D LORD at Kennebunkport ME [3 Apr 1838]
Charles H of Frankfort ME & Abigail DAVIS of Brooks ME at Belfast ME [24 Jan 1834]
Charles W of Hartford ME & Caroline M AUSTIN at Canton ME [27 Nov 1845]
Charlotte & Ezekiel HACKETT at Phillips ME [5 Dec 1834]
David D & Mary E KING at Hallowell ME [22 Aug 1840]
Deborah W & Capt Columbus CROCKETT of Abbot ME at New Sharon ME [16 Apr 1846]
Diantha & Samuel MASON of Augusta ME at Bangor ME [1 Feb 1849]
Edward P & Hannah GODDING at Pownal ME [22 Feb 1844]
Elbridge & Rebecca BOWEN at Bath ME [18 Dec 1845]
Ellen & William WELCH at Calais ME [2 Jul 1842]
Emeline B of Dresden ME & Henry Y BROWN at Hallowell ME [25 Feb 1847]
Hannah of Frankfort ME & James BEALS of Monroe ME at Prospect ME [11 Jul 1844]
Hannah & Chandler R MERRILL both of Frankfort ME at Belfast ME [15 Jul 1843]
Horatio & Jane HARLOW at Minot ME [19 Dec 1837]
Isaac & Maria WOODWORTH at Eastport ME [27 Jun 1844]
Isabella S Mrs & Capt Jesse DUSTON [22 Apr 1847]
J C of Philadelphia PA & E L ALLEN d/o the late Joseph ALLEN Esq at Frankford PA by Rev William D HOWARD [25 Jan 1849]
J & Miss A M SHERMAN at East Thomaston ME [13 Apr 1848]
Jefferson C & Jane P STAFFORD at Greene ME [25 Jan 1849]
John H Esq & Harriet SNOW at Topsham ME [24 Dec 1846]
Joshua of Waldo Plantation ME & Miss Dorothy WENTWORTH at Knox ME [26 Aug 1836]
Julia A of Farmington ME & Samuel C CARLTON of Philips ME at Farmington ME [12 Nov 1842]
Loammi B of Jay ME & Laura Jane F DOLLEY at Weld ME [21 Oct 1847]
Lucinda P & Hiram WIGGIN at Thompson CT [20 Jul 1848]
Lucy A & Joseph T HUSTON, preceptor of Bath Academy at Bath ME [19 Dec 1834]
Lydia F & Daniel W BARNES at Bowdoinham ME [18 Sept 1851]
Lydia & Henry MANNING at Newfield ME [1 Feb 1844]

THOMPSON (cont.) Lydia & Richard T BARNES at Gardiner ME [3 Apr 1845]
M E W Miss & Mr H Q COTTON at West Camden ME [24 Aug 1848]
Margaret C & Mr W WILLIAMSON at Union ME [17 Aug 1848]
Mary D, formerly of Turner ME, & Leonard O FAIRBANKS formerly of (Winthrop) ME at Nashua village NH [12 Oct 1833]
Mary S & William K WYMAN at Livermore ME [26 Mar 1846]
Mehitable Mrs (ae 68y) & Alfred H COWE (ae 18y) at Ogdensburg NY [20 Aug 1846]
N T Capt & Minerva H ALEXANDER at Bowdoin ME [17 Sept 1846]
Nahum & Lucinda WHITTEN at Waterboro ME [24 Apr 1835]
Oliver & Mary Alice RICKER at China ME [9 Dec 1836]
Olivia S & James S DUSTON at Bath ME [30 Sept 1847]
Philena N & Phineas EAMES at Embden ME [27 Dec 1849]
Priscilla M & William M BLANCHARD of Cumberland ME [24 Apr 1845]
Rebecca J of Farmington ME & G W JOHNSON of Gardiner ME at Farmington ME by E C ROLFE Esq [2 Jul 1846]
Robert C of Exeter & Mary A FOGG at Hampton NH [3 Jun 1852]
Robert Esq of Industry ME & Fanny LANE at Fayette ME [26 Sept 1840]
Rosana & Chester HART of St George ME at Thomaston ME [23 Dec 1836]
S B & Asa KNAPP of Leeds ME at Kingfield ME [30 Dec 1847]
Sabrina M & Albert L SCRIBNER both of Unity ME at Thorndike ME [2 Oct 1851]
Salome & Isaac SAYER at Limerick ME [16 Jul 1846]
Samuel & Sophia CHICK at Topsham ME [11 Jan 1844]
Sarah E & Moses B BARTLETT Esq at Brunswick ME [10 Jul 1845]
Sarah & Edwin McALLISTER at Thomaston ME [31 Aug 1848]
Sidney P of Troy NY & Miss C E SMITH at Waterville ME [29 Jun 1848]
Susan E & George W PUTNAM at York ME [30 Sept 1847]
Wealthy of Bath ME & William PARKS Esq of Ionia at Waconsta MI [8 Feb 1844]
Wildes T Capt of Brunswick ME & Wealthy M ROBINSON [19 Sept 1834]
Wildes T Capt of New York, formerly of Bath ME & Miss Abby L DAVIS of St Louis MO? [20 Aug 1846]
William Esq publisher of the *Democrat* & Rosanna G OSGOOD of Exeter ME at Bangor ME [30 Apr 1846]
William W & Abigail B CLARK at Jay ME [3 Apr 1841]

THOMS Amos & Rosalinda SYLVESTER both of Leeds ME at Wayne ME [29 Jan 1846]
Charles A of Leeds ME & Miss Abigail C MITCHELL of Lowell MA at Leeds ME by Rev Walter FOSS [8 Jan 1846]
Esther F & Harrison TAYLOR at Augusta ME [26 Mar 1846]
Harriet N & Loyal DUNLAP of Vassalboro ME at Augusta ME [17 Sept 1846]
Mary Ellen & Albus K QUIMBY at Augusta ME on 3d Jul by Rev A DALTON [15 Jul 1852]
Sarah Ann of Ossipee NH & Samuel S ROLLINS of Great Falls NH [20 Feb 1845]

THORN - THORNE
Edward B of Augusta ME & Elizabeth SMITH at Hallowell ME on 14th inst by J W PATTERSON Esq [25 Jul 1844]
Ira & Louisa HARLOW of Peru ME at Canton ME [14 Feb 1850]

THORNE (cont.) James H & Mary J NORRIS both of Wayne ME by Rev Mr Morse at Winthrop ME [7 Dec 1848]
 Jane & Jeremiah A NILES at Webster ME [5 Apr 1849]
 Jermiah & Hannah GREEN at Vassalboro ME on 18th Oct by by O A WEBBER Esq [4 Nov 1847]
THORNBURN Sophia B & Francis W DELESDENIER of Calias ME? at New York [20 Nov 1835]
THORNDIKE Bethia & Selah G at Thomaston ME [5 Aug 1847]
 Caroline & Medafer HASKELL of Bangor ME, merchant at Camden ME [26 Dec 1834]
 Catherine & Captain Isaac PENDLETON at Camden ME [22 Apr 1852]
 Eliza & Lory A KALLOCH at Warren ME [12 Mar 1846]
 Joshua K & Elvira P SNOW at Thomaston ME [8 Jan 1846]
 Lucy W & Daniel BROWN Jr of Dover ME at Foxcroft ME [1 Feb 1849]
 William H Capt & Melinda ACHORN at Thomaston ME [5 Aug 1847]
THORNTON Milledge & Sarah WHALING of West Isles at Lubec ME [5 Mar 1846]
 Sarah C S G & Mr J G CHASE of Springfield MA at Saco ME [14 May 1846]
THORP Cyrus of Wiscasset ME & Harriet M ROBINSON at Alna ME [9 Oct 1851]
 James & Eunice ROGERS of Cornwallis Nova Scotia Canada at Eastport [12 Sept 1844]
 Stillman of Portland ME & Mary E LEE at Brunswick ME [9 Nov 1833]
THRASHER Sarah F & George LORD [28 May 1836]
THRELDKELD L T & Mary S BUTLER at Shelbyville KY [12 Aug 1847]
THUNDERER Theodore & Jane M COCHRAN at Shirley [11 Jul 1844]
THURLO Moody E of Calais ME? & Martha C HUTCHINSON of Readfield ME at Mount Vernon ME [27 May 1836]
THURLOW Amos Jr & Sylvia E WHITMAN at Woodstock ME [23 Oct 1851]
 Ann E & William J FARRIN at Litchfield ME [31 Aug 1848]
 Betsy & Avery STINSON at Deer Isle by Joseph STINSON Esq [21 Oct 1836]
 Elisha & Elizabeth JOURDAN at Litchfield ME [18 Jul 1837]
 Kingsbury of Litchfield ME & Miss Jane WHITE of Bowdoin ME on 19th ult [9 Oct 1841]
 Lucy of Poland ME & Benjamin BACON Esq of Greenwood ME at Poland ME [21 Mar 1840]
THURSTIN Emily & Mr WATERMAN at Windsor ME [4 Jul 1837]
THURSTON Betsey A & Seth WEBB at Harmony ME [16 Mar 1848]
 Brown of Portland ME & Harriet CHAPMAN of Gilead ME at Gilead ME on 19th ult by Rev David THURSTON [13 Aug 1842]
 Caroline of Madison ME & Matthew BENSON at Solon ME [2 Apr 1846]
 Clarinda & William PAUL at Peru ME [23 May 1840]
 Dennis & Sarah SIMPSON at Avon ME [29 Nov 1849]
 Eli of this town (Hallowell) ME & Miss M Caroline eldest d/o Philo SANFORD Esq at Wrentham MA on 20th inst by the Rev Mr FISK [5 Jul 1838]
 Elisha AB principal of the Charleston Academy & Angeline R MONTGOMERY of Cushing ME at Thomaston ME [2 Sept 1843]

THURSTON (cont.) Elizabeth, d/o Rev D THURSTON of Winthrop ME at the Congregational meeting house on Thurs evening last by Rev Mr Thurston [22 Jun 1839]
   Mitty A & Job BALLARD at Parsonsfield ME [16 Jul 1846]
   Nahum Jr & Miss Ann Elizabeth COLE at Union ME on 6th Oct by Rev Mr HAWES [28 Oct 1847]
   Richard B of Waterville ME & Miss Jane M PIERCE at Friendship PA [1 Jul 1847]
   Samuel D of Bangor ME & Susan D PEIRCE of Friendship PA at Waterville ME [1 Jun 1848]
   Sarah & William POTE at Belfast ME [30 Jan 1845]
   Stephen & Hannah WHITTEN at Parsonsfield ME [11 Mar 1847]
   True W of Peru ME & Rachel F WELCH at Monmouth ME [16 Apr 1846]
THWING Eliza & John GIBBS at Wiscasset ME [30 Sept 1847]
   Rachel & Japheth BEALE at Augusta ME by Rev Stephen ALLEN of Farmington ME [3 Jul 1851]
TIBBETTS - TEBBETTS - TIBBETS - TEBBETS
   Adeline B & John S RIPLEY at this town (Augusta) ME by Asaph B NICHOLS Esq [10 Dec 1846]
   Andrew R & Jane H FOSS at Saco ME [11 Nov 1847]
   Cyrus Rev of Hampton Falls NH & Eliza W LAWSON at Augusta ME [24 Jun 1847]
   Enoch H & Catherine R SEWALL at Hampden ME [22 Feb 1849]
   Fanny W & Ambrose H STURGESS of Cherryfield ME at Columbia ME [30 Sept 1847]
   J G & Clara A BUCKMAN at Lisbon ME [6 Aug 1846]
   John A of New Sharon ME & Sarah Jane WHITTEMORE at Augusta ME on 21st inst by Rev Mr MORSE [28 Jan 1847]
   John C of this town (Augusta) ME & Caroline A BLAKE by Rev Mr FIELD at Hallowell on 25 Oct [2 Nov 1848]
   Jonas C & Almira S MERRILL at Saco ME [17 Sept 1846]
   Lavina of Brownville ME? & Valentine C TARBOX of Ellsworth ME? at Providence RI [24 Jul 1851]
   Louisa L & John WHITE both of Exeter ME at Corinth ME [20 Nov 1851]
   Lydia A & Simon J LOCKE at Saco ME [3 Jun 1847]
   Lydia M & Darius L ROBERTS at Sedgwick Bay [27 Jul 1848]
   Mary Ann of Lisbon ME & Maj George EARLE of Brunswick ME at Topsham ME by Rev Mr Wheeler [3 Jun 1832]
   Mary J of Belgrade & Levi A WEEKS at Sidney ME on June 12 [3 Jul 1851]
   Mehitable & Samuel C BOVEY at Bath ME [28 Jan 1847]
   Moses of Orono ME & Nancy J TIBBETTS of Harmony ME at Dexter ME [17 Jul 1845]
   Roxana & William RINES of Westport ME at Bath ME [1 May 1845]
   Samuel of Monmouth ME & Mehitable RICE d/o John RICE at Hallowell ME [5 Dec 1840]
   Samuel & Mehitable d/o John RICE at Hallowell ME [25 Apr 1840]
   Sarah of Augusta & William ANDERSON of this town (Hallowell) at Hallowell ME on 21st ult by E K BUTLER Esq [2 Jan 1838]
   Sarah of Belgrade ME & Aaron EASTY of East Winthrop ME at Readfield ME on Sunday the 15th inst by David FULLER Esq [21 Aug 1841]

TIBBETTS (cont.) Sarah Richardson & Hall CHASE, M.D., of Waterville ME at Topsham ME [19 Sept 1844]
  Vesta J & Leonard P BICKFORD [20 Nov 1845]
TIFFANY D P & Lucy W MOORE at Sindey ME [6 May 1843]
TIGHE Lucy Jane & John C PARSHLEY at Bath ME on Sunday morning last [27 Jane 1840]
TILDEN Isabella K of Belfast ME & George W HARMON of Boston MA (printer) at Belfast ME on Thurs last [10 Jun 1843]
TILLSON Eliza & Asa W CUMMINGS of Sidney ME at Readfield ME [29 Apr 1833]
TILSON Davis & Margaret ACHORN at Rockland ME [19 Aug 1852]
  Josiah (ae 78y) & Mrs Millet (ae 78y) at Hartford ME [28 May 1846]
TILTON Eliza & Mr M CHASE at Livermore ME [14 Nov 1840]
  Hannah of London NH & William W CLEAVES at Exeter by Chandler EASTMAN Esq [4 Sept 1835]
  Hebron of Waterville ME & Emeline WELD of Nauvoo at Chicago IL [27 Jul 1848]
  Horatio G of Norridgewock ME & Maria STACKPOLE of Vassalboro ME at Portsmouth NH [18 Mar 1852]
  Jacob & Caroline M d/o Dean HOWARD of Winthrop ME at Mt Vernon ME on Thurs the 11th inst by Rev David THURSTON of Winthrop [20 Nov 1841]
  Joseph & Angeline NORCOSS at Farmington ME [13 Mar 1845]
  Josiah & Dianthe SMITH at Monmouth ME [18 Jan 1840]
  Josiah & Sophia Jane SHOREY at Monmouth ME by J M HEATH Esq [13 Dec 1849]
  Luther of Lowell MA & Cynthia N TOREY at China ME on 13th June [23 Jun 1852]
  Salathiel & Miss Julianna HINDS at Livermore ME [5 Oct 1839]
  Sarah & William LEE at Lee on Jul 18th by J H PERKINS Esq [5 Aug 1852]
TIMBERLAKE Almira & Rev Nathan A SOULE at Livermore ME [30 Jul 1846]
  Lois & Silvin SHIRTLIFF by Maj Isaac STRICKLAND at Livermore ME on 5th inst by Maj Isaac STRICKLAND [13 Nov 1835]
  Malansa & David BRYANT at Turner ME [2 Jan 1845]
TIMLIN John of Portland ME & Eliza R MARSTON of Winthrop ME at Hallowell ME on 22d inst by Stewart FOSTER Esq [5 Jun 1845]
TINKER David & Sophia WENTWORTH both of Campobello at Eastport ME [11 Dec 1845]
TINKHAM Betsey & Levi M HAHN at (Winthrop) ME [19 Sept 1840]
  Abiel W & Margaret W ATHERTON at Portland ME [7 Jan 1847]
  Amaziah F of Augusta ME & Mary E WEBB of China ME at Albion ME [14 Jan 1847]
  David W & Eliza Ann W HIGGINS at Hallowell ME [4 Mar 1836]
  Francis F of Albion ME & Eunice ROGERS of Newburg ME at Dixmont ME by A T C DODGE Esq [21 Mar 1850]
  Jemima Wilbur, d/o Pardon TINKHAM Esq, & David S ABBOTT at Albion ME on 1st ult [4 Feb 1843]
  John A & Rozilla RICE at Monmouth ME on Thanksgiving by Elder J PRESCOTT [7 Dec 1839]

TINKHAM (cont.) John I & Mary S BLAKE at Winthrop ME by Rev Mr INGRAHAM of Augusta ME [25 Jan 1840]
    L G of Sidney & Mr B F BUCHNAM by Rev Mr TILLEY at Sidney ME [7 Jan 1847]
    Mary E & Cyrus NOWELL at Calais ME [26 Sept 1840]
    Mary M & Samuel SHACKFORD at Eastport ME [7 Aug 1851]
    Mary & Levi HASKELL at Winthrop ME on Thurs evening last by Rev David THURSTON [28 Dec 1833]
    Orin Deacon of Norridgewock ME & Mrs D W CRAINE at Fayette ME [13 Jul 1848]
    Orville W of Norridgewock ME & Clarissa HOLBROOK of Starks ME at Bloomfield ME [21 Jun 1849]
    Sarah Jane of Wiscasset ME & M A CHANDLER of Augusta ME at Wiscasset ME by Rev Seneca WHITE [10 Oct 1834]
    Smith Esq of Eastport ME & Caroline BREWER at Robbinston ME [13 Jul 1848]
TIRRILL Lucy D & Daniel M TRUSSELL at Belfast ME [20 Jul 1848]
TIRRELL Gideon of Clarkeville NH & Sabre T QUINCY at Farmington ME [2 Apr 1846]
TITCOMB Benjamin of New Portland ME & Ann WILLIAMS at North Anson ME [9 Apr 1846]
    Charlotte & Willard S SIMMONS at North Yarmouth ME [2 May 1834]
    Deborah & Daniel BURNS at Hallowell ME [13 Jan 1837]
    George of Portland ME & Cordelia A SAWYER at Saco ME [18 Feb 1847]
    Harriet, d/o Rev Benjamin TITCOMB, & Gen Richard T DUNLAP at Brunswick ME on the 29th ult [8 Jan 1836]
    Helen & Aaron D BLUNT at Norridgewock ME on 25th June [8 Jul 1852]
    John H of Boston MA & Nancy G DOLE at Hallowell ME [5 Sept 1840]
    Joseph Jr & Elizabeth K WENDALL at Farmington ME [5 Dec 1844]
    Joseph & Joann L RING at North Yarmouth ME [30 Dec 1836]
    Lewis H of this town (Augusta ME) & Julia Maria d/o Gen S G LADD of Farmington on 6th inst by Rev Isaac ROGERS [8 Oct 1846]
    Mary & George T ROBERTS at Kennebunk ME [23 Mar 1839]
    Masiah B & Nathaniel JORDAN at North Yarmouth ME [7 Mar 1837]
    Miranda & Lemont P CARR at Bowdoin ME [28 Oct 1847]
    Nancy of Cumberland ME? & John POOR of Newburyport MA both "deaf & dumb" at Falmouth ME [30 Sept 1843]
    Samuel Jr Esq & Julia, d/o Artemas KIMBALL at Augusta ME on Thurs evening last by Rev Mr JUDD [27 Feb 1845]
    Sarah Ann & Elias W MERRILL of Webster ME at North Yarmouth ME [12 Dec 1840]
    Sarah D & Hiram CHASE at Anson ME [22 Feb 1844]
    Wingate & Miss Lucady FOGG at Parsonfield ME [17 Apr 1835]
TITFORD Ellis & Frances at Topsham ME [10 Sept 1846]
TITUS Huldah E & Corydon C HANNAFORD at Monmouth ME by Rev D B RANDALL [3 Apr 1841]
TOBEN Clarissa & Samuel BROWN at Wayne ME [23 May 1844]
TOBEY Albert & Elizabeth L FOWLER at Fairfield ME [17 Jan 1850]
    Ann & Benjamin WING at Vassalboro ME on 16th June by Edward GRAY Esq [8 Jul 1852]
    Charles E & Louisa LAWRENCE at Fairfield ME [6 Feb 1838]

TOBEY (cont.) Edward T of Waterville ME & Mary E TOBEY at Fairfield ME [22 Nov 1849]
    Hannah M & Capt William JOHNSON at Machiasport ME [19 Jul 1849]
    Harvey & Sarah Jane WOODBRIDGE at Hallowell ME [12 Mar 1846]
    Julia A & H H CAMPBELL Dr both of Fairfield ME at Waterville ME [17 Jul 1851]
    Mary A & Hiram HINKLEY both of (Augusta) ME at Hallowell ME by Rev S W FIELDS [9 Aug 1849]
    Mary I Mrs & Thomas M ATKINSON at Mercer ME on 14 Jan [29 Jan 1852]
    Stephen L of Waterville ME & Carline E BAKER at New Sharon ME [5 Aug 1843]
    Stephen L & Mary Ann HIGHT at Athens ME [29 Nov 1849]
    William 2d & Miss Ruth NORTON at Norridgewock ME [14 Sept 1833]
TOBIN Nancy K & Rev James P STONE at Belfast ME [25 Oct 1849]
TOBY Elbridge of Whitefield ME & Harriet A WOODBRIDGE at Hallowell ME [30 Nov 1839]
    Elijah & Mrs Hannah E NOBLE of New Sharon ME at Farmington Falls ME [29 Apr 1847]
    Erastus of Patricktown Plt ME & Jane W DUDLEY of China ME at China ME [11 Nov 1836]
    John Y & Malvina B TOWNS by Rev Mr DILLINGHAM at (Augusta) ME [30 Mar 1848]
    Mary I Mrs & Thomas M ATKINSON at Mercer ME [12 Feb 1852]
    Nathaniel & Mrs Betsey Ann MILLER both of Waldoboro ME by Rev H W LATHAM at North Waldoboro on 27 Dec [8 Jan 1852]
TODD Hannah M & Edward P NORTON at Bath ME [11 Jul 1834]
    James & Margaret E AMES at Belfast ME [8 Jul 1836]
    John W & Deborah CHASE at Bangor ME [26 Aug 1843]
    Mary A of Portsmouth NH & Mr I W BEARD of Portsmouth NH [23 Sept 1836]
    Priscilla L & Charles E HILTON on 22d ult [4 Nov 1843]
    Sarah H Mrs & Joseph D LORD at Hallowell ME on Thurs evening last [9 Mar 1839]
    Rebecca M, widow of the late Dudley TODD Esq, & Capt Bartlett Weeks VARNUM at Wayne ME [12 Feb 1836]
    Samuel A of Ripley ME & Maoma PLUMER at Alna ME [28 Feb 1834]
TOLMAN Aaron & Betsey THOMPSON at Industry ME [8 Oct 1842]
    Julia & Amos BARRETT of Camden ME at Rockland ME [6 Mar 1851]
    Maria & Robert THOMAS at Thomaston ME [15 Aug 1840]
    Marietta & J S ALLEN at Thomaston ME [9 Oct 1845]
    Mary & Cephas STARRETT at Thomaston ME [30 May 1837]
    Samuel Capt & Rebecca CARROL at West Camden ME [27 Sept 1849]
    Silstina & Aaron HEMENWAY at Camden ME [11 Dec 1851] & [4 Dec 1851]
    William & Sarah DAVIS at Thomaston ME [10 Oct 1844]
TOMAZO Peter & Mrs Mary MONTAIR at Bath ME [12 Jul 1849]
TOMPKINS Benjamin & Miss Olive S MOSIER at Montville both of Unity ME [3 Jan 1850]
    Jacob Capt & Rachel Amelia GRAVES at Bangor ME [19 Aug 1847]
    William O of Bangor ME & Miss Mary L LAKEMAN at Hallowell ME [21 Oct 1847]

TONNEY Amaziah of Carmel ME & Charlotte GETCHELL at Belfast ME [25 Apr 1850]
TOOTHAKER Abraham C & Merriam C GILBERT of Greene ME at Brunswick ME [4 Feb 1847]
  Joanna & John MERRIT at Brunswick ME [8 Oct 1846]
  John Capt & Malvina M MARINER at Belfast ME [1 Jul 1852]
  Martha & John BIBBER at Yarmouth ME on 9th inst by E G BUXTON Esq [13 Sept 1849]
  Olive E & William WRIGHT at Madrid ME [27 Nov 1845]
  Phebe A & Silas S LEMONT of Gardiner ME at Litchfield ME [15 Apr 1847]
  William H & Olive DAWES at Bowdoin ME both of Richmond ME [10 Jun 1847]
TORN Samuel & Emma DOLLOFF both of Paris ME [17 Aug 1839]
TOREY/TORRY Cynthia N & Luther TILTON at China ME on 13th June [23 Jun 1852]
  Erastus & Mary P REYNOLDS at Bangor ME [2 Oct 1835]
  Nabby Mrs & David HOUSE both of Turner ME at Buckfield ME [3 Apr 1851]
  R S & Jane H HIGGINS of Hampden ME at Dixmont ME [4 Mar 1843]
  Sarah E & William H DUTTON at Belfast ME [6 Jul 1848]
TORSEY A M Henry P Rev principal of Maine Wesley Sem at Hallowell ME & Emma J ROBINSON preceptress of same [28 Dec 1848]
  Cynthia "Whereas Cynthia my wife left my bed & board..." William TORSEY at Winthrop ME [3 Oct 1840]
  Henry A of Winthrop ME & Judith B DAY at Leeds ME [13 Feb 1838]
  Louisa & Caleb S of Leeds ME at Winthrop ME [6 Feb 1838]
  Sophia Ann & D N HILL both of Bath ME at Bath ME [11 Dec 1845]
  William of Winthrop ME "Whereas Cynthia my wife left my bed & board..." Cynthia TORSEY at Winthrop ME [3 Oct 1840]
TORREY Charles & Ruth TURNER at Turner ME [4 Apr 1837]
  Sally & William S YOUNG at Turner ME [13 Nov 1838]
  Sally M of Plymouth ME & William CARLTON of Troy ME at Dixmont ME [7 Oct 1847]
TOTMAN Emily & Nathaniel HILL at Bath ME [20 Jan 1848]
TOURTLOTTE/TOURTILOTTE Abraham Jr & Miss Lucinda PUSHAW at Ellsworth ME [28 Dec 1839]
  Jane & George HAMILTON at Ellsworth ME [4 Dec 1851]
TOWER Charles F of Roxbury MA & Harriet N BISBEE at Waterville ME [5 Aug 1847]
  Peter Jr & Miss Huldah FROHOCK at Belmont ME [26 Dec 1837]
  Rebecca & Edward H TREAT of Enfield at Foxcroft ME [11 Nov 1847]
  Reuel of Sweden & Miss Zoa BRADFORD at Turner ME [22 Jan 1852]
TOWL Sybil & William BRAN at Gardiner ME [5 Dec 1844]
TOWLE Aaron of the firm of CARR & TOWLE of this town (Winthrop) ME & Rachel OWEN at Wayne ME, "OWEN (Owing) away we now must take From her, most happy soul! Since, with a slice of Bridal Cake, She paid the Printer's TOWLE (toll)" [20 Nov 1838]
  David E & Eliza A REED, d/o John REED at Augusta ME [16 May 1834]
  Delphina P & John E ELLIOT at Levant ME [24 May 1849]

TOWLE (cont.) Eliza A & Conelius B MORTON at Augusta ME on Monday last by Rev Mr JUDD [27 May 1843]
   John T & Catherine FULLER at Hallowell ME [16 Oct 1851]
   Josiah E of Monmouth ME & Emeline H ALLEN of Litchfield ME [8 Jul 1843]
   Mary A & Josiah WOOD of China ME at Gardiner ME [6 May 1847]
   Mary Jane & Benjamin JONES of Gardiner ME at Dixmont ME [21 Mar 1850]
   Mary of Farmington ME & Thomas CURRIER Esq of Skowhegan ME at Avon ME by Rev S B WITHERELL [27 Mar 1838]
   Paul of Exeter & Matilda HUTCHINGS at Atkinson ME [17 Jul 1845]
   Sarah & John G BISHOP at Hallowell ME on 21st Jan by Rev S W FIELD [31 Jan 1850]
   William H & Mary Ann HARDY at (Winthrop) ME on Monday evening last by Rev Mr CALDWELL [27 Feb 1835]
TOWN Betsey H & Newton SMITH both of Norway ME [4 Dec 1845]
   James D & Eunice HOUGHTON at Gardiner ME both of Gardiner [17 Sept 1842]
   Jonathan G & Abigail D CROCKETT at Norway ME [19 Mar 1846]
   Sophia S & William F M REED of Hampden ME at Augusta ME [22 Apr 1847]
TOWNE Bertha & Benjamin O CUTTER of Sebec ME at Dover ME [15 Aug 1844]
   Elizabeth & Jason HASSELL at Sebec ME [21 Jan 1847]
   Fanny B Mrs & Thomas B LITTLE Esq of Lewiston Falls (Danville-Auburn-Minot) ME at Bethel ME [18 Jan 1845]
   Joseph L & Harriet TURNER at Waterville ME [22 Jul 1852]
   William of Foxcroft ME & Mercy J WELLS at Sebec ME [22 May 1851]
TOWNES Lydia R & Benjamin at Solon ME both of Bingham ME [15 Aug 1844]
TOWNS Malvina B & John Y TOBY at (Augusta) ME [30 Mar 1848]
   Mary F & Jas W BROCK both of Kennebec ME at Augusta ME on 25th Sept by Rev H M BLAKE [16 Oct 1851]
   Susan & Benjamin G DENNISON at Brunswick ME [6 Nov 1838]
TOWNSEND Anne P & Columbus HAINES Esq of East Livermore ME at Sidney ME [9 Dec 1847]
   Asa of Wilton ME & Olive HARDY at Carthage ME [9 May 1837]
   Asa S of Sidney ME & Nancy C HAYES at Hallowell ME on Jan 1 by Rev W A P DILLINGHAM [7 Feb 1850]
   Caroline P & Rev W A P DILLINGHAM, pastor of the Universalist Church in Augusta, at Sidney ME on Oct 21st by Rev William A DREW [4 Nov 1847]
   Dorcas Ann & J F DEERING at Saco ME [20 Jul 1848]
   Elijah L of Danville ME & Miss Drusilla BISHOP of this town (Winthrop ME) at Winthrop on the 1st inst by Rev Asbury CALDWELL [9 Sept 1836]
   Isaac Jr of Union ME & Fanny JOY at Belfast ME [22 Jan 1846]
   Isaac S of Wilton ME & Drusilla DRURY at Jay ME [11 Feb 1843]
   Lucy & James F MARS at Brunswick ME [28 Mar 1837]
   Mercy H & Isiah RANDALL Jr at Saco ME [25 Dec 1845]
   S W Townsend & Roxana BRAN at Gardiner ME [26 Apr 1849]

TOWNSEND (cont.) Salmon Jr of Turner ME & Francina G CROCKETT at Greene ME [12 Mar 1846]
Sarah H & Timothy R ELLIS at Sidney ME [10 Apr 1841]
True W & Mary Jane ODIORNE at Gardiner ME [3 Feb 1848]

TOZER - TOZIER
B Franklin, printer formerly of Dover ME & Miss Hannah W YOUNG at Waterville ME by Rev C I EAMES [30 Oct 1841]
Franklin of Waterville ME & Marion W NORCOSS at Hallowell ME [23 Dec 1843]
George A of Plymouth ME & Mary G SMALL at Troy ME [19 Feb 1852]
Isaac B & Mary B BATES at Waterville ME on Thanksgiving evening by Rev S F SMITH [4 Dec 1841]
Lucinda W of Monmouth ME & Ezra H NORCROSS of Winthrop ME at Augusta ME on Feb 1st by Rev Mr JUDD [19 Feb 1842]
Lucretia A & Richard MILLS at Waterville ME [1 Jun 1848]
Lucretia A & Richard RICE at Waterville [8 Jun 1848]
Margaret Ann & Harrison MARSHALL at Waterville ME [26 Dec 1840]
Oliver C & Ellen COLBY at Waterville ME [16 Jan 1851]
Sophia B of Waterville ME & John WATSON of Wiscasset ME at Detroit ME [30 Dec 1847]

TRACE Amasa of Farmington ME & Helen S DOW of Leicester VT at Thompson CT [2 Mar 1848]
Ichabod B & Augusta J MERRILL by F Davis Esq at (Augusta) ME on 3d Jan [8 Jan 1852]
Melissa D & Joel T BROWN at Lewiston ME [14 Aug 1851]
Peleg H & Mary E HUBBARD at Palmyra ME [13/20 Jan 1848]
Sylvinia Ann & Joseph LITTLEFIELD at Durham ME [20 Apr 1848]
Vaieletta & Benjamin CHICK at Farmington ME [6 Jan 1848]

TRACY Linsey & Belinda TUCKER of Township #7 ME at Gouldsboro ME [11 Mar 1847]
Lydia & Abel P CORBETT at Farmington ME [19 Jul 1849]
Samuel & Lydia CURTIS at Amity ME on 18 Oct by Milo WALTON Esq [5 Dec 1846]

TRAFTON C T of South Berwick ME & Susan M WALKER at Kennebunk ME [5 Mar 1846]
Calvin & Sarah Jane TRAFTON at Chesterville ME [11 Mar 1852]
Edmund 2nd of Cornish ME & Lydia S PIKE formerly of Bridgton ME at Portland ME [4 Jun 1846]
Harriet A & Jonathan PRESCOTT Jr of Easton MA at Gardiner ME [4 Nov 1847]
Ira of Gardiner ME & Julia DICKERSON at Georgetown ME [24 Sept 1846]
Ivory & Sally M WALLS at Gouldsboro ME [12 Aug 1847]
Lewis G & Miss Catherine MERRILL at Biddeford ME [13 Sept 1849]
Mark, M.D., of Evansville IA & Miss M E PIERCE at Townsend [1 Jun 1848]
Martha A, d/o Gen Mark TRAFTON of Bangor ME, & Ebenezer WEBSTER Jr Esq at Orono ME [17 Aug 1839]
Sarah Jane & Calvin TRAFTON at Chesterville ME [11 Mar 1852]
William of Shapleigh ME & Ruth W HASKELL at Livermore ME [3 Jul 1841]

TRASK Alvan Esq of Bradford ME & Elizabeth C HILL of Bangor ME at Bangor ME [4 Jul 1840]
Amos of Lowell MA & Almeda S SAWTELLE d/o Asa C SAWTELLE of Sidney ME at Waterville ME on 26th May at the Rev Mr WESTON's [10 Jun 1852]
Ansel G & Elizabeth M SMALL both of Westbrook ME at Gorham ME [23 May 1857]
Ebenezer Capt of Edgecomb ME & Marietta M DODGE of Wiscasset ME [15 Apr 1843]
Eliza & Warren CARLTON at Alna ME [5 Feb 1842]
James W & Susan BRANN at East Hallowell ME both of Gardiner ME [27 Sept 1849]
Jonathan T & Triphena A SWIFT both of Hallowell ME at Mt Vernon ME on 20th Jan by L VEAZIE Esq [7 Feb 1850]
Lydia Jane & Thomas J HANNIFORD at Wiscasset ME [13 May 1847]
Lyman of Belgrade ME & Mary E SAUNDERS at Augusta ME [29 Jul 1847]
Mary Ann & William CLARRY at Hallowell ME [23 Apr 1846]
Mary Mrs (ae 64y) & Daniel GREEN (ae 83y) both of Augusta ME at Hallowell ME [23 Oct 1845]
Nancy TRASK & Joseph M NILES of Lisbon ME at Leeds ME by Rev Walter FOSS [19 Feb 1846]
Peter H of Bath ME & Rachel L FOGG of Bath at Boston MA [23 Jan 1851]
Peter of Mexico ME & Betsey C ROLFE at Rumford ME [6 Jun 1844]
Susan K & Joshua JONES at Jefferson ME [2 Mar 1848]
Susan T & Thomas F BELL at Augusta ME on 18th inst by Rev C F ALLEN [29 Nov 1849]
Susannah & Joshua MARTIN at Hallowell ME [4 Feb 1843]

TREADWELL Alexander Philip Socrates Amelius Ceaser Hannibal Marcellus George Washington & Caroline Sophia Maria Julianne Worthley Montague Joan of Arc WILLIAMS both of New Orleans [1 Aug 1837]
Susan G & George W NICHOLS, printer of Thomaston ME at Salem MA [14 Nov 1834]
Theodore of Frankfort ME & Emily A ROGERS of Brownville ME at Atkinson ME [17 Jul 1851]
Thomas J & Sarah J SMITH both of Brewer Village ME at East Orrington ME [22 Apr 1847]

TREAT Arthur of Frankfort ME & Miss Harriet WYLLIE at Warren ME [25 Jun 1842]
Edward H of Enfield & Rebecca TOWER at Foxcroft ME [11 Nov 1847]
Eliza G & Capt Paron C KILBURN of Bucksport ME at Frankfort ME [23 Mar 1839]
Henry & Miss Caroline BOYD at Frankfort ME [28 Jul 1849]
Joseph 2d & Harriet Maria PENDLETON at Camden ME [21 Jun 1849]
Nancy & Capt Stephen ELLIS at Prospect ME [20 Apr 1848]
Phebe & Andrew J CLIFFORD both of Prospect ME at Belfast ME [4 Dec 1851]
William A & Mary E DORR at Brewer ME [25 Dec 1851]
William Dr formerly of Gardiner ME & Miranda FINCH at Buffalo NY [24 Jul 1851]

TRECARTIN George & Eleanor Jane HOOPER of Deer Island both of Deer Island Washington Co ME at St Andrews New Brunswick Canada [21 Aug 1851]

Margaret E & Joseph BLATCHFORD Jr at Eastport ME [7 Mar 1850]

Sarah A & Nahum DINSMORE at Eastport ME [25 Apr 1844]

TREVETT Abigail L & Rev Francis A BEAN at Frankfort ME [22 Feb 1844]

Theodore S of Bath & Ann RICHARDS at East Winthrop ME [13 Nov 1845]

Theodore S & Mrs Almira MT HYDE at Bath ME [27 May 1847]

TREWORGY Abigail B & Samuel P HALL at Ellsworth ME [28 Dec 1839]

Phebe E of Bradford ME & William G BRADLEY at Bluehill ME [7 Mar 1840]

TRICKEY A A & Mr B E PENDLETON of Belfast ME at Saco ME [3 Jul 1845]

TRIMM Pamela A of Belfast ME & Augustine WOOD at Boston MA [9 Jan 1845]

TRIPP Eliza A & Capt F COCKRAN both of Searsport ME at Frankfort ME [25 Sept 1851]

Jane H & Nathaniel MADDOX Jr both of Appleton ME at Belfast ME [10 Aug 1839]

Robert (ae 18y) & Diana EMERY (ae 16y) at Harmony ME [8 Feb 1844]

TROOP Alex 2d & Louisa BLANCHARD at Pittston ME [25 Jan 1849]

TROTT Abigail & John McDUFFIE at (Winthrop) ME on Monday last [15 Aug 1840]

Freeman & Julia KENSINGTON at Gardiner ME [1 Jan 1846]

Jane of Woolwich ME & Joseph J PREBLE at Richmond ME [15 Nov 1849]

Mitchell L & Jane F BAKER at Bath ME [12 Dec 1837]

TROTTER William & Margaret J WEBBER at Augusta ME at St Mark's Church by Rev Mr BURGESS [3 Jun 1847]

TROWBRIDGE Lucy H & Samuel W SANFORD at Bath ME [25 Mar 1847]

TRUE Abba & Rev J K L STAPLES of Gardiner ME at Montville ME [12 Jul 1849]

Albion & Emily BAKER at Albion ME [14 Mar 1850]

Alfred R & Frances B PRATT at North Yarmouth ME [7 Nov 1837]

Angeline & Capt Benjamin LARRABEE at Portland ME [8 Feb 1844]

Caleb of Industry ME & Diana SNELL at Starks ME [17 Jul 1838]

Clark P & Sarah E DANFORTH at Norway ME [15 Jan 1852]

D M & Antoinette COX at Searsmont ME [5 Jul 1849]

Jacob B & Susan CUMMINGS of Hallowell ME at Augusta ME on 19 Nov by Rev J STEVENS [27 Nov 1851]

Jacob of Sangerville ME & Theodosia W RANDALL of Wellington ME on the 2d inst by B BURSLEY Esq [18 Jun 1842]

Jennett & Oren THOITS at Pownal ME [6 May 1847]

John, merchant & Mary H ABBOT at Bangor ME [12 Feb 1846]

Lenora S & James M SNELL of Starks ME at Industry ME [1 Jan 1846]

Lyman C of Falmouth ME & Mary B TRUE at Philips ME [14 Sept 1839]

Maria Antoinette & Robert B MOORES at Mercer ME [27 Feb 1845]

Mary B & Elijah VOSE Esq at Union ME [24 Jun 1843]

Mary B & Lyman C TRUE of Falmouth ME at Philips ME [14 Sept 1839]

Samuel P & Ruth CARVER, d/o John CARVER Esq at Leeds ME by Elder W FOSS [27 Nov 1841]

TRUE (cont.) Sarah Ann & Francis W HILL at Exeter ME [23 Jan 1845]
TRUFANT Allen L Miss Joann WING at Winthrop ME on 25th June by Rev Mr CALDWELL [17 Jul 1835]
    Allen L & Miss Delia JOY at Winthrop ME [7 May 1846]
    David H of New Orleans LA & Susan J FOOTE at Bath ME [13 Aug 1846]
    Gilbert C of Bath ME & Sarah F BOYD at Wiscasset ME [28 Aug 1835]
    Hannah C & Samuel M SEWALL of Sangerville ME at Winthrop ME on 16th Oct by Rev P JAQUES [30 Oct 1851]
    Joann of (Winthrop) ME & Abel C CROSBY of Milford NH at Winthrop ME on Thanksgiving evening by Rev Mr THURSTON [26 Nov 1842]
TRULL Caroline B & Albion K LOUIS at Bath ME [5 Jul 1849]
    Herbert of Tewksbury MA formerly of Bloomfield ME [30 May 1840]
    Mary E & Ira MASON at Bath ME [5 Jul 1849]
TRUNDY Caroline P & Leonard LEIGHTON at Wiscasset ME [6 Jul 1848]
TRUSSELL Daniel M & Lucy D TIRRILL at Belfast ME [20 Jul 1848]
    Harriet M & William L HATCH at Thomaston ME [26 Feb 1852]
TRYON Sarah P & Oren FRANCIS at Hallowell ME by Rev M FULLER [1 May 1845]
TUBBS Mary A of Norway ME & William P BUCK at Paris ME [2 Dec 1847]
    Orren of Paris ME & Elizabeth B HALL of Norway ME at Mechanic Falls (Poland-Minot) ME [23 Nov 1848]
    Orrin of Paris & Elizabeth B HORR of Norway at Mechanic Falls (Poland-Minot) ME [14 Dec 1848]
TUCK Caroline & Rev L C STEVENS of Waldoboro ME at Fayette ME on 20th June by Rev A DRINKWATER [8 Jul 1852]
    Parker Esq & Lucy Ann d/o Rev James WILLIAMS at Readfield ME on 6th inst by Rev W C LARRABEE [25 Jan 1840]
    Sarah H & Lorenzo H D SHEPHERD at Biddeford ME [27 Jul 1848]
TUCKER Belinda of Township # 7 ME & Linsey TRACY at Gouldsboro ME [11 Mar 1847]
    Cornelia & James GETCHELL at Bath ME [27 May 1836]
    Edith of Robinson & Park DAVIDSON at Calais ME [2 Jul 1846]
    Francis A & Mrs Lydia M DRAKE at Guilford ME [3 Jun 1852]
    Hannah M & Daniel CLEAVES Esq of Biddeford ME [25 Sept 1835]
    Isaac Jr of Buckfield ME & Esther A DEAN at Paris ME [19 Jul 1849]
    Isaac N & Miss Sarah C STEWART at Gardiner ME [29 Jan 1836]
    Jeremiah 2d & Mary TUCKER at Norway ME [7 Nov 1837]
    John C & Everline CLARK at Palermo ME [27 Jul 1848]
    Josiah W of Mercer ME & Mary Ann GORDEN at Vienna ME [28 Feb 1850]
    Louisa & George BARNES both of Hartland ME [21 Aug 1838]
    Marcia H of Fairfield ME & Mr G Alfred PHILLIPS of Waterville ME at Providence RI [26 Jun 1851]
    Mary & Jeremiah TUCKER 2d at Norway ME [7 Nov 1837]
    Thomas J & Sarah E WHITE of Georgetown ME at Bath ME [30 Jan 1845]
TUFT Sarah C & George GRIFFIN at Boston MA [28 Sept 1833]
TUFTS George & Lydia A HOLT at Norway ME [20 Jun 1844]
    George W of Danvers MA & Harriet T MERRILL at Levant ME [21 May 1846]
    Samuel N & Angeline MORTON at Winthrop ME [18 Dec 1838]

TUFTS (cont.) Sarah A & Ira H FOSS at Saco ME [5 Jul 1849]
   Susan & Benjamin BRACKETT at New Gloucester ME [9 Aug 1849]
   William of New Gloucester ME & Eliza LIBBY at Pownal ME [17 Jun 1836]
TUKEY Albert & Mary J COOLBROTH at Portland ME [14 Aug 1835]
   George & Eliza Ann HISCOCK, d/o Col William HISCOCK at Nobleboro ME by the Rev Mr SCAMMON [25 Dec 1838]
TULLOCK Arthur & Hannah BISBEE at Bath ME [4 Sept 1845]
TUPPER Mary E & Thomas N LORD at Hallowell ME on 3rd inst by Rev Mr THURSTON [18 Sept 1835]
   Olive & George BURRILL at Canaan ME [29 Apr 1836]
   Rebecca P & Charles LITTLEFIELD at Belgrade ME [22 Feb 1844]
TURNER Ann & Austin BUCK at Belfast ME [24 Jan 1834]
   Barton & Mrs Sylva HILTON at Wiscasset ME [25 Feb 1843]
   Belzorah & Ira H BROWN at Palermo ME [30 May 1844]
   Benjamin of Patricktown Plt ME & Miss Maria JONES at Washington ME [11 Mar 1847]
   Betsey of Bangor ME & William HASEY of Albion ME at Augusta ME on Dec 19th [2 Jan 1851]
   Betsey of Foxcroft ME & James R CROMMETT of Sebec ME at Bangor ME [19 Dec 1844]
   Caroline B & Capt Henry D GARDINER of Nantucket at Whitefield ME [28 Jan 1847]
   Catharine of Perkins ME & John HANSON at Bath ME [25 Jan 1849]
   Catherine S & Caleb B SEWALL at Quincy IL [11 Sept 1845]
   Charles K & Lucinda H PAGE both of Norridgewock ME at Skowhegan ME [4 Jun 1846]
   David & Mrs Catherine W JONES of Washington ME at Palermo ME [11 Jun 1846]
   Dorcas & William CHANEY at Whitefield ME by James MERRILL Esq [8 Oct 1842]
   Eliza & Elias MONK at Buckfield ME [13 Mar 1845]
   Elizabeth of St Ann's Jamaica & Capt George G CHURCH of Gardiner ME at New York City [31 Jan 1850]
   Elvira, d/o Rev Richard TURNER of Windsor ME, & Capt Hartwell GARDINER of Vassalborough ME at Windsor ME [4 Jul 1837]
   Ephraim of Milo ME & Miss Julia A MANSFIELD at Foxcroft ME [16 Sept 1843]
   Hannah N & John BRACKETT & at Levant ME [21 Aug 1851]
   Hannah & Solomon L LOTHROP at Leeds ME [2 May 1840]
   Harriet M & Almon C PRAY at Auburn ME [1 Feb 1849]
   Harriet & Joseph L TOWNE of Lewiston ME at Waterville ME [22 Jul 1852]
   Henry A & Salina A NEWELL at Whitefield ME on 23 Aug by Hiram GLIDDEN Esq [27 Sept 1849]
   Henry P & Caroline Amelia LAKE both of Bucksport ME at Ellsworth ME [25 Dec 1851]
   John A & Phebe BRADLEY at Vassalboro ME on 14 Oct by Edward GRAY Esq [30 Oct 1851]
   John Jr & Frances Elizabeth BRIGGS at Livermore ME by Isaac STRICKLAND Esq [14 Nov 1837]
   John & Phebe BRADLEY at Vassalboro ME [13 Nov 1851]

TURNER (cont.) Joshua Capt & Betsey LOTHROP at Leeds ME on Weds the 28th inst [26 Oct 1833]
    Julia A of Norridgewock ME & Joseph P BUSWELL of Solon ME at Skowhegan ME [4 Jan 1844]
    Lydia & Charles BROWN of Carroll at Leeds ME on 5 Oct [16 Oct 1851]
    Mary Ann & Robert FOLLEY at (Augusta) ME on 16th May [27 May 1852]
    Mary J & Capt Charles R WORMELL of Belfast ME at Waterville ME [28 Feb 1850]
    Nehemiah (ae 60) of Palermo ME & Eliza WILLIAMS (ae 16) at Palermo ME on 23d ult [11 Apr 1840]
    Olive & William R WRIGHT of Lewiston ME [7 Oct 1847]
    Philip & Mary L HOWARD at Leeds ME [18 Jul 1834]
    Rebecca A & Edwin MOORE at China ME [11 Mar 1852]
    Ruth & Charles TORREY at Turner ME [4 Apr 1837]
    Silas L W & Eliza L W HILL at Norridgewock ME [23 Jul 1842]
    William E & Celia C ROBINSON at Dover ME [28 Sept 1848]
    William G & Ann C ROBB both of Leeds ME at Leeds on the 26th ult [25 Dec 1835]

TUSHNOE Moses & Sarah B DOUGLAS at Hallowell ME [1 Jan 1846]

TUTHILL Horatio of Providence RI & Julia A MYRICK at Kennebec ME on 31st Mar by I N WADSWORTH Esq [24 Apr 1851]

TUTTLE Abner Jr & Olive A LIBBY both of North Yarmouth ME on the 7th by E G BUXTON Esq [9 Mar 1842]
    Allen of Buckfield ME & Almeda ROBINSON at Sumner ME on 9th Feb [21 Feb 1850]
    Arabel & Cyrus GOSS of Foxcroft ME at Garland ME on 28th Mar [14 May 1842]
    Aunt & Adam MOTT at Temple ME "Their entire weight is said to be 580 lbs - the gentleman weighing 340 & the lady 240 lbs" [18 May 1848]
    Azel S of Paris & Isabella WING at Wayne ME [7 May 1846]
    Chandler & Martha L BALLARD d/o Ephraim BALLARD Esq both of (Augusta) ME by Rev Charles WILLETT at Thompson CT on 14th inst [26 Oct 1848]
    (Ezra of Georgetown MA, m int 11 Feb 1842, see "Vital Records of Charlestown MA," p. 674, *NEHGS*, 1984) & Mary d/o John SAVAGE of Jay ME at Charlestown MA [16 Apr 1842]
    Frances A of Canaan ME & Dr William W COOPER of Henderson Co KY at Bracken Co OH [21 Jan 1847]
    Hiram & Sophia A ATWOOD at Canaan ME [10 Sept 1846]
    John & Harriet HODGDON at Saco ME [23 Aug 1849]
    Rheasylvia A & Samuel ROWE at Palmyra ME [27 Mar 1851]
    Robert B & Ellen A PHILBRICK at Skowhegan ME [20 Apr 1839]
    Samuel F of Portland ME & Cordelia HOLLAND at Belfast ME [7 Sept 1833]
    Sophia H & Daniel W SPENCER at Somersworth NH [30 Sept 1847]
    William H of Freeman ME & Charity FURBUSH at North Anson ME [15 Mar 1849]

TUYKE Anna of Algiers LA & Samuel S WATERS of Waterville MA at Cincinnati OH [22 Feb 1849]

TWEED Harrison Esq of Calais ME & Miss H A POND, d/o Col Asa POND of Ellsworth ME [17 Sept 1842]

TWIGGS Emelina E & John SMITH both of Hermon ME at Bangor ME [13 May 1847]
TWING Charles G & Julia A KIMBALL at China ME [25 Dec 1851]
TWITCHELL Almira & Benjamin C CUMMINGS at Paris ME [18 Dec 1835]
    Alphin of Orono ME & Roxanna A TWITCHELL of Bethel at Bethel ME [24 Jul 1835]
    Eliza & Noble BLOSSOM at Portland ME on Thurs evening by E WILEY [2 Oct 1835]
    Franklin & Lydia HALL at Paris ME [8 Apr 1852]
    L G & Calvin BUCKNAM of Hebron ME at Paris ME [29 Mar 1849]
    M & William W COZZENS of Bangor ME at Waterville ME [7 Jun 1849]
    Roxanna A of Bethel ME & Alphin TWITCHELL of Orono ME at Bethel [24 Jul 1835]
TWOMBLY Susan H & William H JOHNSON at Hallowell ME [27 Sept 1849]
TWYCROSS Thomas J & Margaret O GOODWIN at Dresden ME on 2d inst by Rev Mr DONNELS [18 Jul 1844]
TYLER Caroline & George L HUTCHINSON at Gardiner ME [3 Dec 1846]
    Charles C, publisher of *Eastport Sentinel* & Hannah S BURPEE at Machias ME [2 May 1844]
    George W & Miss Diantha LITTLEFIELD d/o the late A Z LITTLEFIELD of Skowhegan ME at Sheboyan Falls WI [4 Mar 1847]
    Hannah & Alvan MERRILL at Windsor ME [15 Feb 1849]
    John & Phebe A COLSON at Frankfort ME [27 May 1852]
    Lucinda E & William M HOPKINS of Vinalhaven ME at China ME on Jan 17th by William PERCIVAL Esq [24 Jan 1850]

- U -

ULMER Edward & Lucinda OVERLOCK at Rockland ME [7 Aug 1851]
    Enos C & Miss Catharine FIELD at Thomaston ME by J H BECKETT Esq [15 Jul 1836]
    Ephraim J & Delphus DEAN at Rockland ME [27 Mar 1851]
    Ephraim J & Martha J PROCTOR at Thomaston ME [27 May 1847]
    James of Thomaston ME & Mrs Phebe MOORE at Union ME [27 May 1847]
    Joseph & Ann FALES at Thomaston ME [3 Oct 1837]
    Lucy Mrs & Capt Daniel SANBORN at Thomaston ME [28 Oct 1847]
    Maria S & Allen P FARRINGTON at Thomaston ME [23 Sept 1847]
ULRICK Sarah L & Theodore FRENCH of Thomaston ME at Portland ME [23 Oct 1845]
UMBERHIND Mary E & Lewis W PRINCE of Industry ME at Richmond ME [18 Mar 1847]
UNDERWOOD Mary A both of Fayette ME & Marshall LANE at Chesterville ME by Rev J H CONANT [6 Mar 1851]
    Sarah P & Capt Nahum B HOWE at Readfield ME [15 Aug 1837]
UPHAM Edward S of Gardiner ME & Mary P KELLEY of Sidney ME at Sidney ME on 27 Feb 1851 [6 Mar 1851]
    Edwin E of Readfield ME & Anna L T LOVEJOY of Sidney ME at Sidney on 14th inst by Rev William TILLY [21 May 1846]
    Henry B of Trenton MI & Mary E KITTREDGE Dexter ME [12 Jun 1851]

UPHAM (cont.) William L & Joanna STAIN of Readfield ME at Hallowell ME [11 May 1848]
UPSHUR Susan Brown, only d/o the late Hon A P UPSHUR, & Lieut T L RIGGOLD US Army at Northampton Co, VA [27 Aug 1846]
UPTON B F (Mr) of Bath ME & Sarah FOSTER at Topsham ME [24 Jul 1851]
Ellen Frances & Joseph V EATON at Winthrop ME [29 Apr 1852]
Henry of Norway ME & Harriet BAKER of Waterford ME at Bridgton ME [15 Apr 1847]
Polly & James BENNETT of Greenwood ME at Norway ME [6 Jun 1844]
William B & Rebecca C at Norway [25 Oct 1849]
USHER Abijah of Hollis ME & Mrs Sarah BRADLEY at Fryeburg ME [27 Nov 1845]
Elizabeth R & William Edgecomb at Limington ME [21 Sept 1848]
Sarah E & Joseph RIDLON Jr of Georgetown ME at Hollis ME [10 Apr 1845]
VAILLIEUX Bazelice & Mr J BLAIR at Bloomfield ME [24 May 1849]
VALENTINE Ellen & Capt James McMASTERS at Eastport ME [14 May 1846]
Nelson & Rachel COBB at Poland ME [25 Jun 1846]
Sarah B & Harvey HOWARD at Bangor ME [4 Sept 1845]
VANCE Charlotte H of this town (Augusta ME) & Lot M MORRILL Esq of Readfield ME at New York [5 Dec 1844]
VAN HORN Catherine A & Henry MOORE at Eastport ME [31 Jul 1851]
VANNAH Isaac G & ELiza C RAFTER both of Gardiner ME at Whitefield ME [8 Feb 1849]
VARIEL Samuel & Lydia CRAM both of (Augusta) ME by E CLOUGH Esq at Mt Vernon ME on 8th inst [19 Oct 1848]
VARNEY Gustavus B & Margaret HUBBARD at Gardiner ME [16 Jan 1851]
Hannah & Jonas Parker of Norridgewock ME at Bloomfield ME [4 Dec 1851]
Levi S & Addy SMITH at Bloomfield ME [6 May 1852]
Charity & William HASKELL of Auburn ME at Windham ME [16 Apr 1846]
Emma A of Thomaston ME & Capt W D PIERCE at East Thomaston ME [28 Jun 1849]
James & Elizabeth G WING at Brunswick ME [21 Oct 1843]
John C & Margaret A J BROOK at Dover [8 Feb 1844]
John E of Augusta ME & Eliza Ann CROSBY of Readfield ME at Readfield by William C FULLER Esq [25 Mar 1843]
John P of Fairfield ME & Ruth T PARKER of Skowhegan ME by Moses LITTLEFIELD Esq [9 Oct 1845]
Lavina of China ME & Jethro G WORTH of Vassalboro ME [18 Sept 1835]
Lydia & Obed VARNEY at Skowhegan ME both of Fairfield ME [31 Oct 1837]
Lydia W & Parker D SHAW of Brunswick ME at China ME on 14th Oct by William PERCIVAL Esq [18 Oct 1849]
Obed & Lydia VARNEY both of Fairfield ME at Skowhegan ME [31 Oct 1837]
Samuel of Levant ME & Lucy J WHITE at Montville ME [30 Jan 1845]
Susan & Morrell ELDER of Gray ME at Windham ME [18 Jun 1846]

VARNUM Bartlett Weeks Capt & Rebecca M TODD wid/o the late Dudley TODD Esq at Wayne [12 Feb 1836]
   Esther W & Henry HIGGINS at Richmond ME [23 Sept 1847]
   William J W of Wayne ME & Margaret A BROWN of Wayne ME at Leeds ME on Dec 31st by Rev Walter FOSS [9 Jan 1851]
   William & Sarah DINSMORE at Anson ME [29 Jul 1833]
VARRELL Davis E & Sarah P BECKET at Lewiston ME [13 Mar 1851]
VASTONE William M & Almira H FALES at Thomaston [5 Aug 1847]
VAUGHAN Caroline V & Rev Frederic GARDINER of Saco ME at Gardiner ME [3 Sept 1846]
   Cephas R & Lucinda H BOSWORTH both of Norridgewock ME at Madison ME [10 Feb 1848]
   George & Catherine EDGECOMB at Bath ME [24 Jul 1845]
   Hannah & Miles S COBB of Searsmont ME at Union ME [3 Apr 1835]
   Samuel an English merchant in London & [lady] HALLOWELL sis/o the late Mr HALLOWELL [see story about the VAUGHAN family] at Hook part of Hallowell ME "some four or five years before the close of the eighteenth century" (1795-1796) [30 Oct 1851]
VEAZIE Lorena & Noah ROBERTS at Isleboro ME [20 Jul 1848]
   Samuel M & Mary K SEARS at Rockland ME [1 Jan 1852]
VICKERY James & Catherine B SANBORN at Belfast ME [3 Oct 1840]
   Mary & Capt William HANDY at Norridgewock [5 Oct 1848]
   Phebe & Zalmunna WASHBURN at China ME on 27th March 1851 by Zebah WASHBURN Esq [10 Apr 1851]
   Sarah R & John NEAL both of Belmont ME at Montville ME [7 May 1846]
VIDETTO J W & Miss M CLARK at Stetson ME [27 Jul 1848]
VIGOREAU Peter M of Gardiner ME & Harriet E HATCH at Bath ME [14 Jan 1847]
VIGOREUX Catharine A & John R BEALS at Gardiner ME [14 Sept 1848]
VIGOUREAUX Sarah A & Thomas D WILDER at Gardiner ME [5 Sept 1844]
VILES Alfred Jr & Abigail W HOLBROOK of Starks ME at Mercer ME [18 Feb 1847]
   Jotham S of Starks ME & Mary Ann LEACH by B F CHANDLER Esq at (Augusta) ME on 1st Oct [12 Oct 1848]
   Sanborn L of Industry ME & Philena LUCE at North Anson ME [15 Jul 1852]
   Susan F & Joel S YEATON of New Portland ME at Anson ME [18 Oct 1849]
   Susan & Levi BUTLER at Norridgewock ME [4 Oct 1849]
VINAL George Esq of Bangor ME & Mary M MITCHELL at Dover ME [22 Jun 1848]
   John & Margaret NOYES at Jefferson ME [3 Sept 1846]
   Nancy & Daniel Dea PERKINS at Dixmont ME [30 Mar 1848]
   William & Ann M LIGHT at Hope ME on May 18 [29 May 1851]
VINING Caroline & Richard DYER at Durham ME [2 May 1844]
   Daniel & Sally EASTERBROOK at Calais ME [14 Mar 1837]
   Eulalia L & Charles H THOMAS at China ME on 22 Oct [2 Nov 1848]
   Keziah M & Jeremiah R NORTON of Strong ME at Avon ME [3 Apr 1841]
   Mary J & Ira CLOUGH at Windsor ME by J B SWANTON Esq [14 Feb 1837]
VIRGIN Hannah & Moses LUFKIN at Rumford ME [18 Mar 1833]

Marriage Notices from the "Maine Farmer"

VIRGIN (cont.) & Daniel FARNUM at Rumford ME [18 Mar 1833]
VIVUAN Aroline[sic] P of Vassalboro ME & Ephraim Q PATTERSON of Bangor ME at Salem [31 Jul 1851]
VOCE Mary & Justus at Bath ME [4 Sept 1845]
VOSE Elijah Esq & Mary B TRUE [24 Jun 1843]
 James of Thomaston ME & Sophia ANDREWS of Warren ME at Cushing ME [4 Feb 1833]
 John W & Abigail C STINCHFIELD both of Winthrop ME at Wayne ME [24 Dec 1846]
 Rufus C & Miss Eliza T AYER at Palermo ME [13 Jun 1837]
 Thomas of Robbinston ME & Ruth H CARPENTER at Milltown ME [3 Jan 1850]
 William H of Thomaston ME & Charlotte PITCHER at Belfast ME [24 Jun 1843]

- W -

WADE Abby J & Alfred J STEPHENSON at Sangerville ME by Rev Charles DUREN [26 Feb 1842]
 Abigail & John McINTOSH at Belfast ME [11 Feb 1847]
 Climena & T O SAUNDERS at Waterville ME [22 Feb 1849]
 Emily & Cyrus C RICE at Union ME on 17 Oct [26 Oct 1839]
 Elvira F & James PERKINS at Augusta ME on Nov 25th by J J EVELETH Esq [2 Dec 1847]
 Harriet P & Freeman WHITCOMB of Dresden ME at Augusta ME on 19th inst by Rev Mr WILLIAMS [27 Nov 1845]
 Isabella & Capt Robert T SOULE of Bath ME at Freeport ME [29 May 1845]
 James N & Mary E LEIGHTON at Augusta ME [15 Jan 1846]
 John A & Diana COOMBS at Lincolnville ME [16 Jul 1842]
 John F & Mary Ann SMITH of Hallowell ME at Augusta ME by J J EVELETH Esq [4 Apr 1844]
 Olive & William J BOWMAN at Augusta ME on 7th inst by J J EVELETH Esq [15 Aug 1844]
 Paulina S & Henry F HAGGET at Norridgewock ME [14 Jan 1847]
 Richard H of Dresden ME & Mary F MILLER at Wiscasset ME [2 Nov 1833]
 Selden & Harriet E BLACKWELL at Skowhegan ME both of Norridgewock ME [15 Aug 1844]
 Susan & Bryant BRANCH of Belgrade ME at Smithfield ME [14 Oct 1843]
 Caroline & John N HOVEY at (Augusta) ME [24 Feb 1848]
 Rachel & John LARRABEE formerly of Mt Vernon ME at Greenbush WI [25 Dec 1851]
WADLEIGH Benjamin & Mrs Mary WING at Mount Vernon ME [17 Oct 1844]
 Frederic Augustus, Rector of Christ Church, Guilford VT & Mary Jane HUTCHINSON of Fayette at St Mark's Church in Augusta on Monday evening of last week by Rev Mr FREEMAN [14 Oct 1843]
 George W & Abigail S EDGECOMB at Parsonsfield ME [7 Oct 1847]
 Ira Esq of Oldtown ME & Mrs Catherine M FULLER d/o Hon Nathan WESTON at Augusta ME on Christmas evening at St Mark's Church by Rev Mr BURGESS [2 Jan 1845]

WADLEY William & Miss Susan GOUD at Belgrade ME on Oct 31st [20 Nov 1845]
WADLIN Catherine C of Belfast ME & Capt H J ANDERSON at Brooklyn NY [5 Jul 1849]
   William T & Amenda M KENNISON at Biddeford ME [27 Jul 1848]
WADSWORTH Abby & William MACE of Readfield ME at Winthrop ME on Feb 29th by Rev MERRIAM [11 Mar 1843]
   Ann M & E E PINKHAM at Hallowell ME [15 Mar 1849]
   Harriet & Ebenezer MARROW at Winthrop ME on Sunday morning last by Rev Mr INGRAHAM [8 May 1838]
   Isaac N of Hallowell ME & Mary Ann BRIGGS at Winthrop ME [10 Feb 1848]
   Mary & Farnham RICHARDS at Lincolnville ME [9 May 1844]
   Samuel & Lois WHITNEY at Lincolnville ME [27 Jun 1840]
   Sarah E & Sullivan KILBRITH at the Cross Roads in Hallowell ME of Hartford ME [27 Jun 1844]
WAGG Ann S & William D ROAK at Durham ME [15 Jul 1843]
WAIRE Eleanor S of Gardiner ME & Levi B GREEN of Brunswick ME at Gardiner [24 Jun 1833]
   George & Mehitable E SMITH at Gardiner ME [17 Apr 1845]
WAIT - WAITE
   Alexander M of Falmouth ME & Mary E SWEET of Westbrook ME at Westbrook ME [11 Jul 1840]
   David & Martha CARR of Bowdoinham ME at Bowdoin ME [18 Apr 1837]
   Emily E eldest d/o Silas L WAITE Esq & Theodore D MERRILL at Sidney ME on 31st Aug by Rev Mr JUDD [4 Sept 1851]
   G N Mr & Miss M A WEBBER both of Gardiner ME at Hallowell ME [1 Jun 1848]
   George C form/o (Augusta) now of Middleton Plt NJ & Julia STOUT at Washington NJ on 27th ult [10 Feb 1848]
   Hannah & Thomas B JACKINS at Gardiner ME [21 Feb 1850]
   Rebecca & John L DUTTON at (Augusta) ME [4 May 1848]
   Sarah A of Jay ME & William CLAYTON of Dixfield ME at Jay ME the 10th inst by Rev A SANDERSON [25 Jun 1842]
WAKEFIELD Edward B & Mary STAPLES at Biddeford ME [9 Apr 1846]
   Elizabeth C & M C ANDREWS at Thomaston ME [4 Jun 1846]
   Franklin & Matilda DAVIS both of West Gardiner ME at China ME on 22 Feb [11 Mar 1852]
   Hannah of Smithfield ME & Barnabas ALLEN of Saint Stevens NB Canada at Norridgewock ME [1 Oct 1846]
   Henry D & Mary A BROWN at Gardiner [31 May 1849]
   Henry M & Sarah SMITH at Gardiner ME [1 Nov 1849]
   Joana A & Solomon SMITH at Gardiner ME [27 May 1833] & [3 Jun 1833]
   Laura M & Orren DILL at Gardiner ME [26 Feb 1846]
   Mercey & Moses GLASS of Woolwich ME at Gardiner ME [22 Nov 1849]
   Sarah Elizabeth & Daniel P SHAW Esq of Sanford ME at Kennebunkport ME [9 Oct 1851]
   Thankful Mrs & Capt Henry E JENKS at Bath ME [21 Sept 1833]
   Urania H & William P BROWN at Saco ME [17 Dec 1846]
   William H & Eunice D HINKLEY at Sangerville ME [25 Apr 1850]
WALCH Martha J & Arthur BROWN at Bath ME [11 Jun 1846]

Marriage Notices from the "Maine Farmer"

WALDEN Elbridge G & Miss Mary B HIGGINS at Hampden ME [30 Oct 1838]
WALDRON Abigail C I & John C MERRY at Eastport ME [23 Jul 1846]
    Augusta Ann of Dover NH Alonzo Garcelon, M.D., of Lewiston ME at Great Falls NH [25 Sept 1841]
    Cyrus & Miss Philanda HOLT at Sebasticook ME on Oct 26th [8 Nov 1840]
    Francis A of Portland ME at Harriet FURBUSH at Brunswick ME [30 Jul 1846]
    Howard D & Caroline B BAKER at Buckfield ME [23 Aug 1849]
    Ira of South Berwick ME & Mary WINGATE at Great Falls NH [3 Aug 1848]
    Ira & Lucinda HOLT at Sebasticook ME [8 Mar 1849]
    M E A C P Mrs formerly of Bath ME & Mr J W L BROWN at New York [19 Nov 1846]
    Olive J of Buckfield ME & James M WISWELL at East Machias ME [12 Mar 1846]
    W H (William H) of Lewiston ME & Jane A HITCHCOCK (of Strong ME) at Boston [31 May 1849]
WALES Charlotte W d/o Benjamin WALES Esq & Frederick ALLEN, M.D., at Hallowell ME [18 Jun 1842]
    Eliza E of Saco ME & Daniel B ROSS at Biddeford ME [5 Jul 1849]
    Julia M A & Joseph WHEELER at Belfast ME on 12th inst by Rev D FORBES [25 Jun 1842]
WALKER Abel & Isabella MARTIN at Lincolnville ME [25 Mar 1836]
    Abigail & Priam RICHARDSON at Litchfield ME [15 Nov 1839]
    Asa Esq editor of the Bangor (ME) *Gazette* & Emeline B LINCOLN [20 Aug 1846]
    B F & Mary A SMITH at Livermore ME [18 Jan 1844]
    Betsey & Isaac NOYES at Livermore ME [27 Apr 1839]
    Caroline & Theodore NOTT of Winthrop ME at East Dixfield ME [25 Sept 1845]
    Charles of Pownal ME & Julia Ann WALKER of Brunswick ME [11 Jan 1840]
    Cynthia & Abel W SPAULDING at Embden ME [5 Feb 1846]
    Daniel S & Louisa HERRIN at Knox ME [23 Jan 1851]
    Echsa Mrs & Joseph HOUSTON at Dover ME [5 Sept 1844]
    Elliot Esq of Corinna ME & Sophronia B COFFIN at Waterville ME [19 Aug 1852]
    Elvira Mrs & William F DEARBORN at Monmouth ME [18 Jul 1837]
    Eunice M & Capt Charles N LEACH of Portland ME at North Yarmouth ME [2 Jan 1845]
    Fannie W & Alfred LADD at Boston MA [15 Jun 1848]
    Hannah & Isaac CHAPAM at Saco ME [16 Jan 1838]
    James of Alna ME & Nancy E COTTLE at East Mt Vernon ME [24 Aug 1839]
    John B, M.D., & Burtha E RUST at Washington [28 Jun 1849]
    Joshua & Mrs Miriam NEAL of Gardiner ME at Litchfield ME [15 Aug 1837]
    Julia Ann of Brunswick ME & Charles WALKER of Pownal ME [11 Jan 1840]
    Louisa Mrs of Solon ME & Alvah LORD of Athens ME [27 Aug 1846]

WALKER (cont.) & W R EDDY of Skowhegan ME at Madison ME [30 Apr 1846]
   Mark G & Martha HOYT of Phillips ME at Weld ME [10 Jun 1852] & by Kendall WRIGHT Esq at Weld ME [3 Jun 1852]
   Mary A of Fairfield ME & Moses WELCH at Waterville ME [20 Mar 1851]
   Miram & William KNIGHTS at Brunswick ME [22 Aug 1834]
   O B Rev of Baring & Julia WORKS at Norridgewock ME [23 Feb 1839]
   Olive Ann & Mr J WOODBURY at Exeter ME [5 Jul 1849]
   Orin & Selome A DURGIN at Stoneham [27 Jul 1848]
   Orrinda P & Timothy D MANNING at Thomaston ME [10 Oct 1844]
   Paulina & Noah MERRILL of Skowhegan ME at Anson ME [30 Jan 1851]
   Peter Esq of Brighton & Nancy J KELLY at Mayfield [30 Oct 1851]
   Rosetta A & Aaron P McFARLAND at Liberty ME [17 Aug 1848]
   Sarah A H & Alden FULLER of Minot ME at Paris ME [2 Aug 1849]
   Sarah A of Belfast ME & Mr E H ELLIS of Waldo ME by Rev D FORBES [25 Jan 1842]
   Sarah E & J M SMITH at Norridgewock ME [7 Dec 1848]
   Sarah G & Allen WOOD at Brunswick ME [15 May 1851]
   Sarah G & Bradbury PERKINS at Cornville ME [20 Feb 1851]
   Solon G of Paris ME & Vesta CHANDLER at Paris ME [18 Jul 1840]
   Sophia W & Levi W WESTON at Solon ME [4 Mar 1852]
   Susan M & Mr C T TRAFTON of South Berwick ME at Kennebunk ME [5 Mar 1846]
   Sylvester & Emily A PERHAM at Jay ME by M STONE Jr both of Wilton ME [19 Aug 1852]
   Willard & Miss Jane HAM at Bath ME [24 Oct 1834]
   William Capt & Caroline CLOUGH at Bluehill ME [29 Jul 1836]
   William Eugene of Portland ME & Phebe LANDERKIN at Gardiner ME [18 Apr 1850]
   William L Esq of Newport ME & Sarah R eldest d/o Greenwood C CHILD Esq at Augusta ME on 25th ult by Rev Mr Mr JUDD [15 Aug 1844]
   William & Mrs Susan Jane STONE at Thorndike ME [25 Feb 1847]
WALL Albion Capt & Mrs Keturah S HARTHORN at St George ME [6 Mar 1838]
   Amos H of Bath ME & Miss Rebecca H JACKSON at Phipsburg ME [30 Jul 1846]
   Elmira B & John P STOVER at Thomaston ME [16 Mar 1848]
   Granville of Monroe ME & Harriet JORDAN of Etna ME by J C FRIENDS Esq [5 Feb 1839]
   Timothy of Bangor ME & Miss M J COCHRAN at Ellsworth ME [3 Aug 1848]
WALLACE Esther A & James MOODY at Lincolnville ME [13 May 1852]
   Almira & David DOUGHTY of Cumberland ME at Phipsburg ME [15 Jan 1836]
   Lowell B Capt & Miss Ruby WALLACE at Phipsburg ME [22 Feb 1844]
   Maria & Richard CROOT both of Bloomfield ME at Skowhegan ME [8 May 1845]
   Ruby & Capt Lowell B WALLACE at Phipsburg ME [22 Feb 1844]
   William H & Miss Elmira F BENJAMIN at Waldoboro ME [28 May 1846]
WALLIS James D & Miss Wealthy L BLAISDELL at Phipsburg ME [12 Feb 1846]
   Palmer & Mary E MORRISON at Phipsburg ME [5 Mar 1846]

WALLS Sally M & Ivory TRAFTON at Gouldsboro ME [12 Aug 1847]
WALSH Lucretia & Mr W C McINTOSH at Thomaston ME [22 Oct 1846]
WALTER Almira & Mr Joseph SHUMAN at Waldoboro ME by Reuben ORFF Esq [23 Dec 1847]
   Betsey & Elisha PARK at Chesterville ME [27 Nov 1845]
   Cornelia M & William RICHARDS at Boston MA [7 Oct 1847]
   Elizabeth C & Benjamin BATCHELDER at Union meeting house in Fayette ME by Rev George BATES [11 Nov 1843]
   Eunice B & James R BYRAM at Gardiner ME [17 Sept 1842]
   John of Starks ME & Emily A WARD at Madison ME [7 Feb 1850]
   Martha Ann & Mark WARREN of Brooks ME at Belfast ME [15 Feb 1849]
   S B & E F PETTENGILL at East Livermore ME of Fayette ME [8 Aug 1844]
   Samuel M & Mary Jane MINK at North Waldoboro ME on 5 Jul by Reuben ORFF Esq [12 Jul 1849]
   Sylvanus B of Mercer ME & Martha T CHAPMAN of Starks ME at Smithfield ME [11 Nov 1843]
WALTZE Orrin & Susan W KELSEY by Rev Mr HAWES at (Augusta) ME on Sept 26th [5 Oct 1848]
WALWRIGHT Robert M A Lt of the US Army (Ordance Corps) now in command at US Arsenal in Augusta ME of the city of Washington & Ann Eliza CHILD eld/o James L CHILD Esq of Augusta ME at Augusta ME by Rev Dr TAPPAN [9 Sept 1843]
WARD Anna P of China ME & David S PATTERSON at Vassalboro ME on 5 Oct by Edward GRAY Esq [16 Oct 1851]
   Annette & Asel STANLEY of Vassalboro ME at China ME on 19th Mar by Rev B F SHAW [3 Apr 1851]
   Cynthia & Wallace HUTINGTON of Windham CT at Brunswick ME [19 Nov 1846]
   Deborah Ann & Mr B F FORD of Mayfield at Brighton ME [8 May 1851]
   Elmira & Henry WASHBURN at China ME [30 Jan 1851]
   Emily A & John WALTON of Starks ME at Madison ME [7 Feb 1850]
   Eunice C d/o Edmund WARD of China ME & Rev Franklin MERRIAM of Winthrop ME at China ME on the 15th inst by Rev B F SHAW [18 Sept 1845]
   Hartwell O & Hannah S FRY at China ME on Christmas Eve by Rev B F SHAW [10 Jan 1850]
   James of Vassalboro ME & Margaret SEEKINS of Windsor ME [19 Sept 1837]
   Jane H & Wilmot W PLUMMER of Addison ME at Cherryfield ME [29 Jul 1852]
   Levi & Lydia FOSTER d/o Daniel FOSTER at (Augusta) ME [16 Mar 1848]
   Lewis & Paulina C CHURCHILL at Augusta ME on 19th Aug by Asaph R NICHOLS Esq [28 Aug 1851]
   Louisa & William JACKSON at Augusta ME on 31 Dec by Rev Z THOMPSON [9 Jan 1851]
   Maria M & Jefferson F WYMAN at China ME [23 Sept 1847]
   Philena & Ebenezer F STEVENS at N Anson ME [28 Dec 1848]
   Roxana & Charles G CLAPHAM [1 Aug 1834]
   Rufus of Wellington & Mary Ann SMITH at Brighton [27 Mar 1847]
   Thomas D & Sarah B CROSMAN at China ME [30 Sept 1836]
   Thomas of Freeport ME & Jane SPRINGER at Brunswick ME [8 Mar 1849]

WARD (cont.) William S & Abba Jane PEACOCK at Richmond ME [5 Mar 1846]
WARDWELL Abby & Robert RANKIN at Richmond VA [19 Feb 1846]
  Burnham & Sarah L GOODALE both of Bucksport ME at Bangor ME [27 Jul 1848]
  Caroline H of Rumford & Stephen BARKER Jr of Methuen MA at New York [14 Jan 1847]
  Jarvis C of Rumford ME & Mrs Maria L HARLOW of Canton ME at Roxbury MA [29 Jan 1852]
  Peter C of Otisfield ME & Henrietta SNELL at Poland ME [7 Jan 1847]
  Temperance A & John B MILLER of Albany at Otisfield ME [7 Jan 1847]
WARE Elizabeth S of Augusta ME & Uriah FOSTER of Clinton ME at Augusta ME on 27th ult by Rev Mr MORSE [4 Jun 1846]
  Harriet & James RANGERLY Jr at Farmington by Robert GOODENOW Esq [16 Jan 1838]
  James & Mary E PERRY by Rev A DALTON at (Augusta) ME on 23d May [3 Jun 1852]
  John Esq of Athens ME & Sarah Maria SCOTT at Wayne ME [22 Jan 1842]
  Margaret & Charles W McCAUSLAND at Gardiner ME [22 Mar 1849]
  Martha Ann & Seth GARLAND both of Augusta ME at Farmington ME on 24th Nov by Rev Mr ALLEN [6 Dec 1849]
  Mary Jane & Franklin PRESCOTT at Augusta ME on 13th inst [26 Mar 1846]
  Parthene B & Edward C GOLDTHWAIT both of Augusta ME at Winslow ME on 18 Jan by Rev A MOORE [5 Feb 1846]
WARES Hiram & Sophronia COOK at Pittston ME [3 Jul 1851]
WARING Hart E, Missionary for Java (Indonesia) & Adelaide FORBES at New York [25 Apr 1837]
WARMELL Joseph of Boston & Hannah CARPENTER at Eastport ME [27 Feb 1845]
WARNER Ardelia L & Edward DANA Jr at Augusta ME [17 Dec 1846]
  Asborough & Mrs Mary Ann GARDINER at Augusta ME on 25th ult by Rev A MOORE [12 Dec 1844]
  Lucinda ae 12y 6m & Josiah W REED ae 42 at Rowe [6 May 1833]
  Lucy & Thomas SMITH at Augusta ME [15 Aug 1837]
  Mary A & Simeon S LAMKIN at Jay ME on Mar 20th [8 Apr 1852]
WARREN Augustus A & Delia JONES at Kittery ME [4 Sept 1851]
  Caroline C, eld d/o Col H I WARREN of Pownal ME, & Dr David Y PIERCE of Bowdoin ME at Pownal ME on the 24th inst by Rev Jabez WOODMAN [2 Jan 1841]
  Charles & Abby A NELSON at Winthrop ME [1 Jul 1847]
  Cornelia B & David Y PIERCE, M.D., at New Gloucester ME both of New Gloucester [31 May 1849]
  David T formerly of Winthrop ME & Miss Lydia DOWNES, d/o Capt Alexander D BUNKER at Nantucket MA by Rev Mr EDES [28 Sept 1839]
  Edmund C of Vassalboro ME & Melinda C HAMLEN at Winslow ME [16 Nov 1848]
  Edward R of New Castle ME & Mary HATHORNE of Woolwich ME at Bath ME [11 Dec 1835]
  Eliza & George A FAIRFIELD at Skowhegan ME [24 Oct 1837]

WARREN (cont.) Emeline G, d/o Edmund WARREN of New York City, & Charles L THOMAS merchant of Tremont IL and formerly of Winthrop ME at New York City on Sunday evening the 4th inst by Rev Dr HAWKES [16 Dec 1836]
    Esther P & Sylvester PAUL at Biddeford ME [20 Jul 1848]
    George & Julia T HUTCHINSON at Gardiner ME [25 Mar 1836]
    Hannah, d/o Josiah WARREN, & Benjamin ADAMS all of Norridgewock ME at Norridgewock [27 Mar 1838]
    Hiram of Minot ME & Charlotte ROBBINS of Turner ME at Turner [28 Oct 1836]
    J C C Mr & Elizabeth A BROWN at Waterford ME at Waterford [31 Aug 1848]
    J W of Newburgh NY at Cornville ME? & Joanna BUTLER [22 Jul 1847]
    James C Esq of Detroit ME & Rachel LANE at Webster ME [8 Feb 1849]
    Jesse of Hollis ME & Pamelia of Kennebunkport ME [8 Apr 1836]
    John C & Hannah C PRATT at Paris ME [17 Sept 1846]
    John & Mary MELLUS at Hallowell ME [24 Aug 1833]
    John & Mary WEBBER at Gardiner ME [14 May 1846]
    Laura Ann J & Chester CHAMBERLAIN of Foxcroft ME at Sangerville ME [27 Apr 1839]
    Lucy E & Mr D P CLARK of Unity ME at Freedom ME [12 Aug 1852]
    Mark of Brooks ME & Martha Ann WALTON at Belfast ME [15 Feb 1849]
    Martha A & Hosea B REED printer of Augusta ME at Standish ME on 25th Mar by James FOSS Esq [4 Apr 1850]
    Mary D & Calvin H CRAM Esq merchant at Portland ME on 10th inst [21 Sept 1839]
    Mary T & Clark STANLEY of Waterville ME at Ellsworth ME [29 Jan 1839]
    Mason P & Julia Ann B SHAW both of Nashua NH, formerly of Winthrop ME at Nashua NH on 4 Mar by Rev Mr RICHARDS [6 Mar 1841]
    O M of Hallowell ME & Sarah G WORTHING at Palermo ME [20 Sept 1849]
    Samuel of Polkton MI & Catharine Elizabeth KNOWLTON at Chesterville ME [17 Aug 1848]
    Samuel & Irene B GAGE at Waterford ME [22 Jan 1846]
    Sullivan of Parkman ME & Mrs Sarah CAMPBELL at Sangerville ME [20 Mar 1841]
    William & Mrs WING at Skowhegan ME [17 Sept 1846]

WASGATT Nancy D & Dr J W HINCKLEY at Mt Desert ME [29 Apr 1852]

WASHBURN Alonzo & Jane C STRICKLAND at Livermore ME [25 Apr 1850]
    Asenath & Orin HASKELL at Livermore ME by Aaron BARTON Esq [7 Aug 1838]
    Augustus V & Lucy Ann B CHURCHILL at Buckfield ME [13 Feb 1851]
    Bethuel & Sarah C BREWSTER at Parkman ME [30 Apr 1846]
    H G O & Charlotte M FURBER at Belfast ME [3 Oct 1844]
    Harrison G O of Belfast ME & Hannah E DENNESS of Hallowell ME at Hallowell [7 Nov 1834]
    Henry Jr & Elizabeth L GRANT [25 Feb 1843]
    Henry & Elmira WARD at China ME [30 Jan 1851]
    Judson R Capt & Miss Sarah L BISKEY [20 Mar 1845]
    Julia C, d/o J C WASHBURN Esq, & John G STEARNS at Calais ME [26 Dec 1840]
    Maria & Joseph HADLOCK of Falmouth ME at Paris ME [19 Nov 1846]

WASHBURN (cont.) Rhoda Ann & Isaac J CORBETT of Brunswick ME at Gardiner ME [24 Oct 1844]
   Sarah E & Benjamin ROBINSON at Thomaston ME [2 Jan 1845]
   Sullivan of Gardiner ME & Dorcas RICHARDSON at Litchfield ME [21 Aug 1842]
   Thomas T WASHBURN Esq of Orono ME & Marcia PERKINS at Bridgewater ME [22 Jul 1836]
   Zalmunna & Phebe VICKERY at China ME on 27th March 1851 by Zebah WASHBURN Esq [10 Apr 1851]
WASS William Capt & Sarah M SMILEY at Hallowell ME [8 Aug 1840]
   Nathaniel N & Clorinda C at Addison Point [14 Oct 1847]
   Sarah M Mrs & George HODGES at Hallowell ME [15 Jan 1842]
WASSON Susan Ann of Anson ME & Jefferson CLEAVELAND of Embden ME at Norridgewock ME [18 Apr 1837]
   Mary A & Albert C CARR both of Readfield ME at E Windsor ME on May 6 by Rev S POWERS [3 Jul 1851]
WATERHOUSE A Mr of Durham ME & Caroline W DAWES at New Gloucester ME [19 Dec 1844]
   Betsey & Moses HANSON of Windham ME at Westbrook ME [24 Jun 1836]
   Clarissa & Simon WATERHOUSE at Troy ME? [21 May 1842]
   Isaac C & Martha C LORD at Hallowell ME [13 Feb 1851]
   Lydia M & Lewis C MORRILL [19 Apr 1849]
   Olive & Jonathan M HEATH at Monmouth ME [14 Dec 1839]
   Samuel R of Richmond ME & Lydia A HIGGINS of Bowdoin ME at Litchfield ME [20 Jan 1848]
   Simon of Detroit & Clarissa WATERHOUSE at Troy ME? [21 May 1842]
   Theophilus Jr of Standish ME & Elizabeth FROST at Gorham ME [13 Mar 1845]
WATERMAN Charles & Caroline D BURRILL at Sangerville ME [15 Aug 1844]
   Helen R of Appleton ME & Wilson RICHARDS of Liberty ME at South Montville ME on 27th Jan [7 Feb 1850]
   Orren & Lydia HOWARD at (Winthrop ME) by Rev Mr BAILEY [11 Jun 1842]
   Robert of Belfast & Mary RICH at Brooks ME [13 May 1847]
   Samuel H & Olive F ADAMS at Thomaston ME [11 Feb 1847]
   Susan S & Levi FISHER of Charlotte Washington Co ME at Belfast ME [5 Dec 1844]
WATERS Clarendon & Lucy COOLIDGE at Livermore ME [24 Jul 1835]
   Horace of Augusta ME & Miss Ann Elizabeth LEEDS of Brookline MA [30 May 1840]
   Julia E d/o F G WATERS Esq of Bath ME & Rev Thomas SEWALL s/o Prof Thomas SEWALL of Washington DC at Baltimore MD on 19th inst by the Rev Dr DORSEY [28 Nov 1844]
   Samuel S of Waterville ME & Anna TUYKE of Algiers LA at Cincinnati OH [22 Feb 1849]
WATSON Ansyl G & Sarah F McCORD Mrs at (Augusta) ME on July 7 by Frances DAVIS Esq [10 Jul 1851]
   Benjamin of Farmington & Sarah SMITH at Lowell MA [18 May 1848]
   Caroline S of Dover & Timothy E ROLLINS of Camden NJ [3 Jul 1845]

WATSON (cont.) Cyrus S of Susan B OSBORN at Williams College Grant (Littleton or Houlton ME), Aroostook Co [28 Oct 1847]
Dorinda of Fayette ME & Samuel SIMPSON of Alna ME at Fayette ME by Rev P POND [3 Jul 1841]
Eunice C & Matthias V BRADBURY at Parkman ME [9 Jan 1845]
Francis M & Mary Jane JOSSELYN at Augusta ME [2 May 1837]
John of Wiscasset ME & Sophia B TOZER of Waterville ME at Detriot ME [30 Dec 1847]
John & Rebecca RUSSELL at Hallowell ME by Rev Mr FULLER [27 Mar 1845]
Lucy Ann & Josiah BAKER at Portland ME [25 Jul 1834]
Mary T & Asa A MACOMBER at Harmony ME by Elder BAILEY of Cornville ME [18 Apr 1844]
Nancy & William NEWCOMB at Foxcroft ME [8 Jan 1852]
Samuel A & Joan H ROLLIN at Parkman ME [9 Jan 1845]
Sarah & Ichabod ROLLIN Jr at Parkman ME [9 Jan 1845]
Sewall Esq of Augusta ME & Mrs Alice R DELANO d/o the late Benjamin RIGGS Esq at Georgetown ME [24 Dec 1846]
Sewall N of Fayette ME & Rhoda P CLOUGH d/o Elijah CLOUGH Esq of Mt Vernon ME at Readfield ME on 7 Jul by Rev A DRINKWATER [5 Aug 1847]
Woodman H (Rev) of Holden ME & Mary L COLCORD at at Hallowell ME [5 Aug 1843]

WATT James C & Sophronia M ALLEN at Lubec ME [10 Jan 1850]

WATTON Margaret A & William W MILLER of Cushing ME at Waldoboro ME [18 Jul 1844]

WATTS Catherine M & Stephen S LEATHERS at Knox ME [27 May 1852]
Elizabeth C & Mr L JORDAN at Wales ME [10 Aug 1848]
Emma & Capt Gorham METCALF at Hallowell ME [18 Nov 1847]
Isaac Capt & Catherine at Waldoboro ME [21 May 1846]
John B of Thomaston ME & Eliza C DAVIS at Boston MA [25 Sept 1851]
Lawson L & Ann C GIBBS of Livermore ME at Hallowell ME [5 Sept 1844]
M L & Capt Thomas SNOW of Brunswick ME at Hallowell ME [21 Oct 1847]
Samuel Jr Capt of Hallowell ME & Amy Jane BUDDINGTON of Strafford CT at London England [16 Mar 1848]

WAUGH Almira & Ezekiel D BLOOD at Readfield ME [27 Feb 1841]
Asa & Rachel D ELA at Starks ME [22 Nov 1849]
Caroline A & Henry PACKARD at East Winthrop ME on Monday evening last by Rev F MERRIAM [4 Jun 1846]
David F of Mercer ME & Sabra W SHAW of Boston MA at Norridgewock ME [4 Oct 1849]
Elizabeth Ann & Charles B HOWARD of Livermore ME at Readfield ME [22 Jan 1842]
Elizabeth & Daniel A FAIRBANKS at Winthrop ME by Rev Mr THURSTON [7 May 1846]
Harrison & Sophia A STERRY by L G SMITH Esq at Starks ME on 29th Mar [13 Apr 1848]
Manchester F of Mercer ME & Emily N SHAW of Industry ME at the meeting house on 16th ult by Rev John PERHAM [20 Jun 1844]
Mary & Ezekiel RACKLIFF at Starks ME [2 Jul 1846]
Roxanna B & Albert SMITH at Thomaston ME [14 May 1846]

WAYNE Loanthe & Paul D HATHORN at Milford [13 Jan 1848]
WEAVER Margaret & Solomon CREAMER at Waldoboro ME [26 Feb 1846]
   Mary C of Washington ME? & Benjamin L LAW Jr of Union ME at N Waldoboro ME on Dec 4th by Reuben ORFF Esq [11 Dec 1851]
   Sheffel Capt, a pensioner of the Revolution, & Hannah d/o Mr Benjamin DURFEE, another hero of the Revolution at Fall River [14 Mar 1834]
WEBB Albert J of Winthrop ME & Harriet FARRELL at Washington DC [17 Dec 1846]
   Albion of Knox ME & Margaret S STEVENS at Montville ME [19 Feb 1852]
   Ann J of Warren & Nathan G CLARY at Wilton ME [17 Jun 1847]
   Catherine & William SPROUL Jr of Waldoboro ME at Warren ME [12 Dec 1837]
   Clemantine B & Capt Orrin FALES at Thomaston ME [8 Jul 1847]
   Ezekiel T of Woolwich ME & Harriet DEERING of Bath ME at Bath by Rev John DEERING [16 Jan 1841]
   Flavis H Mrs & Lorenzo OAK at Garland ME [12 Sept 1844]
   Harriet F & Capt James T SPRAGUE all of Thomaston ME at Thomaston [30 Sept 1847]
   James L & Mrs Susan KNIGHT at Deer Isle ME [15 Jul 1843]
   John Capt & Harriet P HATCH at Dresden ME [4 Jan 1849]
   John S & Mary A PARKMAN at Skowhegan ME [9 Aug 1849]
   Joseph C Bloomfield ME & Betsey E BURGESS by Joseph GERRY Esq at Fairfield ME on Oct 17th [14 Dec 1848]
   Marion & Christopher PRINCE at Thomaston ME [14 May 1846]
   Mary E of China ME & Amaziah F TINKHAM of Augusta ME at Albion ME [14 Jan 1847]
   Pamelia of Portland ME & Henry FAIRBANKS of Monmouth ME at Portland ME [19 Oct 1833]
   Samuel Esq & Mrs Cynthia HEMINGWAY at Brunswick ME [1 Feb 1849]
   Sarah A of China ME & John C KNOLTON of Montville ME at China ME [26 Nov 1842]
   Seth Jr of Plt # 7 & Betsey A THURSTON at Harmony ME [16 Mar 1848]
   Seth & Deborah BABBAGE at Deer Isle ME [18 Feb 1847]
   Silas L & Harriet Ann NEWMAN at Winthrop ME on Wednesday evening Jan 22d by Rev David THURSTON [6 Feb 1845]
   William F of Prospect ME & Susan J RIDLEY at Monroe ME [30 Sept 1847]
   William & Lucinda SINCLAIR at Bath ME [31 Jul 1835]
WEBBER Amanda M d/o Oliver A WEBBER Esq & Michael KENNEDY Jr of Troy VT at Vassalboro ME on 7 Apr 1851 by Rev Dr TAPPAN of Augusta ME. "We don't exactly like to have the Vermonters carry our Kennebec girls out of the State and away off beyond the Green Mountains but if they will go God bless them and Vermont too." [10 Apr 1851]
   Caroline A & Myron PARDEE Esq of Oswego NY at St Mark's Church in Augusta ME [19 Aug 1847]
   Caroline S & Joseph A SHAW at Augusta ME on 17th inst [21 Sept 1848]
   Celia F & William B COOMBS at China ME on 3d March [11 Mar 1852]
   Charels M of Gardiner ME & Emeline T JONES of Pittston ME at New York City [28 Oct 1847]

WEBBER (cont.) Charles C & Sarah LITTLEFIELD both of York ME at Kennebunk ME [10 Oct 1837]
   Cornelius S & Sarah T WINSLOW at Bangor ME [18 Jul 1844]
   Elias & Adelade FRETHY at Hallowell ME [18 Dec 1851]
   Harriet & William WEST at Wiscasset ME [25 Jun 1842]
   Jane & Capt Thomas PIERCE at Boothbay ME both of Bristol ME [15 Jan 1842]
   Jeremiah & Rebecca J HOLLAND at Lewiston ME [21 Jun 1849]
   Levi M of China ME & Tryphena M CARTER by Rev Mr DOBLE at Etna ME on New Year's Day [8 Jan 1852]
   Levi & Sarah LANGDON at Ellsworth ME [12 Sept 1840]
   M A Miss & Mr G N WAIT at Hallowell ME [1 Jun 1848]
   Margaret J & William TROTTER at Augusta ME at St Mark's Church by Rev Mr BURGESS [3 Jun 1847]
   Mary & John WARREN at Gardiner ME [14 May 1846]
   Oliver A Esq of Vassalboro ME & Sarah H BRYANT at Gardiner ME on Feb 6 by Rev Josiah W PEET [8 Feb 1849]
   Samuel & Emeline N SWAN at Gardiner ME [12 Aug 1847]

WEBSTER Clement, junior editor of the *York County Herald* (York Co ME?) & Miss Catherine P LITTLEFIELD of Providence RI at Saco ME on 15th inst by Rev Mr HORTON [25 May 1839]
   Ebenezer Jr Esq & Martha A d/o Gen Mark TRAFTON of Bangor ME at Orono ME [17 Aug 1839]
   George of Bath ME & Elizabeth GROUSE at Brunswick ME [18 Sept 1845]
   Harriet W d/o Dr J W WEBSTER & Mr S W DABNEY of Fayal Azores at Cambridge MA [17 Apr 1851]
   Isaac of No 4 Aroostook Co (ME) & Miss Rebecca WEBSTER at Glenburg ME [3 Aug 1839]
   James of Orono ME & Ann B BAKER of Augusta ME at Albion ME on 30th Dec by Rev Z MANTER [23 Jan 1851]
   John M & Sarah H HUSSEY of Dover NH at Augusta ME [10 Apr 1841]
   Laura Ann & Daniel L HURD at Augusta ME on the 5th inst [25 Sept 1845]
   Lucy W & Horace L BROWN, M.D., of Dunham Canada East [29 Feb 1844]
   Mary Augusta & Daniel C STANWOOD of Augusta ME at Salem MA [18 Nov 1836]
   Mary C, youngest d/o Ebenezer WEBSTER Esq of Portland ME & John RANGELY of Farmington ME at Portland ME on Weds evening last by Rev Mr CHICKERING [16 Oct 1838]
   Mercy E & Francis REED at Bath ME [23 Jul 1846]
   Rebecca & Isaac WEBSTER of No 4 Aroostook Co ME at Glenburg ME [3 Aug 1839]
   Sophronia & Capt Amos T CHASE both of Portland ME at New Gloucester ME [4 Sept 1838]
   Sullivan Capt & Eliza W LOPANS both of Mt Desert ME at Boston MA [8 Aug 1840]

WEDGEWOOD Edwin W Esq & Esther A CHICK at Cornish ME [17 Apr 1851]
   Ursula & Randall MAYO at Brownville ME [11 Oct 1849]

WEEKES - WEEKS
  Abby C & Thomas C HOYT at Jefferson ME on 30th Dec [8 Jan 1852]
  Alathea & Henry HEDGE at Vassalboro ME [8 Nov 1849]
  Braddock & Clarissa Ann WHITE at Wayne ME on Monday evening last by Rev G BAILEY of Winthrop ME [10 Apr 1841]
  Catharine P & John LORD 3rd at Parsonsfield ME [11 Mar 1847]
  Charles S of Vassalboro ME & Octavia F HALL at China ME [10 Apr 1851]
  Edward & Maria FITCH at Vassalboro ME [18 Jul 1840]
  Edwin & Lucy E WHITTUM at Vassalboro ME [13 Mar 1851]
  Elizabeth J & Thomas FARNHAM Jr at Hallowell ME [15 Mar 1849]
  Ephraim B & Caroline HODGKINS at Jefferson ME [3 & 17 Apr 1851]
  Erastus F & Jenetta G RICHARDSON at Jefferson ME [3 Sept 1846]
  Esther & William T WINSLOW at Vassalboro ME on Nov 14th [30 Nov 1848]
  George, merchant, & Caroline HASKELL at Jefferson ME [7 Mar 1837]
  George W of Boston MA & Susan Emma MAYO [27 Nov 1845]
  H Augusta & Simon NOWELL of Fairfield ME at Waterville ME [11 Oct 1849]
  James F, printer formerly of Augusta ME & Rebecca T LARGE at Davertown OH [1 May 1838]
  John B of Vassalboro ME & Emily E SMILEY at Sidney ME [9 Dec 1847]
  Leander & Mary J ROSS at Jefferson ME on 17th inst [28 Jan 1847]
  Levi A & Mary J TIBBETTS of Belgrade ME at Sidney ME on June 12 [3 Jul 1851]
  Lucy A & Henry W BARNEY at Gardiner ME by Rev J P WESTON [19 Jun 1845]
  Margaret J & Briggs T CARTER, M.D., at Jefferson ME [3 Sept 1846]
  Mary F & Charles SPEAR of Bangor ME at Portland ME [21 Nov 1844]
  Nancy B & Bradbury LIBBY at Sidney ME on 19th inst both of (Augusta ME) [26 Nov 1846]
  Newell & Mary Jane LONG at Abbot ME [28 Jan 1847]
  Noah F & Miss Phebe G STONE at Hallowell ME [25 Apr 1850]
  Paulina & Scott MORSE of Bath ME at Phipsburg ME [25 Apr 1844]
  Philander of Farmington ME & Lydia DAVIS of Industry ME [7 Jan 1843]
  Polly, wid/o Dr WEEKES of Northam, England (ae 70), & Mr William ASKEY of Salem (ae 84) at Salem on Tues evening on Dec 22d [16 Jan 1841]
  Rachel of Alna ME & Robert L KINCAID of Whitefield ME at Hallowell ME [1 Mar 1849]
  Roxana & William A BRAINARD at New Sharon ME [6 May 1847]
  Samuel D m Linda M RAWSON at Paris ME [22 May 1851]
  Samuel & Lavina PEACOCK at Gardiner ME [4 Feb 1833]
  Sarah A & Henry W BURRILL at Corinna ME [20 Apr 1848] & [7 Apr 1848]
  Sarah A & Mr F REED at Bath ME [13 Nov 1851]
WEIR Rachel M & Abel W BOSWORTH formerly of Norridgewock ME at Mobile AL? [14 Mar 1844]
WELCH A K P of Monmouth ME & Miss Julia A GOFF at Auburn ME [12 Mar 1846]
  Ann R & John C WOOD at Vassalboro ME on Dec 11 by Oliver WEBBER Esq [18 Dec 1851]

WELCH (cont.) Esther J & Charles SMALL at Chelsea ME? [12 Jun 1851]
John A of Monmouth ME & Rosanna S HILLMAN at Albany NY [24 Aug 1848]
Martha A & Ephraim DURGIN at Limerick ME [13 Jan 1848]
Moses & Mary A WALKER of Fairfield ME at Waterville ME [20 Mar 1851]
Philena & Jonathan B SMITH at Winthrop ME [30 Mar 1848]

WELCOMBE Isaac of Hallowell ME & Mary DECKER of Gardiner ME at Gardiner ME [15 Jan 1846]

WELD C S (Miss) & Amos DAVIS at Brunswick ME [2 Nov 1848]
Charles 2d & Miss Mary Ann LASH at Waldoboro ME [19 Dec 1837]
Emeline & Hebron TILTON at Chicago IL [27 Jul 1848]
George R of Livermore ME & Mary Ann NEWMAN at Dixfield ME [14 Jan 1847]
Hannah P formerly of Bloomfield ME & Daniel MITCHELL at Dover ME [6 Nov 1838]
Harriet Mrs & Hon Nathan CUTLER of Farmington ME at Brunswick ME [19 Jun 1838]
Henry H of Wyolusing PA & Ellen S LADD d/o Gen S G LADD at Farmington ME on 12th inst by Rev Isaac ROGERS [18 Oct 1849]
Ruby J & Silas R WYMAN at Cornville ME [12 Feb 1852]

WELLINGFORD Helen M of Kennebunk ME & Dr Joseph C HOOPER of Frankfort ME at Bangor ME [25 Sept 1845]

WELLINGTON Fannie & Timothy HEMLEN at Albion ME [30 Jan 1851]
Fanny & T A HAMLIN at Albion ME on Jan 2 [23 Jan 1851]
Mary A & Mr E STACKPOLE of Houlton ME at Albion ME [6 May 1836]
Nathan Capt of Livermore ME & Olive WOOD of this town at Winthrop on Wednesday last by Rev Mr THURSTON [23 Jan 1841]

WELLMAN Ephraim F & Mary Jane DOW both of Strong ME at Farmington ME [5 Mar 1846]
Jacob formerly of Farmington ME & Louisa M PHELPS at New York [20 Jul 1848]
Sarah & William N DOW at Strong ME by Samuel PATTERSON Esq [18 Mar 1833]
Thomas H & Lucy S BELCHER at Belmont ME [24 Oct 1844]

WELLS Clarinda & Mr Z S PURINGTON of Gardiner ME at Georgetown MA [6 Dec 1849]
Hannah B & Howard DEARBORN at Hallowell ME [30 Aug 1849]
Helena & Timothy C SPAULDING at Embden ME [15 May 1845]
Joseph R & Mrs Mary J CROSS at Gardiner ME [25 Jan 1849]
Joshua Jr & Mary S GILMAN at Mt Vernon ME [15 Jan 1836]
Mary A & Henry AMES both of Belfast at Belfast by Rev S G SARGENT [3 Dec 1842]
Mercy J m Willam TOWNE of Foxcroft ME at Sebec ME [22 May 1851]
Moses & Maria Louisa CROWELL at Augusta ME [4 Jul 1837]
Moses & Nancy BRAZIER at Phillips ME [22 Apr 1833]
Sally D & Elisha THOMAS of Rumford ME at Vienna ME [18 Jan 1844]
Sannah & Isaiah LEWIS at Bristol ME [8 Apr 1847]
William & Sarah E LUNT of Calais ME at Belfast ME [30 Jan 1845]
Zenobia, d/o Daniel WELLS Esq of Clinton ME at Skowhegan ME & Harford MERROW of Canaan ME [7 Oct 1847]

WELMAN Hannah F & Richard C MOODY at Pittston ME [28 Aug 1851]

WELLSBY William & Maria LERMOND of Warren ME at Thomaston ME [20 Feb 1845]

WELSH Charlotte & William C BARNES at Atkinson ME [28 Feb 1850]
   Eben S of Monmouth ME & Sarah M CAPEN at Gardiner ME [3 Jun 1847]
      Edward Jr & Miss Elvina L FELT at Hallowell ME [27 Nov 1845]
      Ezekiel H & Lucy P SEWALL at Bath ME [10 Jan 1850]
      Harriet A P & Rev H R NYE of Bangor ME at Lowell MA [28 Aug 1845]
      Mark Capt & Miss Frances E MAHONEY at Northport [14 Jan 1847]
      Milton of Monmouth ME & Caroline F KIMBALL of Turner ME at Livermore ME [23 Sept 1847]
      Mima Ann & Francis H FASSETT at Bath ME [26 Aug 1847]
      Rachel F & True W THURSTON of Peru ME at Monmouth ME [16 Apr 1846]
      Sarah C & Alanson STARKS Esq of Augusta ME at Monmouth ME [24 Dec 1846]
      Sophia & Eldon D MOODY at Monmouth ME [3 Jun 1843]
      William H of Bradford ME? & Miss Priscilla STAPLES at Lisbon ME [23 Aug 1849]
      William & Ellen THOMPSON at Calais ME [2 Jul 1842]

WELT Dorothy & Solomon SHUMAN at Waldoboro ME [25 Dec 1835]
   Horace & Aroline [sic] E HEAD at Waldoboro ME by Newall W LUDWIG Esq [21 Sept 1839]
   Elizabeth K & Joseph TITCOMB Jr at Farmington ME [5 Dec 1844]
   Julia A & F G BUTLER Esq at Farmington ME [21 Aug 1842]
   Susan L & John J LOOK at Farmington ME [10 May 1849]

WELTS Amos & Emily J ALLEN at East Winthrop on 10th Mar [18 Mar 1852]
   Edward P & Elizabeth SHAW both of Mercer ME at Bloomfield ME [10 Jun 1852]

WENHENBURG Emma A & Mr W Arnold KNIGHT at Portsmouth NH on 6th Mar [18 Mar 1852]

WENTWORTH Abram P & Lucinda C PENDLETON both of Searsport ME at Waldo ME [28 May 1846]
   Albion K & Margaret S HARTSHORN at Belfast ME [27 Nov 1851]
   Almond & Delinda WENTWORTH at Belfast ME [27 May 1843]
   Amanda D & George W SNOW Esq at Bangor ME [2 Dec 1847]
   Bartholemew of South Berwick ME & Miss Harriet M ROBERTS of Alfred ME [1 May 1838]
   C O & Mr John F LORD of Kennebunkport ME at Kennebunk ME [25 Dec 1845]
   Charlotte Mrs of Brighton ME & George ROWELL at Solon ME [13 Feb 1851]
   Delinda & Almond WENTWORTH at Belfast ME [27 May 1843]
   Dorothy & Joshua THOMPSON of Waldo Plt ME at Knox ME [26 Aug 1836]
   George P & Harriet F JORDAN at Augusta ME on 19 Sept by Rev J STEVENS [25 Sept 1851]
   George W of Gardiner & Lydia H FOSTER at Winthrop [24 Aug 1848]
   Hester Ann & Dr William SNOW of Fairfield ME at Readfield ME [29 Apr 1847]

WENTWORTH (cont.) Jane & Stephen WENTWORTH at Eastport ME all of Deer Island ME [2 Jan 1845]
   Lucy Ann & Howard SMITH at Webster ME [18 Mar 1852]
   Lydia C of Belfast ME & Capt James N CARVER at Searsport ME [8 May 1845]
   Martha C of Deer Island ME & Stephen O BRIDGES at Eastport ME [2 Jan 1845]
   Mary H & Warwick GOOCH at Kennebunk ME [5 Feb 1852]
   Mary & Richard ROBINSON at Thomaston ME [12 Sept 1840]
   Mary & William H HUGHES at Waterville ME both of Winslow ME [12 Aug 1847]
   Melvira & Nicholas PINKHAM of Turner ME at Auburn ME [20 Feb 1851]
   Nancy & Elijah NICKERSON at Webster ME [9 Jan 1851]
   Noah & Elizabeth BLAISDELL at Rome ME on 12th ult by M A CHANDLER Esq [1 Feb 1849]
   Noah & Urrilla I WOOD at Vassalboro ME on the 8th inst by Oliver WEBBER Esq [16 Jan 1845]
   Octava & Benjamin CLEAVELAND Jr at Embden ME [19 Aug 1843]
   Owen of Kennebunk ME & Mary Ann KNOWLES at Corinna ME [1 Nov 1849]
   Sophia & David TINKER at Eastport ME both of Campobello New Brunswick Canada at Eastport ME [11 Dec 1845]
   Stephen & Jane WENTWORTH at Eastport ME all of Deer Island ME [2 Jan 1845]
   Susan & Calvin WOODBURY both of Bridgeton ME at Gorham ME [11 Dec 1851]
   Thomas B & Sarah FERNALD both of Parsonsfield ME at Limerick ME [14 Feb 1850]
   William Dr & Miss Sophronia C LAWRENCE at Cornville ME [28 Mar 1837]
   William F & Miss A W HALL of Berwick at Lebanon ME [27 Jul 1848]
WERTZ John, Revolutionary soldier, (ae 78) & Widow BURGESS (ae 78) at Allentown PA on 30th ult [10 Aug 1833]
WEST Alfred Capt & Isabella ROBERT at Wiscasset ME [17 Jul 1845]
   Ann Matilda & Abel G MARSTON of Andover ME [14 Jan 1847]
   Ann Myra & Zaccheus R MORGAN at Winthrop ME on Sunday evening last by Rev Mr CALDWELL [12 Jun 1835]
   Frances A & Capt William J ROGERS at Belfast ME [8 Feb 1849]
   Francis Miss, d/o late Col A W ATHERTON, & Rev Richard PIKE of Dorchester MA at Portland on Weds evening by the Rev Dr NICKOLS [11 Mar 1843]
   Gustavus O of Hallowell & Sarah B LEWIS at Vassalborough [8 Apr 1833]
   Hosea & Mehitable Ann BOYNTON at Hallowell ME [22 Jun 1848]
   James G & Martha F M FOSTER at Belfast ME [27 May 1852]
   James M of Waterville & Angerone M SOULE at Augusta [17 Jul 1838]
   Lewis N & Rachel J HODSDON at Pownal ME [24 May 1849]
   Luther & Mrs Mary O DANFORTH at Belfast ME [9 Apr 1846]
   Mary D & Isaiah C HOUSE at Farmington ME [7 Dec 1839]
   William W of Belfast ME & Miss Martha P NASH at Portland ME [19 Dec 1844]
   William & Harriet WEBBER at Wiscasset ME [25 Jun 1842]

WESTCOTT Lucy J & De Witt C FOLSOM & both of Bucksport ME at Providence RI [6 Nov 1851]

WESTON Abigail & Charles BIGELOW at Nashua NH [9 Mar 1848]

Angelica B & John H SINGLETON of Thomaston ME at Warren ME [16 Aug 1849]

Augusta M & Henry P HUMPHREY both of Gray ME at Portland ME [23 Jan 1845]

Bethiah K & Philander S PERCIVAL at Augusta ME on Tuesday last by Rev Mr BURGESS both of Augusta ME [30 Sept 1847]

Betsey C & Ira H HALL at Norridgewock ME [7 Dec 1848]

Bridget & Charles H PARTRIDGE of Gardiner ME at Madison ME [3 Aug 1841]

Caroline A & John A MACOMBER at Durham ME [11 Jun 1846]

Charles H & Susan A LAUGHTON at Norridgewock ME [7 Dec 1848]

Clarissa & Lorenzo McINTIRE of Norridgewock ME at Bloomfield ME [27 Dec 1849]

Daniel C Esq of Augusta ME & Mary Catherine, eldest d/o Col W A S NORTH at D(?)anbesbury NY on the 4th inst by Rev Mr THOMAS [22 Oct 1842]

Daniel of Livermore ME & Laura A GLASS of Turner ME at Turner ME on 9 Oct by E MARTIN Esq [17 Oct 1834]

Edward P, principal of Lewiston Falls Academy (later called Edward Little High School of Danville, now Auburn ME), & Miss Eliza BURBANK at Bethel ME [20 Mar 1841]

Elizabeth, d/o Stephen WESTON, & Aaron HEALY of New YORK at Skowhegan ME [17 Oct 1844]

Enoch of Madison ME & Eliza HAYES of Industry ME [2 Oct 1845]

Esther T & Lewis W HAUGHTON, M.D., of Waterford ME at Otisfield ME [29 Jan 1842]

George M Esq of Augusta ME & Bethsheba MOORE of Orono ME at Orono [30 May 1844]

Gratia Ann & John BURNS 3rd of Madison ME at Bloomfield ME [16 Oct 1851]

Isaiah of Cornville ME & Martha COLLINS of Bingham ME at Bingham [19 Feb 1846]

John B Elder & Nancy M McDONALD at Skowhegan ME [29 Mar 1849]

John & Susan McINTIRE at Bloomfield ME [18 Dec 1851]

Levi W of Bloomfield ME & Sophia W WALKER of Madison ME at Solon ME [4 Mar 1852]

Louisa Mathda & Charles Henry DAVISON at New York City on 2d June [10 Jun 1852]

Marcia Ann & Alden FLINT of Montville ME at Madison ME [25 Apr 1844]

Mary A of Augusta ME & Mr W H FISHER of Bremen ME at Boothbay ME [11 Sept 1851]

Mary P Mrs & Jacob HAYNES of Industry ME at Madison ME [12 Sept 1844]

Nathaniel C of Hallowell ME & Nancy B CASE at Readfield ME on 21st inst by Rev John ALLEN [30 Dec 1847]

Rebecca & Jonathan PIPER of Madison ME at Bloomfield ME [24 Jun 1847]

Simeon of Mt Vernon ME & Lovina BLANCHARD at Wilton ME [3 Jun 1847]

WETHERBEE Thomas S & Mary J McADAMS at Dexter ME [22 Jan 1846]
  Walter H & Sophia B HUME at Augusta ME on 16th ult by A R NICHOLS Esq [10 Jun 1847]
WETHERBY Martha Ann of Charlestown MA & Mr Whitney FARMER of Hallowell ME at Gardiner ME [5 Mar 1846]
WETHERN C P & Mr Lorenzo D NEWELL at New Portland ME [25 Dec 1841]
  Amos F of N Portland ME & Julia A PULLEN at Kingfield ME [4 May 1848]
WEYMAN Thomas of China ME & Louisa HOWES of Vassalboro ME [27 Feb 1838]
WEYMOUTH Catherine & Mr N C POOL at Abbot ME [26 Mar 1846]
  Charlotte W & James H WHITNEY at Dover ME [9 May 1844]
  Daniel L of Topsham ME & Miss Evelina HERRICK at Lisbon ME [12 Aug 1836]
  F H & Miss Julia E BROWN at Gardiner ME [20 Dec 1849]
  Kezia M & Harrison BRAY at Freeman ME both of Dedham MA [28 Feb 1850]
  Mary L of Gardiner ME & Francis J DAY of Hallowell ME at Providence RI [18 Dec 1851]
  Phineas D & Lydia L BISBEY at Biddeford ME [20 Jul 1848]
  Samuel of Orono ME & Emily L HANSCOM at (Augusta) ME [20 May 1852]
WHALAND Martha A Mrs & Winter MAYERS at Bath ME [17 Feb 1848]
WHALEN Ann & Benjamin NODDING at Eastport ME both of West Isles ME [19 Dec 1844]
  Daniel & Martha Ann DUNHAM at Bath ME on the 24th by Rev J T GILMAN [5 Feb 1842]
  Patrick & Eliza LASLEY at Eastport ME both of Deer Island ME [2 Jan 1841]
WHALING Sarah of West Isles NB (Canada?) & Milledge THORNTON at Lubec ME [5 Mar 1846]
WHARF - WHARFF
  A M Miss & William HEDGEWOOD at Lewiston ME on 1st Jan [5 Feb 1852]
  Abigail & V R LOVEJOY of Gardiner ME at Litchfield ME [21 Jan 1833]
  Joseph Capt of Gardiner ME & Mrs Alice MORRILL of East Livermore ME at Wayne ME on Mar 10th [28 Mar 1850]
  Rachel Ann & Albert FOLSOM at Augusta ME [22 Oct 1846]
WHEELWRIGHT John B Rev of Whitneyville & Helen A BARTON at Sidney ME [1 Jun 1848]
WHEELDEN Mary E & Lewis W DOWNS at Orrington ME [11 Nov 1847]
  Grace & Lewis BAKER of Hampden ME at Charleston ME? [20 Mar 1851]
WHEELER Albert G of Farmington & Fanny O RACLIFF at Industry ME [3 Jul 1841]
  Amos of Sidney ME & Abby A SNELL at Winthrop ME [24 Jun 1847]
  Angellia & Capt Rufus GILCHREST at Thomaston ME [11 Jul 1844]
  Cyrus & Miss Lucinda BLAKE at Sidney ME by William HAMLEN both of Waterville ME [9 Jan 1838]
  James B & Clarinda McINTIRE at Bloomfield ME [29 Jun 1848]
  James P & Maria H STORER at Eastport ME [1 Apr 1836]

WHEELER (cont.) Joseph & Julia M A WALES at Belfast ME on 12th inst by Rev D FORBES [25 Jun 1842]
    Julia A & Sumner C PEARSON of Belmont ME at Boston MA [25 Sept 1851]
    Malvina & Barney HINCKLEY at San Francisco CA on Nov 5th [15 Jan 1852]
    Maria, d/o Heber WHEELER Esq. & Hugh DEMPSEY of Waterville ME at Norridgewock ME [23 Sept 1847]
    Martha A & Horatio CUSHING Esq at Waterville ME [2 Sept 1847]
    Mary E & Columbus FOSTER at La Grange ME [17 Jan 1850]
    Mary J & John BUBRE at Webster ME [15 Apr 1852]
    Rachael R & David LIMIKEN [sic] at Thomaston ME both of St George ME [23 Jan 1845]
    Rebecca A & John BURRILL of Boston ME at Worcester MA [21 Mar 1837]
    S B Miss & Mr J S McCLUER [sic] of Lawrence MA at Farmington ME [11 Sept 1851]
    Sarah, d/o Heber WHEELER Esq. & John HILTON at Norridgewock ME on 27th June by the Rev BRONSON [15 Jul 1852]
    Solomon A of Vassalboro ME & Mrs Serena PREBLE at Winslow ME [16 Nov 1848]
    W H H of Canton ME & Mahala L BARNARD at Dixfield ME [28 Aug 1842]
    William H & Sarah W WINSLOW both of Augusta ME at Augusta on Sunday last at the Methodist Chapel by the Rev Mr FULLER [22 May 1838]
    William Q of Norridgewock ME & Martha Jane McCRILLIS of Cornville ME at Skowhegan ME [10 Jun 1847]
WHEELOCK Frances A & Francis H McINTIRE at Newburyport MA [8 Jan 1852]
    Mary V of Readfield ME & Leonard STURDEVANT of New Orleans MA? [16 Jul 1842]
WHELPLEY Abba & Gerry FULLER of Nashville TN at Eastport ME [27 Mar 1845]
    Henry of Eastport ME & Zavilla MOORE [21 Mar 1844]
WHIBLEY George & Julia Ann MORRISON at Solon ME all of East Madison ME [12 Mar 1846]
WHIDDEN Charles R Esq & Miss Mila Frances SMITH at Calais ME [28 Aug 1845]
    Ira & Elizabeth HUNTER at Clinton ME by Samuel HAINS Esq [5 Mar 1842]
WHIPPLE Heman & Jane LOWELL of Concord at Solon ME [13 Jul 1848]
WHITAKER Caroline T & Thomas F BRADSTREET Esq of Jefferson ME at Albion ME [24 Jun 1843]
    John W & Martha C CROSBY of Madison ME at Belfast ME [8 Jan 1846]
    Priscilla H at Houlton ME & C L FRANCIS of Norway ME at Houlton ME [6 Sept 1849]
WHITCOMB Francis E & Lydia Ann MILLS at Boston MA [30 May 1844]
    Freeman of Dresden ME & Harriet P WADE at Augusta ME on 19th inst by Rev Mr WILLIAMS [27 Nov 1845]
    John of Waldo Plt ME & Miss Sybil CHALMERS at Albion ME [2 Apr 1842]

WHITCOMB (cont.) Judith & Benjamin PARKER both of Bloomfield ME at Skowhegan ME [28 Nov 1837]
   Lois H & Royal HOOCH at Moscow ME [21 May 1846]
   Mary E & Alpheus SHERMAN of Thomaston ME at Yarmouth ME [25 Sept 1851]
   Rebecca & John W LINNELL both of Mercer ME at Mercer by Hartley KIMBALL Esq [25 May 1839]
   Sarah & William RYAN at Belmont ME both of Waldo ME [25 Feb 1847]
   Sylvia of Hampden ME & Royal ROOCH at Moscow ME by J D HILL Esq [11 Nov 1847]

WHITE Abby B of Windsor ME & Anthony HATTER of Strawsburg [sic], France at Boston MA [5 Aug 1843]
   Ammi M of Springfield MA & Margaret ELLIOT at Bath ME [5 Nov 1846]
   Ann Mrs, widow of the late Hon Benjamin WHITE, & Col James R BACHELDER of Readfield ME at Monmouth ME on Sunday last by David WHITE Esq [1 Jan 1836]
   B F of Gardiner ME & Victoria LILLY of Dresden ME at Dresden [25 Sept 1845]
   Betsey Mrs & David LINN Jr at Augusta ME on Apr 4th by Anson CHURCH Esq [11 Apr 1850]
   Clarissa Ann & Braddock WEEKS at Wayne ME on Monday evening last by Rev G BAILEY of Winthrop ME [10 Apr 1841]
   D N Mr of Dixfield ME & Sarah WYMAN at Livermore ME [13 Jul 1848]
   Daniel of Orono ME & Eliza Ann HOWARD at Vassalboro ME [29 Feb 1844]
   Daniel of Orono ME & Phebe SYLVESTER of Norridgewock ME [21 Mar 1834]
   E Miss & Thomas B TENNEY at Palmyra ME [1 May 1851]
   Edward J Jr & Amanda Augusta JUNKINS at Monmouth ME [8 Feb 1844]
   Eliza of Orland ME & Henry P BLOOD of Bucksport ME at Atkinson ME [13 May 1847]
   Eliza & Stephen HIGGINS at Augusta ME on 4th Jul by Thomas J DUDLEY Esq [8 Jul 1852]
   Eliza & William A WINGATE of Bangor ME at Frankfort ME [2 May 1857]
   Elizabeth A & Theodore RICHARDSON at Readfield ME [7 Dec 1848]
   Elizabeth M & Thomas B MERRICK at Hallowell ME by Rev Mr COLE [21 Dec 1839]
   Elizabeth & Edward H C HOOPER of Biddeford ME at Hallowell ME [19 Aug 1847]
   Emeline & John M DAVENPORT at Hallowell ME [9 May 1844]
   Emily of Augusta ME & William CREWS Esq of South Bend IA at Manchester NH on 18 Oct by Rev Mr CLARKE [30 Oct 1851]
   George of Herman ME & Damaris RIPLEY of Appleton ME at Union ME [25 Jan 1849]
   George W of Montville ME & Abby P CURRIER at Hallowell ME [18 Jul 1844]
   George & Lydia ELLINGWOOD at Frankfort ME [22 Jun 1848]
   Hiram & Martha A NEWCOMB at Gardiner ME [16 Jan 1845]
   Isaac D & Rebecca E DURGIN at Parsonsfield ME [27 Jan 1848]
   Isaac & Clarissa G McKENNEY at West Bath ME [26 Mar 1846]
   Isabel B & John W S CARD of Woolwich ME at Dresden ME [1 Nov 1849]

WHITE (cont.) James W & Sarah J GILMORE at Belfast ME [23 Dec 1847]
Jane M of Portland ME & G C NEALLY at Monroe ME [28 Oct 1842]
Jane of Bowdoin ME & Kingsbury THURLOW of Litchfield ME at Bowdoin ME [9 Oct 1841]
Job L & Eliza NASON at Wiscasset ME [25 Jun 1842]
Joel & Marinda KEENE by Rev Mr MORSE at Winthrop ME [2 Mar 1848]
John & Louisa L TIBBETTS both of Exeter ME at Corinth ME [20 Nov 1851]
John & Rachel Ann PRATT at Weld ME [18 Jan 1844]
Joseph N of Jay ME & Lucinda YOUNG at East Livermore ME [12 Mar 1846]
Joshua & Martha A FLAGG at Auburn ME [23 Oct 1851]
Julia M of Hallowell ME & Edwin H RIPLEY of Bath ME at Hallowell ME by Rev George SHEPPARD at Hallowell [11 Mar 1836]
L M Miss & R W JEWELL at Bath both of Bath ME [2 Oct 1845]
Lucy C & John S CASE at Rockland ME [19 Aug 1852]
Lucy J & Samuel VARNEY of Levant ME at Montville ME [30 Jan 1845]
Lucy L & W M E BROWN Esq at Solon ME [2 Jul 1846]
Maria G & Rufus A SAMPSON at Topsham ME [2 Oct 1851]
Martha E & George S MAYNARD at Gardiner ME [28 Feb 1850]
Mary A & Willard HOULTON Esq at Houlton ME [22 Apr 1843]
Mary D & Artemas LATHAM formerly of Gray ME at Greenfield ME [27 Jun 1844]
Mary E & John CUMMINGS of Freedom ME at Readfield ME [21 Feb 1850]
Mary Jane & Josiah GOODWIN at Portsmouth NH [20 May 1852]
Mary P & Adam J BOYD at East Machias ME [26 Aug 1847]
Mary & William A GAFFREY at Waterville ME [16 Dec 1847]
Melinda A & John C BARNES at Solon ME [1 Jan 1846]
Melissa & Humphrey M EATON at Dixfield ME [4 Jul 1840]
Nancy J & Normon SOULE of Dexter ME at St Albans ME [14 Aug 1845]
Nancy & Larned CUMMINGS of Sumner ME at Dixfield ME [6 Jun 1837]
Rand & Eliza HOLMAN at Dixfield ME [6 Sept 1849]
Randle & Mrs Elenor PIGGOT at Portland ME [16 May 1844]
Robert of Belfast ME & Eliza A SIMONTON at Camden ME [23 Oct 1845]
S A Maria & John A RIGGS at Georgetown [28 Jun 1849]
Sarah Arabella & Augustus S at Dexter ME [7 Nov 1844]
Sarah E of Georgetown ME & Thomas J TUCKER at Bath ME [30 Jan 1845]
Sarah O & Alonzo TENNEY at Hallowell ME on 2nd inst by Rev D FORBES [18 Apr 1840]
Sarah P & Capt Thomas E DRINKWATER of Belfast ME at Biddeford ME [15 Jan 1846]
Sophronia & Henry STEVENS at Winthrop ME [5 Oct 1848]
Sylvinia R of East Readfield ME & John C CUMNER of Tory NY at New York City on 17 Aug [4 Sept 1851]
Thomas Esq & Abigail HOWARD of Phillips ME at Winthrop ME on 7th inst by Rev David THURSTON [11 Mar 1847]
Thomas H & Frances E R ROWE both of Readfield ME at Augusta ME on 1st Jan by Asaph R NICHOLS [10 Jan 1850]
Thomas P & Eliza F BOARDMAN at Hope ME [26 Feb 1852]

WHITE (cont.) Thomas & Elizabeth D MOSHER both of Augusta ME at Providence RI on 19th Sept [2 Oct 1851]
    William A & Nancy A PITCHER at Belfast ME [19 Mar 1846]
WHITEHEAD T J Mr Esq of Paris ME & Caroline B JORDAN at Oxford ME [20 Apr 1848]
WHITEHOUSE Ambrose & Susannah WILLIAMSON at Hallowell ME [27 Nov 1841]
    Amelia of Smithfield & Thomas KEATING at Augusta ME on 5 Jan by Rev Z THOMPSON [23 Jan 1851]
    Betsey N & Horace C TAYER at Thompson CT on 26th ult [11 Nov 1847]
    Hiram of Unity ME & Martha DUNLAP of Brunswick ME on 29th ult [8 Jan 1836]
    Martha W & Amasa TAYLOR Jr at Vassalboro ME by Rev Mr YOUNG [16 Jan 1845]
    Mary J & Joseph E MERRILL at Paris ME [27 Jan 1848]
    Owen C & Lucy Ann YOUNG by Rev Mr YOUNG at (Augusta) on 17th inst [25 May 1848]
    Paul W of Vassalboro & Huldah E PRATT by Benjamin A G FULLER Esq at (Augusta) on Monday last [12 Oct 1848]
    Reuben & Emeline DAVIS at Wellington ME [23 Jun 1852]
    Samuel H & Miss Melinda A YOUNG at Mercer ME by William BLANDING Esq [26 Aug 1847]
    Seth C & Harriet A HALLETT, d/o the late Elisha HALLETT Esq at Augusta ME by the Rev Mr WEBB [26 Aug 1852]
WHITEN Ebenezer & Mrs Mary RICKER at Waterboro Center ME [6 Sept 1849]
WHITHAM Nancy & Benjamin A CHAPLES at Thomaston ME [23 Dec 1847]
WHITING Charles F & Sarah M FULLER at East Winthrop ME [19 Feb 1852]
    Alvira & Sumner PULLEN of Livermore ME on the 19th inst by Rev Mr HOUGHTON [28 Nov 1834]
    Elizabeth A, recently principal of one of the public schools in Winthrop ME & d/o Calvin WHITING Esq, & Rev Elbridge W LOCKE of New Gloucester ME at Portland ME by Rev C C BURR [16 May 1840]
    Elizabeth A & Augustus PARLIN of Winthrop ME at Union ME [27 Jun 1844]
    Henry & Mary C COVAL at Fairfield ME [11 Jan 1844]
    Maria & Mr J A SARGENT at Portland ME [9 May 1844]
    Leonard J Capt of New Orleans MA? & Miss Frances A WHITNEY at Castine ME [28 Oct 1847]
    Philander of Newport ME & Esther F BURRELL of Corinna ME [13 Jul 1839]
    Urania, d/o Capt Jonathan WHITING, & Harrison PARLIN at Winthrop ME on Thursday evening on 31 Dec by Rev Franklin MERRIAM [9 Jan 1841]
WHITMAN Calvin W of Hebron ME & Maria A SHURLIFF at Livermore ME [27 Nov 1851]
    Eliza B Mrs & Zibeon FIELD at Chesterville ME [16 Mar 1848]
    Ezra Jr & Hannah SINCLAIR at Winthrop ME on Sat evening on 31 Dec by Rev David THURSTON [13 Jan 1837]
    Francis H of Norway ME & Martha B MAYBERRY at Otisfield ME [7 Nov 1844]

WHITMAN (cont.) Isaiah J Esq & Mrs Mary CONNER of this city (Augusta) ME at Dover NH 1st Jan by Elder A KAVANAGH [11 Apr 1850]
 Joshua S & Sophia DACY at Norway ME both of Greenwood ME [19 Mar 1846]
 Lucy & Charles SPRADFORD at Skowhegan ME [23 Jan 1845]
 Oren & Lucy S HOWE at Turner ME on 29 Nov by Rev Mr BATES [24 Dec 1842]
 Sally G & Everet JONES at Turner ME [13 Nov 1835]
 Sarah of Turner ME & Horatio MERRILL of Columbia CT at Turner ME [1 Feb 1849]
 Sylvia E & Amos THURLOW Jr at Woodstock ME [23 Oct 1851]
 Velona Mrs & Francis E SHAW of Buckfield ME at Auburn ME by John E BRIGGS Esq [5 Jun 1845]
 William S & Amanda P ROWE at China ME [8 Jul 1847]
WHITMORE Elizabeth D & Johnson RIDOUT Jr at Bath ME [11 Dec 1845]
 Emily L of China ME & Mr Ensign L WORTHING of Palermo ME at Belfast ME [18 Apr 1850]
 Joel A of Bangor ME & Emily A BRETTUN at Livermore ME [12 Oct 1848]
 John T of Bowdoinham ME & Adeline COOPER at Pittston ME [22 May 1845]
 Minerva H & William G PERCY of Phipsburg ME at Bowdoinham ME [16 Sept 1847]
WHITNEY Abigail of Lisbon ME & Benjamin LOTHROP of Canton ME at Lisbon ME [7 Mar 1834]
 Albion P & Miss Susan D EASTMAN at Limestone River Plt, Aroostook Co, ME [7 Mar 1850]
 Amarose & Mary Jane COUCH at Augusta ME [30 Aug 1849]
 Ann L & Mr E M STEDMAN of Winthrop ME at Canton ME [23 Apr 1846]
 Caroline M & Augustus S FRENCH at Dexter ME on 14th inst [30 Mar 1848]
 Charles Capt 2nd & Sophia L MILLER at Hampden ME [19 Aug 1843]
 Charles T of Plymouth ME & Martha C TAYER at Waterville ME [3 May 1849]
 Ebenezer of Phillips ME & Mrs Dorcas PARLIN at Jay ME [11 Feb 1843]
 Fanny & Charles BOOKER at Augusta ME on 10th inst by John A PETTINGILL Esq [14 Mar 1850]
 Frances A & Capt Leonard J WHITING of New Orleans MA? at Castine ME [28 Oct 1847]
 Frances A & John H COOK at Hallowell ME [16 Sept 1847]
 George C & Emeline B LACROIS both of Winthrop ME at Augusta ME on Monday last by the Rev William A DREW [17 Aug 1833]
 Hannah & Capt John R KINGSBURY of Bradford ME at Dexter ME [11 Apr 1850]
 Hannah & Capt Samuel GILL Jr at Augusta ME [27 May 1847]
 Henry P & Miss Margaret H BOHANAN at Alexander ME [14 Feb 1850]
 James H & Charlotte W WEYMOUTH at Dover ME [9 May 1844]
 Jane & Charles CUMMINGS of Solon ME at Hallowell ME [31 May 1849]
 John & Jane KIFF at Belmont ME [7 Aug 1835]
 Josiah T m Mary MOORE at Moose River ME? [4 Jun 1851]
 Leafy, d/o Daniel WHITNEY, & Reuben RICH of Otisfield ME at Oxford ME by Rev Dan PERRY [10 Jun 1833]
 Levi & H E W MASON both of Milltown ME at Milltown [20 Feb 1845]

WHITNEY (cont.) Lewis & Cynthia B BLETHEN at Durham ME [2 May 1844]
Lois & Samuel WADSWORTH at Lincolnville ME [27 Jun 1840]
Lydia A & George PRATT of Medford MA at Belmont ME [14 Aug 1851]
Lydia P & Joseph B OSMAR at Foxcroft ME [15 Aug 1844]
Maria R & Joseph C STAFFORD of Boston MA at Thomaston ME [31 Oct 1844]
Mary Ann of Lewiston ME & Micah HIGGINS of Portland ME [11 Jun 1846]
Mary E Mrs & Capt Lincoln PATTEN of Topsham ME at Bowdoinham ME [17 Jul 1851]
Mary S & Capt Gilbert M LEIGHTON at Freeman ME [18 May 1848]
Mary & Nathaniel HALE at Bridgton ME? [16 Apr 1846]
Melissa & Hiram H GUFF of Hallowell ME at Cabotville MA [28 Oct 1847]
Michael L & Betsey A HUMPHREY at North Yarmouth ME [13 Jan 1848]
Nancy B L & Peter REDMOND at Moose River Somerset Co ME [25 Jan 1849]
Nancy F & Hon B D EASTMAN at Limestone River Plt, Aroostook Co ME [7 Mar 1850]
Orrin of Letter D Plt ME & Miss Hannah FAIRBANKS, d/o Dennis FAIRBANKS Esq of the former place at Presque Isle Plt ME on Nov 7th by John B WING Esq [1 Jan 1842]
Parthenia & Augustus B FOSS of Lowell MA at Freedom ME [8 Jul 1847]
Priscilla & Edward HATHAWAY at Frankfort ME [14 Mar 1837]
Robert P & Ruth F SPRAGUE at Topsham ME [25 Jun 1846]
Samuel Capt of New Orleans MA? & Rebecca W HOWE of Castine ME at Lincolnville ME [5 Dec 1844]
Thomas R & Emeline H WYMAN both of Sidney ME at Hallowell ME [13 Nov 1845]
William & Charity MORRISON at West Bath ME [15 Feb 1849]

WHITTAKER Mary A & Dyer P JORDAN at Ellsworth ME [27 Mar 1841]

WHITTEMORE Franklin B & Louisa D PAINE at Jay ME [1 Nov 1849]
John W & Miss M E JACKSON at Montville ME [29 Jul 1852]
Julia A of West Cambridge MA & Hon Drummond FARNSWORTH of Norridgewock ME at New York [18 Jun 1846]
Sarah Jane & John A TIBBETTS of New Sharon ME at Augusta ME on 21st inst by Rev Mr MORSE [28 Jan 1847]
Simon G & Jane ARNOLD both of Foxcroft ME at Dover ME [23 May 1844]
Hannah & Stephen THURSTON at Parsonsfield ME [11 Mar 1847]
John & Hannah LARSOETL at Burnham ME [8 Jul 1836]
John R & Miss Caroline S AMES at Hallowell ME [1 Apr 1847]
Lucinda & Nahum THOMPSON at Waterboro ME [24 Apr 1835]
Mary Ann & Joseph SPRAGUE at Bangor ME [14 MAr 1834]
Mary W & Alden W PHILBROOK at Augusta ME [14 May 1846]
Susan of Montville ME & Benjamin F MELVIN of Hope ME at Freedom ME [27 May 1847]
Thomas of Augusta ME & Elizabeth M LITTLEFIELD at Hallowell ME [22 Feb 1840]

WHITTEN John R & Eliza W NORTON at Skowhegan ME [17 Jun 1852]

WHITTIER Benjamin of Monroe ME & Hannah M JOHNSON at Farmington ME [13 Jun 1844]

WHITTIER (cont.) Caroline E & William WOODS at Farmington ME on 1st Jul by Rev Mr ABBOTT [10 Jul 1841]
 Charles T & Frances P McQUESTEN at Bangor ME [16 May 1844]
 Emily Ann & George M ATWOOD at Readfield ME [6 Nov 1838]
 Frances M H of Vassalboro ME & John S CLARK at Sebasticook ME [4 Feb 1847]
 George B & Hannah WHITTIER at Vienna ME [12 Mar 1846]
 Hannah & George B WHITTIER at Vienna ME [12 Mar 1846]
 Isaac N & Miss Priscilla CONNER of New Sharon ME [2 Mar 1839]
 James of Oldtown ME & Eliza W CHAMBERLAIN at Bradford ME [16 Dec 1847]
 James P & Augusta Ann STEVENS P WHITTIER at Dover ME [30 Jul 1846]
 Joseph R Jr & Lydia A MAXCY by the Rev A KALLOCH at this town (Augusta) ME on 19th inst [23 Aug 1849]
 Lucy & George M ATWOOD at Gardiner ME [30 Jan 1845]
 Lydia H & Peleg T JONES Esq at Lincoln ME [6 May 1847]
 Mary E & Nathaniel PATTERSON at Belfast ME [27 May 1852]
 Mary & Henry DUDLEY of Mt Vernon ME at Readfield ME by Josiah WHITTIER Esq [18 Jul 1834]
WHITTER Mary A & John B WRIGHT of Mt Vernon ME at Readfield ME [9 Dec 1847]
 Mary M of Readfield ME & Mr McCobb CUSHING at Augusta ME by Loring CUSHING Esq [1 May 1845]
 Newman T of Rome ME & Sarah A HILL at Augusta ME on 25th Sept by Rev William A DREW [27 Sept 1849]
 Persis formerly of Winthrop ME & Jona CLARK of Tewsbury MA at Methuen MA [4 Feb 1843]
 R Brenda & William ABBOT of Farmington ME at Hallowell ME on 29th Nov by Rev J COLE [6 Dec 1849]
 Relief & John RAMFORD of Fayette ME at Readfield ME [24 Apr 1845]
 Sarah W & William K DUDLEY at Readfield ME on the 4th inst by Daniel CRAIG Esq [11 Dec 1845]
 Sewall C & Abigail LORD at Mt Vernon ME on 10th inst [16 Nov 1839]
WHITTIMORE Harriet P & Darillus MORRISON at Livermore ME [13 Jun 1840]
WHITTING Mary H Mrs of Charleston MA & Ebenezer SHAW of China ME at Boston MA [27 May 1843]
WHITTUM Lucy E & Edwin WEEKS at Vassalboro ME [13 Mar 1851]
WHORFF James & Sarah MOORE at Madison ME [17 May 1849]
 John Jr & Emma ADAMS at Madison ME [14 Oct 1836]
WIATT John Capt & Elisha JOHNSON at Gardiner ME [28 Oct 1847]
WICKER James C of Utica NY & Maria P SMITH at Hallowell ME [27 May 1847]
WIGAND Henry of Cleveland OH & Lucy Ann McLAUGHLIN formerly of Portland ME at New York City on 16th July [6 Aug 1846]
WIGGIN Ann E & Joseph DOWNS at Albion ME [17 Sept 1846]
 Ann M & John C DAVIS at Lewiston ME [8 Feb 1849]
 Harriet M of Brooks ME & Albert MORTON of Thomaston ME at Belfast ME [18 Dec 1845]
 Jacob L & Olive NASON late of Albion ME at China ME by Rev H PROCTOR [11 Sept 1841]

Marriage Notices from the "Maine Farmer" 449

WIGGIN (cont.) John of Augusta ME & Ann M BUCKMINSTER at Saco ME [19 Nov 1846]
   William H of Lowell MA & Zilpha S ROBBINS [4 Jan 1849]
   Hiram of Boston & Lucinda P THOMPSON of Augusta ME at Thompson CT [20 Jul 1848]
   Lot & Mrs Caroline O HALL at Limerick ME [23 Nov 1848]
WIGGINS Ruby & Thos T STINSON at Albion ME on 21 Nov [30 Nov 1848]
   Thomas H of Wellington ME & Achsah R CAMPBELL of Bridgton ME at Bowdoinham ME [15 Jun 1848]
   Henry L K, M.D., & Harriet A PARKER at Greene ME [19 Aug 1847]
WIGHT Daniel M of Letter B ME & Bosette M EMERY of Poland ME at Letter B ME on ult by John J BRAGG Esq [29 Jul 1843]
   Sarah A & Jeremiah CLOUGH at Monmouth ME [20 Jan 1848]
   Selvia & Ethan WILLIS at Gilead ME [8 Apr 1852]
WILBER - WILBUR
   Benjamin & Mary HEATH at Strong ME [21 Jan 1833]
   Caleb of New Sharon ME & Nancy P HINCKLEY at Mercer ME [20 Jan 1837]
   David & Louisa J GARDINER at Pembroke [22 Jan 1852]
   Delany S & Mr E J TENNEY at East Livermore ME [29 Jun 1848]
   Horatio & Lucy H MORSE at Livermore ME [16 Apr 1846]
   Israel of Augusta ME & Areneth ALLEN of Winthrop ME at Winthrop on 22d ult by Elder Samuel FOGG [6 Jun 1834]
   Jacob B & Nancy LOCKE at Newcastle ME [13 May 1852]
   Jemima, d/o Pardon TINKHAM, & David S ABBOT at Albion ME on 1st ult [4 Feb 1843]
   Mary A & Francis C HEWEY of Andover ME at Phillips ME [4 Oct 1849]
   Nancy C & Gilbert STETSON at Phillips ME [30 Dec 1847]
   Rufus P & Harriet N Sawyer at Portland ME [12 Aug 1836]
WILCOX Almira M & Jonah HOLT Esq at Bluehill ME [29 Mar 1849]
   Arabella & Greenleaf M BLAKE at Monmouth ME [30 Dec 1836]
   Charles C of New Vineyard ME & Hannah SKILLINGS at Strong ME [17 Jan 1850]
   Mary T & Sanford S WINSLOW at Monmouth ME [5 Dec 1837]
   Peleg & Sarah GILMAN at Monmouth ME [3 Jun 1843]
WILD Paul & Sarah E HUTCHINS at East Winthrop ME by Rev F MERRIAM [16 Jul 1846]
WILDER Edwin E of Bridgton ME & Philomelia GREENWOOD at Farmington ME [5 Aug 1847]
   Lucy Ann & Samuel MORTON at Wiscasset ME [27 Mar 1845]
   Mary S & David CLAPP of Nobleboro ME at Wiscasset ME [14 Nov 1844]
   Samuel C & Emeline K HOLMAN at Temple ME [22 Jul 1852]
   Thomas D & Sarah A VIGOUREAUX at Gardiner ME [5 Sept 1844]
WILDES Esther A & James NORTON at Bath ME [27 Aug 1846]
   Parker E printer of Boston MA & Ellen S PAGE of Dorchester both formerly of (Augusta) ME by Rev Mr MEANS at Dorchester MA on 22d Oct [9 Nov 1848]
WILEY Abigail P of Newburgh ME & Stephen HUSSEY of Dover ME at Dixmont ME [5 Nov 1846]
   Caleb W & Georgianna NUTTING at Calais ME [25 Jun 1846]
   Rebecca W & Albion E HEWITT at Thomaston ME [12 Apr 1849]

WILKINS David Jr & Mary A LANE both of Parkman ME at Sangerville ME [24 Jul 1845]
 Ellen & Veris GREENWOOD at Greene ME [25 Jan 1849]
 George Esq of Brownville ME at Hampden ME & Mrs Jane N MILLER at Hampden ME [6 Mar 1845]
WILKINSON L D Esq & Miss Frances M ELDER at Saco ME [12 Apr 1849]
WILLAH Mrs & Mr Thomas WISEMAN of Fulford at York ME [16 Sept 1847]
WILLARD Caleb of New Sharon ME & Nancy N HINKLEY at Mercer ME [18 Apr 1837]
 Emma, principal of the Female Seminary in Albany, at Albany NY & Dr C C Yates of New York. The ceremony was performed in the presence of her pupils some hundred and fifty or two hundred in number. [2 Oct 1838]
 Ephraim G & Susan C PAGE both of Brownville ME at Brownville ME on 16th inst by E A JENKS Esq [25 May 1839]
 George W & Martha ABBOT at Bangor ME [11 Jul 1844]
WILLETT Elizabeth A & John M MARTIN at Bristol ME [20 Apr 1848]
 Ephraim of Damariscotta ME & Nancy COOPER at Hallowell ME [20 Nov 1851]
 Thomas B of Brunswick ME & Louisa LOWELL of Saco ME [14 Jan 1847]
WILLEY Betsey & Sewall DALLIFF at Augusta ME on 4 Jul [22 Jul 1847]
WILLIAMS Albert J Waterville ME & Julia F CURRY at Eastport ME [2 Mar 1848]
 Albert & Ellen ATKINSON at North Anson ME [15 Jul 1852]
 Ann & Benjamin TITCOMB of New Portland ME at North Anson ME [9 Apr 1846]
 Benjamin Esq of Solon ME & Lorene A BATES at Anson ME [25 Apr 1840]
 Caroline Sophia Maria Julianna Worthley Montague Joan of Arc & Alexander Philip Socrates Amelius Ceasar Hannibal Marcellus George Washington TREADWELL at New Orleans [1 Aug 1837]
 Catherine & William GAY at Augusta ME [4 Apr 1840]
 Charles & Sarah BOWDEN both of Augusta ME at China ME by Charles A RUSS Esq [14 Jan 1843]
 Delia & William H DOW of Waterville ME at Bath ME [20 Jun 1834]
 Elijah & Catharine MORRISON at Portland ME [23 Jan 1845]
 Eliza J Mrs & William BRIDGE Esq at Augusta ME [9 Jan 1841]
 Eliza of Windsor ME (ae 16) & Nehemiah TURNER (ae 60) of Palermo ME on 23d ult [11 Apr 1840]
 Elizabeth B & Horace EMERY at Skowhegan ME [29 Jun 1848]
 Elizabeth & Capt Samuel ROBINSON at Oxford ME [15 Jan 1836]
 Elizabeth & Col Alfred REDINGTON at Augusta ME [13 Jan 1837]
 Emeline & Henry W CLARK at Augusta ME [11 Jul 1844]
 Evelina H & George R WILLIAMS both of Phippsburg ME at Litchfield ME [20 Feb 1851]
 George formerly of Boston MA & Sarah C BOLDEN of Bath ME at Bath ME on 31st ult by Rev Mr ELLINGWOOD [15 Apr 1843]
 George H of Wayne ME & Lucy WONSON of Gloucester MA on 28th ult [13 Aug 1842]
 George R & Evelina H WILLIAMS both of Phippsburg ME at Litchfield ME [20 Feb 1851]

WILLIAMS (cont.) H C of Waterville ME & Caroline R WOOD of Norridgewock ME at Norridgewock [16 Dec 1843]
    Hannah & Marcellus STEWARD at Skowhegan ME both of Anson ME [18 Jul 1844]
    Helen Augusta, d/o Reuel WILLIAMS, & Dr John T GILMAN of Portland ME at Augusta ME [5 Sept 1837]
    Henry G & Olive B STEDMAN at Sidney ME on 29th ult by Rev John ALLEN [14 Jun 1849]
    Henry & Martha P McQUILLAN at Portland ME [12 Apr 1849]
    Hiram B of Belfast ME & Nancy H CROCKETT at Thomaston ME [27 Nov 1845]
    Horace & Isabella H, d/o John PERRY Esq, at Stillwater-Orono ME [11 Jul 1834]
    Isabel E & Jonas B HUTCHINGS at Harmony ME both of Lincoln ME [7 Mar 1850]
    J J & Mahalia L BOYNTON both of Hallowell ME at (Augusta) ME on 23d inst [1 Jun 1848]
    James of Winthrop ME & Eliza A TENNEY at Raymond ME [25 Jan 1844]
    Jane Elizabeth, d/o Hon Ruel WILLIAMS, & Rev Sylvester JUDD at Augusta ME on 31st by Rev John H INGRAHAM [11 Sept 1841]
    Jarvis of Biddeford ME & M A d/o Johnson LUNT Esq at Augusta ME on Monday morning last by Rev Mr JUDD [16 Jan 1845]
    Joanna K & Almon CASWELL at Mercer ME on 10th June [23 Jun 1852]
    Joel & Betsey PHILBRICK at Skowhegan ME [9 Jan 1837]
    John H & Mary Adelaide DIX by Rev Dr NICHOLS at Portland ME [29 Aug 1840]
    John of Calais & Ellen OSBORNE at Eastport ME [5 Oct 1839]
    Joseph H Esq of Augusta ME & Apphia P d/o Sylvester JUDD at Northampton MA [8 Oct 1842]
    Joseph of Winthrop ME & Mary A HAWES of Newton ME at Boston ME on 6th Sept by Rev Mr DRIVER [17 Sept 1842]
    Joseph & Jane Augusta BRADLEY both of Harpswell ME at Bath ME [23 Jul 1846]
    Judson of Waterville ME & Susan F B BEMENT at Dexter ME [21 Oct 1847]
    Julia A & Col Cyrus BRYANT of Anson ME at Hartland ME [23 Jan 1841]
    Lois W, d/o Rev James WILLIAMS, & Nathan BISHOP at Readfield ME of Fayette ME [25 Apr 1834]
    Lucy Ann, d/o Rev James WILLIAMS, & Parker TUCK Esq Attorney at Law of Ellsworth ME at Readfield ME on 6th inst by Rev W C LARRABEE [25 Jan 1840]
    Lucy & William WOART Esq at Augusta ME [23 May 1844]
    Luther M & Jane F HAMLEN at Vassalboro ME on 13th inst [28 Mar 1834]
    Margaret G & Charles C RICHARDSON at Bath ME [22 Jan 1836]
    Maria of Strong ME & Mr J N GOODENOUGH of Boston MA at Farmington ME [23 Oct 1851]
    Martha J of Orrington ME & Spencer PERKINS of Old Town ME at Bangor ME [12 Apr 1849]
    Mary C & Erastus HASKELL at East Thomaston ME on 18th inst [25 May 1848]

WILLIAMS (cont.) Mary Jane of Natchez (MS)? & Hon Sargent S PRENTISS of Vicksburg (Mississippi)? at Natchez [23 Apr 1842]
  Mary of Mercer ME & Nathan BACHELLER of Machias ME at Mercer ME by Rev Mr FARRINGTON [14 May 1842]
  Mary Sawtelle & Newton EDWARDS at (Augusta) ME at St Mark's Church on 30th Aug [14 Sept 1848]
  Mary & Col John CURRIER at Readfield ME on 2d inst [14 Dec 1839]
  Mercy & Perley G GRAVES at Thomaston ME [5 Jun 1845]
  Miles C & Almira PIERCE d/o Capt Thomas PIERCE by Rev A DRINKWATER at Readfield ME [1 Aug 1840]
  Nathan Capt & Maria N SPALDING of South Thomaston ME at East Thomaston ME [28 Jun 1849]
  Norman S & Martha Ann HAYNES both of Monson ME at Abbott ME [13 Jun 1844]
  Orrilla & Benjamin L STETSON of North Wayne ME at Winthrop ME by Rev C FULLER [6 Sept 1849]
  Otis, a printer, & Jerusha W ROBBINS, a printeress, both of Winthrop ME at Winthrop, on Thanksgiving day eve, by the Rev B F ROBBINS [2 Dec 1847]
  Rebecca of Boston MA & John ROBERTSON of Manchester, England at New York [24 Aug 1833]
  Richmond L & Miss Susan A EMERY both of Athens ME at Skowhegan ME [4 Feb 1847]
  Rosilla A & Leonard FOSTER of Leeds ME at Turner ME [19 Jun 1838]
  Samuel of Bowdoin ME & Charity SMALL Mrs at Topsham ME [17 Jul 1851]
  Thomas (ae 17) & Bulah BARNES (ae 14) at Union Vale NY [21 Sept 1833]
  William J & Miss S A FULTON at Bowdoinham ME [9 Nov 1848]
  William & Mary HILTON at Windsor ME [4 Jul 1837]
  Zilpha Ingraham & John L CUTLER at (Augusta) ME on 18th Oct [26 Oct 1848]
WILLIAMSON Elias W & Eliza A FISHER at Augusta ME on 3 Nov by Rev C F ALLEN [15 Nov 1849]
  Mary T & Aaron B DANFORTH at Augusta ME on 23 Jan by Asaph R NICHOLS Esq [30 Jan 1851]
  Mary & James L BOYNTON at Hallowell ME [27 Nov 1841]
  Susannah & Ambrose A WHITEHOUSE at Hallowell ME [27 Nov 1841]
  W & Margaret C THOMPSON at Union ME [17 Aug 1848]
  Warren Col of Gardiner ME & Mrs Chaarlotte S EGAN at Pittston ME [24 Dec 1846]
WILLIS Caroline N of Strong ME & William H EDDY of Boston MA [18 Dec 1845]
  Catharine & Lorenzo CARVER at Thomaston ME [2 Dec 1847]
  Eri & Mary Ann Lombard at Augusta ME [12 Sept 1837]
  Ethan of Reading MA & Selvia WIGHT at Gilead Oxford Co ME [8 Apr 1852]
  Harriet Susan & Thomas S EDMUNDS of Lowell at Framingham MA [13 Jun 1840]
  Joseph & Lydia E COLE d/o late William COLE Esq at Brunswick ME on 26th ult all of Buckfield [9 Oct 1841]

WILLIS (cont.) N P Esq of New York & Cornelia GRINNELL at New Bedford MA [22 Oct 1846]
Susan Harriet & Philip D EDMUND of Lowell at Farmington MA [13 Jun 1840]
WILLITS Mrs M A & Moses ATKINSON at Canaan ME [30 Oct 1851]
WILLISTON George & Jane TAYLOR at Brunswick ME [21 Dec 1833]
WILSHIRE Eleanor of Palmyra ME & Augustus TAYLOR at (Augusta) ME on July 8 by Rev FOSTER [17 Jul 1851]
Mary Jane & William H MOORE at Bangor ME both of Orono ME [18 Jul 1844]
WILSON Amanda B & Ezra B RICHARDSON at Hallowell ME [2 Aug 1849]
Arthur L & Henrietta POTTER both of Topsham ME at Topsham [7 Nov 1840]
Benjamin B of Topsham ME & Prescilla BUZZELL at Winthrop ME [1 Jan 1846]
Catherine C & Rufus H LONGLEY of Kingfield ME at Augusta ME [22 Aug 1834]
Charles O & Ellen S KNOX at Portland ME [27 Mar 1845]
Charles & Mary BRACE at Bath ME [7 Sept 1833]
Christiana G & George BRAGG at Albion ME [9 Sept 1847]
David & Mrs Dorcas SMITH at Edgecomb ME [14 Mar 1837]
Elbridge G of Gardiner ME & Lucy Ann DUNN d/o John DUNN Esq at Hallowell ME [27 Nov 1835]
Eph of Monmouth ME & Julia A BABB at Litchfield ME [8 Feb 1849]
Eunice Maria & Dexter GOSS of Danville ME at Lewiston ME [4 Jan 1844]
Franklin & Eliza A FIELD at (Augusta) ME on 18th inst [27 Jan 1848]
George of Westbrook ME & Phebe WINSLOW of Falmouth ME [3 Dec 1842]
Gustavus G & Rachel SOULE both of Skowhegan ME at Norridgewock ME [27 Apr 1848]
Harvey S & Rebecca STROUT at Bradford ME [2 Jul 1849]
Hubbard of Hookset NH & Lydia SARGENT of Wilton ME [12 Nov 1842]
Jacob & Mary B HENRY both of (Augusta) ME by John NEAL Esq at Litchfield ME on 26th Aug [14 Sept 1848]
James G Esq of Hastings NY & Mrs Judith F JONES d/o P C JOHNSON Esq formerly of (Augusta ME) at New York City [16 Oct 1851]
Jefferson & Sarah ALLEN at Brunswick ME [11 Feb 1847]
Joel C & Sarah Jane BAKER at Minot ME [8 Jan 1839]
John of Freedom ME & Rosilla HAGMAN at Anson ME [1 Nov 1849]
John R Esq of Cincinnati OH at Lisbon ME & Joanna T ATTWOOD of Durham ME [18 Sept 1845]
Louisa Mrs. (the young lady whose husband was murdered about two years ago) of Harpswell ME, & Lorenzo ALEXANDER of Brunswick ME at Harpswell ME [19 Dec 1844]
Lucetta A & James O CUNNINGHAM at Belfast ME by Rev W FROTHINGHAM [3 Dec 1842]
Margaret & Darby KENNEY at Dixfield ME [7 Mar 1850]
Marinda & Nathaniel W BLETHEM at Belfast ME [30 Sept 1847]
Mary Ann & Capt Marlboro SYLVESTER at Hallowell ME on 11th inst [18 Sept 1845]
Mary Jane & Joseph GREENE at Belfast ME [30 Aug 1849]

WILSON (cont.) Mary N & John W CLARK at Bingham ME [1 Jun 1848]
Newell & Priscilla GILES at Ellsworth ME [4 Dec 1851]
Obed of Bingham & Martha COX of this town (Winthrop) ME at Hallowell ME on Thurs evening last [7 Mar 1837]
Otis D & Grace A PENDLETON of Northport ME at Belmont ME [13 May 1852]
Parker L & Sarah F GUPPY at Corinth ME [6 Feb 1851]
Philena P & Luther D AUSTIN at Augusta ME [4 Nov 1847]
Rachel of Skowhegan ME & Bryce JEWETT at Unity ME [2 Oct 1851]
Rebecca & George W HASTY at Baring [25 Dec 1845]
Sarah & John REGAN at Eastport ME of Plennfield NB (Canada) at Eastport ME [12 Sept 1844]
Susan G & Charles H CHAMBERLAIN at Livermore ME [8 Jun 1848]
Susan & James G MORSE at Belfast ME [18 Jun 1846]
William & Jane PORTERFIELD at Bristol ME [25 Feb 1847]
Zacheus of Parsonsfield ME & Nancy J DOE of Limerick ME at East Parsonsfield ME [13 Mar 1851]

WINCHENBAUCH Horace Capt & Hannah Elizabeth ANDERSON of Warren ME at Waldoboro ME by Rev John DODGE [14 Jan 1843]
Lewis Capt & Mary E DEMUTH at Waldoboro ME [3 May 1849]

WINCHESTER Frances A & Jacob ODELL at Eastport ME [25 Sept 1835]

WINE Joseph & Mary D SIMPSON at Bath ME [15 Apr 1852]

WING Alexander of Peru ME & Mrs Sarah P DEROUT of Winthrop ME on 6 Jan by Thomas PHILLIPS Esq [7 Feb 1834]
Ann C & B F KING of Winthrop ME at Wayne ME [24 Dec 1846]
Augustus K of Brunswick ME & Miss BAILEY at Phillips ME [3 Feb 1848]
B C of Bangor ME & Elvina Z CHANDLER of Winthrop ME by Rev B F ROBBINS [21 May 1846]
Benjamin Franklin & Miss Eliza Ann PERKINS at Winthrop ME on Sunday evening on 24 Apr by Rev David THURSTON [7 May 1842]
Benjamin & Anna TOBEY at Vassalboro ME on 16th June by Edward GRAY Esq [8 Jul 1852]
Betsey R, d/o Ichobod WING Esq late of Winthrop ME & John ABBOTT at Belgrade by Rev J SPAULDING [7 Nov 1834]
Catharine & Cromwell BIXBY at Skowhegan ME [26 Oct 1848]
Cementha & George STUART at Vassalboro ME [26 Feb 1836]
Charles A & Sarah BELCHER at Winthrop ME on 18th inst by Rev David THURSTON [27 Nov 1841]
Clara H & Augustus T BECKFORD printer at Bangor ME [14 Jan 1847]
Cynthia S & Daniel FICKETT of Harrington ME at Bangor ME [3 Apr 1845]
Cynthia & Asa WYMAN Esq of Milburn at Winthrop ME [17 Oct 1834]
Daniel R of Gardiner ME & Ann E BURLEIGH at Fairfield ME [13 Feb 1845]
Daniel R of Monmouth ME & Abigail ESTES at Vassalboro ME on 3rd inst by Rev N GUNNISON [14 Mar 1850]
Eli L of Chesterville ME & Ruth P ORMSBY at Augusta ME on 17th inst by Rev J W SAWYER [25 Nov 1847]
Elizabeth G & James VARNEY at Brunswick ME [21 Oct 1843]
Florentine A & Ira BEAN at Livermore ME [10 Jun 1847]
Harriet & George W BRIGGS at Brunswick ME [22 Oct 1846]
Hiram L & Margaret A HATCH at Bath ME [15 Nov 1849]

WING (cont.) Isabella & Azel S TUTTLE of Paris ME at Wayne ME [7 May 1846]
- J Gancelo & Achsah C SWAIN of Chesterville ME at Farmington ME [17 Jan 1850]
- James Capt & Roana S DAILEY at Wayne ME [6 Feb 1838]
- James M & Mary BOWLES both of Winthrop ME at Wayne ME [23 Jul 1846]
- Jason & Sabra C KING both of Wayne ME at Winthrop ME on Wednesday last by Rev J H INGRAHAM at Winthrop on Wednesday last [14 Nov 1847]
- Joann & Allen L TRUFANT at Winthrop ME on 25 June by Rev Mr CALDWELL [17 Jul 1835]
- John B Esq of Letter D Plt (Fort Fairfield) ME & Sarah P CLARK at Sangerville ME [8 Apr 1843]
- John C & Miss Lydia SMALL at Brunswick ME [18 Mar 1847]
- Joseph M & Emeline C TALBOT formerly of Portland ME at Bangor ME [22 Apr 1836]
- Levi of Greene ME & Mary MOTT d/o Adam MOTT of Wilton ME at the Friends meeting house in Wilton ME [19 Dec 1840]
- Lydia J & Elisha D SOULE at Skowhegan ME by M LITTLEFIELD [15 Jul 1852]
- Lyman of Monmouth ME & Emmy GREENLIEF at Readfield ME by Jonathan G HUNTON Esq [28 Dec 1833]
- Lyman S of Monmouth ME & Mary B YORK at Peru ME [23 May 1840]
- Mary A both of Belgrade ME & Evander L DAVIS at Sidney ME on 23 Oct [13 Nov 1851]
- Mary Jane & Joseph GOLDES at Augusta ME on 30th ult [10 Dec 1846]
- Mary Mrs & Benjamin WADLEIGH at Mount Vernon ME [17 Oct 1844]
- Mrs & William WARREN at Skowhegan ME [17 Sept 1846]
- Nancy N & George L MELLEN of Paris ME at Portland ME [22 Jul 1852]
- Obed Jr of Wayne ME & Alice HUNTON at Livermore ME on the 1st inst by Lewis HUNTON Esq [9 Jan 1835]
- Parinthia A & John JACOBS 2d both of Mt Vernon ME at Readfield ME by Rev Benjamin P REED [9 Dec 1847]
- Richard M of Fayette ME & Patience BESSE at Wayne ME [8 Jul 1847]
- Roxana F & Allen HOUSE Jr at Wayne ME [13 Mar 1835]
- Sarah E of Bangor ME & Daniel W AMES of Oldtown ME at Lowell [25 Sept 1851]
- Sarah of Wayne ME & Andrew CAMPBELL of Brunswick ME at Wayne by Moses WING Esq [29 Jun 1839]
- Silvina P of Wayne ME & Samuel M INGALS of Mt Vernon ME at Wayne by Alonzo WING Esq [28 Dec 1833]
- Sophia Mrs & George WINSLOW of Mercer ME at Belgrade ME [1 Apr 1847]
- Susan A & Samuel A FROST (she is 14 years old) at Winthrop [15 May 1851]
- William & Mary MANNERS at Augusta ME on Feb 16th 1851 [27 Feb 1851]
- William & Mrs Harriet N NORRIS at Wayne ME [29 May 1845]

WINGATE Albert of Hallowell ME & Rhoda MITCHELL of Carthage ME at Carthage by Rev R MOORE [9 Jul 1842]

WINGATE (cont.) Andrew T of Boston MA & Sarah C HAMLIN of Hampden ME at New York [16 Oct 1845]
    Charles J & Mary P d/o Capt William ROBINSON at Augusta ME [30 Nov 1833]
    Elizabeth G & William A SAMPSON at Hallowell ME [11 May 1848]
    H F & Laura A LEADBETTER at Hallowell ME [10 Dec 1846]
    Mary & Ira WALDRON at Great Fall NH [3 Aug 1848]
    Mary A & William NASON at this town (Hallowell) ME on Tues last by Rev B TAPPAN [19 Sept 1837]
    Mary C & William A WOODBRIDGE at Hallowell ME [30 Sept 1843]
    Mary S & Dr M C RICHARDSON at Hallowell ME [20 Sept 1849]
    Sophia P & Jonathan HALLATT of West Waterville ME at Hallowell ME [14 Feb 1850]
    William A of Bangor ME & Eliza WHITE at Frankfort ME [2 May 1837]
WINN George & Susan J REED both of Benton ME? at Lowell MA [4 Dec 1851]
    James a of Great Falls NH m Sarah M DAME at Farmington ME/NH? [29 May 1851]
    Mary of Waterville ME & Julius HENLE at Albany NY [30 Jan 1851]
    Temperance & John GRAY of South Berwick ME at York ME [29 Jul 1847]
WINNETT John of Randolph MA & Harriet P FIELD at Gardiner ME [8 Jul 1847]
WINSLOW Abigail A, d/o Stephen WINSLOW, & David L GUPTIL at Augusta ME on Sunday last at the Methodist Chapel by Rev Mr FULLER [10 Apr 1838]
    Abigail of Cumberland ME & George H LOW of North Yarmouth ME at Cumberland [15 Apr 1836]
    Abigail V & Gen WINSLOW both of North Yarmouth ME at Cumberland ME [22 May 1845]
    Asa W & Mary C KALER at Waldoboro ME [11 Nov 1847]
    Bradford & Mrs Hannah AMES at Damariscotta ME [1 Apr 1852]
    Cecelia & Charles ALEXANDER at Bath ME [5 Jun 1845]
    Charles H of Hallowell ME & Martha NOYES at Pittston ME [21 Feb 1837]
    David of Westbrook ME & Patience BUFFUM at Durham ME [13 May 1847]
    Elizabeth S & Alvin AIKEN at (Augusta) ME on 28 Sept [12 Oct 1848]
    Emily of Falmouth ME & John COLLINS of Kennebec ME at Portland ME [11 Sept 1851]
    Emily & Robert DUSTIN Jr at Vassalboro ME on 17th Dec by John MARBLE Jr [27 Dec 1849]
    Fanny & Caleb SMITH at Livermore ME [10 Jan 1850]
    Gardiner & Susan P JORDAN at Thomaston ME [14 Nov 1844]
    Gen & Abigail V both of North Yarmouth ME at Cumberland ME [22 May 1845]
    George of Mercer ME & Mrs Sophia WING at Belgrade ME [1 Apr 1847]
    George of Nobleboro ME & Lucy Ann COLE at Waldoboro ME [4 Nov 1847]
    Hannah & Elijah MATTHEWS at Hallowell ME [23 Dec 1843]
    Harriet J & Capt Thaddeus JONES of Bangor ME at Westbrook ME [4 Nov 1843]

Marriage Notices from the "Maine Farmer"

WINSLOW (cont.) Harriet N & Asa SWAN at Bath ME [2 Mar 1848]
Harriet S & Leonard C JONES at Hallowell ME [4 Dec 1851]
Horatio N & Mary T BRIMIGINE at Bath ME [28 Feb 1837]
J W Esq of Readfield ME & Miss Deborah M d/o E C STODDER Esq late of Nashville TN at Readfield ME on 30th Oct by Rev F MERRIAM of Winthrop [4 Nov 1843]
James H & Patience A BRAILEY at Thomaston ME [14 Nov 1844]
John T of Westbrook ME & Mary Ann NOYES at Portland ME [11 Jan 1844]
John & Louisa FULLER at Winthrop ME on 8th May by Rev Mr BARNARD [5 Jun 1845]
Jonathan Esq & Mrs Lucy ERSKINE at Albion ME [4 Apr 1850]
Joseph of Portland ME & Flora DAVIS at Hallowell ME [28 Nov 1844]
Lucy & William H HERSEY both of Winthrop ME at E Windsor ME on June 25 by Rev S POWERS [3 Jul 1851]
Luther P of Paris ME & Mary L HOMER of Portland ME at Portland [2 May 1844]
Lydia A & Timothy S CROOKER at Bath ME [9 Jul 1846]
Mary C & Noah HANSON of Portland ME at Windham ME [25 Nov 1847]
Mary F & John C ANDERSON at Bath ME [5 Dec 1844] Nancy W & Ebenezer MURCH Jr of Plymouth ME at Dixmont ME [27 Nov 1851]
Penelope P & George W NICHOLS, senior editor & proprietor of the *Lincoln Patriot* at Marshfield MA [6 Nov 1838]
Phebe of Falmouth ME & George WILSON of Westbrook ME [3 Dec 1842]
Phebe & Levi HUNTINGTON at Gardiner ME by Authur PLUMER Esq [4 Feb 1833]
Samuel of Avon ME & Prudence L AMES at Freeman ME [18 May 1848]
Sanford S & Mary T WILCOX at Monmouth ME [5 Dec 1837]
Sarah G & John M WOOD at Bath ME [12 Aug 1847]
Sarah T & Cornelius S WEBBER at Bangor ME [18 Jul 1844]
Sarah W & William H WHEELER at Augusta ME on Sunday last at the Methodist Chapel by the Rev Mr FULLER [22 May 1838]
Sobrina & John HOWARD at Phillips ME [22 Apr 1833]
Steven of Augusta ME & Elizabeth BASS at Bath ME [14 Oct 1836]
Thomas J & Lydia W PARIS at Bath ME [26 Dec 1844]
Thomas & Mary Jane BERRY at Bath ME [13 Jan 1848]
William T & Esther WEEKS by David G ROBINSON Esq at Vassalboro ME on Nov 14th [30 Nov 1848]

WINTER Elisha Esq of Dixfield ME & Anna B MITCHELL at Carthage ME [10 Jun 1852]
Elisha & Anna B MITCHELL at Carthage ME [17 Jun 1852]
Hannah G & Nathan CARVER Jr of Livermore ME at Wilton ME [30 Apr 1846]
Mary, d/o Samuel WINTER, & Daniel WOODWARD Jr at Hallowell ME [26 Oct 1839]
Olive & Dr Luther LAMB at Carthage ME [12 Nov 1846]
Samuel Jr of Pittston ME & Miss Hannah CROSS of Augusta ME at China ME [25 Nov 1843]
Thomas & Laura Ann GREELEY at Gardiner ME [8 Aug 1844]

WINTERS Abigail Matilda & Benjamin B BRANN at Waterville ME [3 Jun 1852]

WISE Mary J & John W ADAMS at Litchfield ME [27 Jul 1848]

WISE (cont.) Lucy E & Jacob H GEORGE of Prospect ME at Belfast ME [1 Jul 1852]

WISEMAN Thomas of Fulford & Mrs WILLAH of York ME at York [16 Sept 1847]

WISWELL James M & Olive J WALDRON of Buckfield ME at East Machias ME [12 Mar 1846]

WITCOMB Elezer & Miss Submittance CROSS at Belmont ME [26 Aug 1836]

WITHAM Allen & Alice MOORE at Gardiner ME [29 Feb 1844]
   Angeline & Jahn LUNT at Bangor ME [28 Jan 1847]
   Hannah E & Jacob NASON at Biddeford ME [13 Apr 1848]
   Harriet S & Daniel L PUMMER at China ME [8 Feb 1840]
   Isreal & Susan EASTMAN [23 Apr 1846]
   John & Mary LEIGHTON at Washington ME [11 Mar 1847]
   Joseph & Nancy H YOUNG by Rev S WILLIAMSON at Starks ME [23 Jun 1852]
   Lucretia & Moses JORDAN at Kingfield ME by Rev J TRUE [30 Mar 1839]
   Mary T of Phillips ME & Charles H CROSSMAN of Gardiner ME at Augusta ME on 9th inst by Lot M MORRILL Esq [14 Jun 1849]
   N of Oldtown ME & Mary F McKENNA at Levant ME [3 May 1849]
   Nathan & Maomi LUFKIN at Chesterville ME [7 Mar 1837]
   Ruth & Levi CLARK of Sebec ME at Milo ME [24 Sept 1846]
   S P & Louisa J LADD at Gardiner ME [12 Jun 1851]
   Sarah & Joseph LANE at Poland ME [26 Mar 1846]
   Stephen E of New Gloucester ME & Mary A HASKELL of Monmouth ME at Monmouth ME [4 Jul 1840]
   William L & Sarah P ROLLINS at Gardiner ME [9 Apr 1846]
   William & Hepsibeth KENDALL at Lyman ME [9 Jul 1846]

WITHEE Lucy R & Asa BLACKWELL at Norridgewock ME [17 Apr 1838]

WITHEREL Josiah S & Sarah G MOORE at Abbot ME [1 Aug 1834]

WITHERLY E N Capt & Caroline KNIGHT at Lincolnville ME [23 Oct 1841]

WITT Elizabeth P & Hiram LOVEJOY of Greenwood ME at Norway ME [23 Jan 1845]
   Thomas of Norway ME & Rachel L PORTER of Paris ME [18 Dec 1845]

WIXSON Rosanna, formerly of Augusta ME, & Mr S O MORSE of Charlestown at South Andover MA [28 May 1846]

WOART William Esq & Lucy WILLIAMS at Augusta ME by Rev TAPPAN [23 May 1844]

WOLCOTT Cyrenius B of Holyoke MA & Harriet N ABBOTT of (Augusta) ME by Rev Mr WEBB at (Augusta) ME on 11th Feb [19 Feb 1852]

WOLTZE Rooxby [sic] & John STORRER at Waldoboro ME [6 Jan 1837]

WONSON Lucy of Gloucester MA on 28th ult & George H WILLIAMS of Wayne ME [13 Aug 1842]

WOOD Abiel Jr (Rev), Pastor of the Baptist Church in Wiscasset ME, & Catherine Jane FELKER [8 Aug 1834]
   Abigail, d/o Elijah WOOD Esq, & Charles B STINCHFIELD of St Albans ME at Winthrop ME on Thurs last by the Rev Mr THURSTON [23 Nov 1839]
   Allen & Sarah G WALKER at Brunswick ME [15 May 1851]
   Almira & Jonathan S HARDY of Starks ME at Norridgewock ME [23 Jul 1842]

WOOD (cont.) Amasa & Sarah SHAW at Winthrop on Thurs morning last by Elder HOUGHTON [28 Dec 1833]
Ambrose B of Sidney ME & Elizabeth WOOD of Canton ME on New Years's Day [6 Feb 1841]
Armida F of Winthrop ME & Ichabod C NORRIS of Livermore ME at Winthrop ME by Rev Mr THURSTON [23 Jan 1841]
Augustine W & Pamela A TRIMM of Belfast ME at Boston ME [9 Jan 1845]
Barzilla D & Sarah Jane REYNOLDS at Sidney ME [8 May 1851]
Betsey of Mercer ME & James F COLLINS of Anson ME [6 Nov 1838]
Caroline R of Norridgewock ME & Mr H C WILLIAMS of Waterville ME [16 Dec 1843]
Catherine S & Edwin CHAPIN of Belchertown MA at Camden ME [22 Oct 1842]
Cyrus Capt & Mrs Roxanna HINKLEY at New Sharon ME [24 Aug 1839]
Cyrus K Capt of Kingfield ME & Martha K DRESSER at Turner ME [9 Mar 1848]
Edward B & Harriet Ann O JORDAN at Freeport ME [21 Jan 1847]
Elizabeth of Canton ME & Ambrose B WOOD of Sidney ME at Canton ME on New Year's Day [6 Feb 1841]
George N & Mrs Ann PEDER at (Augusta) ME on 9th June [17 Jun 1852]
Hannah W of Winthrop ME & Hiram H LEAVITT of Dexter ME at Winthrop ME on 12th June by Rev Mr THURSTON [5 Sept 1844]
Harriet & Ransom BISHOP at Winthrop ME on 17th inst [25 Dec 1838]
Horace & Cordelia SOUTHARD at Waterville ME [3 Jun 1852]
Isaac & Betsey DUNBAR at Belfast ME [10 Jul 1838]
James 2d & Elizabeth BLACKWELL both at Norridgewock ME on 25th [13 Feb 1841]
James B & Ruth CUTLER at Norridgewock ME [2 Oct 1845]
Jane & Gen Alden BLOSSOM at Turner ME [10 Apr 1851]
John C & Ann R WELCH at Vassalboro ME on Dec 11 by Oliver WEBBER Esq [18 Dec 1851]
John M & Sarah G WINSLOW at Bath ME [12 Aug 1847]
John N & Mary Jane PRATT at Augusta ME on 4th inst by Rev W A P DILLINGHAM [13 Sept 1849]
John & Rachel AMES at Hallowell ME [29 Apr 1847]
Joseph & Sirmantha SNELL at Winthrop ME on Sunday last by Rev Mr INGRAHAM [30 Sept 1836]
Josiah of China ME & Mary A TOWLE at Gardiner ME [6 May 1847]
Lewis & Ann A SNELL d/o John E SNELL of Augusta ME by Rev Mr QUINBY [23 Nov 1839]
Lydia & Anson HERRICK, publisher of the *Maine Free Press* at Hallowell ME at Wiscasset ME [27 May 1833]
Manuel S of Vassalboro ME & Miss Emeline PREBLE at Winslow ME [8 Jun 1846]
Mary & Samuel CORDIS at Winthrop ME on Thurs morning last by Rev David THURSTON [10 Oct 1834]
Olive of Winthrop ME & Capt Nathan WELLINGTON of Livermore ME at Winthrop ME on Wed last by Rev Mr THURSTON [23 Jan 1841]
Polly & Capt David FRENCH of Mt Vernon ME at New Sharon ME [8 Jul 1833]

WOOD (cont.) Priscilla C, d/o Deacon Enoch WOOD, & John LOVERING at Winthrop ME on 2d Apr by Rev Josiah HOUGHTON [10 Apr 1835]
    Quincy P of Anson ME & Lovina JEWETT, d/o Deacon Nathan JEWETT of Solon ME on Thurs last by Rev Mr LORING [13 Mar 1838]
    R N Miss & Mr M FRINGENI at Windham ME [10 Aug 1848]
    Rachel & George HINGE at St Louise KY [14 Aug 1845]
    Richard & Sarah HIGGINS of Pittsfield ME at Winslow ME [26 Aug 1847]
    Rufus H of New York & Harriet MOSES at Bath ME [31 Aug 1848]
    Samuel of Hallowell ME & Sarah ABBOT at Litchfield ME [23 May 1837]
    Samuel of Wilton ME & Sarah NELSON of Winthrop ME at Readfield ME [2 Mar 1839]
    Sarah C, d/o Elijah WOOD Esq of Winthrop ME, & Philander MORTON, merchant of Hallowell ME at Winthrop ME on Weds last by Rev D D TAPPAN [24 Oct 1837]
    Sarah P & Erastus Jr at Wiscasset ME [8 Jul 1847]
    Stiley & Jonathan LEATHER, "A Clergyman in Lowell, says the *Dedham Patriot*, lately turned WOOD into LEATHER" They were married on Thanksgiving day by Rev Mr THURSTON, "So they are both LEATHER now, and we suppose he is to be the upper LEATHER, though if she is to be reckoned the sole LEATHER we hope she is not to be hammered." [9 Jan 1838]
    Susan M & John C GRAHAM at Rumford ME [4 May 1848]
    Thomas C of Winthrop ME & Miss STOCKIN at North Yarmouth ME [1 Aug 1837]
    Urrilla I & Noah WENTWORTH at Vassalboro ME on the 8th inst by Oliver WEBBER Esq [16 Jan 1845]

WOODARD Franklin M & Prudentia F MILLS at Newport ME? [2 Apr 1846]
    Hannah & Jesse LINCOLN at Topsham ME [20 Apr 1848]
    John of Lisbon ME & Mary Ann HIGGINS at Topsham ME [3 May 1849]

WOODBRIDGE Ann E & Mr E L NORCROSS at Hallowell ME [19 Dec 1846]
    Harriet A & Elbridge TOBY at Hallowell ME [30 Nov 1839]
    James A & Frances ALBEE at Hallowell ME [30 May 1844]
    Martha Ann & Joseph A PLUMMER of Alna ME at Newcastle ME [13 Dec 1849]
    Mary Ann of Hallowell ME & Ebenezer C BANKS of Livermore ME at Hallowell ME [13 Nov 1841]
    Mary F & James M LASSELL both of Norway ME at Cambridge MA [2 Jan 1845]
    Sarah Jane & Harvey TOBEY at Hallowell ME [12 Mar 1846]
    William A & Mary C WINGATE at Hallowell ME [30 Sept 1843]

WOODBURY Calvin & Susan WENTWORTH both of Bridgeton ME at Gorham ME [11 Dec 1851]
    Charles & Catherine M BEMIS both of Paris ME at Norway ME [5 Mar 1846]
    Clarinda V & Shepherd MORRILL of Orneville at Bradford [5 Aug 1847]
    Eben & Mrs Louisa M DAVIS at Houlton ME [16 Sept 1843]
    George S & & Jane WYMAN at Dover ME [4 Mar 1843]
    Harriet Ann & nathan HARRIS, M.D., of Addison ME at Minot ME [4 Sept 1845]
    Helen A & Josiah D PULSIFER at Minot ME [8 Jun 1848]
    J B of Portland ME & Miss P W HEALY at Thomaston ME [28 Aug 1845]
    J Jr & Olive Ann WALKER at Exeter ME [5 Jul 1849]

WOODBURY (cont.) James of Litchfield ME & Mary Ann HASKELL of Gardiner ME [20 Mar 1841]
    Mary Ann & Jesse DAVIS of Webster ME at Litchfield ME [20 Mar 1845]
    Rebecca P of Monmouth ME & Elbridge H STEVENS of this town (Winthrop ME) on 14th inst by Rev Mr ROBINSON [24 Sept 1842]
    Sarah P & Silas B JONES at Bangor ME [3 Feb 1848]
    William W, prinicipal of Augusta High School & Miss Climena HALLET at Augusta ME [27 Nov 1841]
    Williams S & Abigail B FOLSOM at Monmouth ME on Monday evening last [11 Nov 1843]

WOODCOOK Clementine B & James O CUSHING at Thomaston ME [1 Jan 1846]
    Elizabeth C & Henry BAKER both of Sidney ME at Waterville ME [15 Mar 1849]
    Lucy A & Charles at Gardiner ME [12 Apr 1849]
    M P & Lucy A HOWARD at Searsmont ME [17 Apr 1851]

WOODHOUSE George (Dr) of Meredith NH & Miss Elizabeth A CLEAVELAND at Brunswick ME [25 Nov 1847]

WOODMAN Andrew J of Saco ME & Abby A HALEY at Cornish ME [13 Feb 1851]
    Charles & Caroline COWAN at Sidney ME [23 Sept 1843]
    Cynthia Bray, d/o Gen WOODMAN of Naples ME, & Israel JORDAN of Casco ME at Naples ME on 23d inst [4 Mar 1847]
    Cyrus of Wisconsin & Miss Charlotte FLINT both of Maine at Tremont IL [19 Feb 1842]
    David & Miss Martha SINNOTT at Saco ME [15 Mar 1849]
    Jane & Daniel M OWEN at Hollis ME? on 16th inst [28 Oct 1842]
    Joanna & Samuel GIBSON at Fairfield ME [21 Feb 1850]
    John of Norway ME & Mary J MORSE of Norway ME at Providence RI [16 Jan 1851]
    John & Mrs Dorcas STURTEVANT at Winslow ME [25 Oct 1849]
    Lucius of New Gloucester ME & Olive M STINCHFIELD at Danville ME [1 Aug 1844]
    Lydia H & Mr H BURRELL at Fairfield ME [9 Nov 1848]
    Martha W & Jeremiah M MASON of Limington ME at Buxton ME [23 Aug 1849]
    Mary L & Nathaniel HANSON at Hollis ME [11 Jul 1840]
    Octavia & Col Enoch SCALES at Wilton ME [30 Aug 1849]
    Olivia B of Wilton ME & Samuel L HAZARD of Boston MA at Wilton ME by A S C STRICKLAND Esq on Sunday evening Feb 9th [14 Mar 1840]
    Roxana T & Horace D MARBLE at Wilton ME [30 Aug 1849]
    Sarah of Searsmont ME & George CURRIER of Lynn MA at Searsmont ME [10 Jul 1845]

WOODS Deborah Jane & Bartlett BRIGGS at Belfast ME both of Belmont ME [31 Jul 1845]
    Franklin J & Mary C BENNETT by Asaph R NICHOLS Esq at (Augusta) ME on 23 Feb [26 Feb 1852]
    Greenlief F & Louisa B SPENCER both of Unity ME at Waldo ME [25 Oct 1849]
    Harriet of Bloomfield ME & Niles HASKELL of Newburyport MA at Bloomfield [16 May 1844]
    John of Bloomfield & Mrs Sarah ROBINSON at Cambridge [14 Feb 1850]

WOODS (cont.) Lovina & Jotham W MITCHELL at Bloomfield [21 Mar 1850]
    Nathan P of Bloomfield ME & Ann Cornelia CASS at Cornville ME [17 Jul 1851]
    Noah Esq of Gardiner ME & Miss Harriet E BLISH at Hallowell ME [15 Oct 1846]
    Noah Esq & Sarah BALLARD both of Gardiner ME at Norridgewock ME [22 Feb 1844]
    Samuel Jr & Mary S LOCKE by Rev James PEARL of Mt Vernon ME at (Augusta) ME on 29 Feb [11 Mar 1852]
    Sarah & Hartford JOY of Detroit at Hallowell ME [21 Feb 1837]
    William of Calais & Mary A PORTER at Lubec ME [14 Nov 1844]
    William & Caroline E WHITTIER both of Farmington ME on July 1st by Rev Mr ABBOT [10 Jul 1841]
WOODSIDE Anstress M & Thomas M CURTIS of Freeport ME at Brunswick ME [7 Jan 1847]
    Eliza Ann & Jedediah MARRINER at Bath ME both of Brunswick ME [25 Nov 1843]
    Owen & Rebecca M PAGE d/o the late Dr William PAGE at Brunswick ME [21 Dec 1833]
    Salome G & Jeremiah HUNT Jr at Brunswick ME [1 Apr 1843]
WOODSOM - WOODSUM
    Cyrus & Sylvia W BICKNELL at Hallowell ME [1 Jan 1846]
    Elisha of Mercer ME & Harriet SAWTELLE at Sidney ME [25 Sept 1845]
    Katherine P & Washington J BRAGG, M.D., at Hartford ME on 18th inst by Rev Cyril PEARL [5 Jun 1842]
    Mary E & Ancel SHOREY at Waterville ME [5 Aug 1847]
    William N & Mary S BILLINGS at Albion ME [4 Jan 1849]
    Zeorah B Mrs & Josiah BEAN at Old Town ME [12 Apr 1849]
    Zeruiah S & Eben TAYLOR of Hermon ME at Albion [15 Mar 1849]
WOODWARD Caroline & Mr A J HOPKINSON at Whitefield ME [19 Apr 1849]
    Daniel Jr & Mary d/o Samuel WINTER at Hallowell ME [26 Oct 1839]
    Emily & Randolph HEATH at Augusta ME on Thurs evening last by Rev C FULLER [31 Dec 1842]
    George S Rev of Philadelphia PA & Miss C A SMITH of Readfield ME by Rev Dr TAPPAN at (Augusta) ME on 30 Oct [9 Nov 1848]
    Gilbert A of North Bridgewater MA & Eunice C PERKINS d/o Capt Luther PERKINS by Rev Mr THURSTON at Winthrop ME on 1st inst [13 Jul 1848]
    Henry & Sarah B CARR d/o Deacon Daniel CARR of Winthrop ME at Winthrop ME on 20th Feb 1851 by Rev Daniel THURSTON [27 Feb 1851]
    Jordon & Deborah SNOW at Brunswick ME [28 Feb 1834]
    Joseph of Lisbon ME & Mrs Dolly COWING at Lewiston ME [18 Feb 1847]
    Mary & Capt Isaac LINSCOTT at Brunswick ME [10 Sept 1846]
    Michael & Mrs Joanna STEVENS at Gardiner ME [28 Jun 1849]
WOODWORTH Maria & Isaac at Eastport ME [27 Jun 1844]
    Sylvia (ae 17) & Deacon William PURINGTON (ae 54) at Bowdoinham ME [21 Dec 1833]
WOOSTER John Capt & Miss Mary Ann DAVIS at Lubec ME [19 Feb 1846]
WORCESTER Joseph & Miss Velina CUTLER at Thomaston ME [19 Aug 1836]

WORCESTER (cont.) Miriam, d/o Rev Thomas WORCESTER, & Rev Samuel F DIKE of Bath ME at Boston morning on 10th inst [23 Apr 1842]
WORK Joseph & Nancy SPRINGER at Bath ME [25 Dec 1838]
   Lewis M & Emily P SAMPSON at Topsham ME [28 Oct 1847]
   Nancy (ae 19) & Lithgow HUNTER (ae 89) at Topsham ME [26 Nov 1846]
   Julia of Norridgewock ME & Rev O B WALKER of Baring at Norridgewock ME [23 Feb 1839]
   Louisa F & John ELLIS of Smithfield ME at Mercer ME [19 Aug 1843]
WORKS Sarah L & Joseph COUSINS at Guilford ME? [3 Apr 1851]
WORMELL Eliza J & Sylvanus H LONG at Thomaston ME [4 May 1848]
   Charles R Capt of Belfast ME & Miss Mary J TURNER at Waterville ME [28 Feb 1850]
WORMWOOD Esther of Kennebunk ME & Rufus A COBB of New Gloucester ME at Kennebunk ME [19 Feb 1836]
   T G & Margaret HOLMAN both of Bath ME at Phipsburg ME [22 Apr 1852]
WORRY Assenath & James GROWS at Bath ME [17 May 1849]
WORTH Eliza A & Albert H CLARK at China ME [11 Feb 1847]
   Jethro G of Vassalboro ME & Lavina VARNEY of China ME [18 Sept 1835]
   Lovina Mrs & Asa BRADLEY at Vassalboro ME on 25 Jan [12 Feb 1852]
   Mary Ann C & Samuel GERREL of Orono ME at Corinth ME [12 Oct 1833]
   Samuel K & Adaline P DOE at Vassalboro ME by Jno MOWER Esq [26 Jul 1849]
WORTHEN Harriet E & Columbus G PARMENTER at China ME [26 Nov 1842]
WORTHING Elizabeth & Albion MOORE at Orono ME [25 Oct 1849]
   Ensign L of Palermo ME & Miss Emily L WHITMORE of China ME at Belfast ME [18 Apr 1850]
   Sally A of China ME & Everett H BRIDGHAM of Leeds ME at Vassalboro ME [22 Jul 1847]
   Sarah G & Mr O M WARREN of Hallowell ME at Palermo ME [20 Sept 1849]
WORTHLEY Adaline & William SWAIN at Skowhegan ME [2 Dec 1847]
   Samuel D & Philena S CONY at Strong ME [20 May 1847]
WOTTON Emma & Charles FIELD of Lisbon ME at Bath ME [4 Dec 1851]
   Lucy & Samuel ROKES both of WARREN at Waldoboro ME [14 Mar 1844]
WRENN Caroline & John HICKS at Gardiner ME on Jan 16th [30 Jan 1851]
WRIGHT see RUDGE and KENT
   A J Mr & Adelia BRAN at Gardiner ME [20 Feb 1851]
   Algernon S of Lawrence MA & Cordelia SWIFT at Wayne by Rev C FULLER [18 Oct 1849]
   Benjamin F & Miss Mary E BEAL both of Greene ME at Webster ME [8 Feb 1849]
   Betsey & Nathan of Pittsfield ME at Greene ME [9 Apr 1846]
   Charlotte & Elbridge G LORD at Bangor ME on 20th ult [12 Oct 1839]
   Cordelia & William H SMITH at Hallowell ME on 24th inst [4 Sept 1845]
   David & Almira BAILEY at Windsor ME [25 Mar 1847]
   Elbridge G Capt & Hannah PORTER at Mt Vernon ME by Dudley FOGG [25 Apr 1840]

WRIGHT (cont.) Emily & Samuel J BOND at Jefferson ME [19 Mar 1846]
  John B of Mt Vernon ME & Mary A WHITTIER at Readfield ME [9 Dec 1847]
  Joseph of Monmouth ME & Mary DAVIS at Lewiston ME [10 Jan 1850]
  Josiah & Mary YOUNG at Avon ME [21 Jan 1833]
  Josiah (Jr) of Guilford ME & Miss L G CHANDLER at Foxcroft ME [23 Nov 1848]
  Lewis E of Woolwich ME & Mary A GREENLEAF at Westport ME [26 Mar 1846]
  Mary McClara & Cyrus K KELLEY, M.D., of St Johnsbury VT at Bethel ME [19 Jun 1845]
  Mary & Dennis DAGGETT of Phillips ME at Guilford ME [6 Mar 1845]
  Mary & Jesse CHANDLER at Temple ME [11 Mar 1852]
  Mary & Jothan S PERKINS at Newcastle ME [17 May 1849]
  Nancy & John BURTON at Clinton ME [22 Nov 1849]
  Octavius of Lewiston ME & Miss Maria RICE of (Hallowell) ME at Augusta [27 Jun 1837]
  Octavus Dr & Miss Abby S PISHON at Clinton ME [29 Oct 1846]
  Octavus L of Brewer ME & Jane NOYES, youngest d/o William D CHASE of Portland ME at Parkman ME [3 Jun 1843]
  Olive of Livermore ME & John M CLARK of Sidney ME at Livermore ME [25 Apr 1844]
  Orlaney & Levi RICHARDS at Nashville NH on 25th Apr [6 Jul 1848] & [3 Aug 1848]
  Otis A of Webster ME & Miss M Ann GRAFFAM at Lewiston ME [20 Dec 1849]
  Royal & Miss Mary C ROBINSON at Newcastle ME [27 Nov 1845]
  Sarah Jane of Lewiston ME & James HAMILTON Jr of Elmira Chemung Co, NY at Lewiston ME [20 Sept 1847]
  Susan B & Eben M DILL of Webster ME at Lewiston ME [28 Oct 1847]
  Washington & Miss Aurelia H GLOVER at Minot ME [4 May 1839]
  William R of Lewiston ME & Olive TURNER at Turner ME [7 Oct 1847]
  William & Olive E TOOTHAKER at Madrid ME? [27 Nov 1845]
WYATT Lorenzo D & Almira DENNISON at Brunswick ME on Sunday evening last [4 Mar 1836]
WYER John & Rebecca S BREED at Vassalboro ME by Edward GRAY Esq [18 Jan 1849]
  Margaret & Arthur GRAY of Naples ME at Harpswell ME [5 Apr 1849]
  Margaret L & Henry POOR at Portland ME by Rev Dr TYLER [11 Mar 1833]
  Paulina & James THOMAS at Harpswell ME [24 Jun 1843]
WYERS Nancy & Cyrus BRAN at Gardiner ME [16 Oct 1835]
WYLIE Alice H & Thomas OLIVER Esq at Winnegance [21 Aug 1851]
  Harriet of Warren ME & Arthur TREAT of Frankfort ME at Warren ME [25 Jun 1842]
  Lavinia C & David LEMONT at Bath ME [13 Nov 1851]
WYMAN A H of Bloomfield ME & Sarah C BLUNT at Norridgewock ME [1 Jan 1852]
  Almeday & William MOORE Esq at Skowhegan ME [9 May 1837]
  Amos of Hallowell ME & Cordelia RICHARDS at Winthrop ME [14 Oct 1847]
  Ann & Samuel H JACOBS at Fairfield [25 Apr 1850]

WYMAN (cont.) Asa Esq of Milburn & Mrs Cynthia WING at Winthrop ME [17 Oct 1834]
    Charles & Mary B SWIFT at Bloomfield ME at Norridgewock ME [27 Dec 1849]
    David Jr & Lydia R MAINES at Brighton ME [20 Mar 1851]
    Ebenezer & Elizabeth B GAGE at Newport ME [14 May 1842]
    Elizabeth of New Sharon ME & Richard C DODD of this town (Winthrop) ME at New Sharon ME on Sunday last by Samuel WAYMAN Esq [22 May 1835]
    Elizabeth & Frederick W BARTLETT of Harmony ME at Bloomfield ME [25 Jul 1844]
    Emeline H & Thomas R WHITNEY both of Sidney ME at Hallowell ME [13 Nov 1845]
    Frances J & Palmer DULY at Phipsburg ME [11 Jan 1844]
    Freelove & Albert N MERRILL at Brighton ME [15 Feb 1849]
    George W of Brighton ME & Corrussan D SMITH at Biddeford ME [5 Aug 1852]
    Henry A Esq of Skowhegan ME & Fanny F RUSSELL at New Sharon ME [7 Jun 1849]
    Howard B of Sidney ME & Maria B ATKINSON at Madison ME [30 Nov 1848]
    Isaiah Jr formerly of Phipsburg ME & Caroline SMITH formerly of Harrison ME at Boston on 23rd ult by Rev J V HIMES [15 Jan 1842]
    Jacob & Miss Martha BRAGG at Winslow ME on Sat evening by David G ROBINSON Esq [3 Apr 1845]
    Jane & George S WOODBURY at Dover [4 Mar 1843]
    Jefferson F & Maria M WARD at China ME [23 Sept 1847]
    Jeremy & Maria MURPHY at Jefferson ME [5 Jun 1835]
    John R & Caroline H FOGG at Fairfield ME [16 Aug 1849]
    John R & Miss Caroline H FOGG at Fairfield ME [2 Aug 1849]
    John & Nancy P DAVIS at Bangor ME [11 Jul 1844]
    Jonas P & Tryphosa HOSKINS at Bangor ME [25 Dec 1851]
    Keziah Ann & Nathaniel C GREEN at Lexington [4 Jan 1849]
    Louisa & James LANE Jr of Fayette ME at Livermore Falls ME [6 May 1843]
    Lydia M & William H GILMAN at Phipsburg ME [20 Nov 1851]
    Mary Ann & Gen Charles N BODFISH at Norridgewock ME [13 Nov 1838]
    Mary E & Walter BEEDLE at Richmond ME [15 Mar 1849]
    Nancy S & Amaziah D MURRAY both of Bloomfield (ME) [29 Jul 1847]
    Ora C & Lucy P HALLOWELL at Windsor ME [7 Mar 1844]
    Pemelia & Joseph BARETT Esq of Canaan ME at Skowhegan ME [25 Nov 1836]
    Prescott J & Mary E SWAN at Augusta ME last by Rev B TAPPAN [13 Nov 1838]
    Rebecca R & Dr Reuben HUSSEY at Ripley ME [30 Mar 1848]
    Rhoda of Fayette ME & William H SEARS at Livermore ME [21 Dec 1839]
    Sarah S of Boothbay ME & George A LORING of Richmond ME at Lexington [4 Jan 1849]
    Sarah & Mr D N WHITE at Livermore ME [13 Jul 1848]
    Silas R & Ruby J WELD at Cornville ME [12 Feb 1852]

WYMAN (cont.) Susan E , only d/o Samuel WYMAN Esq of New Sharon ME, & Stephen MARSTON of Mt Vernon ME at New Sharon ME on Tuesday 29 Sept by Rev J T HAWES [15 Oct 1846]
  Susan J & Lucinda K PARKARD at China ME [29 Apr 1852]
  Susanna S & Albion P KNOX at Peru ME on Dec 7th by Jonas GREENE Esq [18 Dec 1851]
  Sylvanus B & Dolly L BEAN at Livermore ME [29 May 1838]
  William K & Mary S THOMPSON at Livermore ME [26 Mar 1846]
  William & Julia NORCROSS of Hallowell ME at Augusta ME [15 Aug 1834]
WYSE F O Maj of US Army & Miss Mary Eliza POPE, d/o Capt J POPE, US Navy, at Augusta on Tues morning on 6 Jul by the Rev Mr PUTNAM [15 Jul 1852]

- *y* -

YALE John & Phebe JACKSON [2 May 1844]
YALLALEE A W & S L HAINES Esq at Bangor ME [27 May 1847]
  Charles, a printer of Bangor ME & Hannah HIGHT at Norridgewock ME [6 Aug 1846]
  C C of New York & Mrs Emma WILLARD, principal of the Female Seminary in Albany [2 Oct 1838]
  Edward M of the Ellsworth Herald Office & Roseann SKILLIN at Ellsworth on 19 June [1 Jul 1852]
YATES Mary & Milton W CHAPMAN of Bethel ME at Paris ME [10 Jun 1847]
YEATES Margaret of Winthrop ME & Jonathan NEWALL Esq at Waldoboro ME on Thurs morning last [9 May 1840]
YEATON Charlotte of Northport ME & James ROBINSON at Belfast ME [16 Sept 1843]
  Cyrus of Pittston ME & Lucy H REED of Dresden ME [8 Jan 1846]
  James E of Richmond ME & Ellen NEAL at Hallowell ME [25 Dec 1845]
  Joel S of NEW Portland ME & Susan F VILES at Anson ME [18 Oct 1849]
  John of Stafford NH & Susan F HALEY of Webster ME at Dorchester MA [18 Dec 1845]
  Loammi B of Richmond ME & Eliza Ann BROWN at Augusta ME [7 Mar 1844]
  Reuben H of Belgrade ME & Mrs Charlotte N JONES by Elder J SPAULDING at Mercer ME on 21 Mar [20 May 1852]
  Sarah E & Alden FLY of Damariscotta ME at Chelsea [4 Mar 1852]
  William Jr Capt & Eliza J SAWYER of Vinalhaven ME at Northport ME [11 Feb 1847]
YORK Abigail & Hollis BOND at Brewer ME [13 May 1852]
  Henry & Mary PAUL at South Thomaston ME [16 Aug 1849]
  Joel M Esq & Sarah A McPHETRES at Bangor ME [14 Aug 1841]
  Louisa & Richard PERKINS Jr at Ellsworth ME [11 Nov 1847]
  Mary B & Lyman S WING of Monmouth ME at Peru ME [23 May 1840]
  Mary Jane of Exeter NH & Charles PARSHLEY at Brunswick ME [8 Oct 1846]
  Mary & Capt James ESTES at Bethel ME both of Bethel ME [23 Nov 1839]
  Mrs Mary & Charles P HOWARD at Waterford ME [13 May 1852]

YORK (cont.) Samuel Capt of Falmouth ME & Miss Mary HODSDON of Turner ME [6 Apr 1839]
Sarah A & Stephen KNIGHT at Bingham ME [15 May 1845]
Sarah & Joseph W KIDDER at Skowhegan ME by M Littlefield Esq [10 Jul 1851]

YOUNG Mr & Mrs Mary GATCOMB at Grand Menan (Grand Manan Island of the Bay of Fundy Canada) [11 Feb 1847]
Abba & John DOW at Biddeford ME [4 Mar 1852]
Ann & George W LERMOND at Thomaston ME [8 May 1845]
Benjamin Jr & Ruth B BENSON both of Hartford ME at Paris ME [31 Jul 1845]
Betsey M (ae 74) & Lewis OGIER of Camden ME (ae 84) at Lincolnville ME [4 Jul 1844]
Caroline of Gouldsboro ME & Elisha FARROW at Steuben ME [28 Jan 1847]
Catherine of Greenwood ME & Moses S KIMBALL of Bethel ME at Norway ME [19 Dec 1844]
Charlotte & Daniel SHOREY of South Berwick ME at York ME [20 Aug 1846]
Daniel A & Lucy W ABBOTT of Lowell MA at Farmington [26 Aug 1852]
Daniel & Judith SYLVESTER of Freedom ME at Waldoboro ME [5 Mar 1846]
Ebenezer & Sarah MITCHELL at Thomaston ME [4 May 1839]
Edward & Julia SOIETT at Bath ME [18 May 1848]
Eliza A & Ebed LINCOLN Jr at Bath ME [8 Apr 1836]
Elizabeth C & Mansfield H PETTINGILL at Augusta ME on 1st inst [9 Jan 1845]
George F & Esther A MOODY at Pittston ME [7 Dec 1848]
Hannah W & Mr B Franklin TOZIER, printer, formerly of Dover at Waterville ME by Rev C I EAMES [3 Oct 1841]
Hannah & Charles DUDLEY at Livermore Falls ME [19 Dec 1844]
Harriet & David BLIN at Pittston ME [5 Oct 1848]
Hester Ann & Timothy NICKLES at Wayne ME both of Fayette ME [25 Feb 1847]
Hiram of Bethel ME & Olive D BACON of Greenwood ME at Norway ME [21 Aug 1845]
Hiram S of Fayette ME & Olive S PRESCOTT at Vienna ME [5 Apr 1849]
Irene D & Edmund CURTIS of Woodstook ME [26 Feb 1846]
Jabez & Nancy S BURLEY at Linneus Aroostook Co ME on May 22d [16 Jul 1842]
Jane S & Mr S A HOWES at Belfast ME [5 Nov 1846]
Jeremiah & Sarah E JOHNSON at Vassalboro ME on 30 Sept by J MARTIN Esq [9 Oct 1851]
Joshua Esq of Mercer ME & Eleanor GROVE at Wiscasset ME on 19th inst [22 Nov 1849]
Julia B & Levi J HICKS at Augusta ME [14 Oct 1843]
Leander & Mary Ann STEWART at Warren ME [3 Feb 1848]
Levi L & Emily SANFORD both of Augusta ME at Belgrade ME on 10th inst [15 Oct 1846]
Louisa P & Isaac B GORHAM at Norway ME [10 Oct 1840]
Lucinda L & James N DIGGINS of Wayne ME at East Livermore ME [1 May 1845]

YOUNG (cont.) Lucinda & Joseph N WHITE of Jay ME at East Livermore ME [12 Mar 1846]
Lucy Ann & Owen C WHITEHOUSE at (Augusta) ME on 17th inst [25 May 1848]
Lucy E & Amos P KNOWLES at Lincolnville ME [14 Aug 1851]
Lydia & Henry ATKINS at Corinna ME [28 Mar 1850]
Mary Ann & Cyrus H SHAW at Thomaston ME [22 Jan 1852]
Mary M of Palermo & Fenno B SWAN at Gardiner [10 Jul 1851]
Mary & Josiah WRIGHT at Avon ME [21 Jan 1833]
Melinda A & Samuel H WHITEHOUSE at Mercer ME by William BLANDING Esq [26 Aug 1847]
Mercy J & William BARTLETT, editor of the *Mercury* at Bangor ME [22 Apr 1847]
Mercyette of Winthrop ME & Charles C DREW at Lowell on 28 Dec [16 Jan 1851]
Moses A & Maria F CLOUDMAN both of Norway ME at South Paris ME [22 Jan 1846]
Nancy H & Joseph WITHAM at Starks ME [23 Jun 1852]
Nancy M Mrs & Alexander GARDNER both of Augusta ME at China ME on Sunday last by Eld William BOWLER [20 Feb 1851]
Nancy & Charles KEENE at Augusta ME on 24th June [5 Jul 1849]
Oliver & Mary H BAKER at the Forks ME [13 Dec 1849]
Phebe S G & Charles PLUMMER at Belfast ME [26 Dec 1844]
S J of Greenwood & Mr Kingsbury CURTIS of Paris ME [8 Jan 1846]
Sally & Patric DOYLE at Newcastle ME "after a courtship of 25 yrs" [11 Jan 1844]
Solomon & Ellen ROLLE at Falmouth ME [11 Jan 1844]
Thankful Mrs (ae 69) & Joseph SYLVESTER (ae 82) at Freeport ME [12 Jun 1845]
William L & Amanda M COLCORD at Prospect ME [10 Oct 1844]
William Dr of Farmington ME & Sarah J BANGS at Phillips ME [3 Jul 1851]
William of Washington ME & Hannah BOND at Jefferson ME [18 Jan 1840]
William S & Sally TORREY at Turner ME [13 Nov 1838]
William & Margaret SPENCE of St James at Calais ME [21 Aug 1845]
Zenette S of Fayette ME & Ansel SEAVEY of Starks ME at Wayne ME by N B FROST Esq [25 Feb 1847]

MINISTERS AND JUSTICES OF THE PEACE

Below is a listing of the ministers and justices of the peace who are named in this publication. The number in parentheses ( ) stands for the approximate number of issues in which he was named. We also give the location of marriages and the span of time the records were reported. Ministers named in *Marriages & Divorce Records from Maine Freewill Baptist Publications, 1819-1851* are marked with an asterisk (*).

ABBOTT Ambrose H Esq China & Rumford ME 1840 & 1851
ABBOTT Howard G Esq Vassalboro ME 1849
ABBOTT J R Esq Augusta ME 1847
ABBOTT Jacob Rev (Cong) Farmington ME (2) 1841
ABBOTT Nathan Esq Rumford ME 1839
ADAMS Aaron Chester Rev (Cong) Gardiner ME 1840
ADAMS Dr Rev Boston MA 1851
ADAMS George Eliashib Rev (Cong) Brunswick ME 1836 & 1837 [see "Record of Marriages Performed by George E Adams, 1st Parish Congregational Church in Brunswick ME 1829-1870]
ADAMS Jonathan Rev Deer Isle ME 1851
ADAMS Thomas Rev (Cong) (4) Augusta & Vassalboro ME 1839-1842
ADLAM S Rev Hallowell ME 1841 & 1845
ADLUM S Rev Augusta ME 1844
* **ALBEE** Hiram Rev Hallowell ME 1845 & 1848
* **ALLEN** C F Rev Augusta ME (Meth) (4) 1849-1851
* **ALLEN** John Rev Augusta ME (Meth) (4) Readfield, Sidney & Winthrop ME 1838-1849
ALLEN N Rev Readfield ME 1841
ALLEN Rev Augusta ME (3) 1848 Farmington ME 1849
ALLEN Stephen Rev (Meth) (3) Augusta & Farmington 1847-1851

ATKINS C Rev Mt Vernon ME 1838
BABCOCK William R Rev (Epis) Gardiner ME 1841 1851
BACON Henry Providence RI 1848
BAILEY Elder Harmony ME 1844
BAILEY Giles Rev (Univ) (3) Wayne & Winthrop ME 1840-1842
BAKER C Rev (Meth) Portland ME 1835
BAKER Elias Esq Windham ME 1842
BALKHAM Uriah Rev Dr (Cong) Wiscasset ME 1852
BARNARD A F Rev (Meth) (2) Winthrop ME 1845
BARROWS Allen Rev (Bapt) Leeds ME 1852
BARRY Rev Vassalboro ME 1838
BARTLETT B Esq Rumford ME 1835
BARTON Aaron Esq (2) East Livermore ME 1851 & Livermore ME 1838
BATES George Rev (Univ) (4) Fayette, Turner & Winthrop ME 1836-1846
BEAN Shepherd Esq (2) Lee ME 1848 1852
BECKETT J H Esq Thomaston ME 1836 Union ME 1836
BENSON G A (Gustavus Adolphus?) Esq Winthrop ME 1849
BENSON Samuel Page Esq (5) Readfield & Winthrop ME 1834-1843
BILLINGS J Rev Mt Vernon ME 1852
BLACKER Robert Rev (Univ) Livermore ME 1847

BLAKE Edward Esq (4) Augusta & Hartford ME 1837-1850
BLAKE H M Rev (Meth) (4) Augusta ME 1851 1852
BLAKE John L Hon Phillips ME 1843
BLANDING William Esq Mercer ME 1847
BOWLER William Eld (4) Albion, China & Windsor ME 1836-1851
BOWLES Isaac Esq Wayne ME 1835 & Winthrop 1838
BRAGDON (C P) Rev (Meth) Brunswick 1838 & Hallowell 1841
BRAGG John J Rev Letter B ME 1843
BRAN Thomas Esq Patricktown Plantation ME 1849
BRAY Jacob Rev Bridgeton ME 1851
BRAY S Rev (Meth) (2) Vassalboro ME 1851 1852
BRIGGS John E Esq Auburn ME 1845
BROWN George P Esq Dixmont ME 1840
BROWN S P Esq Winthrop ME 1851
BURGESS Alexander Rev (Epis) (12) Augusta ME 1845-1850
BURGESS Bishop George (Epis) Gardiner 1848
BURGIN Jeremiah Eastport ME 1845
BURR Charles C Rev Portland ME (3) 1840 Hallowell ME 1838 North Yarmouth ME 1838
BURRILL S Esq Albion ME 1846
BURRILL Thomas Esq Albion ME 1847 1851
BURSLEY B Esq Wellington ME 1842
BUTLER E K Esq Hallowell ME 1838
BUTLER Nathaniel (Bapt) Rev Turner ME 1848
BUXTON E G Esq North Yarmouth & Yarmouth ME (3) 1842-1849
BUXTON Rev Albion ME 1849
CALDWELL Asbury Rev (Meth) (3) Winthrop ME 1835 1836
CARLTON Rowland Esq Sedwick ME 1838
CARR William C Esq North Palermo ME 1852
CARTER Silas Augusta ME 1838 1838
CAVERNO Rev Brewer ME 1843
CHANDLER B F Esq Augusta ME 1848
CHANDLER M A Esq (3) Belgrade & Rome ME 1849-1851
CHAPIN E H Rev New York City 1852
CHAPMAN Rev Camden ME 1859
CHASE B Rev Rumford ME 1852
CHASE Mr Esq Turner ME 1849
CHEEVER George B Rev New York City NY 1851
* **CHICKERING** John W Rev (Cong) Portland ME 1838 & 1842
CHURCH Anson Esq (4) Augusta ME 1846-1850
CHURCH G Rev Wayne ME 1841
CILLEY W S Rev Dexter ME 1848
CLAPP J Rev New Orleans 1837
CLAPP Joel Rev (Epis) (3) Gardiner ME 1834-1838
CLARKE Rev Manchester NH 1851
CLEAVLAND J Rev (Meth) Winthrop ME 1840
CLINCH Rev Boston MA 1852
CLOUGH E Esq Mt Vernon ME 1848
COLE Albert Rev (Cong) (2) Vassalboro ME 1849 Winslow ME 1849 [NB "A bishop of the whole Saco Valley (ME) region, attended 944 funerals, 233 in Cornish, 127 in Hiram, 126 in Limington, 117 in Baldwin, 77 in Parsonsfield, 54 in Limerick, 61 in Porter, 39 in Sebago & 15 in other towns. He performed 356 marriages, 242 in his own home in 20 years; in Cornish 68; in Parsonsfield 38; in

COLE Albert, (cont.) Baldwin 36; in Hiram 35; in Limington 32; in Limerick 25 & couples from 18 other towns." see *Baptismal, Marriage & Funeral Records Records of Albert Cole 1818-1881 of Cornish ME* by Ancient Landmarks Society of Parsonsfield ME 1983]

COLE Jonathan Rev (2) (Unitarian) Hallowell ME 1837-1849

COLE Rev (4) Hallowell ME 1837-1843

CONANT Joseph H Rev (Cong) Chesterville ME 1851

* **CONE** C C Rev (Meth) Bowdoinham ME 1841

COOMBS A Esq Windsor ME 1852

CRAIG Daniel Esq (3) Readfield ME 1838-1848

CROSBY Lemuel Esq Freeman ME 1851

CROSON William Esq Warren Co OH 1839

CROSS Isaac Esq Turner ME 1835

CROSS Rev Hallowell ME 1838

CROWELL T Esq Honolulu Sandwich Islands 1851

CUMMINGS A W Rev Readfield ME 1848

CUNNINGHAM E Esq Edgecomb ME 1833

CURLEY J A Rev Cincinnati OH 1844

CURRIER J Esq Mt Vernon ME 1838 1840

CUSHING Loring Esq (4) Augusta & Sidney ME 1844-1847

CUSHMAN David Quimby Rev (Cong) Boothbay ME 1841

CUTLER Elibridge G (Cong) Rev Belfast ME 1843

DALTON Asa Rev (Bapt) (3) Augusta ME 1852

DAVIES J Esq Belgrade ME 1847

DAVIS Abner Rev Brownfield ME 1841

DAVIS C B Paris ME 1851

DAVIS Frances Esq Augusta ME (2) 1851 1852

DAVIS Jesse Esq Webster (now Sabattus) ME (3) 1848 1851

DAVIS Joshua Esq Sidney ME 1844

DAVIS Timothy Rev (Cong) Litchfield ME 1849 1849

DAY Josiah Leeds ME 1849

DAY Rufus Rev (Meth) Monmouth ME 1850

DEERING John Rev Bath ME 1841

DENNET John Esq Paris ME 1845

DIELL Rev Oahu Sandwich Islands (Hawaii) 1834

DILLINGHAM W A P Rev (4) Augusta & Hallowell ME 1847-1850

DODGE A T C Esq Dixmont ME 1850

DODGE John Rev Waldoboro ME 1843

DONNELS Moses Rev (Meth) Dresden ME 1844

DORSEY Dr Rev Baltimore MD 1844

DOW Joseph Esq (3) Phillips ME 1847-1848

DOWNING Isaac Rev (Meth) Monmouth ME 1841

DREW William A Rev (Univ)(28) 1833-1852

DRINKWATER Arthur Rev (Bapt) (5) Bloomfield, Fayette, Mt Vernon, & Readfield ME 1834-1852

DRIVER Rev Boston MA 1842

* **DUDLEY** Thomas Elder (FWB) (3) Augusta ME 1851-1852

DUNBAR Levi Esq Etna ME 1849

DUNN John Esq Hallowell ME 1838

DUREN Charles Rev (Cong) Sangerville ME 1842

* **DWIGHT** Edward S Rev Saco ME 1852

* **DWIGHT** William T Rev (Cong) Portland ME 1838

EAMES C I Rev Waterville ME 1841

EASTMAN Chandler Esq Exeter NH? 1835
EASTMAN Samuel Esq Strong ME 1847
EDDY Rev Lowell MA 1851
EDES Rev Nantucket MA 1839
* **EDGECOMB** Joseph Rev (FWB)(3) Mt Vernon ME 1846-1851 [NB "baptized 325, married 240 couples & attended 1200 funerals" p180 *FWBC*]
ELDRED Thomas Esq Belgrade ME 1845
ELLINGWOOD John W Rev (Cong) Bath ME 1843
ELLIOT T Rev (Univ) Winthrop ME 1851
ELLIS Sumner Rev Boston MA 1852
EMERSON Myric Esq Orono ME 1843
ESTES J D Esq China ME 1851
EVANS Daniel Jr Mayfield ME 1842
EVELETH J J Esq (5) Augusta ME 1844-1847
FAIRBANKS Levi Esq Monmouth ME 1835 1836
FALES Thomas F Rev (Epis) Brunswick ME 1845
FARMER Rev Belgrade ME 1833
FARRINGTON Rev Mercer ME 1842
FARRINGTON W F Rev (Meth) Portland ME 1843
FESSENDEN Samuel C Rev (Cong) E Thomaston ME 1839
FESSENDEN Samuel Esq Portland Jail ME 1843
FIELD S W Rev (2) Hallowell & Augusta ME 1848-1850
* **FILES** Allen Rev (FWB) Winthrop ME 1839
FISK Rev Wrentham MA 1838
FOGG Dudley Esq (3) Mt Vernon ME 1835-1840
FOGG Rev Woolwich ME 1852
FOGG Samuel Eld (2) (Bapt) Winthrop ME 1834-1841
FOLLETT J M Jay ME 1847

FORBES Darius Rev (4) Belfast, Hallowell, Waldo & Pittston ME 1839-1842
FOREST Rev Winooski 1838
FOSS James Esq Standish ME 1850
FOSS Walter Elder (Bapt) (13) Leeds 1836-1852 Hartford, Monmouth, Wayne, & Webster ME 1836-1852
FOSTER Benjamin Monmouth ME 1848
FOSTER Frederic Rev (Univ) (4) Winthrop ME 1843-1849
FOSTER Oliver Esq Winthrop ME 1834
FOSTER Rev Augusta & Hallowell ME (2) 1851
FOSTER Stewart Esq (2) Hallowell ME 1840-1845
FOX Thomas B Rev Newburyport MA 1837
FREEMAN E/F Rev Augusta ME 1843 & 1846
FREEMAN Fredrick Sandwich MA 1847
FREEMAN Rev (3) Augusta & Pittston ME 1841-1846
FRENCH William R Rev (Univ) Lewiston ME 1847
FRIENDS J C Esq Etna/Monroe ME 1839
FROST N B Esq Wayne ME 1847
FROTHINGHAM William Rev (Cong) (2) Belfast ME 1842-1843
FULLER Benjamin A G Augusta ME 1846 & 1848
FULLER C Rev (Meth) (16) Augusta, Hallowell, Leeds, North Wayne, Winthrop ME 1842-1852
FULLER D Bin Esq (3) Albion ME 1848-1851
FULLER Daniel Rev (Meth) (4) Winthrop ME 1833-1834
FULLER David Esq Readfield ME 1841
FULLER Edward Esq Readfield (2) 1837 & 1851

Marriage Notices from the "Maine Farmer"

FULLER Francis Esq Winthrop ME 1849
FULLER Jona H Esq Unity ME 1850
FULLER M Rev (2) Augusta & Hallowell ME 1844-1845
FULLER Mr (2) Augusta ME 1843 & 1838
FULLER Rev Falmouth ME 1845
FULLER Simon Dr Rumford ME 1839
FULLER William C Esq (2) Readfield & Winthrop ME 1835 & 1843
GARDINER Calvin Rev (Uv)(5) Sidney, Winslow, Hallowell, Waterville ME 1838-1849
GARDINER William Esq No 11 (Ashland) Aroostook Co ME 1847
GARLAND Edmund F Esq No 11 Range 5th (Ashland) Aroostook Co ME 1849
GERRY Joseph Esq Fairfield ME 1848
GERRY Joseph Rev (Meth) (2) Jay & Fayette ME 1852
GILLETT Eliphalet Rev (Cong) (2) Augusta & Hallowell ME 1837 & 1848
GILMAN J T Rev (3) Bath ME 1841-1852
GLIDDEN Hiram Esq Whitefield ME 1849
GOLDTHWAIT Rev Vassalboro ME 1848
GOODENOW Robert Esq Farmington ME 1838
GOULD Daniel Rev Dixfield ME 1835
GRANT William O Rev (Bapt) (4) Bowdoin, Hallowell & Litchfield ME 1838-1845
GRAY Dr Rev Jamaica Plain NY 1841
GRAY Edward Esq (3) Vassalboro ME 1849-1852
GREELEY Joseph Esq (2) China ME 1845 & 1849
GREEN L H Esq Gardiner ME 1848
GREENE Jonas Esq Peru ME 1851
GREENOUGH John Jr Rev Old Town ME 1847
GUNNISON N Rev (Univ) (3) Augusta & Vassalboro ME 1844 & 1850
GURLEY Rev Cincinnati OH 1844
HACKETT Simeon Rev (Cong) Temple ME 1840 & 1852
HAINES Columbus Esq East Livermore ME 1844
HAINES Samuel Esq Clinton ME 1842
HALL I C Esq Montville ME 1852
HAM John Esq Sidney ME 1842
HAMLEN William Esq Sidney ME 1837 & 1838
HAMMOND E F Esq Atkinson ME 1849
HAMMOND William Esq Guilford ME 1838
HARLOW William Rev (Cong) Harpswell ME 1833
HASKELL James B Esq (3) China ME 1847-1850
* **HATHAWAY** George W Rev (Cong) Bloomfield ME 1851
HAWES H Rev Augusta ME 1849
HAWES J T Rev New Sharon ME 1846 & 1849 (Cong in Topsham in 1833)
HAWES Rev Augusta & Union ME 1847 & 1849
HAWKES Joseph Rev (Meth) Bowdoinham ME 1846
HAWKES Rev New York City 1836
HAZE Elder Winthrop ME 1836
HAZE Robert Elder Buckfield ME 1850
HEALD Solomon Esq Lovell ME 1848
HEARSEY John Esq Canton Point ME 1840
HEATH Jonathan M Esq Monmouth ME 1849
HERSEY William R Esq Lincoln ME 1846
HILL J D Esq Moscow ME 1847
HILL Theodore Rev Mt Vernon ME 1850

HILLMAN A P Rev (Meth) Winthrop ME 1839
HINES J V Rev Boston MA 1842
HINKLEY Ariel Esq Belgrade ME 1848
HINKLEY Smith Rev (Bapt) Monmouth ME 1843
HOBART Caleb Rev (Cong) North Yarmouth ME 1835 & 1842
HOBART J Rev Providence RI 1851
HOBART N Rev (Meth) Cornish ME 1849
HOBART Rev Dr New York ME 1851
HOLLAND C Hon Canton ME 1850
HOLMES Aaron Esq Jay ME 1842
HOLMES M H Esq Swanville ME 1851
HOMANS John Esq Vassalboro ME 1851
HORTON Rev Saco ME 1839
HOUGHTON Josiah Rev (Bapt) (4) Fayette, Livermore, & Winthrop ME 1833-1842
HOWARD M Rev Gardiner ME 1842
HOWARD Oakes Esq (3) Winthrop 1838-1846
HOWARD Rev (2) Augusta & Brunswick ME 1841-1843
HOWARD William D Rev Frankford PA 1849
HUNTON Jonathan G Esq (Gov of Maine) Readfield ME 1833
HUNTON Lewis Esq (3) Livermore ME 1834-1848
HUNTON Mr Esq Lewiston ME 1834
HYDE William Lyman Rev (Cong) Gardiner ME 1852
INGERHAM John H/E Elder (Bapt) (16) Augusta, Hallowell, Mt Vernon, Winthrop ME 1836-1851
JACK Robert Esq Lisbon ME 1852
JAQUES Parker Rev (2) (Meth) Winthrop ME 1851-1852
JENKS E A Esq Brownville ME 1839
JEWETT Henry C Rev (Cong) Winslow ME 1836
JOHNSTON Rev Alexandria DC 1841
JONES Elijah Rev (Cong) Auburn ME 1842
JONES Rev Hope ME 1837
JONES Thomas Esq Norridgewock ME 1846
JUDD Sylvester Rev (Univ) (16) Augusta & Sidney ME 1843-1852
KALLOCH A Rev Augusta ME 1849
KALLOCH I S Rev (Bapt?) Warren ME 1849
* **KALLOCH** Rev Augusta (3) ME 1848-1849
KALLOCH Rev Dexter ME 1849
KAVANAGH A Elder Dover NH 1850
KEELER S H Rev (Cong) Calais ME 1840
KEENE Waite W Esq (2) Bremen ME 1838-1839
KELLAR Cyrus Esq Searsmont ME 1839
KELLEY Erastus? W Esq Winthrop ME 1850
KENT Cephas H Rev (Cong) Freeport ME 1836
KIMBALL Hartley Esq (2) Mercer ME 1839
KIMBALL S Esq West Waterville ME 1849
KING Amos S Esq Phillips ME 1849
KNOX George Rev (Bapt) Brunswick & Topsham ME 1833 & 1842
LARRABEE W C Rev Readfield ME 1840
LATHAM H W Rev (Meth) (2) North Waldoboro ME 1851 1852
LAUGHTON Shepherd Esq Pittston ME 1841
LAURENCE Rev Sumner ME 1839
LAWRENCE Ephraim Esq Gray ME 1835

LEATHHEAD John Esq Anson ME 1836
LEIGHTON S S Rev Leeds ME 1845
LEWIS E Elder Clinton ME 1840
* **LEWIS** Daniel B Rev (FWB) Readfield ME 1851
LEWIS Samuel Rev Waterville ME 1839
LINSCOTT J A (2) Hon Phillips ME 1849-1851
LITTLEFIELD Moses Esq (4) Skowhegan ME 1845-1852
LOMBARD B L Elder Wayne ME 1849
LOMBARD Benjamin Esq Wayne ME 1841
LORD Rev (Unitarian) Plymouth MA 1843
LORD Thomas N Rev (Cong) Topsham & Thomaston ME 1838-1841
LORING Asa T Rev (Cong) Phippsburg ME 1845
LORING Rev Anson/Solon ME 1838
LOVEJOY H B Esq (2) Fayette ME 1851
LOW Robert Rev Hallowell ME 1834
* **LOWELL** Tallman Esq Phipsburg ME 1852
LUDDEN J B Esq (3) Lee ME 1851
LUDWIG Newall W Esq Waldoboro ME 1839
LUNT Orrington Esq Bowdoinham ME 1838
LYON Eliab Jr Esq Readfield ME 1840
MACOMBER James H Esq (3) Milo ME 1848-1851
MALTHY John Mr Rev (Cong) Bangor ME 1840
MANTER Z Rev (Meth?) Albion ME 1851
MARBLE John Jr (2) Vassalboro ME 1849
MARSTON James R Esq (2) Mt Vernon ME 1848-1849
MARSTON Joseph Esq Waterville ME 1845

MARTIN Ezekiel Esq (3) Turner ME 1833-1835
MARTIN J Esq (2) Turner & Vassalboro ME 1834-1851
MARTIN Jesse Rev China ME 1848
MATHER (William L?) Rev (Cong?) Wiscasset ME 1842
MAXIM Ephraim Esq Wayne ME 1850
MAY John Esq (4) Winthrop ME 1834-1852
MAY Seth Esq Winthrop ME 1837
MAYHEW Nathan Elder Jay ME 1852
MAYO Elder Carthage ME 1843
McGEHEE John Esq Columbia Co GA 1836
McKEEN Silas Rev (Cong) Belfast ME 1836
MEANS Rev Dorchester MA 1848
MEDBURY Rev Newburyport MA 1848
MEGQUIRE Charles Esq Gray ME 1843
MEIGS Eben Esq China ME 1848
MERRIAM Franklin Rev (Bapt) (15) Belgrade, East Winthrop, Readfield, Winthrop ME 1841-1847
MERRILL James Esq Whitefield ME 1842
MERRILL Lot M Esq (2) Augusta ME 1849-1851
METOIE E M Rev 1837
MILES Rev Hallowell ME 1834
MILLETT Rev Wayne ME 1845
MILNER Reuben Rev Canton ME 1835
MITCHELL Rev Hampden ME 1847
MOODY Dudley Esq Kent's Hill, Readfield ME 1840
MOODY Samuel Lisbon ME 1840
MOORE Asahel Rev (Meth) (5) Augusta & Winslow ME 1844-1846
MOORE R Rev Carthage ME 1842
MOORE Samuel Esq Steuben ME 1842

MORRILL Lot M Esq (2) Augusta ME 1849
MORRILL Rev Livermore & Vassalboro ME 1843 & 1848
MORSE Rev (6) Augusta & Winthrop ME 1847
MORSE S W Rev (5) Augusta & Winthrop ME 1846-1848
MORSE (Charles W) Rev (Meth) Readfield ME 1848
MOWER John/Jonathan Esq (3) Vassalboro ME 1849-1852
MUGFORD Caleb Rev (3) (Meth) Hallowell & Readfield ME 1841-1851
MULLIKEN George Esq Augusta ME 1851
NASON N F Elder Palmyra ME 1849
NASON S S Elder (3) Albion & Troy ME 1850
NASON William H Esq Plymouth ME 1838
NEAL John Esq Litchfield ME 1848
NICHOLS Asaph R Esq (15) Augusta & Readfield ME 1846
NICHOLS Dr Rev Portland ME 1840
NICHOLS Joseph Esq Waterville ME 1849
NICHOLS Mr Rev North Yarmouth ME 1833
NICKELS I Rev Dr (Uni) Portland ME 1843
NICKERSON S H Esq Frankfort ME 1842
NORRIS T C Esq Hallowell & Vienna ME 1833 & 1851
NORTH James W Esq Sebasticook ME 1842
NORTON Mr Saco ME 1839
NORTON Rev Harpswell ME 1838
NOTT Rev Bath ME 1842
NUTTER David Elder 1852
ORFF Reuben Esq (9) North Waldoboro ME 1847-1851
O'REILLY Rev (Roman Cath) Augusta ME 1851
PACKARD L Rev Readfield ME 1846

PACKARD Rev Cornville ME 1851
PALMER A Rev Winslow ME 1852
PALMER R Bath ME 1842
PARKARD Rev China ME 1852
PARKER Jeremiah Esq Gorham ME 1843
PARKER Theodore Rev Boston MA 1851
PARLIN I Esq Weld ME 1849
PATTERSON J W Esq (3) Augusta & Hallowell ME 1839-1846
PATTERSON Samuel Strong ME 1833
PEABODY Mr Rev Portsmouth NH & Worcester MA 1838 & 1852
PEARL Cyril Rev (2) (Cong) Gorham & Hartford ME 1840-1842
PEARL James Elder Mt Vernon ME 1848
PEET Josiah Wheelock Rev (5) (Cong) Gardiner & Norridgewock ME 1840-1851
PERCIVAL William 2nd Esq (9) China & Windsor ME 1846-1851
PERHAM John Rev (Cong) (2) Industry & Wilton ME 1844
PERKINS J H Esq Lee ME? 1852
PERRY Dan Rev (Meth) Oxford ME 1833
PERRY J A Rev Machias ME 1844 1844
PETTINGILL John A Esq (3) Augusta ME 1848-1850
PHILLIPS Thomas Esq Winthrop ME 1834
PIERCE Alfred Esq Greene ME 1834
PIERCE Mr Leeds ME 1835
PIERCE W Rev Portland ME 1842
PIKE Charles Esq Kingfield ME 1834
PIKE D T Esq Augusta ME 1838 & 1849
PILLSBURY E P Esq (3) Kingfield ME 1846-1852
PINEO Dan Esq Topsfield ME 1851
PINGRESS A Rev Belfast ME 1843
PINKHAM Mr Sedgwick ME 1839

PLUMMER Henry Rev Haverhill MA 1851
POMROY Swan L Rev (Cong) Bangor ME 1843
POND Dr Rev Bucksport ME 1843
POND Enoch Rev Bucksport ME 1843
POND P Rev Fayette ME 1841
POOLE W Rev (Bapt) Readfield ME 1845
POWERS S Rev East Windsor ME 1851
POWERS Sampson Rev (Bapt) East Winthrop ME 1851
PRESCOTT Jedediah B Rev (10) Monmouth ME 1834-1852
PRINCE Job Esq (3) Turner ME 1847-1850
PRINCE W Rev Portland ME 1842
PROCTOR H Rev China ME 1841
PUTNAM Rev (2) Augusta ME 1852
QUINBY Edwin F North Yarmouth ME 1843
QUINBY George W Rev (Univ) (4) Livermore, Litchfield, Canton & Winthrop ME 1838-1847
RANDALL Daniel B Rev (Meth) Monmouth & Winthrop ME 1841 & 1842
REDMAN John R Hon Brooksville ME 1838
REED Andrew Esq Phipsburg ME 1838
REED Benjamin P Rev Readfield ME 1847
REED John Esq Byron ME 1838
RICE Allen Esq Hallowell ME 1845
RICHARD Rev Nashua NH 1841
RICHARDSON C T Esq Turner ME 1843
ROBBINS B F Rev (Uv) (4) Winthrop ME 1846-1846
ROBINSON David G Esq (3) Albion, Vassalboro & Winslow ME 1845-1848
ROBINSON Ezekiel Rev (Meth) (10) Fayette, Readfield, Pittston & Winthrop 1837-1843
ROBINSON Jesse Esq Dixmont ME 1838
ROBINSON Nathaniel Rev Dover ME 1842
ROBINSON Rev (3) Monmouth, Pittston, Wayne, Winthrop ME 1833-1843
ROBINSON Z Esq Sumner ME 1850
ROGER Samuel L Phipsburg ME 1842
ROGERS George Esq Topsham ME 1833
* **ROGERS** Isaac Rev (Cong) (4) Farmington ME 1842-1847
ROGERS Mr Rev Boston MA 1842
ROGERS Samuel L Esq Philpsburg ME 1842
ROLFE E C Esq Farmington ME 1846
ROLLINS Isaiah Esq Belgrade ME 1848
ROSE Hiram Esq Newport ME 1848
RUSS Charles A Esq (3) China & Windsor ME 1838-1843
RUSSELL Elder Cornville ME 1851
RUST Rev Portsmouth NH 1852
RYAN Rev Jefferson ME 1844
SADLER Rev Portland ME 1842
SAFFORD John Esq Monmouth ME 1849
SANBORN Mr Rev Gardiner ME 1835
SANDERSON A Rev A Jay ME 1842
SARGENT Sylvanus G Rev (Bapt)(3) Belfast 1842-1843
SARGENT Walter Rev Mt Vernon ME 1842
SAWYER J W Rev Augusta ME 1847
SAWYER John S Esq Bangor ME 1841
SAYWARD John S Esq (2) Bangor ME 1841 & 1842
SCAMMEN C Rev (Meth?) New Sharon ME 1841
SCAMMON E Rev (Meth?) Pittston ME 1845
SCAMMON Rev Nobleboro ME 1838

SEAMMON E Rev Pittston ME 1845
SEARLS T Esq Hallowell ME 1850
SEARS Mr Esq Lagrange ME 1842
SEARSLES T Esq Hallowell ME 1850
SEWALL Jothan Jr Rev (Cong) Fayette ME 1834
SHARP Rev Dr Boston MA 1833
SHAW B F Rev (Bapt) (3) Winthrop, China & Vassalboro ME 1845-1851
SHELDON N W Rev Vassalboro & Waterville ME 1845 & 1848
SHEPHERD Rev Stratford 1837
SHEPPARD George Rev (Cong) Hallowell ME 1836
SIKES Oren S Rev Mercer ME 1844 [see also SYKES]
SMALL Joel Esq (2) Wales ME 1839-1846
SMART Edward Esq Etna ME 1843
SMITH C H Rev Lowell MA 1845
SMITH Daniel Talcott Prof (Cong) Bangor ME 1847
SMITH E Esq Augusta ME 1848
SMITH G H Rev Lowell MA 1845
SMITH George Esq Wayne ME 1835
SMITH J Palermo ME 1849
SMITH James Rev Fayette ME 1849
SMITH L C Esq/ L G Esq (3) Starks ME 1836-1849
SMITH Rev Waterville ME 1836
SMITH S F Rev Waterville ME 1841
SNOW George W Esq Bangor ME 1847
* **SPAULDING** Joel Elder (FWB, "During the year(s) spent in Maine he baptised about 250 converts" (3) Bath, Belgrade, Mt Vernon & Mercer ME 1834-1852
SPENCER George S G Rev Augusta ME 1850
SPRING C H Montville ME 1839
SPRINGER J Esq Augusta ME 1844

SPRINGER Moses (2) Gardiner ME 1837
STANDWOOD Daniel Esq Bath ME 1833 1839
STAPLES Rev Phipsburg ME 1849
STARKS Alanson Esq Augusta ME 1845
STARR Robert C Rev (Bapt) Wayne & Winthrop ME 1841 & 1843
STARR Robert C Esq Wayne ME 1843 1842
STEARNS Rev (3) Bath ME 1833-1839
STEELE J P Rev Hallowell ME 1851
STEVENS D T Rev (Univ) Minot ME 1839
STEVENS H Esq Pittston ME 1835
* **STEVENS** John Rev (FWB) (5) Augusta ME 1851
STEVENS L C Rev Fayette ME 1840
STEVENS R Esq Pittston ME 1835
STEWART Mr Esq Hallowell ME 1845
STICKNEY Amos Esq Vassalboro ME 1837
STINCHFIELD B H Rev Wayne ME 1843
STINCHFIELD Rufus H (Meth) Wayne ME 1842
STINCKNEY Amos Esq Vassalboro ME 1837
STINSON Joseph Esq Deer Isle ME 1836
STOCKBRIDGE J C Rev Fairfield ME 1847
STONE M Jr Esq Jay & Wilton ME 1852
STONE Rev Biddeford ME 1845 1845
STORER H Esq Cathage ME 1839
STOW Rev Boston MA 1842 1842
STREETER Rev Boston MA 1839
STRICKLAND A S C Esq Wilton ME 1840
STRICKLAND Isaac Maj Esq (3) Livermore ME 1835-1837
STROUT Stephen Esq Freedom ME 1847

SWAN Rev Kennebunk ME 1851
SWANTON J B Esq (4) Windsor ME 1834-1837
SWEAT T J Rev Windsor/Vassalboro ME 1847
SYKES Rev Greene ME 1841 [see also SIKES]
TALBOT Archibald Esq Phillips ME 1843
TALBOT Charles J Esq Phillips ME 1847
TAPPAN Benjamin Rev Dr (Cong) (6) Augusta & Hallowell ME 1838-1851
TAPPAN Daniel D (8) Augusta, Hallowell & Winthrop ME 1837-1852
TAPPAN O O Rev Winthrop ME 1837
TAPPAN Rev (3) Augusta, Hallowell, Hampden ME 1838 - 1843
THING Ira Dr Mt Vernon ME 1850
THOMAS Rev D?anbesbury NY 1842
THOMAS W O Rev Rockland ME 1852
THOMPSON Rev Falmouth ME 1843
* **THOMPSON** Zenas Rev (14) (Univ) Augusta ME 1851 & 1852
THURSTON D Rev (5) Canton, Monmouth, Winthrop ME 1836-1849
THURSTON Daniel (2) Winthrop ME 1851
THURSTON David (20) Gilead, Hallowell, Monmouth, Mt Vernon, Readfield, Winthrop ME 1833-1847
THURSTON Eli Rev (4) (Cong) Hallowell ME 1838-1849
THURSTON J S Rev Mercer ME 1845
THURSTON Rev (13) Augusta, Gardiner, Hallowell & Winthrop ME 1834-1850
TILLEY William Rev (5) (Bapt) Sidney ME 1845-1851

TILTON Recorder New York City 1852
TILTON Rev New Sharon ME 1849
TILTON Rev North Wayne ME 1849
TINKHAM Pardon Esq Albion ME 1850-1851
TITCOMB Benjamin Rev Brunswick ME 1836
TITCOMB E Esq1851
TITCOMB Samuel Jr Esq (3) Augusta & Mt Vernon ME 1845-1848
* **TOBIE** Elisha M Rev (FWB) Hallowell ME 1837
TOBIE Rev Hallowell ME 1838
TRASK E Rev (3) Nobleboro ME 1838
TRENCH J Esq Norridgewook ME 1847
TRIPP Rev Harmony ME 1842
TRUE John Rev Freedom ME 1842
TWOMBLY Rev Lowell MA 1851
TYLER Bennet Dr Rev (Cong) Portland ME 1833
TYLER/TYLOR Isaac Esq (5) Weld ME 1845-1851
VARNEY James L Esq Augusta & Rome ME 1844 & 1845
VARNUM William Esq (2) Anson & Solon ME 1834 & 1843
VEAZIE L Esq Mt Vernon ME 1850
VICKERY Isaiah Parkman ME 1849
VINTON Rev Newport RI 1842
VIRGIN P C Esq Rumford ME 1835
WADSWORTH I N Esq Kennebec ME 1851
WALTON Milo Esq (2) Amity ME 1846
WARD William Rev (Bapt) Belgrade ME 1848
WARREN E R Livermore/Winthrop & Vassalboro ME 1836-1839
WARREN Rev Augusta ME 1844

WASHBURN O W Esq Albion & China ME 1848 & 1851
WASHBURN Ruel Esq Canton ME/Livermore ME 1835
WASHBURN Zehah Esq China ME 1851
WASHINGTON Zehah Esq China ME 1851
WATERHOUSE S Rev Scarboro ME 1852
* **WATERMAN** Dexter Rev (FWB) (2) Jay & Strong ME 1843
WATSON John L Rev Boston MA 1844
WATSON Milo Amity ME 1846
WAYMAN Samuel Esq New Sharon ME 1835
WEBB Edwin B Rev (6) (Cong) Augusta ME 1851 & 1852
WEBBER George Rev (Meth) Readfield ME 1838
WEBBER Oliver A Esq (3) Vassalboro ME 1845-1851
WEBBER Rev Bangor ME 1842
WEBBER Rev (4) Hallowell & Readfield ME 1837
WEBSTER Rev Hallowell ME 1838
WENTWORTH L Rev (3) China & Vassalboro ME 1851-1852
WEST Ammi Esq Greene ME 1847
WEST J D Elder Augusta ME 1852
WESTON George M Esq Augusta ME 1845
WESTON Isaac? Rev (Cong) Cumberland ME 1835
WESTON James Partelow Rev (Univ) Gardiner ME 1845
WESTON Rev Waterville ME 1852
WETHERBEE S F Rev (Meth) Corinna ME 1848
WHEELER Rev Topsham ME 1832 & 1843
WHEELWRIGHT J B Rev Weld ME 1851
WHITE David Esq (2) Monmouth ME 1836
WHITE Rev New York City 1841
WHITE Seneca Rev (Cong) Unity & Wiscasset ME 1834 & 1842
WHITEHOUSE Rev (2) Augusta & Jefferson ME 1844

WHITING Elias Esq Winthrop ME 1836
WHITTIER Josiah Esq Readfield ME 1834
WILEY E Portland ME 1835
WILLETT Charles Rev Thompson CT 1848
WILLIAMS John Esq Bangor ME 1843
WILLIAMS N W Rev (2) Augusta ME 1844 & 1845
WILLIAMS Rev (4) Augusta & New Sharon ME 1844-1846
WILLIAMS Thomas Rev (Cong) Poland ME 1841 & 1842
* **WILLIAMSON** Stephen Elder (FWB) Augusta & Starks ME 1851 & 1852
WILLIS L Rev Lynn MA 1840
WILSON Obid Rev Skowhegan ME 1839
WING Alonzo Esq Mt Vernon ME 1833
WING John B Esq Presque Isle Plantation ME 1842
WING Moses Esq Wayne ME 1839
WINSLOW Rev New Portland ME 1848
WISWELL Luther Rev (Cong) Dixmont ME 1839
WITHERELL S B Rev Avon ME 1838
WOART William Esq Augusta ME 1847
WOOD Elijah Jr Esq Hartland ME 1836
WOODMAN Jabez Rev Pownal/Bowdoin ME 1841
WOODS John A Esq Farmington ME 1840
WORCESTER Rev Bath ME 1837
WORTHING Clifford S Esq Palermo ME 1845
WRIGHT Kendall Esq (2) Weld ME 1852
WRIGHT Rev Poland ME 1841
WYMAN Samuel Esq New Sharon ME 1835
YOUNG Rev Augusta & Vassalboro ME 1845 & 1848

Marriage Notices from the "Maine Farmer"

The Quakers (Society of Friends) do not have ministers [see p 743 *Vital Records from Maine Newspapers 1785-1820* for information on Quaker records]. Listed below are the surnames, place & year of Quaker marriages listed in this volume.

BAILEY-JONES Winthrop 1840
BRIGGS-ROBBINS Winthrop 1840
DEAN-JEPSON Wilton 1844
DUNHAM-ESTES Leeds 1837
ESTES-DUNHAM Leeds 1837
FARR-JONES Hallowell 1840
HUSSEY-MORRILL Portland 1838
JEPSON-DEAN Wilton 1844
JONES-BAILEY Winthrop 1840
JONES-FARR Hallowell 1840
MORRILL-HUSSEY Portland 1838
MOTT-WING Wilton 1840
ROBBINS-BRIGGS Winthrop 1840
WING-MOTT Wilton 1840

Marriage Notices from the "Maine Farmer" 483

NAME OF TOWNS, CITIES, OR PLACES NAMED IN THIS VOLUME

Abbott ME
Abington MA
Albany NY
Albion ME
Alexander ME
Alfred ME
Allentown PA
Alstead NH
Amherst ME or MA
Amity ME
Andover ME
Appleton ME
Arrowsic ME
Athens ME
Athol MA
Atkinson ME
Auburn ME
Augusta ME
Avon ME
Baltimore MD
Bangor ME
Barnstable MA
Bartlett NH
Bath ME
Belchertown
Belfast ME
Belgrade ME
Belmont ME
Benton ME
Bethel ME
Beverly MA
Biddeford ME
Bingham ME
Bloomfield ME
Bluehill ME
Boothbay ME
Boston MA
Bowdoin ME
Bowdoinham ME
Boxford MA
Bracken Co OH
Bradford ME
Bremen ME
Brewer ME
Bridgeton ME
Bridgewater MA
Bristol ME
Brookline MA
Brooklyn NY
Brooks ME

Brooksville ME
Brownfield ME
Brownville ME
Brunswick ME
Buckfield ME
Bucksport ME
Buffalo NY
Burlington IA
Burlington VT
Buxton ME
Calais ME
California
Cambridgeport MA
Camden ME
Campobello Maine/Canada border
Canaan ME
Canadaigua NY
Canterbury CT
Canterbury NH
Canton ME
Cape Elizabeth ME
Carlton MA
Carmel ME
Carroll Penobscot Co ME
Carthage ME
Casco ME
Castine ME
Charleston MA
Charlestown ME
Charlton ME
Chelmsford MA
Cherryfield ME
Chesterville ME
Chicago IL
China ME
Cincinnati OH
Clark Co VA
Clinton ME
Cohasset MA
Collinsville IL
Columbia ME
Columbia SC
Columbia TN
Concord ME
Concord NH
Conway NH
Corinna ME
Corinth ME
Cornish ME
Cornville ME

Cranston RI
Creniton England
Crystal Plt, Aroostook Co ME
Cumberland ME
Cushing ME
Damariscotta ME
Danville ME
Davertown OH
Dayton OH
Dedham MA
Deer Island of Eastport ME
Deer Isle ME
Dennis MA
Dennysville ME
Dexter ME
Dixfield ME
Dixmont ME
Dover ME
Dover NH
Dracut MA
Dresden ME
Dublin NH
Dunham (Canada East)
Durham (Canada East)
Durham ME
East Abbington MA
East Cambridgeport MA
East Corrinth ME
East Dixfield ME
East Eddington ME
East Livermore ME
East Machias ME
East Orrington ME
East Thomaston ME
East Vassalboro ME
Easton MA
Eastport ME
Eaton NH
Eddington ME
Edgartown MA
Edgecomb ME
Edinburgh Scotland
Ellsworth ME
ELmira, Chemung Co NY
Embden ME
Etna ME
Exeter ME
Fairfield ME
Fairhaven MA
Falmouth ME
Farmington ME
Fayal Azores

Fayette ME
Fort Fairfield ME
Foxcroft ME
Framington MA
Frankfort ME
Frankfort PA
Freedom ME
Freeman ME
Freeport IL
Freeport ME
Friendship PA
Fryeburg ME
Ft Wayne Indiana
Galveston TX
Gardiner ME
Garland ME
Georgetown ME
Gilead ME
Gilford NH
Glasgow Scotland
Glenburn ME
Gloucester MA
Gloucester RI
Goose River ME
Gorham ME
Gouldsboro ME
Gray ME
Great Falls NH
Green Bay WI
Greenbush WI
Greene ME
Greenfield MA
Greenwood ME
Guilford ME
Hallowell ME
Hampden ME
Hampton Falls NH
Harlem Co NY
Harmony ME
Harpswell ME
Harrington ME
Harrison ME
Hartford ME
Hartland ME
Hebron ME
Hempstead Harbor LI
Henriville (Lower Canada)
Hermon ME
Hiram ME
Holden MA
Hollis ME

Marriage Notices from the "Maine Farmer" 483

NAME OF TOWNS, CITIES, OR PLACES NAMED IN THIS VOLUME

Abbott ME
Abington MA
Albany NY
Albion ME
Alexander ME
Alfred ME
Allentown PA
Alstead NH
Amherst ME or MA
Amity ME
Andover ME
Appleton ME
Arrowsic ME
Athens ME
Athol MA
Atkinson ME
Auburn ME
Augusta ME
Avon ME
Baltimore MD
Bangor ME
Barnstable MA
Bartlett NH
Bath ME
Belchertown
Belfast ME
Belgrade ME
Belmont ME
Benton ME
Bethel ME
Beverly MA
Biddeford ME
Bingham ME
Bloomfield ME
Bluehill ME
Boothbay ME
Boston MA
Bowdoin ME
Bowdoinham ME
Boxford MA
Bracken Co OH
Bradford ME
Bremen ME
Brewer ME
Bridgeton ME
Bridgewater MA
Bristol ME
Brookline MA
Brooklyn NY
Brooks ME

Brooksville ME
Brownfield ME
Brownville ME
Brunswick ME
Buckfield ME
Bucksport ME
Buffalo NY
Burlington IA
Burlington VT
Buxton ME
Calais ME
California
Cambridgeport MA
Camden ME
Campobello Maine/Canada border
Canaan ME
Canadaigua NY
Canterbury CT
Canterbury NH
Canton ME
Cape Elizabeth ME
Carlton MA
Carmel ME
Carroll Penobscot Co ME
Carthage ME
Casco ME
Castine ME
Charleston MA
Charlestown ME
Charlton ME
Chelmsford MA
Cherryfield ME
Chesterville ME
Chicago IL
China ME
Cincinnati OH
Clark Co VA
Clinton ME
Cohasset MA
Collinsville IL
Columbia ME
Columbia SC
Columbia TN
Concord ME
Concord NH
Conway NH
Corinna ME
Corinth ME
Cornish ME
Cornville ME

Cranston RI
Creniton England
Crystal Plt, Aroostook Co ME
    Cumberland ME
Cushing ME
Damariscotta ME
Danville ME
Davertown OH
Dayton OH
Dedham MA
Deer Island of Eastport ME
Deer Isle ME
Dennis MA
Dennysville ME
Dexter ME
Dixfield ME
Dixmont ME
Dover ME
Dover NH
Dracut MA
Dresden ME
Dublin NH
Dunham (Canada East)
Durham (Canada East)
Durham ME
East Abbington MA
East Cambridgeport MA
East Corrinth ME
East Dixfield ME
East Eddington ME
East Livermore ME
East Machias ME
East Orrington ME
East Thomaston ME
East Vassalboro ME
Easton MA
Eastport ME
Eaton NH
Eddington ME
Edgartown MA
Edgecomb ME
Edinburgh Scotland
Ellsworth ME
ELmira, Chemung Co NY
Embden ME
Etna ME
Exeter ME
Fairfield ME
Fairhaven MA
Falmouth ME
Farmington ME
Fayal Azores

Fayette ME
Fort Fairfield ME
Foxcroft ME
Framington MA
Frankfort ME
Frankfort PA
Freedom ME
Freeman ME
Freeport IL
Freeport ME
Friendship PA
Fryeburg ME
Ft Wayne Indiana
Galveston TX
Gardiner ME
Garland ME
Georgetown ME
Gilead ME
Gilford NH
Glasgow Scotland
Glenburn ME
Gloucester MA
Gloucester RI
Goose River ME
Gorham ME
Gouldsboro ME
Gray ME
Great Falls NH
Green Bay WI
Greenbush WI
Greene ME
Greenfield MA
Greenwood ME
Guilford ME
Hallowell ME
Hampden ME
Hampton Falls NH
Harlem Co NY
Harmony ME
Harpswell ME
Harrington ME
Harrison ME
Hartford ME
Hartland ME
Hebron ME
Hempstead Harbor LI
Henriville (Lower Canada)
Hermon ME
Hiram ME
Holden MA
Hollis ME

Marriage Notices from the "Maine Farmer"   485

Honolulu, Sandwich Islands (Hawaii) USA
Hook, part of Hallowell ME
Hope ME
Hopkinton NH
Houlton Aroostook Co ME
Industry ME
Jackson, Jackson Co OH
Jarvis Gore (Bradley, Eddington, &/or Clifton SE Penobscot Co ME)
Java (Indonesia)
Jay ME
Jefferson ME
Kenduskeag ME
Kennebunkport ME
Kilmarnock ME
Kingfield ME
Kittery ME
Knox ME
LaGrange ME
Lake Village NH
Lana
Lawrence MA
Lawrence MA
Leicester MA
Letter B ME
Letter D Plt, Aroostook Co ME
Letter E ME
Levant ME
Lewiston Falls ME
Lewiston ME
Liberty ME
Limerick ME
Limeston River Plt, Aroostook Co ME
Limington ME
Lincoln ME
Lincolnville ME
Linneus, Aroostook Co ME
Lisbon ME
Litchfield ME
Livermore ME
London
London NH
Lowell MA
Lubec ME
Lyman ME
Lynn MA
Machiasport ME
Madison ME
Madrid ME
Matagorda TX
Mattapoisett MA?
Maumee City OH
Maxfield Penobscot Co ME
Mechanic Falls ME
Mercier ME
Meredith NH
Methuen MA
Milford ME
Milltown ME
Milo ME
Minot ME
Minudia, Nova Scotia Canada
Mobile AL
Monmouth ME
Monroe ME
Monson ME
Montgomery AL
Montpelier VT
Montville ME
Moulton NH
Mt Vernon ME
Muscatine Iowa
N Salem MA
Nantucket MA
Nashville TN
Nemours DEL
New Bedford MA
New Boston NH
New Brunswick Canada
New Gloucester ME
New Orleans LA
New Portland ME
New Sharon ME
New York NY
Newbury MA
Newcastle ME
Newfield ME
Newport ME
Newry ME
Nobleboro NH
Norridgewock ME
North Anson ME
North Bridgewater MA
North Palermo ME
North Waldoboro ME
North Wayne ME
North Yarmouth ME
Northam England
Northampton Co VA
Northborough MA
Norway ME

Nottingham England
Number 11 Aroostook Co ME
Number 11 Range 5 Aroostook Co ME
Number 12 Range 6 Aroostook Co ME
Number 6 (Berlin) ME
Oahu, Sandwich Islands (Hawaii) USA
Ogdensburg NY
Old Town ME
Orland ME
Orneville ME
Orono ME
Oxford MA
Oxford ME
Palermo ME
Palmyra ME
Paris ME
Park Hill, Cherokee Nation
Parkman ME
Parma Centre NY
Parsonsfield ME
Passadumkeag ME
Patrickstown Plt ME
Penobscot ME
Perry ME
Peru ME
Philadelphia PA
Phillips ME
Phipsburg ME
Pittsfield NH
Pittston ME
Plainfield MI
Pleasant Ridge ME
Plennfield, New Brunswick Canada
Plymouth ME
Poland ME
Porter ME
Portland ME
Portsmouth NH
Pownal ME
Presque Isle Plt Aroostook Co ME
Prospect ME
Providence RI
Providence RI
Quebec Canada
Quincy IL
Raymond ME
Readfield ME
Reading MA
Richmond ME
Richmond VA
Robbinston ME
Rockland ME
Rockport MA
Rollinsford NH
Rome ME
Roxbury MA
Rumford ME
Sacarappa ME
Saco ME
Salem MA
Salem ME
San Francisco CA
Sandwich MA
Scarborough ME
Searsmont ME
Sebasticook ME
Sebec ME
Sheboyan Falls WI
Shelbyville KY
Shirley ME
Sidney ME
Skowhegan ME
Smithfield ME
Solon ME
South Andover MA
South Bend IA [sic]
South Berwick ME
South Manchester CT
South Paris ME
South Prospect ME
South Solon ME
South Windham ME
Springfield MA
St Albans ME
St Andrews, New Brunswick Canada
St Ann's Jamaica
St George ME
St John, New Brunswick Canada
St Petersburg Russia
Standish ME
Starks ME
Stetson ME
Steuben ME
Strawsburg [sic] France
Strong ME
Sturbridge MA
Sumner ME
Swanville ME
Tauton MA

Tawmorth NH
Temple ME
The Forks of the Kennebec River
    Maine
Thetford VT
Thomaston ME
Thompson CT
Thorndike ME
Tingsbury MA
Tisbury MA
Tiverton RI
Topsham ME
Toronto Upper Canada
Tremont IL
Troy ME
Troy VT
Turner ME
Union ME
Union Vale NY
Unity ME
Vassalboro ME
Venice Italy
Vienna ME
Vinalhaven ME
Waconsta MI
Wakefield ME
Waldo Plt ME
Warren ME
Washington City
Washington DC
Waterboro (Canada West)
Waterborough ME
Watertown MA
Waterville ME
Wayne ME

Webster (Sabattus) ME
Weld ME
Wellington
Wells ME
West Bath ME
West Cambridge MA
West Camden ME
West Gardiner ME
West Minot ME
West Sumner ME
West Troy NY
West Waterville ME
Westbrook ME
Westfield MA
Weston ME
Westport ME
Whitefield ME
Wilbraham MA
Williamsburg ME
Wilson ME
Wilton ME
Windham ME
Windsor ME
Windsor VT
Winslow ME
Winthrop ME
Wiscasset ME
Woodford VT
Woodstock ME
Woolwich ME
Worcester MA
Wren Co OH
Yarmouth ME
Yazoo City MS
York ME

www.ingramcontent.com/pod-product-compliance
Lightning Source LLC
Chambersburg PA
CBHW071933240426
43668CB00038B/1258